~~344~~, ~~407~~ 408, 451

Monda[illegible] 27-30

(301) 11-15

(306) 33-40

(318) ~~13-21~~

pg) 21-38
306

321-322 (read)

(324) 9-16

77-78
1-16

135

Thursday

322-324
(1-8) (1-15)

25-30 (420)

16-24 (419)

chapter test

pg 160
pg 242

pg 282

[redacted]

Structure and Method *Book 1*

Algebra

Structure and Method
Book 1

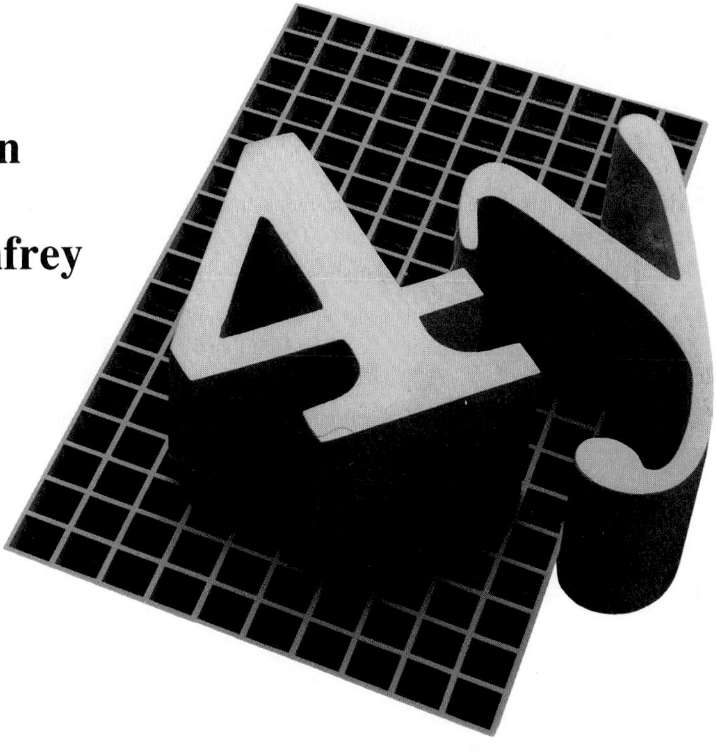

Richard G. Brown
Mary P. Dolciani
Robert H. Sorgenfrey
William L. Cole

Contributing Authors
Cleo Campbell
Joan MacDonald Piper

Teacher Consultants
Alma Cantu Aguirre
Gail Girvan Gismondi
Celia Lazarski
Ron Pelfrey
Edward M. VanderTook

McDougal Littell
A HOUGHTON MIFFLIN COMPANY
Evanston, Illinois • Boston • Dallas

Authors

Richard G. Brown, Mathematics Teacher, Phillips Exeter Academy, Exeter, New Hampshire

Mary P. Dolciani, formerly Professor of Mathematical Sciences, Hunter College of the City University of New York

Robert H. Sorgenfrey, Professor Emeritus of Mathematics, University of California, Los Angeles

William L. Cole, Associate Professor of Mathematics Education, Michigan State University

Contributing Authors

Cleo Campbell, Coordinator of Mathematics, Anne Arundel County Public Schools, Annapolis, Maryland

Joan MacDonald Piper, Mathematics Editor, Westborough, Massachusetts, and former Mathematics Teacher, Concord Academy, Concord, Massachusetts

Teacher Consultants

Alma Cantu Aguirre, Mathematics Department Chairperson, Thomas Jefferson High School, San Antonio, Texas

Gail Girvan Gismondi, Mathematics Teacher, Log College Middle School, Warminster, Pennsylvania

Celia Lazarski, Mathematics Teacher, Glenbard North High School, Carol Stream, Illinois

Ron Pelfrey, Mathematics Coordinator, Fayette County School, Lexington, Kentucky

Edward M. VanderTook, former Assistant Director for Instruction, Math/Science/Computer Unit, Tucson Unified School District, Tucson, Arizona

The authors wish to thank **David L. Myers**, Computer Coordinator and Mathematics Teacher, Winsor School, Boston, Massachusetts, for writing the Portfolio Projects.

2011 Impression

Copyright © 2000, 1997, 1994, 1992, 1990 by Houghton Mifflin Company. All rights reserved. No part of this work may be reproduced or transmitted in any form or by any means, electronic or mechanical, including photocopying and recording, or by any information storage or retrieval system without the prior written permission of McDougal Littell Inc. unless such copying is expressly permitted by federal copyright law. Address inquiries to Manager, Rights and Permissions, McDougal Littell Inc., P.O. Box 1667, Evanston, IL 60204.

Printed in U.S.A.

ISBN 978-0-395-97722-4

17 18 19 20 0914 13 12 11 10 09

Contents

6 Fractions

7 Applying Fractions

8 Introduction to Functions

9 Systems of Linear Equations

10 Inequalities

11 Rational and Irrational Numbers

12 Quadratic Functions

Using Technology with This Course

There are three types of optional technology material in this text: Computer Key-In features, Computer Exercises, and suggestions for using graphing calculators and software to explore concepts and confirm results.

The Computer Key-In features can be used by students without previous programming experience. They include a program that students can run to explore an algebra topic covered in the chapter. Some writing of programs may be required in some of these features.

The optional Computer Exercises are designed for students who have some familiarity with programming in BASIC. Students are usually asked to write one or more programs related to the lesson just presented.

The suggestions for applying computer graphing techniques are appropriate for use with a graphing calculator or with graphing software such as *Algebra Plotter Plus* or *McDougal Littell Mathpack*.

Calculator Key-In features and certain exercise sets also suggest appropriate use of scientific and graphing calculators with this course.

Reading Your Algebra Book

An algebra book requires a different type of reading than a novel or a short story. Every sentence in a math book is full of information and logically linked to the surrounding sentences. You should read the sentences carefully and think about their meaning. As you read, remember that algebra builds upon itself; for example, the method of multiplying binomials that you'll study on page 200 will be useful to you on page 544. Be sure to read with a pencil and paper: Do calculations, draw sketches, and take notes.

Vocabulary

You'll learn many new words in algebra. Some, such as *polynomial* and *parabola,* are mathematical in nature. Others, such as *power* and *proof,* are used in everyday speech but have different meanings when used in algebra. Important words whose meanings you'll learn are printed in **heavy type.** They are also listed at the beginning of each Self-Test. If you don't recall the meaning of a word, you can look it up in the Glossary or the Index at the back of the book. The Glossary will give you a definition, and the Index will give you page references for more information.

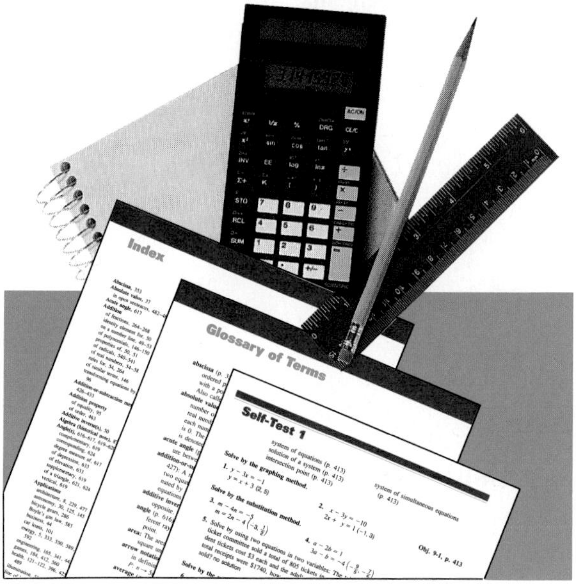

Symbols

Algebra, and mathematics in general, has its own symbolic language. You must be able to read these symbols in order to understand algebra. For example, $|x| > 2$ means "the absolute value of x is greater than 2." If you aren't sure what a symbol means, check the list of symbols on page xvi.

Diagrams

Throughout this book you'll find many diagrams. They contain information that will help you understand the concepts under discussion. Study the diagrams carefully as you read the text that accompanies them.

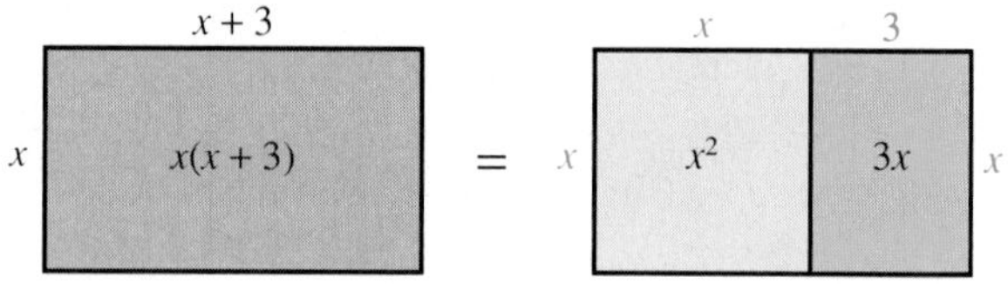

Displayed Material

Throughout this book important information is displayed in gray boxes. This information includes properties, definitions, methods, and summaries. Be sure to read and understand the material in these boxes. You should find these boxes useful when reviewing for tests and exams.

If a is a real number and m and n are positive integers, then $\boldsymbol{a^m \cdot a^n = a^{m+n}}$.

This book also contains worked-out examples. They will help you in doing many of the exercises and problems.

Example Simplify $x^3 \cdot x^5$.

Solution $x^3 \cdot x^5 = x^{3+5} = x^8$ ***Answer***

Reading Aids

Throughout this book you will find sections called Reading Algebra. These sections deal with such topics as independent study and problem solving strategies. They will help you become a more effective reader and problem solver.

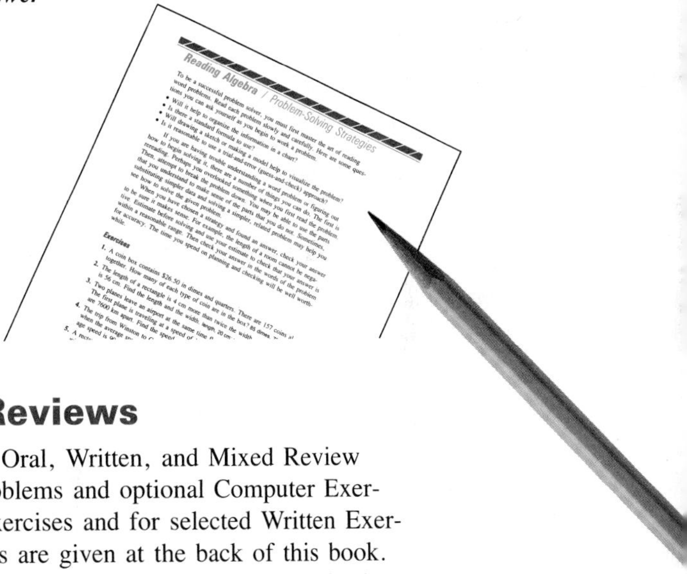

Exercises, Tests, and Reviews

Each lesson in this book is followed by Oral, Written, and Mixed Review Exercises. Lessons may also include Problems and optional Computer Exercises. Answers for all Mixed Review Exercises and for selected Written Exercises, Problems, and Computer Exercises are given at the back of this book.

Within each chapter you will find Self-Tests that you can use to check your progress. Answers for all Self-Tests are also given at the back of this book.

Each chapter concludes with a Chapter Summary that lists important ideas from the chapter, a Chapter Review in multiple-choice format, and a Chapter Test. Lesson numbers in the margins of the Review and Test indicate which lesson a group of questions covers.

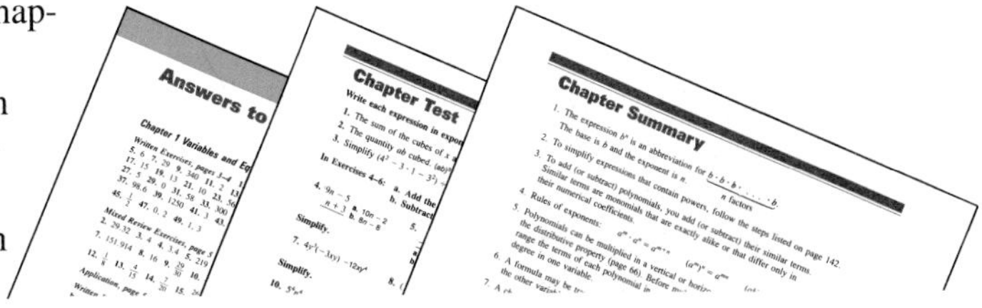

Reading Algebra/*Symbols*

		Page
$\cdot$	$\times$ (times)	1
$=$	equals, is equal to	2
$\neq$	is not equal to	2
$(\ )$	parentheses—a grouping symbol	2
$[\ ]$	brackets—a grouping symbol	6
π	pi, a number approximately equal to $\frac{22}{7}$	8
$\in$	is a member of, belongs to	10
$\therefore$	therefore	11
$\stackrel{?}{=}$	is this statement true?	27
$-$	negative	31
$+$	positive	31
$<$	is less than	32
$>$	is greater than	32
$-a$	opposite or additive inverse of *a*	36
$\|a\|$	absolute value of *a*	37
$\frac{1}{b}$	reciprocal or multiplicative inverse of *b*	79
$\emptyset$	empty set, null set	117
$a:b$	ratio of *a* to *b*	287

		Page
(a, b)	ordered pair whose first component is *a* and second component is *b*	349
$f(x)$	*f* of *x*, the value of *f* at *x*	379
$\geq$	is greater than or equal to	457
$\leq$	is less than or equal to	457
$\cap$	the intersection of	476
$\cup$	the union of	476
$\approx$	is approximately equal to	514
$\sqrt{\ }$	principal square root	517
$P(A)$	probability of event *A*	603
$\overleftrightarrow{AB}$	line *AB*	616
$\overline{AB}$	segment *AB*	616
AB	the length of $\overline{AB}$	616
$\overrightarrow{AB}$	ray *AB*	616
$\angle$	angle	616
$^\circ$	degree(s)	617
$\triangle$	triangle	621
$\sim$	is similar to	624
$\cos A$	cosine of *A*	627
$\sin A$	sine of *A*	627
$\tan A$	tangent of *A*	627

Reading Algebra/*Table of Measures*

Metric Units			
Length	10 millimeters (mm)	=	1 centimeter (cm)
	100 centimeters 1000 millimeters	=	1 meter (m)
	1000 meters	=	1 kilometer (km)
Area	100 square millimeters (mm^2)	=	1 square centimeter (cm^2)
	10,000 square centimeters	=	1 square meter (m^2)
Volume	1000 cubic millimeters (mm^3)	=	1 cubic centimeter (cm^3)
	1,000,000 cubic centimeters	=	1 cubic meter (m^3)
Liquid Capacity	1000 milliliters (mL)	=	1 liter (L)
	1000 cubic centimeters	=	1 liter
Mass	1000 milligrams (mg)	=	1 gram (g)
	1000 grams	=	1 kilogram (kg)
Temperature in degrees Celsius (°C)	0°C	=	freezing point of water
	100°C	=	boiling point of water

United States Customary Units			
Length	12 inches (in.)	=	1 foot (ft)
	36 inches 3 feet	=	1 yard (yd)
	5280 feet 1760 yards	=	1 mile (mi)
Area	144 square inches ($in.^2$)	=	1 square foot (ft^2)
	9 square feet	=	1 square yard (yd^2)
Volume	1728 cubic inches ($in.^3$)	=	1 cubic foot (ft^3)
	27 cubic feet	=	1 cubic yard (yd^3)
Liquid Capacity	16 fluid ounces (fl oz)	=	1 pint (pt)
	2 pints	=	1 quart (qt)
	4 quarts	=	1 gallon (gal)
Weight	16 ounces (oz)	=	1 pound (lb)
Temperature in degrees Fahrenheit (°F)	32°F	=	freezing point of water
	212°F	=	boiling point of water

Time		
60 seconds (s)	=	1 minute (min)
60 minutes	=	1 hour (h)

1 Introduction to Algebra

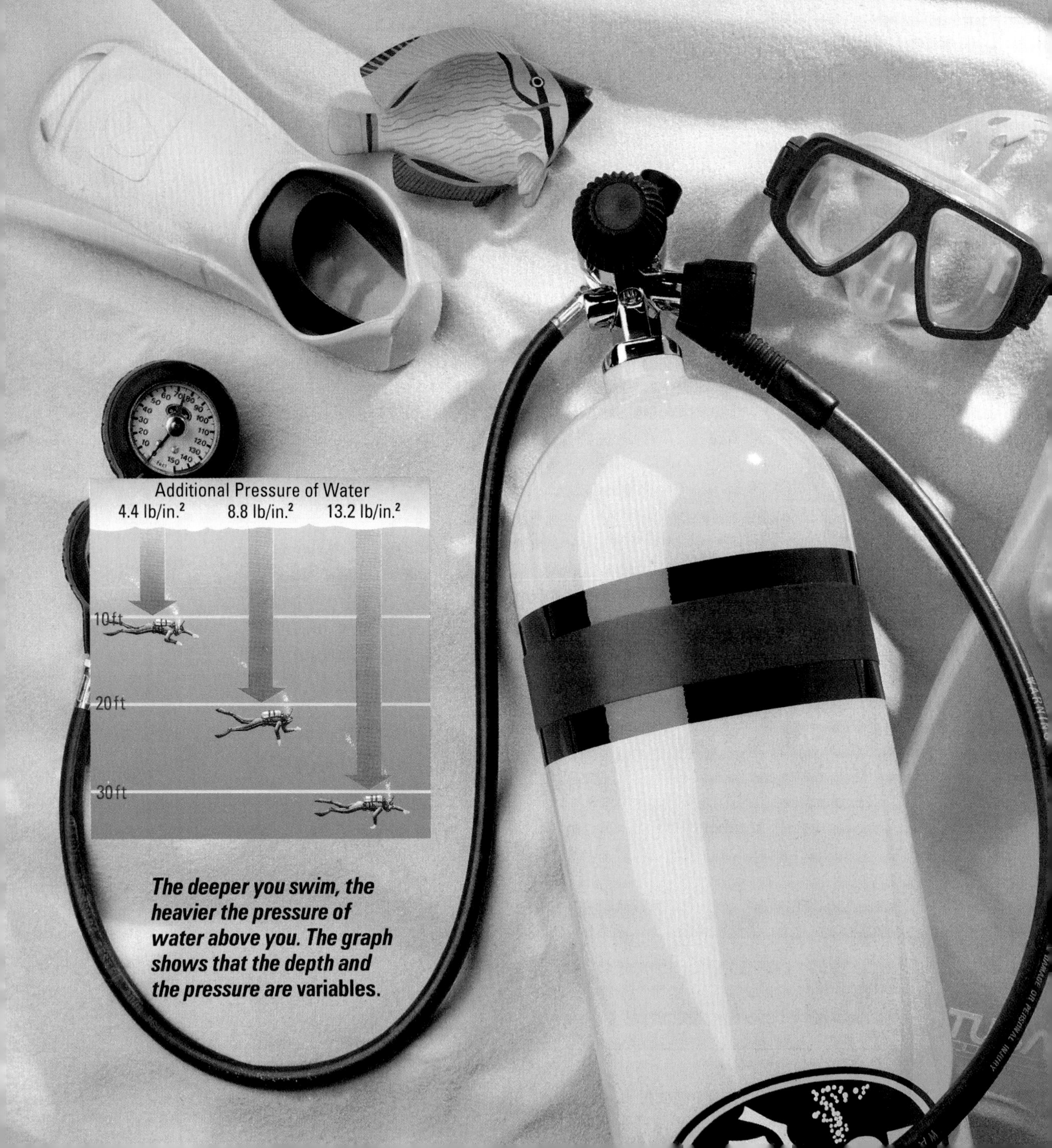

The deeper you swim, the heavier the pressure of water above you. The graph shows that the depth and the pressure are **variables.**

Variables and Equations

1-1 Variables

Objective To simplify numerical expressions and evaluate algebraic expressions.

When you go to an ocean beach, you may find small shops that rent recreational equipment, such as scuba gear, surfboards, and snorkeling gear. Suppose the rental charge for snorkeling gear is \$4.50 per hour. The amount you'll pay for using the gear depends on the amount of time you have it.

Number of hours	Rental charge
1	$\$4.50 \times 1 = \$4.50$
2	$\$4.50 \times 2 = \$9.00$
3	$\$4.50 \times 3 = \$13.50$
4	$\$4.50 \times 4 = \$18.00$

The rental charge follows this pattern:

$$\begin{aligned}\text{Rental charge} &= \$4.50 \times \text{number of hours}\\ &= \$4.50 \times h\end{aligned}$$

The letter h stands for the hours shown in the table: 1, 2, 3, or 4. Also, h can stand for other hours not in the table. We call h a *variable*.

A **variable** is a symbol used to represent one or more numbers. The numbers are called **values of the variable.** An expression that contains a variable, such as the expression $4.50 \times h$, is called a **variable expression.** An expression, such as 4.50×4, that names a particular number is called a **numerical expression,** or **numeral.**

Another way to indicate multiplication is to use a raised dot, for example, $4.50 \cdot 4$. In algebra, products that contain a variable are usually written without the multiplication sign because it looks too much like the letter x, which is often used as a variable.

$19 \times n$ can be written as $19n$.

$a \times b$ can be written as ab.

$\frac{1}{2} \times x$ can be written as $\frac{1}{2}x$.

The number named by a numerical expression is called the **value of the expression.** Since the expressions $4 + 2$ and 6 name the same number, they have the same value. To show that these expressions have the same value, you use the equals sign, $=$.

You write $4 + 2 = 6$

and say "four plus two *equals* (or *is equal to* or *is*) six." The *simplest,* or most common, name for the number six is 6.

The symbol $\neq$ means "is not equal to." You write

$$4 + 2 \neq 5$$

to show that the expressions $4 + 2$ and 5 do not have the same value.

Replacing a numerical expression by the simplest name for its value is called **simplifying the expression.** When you simplify a numerical expression, you use the following principle.

Substitution Principle

An expression may be replaced by another expression that has the same value.

Example 1 Simplify each expression. **a.** $(42 \div 6) + 8$ **b.** $54 \div (8 - 2)$

Solution The parentheses ( ) show how the numerals in the expression are to be grouped. The expression within the parentheses is simplified first.

a. $(42 \div 6) + 8 = 7 + 8 = 15$ ***Answer***
Note that to read the symbols "$(42 \div 6) + 8$," you may say "the *quantity* forty-two divided by six, plus eight."

b. $54 \div (8 - 2) = 54 \div 6 = 9$ ***Answer***

Replacing each variable in a variable expression by a given value and simplifying the result is called **evaluating the expression** or **finding the value of the expression.**

Example 2 Evaluate each expression if $a = 5$. **a.** $7a$ **b.** $(3a) + 2$

Solution

a. Substitute 5 for a.
$7a = 7 \cdot 5$
$= 35$ ***Answer***

b. Substitute 5 for a.
$(3a) + 2 = (3 \cdot 5) + 2$
$= 15 + 2 = 17$ ***Answer***

In Examples 1 and 2 the parentheses show how the variables and numbers in the expression are to be grouped. Notice that *expressions within parentheses should be simplified first.*

Example 3 Evaluate $(5x) - (3 + y)$ if $x = 12$ and $y = 9$.

Solution First replace x with 12 and y with 9, and insert the necessary multiplication symbol.

Then simplify the result.

$$(5x) - (3 + y)$$
$$(5 \cdot 12) - (3 + 9)$$
$$60 - 12 = 48$$ ***Answer***

Oral Exercises

Tell whether each statement is true or false. Give a reason for your answer.

Sample **a.** $7 \cdot 5 = 20 + 15$ **b.** $3 \cdot 4 = 3 + 4$ **c.** $2 + 2 \neq 2 \cdot 2$

Solution **a.** True, because the value of both $7 \cdot 5$ and $20 + 15$ is 35.

b. False, because $3 \cdot 4 = 12$, but $3 + 4 = 7$.

c. False, because the value of both $2 + 2$ and $2 \cdot 2$ is 4.

1. $6 \cdot 3 = 3 \cdot 6$

2. $4 \cdot 0 = 0 \cdot 6$

3. $8 \div 1 \neq 1 \div 8$

4. $54 \times \frac{1}{2} \neq 54 \times 0.5$

5. $3 \cdot (4 \cdot 2) = (3 \cdot 4) \cdot 2$

6. $(14 - 3) - 1 = 14 - (3 - 1)$

7. $\frac{(8 - 2)}{2} = 8 - 1$

8. $0.23 \times 5 = 2.3 \times 0.5$

Simplify each expression.

9. $9 + (5 \cdot 4)$

10. $(9 + 5) \cdot 4$

11. $18 - (4 \cdot 4)$

12. $(17 - 3) \cdot 3$

13. $\frac{(22 - 7)}{5}$

14. $\frac{(13 + 11)}{(6 - 2)}$

Evaluate each expression if $a = 1$, $b = 2$, and $c = 3$.

15. $7b$

16. $6a$

17. $c - 3$

18. $9 - b$

19. $\frac{2}{b}$

20. $(5c) - 4$

21. $b + (ac)$

22. $a + (bc)$

23. $3 \cdot (a - 1)$

24. $2 \cdot (b + 2)$

25. $(a + b) \div c$

26. $a \div (c - b)$

Written Exercises

Simplify each expression.

A **1.** $(8 - 3) + 3$

2. $9 + (18 - 2)$

3. $5 \cdot (11 + 1)$

4. $(13 - 6) - 7$

5. $(6 + 12) \div 3$

6. $6 + (12 \div 3)$

Simplify each expression.

7. $29 - (0 \cdot 9)$
8. $5 - (16 \div 4)$
9. $(8 \cdot 17) + (12 \cdot 17)$
10. $(12 \cdot 11) - (2 \cdot 11)$
11. $(26 + 4) \div (30 \div 2)$
12. $(40 \div 10) \div (1 \cdot 4)$

Evaluate each expression if $x = 2$, $y = 3$, and $z = 4$.

13. $5x$
14. $6y$
15. xy
16. yz
17. $(4x) + 7$
18. $(3y) - 9$
19. $(5z) - 7$
20. $(8x) + 7$
21. $(2x) + (2y)$
22. $(3z) - (4x)$
23. $8 \cdot (y + z)$
24. $7 \cdot (y - x)$
25. $\frac{1}{2} \cdot (z - x)$
26. $\frac{2}{3} \cdot (y + 6)$
27. $\frac{(y + x)}{(y - x)}$
28. $\frac{(z + y)}{(z - y)}$
29. $(4x) - 8$
30. $4z - (8x)$
31. $(5yz) - x$
32. $8 + (9xy)$

Evaluate each expression in color for the given values of the variables.

B 33. Area of a rectangle: lw
if $l = 25$ and $w = 12$

34. Perimeter of a rectangle: $(2l) + (2w)$
if $l = 25$ and $w = 12$

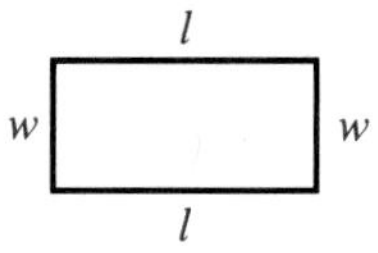

Exs. 33 and 34

35. Perimeter of a triangle: $(a + b) + c$
if $a = 10$, $b = 24$, and $c = 26$

36. Area of a right triangle: $\frac{1}{2} \cdot (ab)$
if $a = 10$ and $b = 24$

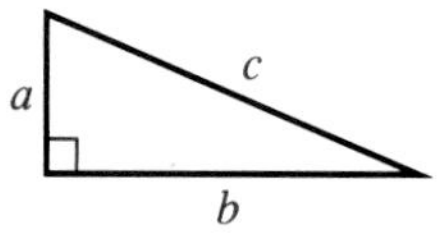

Exs. 35 and 36

37. Temperature in degrees Fahrenheit, given degrees Celsius:
$(1.8C) + 32$ if $C = 37$

38. Distance in meters traveled by an object falling for t seconds:
$\left(\frac{1}{2} \cdot g\right)(t \cdot t)$ if $g = 9.8$ and $t = 16$

39. Simple interest on a loan of P dollars: Prt
if $P = 5000$ (dollars), $r = 0.125$ (12.5% per year), and $t = 2$ (years)

40. Cost in cents of electricity to operate an electric light for one hour:
$\frac{(p \cdot c)}{1000}$ if $p = 75$ (watts) and $c = 9.5$ (cents) per kilowatt hour

For each variable find a value that will make a true statement. If possible, find more than one value.

41. $4n = 12$
42. $8x = 16$
43. $y + 3 = 3 + y$
44. $m + 5 = 5$
45. $6\frac{1}{2} - y = 3 \cdot 2$
46. $\frac{3}{4} + y = 0.75 + y$

C 47. $a \cdot a = 2a$
48. $z \cdot 8 = z$
49. $(b \cdot b) + 3 = 4b$

Mixed Review Exercises

Perform the indicated operation.

1. $(0.3) \cdot (1.2)$ **2.** $21.25 + 8.07$ **3.** $1.6 \div 0.4$ **4.** $7.2 - 3.8$

5. $212.1 + 6.9$ **6.** $6.32 - 4.7$ **7.** 72.34×2.1 **8.** $33.6 \div 2.1$

9. $\frac{2}{3} + \frac{3}{10}$ **10.** $\frac{5}{7} \times \frac{14}{16}$ **11.** $\frac{1}{2} \div \frac{3}{8}$ **12.** $\frac{3}{8} - \frac{1}{4}$

13. $\frac{7}{20} \times \frac{16}{21}$ **14.** $\frac{5}{12} - \frac{1}{15}$ **15.** $\frac{4}{7} + \frac{2}{3}$ **16.** $\frac{4}{7} \div \frac{3}{14}$

Application / *Energy Consumption*

Power is associated with the flow of electricity in a circuit. Your electric company determines your monthly electric bill based on how much electricity you have used. Electrical power is measured in watts (W).

When p watts are used for t hours, the amount of energy measured in watt-hours is represented by the expression $p \cdot t$. The electric meter for your home measures the amount of electricity you use in units called *kilowatt-hours* (kW · h). A kilowatt is 1000 watts.

To find the number of kilowatt-hours an appliance uses, use the expression $p \cdot t$ to determine the number of *watt-hours* used and then divide by 1000. You can get an idea of what 1 kW · h of electricity is by thinking of a 100-watt light bulb. To use 1 kW · h of electricity, you need to burn the 100-watt light bulb for 10 hours.

Example An air conditioner uses 1330 watts for 6 hours. How many kilowatt-hours does it use?

Solution In the expression $p \cdot t$, $p = 1330$ and $t = 6$.

$1330 \cdot 6 = 7980$ (watt-hours)

$7980 \div 1000 = 7.98$ (kW · h) ***Answer***

Exercises

1. An iron using 1008 watts is plugged in for 2 hours. How many kilowatt-hours are used?
2. A clothes dryer uses 4856 watts. How many kilowatt-hours are used if it runs for 10 hours?

1-2 Grouping Symbols

Objective To simplify expressions with and without grouping symbols.

Parentheses have been used to show you how to group the numerals in an expression. Different groupings may produce different numbers.

$(150 \div 10) + 5$ means $15 + 5$, or 20.
$150 \div (10 + 5)$ means $150 \div 15$, or 10.

A **grouping symbol** is a device, such as a pair of parentheses, used to enclose an expression that should be simplified first. Multiplication symbols are often left out of expressions with grouping symbols.

Example 1 Simplify: **a.** $6(5 - 3)$ **b.** $6(5) - 3$

Solution **a.** $6(5 - 3)$ stands for $6 \times (5 - 3)$.
The parentheses tell you to simplify $5 - 3$ first. Then multiply by 6.
$6(5 - 3) = 6(2) = 12$ ***Answer***

b. $6(5)$ stands for 6×5.
$6(5) - 3 = 30 - 3 = 27$ ***Answer***

In Example 1, note that $6(5)$ stands for 6×5. Other ways to write this product using parentheses are $(6)5$ and $(6)(5)$.

In a fraction such as $\frac{12 + 4}{15 - 7}$ the bar is a grouping symbol as well as a division sign.

Example 2 Simplify $\frac{12 + 4}{15 - 7}$.

Solution $\frac{12 + 4}{15 - 7} = \frac{16}{8} = 16 \div 8 = 2$ ***Answer***

Throughout your work in algebra you will use these symbols:

Grouping Symbols

Parentheses	Brackets	Fraction Bar
$6(5 - 3)$	$6[5 - 3]$	$\frac{12 + 4}{15 - 7}$

If an expression contains more than one grouping symbol, *first simplify the expression in the innermost grouping symbol.* Then work toward the outermost grouping symbol until the simplest expression is found.

Example 3 Simplify $18 - [52 \div (7 + 6)]$.

Solution
$$18 - [52 \div \underbrace{(7 + 6)}]$$
$$18 - [\underbrace{52 \div 13}]$$
$$\underbrace{18 - 4}$$
$$14 \quad \textit{Answer}$$

When there are no grouping symbols, simplify in the following order:

1. Do all multiplications and divisions in order from left to right.
2. Do all additions and subtractions in order from left to right.

Example 4 Simplify: **a.** $29 + 15 \cdot 4$ **b.** $19 - 7 + 12 \cdot 2 \div 8$

Solution

a.
$$29 + \underbrace{15 \cdot 4}$$
$$\underbrace{29 + 60}$$
$$89$$
Answer

b.
$$19 - 7 + \underbrace{12 \cdot 2} \div 8$$
$$19 - 7 + \underbrace{24 \div 8}$$
$$\underbrace{19 - 7} + 3$$
$$\underbrace{12 + 3}$$
$$15 \quad \textit{Answer}$$

Example 5 Evaluate $\frac{4x + 5y}{3x - y}$ if $x = 3$ and $y = 8$.

Solution Replace x with 3 and y with 8. Then simplify the result.

$$\frac{4x + 5y}{3x - y} = \frac{4 \cdot 3 + 5 \cdot 8}{3 \cdot 3 - 8} = \frac{12 + 40}{9 - 8} = \frac{52}{1} = 52 \quad \textit{Answer}$$

You may wish to use a calculator to evaluate some expressions. If you do, be sure to read the Calculator Key-In on page 13 first.

Oral Exercises

Describe the operation(s) for each expression.

Sample $3(x + 1) + 5$

Solution 1 Multiply 3 by the sum of x and 1; then add 5 to the product.

Solution 2 Add x and 1; multiply the sum by 3; then add 5 to the product.

1. $7y$ **2.** $z - 2$ **3.** $9x + 4$ **4.** $8z - 5$ **5.** $4(z + 6)$

6. $4(2x - 1)$ **7.** $\frac{z}{x + y}$ **8.** $\frac{z - y}{x}$ **9.** $\frac{13 - x}{y}$ **10.** $\frac{6x + 9}{8 + z}$

11–20. In Exercises 1–10, evaluate each expression if $x = 1$, $y = 3$, and $z = 7$.

Written Exercises

Simplify each expression.

A

1. a. $8 + 3 \cdot 4$
   b. $(8 + 3)4$
2. a. $9 + 5 \cdot 2$
   b. $(9 + 5)2$
3. a. $6 - 3 \div 3$
   b. $(6 - 3) \div 3$
4. a. $5 + 10 \div 5$
   b. $(5 + 10) \div 5$
5. $\dfrac{6 + 5 \cdot 3}{6 + 1}$
6. $\dfrac{8 + 3 \cdot 2}{4 + 3}$
7. $\dfrac{3(12 - 8)}{2 \cdot 5 - 4}$
8. $\dfrac{8 \cdot 5 + 2 \cdot 7}{2(7 - 4)}$

Evaluate each expression if $t = 6$, $x = 3$, $y = 4$, and $z = 5$.

9. a. $2x + 7$
   b. $2(x + 7)$
10. a. $5y - 3$
    b. $5(y - 3)$
11. a. $18 - 4x$
    b. $(18 - 4)x$
12. a. $7z + 8$
    b. $7(z + 8)$
13. a. $xy + z$
    b. $x(y + z)$
14. a. $zt - y$
    b. $z(t - y)$
15. a. $4xz + 3y$
    b. $4(xz + 3y)$
16. a. $9xyz - t$
    b. $9x(zy - t)$
17. $5(3y - 4x)$
18. $6y - 2xy$
19. $xyz - 4z$
20. $(y \cdot y + z) \cdot z$
21. $\dfrac{9x + z}{x + z}$
22. $\dfrac{4y - 2t}{y + 2t}$
23. $\dfrac{10t - z}{10(t - z)}$
24. $\dfrac{2(y + x)}{2y + x}$

B

25. $2[x + 4(y + z)]$
26. $3[z + 5(2y - x)]$
27. $[(5y + 6z) - 3t] \div y$
28. $2t - [7z \div (y + x)]$

Evaluate each expression in color for the given values of the variables.

29. Perimeter of a parallelogram: $2(a + b)$
    if $a = 7.5$ and $b = 19.5$

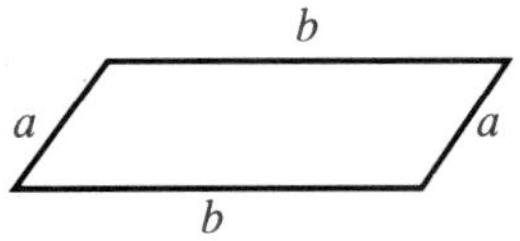

Ex. 29

30. Perimeter of an isosceles trapezoid: $2a + b + c$
    if $a = 20$, $b = 16$, and $c = 48$

Exs. 30-31

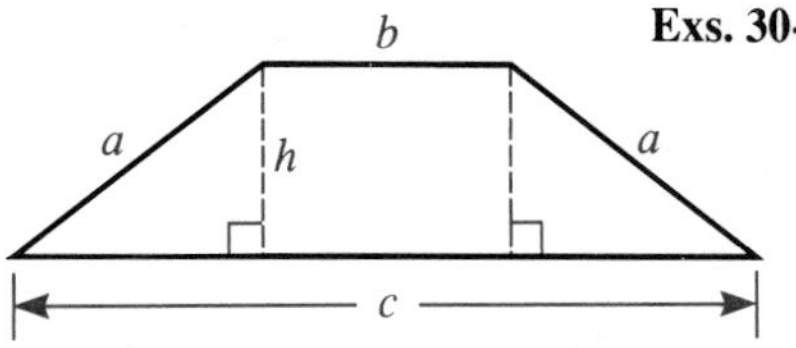

31. Area of a trapezoid: $\frac{1}{2}h(b + c)$
    if $h = 12$, $b = 16$, and $c = 48$

32. Area of a circle: $(\pi r)r$ if $r = 28$
    Use $\frac{22}{7}$ as an approximate value for π.

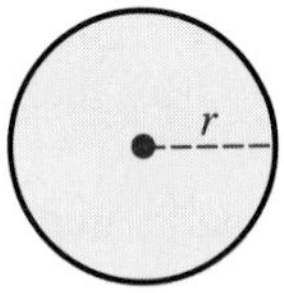

Ex. 32

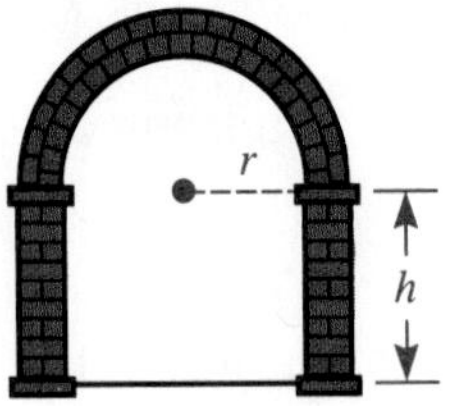

Ex. 33

33. Perimeter of a Norman window: $2(r + h) + \pi r$
    if $r = 2.00$ and $h = 3.00$
    Use 3.14 as an approximate value for π.

34. Surface area of a rectangular solid: $2(lw + wh + lh)$
if $l = 14$, $w = 12$, and $h = 10$

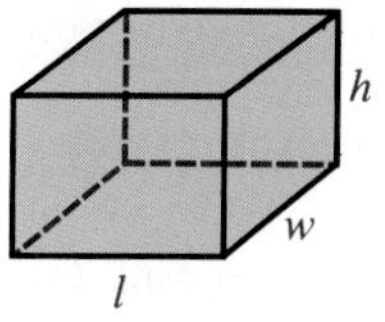

Simplify the expression on each side of the $\underline{\ ?\ }$. Then complete using one of the symbols = or ≠ to make a true statement.

35. $\frac{24 \cdot 8}{12 + 4} \ \underline{\ ?\ }\ \frac{12 \cdot 4}{6 + 2}$

36. $\frac{23 + 19}{7 \cdot 2} \ \underline{\ ?\ }\ 54 \div 9 - 3$

37. $2[3(12 - 7)] \ \underline{\ ?\ }\ 5 \cdot 5 + 5$

38. $3[36 \div (3 + 6)] \ \underline{\ ?\ }\ 30 - [(36 \div 3) + 6]$

Insert grouping symbols in the expression $5 \cdot 8 - 6 \div 2$ so that its value is:

C **39.** 5 **40.** 17 **41.** 25 **42.** 37

Insert grouping symbols in $5 \cdot 2 + 8 - 4 \div 2$ so that its value is:

43. 15 **44.** 16 **45.** 7 **46.** 12

Mixed Review Exercises

Simplify.

1. $(10 - 4) \div 2$
2. $40 \cdot 10 + 18 \cdot 2$
3. $8 \times (26 - 8)$
4. $7 + 15 \div 3$
5. $(28 + 4) \div (16 \div 2)$
6. $(6 + 5) \cdot (8 - 3)$

Evaluate if $a = 3$, $b = 2$, $x = 8$, and $y = 5$.

7. $x + ay$
8. $(5 - a)y$
9. $3a - 2b$
10. $\frac{1}{4}x + 3$
11. $\frac{1}{2}axy$
12. $x \cdot (2a - b)$

Challenge

Notice that:

$$2(1 + 2 + 3) = 3 \cdot 4$$
$$2(1 + 2 + 3 + 4) = 4 \cdot 5$$
$$2(1 + 2 + 3 + 4 + 5) = 5 \cdot 6$$

If this pattern continues to hold, predict the value of:

a. $2(1 + 2 + 3 + 4 + 5 + 6 + 7 + 8 + 9 + 10)$.

b. the sum of the integers from 1 to 100.

1-3 Equations

Objective To find solution sets of equations over a given domain.

An **equation** is formed by placing an equals sign between two numerical or variable expressions, called the **sides** of the equation.

$$\underbrace{11-7}=\underbrace{4} \qquad \underbrace{5x-1}=\underbrace{9} \qquad \underbrace{y+2}=\underbrace{2+y}$$

the two sides   the two sides   the two sides

Sentences containing variables (like the equations $5x - 1 = 9$ and $y + 2 = 2 + y$) are called **open sentences.** The given set of numbers that a variable may represent is called the **domain** of the variable.

A variable in an equation can be replaced by any of the numbers in its domain. The resulting equation may be either true or false.

You may use *braces* { } to show a set of numbers. A short way to write "the set whose members are 1, 2, and 3" is {1, 2, 3}.

Example 1 The domain of x is {1, 2, 3}.
Is the equation $5x - 1 = 9$ true when $x = 1$? when $x = 2$? when $x = 3$?

Solution Replace x in turn by 1, 2, and 3.

x	$5x - 1 = 9$	
1	$5 \cdot 1 - 1 = 9$	False
2	$5 \cdot 2 - 1 = 9$	True
3	$5 \cdot 3 - 1 = 9$	False

In Example 1, when x is replaced by 2, the resulting equation is true. Any value of a variable that turns an open sentence into a true statement is a **solution,** or **root,** of the sentence and is said to **satisfy** the sentence.

The set of all solutions of an open sentence is called the **solution set** of the sentence. Finding the solution set is called **solving** the sentence. In Example 1, there is only one solution. For the equation $5x - 1 = 9$ you may say either "The solution is 2," or "The solution set is {2}."

Some equations have more than one solution, and some equations have no solutions. The sentence $y + 2 = 2 + y$ is true no matter what number is substituted for y. Therefore the solution set is the set of *all* numbers. If you are asked to solve this equation *over the domain* {0, 1, 2, 3}, you state that the solution set is the domain itself, {0, 1, 2, 3}.

Here is another way to show that the domain of a variable y is {0, 1, 2, 3}:

$$y \in \{0, 1, 2, 3\}$$

(Read "y belongs to the set whose members are 0, 1, 2, and 3.")

Example 2 Solve $y(4 - y) = 3$ if $y \in \{0, 1, 2, 3\}$.

Solution

y	$y(4 - y) = 3$	
0	$0 \cdot (4 - 0) = 3$	False
1	$1 \cdot (4 - 1) = 3$	True
2	$2 \cdot (4 - 2) = 3$	False
3	$3 \cdot (4 - 3) = 3$	True

The solutions are 1 and 3.
$\therefore$ (read "therefore") the solution set is $\{1, 3\}$.
Answer

Example 3 Solve over the domain $\{6, 8, 12\}$:
Five more than twice a number is 29. What is the number?

Solution Use mental math to see which members of the given domain are solutions.

Number	Five more than twice a number is 29.	
6	Five more than twice 6 is 29.	False
8	Five more than twice 8 is 29.	False
12	Five more than twice 12 is 29.	True

$\therefore$ the number is 12. ***Answer***

Oral Exercises

Solve each equation if $x \in \{0, 1, 2, 3, 4, 5, 6\}$. If there is no solution over the given domain, say "No solution."

1. $x + 2 = 6$ **2.** $x - 1 = 4$ **3.** $2x = 6$ **4.** $x + 5 = 1$

5. $x - 3 = 3$ **6.** $x + 1 = 5$ **7.** $x + 4 = 4 + x$ **8.** $x + 4 = x$

Solve each problem over the domain $\{1, 3, 5, 7, 9\}$. Use mental math.

9. Three more than twice a number is 13. What is the number?

10. Eight times the sum of 4 and a number is 56. What is the number?

Written Exercises

Solve each equation if $x \in \{0, 1, 2, 3, 4, 5\}$.

A **1.** $x + 5 = 9$ **2.** $6 + x = 11$ **3.** $x - 2 = 3$ **4.** $x - 3 = 1$

5. $7 - x = 2$ **6.** $6 - x = 3$ **7.** $2x = 8$ **8.** $5x = 10$

9. $8x = 16$ **10.** $2x = 10$ **11.** $3x = 0$ **12.** $0 = 4x$

13. $x \div 3 = 1$ **14.** $x \div 2 = 2$ **15.** $\frac{1}{2}x = 2$ **16.** $\frac{1}{3}x = 1$

17. $x \cdot x = 1$ **18.** $9x = 9$ **19.** $x - x = 0$ **20.** $x \cdot x = 25$

Solve each problem over the domain {0, 2, 4, 6, 8}.

21. Eight times a number is 32. What is the number?

22. Twelve more than a number is 20. What is the number?

23. A number divided by four is 2. What is the number?

24. Three less than a number is 3. What is the number?

B **25.** Three more than twice a number is 7. What is the number?

26. Four times a number is 6 more than the number. What is the number?

Solve each equation over the domain {0, 1, 2, 3, 4, 5, 6, 7, 8, 9}.

27. $2a + 9 = 17$ **28.** $3b - 4 = 11$ **29.** $10 = 8c - 6$

30. $13 = 6d - 5$ **31.** $9 + 9r = 81$ **32.** $5 + 5n = 50$

33. $2x = x + 7$ **34.** $3w = w \cdot 3$ **35.** $2f = f \cdot f$

36. $y(8 - y) = 0$ **37.** $(6 - v)(1 + v)v = 0$ **38.** $27k = (3k)(3k)(3k)$

Suppose the domain for each equation is {1, 2, 3, 4,...}. (The dots show that the set goes on without end.) Determine the number of solutions for each equation. Write "None," "One," or "More than one." For those equations with one solution, try to determine what the solution is.

C **39. a.** $x + 3 = 3 + x$ **b.** $x + 4 = x + 3$ **c.** $x + 4 = 8$

40. a. $x - x = 1$ **b.** $x + x = 2x$ **c.** $x - x = 2x$

41. a. $4x = 8$ **b.** $4 \cdot x = x \cdot 4$ **c.** $4x = 4x + 1$

42. a. $3 \cdot x = x \cdot 3$ **b.** $x - 3 = x$ **c.** $x - 3 = 3 - x$

Write two different equations for which the solution set over the domain {0, 1, 2, 3, 4} is the given set.

43. {3} **44.** {0} **45.** {0, 1, 2, 3, 4} **46.** {0, 3}

Mixed Review Exercises

Simplify.

1. $11 \cdot 9 + 3 \cdot 11$ **2.** $7 + (15 \div 5)$ **3.** $(17 - 8) \div 3$

4. $(3 + 2 \cdot 2) \div 8$ **5.** $7 - 4 \div 2 \div 2$ **6.** $42 \div 7 \div (2 + 1)$

Evaluate if $a = 3$, $x = 2$, $y = 5$, and $z = 4$.

7. $3x + 4z$ **8.** $6 \cdot (z - x)$ **9.** $4(yz + 2)$

10. $5xz + 3y$ **11.** $axz \div (2y)$ **12.** $2y - [4a \div (x + 1)]$

Calculator Key-In

Does your calculator follow the steps for simplifying an expression stated on page 7? Experiment with your calculator by entering the following example exactly as it appears here: $8 + 3 \times 4 =$

If your calculator displays the answer 20, it followed the order of operations you learned: multiplication before addition. Your calculator has an algebraic operating system. The answer 20 is correct.

If your calculator displays the answer 44, it performed the addition and the multiplication in the order in which you pressed the keys. One way to get the correct answer on your calculator is to multiply 3 and 4 first and then add 8, just as you would if you were using pencil and paper.

Exercises

Use a calculator to simplify each expression.

1. $21 - 2.8 \times 7.5$

2. $0.8 + 1.2 \div 0.4$

3. $0.75 \div 0.25 \times 0.5 - 1.4$

4. $0.45 \times 369 + 0.55 \times 369$

5. $364 \div 13 \times 15{,}873 - 5291 \times 7 \times 3$

6. $432 \times 0.25 - 24 \div 0.25$

7. Evaluate $C = 5(F - 32) \div 9$ for each value of F:
a. $F = 212$ **b.** $F = 32$ **c.** $F = 98.6$

Self-Test 1

Vocabulary

variable (p. 1)
value of a variable (p. 1)
variable expression (p. 1)
numerical expression (p. 1)
value of a numerical expression (p. 1)
simplify an expression (p. 2)
substitution principle (p. 2)
evaluate an expression (p. 2)
grouping symbol (p. 6)
equation (p. 10)
side of an equation (p. 10)
open sentence (p. 10)
domain of a variable (p. 10)
solution or root (p. 10)
satisfy an open sentence (p. 10)
solution set (p. 10)
solve an open sentence (p. 10)

Evaluate if $x = 4$, $y = 2$, and $z = 5$.

1. $(5x + y)(z - 4)$ **2.** $3x(y + z)$ **Obj. 1-1, p. 1**

3. $8x - 3(z - y)$ **4.** $\frac{2(x + 5)}{4y - z}$ **Obj. 1-2, p. 6**

Solve if $x \in \{0, 1, 2, 3, 4, 5\}$.

5. $12 - 2x = 2$ **6.** $2x = x + 3$ **Obj. 1-3, p. 10**

Check your answers with those at the back of the book.

Applications and Problem Solving

1-4 Translating Words into Symbols

Objective To translate phrases into variable expressions.

To solve problems using algebra, you must often translate phrases about numbers into expressions containing variables.

	Phrase	Translation
Addition	The *sum of* 8 and x A number *increased* by 7 5 *more than* a number	$8 + x$ $n + 7$ $n + 5$
Subtraction	The *difference* between a number and 4 A number *decreased* by 8 5 *less than* a number 6 *minus* a number	$x - 4$ $x - 8$ $n - 5$ $6 - n$
Multiplication	The *product of* 4 and a number Seven *times* a number One third *of* a number	$4n$ $7n$ $\frac{1}{3}x$
Division	The *quotient of* a number and 8 A number *divided* by 10	$\frac{n}{8}$ $\frac{n}{10}$

Caution: Be careful with phrases involving subtraction.
The phrase "5 less than x" is translated $x - 5$ and *not* $5 - x$.
The phrase "5 more than x" can be translated as either $5 + x$ or $x + 5$.

Example 1 Translate each phrase into a variable expression.

a. 3 less than half of x **b.** Half the difference between x and 3

Solution **a.** $\frac{1}{2}x - 3$ **b.** $\frac{1}{2}(x - 3)$

Notice that the answer to Example 1 (b) is $\frac{1}{2}(x - 3)$, *not* $\frac{1}{2}(3 - x)$. In this book when we say "the difference between x and y," we mean $x - y$. Also, "the quotient of x and y" means $\frac{x}{y}$, or $x \div y$.

Example 2 If the length of a board in centimeters is l, then the length of a board 7 cm *shorter* is $l - 7$, and the length of a board 6 cm *longer* is $l + 6$.

Formulas are often used in algebra. **Formulas** are equations that state rules about relationships. Here are four useful formulas:

$A = lw$	**Area of rectangle** = length of rectangle × width of rectangle
$P = 2l + 2w$	**Perimeter of rectangle** = (2 × length) + (2 × width)
$D = rt$	**Distance traveled** = rate × time traveled
$C = np$	**Cost** = number of items × price per item

Example 3 Find the area and perimeter of a rectangle with length 10 and width w.

Solution

$$\begin{aligned} \textit{Area} &= \text{length} \times \text{width} \\ &= 10 \cdot w \\ &= 10w \quad \textbf{\textit{Answer}} \end{aligned}$$

$$\begin{aligned} \textit{Perimeter} &= (2 \times \text{length}) + (2 \times \text{width}) \\ &= (2 \cdot 10) + (2 \cdot w) \\ &= 20 + 2w \quad \textbf{\textit{Answer}} \end{aligned}$$

Example 4 You and your friends buy 2 pizzas at p dollars each and 4 salads at s dollars each. How much do you and your friends spend?

Solution

Cost = number × price

Pizza cost = $2p$ Salad cost = $4s$

Total cost = $2p + 4s$

You spend $(2p + 4s)$ dollars. ***Answer***

Example 5 You travel $(h + \frac{1}{2})$ hours at 80 km/h. How far do you travel?

Solution

Distance = rate × time

$= 80(h + \frac{1}{2})$

You travel $80(h + \frac{1}{2})$ km. ***Answer***

Oral Exercises

Translate each phrase into a variable expression. Use *n* for the variable.

1. Eight times a number
2. The product of three and a number
3. Five more than a number
4. One fourth of a number
5. A number decreased by four
6. A number divided by five
7. Nine less than half a number
8. Nine more than twice a number

Complete each statement with a variable expression.

9. A rectangle has width 6 units and length x units. Its area is __?__ square units.
10. A rectangle has width y and length 13. Its perimeter is __?__.
11. You travel for $(t - 2)$ hours at 75 km/h. You travel __?__ km.
12. You buy $(m + 5)$ bagels at 35 cents each. The cost is __?__ cents.
13. Al earns $(p + 3)$ dollars per hour. In 8 hours, he earns __?__ dollars.
14. Our house is y years old. Four years ago it was __?__ years old.
15. The Golden Gate Bridge was built n years ago. Three years from now it will have been standing __?__ years.
16. A sports arena was d years old 15 years ago. It is now __?__ years old.
17. Nine years from now Fenway Park will be g years old. It is now __?__ years old.
18. Mike jogs for half an hour at y mi/h. He jogs __?__ mi.
19. Workers on an assembly line produce $(x + 10)$ cars each day. In 5 days they produce __?__ cars.
20. A conveyor belt moves at n yd/min. In 10 minutes it moves __?__ yd.

Written Exercises

Translate each phrase into a variable expression.

A

1. 8 more than a number
2. Four times a number
3. A number decreased by 11
4. The sum of 3 and a number
5. Half of a number
6. A number increased by 10
7. The quotient of 17 and d
8. A number divided by 3
9. The product of 11 and x
10. The difference between a number and 2
11. 7 more than twice y
12. 4 less than five times a number
13. 8 less than half of n
14. 11 more than one third of a number
15. 5 plus the quotient of a number and 8
16. 10 times the sum of a number and 9

Match each phrase in the first column with the corresponding variable expression in the second column.

17. Seven decreased by three times a number	**a.** $2(x + 3)$
18. Twice the sum of a number and three	**b.** $3x + 1$
19. Five times the sum of a number and two	**c.** $3x - 7$
20. The difference between three times a number and one	**d.** $3x - 1$
21. Six times the difference of a number and five	**e.** $5x + 2$
22. Five less than six times a number	**f.** $2x + 3$
23. One more than three times a number	**g.** $5(x + 2)$
24. Twice a number, increased by three	**h.** $6(x - 5)$
25. Seven less than three times a number	**i.** $7 - 3x$
26. Two increased by five times a number	**j.** $6x - 5$

Complete each statement with a variable expression.

27. Leann is 3 cm taller than Fred.
If Fred's height is f cm,
then Leann's height is __?__ cm.

28. Adam is 9 in. shorter than Jeff.
If Jeff's height is j in.,
then Adam's height is __?__ in.

29. Maria has \$10 more than Luisa.
If Maria has m dollars,
then Luisa has __?__ dollars.

30. Dale has twice as much money as Leo.
If Dale has d dollars,
then Leo has __?__ dollars.

31. The sum of two numbers is 17.
If one number is x,
then the other number is __?__.

32. The product of two numbers is 18.
If one number is y,
then the other number is __?__.

B **33.** Seiji is 3 in. taller than Dan.
a. If Seiji's height is s in.,
then Dan's height is __?__ in.
b. If Dan's height is d in.,
then Seiji's height is __?__ in.

34. Ruth weighs 5 lb less than Erin.
a. If Ruth's weight is r lb,
then Erin's weight is __?__ lb.
b. If Erin's weight is e lb,
then Ruth's weight is __?__ lb.

35. There are 12 fewer boys than girls.
a. If the number of girls is g,
then there are __?__ boys.
b. If the number of boys is b,
then there are __?__ girls.

36. Two numbers differ by 12.
a. If the smaller number is s,
then the larger number is __?__.
b. If the larger number is l,
then the smaller number is __?__.

Answer each question. Use the formulas on page 15.

37. I drove for 3 hours at r mi/h. How far did I go?

38. Dick drove for h hours at 85 km/h. How far did he go?

39. Pencils cost p cents each. How much will 5 pencils cost?

40. Yogurt costs 75 cents per container. How much will x containers cost?

41. Sketch a rectangle having length l and width 5. What is its area?

Answer each question. Use the formulas on page 15.

42. Sketch a rectangle having length 7 and width w. What is its perimeter?

43. Pencils cost p cents each and notebooks cost n cents each. How much will 3 pencils and 2 notebooks cost?

44. Shirts cost 20 dollars each and ties cost 12 dollars each. How much will s shirts and t ties cost?

45. How many minutes are in 3 hours? In h hours?

46. How many days are in 4 weeks? In w weeks?

47. How many years are in 36 months? In m months?

48. How many minutes are in 330 seconds? In s seconds?

Complete each statement with a variable expression.

49. Oranges sell for c cents per pound at Carl's Convenience Store. They cost 5 cents per pound less at the local supermarket. Ten pounds of oranges cost _?_ cents at Carl's and _?_ cents at the supermarket.

50. Vera drove at the rate of r km/h. Kim's average speed was 3 km/h faster. In two hours, Vera traveled _?_ km and Kim traveled _?_ km.

51. The difference between two numbers is five. The greater number is n. The smaller number is _?_.

52. The difference between two numbers is eight. The smaller number is m. The larger number is _?_.

C **53.** An apple has 29 more calories than a peach and 13 fewer calories than a banana. If a peach has p calories, then there are _?_ calories in a fruit salad made with one apple, two peaches, and one banana.

54. A cup of peanuts contains 8 more grams of carbohydrates than a cup of walnuts and 1 less gram than a cup of almonds. If a cup of walnuts contains w grams of carbohydrates, then a mix of one cup each of peanuts, walnuts, and almonds contains _?_ grams of carbohydrates.

Mixed Review Exercises

Evaluate if $t = 2$, $x = 3$, $y = 4$, and $z = 5$.

1. $7x - 2y$ **2.** $4 + 3yz$ **3.** $(2x - t) \cdot 3$

4. $4z + 3x - t$ **5.** $txy + 2$ **6.** $ty + z + x$

Solve if $x \in \{0, 1, 2, 3, 4\}$.

7. $x + 4 = 8$ **8.** $3x = 12$ **9.** $4x = 4$ **10.** $5x = 0$

11. $2x + 1 = 7$ **12.** $5 = 3x - 1$ **13.** $x \div 2 = 2$ **14.** $2x = x + 3$

1–5 Translating Sentences into Equations

Objective To translate word sentences into equations.

Applications of algebra frequently require you to translate word sentences about numbers into equations. Sometimes you can translate the words in order. You may need grouping symbols.

Example 1 Twice the sum of a number and four is ten.

Translation $2 \cdot (n + 4) = 10$

Example 2 When a number is multiplied by four and the result decreased by six, the final result is 10.

Translation $4x - 6 = 10$

Caution: Be careful when the words "less than" are used. You may not be able to translate the words in order.

Example 3 Three less than the number x is 12.

Translation $x - 3 = 12$

Sometimes you will need to use a formula in order to write an equation. Examples 4 and 5 illustrate how this may be done.

Example 4 Use the figure and the information below it to write an equation involving x.

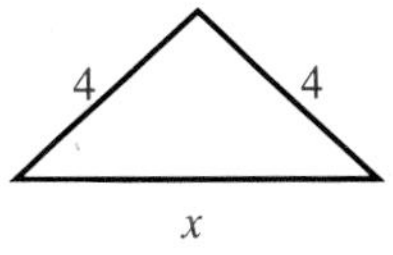

Perimeter = 14

Solution Perimeter = the sum of the lengths of the sides.

$14 = 4 + 4 + x$

$14 = 8 + x$ ***Answer***

Example 5 **a.** Choose a variable to represent the number described by the words in parentheses.

b. Write an equation that represents the given information.

The distance traveled in 3 hours of driving was 240 km. (Hourly rate)

Solution 1 **a.** Let r = the hourly rate.

b. Since rate × time = distance, $r \cdot 3 = 240$, or $3r = 240$.

Solution 2 **a.** Let $r =$ the hourly rate.
b. Since the hourly rate is the number of miles traveled in one hour, $r = \frac{240}{3}$.

Notice that the equations obtained in the Solutions to Example 5 are not the same. As soon as you become more familiar with algebra, you will see that these equations have the same solution set.

Oral Exercises

Translate each sentence into an equation.

1. Twelve more than the number p is 37.
2. Eight is 5 less than twice the number r.
3. Forty decreased by the number m is 24.5.
4. The number a increased by 2.3 is 8.3.
5. The sum of one third of the number s and 12 is 23.
6. The product of 58 and the number n is 1.
7. The quotient of the number b and 4 is 8.
8. Three fourths of the number h is 192.
9. The product of 12 and the quantity 1 less than the number d is 84.
10. The product of 7 and the sum of twice the number x and 3 is 126.

Use the figure and the information below it to write an equation involving x.

11.

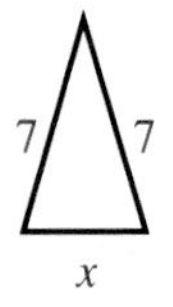

Perimeter = 18

12.

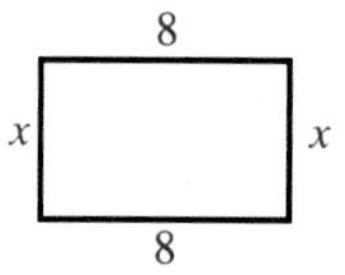

Perimeter = 26

13.

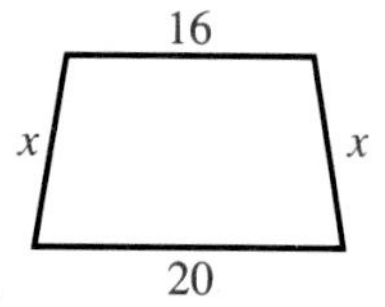

Perimeter = 60

Written Exercises

Tell whether equation (a) or equation (b) is a translation of the given statement.

A 1. One third of a number is seven. **a.** $\frac{1}{3} \cdot n = 7$ **b.** $\frac{1}{3} \cdot 7 = n$

2. Six less than a number is twelve. **a.** $6 - n = 12$ **b.** $n - 6 = 12$

3. Half of the sum of three and a number is four **a.** $\frac{1}{2}(3 + n) = 4$ **b.** $\frac{1}{2} \cdot 3 + n = 4$

4. Four less than twice a number is nine. **a.** $2x - 4 = 9$ **b.** $4 - 2x = 9$

5. Twice a number is 18 more than five times the number. **a.** $2x + 18 = 5x$ **b.** $2x = 18 + 5x$

6. A number is 9 more than one third of itself. **a.** $n = 9 + \frac{1}{3}n$ **b.** $n = \frac{1}{3}(n + 9)$

7. Eleven less than twice n is seven more than n. **a.** $(11 - 2)n = 7 + n$ **b.** $2n - 11 = 7 + n$

8. Ten times x is twice the sum of x and eight. **a.** $10x = 2x + 8$ **b.** $10x = 2(x + 8)$

Match the sentence in the first column with the corresponding equation in the second column.

9. Three less than twice a number is eight.
10. Three times the quantity two less than x is eight.
11. Two less than the product of three and x is eight. b
12. Two times the number which is three less than x is eight.
13. Three times two decreased by x is eight.
14. Three diminished by twice a number is eight.
15. Two decreased by three times a number is eight. h
16. Three times the number which is x less than two is eight.

a. $3(x - 2) = 8$
b. $3x - 2 = 8$
c. $3(2 - x) = 8$
d. $3 \cdot 2 - x = 8$
e. $2x - 3 = 8$
f. $2(x - 3) = 8$
g. $3 - 2x = 8$
h. $2 - 3x = 8$

Use the figure and the information below it to write an equation involving x.

17.

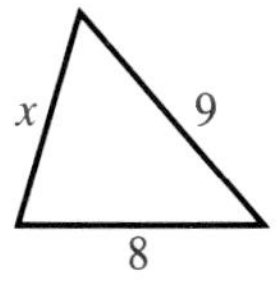

Perimeter = 24

18.

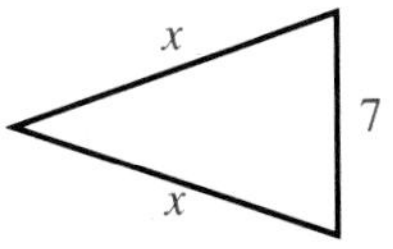

Perimeter = 29

19.

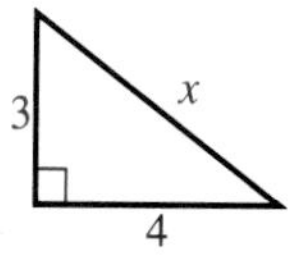

Perimeter = 12

20.

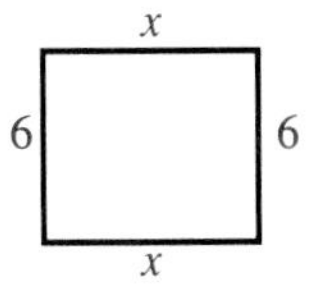

Rectangle
Perimeter = 26

21.

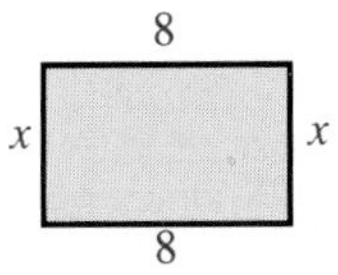

Rectangle
Area = 40

22.

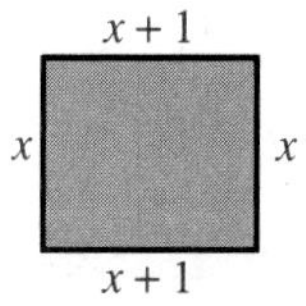

Rectangle
Area = 42

In Exercises 23–36,
a. Choose a variable to represent the number described by the words in parentheses.
b. Write an equation that represents the given information.

B **23.** The perimeter of a square is 116 m. (Length of a side)

24. A dozen eggs cost $1.19. (Cost of one egg)

25. Seven years from now a coin will be 50 years old. (Coin's age now)

26. Nine days ago a new radio station had been on the air for 13 days. (Station's age now)

27. A bookstore has sold all but 12 of the dictionaries in a shipment of 120 dictionaries. (Number of dictionaries sold)

28. A student solved all but the last four exercises in a homework assignment of 30 exercises. (Number of exercises solved)

29. One eighth of a pizza sold for $.95. (Cost of the whole pizza)

30. A sixteen-year-old building is one fourth as old as a nearby bridge. (Bridge's age now)

31. A train traveled 462 km at a rate of 132 km/h. (Number of hours traveled)

32. A rectangular floor is tiled with 928 square tiles. The floor is 32 tiles long. (Number of tiles in the width)

33. In the floor plan of a house, dimensions are shown $\frac{1}{100}$ of actual size. The length of the family room in the plan is 8.5 cm. (Actual length of the room)

34. A season ticket good for 39 basketball games costs $1092. (Cost of one admission with this ticket)

C **35.** Each car in a fleet of 24 rental cars is either red or blue. There are 3 more blue cars than twice the number of red ones. (Number of red cars)

36. The sum of three numbers is 120. The second of the numbers is 8 less than the first, and the third is 4 more than the first. (First number)

Mixed Review Exercises

Solve if $x \in \{0, 1, 2, 3, 4, 5, 6\}$.

1. $3 + x = 7$ **2.** $2 = x - 4$ **3.** $5x = 25$ **4.** $3 = x \div 2$

5. $3x + 1 = 10$ **6.** $4x = x + 6$ **7.** $x + 5 = 2x$ **8.** $4x = x \cdot 4$

Translate each phrase into a variable expression.

9. A number decreased by 5 **10.** 5 more than a number

11. The quotient of 5 and a number **12.** Twice the sum of 5 and a number

1-6 Translating Problems into Equations

Objective To translate simple word problems into equations.

A word problem describes a situation in which certain numbers are related to each other. Some of these numbers are given in the problem and are considered to be known numbers. Other numbers are at first unknown. You must determine their values by using the facts of the problem.

Simple word problems often give two facts involving two unknowns. The following steps can be used to translate such problems into equations. (In a later section, you will learn to find the solution of the problem by solving the equation.)

Step 1 **Read the problem carefully.**
- Decide what the unknowns are.
- Decide what the facts are.

Step 2 **Choose a variable and represent the unknowns.**
- Choose a variable for one unknown.
- Write an expression for the other unknown using the variable and one of the facts.

Step 3 **Reread the problem and write an equation.**
- Use the other fact from the problem to write an equation.

Example 1 Translate the problem into an equation.

(1) Marta has twice as much money as Heidi.
(2) Together they have \$36.
How much money does each have?

Solution Use the three steps shown above.

Step 1 The unknowns are the amounts of money Marta and Heidi have. Each of the numbered sentences gives you a fact.

Step 2 Choose a variable: Let h = Heidi's amount.
Use h and sentence (1): Then $2h$ = Marta's amount.

Step 3 Use sentence (2) to write an equation: $h + 2h = 36$

If a word problem involves lengths or distances, a sketch can help you to analyze the problem. Example 2 illustrates this.

Example 2 Translate the problem into an equation.

(1) A wooden rod 60 in. long is sawed into two pieces.
(2) One piece is 4 in. longer than the other.
What are the lengths of the pieces?

Solution Use the three steps shown on page 23.

Step 1 The unknowns are the lengths of the pieces.
Sentences (1) and (2) each give a fact.

Step 2 Choose a variable:
Let x = the shorter length.

Use x and sentence (2):
Then $x + 4$ = the longer length.

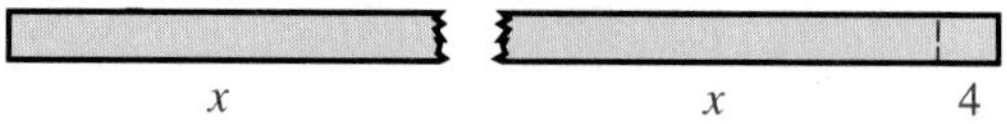

Step 3 Use sentence (1) to write an equation: $x + (x + 4) = 60$

Problems

Translate each problem into an equation.

A

1. (1) Luke has $5 more than Sam.
(2) Together they have $73.
How much money does each have?

2. (1) Lyn has twice as much money as Jo.
(2) Together they have $63.
How much money does each have?

3. (1) There were 12 people on the jury.
(2) There were 4 more men than women.
How many men were there?

4. (1) State College has 620 students.
(2) There are 20 more women than men.
How many women are there?

5. (1) Lee bicycled 3 km farther than Wing.
(2) The sum of the distances they bicycled was 25 km.
How far did each bicyclist go?

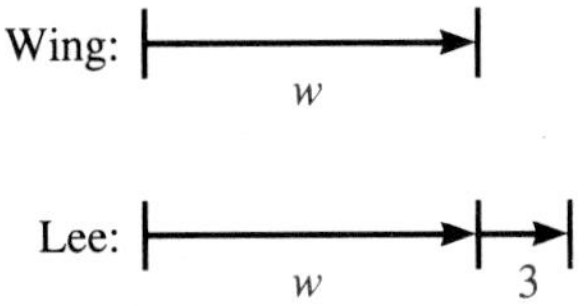

6. (1) Brenda drove three times as far as Jan.
(2) Brenda drove 24 miles more than Jan.
How far did Jan drive?

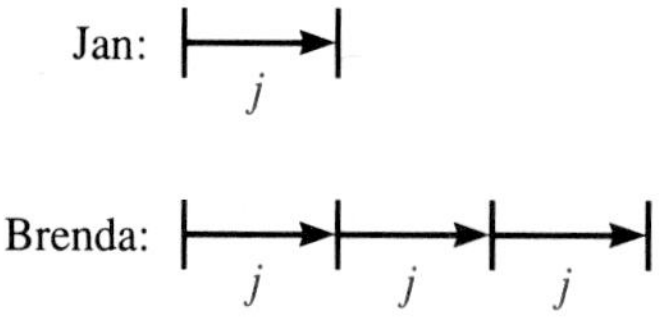

7. (1) Lisa walked 8 km more than Tim.
(2) Lisa walked twice as far as Tim.
How far did each walk?

8. (1) The Ravens won twice as many games as they lost.
(2) They played 96 games.
How many games did they win?

9. (1) Shelley made five more sales calls than Clark.
(2) Shelley and Clark made a total of 33 sales calls.
How many sales calls did each make?

10. (1) Skip had eight fewer job interviews than Woody.
(2) Together they had 20 interviews.
How many interviews did each have?

11. (1) Amanda spent $2 more than Barry on school supplies.
(2) Together they spent $34.
How much money did each spend?

12. (1) The number of items on two grocery lists differs by 7.
(2) The total number of items is 33.
How many items are on each list?

Translate each problem into an equation. Drawing a sketch may help you.

B **13.** A ribbon 9 feet long is cut into two pieces. One piece is 1 foot longer than the other. What are the lengths of the pieces?

14. The height of a tower is three times the height of a certain building. If the tower is 50 m taller than the building, how tall is the tower?

15. The length of a rectangle is twice its width. If the perimeter is 60, find the dimensions of the rectangle.

16. The length of a rectangle is one unit more than its width. If the area is 30 square units, find the dimensions of the rectangle.

17. The sides of a triangle have lengths 7, x, and $x + 1$. If the perimeter is 30, find the value of x.

18. A triangle has two equal sides and a third side that is 15 cm long. If the perimeter is 50 cm, how long is each of the two equal sides?

Translate each problem into an equation. Note that Problems 19–22 involve three facts about three unknowns.

Sample Ling is three times as heavy as her packed suitcase. Her suitcase is 20 lb heavier than her knapsack. The weights of Ling, her suitcase, and her knapsack total 170 lb. How much does each weigh?

Solution

Step 1 The unknowns are the weights of Ling, her suitcase, and her knapsack. We know three facts that relate these weights to each other.

Step 2 Let k = the knapsack weight.
Then $k + 20$ = the suitcase weight, and $3(k + 20)$ = Ling's weight.

Step 3 $k + (k + 20) + 3(k + 20) = 170.$

C **19.** A hockey team played 12 games. They won two more than they lost. They lost one more than they tied. How many games did they win, lose, and tie?

20. Tina, Dawn, and Harry have $175 together. Tina has three times as much money as Dawn. Dawn has twice as much money as Harry. How much money does each have?

21. A board ten feet long is cut into three pieces. One piece is one foot longer than the shortest piece and two feet shorter than the longest piece. How long is each piece?

22. Terri has $\frac{1}{4}$ as many Canadian stamps as her father has in his collection. She has $\frac{1}{7}$ as many Canadian stamps as her grandfather has. How many stamps do they each have if together they have 120 Canadian stamps?

Mixed Review Exercises

Solve if $x \in \{0, 1, 2, 3, 4, 5, 6\}$.

1. $2x + 3 = 5$
2. $x \div 2 = 1$
3. $16 = 4x$
4. $3 = 2x - 5$
5. $6 + 6x = 36$
6. $7 = 2x - 3$
7. $3x = x + 4$
8. $x \cdot x = 16$

Translate each phrase into a variable expression.

9. One third of a number
10. 2 less than 4 times a number
11. 5 more than twice a number
12. 4 less than one fourth of a number

Reading Algebra / Problem Solving

Accurate reading is a vital part of problem solving. When you read a problem, do so slowly and carefully to be sure you fully understand every word, fact, and idea. Look up any words that you do not know in a dictionary or in the glossary at the back of this book. Remember that more information than you need may be given.

When you have read the problem carefully and answered the questions, check your answers with those printed at the back of the book or with your teacher. If your answer is wrong, reread the problem and try to find your error. Good problem solvers learn from their mistakes as well as their successes.

A good way to find your error is to explain to a classmate how you reached your answer. Explaining to someone else—or even explaining aloud to yourself—often helps you clarify your own thinking.

Exercises

One day a cafeteria served twice as much milk as apple juice and three times as much milk as fruit punch. A total of 660 cartons of the three drinks was served. This is 100 more than 80% of the usual number served.

1. What given information do you need in order to find the number of cartons of milk served?

2. Which is greater, the number of cartons of apple juice served, or the number of cartons of fruit punch served?

3. Rob found the number of cartons of milk served by using the equation $x + 2x + 3x = 660$, where x represents the number of cartons of milk served. Was this method correct? Explain.

1-7 A Problem Solving Plan

Objective To use the five-step plan to solve word problems over a given domain.

To solve a word problem using algebra you can use the five-step plan below. Notice that you already know how to do the first three steps!

Plan for Solving a Word Problem

Step 1 Read the problem carefully. Decide what unknown numbers are asked for and what facts are known. Making a sketch may help.

Step 2 Choose a variable and use it with the given facts to represent the unknowns described in the problem.

Step 3 Reread the problem and write an equation that represents relationships among the numbers in the problem.

Step 4 Solve the equation and find the unknowns asked for.

Step 5 Check your results with the words of the problem. Give the answer.

In this section you will be asked to check which number in a given domain satisfies the equation you write for Step 3. Later you will learn how to solve an equation (Step 4) using other algebraic methods.

Example 1 Solve using the five-step plan. Write out each step. A choice of possible numbers for one unknown is given.

Phillip has \$23 more than Kevin. Together they have \$187. How much money does each have?
Choices for Kevin's amount: 72, 78, 82

Solution

Step 1 The unknowns are the amounts of money that Phillip and Kevin have.

Step 2 Let k = Kevin's amount. Then $k + 23$ = Phillip's amount.

Step 3 $k + (k + 23) = 187$

Step 4 Replace k in turn by 72, 78, and 82.

k	$k + (k + 23) = 187$	
72	$72 + (72 + 23) \stackrel{?}{=} 187$	False
78	$78 + (78 + 23) \stackrel{?}{=} 187$	False
82	$82 + (82 + 23) \stackrel{?}{=} 187$	True

Kevin's amount: $k = 82$ Phillip's amount: $k + 23 = 82 + 23 = 105$

Step 5 Check the results of Step 4 with the words of the problem.

Phillip has \$23 more than Kevin. $105 \stackrel{?}{=} 23 + 82$

$105 = 105 \checkmark$

Together they have \$187. $105 + 82 \stackrel{?}{=} 187$

$187 = 187 \checkmark$

$\therefore$ Kevin has \$82 and Phillip has \$105. ***Answer***

Problems

Solve using the five-step plan. Write out each step. A choice of possible numbers for one unknown is given. In Problems 11–16, drawing a sketch may help you.

A

1. An oil painting is 16 years older than a watercolor by the same artist. The oil painting is also three times older than the watercolor. How old is each?
   Choices for the watercolor's age: 4, 8, 12
2. The gym is 21 years newer than the auditorium. The gym is also one fourth as old as the auditorium. How old is each building?
   Choices for the auditorium's age: 26, 27, 28
3. Two numbers differ by 57. Their sum is 185. Find the numbers.
   Choices for the smaller number: 54, 64, 74
4. One number is four times another number. The larger number is also 87 more than the smaller number. Find the numbers.
   Choices for the smaller number: 29, 30, 33
5. A bus went 318 km farther than a car. The car went one third as far as the bus. How far did each vehicle travel?
   Choices for the car's distance: 147, 151, 159
6. A clown weighs 60 lb more than a trapeze artist. The trapeze artist weighs two thirds as much as the clown. How much does each weigh?
   Choices for the weight of the trapeze artist: 110, 120, 125
7. The U.S. Senate has 100 members, all Democrats or Republicans. Recently there were 12 more Democrats than Republicans. How many Senators from each political party were there at that time?
   Choices for the number of Republicans: 38, 42, 44
8. The ninth grade class has 17 more girls than boys. There are 431 students in all. How many boys are there? How many girls are there?
   Choices for the number of boys: 191, 202, 207
9. Elena has one and a half times as much money as Ramon. Together they have \$225. How much money does each have?
   Choices for Ramon's amount: 80, 90, 95
10. Western State College is 18 years older than Southern State. Western is also $2\frac{1}{2}$ times as old as Southern. How old is each?
    Choices for Southern State's age: 12, 14, 18

B **11.** The height of the flagpole is three fourths the height of the school. The difference in their heights is 4.5 m. What is the height of the school? Choices for school's height: 18, 20, 24

12. Leah and Barb started at school and jogged in opposite directions. After 30 min they were 10.5 km apart. Barb had traveled 1.5 km farther than Leah. How far did each jog? Choices for Leah's distance: 4.5, 4.6, 4.7

13. A rectangle is 12 m longer than it is wide. Its perimeter is 68 m. Find its length and width. Choices for the width: 10, 11, 12

14. The length of a rectangle is $3\frac{1}{2}$ times its width. Its perimeter is 108 cm. Find its length and width. Choices for the width: 12, 18, 24

15. A rectangle is 15 ft longer than it is wide and its area is 324 ft^2. Find its length and width. Choices for the width: 10, 12, 16

C **16.** A rectangle and a square have the same width but the rectangle is 5 m longer than the square. Their total area is 133 m^2. Find the dimensions of each figure. Choices for the square's width: 6, 7, 8

17. Luis weighs 5 lb more than Carla. Carla weighs 2 lb more than Rita. Together their weights total 333 lb. How much does each weigh? Choices for Luis's weight: 110, 115, 120

18. Tony has twice as much money as Alicia. She has $16 less than Ralph. Together they have $200. How much money does each have? Choices for Ralph's amount: 59, 62, 63

Mixed Review Exercises

Simplify.

1. $\frac{7 \cdot 2 + 6 \cdot 6}{10 - 6 + 1}$

2. $(30 - 4 + 4 \div 2) \div (21 \div 3)$

3. $30 - (12 \div 3 + 2)$

4. $6 \cdot 17 + 17 \cdot 3$

Translate each sentence into an equation.

5. Six times a number is 36.

6. Six is two less than a number.

7. Two more than twice a number is ten.

8. One third of a number is six.

Self-Test 2

Vocabulary formula (p. 15)

1. A variable expression for eight times the sum of a number n and four is __?__. **Obj. 1-4, p. 14**

Translate into an equation.

2. Twice a number x is two more than x. **Obj. 1-5, p. 19**

3. A rope 11 ft long is cut so that one piece is 2 ft longer than twice the other piece. What are the lengths of the pieces? **Obj. 1-6, p. 23**

4. Use the five-step plan to solve the following problem. **Obj. 1-7, p. 27**

A rectangle has an area of 55 ft^2.
Its length is 6 ft more than its width.
Find the length and the width.
Choices for the width: 5, 7, 9

Check your answers with those at the back of the book.

Biographical Note / *Maria Mitchell*

Maria Mitchell (1818–1889) was the first woman in the United States to be recognized for her work in astronomy. Born on the island of Nantucket, off the coast of Massachusetts, Mitchell helped her father with calculations needed to rate the chronometers of whaling ships.

Mitchell became the librarian of the Nantucket Atheneum in 1836 and continued to study mathematics and astronomy. On October 1, 1847, while conducting telescope observations, Mitchell discovered a new comet that was later named for her. She gained worldwide recognition for this discovery.

In 1865 Mitchell became the first professor of astronomy and the director of the observatory at Vassar College. In 1869 she became the first woman elected to the American Philosophical Society for her scientific achievements.

Numbers on a Line

1-8 Number Lines

Objective To graph real numbers on a number line and to compare real numbers.

The numbers used in elementary algebra can be pictured as points on a *number line* as shown below. The point labeled zero is called the **origin.** The origin separates the line into a **positive side** and **negative side.** For a horizontal line, the side to the right of the origin is the positive side.

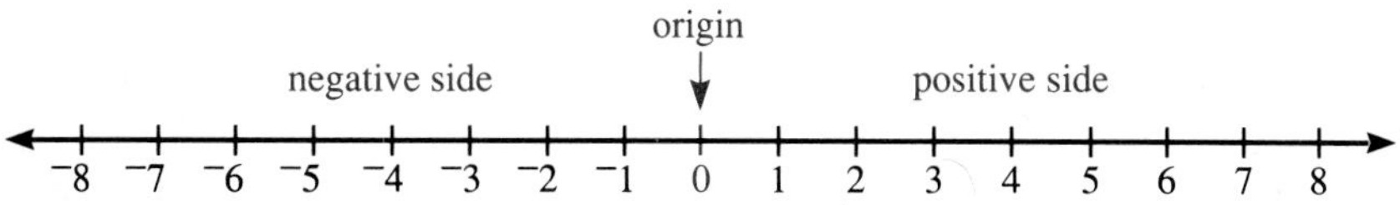

Equal units of distance are marked on both sides of the origin. The endpoints of successive units are paired with *negative and positive integers.* The number $^-1$ is read "negative one." The number "positive one" can be written either as 1 or $^+1$. Zero is neither positive nor negative.

Positive integers: $\{1, 2, 3, 4, \ldots\}$

Negative integers: $\{^-1, {}^-2, {}^-3, {}^-4, \ldots\}$

The three dots are read "and so on." They indicate that the list continues without end. The positive integers, negative integers, and zero make up the set of **integers.**

Integers: $\{\ldots, {}^-3, {}^-2, {}^-1, 0, 1, 2, 3, \ldots\}$

The set of **whole numbers** consists of zero and all positive integers.

Whole numbers: $\{0, 1, 2, 3, \ldots\}$

A number line contains points corresponding to fractions and decimals as well as integers. A **positive number** is a number paired with a point on the positive side of a number line. A **negative number** is a number paired with a point on the negative side of a number line. For example:

A is 1.5 units from 0 on the positive side.
The *positive* number 1.5 is paired with A.

B is 1.5 units from 0 on the negative side.
The *negative* number $^-1.5$ is paired with B.

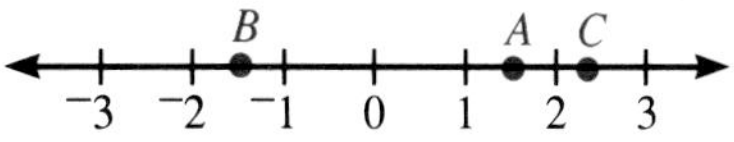

On a number line, the point paired with a number is called the **graph** of the number. The number paired with a point is called the **coordinate** of the point. Point C, above, is the graph of $2\frac{1}{3}$, and $2\frac{1}{3}$ is the coordinate of C.

Any number that is either positive, negative, or zero is called a **real number.** When you graph real numbers, you take the following for granted.

1. Each real number is paired with exactly one point on a number line.
2. Each point on a number line is paired with exactly one real number.

Thus, the graphs of *all* the real numbers make up the entire number line:

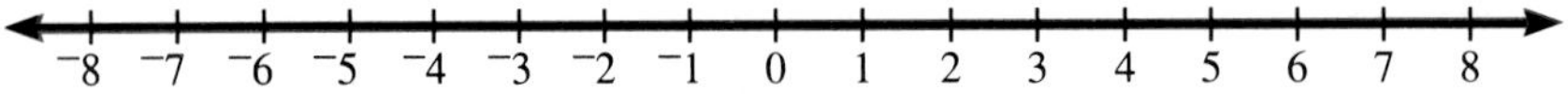

The arrowheads indicate that the number line and the graphs go on without end in both directions.

Because positive and negative numbers suggest opposite directions, they are sometimes called *directed numbers*. You use them for measurements that have *direction* as well as size.

Example 1 Write a number to represent each situation.

a. A temperature rise of 6°: 6
A temperature drop of 6°: $^{-}6$

b. 7.3 km north: 7.3
7.3 km south: $^{-}7.3$

c. A wage increase of \$15: 15
A wage decrease of \$15: $^{-}15$

Inequality symbols are used to show the *order* of two real numbers.

$<$ means "is less than" $\qquad 3 < 7$

$>$ means "is greater than" $\qquad 7 > 3$

The greater number is always placed at the greater (or open) end of the inequality symbol. The statements $3 < 7$ and $7 > 3$ give the same information and are interchangeable.

On a horizontal number line, such as the one above, the numbers increase from left to right and decrease from right to left. By studying the number line, you can see that the following statements are true.

$^{-}5 < ^{-}2 \qquad ^{-}5 < 0 \qquad ^{-}5 < 3$

$^{-}2 > ^{-}5 \qquad 0 > ^{-}5 \qquad 3 > ^{-}5$

Example 2 Graph the numbers $^{-}1$, 2.5, 0, $^{-}3$, $\frac{7}{3}$, and $^{-}3.75$ on a number line. Then list them in increasing order.

Solution

From least to greatest: $^{-}3.75$, $^{-}3$, $^{-}1$, 0, $\frac{7}{3}$, 2.5

Oral Exercises

Exercises 1–16 refer to the number line below.

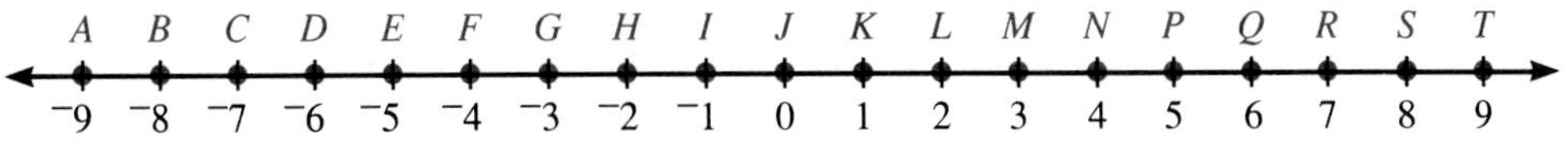

Name the point that is the graph of the given coordinate.

Sample 1 $^{-}7$ **Solution** Point C

1. 8 **2.** 0 **3.** $^{-}1$ **4.** $^{-}6$ **5.** 4 **6.** $^{-}4$

State the coordinate of the given point.

7. G **8.** R **9.** T **10.** H **11.** B **12.** J

Sample 2 The point halfway between P and Q **Solution** 5.5

13. The point halfway between L and M

14. The point halfway between D and E

15. The point one third of the way from E to K

16. The point one fourth of the way from I to A

Read aloud each inequality statement. Tell whether it is true or false.

17. $2 < 5$ **18.** $^{-}4 < 0$ **19.** $^{-}3 > {}^{-}2$ **20.** $^{-}5 < \frac{1}{4}$

21. $8 > {}^{-}9$ **22.** $^{-}3 > {}^{-}4$ **23.** $7 > 0$ **24.** $^{-}2 < {}^{-}2.01$

Written Exercises

Write a number to represent each situation. Then write the opposite of that situation and write a number to represent it.

A

1. Five steps down

2. Two rooms to the right

3. 190 m above sea level

4. Nine degrees below freezing (0° C)

5. A profit of \$18

6. Four losses

7. 15 km west

8. Latitude of 41° north

9. Receipts of \$85

10. A bank withdrawal of \$25

11. One foot below ground

12. 3 bonus points

13. A loss of \$50

14. 10 lb lost

Translate each statement into symbols.

15. Six is greater than negative nine.

16. Negative eleven is less than negative one.

17. Negative eight is greater than negative ten.

18. Ten is greater than seven.

19. Six is less than six and five tenths.

20. Zero is greater than negative three tenths.

21. Negative thirteen is less than zero.

22. One eighth is less than one seventh.

List the letters of the points whose coordinates are given.

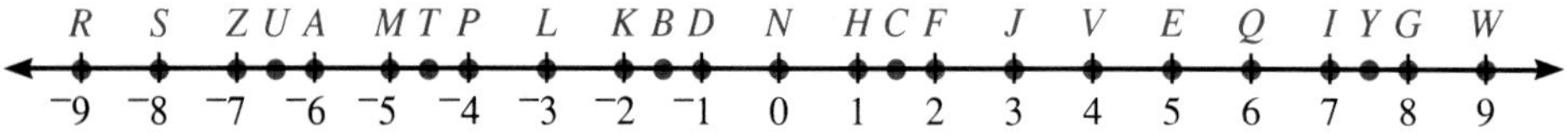

23. $^{-}8, 2$ **24.** $^{-}5, 4$ **25.** $0, ^{-}9$ **26.** $^{-}6, 8$

27. $6, ^{-}6, ^{-}6\frac{1}{2}$ **28.** $1, ^{-}1, ^{-}1\frac{1}{2}$ **29.** $^{-}5, ^{-}4\frac{1}{2}, ^{-}4$ **30.** $^{-}8, ^{-}7, 7\frac{1}{2}$

State two inequalities, one with > and one with <, for the coordinates of the points shown in color.

Sample

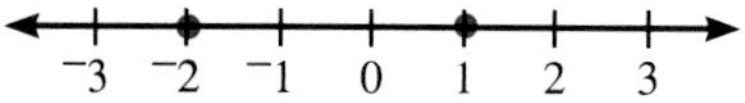

Solution $^{-}2 < 1, 1 > ^{-}2$

31.

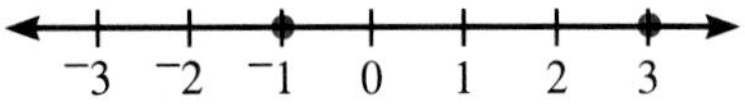

32.

33.

34.

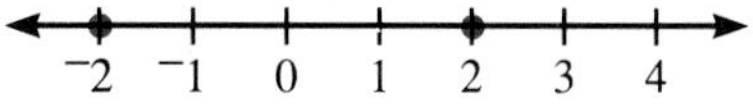

35.

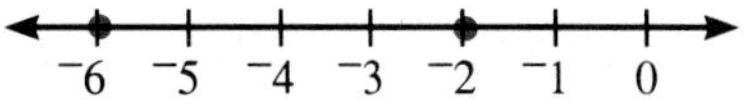

36.

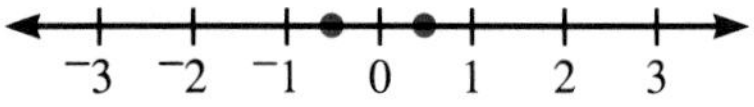

37.

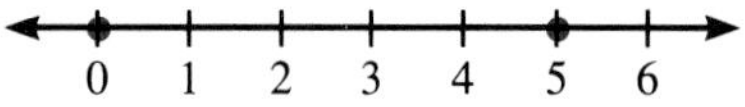

38.

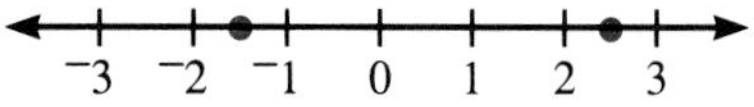

Complete using one of the symbols < or > to make a true statement.

39. $^{-}4$ _?_ 0 **40.** 0 _?_ $^{-}5$ **41.** 6 _?_ $5 + 4$ **42.** $8 - 7$ _?_ $^{-}1$

43. 0 _?_ $^{-}1$ **44.** 0×0 _?_ 1 **45.** $^{-}3.1$ _?_ $^{-}3.2$ **46.** $-\frac{2}{5}$ _?_ $-\frac{1}{5}$

Graph the given numbers on a number line. Draw a separate line for each exercise. Then list the numbers in increasing order.

B **47.** $1, 2, ^{-}2, ^{-}1$ **48.** $3, ^{-}3, 6, ^{-}6$ **49.** $0, 1.5, ^{-}1, ^{-}0.5$

50. $^{-}1, ^{-}2, ^{-}1.5, 0$ **51.** $^{-}1\frac{2}{3}, ^{-}3, 0, \frac{^{-}1}{3}$ **52.** $0, ^{-}4, 1, \frac{1}{2}$

53. $^{-}1\frac{1}{4}, \frac{3}{4}, \frac{^{-}1}{4}, 2\frac{1}{4}$ **54.** $\frac{5}{3}, \frac{10}{3}, \frac{2}{3}, \frac{^{-}2}{3}$

55. Freida is taller than Cora but shorter than Stu.
Stu is taller than Freida but shorter than Janelle.
List the names of these people in order from shortest to tallest.

56. Jack and Nick are both older than Mona.
Pete is older than Jack but younger than Nick.
List the names of these people in order from oldest to youngest.

C **57.** On a number line, point M has coordinate 2 and point T has coordinate 5. What is the coordinate of the point between M and T that is half as far from M as it is from T?

58. On a number line, point C has coordinate $^{-}2$ and point D has coordinate 4. What is the coordinate of the point between C and D that is twice as far from C as it is from D?

Mixed Review Exercises

Evaluate if $a = 2$, $b = 5$, $c = 4$, $x = 3$, and $y = 7$.

1. $3ab - 2x$

2. $4x(y - b)$

3. $a \cdot (3y \div 7)$

4. $\frac{1}{5}(4c - 1)$

5. $3y - (2a + c \div 2)$

6. $\left(\frac{1}{2}ac\right) + (5 - x)b$

Translate each sentence into an equation.

7. Thirty decreased by a number is twelve.

8. Four more than a number is two.

9. The product of a number and 6 is 2.

10. One fourth of a number is one.

Challenge

1, 3, 6, 10, 15, . . . are called triangular numbers because they can be represented by dots arranged to form equilateral triangles.

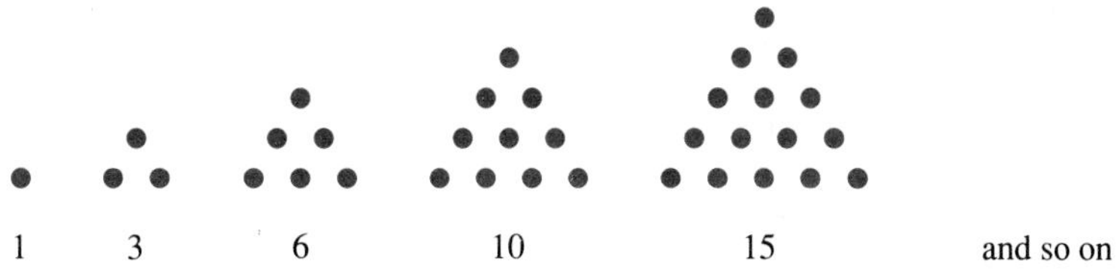

1. Find the next five triangular numbers.

2. Let n represent the position of a particular triangular number in the list ($n = 1$ for 1, $n = 2$ for 3, and so on). Show that for $n = 1, 2, \ldots, 10$, the nth triangular number $= \frac{n(n + 1)}{2}$.

1-9 Opposites and Absolute Values

Objective To use opposites and absolute values.

The paired points on the number line below are the same distance from the origin but on opposite sides of the origin. The origin is paired with itself.

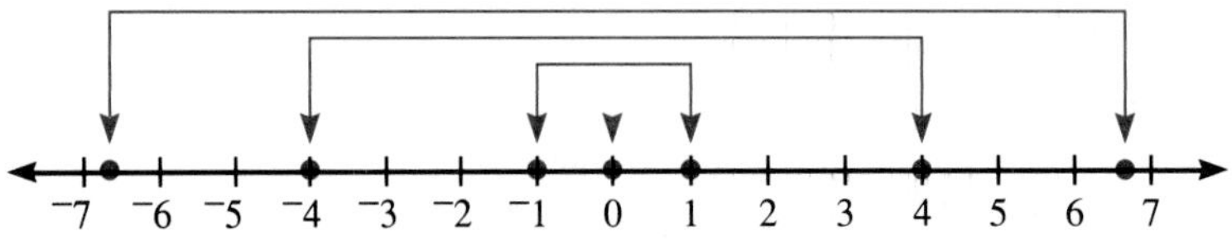

The coordinates of the paired points can also be paired:

0 with 0 $\quad$ $^{-}1$ with 1 $\quad$ $^{-}4$ with 4 $\quad$ $^{-}6.8$ with 6.8

Each number in a pair such as 4 and $^{-}4$ is called the **opposite** of the other number. The opposite of a is written $-a$. For example:

$-4 = {}^{-}4$, read "The opposite of four equals negative four."
$-({}^{-}4) = 4$, read "The opposite of negative four equals four."
$-0 = 0$, read "The opposite of zero equals zero."

The numerals -4 (lowered minus sign) and $^{-}4$ (raised minus sign) name the same number. Thus, -4 can mean "negative four" or "the opposite of four."

To simplify notation, lowered minus signs will be used to write negative numbers throughout the rest of this book.

Caution: $-a$, read "the opposite of a," is not necessarily a negative number. For example, if $a = -2$, then $-a = -(-2) = 2$.

1. If a is positive, then $-a$ is negative.
2. If a is negative, then $-a$ is positive.
3. If $a = 0$, then $-a = 0$.
4. The opposite of $-a$ is a; that is, $-(-a) = a$.

Example 1 Simplify: **a.** $-(7 + 9)$ **b.** $-(-1.8)$

Solution **a.** -16 **b.** 1.8

Example 2 Evaluate $-n + 14$, if $n = -8$.

Solution

$$\begin{aligned} -n + 14 &= -(-8) + 14 \\ &= 8 + 14 \\ &= 22 \quad \textbf{\textit{Answer}} \end{aligned}$$

In any pair of nonzero opposites, such as -4 and 4, one number is negative and the other is positive. The positive number of any pair of opposite nonzero real numbers is called the **absolute value** of each number in the pair.

The absolute value of a number a is denoted by $|a|$.

1. If a is positive, $\mathbf{|a| = a.}$ Example: $|8| = 8$
2. If a is negative, $\mathbf{|a| = -a.}$ Example: $|-8| = -(-8) = 8$
3. If a is zero, $\mathbf{|a| = 0.}$ Example: $|0| = 0$

The absolute value of a number may also be thought of as *the distance between the graph of the number and the origin on a number line*. The graphs of both 4 and -4 are 4 units from the origin.

Example 3 Simplify: **a.** $|-7| + |5|$ **b.** $|-15| + 8|-3|$

Solution **a.** $|-7| + |5| = 7 + 5$
$= 12$ ***Answer***

b. $|-15| + 8|-3| = 15 + 8(3)$
$= 15 + 24$
$= 39$ ***Answer***

Example 4 Solve $|x| = 3$.

Solution Think of which numbers are 3 units from the origin. They are 3 and -3, so the replacements for x that make $|x| = 3$ true are 3 and -3. Therefore $x = 3$ or $x = -3$.

$\therefore$ the solution set is $\{3, -3\}$. ***Answer***

Oral Exercises

Name the opposite and the absolute value of each number.

1. 7 **2.** 5 **3.** -1 **4.** -9 **5.** 24

6. -56 **7.** 0 **8.** 0.3 **9.** 6.5 **10.** $-2\frac{1}{3}$

Read each expression aloud. Then simplify.

11. $-(-2)$ **12.** $-\left(-\frac{1}{2}\right)$ **13.** $|12|$ **14.** $-(9 + 8)$

15. $-(9 - 8)$ **16.** $-[-(-8)]$ **17.** $-[-(-0)]$ **18.** $|-14|$

19. $|-3.4|$ **20.** $-|-4|$ **21.** $-|0|$ **22.** $6 - |-6|$

Complete each statement.

23. If n is a negative number, then $-n$ is a _?_ number.

24. If n is a positive number, then $-n$ is a _?_ number.

25. The only number whose absolute value is zero is _?_.

26. A real number that is its own opposite is _?_.

27. How many solutions are there for the equation $|x| = -7$? Explain.

Written Exercises

Simplify.

A

1. $-(7 + 5)$ **2.** $-(8 - 2)$ **3.** $-(13 - 13)$

4. $-(0 + 0)$ **5.** $[-(-9)] + 10$ **6.** $[-(-7)] + 1$

7. $6 + [-(-2)]$ **8.** $3 - [-(-1)]$ **9.** $8 + |-3|$

10. $|-11| + 4$ **11.** $|-8| + |6|$ **12.** $|2| + |-9|$

13. $\left|-\frac{3}{2}\right| + |0|$ **14.** $|-1| - |0|$

15. $|-0.7| + |-3.3|$ **16.** $|-2.8| + |2.8|$

17. $\left|\frac{1}{2}\right| + \left|-\frac{1}{2}\right|$ **18.** $\left|-\frac{3}{4}\right| - \left|\frac{1}{4}\right|$

19. $|6| - |6|$ **20.** $|6| - |-6|$

Complete using one of the symbols >, <, or = to make a true statement.

21. $-(-8)$ _?_ (-8) **22.** $-(-2)$ _?_ $|-3|$

23. $|-8|$ _?_ $|-10|$ **24.** $|-15|$ _?_ $|-6|$

25. $-|-8|$ _?_ -8 **26.** -3 _?_ $-|-3|$

Translate each statement into symbols.

27. The absolute value of negative five is greater than two.

28. Four is less than the absolute value of negative ten.

29. The opposite of negative two is greater than the opposite of negative one.

30. The opposite of eight is less than the opposite of four.

Solve each equation over the set of real numbers. If there is no solution, explain why there is none.

B

31. $|n| = 0$ **32.** $|p| = 2$ **33.** $|t| = \frac{1}{2}$ **34.** $|z| = 0.3$

35. $|a| = -2$ **36.** $|b| = -9$ **37.** $|-q| = 1$ **38.** $|-x| = 5$

Evaluate each expression if $a = 1.5$, $b = -2$, and $c = -1.7$.

39. $|a| + |b|$

40. $a + |-b|$

41. $4a - |b| - |c|$

42. $2|b| - |a| + |c|$

43. $(a + 8.5) - [(-b) + |c|]$

44. $(10.5 - a) - [|c| + (-b)]$

C 45. Two of the following statements are true and one is false. Which one is false? Explain why you think it's false.
 a. The absolute value of every real number is a positive number.
 b. There is at least one real number whose absolute value is zero.
 c. The absolute value of a real number is never a negative number.

Mixed Review Exercises

Simplify.

1. $6 - (2 + 3)$
2. $6 - 2 + 3$
3. $6 \div (2 + 1)$
4. $(4 - 2) \cdot (5 - 1)$
5. $7 - 2 \cdot 3$
6. $15 - 6 \div (2 + 1)$

Write a number to represent each situation. Then write the opposite of that number.

7. Three steps down
8. A bank withdrawal of $50
9. A profit of $1000
10. A pay raise of $.50 per hour

Self-Test 3

Vocabulary
origin (p. 31)
positive side (p. 31)
negative side (p. 31)
positive integer (p. 31)
negative integer (p. 31)
integers (p. 31)
whole numbers (p. 31)
positive number (p. 31)
negative number (p. 31)
graph (p. 31)
coordinate (p. 31)
real number (p. 32)
inequality symbols (p. 32)
opposite (p. 36)
absolute value (p. 37)

1. Graph the given numbers on the same number line: 2, $^{-}3$, 3, $^{-}2$ **Obj. 1-8, p. 31**

Simplify.

2. $-(4 + 3)$
3. $|-11| + |3|$ **Obj. 1-9, p. 36**
4. $-[-(-3)]$
5. $\left|-\frac{1}{3}\right| + \left|\frac{1}{3}\right|$

Check your answers with those at the back of the book.

Career Note / *Bilingual Math Teacher*

Math teachers with Spanish-speaking students might assign this problem:

Cuarenta obreros construyen en 28 días 1220 m de un camino. ¿Que longitud construiran 24 obreros en 28 días?

Here is a translation:

Forty workers construct 1220 m of road in 28 days. How many meters will 24 workers construct in 28 days?

Can you follow the solution below?

Solución:

40 obr. 1220 m

1 obr. $\frac{1220 \text{ m}}{40}$

24 obr. $\frac{1220 \text{ m} \times 24}{40} = 732 \text{ m}$

Bilingual teachers are fluent in two languages. For certification in public schools, a bachelor's degree with courses in education and mathematics is required.

Chapter Summary

1. A numerical expression represents a particular number. To simplify a numerical expression, replace it with the simplest name for its value.
2. A variable expression is evaluated by replacing each variable with a given value and simplifying the resulting numerical expression.
3. Grouping symbols are used to enclose an expression that should be simplified first. (When there are no grouping symbols, follow the steps listed on page 7.)
4. Replacing each variable in an open sentence by each of the values in its domain is a way to find solutions of the open sentence.
5. A word problem can often be solved by writing an equation based on the given facts and then solving the equation as outlined on page 27.
6. The positive numbers, the negative numbers, and zero make up the real numbers. These numbers can be paired with the points on a number line, thereby showing their order.
7. The opposite of a number a is written as $-a$. The positive number of any pair of opposite nonzero real numbers is called the absolute value of each number in the pair. The absolute value of a is written as $|a|$.

Chapter Review

Write the letter of the correct answer.

1. Simplify $36 \div (9 \cdot 4)$. **1-1**
a. 19 **b.** 0 **c.** 81 **d.** 1

2. Evaluate $(x + y) - 3z$ if $x = 7$, $y = 8$, and $z = 0$.
a. 12 **b.** 0 **c.** 15 **d.** 5

3. Evaluate $\frac{3x - y}{3(x - y)}$ if $x = 5$ and $y = 3$. **1-2**
a. 1 **b.** 2 **c.** 3 **d.** 6

4. Solve $9 = 3c - 6$ over the domain $\{0, 1, 2, 3, 4, 5\}$. **1-3**
a. $\{0\}$ **b.** $\{1\}$ **c.** $\{2\}$ **d.** $\{5\}$

5. Translate the following phrase into a variable expression. **1-4**
The difference of seven times n and three.
a. $7(n - 3)$ **b.** $3 + 7n$ **c.** $7n - 3$ **d.** $7(3 - n)$

6. Translate the following sentence into an equation. **1-5**
The product of nine and four less than n is twenty-seven.
a. $9n - 4 = 27$ **b.** $9(n - 4) = 27$
c. $9(4 - n) = 27$ **d.** $9 + 4 - n = 27$

7. Use the figure and the information beside it to write an equation involving x.
a. $14 + x + x = 28$ **b.** $x + 7 = 28$
c. $7x = 28$ **d.** $(7 + x)(7 + x) = 28$

8. Translate the following problem into an equation. **1-6**
(1) Katie spent \$1 more than Mark. (2) Together they spent \$5.
How much did Mark spend?
a. $m = m + 1$ **b.** $5 = k + (k + 1)$
c. $k + 1 = 5$ **d.** $(m + 1) + m = 5$

9. Wilt weighs $1\frac{1}{2}$ times as much as Anita. Together they weigh 250 lb. Find Anita's weight. Choices for Anita's weight: 90, 100, 105, 150 **1-7**
a. 90 lb **b.** 100 lb **c.** 105 lb **d.** 150 lb

10. If a surplus of 12 items is represented by 12, determine the opposite of that number and describe the measurement indicated by that opposite. **1-8**
a. 12; a gain of 12 items. **b.** $\frac{1}{12}$; each item is $\frac{1}{12}$ of the total.
c. $|12|$; there are 12 items. **d.** -12; a shortage of 12 items.

11. Solve $|m| = 4$ over the set of real numbers. **1-9**
a. no solution **b.** $\{-4\}$
c. $\{4\}$ **d.** $\{-4, 4\}$

12. Which of the following is a true statement?
a. $-5(0) > |-5| + 0$ **b.** $6 < -(-6)$
c. $-\frac{3}{4} > -\frac{5}{4}$ **d.** $6 - |-4| > 9$

Chapter Test

Simplify.

1. $5 + (15 \div 5)$ **2.** $(4 + 12) \cdot 3$ 1-1

3. $(64 \div 4) + 2$ **4.** $(12 - 7) \cdot 9$ 1-2

Evaluate.

5. $7x(y - z)$ if $x = 5$, $y = 8$, and $z = 6$.

6. Circumference of a circle: $2\pi r$
if $r = 49$
Use $\frac{22}{7}$ as an approximate value for π.

Solve if $x \in \{0, 1, 2, 3, 4, 5, 6\}$.

7. $56 = 14 + 7x$ **8.** $x \cdot x = 0$ **9.** $\frac{1}{2}x = \frac{x}{2}$ 1-3

10. Inga lives 3 miles more than twice as far from school as Brent does. If Brent lives b miles from school, then Inga lives _?_ miles from school. 1-4

11. Use the figure and the information below it to write an equation involving x. 1-5

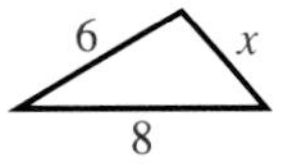

Perimeter = 18

12. Translate the following problem into an equation. 1-6
(1) Together Jon and Amy spent \$29 on a birthday gift.
(2) Jon spent \$5 more than Amy.
How much did each spend?

13. Kirsten built a rectangular corral with a fence on three sides. A side of the barn served as a short side of the corral. She used 130 m of fencing. The length of the corral was 20 m longer than the width. Find the dimensions of the corral. Choices for the width: 25, 30, 35 1-7

Graph the given numbers on a number line. Draw a separate line for each exercise. Then list the numbers in increasing order.

14. $2, 5, -2, -5$ **15.** $0, \frac{1}{4}, -3, 1$ 1-8

Simplify.

16. $|-2.1| + 3.2$ **17.** $-(-2.75)$ **18.** $-|4 + 1.5|$ 1-9

Complete using one of the symbols >, <, or = to make a true statement.

19. $-(-5)$ _?_ -4 **20.** $-|-10|$ _?_ $|8|$

Maintaining Skills

Perform the indicated operations.

Sample 1

$$\begin{array}{r} {}^{12\ \ 1} \\ 729.35 \\ 84. \\ +\ 68.29 \\ \hline 881.64 \end{array}$$

Sample 2

$$\begin{array}{r} 625.3 \\ \times\ 32.1 \\ \hline 6253 \\ 12506 \\ 18759 \\ \hline 20072.13 \end{array}$$

1. $\begin{array}{r} 0.0056 \\ 2.3 \\ 18.232 \\ +\ 9.41 \\ \hline \end{array}$

2. $\begin{array}{r} 42.31 \\ 8.79 \\ +\ 13.26 \\ \hline \end{array}$

3. $\begin{array}{r} 22.6 \\ 153.3 \\ +\ 201.8 \\ \hline \end{array}$

4. $\begin{array}{r} 27 \\ 6.25 \\ 108.1 \\ +\ 35.72 \\ \hline \end{array}$

5. $\begin{array}{r} 318 \\ \times\ 5.2 \\ \hline \end{array}$

6. $\begin{array}{r} 208.2 \\ \times\ 10.3 \\ \hline \end{array}$

7. $\begin{array}{r} 7.51 \\ \times\ 2.2 \\ \hline \end{array}$

8. $\begin{array}{r} 0.876 \\ \times\ 0.09 \\ \hline \end{array}$

9. $\begin{array}{r} 824.2 \\ \times\ 1.2 \\ \hline \end{array}$

10. $\begin{array}{r} 0.222 \\ \times\ 11.1 \\ \hline \end{array}$

11. $\begin{array}{r} 35.83 \\ +\ 9.96 \\ \hline \end{array}$

12. $\begin{array}{r} 20.05 \\ +\ 8.87 \\ \hline \end{array}$

Rewrite the fractions using their least common denominator.

Sample 3 $\frac{7}{8}$ and $\frac{2}{3}$

Solution The least common denominator is 24.

$$\frac{7}{8} = \frac{7}{8} \cdot \frac{3}{3} = \frac{21}{24} \qquad \frac{2}{3} = \frac{2}{3} \cdot \frac{8}{8} = \frac{16}{24}$$

13. $\frac{5}{8}$ and $\frac{3}{4}$

14. $\frac{2}{3}$ and $\frac{3}{5}$

15. $\frac{2}{7}$ and $\frac{2}{3}$

16. $\frac{5}{12}$ and $\frac{3}{2}$

Perform the indicated operations.

Sample 4 $\frac{3}{7} + \frac{2}{3}$

Solution $\frac{3}{7} + \frac{2}{3} = \frac{3}{7} \cdot \frac{3}{3} + \frac{2}{3} \cdot \frac{7}{7} = \frac{9}{21} + \frac{14}{21} = \frac{23}{21}$

Sample 5 $\frac{2}{5} \cdot \frac{7}{8}$

Solution $\frac{2}{5} \cdot \frac{7}{8} = \frac{\overset{1}{\cancel{2}} \cdot 7}{5 \cdot \underset{4}{\cancel{8}}} = \frac{7}{20}$

17. $\frac{3}{5} + \frac{4}{9}$

18. $\frac{2}{7} + \frac{1}{4}$

19. $\frac{3}{8} + \frac{5}{9}$

20. $\frac{7}{10} + \frac{2}{5}$

21. $\frac{5}{13} \cdot \frac{3}{4}$

22. $\frac{5}{9} \cdot \frac{3}{5}$

23. $\frac{10}{11} \cdot \frac{11}{12}$

24. $\frac{5}{6} \cdot \frac{15}{16}$

25. $\frac{2}{3} + \frac{3}{7}$

26. $\frac{9}{10} \cdot \frac{5}{3}$

27. $\frac{7}{8} \cdot \frac{14}{16}$

28. $\frac{9}{13} + \frac{2}{5}$

2 Working with Real Numbers

Cash registers fill and empty. The activity can be recorded and graphed on a computer. Positive and negative numbers show gains and losses.

Addition and Subtraction

2-1 Basic Assumptions

Objective To use number properties to simplify expressions.

This chapter develops rules for working with positive and negative numbers. The two principal operations are addition and multiplication. Subtraction is related to addition. Later in this chapter you will see that division is related to multiplication.

The rules for working with real numbers are based on several properties that you can accept as facts.

Closure Properties

For all real numbers a and b:

$\boldsymbol{a + b}$ is a unique real number.

$\boldsymbol{ab}$ is a unique real number.

The sum and product of any two real numbers are also real numbers. Moreover, they are *unique*. (This means there is one and only one possible answer when you add or multiply two real numbers.)

Commutative Properties

For all real numbers a and b:

$\boldsymbol{a + b = b + a}$ Example: $2 + 3 = 3 + 2$

$\boldsymbol{ab = ba}$ Example: $4 \cdot 5 = 5 \cdot 4$

The order in which you add or multiply two numbers does not affect the result.

Associative Properties

For all real numbers a, b, and c:

$\boldsymbol{(a + b) + c = a + (b + c)}$ Example: $(5 + 6) + 7 = 5 + (6 + 7)$

$\boldsymbol{(ab)c = a(bc)}$ Example: $(2 \cdot 3)4 = 2(3 \cdot 4)$

When you add or multiply any three real numbers, the grouping (or association) of the numbers does not affect the result.

In the sum $a + b$, a and b are called **terms.** In the product ab, a and b are called **factors.** To find the sum or product of several numbers, you work with two numbers at a time. Examples 1 and 2 show how the commutative and associative properties can sometimes help you to simplify expressions.

Example 1 Simplify $43 + 78 + 7$.

Solution The rule for order of operations tells you to add from left to right: $(43 + 78) + 7$. For mental math it is easiest to add 43 and 7 first. The steps you do almost without thinking about them are shown below. Each step is justified by a property.

$(43 + 78) + 7 = (78 + 43) + 7$	Commutative property of addition
$= 78 + (43 + 7)$	Associative property of addition
$= 78 + 50$	Substitution of 50 for $43 + 7$
$= 128$	Substitution of 128 for $78 + 50$

Example 2 Simplify: **a.** $7 + 9m + 5$ **b.** $(2x)(3y)(4z)$

Solution **a.** $7 + 9m + 5 = 9m + (7 + 5)$
$= 9m + 12$ ***Answer***

b. $(2x)(3y)(4z) = (2 \cdot 3 \cdot 4)(xyz)$
$= 24xyz$ ***Answer***

To simplify expressions, you often use the properties listed below.

Properties of Equality

For all real numbers a, b, and c:

Reflexive Property	$a = a$
Symmetric Property	If $a = b$, then $b = a$.
Transitive Property	If $a = b$ and $b = c$, then $a = c$.

Throughout the rest of this book, the domain of each variable is the set of real numbers unless otherwise specified.

Oral Exercises

Simplify each expression. Use the commutative and associative properties to reorder and regroup.

1. $(5 \cdot 83) \cdot 2$
2. $(47 + 39) + 3$
3. $17 + 89 + 3 + 11$
4. $4 + 5x + 2$
5. $9 + 3y + 4$
6. $a + 1 + b + 2$
7. $2(7a)$
8. $(5n)4$
9. $(3x)(2y)$
10. $(5a)(4b)$
11. $(3p)(5q)(2r)$
12. $r(3s)(4t)$

Name the property illustrated.

13. $3(14) = (14)3$

14. $(74 + 99) + 1 = 74 + (99 + 1)$

15. $\frac{1}{6} + 9 = 9 + \frac{1}{6}$

16. $\frac{1}{5}(15w) = \left(\frac{1}{5} \cdot 15\right)w$

17. $2.1 + y = y + 2.1$

18. $3(8 \cdot 0) = (3 \cdot 8)0$

19. If $7m = 35$, then $35 = 7m$.

20. If $3 + p = 12$, then $12 = 3 + p$.

21. Every real number is equal to itself.

22. $(5 + q) + (-3) = (q + 5) + (-3)$

23. If $w + 2 = 7$ and $7 = 5 + 2$, then $w + 2 = 5 + 2$.

24. There is only one real number that is the sum of 0.4 and 2.6.

25. $(r + 37) + 23 + s = r + (37 + 23) + s$

Written Exercises

Simplify.

A

1. $275 + 52 + 25 + 8$

2. $803 + 26 + 47 + 24$

3. $2 \cdot 21 \cdot 5 \cdot 3$

4. $50 \cdot 3 \cdot 3 \cdot 20$

5. $25 \cdot 74 \cdot 2 \cdot 2$

6. $8 \cdot 17 \cdot 9 \cdot 25$

7. $6\frac{1}{2} + 4\frac{1}{3} + 1\frac{1}{2} + \frac{2}{3}$

8. $56\frac{7}{8} + \frac{3}{5} + \frac{1}{8} + 4\frac{2}{5}$

9. $0.1 + 1.8 + 5.9 + 0.2$

10. $4.75 + 2.95 + 1.05 + 10.25$

11. $3 + 7y + 4$

12. $8 + 9z + 4$

13. $5 + 2x + 1$

14. $5 + 3w + 2$

15. $2(5a)$

16. $3(4n)$

17. $(7y)(5z)$

18. $(6m)(4n)$

19. $(8x)(2y)(3z)$

20. $(3p)(4q)(6r)$

Sample $5x + 3 + 4y + 7 = 5x + 4y + (3 + 7)$
$= 5x + 4y + 10$ ***Answer***

21. $a + 3 + b + 4$

22. $7 + x + y + 4$

23. $4a + 5 + 3n + 1$

24. $9m + 2 + 7n + 3$

B

25. $5 + 7x + 3 + 4y + z$

26. $8p + 4 + 3q + 87 + 96$

27. $(25b)(25c)(4d)(4e)$

28. $(5a)(5b)(5c)(2d)$

Name the property illustrated.

29. $pq = qp$

30. $(25 + 84) + 16 = 25 + (84 + 16)$

31. $x + y = y + x$

32. If $3.2 = 8y$, then $8y = 3.2$.

33. $(3r)s = 3(rs)$

34. If $x = -3$ and $-3 = z$, then $x = z$.

Name the property that justifies each step.

35. $57 + (25 + 13) = 57 + (13 + 25)$ **a.** ?
$= (57 + 13) + 25$ **b.** ?
$= 70 + 25$ **c.** ?
$= 95$ **d.** ?

36. $25 \cdot (37 \cdot 8) = 25 \cdot (8 \cdot 37)$ **a.** ?
$= (25 \cdot 8) \cdot 37$ **b.** ?
$= 200 \cdot 37$ **c.** ?
$= (100 \cdot 2) \cdot 37$ **d.** ?
$= 100 \cdot (2 \cdot 37)$ **e.** ?
$= 100 \cdot 74$ **f.** ?
$= 7400$ **g.** ?

C **37. a.** Find the values of $(7 - 4) - 2$ and $7 - (4 - 2)$.
b. Is subtraction of real numbers associative?

38. a. Find the values of $(48 \div 8) \div 2$ and $48 \div (8 \div 2)$.
b. Is division of real numbers associative?

39. Is division of real numbers commutative? Give a convincing argument to justify your answer.

40. A set of numbers is said to be *closed* under an operation if the result of combining *any* two numbers in the set results in a number that is also in the set. Decide whether or not each set is closed under the operation.
a. {positive integers}; $\div$
b. {odd integers}; $\times$
c. {odd integers}; $+$
d. {integers ending in 4 or 6}; $\times$

Mixed Review Exercises

Evaluate if $a = 3$, $x = 5$, $y = 2$, and $z = 6$.

1. $\dfrac{2a - y}{4y - z}$

2. $5z(x - y)$

3. $\dfrac{3a + x}{4z - (y + 1)}$

Evaluate if $a = -4$, $b = 2$, and $x = -3$.

4. $|a| + |x| - b$

5. $2|a| + 7|x|$

6. $2|x| - |b| + |a|$

7. $10|x| - 3|b|$

8. $2|b| + 3|a|$

9. $|-x - 1| - |b - 1|$

Challenge

Change for a dollar consisted of 15 coins (pennies, nickels, and dimes only). At least one of each type of coin was used. How was this done?

2-2 Addition on a Number Line

Objective To add real numbers using a number line or properties about opposites.

You already know how to add two positive numbers. You can use a number line to help you find the sum of *any* two real numbers. Moves to the left represent negative numbers; moves to the right represent positive numbers.

To find the sum of -3 and -6, first draw a number line. Then, starting at the origin, move your pencil 3 units to the left along your number line. From that position, move your pencil 6 more units to the left. Together, the two moves result in a move of 9 units to the left from the origin. The arrows in the diagram below show the moves.

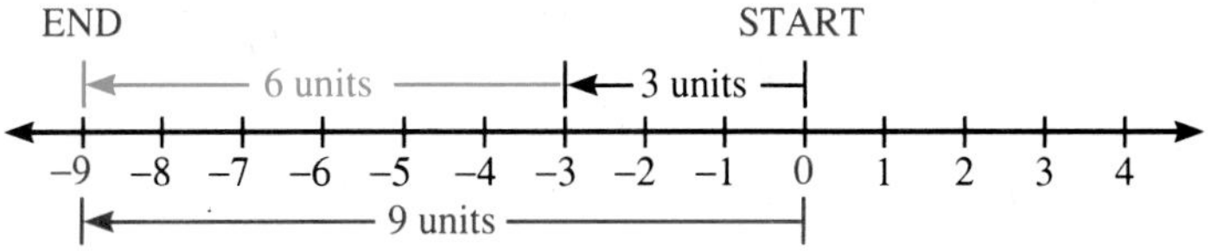

This shows that $-3 + (-6) = -9$.

Note the use of parentheses in "$-3 + (-6)$" to separate the plus sign that means "add" from the minus sign that is part of the numeral for negative six.

To find the sum $-3 + 6$, first move 3 units to the left from the origin. Then, from that position, move 6 units to the right. The two moves result in a move of 3 units to the right of the origin, as shown below.

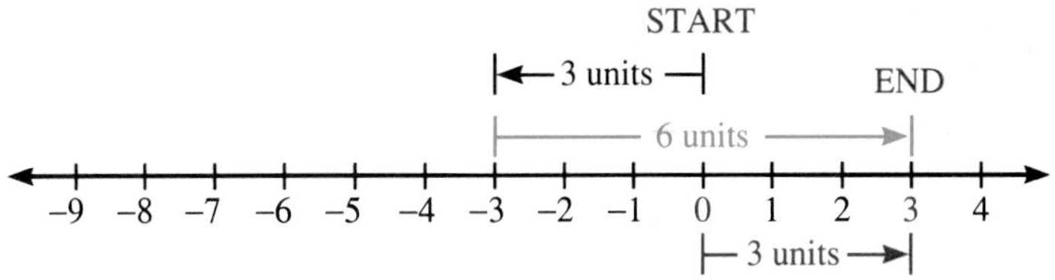

This shows that $-3 + 6 = 3$.

Example 1 Simplify $3 + (-6)$.

Solution

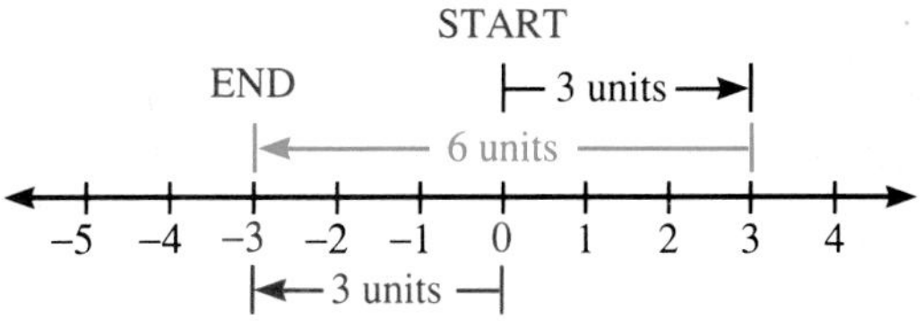

$3 + (-6) = -3$ ***Answer***

Can you visualize $-3 + 0$ on a number line? Think of "adding 0" to mean "moving no units." Then you can see that

$$-3 + 0 = -3 \quad \text{and} \quad 0 + (-3) = -3.$$

These equations illustrate the special property of zero for addition of real numbers: When 0 is added to any real number, the sum is *identical* to that number. We call 0 the **identity element for addition.**

Identity Property of Addition

There is a unique real number 0 such that for every real number a,

$$\mathbf{a + 0 = a \quad \text{and} \quad 0 + a = a.}$$

Think of adding a pair of opposites, such as 5 and -5, on a number line as shown below.

Example 2 Simplify: **a.** $5 + (-5)$ **b.** $-5 + 5$

Solution **a.**

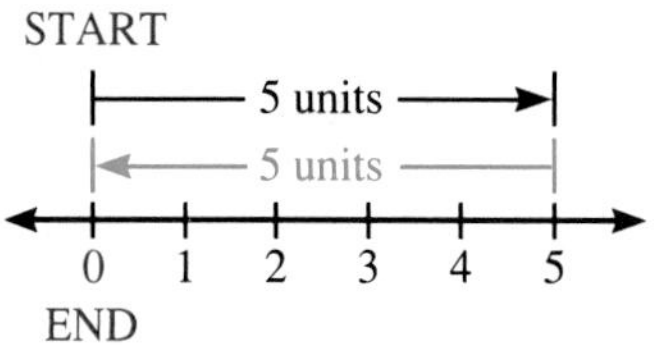

$5 + (-5) = 0$
Answer

b.

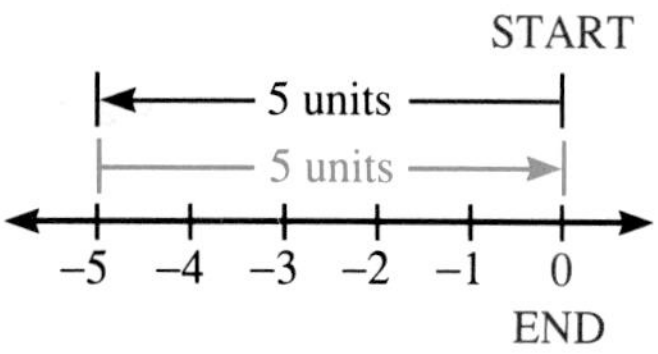

$-5 + 5 = 0$
Answer

The following property is a formal way of saying that the sum of any number and its opposite is zero.

Property of Opposites

For every real number a, there is a unique real number $-a$ such that

$$\mathbf{a + (-a) = 0 \quad \text{and} \quad (-a) + a = 0.}$$

A number and its opposite are called **additive inverses** of each other because their sum is zero, the identity element for addition. Thus, the numeral -5 can be read "negative five," "the opposite of five," or "the additive inverse of five."

From the properties of addition, we can prove the following property of the opposite of a sum. (See Exercise 39.)

Property of the Opposite of a Sum

For all real numbers a and b:

$$-(a + b) = (-a) + (-b)$$

The opposite of a sum of real numbers is equal to the sum of the opposites of the numbers.

Example 3 Simplify: **a.** $-8 + (-3)$ **b.** $14 + (-5)$

Solution **a.** $-8 + (-3) = -(8 + 3)$
$= -11$
Answer

b. $14 + (-5) = (9 + 5) + (-5)$
$= 9 + [5 + (-5)]$
$= 9 + 0$
$= 9$
Answer

Oral Exercises

Give an addition statement illustrated by each diagram.

1.

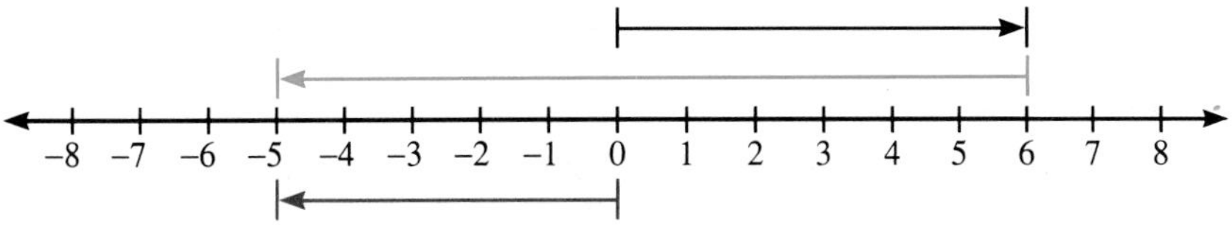

2.

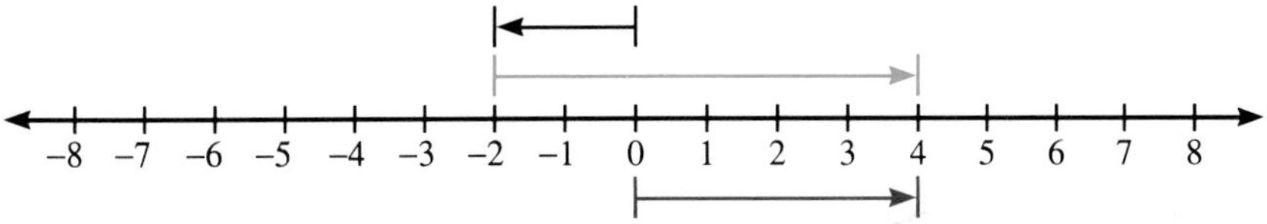

3.

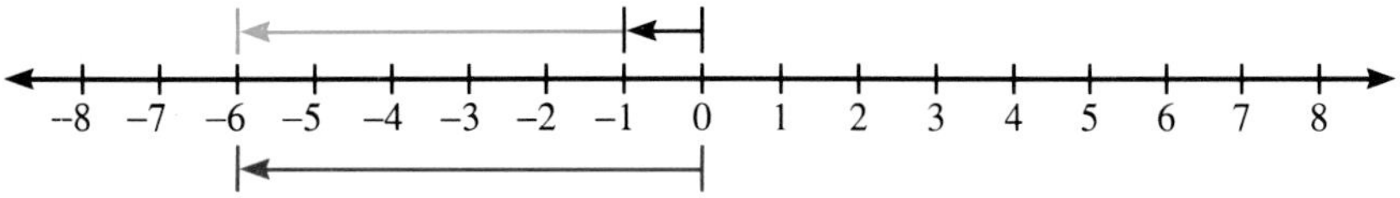

4.

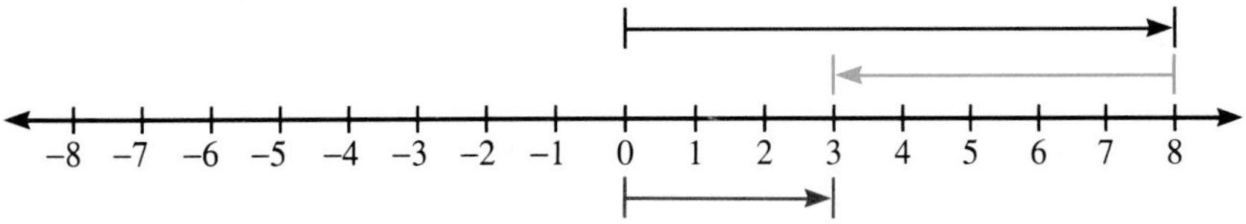

Simplify each expression. If necessary, think of moves along a number line.

5. $-2 + 0$
6. $0 + (-5)$
7. $-6 + 6$
8. $1 + (-1)$
9. $-4 + (-8)$
10. $-7 + (-1)$
11. $5 + (-1)$
12. $-4 + 9$
13. $-8 + 7$
14. $6 + (-4)$
15. $13 + (-18)$
16. $-1 + (-99)$
17. $102 + (-2)$
18. $-100 + 1$
19. $-10 + 0$
20. $-45 + 45$

Written Exercises

Simplify each expression. If necessary, draw a number line to help you.

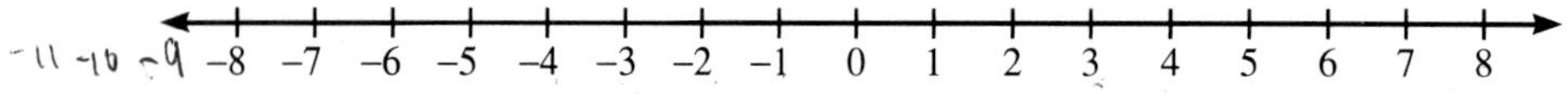

A

1. $(-4 + 8) + 7$
2. $(-5 + 8) + 2$
3. $(-9 + 11) + (-2)$
4. $(-3 + 5) + (-2)$
5. $[3 + (-10)] + 6$
6. $[5 + (-15)] + 7$
7. $[-9 + (-8)] + 9$
8. $[-5 + (-23)] + 5$
9. $22 + [6 + (-11)]$
10. $32 + [8 + (-16)]$
11. $-26 + [-2 + (-8)]$
12. $-5 + [-12 + (-18)]$
13. $[37 + (-7)] + [1 + (-1)]$
14. $(-3 + 3) + [8 + (-12)]$
15. $[0 + (-8)] + [-7 + (-23)]$
16. $(-4 + 4) + [18 + (-8)]$
17. $-3 + (-4) + (-6)$
18. $-5 + (-7) + (-9)$
19. $-4 + (-10) + 9 + (-6)$
20. $-17 + 12 + (-4) + (-13)$
21. $-3.2 + (-4.6) + 5.4$
22. $5.9 + (-3.2) + (-7.8)$
23. $-\frac{3}{2} + 5 + \left(-\frac{7}{2}\right)$
24. $-\frac{9}{5} + (-3) + \left(-\frac{6}{5}\right)$

Simplify.

Sample $2 + (-3) + n + 7$

Solution Use the commutative and associative properties to reorder and regroup.

$$\begin{aligned} 2 + (-3) + n + 7 &= -1 + n + 7 \\ &= n + (-1) + 7 \\ &= n + 6 \quad \textit{Answer} \end{aligned}$$

25. $3 + x + (-8)$
26. $y + (-2) + 7$
27. $2n + 5 + (-5)$
28. $8 + 3n + (-12)$
29. $13 + 5n + (-21)$
30. $-7 + (-z) + 12$

B **31.** $3a + (-7) + 4b + (-6)$

32. $-2 + 4n + 9 + (-7)$

33. $7x + (-3) + (-y) + (-7)$

34. $-8 + 7c + 11 + (-3)$

C **35.** $b + [a + (-b)]$

36. $-m + (k + m)$

37. $-m + [-h + (m + h)]$

38. $[a + (-b)] + [b + (-a)]$

39. a. Show that $(a + b) + [(-a) + (-b)] = 0$.

b. The opposite of $(a + b)$ is $-(a + b)$. What property tells you that $(a + b) + [-(a + b)] = 0$?

c. Explain how the equation in part (a) and the equation in part (b) can be used together to prove the property of the opposite of a sum.

Mixed Review Exercises

Simplify.

1. $7 + 21 \div 7$

2. $|-6| + |3|$

3. $6 - [-(-2)]$

4. $\frac{4 + (3 \cdot 2)}{2}$

5. $\left|\frac{1}{3}\right| + \left|-\frac{1}{3}\right|$

6. $\left|-\frac{2}{3}\right| - \left|\frac{1}{3}\right|$

7. $63 + 25 + 17 + 15$

8. $25 \cdot 5 \cdot 20$

9. $(4a)(2b)(3c)$

10. $5\frac{2}{3} + 3\frac{1}{4} + 2\frac{1}{3} + 6\frac{3}{4}$

11. $0.7 + 2.4 + 6.3$

12. $2 \cdot 17 \cdot 5$

Challenge

Recall (page 35) that the triangular numbers are 1, 3, 6, 10, 15, and so on. 1, 4, 9, 16, 25, . . . are called square numbers because they can be represented by dots arranged to form squares.

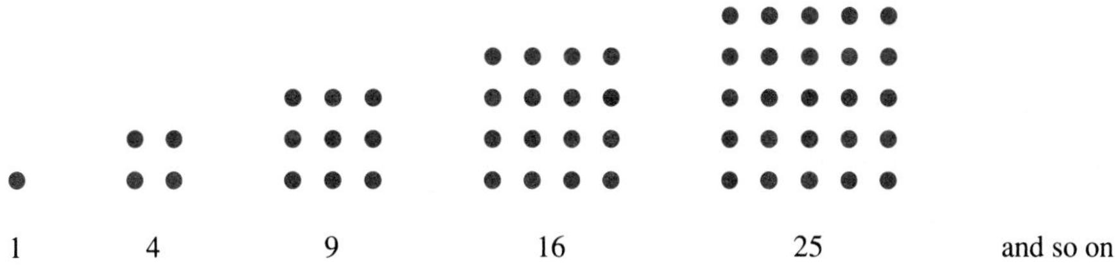

1. What are the next two square numbers after 25?

2. Verify that each square number from 4 to 100 is the sum of two consecutive triangular numbers.

3. Illustrate Exercise 2 by dividing the square array of dots shown above for 25 into two triangular arrays.

2-3 Rules for Addition

Objective To add real numbers using rules for addition.

Perhaps you have already discovered these rules for adding positive and negative numbers without using a number line.

Rules for Addition	*Examples*
1. If a and b are both positive, then $a + b = \lvert a\rvert + \lvert b\rvert$.	$3 + 7 = 10$
2. If a and b are both negative, then $a + b = -(\lvert a\rvert + \lvert b\rvert)$.	$-6 + (-2) = -(6 + 2) = -8$
3. If a is positive and b is negative and a has the greater absolute value, then $a + b = \lvert a\rvert - \lvert b\rvert$.	$8 + (-5) = 8 - 5 = 3$
4. If a is positive and b is negative and b has the greater absolute value, then $a + b = -(\lvert b\rvert - \lvert a\rvert)$.	$4 + (-9) = -(9 - 4) = -5$
5. If a and b are opposites, then $a + b = 0$.	$2 + (-2) = 0$

A positive and a negative number are said to have *opposite* signs. The rules for adding two nonzero numbers can be restated as follows:

If the numbers have the *same* sign, add their absolute values and prefix their common sign.

If the numbers have *opposite* signs, subtract the lesser absolute value from the greater and prefix the sign of the number having the greater absolute value.

Example 1 shows two methods for adding several numbers.

Example 1 Simplify $7 + (-9) + 15 + (-12)$.

Solution 1 Add the numbers in order from left to right.

$$\underbrace{\underbrace{\underbrace{7 + (-9)}_{-2} + 15}_{13} + (-12)}_{1}$$

1 ***Answer***

Solution 2

1. Add positive numbers.

$$\begin{array}{r} 7 \\ \underline{15} \\ 22 \end{array}$$

2. Add negative numbers.

$$\begin{array}{r} -9 \\ \underline{-12} \\ -21 \end{array}$$

3. Add the sums.

$$\begin{array}{r} 22 \\ \underline{-21} \\ 1 \end{array}$$

Answer

Example 2 Add.

$$\begin{array}{r} -291 \\ 379 \\ 185 \\ \underline{-462} \end{array}$$

Solution

1. Add positive numbers.

$$\begin{array}{r} 379 \\ \underline{185} \\ 564 \end{array}$$

2. Add negative numbers.

$$\begin{array}{r} -291 \\ \underline{-462} \\ -753 \end{array}$$

3. Add the sums.

$$\begin{array}{r} -753 \\ \underline{564} \\ -189 \end{array}$$

Answer

Oral Exercises

Add.

1. $\begin{array}{r} 7 \\ \underline{7} \end{array}$ **2.** $\begin{array}{r} -4 \\ \underline{-3} \end{array}$ **3.** $\begin{array}{r} -9 \\ \underline{6} \end{array}$ **4.** $\begin{array}{r} 13 \\ \underline{-8} \end{array}$ **5.** $\begin{array}{r} -12 \\ \underline{-27} \end{array}$ **6.** $\begin{array}{r} -1 \\ \underline{10} \end{array}$

7. $\begin{array}{r} -16 \\ \underline{7} \end{array}$ **8.** $\begin{array}{r} -4 \\ \underline{-19} \end{array}$ **9.** $\begin{array}{r} -13 \\ \underline{53} \end{array}$ **10.** $\begin{array}{r} 35 \\ \underline{-75} \end{array}$ **11.** $\begin{array}{r} -98 \\ \underline{36} \end{array}$ **12.** $\begin{array}{r} 65 \\ \underline{-37} \end{array}$

Simplify.

13. $-8 + (-13)$

14. $-18 + 8$

15. $14 + (-15)$

16. $15 + (-9)$

17. $3 + (-12)$

18. $-5 + 22$

19. $4 + (-1) + (-3)$

20. $-4 + (-9) + 9$

21. $-3 + (-6) + 9$

Written Exercises

Add.

A

1. $\begin{array}{r} -7 \\ \underline{6} \end{array}$ **2.** $\begin{array}{r} -5 \\ \underline{-6} \end{array}$ **3.** $\begin{array}{r} -34 \\ \underline{75} \end{array}$ **4.** $\begin{array}{r} 58 \\ \underline{-72} \end{array}$ **5.** $\begin{array}{r} 148 \\ -72 \\ -73 \\ \underline{-31} \end{array}$ **6.** $\begin{array}{r} -173 \\ 412 \\ -58 \\ \underline{-93} \end{array}$

Simplify.

7. $-12 + 7 + (-14) + 29$
8. $-16 + (-9) + 8 + 25$
9. $109 + (-56) + (-91) + 26$
10. $-206 + (-75) + 153 + 37$
11. $-[24 + (-5)] + [-(-2 + 6)]$
12. $[-7 + (-1)] + [-(-7 + 1)]$
13. $3.7 + 4.2 + (-2.3) + 0 + 6.4 + 12.8$
14. $-7.2 + 11.4 + (-8.1) + (-9.7) + 0.6$
15. $27 + 43 + (-14) + (-57) + 5 + (-36) + (-14)$
16. $46 + (-33) + 18 + 0 + (-93) + (-2) + (-34)$
17. $-\frac{1}{3} + \left(-1\frac{2}{3}\right) + 2$
18. $3 + \left(-\frac{5}{2}\right) + \left(-\frac{7}{2}\right)$
19. $-1\frac{3}{4} + 2\frac{1}{4}$
20. $-3\frac{2}{5} + \left(-1\frac{4}{5}\right)$
21. $-\frac{7}{8} + \left(-\frac{11}{8}\right)$
22. $\frac{16}{3} + \left(-\frac{10}{3}\right)$

Sample $5 + (-7) + (-x) + (-10) = -x + 5 + (-7) + (-10) = -x + (-12)$

23. $-3 + x + (-5) + 4$
24. $2 + (-9) + (-y) + (-11)$
25. $-4 + a + 4 + (-a)$
26. $21 + 4b + (-17) + (-12)$
27. $-[8 + (-5)] + (-c) + 3$
28. $-(-9) + 2y + (-9) + 6$
29. $x + 5 + [(-x) + (-14)]$
30. $4x + [8 + (-5) + (-7)]$

Evaluate each expression if $x = -3$, $y = 6$, and $z = -4$.

B 31. $x + y + (-1)$
32. $-21 + x + z$
33. $-15 + (-x) + y$
34. $-z + (-8) + y$
35. $1 + (-y) + z$
36. $-y + (-11) + x$
37. $|x + y + z|$
38. $|x + (-y) + z|$
39. $-|x + z + (-8)|$

Simplify.

C 40. $-b + [-a + (a + b)]$
41. $-(-x + y) + y$
42. $r + s + [-(r + s + t)]$
43. $a + [-(a + b)]$

Problems

a. **Write a positive number or a negative number to represent each situation.**
b. **Compute the sum of the numbers.**
c. **Answer each question.**

Sample A helicopter flying at an altitude of 2860 ft descended 120 ft and then rose 350 ft. What was its new altitude?

Solution **a.** 2860, −120, 350 **b.** $2860 + (-120) + 350 = 3090$ **c.** 3090 ft

A 1. An elevator started at the eighteenth floor. It then went down seven floors and up nine floors. At what floor was the elevator then located?

2. A submarine descended to a level 230 m below the surface of the ocean. Later it ascended 95 m and then dove 120 m. What was the new depth of the submarine?

3. Moira has $784 in her checking account. She deposits $96 and then writes two checks, one for $18 and the other for $44. What is the new balance in the account?

4. On five plays a football team lost 3 yards, gained 15, gained 8, lost 9, and lost 4. What was the net yardage on the plays?

5. In September, the Drama Club treasury contained $698. The club then presented a fall play, for which they paid a royalty of $250. Scenery and costumes cost $1684, and programs and other expenses totaled $1316. The sale of tickets brought in $3700. How much money was in the treasury after the play was presented?

6. The stock of the Computer Research Corporation opened on Monday at $32 per share. It lost $5 that day, dropped another $3 on Tuesday, but then gained $4 on Wednesday and $2 on Thursday. On Friday it was unchanged. What was its closing price for the week?

7. During a four-day period at the Hotel Gran Via, the numbers of guests checking in and out were as follows: 32 in and 27 out, 28 in and 31 out, 12 in and 18 out, and 16 in and 25 out. How did the number of guests in the hotel at the end of the fourth day compare with the number at the start of the four-day period?

8. During their first year after opening a restaurant, the Habibs had a loss of $14,250. In their second year of operation, they broke even. During their third and fourth years, they had gains of $18,180 and $29,470, respectively. What was the restaurant's net gain or loss over the four-year period?

9. A delivery truck traveled 5 blocks west, 3 blocks north, 8 blocks east, and 12 blocks south. After this, where was the truck relative to its starting point?

10. During an unusual storm, the temperature fell 8° C, rose 5° C, fell 4° C, and then rose 6° C. If the temperature was 32° C at the outset of the storm, what was it after the storm was over?

B 11. The lowest point in Death Valley is 86 m below sea level. A helicopter flying at an altitude of 41 m above this point climbed 28 m and then dropped 37 m. At what altitude relative to sea level was it then flying?

12. The rim of a canyon is 156 ft below sea level. If a stranded hiker 71 ft below the rim fired a warning flare that rose 29 ft, to what altitude relative to sea level would the flare rise?

13. Leaving Westwood at 1:00 P.M., Coretta flew to Bay View. The flight took 1.5 hours, but the time zone for Bay View is 2 hours earlier than Westwood's zone. What time was it in Bay View when Coretta landed?

14. A passenger on a train traveling at 135 km/h walks toward the back of the train at a rate of 7 km/h. What is the passenger's rate of travel with respect to the ground?

Solve.

C 15. Wes charged $175 for clothing and $287 for camera equipment. He then made two payments of $50 each to his charge account. The next bill showed that he owed a balance of $495.25, including $11.50 in interest charges. How much did Wes owe on the account before making his purchase?

16. The volume of water in a tank during a five-day period changed as follows: up 375 L, down 240 L, up 93 L, down 164 L, and down 157 L. What was the volume of water in the tank at the beginning of the five-day period if the final volume was 54 L?

Mixed Review Exercises

Simplify.

1. $5 - 9 \div 3$
2. $3 \cdot 5 \cdot 4 \cdot 20$
3. $(6 - 4 \div 2) \cdot 3 + 1$
4. $|-7| - 6$
5. $|-1.2| + 1.2$
6. $|-15| - |-6|$
7. $\frac{7 \cdot 6 + 3 \cdot 7}{(5 + 2)}$
8. $6\frac{1}{7} + 5\frac{2}{3} + 8\frac{6}{7}$
9. $3.2 + 1.0 + 4.8$
10. $[15 + (-5)] + 6$
11. $(-8 + 4) + (-6)$
12. $-3 + (-9) + 6 + (-5)$

Calculator Key-In

Most calculators have a change-sign key, +/−, that will change a number from positive to negative or from negative to positive. When adding two or more positive and negative numbers, you can add in the usual order, making a number negative by hitting the change-sign key after entering the number.

Exercises

Use your calculator to find the sum.

1. $198 + (-217)$
2. $-612 + 38$
3. $-418 + 27$
4. $-115.8 + 22.4$
5. $13.8 + (-21.9)$
6. $-319.2 + 45.5$

2-4 Subtracting Real Numbers

Objective To subtract real numbers and to simplify expressions involving differences.

The first column below lists a few examples of the subtraction of 2. The second column lists related examples of the addition of -2.

Subtracting 2	Adding -2
$3 - 2 = 1$	$3 + (-2) = 1$
$4 - 2 = 2$	$4 + (-2) = 2$
$5 - 2 = 3$	$5 + (-2) = 3$
$6 - 2 = 4$	$6 + (-2) = 4$

Comparing the entries in the two columns shows that subtracting 2 gives the same result as adding the opposite of 2. This suggests the following:

Definition of Subtraction

For all real numbers a and b, the **difference** $a - b$ is defined by

$$\mathbf{a - b = a + (-b).}$$

To subtract b, add the opposite of b.

Example 1 Simplify.

a. $3 - 12$ **b.** $-7 - 1$ **c.** $-4 - (-10)$ **d.** $y - (y + 6)$

Solution

a. $3 - 12 = 3 + (-12) = -9$

b. $-7 - 1 = -7 + (-1) = -8$

c. $-4 - (-10) = -4 + 10 = 6$

d. $y - (y + 6) = y + [-(y + 6)] = y + (-y) + (-6) = -6$

Note that in part (d), the property of the opposite of a sum is used. The opposite of $(y + 6)$ is $-y + (-6)$.

Using the definition of subtraction, you may replace any difference with a sum. For example,

$$12 - 8 - 7 + 4 \quad \text{means} \quad 12 + (-8) + (-7) + 4.$$

As shown at the right, you may simplify this expression by grouping from left to right. This method is convenient if you are doing the work mentally or with a calculator.

$$\underbrace{\underbrace{\underbrace{12 + (-8)}_{4} + (-7)}_{-3} + 4}_{1}$$

For written work, you may want to group positive terms and negative terms:

$$\begin{aligned} 12 - 8 - 7 + 4 &= 12 + (-8) + (-7) + 4 \\ &= (12 + 4) + [(-8) + (-7)] \\ &= 16 + (-15) = 1 \end{aligned}$$

Certain sums are usually replaced by differences. For example,

$9 + (-2x)$ is usually simplified to $9 - 2x$.

Example 2 Simplify: **a.** -30 decreased by -19
b. The opposite of the difference between a and b

Solution **a.** First write the expression: $-30 - (-19)$
Then simplify: $-30 - (-19) = -30 + 19 = -11$ ***Answer***

b. First write the expression: $-(a - b)$. Then simplify:

$-(a - b) = -[a + (-b)]$	(Definition of subtraction)
$= (-a) + [-(-b)]$	(Property of the opposite of a sum)
$= -a + b$ ***Answer***	(Property of opposites)

The property of the opposite of a sum and the definition of subtraction produce this useful result: *When you find the opposite of a sum or a difference, you change the sign of each term of the sum or difference.*

$$\begin{aligned} -(a + b) &= (-a) + (-b) \\ &= -a - b \end{aligned} \qquad \begin{aligned} -(a - b) &= (-a) - (-b) \\ &= -a + b \end{aligned}$$

Now that you understand the reasoning behind each step, you can simplify some expressions mentally and write only the results, as shown in Example 3.

Example 3 Simplify: **a.** $-(x - 4)$ **b.** $-(-c + 5 - n)$ **c.** $x - (y - 2)$

Solution **a.** $-x + 4$ **b.** $c - 5 + n$ **c.** $x - y + 2$

Caution: Subtraction is *not* commutative.
$8 - 3 = 5$ but $3 - 8 = -5$

Subtraction is *not* associative.
$(6 - 4) - 3 = -1$ but $6 - (4 - 3) = 5$

Oral Exercises

Simplify.

1. $2 - 4$	**2.** $19 - 12$	**3.** $7 - 5$	**4.** $7 - 27$
5. $0 - 8$	**6.** $0 - (-6)$	**7.** $-16 - 0$	**8.** $-8 - 2$
9. $3 - (-1)$	**10.** $7 - (-3)$	**11.** $-9 - (-13)$	**12.** $-6 - (-4)$
13. $x - (x + 1)$	**14.** $n - (n + 4)$	**15.** $-(a - 3)$	**16.** $-(w - 5)$

Written Exercises

Simplify.

A

1. $25 - 213$
2. $154 - 281$
3. $39 - (-32)$
4. $47 - (-49)$
5. $-19 - (-3)$
6. $-25 - (-9)$
7. $-2.8 - 4.4$
8. $-5.1 - 6.7$
9. $174 - (-24)$
10. $-106 - (-95)$
11. $1.91 - (-1.03)$
12. $2.95 - (-2.55)$
13. -21 decreased by 6
14. -6 decreased by -32
15. 24 less than -1
16. 15 less than -3
17. $132 - (72 - 61)$
18. $275 - (80 - 65)$
19. $234 - (56 - 87)$
20. $193 - (30 - 75)$
21. $(22 - 33) - (55 - 66)$
22. $(42 - 50) - (73 - 60)$
23. $(3 - 8) - (-15 + 19)$
24. $(42 - 33) - (-7 + 12)$
25. $106 - 492 + 776$
26. $910 - 939 - 201$
27. $12 - (-9) - [5 - (-4)]$
28. $-15 - 6 - [-7 - (-10)]$
29. $4 - 5 + 8 - 17 + 31$
30. $18 - 14 + 15 + 7 - 26$
31. $-6 - 19 + 4 - 8 + 20$
32. $-11 - 43 + 1 - 9 + 30$
33. The difference between 81 and -6, decreased by -29
34. -54 decreased by the difference between -37 and 15
35. -46 decreased by the difference between -23 and -61
36. The difference between -59 and 12, decreased by 72
37. $-(x - 7)$
38. $-(4 - y)$
39. $x - (x + 5)$
40. $8 - (y + 8)$
41. $5 - (b - 7)$
42. $n - (4 + n)$

Simplify.

B

43. The sum of 8 and y subtracted from z
44. The opposite of the sum of -7 and y
45. Five less than the difference between 7 and z
46. The opposite of the difference between x and 4
47. $7 + y - (7 - y) - y$
48. $s - (-3) - [s + (-3)] - 3$
49. $h + 8 - (-9 + h)$
50. $-(10 - k) - (k - 12)$
51. $(\pi + 2)$ subtracted from $(\pi - 17)$
52. $(7 - 2\pi)$ subtracted from $(11 - 2\pi)$

Evaluate each expression if $a = -4$, $b = 5$, and $c = -1$.

53. $c - |a - b|$
54. $b - c - |a|$
55. $|c - a| - b$
56. $|b - c| - a$
57. $a - |c| - (|a| - b)$
58. $|c| - b - (|a| - c)$
59. $(a - |c|) - |a| - b$
60. $(|c| - b) - |a| - c$

In Exercise 61, name the definition or property that justifies each step.

C **61. a.** $b + (a - b) = b + [a + (-b)]$ **a.** ___?___
$= b + [(-b) + a]$ **b.** ___?___
$= [b + (-b)] + a$ **c.** ___?___
$= 0 + a$ **d.** ___?___
$= a$ **e.** ___?___

b. Use the result of part (a) to complete the following sentence:
$a - b$ is the number to add to b to obtain ___?___.

62. Suppose you are told that $b - a$ *is the opposite of* $a - b$. Explain how adding $b - a$ to $a - b$ can convince you that this statement is true.

Problems

Express the answer to each question as the difference between two real numbers. Compute the difference. Answer the question and interpret the sign of the answer.

Sample If astronauts traveled from the sunny side of the moon to the dark side, they would find the temperature 220° C lower than on the sunny side. If the temperature on the sunny side was 90° C, what was it on the dark side?

Solution $90 - 220 = -130$
The temperature on the dark side of the moon is 130 degrees *below* 0° C.

A **1.** Mars is 141.5 millions of miles from the sun. Earth is 48.6 millions of miles closer to the sun than Mars is. How far is Earth from the sun?

2. The highest recorded weather temperature on Earth is 58.0° C. The difference between that record and the lowest recorded weather temperature is 146.3° C. What is the record low?

3. The Roman poet Virgil was born in 70 B.C. How old was he on his birthday in 42 B.C.?

4. Pythagoras, the Greek mathematician, was born in 582 B.C. and died on his birthday in 497 B.C. How old was he when he died?

5. Krypton boils at 153.4° below 0° C and melts at 157.2° below 0° C. What is the difference between its boiling and melting points?

6. Including the wind-chill factor, the temperature at Council Bluffs was eight degrees below zero Celsius at midnight and seventeen below zero at dawn. What was the change in temperature?

7. Becky Kasai took the subway from a stop 52 blocks east of Central Square to a stop 39 blocks west of Central Square. How many blocks did she ride?

8. Glynis drove a golf ball from a point 126 yd north of the ninth hole to a point 53 yd south of the hole. How far did the ball travel?

9. Find the difference in altitude between Mt. Rainier, Washington, 4392 m above sea level, and Death Valley, California, 86 m below sea level.

10. The difference in altitude between the highest and lowest points in Louisiana is 164.592 m. If Driskill Mountain, the highest point, is 163.068 m above sea level, what is the altitude of New Orleans, the lowest point?

B 11. In 1972, the Apollo space mission land rover weighed about 475 lb on Earth. Because of low gravity, it weighed 396 lb less on the moon. How much did the land rover weigh on the moon?

12. Alonzo has \$22; Brad has \$29; Caryl has \$2; and Diane has \$13. Alonzo owes Brad \$15 and Caryl \$3. Brad owes Caryl \$18 and Diane \$7. Diane owes Caryl \$11 and Alonzo \$5. When all debts are paid, how much money will each have?

Mixed Review Exercises

Simplify.

1. $|-9| + |7|$
2. $18 \cdot 3 \cdot 5 \cdot 2$
3. $4 + 7x + 3y + 5$
4. $\left|-\frac{2}{5}\right| - \left|\frac{1}{5}\right|$
5. $-\frac{5}{4} + \left(-\frac{7}{4}\right)$
6. $1\frac{1}{3} + \left(-3\frac{2}{3}\right)$
7. $[6 + (-12)] + 9$
8. $4.2 - 0.5 + (-3.2)$
9. $-6 + [-8 + (-4)]$
10. $-3.2 + 74 + (-2.8)$
11. $-41 + (-28) + 32 + 49$
12. $3 + (-7) + (-12) + (-x)$

Self-Test 1

Vocabulary

closure properties (p. 45)
commutative properties (p. 45)
associative properties (p. 45)
terms (p. 46)
factors (p. 46)
reflexive property (p. 46)
symmetric property (p. 46)
transitive property (p. 46)
identity element for addition (p. 50)
identity property of addition (p. 50)
property of opposites (p. 50)
additive inverses (p. 50)
property of the opposite of a sum (p. 51)
difference (p. 59)
subtraction (p. 59)

(Self-Test continues on next page.)

Simplify.

1. $9 \cdot 4 \cdot 7 \cdot 25$		2. $82 + 31 + x + 18$	**Obj. 2-1, p. 45**
3. $3 + (-4)$	4. $(-5 + 6) + 4$	5. $4 + 2x + (-5)$	**Obj. 2-2, p. 49**
6. $-13 + (-7)$		7. $-201 + (-19) + 20 + 180$	**Obj. 2-3, p. 54**
8. $12 - 26$		9. $9 - (y - 9)$	**Obj. 2-4, p. 59**

Check your answers with those at the back of the book.

Reading Algebra / Independent Study

When you read an algebra textbook, it helps to know the goals of a lesson. The lesson title and the lesson objective (directly below the title) give you a good idea of what you should know when you have finished reading.

Have you noticed that it's useful to skim each lesson first? As you read, look for important words, phrases, and ideas that are in **heavy type,** in *italics,* or in boxes. You need to know the highlighted ideas in order to understand the lesson. The glossary and index can help you find more information about important ideas.

Working through each example in a lesson can help you do some of the Oral and Written Exercises on your own. Doing the exercises will let you know whether you understand the lesson objectives.

The Self-Tests, with answers at the back of the book, will help you review a group of lessons. The Chapter Reviews, Chapter Tests, Cumulative Reviews, Mixed Reviews, and Mixed Problem Solving Reviews will also give you a good idea of your progress. If you do not understand a concept, and re-reading doesn't seem to help, it is a good idea to make a note of the concept so that you can discuss it with your teacher.

Exercises

Skim through Lessons 4-2 and 4-3 (pages 146–154). Then answer the following questions.

1. What should you be able to do when you have finished reading the text of these lessons?
2. What new words or phrases are introduced?
3. What is a monomial? a polynomial? Find the definitions of these words in your book.
4. Suppose that you had forgotten the definition of the term *variable*. Where could you look it up? On what page of your textbook is this word first used?
5. Lesson 4-2 covers adding and subtracting polynomials. Where could you find information about addition and subtraction in general?

2-5 The Distributive Property

Objective To use the distributive property to simplify expressions.

The cost of a certain model of cross-country skis is \$90. A pair of ski poles costs \$12. When Rita bought her family 4 sets of skis and poles, the total cost could have been calculated in two ways:

(1) Total cost:
$4 \times$ (cost of one set of skis and poles)
$4 \times (90 + 12) = 4 \times 102 = \$408$

(2) Total cost:
($4 \times$ cost of skis) + ($4 \times$ cost of poles)
$(4 \cdot 90) + (4 \cdot 12) = 360 + 48 = \$408$

Either way you compute it, the total cost is the same:

$$4(90 + 12) = (4 \cdot 90) + (4 \cdot 12)$$

Note that 4 is *distributed* as a multiplier of each term of the sum 90 + 12. This example illustrates another important property that we use when working with real numbers.

Distributive Property (of multiplication with respect to addition)

For all real numbers a, b, and c:

$$a(b + c) = ab + ac \quad \text{and} \quad (b + c)a = ba + ca.$$

Example 1 shows how the distributive property can make mental math easier.

Example 1

a. $5 \cdot 83 = 5(80 + 3)$
$= (5 \cdot 80) + (5 \cdot 3)$
$= 400 + 15$
$= 415$ ***Answer***

b. $6(9.5) = 6(9 + 0.5)$
$= (6 \cdot 9) + (6 \cdot 0.5)$
$= 54 + 3$
$= 57$ ***Answer***

c. $8\left(2\frac{1}{4}\right) = 8\left(2 + \frac{1}{4}\right)$
$= (8 \cdot 2) + \left(8 \cdot \frac{1}{4}\right)$
$= 16 + 2 = 18$ ***Answer***

Example 2 **a.** $5(x + 2) = 5 \cdot x + 5 \cdot 2$
$= 5x + 10$ ***Answer***

b. $(6y + 7)4 = 6y \cdot 4 + 7 \cdot 4$
$= 24y + 28$ ***Answer***

Multiplication is distributive with respect to subtraction as well as addition. For example,

$$2(8 - 3) = 2 \cdot 8 - 2 \cdot 3 = 16 - 6 = 10 \quad \text{and} \quad 4(x - 6) = 4 \cdot x - 4 \cdot 6 = 4x - 24.$$

This principle is stated in general below and will be proved in the next lesson. (See Exercise 60, page 73.)

Distributive Property (of multiplication with respect to subtraction)

For all real numbers a, b, and c:

$$a(b - c) = ab - ac \quad \text{and} \quad (b - c)a = ba - ca.$$

By applying the symmetric property of equality, the distributive properties of multiplication can also be written in the following forms:

$$ab + ac = a(b + c) \qquad ba + ca = (b + c)a$$
$$ab - ac = a(b - c) \qquad ba - ca = (b - c)a$$

For example, the diagram below illustrates that

$$(3 \cdot 4) + (3 \cdot 2) = 3(4 + 2).$$

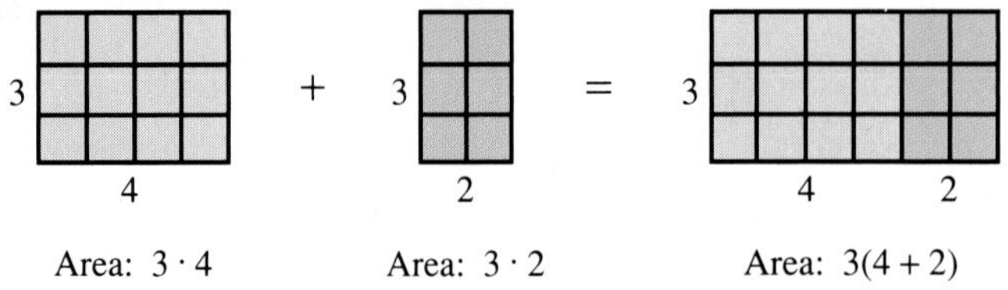

Example 3 Simplify $75 \cdot 17 + 25 \cdot 17$.

Solution
$$75 \cdot 17 + 25 \cdot 17 = (75 + 25)17 = (100)17 = 1700$$ ***Answer***

Example 4 Show that $9x + 5x = 14x$ for every real number x.

Solution

$9x + 5x = (9 + 5)x$	Distributive property
$= 14x$	Substitution principle

The properties of real numbers and equality guarantee that for all values of the variable x, $9x + 5x$ and $14x$ represent the same number. Therefore the two expressions are **equivalent.**

The expression $9x + 5x$ has two terms. The expression $14x$ has one term. Replacing an expression containing variables by an equivalent expression with as few terms as possible is called **simplifying the expression.**

Example 5 Simplify: **a.** $8y - 6y$ **b.** $3n + 7n - 4n$ **c.** $8(n - 1) + 3n$

Solution

a. $8y - 6y = (8 - 6)y$
$= 2y$ ***Answer***

b. $3n + 7n - 4n = 10n - 4n$
$= 6n$ ***Answer***

c. $8(n - 1) + 3n = 8 \cdot n - 8 \cdot 1 + 3n$
$= 8n - 8 + 3n$
$= 11n - 8$ ***Answer***

Oral Exercises

Use the distributive property and mental math to simplify each expression.

1. $2(30 + 5)$ **2.** $7(40 + 1)$ **3.** $4(20 - 1)$ **4.** $5(60 - 2)$

5. $3 \cdot 99$ **6.** $8 \cdot 3\frac{1}{4}$ **7.** $10\left(3\frac{1}{5}\right)$ **8.** $5(7.2)$

For each expression give an equivalent expression without parentheses.

9. $5(a + 2)$ **10.** $3(x + 4)$ **11.** $6(n + 3)$ **12.** $4(a - 1)$

13. $5(2t - 3)$ **14.** $9(3n - 2)$ **15.** $8(b - c)$ **16.** $7(m + n)$

Simplify.

17. $6x + 16x$ **18.** $12y + 8y$ **19.** $2a + 5a$

20. $3b + b$ **21.** $(-2)x + (-6)x$ **22.** $(-3)y + (-8)y$

23. $11k - 15k$ **24.** $2c - 4c$ **25.** $3(1 + z) + 7$

Written Exercises

Simplify.

A **1.** $8(30 + 1)$ **2.** $7(60 + 2)$ **3.** $5(70 - 2)$ **4.** $9(20 - 1)$

5. $4(50 - 3)$ **6.** $6(80 + 5)$ **7.** $4 \cdot 52$ **8.** $6 \cdot 64$

9. $4(9.5)$ **10.** $6(9.9)$ **11.** $14\left(1\frac{1}{7}\right)$ **12.** $15\left(4\frac{3}{5}\right)$

Simplify.

13. $30 \cdot 18 + 70 \cdot 18$
14. $11 \cdot 43 + 89 \cdot 43$
15. $(13 \cdot 27) - (13 \cdot 27)$
16. $(64 \cdot 81) + (36 \cdot 81)$
17. $(0.75)(32) + (0.25)(32)$
18. $(3.6)(25) - (1.6)(25)$
19. $5a + 2a$
20. $7x + 6x$
21. $13y - 4y$
22. $2n + (-8)n$
23. $(-3)p + 7p$
24. $(-8)n - 7n$

For each expression write an equivalent expression without parentheses.

25. $3(x + 2)$
26. $5(a + 7)$
27. $4(n - 2)$
28. $8(b - 5)$
29. $6(3n + 2)$
30. $7(5n + 3)$
31. $3(j - k)$
32. $2(3x - y)$
33. $(3n + 7)2$
34. $(4x + 3)3$
35. $(2x + 3y)5$
36. $(6m + 7n)2$

Simplify.

37. $3a + 7 + 5a$
38. $6n + 1 + 3n$
39. $8n - 5 + 4n$
40. $3p + 8 - 3p$
41. $8y - 7y + 4$
42. $y + 9z - 6z$

Sample $8x + y + 2x + 6y = (8x + 2x) + (y + 6y)$
$= 10x + 7y$ ***Answer***

43. $2a + b + 5a + 3b$
44. $4c + d + 3c + 2d$
45. $3s + 5t - t - 2s$
46. $5d - 3e + 4e - d$
47. $7x + 5y - x - 5y$
48. $6g - 3f + 8f - g$

B

49. $4(x + 3) + 3$
50. $3(n - 1) + 4$
51. $3(a - 7) - 4$
52. $2(n - 8) + 9$
53. $7 + 2(5 - x)$
54. $8 + 3(4 - y)$
55. $2 + (x + 3)5$
56. $(y - 5)6 + 15$
57. $5(y + 3) + 7y$
58. $9(n - 3) + 4n$
59. $3(2x + y + 1)$
60. $5(7y - 3z + 4)$
61. $9(a + b) + 4(3a + 2b)$
62. $8(k + m) + 15(2k + 5m)$
63. $6(r + 5) + 9(r - 2) - 4r$
64. $4(n + 7) + 5(n - 3) - 2n$
65. $7(c + 2d + 8) + 3(9c - 2)$
66. $4(5x + 3y + 6) + 14(2y - 1)$

In Exercises 67–70, represent each word phrase by a variable expression. Then simplify it.

67. Five times the sum of c and d, increased by twice the sum of $3c$ and d
68. Twice the sum of eleven and x, increased by three times the difference between x and seven
69. Eight more than the sum of -5 and $15y$, increased by one half of the difference between $12y$ and 8
70. Six more than three times the sum of a and b, increased by five less than b

Use the 5-step plan to solve each problem over the given domain.

C **71.** If a number is increased by 17 and this sum is multiplied by 4, the result is 77 more than the number. Find the number.
Domain: $\{2, 3, 4\}$

72. If five is subtracted from twice a number and this difference is tripled, the result is one more than four times the number. Find the number.
Domain: $\{8, 9, 10\}$

Simplify.

73. $8[5x + 7(3 + 4x)] - 16x - 8$

74. $-24 + 3[4y + 2(5y - 8)] - 9y$

75. $12(3n + 2p) + 11[n + 3(2n - p - 3)]$

76. $9[7(3a + 2b - 4) + 12(a - 2)] + 3(5a - 8b)$

77. $3[4y - 2(x + 3) + (2 - y)]$

78. $9[4(2n + r) - 11r] + 3(r - n)$

Mixed Review Exercises

Evaluate if $a = -3$, $b = -2$, $c = 2$, $x = 4$, and $y = 5$.

1. $5x + 2y - c$
2. $(c \cdot c + x) \div 2$
3. $2y - (4x \div c)$
4. $|a| + |b| + (-c)$
5. $c + |-y| + |b|$
6. $3|a| - |b|$
7. $-(-b + x) + y$
8. $b + y + (-2)$
9. $a + x + (-y)$
10. $x - (a - b)$
11. $-a - b + y$
12. $|b + a| - y$

Challenge

1. Copy the diagram.

2. Find each product and write it in the appropriate box. A calculator may be helpful.

a. $142{,}857 \cdot 1$
b. $142{,}857 \cdot 2$
c. $142{,}857 \cdot 3$
d. $142{,}857 \cdot 4$

3. Predict the following products from the pattern you see in Exercise 2.

a. $142{,}857 \cdot 5$
b. $142{,}857 \cdot 6$

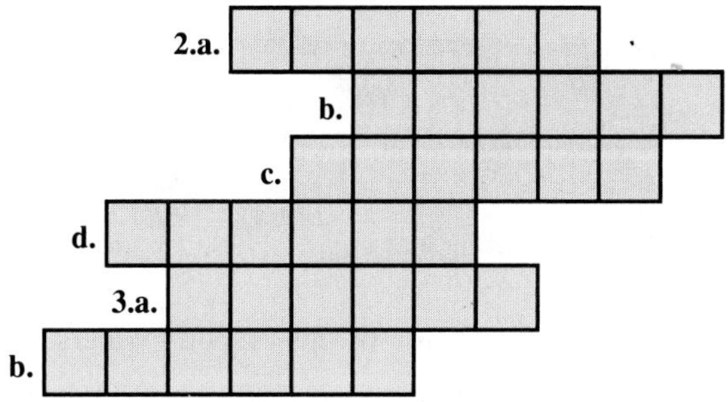

2-6 Rules for Multiplication

Objective To multiply real numbers.

When you multiply any given real number by 1, the product is equal to the given number. For example:

$$4 \cdot 1 = 4 \quad \text{and} \quad 1 \cdot 4 = 4$$

The **identity element for multiplication** is 1.

Identity Property of Multiplication

There is a unique real number 1 such that for every real number a,

$$\boldsymbol{a \cdot 1 = a} \quad \text{and} \quad \boldsymbol{1 \cdot a = a.}$$

The equations $4 \cdot 0 = 0$ and $0 \cdot 4 = 0$

illustrate the *multiplicative property of zero:* When one (or at least one) of the factors of a product is zero, the product itself is zero.

Multiplicative Property of Zero

For every real number a:

$$\boldsymbol{a \cdot 0 = 0} \quad \text{and} \quad \boldsymbol{0 \cdot a = 0}$$

Would you guess that $4(-1) = -4$? You can verify this product by noticing that

$$4(-1) = (-1) + (-1) + (-1) + (-1) = -4.$$

Multiplying *any* real number by -1 produces the opposite of the number. (See Exercise 59, page 73.)

Multiplicative Property of −1

For every real number a:

$$\boldsymbol{a(-1) = -a} \quad \text{and} \quad \boldsymbol{(-1)a = -a}$$

A special case of this property occurs when the value of a is -1.

$$(-1)(-1) = 1$$

Using the multiplicative property of -1 with the familiar multiplication facts for positive numbers and properties that you have learned, you can compute the product of *any* two real numbers.

Example 1 Multiply: **a.** $4(7)$ **b.** $(-4)(7)$ **c.** $4(-7)$ **d.** $(-4)(-7)$

Solution

a. $4(7) = 28$ ***Answer***

b. $(-4)(7) = (-1)4(7)$
$= (-1)28$
$= -28$ ***Answer***

c. $4(-7) = 4(-1)(7)$
$= 4(7)(-1)$
$= 28(-1)$
$= -28$ ***Answer***

d. $(-4)(-7) = (-1)4(-1)7$
$= (-1)(-1)4(7)$
$= 1(28)$
$= 28$ ***Answer***

Property of Opposites in Products

For all real numbers a and b:

$$(-a)(b) = -ab \qquad a(-b) = -ab \qquad (-a)(-b) = ab$$

Practice in computing products will suggest to you the following rules for multiplication of positive and negative numbers.

Rules for Multiplication

1. If two numbers have the *same* sign, their product is *positive*.
   If two numbers have *opposite* signs, their product is *negative*.
2. The product of an *even* number of negative numbers is *positive*.
   The product of an *odd* number of negative numbers is *negative*.

Example 2

a. $4(-6)(-7)(-5)$ is negative because it has 3 negative factors.
b. $(-2)(-8)(-7)(5)(-6)$ is positive because it has 4 negative factors.
c. $(-9)(3)(0)(-5)$ is zero because it has a zero factor.

Example 3 Simplify: **a.** $(-3x)(-4y)$ **b.** $4p + (-5p)$

Solution

a. $(-3x)(-4y) = (-3)x(-4)y$
$= (-3)(-4)xy$
$= 12xy$ ***Answer***

b. $4p + (-5p) = [4 + (-5)]p$
$= (-1)p$
$= -p$ ***Answer***

Example 4 Simplify: **a.** $-2(x - 3y)$ **b.** $3p - 4(p - 2)$

Solution

a. $-2(x - 3y) = -2x - (-2)(3y)$
$= -2x - (-6y)$
$= -2x + 6y$
Answer

b. $3p - 4(p - 2) = 3p - (4p - 4 \cdot 2)$
$= 3p - (4p - 8)$
$= 3p - 4p + 8$
$= -p + 8$ ***Answer***

Oral Exercises

Simplify.

1. $(-3)(-1)$ **2.** $10(-8)$ **3.** $(-3)(-9)$ **4.** $(-8)(-5)$

5. $(-1)(6)(-6)$ **6.** $2(-6)(-1)$ **7.** $(-1)(-3)(-5)$ **8.** $(-2)(-4)(-6)$

9. $7(0)(-12)$ **10.** $(-11)(-7)(0)$ **11.** $(-6)(-10g)$ **12.** $(-7)(12p)$

13. $(-3p)(-4q)$ **14.** $(4e)(-6f)$ **15.** $(-9v)(2w)$

16. $-2ab - 3ab$ **17.** $7c + (-7c)$ **18.** $-7rs + 2rs$

19. $-5wz + (-4wz)$ **20.** $8u + (-8u)$ **21.** $-9xy + 8xy$

22. $-3(x - y)$ **23.** $-2(a - 5b)$ **24.** $-2(c + 5d)$

25. $-4(3b - 5)$ **26.** $(x - 7)(-2)$ **27.** $(-m - n)(-9)$

28. $1 - 2(g + h)$ **29.** $5 - 2(a - b)$ **30.** $-(x - 7) + 4$

Written Exercises

Multiply.

A

1. $(-37)(-2)$ **2.** $23(-5)$ **3.** $(-4)(10)(-12)$

4. $(-6)(-9)(20)$ **5.** $(-3)(-7)(-4)$ **6.** $(-2)(-8)(-4)$

7. $(-17)(-18)(0)$ **8.** $54(-47)(0)$ **9.** $5(-3)(-10)(-2)$

10. $(-4)(25)(-2)(-3)$ **11.** $(-6)(-1)(-7)(-10)$ **12.** $(-9)(-5)(-1)(-3)$

13. $(-2a)(-3b)$ **14.** $(-5x)(-3y)$ **15.** $2p(-7q)$

16. $(-4e)(5t)$ **17.** $(-7a)(-5c)4$ **18.** $(-x)(-3y)(-z)$

19. $-2(x - 3y)$ **20.** $-5(c + 2d)$ **21.** $-7(3m + 4n)$

22. $-9(-5y - 8)$ **23.** $(5x - 3)(-7)$ **24.** $(-4 + 7y)(-2)$

25. $(-1)(a + b - 3)$ **26.** $(-1)(2n - y - 5)$ **27.** $(-1)(a - b - c)$

28. $(-1)(-x - y + 7)$ **29.** $-[(-2)(a + b)]$ **30.** $-[(-3)(x - y)]$

Simplify.

31. $5x - 7x + 8 + 2x$ **32.** $3y - 7 - 8y + 5$

33. $14p - 7c - 9c + 11p$ **34.** $-y - 3z + 4y - 9z - y$

B

35. $3.4y + 1.6s - (-1.9y) - 3.6s$ **36.** $-0.8c + 4.1h - (-3.2c) - 0.1h$

37. $-8x - 7x - 5x$ **38.** $-34n + 18n - 4n$

39. $-8(-19) - 7(-19) - 5(-19)$ **40.** $-34 \cdot 9 + 18 \cdot 9 - 4 \cdot 9$

41. $88(-57) + 13(-57) + (-1)(-57)$ **42.** $-63 \cdot 81 + 56 \cdot 81 - 13 \cdot 81$

43. $-m + \frac{2}{3}m - \frac{1}{2}n + \frac{5}{2}n$ **44.** $-5a - \left(-\frac{1}{2}b\right) + 3\frac{1}{2}a - \frac{1}{2}b$

45. $7 - 3(r + s)$

46. $2 + 6(m - n)$

47. $2(x + 5y) + (-3)(7x - y)$

48. $8(t - u) + 5(2t - 3u)$

49. $-2(2q + w) - 7(w - q)$

50. $-3(7c + d) - 2(10d - c)$

51. $-4(-e + 3f) - 3[e + (-5f)]$

52. $-6[v + (-9w)] + (-5)(3v - w)$

C **53.** $2[-7(r + 2s) - r] - 3(s + 2r)$

54. $4[2(-5x + y) - y] - 10(y - 4x)$

55. $-15 + (-3)[2(g - 7) - 2(1 - g)]$

56. $-50 + (-2)[3(1 - f) - 3(-2 + f)]$

Write your answer as a variable expression.

57. Sal owned 500 shares of Acme Tube. On Monday morning each share of the stock had gained p points. On Tuesday each share lost one more than twice as many points as it had gained the day before. How much did the total value of Sal's shares of Acme Tube change between the opening of trading on Monday and the closing on Tuesday?

58. A discount store bought 12 dozen radios, each to be sold at \$15 above cost. The store sold x of the radios at that price. Each of the remaining radios was sold at \$4 below cost. If the store paid \$11 for each radio, what was the total income from the sale? (*Hint:* Income = Sales − Cost)

59. To show that $a(-1)$ is the opposite of a for every real number a, you can show that the sum of $a(-1)$ and a is zero as follows. Name the property that justifies each step.

$a(-1) + a$	$= a(-1) + a(1)$	**a.** ?
	$= a[(-1) + 1]$	**b.** ?
	$= a(0)$	**c.** ?
	$= 0$	**d.** ?

Since the unique opposite of a is $-a$, $a(-1) = -a$.

60. Name the property or definition that justifies each step.

$a(b - c)$	$= a[b + (-c)]$	**a.** ?
	$= a(b) + a(-c)$	**b.** ?
	$= ab + (-ac)$	**c.** ?
	$= ab - ac$	**d.** ?

Mixed Review Exercises

Translate each sentence into an equation.

1. Four times a number is 44.

2. The sum of n and 2 is 32.

3. Half of a number is twelve.

4. Seven more than twice a number is 11.

Simplify.

5. $120 - (14 - 6)$

6. $191 - (9 - 12)$

7. $3 + (-2) + (-y) + 11$

8. $4(30 + 2)$

9. $3n + (-7n)$

10. $4(n + 2) + 8$

Application / *Understanding Product Prices*

You may have noticed the Universal Product Code (UPC) on items in your supermarket. This code is a series of bands of alternating light and dark spaces of varying widths that represent the numbers printed underneath. Many supermarkets have installed electronic check-out counters that contain scanners. These scanners read the UPC on items and send the information to a central computer. The computer "looks up" the price of the item and subtracts the item from the store's inventory of products. The product name and price are then printed on the sales slip. The customer benefits by having a record of the transaction and the store benefits by having up-to-date inventory records.

0 39800 00320

Manufacturer Code   Product Code

Consumers must make many choices while shopping. Quality, price, and convenience are all important considerations. Sometimes it is difficult to compare the prices of products in different-sized packages. Unit pricing can help you make the comparison. The unit price of an item is its price per unit of measure. Unit prices are often posted on the shelves with the products. The product with the lowest unit price is the best buy provided the quality and the quantity meet your needs.

Example Find the unit price per liter of lowfat milk: \$.95 for 950 mL.

Solution 1 L = 1000 mL, so 950 mL = $\frac{950}{1000}$ L = 0.95 L.

\$.95 ÷ 0.95 L = \$1.00 per liter

Exercises

Find the unit price per liter of each item. A calculator may be helpful.

1. Shampoo: \$2.40 for 480 mL
2. Chicken noodle soup: \$.63 for 315 mL
3. Soy sauce: \$1.98 for 600 mL
4. Grapefruit juice: \$1.44 for 1440 mL

2-7 Problem Solving: Consecutive Integers

Objective To write equations to represent relationships among integers.

When you want to be served at a bakery, a deli, or a pizza parlor you often must take a number. The numbers help the clerks keep track of who is next in line.

When you count by ones from any number in the set of integers,

$$\{\ldots, -3, -2, -1, 0, 1, 2, 3, \ldots\},$$

you obtain **consecutive integers.** For example, -2, -1, 0, 1, and 2 are five consecutive integers. Those integers are listed in *natural order,* that is, in order from least to greatest.

Example 1 An integer is represented by n.

a. Write the next three integers in natural order after n.
b. Write the integer that immediately precedes n.
c. Write an equation that states that the sum of four consecutive integers, starting with n, is 66.

Solution

a. $n + 1, n + 2, n + 3$
b. $n - 1$
c. $n + (n + 1) + (n + 2) + (n + 3) = 66$

Ten is called an *even* integer because $10 = 2 \cdot 5$. An integer that is the product of 2 and any integer is an **even integer.** In natural order, they are

$$\ldots, -6, -4, -2, 0, 2, 4, 6, \ldots$$

An **odd integer** is an integer that is not even. In natural order, the odd integers are

$$\ldots, -5, -3, -1, 1, 3, 5, \ldots$$

If you count by *twos* beginning with any even integer, you obtain **consecutive even integers.** For example:

Three consecutive even integers: 8; $8 + 2$, or 10; $10 + 2$, or 12

If you count by *twos* beginning with any odd integer, you obtain **consecutive odd integers.** For example:

Three consecutive odd integers: 9; $9 + 2$, or 11; $11 + 2$, or 13

Thus, in natural order, $n, n + 2, n + 4$

are said to be consecutive even integers if n is even, and consecutive odd integers if n is odd.

Example 2 Solve over the given domain: The sum of three consecutive odd integers is 100 more than the smallest integer. What are the integers?
Domain for the smallest integer: $\{27, 37, 47\}$

Solution

Step 1 The unknowns are the 3 consecutive odd integers.

Step 2 Let n = the smallest integer, $n + 2$ = the middle integer, and $n + 4$ = the largest integer.

Step 3 $\underbrace{\text{The sum}}_{n + (n + 2) + (n + 4)} \underset{=}{\text{is}} \underbrace{\text{100 more than the smallest integer}}_{n + 100}$.

$$n + (n + 2) + (n + 4) = n + 100$$

Step 4

n	$n + (n + 2) + (n + 4) = n + 100$	
27	$27 + 29 + 31 = 27 + 100$	False
37	$37 + 39 + 41 = 37 + 100$	False
47	$47 + 49 + 51 = 47 + 100$	True

Step 5 Are 47, 49, and 51 consecutive odd integers whose sum is 147?
The check is left to you. $\therefore$ the integers are 47, 49, and 51. ***Answer***

Oral Exercises

1. If $w = 3$, what are the values of $w + 1$, $w + 2$, and $w + 3$?

2. If $r = 1$, what are the values of $r - 1$, $r - 2$, and $r - 3$?

3. The smallest of four consecutive integers is -1. What are the other three integers?

4. The greatest of four consecutive integers is 12. What are the other three integers?

5. If $x = 15$, represent 14 and 16 in terms of x.

6. If $p = 20$, represent 18 and 22 in terms of p.

7. If $k = 11$, represent 7, 9, and 13 in terms of k.

8. If $e = 12$, represent 8, 10, 14, and 16 in terms of e.

9. If m is an odd integer, is $m + 1$ odd or is it even? $m + 2$? $m - 1$?

10. If m and n are even, is $m + n$ odd or is it even? $m - n$? mn?

11. If m and n are odd, is $m + n$ odd or is it even? $m - n$? mn?

12. If m is odd and n is even, is $m + n$ odd or is it even? $m - n$? mn?

13. If n is an integer, is $2n$ odd or even? What are the next two even integers greater than $2n$? What is the next smaller even integer?

14. If n is an integer, is $2n + 1$ odd or even? What are the next two odd integers greater than $2n + 1$? What is the next smaller odd integer?

Written Exercises

Write an equation to represent the given relationship among integers.

Sample The product of two consecutive integers is 8 more than twice their sum.

Solution Let x = the first of the integers.
Then $x + 1$ = the second integer.

$$\underbrace{\text{Their product}}_{x(x+1)} \underset{=}{\text{is}} \underbrace{\text{8 more than twice their sum.}}_{2[x+(x+1)]+8}$$

$\therefore$ the equation is $x(x + 1) = 2[x + (x + 1)] + 8$. ***Answer***

A

1. The sum of two consecutive integers is 43.

2. The sum of three consecutive integers is 69.

3. The sum of four consecutive integers is -106.

4. The sum of four consecutive integers is -42.

5. The sum of three consecutive odd integers is 75.

6. The sum of three consecutive odd integers is 147.

7. The product of two consecutive even integers is 168.

8. The product of two consecutive odd integers is 195.

9. The sum of four consecutive even integers is -100.

10. The greater of two consecutive even integers is six less than twice the smaller.

11. Four cousins were born at two-year intervals. The sum of their ages is 36.

12. The smaller of two consecutive even integers is five more than one half of the greater.

Solve each problem over the given domain.

B

13. The sum of three consecutive odd integers is 40 more than the smallest. What are the integers?
Domain for the smallest: $\{13, 17, 25\}$

14. The sum of three consecutive even integers is 30 more than the largest. What are the integers?
Domain for the smallest: $\{14, 18, 20\}$

15. Find two consecutive integers whose product is 5 less than 5 times their sum.
Domain for the smallest: $\{0, 6, 9\}$

16. Find two consecutive odd integers whose product is 1 less than 6 times their sum.
Domain for the smallest: $\{-1, 1, 11\}$

Write an equation to represent the given relationship among integers. Use this definition:

The product of any real number and an integer is called a ***multiple*** *of the real number.*

C **17.** The lengths in feet of three ropes are consecutive multiples of 3. If each rope were 4 ft shorter, the sum of their lengths would be 42 ft.

18. Jim weighs more than Joe but less than Jack. Their weights in kilograms are consecutive multiples of 7. If they each weighed 5 kg less, the sum of their weights would be 195 kg.

Mixed Review Exercises

Simplify.

1. $(40 - 7) - (55 - 20)$

2. $-5.3 + 2.1 - 1.7$

3. $-4 + 2c + (-1) + 8$

4. $\frac{6}{5} + \left(-\frac{9}{5}\right)$

5. $3\frac{1}{3} + 12 + 2\frac{2}{3}$

6. $6\left(\frac{2}{5}\right) - 5\left(\frac{2}{5}\right) + 3\left(\frac{1}{5}\right)$

7. $-(11 - x) - (x - 13)$

8. $15a - 3a + 7a$

9. $12 + 5y + 6 + (-2)$

10. $(-1)(x + y - z)$

11. $-[-6(a - b)]$

12. $3(-5 + y)$

Self-Test 2

Vocabulary

distributive property (p. 65)
equivalent expressions (p. 67)
simplify a variable expression (p. 67)
identity element for multiplication (p. 70)
identity property of multiplication (p. 70)
multiplicative property of zero (p. 70)
multiplicative property of -1 (p. 70)
property of opposites in products (p. 71)
consecutive integers (p. 75)
natural order (p. 75)
even integer (p. 75)
odd integer (p. 75)
consecutive even integers (p. 75)
consecutive odd integers (p. 75)

Simplify.

1. $x + 2y + 3x + 4y$

2. $4(y - 2) + 1$ **Obj. 2-5, p. 65**

3. $(-2)a + 4a$

4. $2(x + 3) - 2$

5. $(-5)(3)(-6)(-2)$

6. $(-4x)(-2y)(7)$ **Obj. 2-6, p. 70**

7. $-3(a + b - c)$

8. $18 \cdot 12 + 18 \cdot 10$

9. If $x = 30$, represent 29 and 31 in terms of x. **Obj. 2-7, p. 75**

10. Write an equation to represent the given relationship among the integers: The greater of two consecutive odd integers is one less than twice the smaller.

Check your answers with those at the back of the book.

2-8 The Reciprocal of a Real Number

Objective To simplify expressions involving reciprocals.

Two numbers whose product is 1 are called **reciprocals,** or **multiplicative inverses,** of each other. For example:

1. 5 and $\frac{1}{5}$ are reciprocals because $5 \cdot \frac{1}{5} = 1$.
2. $\frac{4}{5}$ and $\frac{5}{4}$ are reciprocals because $\frac{4}{5} \cdot \frac{5}{4} = 1$.
3. -1.25 and -0.8 are reciprocals because $(-1.25)(-0.8) = 1$.
4. 1 is its own reciprocal because $1 \cdot 1 = 1$.
5. -1 is its own reciprocal because $(-1)(-1) = 1$.
6. 0 has no reciprocal because 0 times *any* number is 0, *not* 1.

The symbol for the reciprocal, or multiplicative inverse, of a nonzero real number a is $\frac{1}{a}$. Every real number except 0 has a reciprocal.

Property of Reciprocals

For every *nonzero* real number a, there is a unique real number $\frac{1}{a}$ such that

$$\mathbf{a \cdot \frac{1}{a} = 1 \quad \text{and} \quad \frac{1}{a} \cdot a = 1.}$$

Look at the following product:

$$(-a)\left(-\frac{1}{a}\right) = (-1a)\left(-1 \cdot \frac{1}{a}\right) = (-1)(-1)\left(a \cdot \frac{1}{a}\right) = 1 \cdot 1 = 1$$

Therefore, $-a$ and $-\frac{1}{a}$ are reciprocals.

Property of the Reciprocal of the Opposite of a Number

For every *nonzero* number a,

$$\mathbf{\frac{1}{-a} = -\frac{1}{a}.}$$

Read, "The reciprocal of $-a$ is $-\frac{1}{a}$."

Now look at this product:

$$(ab)\left(\frac{1}{a}\cdot\frac{1}{b}\right) = \left(a\cdot\frac{1}{a}\right)\left(b\cdot\frac{1}{b}\right) = 1\cdot 1 = 1$$

Therefore, ab and $\frac{1}{a}\cdot\frac{1}{b}$ are reciprocals.

Property of the Reciprocal of a Product

For all *nonzero* numbers a and b,

$$\mathbf{\frac{1}{ab} = \frac{1}{a}\cdot\frac{1}{b}}.$$

The reciprocal of the product of two nonzero numbers is the product of their reciprocals.

Example 1 Simplify: **a.** $\frac{1}{4}\cdot\frac{1}{-7}$ **b.** $4y\cdot\frac{1}{4}$ **c.** $(-6ab)\left(-\frac{1}{3}\right)$

Solution **a.** $\frac{1}{4}\cdot\frac{1}{-7} = \frac{1}{4(-7)} = \frac{1}{-28} = -\frac{1}{28}$ ***Answer***

b. $4y\cdot\frac{1}{4} = \left(4\cdot\frac{1}{4}\right)y = 1y = y$ ***Answer***

c. $(-6ab)\left(-\frac{1}{3}\right) = (-6)\left(-\frac{1}{3}\right)(ab) = 2ab$ ***Answer***

Example 2 Simplify $\frac{1}{3}(42m - 3v)$.

Solution

$$\begin{aligned}\frac{1}{3}(42m - 3v) &= \frac{1}{3}(42m) - \frac{1}{3}(3v)\\ &= \left(\frac{1}{3}\cdot 42\right)m - \left(\frac{1}{3}\cdot 3\right)v\\ &= 14m - v\end{aligned}$$

Answer

Oral Exercises

State the reciprocal in simplest form.

1. 7 **2.** 1 **3.** -1 **4.** $\frac{1}{11}$

5. -2 **6.** $\frac{3}{4}$ **7.** 0.25 **8.** $-\frac{1}{8}$

9. $-\frac{13}{5}$ **10.** $-\frac{2}{3}$ **11.** $\frac{1}{w}$, $w \neq 0$ **12.** $-\frac{1}{s}$, $s \neq 0$

Simplify.

13. $\frac{1}{6} \cdot \frac{1}{10}$ **14.** $\frac{1}{-2} \cdot \frac{1}{-12}$ **15.** $\frac{1}{6} \cdot \frac{1}{-4}$ **16.** $\frac{1}{-x} \cdot \frac{1}{y}$, $x \neq 0$, $y \neq 0$

17. $(3a)\frac{1}{3}$ **18.** $\frac{1}{5}(5x)$ **19.** $6w \cdot \frac{1}{6}$ **20.** $\frac{1}{-3}(3ab)$

21. $\frac{1}{2}(10z + 12)$ **22.** $\frac{1}{7}(21g - 14)$ **23.** $-\frac{1}{4}(16m + 32)$ **24.** $-\frac{1}{6}(54t - 18)$

25. **a.** $\frac{1}{\frac{2}{3}}$ represents the reciprocal of __?__. **b.** In simplest form $\frac{1}{\frac{2}{3}} =$ __?__.

Written Exercises

Simplify each expression.

A **1.** $\frac{1}{5}(-20)$ **2.** $-\frac{1}{12}(48)$ **3.** $-1000\left(\frac{1}{100}\right)$

4. $-70\left(\frac{1}{7}\right)$ **5.** $96\left(-\frac{1}{8}\right)\left(-\frac{1}{12}\right)$ **6.** $-63\left(-\frac{1}{3}\right)\left(-\frac{1}{21}\right)$

7. $\frac{1}{-3}(36)\left(\frac{1}{4}\right)$ **8.** $-150\left(\frac{1}{2}\right)\left(-\frac{1}{3}\right)$ **9.** $4r\left(-\frac{1}{4}\right)$

10. $33p\left(-\frac{1}{11}\right)$ **11.** $\frac{1}{x}(5x)$, $x \neq 0$ **12.** $7t\left(\frac{1}{t}\right)$, $t \neq 0$

13. $12xy\left(\frac{1}{3}\right)$ **14.** $15mn\left(\frac{1}{5}\right)$ **15.** $8ab\left(-\frac{1}{4}\right)$

16. $9cd\left(\frac{1}{-3}\right)$ **17.** $(-4pg)\left(\frac{1}{-2}\right)$ **18.** $(-36ac)\left(\frac{1}{-9}\right)$

B **19.** $\frac{1}{2}(-16a + 20)$ **20.** $\frac{1}{3}(18b - 39)$

21. $-\frac{1}{5}(-45c + 10d)$ **22.** $-\frac{1}{8}(56g - 72h)$

23. $(-42m - 91k)\left(-\frac{1}{7}\right)$ **24.** $(-39n - 52p)\left(-\frac{1}{13}\right)$

25. $\frac{1}{2}(8u + 10v) - \frac{1}{3}(15u - 3v)$ **26.** $\frac{1}{5}(-5a + 20b) - \frac{1}{2}(2b - 6a)$

27. $6\left(\frac{1}{3}x - \frac{1}{2}y\right) + 42\left(-\frac{1}{3}y - \frac{1}{7}x\right)$ **28.** $-8\left(-\frac{1}{8}p + q\right) + \frac{1}{9}(63p - 9q)$

29. $-\frac{1}{8}(48m - 16) - \frac{1}{4}(84m + 8)$ **30.** $-5\left(4 - \frac{1}{2}n\right) + \frac{1}{16}(-32n + 8)$

C **31.** $-\frac{1}{12}(6r + 4s) + 7\left(\frac{1}{21}s - \frac{1}{14}r\right)$ **32.** $-\frac{1}{20}(5z - 4w) - 6\left(-\frac{1}{30}w - \frac{1}{24}z\right)$

33. $-3\left[\frac{1}{4}(12n + 1) - \frac{1}{4}\right] + 10n$ **34.** $3s + \left(-\frac{1}{2}\right)\left[6 + 24\left(-\frac{1}{3} + \frac{1}{4}s\right)\right]$

Use the five-step plan for solving each problem over the given domain.

35. The sum of a number and its reciprocal is $\frac{13}{6}$. Find the number.

Domain: $\left\{\frac{2}{3}, \frac{3}{4}, \frac{5}{4}, \frac{3}{2}\right\}$

36. A number is $2\frac{1}{10}$ more than its reciprocal. Find the number.

Domain: $\left\{\frac{2}{5}, \frac{3}{5}, \frac{5}{4}, \frac{5}{2}\right\}$

Mixed Review Exercises

Translate each sentence into an equation.

1. Four more than five times a number is 24.
2. Fifteen less than a number is 250.
3. The sum of two consecutive integers is 67.
4. The product of two consecutive integers is 42.

Simplify.

5. $(-12)(-5)(-2)$ **6.** $-36(25)(-2)$ **7.** $(3)(-7)(-2)$

8. $-7(5a - 2d)$ **9.** $-4(2 + x) - 3(x - 2)$ **10.** $8(x - 1) + 5(2 - x)$

Calculator Key-In

Use the reciprocal key on a calculator to find the reciprocal of each number.

1. 0.0625 **2.** −32 **3.** 3125 **4.** 0.000064

5. For each number in Exercises 1–4, press the reciprocal key twice. Your results illustrate the property: The reciprocal of the reciprocal of a number is __?__.

6. a. Copy and complete the table.

a	b	$\frac{1}{ab}$	$\frac{1}{a} \cdot \frac{1}{b}$
4	16	?	?
−32	−0.5	?	?
0.234	0.654	?	?
555	222	?	?

b. What property does your completed table illustrate?

2-9 Dividing Real Numbers

Objective To divide real numbers and to simplify expressions involving quotients.

Dividing by 2 is the same as multiplying by $\frac{1}{2}$: $8 \div 2 = 4$ and $8 \cdot \frac{1}{2} = 4$.

Dividing by 5 is the same as multiplying by $\frac{1}{5}$: $15 \div 5 = 3$ and $15 \cdot \frac{1}{5} = 3$.

The examples above illustrate how division is related to multiplication.

Definition of Division

For every real number a and every *nonzero* real number b, the **quotient** $a \div b$, or $\frac{a}{b}$, is defined by:

$$\boldsymbol{a \div b = a \cdot \frac{1}{b}}.$$

To divide by a nonzero number, multiply by its reciprocal.

You can use the definition of division to express any quotient as a product.

Example 1 **a.** $\frac{24}{6} = 24 \div 6 = 24 \cdot \frac{1}{6} = 4$

b. $\frac{24}{-6} = 24 \div (-6) = 24\left(-\frac{1}{6}\right) = -4$

c. $\frac{-24}{6} = -24 \div 6 = -24 \cdot \frac{1}{6} = -4$

d. $\frac{-24}{-6} = -24 \div (-6) = (-24)\left(-\frac{1}{6}\right) = 4$

The four quotients in Example 1 illustrate the following rules.

Rules for Division

If two numbers have the *same* sign, their quotient is *positive*.
If two numbers have *opposite* signs, their quotient is *negative*.

Example 2 **a.** $(-9) \div \left(-\frac{10}{3}\right) = (-9)\left(-\frac{3}{10}\right) = \frac{27}{10}$ ***Answer***

b. $\frac{-3}{-\frac{1}{3}} = (-3) \div \left(-\frac{1}{3}\right) = (-3)(-3) = 9$ ***Answer***

Example 3 $\frac{45x}{-9} = 45x\left(-\frac{1}{9}\right) = 45\left(-\frac{1}{9}\right)x = -5x$ ***Answer***

Example 4 $\frac{w}{13} \cdot 13 = w \cdot \frac{1}{13} \cdot 13 = w \cdot 1 = w$ ***Answer***

Here are some important questions and answers about division of real numbers:

1. Why can you never divide by zero? Dividing by 0 would mean multiplying by the reciprocal of 0. But 0 has no reciprocal (page 79). Therefore, *division by zero has no meaning in the set of real numbers.*
2. Can you divide zero by any number other than zero? Yes, for example,

$$\frac{0}{5} = 0 \cdot \frac{1}{5} = 0 \quad \text{and} \quad 0 \div (-2) = 0 \cdot \left(-\frac{1}{2}\right) = 0.$$

   When zero is divided by any nonzero number, the quotient is zero.

3. Is division commutative? No, for example,

$$8 \div 2 = 4 \quad \text{but} \quad 2 \div 8 = 0.25.$$

4. Is division associative? No, for example,

$$(12 \div 3) \div 2 = 4 \div 2 = 2 \quad \text{but} \quad 12 \div (3 \div 2) = 12 \div 1.5 = 8.$$

The following properties of division will be proved in Exercises 34 and 35 on page 86.

For all real numbers a, b, and c such that $c \neq 0$,

$$\frac{a+b}{c} = \frac{a}{c} + \frac{b}{c} \quad \text{and} \quad \frac{a-b}{c} = \frac{a}{c} - \frac{b}{c}.$$

Oral Exercises

Read each quotient as a product. Then simplify.

Sample $8 \div \left(-\frac{1}{6}\right)$ **Solution** Eight times negative six; -48

1. $\frac{-21}{3}$ **2.** $\frac{0}{8}$ **3.** $-25 \div 5$ **4.** $18 \div (-18)$

5. $\frac{0}{-9}$ **6.** $\frac{-6}{-6}$ **7.** $\frac{-2}{2}$ **8.** $\frac{49}{-7}$

9. $\frac{38}{-2}$ **10.** $\frac{-56}{-8}$ **11.** $\frac{4}{-64}$ **12.** $\frac{-8}{72}$

Simplify.

13. $x \div 1$ **14.** $x \div (-1)$ **15.** $8a \div (-2)$ **16.** $(-18b) \div 3$

17. $(-60a) \div (-5)$ **18.** $(-48b) \div (-6)$ **19.** $\frac{a}{a}$, $a \neq 0$ **20.** $\frac{-a}{a}$, $a \neq 0$

21. $6 \cdot \frac{n}{6}$ **22.** $\left(-\frac{s}{4}\right)(-4)$ **23.** $2\left(\frac{y}{-2}\right)$ **24.** $-3 \cdot \frac{n}{3}$

Written Exercises

Simplify.

A

1. $-48 \div 6$ **2.** $-64 \div 4$ **3.** $-12 \div (-3)$ **4.** $-24 \div (-8)$

5. $8 \div \left(-\frac{1}{2}\right)$ **6.** $12 \div \left(-\frac{1}{3}\right)$ **7.** $0 \div \frac{3}{4}$ **8.** $-6 \div \left(-\frac{1}{4}\right)$

9. $\frac{-6}{-\frac{1}{6}}$ **10.** $\frac{-8}{-\frac{1}{3}}$ **11.** $\frac{-7}{\frac{1}{5}}$ **12.** $\frac{9}{-\frac{1}{9}}$

13. $3 \cdot \frac{x}{3}$ **14.** $\frac{-w}{4} \cdot 4$ **15.** $(-4)\left(\frac{-y}{2}\right)$ **16.** $(-8)\left(\frac{x}{-2}\right)$

17. $\frac{156a}{12}$ **18.** $\frac{384b}{-8}$ **19.** $\frac{-54x}{6}$ **20.** $\frac{-144y}{-24}$

In Exercises 21–24, find the average of the given numbers. (The *average* is the sum of the numbers divided by the number of numbers.)

Sample 1 15, −3, −14, −2

Solution $\frac{15 + (-3) + (-14) + (-2)}{4} = \frac{-4}{4} = -1$ *Answer*

21. −12, 4, −11, −7 **22.** 18, −21, −7, 2

23. 18, −17, −22, 16, 0 **24.** 18, −17, −22, 16

Evaluate each expression if $a = -3$, $b = -1$, $c = 2$, and $d = 6$.

Sample 2 $\frac{abd}{a + c} = \frac{(-3)(-1)(6)}{-3 + 2} = \frac{3(6)}{-1} = \frac{18}{-1} = -18$ *Answer*

B

25. $\frac{b + 5c}{3 - d}$ **26.** $\frac{bcd}{(1 - b)a}$ **27.** $\frac{abc}{(1 - c)d}$

28. $\frac{7a + d}{a + c}$ **29.** $\frac{a - 2d}{b + 3c}$ **30.** $\frac{4a - d}{abc}$

31. $\frac{a - 3b}{bcd}$ **32.** $\frac{abc - d}{abc}$ **33.** $\frac{(c + a)(c - a)}{b + d}$

In Exercises 34 and 35, assume that a, b, and c are any real numbers and $c \neq 0$.

C **34.** Name the property or definition that justifies each step.

$$\frac{a+b}{c} = (a+b) \cdot \frac{1}{c} \qquad \textbf{a. } \underline{\ ?\ }$$

$$= \left(a \cdot \frac{1}{c}\right) + \left(b \cdot \frac{1}{c}\right) \qquad \textbf{b. } \underline{\ ?\ }$$

$$= \frac{a}{c} + \frac{b}{c} \qquad \textbf{c. } \underline{\ ?\ }$$

35. Show that $\frac{a-b}{c} = \frac{a}{c} - \frac{b}{c}$. Use the fact that multiplication is distributive with respect to subtraction. (*Hint:* See Exercise 34.)

Mixed Review Exercises

Solve if $x \in \{0, 1, 2, 3, 4, 5, 6\}$.

1. $x + 3 = 8$

2. $\frac{1}{3}x = 2$

3. $x - 1 = 2$

4. $3x = 6$

5. $2x + 1 = 5$

6. $x \div 4 = 1$

Solve over the domain $\{0, 1, 2, 3, 4, 5\}$.

7. $\frac{1}{5}n = 1$

8. $5y - 1 = 14$

9. $x + 2 = 5$

10. $2x = 4$

11. $x \cdot x \cdot x = 1$

12. $5n = n \cdot 5$

Self-Test 3

Vocabulary

reciprocals (p. 79)
multiplicative inverse (p. 79)
property of reciprocals (p. 79)
property of the reciprocal of the opposite of a number (p. 79)
property of the reciprocal of a product (p. 80)
division (p. 83)
quotient (p. 83)

State the reciprocal of each expression or number. **Obj. 2-8, p. 79**

1. $3y,\ y \neq 0$

2. $-\frac{1}{2}$

Simplify. **Obj. 2-9, p. 83**

3. $-30\left(\frac{1}{3}\right)$

4. $\frac{1}{6}(24)(-12)$

5. $-81 \div 3$

6. $-36 \div (-2)$

7. $4 \div \frac{1}{2}$

8. $\frac{-48x}{12}$

Check your answers with those in the back of the book.

Computer Key-In

The program below will find the sum of a list of numbers that does not include zero.

```
10 PRINT "TO FIND THE SUM OF SEVERAL"
20 PRINT "NUMBERS (<>0)."
30 PRINT "(TO END, TYPE 0.)"
40 LET S=0
50 PRINT "NUMBER";
60 INPUT N
70 IF N=0 THEN 100
80 LET S=S+N
90 GOTO 50
100 PRINT "SUM=";S
110 END
```

Line 80 is not an equation. It adds each new value of N to S. It means "Take the value of S, add the value of N to it, and then put the new value into S."

Lines 50–90 form a *loop*. Line 90 sends the program back to line 50 for the next value of N to be INPUT. Lines 50–90 will be repeated until line 70 ends the INPUT when 0 is entered. After all of the numbers in the list are INPUT, line 100 prints the final value of S.

Exercises

Use the program above to find the sum of the numbers in each list.

1. 2, −4, 6, −8, 10, −12

2. 1, 4, 9, 16, 25, 36, 49, 64, 81, 100

3. 2.25, 3.42, 5.15, 1.98, 4.82

4. 12.95, 27.59, 21.76, 38.25, 47.34

Add the three lines below to your program so that it will compute the average of the numbers in the list. The variable C acts as a counter. (You can then type LIST to get a clean copy of the modified program.)

```
45 LET C=0
85 LET C=C+1
105 PRINT "AVERAGE=";S/C
```

5–8. Find the average of the numbers in each list in Exercises 1–4.

Historical Note / *Why We Call It "Algebra"*

The word "algebra" comes from the title of a ninth-century mathematical book by the mathematician and astronomer Muhammed ibn-Musa al-Khwarizmi. The book, *hisab al-jabr w' al muqabalah* ("the science of reduction and comparison"), deals with solving equations. While the entire work may not have been original, it was the first time that algebra was systematically discussed as a separate branch of mathematics.

Al-Khwarizmi's book made its way into Europe and was translated into Latin in the twelfth century as *Ludus algebrae et almucgrabalaeque*. The title was eventually shortened to "algebra."

Chapter Summary

1. A number line can be used to find the sum of two real numbers.
2. Opposite and absolute values are used in the rules for adding real numbers (page 54) and multiplying real numbers (page 71).
3. Real-number properties are statements about numbers that are accepted as true and that form the basis for computation in arithmetic and in algebra. The statements in the chart below are true for all real values of each variable except as noted.
4. Useful properties about addition and multiplication:

   Property of the opposite of a sum: $-(a + b) = (-a) + (-b)$

   Multiplicative property of zero: $a \cdot 0 = 0 \cdot a = 0$

   Multiplicative property of -1: $a(-1) = (-1)a = -a$

   Property of opposites in products: $(-a)(b) = -ab$
   $a(-b) = -ab$
   $(-a)(-b) = ab$

   Property of the reciprocal of a product: $\frac{1}{ab} = \frac{1}{a} \cdot \frac{1}{b};\ a \neq 0,\ b \neq 0$

5. Subtraction and division are defined as follows: $a - b = a + (-b)$
   $a \div b = \frac{a}{b} = a \cdot \frac{1}{b};\ b \neq 0$

Properties of Real Numbers

Equality:	Reflexive property	$a = a$
	Symmetric property	If $a = b$, then $b = a$.
	Transitive property	If $a = b$ and $b = c$, then $a = c$.
	Substitution principle	If $a = b$, then b may be substituted for a in any expression.

	Addition	Multiplication
Properties of closure	$a + b$ is a unique real number.	ab is a unique real number.
Commutative properties	$a + b = b + a$	$ab = ba$
Associative properties	$(a + b) + c = a + (b + c)$	$(ab)c = a(bc)$
Identity properties	$a + 0 = 0 + a = a$	$a \cdot 1 = 1 \cdot a = a$
Property of opposites	$a + (-a) = (-a) + a = 0$	
Property of reciprocals		$a \cdot \frac{1}{a} = \frac{1}{a} \cdot a = 1,\ a \neq 0$
Distributive property	$a(b + c) = ab + ac$ and $(b + c)a = ba + ca$ $a(b - c) = ab - ac$ and $(b - c)a = ba - ca$	

Chapter Review

Give the letter of the correct answer.

1. Simplify $125 + 62 + 75 + 38$. 2-1
a. 310 **b.** 301 **c.** 290 **d.** 300

2. Simplify $(16p)(5q)$.
a. $21pq$ **b.** $80pq$ **c.** $21p + q$ **d.** $80(p + q)$

3. Simplify $13 - 5x + (-17)$. 2-2
a. $-22x$ **b.** $-5x - 4$ **c.** -9 **d.** $5x + 30$

4. Simplify $33 + [7 + (-12)]$
a. 52 **b.** -52 **c.** 28 **d.** -28

5. Simplify $[-6 + (-1)] + [-(-6 + 1)]$. 2-3
a. -12 **b.** -2 **c.** 0 **d.** 2

6. Ten passengers got on an empty bus. Then 3 more passengers got on, 5 got off, and 2 more got on. How many passengers were left inside?
a. 10 **b.** 9 **c.** 8 **d.** 20

7. Simplify $x + 9 - (x - 7)$. 2-4
a. 2 **b.** 16 **c.** $2x + 16$ **d.** $2x + 2$

8. Simplify $(23 \cdot 32) - (13 \cdot 32)$. 2-5
a. 360 **b.** 330 **c.** 320 **d.** 640

9. Simplify $3 + 7(r - 4)$.
a. $10r - 40$ **b.** $10r - 28$ **c.** $7r - 25$ **d.** $7r - 31$

10. Simplify $(-2)(6)(-1)(8)$. 2-6
a. 96 **b.** -48 **c.** 48 **d.** -96

11. Simplify $2(3c - 2d) - 4(c - 3d)$.
a. $2c - 14d$ **b.** $10c + 10d$ **c.** $10c - 14d$ **d.** $2c + 8d$

12. Choose the equation that represents the following: The smaller of two consecutive even integers is eight less than twice the greater. 2-7
a. $x = 8 - 2(x + 2)$ **b.** $x = 2(x + 2) - 8$
c. $x + 2 = 8 - 2(x + 2)$ **d.** $x + 2 = 2(x + 2) - 8$

13. Simplify $(-63st)\left(-\frac{1}{9}\right)$. 2-8
a. $7s + 1$ **b.** $-7st$ **c.** $7st$ **d.** $7s - t$

14. Simplify $12\left(\frac{1}{4}x + \frac{1}{3}\right) - \frac{1}{2}(12x - 6)$.
a. $-3x + 7$ **b.** $3x + 7$ **c.** 4 **d.** $-5x + 3$

15. Simplify $\frac{72x}{-9}$. 2-9
a. $-648x$ **b.** $8x$ **c.** -8 **d.** $-8x$

16. Evaluate $\frac{a + 15b}{c}$ if $a = -6$, $b = 9$, and $c = -3$.
a. -43 **b.** 137 **c.** -13 **d.** -47

Chapter Test

Simplify.

1. $16 + p + q + 5$	**2.** $25 \cdot 12 \cdot 4$	**2-1**
3. $-5 + [-9 + (-9)]$	**4.** $3n - 6 + (-9)$	**2-2**
5. $\left(-1\frac{3}{5}\right) + \frac{2}{5} + 1$	**6.** $-7 + 5 - 4$	**2-3**

7. Samantha left home with \$42.51. The subway fare was \$1.20. At the station she bought a magazine for \$1.95. Lunch cost \$4.36. After work she bought a skirt on sale for \$26.00. Her subway fare home was also \$1.20. At the station Shelly gave Samantha \$5 to pay back a loan. How much money did Samantha have at the end of the day?

Simplify.

8. $(25 - 31) - (-6 + 11)$	**9.** $x - (-8) - [x + (-8)]$	**2-4**

10. Kara left home $2\frac{2}{3}$ hours before she arrived at the airport. How long had she been gone from home when she had been at the airport for $1\frac{2}{3}$ hours?

Simplify.

11. $(23)(0.25) - (7)(0.25)$	**12.** $(6x + 3)4$	**2-5**
13. $5(b - 1) + 8$	**14.** $7(2c - 4d + 6)$	
15. $-16(-3)$	**16.** $(-11 + 11)19$	**2-6**
17. $(-9)(8)(-1)(-3)$	**18.** $7x - y + 2x + 3y$	

19. Write an equation to represent the following relationship among integers: The sum of three consecutive even integers is 30 more than the smallest integer. **2-7**

20. State the reciprocal of -1.	**21.** State the reciprocal of $\frac{5}{7}$.	**2-8**

Simplify.

22. $\left(-\frac{1}{17}\right)(85)\left(\frac{1}{5}\right)$	**23.** $-\frac{1}{7}(-56m + 49n)$	
24. $\dfrac{-13}{\frac{1}{6}}$	**25.** $\dfrac{343w}{-7}$	**2-9**

Cumulative Review *(Chapters 1 and 2)*

Simplify.

1. $(56 \div 7) - (26 \div 13)$

2. $\frac{12 + 72}{6 + 8}$

3. $|-12| - |-6|$

4. $-|20| \div |-4|$

5. $38 + [(-3) + 16]$

6. $3[27 \div (12 \div 4)]$

7. $2 + 10 \cdot 15 \div 5$

8. $2\frac{5}{9} + 7\frac{1}{8} + 8\frac{4}{9}$

9. $-120 - (-17)$

10. $6(2x + 3) - 3(7 - 3x)$

11. $3(x + 2y) + 5(2x + y)$

12. $(-9)(-5)(4) - 9(5)$

13. $-18 - 4 - [(-6) + 12]$

14. $\frac{1}{12}(-552xy) \div (-23)$

15. $\frac{6}{7}(4a - 3b) - \frac{3}{7}(8a - 6b)$

Evaluate each expression if $x = -3$, $y = 4$, and $z = 5$.

16. $-z + (-x + 7)$

17. $x - |y| + |z|$

18. $\frac{(x + 6)(z - y)}{(x + y)}$

Write the numbers in order from least to greatest.

19. $0, -2, 4, \frac{1}{2}, -\frac{1}{2}, -3$

20. $-5, |5|, -\frac{1}{3}, -\frac{2}{3}, |-3|$

21. Graph the numbers $-4, 4, 3, 2, -\frac{1}{2}$, and 0 on a number line.

Solve.

22. $|y| = 7$

23. $|-x| = 10$

24. $-|y| = -3$

25. $c + 12 = 0$

26. $b \cdot 1 = 9$

27. $a + 25 = 25$

Solve if $x \in \{-5, -3, 0, 3, 5\}$.

28. $4x + 2 = 14$

29. $\frac{1}{3}x - 2 = -3$

30. $6 = 2x - 4$

Translate each phrase or sentence into a variable expression or an equation.

31. Five more than the product of seven and y

32. Two less than the sum of x and the opposite of a, decreased by three times y.

33. The opposite of x is four less than eight.

34. The sum of two consecutive integers is one less than twice the greater integer.

Solve.

35. Paul got into an elevator on the fourth floor. Before he got out, the elevator went up seven floors and down eight floors. On what floor did he get out?

Maintaining Skills

Perform the indicated operations.

Sample 1

$$\begin{array}{r} \overset{8}{\cancel{9}}\overset{11}{\cancel{1}}7.\overset{2}{\cancel{3}}\overset{18}{\cancel{8}} \\ -\ \ 55.19 \\ \hline 862.19 \end{array}$$

Sample 2

$$\begin{array}{r} 2.75 \\ 2.6\overline{)7.150} \\ \underline{5\,2} \\ 1\,95 \\ \underline{1\,82} \\ 130 \\ \underline{130} \\ 0 \end{array}$$

1. $\begin{array}{r} 49.92 \\ -\ 38.6 \\ \hline \end{array}$

2. $\begin{array}{r} 575.25 \\ -\ \ \ 9.009 \\ \hline \end{array}$

3. $\begin{array}{r} 337.14 \\ -\ \ 45.32 \\ \hline \end{array}$

4. $\begin{array}{r} 700.07 \\ -\ \ 38 \\ \hline \end{array}$

5. $\begin{array}{r} 3.4276 \\ -\ 0.828 \\ \hline \end{array}$

6. $\begin{array}{r} 16.8 \\ -\ \ 9.25 \\ \hline \end{array}$

7. $\begin{array}{r} 5.52 \\ -\ 4.763 \\ \hline \end{array}$

8. $\begin{array}{r} 877.3 \\ -\ \ 94.3 \\ \hline \end{array}$

9. $0.02\overline{)1.10}$

10. $0.8\overline{)0.036}$

11. $5.1\overline{)3376.2}$

12. $1.9\overline{)860.7}$

13. $3.4\overline{)0.0085}$

14. $0.05\overline{)2.367}$

15. $0.25\overline{)48}$

16. $0.34\overline{)1156}$

Express each fraction in simplest form.

Sample 3 $\frac{16}{24}$

Solution $\frac{16}{24} = \frac{2 \cdot 8}{3 \cdot 8} = \frac{2}{3}$

17. $\frac{14}{49}$

18. $\frac{21}{24}$

19. $\frac{39}{52}$

20. $\frac{27}{54}$

21. $\frac{63}{81}$

22. $\frac{27}{33}$

Perform the indicated operations. Express the answers in simplest form.

Sample 4 $\frac{5}{6} - \frac{2}{13}$ Note that the least common denominator is 78.

Solution $\frac{5}{6} - \frac{2}{13} = \left(\frac{5}{6} \cdot \frac{13}{13}\right) - \left(\frac{2}{13} \cdot \frac{6}{6}\right) = \frac{65}{78} - \frac{12}{78} = \frac{65 - 12}{78} = \frac{53}{78}$

Sample 5 $\frac{7}{18} \div \frac{14}{15}$

Solution $\frac{7}{18} \div \frac{14}{15} = \frac{7}{18} \cdot \frac{15}{14} = \frac{\overset{1}{\cancel{7}} \cdot \overset{5}{\cancel{15}}}{\underset{6}{\cancel{18}} \cdot \underset{2}{\cancel{14}}} = \frac{5}{12}$

23. $\frac{2}{3} - \frac{1}{6}$

24. $\frac{5}{7} - \frac{2}{3}$

25. $\frac{3}{4} - \frac{15}{21}$

26. $\frac{3}{4} - \frac{5}{12}$

27. $\frac{4}{5} - \frac{2}{11}$

28. $\frac{3}{7} - \frac{11}{28}$

29. $\frac{5}{6} \div \frac{5}{2}$

30. $\frac{12}{21} \div \frac{8}{14}$

31. $\frac{21}{25} \div \frac{9}{20}$

32. $\frac{10}{7} \div \frac{7}{10}$

33. $\frac{24}{25} \div \frac{5}{6}$

34. $\frac{24}{25} \div \frac{6}{5}$

Preparing for College Entrance Exams

Strategy for Success

Familiarize yourself with the test you will be taking well before the test date. This will help you to become comfortable with the types of questions and directions that may appear on the test. Sample tests, with explanations, are available for many standardized tests. The Preparing for College Entrance Exams tests at the end of even-numbered chapters in this book will give you helpful hints and practice in taking such tests.

Decide which is the best of the choices given and write the corresponding letter on your answer sheet.

1. Write an expression that corresponds to the following word sentence.
The sum of two consecutive even integers is 20 less than their product.
(A) $n(n + 1) = n + (n + 1) - 20$ **(B)** $n + (n + 1) = n(n + 1) - 20$
(C) $n(n + 2) = n + (n + 2) - 20$ **(D)** $n + (n + 2) = n(n + 2) - 20$

2. Michael's weight is 85 lb less than twice the weight of his sister Stacy. Which equation represents the relationship between Michael's weight, m, and Stacy's weight, s?
(A) $s = 2m - 85$ **(B)** $s = 2m + 85$ **(C)** $m = 2s + 85$ **(D)** $m = 2s - 85$

3. Simplify the expression $73(19 + 31) - 48(24 + 26)$.
(A) 1250 **(B)** 6050 **(C)** 1200 **(D)** 1750

4. On a number line, point A has coordinate -4 and point B has coordinate 8. What is the coordinate of the point one fourth of the way from A to B?
(A) 2 **(B)** -2 **(C)** -1 **(D)** 5 **(E)** 6

5. The operation $*$ is defined for all real numbers a and b by $a * b = ab + a + b$. Which of the following properties does $*$ have?
I. Closure II. Commutativity
(A) I only **(B)** II only **(C)** I and II
(D) None of the above

6. Suppose x is a nonzero real number. Which of the following is (are) always true?
I. $\frac{1}{|x|} > 0$ II. $|x| > x$ III. $|x| > -x$
(A) I only **(B)** II only **(C)** III only
(D) II and III only **(E)** I and III only

7. a, b, c, and d are positive numbers. Which of the following guarantees that $\frac{a - b}{c - d} < 0$?
(A) $a > b$ and $c > d$ **(B)** $a < b$ and $c < d$ **(C)** $a > b$ and $c < d$
(D) $|a - b| > 0$ and $|c - d| > 0$ **(E)** $|a - b| > 0$ and $|c - d| < 0$

3 Solving Equations and Problems

The mobile is in balance, as are the weights in the pans. If a weight is removed from just one side, the balance will be upset. We use the idea of balance to solve equations.

Transforming Equations

3-1 Transforming Equations: Addition and Subtraction

Objective To solve equations using addition or subtraction.

Two soccer teams are tied at half time: 2 to 2. If each team scores 3 goals in the next half, then the score will still be tied:

$$2 + 3 = 2 + 3$$

Two sporting goods stores charge \$36 for a soccer ball. If, during a spring sale, each store reduces the price by \$5, both stores will still be charging the same price:

$$36 - 5 = 36 - 5$$

The examples above illustrate the following properties of equality.

Addition Property of Equality

If a, b, and c are any real numbers, and $a = b$, then

$$\boldsymbol{a + c = b + c} \quad \text{and} \quad \boldsymbol{c + a = c + b}.$$

If the same number is added to equal numbers, the sums are equal.

Subtraction Property of Equality

If a, b, and c are any real numbers, and $a = b$, then

$$\boldsymbol{a - c = b - c}.$$

If the same number is subtracted from equal numbers, the differences are equal.

Notice that the subtraction property of equality is just a special case of the addition property, since subtracting the number c is the same as adding $-c$. The addition property of equality guarantees that if $a = b$,

$$a + (-c) = b + (-c)$$

or $$a - c = b - c.$$

Examples 1 and 2 show how to use the addition and subtraction properties of equality to solve some equations. You add the same number to, or subtract the same number from, each side of the given equation in order to get an equation with the variable alone on one side.

Example 1 Solve $x - 8 = 17$.

Solution

$$x - 8 = 17 \qquad \{\text{Copy the equation.}$$

$$\left.\begin{aligned} x - 8 + 8 &= 17 + 8 \\ x &= 25 \end{aligned}\right\} \text{Add 8 to each side and then simplify.}$$

Because errors may occur in solving equations, you should check that each solution of the final equation satisfies the *original equation*.

Check: $x - 8 = 17 \leftarrow$ original equation

$25 - 8 \stackrel{?}{=} 17$

$17 = 17 \ \checkmark$ $\quad \therefore$ the solution set is $\{25\}$. ***Answer***

The properties of real numbers guarantee in Example 1 that if the original equation, $x - 8 = 17$, is true for some value of x, then the final equation, $x = 25$, is also true for that value of x, and vice versa. Therefore the two equations have the same solution set, $\{25\}$.

Example 2 Solve $-5 = n + 13$.

Solution

$$-5 = n + 13$$

$$\left.\begin{aligned} -5 - 13 &= n + 13 - 13 \\ -18 &= n \end{aligned}\right\} \text{Subtract 13 from each side and then simplify.}$$

Check: $-5 = n + 13$

$-5 \stackrel{?}{=} -18 + 13$

$-5 = -5 \ \checkmark$ $\quad \therefore$ the solution set is $\{-18\}$. ***Answer***

Equations having the same solution set over a given domain are called **equivalent equations** over that domain. In Example 1, the equations $x - 8 = 17$ and $x = 25$ are equivalent equations. In Example 2, the equations $-5 = n + 13$ and $-18 = n$ are equivalent equations.

It is often possible to change, or *transform*, an equation into a simpler equivalent equation by using substitution or the addition and subtraction properties. The goal is to obtain a simpler equation whose solution or solutions can be easily seen.

Transforming an Equation into an Equivalent Equation

Transformation by Substitution
Substitute an equivalent expression for any expression in a given equation.

Transformation by Addition
Add the same real number to each side of a given equation.

Transformation by Subtraction
Subtract the same real number from each side of a given equation.

Oral Exercises

Describe how to change each equation to produce an equivalent equation with the variable alone on one side. Then state this equivalent equation.

Sample 1 $x - 3 = 5$ **Solution** Add 3 to each side; $x = 8$

Sample 2 $z + 5 = 4$ **Solution** Subtract 5 from each side; $z = -1$

1. $x + 5 = 9$ **2.** $x + 3 = 8$ **3.** $t - 2 = 7$

4. $w - 11 = 4$ **5.** $a + 9 = 1$ **6.** $b + 7 = 6$

7. $6 + n = 0$ **8.** $-4 + y = 0$ **9.** $-5 + m = 5$

10. $-1 + r = -1$ **11.** $-8 + t = -8$ **12.** $-5 = u + 9$

13. $-5 = t - 9$ **14.** $4 = -2 + s$ **15.** $-1 = 5 + k$

16. $z - \frac{1}{4} = \frac{1}{4}$ **17.** $\frac{4}{5} = \frac{1}{5} + d$ **18.** $h + 1.7 = -2.1$

19. $x + 3.2 = 4.5$ **20.** $-4.2 = z + 2.1$ **21.** $-1 + x = \frac{1}{3}$

Written Exercises

Solve.

A **1.** $x - 7 = 13$ **2.** $y - 9 = 17$ **3.** $z + 8 = 31$

4. $x + 15 = 27$ **5.** $-52 + m = 84$ **6.** $-49 + n = 63$

7. $t - 25 = -18$ **8.** $x - 26 = 18$ **9.** $p + 18 = -32$

10. $y + 32 = -45$ **11.** $0 = 38 + k$ **12.** $0 = z - 14$

13. $-19 + a = 23$ **14.** $-32 + b = 82$ **15.** $c + 9 = 5$

16. $x - 8 = 25$ **17.** $f + 7 = 9 - 2$ **18.** $g - 6 = 14 - 8$

19. $z - 57 = -67$ **20.** $x - 97 = -105$ **21.** $-0.7 + k = -1.7$

22. $-1.8 + h = -3.8$ **23.** $4.5 = x + 1.6$ **24.** $3.9 = y + 1.2$

Sample 1 $-x + 7 = 2$

Solution

$$-x + 7 - 7 = 2 - 7$$
$$-x = -5$$
$$x = 5$$

{Remember that the opposite of $-x$ is x and the opposite of -5 is 5.

$\therefore$ the solution set is $\{5\}$. ***Answer***

B **25.** $-x + 6 = 4$ **26.** $-y + 5 = 17$ **27.** $21 - x = 28$

28. $9 - y = 16$ **29.** $8 = -x + 18$ **30.** $11 = 32 - y$

Solve.

31. $-8 - y = 9$
32. $7 = -12 + e$
33. $13 = -y + 8$
34. $(c + 2) + 8 = 4$
35. $(r + 4) + 2 = 1$
36. $2 = 10 + (x - 2)$
37. $8 = 16 + (y - 1)$
38. $-2 + (1 + p) = 5$
39. $-3 + (1 + n) = 9$
40. $(a - 3) + 19 = 125$
41. $(b - 6) + 14 = 100$
42. $4 - (1 + x) = 5$
43. $2 - (3 + y) = 6$
44. $1 = -2 - (4 - w)$
45. $11 = 7 - (1 - q)$

Sample 2 $|x| + 4 = 13$

Solution

$|x| + 4 - 4 = 13 - 4$
$|x| = 9$
$x = 9$ or $x = -9$ $\therefore$ the solution set is $\{9, -9\}$ ***Answer***

C **46.** $|y| - 2 = 8$
47. $|z| + 10 = 28$
48. $-7 + |s| = 0$
49. $6 + |t| = 14$
50. $|x| + (-2) = 4$
51. $|y| + (-1) = 1$
52. $0 = -5 + |r|$
53. $2 = 6 + |t|$
54. $-(|a| - 9) = 1$
55. $-(|x| + 2) = -6$
56. $4 - (2 - |n|) = 2$
57. $7 - (3 - |m|) = 8$
58. $9 - (|s| + 7) = 4$
59. $-3 + (15 - |a|) = 12$
60. $(|e| - |-8|) + 15 = 7$

Problems

Write an equation based on the facts of the problem. Then solve the equation and answer the question asked in the problem.

Sample 1 37 less than a number is -19. What is the number?

Solution

$n - 37 = -19$
$n = 18$ $\therefore$ the number is 18. ***Answer***

A **1.** Fifty-one more than a number is -12. What is the number?
2. Twenty-two less than a number is -7. What is the number?
3. If a number is increased by 28, the result is 7. What is the number?
4. If a number is decreased by 8, the result is -21. What is the number?
5. If -8 is subtracted from a number, the result is 84. What is the number?
6. If -15 is subtracted from a number, the result is -29. What is the number?

Sample 2 Wylie hiked into the Grand Canyon from its South Rim, which is 6876 ft above sea level. Walking along the 7.8 mi Bright Angel Trail, he reached the Colorado River in 4 h. At that point he was 2460 ft lower in the Canyon than at his starting point. How far above sea level is the Colorado River at this point?

Solution

Step 1 You are asked to find the river's elevation above sea level at the point where it crosses the Bright Angel Trail. Make a sketch to show the given information.

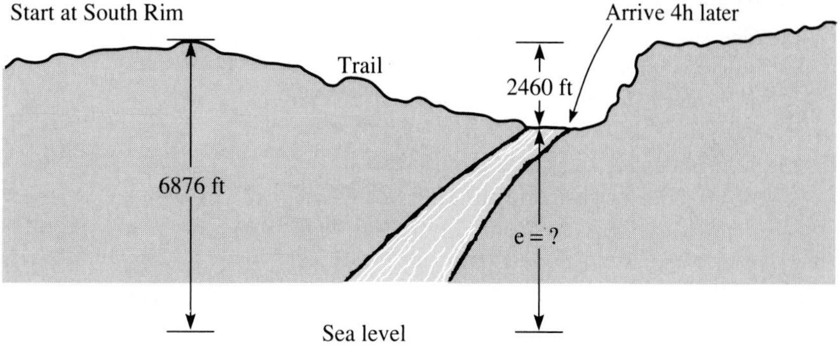

Step 2 Let e = the elevation of the river.

Step 3 $$e + 2460 = 6876$$

Step 4 $$e + 2460 - 2460 = 6876 - 2460$$
$$e = 4416$$

Step 5 *Check:* The check is left to you.

∴ the Colorado River is 4416 ft above sea level at the point where it meets the trail. ***Answer***

Notice that two of the given facts were not used in solving the problem: the length of the trail and the time spent hiking.

7. A lion can run 18 mi/h faster than a giraffe. If a lion can run 50 mi/h, how fast can a giraffe run?

8. Corita ran the 400-meter dash in 56.8 s. This was 1.3 s less than her previous time. What was her previous time?

9. The desert temperature rose 25° C between 6 A.M. and noon. If the temperature at noon was 18° C, what was the temperature at 6 A.M.?

10. The temperature at the summit of Mt. Mansfield dropped 17° F between 4 P.M. and 11 P.M. If the temperature at 11 P.M.was −11° F, what was the temperature at 4 P.M.?

11. Enrico paid $4.75 for a sandwich, a drink, and frozen yogurt. He remembered that the drink and the yogurt were each $1.15 and that the sandwich had too much mustard, but he forgot the price of the sandwich. How much did the sandwich cost?

12. Ruth Panoyan had 45 sheets of graph paper. She gave five sheets to each of the six students she tutored and put the remaining sheets in her desk. How many did she put in her desk?

Write an equation based on the facts of the problem. Then solve the equation and answer the question asked in the problem.

B **13.** A factory hired 130 new workers during a year in which 27 workers retired and 59 left for other reasons. If there were 498 workers at the end of the year, how many were there at the beginning of the year?

14. During one day of trading in the stock market, an investor lost \$2500 on one stock, but gained \$1700 on another. At the end of trading that day, the investor's holdings in those two stocks were worth \$52,400. What were they worth when the market opened that day?

15. Longitudes are measured east and west of the Greenwich meridian. How many degrees east of New York City is Nairobi, Kenya? (In the diagram, measurements are given to the nearest degree.)

16. Latitudes are measured north and south of the equator. How many degrees south of New York City is Nairobi?

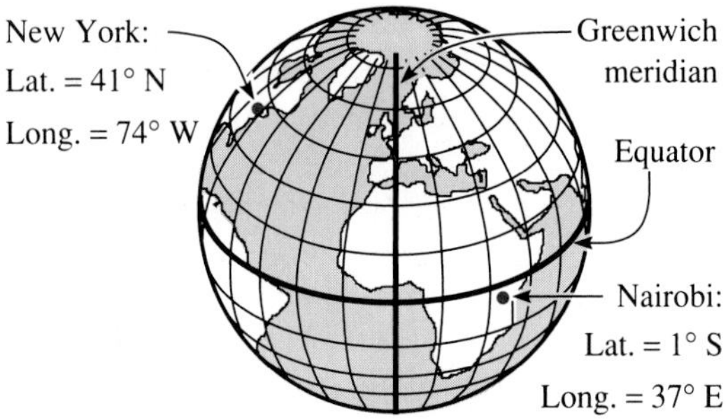

17. Gino paid \$3.23 for two tubes of toothpaste. He paid the regular price of \$1.79 for one tube. However, he bought the other one for less because he used a discount coupon. How much was the coupon worth?

18. Kerry bought a picture frame on sale for \$4.69. A week later, she returned to buy another frame. However, she had to pay the regular price for the second one. If the two frames cost Kerry \$10.64, how much had the store reduced the price for the sale?

C **19.** At 8:00 P.M. a scavenger hunt started at the town hall. Team 1 drove 5 km east to the golf course, while Team 2 drove 12 km west to the beach. By the time Team 2 had found some seaweed at the beach, Team 1 had already found an orange golf ball and driven 3 km back toward town hall. How far apart were the two teams at this point?

20. After traveling 387 miles from Los Angeles to San Francisco, Rick noted that his car's odometer read exactly 27972. This number reads the same backwards as forwards. What is the next such number and how far will he have to drive to get it to appear on the odometer?

Mixed Review Exercises

Evaluate if $a = 4$, $b = -6$, $c = -7$, and $d = 5$.

1. $a - |c - b|$

2. $(|b| - a) - (|d| - a)$

3. $2|a| - (-a)$

4. $\frac{b - 2c}{b + 2d}$

5. $\frac{4d + c + 1}{abc}$

6. $\frac{3ab}{c + d}$

Simplify.

7. $(-6)(-7)(10)$
8. $(-9 \cdot 12) + (-9 \cdot 18)$
9. $148a \div (-37)$
10. $96\left(-\frac{1}{24}\right)\left(-\frac{1}{4}\right)$
11. $-\frac{12b}{5} \cdot (-5)$
12. $\frac{1}{7}(21a - 7b) - \frac{1}{3}(12b - 6a)$

Application / *Car Loans*

A car is an expensive purchase. Most people do not have the money to pay for a car with cash. Instead, they pay part of the cash price as a *down payment* and borrow the rest by taking out a loan. The car buyer must pay the lender the amount of money borrowed, which is called the *principal,* plus *interest*.

Example Miriam bought a \$3600 used car. She made a \$630 down payment and got a loan for 36 months with payments of \$95 per month.

a. Find the total amount paid for the car.
b. Find the amount of interest Miriam had to pay.

Solution

a. Total paid = down payment + total of the monthly payments
= 630 + 36(95)
= 630 + 3420
= 4050 ∴ the total paid was \$4050. ***Answer***

b. Interest = total paid − cash price
= 4050 − 3600
= 450 ∴ Miriam had to pay \$450 in interest. ***Answer***

Exercises

a. Find the total amount to be paid on each vehicle.
b. Find the amount of interest the buyer would be paying.

1. Sean bought a \$3000 used car by making a \$480 down payment and getting a loan for two years with payments of \$115 per month.
2. The Valley Fruit Stand got a three-year loan at \$154 per month to pay for a \$5500 used truck. The down payment was \$451.
3. A \$4500 station wagon was advertised in the Daily Gazette. The buyer paid \$498 down and made 48 monthly payments of \$95 per month.
4. Linda bought a used car with a cash price of \$10,000. She made a down payment of \$620 and paid \$220 per month for four years.

3-2 Transforming Equations: Multiplication and Division

Objective To solve equations using multiplication or division.

At a hardware store, small construction supplies are often sold by the pound rather than by the number of items.

Suppose a pound of roof nails costs the same as a pound of floor nails. You would expect to pay the same price for *two* pounds of roof nails as for *two* pounds of floor nails, and the same price for *one-half* pound of roof nails as for *one-half* pound of floor nails.

This is an example of the multiplication and division properties of equality.

Multiplication Property of Equality

If a, b, and c are any real numbers, and $a = b$, then

$$ca = cb \qquad \text{and} \qquad ac = bc.$$

If equal numbers are multiplied by the same number, the products are equal.

Division Property of Equality

If a and b are any real numbers, c is any nonzero real number, and $a = b$, then

$$\frac{a}{c} = \frac{b}{c}.$$

If equal numbers are divided by the same *nonzero* number, the quotients are equal.

These properties give you two more ways to transform an equation into an equivalent equation. The others that you have already studied are listed on page 96.

Transforming an Equation into an Equivalent Equation

Transformation by Multiplication:
Multiply each side of a given equation by the same *nonzero* real number.

Transformation by Division:
Divide each side of a given equation by the same *nonzero* real number.

Example 1 Solve $6x = 222$.

Solution

$$6x = 222$$
$$\frac{6x}{6} = \frac{222}{6}$$
$$x = 37$$

$\left\{\text{To get } x \text{ alone on one side, divide each side by 6 (or multiply by } \tfrac{1}{6}\text{, the reciprocal of 6).}\right.$

Check:

$$6x = 222$$
$$6(37) \stackrel{?}{=} 222$$
$$222 = 222 \quad \checkmark$$

$\therefore$ the solution set is $\{37\}$. ***Answer***

Example 2 Solve $8 = -\frac{2}{3}t$.

Solution

$$8 = -\frac{2}{3}t$$
$$-\frac{3}{2}(8) = -\frac{3}{2}\left(-\frac{2}{3}t\right)$$
$$-12 = t$$

$\left\{\text{To get } t \text{ alone on one side, multiply each side by } -\tfrac{3}{2}\text{, the reciprocal of } -\tfrac{2}{3}.\right.$

Check:

$$8 = -\frac{2}{3}t$$
$$8 \stackrel{?}{=} -\frac{2}{3}(-12)$$
$$8 = 8 \quad \checkmark$$

$\therefore$ the solution set is $\{-12\}$. ***Answer***

Example 3 Solve: **a.** $\frac{m}{3} = -5$ **b.** $\frac{1}{4}s = 6\frac{1}{4}$

Solution

a.

$$3\left(\frac{m}{3}\right) = 3(-5)$$
$$m = -15$$

$\therefore$ the solution set is $\{-15\}$. ***Answer***

b.

$$\frac{1}{4}s = \frac{25}{4}$$
$$4\left(\frac{1}{4}s\right) = 4\left(\frac{25}{4}\right)$$
$$s = 25$$

$\therefore$ the solution set is $\{25\}$. ***Answer***

You know that zero cannot be a divisor (page 84). Do you know why zero is not allowed as a multiplier in transforming an equation? Look at the following equations.

(1) $5z = 45$
(2) $0 \cdot 5z = 0 \cdot 45$
(3) $(0 \cdot 5)z = 0 \cdot 45$
(4) $0 \cdot z = 0$

Equation (1) had just one root, namely 9. Equation 4 is satisfied by *any* real number. Since they do not have the same solution set, Equations (1) and (4) are *not* equivalent (see page 96). *In transforming an equation, never multiply by zero.*

Oral Exercises

Describe how you could produce an equivalent equation with the variable alone on one side. Then state the equivalent equation.

1. $8x = 16$ **2.** $5y = 15$ **3.** $3a = -12$

4. $-8a = 32$ **5.** $\frac{1}{2}b = 4$ **6.** $\frac{1}{3}t = 7$

7. $-\frac{1}{10}r = 5$ **8.** $-\frac{9}{5}m = 9$ **9.** $5 = \frac{5}{3}y$

10. $-7 = -\frac{7}{2}x$ **11.** $0 = -4k$ **12.** $x \div 8 = -1$

13. $n \div (-5) = 4$ **14.** $\frac{d}{2} = -6$ **15.** $-4 = \frac{x}{3}$

16. $-11f = -88$ **17.** $-25p = -75$ **18.** $7 = -\frac{u}{2}$

Written Exercises

Solve.

A

1. $4x = 44$ **2.** $5y = 65$ **3.** $6y = -18$ **4.** $3t = -27$

5. $-8c = 72$ **6.** $-6p = 42$ **7.** $-12a = -36$ **8.** $-9z = -63$

9. $\frac{1}{2}x = 12$ **10.** $\frac{1}{3}y = 18$ **11.** $\frac{x}{5} = -7$ **12.** $\frac{c}{4} = -9$

13. $-\frac{1}{8}b = 8$ **14.** $-\frac{1}{5}t = 17$ **15.** $\frac{2}{3}x = 12$ **16.** $\frac{5}{2}y = 10$

17. $\frac{3}{4}d = -60$ **18.** $\frac{5}{8}c = -20$ **19.** $-\frac{2}{3}t = 22$ **20.** $-\frac{2}{11}p = 14$

21. $600 = -25x$ **22.** $-324 = -18c$ **23.** $-17d = 0$ **24.** $252 = -14y$

25. $99 = -\frac{11}{5}x$ **26.** $24 = -\frac{3}{7}t$ **27.** $-6 = \frac{x}{3}$ **28.** $21 = \frac{c}{7}$

B

29. $\frac{1}{3}y = 2\frac{1}{3}$ **30.** $\frac{1}{2}t = 3\frac{1}{2}$ **31.** $-1 = 2.5z$ **32.** $0 = -4.5y$

33. $\frac{2}{5}a = 6\frac{2}{5}$ **34.** $\frac{3}{2}b = -14\frac{1}{2}$ **35.** $-\frac{y}{3} = 3\frac{2}{3}$ **36.** $-\frac{x}{2} = 11\frac{1}{2}$

37. $-\frac{y}{12} = \frac{1}{4}$ **38.** $-\frac{n}{4} = -\frac{3}{2}$ **39.** $0 = -\frac{x}{5}$ **40.** $-\frac{5}{3}x = 10$

C

41. $2|x| = 18$ **42.** $3|y| = 33$ **43.** $-7|t| = 42$ **44.** $-32 = 8|k|$

45. $\frac{|x|}{5} = 2$ **46.** $\frac{|a|}{8} = 4$ **47.** $3 = \frac{|n|}{7}$ **48.** $6 = \frac{|m|}{2}$

49. $\frac{5|c|}{3} = 10$ **50.** $\frac{4}{7}|x| = 16$ **51.** $7 - \frac{3|a|}{2} = 1$ **52.** $10 - \frac{4}{3}|b| = -2$

Problems

Write an equation based on the facts of each problem. Then solve the equation and the problem.

A

1. Five times a number is -375. Find the number.
2. Negative nine times a number is -108. Find the number.
3. One third of a number is -7. Find the number.
4. Three quarters of a number is 21. Find the number.
5. One hundred twenty seniors are on the honor roll. This represents one third of the senior class. How many seniors are there?
6. Two hundred twenty-five students play a team sport at Lincoln High School. These students represent $\frac{3}{8}$ of the total student population. How many students attend the school?
7. The perimeter of a square parking lot is 784 m. How long is each side of the lot?
8. The distance around the United States Pentagon building is one mile. How long is each side? (*Hint:* A regular pentagon has five equal sides.)

9. Luis ate three of the eight pizza slices. He paid \$2.70 as his share of the cost. How much did the whole pizza cost?
10. A restaurant charges \$2.50 for one eighth of a quiche. At this rate, how much does the restaurant receive for the whole quiche?
11. The Eagles won three times as many games as they lost. They won 21 games. How many games did they lose?
12. Buena Vista High School has five times as many black-and-white monitors as color monitors. The school has 40 black-and-white monitors for computers. How many color monitors does the school have?
13. How many apples, averaging 0.2 kg each, are included in a 50 kg shipment of apples?
14. A 75-watt bulb consumes 0.075 kW · h (kilowatt-hours) of energy when it burns for one hour. How long was the bulb left burning if it consumed 3.3 kW · h of energy?

B

15. A hard-cover book sells for \$16.50. The same title in paperback sells for \$4.95. How many hard-cover books must a dealer sell to take in as much money as he/she does for 30 paperback copies?
16. A certain real-estate agent receives \$6 for every \$100 of a house's selling price. How much was a house sold for if the agent received \$10,725?

17. An employer said that each worker received \$24 in fringe benefits for every \$100 in wages. At this rate, what wages were earned by a worker whose fringe benefits were valued at \$5100?

18. One kilogram of sea water contains, on average, 35 g of salt. How many grams of sea water contain 4.2 g of salt?

C **19.** Raul drove $\frac{1}{4}$ mi from Exit 27 to Exit 28 in 18 s. At what rate was he traveling in mi/s? At what rate was he driving in mi/h? (*Hint:* rate · time = distance)

20. A police helicopter clocked a truck over a stretch of highway $\frac{1}{5}$ mi long. The truck traveled the distance in 10 s. At what rate was the truck traveling in mi/s? At what rate was it traveling in mi/h?

Mixed Review Exercises

Evaluate if $a = 2$, $b = -3$, and $c = 4$.

1. $7a - 2b$ **2.** $(3a - 2b)c$ **3.** $|b| + |c| - (-c)$

4. $|a| - |b + c|$ **5.** $\frac{-(5ab)}{2c}$ **6.** $\frac{2 + a}{c}$

Simplify.

7. $7a + 6 + 9a$ **8.** $5n - 9 + 9$ **9.** $10p - p + 2$

10. $-4(m + 2)$ **11.** $(x + 7)8$ **12.** $3(2y - 5)$

Calculator Key-In

Use the division key on a calculator to find a decimal equal to each expression.

Sample 1 $\frac{-36}{8}$ ***Solution*** $\frac{-36}{8} = -36 \div 8 = -4.5$

1. $\frac{3}{4}$ **2.** $\frac{-5}{8}$ **3.** $\frac{7}{-35}$ **4.** $\frac{-3}{-20}$ **5.** $\frac{1}{40}$

6. $\frac{-11}{4}$ **7.** $\frac{12}{-50}$ **8.** $\frac{-7}{-8}$ **9.** $\frac{31}{32}$ **10.** $\frac{43}{-64}$

11–20. Use the multiplication and reciprocal keys on a calculator to find a decimal equal to each expression in Exercises 1–10. (See Sample 2.) Are your answers the same as before?

Sample 2 $\frac{-36}{8}$ ***Solution*** $\frac{-36}{8} = -36 \cdot \frac{1}{8} = -4.5$

3-3 Using Several Transformations

Objective To solve equations by using more than one transformation.

If you start with n, multiply by 5, and subtract 9, you get the expression $5n - 9$. If you start with $5n - 9$, add 9, and divide by 5, you're back to n.

$$n \xrightarrow{\times 5} 5n \xrightarrow{-9} 5n - 9$$

$$5n - 9 \xrightarrow{+9} 5n \xrightarrow{\div 5} n$$

The addition of 9 "undoes" the subtraction of 9. We call addition and subtraction **inverse operations.** The diagram also shows that division by 5 "undoes" multiplication by 5. Multiplication and division are also inverse operations.

For all real numbers a and b,

$$\mathbf{(a + b) - b = a} \quad \text{and} \quad \mathbf{(a - b) + b = a.}$$

For all real numbers a and all *nonzero* real numbers b,

$$\mathbf{(ab) \div b = a} \quad \text{and} \quad \mathbf{(a \div b)b = a.}$$

Example 1 Solve $5n - 9 = 71$.

Solution

Use inverse operations:

$$5n - 9 = 71$$

$$5n - 9 + 9 = 71 + 9$$

To undo the subtraction of 9 from $5n$, add 9 to each side.

$$5n = 80$$

$$\frac{5n}{5} = \frac{80}{5}$$

To undo the multiplication of n by 5, divide each side by 5.

$$n = 16$$

$\therefore$ the solution set is $\{16\}$. ***Answer***

Example 2 Solve $\frac{1}{2}x + 3 = 9$.

Solution

$$\frac{1}{2}x + 3 = 9$$

$$\frac{1}{2}x + 3 - 3 = 9 - 3$$

To undo the addition of 3 to $\frac{1}{2}x$, subtract 3 from each side.

$$\frac{1}{2}x = 6$$

$$2\left(\frac{1}{2}x\right) = 2 \cdot 6$$

To undo the multiplication of x by $\frac{1}{2}$, multiply each side by 2, the reciprocal of $\frac{1}{2}$.

$$x = 12$$

$\therefore$ the solution set is $\{12\}$. ***Answer***

Example 3 Solve $\frac{w-5}{9} = 2$.

Solution 1

$$\frac{w-5}{9} = 2$$
$$9\left(\frac{w-5}{9}\right) = 9 \cdot 2$$
$$w - 5 = 18$$
$$w - 5 + 5 = 18 + 5$$
$$w = 23$$

$\therefore$ the solution set is $\{23\}$. ***Answer***

Solution 2 (condensed)

$$\frac{w-5}{9} = 2$$
$$w - 5 = 18$$
$$w = 23$$

$\therefore$ the solution set is $\{23\}$. ***Answer***

Examples 4 and 5 show that it is sometimes necessary to use the distributive property and simplify one or both sides of an equation as the first step in solving it.

Example 4 Solve $32 = 7a + 9a$.

Solution 1

$$32 = 7a + 9a.$$
$$32 = 16a$$
$$\frac{32}{16} = \frac{16a}{16}$$
$$2 = a$$

$\therefore$ the solution set is $\{2\}$. ***Answer***

Solution 2 (condensed)

$$32 = 7a + 9a$$
$$32 = 16a$$
$$2 = a$$

$\therefore$ the solution set is $\{2\}$. ***Answer***

Example 5 Solve $4(y + 8) - 7 = 15$.

Solution 1

$$4(y + 8) - 7 = 15$$
$$4y + 32 - 7 = 15$$

{Use the distributive property and simplify the left side.

$$4y + 25 = 15$$
$$4y + 25 - 25 = 15 - 25$$
$$4y = -10$$
$$\frac{4y}{4} = \frac{-10}{4}$$
$$y = -\frac{10}{4} = -\frac{5}{2}$$

$\therefore$ the solution set is $\left\{-\frac{5}{2}\right\}$. ***Answer***

Solution 2 (condensed)

$$4(y + 8) - 7 = 15$$
$$4y + 32 - 7 = 15$$
$$4y + 25 = 15$$
$$4y = -10$$
$$y = -\frac{10}{4} = -\frac{5}{2}$$

$\therefore$ the solution set is $\left\{-\frac{5}{2}\right\}$. ***Answer***

At the top of the next page you will find two helpful tips for solving an equation in which the variable is on one side.

1. Simplify each side of the equation as needed.
2. If the side containing the variable involves a certain order of operations, apply the inverse operations in the opposite order.

Oral Exercises

Describe how you would solve each equation.

Sample 1 $\frac{1}{5}x + 2 = -1$

Solution First subtract 2 from each side; then multiply each side by 5.

Sample 2 $14 = \frac{2m}{3}$

Solution 1 Multiply each side by 3; then divide each side by 2.

Solution 2 Multiply each side by $\frac{3}{2}$.

1. $5y + 3 = 18$ **2.** $3y - 4 = 14$ **3.** $\frac{1}{4}a - 2 = -3$

4. $-\frac{1}{2}b + 9 = 5$ **5.** $-6 + \frac{y}{5} = 5$ **6.** $4 = -4 - \frac{x}{3}$

7. $\frac{3n}{4} = -12$ **8.** $\frac{-5z}{9} = 30$ **9.** $5x + 4x = 18$

10. $-4n + 7n = -36$ **11.** $\frac{7}{8}s + 2 = 16$ **12.** $1 - \frac{4}{5}n = -19$

13. $\frac{y - 2}{3} = 7$ **14.** $\frac{2}{3}w + 4 = 5$ **15.** $1 - \frac{2}{9}v = 4$

16. $5 = c + 8c - 4$ **17.** $10p - p + 2 = -7$ **18.** $-4(m + 12) = 36$

Written Exercises

Solve.

A **1.** $2x - 1 = 11$ **2.** $3y - 8 = 16$ **3.** $4n + 9 = -3$

4. $5c + 7 = -28$ **5.** $-2x + 5 = 19$ **6.** $-8y - 11 = 13$

7. $\frac{1}{2}x + 7 = 6$ **8.** $\frac{2}{3}p - 7 = 17$ **9.** $\frac{2x}{3} = 8$

10. $\frac{4y}{5} = 28$ **11.** $\frac{x + 5}{3} = 7$ **12.** $\frac{z - 5}{4} = 8$

Solve.

13. $\frac{1-x}{2} = 7$

14. $\frac{5-n}{3} = 4$

15. $7x - 4x = 54$

16. $3y - 7y = 28$

17. $-3n - 5n = 0$

18. $2a - 11a = -27$

19. $y - 7 + 4y = 13$

20. $2x + 5 - 7x = 15$

21. $0 = n - 15 - 4n$

22. $0 = p + 18 + 5p$

23. $2(x - 4) = 22$

24. $3(y - 7) = 27$

25. $35 = 5(n + 2)$

26. $20 = 4(x + 3)$

27. $y + 5 - 4y = -10$

28. $4w - 3w + 2w = 24$

29. $15 = 8x - 5 + 2x$

30. $32 = 2n - 3n + 5n$

B

31. $-\frac{1}{2}(x + 4) = 16$

32. $\frac{3}{5}(x + 2) = 12$

33. $21 = -\frac{3}{2}(x - 2)$

34. $66 = -\frac{6}{5}(s + 3)$

35. $3(a - 5) + 19 = -2$

36. $2(b + 8) - 9 = 5$

37. $-3 = 4(k + 7) - 15$

38. $3 = 7(h - 2) + 17$

39. $4c + 3(c - 2) = -34$

40. $d + 4(d + 6) = -1$

41. $\frac{2x - 1}{3} = 5$

42. $\frac{4y + 3}{7} = 9$

43. $0 = \frac{8 - 2x}{5}$

44. $7 = \frac{4 + 9y}{7}$

45. $1 - \frac{3}{4}(v + 2) = -5$

46. $9 - \frac{4}{5}(u - 3) = 1$

47. $-9 - 3(2q - 1) = -18$

48. $-10 + 4(3p + 10) = 18$

49. $-2 = 4(s + 8) - 3s$

50. $-7 = 3(t - 5) - t$

51. $(x - 13) - (x - 5) + 2x = 0$

52. $(5 - y) + (6 - y) - (5 - y) = 0$

53. $b - (1 - 2b) + (b - 3) = -4$

54. $(c + 3) - 2c - (1 - 3c) = 2$

C

55. $5m - 3[7 - (1 - 2m)] = 0$

56. $\frac{1}{5}[4(k + 2) - (3 - k)] = 4$

57. $5(g - 7) + 2[g - 3(g - 5)] = 0$

58. $7n + 2[3(1 - n) - 2(1 + n)] = 14$

59. $3|n| - (2|n| - 2) = 9$

60. $(9|x| + 3) - 5|x| - 3 = 12$

Mixed Review Exercises

Solve.

1. $\frac{1}{7}x = -23$

2. $\frac{x}{8} = \frac{3}{4}$

3. $\frac{1}{5}x = 3\frac{1}{5}$

4. $-3 + x = 1$

5. $2x + 7 = 13$

6. $51 = y + 17$

7. $-12 + x = -20$

8. $32 - x = 36$

9. $-0.25x = 1$

10. $2.3 = x + 1$

11. $0 = 3x$

12. $18y = 360$

Computer Exercises

1. Write a BASIC program to solve an equation of the form $Ax + B = C$, where the values of A, B, and C are entered with INPUT statements. Use the program to solve the following equations.

   a. $7x + 8 = 64$ **b.** $3x - 2 = -8$ **c.** $\frac{2}{5}x + 11 = 7$

   d. $\frac{3}{2}x + 4 = 13$ **e.** $\frac{1}{4}x - 9 = 0$ **f.** $\frac{3}{10}x + 10.7 = 14$

2. Use the program from Exercise 1 to solve $0x + 9 = 12$. What happens? What is the correct solution? Modify the program from Exercise 1 to print an appropriate response if the value of A is 0.

3. Modify the program from Exercise 1 to solve an equation of the form $A|x| + B = C$. Use this program to solve the following equations.

   a. $|x| + 8 = 10$ **b.** $|x| + 10 = 8$ **c.** $6|x| + 2 = 5$

Self-Test 1

Vocabulary equivalent equations (p. 96)
transformation by substitution (p. 96)
transformation by addition (p. 96)
transformation by subtraction (p. 96)
transformation by multiplication (p. 102)
transformation by division (p. 102)
inverse operations (p. 107)

Solve.

1. $n - 32 = 6$ 2. $19 + y = 61$ **Obj. 3-1, p. 95**

3. $625 = 5y$ 4. $-\frac{1}{2}x = 5\frac{1}{2}$ **Obj. 3-2, p. 102**

5. A rectangle is three times as long as it is wide. If its perimeter is 48 cm, find its dimensions. Draw a diagram first.

6. $3x - 4 = 17$ 7. $\frac{1}{2}y + 4 = 16$ **Obj. 3-3, p. 107**

Check your answers with those at the back of the book.

Calculator Key-In

You can use a calculator to check whether 16 is a solution of $5n - 9 = 71$. If it is, the calculator will display 71 when you enter $5 \times 16 - 9$.

Exercises

Is the given number a solution of the equation?

1. $6x - 7 = 21$; 3.5 2. $22x + 5 = 60$; 2.5 3. $3.9x - 11.2 = 4.6$; 4.2

Solving Problems

3-4 Using Equations to Solve Problems

Objective To use the five-step plan to solve word problems.

The skills that you have gained in solving equations can often help you to solve word problems. Use the five-step plan on page 27 as a guide.

Example 1 Lynne took a taxicab from her office to the airport. She had to pay a flat fee of \$2.05 plus \$.90 per mile. The total cost was \$5.65. How many miles was the taxi trip?

Solution

Step 1 The problem asks for the number of miles traveled in the taxi.

Step 2 Let m = the number of miles.
Then $90m$ = the mileage cost in cents.

Step 3 Flat fee + mileage cost = total cost
$$205 + 90m = 565$$

Step 4 Solve.
$$90m = 360$$
$$m = 4$$

Step 5 *Check:* 4 miles at \$.90 per mile: 4(\$.90) = \$3.60
Flat fee + mileage cost: \$2.05 + \$3.60 = \$5.65 ✓

∴ the taxi trip was 4 mi. ***Answer***

Example 2 shows that some word problems can be solved more easily if you first draw a diagram.

Example 2 The perimeter of a trapezoid is 90 cm.
The parallel bases are 24 cm and 38 cm long.
The lengths of the other two sides are consecutive odd integers.
What are the lengths of these other two sides?

Solution

Step 1 Draw a diagram to help you understand the problem.

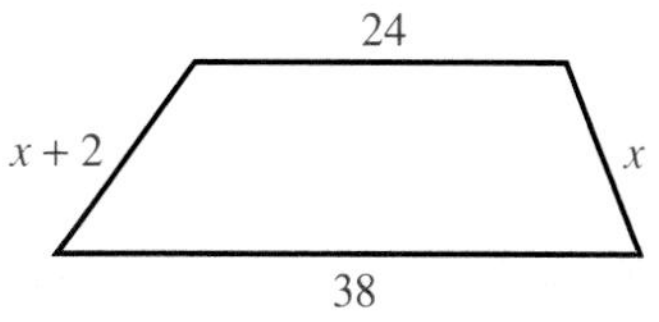

Step 2 Use x and $x + 2$ to represent the unknown lengths of the sides.

Step 3

$$\text{perimeter} = 90$$
$$38 + x + 24 + (x + 2) = 90$$

Step 4

$$2x + 64 = 90$$
$$2x = 26$$
$$x = 13 \text{ and } x + 2 = 15$$

Step 5 *Check:* Is the sum of the lengths of the sides 90 cm?

$38 + 13 + 24 + 15 = 90$ ✓

$\therefore$ the required lengths are 13 cm and 15 cm. ***Answer***

Problems

Solve each problem using the five-step plan to help you.

A

1. The sum of 38 and twice a number is 124. Find the number.
2. Five more than three times a number is 197. Find the number.
3. Four less than half of a number is 17. Find the number.
4. When one third of a number is decreased by 11, the result is 38. Find the number.
5. Four more than two thirds of a number is 22. Find the number.
6. Eight less than three quarters of a number is 91. Find the number.
7. Find three consecutive integers whose sum is 171.
8. Find three consecutive odd integers whose sum is 105.
9. Find four consecutive even integers whose sum is 244.
10. Find five consecutive integers whose sum is 195.
11. Burt's Burger Barn sold 495 hamburgers today. The number sold with cheese was half the number sold without cheese. How many of each kind were sold?
12. A company added a new oil tank that holds 350 barrels of oil more than its old oil tank. Together they hold 3650 barrels of oil. How much does each tank hold?
13. Brian has \$88 in his savings account. If he saves \$3.50 per week, how long will it take him to have \$200 in his account?
14. A 1000 L tank now contains 240 L of water. How long will it take to fill the tank using a pump that pumps 25 L per minute?

Solve each problem using the five-step plan. In Exercises 15–26, draw a diagram to help you.

15. The perimeter of a rectangle is 332 cm and the width is 76 cm. Find the rectangle's length.

16. The perimeter of a rectangle is 408 cm and the length is 134 cm. Find the rectangle's width.

17. In an isosceles triangle, there are two sides, called *legs,* with the same length. The third side is called the *base*. If an isosceles triangle has perimeter 345 cm and base length 85 cm, what is the length of each leg?

18. The length of a rectangle is 7 cm more than the width. The perimeter is 78 cm. Find the rectangle's dimensions.

19. The width of a rectangle is 15 cm less than the length. The perimeter is 98 cm. Find the rectangle's dimensions.

20. The longest side of a triangle is twice as long as the shortest side and the remaining side is 25 cm. If the perimeter is 70 cm, find the lengths of the sides of the triangle.

21. A rectangle's length is 8 cm more than three times its width. If the perimeter is 128 cm, find the length and the width.

22. A triangle has sides with lengths in centimeters that are consecutive even integers. Find the lengths if the perimeter is 186 cm.

B **23.** In any triangle, the sum of the measures of the angles is 180°. In $\triangle ABC$, $\angle A$ is three times as large as $\angle B$ and also 16° larger than $\angle C$. Find the measure of each angle.

24. In any triangle, the sum of the measures of the angles is 180°. In $\triangle ABC$, $\angle A$ is twice as large as $\angle B$. $\angle B$ is 4° larger than $\angle C$. Find the measure of each angle.

25. In $\triangle ABC$, $\overline{AB}$ is 9 cm shorter than $\overline{AC}$, while $\overline{BC}$ is 3 cm longer than $\overline{AC}$. If the perimeter of the triangle is 48 cm, find the lengths of the three sides.

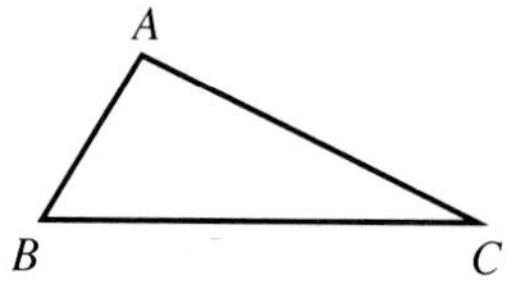

26. In isosceles trapezoid $ABCD$, the longer base, $\overline{AB}$, is one and one half times as long as the shorter base, $\overline{CD}$. The other two sides, $\overline{AD}$ and $\overline{BC}$, are both 13 cm long.

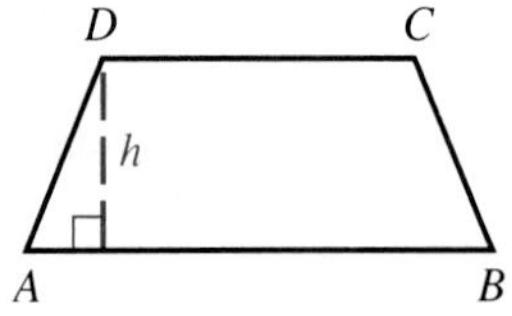

a. If the perimeter is 76 cm, find the lengths of $\overline{AB}$ and $\overline{CD}$.

b. If the height of the trapezoid is 12 cm, find its area.
(*Hint:* Area $= \frac{1}{2} \times$ height $\times$ sum of base lengths)

27. Theo has \$5 more than Denise and Denise has \$11 more than Rudy. Together they have \$45. How much money does each have?

28. Chandra has twice as much money as Nora. Nora has \$6 less than Lian. Together they have \$54. How much money does each have?

29. In one day, Machine A caps twice as many bottles as Machine B. Machine C caps 500 more bottles than Machine A. The three machines cap a total of 40,000 bottles in a day. How many bottles does each of the machines cap in one day?

30. The total cost of a sandwich, a glass of milk, and an apple is \$3.50. The milk costs one and a half times as much as the apple. The sandwich costs \$1.40 more than the apple. What is the price of each?

C 31. With the major options package and destination charge, a sports car cost \$24,416. The base price of the car was ten times the price of the major options package and fifty times the destination charge. What was the base price of the car?

32. On the first of three tests, Keiko scored 72 points. On the third test, her score was 1 point more than on the second. Her average on the three tests was 83. What were her scores on the second and third tests?

33. The absolute value of the sum of -7 and twice a number is 23. Find the number. (*Hint:* There are two answers.)

Mixed Review Exercises

Solve.

1. $-5 + y = 1$	**2.** $x - 1.5 = -3$	**3.** $y + 8 = 21$	**4.** $\frac{2}{5}y = 2$
5. $-21 = \frac{c}{3}$	**6.** $-\frac{1}{5}x = 20$	**7.** $41 = y + 11$	**8.** $x - 20 = 37$
9. $0 = 1.75y$	**10.** $5y + 6 = 16$	**11.** $2x - 5 = 15$	**12.** $2(a - 3) + 6 = -3$

Historical Note / *Variables*

Until the sixteenth century, unknown quantities were represented by words such as "heap," "root," or "thing." Eventually, abbreviations for such words, as well as drawings of squares and cubes, were used to symbolize unknowns.

In the late sixteenth century, a French lawyer, Francois Vietá, who enjoyed studying algebra during his leisure hours, began using vowels for unknowns. An English mathematician, Thomas Harriot, later adopted lowercase letters to stand for variables. In 1637, René Descartes, a French mathematician and philosopher, began using the final letters of the alphabet to represent unknowns.

3-5 Equations with the Variable on Both Sides

Objective To solve equations with the variable on both sides.

In the first four lessons of this chapter, the variable appeared on just one side of a given equation. In this lesson, the variable may occur on both sides of the equation. Since variables represent numbers, you may transform an equation by adding a variable expression to each side or by subtracting a variable expression from each side. Then solve the resulting equation as you have in earlier lessons.

Example 1 Solve $6x = 4x + 18$.

Solution 1

$$6x = 4x + 18$$
$$6x - 4x = 4x + 18 - 4x \qquad \text{Subtract } 4x \text{ from each side.}$$
$$2x = 18$$
$$\frac{2x}{2} = \frac{18}{2}$$
$$x = 9$$

Solution 2 (condensed)

$$6x = 4x + 18 \qquad \textit{Check: } 6 \cdot 9 \stackrel{?}{=} 4 \cdot 9 + 18$$
$$2x = 18 \qquad 54 \stackrel{?}{=} 36 + 18$$
$$x = 9 \qquad 54 = 54 \ \checkmark$$

$\therefore$ the solution set is $\{9\}$. ***Answer***

Example 2 Solve $3y = 15 - 2y$.

Solution

$$3y = 15 - 2y \qquad \text{Add } 2y \text{ to both sides.}$$
$$5y = 15$$
$$y = 3$$

$\therefore$ the solution set is $\{3\}$. ***Answer***

Example 3 Solve: **a.** $\frac{4}{5}x + 3 = x$ **b.** $\frac{8 + x}{9} = x$

Solution

a.

$$3 = x - \frac{4}{5}x$$
$$3 = x\left(1 - \frac{4}{5}\right)$$
$$3 = \frac{1}{5}x$$
$$15 = x$$

$\therefore$ the solution set is $\{15\}$. ***Answer***

b.

$$8 + x = 9x$$
$$8 = 8x$$
$$1 = x$$

$\therefore$ the solution set is $\{1\}$. ***Answer***

Example 4 Solve $7(a-2)-6=2a+8+a$.

Solution

$$\begin{aligned} 7(a-2)-6&=2a+8+a \\ 7a-14-6&=2a+8+a \\ 7a-20&=3a+8 \\ 4a-20&=8 \\ 4a&=28 \\ a&=7 \end{aligned}$$

{First use the distributive property and simplify both sides.}

$\therefore$ the solution set is $\{7\}$. ***Answer***

It is possible that an equation may have *no* solution, or that it may be satisfied by *every* real number. Examples 5 and 6 illustrate these cases.

Example 5 Solve $3(1-r)+5r=2(r+1)$.

Solution

$$\begin{aligned} 3-3r+5r&=2r+2 \\ 3+2r&=2r+2 \\ 3+2r-2r&=2r+2-2r \\ 3&=2 \end{aligned}$$

The given equation is equivalent to the false statement $3=2$.
$\therefore$ the equation has no solution. ***Answer***

We call the set with no members the **empty set,** or the **null set.** It is denoted by the symbol $\emptyset$. The solution set of the equation in Example 5 is $\emptyset$.

Example 6 Solve $\frac{1}{3}(12x-21)=4x-7$.

Solution

$$4x-7=4x-7$$

The given equation is equivalent to $4x-7=4x-7$, which is satisfied by every real number. $\therefore$ the solution set is {real numbers}. ***Answer***

An equation that is true for every value of the variable is called an **identity.** The equation in Example 6 is an identity.

Oral Exercises

Solve. If the equation is an identity or if it has no solution, say so.

1. $4x=3x+5$ **2.** $4n+10=5n$ **3.** $8r+1=9r$

4. $2p-1=3p$ **5.** $7+b=b+7$ **6.** $2b=6+2b$

7. $4a=2a+a$ **8.** $8k=k$ **9.** $3s=s-2$

10. $3n+4=3n+5$ **11.** $5(x-2)=5x-10$ **12.** $3(w+1)=2w$

Written Exercises

Solve each equation. If the equation is an identity or if it has no solution, write *identity* or *no solution*.

A

1. $5n = 2n + 6$
2. $8a = 2a + 30$
3. $y = 24 - 3y$
4. $2b = 80 - 8b$
5. $12n = 34 - 5n$
6. $3x = 27 - 15x$
7. $30 = 8 - 2x$
8. $51 = 9 - 3x$
9. $51a - 56 = 44a$
10. $39c + 78 = 33c$
11. $98 - 4b = -11b$
12. $-7a = -12a - 65$
13. $4n + 5 = 6n + 7$
14. $5p - 9 = 2p + 12$
15. $3p - 8 = 13 - 4p$
16. $89 + x = 2 - 2x$
17. $71 - 5x = 9x - 13$
18. $5n + 1 = 5n - 1$
19. $2(x - 6) = 3x$
20. $4(y - 6) = 7y$
21. $8(5 - n) = 2n$
22. $7(2 - m) = 3m$
23. $\frac{1}{2}x + 5 = x$
24. $\frac{2}{3}x - 7 = x$
25. $\frac{4 + y}{5} = y$
26. $\frac{x - 2}{3} = x$
27. $\frac{9 - 2y}{7} = y$
28. $\frac{6 - 4y}{2} = y$
29. $\frac{4n - 28}{3} = 2n$
30. $\frac{23 - 11c}{7} = 5c$

B

31. $\frac{1}{3}(12 - 6x) = 4 - 2x$
32. $\frac{1}{4}(20 - 4a) = 6 - a$
33. $5(2 + n) = 3(n + 6)$
34. $3(30 + s) = 4(s + 19)$
35. $5u + 5(1 - u) = u + 8$
36. $2(g - 2) - 4 = 2(g - 3)$
37. $3(m + 5) - 6 = 3(m + 3)$
38. $3(2 + v) - 4v = v + 16$
39. $3(5y + 2) - y = 2(y - 3)$
40. $4(3y - 1) + 13 = 5y + 2$
41. $6r - 2(2 - r) = 4(2r - 1)$
42. $5x + 2(1 - x) = 2(2x - 1)$
43. $3 + 4(p + 2) = 2p + 3(p + 4)$
44. $4(a + 2) = 14 - 2(3 - 2a)$

C

45. $3x + 2[1 - 3(x + 2)] = 2x$
46. $2[5(w + 3) - (w + 1)] = 3(1 + w)$
47. $5(2m + 3) - (1 - 2m) = 2[3(3 + 2m) - (3 - m)]$
48. $3(r + 1) - [2(3 - 2r) - 3(3 - r)] = 2(r + 5) - 4$

Problems

Solve.

A

1. Find a number that is 96 greater than its opposite.
2. Find a number that is 38 less than its opposite.
3. Find a number whose product with 9 is the same as its sum with 56.
4. Find a number that is 68 greater than three times its opposite.

5. Three times a number, decreased by 8, is the same as twice the number, increased by 15. Find the number.

6. Four times a number, increased by 25, is 13 less than six times the number. Find the number.

7. The greater of two consecutive integers is 15 more than twice the smaller. Find the integers.

8. The greater of two consecutive even integers is 20 more than twice the smaller. Find the integers.

9. Lyle shot three times as many baskets as Cliff, while Kyle shot 12 more baskets than Cliff. If Lyle and Kyle shot the same number of baskets, how many baskets did each of them shoot?

10. Dionne has six steel balls of equal mass. If she puts five of them in one pan of a beam balance and one ball and a 100 g mass in the other pan, the pans balance each other. What is the mass of each steel ball?

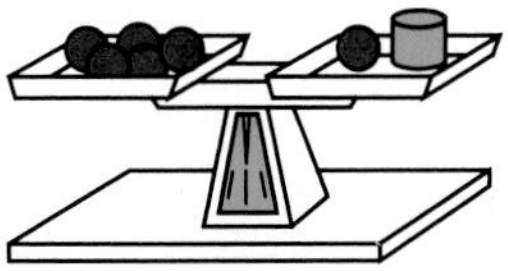

B 11. The sum of two numbers is 15. Three times one of the numbers is 11 less than five times the other. Find the numbers.

12. The difference of two integers is 9. Five times the smaller is 7 more than three times the larger. Find the numbers.

13. The lengths of the sides of a triangle are consecutive even integers. Find the length of the longest side if it is 22 units shorter than the perimeter.

14. The length of a rectangle is twice the width. The perimeter is 84 cm more than the width. Make a diagram and find the rectangle's dimensions.

15. Mei's salary starts at $16,000 per year with annual raises of $1500. Janet's starting salary is $19,300 with annual raises of $950. After how many years will the two women be earning the same salary?

16. A 2000 L tank containing 550 L of water is being filled with water at the rate of 75 L per minute from a full 1600 L tank. How long will it be before the two tanks have the same amount of water?

17. Eric has twice as much money as Marcia, who has $175 less than Laurel. But Laurel has as much money as Eric and Marcia have together. How much money does each person have?

18. A boat weighs 1500 lb more than its motor and 1900 lb more than its trailer. Together the boat and motor weigh five times as much as the trailer. How much does the boat weigh?

19. Show that it is impossible for three consecutive integers to have a sum that is 200 more than the smallest integer.

20. Is it possible for four consecutive even numbers to have a sum that is ten more than the sum of the smallest two numbers? If so, tell how many solution(s) there are. If there are no solutions, tell why not.

Mixed Review Exercises

Simplify.

1. $4 + \left(-\frac{1}{2}\right) + \left(-\frac{3}{2}\right)$

2. $-2\frac{3}{5} + 1\frac{1}{5}$

3. $-212 - (-13)$

4. $17x + (-3)x - 5$

5. $-5y + 6 + 20y + 12$

6. $7(-3)(-10)(-2)$

Solve.

7. $-3 - x = 9$

8. $5 - (1 + z) = 3$

9. $4x = -392$

10. $\frac{1}{2}x = 4\frac{1}{2}$

11. $\frac{x}{7} = 6$

12. $-12\frac{2}{3} = -\frac{1}{3}x$

Computer Exercises

For students with some programming experience.

Write a BASIC program to solve an equation of the form $Ax + B = Cx + D$, where the values of A, B, C, and D are entered with INPUT statements. Be sure that the program prints an appropriate message for identities and for equations having no solution. Use the program to solve the following equations.

1. $3x + 4 = 5x + 10$

2. $\frac{1}{2}x + 1 = -2x + 11$

3. $4x - 7 = 3 + 4x$

4. $\frac{1}{2}x + 5 = 5 + \frac{1}{2}x$

5. $3x - 13 = \frac{2}{5}x$

6. $3 - x = 4x - 3$

Self-Test 2

Vocabulary empty set (p. 117) null set (p. 117) identity (p. 117)

Solve.

1. A \$48 sweater costs \$6 more than twice as much as the shirt that goes with it. How much does the shirt cost? **Obj. 3-4, p. 112**

2. $25 - 4n = n$ **3.** $3(x + 1) = 2(x + 5)$ **Obj. 3-5, p. 116**

4. Hilary has three times as much money as Paul. Jeff has \$4 less than Hilary and \$5 more than Paul. How much money does each have?

Check your answers with those at the back of the book.

Extending Your Problem Solving Skills

3-6 Problem Solving: Using Charts

Objective To organize the facts of a problem in a chart.

Using a chart to organize the facts of a problem can be a helpful problem solving strategy.

Example 1 Organize the given information in a chart:
A roll of carpet 9 ft wide is 20 ft longer than a roll of carpet 12 ft wide.

Solution 1

	Width	Length
First roll	9	l
Second roll	12	$l - 20$

Solution 2

	Width	Length
First roll	9	$l + 20$
Second roll	12	l

Example 2 Solve the problem using the two given facts.
Find the number of Calories in an apple and in a pear.
(1) A pear contains 30 Calories more than an apple.
(2) Ten apples have as many Calories as 7 pears.

Solution

Step 1 The problem asks for the number of Calories in an apple and in a pear.

Step 2 Let $a =$ the number of Calories in an apple.
Then $a + 30 =$ the number of Calories in a pear.

	Calories per fruit ×	Number of fruit =	Total Calories
Apple	a	10	$10a$
Pear	$a + 30$	7	$7(a + 30)$

Step 3 Calories in 10 apples = Calories in 7 pears

$$10a = 7(a + 30)$$

Step 4

$$10a = 7a + 210$$
$$3a = 210$$
$$a = 70 \text{ and } a + 30 = 100$$

(Solution continues on the next page.)

Step 5 Check: (1) 100 Calories is 30 more than 70 Calories. √
(2) Ten apples have $10 \cdot 70$, or 700 Calories and seven pears have $7 \cdot 100$, or 700 Calories. √

∴ there are 70 Calories in an apple and 100 Calories in a pear. ***Answer***

Oral Exercises

Organize the given information by completing each chart.

1. A swimming pool 25 m long is 13 m narrower than a pool 50 m long.

a.

	Length	Width
1st pool	25	?
2nd pool	50	w

b.

	Length	Width
1st pool	25	w
2nd pool	50	?

2. In game 1, Ellen scored twice as many points as Jody. In game 2 Ellen scored ten fewer points than she did in game 1, while Jody scored 12 more points than she did in game 1.

	Game 1 points	Game 2 points
Ellen	?	?
Jody	m	?

3. Use the two given facts to complete the chart. What equation would you write to find the amount of protein in a scrambled egg?
(1) An egg scrambled with butter and milk has one more gram of protein than an egg fried in butter.
(2) Ten scrambled eggs have as much protein as a dozen fried eggs.

	Protein per egg ×	Number of eggs =	Total protein
Scrambled egg	?	10	?
Fried egg	x	?	?

Problems

Solve each problem using the two given facts. If a chart is given, first copy and complete the chart to help you solve the problem.

A **1.** Find the number of full 8 hour shifts that Maria worked last month.
(1) She worked twice as many 6 hour shifts as 8 hour shifts.
(2) She worked a total of 280 hours.

(Chart on next page)

	Hours per shift ×	Number of shifts =	Total hours worked
6 h shift	?	?	?
8 h shift	?	x	?

2. Find the number of round-trip commuter rail tickets sold.
(1) Thirty times as many round-trip tickets as 12-ride tickets were sold.
(2) The total number of tickets sold represented 1440 rides.

	Rides per ticket ×	Number of tickets sold =	Total rides
12-ride ticket	?	n	?
Round-trip ticket	?	?	?

3. Find the total weight of the boxes of pecans in a shipment of 3 lb boxes of pecans and 2 lb boxes of walnuts.
(1) There were 24 fewer 2 lb boxes of walnuts than 3 lb boxes of pecans.
(2) The total weight of the shipment was 462 lb.

	Weight per box ×	Number of boxes =	Total Weight
Pecans	?	?	?
Walnuts	?	?	?

4. Find the amount of time Joel spent watching space adventure movies.
(1) He saw twice as many $1\frac{1}{2}$ h space movies as he did 2 h mysteries.
(2) He spent a total of 15 h watching movies.

	Movie length ×	Number of movies =	Total time
Space movies	?	?	?
Mystery movies	?	?	?

5. Find the number of Calories in an orange and in a peach.
(1) An orange has 30 Calories more than a peach.
(2) Thirteen peaches have as many Calories as 7 oranges.

6. Find the number of Calories in a stalk of celery and in a carrot.
(1) A carrot has 13 Calories more than a celery stalk.
(2) Five carrots and ten celery stalks have only 170 Calories.

Solve. Use a chart to help you solve the problem.

7. The length of a red rectangle is 15 cm more than its width w. A blue rectangle, which is 5 cm wider and 2 cm shorter than the red one, has perimeter 72 cm. Make a sketch of the rectangles expressing all dimensions in terms of w. Then find the dimensions of each rectangle.

Solve. Use a chart to help you solve the problem.

8. The length of a rectangle is twice its width w. A second rectangle, which is 8 cm longer and 3 cm narrower than the first rectangle, has perimeter 154 cm. Make a sketch of the rectangles expressing all dimensions in terms of w. Then find the dimensions of each rectangle.

B **9.** Brian O'Reilly earns twice as much each week as a tutor than he does pumping gas. His total weekly wages are $150 more than that of his younger sister. She earns one quarter as much as Brian does as a tutor. How much does Brian earn as a tutor?

10. Mona Yahuso earns three times as much as an actuary as she does as a writer. Her total income is $40,000 more than that of her brother. He earns half as much as Mona does as an actuary. What is Mona's salary as an actuary?

11. A roll of carpet 9 ft wide is 30 ft longer than a roll of carpet 15 ft wide. Both rolls have the same area. Make a sketch of the unrolled carpets and find the dimensions of each.

12. Leo's garden, which is 6 m wide, has the same area as Jen's garden, which is 8 m wide. Find the lengths of the two rectangular gardens if Leo's garden is 3 m longer than Jen's garden. First make a sketch.

13. In March, Rodney sold twice as many cars as Greg. In April, Rodney sold 5 fewer cars than he did in March, while Greg sold 3 more cars than he did in March. If they sold the same number of cars in April, how many cars did each sell in March?

14. In one basketball game Maria scored three times as many points as Holly. In the next game, Maria scored 7 fewer points than she did in the first game, while Holly scored 9 more points than she did in the first game. If they scored the same number of points in the second game, how many points did each score in the first game?

15. Paula mixed 2 cups of sunflower seeds and 3 cups of raisins to make a snack for a hike. She figured that the mixture would provide her with 2900 Calories of food energy. Find the number of Calories per cup of raisins if it is 400 less than the number of Calories per cup of sunflower seeds.

16. The Eiffel Tower is 497 ft taller than the Washington Monument. If each of the monuments were 58 ft shorter, the Eiffel Tower would be twice as tall as the Washington Monument. How tall is each?

17. The upper Angel Falls, the highest waterfall on Earth, are 750 m higher than Niagara Falls. If each of the falls were 7 m lower, the upper Angel Falls would be 16 times as high as Niagara Falls. How high is each waterfall?

18. Nine cartons of juice cost the same as 5 fruit cups. Also, one fruit cup costs 50¢ more than one bowl of soup, while one bowl of soup costs 50¢ more than one carton of juice. What would be the cost of each item: a carton of juice, a fruit cup, and a bowl of soup?

19. One serving ($\frac{1}{2}$ cup) of cooked peas contains 45 more Calories than one serving of cooked carrots and 50 more Calories than one serving of cooked green beans. If one serving of carrots and three servings of green beans contain the same number of Calories as one serving of peas, how many Calories are there in one serving of peas?

C 20. The cross-country teams of East High and West High run against each other twice each fall. At the first meet, East's score was two thirds of West's score. At the second meet, East's score increased by seven points and West's score decreased by seven points. In the second meet West's score was three less than East's score. How many points did each team score in each meet?

Mixed Review Exercises

Solve.

1. $25z = 600$	**2.** $6 = \frac{2}{5}x$	**3.** $12z - 3z = 0$
4. $195 = 3x$	**5.** $7y + 3 = 24$	**6.** $-12 + 3y = -36$
7. $5x - 2x = 21$	**8.** $4(x + 2) = 6x$	**9.** $7x - 11 = 2x + 44$
10. $41 - x = -1 - 7x$	**11.** $-x = 2x - 54$	**12.** $5(y + 2) - 3(y - 1) = -27$

Career Note / *Astronomer*

Modern astronomers make few direct observations with telescopes. Instead, they use mathematics and physics to explore the nature of the universe. Their theories are described by mathematical equations that are tested on computers using data from observatories.

Observatories often gather data with radio telescopes and spectroscopes. Radio telescopes are used to detect the invisible x rays and radio waves that are emitted by stars. Spectroscopes, on the other hand, are used to separate a star's visible light into its various wave lengths, to form the star's spectral pattern.

With the aid of a computer, as shown in the photo, an astronomer can analyze a star's spectral pattern to determine whether the star is moving toward or away from the Earth.

Most astronomers work in universities or government space centers as teachers or researchers. They are highly trained in mathematics and physics and most have a Ph.D. in astronomy.

3-7 Cost, Income, and Value Problems

Objective To solve problems involving cost, income, and value.

The word problems in this lesson involve cost, income, and value. Organizing the given facts in a chart will help you to solve such problems. The following formulas will be useful in setting up your charts.

Cost = number of items × price per item

Income = hours worked × wage per hour

Total value = number of items × value per item

Example Tickets for the senior class play cost \$6 for adults and \$3 for students. A total of 846 tickets worth \$3846 were sold. How many student tickets were sold?

Solution

Step 1 The problem asks for the number of student tickets sold.

Step 2 Let x = the number of student tickets sold.
Then $846 - x$ = the number of adult tickets sold.

Make a chart.

	Number ×	Price per ticket =	Cost
Student	x	3	$3x$
Adult	$846 - x$	6	$6(846 - x)$

Step 3 The only fact not recorded in the chart is that the total cost of the tickets was \$3846. Write an equation using this fact.

Student ticket cost + adult ticket cost = 3846

$$3x + 6(846 - x) = 3846$$

Step 4

$$3x + 5076 - 6x = 3846$$
$$5076 - 3x = 3846$$
$$-3x = -1230$$
$$x = 410 \leftarrow \text{student tickets}$$
$$846 - x = 436 \leftarrow \text{adult tickets}$$

Step 5 *Check:* 410 student tickets at \$3 each cost \$1230.
436 adult tickets at \$6 each cost \$2616.

The total number of tickets is 410 + 436, or 846.
The total cost of the tickets is \$1230 + \$2616, or \$3846. √

∴ 410 student tickets were sold. ***Answer***

Oral Exercises

Read each problem and complete the chart. Then give an equation that can be used to solve the problem.

1. Marlee makes \$5 an hour working after school and \$6 an hour working on Saturdays. Last week she made \$64.50 by working a total of 12 hours. How many hours did she work on Saturday?

	Hours worked ×	Wage per hour =	Income
Saturdays	s	?	?
Weekdays	?	?	?

2. Ernesto purchased 100 postage stamps worth \$9.90. Half of them were 1¢ stamps, and the rest were 14¢ and 22¢ stamps. How many 22¢ stamps did he buy? (*Hint:* In your equation, use 990¢ instead of \$9.90.)

	Number ×	Price =	Cost
1¢ stamps	?	?	?
14¢ stamps	?	?	?
22¢ stamps	x	?	?

Problems

Solve. Copy and complete the chart first.

A 1. Thirty students bought pennants for the football game. Plain pennants cost \$4 each and fancy ones cost \$8 each. If the total bill was \$168, how many students bought the fancy pennants?

	Number ×	Price =	Cost
Fancy	f	?	?
Plain	?	?	?

2. Adult tickets for the game cost \$4 each and student tickets cost \$2 each. A total of 920 tickets worth \$2446 were sold. How many student tickets were sold?

	Number ×	Price =	Cost
Adult	?	?	?
Student	s	?	?

3. A collection of 40 dimes and nickels is worth \$2.90. How many nickels are there? (*Hint:* In your equation, use 290¢ instead of \$2.90.)

	Number ×	Value of coin =	Total value
Dimes	?	?	?
Nickels	?	?	?

Solve. If a chart is given, copy and complete the chart first.

4. A collection of 52 dimes and nickels is worth \$4.50. How many nickels are there?

	Number ×	Value of coin (¢) =	Total value (¢)
Dimes	?	?	?
Nickels	?	?	?

5. Hans paid \$1.50 each for programs to the game. He sold all but 20 of them for \$3 each and made a profit of \$15. How many programs did he buy? (*Hint:* Profit = selling price − purchase price)

	Number ×	Price (\$) =	Cost (\$)
Bought	?	?	?
Sold	?	?	?

6. Celia bought 12 apples, ate two of them, and sold the rest at 20¢ more per apple than she paid. Her total profit was \$1.00. How much did she sell each apple for?

	Number ×	Price (¢) =	Cost (¢)
Bought	?	?	?
Sold	?	?	?

B 7. I have twice as many nickels as quarters. If the coins are worth \$4.90, how many quarters are there?

8. I have eight more quarters than dimes. If the coins are worth \$6.20, how many dimes are there?

9. The Audio Outlet purchased 60 cassette recorders, gave away three in a contest, and sold the rest at twice their purchase price. If the store's total profit was \$1188, how much did the store sell each recorder for?

10. The Alan Company bought 80 tickets for a jazz concert. After giving away 20 tickets to customers, the company sold the rest to employees at half of the purchase price. If the company absorbed a \$1000 loss on all the tickets, how much did an employee pay for a ticket?

11. A plumber makes \$4.50 per hour more than his apprentice. During an 8-hour day, their combined earnings total \$372. How much does each make per hour? (*Hint:* If you decide to use cents instead of dollars, then use 450 cents per hour and 37200 cents total earnings.)

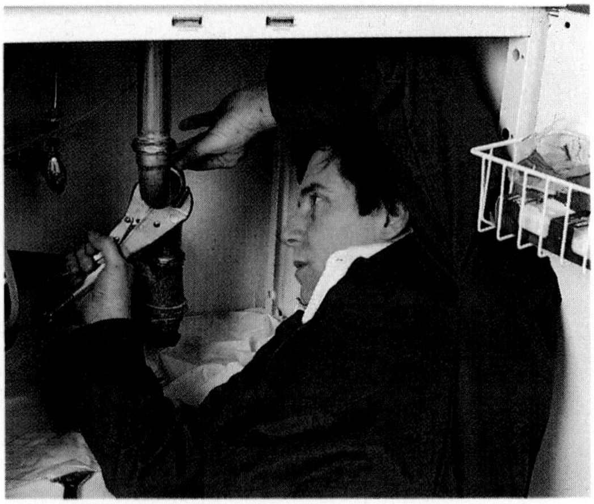

12. Raul works 2 h daily after school, Monday through Friday. On Saturdays he works 8 h at \$2 more per hour than on weekdays. If he makes \$142 per week, how much does he make per hour on weekdays?

13. Warren has 40 coins (all nickels, dimes, and quarters) worth \$4.05. He has 7 more nickels than dimes. How many quarters does Warren have?

14. Jo has 37 coins (all nickels, dimes, and quarters) worth \$5.50. She has 4 more quarters than nickels. How many dimes does Jo have?

15. Rory claims: "I have \$20 in quarters, half dollars, and one-dollar bills. I have twice as many quarters as half dollars, and half as many one-dollar bills as half dollars." Give a convincing argument to explain why he must be wrong.

16. Eleanor claims: "It is possible for 46 pennies and nickels to have a total value of a dollar." Is she right or wrong? Give a convincing argument to justify your answer.

C 17. Nadine has seven more nickels than Delano has dimes. If Delano gives Nadine four of his dimes, then Delano will have the same amount of money as Nadine. How much money do they have together? (Assume that Nadine has only nickels and Delano has only dimes.)

18. Natalie has some nickels, Dirk has some dimes, and Quincy has some quarters. Dirk has five more dimes than Quincy has quarters. If Natalie gives Dirk a nickel, Dirk gives Quincy a dime, and Quincy gives Natalie a quarter, they will all have the same amount of money. How many coins did each have originally?

Mixed Review Exercises

Simplify.

1. $\frac{40 \div 5 + 3}{13 - 2}$ **2.** $36 \div \frac{1}{6}$ **3.** $\frac{1}{3}(39y - 6) + 3$

4. $(-7)(5)(-1)$ **5.** $4(2x + 7) + 5(-x)$ **6.** $7(x + y) + 8(2y + x)$

Evaluate if $a = 4$, $b = 5$, and $x = 8$.

7. $\frac{5a + b}{x - 3}$ **8.** $\frac{ab}{4x}$ **9.** $3(a + b) - x \div 2$

Computer Exercises

For students with some programming experience.

Jane has a total of 12 coins, some of which are nickels and the rest dimes.

1. Write a BASIC program that uses a FOR . . . NEXT loop to print a chart showing every possible combination of dimes and nickels. The chart should also show the total value of the coins for each combination.
2. Modify the program from Exercise 1 to print the chart for K coins. The value of K should be entered with an input statement.

3-8 Proof in Algebra

Objective To prove statements in algebra.

Some of the properties stated earlier in this book are statements we assume to be true. Others are theorems. A **theorem** is a statement that is shown to be true using a logically developed argument. Logical reasoning that uses given facts, definitions, properties, and other already proved theorems to show that a theorem is true is called a **proof.** Example 1 shows how a theorem is proved in algebra.

Example 1 *Prove:* For all numbers a and b, $(a + b) - b = a$.

Proof

Statements	Reasons
1. $(a + b) - b = (a + b) + (-b)$	1. Definition of subtraction
2. $(a + b) + (-b) = a + [b + (-b)]$	2. Associative property of addition
3. $b + (-b) = 0$	3. Property of opposites
4. $a + [b + (-b)] = a + 0$	4. Substitution principle
5. $a + 0 = a$	5. Identity property of addition
6. $(a + b) - b = a$	6. Transitive property of equality

Generally, a shortened form of proof is given, in which only the *key reasons* are stated. (The substitution principle and properties of equality are usually not stated.) The proof shown in Example 1 could be shortened to the steps shown below.

Statements	Reasons
1. $(a + b) - b = (a + b) + (-b)$	1. Definition of subtraction
2. $\qquad = a + [b + (-b)]$	2. Associative property of addition
3. $\qquad = a + 0$	3. Property of opposites
4. $\qquad = a$	4. Identity property of addition

Example 2 *Prove:* For all real numbers a and b such that $a \neq 0$ and $b \neq 0$,

$$\frac{1}{ab} = \frac{1}{a} \cdot \frac{1}{b}. \qquad \textit{(Property of the reciprocal of a product)}$$

Proof Since $\frac{1}{ab}$ is the unique reciprocal of ab, you can prove that $\frac{1}{ab} = \frac{1}{a} \cdot \frac{1}{b}$ by showing that the product of ab and $\frac{1}{a} \cdot \frac{1}{b}$ is 1:

Statements	Reasons
1. $(ab)\left(\frac{1}{a} \cdot \frac{1}{b}\right) = \left(a \cdot \frac{1}{a}\right)\left(b \cdot \frac{1}{b}\right)$	1. Commutative and associative properties of multiplication
2. $\qquad = 1 \cdot 1$	2. Property of reciprocals
3. $\qquad = 1$	3. Identity property of multiplication

Once a theorem has been proved, it can be used as a reason in other proofs. You may refer to the Chapter Summary on page 88 for listings of properties and theorems that you can use as reasons in your proofs in the following exercises.

Oral Exercises

State the missing reasons. Assume that each variable represents any real number.

1. *Prove:* If $a = b$, then $a + c = b + c$.
(Addition property of equality)

Proof:

1. $a + c = a + c$	1. _?_ property of equality
2. $a = b$	2. Given
3. $a + c = b + c$	3. _?_ principle

2. *Prove:* If $a = b$, then $a - c = b - c$.
(Subtraction property of equality)

Proof:

1. $a = b$	1. _?_
2. Since c is a real number, $-c$ is a real number.	2. Property of opposites
3. $a + (-c) = b + (-c)$	3. _?_ property of equality (proved in Oral Exercise 1)
4. $a - c = b - c$	4. Definition of _?_

3. *Prove:* If $a = b$, then $-a = -b$.

Proof:

1. $a = b$	1. _?_
2. $a + (-b) = b + (-b)$	2. _?_ property of equality
3. $a + (-b) = 0$	3. Property of _?_
4. $-a + [a + (-b)] = -a + 0$	4. _?_ property of equality
5. $(-a + a) + (-b) = -a + 0$	5. _?_ property of addition
6. $0 + (-b) = -a + 0$	6. Property of _?_
7. $-b = -a$	7. _?_ property of addition
8. $-a = -b$	8. _?_ property of equality

Written Exercises

Write the missing reasons. Assume that each variable represents any real number.

A **1.** *Prove:* If $a = b$, then $ca = cb$.
(Multiplication property of equality)

Proof:

1. $ca = ca$	1. _?_
2. $a = b$	2. Given
3. $ca = cb$	3. _?_

Write the missing reasons in Exercises 2–8. Assume that each variable represents any real number, except as noted.

2. *Prove:* If $a + c = b + c$, then $a = b$.

Proof:

1. $a + c = b + c$	1. Given
2. $(a + c) + (-c) = (b + c) + (-c)$	2. ?
3. $a + [c + (-c)] = b + [c + (-c)]$	3. ?
4. $a + 0 = b + 0$	4. ?
5. $a = b$	5. ?

3. *Prove:* If $ac = bc$ and $c \neq 0$, then $a = b$.

Proof:

1. $ac = bc$	1. Given
2. $(ac) \cdot \frac{1}{c} = (bc) \cdot \frac{1}{c}$	2. ?
3. $a\left(c \cdot \frac{1}{c}\right) = b\left(c \cdot \frac{1}{c}\right)$	3. ?
4. $a \cdot 1 = b \cdot 1$	4. ?
5. $a = b$	5. ?

4. *Prove:* If $b \neq 0$, then $\frac{1}{b}(ba) = a$ and $(ab)\frac{1}{b} = a$.

Proof:

1. $\frac{1}{b}(ba) = \left(\frac{1}{b} \cdot b\right)a$	1. ?
2. $= 1 \cdot a$	2. ?
3. $= a$	3. ?

From Step 3 prove that $(ab)\frac{1}{b} = a$.

4. $\frac{1}{b}(ba) = a$	4. (Step 3, above)
5. $(ba)\frac{1}{b} = a$	5. ?
6. $(ab)\frac{1}{b} = a$	6. ?

B **5.** *Prove:* $-(-b) = b$

Proof:

1. $b + (-b) = 0$	1. ?
2. $(-b) + [-(-b)] = 0$	2. ?
3. $(-b) + [-(-b)] = b + (-b)$	3. ?
4. $[-(-b)] + (-b) = b + (-b)$	4. ?
5. $-(-b) = b$	5. Proved in Oral Exercise 2

6. *Prove:* $-(a + b) = (-a) + (-b)$
(Property of the opposite of a sum)

Proof: Since $-(a + b)$ is the unique additive inverse of $(a + b)$, we can prove that $-(a + b) = (-a) + (-b)$ by showing that the sum of $(a + b)$ and $[(-a) + (-b)]$ is 0.

(Proof continues on next page.)

1. $(a + b) + [(-a) + (-b)] = [(a + b) + (-a)] + (-b)$ 1. ___?___
2. $= [a + (-a) + b] + (-b)$ 2. ___?___
3. $= [0 + b] + (-b)$ 3. ___?___
4. $= b + (-b)$ 4. ___?___
5. $= 0$ 5. ___?___

7. *Prove:* $-(a - b) = b - a$

Proof:

1. $-(a - b) = -[a + (-b)]$ — 1. Definition of ___?___
2. $= (-a) + [-(-b)]$ — 2. Property of the opposite of a sum (proved in Exercise 6)
3. $= (-a) + b$ — 3. Proved in Exercise ___?___
4. $= b + (-a)$ — 4. ___?___
5. $= b - a$ — 5. ___?___

8. *Prove:* $-(-a - b) = a + b$

Proof:

1. $-(-a - b) = -[-a + (-b)]$ — 1. Definition of ___?___
2. $= -(-a) + [-(-b)]$ — 2. Property of the opposite of a sum (proved in Exercise 6)
3. $= a + b$ — 3. Proved in Exercise ___?___

Write proofs giving statements and reasons.

C **9.** *Prove:* If a and b are any real numbers, c is any nonzero real number, and $a = b$, then $\frac{a}{c} = \frac{b}{c}$. (*Hint:* Use Exercise 1.)

10. *Prove:* If a is any nonzero real number, then $\frac{a}{a} = 1$.

11. *Prove:* If a and b are nonzero real numbers, then $\frac{1}{\frac{a}{b}} = \frac{b}{a}$. (*Hint:* Show that $\frac{a}{b} \cdot \frac{b}{a} = 1$.)

Mixed Review Exercises

Simplify.

1. $12(12 - 7) \div 6 + 4$ **2.** $-4(-16 + 8)$ **3.** $-7x - 2x + 12x$

4. $-\frac{1}{2}(8 + 2a)$ **5.** $\frac{1}{2}(2b - 4) + 3$ **6.** $10 \div \frac{1}{2}$

Evaluate if $a = 5$, $b = 4$, $c = 3$, and $x = 6$.

7. $a(b + x)$ **8.** $3|x - a|$ **9.** $b - |x - a|$

10. $\frac{b + 2a}{|1 - c|x}$ **11.** $\frac{5a + x + 4}{b + c}$ **12.** $\frac{1}{2}(c - a) + x$

Self-Test 3

Vocabulary theorem (p. 130) proof (p. 130)

1. The length of a rectangle is 8 cm more than the width. A second rectangle is 5 cm wider and 6 cm longer than the first rectangle. The second rectangle has a perimeter of 242 cm. Find the dimensions of each rectangle. Make a sketch first. **Obj. 3-6, p. 121**

2. Jeremy had 34 nickels and quarters totaling $4.10. He had two less than twice as many nickels as quarters. How many of each did he have? **Obj. 3-7, p. 126**

3. Write the missing reasons. **Obj. 3-8, p. 130**

1.	$-a + (a + b) = (-a + a) + b$	1. ?
2.	$= 0 + b$	2. ?
3.	$= b$	3. ?

Check your answers with those at the back of the book.

Chapter Summary

1. The addition, subtraction, multiplication, and division properties of equality guarantee that:
   a. Adding the same real number to, or subtracting the same real number from, equal numbers gives equal results.
   b. Multiplying or dividing equal numbers by the same nonzero real number gives equal results.
2. Transforming an equation by substitution, by addition or subtraction, or by multiplication or division (not by zero) produces an equivalent equation. These transformations are used in solving equations.
3. Inverse operations are used in solving equations.
4. Equations can be used to solve word problems. Organizing the facts of a word problem in a chart is often helpful.
5. The following formulas are helpful in setting up charts to solve problems about cost, income, and value.

   Cost = number of items × price per item

   Income = hours worked × wage per hour

   Value = number of items × value per item
6. Theorems are proved by logically developing an argument to support them. In such a proof, each step is justified by a definition, property, or previously proven theorem.

Chapter Review

Write the letter of the correct answer.

1. Solve $20 = 5 + x$. **3-1**

a. 25 **b.** -15 **c.** 15 **d.** -25

2. Solve $y - 17 = 19$.

a. -36 **b.** 2 **c.** 26 **d.** 36

3. Solve $\frac{1}{9}x = 5$. **3-2**

a. $\frac{5}{9}$ **b.** $5\frac{1}{9}$ **c.** $4\frac{5}{9}$ **d.** 45

4. Solve $4n = -2$.

a. 6 **b.** 2 **c.** -2 **d.** $-\frac{1}{2}$

5. Solve $\frac{1}{3}x - 3 = -3$. **3-3**

a. 0 **b.** -18 **c.** 18 **d.** 2

6. Solve $b - 3b = 24$.

a. -8 **b.** -12 **c.** 12 **d.** -6

7. Howard works an 8-hour day at his gas station. He spends twice as much time working on cars as he does waiting on customers. He takes $1\frac{1}{4}$ hours to eat lunch and balance his books. How many hours does he spend waiting on customers? **3-4**

a. 2 h **b.** $2\frac{1}{4}$ h **c.** $1\frac{1}{4}$ h **d.** $4\frac{1}{2}$ h

8. Solve $2m = 1 - m$. **3-5**

a. $\frac{1}{3}$ **b.** 2 **c.** 1 **d.** 3

9. Solve $3w - 13 = \frac{1}{4}(52 - 12w)$.

a. $4\frac{1}{3}$ **b.** -1 **c.** no solution **d.** identity

10. Arthur weighs 34 lb more than Lily. Their combined weight is 180 lb less than four times Lily's weight. How much does Arthur weigh? **3-6**

a. 141 lb **b.** 151 lb **c.** 107 lb **d.** 127 lb

11. Nick worked 16 hours last week. He earned \$5 per hour at a local restaurant and \$5.50 per hour at a grocery store. If he earned a total of \$82, how many hours did he work at the grocery store? **3-7**

a. 8 h **b.** 4 h **c.** 12 h **d.** 2 h

12. Which of the following properties should be given as the reason for the statement $a(bc) = a(cb)$? **3-8**

a. Distributive property **b.** Associative property of multiplication

c. Property of opposites **d.** Commutative property of multiplication

Chapter Test

Solve.

1. $y + 25 = 10$ **2.** $73 = h - 13$ **3-1**

3. $c + 51 = 38$ **4.** $x - 38 = 12$

5. $\frac{1}{13}y = 65$ **6.** $-19v = -114$ **3-2**

7. $-112 = 16e$ **8.** $-\frac{x}{21} = 35$

9. $12y - 7 = 113$ **10.** $\frac{2}{3}x + 6 = 16$ **3-3**

11. $\frac{3x + 90}{5} = 0$ **12.** $-\frac{7}{8}(w - 16) = 70$

13. In the game of basketball you can score one point for a foul shot, two points for a regular shot and three points for an outside shot. Manuel scored 30 points by making eight foul shots and two outside shots. How many regular shots did he make? Use the five-step plan. **3-4**

Solve each equation. If the equation is an identity or if it has no solution, write *identity* or *no solution*.

14. $7(a - 6) = -3 + 6a$ **15.** $6(m - 1) = 6(m + 3)$ **3-5**

Solve. In Exercises 17 and 18, use a chart to help you.

16. Three times a number increased by 44 is the same as the opposite of the number. Find the number.

17. Sean weighs 10 lb more than twice Brad's weight. If Brad gains 10 lb, together they'll weigh 230 lb. How much does each weigh now? **3-6**

18. When Courtney collected her change she realized that she had five times as many dimes as quarters. Her dimes and quarters totaled $5.25. How many quarters did she have? **3-7**

19. Write the missing reasons to justify the multiplicative property of zero. **3-8**

1.	$0 = 0 + 0$	1. ?
2.	$a \cdot 0 = a(0 + 0)$	2. ?
3.	$a \cdot 0 = a \cdot 0 + a \cdot 0$	3. ?
4. But	$a \cdot 0 = a \cdot 0 + 0$	4. Identity property of addition
5.	$\therefore a \cdot 0 + a \cdot 0 = a \cdot 0 + 0$	5. ?
6.	$a \cdot 0 = 0$	6. ?
7.	$0 \cdot a = 0$	7. ?

Cumulative Review *(Chapters 1–3)*

Simplify.

1. $45 - 2(16 - 6)$

2. $\frac{56 \div 7}{16}$

3. $48 \div (9 + 3)$

4. $|-21| - |-14|$

5. $31 - [35 \div 5]$

6. $48 \div 3 + 7(3)$

7. $-55 - (-42 + 7)$

8. $-22 + 31 + (-44) + 50$

9. $1\frac{1}{3} - 10\frac{1}{4} + 12\frac{2}{3}$

10. $2.4 + 5.1 - 6.3$

11. $9 + x - (5 - x) - 6$

12. $4(x + 3y) - 3(x - 4y)$

13. $-5(42)\left(-\frac{2}{5}\right)\left(-\frac{1}{3}\right)$

14. $-5(-a - b) + 5(a + b)$

15. $\frac{85xy}{5y}$; $y \neq 0$

***Evaluate if* $w = 2$, $x = -3$, $y = \frac{1}{2}$, and $z = 3$.**

16. $w - |z - x|$

17. $\frac{4y - x}{w + z}$

18. $-5(x + w)$

19. $-w + 2x + 4y$

State the coordinate of the given point.

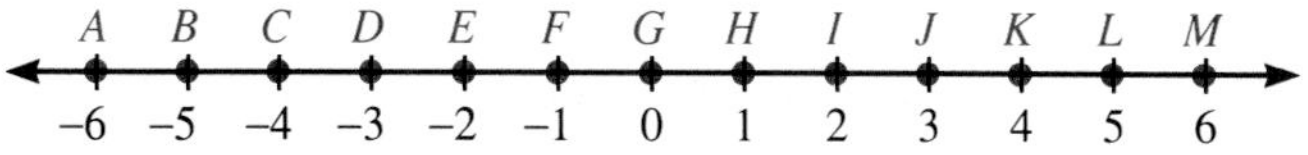

20. The point halfway between *F* and *G*.

21. The point halfway between *B* and *C*.

Solve. If the equation is an identity or has no solution, state that fact.

22. $|x| = 3$

23. $|y| = -2$

24. $x + 7 = 12$

25. $z + 1 = -3$

26. $y + 2 = 9$

27. $(x - 3) + 17 = 30$

28. $\frac{a}{3} = -14$

29. $9 = \frac{1}{2}q$

30. $2x + 6 = -2$

31. $\frac{1}{2}(2x + 4) = 2x$

32. $16 = \frac{3}{4}k + 1$

33. $5(z - 3) = 40$

34. $5y - 2 = 7y + 8$

35. $9(2 - b) = b$

36. $3(x - 4) = 6(x - 3)$

Solve.

37. A honeydew melon costs four times as much as a peach. Together they cost \$1.50. How much does each cost?

38. Find three consecutive integers whose sum is 87.

39. Thirty-eight employees at High Tech Sales ride to work on the subway. This represents $\frac{2}{5}$ of the employees. How many employees are there?

40. Rory has 30 coins (all nickels and dimes). He has five times as many nickels as dimes. How much money does he have?

Maintaining Skills

Express each fraction as a mixed number.

Sample 1 $\frac{35}{13}$

Solution $13\overline{)35}$ with quotient 2; 26; remainder 9

$\therefore \frac{35}{13} = 2\frac{9}{13}$

1. $\frac{25}{12}$ **2.** $\frac{45}{6}$ **3.** $\frac{78}{15}$ **4.** $\frac{86}{20}$

5. $\frac{91}{12}$ **6.** $\frac{83}{7}$ **7.** $\frac{111}{12}$ **8.** $\frac{115}{13}$

Express each mixed number as a fraction.

Sample 2 $5\frac{2}{5}$

Solution $5\frac{2}{5} = 5 + \frac{2}{5} = \frac{25}{5} + \frac{2}{5} = \frac{27}{5}$

9. $4\frac{1}{6}$ **10.** $8\frac{3}{5}$ **11.** $2\frac{7}{9}$ **12.** $12\frac{3}{4}$

13. $3\frac{8}{13}$ **14.** $17\frac{1}{3}$ **15.** $9\frac{11}{12}$ **16.** $10\frac{7}{8}$

Perform the indicated operations. Express the answers in simplest form.

Sample 3 $8\frac{2}{3} + 7\frac{5}{6}$

Solution
$$8\frac{2}{3} + 7\frac{5}{6} = \frac{26}{3} + \frac{47}{6}$$
$$= \frac{52}{6} + \frac{47}{6}$$
$$= \frac{99}{6} = \frac{33}{2} = 16\frac{1}{2}$$

Sample 4 $3\frac{1}{3} \div 7\frac{1}{2}$

Solution
$$3\frac{1}{3} \div 7\frac{1}{2} = \frac{10}{3} \div \frac{15}{2}$$
$$= \frac{\overset{2}{\cancel{10}}}{3} \cdot \frac{2}{\underset{3}{\cancel{15}}} = \frac{4}{9}$$

17. $8\frac{7}{15} + 9\frac{11}{15}$ **18.** $5\frac{7}{9} - 6\frac{4}{9}$ **19.** $7\frac{1}{3} \cdot \left(-\frac{1}{7}\right)$ **20.** $4\frac{2}{5} \div 2\frac{1}{5}$

21. $10\frac{1}{5} \div \frac{2}{5}$ **22.** $20\frac{5}{13} + 8\frac{4}{5}$ **23.** $6\frac{5}{8} - 3\frac{2}{5}$ **24.** $6\frac{3}{5} \div 2\frac{3}{4}$

25. $12\frac{9}{10} - 8\frac{3}{5}$ **26.** $-9\frac{1}{2} + \left(-13\frac{5}{9}\right)$ **27.** $11\frac{4}{7} + 10\frac{1}{5}$ **28.** $8\frac{5}{6} \div 6\frac{5}{8}$

29. $4\frac{10}{11} - 7\frac{1}{2}$ **30.** $12\frac{3}{20} \cdot 1\frac{5}{9}$ **31.** $9\frac{5}{9} - 8\frac{1}{4}$ **32.** $3\frac{9}{10} \cdot 7\frac{1}{13}$

33. $-5\frac{2}{3} \div 3\frac{1}{2}$ **34.** $5\frac{5}{9} \cdot 4\frac{1}{2}$ **35.** $17\frac{3}{4} + 8\frac{1}{3}$ **36.** $10\frac{5}{6} \cdot 3\frac{4}{5}$

Mixed Problem Solving

Solve each problem that has a solution. If a problem has no solution, explain why.

A

1. The sum of twice a number and -6 is 9 more than the opposite of the number. Find the number.

2. Roger spent \$22 on a baseball mitt and softball. If the mitt cost \$2 less than 5 times the cost of the softball, find the cost of each.

3. I drove 450 km in 6 h. Find my rate of travel.

4. The Longs' checking account was overdrawn by \$35.87. They deposited \$580 in the account. Then they wrote checks for \$25 and \$254.09. Find their new balance.

5. Alice bought 12 apples and oranges for \$2.51. If an apple costs 25¢ and an orange costs 18¢, how many of each did she buy?

6. A rectangle has a perimeter of 48 cm. If the width and the length are consecutive odd integers, find the dimensions of the rectangle.

7. The usual July temperature in Windsor, Ontario, 22° C, is 27° above the usual January temperature. Find the usual January temperature.

8. When 7 is decreased by a number, the result is 10. Find the number.

9. Find three consecutive integers such that three times the smallest is equal to the middle number increased by the greatest number.

10. What is the difference between the boiling point of mercury, 357° C, and the melting point, $-39°$ C?

11. Ruwa has \$125 in \$5 bills and \$10 bills. If he has four more \$5 bills than \$10 bills, how many of each does he have?

B

12. A store manager bought c calculators for \$8 each. All but four were sold for \$10 each. The remaining four calculators were not sold. Find the store's profit, in simplified form, in terms of c.

13. At a city zoo, about \$45 of every \$100 spent is used for animal care and supplies. One year \$216,000 was spent on these uses. Find the total zoo budget that year.

14. Denise did $\frac{7}{8}$ of the problems on a quiz correctly and five incorrectly. She did all the problems. How many were there?

15. On Saturday Kim worked three hours more than Ann did. Together, they worked one hour less than three times the hours Ann worked. How many hours did Kim work?

16. A bank contains 44 coins (nickels, dimes, and quarters). There are twice as many dimes as nickels and 8 fewer nickels than quarters. How much money is in the bank?

17. Sara has twice as much money as Miguel. If she had \$6 more, she would have $\frac{4}{3}$ as much money as he has. How much money does each have now?

4 Polynomials

For rectangles, area is the product of length and width. If you're given variable expressions for length and width instead of exact values, you may use exponents to write the product more compactly.

Addition and Subtraction

4-1 Exponents

Objective To write and simplify expressions involving exponents.

The number 25 can be written as $5 \cdot 5$ and is called a *power* of 5. Here is how some powers are defined and written:

First power of 5:	$5^1 = 5$	(read "five to the first power")
Second power of 5:	$5^2 = 5 \cdot 5$	(read "five to the second power" or "five squared" or "the square of five")
Third power of 5:	$5^3 = 5 \cdot 5 \cdot 5$	(read "five to the third power" or "five cubed" or "the cube of five")
Fourth power of 5:	$5^4 = 5 \cdot 5 \cdot 5 \cdot 5$	(read "five to the fourth power")

In the expression 5^4 the number 4 is called the **exponent** and the number 5 is called the **base.** We call 5^4 the **exponential form** of $5 \cdot 5 \cdot 5 \cdot 5$. The exponent tells you the number of times the base is used as a factor.

In general, if b is any real number and n is any positive integer, the ***n*th power of *b*** is written b^n and is defined as follows:

Exponent → n

$$b^n = \underbrace{b \cdot b \cdot b \cdot \ \ldots \ \cdot b}_{n \text{ factors}}$$

Base → b

The expression b^n tells you that b is used as a factor n times.

Example 1 Write each expression in exponential form.

a. $6 \cdot 6 \cdot 6 \cdot 6$ **b.** $a \cdot a \cdot a \cdot a \cdot a \cdot a$ **c.** $-2 \cdot p \cdot q \cdot 3 \cdot p \cdot q \cdot p$

Solution **a.** 6^4 **b.** a^6 **c.** $-6p^3q^2$

Example 2 Find the area of the rectangle.

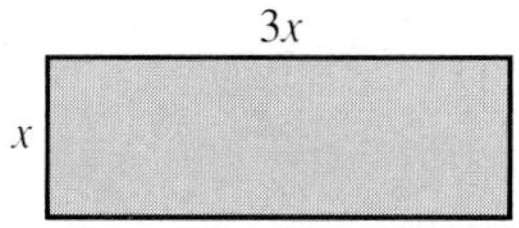

Solution

$$\begin{aligned} \text{Area} &= \text{length} \times \text{width} \\ &= 3x \cdot x \\ &= 3x^2 \quad \textbf{\textit{Answer}} \end{aligned}$$

Caution: Be careful when an expression contains both parentheses and exponents.

$(2y)^3$ means $(2y)(2y)(2y)$. 3 is the exponent of the base $2y$.
$2y^3$ means $2 \cdot y \cdot y \cdot y$. 3 is the exponent of the base y.

Example 3 Evaluate x^3 if $x = -5$.

Solution Replace x with -5 and simplify.

$$x^3 = (-5)^3 = (-5)(-5)(-5)$$
$$= -125 \quad \textit{Answer}$$

The following steps are used to simplify numerical expressions.

Summary of Order of Operations

1. First simplify expressions within grouping symbols.
2. Then simplify powers.
3. Then simplify products and quotients in order from left to right.
4. Then simplify sums and differences in order from left to right.

Example 4 Simplify: **a.** -3^4 **b.** $(-3)^4$ **c.** $(1 + 5)^2$ **d.** $1 + 5^2$

Solution

a. $-3^4 = -(3 \cdot 3 \cdot 3 \cdot 3) = -81$
b. $(-3)^4 = (-3)(-3)(-3)(-3) = 81$
c. $(1 + 5)^2 = 6^2 = 36$
d. $1 + 5^2 = 1 + 5 \cdot 5 = 1 + 25 = 26$

Example 5 Evaluate $(2a + b)^2$ if $a = 3$ and $b = -2$.

Solution

$$\begin{aligned} (2a + b)^2 &= [2 \cdot 3 + (-2)]^2 \\ &= [6 + (-2)]^2 \\ &= 4^2 \\ &= 16 \quad \textit{Answer} \end{aligned}$$

{Replace a with 3 and b with -2, and simplify.

Example 6 Evaluate $\dfrac{(x - y)^3}{2x + y}$ if $x = 2$ and $y = 5$.

Solution

$$\begin{aligned} \frac{(x - y)^3}{2x + y} &= \frac{(2 - 5)^3}{2 \cdot 2 + 5} \\ &= \frac{(-3)^3}{4 + 5} \\ &= \frac{-27}{9} \\ &= -3 \quad \textit{Answer} \end{aligned}$$

{Replace x with 2 and y with 5, and then simplify.

Oral Exercises

State each expression in exponential form.

1. $x \cdot x \cdot x \cdot x$ **2.** $a \cdot a \cdot a \cdot a \cdot a$ **3.** $n \cdot y \cdot y \cdot n$

4. $c \cdot c \cdot y$ **5.** $2 \cdot p \cdot 5 \cdot p$ **6.** $a \cdot 3 \cdot a \cdot a \cdot 2 \cdot a$

7. $(-r)(-r)$ **8.** $-r \cdot r$ **9.** $(-2) \cdot b \cdot (-4) \cdot b$

10. $2 \cdot k \cdot k \cdot (-4) \cdot k$ **11.** $a \cdot a \cdot a \cdot 3 \cdot b \cdot b \cdot b$ **12.** $a \cdot a \cdot b \cdot 5 \cdot b \cdot b \cdot a$

Simplify.

13. 2^5 **14.** 5^2 **15.** $5 \cdot 2^3$ **16.** $(5 \cdot 2)^3$

17. $(-2)^4$ **18.** -2^4 **19.** $(2 + 3)^2$ **20.** $2 + 3^2$

21. An even power of a negative number is a __?__ (positive, negative) number.

22. An odd power of a negative number is a __?__ (positive, negative) number.

Evaluate if $a = 3$ and $x = 2$.

23. ax^2 **24.** $(ax)^2$ **25.** $(a + x)^2$ **26.** $a + x^2$

27. $x^3 - a$ **28.** $(x - a)^3$ **29.** $a^3 + x^3$ **30.** $(a + x)^3$

31. $(x - a)^4$ **32.** $x^4 - a$ **33.** $x - a^4$ **34.** $x^4 - a^4$

35. Study the figures at the right. Explain why the second and third powers of b are called "b squared" and "b cubed."

36. For any positive integer n, $0^n = 0$ and $1^n = 1$. Explain.

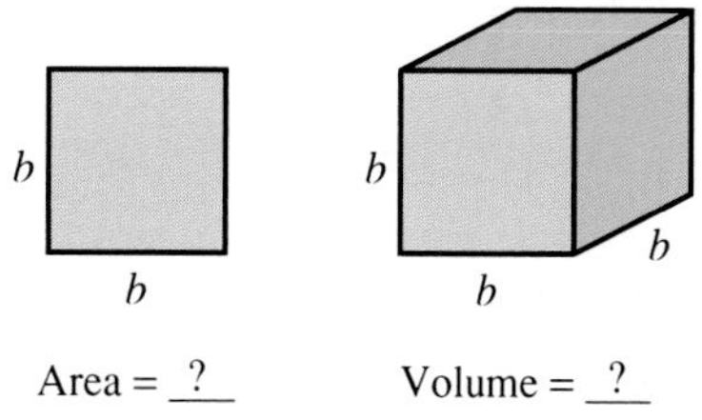

Written Exercises

Find the area of each rectangle.

A **1.**

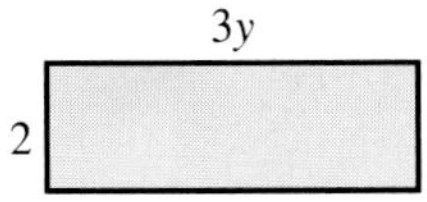

2.

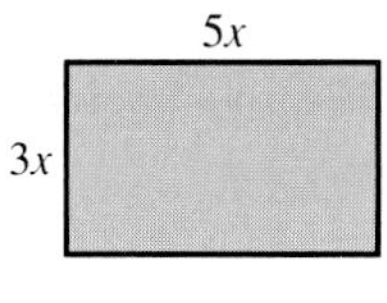

3.

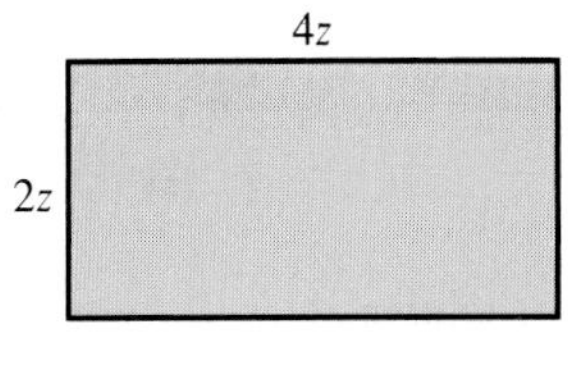

Write each expression in exponential form.

4. $x \cdot x \cdot x \cdot x \cdot x$ **5.** $m \cdot m \cdot m$ **6.** $4 \cdot t \cdot t \cdot t$ **7.** $c \cdot c \cdot 3 \cdot c$

8. $-6 \cdot z \cdot z$ **9.** $y \cdot y \cdot (-5)$ **10.** $-3 \cdot x \cdot 2 \cdot x$ **11.** $7 \cdot n \cdot (-2) \cdot n$

Write each expression in exponential form.

12. $a \cdot a \cdot b \cdot b \cdot b$
13. $c \cdot d \cdot c \cdot c$
14. $m \cdot 8 \cdot m \cdot n \cdot n$
15. $u \cdot v \cdot u \cdot u \cdot 9$
16. $-3 \cdot x \cdot y \cdot x$
17. $r \cdot (-4) \cdot s \cdot s$
18. $e \cdot f \cdot e \cdot g \cdot g$
19. $p \cdot p \cdot q \cdot q \cdot r \cdot s$

Match each phrase with the corresponding algebraic expression.

20. The square of a plus the square of b — **a.** $(a + b)^3$
21. The square of the sum of a and b — **b.** $a^2 + b^2$
22. The cube of the quantity a plus b — **c.** $a^3 + b^3$
23. The sum of the cube of a and the cube of b — **d.** $(a + b)^2$

Simplify.

24. **a.** -6^2 **b.** $(-6)^2$
25. **a.** $(-2)^2$ **b.** -2^2
26. **a.** $2 \cdot 5^2$ **b.** $(2 \cdot 5)^2$
27. **a.** $-4^2 \cdot 3$ **b.** $(-4 \cdot 3)^2$
28. **a.** $5 - 3^4$ **b.** $(5 - 3)^4$
29. **a.** $7 + 3^3$ **b.** $(7 + 3)^3$
30. **a.** $2 \cdot 3 - 5^2$ **b.** $2 \cdot (3 - 5)^2$
31. **a.** $3 \cdot (4 - 5)^2$ **b.** $3 \cdot 4 - 5^2$

Sample $6^3 \div [5^2 - 3^2 - (-2)^2] = 6^3 \div [25 - 9 - 4]$
$= 216 \div 12$
$= 18$ ***Answer***

B

32. $(1 \cdot 10^3) + (4 \cdot 10^2) + (9 \cdot 10) + 2$
33. $(1 \cdot 10^3) + (7 \cdot 10^2) + (7 \cdot 10) + 6$
34. $[2^3 + 3^3] \div [2^3 + (-1)^2]$
35. $[5^3 + (-3)^3] \div 7^2$
36. $[3^3 + (-2)^3 + (-1)^3] \div 3^2$
37. $(3^4 - 2^4) \div [5^3 \div (4^2 + 3^2)]$
38. $3^2 \div (2^2 - 1) - (5^2 - 3^2) \div (-2)^3$
39. $[2^2 \cdot 3^3 - 3 \cdot 2^4] \div [(2 \cdot 3)^2 - 2^4]$

Evaluate if $a = 3$ and $b = -2$.

40. **a.** $ab - a^2$ **b.** $a(b - a)^2$
41. **a.** $4 + ab^2$ **b.** $(4 + ab)^2$
42. **a.** $(2a - b)^3$ **b.** $2a - b^3$
43. **a.** $(a + 2b)^3$ **b.** $a^3 + 2b^3$
44. $\frac{(2a + b)^2}{2a + b}$
45. $\frac{a^3 + 2b^3}{a + 2b}$
46. $\frac{a^4 + b^4}{a + b}$
47. $\frac{4a}{ab + 4}$

Evaluate each expression for the given value of x.

C

48. $(x^2 + 4x + 5)(x^2 + x - 2)$, $x = -3$
49. $(x^2 - 3x + 1)(x^2 + 2x - 8)$, $x = -4$

Mixed Review Exercises

Solve.

1. $-7x = 56$
2. $3(n - 4) = 36$
3. $36 = -3x$
4. $-n + 8 = 6$
5. $x - 5 = |7 - 12|$
6. $-y + 12 = 8$
7. $-\frac{1}{2}(x + 2) = 3$
8. $\frac{1}{5}x = 10$
9. $3k = -\frac{6}{7}$

Computer Exercises

For students with some programming experience.

1. Write a BASIC program that uses a FOR . . . NEXT loop to print out the value of n^n for $n = 1, 2, 3, 4, 5$.
2. The symbol 4! is read "four factorial," and its value is $1 \cdot 2 \cdot 3 \cdot 4 = 24$. Similarly, $6! = 1 \cdot 2 \cdot 3 \cdot 4 \cdot 5 \cdot 6 = 720$. Write a BASIC program that uses a FOR . . . NEXT loop to print out the value of $n!$ for $n = 1, 2, 3, 4, 5$.
3. Study the data in Exercises 1 and 2. For integers greater than 1, which appears to be larger, $n!$ or n^n? Can you explain why?

Calculator Key-In

Your calculator may have a square key, x^2, or a power key, y^x, to help you simplify powers. Simplify each of the following mentally, then use a calculator to check your answers.

Exercises

1. $(0.1)^2$	**2.** $(0.2)^2$	**3.** $(0.5)^2$	**4.** $(1.1)^2$
5. $(0.11)^2$	**6.** $(0.02)^2$	**7.** $(0.3)^3$	**8.** $(0.4)^3$

Biographical Note / *Hypatia*

Hypatia (A.D. 370–415) is regarded as the first woman mathematician because so little is known about women mathematicians who may have lived before her. She was born in Alexandria, Egypt, when the city was one of the greatest centers of learning in the ancient world. Except for one of her papers that was found in the fifteenth century, our knowledge of Hypatia is based on the letters of her contemporaries and students.

Highly regarded as a mathematician and as an astronomer, Hypatia became a professor of mathematics and philosophy at the University of Alexandria. She lectured on Plato, Aristotle, astronomy, geometry, Diophantine algebra, and the conics of Appollonius. She also invented instruments used in the study of astronomy and apparatus for distilling water, measuring the level of water, and determining the specific gravity of liquids.

After her death in A.D. 415, no significant progress in the mathematics taught by Hypatia was made for centuries.

4-2 Adding and Subtracting Polynomials

Objective To add and subtract polynomials.

Each of the following expressions is a *monomial:* 14, z, $\frac{2}{3}r$, $-6x^2y$.

A **monomial** is an expression that is either a numeral, a variable, or the product of a numeral and one or more variables. A numeral, such as 14, is called a **constant monomial,** or a **constant.**

A sum of monomials is called a **polynomial.** A polynomial such as $x^2 + (-4x) + (-5)$ is usually written as $x^2 - 4x - 5$. Some polynomials have special names:

Binomials (two terms)	$2x - 9$	$2ab + b^2$
Trinomials (three terms)	$x^2 - 4x - 5$	$a^2 + 3ab - 4b^2$

A monomial is considered to be a polynomial of one term.

In the monomial $-3xy^2$, the numeral -3 is called the **coefficient,** or **numerical coefficient.** Two monomials that are exactly alike or are the same except for their numerical coefficients are said to be **similar, or like, terms.**

The following monomials are all similar: $-5xy^2$, $16yxy$, xy^2, and $\frac{1}{3}xy^2$. The monomials $-3xy^2$ and $-3x^2y$ are not similar.

A polynomial is **simplified,** or **in simplest form,** when no two of its terms are similar. You may use the distributive property to add similar terms. You may find it helpful at first to copy the polynomial and underline similar terms.

Example 1 Simplify $-6x^3 + 3x^2 + x^2 + 6x^3 - 5$.

Solution

$$\begin{aligned} \underline{-6x^3} + \underline{\underline{3x^2}} + \underline{\underline{x^2}} + \underline{6x^3} - 5 &= (-6 + 6)\underline{x^3} + (3 + 1)\underline{\underline{x^2}} - 5 \\ &= 0x^3 + 4x^2 - 5 \\ &= 4x^2 - 5 \quad \textbf{\textit{Answer}} \end{aligned}$$

Example 2 Write the sum of the areas of the rectangles as a polynomial in simplest form.

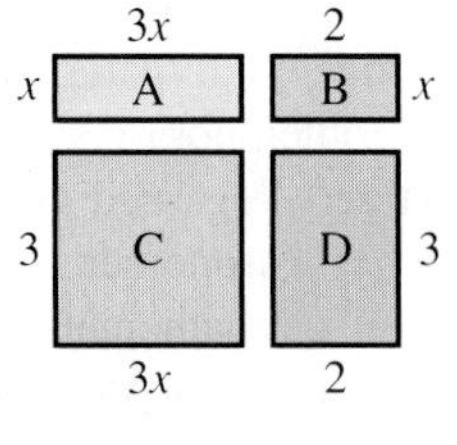

Solution

$$\begin{array}{ccccccc} \text{Area of A} & + & \text{Area of B} & + & \text{Area of C} & + & \text{Area of D} \\ \underbrace{x \cdot 3x} & & \underbrace{x \cdot 2} & & \underbrace{3 \cdot 3x} & & \underbrace{3 \cdot 2} \\ 3x^2 & + & 2x & + & 9x & + & 6 \end{array}$$

$3x^2 + 11x + 6$ ***Answer***

The **degree of a variable in a monomial** is the number of times that the variable occurs as a factor in the monomial. The **degree of a monomial** is the sum of the degrees of its variables. The degree of any nonzero constant monomial, such as 12, is 0.

Example 3 Find the degree of $5x^2yz^4$.

Solution

$$5x^2yz^4$$

The degree of x is 2.
The degree of y is 1.
The degree of z is 4.

$\therefore$ the degree of $5x^2yz^4$ is $2 + 1 + 4 = 7$. ***Answer***

The **degree of a polynomial** is the greatest of the degrees of its terms *after it has been simplified*. Since the polynomial $-6x^3 + 3x^2 + x^2 + 6x^3 - 5$ of Example 1 can be simplified to $4x^2 - 5$, its degree is 2, *not* 3.

To find the sum of two polynomials, you add the similar terms.

Example 4 Add $3x^2y + 4xy^2 - 2y^3 + 3$ and $x^2y + 3y^3 - 4$.

Solution 1 First group similar terms and then combine them.

$$(3x^2y + 4xy^2 - 2y^3 + 3) + (x^2y + 3y^3 - 4) =$$
$$(3x^2y + x^2y) + (4xy^2) + (-2y^3 + 3y^3) + (3 - 4) =$$
$$4x^2y + 4xy^2 + y^3 - 1 \quad \textbf{\textit{Answer}}$$

Solution 2 You can also align similar terms vertically and then add.

$$\begin{array}{r} 3x^2y + 4xy^2 - 2y^3 + 3 \\ \underline{x^2y \qquad\qquad + 3y^3 - 4} \\ 4x^2y + 4xy^2 + \;\; y^3 - 1 \end{array}$$

Subtracting polynomials is like subtracting real numbers. To subtract a real number, you add the opposite of that number. To subtract a polynomial, you add the opposite of *each* term of that polynomial and then simplify.

Example 5 Subtract $-a^2 - 5ab + 4b^2 - 2$ from $3a^2 - 2ab - 2b^2 - 7$.

Solution 1 Add the opposite of $-a^2 - 5ab + 4b^2 - 2$ to $3a^2 - 2ab - 2b^2 - 7$.

$$(3a^2 - 2ab - 2b^2 - 7) - (-a^2 - 5ab + 4b^2 - 2) =$$
$$3a^2 - 2ab - 2b^2 - 7 + a^2 + 5ab - 4b^2 + 2 =$$
$$(3a^2 + a^2) + (-2ab + 5ab) + (-2b^2 + -4b^2) + (-7 + 2) =$$
$$4a^2 + 3ab - 6b^2 - 5 \quad \textbf{\textit{Answer}}$$

Solution 2 You can also align similar items vertically.

$$\begin{array}{r} 3a^2 - 2ab - 2b^2 - 7 \\ \underline{-a^2 - 5ab + 4b^2 - 2} \end{array} \rightarrow \left\{\begin{array}{l}\text{Change to the} \\ \text{opposite and add.}\end{array}\right\} \rightarrow \begin{array}{r} 3a^2 - 2ab - 2b^2 - 7 \\ \underline{+a^2 + 5ab - 4b^2 + 2} \\ 4a^2 + 3ab - 6b^2 - 5 \end{array}$$

Oral Exercises

Name the similar monomials.

1. $-2x,\ 2xy,\ 4y,\ x,\ -xy,\ -y$
2. $-st^2,\ 2s^2t,\ 3t^2s,\ -s^2t$
3. $3a^4,\ -4a^3,\ a^2,\ 5a^3,\ 3a^2$
4. $x^2y^2,\ x^2,\ y^2,\ -3x^2y^2,\ -4x^2$

In Exercises 5–10, (a) state the degree of each variable in the monomial, and (b) state the degree of the monomial.

5. $-5xy^4z^3$
6. $7ab^3c$
7. $-10xyz$
8. $-3a^5bc^2$
9. $n^2p^2q^2$
10. $-2u^4v^6w^2$

State the degree of each polynomial. If the polynomial is a binomial or a trinomial, say so.

11. $3x^2 - 7x + 4$
12. $-2x^2 - 4x^3 + 6x - 5$
13. $x^3 - x^5$
14. $p^2q^3 - 3pq^4$
15. $r^2s - 3rs^3 + 2r^3s^2 + s^4$
16. $2s^2t + 3st^2 - s^2t^2$

Add.

17. $\begin{array}{r} 2x - 5 \\ x + 3 \\ \hline \end{array}$

18. $\begin{array}{r} 4m - 3 \\ 3m + 1 \\ \hline \end{array}$

19. $\begin{array}{r} 5n + 6 \\ -2n + 1 \\ \hline \end{array}$

20. $\begin{array}{r} 4y - 2 \\ -3y - 9 \\ \hline \end{array}$

21. $\begin{array}{r} 3x^2 - 2x + 1 \\ x^2 - 2x + 3 \\ \hline \end{array}$

22. $\begin{array}{r} 3y^2 \qquad\quad - 5 \\ 2y^2 - 3y + 4 \\ \hline \end{array}$

23. $\begin{array}{r} 6a - 4b + c \\ 4a + 4b + c \\ \hline \end{array}$

24. $\begin{array}{r} 1 - 2y + 3y^2 \\ 3 - 2y + \ \ y^2 \\ \hline \end{array}$

25. $\begin{array}{r} 3x^3 - 2x^2y + xy^2 \\ x^3 + \ \ x^2y - xy^2 \\ \hline \end{array}$

26–34. In Exercises 17–25, subtract the lower polynomial from the upper one.

Simplify.

35. $(3x - 2y + 5) + (x + 2y - 2)$
36. $(2p - q + 1) + (-p - q + 3)$
37. $(5r - 2y) - (2r - 3y)$
38. $(3x + 3y - 5) - (2x - 2y + 5)$

Written Exercises

Copy each polynomial and underline similar terms as was done in Example 1, page 146. Then simplify the polynomials.

A

1. $3x - 2y - x - 3y$
2. $6m - 6n - 4m + n$
3. $3x^2 - 2x - 2x^2 - 4x - 3$
4. $n^2 - 4n - 3n^2 + 7n + 5n^2$
5. $a^2 + 3ab - 4ab + 3a^2$
6. $p^2q - q^3 - 3p^2q + 4q^3$
7. $r^2s - 3rs^2 + 4s^3 - 2r^2s - 3s^2$
8. $-3x^2 + 7x^2y - x^3 + xy^2 + 4x^3 - 3x^2y$

Add.

9. $\begin{array}{r} 5y - 3 \\ \underline{2y + 9} \end{array}$

10. $\begin{array}{r} 4x + 7 \\ \underline{x - 2} \end{array}$

11. $\begin{array}{r} 3y + 8 \\ \underline{2y - 5} \end{array}$

12. $\begin{array}{r} 7n - 6 \\ \underline{n + 4} \end{array}$

13. $\begin{array}{r} 2r - 3x + 5 \\ \underline{-r + 3x - 2} \end{array}$

14. $\begin{array}{r} -2p + 4q - 7 \\ \underline{-4p - 2q + 5} \end{array}$

15. $\begin{array}{r} 2x^2 - 3x - 4 \\ \underline{3x^2 + 4x - 6} \end{array}$

16. $\begin{array}{r} 4 - 3n - 5n^2 \\ \underline{-2 + n - 3n^2} \end{array}$

17. $\begin{array}{r} 4x^2 - 3xy - 5y^2 \\ \underline{2x^2 + xy - 3y^2} \end{array}$

18. $\begin{array}{r} 8p^2 - 5pq + 6q^2 \\ \underline{-2p^2 + 5pq - 4q^2} \end{array}$

19. $\begin{array}{r} 3a - 7b - 5c + 2 \\ -a + 4b + c - 5 \\ \underline{2a \qquad + 3c + 3} \end{array}$

20. $\begin{array}{r} 7x - 6y + 4z - 1 \\ -3x + 3y - 5z + 3 \\ \underline{-2x - y + z - 4} \end{array}$

21–30. In Exercises 9–18, subtract the lower polynomial from the upper one.

Simplify.

Sample 1 $(4x^2 + 2x - 5) + (-x^2 + 3x + 5) = (4x^2 - x^2) + (2x + 3x) + (-5 + 5)$
$= 3x^2 + 5x$ ***Answer***

31. $(2x - 5y + 2) + (5x + 6y - 7)$

32. $(2p - 7q - 4) + (3q + 2p - 1)$

33. $(2x - 5) - (x - 2)$

34. $(3m + 5) - (-2m + 3)$

35. $(5x - 3t - 7) - (x - 2t - 3)$

36. $(a - 3b + 5) - (-a + 2b + 3)$

37. $(3n^2 + 5n - 6) + (-n^2 - 3n + 3)$

38. $(y^2 + 6y - 5) + (-y^2 - 3y - 1)$

39. $(3x^2 - 4x - 2) - (-x^2 - 4x + 7)$

40. $(y^2 - 3y - 5) - (-y^2 - 7y + 4)$

B **41.** $(u^3 - 3u^2v + 2uv^2) + (3u^2v - 2uv^2 - v^3)$

42. $(2x^2y - 3xy^2 - y^3) + (2x^2y - xy^2)$

43. $(3a^3 - 2ab^2) - (a^3 - 4ab^2 - b^3)$

44. $(2p^2q - 3pq^2 + q^3) - (-p^2q + q^3)$

Solve.

Sample 2

$$\begin{aligned} 9x - (3x - 8) &= 20 \\ 9x - 3x + 8 &= 20 \\ 6x + 8 &= 20 \\ 6x &= 12 \\ x &= 2 \end{aligned}$$

$\therefore$ the solution set is $\{2\}$. ***Answer***

45. $7x - (3x - 2) = 10$

46. $z - (4z - 5) = 8$

47. $(11n - 5) - (3n - 2) = -19$

48. $(2x + 3) - (5x - 7) = 1$

49. $(4y - 3) - (4 - y) = 3(y + 3)$

50. $3(n - 2) - 2(3 - n) = 4(n - 3)$

51. $2 - 3x = 8(5 - x) - (x - 10)$

52. $3(4u - 6) = 2(4u - 3) - (u - 8)$

C **53.** $(2y^2 - y + 6) - 2(y^2 - 3y + 5) = 11$

54. $y(2 - y) = 6 - (y^2 + 3y - 4)$

55. $x(3 - x) = x - (x^2 - 2x + 4)$

56. $3 - 2x(x - 1) = x(3 - 2x) - (x - 3)$

Problems

Write the sum of the areas of the rectangles as a polynomial in simplest form.

A **1.**

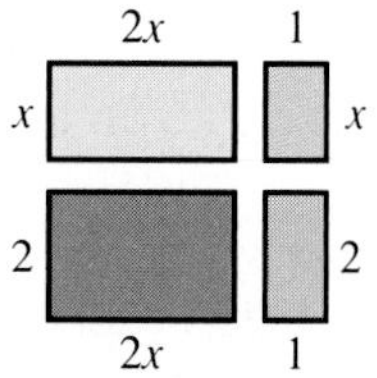

2.

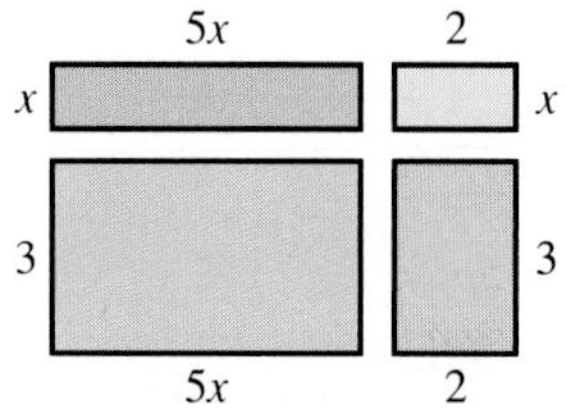

3.

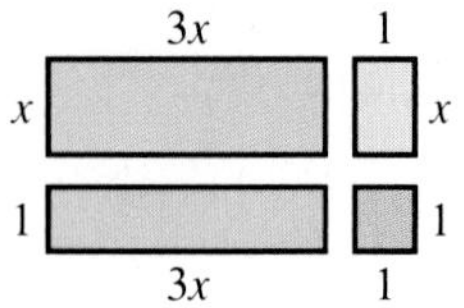

4.

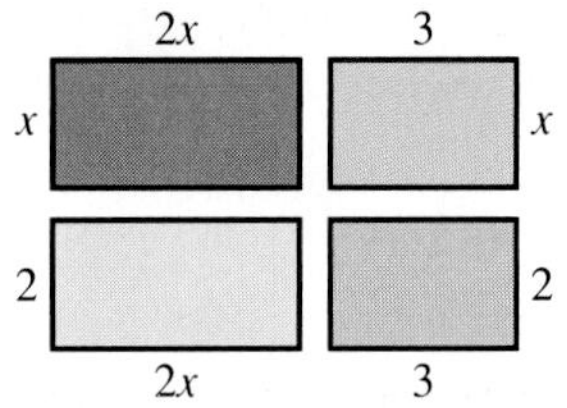

Solve.

5. Find two consecutive integers whose sum is the square of 7.

6. Find three consecutive integers whose sum is the square of 6.

7. Find four consecutive integers whose sum is twice the cube of 5.

8. Find two consecutive odd integers whose sum is the cube of 4.

9. The greater of two consecutive integers is 10 less than twice the smaller. Find the integers.

10. The greater of two consecutive even integers is 10 less than twice the smaller. Find the integers.

B **11.** Find three consecutive odd integers such that twice the smallest is 3 more than the greatest integer.

12. Find four consecutive integers such that the sum of the two greatest is 17 less than twice the sum of the two smallest.

13. Find four consecutive even integers such that the fourth is the sum of the first and second.

14. Find four consecutive odd integers such that the sum of the two greatest is four times the smallest.

Mixed Review Exercises

Simplify.

1. -5^2 **2.** $(-5)^2$ **3.** $(2^3 + 3^2)$ **4.** $(4 - 6)^2$

Solve.

5. $2(y + 3) - 4 = 3(5 - y)$ **6.** $15 = 2(n + 3)$ **7.** $5(x + 12) = 15 - 2(2x - 2)$

8. $-\frac{4}{3}(n + 5) = 10$ **9.** $c - 3 = |2 - 9|$ **10.** $\frac{2}{5}(2y + 1) = y - 3$

Computer Exercises

For students with some programming experience.

Write a BASIC program to add two polynomials. Using INPUT statements, ask the user to enter the degree of each polynomial. Then ask the user to enter the coefficients of each polynomial in order from least to greatest degree. Store the set of coefficients of each polynomial in an array. Use your program to find the sum of each of the following pairs of polynomials.

1. $3 + 4x + 5x^2$ and $1 + 7x - 2x^2$ **2.** $-5 - 6x^2$ and $2x^2 + x^4$

3. $4x + 9x^2$ and $5x^3$ **4.** $7 + 2x + x^3$ and $-3 + 4x + x^2$

Self-Test 1

Vocabulary

power (p. 141)
base (p. 141)
exponent (p. 141)
exponential form (p. 141)
monomial (p. 146)
constant (p. 146)
polynomial (p. 146)
binomial (p. 146)
trinomial (p. 146)
coefficient (p. 146)
similar or like terms (p. 146)
polynomial in simplest form (p. 146)
degree of a monomial (p. 146)
degree of a polynomial (p. 147)

Write in exponential form.

1. $n \cdot m \cdot n \cdot n$ **2.** $5 \cdot x \cdot (-3) \cdot x$ **3.** $-2 \cdot y \cdot y \cdot 4$ **Obj. 4-1, p. 141**

Simplify.

4. $(-2)^4$ **5.** -2^4 **6.** $(3 - 6)^3$

7. $3 - 6^3$ **8.** $2 \cdot (4 - 6)^3$ **9.** $[7^2 + (-1)^4] \div 5^2$

In Exercises 10–12, (a) add the polynomials, and (b) subtract the lower polynomial from the upper one.

10. $\begin{array}{r} 7x + 5 \\ \underline{3x - 1} \end{array}$ **11.** $\begin{array}{r} 5x^2 + 6x - 8 \\ \underline{x^2 - 6x - 4} \end{array}$ **12.** $\begin{array}{r} x^2y - 3xy^2 + 7 \\ \underline{-x^2y + 3xy^2 - 4} \end{array}$ **Obj. 4-2, p. 146**

13. Find three consecutive even integers such that the greatest is 8 less than twice the smallest.

Check your answers with those at the back of the book.

Multiplication

4-3 Multiplying Monomials

Objective To multiply monomials.

Study the following examples. Remember that an exponent indicates the number of times the base is used as a factor.

$$x^3 \cdot x^5 = \underbrace{\overbrace{(x \cdot x \cdot x)}^{3 \text{ factors}} \cdot \overbrace{(x \cdot x \cdot x \cdot x \cdot x)}^{5 \text{ factors}}}_{8 \text{ factors}} = x^8$$

$$a^m \cdot a^n = \underbrace{\overbrace{(a \cdot a \cdot \ \ldots \ \cdot a)}^{m \text{ factors}} \cdot \overbrace{(a \cdot a \cdot \ \ldots \ \cdot a)}^{n \text{ factors}}}_{m + n \text{ factors}} = a^{m+n}$$

The following general rule applies when two powers to be multiplied have the *same base*.

Rule of Exponents for Products of Powers

For all positive integers m and n:

$$a^m \cdot a^n = a^{m+n}.$$

To multiply two powers having the same base, you add the exponents.

Example 1 Simplify: **a.** $x^3 \cdot x^5$ **b.** $b^7 \cdot b^4$

Solution **a.** $x^3 \cdot x^5 = x^{3+5} = x^8$ **b.** $b^7 \cdot b^4 = b^{7+4} = b^{11}$

When you multiply two monomials, you use the rule of exponents along with the commutative and associative properties of multiplication.

Example 2 Simplify $(3n^2)(4n^4)$.

Solution

$(3n^2)(4n^4) = (3 \cdot 4)(n^2 \cdot n^4)$ — {Commutative and associative properties of multiplication

$= 12n^6$ — {Rule of exponents for products of powers

Example 3 $(-3a^3b^2)(5ab^4) = (-3 \cdot 5)(a^3 \cdot a)(b^2 \cdot b^4)$
$= -15a^4b^6$ ***Answer***

Example 4 $\frac{20x^2y}{3} \cdot \frac{12x^3y^5}{5} = \left(\frac{20}{3} \cdot \frac{12}{5}\right)(x^2 \cdot x^3)(y \cdot y^5)$
$= 16x^5y^6$ ***Answer***

Example 5 $(3x^4y^6)(-2x^2y) + (8x^3y^2)(x^3y^5) = -6x^6y^7 + 8x^6y^7$
$= 2x^6y^7$ ***Answer***

Oral Exercises

Simplify.

1. $x^2 \cdot x^5$
2. $t^4 \cdot t^3$
3. $y^2 \cdot y \cdot y^3$
4. $c \cdot c^6 \cdot c^3$
5. $(2s)(5s)$
6. $(3t)(4t)$
7. $(ab^2)(a^2b)$
8. $(x^2y)(xy^3)$
9. $(2x^2)(3x^3)$
10. $(4x^4)(5x^5)$
11. $(2ab^3)(a^3b)$
12. $(3mn)(mn^4)$
13. $(5x^5y)(3x^2y^2)$
14. $(4y^6z)(2yz^4)$
15. $(-3s)(7s^2)$
16. $(-c^3)(-3c^2)$
17. $(x^2y^3)(x^3y)$
18. $(r^2s^2)(2rs^3)$
19. $(-t^3)(-t)^3$
20. $(-x^2)(-x)^2$

Written Exercises

Simplify.

A

1. $n^3 \cdot n^5$
2. $a^2 \cdot a^2$
3. $x^3 \cdot x^4 \cdot x^2$
4. $n^2 \cdot n^2 \cdot n$
5. $(2x^2)(5x^5)$
6. $(5a^5)(6a^6)$
7. $(m^2n)(mn^4)$
8. $(y^3z)(y^2z^3)$
9. $(2ab)(3ab^5)$
10. $(5x^2y)(3x^3y^4)$
11. $(4x^5)(-3x^2)$
12. $(5y^3)(-2y^4)$
13. $(-3xy^3)(-2x^3y)$
14. $(3r^2s^3)(-5r^3s)$
15. $(5a^2b^3c)(2ab^4c^2)$
16. $(3y^3z)(4y^4z^2)$
17. $(2p^2q)(3pq)(4q)$
18. $(ab^2)(5a^2b^3)(3a^3)$
19. $(-x^2y^3)(3xy^2)(-2x^3y)$
20. $(-r^2s)(-3rs^3)(-s^2)$
21. $\left(\frac{2}{3}t^4\right)\left(\frac{3}{2}t^2\right)$
22. $\left(\frac{2}{7}a^2\right)(21a^5)$
23. $\frac{15a^3b}{2} \cdot \frac{8ab^2}{10}$
24. $\frac{4h^3k^2}{7} \cdot \frac{21hk^5}{2}$
25. $(3x^3)\left(\frac{1}{6}x^2\right)(8x)$
26. $(8c^2)(-d)\left(-\frac{1}{4}cd^2\right)$
27. $(3p^3q)\left(-\frac{5}{6}q^3\right)(-p^4)$
28. $(-a^3b)(-a^2b^2)(-ab^3)$
29. $(4xy)(2xy^3)(-2y^2)$
30. $(5b^4)(-3a^2b)(-a^3)$

Simplify.

B **31.** $(5x^2)(2x^3) + (3x)(4x^4)$

32. $(2y)(4y^3) + (3y^2)(5y^2)$

33. $(3a^5)(5a^3) - (6a^2)(a^6)$

34. $(6s^5)(2s^2) - (3s^4)(4s^3)$

Find the perimeter and the area of each shaded region.
(Area of rectangle = length × width.)

35.

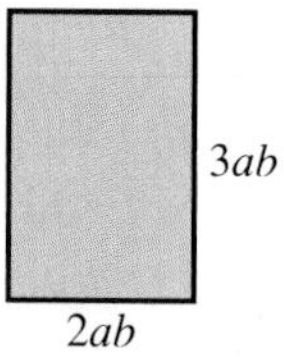

36.

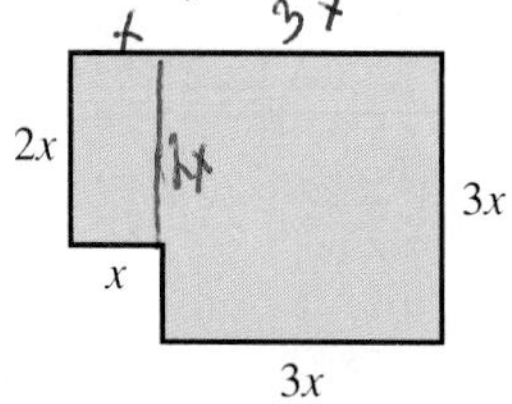

37.

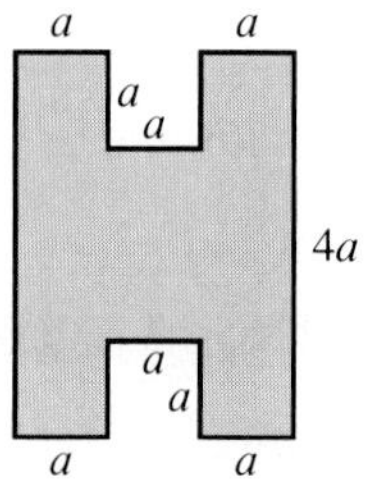

Find the total surface area of each solid.
(The total surface area of a solid is the sum of the areas of all its faces.)

38.

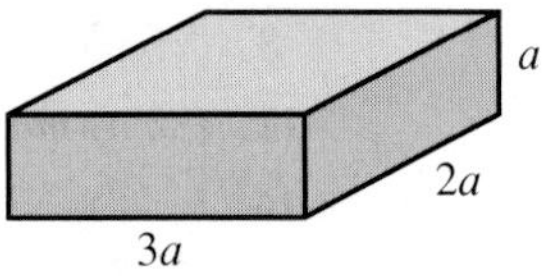

39.

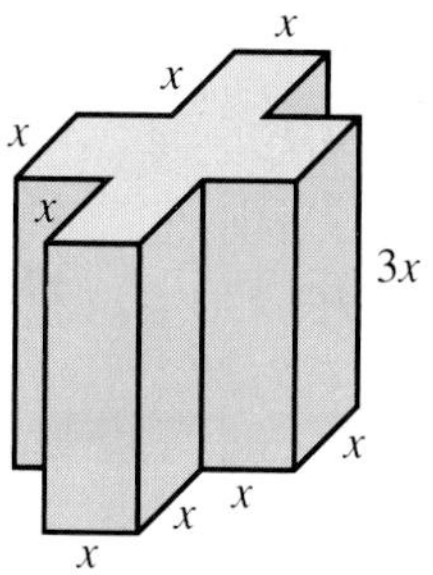

40.

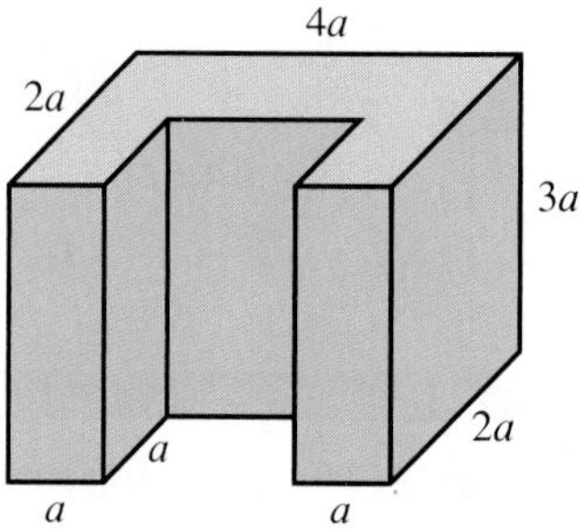

Simplify.

C **41.** $a^m \cdot a^m$

42. $x^{3n} \cdot x^n$

43. $3^p \cdot 3^q$

44. $5^x \cdot 5^4$

45. $4^2 \cdot 4^{x-2}$

46. $(-2)(-2)^{x-2}$

47. $a^x \cdot a^3$

48. $x^2 \cdot x^n$

49. $2^{x-1} \cdot 2^{x+4}$

50. $5^{2n} \cdot 5^{n+2} \cdot 5^n$

51. $(nx^5)(5x^5)$

52. $(3t^k)(kt^3)$

Mixed Review Exercises

Simplify.

1. $4 + 2^2$

2. $(4 + 2)^2$

3. $3p^2 + 4q^2 - 2p^2q - q^2$

4. $3 \cdot 7^2$

5. $(3 \cdot 7)^2$

6. $3x^2 - 4x + 5 + 6x + 4x^2$

Solve.

7. $4(y + 3) = 3y$

8. $15z = 30 + 10z$

9. $7n - 5 = 2n$

10. $\frac{n}{5} + 3 = 6$

11. $2(x - 4) = 6$

12. $\frac{y}{2} - 1 = 3$

4-4 Powers of Monomials

Objective To find powers of monomials.

To find a power of a monomial that is already a power, you can use the definition of a power and the rule of exponents for products of powers.

Example 1 $(x^5)^3 = x^5 \cdot x^5 \cdot x^5 = x^{5+5+5} = x^{15}$

Notice that $(x^5)^3 = x^{15}$, or $x^{5\cdot 3}$. In general:

$$(a^m)^n = \overbrace{a^m \cdot a^m \cdot \ \ldots \ \cdot a^m}^{a^m \text{ is a factor } n \text{ times}} = a^{\overbrace{m+m+\cdots+m}^{n \text{ terms}}} = a^{mn}.$$

Rule of Exponents for a Power of a Power

For all positive integers m and n:

$$(a^m)^n = a^{mn}$$

To find a power of a power, you multiply the exponents.

Example 2 $(u^4)^5 = u^{4\cdot 5} = u^{20}$

Example 3 $[(-a)^2]^3 = (a^2)^3 = a^6$

To find a power of a product, you can use the definition of a power and the commutative and associative properties of multiplication.

Example 4 Simplify $(2x)^3$.

Solution

$$\begin{aligned}(2x)^3 &= (2x)(2x)(2x)\\ &= (2 \cdot 2 \cdot 2) \cdot (x \cdot x \cdot x)\\ &= 2^3 \cdot x^3 = 8x^3\end{aligned}$$ ***Answer***

Both the 2 and the x are cubed when the product $2x$ is cubed. In general:

$$(ab)^m = \overbrace{(ab)(ab)\cdots(ab)}^{ab \text{ is a factor } m \text{ times}} = \overbrace{(a \cdot a \cdot \ \ldots \ \cdot a)}^{m \text{ factors}}\overbrace{(b \cdot b \cdot \ \ldots \ \cdot b)}^{m \text{ factors}} = a^m b^m$$

Rule of Exponents for a Power of a Product

For every positive integer m:

$$(ab)^m = a^m b^m$$

To find a power of a product, you find the power of each factor and then multiply.

Example 5 Simplify $(-2k)^5$.

Solution $(-2k)^5 = (-2)^5k^5 = -32k^5$ ***Answer***

Example 6 Evaluate if $t = 2$: **a.** $3t^3$ **b.** $(3t)^3$ **c.** 3^3t^3

Solution

a. $3t^3 = 3(2)^3$
$= 3(8)$
$= 24$

b. $(3t)^3 = (3 \cdot 2)^3$
$= 6^3$
$= 216$

c. $3^3t^3 = 3^3 \cdot 2^3$
$= 27 \cdot 8$
$= 216$

In Example 7, both rules of exponents for powers are used.

Example 7 Simplify $(-3x^2y^5)^3$.

Solution $(-3x^2y^5)^3 = (-3)^3(x^2)^3(y^5)^3$
$= -27x^6y^{15}$ ***Answer***

Oral Exercises

Simplify.

1. $(a^2)^4$ **2.** $(x^5)^2$ **3.** $(t^6)^3$ **4.** $(c^4)^4$

5. a. $(t^3)^2$ **b.** $t^3 \cdot t^2$

6. a. $(y^5)^3$ **b.** $y^5 \cdot y^3$

7. a. $x^2 \cdot x^4$ **b.** $(x^2)^4$

8. a. $b^4 \cdot b^3$ **b.** $(b^4)^3$

9. a. $(-z^2)^3$ **b.** $(-z^3)^2$

10. a. $(2a^2)^3$ **b.** $(2a^3)^2$

11. a. $(3a^4)^2$ **b.** $(3a^2)^4$

12. a. $[(-x)^5]^2$ **b.** $[(-x)^2]^5$

13. $(2a^3)^5$ **14.** $(-r^3)^4$ **15.** $(3t^3)^2$ **16.** $(2t^2)^4$

17. $[(-2)^3]^2$ **18.** $[(-1)^7]^3$ **19.** $(-3x^3)^2$ **20.** $(-2x^2)^3$

21. $(a^2b^5)^3$ **22.** $(x^3y^3)^2$ **23.** $(2xy^2)^2$ **24.** $(-a^2b^3)^3$

Give the square and the cube of each expression in simplified form.

25. $-2t^2k$ **26.** $3rs^4$ **27.** $5m^3n$ **28.** $-4x^2y^2$

Written Exercises

Evaluate if $x = 3$ and $y = 2$.

A

1. a. $3x^3$ **b.** $(3x)^3$ **c.** $3^3 \cdot x^3$

2. a. $5y^2$ **b.** $(5y)^2$ **c.** 5^2y^2

3. a. xy^2 **b.** x^2y^2 **c.** $(xy)^2$

4. a. xy^3 **b.** $(xy)^3$ **c.** x^3y^3

Simplify.

5. a. $c^5 \cdot c^2$
   b. $(c^2)^5$
   c. $(c^5)^2$

6. a. $x^4 \cdot x^7$
   b. $(x^4)^7$
   c. $(x^7)^4$

7. a. $(-5a^4)^3$
   b. $-(5a^4)^3$
   c. $-5(a^4)^3$

8. a. $(-2k^5)^6$
   b. $-(2k^5)^6$
   c. $-2(k^5)^6$

9. $(7a)^2$
10. $(-2t)^5$
11. $(-4c)^3$
12. $(5x)^3$
13. $(4k^2)^3$
14. $(6x^3)^2$
15. $(-3y^3)^3$
16. $(-2t^4)^4$
17. $(3a^2b)^3$
18. $(2x^2y)^5$
19. $(2r^3s^4)^4$
20. $(5p^3q^4)^3$

B

21. $(2x)^2(2x)^4$
22. $(3c)^2(3c)^3$
23. $(10b)^3(10b)^3$
24. $\left(\frac{1}{2}y\right)^2(2y)^5$
25. $(3a^2b)^3(2a^3b)$
26. $(2x^2y^3)^4(-xy^2)^2$
27. $\left(\frac{1}{2}p^2q\right)^3(2pq^2)^4$
28. $\left(\frac{1}{10}x^3y\right)^3(10y)^4$
29. $[(2x^2)^2]^2$
30. $[(-x^3)^2]^3$
31. $(3x^2y)^3(2xy)$
32. $(5a^2b)^2(5b)^3$

Find and simplify (a) the sum and (b) the product of the given monomials.

33. $(3x^3)^2,\ (2x^2)^3$
34. $(a^2)^6,\ (-2a^4)^3$
35. $a^2(ab^3)^2,\ b^2(a^2b^2)^2$
36. $p(-pq)^4,\ p^3(2pq^2)^2$
37. $a(-ab^2)^3,\ (2a^2b^3)^2$
38. $(2x)^3(xy)^2,\ (2xy)^2(-x)^3$

Simplify.

C

39. $(x^n)^2$
40. $(a^x)^3$
41. $a^x \cdot a^3$
42. $x^n \cdot x^2$
43. $x^n \cdot x^n$
44. $a^x \cdot a^x \cdot a^x$
45. $z^x \cdot z^x \cdot z^x$
46. $(a^x)^y(a^y)^x$
47. $(2r^n)^3(3r^n)^2$
48. $(2x^n)^3(x^n)^5$
49. $(3x^n)^2(x^2)^n$
50. $(t^m)^n \cdot 3(t^n)^m$

51. a. Find the volumes of the two cubes shown.
    b. Which cube has a larger volume?
    c. The bigger cube is how many times as large as the smaller cube?

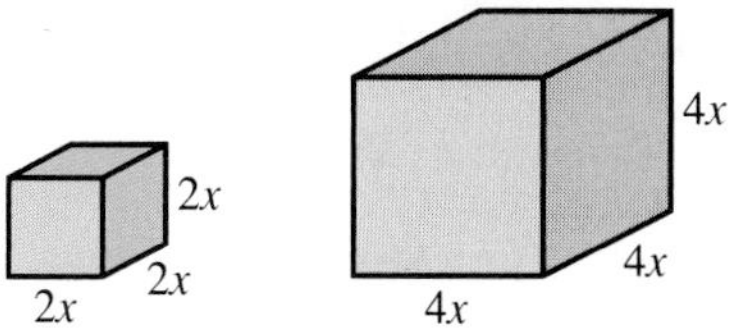

52. a. Which is larger, $(3^3)^3$ or $3^{(3^3)}$?
    b. How many times as large is it?

53. Show that $16^x \cdot (4^x)^2 = (2^x)^8$.

Mixed Review Exercises

Simplify.

1. $(3a^2b)(2ab)(4b)$
2. $(-x^2y)(2xy)(-4y)$
3. $(2x^2y^3)^4$
4. $\left(\frac{1}{2}t^3\right)\left(\frac{2}{3}t^2\right)$
5. $6c - 3a - 2c + a$
6. $(3x + 4y + 2) + (2x + y)$
7. $2 \cdot 3^3 + 2 \cdot 3$
8. $-5^2 \cdot 3$
9. $(4^3 + 6^2) \div 5^2$

4-5 Multiplying Polynomials by Monomials

Objective To multiply a polynomial by a monomial.

You can think of the product $x(x + 3)$ as the area of a rectangle as shown in the diagram below.

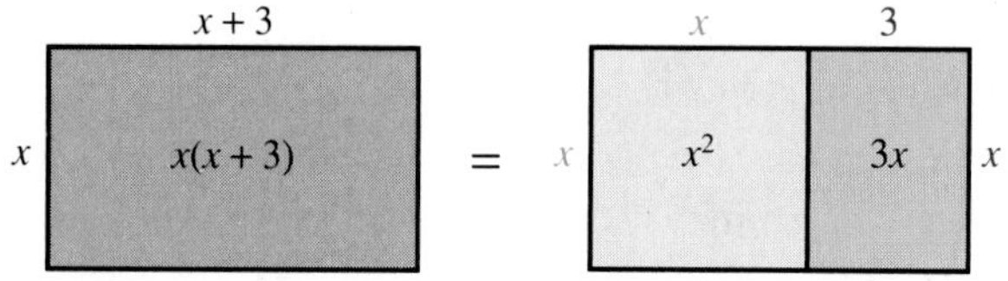

The diagram shows that $x(x + 3) = x^2 + 3x$.

By using the distributive property and the rules of exponents, you can multiply any polynomial by a monomial. You may multiply either horizontally or vertically.

Example 1 Multiply: $x(x + 3)$

Solution 1 $x(x + 3) = x(x) + x(3)$
$= x^2 + 3x$ ***Answer***

Solution 2

$$\begin{array}{l} x + 3 \\ x \\ \hline x^2 + 3x \end{array}$$ ***Answer***

Example 2 Multiply: $-2x(4x^2 - 3x + 5)$

Solution 1 $-2x(4x^2 - 3x + 5) = -2x(4x^2) - 2x(-3x) - 2x(5)$
$= -8x^3 + 6x^2 - 10x$ ***Answer***

Solution 2

$$\begin{array}{l} 4x^2 - 3x + 5 \\ -2x \\ \hline -8x^3 + 6x^2 - 10x \end{array}$$ ***Answer***

Example 3 Multiply: $5xy^2(3x^2 - 4xy + y^2)$

Solution $5xy^2(3x^2 - 4xy + y^2) = 5xy^2(3x^2) - 5xy^2(4xy) + 5xy^2(y^2)$
$= 15x^3y^2 - 20x^2y^3 + 5xy^4$ ***Answer***

Example 4 Solve $n(2 - 5n) + 5(n^2 - 2) = 0$.

Solution

$$\begin{aligned} n(2 - 5n) + 5(n^2 - 2) &= 0 \\ 2n - 5n^2 + 5n^2 - 10 &= 0 \\ 2n - 10 &= 0 \\ 2n &= 10 \\ n &= 5 \end{aligned}$$

$\therefore$ the solution set is $\{5\}$. ***Answer***

Oral Exercises

Multiply.

1. $3(x + 2)$ **2.** $5(t - 2)$ **3.** $4(3r - 1)$ **4.** $6(2 - y)$

5. $z(3 - z)$ **6.** $-x(3 - 2x)$ **7.** $-t(-2 - t)$ **8.** $a(b + 2c)$

9. $2x(3x + 2)$ **10.** $ab(a + b)$ **11.** $a(a^2 - 2a + 3)$ **12.** $c^2(2 - c - c^2)$

Written Exercises

Multiply.

A

1. $4(x - 3)$ **2.** $-3(y + 3)$ **3.** $c(c - 2)$ **4.** $a(4 - 2a)$

5. $3y(y + 5)$ **6.** $4x(2x - 3)$ **7.** $-2r(7 - 3r)$ **8.** $-z(6 - 5z)$

9. $\begin{array}{l} 3y^2 - y - 5 \\ \underline{2y \qquad\qquad} \end{array}$ **10.** $\begin{array}{r} 2k^2 - 3k - 7 \\ \underline{-3k \qquad\qquad} \end{array}$

11. $\begin{array}{l} a^2b - 3ab^2 + 5b^3 \\ \underline{-2ab \qquad\qquad\quad} \end{array}$ **12.** $\begin{array}{l} 2p^3 - 5p^2q - 3pq^2 \\ \underline{3q^2 \qquad\qquad\qquad} \end{array}$

13. $3x(x^2 - 2x + 4)$ **14.** $4t(2t^2 - t - 5)$

15. $pq^2(p^2 - 3pq - 4q^2)$ **16.** $2x^2y(2x^2 - 3xy + y^2)$

17. $\frac{1}{3}x^2(6x^2 - 9xy - 3y^2)$ **18.** $\frac{1}{2}s^2t(4t^2 - 10st + 6s^2)$

Simplify.

Sample

$$\begin{aligned} 4n(n + 5) + n(6 - n) &= 4n(n) + 4n(5) + n(6) - n(n) \\ &= 4n^2 + 20n + 6n - n^2 \\ &= 3n^2 + 26n \end{aligned}$$

Answer

19. $2x(x - 3) + x(5 - x)$ **20.** $3x(5 - 2x) + 6x(x - 2)$

21. $6r^2(2r - 1) - 3r(4r^2 - 5r)$ **22.** $4y(2y^2 - 3y) - 3y^2(y - 4)$

23. $-[6y - 3(5y - 4)]$ **24.** $8n - 2[n - 2(3 - n)]$

25. $a[2a - 3(1 - a)] + 5(a - a^2)$ **26.** $2x[3x - 2(3 + x)] - x^2$

Solve.

27. $2(x - 3) + 5 = 7$

28. $3(z + 3) - 7 = 8$

29. $15 = 3(x - 1) + 2(4 - x)$

30. $0 = 3(1 - 2t) - 5(2 - t)$

B **31.** $y(2 - 3y) + 3(y^2 - 4) = 0$

32. $\frac{1}{2}(12 - 4s^2) - 2s(1 - s) = 8$

33. $2(n - 3) + n(2 - n) = 2 - n^2$

34. $\frac{1}{2}(6c + 4) - 2\left(c + \frac{5}{2}\right) = \frac{2}{3}(9 - 3c)$

35. $\frac{3}{2}(4x - 6) - x(3 - x) = \frac{1}{3}x(3x + 6)$

36. $4(y - 7) - 2y(1 - 3y) = 6y^2$

37. $r^2 - [4 - r(3 - r)] = 2(2r - 3)$

38. $1 = 2x(x - 2) - [5 - 2x(1 - x)]$

39. A rectangular region is divided into two smaller regions with the dimensions shown.

a. Find the sum of the areas of these two regions.

b. Find the product of the length and width of the original rectangle.

c. Compare your answers to parts (a) and (b). What property of real numbers does this diagram illustrate?

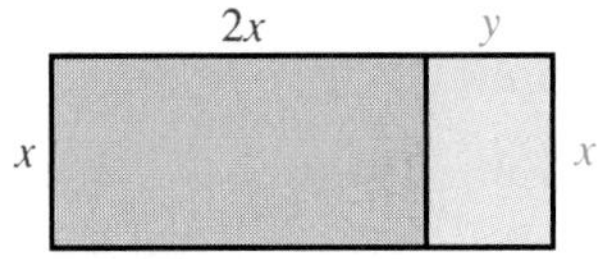

Find the area of each shaded region.

40.

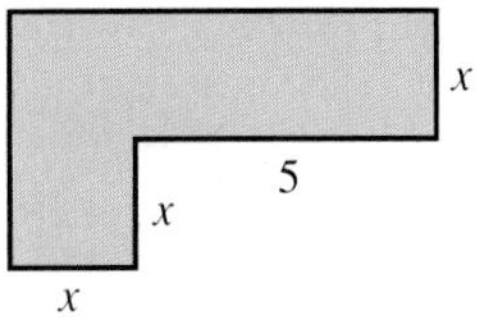

41.

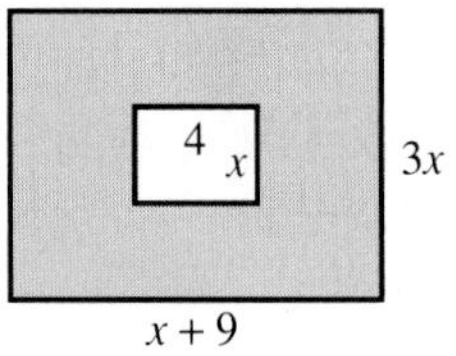

42.

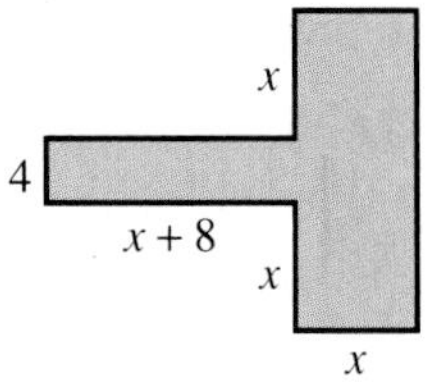

Find the total surface area and the volume of each solid shown.

C **43.**

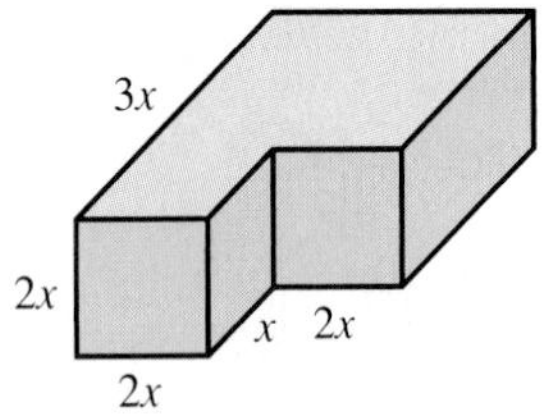

44.

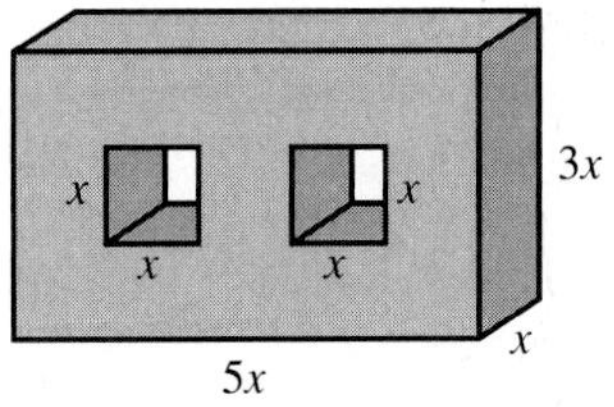

Mixed Review Exercises

Simplify.

1. $(3x^2y)^3$

2. $(-5r^3y^4)^2$

3. $(-3n)^3$

4. $(2a^3y)^3(3a^2y^2)^2$

5. $(2x^2)(3x^3) + (x^4)(4x)$

6. $(5n^4)n^2 - n^3(2n^3)$

7. $(7p - 3q + 5) + (3q + 3p)$

8. $(2x + y - 3) - (y + x - 7)$

9. $(5y^3)^2(3x^2y)^3$

4-6 Multiplying Polynomials

Objective To multiply polynomials.

You have learned how to use the distributive property to multiply a polynomial by a monomial:

$$(2x)(3x + 2) = (2x)3x + (2x)2$$

If you replace $(2x)$ in the example by the polynomial $(2x + 5)$, the distributive property can still be used:

$$\begin{aligned}(2x + 5)(3x + 2) &= (2x + 5)3x + (2x + 5)2\\ &= 6x^2 + 15x + 4x + 10\\ &= 6x^2 + 19x + 10\end{aligned}$$

The product of two polynomials can also be thought of as the area of a rectangle. The diagram also shows that the product of $(2x + 5)$ and $(3x + 2)$ is $6x^2 + 19x + 10$.

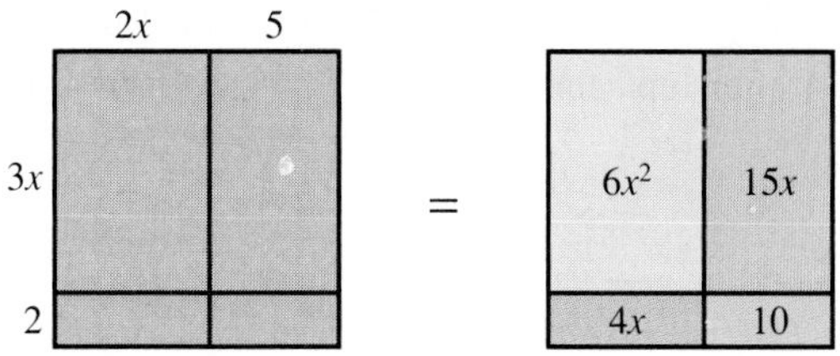

Example 1 Multiply: $(3x - 2)(2x^2 - 5x - 4)$

Solution You can find the product by arranging your work in vertical form.

Step 1 Multiply by $3x$.

$$\begin{array}{r}2x^2 - 5x - 4\\ \underline{3x - 2}\\ 6x^3 - 15x^2 - 12x\end{array}$$

Step 2 Multiply by -2.

$$\begin{array}{r}2x^2 - 5x - 4\\ \underline{3x - 2}\\ 6x^3 - 15x^2 - 12x\\ - 4x^2 + 10x + 8\end{array}$$

Step 3 Add.

$$\begin{array}{r}2x^2 - 5x - 4\\ \underline{3x - 2}\\ 6x^3 - 15x^2 - 12x\\ \underline{- 4x^2 + 10x + 8}\\ 6x^3 - 19x^2 - 2x + 8\end{array}$$ ***Answer***

It often is helpful to rearrange the terms of a polynomial so that the degrees of a particular variable are in either increasing order or decreasing order.

In order of *decreasing* degree of x: $x^4 + 2x^3 - 4x + 2$

In order of *increasing* degree of x: $2 - 4x + 2x^3 + x^4$

In order of *decreasing degree* of x and *increasing degree* of y: $x^3 - 3x^2y + xy^2 + 2y^3$

To see the advantage of rearranging terms, multiply the polynomials in Example 2 as they are given. Then compare your work with the solution of Example 2.

Example 2 Multiply: $(y + 2x)(x^3 - 2y^3 + 3xy^2 + x^2y)$

Solution

$$\begin{array}{r} x^3 - 2y^3 + 3xy^2 + x^2y \\ \underline{y + 2x} \end{array}$$

Rearrange in order of decreasing degree of x.

$$\begin{array}{rrrrr} x^3 & + x^2y & + 3xy^2 & - 2y^3 & \\ \underline{2x + y} & & & & \\ 2x^4 + 2x^3y & + 6x^2y^2 & - 4xy^3 & & \\ x^3y & + x^2y^2 & + 3xy^3 & - 2y^4 & \\ \hline 2x^4 + 3x^3y & + 7x^2y^2 & - xy^3 & - 2y^4 & \end{array}$$

Oral Exercises

Arrange in order of decreasing degree in the variable printed in color.

1. $5 + 2x^2 - 3x$, x
2. $3n - 4n^2 + n^3 - 3$, n
3. $a^2b - 2ab^2 + a^3 + 3b^3$, a
4. $xy^2 - 3x^2y + 2x^3y - 2y$, x

5–8. Repeat Exercises 1–4 after replacing "decreasing" by "increasing."

Complete.

9. $(2x + 3)(4x + 1) = (\underline{\ ?\ })4x + (\underline{\ ?\ })1$
10. $(t - 5)(2t - 3) = (\underline{\ ?\ })2t - (\underline{\ ?\ })3$
11. $(a^2 + 2a + 3)(a - 2) = (\underline{\ ?\ })a - (\underline{\ ?\ })2$
12. $(y^2 - y + 6)(2y + 3) = (\underline{\ ?\ })2y + (\underline{\ ?\ })3$
13. $(x + 2)(x + 3) = (x + 2)x + (x + 2)3 = (\underline{\ ?\ })x^2 + (\underline{\ ?\ })x + (\underline{\ ?\ })$
14. $(x - 3)(x + 5) = (x - 3)x + (x - 3)5 = (\underline{\ ?\ })x^2 + (\underline{\ ?\ })x - (\underline{\ ?\ })$

Written Exercises

Multiply. Use the vertical form.

A

1. $\begin{array}{r} 3x - 5 \\ \underline{2x + 1} \end{array}$
2. $\begin{array}{r} 5t - 1 \\ \underline{2t - 3} \end{array}$
3. $\begin{array}{l} a^2 - 3a + 4 \\ \underline{2a + 3\quad\quad} \end{array}$
4. $\begin{array}{l} r^2 + 2r - 5 \\ \underline{3r - 2\quad\quad} \end{array}$
5. $\begin{array}{r} 3x - 2y \\ \underline{2x + 5y} \end{array}$
6. $\begin{array}{r} 2a - 5b \\ \underline{a - 3b} \end{array}$
7. $\begin{array}{l} c^2 + 2cd - 3d^2 \\ \underline{c - 2d\quad\quad\quad} \end{array}$
8. $\begin{array}{l} 2x^2 - 3xy - y^2 \\ \underline{2x + y\quad\quad\quad} \end{array}$

Multiply. Use the horizontal form.

9. $(y + 3)(y + 2)$
10. $(n + 7)(n + 5)$
11. $(a + 4)(a - 1)$
12. $(r - 3)(r + 6)$
13. $(2x - 1)(x - 5)$
14. $(3a - 2)(a - 3)$
15. $(3z - 2)(2z + 3)$
16. $(5k + 2)(2k - 3)$

17. $(4s - 5)(4s + 5)$

18. $(3x + 7)(3x - 7)$

19. $(a + 2)(a^2 + 3a + 5)$

20. $(x + 3)(x^2 + 2x + 4)$

21. $(m - 1)(m^2 + 2m + 6)$

22. $(y - 5)(y^2 - 3y - 7)$

23 $(2x - 1)(x^2 - x + 3)$

24. $(3s + 2)(2s^2 - 2s + 1)$

25. $(3z - 2)(3z^2 - z + 4)$

26. $(2n - 5)(2n^2 - 3n - 2)$

In each of the following figures, a rectangle has been divided into four smaller rectangles. (a) Find the sum of the areas of the four smaller rectangles. (b) Find the product of the length and width of the original rectangle. (c) Compare your answers to parts (a) and (b).

27.

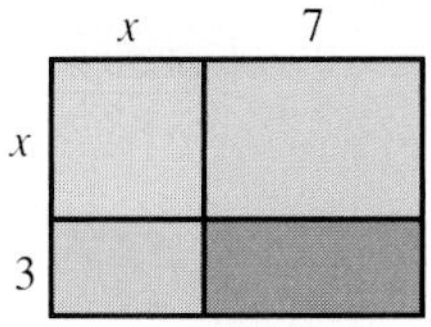

28.

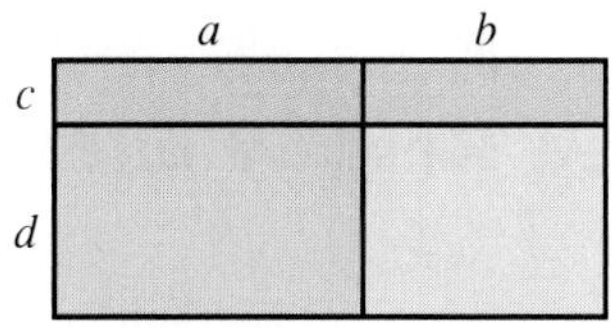

Multiply using either the horizontal or vertical form. Arrange the terms in each factor in order of decreasing or increasing degree of one of the variables.

B 29. $(2 + y)(y^2 - 2y + 3)$

30. $(5 + x)(x^2 - 5x + 4)$

31. $(2y - 3)(2y - 4 + y^2)$

32. $(3y - 4)(y - 2y^2 + 6)$

33. $(2 - 3x)(x^2 - 2x + 5)$

34. $(1 - 2a)(a^2 - 4 + 3a)$

35. $(2r - s)(s^2 + 4r^2 - 4rs)$

36. $(y - 2x)(2x^2 + y^2 - 3xy)$

Solve.

Sample $(x + 4)(x + 3) = (x + 1)(x + 5)$

Solution

$x^2 + 7x + 12 = x^2 + 6x + 5$

$7x + 12 = 6x + 5$ {Subtract x^2 from both sides.

$x + 12 = 5$ {Subtract $6x$ from both sides.

$x = -7$ {Subtract 12 from both sides.

$\therefore$ the solution set is $\{-7\}$. ***Answer***

37. $(x + 2)(x - 5) = (x - 1)(x - 3)$

38. $(x - 3)(x + 7) - (x + 1)(x + 5) = 0$

39. $(2x - 5)(x - 4) + 2x(1 - x) = 0$

40. $(3x + 5)(2x - 3) = (x - 1)(6x + 5)$

41. $(x - 3)(x^2 - 2x + 6) = x(x^2 - 5x + 9)$

42. $(2n - 3)(n^2 + 3n - 2) = (n - 1)(2n^2 + 5n - 4)$

Express as a polynomial.

43. The square of $x^2 - 3x + 5$

44. The square of $n^2 + 2n - 1$

45. The cube of $x + 5$

46. The cube of $a - 3$

47. Given that $(2 - y)^3 = 8 - 12y + 6y^2 - y^3$, find $(2 - y)^4$.

48. Subtract the product of $2x - y$ and $x - 2y$ from $x^2 + y^2$.

49. When a certain polynomial is divided by $x - 3$, the quotient is $x^2 + x - 2$. Find the polynomial.

C **50.** **a.** Multiply:

(1) $(x + 1)(x^2 - x + 1)$

(2) $(x + 1)(x^3 - x^2 + x - 1)$

(3) $(x + 1)(x^4 - x^3 + x^2 - x + 1)$

b. Using your answers in part (a), predict each product:

(4) $(x + 1)(x^5 - x^4 + x^3 - x^2 + x - 1)$

(5) $(x + 1)(x^6 - x^5 + x^4 - x^3 + x^2 - x + 1)$

Mixed Review Exercises

Solve.

1. $3(x - 1) = 6$ **2.** $4(x + 2) - 3 = 21$ **3.** $6(2a + 2) = 3(a + 10)$

Evaluate if $w = 3$, $x = -1$, and $y = 4$.

4. $w + |-x| + (-y)$ **5.** $w + x + 3$ **6.** $w - |x - y|$

7. $(w + y)^2$ **8.** $(-x^8)x^2$ **9.** xw^3

Self-Test 2

Simplify.

1. $3x^2x^4$ **2.** $(-6a^7)(-9a)\left(\frac{1}{3}a\right)$ **Obj. 4-3, p. 152**

3. $126a\left(-\frac{1}{9}a\right)\left(\frac{1}{7}a^3\right)$ **4.** $(ab^2)(a^2b)(a^2b^2)$

5. $(5xy^2)^3$ **6.** $(-2x^2y)^3$ **Obj. 4-4, p. 155**

7. $-(2x^2y)^3$ **8.** $(-3x^3)^2$

9. $-2n(5 - n)$ **10.** $\frac{1}{7}xy^2(56x^2 - 49xy + y^2)$ **Obj. 4-5, p. 158**

11. Solve $4 - \frac{2}{3}(6a - 15) = -38$.

Multiply.

12. $\begin{array}{r} 4x - 5 \\ \underline{3x + 2} \end{array}$ **13.** $\begin{array}{r} a^2 + 3a + 2 \\ \underline{5a - 4} \end{array}$ **Obj. 4-6, p. 161**

14. $(6a - 5)(a - 9)$ **15.** $(9 - 7y)(7 - 6y + 8y^2)$

Check your answers with those at the back of the book.

Problem Solving

4-7 Transforming Formulas

Objective To transform a formula.

Formulas are used in many applications of mathematics. Example 1 uses a formula from automotive engineering. It is often helpful to transform such a formula to express a particular variable in terms of the other variables.

Example 1 A formula for the total piston displacement of an automobile engine is $P = 0.7854d^2sn$, where d is the diameter of each cylinder, s is the length of the stroke, and n is the number of cylinders. Solve this formula for the variable s in terms of P, d, and n.

Solution $P = 0.7854d^2sn$

To get s alone on one side, divide both sides by $0.7854d^2n$.

$$\frac{P}{0.7854d^2n} = s \quad \textbf{Answer}$$

Note that the formula obtained for s in Example 1 is meaningful only if $d \neq 0$ and $n \neq 0$. (Of course, neither n nor d will be zero, since the engine must have cylinders and each cylinder must have a diameter.)

Example 2 Solve the formula for the variable shown in color: $A = s^2 + 2rs$, r

Solution

$$A = s^2 + 2rs$$
$$A - s^2 = 2rs$$
$$\frac{A - s^2}{2s} = r \quad \textbf{Answer}$$

{ To get r alone on one side first get $2rs$ alone on one side. Then divide by $2s$.

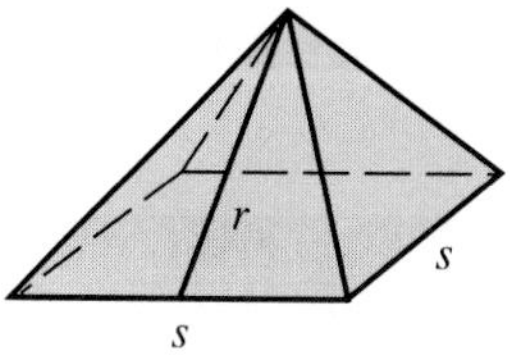

Total Surface Area:
$A = s^2 + 2rs$

The formula obtained in Example 2 is meaningful if $s \neq 0$. (Since s is the length of a side, $s > 0$.)

Oral Exercises

Solve each equation for the variable shown in color.

1. $b = ax$; x
2. $b = x + a$; x
3. $c = ax - b$; x
4. $s = a + b + c$; c
5. $a = \frac{x}{b^2}$; x
6. $C = \frac{mv^2}{r}$; r
7. $V = Bh$; B
8. $d = rt$; r
9. $E = mc^2$; m
10. $F = \frac{mv^2}{r}$; r
11. $A = \frac{1}{2}bh$; b
12. $R = \frac{kl}{d^2}$; l

Written Exercises

Solve the given formula for the variable shown in color. State the restrictions, if any, for the formula obtained to be meaningful.

A

1. $C = 2\pi r$; r
2. $F = ma$; a
3. $s = \frac{v}{r}$; r
4. $d = \frac{m}{v}$; v
5. $I = Prt$; P
6. $A = P + Prt$; t
7. $A = 2a^2 + 4ah$; h
8. $s = vt + 16t^2$; v
9. $A = \frac{1}{2}h(a + b)$; h
10. $S = \frac{n}{2}(a + l)$; n
11. $p = 2(l + w)$; w
12. $A = P(1 + rt)$; r
13. $m = \frac{x + y}{2}$; y
14. $a = \frac{v - u}{t}$; v

B

15. $S = \frac{n}{2}(a + l)$; a
16. $C = \frac{5}{9}(F - 32)$; F
17. $a = \frac{v - u}{t}$; t
18. $m = \frac{x + y + z}{3}$; y
19. $v^2 = u^2 + 2as$; s
20. $s = \frac{n}{2}(a + l)$; l
21. $S = \frac{a}{a - r}$; r
22. $l = a + (n - 1)d$; n
23. $F = \frac{fg}{f + g - d}$; d
24. $S = \frac{a - rl}{1 - r}$; l
25. $a = \frac{180(n - 2)}{n}$; n
26. $S = \frac{r}{1 - r}$; r

C

27. $r = \frac{ab}{a + b}$; a
28. $F = \frac{fg}{f + g - d}$; f
29. $C = K\left(\frac{Rr}{R - r}\right)$; R

Mixed Review Exercises

Simplify.

1. $(y - 5)(y + 3)$
2. $(3n - 2)(2n - 4)$
3. $a[2a - 4(2 + a)]$
4. $xy(2x + 3y)$
5. $4x(x^2 - 3x + 2)$
6. $(-3x^3)^3$
7. $n^2 \cdot n^2 \cdot n^2$
8. $(3a^2)^2 \cdot 4a^3b$

4-8 Rate-Time-Distance Problems

Objective To solve some word problems involving uniform motion.

An object is in **uniform motion** when it moves without changing its speed, or rate. The examples illustrate three types of problems involving uniform motion. Each is solved by using a chart, a sketch, and the distance formula:

$$\text{Distance} = \text{rate} \times \text{time}$$
$$D = rt$$

Example 1 (Motion in opposite directions) Bicyclists Brent and Jane started at noon from points 60 km apart and rode toward each other, meeting at 1:30 P.M. Brent's speed was 4 km/h greater than Jane's speed. Find their speeds.

Solution

Step 1 The problem asks for Brent's speed and Jane's speed. Draw a sketch.

Step 2 Let r = Jane's speed. Then $r + 4$ = Brent's speed.

Make a chart organizing the given facts and use it to label your sketch.

Notice that the time from noon to 1:30 P.M. is 1 h 30 min, or 1.5 h.

	Rate	× Time =	Distance
Brent	$r + 4$	1.5	$1.5(r + 4)$
Jane	r	1.5	$1.5r$

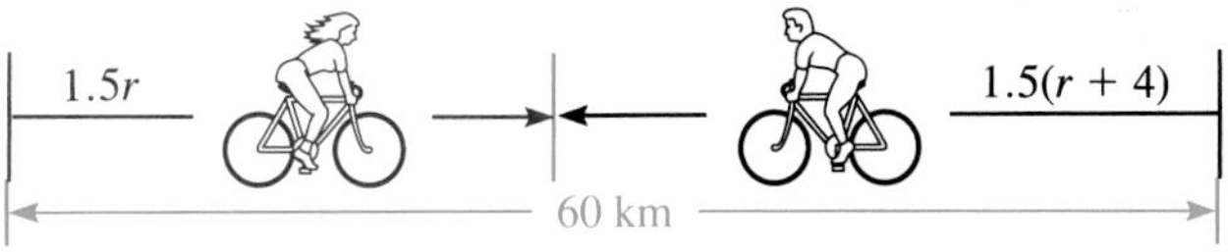

Step 3 The sketch helps you write the equation:

$1.5(r + 4) + 1.5r = 60$

Step 4
$$\begin{aligned} 1.5r + 6 + 1.5r &= 60 \\ 3r + 6 &= 60 \\ 3r &= 54 \\ r &= 18 \leftarrow \text{Jane's speed} \\ r + 4 &= 22 \leftarrow \text{Brent's speed} \end{aligned}$$

Step 5 *Check:* In 1.5 h Jane travels $1.5 \cdot 18 = 27$ (km).
Brent travels $1.5 \cdot 22 = 33$ (km). $27 + 33 = 60$ (km) ✓

∴ Brent's speed was 22 km/h, and Jane's speed was 18 km/h. ***Answer***

Example 2 (Motion in the same direction) A helicopter leaves Central Airport and flies north at 180 mi/h. Twenty minutes later a plane leaves the airport and follows the helicopter at 330 mi/h. How long does it take the plane to overtake the helicopter?

Solution

Step 1 The problem asks for the plane's flying time before it overtakes the helicopter. Draw a sketch.

Step 2 Let t = plane's flying time.

Make a chart organizing the given facts and use it to label your sketch.

Notice that 20 min must be written as $\frac{1}{3}$ h because the speeds are given in miles per hour.

	Rate ×	Time =	Distance
Helicopter	180	$t + \frac{1}{3}$	$180\left(t + \frac{1}{3}\right)$
Plane	330	t	$330t$

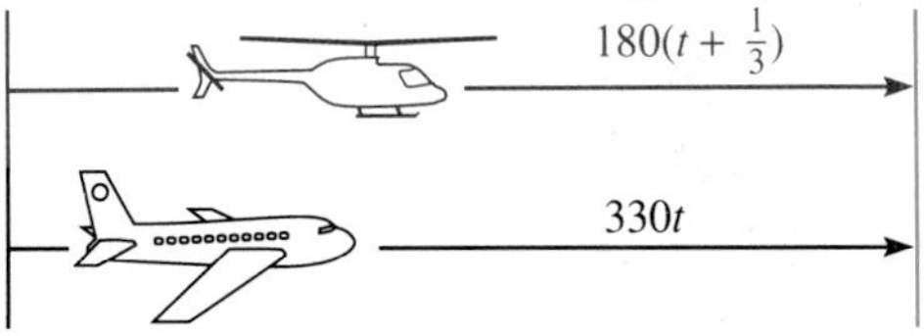

Step 3 When the plane overtakes the helicopter, the distances will be equal.

$$330t = 180\left(t + \frac{1}{3}\right)$$

Step 4

$$330t = 180t + 60$$
$$150t = 60$$
$$t = \frac{2}{5}$$

Step 5 *Check:* The helicopter travels at 180 mi/h for $\frac{1}{3}$ h before the plane leaves the airport and $\frac{2}{5}$ h after the plane leaves the airport.

The helicopter covers $\frac{1}{3} \cdot 180 + \frac{2}{5} \cdot 180 = 132$ (mi).

In $\frac{2}{5}$ h the plane travels $\frac{2}{5} \cdot 330 = 132$ (mi). $\surd$

$\therefore$ the plane overtakes the helicopter in $\frac{2}{5}$ h, or 24 min. ***Answer***

Caution: Some problems, such as the one in Example 2, give the time in *minutes,* and the speed in *hours*. Be sure to write the time in terms of hours when you use the given facts.

Example 3 (Round trip) A ski lift carried Maria up a slope at the rate of 6 km/h, and she skied back down parallel to the lift at 34 km/h. The round trip took 30 min. How far did she ski and for how long?

Solution

Step 1 The problem asks for Maria's skiing distance and time. Draw a sketch.

Step 2 Let t = Maria's skiing time. Make a chart.

Notice that 30 min = 0.5 h.

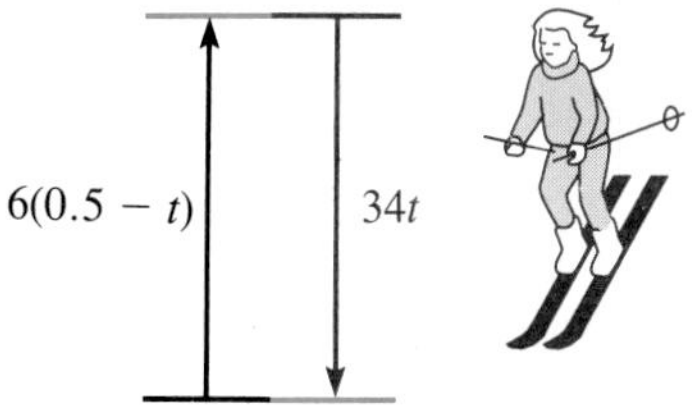

	Rate ×	Time =	Distance
Up	6	$0.5 - t$	$6(0.5 - t)$
Down	34	t	$34t$

Step 3 In round-trip problems, the two distances are equal.

$$34t = 6(0.5 - t)$$

Step 4

$$34t = 3 - 6t$$
$$40t = 3$$
$$t = \frac{3}{40} = 0.075 \text{ and } 34t = 34(0.075) = 2.55 \text{ (km)}$$

Step 5 The check is left to you.

$\therefore$ Maria skied for 0.075 h, or 4.5 min, for a distance of 2.55 km. ***Answer***

A calculator is helpful for solving problems such as the one above.

Oral Exercises

Classify each problem as involving (1) motion in opposite directions, (2) motion in the same direction, or (3) a round trip. Then complete the table and give an equation.

1. At noon a private plane left Austin for Los Angeles, 2100 km away, flying at 500 km/h. One hour later a jet left Los Angeles for Austin at 700 km/h. At what time did they pass each other?

	Rate ×	Time =	Distance
Plane	?	t	?
Jet	?	?	?

2. At 8:00 A.M. the Smiths left a campground, driving at 48 mi/h. At 8:20 A.M. the Garcias left the same campground and followed the same route, driving at 60 mi/h. At what time did they overtake the Smiths?

	Rate ×	Time =	Distance
Smiths	?	t	?
Garcias	?	?	?

3. Kwan hiked up a hill at 4 km/h and back down at 6 km/h. His total hiking time was 3 h. How long did the trip up the hill take him?

	Rate	× Time	= Distance
Up	?	?	?
Down	?	?	?

4. Jenny had driven for 2 h at a constant speed when road repairs forced her to reduce her speed by 10 mi/h for the remaining 1 h of her 152 mi trip. Find her original speed.

	Rate	× Time	= Distance
At original speed	?	?	?
At slower speed	?	?	?

Problems

A **1–4.** Complete the solutions of Oral Exercises 1–4.

Solve.

5. Two jets leave Denver at 9:00 A.M., one flying east at a speed 50 km/h greater than the other, which is traveling west. At 11:00 A.M. the planes are 2500 km apart. Find their speeds.

6. At 7:00 A.M. Joe starts jogging at 6 mi/h. At 7:10 A.M. Ken starts off after him. How fast must Ken run in order to overtake him at 7:30 A.M.?

7. At 9:30 A.M. Andrew left Exeter for Portsmouth, cycling at 12 mi/h. At 10:00 A.M. Stacy left Portsmouth for Exeter, cycling at 16 mi/h. The distance from Exeter to Portsmouth is 20 mi. Find the time when they met.

8. It takes a plane 40 min longer to fly from Boston to Los Angeles at 525 mi/h than it does to return at 600 mi/h. How far apart are the cities?

9. A bus traveled 387 km in 5 h. One hour of the trip was in city traffic. The bus's city speed was just half of its speed on open highway. The rest of the trip was on open highway. Find the bus's city speed.

10. It took Cindy 2 h to bike from Abbott to Benson at a constant speed. The return trip took only 1.5 h because she increased her speed by 6 km/h. How far apart are Abbott and Benson?

B **11.** Jerry spent 2.5 h biking up Mount Lowe, rested at the top for 30 min, and biked down in 1.5 h. How far did he bike if his rate of ascent was 3 km/h less than his rate of descent?

12. Jan can run at 7.5 m/s and Mary at 8.0 m/s. On a race track Jan is given a 25 m head start, and the race ends in a tie. How long is the track?

13. If Gina leaves now and drives at 66 km/h, she will reach Alton just in time for her appointment. On the other hand, if she has lunch first and leaves in 40 minutes, she will have to drive at 90 km/h to make her appointment. How far away is Alton?

14. An ultralight plane had been flying for 40 min when a change of wind direction doubled its ground speed. The entire trip of 160 mi took 2 h. How far did the plane travel during the first 40 min?

15. A ship must average 22 knots (nautical miles per hour) to make its 10-hour run on schedule. During the first four hours bad weather caused it to reduce speed to 16 knots. What should its average speed be for the rest of the trip to maintain its schedule?

16. Jamie ran two laps around a track in 99 s. How long did it take him to run each lap if he ran the first lap at 8.5 m/s and the second at 8.0 m/s?

In Exercises 17 and 18, cars *A* and *B* travel the same road. *A*'s speed is r km/h, and *B*'s speed is s km/h ($r < s$). When will *B* overtake *A* in each situation? Let t = *A*'s time.

C 17. *A* and *B* start at the same time, but *A* starts p km in front of *B*.

18. *A* and *B* start at the same place, but *A* starts q hours before *B*.

Suppose that cars *A* and *B* described above are d km apart.

19. If *A* and *B* start toward each other at the same time, how much later will they meet?

20. If *A* and *B* drive in opposite directions, how far apart will they be after t hours?

Mixed Review Exercises

Solve.

1. $64 = -8x$
2. $4(x + 2) = 32$
3. $(x - 6)(x + 9) = (x + 6)(x - 2)$
4. $-5x = -\frac{10}{18}$
5. $x - 7 = |2 - 10|$
6. $(x - 4)(x + 3) = (x - 6)(x + 4)$
7. Solve for x: $\frac{bx - 6}{2} = 3$
8. Solve for x: $a = 3x + 5$

4-9 Area Problems

Objective To solve some problems involving area.

To solve some problems involving area, you'll need to multiply, and add or subtract, polynomials. Sketches are especially helpful in solving such problems. The units of measure that you'll use most often are square centimeters (cm^2), square meters (m^2), square inches ($in.^2$), and square feet (ft^2).

A photograph 8 in. wide and 10 in. long is surrounded by a border 2 in. wide. To find the area of the border, subtract the areas of the rectangles.

Area of border = Area of outer rectangle − Area of inner rectangle

$= (10 + 4)(8 + 4) - (10)(8)$

$= (14)(12) - (10)(8)$

$= 168 - 80 = 88$

Therefore the area of the border is 88 $in.^2$.

Example 1 Hector Herrera made a rectangular fish pond surrounded by a brick walk 2 m wide. He had enough bricks for the area of the walk to be 76 m^2. Find the dimensions of the pond if it is twice as long as it is wide.

Solution

Step 1 The problem asks for the dimensions of the pond. Make a sketch.

Step 2 Let x = the width of the pond. Then $2x$ = the length of the pond. Label your sketch.

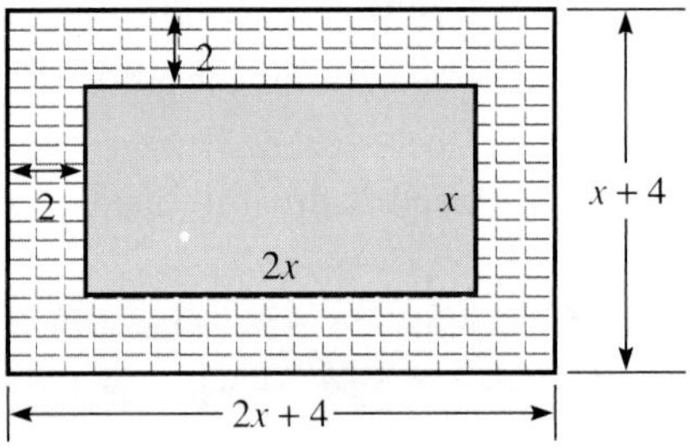

Step 3 Area of walk = Area of pond and walk − Area of pond

$76 = (2x + 4)(x + 4) - (2x)(x)$

Step 4

$76 = 2x^2 + 12x + 16 - 2x^2$

$76 = 12x + 16$

$60 = 12x$

$5 = x$ and $2x = 10$

Step 5 *Check:* If the dimensions of the pond are 5 m and 10 m, the dimensions of the pond and walk are 9 m and 14 m.

Area of pond and walk = $9 \cdot 14 = 126$ (m^2)
Area of pond = $5 \cdot 10 = 50$ (m^2)
Area of walk = $126 - 50 = 76$ (m^2) $\checkmark$

$\therefore$ the dimensions of the pond are 10 m and 5 m. ***Answer***

Oral Exercises

Solve.

1. A rectangle is 5 cm longer than it is wide. If its length and width are both increased by 3 cm, its area is increased by 60 cm^2. Find the dimensions of the original rectangle.

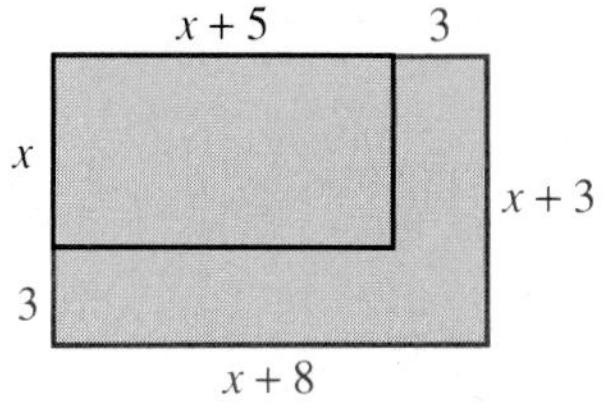

2. A rectangle is 10 m longer than it is wide. If its length and width are both decreased by 2 m, its area is decreased by 48 m^2. Find its original dimensions.

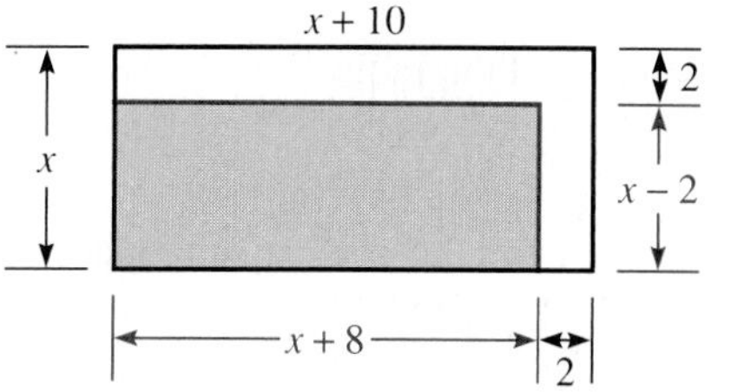

Problems

Solve.

A **1.** A rectangle is three times as long as it is wide. If its length and width are both decreased by 2 cm, its area is decreased by 36 cm^2. Find its original dimensions. Make a sketch as in Oral Exercise 2.

2. A rectangle is twice as long as it is wide. If both its dimensions are increased by 4 m, its area is increased by 88 m^2. Make a sketch as in Oral Exercise 1. Find the dimensions of the original rectangle.

3. A rectangular swimming pool is three times as long as it is wide and is surrounded by a deck 2.5 m wide. Find the dimensions of the pool if the area of the deck is 265 m^2.

4. A poster is 25 cm taller than it is wide. It is mounted on a piece of cardboard so that there is a 5 cm border on all sides. If the area of the border alone is 1350 cm^2, what are the dimensions of the poster?

5. A brick patio is twice as long as it is wide. It is bordered on all sides by a garden 1.5 m wide. Find the dimensions of the patio if the area of the garden is 54 m^2.

6. A house has two rooms of equal area. One room is square and the other room is a rectangle 4 ft narrower and 5 ft longer than the square one. Find the area of each room.

B **7.** A small city park consists of a rectangular lawn surrounded on all sides by a 330 m^2 border of flowers 2.5 m wide. Find the area of the lawn if the entire park is 5 m longer than it is wide.

8. A corner lot that originally was square lost 185 m^2 of area when one of the adjacent streets was widened by 3 m and the other was widened by 5 m. Find the new dimensions of the lot. (*Hint:* Let $x =$ the length of a side of the original square lot.)

9. The area of a circle of radius r is given by the formula $A = \pi r^2$. Use this fact to find a formula for the shaded area in the figure below.

In Problems 10 and 11, refer to Problem 9. Use $\frac{22}{7}$ as an approximation for π.

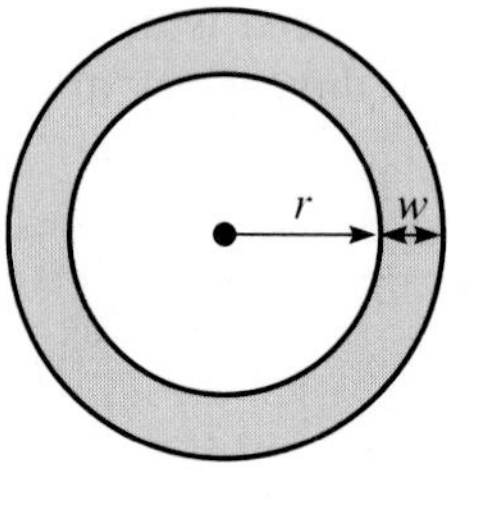

Exs. 9-11

10. Find the radius r if the width w of the shaded region is 2 cm and its area is 176 cm^2.

11. A circular pool is surrounded by a brick walkway 3 m wide. Find the radius of the pool if the area of the walkway is 198 m^2.

C 12. A running track 4 m wide goes around a soccer field that is twice as long as it is wide. At each end of the soccer field the track is a semi-circle with inner radius r. Find a formula for the area of the track in terms of π and r.

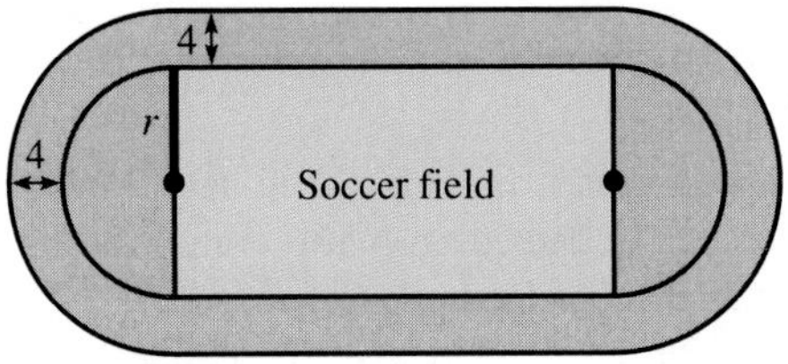

13. a. Suppose that you plan to run once around the track described in Problem 12. If you stay 0.5 m from the inner edge of the track, how far will you run? (*Hint:* The circumference of a circle is $2\pi r$. Your answer will be in terms of π and r.)

b. Suppose that a friend stays 0.5 m from the outer edge of the track. How much farther does your friend run than you do?

Mixed Review Exercises

Simplify.

1. $(-5 + 9) + (-8)$
2. $6(c - 2) + (-3)c + 5$
3. $(4xy^3)^3$
4. $y - (-7) - [y + (-7)]$
5. $5^3 \cdot 2^2$
6. $(7 \cdot 4 + 4 \cdot 5) \div (3 \cdot 2)$
7. $-\frac{9}{4} + \frac{5}{4} + 1$
8. $\left(\frac{1}{2}x^4\right)\left(\frac{2}{5}x^3\right)$
9. $-\frac{x}{11}(-143)$
10. $(-8 + 12) + (-4)$
11. $\left(\frac{1}{3}y^3\right)\left(\frac{3}{5}y\right)$
12. $(3y^2z)^4$

4-10 Problems Without Solutions

Objective To recognize problems that do not have solutions.

Not all word problems have solutions. Here are some reasons for this:

1. Not enough information is given.
2. The given facts lead to an unrealistic result. (The result satisfies the equation used but not the conditions of the problem situation.)
3. The given facts are contradictory. (They cannot all be true at the same time.)

Example 1 For the first 2 h of her trip Ginny Chang drove at her normal speed, but then road repairs forced her to drive 10 mi/h slower than her normal speed. Still, she made the trip in 3 h. Find her normal speed.

Solution

Step 1 The problem asks for Ginny's normal speed.

Step 2 Let r = Ginny's normal speed. Make a chart showing the given facts.

	Rate	× Time	= Distance
First part of trip	r	2	$2r$
Rest of trip	$r - 10$	1	$r - 10$

All the given facts have been used, but *not enough information has been given* to write an equation.

$\therefore$ the problem does not have a solution.

Example 2 A lawn is 8 m longer than it is wide. It is surrounded by a flower bed 5 m wide. Find the dimensions of the lawn if the area of the flower bed is 140 m^2.

Solution When you try to solve this problem by letting the dimensions of the lawn be x and $x + 8$, you will obtain the equation $(x + 10)(x + 18) - x(x + 8) = 140$.

This equation is equivalent to $x = -2$. Since the width of the lawn cannot be negative, *the given facts lead to an unrealistic result.*

$\therefore$ the problem does not have a solution.

Example 3 Raoul says he has equal numbers of dimes and quarters and three times as many nickels as dimes. The value of his nickels and dimes is 50¢ more than the value of his quarters. How many of each kind of coin does he have?

(Solution on next page)

Solution

Step 1 The problem asks for the numbers of nickels, dimes, and quarters.

Step 2 Let x = the number of dimes and x = the number of quarters.
Then $3x$ = the number of nickels.

Step 3 Value of nickels(¢) + Value of dimes(¢) = Value of quarters(¢) + 50

$$15x \quad + \quad 10x \quad = \quad 25x \quad + 50$$

Step 4

$$25x = 25x + 50$$
$$0 = 50$$

The false statement "0 = 50" tells you that the *given facts are contradictory.*

∴ the problem does not have a solution.

Problems

Solve each problem that has a solution. If a problem has no solution, explain why.

A

1. A pool is surrounded by a deck 3.5 m wide. Find the area of the pool if the area of the deck is 301 m^2.
2. A child's bank contains \$6.30 in dimes and quarters. There are twice as many dimes as quarters. How many of each kind of coin are in the bank?
3. In the course of a year, the sum of an investor's gains and losses was \$1000. What were his gains that year? His losses?
4. Kyle spent \$4.95 to buy 15 stamps in 25¢ and 40¢ values. How many of each kind of stamp did he buy?

5. Ben weighs 30 lb more than Ann, and their canoe weighs twice as much as Ben. If their canoe weighed 20 lb less, its weight would equal the sum of Ann's and Ben's weights. How much do Ann, Ben, and the canoe each weigh?
6. The average of four consecutive even integers is 17. Find the integers.
7. A messenger left a construction site and traveled by jeep at 51 km/h. Forty minutes later it was discovered that she had been given the wrong parcel. How fast must a second messenger travel to overtake her in one hour?
8. Jim's sandwich cost the same as the combined cost of his salad and milk. The sandwich cost three times as much as the milk. The salad cost 20¢ more than twice the cost of the milk. How much did Jim's lunch cost?
9. Find three consecutive odd integers whose sum is 24 more than the greatest of the three integers.

10. Janet has \$8.55 in nickels, dimes, and quarters. She has 7 more dimes than nickels and quarters combined. How many of each coin does she have?

11. At noon a train leaves St. Louis for Chicago. At 1:30 P.M. a train on a parallel track leaves Chicago for St. Louis. If the later train travels 5 mi/h faster than the earlier one, when will they pass each other?

12. A rectangle is 8 cm longer than it is wide. If the width is increased by 3 cm and the length is decreased by 3 cm, the area is increased by 4 cm^2. Find the dimensions of the original rectangle.

B **13.** A bus driven at 49 mi/h for 5 h can cover its route on schedule. During the first 1.5 h, traffic forced the driver to reduce his speed to 42 mi/h. What should the speed of the bus be for the rest of the trip to keep on schedule?

14. The edges of one cube are 3 cm longer than the edges of another cube. The total surface area of the first cube exceeds the total surface area of the second cube by 234 cm^2. How long is each edge of the larger cube?

15. Jane says she has \$8.60 in nickels, dimes, and quarters. She has 6 fewer quarters than nickels and 3 more dimes than twice the number of nickels. How many of each kind of coin does she have?

16. At the beginning of the year Alison and Sean together had 24 paperback books. During the year Alison doubled her supply but Sean lost three of his. Together, they had 46 books at the end of the year. How many books did each have at the beginning of the year?

Self-Test 3

Vocabulary uniform motion (p. 167)

1. Solve the formula $\frac{PV}{T} = k$ for V. **Obj. 4-7, p. 165**

Solve each problem. If a problem has no solution, explain why.

2. At 8:00 A.M. two bicyclists are 315 km apart and heading towards each other. At 3:00 P.M. the same day, they both pass Sherwood Park. If the eastbound bicyclist rides at the rate of 20 km/h, find the rate of the westbound bicyclist. **Obj. 4-8, p. 167**

3. A rectangular fish pond is 7 ft longer than it is wide. A wooden walk 1 ft wide is placed around the pond. The area covered by the pond and the walk is 58 ft^2 greater than the area covered by the pond alone. What are the dimensions of the pond? **Obj. 4-9, p. 172**

4. George wants to cash his \$280 paycheck for an equal number of \$5 bills, \$20 bills, and \$50 bills. How many of each kind of bill will he get? **Obj. 4-10, p. 175**

Check your answers with those at the back of the book.

Chapter Summary

1. The expression b^n is an abbreviation for $\underbrace{b \cdot b \cdot b \cdot \ . \ . \ . \ \cdot b}_{n \text{ factors}}$.
   The base is b and the exponent is n.
2. To simplify expressions that contain powers, follow the steps listed on page 142.
3. To add (or subtract) polynomials, you add (or subtract) their similar terms. Similar terms are monomials that are exactly alike or that differ only in their numerical coefficients.
4. Rules of exponents: $a^m \cdot a^n = a^{m+n}$ $\quad (a^m)^n = a^{mn}$ $\quad (ab)^m = a^m b^m$
5. Polynomials can be multiplied in a vertical or horizontal form by applying the distributive property (page 66). Before multiplying, it is wise to rearrange the terms of each polynomial in order of increasing or decreasing degree in one variable.
6. A formula may be transformed to express a particular variable in terms of the other variables.
7. A chart can be used to solve problems about distances or areas. Formulas to use are:

   rate × time = distance
   length × width = area of a rectangle
8. To solve problems involving area, you may find it helpful to make a sketch.
9. Problems may fail to have solutions because of lack of information, contradictory facts, or unrealistic results.

Chapter Review

Give the letter of the correct answer.

1. Express the cube of the sum of a and b in exponential form. **4-1**
a. $a^3 + b^3$ **b.** $(a + b)^3$ **c.** a^3b^3 **d.** $3a^3b^3$

2. Simplify $9 - 4^3$.
a. 125 **b.** -125 **c.** -55 **d.** -7

3. Simplify $(xy^2 + 4x^2y - 6) + (5xy^2 - 5x^2y - 7)$. **4-2**
a. $6xy - 9x^2y - 1$ **b.** $6xy^2 - x^2y - 13$
c. $5xy^2 - 13$ **d.** $6xy^2 - x^2y - 1$

4. Solve $x - (15x - 6) = 104$.
a. $\{-7\}$ **b.** $\left\{-6\frac{1}{8}\right\}$ **c.** $\left\{-6\frac{7}{8}\right\}$ **d.** $\{7\}$

5. Simplify $3x^6\left(-\frac{1}{3}x^6\right)$. **4-3**
a. $-9x^6$ **b.** $-x^6$ **c.** $-x^{36}$ **d.** $-x^{12}$

6. Simplify $(3a^4b)(5a^2b^2)(2a^3)$.
a. $60a^{11}b^3$ b. $30a^{10}b^2$ c. $150a^{10}b^3$ d. $30a^9b^3$

7. Simplify $(-3x^2y^4)^3$. 4-4
a. $9x^5y^7$ b. $-9x^5y^7$ c. $27x^6y^{12}$ d. $-27x^6y^{12}$

8. Simplify $9n^2\left(\frac{1}{3}n\right)^4$.

a. $3n^8$ b. $3n^6$ c. $\frac{1}{9}n^6$ d. $36n^3$

9. Simplify $-6[16a - 8(2a - 2)]$. 4-5
a. 12 b. $-96a$ c. 0 d. -96

10. Solve $6 - 2(n - 3) = 12$.

a. $\{0\}$ b. $\{6\}$ c. $\{-6\}$ d. $\left\{-4\frac{1}{2}\right\}$

11. Multiply $(4x - 3)(x - 4)$. 4-6
a. $4x^2 - 19x - 12$ b. $4x^2 - 7$ c. $4x^2 - 12$ d. $4x^2 - 19x + 12$

12. Multiply $(c - 6)(c^2 + 2c + 3)$.
a. $c^3 + 4c^2 - 15c + 18$ b. $c^3 - 12c - 18$
c. $c^3 - 4c^2 - 9c - 18$ d. $c^3 - 17c - 18$

13. Multiply $(a - b)(a^2 + ab + b^2)$.
a. $a^3 - b^3$ b. $a^3 + a^2b + ab^2$
c. $a - a^2b - ab^2 - b^3$ d. $a^3 + 2a^2b + 2ab^2 - b^3$

14. Solve for b in the equation $c + by = a$. 4-7

a. $b = \frac{c + a}{y}$ b. $b = \frac{a - y}{c}$

c. $b = \frac{a - c}{y}$ d. $b = \frac{a + y}{c}$

15. Solve for y in the equation $\frac{xy + z}{2} = a$.

a. $y = \frac{2a + z}{x}$ b. $y = \frac{2a - z}{x}$

c. $y = 2ax - zx$ d. $y = 2ax + zx$

16. Laurie left home and ran to the lake at 10 mi/h. She ran back home at 8 mi/h. If the entire trip took 27 min, how far did she run in all? 4-8
a. 0.4 mi b. 4 mi c. 4.4 mi d. 2.4 mi

17. A picture is 1 in. longer than it is wide. It is put into a frame $\frac{1}{2}$ in. wide. 4-9
If the area of the frame itself is 8 in.^{2}, how big is the picture?
a. 3 in. by 4 in. b. 4 in. by 5 in. c. 5 in. by 6 in. d. 7 in. by 8 in.

18. Esteban has 16 coins that total $3.00. If he has only nickels and quarters, how many quarters does he have? 4-10
a. No solution—not enough facts b. No solution—facts contradict
c. 5 d. 11

Chapter Test

Write each expression in exponential form.

1. The sum of the cubes of x and y. 4-1
2. The quantity ab cubed.
3. Simplify $(4^2 - 3 \cdot 1 - 3^2) \div [0 - (-2)^2]$.

In Exercises 4–6: a. Add the polynomials.
b. Subtract the lower polynomial from the upper one.

4. $\begin{array}{r} 9n - 5 \\ \underline{n + 3} \end{array}$

5. $\begin{array}{r} 6x^2 - 5x - 1 \\ \underline{-6x^2 + 5x + 1} \end{array}$

6. $\begin{array}{r} x^2 + 2xy + 3y^2 \\ \underline{5x^2 - xy - y^2} \end{array}$ 4-2

Simplify.

7. $4y^3(-3xy)$
8. $(12a^2)\left(\frac{2}{3}a^3\right)$
9. $7^2 \cdot 7x^3$ 4-3

Simplify.

10. 5^4n^4
11. $(2x^3)^5$
12. $4n^3\left(\frac{1}{2}n\right)^4$ 4-4

Multiply.

13. $2x(5 - 4x)$
14. $-3xy(7x^2 - 8xy + 9y^2)$ 4-5
15. Solve $\frac{5}{6}(12x - 6) - 4(3x - 1) = 0$.

Multiply.

16. $(3x + 2)(2x + 1)$
17. $(c + 3)(4c^2 - 6c + 1)$ 4-6

Solve for the variable shown in color.

18. $F = \frac{9}{5}C + 32$; C
19. $D = \frac{a}{2}(2t - 1)$; a 4-7

Solve each problem that has a solution. If a problem has no solution, explain why.

20. Lee and Jessie swam towards each other from opposite sides of a lake that is 3.9 km wide. They began swimming at 2:00 P.M. and met at 2:30 P.M. Lee's speed was 1 km/h greater than Jessie's speed. Find their speeds. 4-8
21. A rectangle is 4 cm longer than it is wide. If the length and width are both decreased by 2 cm, the area is decreased by 24 cm^2. Find the dimensions of the original rectangle. 4-9
22. Roy says he has more nickels than dimes. If he has \$5.20, how many of each coin does he have? 4-10

Cumulative Review *(Chapters 1–4)*

Simplify.

1. $(6x + 3) + (4x + 2)$
2. $\frac{1}{2}(101 - 43)$
3. $-2.2 + 3.8 - 5.6 + 4$
4. $15s - (2s - 9)$
5. $-7 - (-20) \div 2$
6. $-\frac{3}{5} + 4\frac{5}{8} - \frac{2}{5} + 7\frac{1}{8}$
7. $3^3 + 42 \div 3 + 4$
8. $(9a - 5) + (4a + 7)$
9. $-3|6 - 12|$
10. $(5x - 2)(2x + 3)$
11. $(4a^3)(5a)^2$
12. $5(3z^2 - 2z + 4)$
13. $-4x^2(3x^2 - 2x - 5)$
14. $(3y^3)(2y^2) - 2(y)(y^4)$
15. $(5 - 4x)(3 + 2x)$

Evaluate each expression if $w = \frac{1}{5}$, $x = -1$, $y = -3$, and $z = 2$.

16. $w(3y + x)$
17. $(xz - y)^5$
18. $w(z - (-y))$
19. $z(x - 2y)$

Solve. If the equation is an identity or has no solution, state that fact.

20. $|-x| = 9$
21. $|y - 1| + 4 = 0$
22. $5 = |x| + 5$
23. $c - (-4) = -8$
24. $3x - 2 = x + 6$
25. $42z = -42$
26. $0 = \frac{1}{3}n + 2$
27. $-10 = 4m + 2$
28. $\frac{1}{4}x = 20$
29. $3(2 + x) = -4(x - 5)$
30. $(11x - 3) - (4 + 2x) = 11$
31. $(2n + 9) + (5n - 4) = 6n + 9$
32. $(4y - 2) + (4 - 2y) = 30$
33. $2(c - 1) - 7 = 1$
34. $(2x - 3)(3x + 1) = (3x - 4)(2x + 2)$

Solve each equation for the variable shown in color.

35. $am - bn = c$; m
36. $by - ax = 0$; x

Solve.

37. One third of the sum of two consecutive odd integers is five less than the smaller integer. Find both integers.
38. Randy and Amy left school at the same time and began walking in opposite directions. Randy walked at a rate of 3.6 km/h and Amy walked at a rate of 4.2 km/h. How far apart were they after 10 min?
39. Jessica has 16 dimes and quarters. Whitney has twice as many dimes and $\frac{1}{3}$ as many quarters as Jessica has. If they both have the same amount of money, what coins does each have?
40. A rectangular piece of plywood is trimmed to make a square by cutting a 4-cm strip off the top and a 2-cm strip off one side. If the area of the original piece is 74 cm^2 greater than the area of the square, find the dimensions of the rectangle.

Maintaining Skills

Simplify.

Sample 1 $614 - (821 - 911)$

Solution $614 - (821 - 911) = 614 - (-90) = 614 + 90 = 704$ ***Answer***

1. $1921 + (-876)$
2. $181 + 97 - 64$
3. $(55 - 82) + (91 - 108)$
4. $-78 - 84 - (-92)$
5. $(28 - 86) - (46 - 81)$
6. $284 - (93 - 165)$
7. $35 - (58 + 62)$
8. $-325 + (-726) + 922$
9. $\frac{7}{8} - \left(-\frac{1}{4} + \frac{1}{2}\right)$
10. $\left(\frac{3}{5} - \frac{2}{3}\right) - \frac{5}{9}$
11. $17.6 - (8.05 - 9.6)$
12. $112.72 + (92.04 - 87.6)$

Sample 2 $-53(28) + 27(-40)$

Solution $-53(28) + 27(-40) = -1484 + (-1080) = -2564$ ***Answer***

Sample 3 $(-814 + 776) \div (-19)$

Solution $(-814 + 776) \div (-19) = -38 \div (-19) = 2$ ***Answer***

13. $-12(-16) + 5(-24)$
14. $27(20) - 60(48)$
15. $-65 - (412 - 385)$
16. $-4(-50) + 8(-25)$
17. $9.25(-2.3)$
18. $-6.06(-5.4)$
19. $-82.05 \div (-25)$
20. $-\frac{24}{35} \div \frac{9}{14}$
21. $7.24 \div (-0.25)$
22. $-\frac{12}{25} \cdot \left(-\frac{35}{42}\right)$
23. $-\frac{18}{35} \cdot \frac{49}{54}$
24. $-\frac{15}{64} \cdot \left(-\frac{40}{27}\right)$
25. $-2\frac{3}{8} \div \left(-2\frac{1}{8}\right)$

Sample 4 $82 + (-14)^2 \div 7 + 6$

Solution
$$\begin{aligned} 82 + (-14)^2 \div 7 + 6 &= 82 + 196 \div 7 + 6 \\ &= 82 + 28 + 6 \\ &= 116 \end{aligned}$$
Answer

26. $7 \cdot 8^2 - 6 \cdot 3 - 12 \div 2$
27. $(29 + 7) \div 3^2 + 13 - 2^2$
28. $(0.6)^2 - 1.2^2 \div 8 + 0.27 \div 0.3$
29. $-2(0.35 + 0.55)^2 \div 1.8 \div 2$
30. $1\frac{4}{5} \div 9 \cdot \frac{1}{2} - \left(\frac{1}{3} + \frac{1}{2}\right)^2$
31. $-\frac{5}{7}\left[-\left(1\frac{1}{3} - \frac{3}{4}\right)\right] + \frac{1}{3} \div 4$

Preparing for College Entrance Exams

Strategy for Success

If you cannot solve a problem quickly, go on to others that may be easier for you. If time permits, you can return and try the problem again. Also, while working on other problems you may get an idea that will help you with a problem that you skipped.

Decide which is the best of the choices given and write the corresponding letter on your answer sheet.

1. *PQRS* is a rectangle. Each of the longer sides is 1 cm shorter than twice a shorter side. The perimeter of the rectangle is 28 cm. Find the length of a longer side.
(A) 7 cm **(B)** 9 cm **(C)** 5 cm **(D)** 11 cm

2. Twice the sum of two consecutive integers is 10 less than 5 times the smaller integer. Find the greater integer.
(A) 12 **(B)** 14 **(C)** 13 **(D)** -6 **(E)** -8

3. The cost of a cup of soup, a sandwich, and a salad is \$4.70. The sandwich costs twice as much as the soup. The salad costs 30¢ more than the soup. What is the cost of the soup?
(A) \$1.25 **(B)** \$1.10 **(C)** \$1.15 **(D)** \$1.20

4. The Metro Theater has three times as many reserved seats as general admission seats. Reserved seats cost \$5 more than general admission seats. Which of the following is (are) sufficient to determine the amount of money collected on a sellout day?
I. the number of general admission seats
II. the cost of a general admission seat III. the total number of seats
(A) I only **(B)** II only **(C)** III only **(D)** I and II only

5. Evaluate the expression $(a + b)^2 \div (2a) - b^2$ if $a = 6$ and $b = 4$.
(A) $-\frac{23}{3}$ **(B)** -13 **(C)** -25 **(D)** $\frac{25}{16}$

6. Find $(2n^3)^2$ if $(n + 2)(n + 3) = (4 - n)(12 - n)$.
(A) 144 **(B)** 128 **(C)** 256 **(D)** 784

7. Solve for p in the equation $q = 1 + \frac{p}{100}$.
(A) $p = 100q - 1$ **(B)** $p = \frac{q - 1}{100}$ **(C)** $p = 100(q - 1)$ **(D)** $p = 1 + \frac{q}{100}$

8. On a 25 km trip to a park, Megan rode her bike for 20 min, then walked the rest of the way. Her walking speed was 18 km/h slower than her biking speed. How long did the trip take?
(A) 30 min **(B)** 40 min **(C)** 50 min **(D)** Cannot be determined.

5 Factoring Polynomials

Breaking a polynomial into its factors is like pulling a wooden puzzle apart to reveal its different components. The diagram shows that
$a^3 + 3a^2b + 3ab^2 + b^3 = (a + b)^3$.

Quotients and Factoring

5-1 Factoring Integers

Objective To factor integers and to find the greatest common factor of several integers.

When you write $56 = 8 \cdot 7$ or $56 = 4 \cdot 14$,

you have *factored* 56. In the first case the factors are 8 and 7. In the second case the factors are 4 and 14. You could also write $56 = \frac{1}{2} \cdot 112$ and call $\frac{1}{2}$ and 112 factors of 56. Usually, however, you are interested only in factors that are integers. To **factor** a number *over* a given set, you write it as a product of numbers in that set, called the **factor set.** In this book *integers will be factored over the set of integers* unless some other set is specified. The factors are then *integral* factors.

You can find the *positive factors* of a given positive integer by dividing it by positive integers in order. Record only the integral factors. Continue until a pair of factors is repeated.

Example 1 Give all the positive factors of 56.

Solution Divide 56 by 1, 2, 3, ... Stop

$$56 = 1 \cdot 56 = 2 \cdot 28 = 4 \cdot 14 = 7 \cdot 8 \; (= 8 \cdot 7)$$

$\therefore$ the positive factors of 56 are 1, 2, 4, 7, 8, 14, 28, and 56.

A **prime number,** or **prime,** is an integer greater than 1 that has no positive integral factor other than itself and 1. The first ten prime numbers are:

2, 3, 5, 7, 11, 13, 17, 19, 23, 29

To find the **prime factorization** of a positive integer, you express it as a product of primes. Example 2 shows a way to organize your work.

Example 2 Find the prime factorization of 504.

Solution Try the primes in order as divisors. Divide by each prime as many times as possible before going on to the next prime.

$$\begin{aligned} 504 &= 2 \cdot 252 \\ &= 2 \cdot 2 \cdot 126 \\ &= 2 \cdot 2 \cdot 2 \cdot 63 \\ &= 2 \cdot 2 \cdot 2 \cdot 3 \cdot 21 \\ &= 2 \cdot 2 \cdot 2 \cdot 3 \cdot 3 \cdot 7 \\ &= 2^3 \cdot 3^2 \cdot 7 \quad \textbf{\textit{Answer}} \end{aligned}$$

Exponents are generally used for prime factors that occur more than once in a factorization. The prime factorization of an integer is *unique* (there is only one) except for the order of the factors.

A factor of two or more integers is called a **common factor** of the integers. The **greatest common factor (GCF) of two or more integers** is the greatest integer that is a factor of all the given integers.

Example 3 Find the GCF of 882 and 945.

Solution First find the prime factorization of each integer. Then form the product of the *smaller* powers of each common prime factor.

$$882 = 2 \cdot 3^2 \cdot 7^2 \qquad 945 = 3^3 \cdot 5 \cdot 7$$

The common prime factors are 3 and 7.
The smaller powers of 3 and 7 are 3^2 and 7.

$\therefore$ the GCF of 882 and 945 is $3^2 \cdot 7$, or 63. ***Answer***

Oral Exercises

Give all the positive factors of each number.

1. 12 **2.** 15 **3.** 37 **4.** 1 **5.** 30 **6.** 41

State whether or not the number is prime. Give the prime factorization of the number.

7. 31 **8.** 32 **9.** 46 **10.** 51 **11.** 81 **12.** 39
13. 36 **14.** 100 **15.** 45 **16.** 47 **17.** 71 **18.** 98

Find the GCF of each pair of numbers.

19. 15 and 25 **20.** 12 and 18 **21.** 22 and 35 **22.** 23 and 46

Written Exercises

Sample List all pairs of factors of each integer. **a.** 20 **b.** -20

Solution

a. (1)(20) $(-1)(-20)$
(2)(10) $(-2)(-10)$
(4)(5) $(-4)(-5)$

b. $(1)(-20)$ $(-1)(20)$
$(2)(-10)$ $(-2)(10)$
$(4)(-5)$ $(-4)(5)$

List all pairs of factors of each integer.

A **1.** 13 **2.** 22 **3.** 24 **4.** 18 **5.** 29
6. 49 **7.** 40 **8.** 101 **9.** -121 **10.** -52

11. −33 **12.** −48 **13.** 53 **14.** 67 **15.** 26
16. 64 **17.** 68 **18.** 83 **19.** 38 **20.** 74

Find the prime factorization of each number. A calculator may be helpful.

21. 16 **22.** 34 **23.** 69 **24.** 65
25. 75 **26.** 88 **27.** 27 **28.** 54
29. 99 **30.** 120 **31.** 104 **32.** 128

B **33.** 125 **34.** 200 **35.** 450 **36.** 476
37. 1089 **38.** 840 **39.** 782 **40.** 2310

Find the GCF of each group of numbers. A calculator may be helpful.

41. 66, 90 **42.** 132, 220 **43.** 182, 196
44. 132, 242 **45.** 330, 945 **46.** 348, 426

C **47.** 1176, 1617 **48.** 1925, 6300 **49.** 56, 98, 126
50. 105, 126, 210 **51.** 141, 198, 364 **52.** 90, 126, 252

Mixed Review Exercises

Simplify.

1. $\frac{1}{3}(6x + 3) + 2\left(\frac{1}{2}x - 1\right)$ **2.** $(5 + 4)^2$ **3.** $3^2 + (2 + 1)^2$
4. $3x - 4 - (2x + 6)$ **5.** $3ab(2a^2)3a$ **6.** $3x^3(4y)2y$
7. $(3x)^3x$ **8.** $2n(3n^2 - 4n) + 8n^2$ **9.** $(-2)^5x^5$
10. $x(x^2 + 3) - x^2(x - 2)$ **11.** $(2y + 5)(y + 3)$ **12.** $(x - 4)(3x + 4)$

Computer Exercises

1. Write a BASIC program that uses the INT function to determine whether an integer entered with an INPUT statement is even or odd.
2. Write a BASIC program that uses the INT function to determine whether one integer is a factor of another integer. Each integer should be entered with an INPUT statement.
3. Write a BASIC program that uses the INT function and a FOR . . . NEXT loop to determine whether a number is *composite*. (A composite number is a number, such as 4, 6, 8, 9, and 10, that has two or more prime factors. Use a flag (F) to indicate whether the number is prime (F=0) or composite (F=1). When running your program, enter only integers greater than one.

Computer Key-In

The BASIC function INT( ) will give the greatest integer less than or equal to whatever number appears inside the parentheses.

INT(4)=4 INT(4.9)=4 INT(−4.9)=−5

This function can be used to find factors of a number.

INT(12/3)=12/3, so 3 is a factor of 12.
INT(12/5)≠12/5, so 5 is not a factor of 12.

The following program will PRINT pairs of positive integral factors of a positive integer.

```
10 PRINT "TO FIND POSITIVE INTEGRAL FACTORS"
20 PRINT " OF A POSITIVE INTEGER."
30 INPUT "ENTER A POSITIVE INTEGER > 1: "; W
40 FOR F=1 TO W/2
50 LET Q=W/F
60 IF Q<>INT(Q) THEN 80
70 PRINT F; " AND "; Q; " ARE FACTORS OF "; W
80 NEXT F
90 END
```

(Line 40: No additional factors will be found between W/2 and W.)

Exercises

1. Run the program for the following values of *W*: 30, 31, 36, 119, 323.
2. Explain why no additional factors of *W* will be found between *W*/2 and *W*.
3. Insert a line in the program to test whether the number you INPUT is actually a positive integer. If not, the program should return to line 30.
4. Modify the program to report if the number you INPUT is a prime number. You can do this by adding these four lines to the program:

```
35 LET C=0
75 LET C=C+1
85 IF C>1 THEN 90
86 PRINT W; " IS PRIME."
```

(Type LIST to get a clean copy of the modified program.)

5. RUN the modified program for the following values of *W*: 1, 2, 11, 51, 53.
6. Challenge: Modify the program you used for Exercise 5 so that it will print out all the prime numbers less than 500.

Challenge

The following problem is from the Egyptian Rhind papyrus:

There are seven houses; in each are seven cats. Each cat kills seven mice. Each mouse would have eaten seven ears of spelt [wheat]. Each ear of spelt will produce seven hekats of grain. How much grain was saved?

5-2 Dividing Monomials

Objective To simplify quotients of monomials and to find the GCF of several monomials.

There are three basic rules used to simplify fractions whose numerators and denominators are monomials. The property of quotients (proved in Exercise 61, page 193) allows you to express a fraction as a product.

Property of Quotients

If a, b, c, and d are real numbers with $b \neq 0$ and $d \neq 0$, then

$$\frac{ac}{bd} = \frac{a}{b} \cdot \frac{c}{d}.$$

Example 1 $\frac{15}{21} = \frac{3 \cdot 5}{3 \cdot 7} = \frac{3}{3} \cdot \frac{5}{7} = 1 \cdot \frac{5}{7} = \frac{5}{7}$

You obtain the following *rule for simplifying fractions* if you let $a = b$ in the property of quotients. (This rule is proved in Exercise 62, page 193.)

If b, c, and d are real numbers with $b \neq 0$ and $d \neq 0$, then

$$\frac{bc}{bd} = \frac{c}{d}.$$

This rule allows you to divide the numerator and the denominator of a fraction by the same nonzero number. In the examples of this lesson, *assume that no denominator equals zero.*

Example 2 Simplify: **a.** $\frac{35}{42}$ **b.** $\frac{-4xy}{10x}$

Solution **a.** Divide both numerator and denominator by 7. The red marks show this.

$$\frac{35}{42} = \frac{5 \cdot \cancel{7}}{6 \cdot \cancel{7}} = \frac{5}{6}$$

b. Divide both numerator and denominator by $2x$.

$$\frac{-4xy}{10x} = \frac{\cancel{2x} \cdot (-2y)}{\cancel{2x} \cdot 5} = \frac{-2y}{5} \text{ or } -\frac{2y}{5}$$

Example 3 Simplify: **a.** $\frac{c^7}{c^4}$ **b.** $\frac{a^3}{a^8}$ **c.** $\frac{b^5}{b^5}$

Solution **a.** $\frac{c^7}{c^4} = \frac{\cancel{c^4} \cdot c^3}{\cancel{c^4}} = c^3$ **b.** $\frac{a^3}{a^8} = \frac{\cancel{a^3} \cdot 1}{\cancel{a^3} \cdot a^5} = \frac{1}{a^5}$ **c.** $\frac{b^5}{b^5} = b^5 \cdot \frac{1}{b^5} = 1$

The results of Example 3 show that when you *divide powers* with the same base, you can *subtract* the smaller exponent from the greater if they are different. (Remember: when you *multiply* powers, you *add* the exponents.)

Rule of Exponents for Division

If a is a nonzero real number and m and n are positive integers, then:

If $m > n$:	If $n > m$:	If $m = n$:
$\frac{a^m}{a^n} = a^{m-n}$.	$\frac{a^m}{a^n} = \frac{1}{a^{n-m}}$.	$\frac{a^m}{a^n} = 1$.

Example 4 Simplify: **a.** $\frac{x^9}{x^5}$ **b.** $\frac{x^2}{x^7}$ **c.** $\frac{x^3}{x^3}$

Solution **a.** $\frac{x^9}{x^5} = x^{9-5} = x^4$ **b.** $\frac{x^2}{x^7} = \frac{1}{x^{7-2}} = \frac{1}{x^5}$ **c.** $\frac{x^3}{x^3} = 1$

The **greatest common factor (GCF) of two or more monomials** is the common factor with the *greatest coefficient* and the *greatest degree* in each variable.

Example 5 Find the GCF of $72x^3yz^3$ and $120x^2z^5$.

Solution

1. Find the GCF of the numerical coefficients.

   $72 = 2^3 \cdot 3^2$ and $120 = 2^3 \cdot 3 \cdot 5$

   $\therefore$ the GCF of 72 and 120 is $2^3 \cdot 3 = 8 \cdot 3 = 24$.

2. Find the smaller power of each variable that is a factor of *both* monomials.

   The smaller power of x is x^2.
   y is not a common factor.
   The smaller power of z is z^3.

3. Find the product of the GCF of the numerical coefficients and the smaller power of each variable that is a factor of both monomials.

   $24 \cdot x^2 \cdot z^3$

$\therefore$ the GCF of $72x^3yz^3$ and $120x^2z^5$ is $24x^2z^3$. ***Answer***

A quotient of monomials is said to be *simplified* when each base appears only once, when there are no powers of powers, and when the numerator and denominator have no common factors other than 1.

Example 6 Simplify $\frac{35x^3yz^6}{56x^5yz}$.

Solution 1 Use the property of quotients and the rule of exponents for division.

$$\frac{35x^3yz^6}{56x^5yz} = \frac{35}{56} \cdot \frac{x^3}{x^5} \cdot \frac{y}{y} \cdot \frac{z^6}{z}$$
$$= \frac{5}{8} \cdot \frac{1}{x^2} \cdot 1 \cdot z^5$$
$$= \frac{5z^5}{8x^2} \quad \textit{Answer}$$

Solution 2 Find the GCF of the numerator and denominator and use the rule for simplifying fractions.

$$\frac{35x^3yz^6}{56x^5yz} = \frac{\cancel{7x^3yz} \cdot 5z^5}{\cancel{7x^3yz} \cdot 8x^2} = \frac{5z^5}{8x^2} \quad \textit{Answer}$$

Oral Exercises

Find the GCF of the given monomials.

1. $3x^2, 9x^3$
2. $4c^3, 8c$
3. $15a^4, 21a^2$
4. $10b, 25b^5$
5. p^2q^3, p^3q^2
6. $42ab^2c^3, 30a^3b^2c$
7. $7xy^3, 14x^2y^2$
8. $4xy^2, 6x^2y$
9. $6s^2t^2, 9st^3$
10. $14a^3b^4, 21a^2b^5$
11. $20ax^3, 30abx$
12. $25p^2qr, 36pr^3$

Simplify. Assume that no denominator equals 0.

13. $\frac{24}{52}$
14. $\frac{32}{44}$
15. $\frac{10^8}{10^5}$
16. $\frac{10^3}{10^7}$
17. $\frac{10^6}{10^6}$
18. $\frac{6t}{2t}$
19. $\frac{8w}{4w}$
20. $\frac{9c^3}{3c}$
21. $\frac{3a^2}{6a}$
22. $\frac{5w^4}{15w^2}$
23. $\frac{24b^3}{12b^3}$
24. $\frac{12x^5}{-3x^3}$
25. $\frac{-6p^3}{12p^5}$
26. $\frac{8x^2y}{2xy}$
27. $\frac{5x^2y^2}{xy}$
28. $\frac{r^3s^2}{rs^4}$
29. $\frac{mn^5}{m^3n^2}$
30. $\frac{ab^3}{a^5b}$

Sample $\frac{(4n)^2}{(2n)^3} = \frac{16n^2}{8n^3} = \frac{\cancel{8n^2} \cdot 2}{\cancel{8n^2} \cdot n} = \frac{2}{n}$

31. $\frac{(2t)^5}{(2t)^3}$
32. $\frac{(2r)^3}{2r^2}$
33. $\frac{3s^3}{(3s)^2}$
34. $\frac{3x^3y}{(-x)^2y}$
35. $\frac{-x^4y}{(-x^2)^2}$
36. $\frac{-(m^3n)}{(-mn)^3}$

Written Exercises

Simplify. Assume that no denominator equals 0.

A

1. $\frac{42}{63}$
2. $\frac{54}{72}$
3. $\frac{10^4}{10^6}$
4. $\frac{10^9}{10^7}$
5. $\frac{12a}{3a}$
6. $\frac{10m}{5m}$
7. $\frac{6 \cdot 10^5}{3 \cdot 10^3}$
8. $\frac{12 \cdot 10^3}{4 \cdot 10^4}$
9. $\frac{4x^5}{8x}$
10. $\frac{3n^7}{15n^3}$
11. $\frac{12y^3}{4xy}$
12. $\frac{3r^2s}{9rs^2}$
13. $\frac{-9x^2y^3}{12xy^2}$
14. $\frac{-6pq^2}{-15pq}$
15. $\frac{-28cd^3}{-21bd^2}$
16. $\frac{42yz^4}{-48xz^3}$
17. $\frac{xy^2z^3}{x^3y^2z}$
18. $\frac{r^2s^4t}{r^2st^3}$
19. $\frac{32a^2bc^3}{20abc}$
20. $\frac{39x^3y^2z}{52x^2y}$
21. $\frac{(2r)^4}{2r^4}$
22. $\frac{7m^2}{(7m)^2}$
23. $\frac{(3t^2)^3}{(3t^3)^2}$
24. $\frac{(5a^2)^3}{(5a^3)^2}$
25. $\frac{(2ab)^2}{2ab^2}$
26. $\frac{(3mn)^2}{3mn^2}$
27. $\frac{(-z)^9}{(-z)^6}$
28. $\frac{(-a)^7}{(-a)^4}$
29. $\frac{(-xy)^9}{xy^9}$
30. $\frac{(-t^4)^3}{(-t^2)^5}$

Find the missing factor.

Sample $48x^3y^2z^4 = (3xy^2z)(\underline{\ ?\ })$

Solution $\frac{48x^3y^2z^4}{3xy^2z} = 16x^2z^3$

31. $6t^4 = (2t)(\underline{\ ?\ })$
32. $12w^6 = (3w^2)(\underline{\ ?\ })$
33. $9a^3b^4 = (3a^2b^2)(\underline{\ ?\ })$
34. $18pq^3 = (6pq)(\underline{\ ?\ })$
35. $-35x^3y^5 = (7x^2y)(\underline{\ ?\ })$
36. $-28r^4s^3 = (-7r)(\underline{\ ?\ })$
37. $48c^5d^4 = (-3c^3d^2)(\underline{\ ?\ })$
38. $72h^3k = (-8hk)(\underline{\ ?\ })$

B

39. $(3a^3b^2)^3 = (3a^3b^2)^2(\underline{\ ?\ })$
40. $(2s^3t)^5 = (2s^3t)^3(\underline{\ ?\ })$
41. $(x^2y^3)^3 = (x^4y^5)(\underline{\ ?\ })$
42. $(2c^3d^2)^5 = (2c^2d^2)^4(\underline{\ ?\ })$
43. $36r^5s^7 = (2r^3s)(6s^4)(\underline{\ ?\ })$
44. $48p^5q^4 = (2pq^2)(4pq)(\underline{\ ?\ })$
45. $72x^5y^5 = (2x^2y)^2(3y^3)(\underline{\ ?\ })$
46. $75a^6b^5 = (ab)^3(5a)^2(\underline{\ ?\ })$

Find the GCF of each pair of monomials.

47. $48a^2bc^3,\ 72ab^3c^2$
48. $36x^2y^2z^2,\ 24xy^2z^3$
49. $25p^2q^3,\ 15p^2q^2,\ 35pq^4$
50. $56r^4s^3,\ 28r^3s^2,\ 42r^3s$
51. $(x + y)(x - y),\ 2x(x + y)$
52. $4p^2(p - 1),\ 6p(p + 1)^2$

Simplify. Assume that no denominator equals 0.

53. $\frac{(a + b)^3}{(a + b)^2}$
54. $\frac{(w + x)^4}{(w + x)^5}$
55. $\frac{(x + y)(x - y)}{(x + y)^2}$
56. $\frac{(r - s)^2}{(r + s)(r - s)}$

Simplify. Assume that $x \neq 0$, $y \neq 0$, and n is a positive integer.

C 57. $\dfrac{136x^{n+1}}{187x^n}$

58. $\dfrac{143(xy)^n}{117xy^n}$

59. $\dfrac{x^{2n+1}y^{n+1}}{(xy^2)^n}$

60. $\dfrac{(-xy)^{2n+1}}{x^{2n}y^{n+1}}$

Give a reason for each step of the proof. You may use the property of quotients in Exercise 62. Assume that c, d, x, and y are real numbers and that no denominator equals 0.

61. Property of quotients

$\dfrac{ac}{bd} = (ac)\left(\dfrac{1}{bd}\right)$ **a.** ?

$= (ac)\left(\dfrac{1}{b} \cdot \dfrac{1}{d}\right)$ **b.** ?

$= \left(a \cdot \dfrac{1}{b}\right)\left(c \cdot \dfrac{1}{d}\right)$ **c.** ? ; ?

$= \dfrac{a}{b} \cdot \dfrac{c}{d}$ **d.** ?

62. Simplification rule for fractions

$\dfrac{bc}{bd} = \dfrac{b}{b} \cdot \dfrac{c}{d}$ **a.** ?

$= \left(b \cdot \dfrac{1}{b}\right) \cdot \dfrac{c}{d}$ **b.** ?

$= 1 \cdot \dfrac{c}{d}$ **c.** ?

$= \dfrac{c}{d}$ **d.** ?

Mixed Review Exercises

Simplify.

1. $\frac{1}{5}(-25)$

2. $111 \cdot \frac{1}{3}$

3. $423 \div 9$

4. $6n^4\left(\frac{1}{6}n^4\right)$

5. $15 \div \left(-\frac{1}{3}\right)$

6. $8y \cdot \frac{3}{4}y^2$

Evaluate if $x = 4$, $y = 2$, and $z = -3$

7. $\dfrac{xy}{(1 - z)y}$

8. $\dfrac{2x}{y - z}$

9. $7y^3 + 2x$

Calculator Key-In

When you use a calculator to divide one number by another, any remainder is a decimal. Here's how to write the decimal as a fraction:

1. Subtract the whole number part of the quotient from the entire quotient.
2. Multiply the decimal that remains from the subtraction by the divisor and round to the nearest integer. The result is the remainder.
3. Use the remainder as the numerator and the divisor as the denominator to write the decimal as a fraction.

Find the remainder. Then give the value of the decimal as a fraction.

1. $354 \div 13$

2. $621 \div 7$

3. $753 \div 11$

4. $1258 \div 15$

5. $3698 \div 36$

6. $5829 \div 45$

5-3 Monomial Factors of Polynomials

Objective To divide polynomials by monomials and to find monomial factors of polynomials.

On page 86 we proved that if a, b, and c are real numbers and $c \neq 0$, then

$$\frac{a+b}{c} = \frac{a}{c} + \frac{b}{c}.$$

This result is also true when a, b, and c are monomials and $c \neq 0$.

Example 1 Divide: $\frac{5m + 35}{5}$

Solution
$$\frac{5m+35}{5} = \frac{5m}{5} + \frac{35}{5}$$
$$= m + 7 \quad \textit{Answer}$$

To divide a polynomial by a monomial, divide each term of the polynomial by the monomial and add the results.

In the remaining lessons of this book, assume that no divisor equals 0.

Example 2 Divide: $\frac{26uv - 39v}{13v}$

Solution
$$\frac{26uv - 39v}{13v} = \frac{26uv}{13v} - \frac{39v}{13v}$$
$$= 2u - 3 \quad \textit{Answer}$$

Example 3 Divide: $\frac{3x^4 - 9x^3y + 6x^2y^2}{-3x^2}$

Solution
$$\frac{3x^4 - 9x^3y + 6x^2y^2}{-3x^2} = \frac{3x^4}{-3x^2} - \frac{9x^3y}{-3x^2} + \frac{6x^2y^2}{-3x^2}$$
$$= -x^2 + 3xy - 2y^2 \quad \textit{Answer}$$

Example 4 Divide: $\frac{x^3y - 4x + 6y}{xy}$

Solution
$$\frac{x^3y - 4x + 6y}{xy} = \frac{x^3y}{xy} - \frac{4x}{xy} + \frac{6y}{xy}$$
$$= x^2 - \frac{4}{y} + \frac{6}{x} \quad \textit{Answer}$$

We say that one polynomial is **evenly divisible,** or just **divisible,** by another polynomial if the quotient is also a polynomial. Example 3 shows that $3x^4 - 9x^3y + 6x^2y^2$ is divisible by $-3x^2$. Example 4 shows that $x^3y - 4x + 6y$ is *not* divisible by xy because the quotient is not a polynomial.

You *factor* a polynomial by expressing it as a product of other polynomials. Unless otherwise specified, *the factor set for a polynomial having integral coefficients is the set of all polynomials having integral coefficients.*

You can use division to test for factors of a polynomial. Example 3 shows that the divisor, $-3x^2$, is a factor of $3x^4 - 9x^3y + 6x^2y^2$. The quotient is the other factor.

$$3x^4 - 9x^3y + 6x^2y^2 = -3x^2(-x^2 + 3xy - 2y^2)$$

Of course, -3, x, and x^2 (besides $-3x^2$) are all factors of $3x^4 - 9x^3y + 6x^2y^2$, but you should use the *greatest* monomial factor of a polynomial. The **greatest monomial factor of a polynomial** is the GCF of its terms.

Example 5 Factor $5x^2 + 10x$.

Solution

1. The greatest monomial factor of $5x^2 + 10x$ is $5x$.
2. Divide: $\dfrac{5x^2 + 10x}{5x} = \dfrac{5x^2}{5x} + \dfrac{10x}{5x}$ $= x + 2$
3. $\therefore 5x^2 + 10x = 5x(x + 2)$ ***Answer***

Example 6 Factor $4x^5 - 6x^3 + 14x$.

Solution

1. The greatest monomial factor of $4x^5 - 6x^3 + 14x$ is $2x$.
2. Divide: $\dfrac{4x^5 - 6x^3 + 14x}{2x} = \dfrac{4x^5}{2x} - \dfrac{6x^3}{2x} + \dfrac{14x}{2x}$ $= 2x^4 - 3x^2 + 7$
3. $\therefore 4x^5 - 6x^3 + 14x = 2x(2x^4 - 3x^2 + 7)$ ***Answer***

Example 7 Factor $8a^2bc^2 - 12ab^2c^2$.

Solution

1. The greatest monomial factor of $8a^2bc^2 - 12ab^2c^2$ is $4abc^2$.
2. Divide: $\dfrac{8a^2bc^2 - 12ab^2c^2}{4abc^2} = \dfrac{8a^2bc^2}{4abc^2} - \dfrac{12ab^2c^2}{4abc^2}$ $= 2a - 3b$
3. $\therefore 8a^2bc^2 - 12ab^2c^2 = 4abc^2(2a - 3b)$ ***Answer***

With a little practice you will be able to do the division steps mentally. You should check your factorization by multiplying the resulting factors.

Oral Exercises

Divide.

1. $\frac{7x + 14}{7}$
2. $\frac{10y - 5}{5}$
3. $\frac{4u - 6v}{2}$
4. $\frac{14x - 28y + 21z}{7}$
5. $\frac{36m - 48mn}{6m}$
6. $\frac{22ab + 33b}{11b}$
7. $\frac{3c^2d - 12cd^2}{3cd}$
8. $\frac{2a^3b - 6a^2b^2 + 4ab^3}{2ab}$
9. $\frac{x^2y^2 + x^2y + xy^2}{xy}$

Find the greatest monomial factor. Then factor the given polynomial.

10. $4y^2 + 8y$
11. $15x^3 - 10x$
12. $ab^2 - a^2b$
13. $6pq + 9qr$
14. $\pi r^2 - 2\pi r$
15. $2x^2y^2 - 12xy$
16. $xy^2z^3 + x^3y^2z$
17. $uv^2r - u^2vs$

Written Exercises

Divide.

A

1. $\frac{6a + 9}{3}$
2. $\frac{4x - 6}{2}$
3. $\frac{24t - 12}{6}$
4. $\frac{21c + 35}{7}$
5. $\frac{9m - 18n}{9}$
6. $\frac{15a + 25b}{5}$
7. $\frac{12xy + 27y}{3y}$
8. $\frac{24mn - 16n}{8n}$
9. $\frac{10z^2 - 15z - 20}{5}$
10. $\frac{3x^2 - 12x - 18}{3}$
11. $\frac{33y^4 + 11y^3 - 44y^2}{11y}$
12. $\frac{4u^3 + 10u^2 - 6u}{2u}$
13. $\frac{8r^4 - 4r^3 - 6r^2}{-2r^2}$
14. $\frac{9m^5 + 12m^4 - 6m^3}{-m^3}$
15. $\frac{pq^3 - p^3q}{pq}$
16. $\frac{10a^2b - 15ab^2}{5ab}$
17. $\frac{x^2y - xy^2 - xy}{xy}$
18. $\frac{6c^3d - 12cd^3 - 15cd}{3cd}$
19. $\frac{28r^3s^2 + 42r^2s^3 - 56r^3s^3}{-7r^2s^2}$
20. $\frac{30p^4q - 45p^3q^2 + 15p^2q^3}{5p^2q}$

Evaluate by factoring first.

Sample $11^2 - 7 \cdot 11 = 11 \cdot 11 - 7 \cdot 11 = (11 - 7)11 = 4 \cdot 11 = 44$

21. $65 \cdot 3 + 65 \cdot 7$
22. $43 \cdot 13 - 43 \cdot 3$
23. $7 \cdot 19 - 3 \cdot 19 + 6 \cdot 19$
24. $7 \cdot 13 + 8 \cdot 13 + 5 \cdot 13$

25. $83^2 + 83 \cdot 17$

26. $2 \cdot 9 + 9^2$

27. $13^2 - 5 \cdot 13 + 2 \cdot 13$

28. $12 \cdot 13 - 60 + 12^2$

29. $7^2 - 28 + 7 \cdot 17$

30. $11^2 - 6 \cdot 11 + 5 \cdot 11$

Factor.

31. $15a - 25b + 20$

32. $18x - 12y + 36$

33. $6x^2 + 10x$

34. $14c^3 - 21c$

35. $6p^2q - 9pq$

36. $2a^2b^2 + 10ab$

37. $7y^3 - 21y^2 - 14y$

38. $22y^4 - 33y^3 + 11y^2$

B 39. $6ab^2 - 8a^2b$

40. $4x^2y - 16xy^2$

41. $-15x^2y^2 - 6xy^2$

42. $-16x^3y - 24x^4y^3$

43. $5ax^2 + 10a^2x - 15a^3$

44. $14p^3q^3 - 21p^2q^2 + 35pq$

45. $48a^3b^2 + 72a^2b^3$

46. $77r^7s^7 - 84r^8s^4$

47. $96wx^3y^2z^2 - 144w^3xy^2z^2$

48. $84ab^2c^3d^4 + 126a^4b^3c^2$

Simplify.

Sample $\frac{15x - 25y}{5} - \frac{14x - 21y}{7} = (3x - 5y) - (2x - 3y)$

$= 3x - 5y - 2x + 3y$

$= x - 2y$ ***Answer***

49. $\frac{4a - 6}{2} + \frac{3a + 6}{3}$

50. $\frac{14x - 21}{7} - \frac{10x - 25}{5}$

51. $\frac{6p + 9q}{3} - \frac{7p + 21q}{7}$

52. $\frac{a^2b + 2ab^2}{ab} - \frac{2ab - b^2}{b}$

53. $\frac{x^2y - 3x^2y^2}{xy} + \frac{6xy + 9xy^2}{3y}$

54. $\frac{a^3b^4 - a^4b^3}{a^2b^3} - \frac{a^3b^2 - a^2b^3}{a^2b}$

Problems

Sample Write an expression in factored form for the area A of the shaded region.

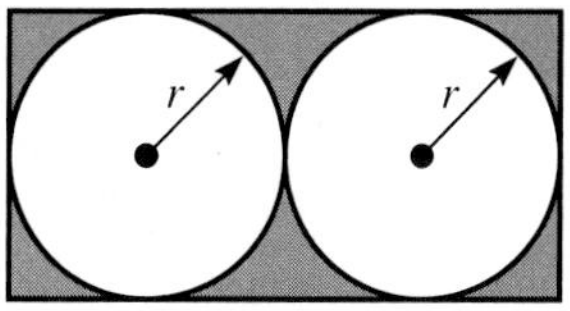

Solution The length of the rectangle equals the length of four radii ($4r$), and the width equals the length of two radii ($2r$).

A = Area of the rectangle − (2 × area of a circle)

$= (4r \cdot 2r) - 2\pi r^2$

$= 2r^2(4 - \pi)$ ***Answer***

Write an expression in factored form for the area A of each shaded region.

A **1.**

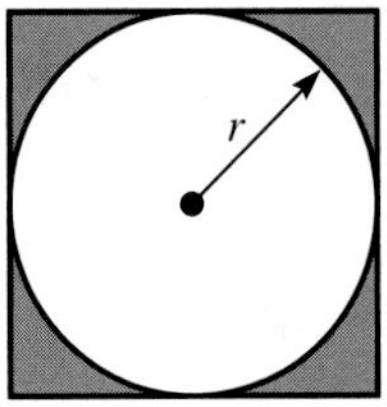

2.

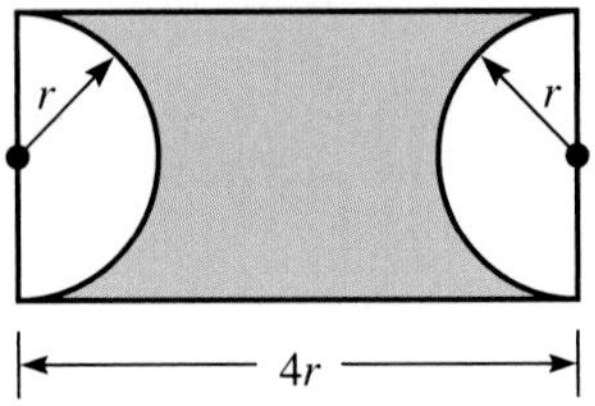

3.

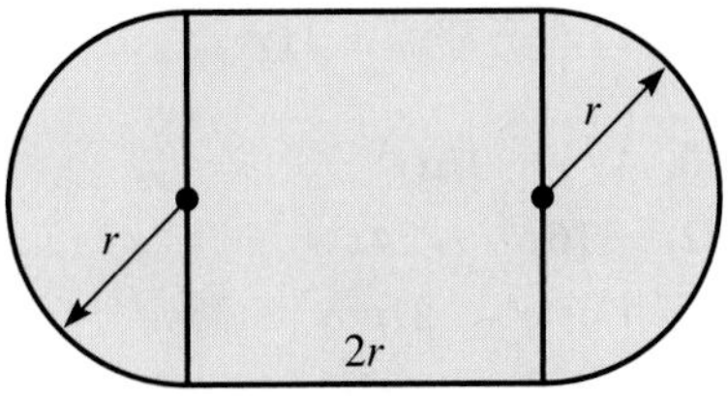

4.

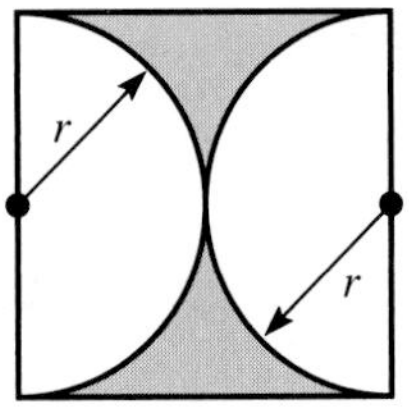

5.

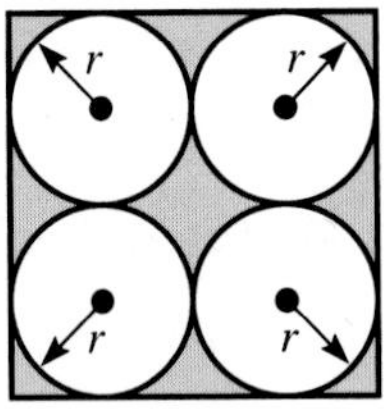

6.

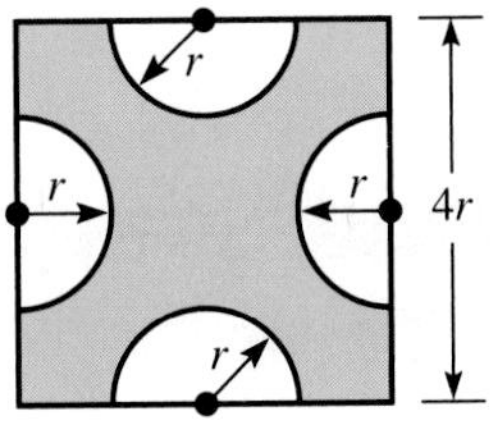

B **7.**

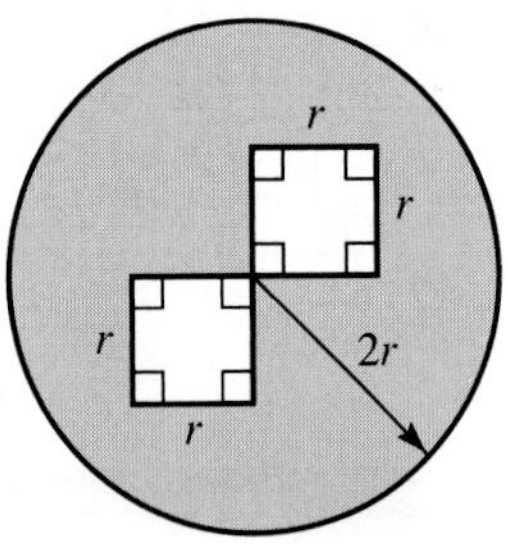

8.

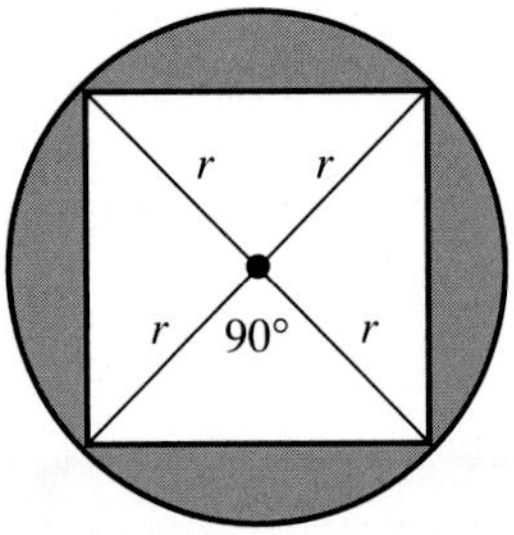

9.

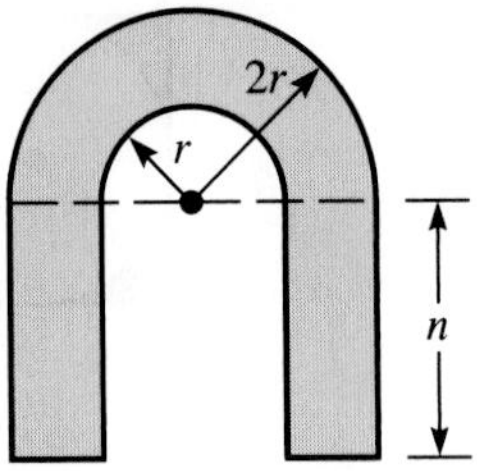

10.

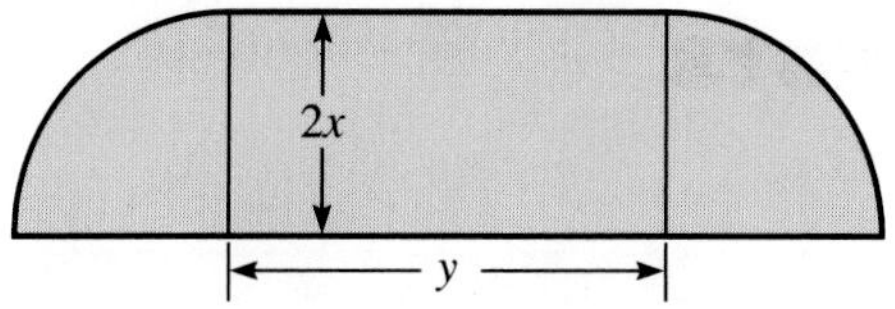

11.

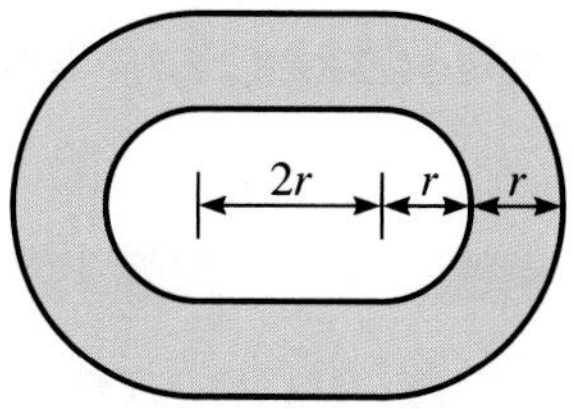

Mixed Review Exercises

Simplify.

1. $7n^3\left(\frac{1}{7}n^3\right)$ **2.** $9x^2\left(\frac{2}{3}x^3\right)$ **3.** $4a^2 - 7a^2c + 2a^2 - 3ac^2$

4. $\frac{3x^3y}{6xy^2}$ **5.** $28 \div \left(-\frac{1}{4}\right)$ **6.** $\frac{(2a^3)^3}{a^4}$

7. $(4a)^4$ **8.** $5(2^2 - 1) + 3^3 \cdot 2$ **9.** $(x - 2)(x^2 + 2x + 5)$

Self-Test 1

Vocabulary factor (p. 185)
factor set (p. 185)
prime number (p. 185)
prime factorization (p. 185)
greatest common factor of two or more integers (p. 186)
greatest common factor of monomials (p. 190)
divisible (p. 195)
greatest monomial factor of a polynomial (p. 195)

1. List all pairs of factors of 45. **Obj. 5-1, p. 185**

2. Find the prime factorization of 54.

3. Find the greatest common factor of 54 and 45.

Simplify.

4. $-\frac{21x^2y^5}{7xy^5}$ **5.** $\frac{10m^3n^8}{75m^5n^2}$ **Obj. 5-2, p. 189**

Find the missing factor.

6. $27x^4 = 3x^2(\underline{\ ?\ })$ **7.** $-35a^2b^5 = (7ab)(\underline{\ ?\ })$

8. Divide: $\frac{21t^4 + 15t^3 - 9t^2}{3t^2}$ **9.** Factor $5m^3 - 20m^2 + 25m$. **Obj. 5-3, p. 194**

Check your answers with those at the back of the book.

Products and Factors

5-4 Multiplying Binomials Mentally

Objective To find the product of two binomials mentally.

The following example shows how the distributive property, $(a + b)c = ac + bc$, is used to multiply $(2x + 5)$ by $(3x - 4)$. Notice how the three terms of the product are formed.

Example 1 Write the product $(2x + 5)(3x - 4)$ as a trinomial.

Solution 1 You can do the work horizontally, as shown below, or vertically, as shown at the right.

$$\begin{aligned}(2x + 5)(3x - 4) &= 2x(3x - 4) + 5(3x - 4)\\ &= 6x^2 - 8x + 15x - 20\\ &= 6x^2 + 7x - 20\end{aligned}$$

$$\begin{array}{r}3x - 4\\ \underline{2x + 5}\\ 6x^2 - 8x \qquad\\ \underline{15x - 20}\\ 6x^2 + 7x - 20\end{array}$$ ***Answer***

Solution 2 First use the following short method to multiply in your head.

Think of the products of these terms:

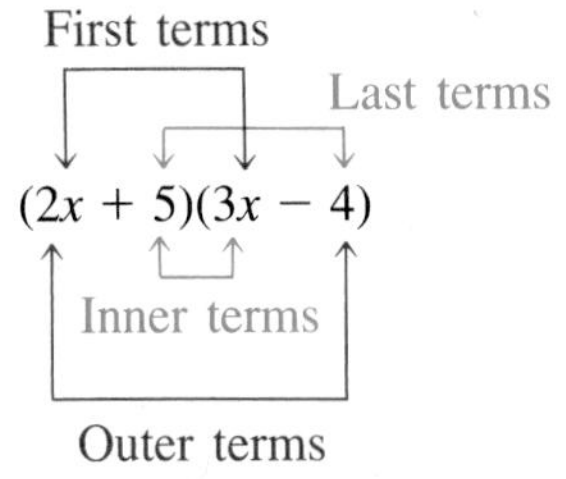

Then write the products:

$6x^2$	$-$	$8x$	$+$	$15x$	$-$	20	$= 6x^2 + 7x - 20$ ***Answer***
First terms		Outer terms		Inner terms		Last terms	

This method is sometimes called the FOIL method.

To write the product $(ax + b)(cx + d)$ as a trinomial:

1. Multiply the first terms of the binomials.
2. Multiply the first term of each binomial by the last term of the other and add these products.
3. Multiply the last terms of the binomials.

Each term of a trinomial like $6x^2 + 7x - 20$ has a standard name. A **quadratic term** is a term of degree two. A **linear term** is a term of degree one. As defined earlier, a *constant term* is one having no variable factor. The trinomial itself is called a **quadratic polynomial** since its term of greatest degree is quadratic.

$$6x^2 + 7x - 20$$

$6x^2$ is the quadratic term.
$7x$ is the linear term.
-20 is the constant term.

Sometimes you may need to evaluate a quadratic polynomial. The Calculator Key-In on page 203 will help you.

Oral Exercises

For each product, state (a) the quadratic term, (b) the two terms that form the linear term, (c) the constant term, and (d) the trinomial product.

Sample $(n - 7)(2n + 5)$

Solution **a.** $2n^2$ **b.** $5n$ and $-14n$ **c.** -35 **d.** $2n^2 - 9n - 35$

1. $(x + 1)(x + 3)$ **2.** $(y + 2)(y + 5)$ **3.** $(t - 2)(t - 3)$
4. $(u - 4)(u - 1)$ **5.** $(s - 6)(s - 3)$ **6.** $(7 - k)(4 - k)$
7. $(y - 3)(y + 5)$ **8.** $(x - 1)(x + 4)$ **9.** $(r + 3)(r - 5)$
10. $(s - 3)(s + 3)$ **11.** $(y + 2)(y + 2)$ **12.** $(x - 7)(x + 5)$
13. $(2y + 3)(y + 1)$ **14.** $(n + 1)(2n + 5)$ **15.** $(x - 3)(2x + 3)$
16. $(3y - 1)(y + 3)$ **17.** $(3r + 1)(r - 2)$ **18.** $(1 - 5x)(5 - x)$

Written Exercises

Write each product as a trinomial.

A **1.** $(x + 5)(x + 8)$ **2.** $(x + 7)(x + 6)$ **3.** $(y - 4)(y - 3)$
4. $(c - 9)(c - 6)$ **5.** $(z + 4)(z - 7)$ **6.** $(y + 6)(y - 2)$
7. $(n - 3)(n + 7)$ **8.** $(u - 10)(u + 9)$ **9.** $(3 + z)(2 + z)$
10. $(4 - x)(1 - x)$ **11.** $(2y + 5)(y + 2)$ **12.** $(r + 4)(2r + 3)$
13. $(7x - 1)(x + 7)$ **14.** $(4k - 1)(k + 4)$ **15.** $(2y + 1)(3y + 2)$
16. $(2n + 1)(5n + 2)$ **17.** $(2 - 3s)(1 - 2s)$ **18.** $(3 - 2r)(2 - 3r)$
19. $(3h - 5)(2h + 1)$ **20.** $(3x + 2)(2x - 3)$ **21.** $(5n + 4)(4n - 5)$

Sample 1 $(3x - 5y)(4x + y) = 12x^2 + (3xy - 20xy) - 5y^2$
$= 12x^2 - 17xy - 5y^2$ ***Answer***

Write each product as a trinomial. See Sample 1 on page 201.

B **22.** $(a + 2b)(a - b)$ **23.** $(3x - y)(x - 2y)$ **24.** $(2r - s)(3r + 2s)$

25. $(4h - k)(2h + 3k)$ **26.** $(2x + 5y)(2x - 3y)$ **27.** $(7a - 2b)(5a - 3b)$

Sample 2 $(m^2 - 5m)(2m^2 + 4m) = (m^2)(2m^2) + (m^2)(4m) + (-5m)(2m^2) + (-5m)(4m)$
$= 2m^4 + 4m^3 - 10m^3 - 20m^2$
$= 2m^4 - 6m^3 - 20m^2$ ***Answer***

28. $(x^2 - 4x)(3x^2 + 2x)$ **29.** $(a^2 + 3b)(3a^2 - b)$ **30.** $(p^2 - q^2)(p^2 + 3q^2)$

31. $(p^3 - 4q^3)(p^3 + 3q^3)$ **32.** $(y^4 - 3y^2)(y^2 + 2)$ **33.** $(x^4 + x^2y^2)(4x^2 - y^2)$

Sample 3 $n(n - 3)(2n + 1) = n[2n^2 + (-6n + n) - 3]$
$= n[2n^2 - 5n - 3]$
$= 2n^3 - 5n^2 - 3n$ ***Answer***

34. $y(2y - 1)(y + 4)$ **35.** $y(4y + 3)(y - 2)$

36. $y^2(1 - 2y)(2 + 3y)$ **37.** $x^2(4 - x)(2 - 3x)$

Solve.

Sample 4 $(x - 4)(x + 9) = (x + 5)(x - 3)$

Solution

$$\begin{aligned} x^2 - 4x + 9x - 36 &= x^2 + 5x - 3x - 15 \\ x^2 + 5x - 36 &= x^2 + 2x - 15 \\ 5x - 36 &= 2x - 15 \\ 3x - 36 &= -15 \\ 3x &= 21 \\ x &= 7 \end{aligned}$$

$\therefore$ the solution set is $\{7\}$. ***Answer***

38. $(x - 2)(x - 3) = (x - 7)(x + 3)$ **39.** $(y + 4)(y - 3) = (y - 2)(y + 5)$

40. $(2n + 5)(3n - 4) = (n + 2)(6n - 7)$ **41.** $(2x - 1)(8x + 3) = (4x + 5)(4x - 5)$

42. $(n + 3)(2n + 3) = (n + 2)^2 + (n - 2)^2$ **43.** $(2x - 3)(x + 3) = (x - 3)^2 + (x + 3)^2$

44. Show that $(ax + b)(cx + d) = acx^2 + (ad + bc)x + bd$.

In Exercises 45 and 46, find the values of *p*, *q*, and *r*.

C **45.** $(px + q)(2x + 5) = 6x^2 + 11x + r$ **46.** $(px + 2)(3x + q) = rx^2 + x - 2$

Write each product as a trinomial. Assume that *n* represents a positive integer.

47. $(x^n - y^n)(2x^n + 3y^n)$ **48.** $(2x^n - y^n)(2x^n + y^n)$

49. Show that the square of any odd integer is odd. (*Hint:* If n is an integer, then $2n$ is an even integer and $2n + 1$ is an odd integer.)

Mixed Review Exercises

Simplify.

1. $(2x^3y)(-4xy^3)$
2. $(5x^2y^5)^3$
3. $(6n + 3)(2n^2 + 3n - 1)$
4. $\frac{10r^2 + 25r - 30}{5}$
5. $\frac{(5y)^4}{5y}$
6. $\frac{15 - 9x - 3x^2}{3}$

Solve.

7. $m = 42 - 2m$
8. $4x - (2x + 5) = 5$
9. $4(n + 3) = 3(5 + n)$
10. $6y + 3 = 63$
11. $2(x + 1) - 3 = 9$
12. $3(y - 3) + 7 = 10$

Computer Exercises

For students with some programming experience.

Write a BASIC program to find the product of $(Ax + B)(Cx + D)$. Enter the values of A, B, C, and D with INPUT statements. Use the program to find the following products. Check the computer's answers by multiplying mentally.

1. $(x + 3)(x + 5)$
2. $(x - 4)(2x + 1)$
3. $(4x + 3)(2x - 5)$
4. $(2x + 7)(2x + 7)$
5. $(3x - 2)(3x + 2)$
6. $(6x - 7)(6x - 7)$
7. $(10x + 4)(5x + 2)$
8. $(8x + 9)(9x - 8)$
9. $(12x - 10)(12x + 10)$

Calculator Key-In

You can use a calculator to evaluate a quadratic polynomial for a given value of the variable. One way is to evaluate the polynomial term by term using the calculator's memory to store the partial sums.

Another way is to express the polynomial in a form that suggests a sequence of steps on the calculator. For example, to evaluate $5x^2 - 3x + 6$ you could first rewrite it as follows.

$$5x^2 - 3x + 6 = (5x - 3)x + 6$$

Then to evaluate the polynomial for a particular value, you can just work through the rewritten expression from left to right substituting the appropriate value for x.

Exercises

Evaluate the quadratic polynomial for the given value of the variable.

1. $4x^2 + 5x - 7;\ 3$
2. $6z^2 + 8z - 9;\ 4$
3. $2x^2 + 4x + 5;\ -3$
4. $y^2 - 4y - 3;\ 2.5$
5. $9k^2 - 35k + 50;\ 10$
6. $40y^2 - 25y + 70;\ 14$
7. $18x^2 - 15x - 10;\ -6$
8. $4y^2 + 4y - 5;\ 0.4$
9. $20z^2 - 15z + 5;\ -0.5$

5-5 Differences of Two Squares

Objective To simplify products of the form $(a + b)(a - b)$ and to factor differences of two squares.

The shaded area below can be thought of as the product $(a + b)(a - b)$. Notice on the right that when you multiply, the product can be simplified to $a^2 - b^2$, the difference of two squares.

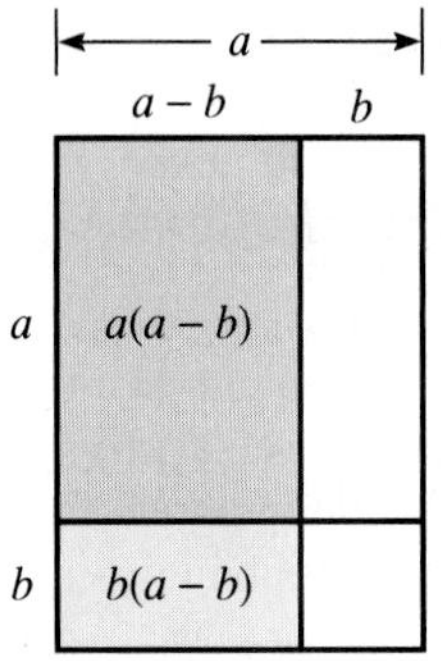

$$\begin{array}{rr} a - b & \\ a + b & \\ \hline a^2 - ab & \\ & ab - b^2 \\ \hline a^2 & - b^2 \end{array}$$

$$(a + b)(a - b) = a^2 - b^2$$

$$\begin{pmatrix}\text{Sum of two}\\ \text{numbers}\end{pmatrix} \times (\text{Their difference}) = \begin{pmatrix}\text{First}\\ \text{number}\end{pmatrix}^2 - \begin{pmatrix}\text{Second}\\ \text{number}\end{pmatrix}^2$$

Example 1 Write each product as a binomial.

a. $(x + 3)(x - 3)$ **b.** $(2n + 5)(2n - 5)$

Solution

a. $(x + 3)(x - 3) = x^2 - 3^2$
$= x^2 - 9$ ***Answer***

b. $(2n + 5)(2n - 5) = (2n)^2 - 5^2$
$= 4n^2 - 25$ ***Answer***

Example 2 Write each product as a binomial.

a. $(a^2 - 2b)(a^2 + 2b)$ **b.** $(xy + z^2)(xy - z^2)$

Solution

a. $(a^2 - 2b)(a^2 + 2b) = (a^2)^2 - (2b)^2$
$= a^4 - 4b^2$ ***Answer***

b. $(xy + z^2)(xy - z^2) = (xy)^2 - (z^2)^2$
$= x^2y^2 - z^4$ ***Answer***

Working in the other direction, if you have the difference of two squares, you can factor the expression:

$$a^2 - b^2 = (a + b)(a - b)$$

Example 3 Factor: **a.** $z^2 - 49$ **b.** $16 - 9x^2$ **c.** $81a^2 - 25x^6$

Solution

a. $z^2 - 49 = z^2 - 7^2$
$= (z + 7)(z - 7)$
Answer

b. $16 - 9x^2 = (4)^2 - (3x)^2$
$= (4 + 3x)(4 - 3x)$
Answer

c. $81a^2 - 25x^6 = (9a)^2 - (5x^3)^2$
$= (9a + 5x^3)(9a - 5x^3)$ ***Answer***

In Examples 3(b) and 3(c) you needed to recognize that both terms of the given binomial were *squares*. A monomial is a *square* if the exponents of all powers in it are even and the numerical coefficient is the square of an integer.

You can use a calculator or the table at the back of the book to see if a given integer is a square. For example, the table shows that 361 is the square of 19.

Example 4 Factor $16r^4 - 625$.

Solution

$16r^4 - 625 = (4r^2)^2 - (25)^2$
$= (4r^2 + 25)(4r^2 - 25)$ {Notice that $4r^2 - 25$ is also a difference of two squares.
$= (4r^2 + 25)(2r + 5)(2r - 5)$
Answer

Oral Exercises

Square each monomial.

Sample 1 $-7x^2$

Solution $(-7x^2)^2 = (-7)^2(x^2)^2 = 49x^4$

1. 8 **2.** $5a$ **3.** $-3t$ **4.** $4x^2$
5. $-5y^3$ **6.** ab **7.** $2pq^2$ **8.** m^8

Find a monomial whose square is the given monomial.

Sample 2 **a.** $36m^2$ **b.** $81x^6y^4$

Solution **a.** $6m$ **b.** $9x^3y^2$

9. $9x^2$ **10.** $16c^2$ **11.** $4a^4$ **12.** $25t^4$
13. x^2y^2 **14.** $4a^2b^2$ **15.** $49p^2q^4$ **16.** $9r^4s^6$

Express each product as a binomial.

17. $(n + 2)(n - 2)$
18. $(r - 5)(r + 5)$
19. $(2x + 5)(2x - 5)$
20. $(4y + 1)(4y - 1)$
21. $(3s - 2)(3s + 2)$
22. $(a - 2b)(a + 2b)$

Tell whether each binomial is the difference of two squares. If it is, factor it.

23. $n^2 - 4$
24. $m^2 - 5$
25. $y^2 - 64$
26. $b^2 + 9$
27. $4x^2 - 1$
28. $x^2 - 9y^2$
29. $a^8 + 36$
30. $a^4 - 9$
31. $a^4 - b^2$
32. $k^3 - 16$

Written Exercises

Write each product as a binomial.

A

1. $(y - 7)(y + 7)$
2. $(m + 8)(m - 8)$
3. $(4 + x)(4 - x)$
4. $(9 - w)(9 + w)$
5. $(5y - 2)(5y + 2)$
6. $(8x - 11)(8x + 11)$
7. $(1 + 3a)(1 - 3a)$
8. $(7 + 2a)(7 - 2a)$
9. $(3x + 2y)(3x - 2y)$
10. $(4w + 6z)(4w - 6z)$
11. $(4s + 5t)(4s - 5t)$
12. $(7p + 5q)(7p - 5q)$
13. $(x^2 - 9y)(x^2 + 9y)$
14. $(2x + n^2)(2x - n^2)$
15. $(2r^2 + 7s^2)(2r^2 - 7s^2)$
16. $(3m^2 - 8n^2)(3m^2 + 8n^2)$
17. $(ab - c^2)(ab + c^2)$
18. $(xy + 3z)(xy - 3z)$

Multiply. Use the pattern $(a + b)(a - b) = a^2 - b^2$.

Sample 1 $57 \cdot 63$

Solution

$$57 \cdot 63 = (60 - 3)(60 + 3)$$
$$= 3600 - 9$$
$$= 3591 \quad \textit{Answer}$$

19. $38 \cdot 42$
20. $53 \cdot 47$
21. $87 \cdot 93$
22. $49 \cdot 51$
23. $91 \cdot 89$
24. $102 \cdot 98$
25. $74 \cdot 66$
26. $25 \cdot 35$

Factor. You may use a calculator or the table of squares.

27. $b^2 - 36$
28. $m^2 - 25$
29. $4c^2 - 81$
30. $9a^2 - 100$
31. $25z^2 - 1$
32. $16x^2 - 9$
33. $169u^2 - 225$
34. $81n^2 - 121$
35. $1 - 9a^2$
36. $144 - y^2$
37. $49a^2 - 9b^2$
38. $64u^2 - 25v^2$

B

39. $16 - c^4$
40. $625x^4 - 1$
41. $u^4 - 81v^4$
42. $81s^4 - 16t^8$
43. $x^8 - y^8$
44. $m^{16} - 1$

Factor out the greatest monomial factor. Then factor the remaining binomial.

Sample 2 $3n^5 - 48n^3 = 3n^3(n^2 - 16)$
$= 3n^3(n + 4)(n - 4)$ ***Answer***

45. $5x^3 - 20x$

46. $2a^4 - 18a^2$

47. $36a^2 - 16a^4$

48. $50r^8 - 32r^2$

49. $uv^3 - u^3v$

50. $27a^3b - 12ab$

51. $2a^5 - 162a$

52. $16x^5y^2 - xy^6$

Factor each expression as the difference of two squares. Then simplify the factors.

Sample 3 $u^2 - (u - 5)^2 = [u - (u - 5)][u + (u - 5)]$
$= 5(2u - 5)$ ***Answer***

53. $(x + 4)^2 - x^2$

54. $t^2 - (t - 1)^2$

55. $(s + 2)^2 - (s - 2)^2$

56. $9(a + 1)^2 - 4(a - 1)^2$

Factor, assuming that *n* is a positive integer.

Sample 4 $x^{2n} - y^6 = (x^n)^2 - (y^3)^2$
$= (x^n + y^3)(x^n - y^3)$ ***Answer***

57. $a^{2n} - b^{2n}$

58. $x^{2n} - 25$

59. $u^{4n} - 4v^{2n}$

60. $45r^{2n} - 5s^{4n}$

61. $x^{4n} - y^{4n}$

62. $a^{4n} - 81b^{4n}$

63. $rt^{4n} - 16r$

64. $x^2 - x^2y^{4n}$

C **65.** Show that the square of the sum of two numbers minus the square of their difference is equal to four times their product.

66. Show that the absolute value of the difference of the squares of two consecutive integers is equal to the absolute value of the sum of the integers.

Mixed Review Exercises

Simplify.

1. $3z(z - 4) + 4z(z + 5)$

2. $(x + 5)(x - 7)$

3. $-2(m + 3) - 5m(m - 2)$

4. $\frac{25a^4b}{5a^2}$

5. $\frac{21a + 3}{3}$

6. $\frac{24n^3x}{6n^2x}$

7. $(a + 1)(2a - 3)$

8. $5b(b - 2)(3b + 1)$

9. $(3x)^2\left(\frac{1}{3}\right)^2x$

10. $\frac{12y^3 + 36y^2 - 6y}{6y}$

11. $\frac{28x^2 + 42x - 14}{14}$

12. $\frac{18x^2y^3z}{x^2y^2z}$

5-6 Squares of Binomials

Objective To find squares of binomials and to factor perfect square trinomials.

The diagram of the areas below helps you to see what happens when you square the binomial $a + b$.

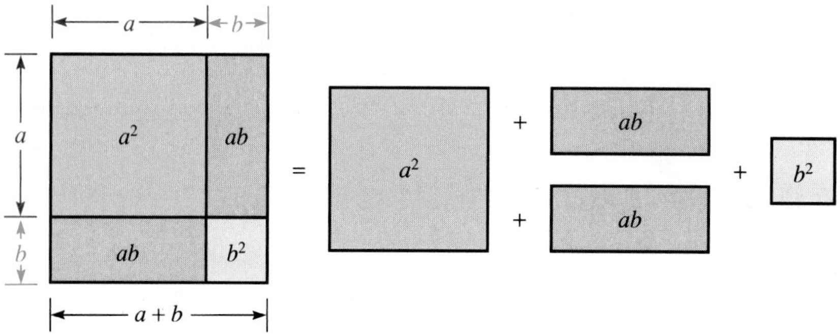

$$(a + b)^2 \quad = \quad a^2 \quad + \quad 2ab \quad + \quad b^2$$

Compare the above result with the algebraic result of multiplying the two binomials.

$$\begin{array}{r} a + b \\ \underline{a + b} \\ a^2 + ab \qquad \\ \underline{\qquad ab + b^2} \\ a^2 + 2ab + b^2 \end{array}$$

1. Square of the first term.
2. Twice the product of the two terms.
3. Square of the last term.

See what happens when you square the binomial difference $a - b$. The middle term in the product has a minus sign. Exercise 64 illustrates this in a diagram.

$$\begin{array}{r} a - b \\ \underline{a - b} \\ a^2 - ab \qquad \\ \underline{\qquad - ab + b^2} \\ a^2 - 2ab + b^2 \end{array}$$

1. Square of the first term.
2. Twice the product of the two terms.
3. Square of the last term.

It will be helpful to memorize these patterns for writing squares of binomials as trinomials.

$$(a + b)^2 = a^2 + 2ab + b^2$$

$$(a - b)^2 = a^2 - 2ab + b^2$$

Example 1 Write each square as a trinomial.
a. $(x + 3)^2$ **b.** $(7u - 3)^2$ **c.** $(4s - 5t)^2$ **d.** $(3p^2 - 2q^2)^2$

Solution **a.** $(x + 3)^2 = x^2 + 2(x \cdot 3) + 3^2$
$= x^2 + 6x + 9$ ***Answer***

b. $(7u - 3)^2 = (7u)^2 - 2(7u \cdot 3) + 3^2$
$= (7u)^2 - 2(21u) + 3^2$
$= 49u^2 - 42u + 9$ ***Answer***

c. $(4s - 5t)^2 = (4s)^2 - 2(4s \cdot 5t) + (5t)^2$
$= (4s)^2 - 2(20st) + (5t)^2$
$= 16s^2 - 40st + 25t^2$ ***Answer***

d. $(3p^2 - 2q^2)^2 = (3p^2)^2 - 2(3p^2 \cdot 2q^2) + (2q^2)^2$
$= 9p^4 - 2(6p^2q^2) + 4q^4$
$= 9p^4 - 12p^2q^2 + 4q^4$ ***Answer***

The patterns given at the bottom of page 208 are also useful for factoring:

$$a^2 + 2ab + b^2 = (a + b)^2$$
$$a^2 - 2ab + b^2 = (a - b)^2$$

The expressions on the left sides of these equations are called **perfect square trinomials** because each expression has three terms and is the square of a binomial. To test whether a trinomial is a perfect square, ask three questions as shown in Example 2.

Example 2 Decide whether each trinomial is a perfect square. If it is, factor it.
a. $4x^2 - 20x + 25$ **b.** $64u^2 + 72uv + 81v^2$

Solution **a.** $4x^2 - 20x + 25$

1. Is the first term a square? Yes; $4x^2 = (2x)^2$
2. Is the last term a square? Yes; $25 = 5^2$
3. Is the middle term, neglecting the sign, twice the product of $2x$ and 5? Yes; $20x = 2(2x \cdot 5)$

$\therefore$ $4x^2 - 20x + 25$ is a perfect square and equals $(2x - 5)^2$. ***Answer***

b. $64u^2 + 72uv + 81v^2$

1. Is the first term a square? Yes; $64u^2 = (8u)^2$
2. Is the last term a square? Yes; $81v^2 = (9v)^2$
3. Is the middle term, neglecting the sign, twice the product of $8u$ and $9v$? No; $72uv \neq 2(8u \cdot 9v)$

$\therefore$ $64u^2 + 72uv + 81v^2$ is not a perfect square. ***Answer***

You may have to rearrange the terms of a trinomial before you test whether it's a perfect square. For example, if you write $x^2 + 100 - 20x$ as $x^2 - 20x + 100$, you can answer "yes" to all three questions.

Oral Exercises

Express each square as a trinomial.

1. $(a + 4)^2$ **2.** $(t - 2)^2$ **3.** $(x - 6)^2$

4. $(z + 7)^2$ **5.** $(2y + 1)^2$ **6.** $(3u - 1)^2$

7. $(5c - 1)^2$ **8.** $(u^2 - 10)^2$ **9.** $(9 - k^3)^2$

Decide whether each trinomial is a perfect square. If it is, factor it.

10. $x^2 + 12x + 36$ **11.** $a^2 + 2a + 1$ **12.** $u^2 - 6u + 9$

13. $y^2 - 4y + 16$ **14.** $n^2 + 10n - 25$ **15.** $4c^2 - 12c + 9$

16. $25x^2 + 10xy + y^2$ **17.** $a^2 - 2ab + 4b^2$ **18.** $v^4 - 14v^2 + 49$

19. Find the square of 21 by thinking of it as $(20 + 1)^2$.

20. Find the square of 29 by thinking of it as $(30 - 1)^2$.

Written Exercises

Write each square as a trinomial.

A

1. $(n + 5)^2$ **2.** $(z + 8)^2$ **3.** $(a - 9)^2$ **4.** $(p - 10)^2$

5. $(4u - 1)^2$ **6.** $(6c - 1)^2$ **7.** $(5n - 4)^2$ **8.** $(3y - 8)^2$

9. $(2r + 9s)^2$ **10.** $(4u + 7v)^2$ **11.** $(5p - 6q)^2$ **12.** $(5a - 8z)^2$

13. $(mn + 2)^2$ **14.** $(pq - 4)^2$ **15.** $(2ab + c^2)^2$ **16.** $(-6rs + s^2)^2$

17. $(-4m^2 - 3n)^2$ **18.** $(-13u + v^2)^2$ **19.** $(9p^3 + 10)^2$ **20.** $(-11t^2 - 2)^2$

Decide whether each trinomial is a perfect square. If it is, factor it. If it is not, write *not a perfect square*.

21. $y^2 + 6y + 9$ **22.** $x^2 - 4x + 4$ **23.** $p^2 - 14p + 49$

24. $a^2 + 16a + 64$ **25.** $121 - 22u + u^2$ **26.** $144 + 12y + y^2$

27. $4x^2 + 9 + 12x$ **28.** $9 + 16c^2 - 24c$ **29.** $25x^2 - 15xy + 36y^2$

30. $49a^2 + 28ab + 4b^2$ **31.** $4s^2 - 36st + 81t^2$ **32.** $9u^2 + 30uv + 100v^2$

Factor.

Sample 1 $63n^3 - 84n^2 + 28n = 7n(9n^2 - 12n + 4)$
$= 7n(3n - 2)^2$

{First factor out the greatest monomial factor.

33. $8x^2 + 8x + 2$

34. $3a^2 - 18a + 27$

35. $9 - 72m + 144m^2$

36. $125u^2 - 50u + 5$

B 37. $x^5 + 2x^4 + x^3$

38. $y^4 - 14y^3 + 49y^2$

39. $a^2b + 6ab^2 + 9b^3$

40. $8u^3 - 24u^2v + 18uv^2$

41. $36p^4 - 48p^3 + 16p^2$

42. $3x^8 + 48x^5 + 192x^2$

Sample 2

$$\begin{aligned} x^2 - y^2 + 6y - 9 &= x^2 - (y^2 - 6y + 9) \\ &= x^2 - (y - 3)^2 \\ &= [x + (y - 3)][x - (y - 3)] \\ &= (x + y - 3)(x - y + 3) \quad \textbf{\textit{Answer}} \end{aligned}$$

{Look for a perfect square trinomial and factor it.}

43. $u^2 - 2u + 1 - v^2$

44. $p^2 + 4p + 4 - q^2$

45. $a^2 - b^2 + 6b - 9$

46. $p^2 - q^2 - 4q - 4$

Decide whether each polynomial is a perfect square. If it is, factor it. If it is not, write *not a perfect square*.

47. $x^6 + 10x^3 + 25$

48. $4 - 4y^2 + y^4$

49. $p^2q^2 - 12pq + 36$

50. $a^4 + 2a^2b^4 + b^8$

51. $121 - 33n^2 + 9n^4$

52. $121c^4 - 264c^2 + 144$

53. $(x + 1)^2 - 2(x + 1) + 1$

54. $(x + 1)^2 + 2(x + 1) + 1$

55. Show that $x^4 - 8x^2 + 16$ can be factored as $(x + 2)^2(x - 2)^2$.

56. Show that $a^4 - 18a^2 + 81$ can be factored as $(a + 3)^2(a - 3)^2$.

57. **a.** Express $(2x - 3y)^2$ and $(3y - 2x)^2$ as trinomials.
b. Explain why $(2x - 3y)^2 = (3y - 2x)^2$ even though $2x - 3y \neq 3y - 2x$.

Solve and check.

58. $(x + 2)^2 - (x - 3)^2 = 35$

59. $(2x + 5)^2 = (2x + 3)^2$

60. $(3x + 2)^2 + (4x - 3)^2 = (5x - 1)^2$

61. $(x + 2)^2 - (x - 2)^2 = (x - 1)^2 - (x - 3)^2$

Copy and cut up the model to show that each diagram illustrates the statement below it.

62.

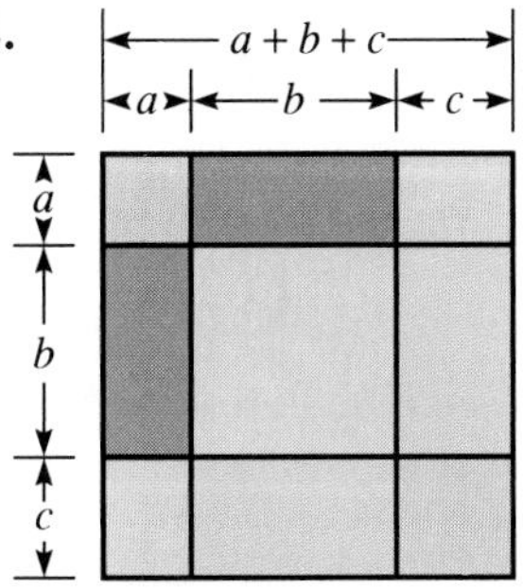

$(a + b + c)^2 =$
$a^2 + b^2 + c^2 + 2ab + 2ac + 2bc$

63.

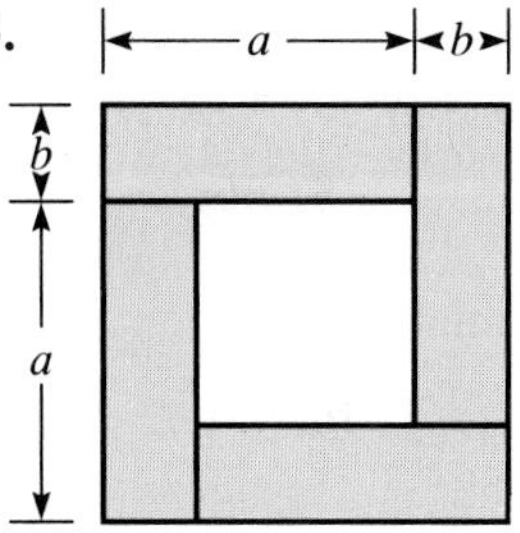

$(a + b)^2 - (a - b)^2 = 4ab$

64.

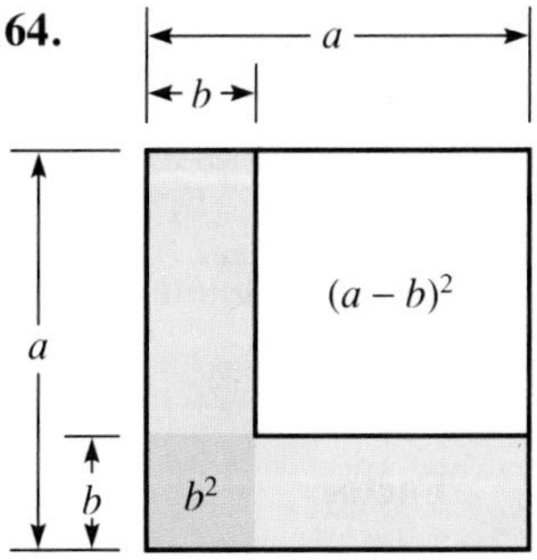

$(a - b)^2 = a^2 - 2ab + b^2$

C **65.** The perimeter of a square garden is 12 m greater than the perimeter of a smaller square garden. The area of the larger garden is 105 m^2 greater than that of the smaller garden. Find the dimensions of the larger garden.

66. The square of a two-digit number ending in 5 always ends in 25. You find the digits preceding the 25 by multiplying the tens' digit by one more than the tens' digit, as shown. **(a)** Use this rule to find the squares of 25, 55, and 95. **(b)** Let $10n + 5$ represent a two-digit number ending in 5. Show that the square of this number equals $100n(n + 1) + 25$.

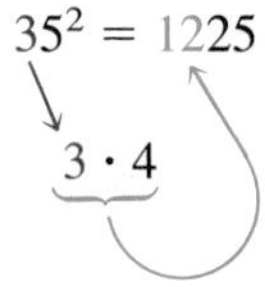

Mixed Review Exercises

Evaluate if $x = 4$ and $y = 2$.

1. $x + y + (-8)$ **2.** $x - |y| - |3|$ **3.** $9 + xy^2$

4. $(9 + xy)^2$ **5.** $(y)^3(-y)^6$ **6.** $(x^2y^2)^2$

Simplify.

7. $(4s + 3)(4s - 3)$ **8.** $(x + 9)(x + 3)$ **9.** $(5 - 3)^3$

10. $5 - 3^3$ **11.** $\frac{(a^6)^2}{(a^5)^3}$ **12.** $\frac{(2xy)^2}{4xy^2}$

Self-Test 2

Vocabulary quadratic term (p. 201) quadratic polynomial (p. 201) linear term (p. 201) perfect square trinomials (p. 209)

Write each product as a polynomial.

1. $(n + 3)(n + 8)$ **2.** $(m - 5)(m - 6)$ **Obj. 5-4, p. 200**

3. $(2y + 7)(3y - 4)$ **4.** $2x(x - 4)(3x - 2)$

5. $(x + 9)(x - 9)$ **6.** $(9a + 2b)(9a - 2b)$ **Obj. 5-5, p. 204**

Factor.

7. $4n^2 - 81$ **8.** $36x^4 - 16$

Write each square as a trinomial.

9. $(2n + 4)^2$ **10.** $(3z - 5k)^2$ **Obj. 5-6, p. 208**

Factor.

11. $9a^2 + 12a + 4$ **12.** $16m^2 - 24mn + 9n^2$

Check your answers with those at the back of the book.

Factoring Patterns

5-7 Factoring Pattern for $x^2 + bx + c$, c positive

Objective To factor quadratic trinomials whose quadratic coefficient is 1 and whose constant term is positive.

In this lesson you will study trinomials that can be factored as a product of the form $(x + r)(x + s)$, where r and s are both positive or both negative. The diagram shows that the product $(x + r)(x + s)$ and the trinomial $x^2 + (r + s)x + rs$ represent the same total area. Notice that the coefficient of the x-term is the *sum* of r and s, and the constant term is the *product* of r and s.

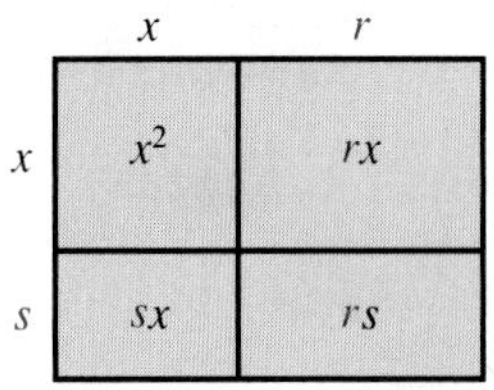

Example 1 $(x + 3)(x + 5) = x^2 + 8x + 15$

sum of 3 and 5 → $8x$; product of 3 and 5 → 15

Example 2 $(x - 6)(x - 4) = x^2 - 10x + 24$

sum of -6 and -4 → $-10x$; product of -6 and -4 → 24

The examples above suggest the following method for factoring trinomials whose quadratic coefficient is 1 and whose constant term is positive.

1. List the pairs of factors whose products equal the constant term.
2. Find the pair of factors in the list whose sum equals the coefficient of the linear term.

Examples 1 and 2 suggest that in Step 1 you need to consider only the factors with the *same sign* as the linear term.

Example 3 Factor $y^2 + 14y + 40$.

Solution

1. Since the coefficient of the linear term is positive, list the pairs of positive factors of 40.
2. Find the factors whose sum is 14: 4 and 10.
3. $\therefore y^2 + 14y + 40 = (y + 4)(y + 10)$ ***Answer***

Factors of 40		Sum of the factors
1	40	41
2	20	22
4	10	14
5	8	13

Example 4 Factor $y^2 - 11y + 18$.

Solution

1. Since -11 is negative, think of the negative factors of 18.
2. Select the factors of 18 with sum -11: -2 and -9
3. $\therefore y^2 - 11y + 18 = (y - 2)(y - 9)$ ***Answer***

A polynomial that cannot be expressed as a product of polynomials of lower degree is said to be **irreducible.** An irreducible polynomial with integral coefficients whose greatest monomial factor is 1 is a **prime polynomial.**

Example 5 Factor $x^2 - 10x + 14$.

Solution

1. The pairs of negative factors of 14 are: $-1, -14$; $-2, -7$.
2. Neither of these pairs has the sum -10.
3. $\therefore x^2 - 10x + 14$ cannot be factored. It is a prime polynomial. ***Answer***

Oral Exercises

The area of each rectangle is represented by the trinomial below it. Use the diagram to factor the trinomial. You may wish to make models from grid paper, using a 10-by-10 square for x^2, a 10-by-1 rectangle for x and a 1-by-1 square for 1.

Sample

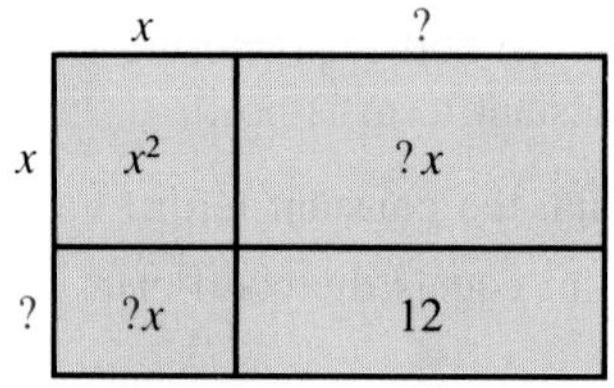

$x^2 + 8x + 12 = (x + ?)(x + ?)$

Solution

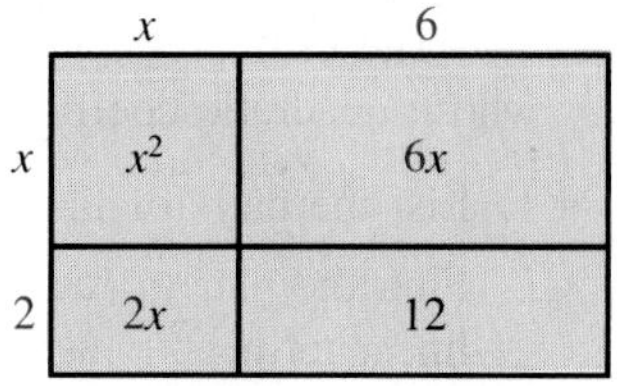

$x^2 + 8x + 12 = (x + 2)(x + 6)$

1.

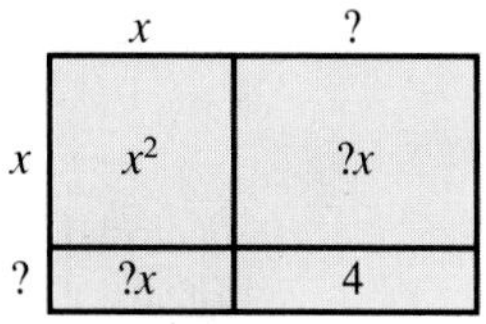

$x^2 + 5x + 4 =$
$(x + ?)(x + ?)$

2.

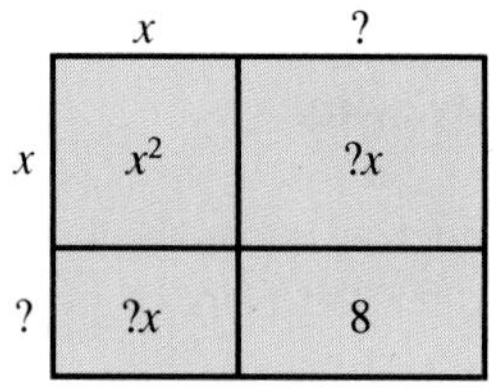

$x^2 + 6x + 8 =$
$(x + ?)(x + ?)$

3.

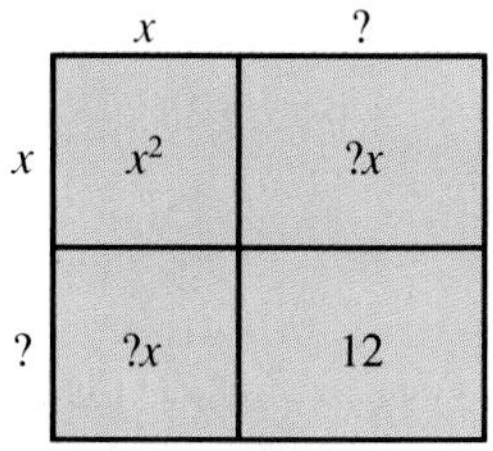

$x^2 + 7x + 12 =$
$(x + ?)(x + ?)$

Find two integers with the given sum and product.

	Example	4.	5.	6.	7.	8.	9.	10.	11.	12.	13.
Sum	$5 = 4 + 1$	5	7	−6	−6	8	10	−9	−11	−10	12
Product	$4 = 4 \cdot 1$	6	6	8	9	15	16	18	24	24	32

For each trinomial tell which two factors of the constant term have a sum equal to the coefficient of the linear term.

Sample $x^2 - 13x + 22$

Solution $(-2)(-11) = 22$ and $-2 + (-11) = -13$
$\therefore$ -2 and -11 are the correct factors. ***Answer***

14. $x^2 + 8x + 7$
15. $z^2 - 6z + 5$
16. $p^2 - 5p + 6$
17. $y^2 + 7y + 12$
18. $c^2 - 15c + 14$
19. $u^2 + 11u + 18$
20. $r^2 + 9r + 20$
21. $s^2 - 12s + 20$
22. $x^2 - 14x + 24$
23. $y^2 + 25y + 24$
24. $x^2 + 11x + 28$
25. $n^2 - 17n + 30$

Written Exercises

Factor. Check by multiplying the factors. If the polynomial is not factorable, write *prime*.

A

1. $x^2 + 5x + 4$
2. $z^2 + 9z + 8$
3. $r^2 - 6r + 8$
4. $c^2 - 10c + 16$
5. $y^2 - 9y + 14$
6. $p^2 - 14p + 13$
7. $q^2 + 16q + 15$
8. $n^2 + 10n + 21$
9. $a^2 - 15a + 26$
10. $s^2 - 12s + 40$
11. $x^2 + 20x + 36$
12. $z^2 + 16z + 39$
13. $u^2 + 12u + 28$
14. $x^2 - 22x + 72$
15. $42 - 23k + k^2$
16. $64 - 20s + s^2$
17. $75 + 20r + r^2$
18. $75 + 27u + u^2$

Sample $x^2 - 10xy + 21y^2$

Solution
$$x^2 - 10xy + 21y^2 = (x - ?)(x - ?)$$
$$= (x - 3y)(x - 7y)$$

Check:
$$(x - 3y)(x - 7y) = x^2 - 3xy - 7xy + 21y^2$$
$$= x^2 - 10xy + 21y^2$$

19. $p^2 + 19pq + 34q^2$
20. $a^2 + 10ab + 24b^2$
21. $c^2 - 16cd + 48d^2$
22. $x^2 - 15xy + 72y^2$
23. $u^2 - 50uv + 49v^2$
24. $h^2 - 14hk + 49k^2$
25. $x^2 - 16xy + 45y^2$
26. $m^2 + 20mn + 51n^2$
27. $a^2 + 17ab + 52b^2$
28. $p^2 + 20pq + 50q^2$
29. $r^2 - 15rs + 54s^2$
30. $a^2 - 12ab + 27b^2$

Factor. Check by multiplying the factors.

B **31.** $y^2 + 20yz + 91z^2$ **32.** $w^2 + 20wm + 96m^2$ **33.** $124 - 35y + y^2$

34. $108 - 24y + y^2$ **35.** $112a^2 - 22ab + b^2$ **36.** $117x^2 - 22xy + y^2$

Find all the integral values of *k* for which the trinomial can be factored.

Sample $x^2 + kx + 28$

Solution 28 can be factored as a product of two integers in these ways:

(1)(28) (−1)(−28)
(2)(14) (−2)(−14)
(4)(7) (−4)(−7)

The corresponding values of k are 29, 16, 11, −29, −16, and −11. ***Answer***

37. $y^2 + ky + 14$ **38.** $x^2 + kx + 10$ **39.** $z^2 + kz + 12$

40. $p^2 + kp + 18$ **41.** $n^2 + kn + 9$ **42.** $r^2 + kr + 20$

Find all *positive* integral values of *k* for which the trinomial can be factored.

43. $n^2 + 6n + k$ **44.** $z^2 + 7z + k$

45. $y^2 + 8y + k$ **46.** $x^2 + 9x + k$

Factor completely.

C **47.** $(y + 2)^2 - 6(y + 2) + 5$ **48.** $(t + 3)^2 + 8(t + 3) + 15$

49. $(y + 3)^2 + 6(y + 3) + 9$ **50.** $z^6 - 17z^4 + 16z^2$

51. $x^4 - 5x^2 + 4$ **52.** $r^4 - 29r^2 + 100$

53. $t^5 - 20t^3 + 64t$ **54.** $(a - 4)^2 + 5(a - 4)(a + 2) + 6(a + 2)^2$

55. Factor $a^{2n} - 30a^n b^{2n} + 209b^{4n}$, where n is a positive integer.

56. Factor $p^{4n} - 30p^{2n}q^n + 221q^{2n}$, where n is a positive integer.

Mixed Review Exercises

Solve.

1. $-13 + x = -9$ **2.** $d + (-5) = -6$ **3.** $-15 + b = 8$

4. $n + 2 = |3 - 6|$ **5.** $19m = 76$ **6.** $3p + 18 = -72$

7. $-\frac{1}{2}x = 12$ **8.** $\frac{r}{3} - 4 = 5$ **9.** $-21x = 252$

Simplify.

10. $(5y + 7)(5y - 7)$ **11.** $(2xy^3)^3$ **12.** $(2x^2)^6$

5-8 Factoring Pattern for $x^2 + bx + c$, c negative

Objective To factor quadratic trinomials whose quadratic coefficient is 1 and whose constant term is negative.

The factoring that you did in the last lesson had this pattern:

$$x^2 + bx + c = (x + r)(x + s)$$

c positive ↑ ↑ ↑ r and s are *both positive* or *both negative*.

The factoring that you will do in this lesson has the following pattern:

$$x^2 + bx + c = (x + r)(x + s)$$

c negative ↑ ↑ ↑ r and s have *opposite* signs.

When you find the product $(x + r)(x + s)$, you obtain

$$x^2 + bx + c = x^2 + (r + s)x + rs$$

Therefore, the method used in this lesson is the same as before. You find two numbers, r and s, whose product is c and whose sum is b. Since c is negative, one of r and s must be negative and the other must be positive.

Example 1 Factor $x^2 - x - 20$.

Solution

1. List the factors of -20 by writing them down or reviewing them mentally.
2. Find the pair of factors with sum -1: 4 and -5.
3. $\therefore x^2 - x - 20 = (x + 4)(x - 5)$ ***Answer***

You can check the result by multiplying $(x + 4)$ and $(x - 5)$.

Factors of -20		Sum of the factors
1	-20	-19
-1	20	19
2	-10	-8
-2	10	8
4	-5	-1
-4	5	1

Example 2 Factor $a^2 + 29a - 30$.

Solution

1. The factoring pattern is $(a + ?)(a - ?)$.
2. Find the pair of factors of -30 with sum 29: 30 and -1.
3. $\therefore a^2 + 29a - 30 = (a + 30)(a - 1)$ ***Answer***

Example 3 Factor $x^2 - 4kx - 12k^2$.

Solution

1. The factoring pattern is $(x + ?)(x - ?)$.
2. Find the pair of factors of $-12k^2$ with a sum of $-4k$: $2k$ and $-6k$.
3. $\therefore x^2 - 4kx - 12k^2 = (x + 2k)(x - 6k)$ ***Answer***

Oral Exercises

Find two integers with the given sum and product.

	Example	1.	2.	3.	4.	5.	6.	7.	8.	9.	10.
Sum	$1 = 3 + (-2)$	2	-3	-2	15	3	-7	1	0	2	-10
Product	$-6 = 3(-2)$	-3	-10	-15	-16	-18	-18	-30	-25	-24	-24

For each trinomial tell which two factors of the constant term have a sum equal to the coefficient of the linear term.

Sample $x^2 - 3x - 28$

Solution $(-7)(4) = -28$ and $-7 + 4 = -3$
$\therefore$ -7 and 4 are the correct factors. ***Answer***

11. $z^2 + 3z - 4$
12. $z^2 - 4z - 5$
13. $c^2 - c - 6$
14. $p^2 + p - 12$
15. $y^2 - 5y - 14$
16. $r^2 - 2r - 8$
17. $x^2 + 2x - 15$
18. $u^2 - u - 2$
19. $k^2 + 8k - 9$

Written Exercises

Factor. Check by multiplying the factors. If the polynomial is not factorable, write *prime*.

A

1. $y^2 + 5y - 6$
2. $v^2 - 3v - 4$
3. $x^2 - 6x - 16$
4. $x^2 + 2x - 8$
5. $c^2 - 4c - 12$
6. $u^2 - 10u - 9$
7. $n^2 + 2n - 6$
8. $a^2 - 5a - 24$
9. $b^2 - 13b - 30$
10. $p^2 + 7p - 18$
11. $y^2 + 12y - 36$
12. $y^2 - 4y - 32$
13. $x^2 - 25x - 54$
14. $t^2 - 16t - 40$
15. $y^2 - 21y - 72$
16. $z^2 + z - 72$
17. $a^2 - ab - 42b^2$
18. $r^2 - 20rs - 44s^2$
19. $u^2 + 9uv - 70v^2$
20. $x^2 - 2xy - 63y^2$
21. $h^2 - 25hk - 54k^2$
22. $m^2 + mn - 56n^2$
23. $p^2 - 16pq - 36q^2$
24. $a^2 - 13ab - 48b^2$

Sample $1 - 10x - 24x^2$

Solution Find two factors of $-24x^2$ whose sum is $-10x$: $2x$ and $-12x$.
$\therefore 1 - 10x - 24x^2 = (1 + 2x)(1 - 12x)$ ***Answer***

B

25. $1 - 2n - 48n^2$
26. $1 + 15c - 34c^2$
27. $x^2 - 10xy - 75y^2$
28. $a^2 + 5ab - 84b^2$

29. $1 + 11pq - 80p^2q^2$
30. $1 - 15mn - 100m^2n^2$
31. $p^2 + 2p - 360$
32. $n^2 + 9n - 400$
33. $-380 + x + x^2$
34. $-800 - 20a + a^2$

Find all the integral values of k for which the given polynomial can be factored.

35. $y^2 + ky - 28$
36. $c^2 + kc - 20$
37. $p^2 + kp - 35$
38. $x^2 + kx - 36$

Find two negative values of k for which the given polynomial can be factored. (There may be many possible values.)

39. $r^2 - 2r + k$
40. $y^2 + 4y + k$
41. $k + 5x + x^2$
42. $k - 7r + r^2$
43. $k + 4t + t^2$
44. $k - 6z + z^2$

Factor completely.

C 45. $x^4 - 3x^2 - 4$
46. $t^4 - 7t^2 - 18$
47. $x^4 - 15x^2y^2 - 16y^4$
48. $(x + 2)^2 - 4(x + 2) - 21$
49. $(y + 3)^2 + 5(y + 3) - 24$
50. $(p + q)^2 - 2(p + q) - 15$
51. $(a + b)^2 - (a + b) - 2$
52. $(p + q)^2 - 2r(p + q) - 15r^2$
53. $(a + b)^2 - c(a + b) - 2c^2$
54. $(a + b)^4 - (a - b)^4$

55. Factor $x^{2n} - 4x^ny^{2n} - 221y^{4n}$, where n is a positive integer.
56. Factor $x^{4n} - 4x^{2n}y^n - 252y^{2n}$, where n is a positive integer.

Mixed Review Exercises

Simplify.

1. $(9x^2y)(3xy^2)(2x^2)$
2. $(3x - 4)(2x + 3)$
3. $-7x(3x^2 - 2x + 4)$
4. $(3x - 4)^2$
5. $(7x^5y^2)^3$
6. $5y(2y^2 + 3y + 5)$
7. $\dfrac{5(xy)^6}{10(xy)^3}$
8. $\dfrac{-4ab}{-12ab^3}$
9. $\dfrac{(-n)^6}{-n^{10}}$
10. $(n + 3p)^2$
11. $(a - 6)(5a + 2)$
12. $(2y + 7)^2$

Factor.

13. $15m - 21n + 9$
14. $121k^2 - 81$
15. $a^2 + 18a + 81$
16. $a^2 - 13ab + 42b^2$
17. $16x^2 + 24x$
18. $64 - n^2$
19. $u^2 - 10u + 25$
20. $44 + 15y + y^2$
21. $7a^2b^3 - 14ab$
22. $49w^4 - 16x^2$
23. $4m^2 + 20m + 24$
24. $c^2 - 11c - 26$
25. $9x^2 - 24xy + 16y^2$
26. $56 - 15z + z^2$
27. $x^2 - 1$
28. $a^2 + 13a - 68$
29. $25w^6 - 144x^6$
30. $25a^2 + 20ab + 4b^2$

5-9 Factoring Pattern for $ax^2 + bx + c$

Objective To factor general quadratic trinomials with integral coefficients.

If $ax^2 + bx + c$ $(a > 1)$ can be factored, the factorization will have the pattern

$$(px + r)(qx + s).$$

Example 1 Factor $2x^2 + 7x - 9$.

Solution

Clue 1 Because the trinomial has a negative constant term, one of r and s will be negative and the other will be positive.

Clue 2 You can list the possible factors of the quadratic term, $2x^2$, and the possible factors of the constant term, -9.

Factors of $2x^2$	Factors of -9	
$2x, x$	$1, -9$	$-1, 9$
	$3, -3$	$-3, 3$
	$9, -1$	$-9, 1$

Test the possibilities to see which produces the correct linear term, $7x$. Making a chart will help you do this.

Possible factors	Linear term
$(2x + 1)(x - 9)$	$(-18 + 1)x = -17x$
$(2x + 3)(x - 3)$	$(-6 + 3)x = -3x$
$(2x + 9)(x - 1)$	$(-2 + 9)x = 7x$
$(2x - 1)(x + 9)$	$(18 - 1)x = 17x$
$(2x - 3)(x + 3)$	$(6 - 3)x = 3x$
$(2x - 9)(x + 1)$	$(2 - 9)x = -7x$

Since $(2x + 9)(x - 1)$ gives the correct linear term,

$2x^2 + 7x - 9 = (2x + 9)(x - 1)$. ***Answer***

Example 2 Factor $14x^2 - 17x + 5$.

Solution

Clue 1 Because the trinomial has a positive constant term and a negative linear term, both r and s will be negative.

Clue 2 List the factors of the quadratic term, $14x^2$, and the negative factors of the constant term, 5.

Factors of $14x^2$	Factors of 5
$x, 14x$	$-1, -5$
$2x, 7x$	$-5, -1$

Test the possibilities to see which produces the correct linear term, $-17x$.

Possible factors	Linear term
$(x - 1)(14x - 5)$	$(-5 - 14)x = -19x$
$(x - 5)(14x - 1)$	$(-1 - 70)x = -71x$
$(2x - 1)(7x - 5)$	$(-10 - 7)x = -17x$
$(2x - 5)(7x - 1)$	$(-2 - 35)x = -37x$

Since $(2x - 1)(7x - 5)$ gives the correct linear term,

$14x^2 - 17x + 5 = (2x - 1)(7x - 5)$. ***Answer***

Remember to check each factorization by multiplying the factors. After some practice you will be able to select the correct factors without writing down all the possibilities.

When the coefficient of the quadratic term is negative, it may be helpful to begin by factoring -1 from each term.

Example 3 Factor $10 + 11x - 6x^2$.

Solution

$10 + 11x - 6x^2 = -6x^2 + 11x + 10$ {Arrange the terms by decreasing degree.

$= (-1)(6x^2 - 11x - 10)$ {Factor -1 from each term.

$= (-1)(2x - 5)(3x + 2)$ {Factor the resulting trinomial.

$= -(2x - 5)(3x + 2)$ ***Answer***

Note: If you factor $10 + 11x - 6x^2$ directly, you will get $(5 - 2x)(2 + 3x)$. Since $(5 - 2x) = -(2x - 5)$, the two answers are equivalent.

Example 4 Factor $5a^2 - ab - 22b^2$.

Solution

$5a^2 - ab - 22b^2 = (a \quad)(5a \quad)$ {Write the factors of $5a^2$.

$= (a + ?)(5a - ?)$ {Test possibilities.

$= (a + 2b)(5a - 11b)$ ***Answer***

Note: If you write $(a - ?)(5a + ?)$ as the second step, you will not find a combination of factors that produces the desired linear term.

Oral Exercises

The area of the rectangle is represented by the trinomial below. Use the diagram to factor the trinomial.

Sample

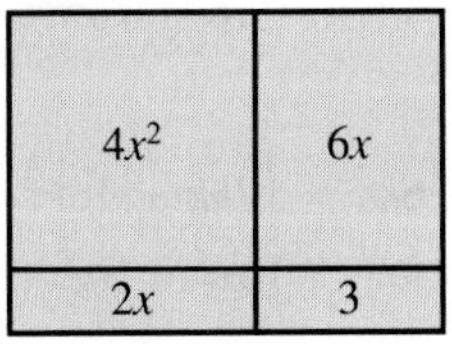

$4x^2 + 8x + 3$

Solution

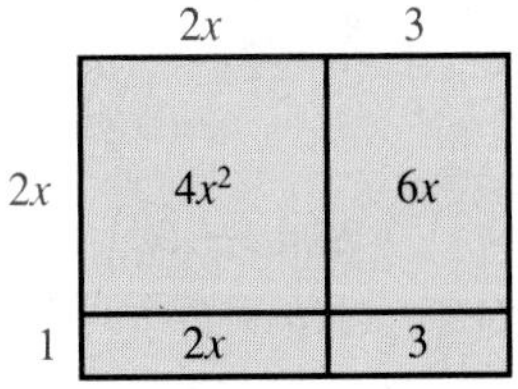

$4x^2 + 8x + 3 = (2x + 3)(2x + 1)$

1.

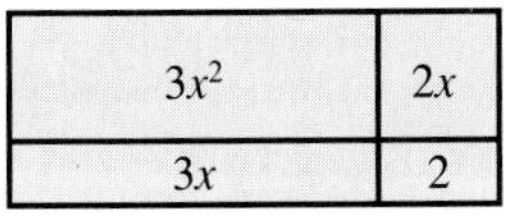

$3x^2 + 5x + 2$

2.

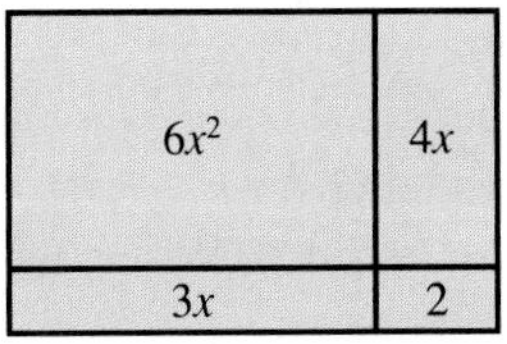

$6x^2 + 7x + 2$

For each quadratic trinomial tell whether its factorization will have the form

$$(px + r)(qx + s),$$
$$(px + r)(qx - s),$$
$$\text{or } (px - r)(qx - s),$$

where p, q, r, and s represent positive integers.

3. $2x^2 + x - 6$

4. $5x^2 - 13x + 6$

5. $4x^2 + 8x + 3$

6. $4x^2 - 4x - 3$

7. $2x^2 - x - 10$

8. $6x^2 + 5x + 1$

9. $3x^2 + 4x - 4$

10. $5x^2 - 11x + 2$

11. $8x^2 - 25x + 3$

12. $9x^2 + 6x - 8$

13. $14x^2 + 13x + 3$

14. $10x^2 - 10x - 9$

Written Exercises

Factor. Check by multiplying the factors. If the polynomial is not factorable, write *prime*.

A

1. $3x^2 + 7x + 2$

2. $2x^2 + 5x + 3$

3. $3c^2 - 8c + 5$

4. $2x^2 - 15x + 7$

5. $5y^2 + 4y - 1$

6. $3a^2 + 4a - 4$

7. $5u^2 - 6u - 2$

8. $3r^2 - 2r - 5$

9. $7x^2 + 8x + 1$

10. $2p^2 + 7p + 3$

11. $5x^2 - 17x + 6$

12. $7m^2 - 9m + 2$

13. $3p^2 + 7p - 6$

14. $4c^2 + 4c - 3$

15. $4y^2 - y - 3$

16. $6a^2 - 5a - 2$

17. $5 + 7x - 6x^2$

18. $9 + 6k - 8k^2$

19. $1 - 5b - 8b^2$

20. $7 - 12s - 4s^2$

21. $3m^2 + 11mn + 6n^2$

22. $2p^2 - 7pq + 6q^2$

23. $2x^2 + xy - 3y^2$

24. $5a^2 - 2ab - 7b^2$

B

25. $9m^2 - 25mn - 6n^2$

26. $6h^2 + 17hk + 10k^2$

27. $6r^2 - 11rp + 5p^2$

28. $4x^2 + 16xy - 9y^2$

29. $21c^2 + 4c - 12$

30. $18z^2 + 19z - 12$

31. $6 + 7a - 20a^2$

32. $8 + 45r - 18r^2$

33. $32n^2 - 4n - 15$

34. $33u^2 - u - 14$

35. $21c^2 + 22c - 24$

36. $35y^2 + 2y - 24$

C

37. $2(a + 2)^2 + 5(a + 2) - 3$

38. $2(x - 1)^2 - 9(x - 1) - 5$

39. $2(a + 2b)^2 + 5(a + 2b)c - 3c^2$

40. $2(x - y)^2 - 9(x - y)z - 5z^2$

41. $4x^4 - 17x^2 + 4$

42. $2x^4 - 15x^2 - 27$

43. $(y^2 + 3y - 1)^2 - 9$

44. $(a^2 - 4a - 1)^2 - 16$

45. Show that $(15x^2 - 14x + 3)(6x^2 + 19x - 7)(10x^2 + 29x - 21)$ is a *perfect square* by showing that it is the square of a polynomial.

46. Factor $90a^{8n+1}b^2 - 25a^{4n+1}b^{2n+2} - 240ab^{4n+2}$, where n is a positive integer.

Mixed Review Exercises

Factor.

1. $x^2 - 225$	**2.** $x^2 - 9x + 20$	**3.** $r^2 - 5r - 14$
4. $c^2 - 6c + 9$	**5.** $9y^2 - 289x^2$	**6.** $4a^4 - 49$
7. $y^2 + 15y + 56$	**8.** $p^2 + 12p + 36$	**9.** $16y^2 + 24y + 9$
10. $m^2 - m - 72$	**11.** $n^2 + 15n + 36$	**12.** $b^2 - 2b - 24$

Self-Test 3

Vocabulary irreducible polynomial (p. 214) prime polynomial (p. 214)

Factor.

1. $a^2 + 12a + 35$	**2.** $x^2 - 10x + 16$	**Obj. 5-7, p. 213**
3. $n^2 - 3n - 28$	**4.** $c^2 + 3cd - 40d^2$	**Obj. 5-8, p. 217**
5. $2r^2 - 7r + 6$	**6.** $3x^2 + 10xy - 8y^2$	**Obj. 5-9, p. 220**

Challenge

According to the legend, the inventor of the game of chess asked to be rewarded by having one grain of wheat put on the first square of a chessboard, two grains on the second, four grains on the third, eight grains on the fourth, and so on. The total number of grains would be $2^{64} - 1$, which is several thousand times the world's annual wheat yield.

1. To find how large 2^{64} is approximately, you could enter the number 2 on the calculator and press the squaring button a number of times. How many times must you press this button?

2. Factor $2^{64} - 1$ as a difference of squares to show that it is divisible by 3, 5, and 17.

General Factoring and Its Application

5-10 Factoring by Grouping

Objective To factor a polynomial by grouping terms.

A key tool in factoring polynomials is the distributive property:

$$ba + ca = (b + c)a$$

This property is valid not only when a represents a monomial, but also when a represents any polynomial. For example:

If $a = x + 2$, you have $b(x + 2) + c(x + 2) = (b + c)(x + 2)$

If $a = 3r - s + 7$, you have $b(3r - s + 7) + c(3r - s + 7) = (b + c)(3r - s + 7)$

Example 1 Factor: **a.** $5(x + y) + w(x + y)$ **b.** $m(m + 4n) - (m + 4n)$

Solution **a.** $(5 + w)(x + y)$ **b.** $(m - 1)(m + 4n)$

Another helpful tool is recognizing factors that are opposites of each other.

Factor	Opposite				
$x - y$	$-(x - y)$	or	$-x + y$	or	$y - x$
$4 - a^2$	$-(4 - a^2)$	or	$-4 + a^2$	or	$a^2 - 4$
$2n - 3k - 1$	$-(2n - 3k - 1)$	or	$-2n + 3k + 1$	or	$3k - 2n + 1$

Example 2 Factor $5(a - 3) - 2a(3 - a)$.

Solution Notice that $a - 3$ and $3 - a$ are opposites.

$$\begin{aligned} 5(a - 3) - 2a(3 - a) &= 5(a - 3) - 2a[-(a - 3)] \\ &= 5(a - 3) + 2a(a - 3) \\ &= (5 + 2a)(a - 3) \quad \textbf{\textit{Answer}} \end{aligned}$$

In Example 3 you first group terms with common factors, and then factor.

Example 3 Factor $2ab - 6ac + 3b - 9c$.

Solution 1

$$\begin{aligned} 2ab - 6ac + 3b - 9c &= (2ab - 6ac) + (3b - 9c) \\ &= 2a(b - 3c) + 3(b - 3c) \\ &= (2a + 3)(b - 3c) \quad \textbf{\textit{Answer}} \end{aligned}$$

Solution 2 $2ab - 6ac + 3b - 9c = (2ab + 3b) - (6ac + 9c)$
$= b(2a + 3) - 3c(2a + 3)$
$= (b - 3c)(2a + 3)$ ***Answer***

Example 4 uses what you know about factoring perfect square trinomials and differences of squares.

Example 4 Factor $4p^2 - 4q^2 + 4qr - r^2$.

Solution $4p^2 - 4q^2 + 4qr - r^2 = 4p^2 - (4q^2 - 4qr + r^2) \longleftarrow$ A trinomial square
$= (2p)^2 - (2q - r)^2 \longleftarrow$ The difference of two squares.
$= [2p + (2q - r)][2p - (2q - r)]$
$= (2p + 2q - r)(2p - 2q + r)$ ***Answer***

In Example 4 you could have tried the grouping $(4p^2 - 4q^2) + (4qr - r^2)$ and factored the groups to obtain $4(p + q)(p - q) + r(4q - r)$. But this doesn't lead anywhere. There are different approaches to factoring a polynomial. You may need to try several before arriving at one that works.

Oral Exercises

Factor.

1. $a(a - 2) + 3(a - 2)$
2. $p(q + 1) - 4(q + 1)$
3. $2r(r - 3) - 5(r - 3)$
4. $x(x + 2y) - (x + 2y)$
5. $u(u + v) - v(u + v)$
6. $h(h - 2) + 2(2 - h)$
7. $x(x - 4) - (4 - x)$
8. $m(n - m) - n(m - n)$
9. $2r(r - s) + s(s - r)$

Written Exercises

Factor. Check by multiplying the factors.

A

1. $3(x + y) + z(x + y)$
2. $7(r - s) + t(r - s)$
3. $e(f - g) - 4(f - g)$
4. $w(x - y) - 8(x - y)$
5. $7(r - s) + t(s - r)$
6. $7(m - n) + p(n - m)$
7. $2a(a + 3) - (3 + a)$
8. $u(v - 2) + 2(2 - v)$
9. $2x(x - y) + y(y - x)$
10. $3p(2q - p) - 2q(p - 2q)$
11. $2u(u - 2v) + v(u - 2v) + (u - 2v)$
12. $a(a - b) + 4b(a - b) - a(a - b)$
13. $x(2w - 3v + u) - (2w - 3v + u)$
14. $r(r - s - 2t) + s(r - s - 2t)$
15. $(s^2 - 2ps + 2s) - (2s - 4p + 4)$
16. $(x^2 - xy + x) - (y - x - 1)$
17. $(3t - 3st) + (rs - r)$
18. $(9p - 3pq) + (2nq - 6n)$
19. $(12x^2 - 8xy) - 5(3xz - 2yz)$
20. $(p^2 - 2pq) - 2(2qr - pr)$

Factor. Check by multiplying the factors.

21. $3a + ab + 3c + bc$

22. $rs + 5r + st + 5t$

23. $x^2 - 2x + xy - 2y$

24. $u^2 - 2u + uv - 2v$

25. $h^2 - hk + hr - kr$

26. $x^2 - 2xy + 4xz - 8yz$

27. $p^3 - 2p^2 + 4p - 8$

28. $3a^3 + a^2 + 6a + 2$

29. $p^2 - 2pq + pr - 2qr$

30. $u^2 - 3uv - 6uw + 18vw$

31. $3hk - 2k - 12h + 8$

32. $3ab - b - 4 + 12a$

33. $4z^3 - 6z^2 - 6z + 9$

34. $3u^3 - u^2 - 9u + 3$

35. $(h^2k^2 + 4k^2) + (h^2k + 4k)$

36. $(a^2b^2 + 2a^2) - (2ab^2 + 4a)$

37. $x^3 - 3x^2 - x + 3$

38. $n^3 + 2n^2 - 4n - 8$

Factor each expression as a difference of squares.

39. $x^2 - (y - z)^2$

40. $(a + 2b)^2 - 9c^2$

41. $(u - 2v)^2 - 4w^2$

42. $4p^2 - (q - 2r)^2$

B **43.** $(a + 2b)^2 - (2b + c)^2$

44. $4(x + y)^2 - (2y - z)^2$

45. $a^2 + 4a + 4 - b^2$

46. $x^2 - 2xy + y^2 - 4$

47. $u^2 - v^2 + 2v - 1$

48. $m^2 - n^2 - 2m + 1$

49. $h^2 - 4k^2 - 4h + 4$

50. $a^2 - b^2 - 2a + 1$

51. $p^2 - q^2 + r^2 - 2pr$

52. $4s^2 - 4t^2 + 4s + 1$

Factor.

53. $x^2 - 4y^2 + 4z^2 - 4xz$

54. $m^2 - 9n^2 + 9 - 6m$

55. $a^2 + b^2 + 2ab + 2a + 2b$

56. $p^2 - q^2 - 2p + 2q$

57. $x^4 - y^4 - 4x^2 + 4$

58. $a^4 + b^4 - c^4 + 2a^2b^2$

59. $p^2 + q^2 - r^2 - 2pq + 2r - 1$

60. $h^2 - 4k^2 + 4h - 8k$

C **61.** Factor $x^4 + 4$ by writing it as $(x^4 + 4x^2 + 4) - 4x^2$, a difference of two squares.

62. Use the method of Exercise 61 to factor **(a)** $64x^4 + 1$ and **(b)** $x^4 + 4a^4$.

63. Factor $a^{2n+1} + b^{2n+1} + a^{2n}b^{2n} + ab$, where n is a positive integer.

Mixed Review Exercises

Solve.

1. $-12 + x = -29$

2. $-n + 10 = 2$

3. $18 + x = 32$

4. $16 = 1 + 3z$

5. $10m - 6m = 36$

6. $5n - 2n + 8 = 9$

7. $14x = 700$

8. $-13n = 156$

9. $9b = 108$

10. $10n = 2n - 24$

11. $19m = 55 + 14m$

12. $10y + 6 = 4(19 - y)$

$2x^3 + 3x^2 + 2x$

5-11 Using Several Methods of Factoring

Objective To factor polynomials completely.

A polynomial is **factored completely** when it is expressed as the product of a monomial and one or more prime polynomials.

Guidelines for Factoring Completely

1. Factor out the greatest monomial factor first.
2. Look for a difference of squares.
3. Look for a perfect square trinomial.
4. If a trinomial is not a square, look for a pair of binomial factors.
5. If a polynomial has four or more terms, look for a way to group the terms in pairs or in a group of three terms that is a perfect square trinomial.
6. Make sure that each binomial or trinomial factor is prime.
7. Check your work by multiplying the factors.

Example 1 Factor $-4n^4 + 40n^3 - 100n^2$ completely.

Solution

$$-4n^4 + 40n^3 - 100n^2 = -4n^2(n^2 - 10n + 25) \leftarrow \text{perfect square trinomial}$$

greatest monomial factor ($-4n^2$)

$$= -4n^2(n - 5)^2 \quad \textbf{Answer}$$

Example 2 Factor $5a^3b^2 + 3a^4b - 2a^2b^3$ completely.

Solution First rewrite the polynomial in order of decreasing degree in a.

$$5a^3b^2 + 3a^4b - 2a^2b^3 = 3a^4b + 5a^3b^2 - 2a^2b^3$$

$$= a^2b(3a^2 + 5ab - 2b^2) \leftarrow \text{trinomial}$$

greatest monomial factor (a^2b)

$$= a^2b(3a - b)(a + 2b) \quad \textbf{Answer}$$

Example 3 Factor $a^2bc - 4bc + a^2b - 4b$ completely.

Solution

$$a^2bc - 4bc + a^2b - 4b = b(a^2c - 4c + a^2 - 4)$$

$$= b[c(a^2 - 4) + (a^2 - 4)] \quad \{\text{Factor by grouping.}$$

$$= b(c + 1)(a^2 - 4) \longleftarrow \text{Difference of squares}$$

$$= b(c + 1)(a + 2)(a - 2)$$

Answer

Oral Exercises

State the greatest monomial factor of each polynomial.

1. $6a^2 - 9ab - 15b^2$
2. $18x - 8x^3$
3. $15r^3 + 20r^2s - 20rs^2$
4. $6ab+9a^2b - 15a^3b$
5. $4(z - 4)^2 - 16$
6. $12x^2y - 36xy^2 + 27y^3$

Factor completely.

7. $10a^2 - 15ab^2$
8. $-4x + 6x^2$
9. $t^3 - 9t$
10. $y^4 + 6y^3 + 9y^2$
11. $p^3 - 2p^2q + pq^2$
12. $u^3v - uv^3$

Written Exercises

Factor completely.

A

1–6. The polynomials in Oral Exercises 1–6.

7. $5a^2 + 10ab + 5b^2$
8. $6c^2 + 18cd + 12d^2$
9. $4m^3 - m$
10. $3xy^2 - 27x^3$
11. $y^4 - 2y^2 - y^3$
12. $-n^4 - 3n^2 - 2n^3$
13. $x^2 - xy - x + y$
14. $-m^2 + mn + 2m - 2n$
15. $-41a + 10 + 21a^2$
16. $80 - 120p + 45p^2$
17. $a^3 - 2a^2b + 3a^2 - 6ab$
18. $8p^3q - 18pq^3$
19. $6u^2v - 11u^2v^2 - 10u^2v^3$
20. $180x^2y - 108xy^2 - 75x^3$
21. $k(k + 1)(k + 2) - 3k(k + 1)$
22. $n(n^2 - 1) + n(n - 1)$
23. $2u^5 - 7u^3 - 4u$
24. $81a + 18a^3 + a^5$
25. $r^2 - 6r - 9s^2 + 9$
26. $x^2 - 4y^2 - 4x + 4$
27. $u^2 - 4v^2 + 3u - 6v$
28. $a^2 - b^2 + ac - bc$
29. $p^2 - 1 - 4q^2 - 4q$
30. $x^2 - 2x - 4y^2 - 4y$

B

31. $100 + 4x^2 - 16y^2 - 40x$
32. $16x^2 + 16y - y^2 - 64$
33. $a^4 - b^4$
34. $m^8 - n^8$
35. $2pq + 2pr + q^2 - r^2$
36. $8a^3 + 4a^2b - 2ab^2 - b^3$
37. $(a + b)^2 - (a - c)^2$
38. $3x^5 + 15x^3 - 108x$
39. $x^3 - x^2y - xy^2 + y^3$
40. $4 - 4x^2 - 4y^2 + 8xy$
41. $a(a + 2)(a - 3) - 8(a - 3)$
42. $x(x + 1)(x - 4) + 4(x + 1)$
43. $16c^{16} - 16$
44. $(u - v)^3 + v - u$
45. $a(a^2 - 9) - 2(a + 3)^2$
46. $(x - 2)(x^2 - 1) - 6x - 6$
47. $9u^2 - 9v^2 - 36w^2 + 36vw$
48. $x^4 - x^2 + 4x - 4$

C **49.** $x^2(x + 2) - x(x + 2) - 12(x + 2)$

50. $(a + b)^3 - 6(a + b)^2 - 7(a + b)$

51. $t^4 - 10t^2 + 9$

52. $16t^4 - 8t^2 + 1$

53. $a^2 + b^2 - c^2 - d^2 - 2ab + 2cd$

54. $(u^2 - v^2)^2 - w^2(u + v)^2$

55. Factor $x^4 + x^2 + 1$ by writing it as $(x^4 + 2x^2 + 1) - x^2$, a difference of squares.

56. Factor $a^4 + a^2b^2 + b^4$. (*Hint:* See Exercise 55.)

57. Factor $a^3 + b^3$ by writing it as $a^3 + a^2b - a^2b - ab^2 + ab^2 + b^3$ and grouping the terms by pairs.

58. Factor $a^3 - b^3$. (*Hint:* See Exercise 57.)

Mixed Review Exercises

Simplify.

1. $\left(-\frac{1}{4}\right)\left(\frac{1}{5}\right)(40)$

2. $\frac{1}{8}(56)$

3. $-\frac{1}{9}(72)\left(-\frac{1}{8}\right)$

4. $\frac{140b}{7}$

5. $52 \div \left(\frac{1}{13}\right)$

6. $625 \div (-5)$

Factor.

7. $x^2 - 12x + 35$

8. $x^2 + 3x - 28$

9. $x^2 - x - 2$

10. $2n^2 + 19n + 9$

11. $3x^2 + 11x + 10$

12. $(3x - 12) - 2n(4 - x)$

Career Note / *Draftsperson*

Manufacturers and construction workers rely on detailed plans of buildings and manufactured products as a guide for production. The plans are prepared by a draftsperson using many different tools. For example, he or she may use a compass, a protractor, a triangle, and a calculator. A draftsperson also makes use of math skills, such as working with fractions, making measurements, and making drawings to different scales.

Today draftspersons use computer-aided design (CAD) systems to allow them to see many variations of a design. They often specialize in a particular field of work, such as mechanical, electrical, aeronautical, or architectural drafting. A draftsperson needs coursework in mathematics, mechanical drawing, and drafting.

5-12 Solving Equations by Factoring

Objective To use factoring in solving polynomial equations.

The multiplicative property of zero can be stated as follows:

If $a = 0$ or $b = 0$, then $ab = 0$. ⟵ statement

The statement above is given in "if-then" form. The **converse** of a statement in "if-then" form is obtained by interchanging the "if" and "then" parts of the statement as shown below.

If $ab = 0$, then $a = 0$ or $b = 0$. ⟵ converse

The converse of a true statement is not necessarily true. You can show that the particular converse displayed above *is* true (Exercise 55, page 233).

The words "if and only if" are used to combine a statement and its converse when both are true. The *zero-product property* stated below combines the multiplicative property of zero and its converse.

Zero-Product Property

For all real numbers a and b:

$ab = 0$ if and only if $a = 0$ or $b = 0$.

A product of factors is zero if and only if one or more of the factors is zero.

The zero-product property is true for any number of factors. You can use this property to solve certain equations.

Example 1 Solve $(x + 2)(x - 5) = 0$.

Solution One of the factors on the left side must equal zero. Therefore,

$$\begin{aligned} x + 2 &= 0 \quad \text{or} \quad & x - 5 &= 0 \\ x &= -2 & x &= 5 \end{aligned}$$

Just by looking at the original equation, you might have seen that when $x = -2$ or $x = 5$ one of the factors will be zero.

Either method gives the solution set $\{-2, 5\}$. ***Answer***

Example 2 Solve $5n(n - 3)(n - 4) = 0$.

Solution

$$\begin{aligned} 5n &= 0 \quad \text{or} \quad & n - 3 &= 0 \quad \text{or} \quad & n - 4 &= 0 \\ n &= 0 & n &= 3 & n &= 4 \end{aligned}$$

$\therefore$ the solution set is $\{0, 3, 4\}$. ***Answer***

A **polynomial equation** is an equation whose sides are both polynomials. Polynomial equations usually are named by the term of highest degree. If $a \neq 0$:

$ax + b = 0$ is a **linear equation.**

$ax^2 + bx + c = 0$ is a **quadratic equation.**

$ax^3 + bx^2 + cx + d = 0$ is a **cubic equation.**

Many polynomial equations can be solved by factoring and then using the zero-product property. Often the first step is to transform the equation into **standard form** in which one side is zero. The other side should be a simplified polynomial arranged in order of decreasing degree of the variable.

Example 3 Solve the quadratic equation $2x^2 + 5x = 12$.

Solution

1. Transform the equation into standard form. $\quad 2x^2 + 5x - 12 = 0$
2. Factor the left side. $\quad (2x - 3)(x + 4) = 0$
3. Set each factor equal to 0 and solve.

$$2x - 3 = 0 \quad \text{or} \quad x + 4 = 0$$
$$2x = 3 \qquad\qquad x = -4$$
$$x = \frac{3}{2}$$

4. Check the solutions in the original equation.

$$2\left(\frac{3}{2}\right)^2 + 5\left(\frac{3}{2}\right) \stackrel{?}{=} 12 \qquad\qquad 2(-4)^2 + 5(-4) \stackrel{?}{=} 12$$
$$2\left(\frac{9}{4}\right) + \frac{15}{2} \stackrel{?}{=} 12 \qquad\qquad 2(16) - 20 \stackrel{?}{=} 12$$
$$\frac{9}{2} + \frac{15}{2} = \frac{24}{2} = 12 \ \checkmark \qquad\qquad 32 - 20 = 12 \ \checkmark$$

$\therefore$ the solution set is $\left\{\frac{3}{2}, -4\right\}$. ***Answer***

Example 4 Solve the cubic equation $18y^3 + 8y + 24y^2 = 0$.

Solution

1. Transform the equation into standard form. $\quad 18y^3 + 24y^2 + 8y = 0$
2. Factor completely.

$$2y(9y^2 + 12y + 4) = 0$$
$$2y(3y + 2)^2 = 0$$

3. Solve by inspection or by equating each factor to 0. $\quad y = 0 \text{ or } y = -\frac{2}{3} \text{ or } y = -\frac{2}{3}$
4. The check is left to you.

$\therefore$ the solution set is $\left\{0, -\frac{2}{3}\right\}$. ***Answer***

The factorization in Example 4 produced two identical factors. Since the factor $3y + 2$ occurs twice in the factored form of the equation, $-\frac{2}{3}$ is a **double** or **multiple root.** Notice that we list it only once in the solution set.

Caution: Never transform an equation by dividing by an expression containing a variable. Notice that in Example 4, the solution 0 would have been lost if both sides of $2y(9y^2 + 12y + 4) = 0$ had been divided by $2y$.

Oral Exercises

Solve.

1. $x(x - 6) = 0$ **2.** $2a(a + 1) = 0$ **3.** $0 = 3p(2p - 1)$

4. $(y - 2)(y + 3) = 0$ **5.** $0 = (3t - 2)(t - 3)$ **6.** $x(2x - 5)(2x + 1) = 0$

Explain how you could solve the given equation. Then solve.

7. $4x^2 - x^3 = 0$ **8.** $a^3 = 4a$ **9.** $k^2 + 4 = 4k$

10. $m^3 - 2m = m^2$ **11.** $9x^2 = x^3$ **12.** $0 = -n^3 + n$

13. Give an example of a true "if-then" statement with a false converse.

Written Exercises

Solve.

A **1.** $(y + 5)(y - 7) = 0$ **2.** $(n + 1)(n + 9) = 0$ **3.** $15n(n + 15) = 0$

4. $2x(x - 20) = 0$ **5.** $(2t - 3)(3t - 2) = 0$ **6.** $(2u + 7)(3u - 1) = 0$

7. $3x(2x + 1)(2x + 5) = 0$ **8.** $n(5n - 2)(2n + 5) = 0$ **9.** $y^2 - 3y + 2 = 0$

10. $p^2 - p - 6 = 0$ **11.** $0 = x^2 + 14x + 48$ **12.** $0 = k^2 - 12k + 35$

13. $m^2 - 36 = 16m$ **14.** $r^2 + 9 = 10r$ **15.** $s^2 = 4s + 32$

16. $x^2 = 20x - 100$ **17.** $y^2 = 16y$ **18.** $9k^2 = 4k$

19. $4x^2 - 9 = 0$ **20.** $25m^2 - 16 = 0$ **21.** $6n^2 + n = 2$

22. $3x^2 + x = 2$ **23.** $4s - 4s^2 = 1$ **24.** $r - 6r^2 = -1$

25. $7x^2 = 18x - 11$ **26.** $2y^2 = 25y + 13$ **27.** $8u^3 - 2u^2 = 0$

28. $10u^3 - 5u^2 = 0$ **29.** $0 = 4y^3 - 2y^2$ **30.** $0 = 10x^3 - 15x^2$

31. $8y^2 - 9y + 1 = 0$ **32.** $6h^2 + 17h + 12 = 0$ **33.** $15u^2 - 14u = 49$

34. $25x^2 - 90x = -81$ **35.** $4p^2 + 121 = 44p$ **36.** $6c^2 - 72 = 11c$

B **37.** $4x^3 - 12x^2 + 8x = 0$ **38.** $2n^3 - 30n^2 + 100n = 0$ **39.** $9x^3 + 9x = 30x^2$

40. $9x^3 + 25x = 30x^2$ **41.** $y^4 - 10y^2 + 9 = 0$ **42.** $u^5 - 13u^3 + 36u = 0$

Sample 1 $(x - 1)(x + 3) = 12$

Solution $x^2 + 2x - 3 - 12 = 0$

$(x - 3)(x + 5) = 0$ $\therefore$ the solution set is $\{3, -5\}$

Solve. See Sample 1 on page 232.

43. $(z + 1)(z - 5) = 16$

44. $(2t - 5)(t - 1) = 2$

45. $(x - 2)(x + 3) = 6$

46. $(a - 5)(a - 2) = 28$

47. $x(x - 6) = 4(x - 4)$

48. $3(m + 2) = m(m - 2)$

Find an equation in standard form with integral coefficients that has the given solution set.

Sample 2 $\left\{\frac{2}{3}, -4\right\}$

Solution

$$\left(x - \frac{2}{3}\right)(x + 4) = 0$$

$$3\left(x - \frac{2}{3}\right)(x + 4) = 0 \quad \text{Multiply by 3 for integral coefficients.}$$

$$(3x - 2)(x + 4) = 0$$

$$3x^2 + 10x - 8 = 0 \quad \textit{Answer}$$

49. $\{2, -3\}$

50. $\{-1, 5\}$

51. $\left\{\frac{5}{2}, -2\right\}$

52. $\left\{-\frac{1}{3}, -1\right\}$

53. $\left\{\frac{1}{3}, \frac{3}{2}\right\}$

54. $\left\{-\frac{5}{2}, \frac{2}{5}\right\}$

C **55.** Supply the missing reasons in the proof of: If $ab = 0$, then $a = 0$ or $b = 0$.

Case 1: If $a = 0$, then the theorem is true; there is nothing to prove.

Case 2: Suppose that $a \neq 0$ and show that then $b = 0$.

a. $ab = 0$	**a.** Given
b. $\frac{1}{a}$ exists	**b.** ?
c. $\frac{1}{a}(ab) = \frac{1}{a}(0)$	**c.** ?
d. $\frac{1}{a}(ab) = 0$	**d.** ?
e. $\left(\frac{1}{a} \cdot a\right)b = 0$	**e.** ?
f. $1 \cdot b = 0$	**f.** ?
g. $b = 0$	**g.** ?

Mixed Review Exercises

Evaluate if $x = 2$ and $y = 4$.

1. $(x - y)^4$

2. $x^4 \cdot y^2$

3. $5x^3$

4. $(5x)^3$

5. $4x + y^2$

6. $4x^2 + y$

7. $4(x + y)^2$

8. $(yx)^2$

9. y^2x^2

Simplify.

10. $(3x^3y)(-2xy^5)$

11. $(9a)^3$

12. $-5(x + 2)$

5-13 Using Factoring to Solve Problems

Objective To solve problems by writing and factoring quadratic equations.

The problems in this lesson all lead to polynomial equations that can be solved by factoring. Sometimes a solution of an equation may not satisfy some of the conditions of the problem. For example, a negative number cannot represent a length or an age. You reject solutions of an equation that do not make sense for the problem.

Example 1 A decorator plans to place a rug in a 9 m by 12 m room so that a uniform strip of flooring around the rug will remain uncovered. How wide will this strip be if the area of the rug is to be half the area of the room?

Solution

Step 1 The problem asks for the width of the strip.

Step 2 Let x = the width of the strip. Then $12 - 2x$ = the length of the rug and $9 - 2x$ = the width of the rug.

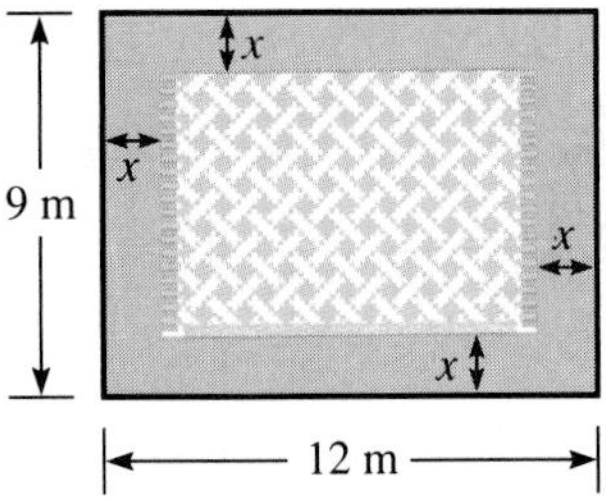

Step 3 $\text{Area of the rug} = \frac{1}{2}(\text{Area of the room})$

$$(12 - 2x)(9 - 2x) = \frac{1}{2} \cdot 9 \cdot 12$$

Step 4

$$108 - 42x + 4x^2 = 54$$
$$4x^2 - 42x + 54 = 0$$
$$2(2x^2 - 21x + 27) = 0$$
$$2[(2x - 3)(x - 9)] = 0$$
$$2x - 3 = 0 \quad \text{or} \quad x - 9 = 0$$
$$x = \frac{3}{2}, \text{ or } 1.5 \qquad x = 9$$

Step 5 *Check:* When $x = 1.5$, the area of the rug is $(12 - 2x)(9 - 2x) = 9 \cdot 6 = 54$ $= \frac{1}{2}(\text{Area of the room})$ ✓

When $x = 9$, the length, $12 - 2x$, and width, $9 - 2x$, are negative. Since a negative length or width is meaningless, reject $x = 9$ as an answer.

∴ the strip around the rug will be 1.5 m wide. ***Answer***

The equation in Step 3 of Example 1 has a root that does not check because this equation does not meet the "hidden" requirements that the rug have positive length ($12 - 2x > 0$) and positive width ($9 - 2x > 0$). Usually it is easier to write only the equation and then check its roots against other conditions stated or implied in the problem.

In the next example both solutions of the equation satisfy the conditions of the problem. You can use the formula

$$h = rt - 4.9t^2$$

to obtain a good approximation of the height h (in meters) of an object t seconds after it is projected upward with an initial speed of r meters per second (m/s).

Example 2 An arrow is shot upward with an initial speed of 34.3 m/s. When will it be at a height of 49 m?

Solution

Step 1 The problem asks for the time when the arrow is 49 m high.

Step 2 Let t = the number of seconds after being shot that the arrow is 49 m high. Let h = the height of arrow = 49 m. Let r = initial speed = 34.3 m/s.

Step 3 Substitute in the formula:

$$h = rt - 4.9t^2$$
$$49 = 34.3t - 4.9t^2$$

Step 4

$$4.9t^2 - 34.3t + 49 = 0$$
$$4.9(t^2 - 7t + 10) = 0$$
$$4.9(t - 2)(t - 5) = 0$$

Completing the solution and checking the result are left for you. A calculator may be helpful.

$\therefore$ the arrow is 49 m high both 2 s and 5 s after being shot. ***Answer***

Problems

Solve.

A

1. If a number is added to its square, the result is 56. Find the number.
2. If a number is subtracted from its square, the result is 72. Find the number.
3. A positive number is 30 less than its square. Find the number.
4. A negative number is 42 less than its square. Find the number.
5. Find two consecutive negative integers whose product is 90.
6. Find two consecutive positive odd integers whose product is 143.
7. The sum of the squares of two consecutive positive even integers is 340. Find the integers.
8. The sum of the squares of two consecutive negative even integers is 100. Find the integers.

Solve.

9. The length of a rectangle is 8 cm greater than its width. Find the dimensions of the rectangle if its area is 105 cm^2.

10. The length of a rectangle is 6 cm less than twice its width. Find the dimensions of the rectangle if its area is 108 cm^2.

11. Find the dimensions of a rectangle whose perimeter is 46 m and whose area is 126 m^2. (*Hint:* Let the width be w. Use the perimeter to find the length in terms of w.)

12. Find the dimensions of a rectangle whose perimeter is 42 m and whose area is 104 m^2.

13. The sum of two numbers is 25 and the sum of their squares is 313. Find the numbers. (*Hint:* Let one of the numbers be x. Express the other number in terms of x.)

14. The difference of two positive numbers is 5 and the sum of their squares is 233. What are the numbers?

15. Originally the dimensions of a rectangle were 20 cm by 23 cm. When both dimensions were decreased by the same amount, the area of the rectangle decreased by 120 cm^2. Find the dimensions of the new rectangle.

16. Originally a rectangle was twice as long as it was wide. When 4 m were added to its length and 3 m subtracted from its width, the resulting rectangle had an area of 600 m^2. Find the dimensions of the new rectangle.

In Exercises 17–23, use the formula $h = rt - 4.9t^2$ where h is in meters and the formula $h = rt - 16t^2$ where h is in feet. A calculator may be helpful.

B 17. A ball is thrown upward with an initial speed of 24.5 m/s. When is it 19.6 m high? (Two answers)

18. A rocket is fired upward with an initial speed of 1960 m/s. After how many minutes does it hit the ground?

19. A batter hit a baseball upward with an initial speed of 120 ft/s. How much later did the catcher catch it?

20. Mitch tossed an apple to Kathy, who was on a balcony 40 ft above him, with an initial speed of 56 ft/s. Kathy missed the apple on its way up, but caught it on its way down. How long was the apple in the air?

21. A signal flare is fired upward with initial speed 245 m/s. A stationary balloonist at a height of 1960 m sees the flare pass on the way up. How long after this will the flare pass the balloonist again on the way down?

22. A ball is thrown upward from the top of a 98 m tower with initial speed 39.2 m/s. How much later will it hit the ground? (*Hint:* Consider the top of the tower as level zero. If h is the height of the ball above the top of the tower, then $h = -98$ when the ball hits the ground.)

23. A rocket is fired upward with an initial velocity of 160 ft/s.
   a. When is the rocket 400 ft high?
   b. How do you know that 400 ft is the greatest height the rocket reaches?

Solve.

24. A garden plot 4 m by 12 m has one side along a fence as shown at the right. The area of the garden is to be doubled by digging a border of uniform width on the other three sides. What should the width of the border be?

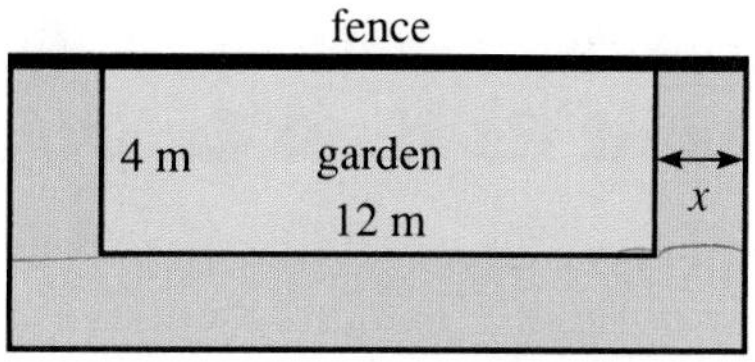

25. Vanessa built a rectangular pen for her dogs. She used an outside wall of the garage for one of the sides of the pen. She had to buy 20 m of fencing in order to build the other sides of the pen. Find the dimensions of the pen if its area is 48 m^2.

26. A rectangular garden 30 m by 40 m has two paths of equal width crossing through it as shown. Find the width of each path if the total area covered by the paths is 325 m^2.

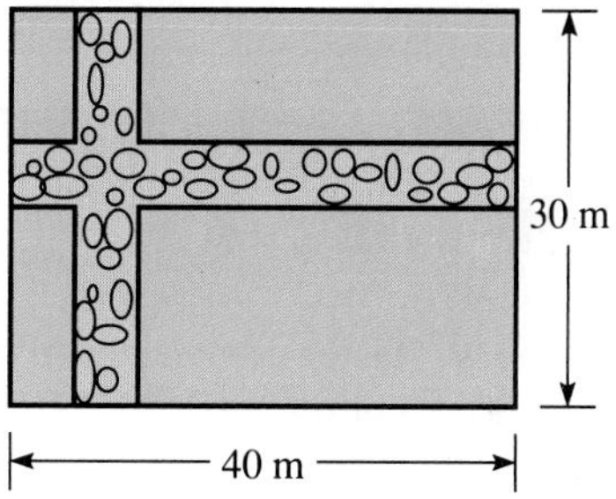

27. A box has a square bottom and top and is 5 cm high. Find its volume if its total surface area is 192 cm^2.

28. The bottom and top of a box are rectangles twice as long as they are wide. Find the volume of the box if it is 4 ft high and has a total surface area of 220 ft^2.

29. A 50 m by 120 m park consists of a rectangular lawn surrounded by a path of uniform width. Find the dimensions of the lawn if its area is the same as the area of the path. (*Hint:* Let x = the width of path.)

C 30. The Parkhursts used 160 yd of fencing to enclose a rectangular corral and to divide it into two parts by a fence parallel to one of the shorter sides. Find the dimensions of the corral if its area is 1000 yd^2.

31. Each edge of one cube is 2 cm longer than each edge of another cube. The volumes of the cubes differ by 98 cm^3. Find the lengths of the edges of each cube.

32. A rectangular sheet of metal is 10 cm longer than it is wide. Squares, 5 cm on a side, are cut from the corners of the sheet, and the flaps are bent up to form an open-topped box having volume 6 L. Find the original dimensions of the sheet of metal. You may wish to make a model. (Recall that $1 \text{ L} = 1000 \text{ cm}^3$.)

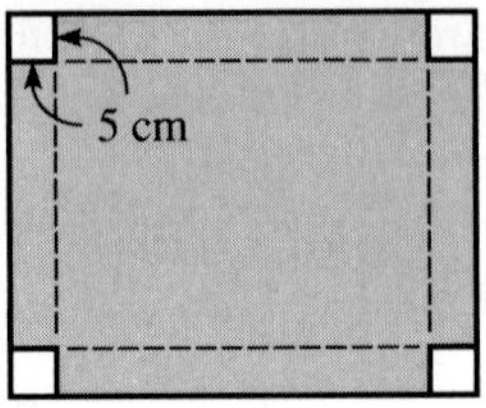

Mixed Review Exercises

Simplify.

1. $(8a^2b)(2ab^2)$ **2.** $(5a^2)^3$ **3.** $3a(4 - 2b)$

4. $(6r)\left(\frac{1}{3}rs^2\right)$ **5.** $\left(\frac{1}{8}\right)(16n - 24p)$ **6.** $(-28x - 14y)\left(-\frac{1}{7}\right)$

7. $(3a + 2)(2a^2 + 5 - 7a)$ **8.** $(3b^2y)^2$ **9.** $6x(x^2 - 8)$

Factor completely.

10. $-28 + 6m + 10m^2$ **11.** $36a^3 - 9ab^2$ **12.** $21n^2 + 22n - 8$

13. $y^4 - y^3 - 12y^2$ **14.** $15m^2 + 26mn + 8n^2$ **15.** $3 + 10x^2 - 17x$

Self-Test 4

Vocabulary factor completely (p. 227)
converse (p. 230)
polynomial equation (p. 231)
linear equation (p. 231)
quadratic equation (p. 231)
cubic equation (p. 231)
standard form of a polynomial equation (p. 231)

Factor completely.

1. $7r - 3rt + 7s - 3st$ **2.** $n^2 - 2n + 1 - 100t^4$ **Obj. 5-10, p. 224**

3. $18a^3 - 12a^2 + 2a$ **4.** $21xy - 18x^2 - 6y^2$ **Obj. 5-11, p. 227**

Solve.

5. $k^2 - 4k = 32$ **6.** $5m^2 + 20m + 20 = 0$ **Obj. 5-12, p. 230**

7. $a^3 = 169a$ **8.** $z^3 = z^2 + 30z$

9. The length of a rectangle is 9 cm more than its width. The area of the rectangle is 90 cm^2. Find the dimensions of the rectangle. **Obj. 5-13, p. 234**

Check your answers with those at the back of the book.

Historical Note / The Sieve of Eratosthenes

Although Eratosthenes (276–194 B.C.) is best known for determining the diameter and circumference of Earth, one of his greatest contributions to mathematics was his sieve, a method of "sifting out" the primes from the set of positive integers.

To use the sieve of Eratosthenes write out the consecutive integers from 2 through any number, say 100. Then, circle 2 and cross out all numbers in the list that are multiples of 2. Next, circle 3 and cross out every number that is a multiple of 3. Continue in this manner until only the circled numbers remain. These are *prime numbers*.

	(2)	(3)	~~4~~	(5)	~~6~~	(7)	~~8~~	~~9~~	~~10~~	(11)	~~12~~	(13)	~~14~~	~~15~~	~~16~~	(17)	~~18~~	(19)	~~20~~
~~21~~	~~22~~	(23)	~~24~~	~~25~~	~~26~~	~~27~~	~~28~~	(29)	~~30~~	(31)	~~32~~	~~33~~	~~34~~	~~35~~	~~36~~	(37)	~~38~~	~~39~~	~~40~~
(41)	~~42~~	(43)	~~44~~	~~45~~	~~46~~	(47)	~~48~~	~~49~~	~~50~~	~~51~~	~~52~~	(53)	~~54~~	~~55~~	~~56~~	~~57~~	~~58~~	(59)	~~60~~
(61)	~~62~~	~~63~~	~~64~~	~~65~~	~~66~~	(67)	~~68~~	~~69~~	~~70~~	(71)	~~72~~	(73)	~~74~~	~~75~~	~~76~~	~~77~~	~~78~~	(79)	~~80~~
~~81~~	~~82~~	(83)	~~84~~	~~85~~	~~86~~	~~87~~	~~88~~	(89)	~~90~~	~~91~~	~~92~~	~~93~~	~~94~~	~~95~~	~~96~~	(97)	~~98~~	~~99~~	~~100~~

Extra / Sums and Differences of Cubes

Both sums and differences of cubes can be factored, as shown by the factoring patterns at the right.

$$x^3 + y^3 = (x + y)(x^2 - xy + y^2)$$
$$x^3 - y^3 = (x - y)(x^2 + xy + y^2)$$

Exercises

1. Verify the factoring pattern for the sum of two cubes by multiplying $(x + y)(x^2 - xy + y^2)$.

2. Verify the factoring pattern for the difference of two cubes by multiplying $(x - y)(x^2 + xy + y^2)$.

Factor.

Sample $m^3 - 27 = m^3 - 3^3 = (m - 3)(m^2 + 3m + 9)$

3. $m^3 + 8$ **4.** $a^3 - 64$ **5.** $n^3 + 125$ **6.** $27 - 216y^3$

7. a. Factor $w^6 - 1$ as a difference of cubes to show that
$$w^6 - 1 = (w - 1)(w + 1)(w^4 + w^2 + 1).$$

b. Factor $w^6 - 1$ as a difference of squares to show that
$$w^6 - 1 = (w - 1)(w + 1)(w^2 + w + 1)(w^2 - w + 1).$$

c. Show that the factorizations given in parts (a) and (b) are equivalent by writing
$$w^4 + w^2 + 1 = (w^4 + 2w^2 + 1) - w^2$$
and then factoring the difference of squares on the right.

Chapter Summary

1. Prime factors of positive integers can be found by using the primes in order as divisors. The *prime factorization* of a positive integer is the expression of the integer as a product of prime factors.
2. The *greatest common factor (GCF) of two or more integers* is the greatest integer that is a factor of all of them. The *greatest common factor of two or more monomials* is the common factor with the greatest coefficient and greatest degree in each variable.
3. The *rule for simplifying fractions* (page 189) and the *rule of exponents for division* (page 190) can be used to simplify quotients of monomials.
4. A method for multiplying binomials mentally is given on page 200.
5. The following factoring patterns are useful in factoring polynomials:

$$a^2 + 2ab + b^2 = (a + b)^2$$
$$a^2 - 2ab + b^2 = (a - b)^2$$
$$a^2 - b^2 = (a + b)(a - b)$$

6. Guidelines for factoring polynomials completely are given on page 227.
7. The *zero-product property* ($ab = 0$ if and only if $a = 0$ or $b = 0$) is useful in solving polynomial equations.

Chapter Review

Write the letter of the correct answer.

1. List all the pairs of integral factors of -111. 5-1

a. $(-1)(-111)$, $(-3)(-37)$ **b.** $(-1)(111)$, $(-3)(37)$ **c.** $(-1)(111)$, $(1)(-111)$, $(3)(-37)$, $(-3)(37)$ **d.** $(1)(111)$, $(-1)(-111)$, $(3)(37)$, $(-3)(-37)$

2. Find the prime factorization of 72.

a. $1 \cdot 2^2 \cdot 3^2$ **b.** $2^2 \cdot 3 \cdot 6$ **c.** $2^2 \cdot 3^3$ **d.** $2^3 \cdot 3^2$

3. Find the GCF of 14 and 42.

a. 2 **b.** 7 **c.** 14 **d.** 42

4. Simplify $\frac{(-5m)^2}{-5m^2}$. 5-2

a. 1 **b.** -1 **c.** 5 **d.** -5

5. Find the missing factor: $-105x^3y^6 = (7xy^2)(\underline{\ ?\ })$

a. $-112x^3y^3$ **b.** $-15y^3y^3$ **c.** $-15x^2y^4$ **d.** $-25x^2y^4$

6. Divide: $\frac{12c^2 - 30c + 6}{6}$ 5-3

a. $2c^2 - 5c$ **b.** $5c^2 - 2c + 16$ **c.** $2c^2 - 5c + 1$ **d.** 2

7. Factor $18x^3 - 63x^2 + 9x$.

a. $9(2x^3 - 7x^2 + x)$ b. $9x(2x^2 - 7x)$
c. $9x(2x^2 - 7x + x)$ d. $9x(2x^2 - 7x + 1)$

8. Express $(k - 1)(k - 1)$ as a polynomial. 5-4

a. $k^2 + 1$ b. $2k + 1$ c. $k^2 - 2k + 1$ d. $k^2 + 2k + 1$

9. Express $(5m + 4n)(m + 4n)$ as a polynomial.

a. $5m^2 + 8n^2$ b. $5m^2 + 16n^2$
c. $5m^2 + 24mn + 8n^2$ d. $5m^2 + 24mn + 16n^2$

10. Express $(2m - 3n)(2m + 3n)$ as a polynomial. 5-5

a. $2m^2 - 3n^2$ b. $4m^2 - 9n^2$
c. $4m^2 + 12mn - 9n^2$ d. $4m^2 - 12mn - 9n^2$

11. Factor $49 - x^4$.

a. $(x^2 + 7)(x^2 - 7)$ b. $(7 + x^2)(7 - x^2)$
c. $(x^4 + 7)(x^4 - 7)$ d. $(7 - x^4)(7 + x^4)$

12. Express $(7r - 3s)^2$ as a polynomial. 5-6

a. $49r^2 + 9s^2$ b. $49r^2 - 9s^2$
c. $49r^2 + 42rs - 9s^2$ d. $49r^2 - 42rs + 9s^2$

13. Factor $a^2 - 2a + 1$.

a. not possible b. $(a - 1)^2$ c. $(a + 1)^2$ d. $(a - 2)^2$

14. Factor $a^2 + ab + b^2$.

a. not possible b. $(a + b)^2$ c. $(a - b)^2$ d. $(a + b)(a - b)$

15. Factor $y^2 - 7y + 12$. 5-7

a. not possible b. $(y - 12)(y - 1)$ c. $(y - 3)(y - 4)$

16. Factor $x^2 + 16x + 48$.

a. $(x + 6)(x + 8)$ b. $(x + 2)(x + 24)$ c. $(x + 4)(x + 12)$

17. Factor $n^2 + 12n - 45$. 5-8

a. $(n - 9)(n + 5)$ b. $(n + 15)(n - 3)$ c. $(n - 15)(n + 3)$

18. Factor $x^2 - 14x - 48$.

a. not possible b. $(x - 16)(x + 2)$ c. $(x + 4)(x - 12)$

19. Factor $8a^2 - 17a + 2$. 5-9

a. $(2a - 2)(4a - 1)$ b. $(8a - 1)(a - 2)$ c. $(8a - 2)(a - 1)$

20. Factor $3(x - 2) - 4x(2 - x)$. 5-10

a. $12x(x - 2)$ b. $(3 + 4x)(x - 2)$ c. $(4x - 3)(x - 2)$

21. Factor $2x^3y - 50xy$ completely. 5-11

a. $2y(x^2 - 25x)$ b. $2xy(x - 5)^2$ c. $2xy(x + 5)(x - 5)$

22. Factor $m^2 - 9n^2 + 2m - 6n$ completely.

a. $(m + 2)(m - 3n)$ b. $(m + 3n + 2)(m - 3n)$ c. $(m + 3n)(m - 3n)(m - 3n)$

23. Solve $5a(3a - 1)(2a + 4) = 0$. 5-12

a. $\{0, \frac{1}{3}, -2\}$ b. $\{0, 3, -2\}$ c. $\{0, 3, -\frac{1}{2}\}$ d. $\{0, \frac{1}{3}, -\frac{1}{2}\}$

24. I am thinking of four consecutive integers. The sum of the squares of the second and third is 61. Find the integers. 5-13

a. $\{4, 5, 6, 7\}$ b. $\{-10, -9, -8, -7\}$
c. no solution d. $\{-4, -5, -6, -7\}$ or $\{4, 5, 6, 7\}$

Chapter Test

List all pairs of integral factors of each integer.

1. -87 **2.** 91 5-1

Give the prime factorization of each number.

3. 420 **4.** 168

Simplify each fraction.

5. $\frac{-70m^5}{-42mn^7}$ **6.** $\frac{(-3x)^4}{-39x}$ 5-2

7. $\frac{49ab^2 - 56ab^8}{7ab^2}$ **8.** $\frac{-65r^6 + 78r^4 - 52r^2}{-13r^2}$ 5-3

Evaluate by factoring first.

9. $97 \times 16 - 97 \times 6$ **10.** $82^2 + 82 \cdot 18$

Write each product as a polynomial.

11. $(5m - 1)(6m - 5)$ **12.** $(7x - y)(8x + 9y)$ 5-4

13. $(7 - 8x)(7 + 8x)$ **14.** $(c^4 + c^2)(c^4 - c^2)$ 5-5

15. $(x - 9)^2$ **16.** $(4m - 6n)^2$ 5-6

Decide whether each trinomial is a perfect square. If it is, factor it. If it is not, write *not a perfect square*.

17. $n^2 + 16k - 64$ **18.** $16x^2 - 8x + 1$ **19.** $a^2 - 9ab + 81b^2$

Factor completely. If the polynomial is not factorable, write *prime*.

20. $b^2 - 3b + 2$ **21.** $x^2 - 2x + 4$ **22.** $a^2 - 6ab + 8b^2$ 5-7

23. $a^2 - 6a - 40$ **24.** $z^2 + z - 3$ **25.** $x^2 + 22xy - 48y^2$ 5-8

26. $4a^2 - a - 5$ **27.** $6y^2 + y - 15$ **28.** $7 - 23r + 6r^2$ 5-9

29. $5(x - y) + z(y - x)$ **30.** $ax + 2x + a + 2$ 5-10

31. $x^4 - 1$ **32.** $x^2y - y^3$ 5-11

33. $9m^3 - 63m^2 + 108m$ **34.** $a^2 + a + ab + b$

Solve.

35. $3x^2 - 41x = -60$ **36.** $5m^2 = 85m$ **37.** $9x^2 = 1$ 5-12

38. The length of a rectangle is 3 cm more than twice the width. The area of the rectangle is 90 cm^2. Find the dimensions of the rectangle. 5-13

Cumulative Review *(Chapters 1–5)*

Simplify. Assume that no denominator equals zero.

1. $-3.3 + (-27.3 + 10.6)$
2. $-\frac{3}{5}\left(-\frac{9}{17}\right) + \frac{8}{5}\left(-\frac{9}{17}\right)$
3. $\frac{-168a}{24}$
4. $(-4)^2 \div 2 + 2 - 8$
5. $(2z - 3) + (3z - 4)$
6. $(3m - 4) - (4m - 5)$
7. $(2a^2b)^3(3a^2b)^3$
8. $\frac{-45r^3st^2}{25rst}$
9. $\frac{27x^3y^2 - 9x^2y + 8xy}{9xy}$
10. $(6rs - 7t)(6rs + 7t)$
11. $(7a + 4)^2$
12. $-t(3t + 5)(2t - 5)$

Evaluate if $w = -\frac{1}{2}$, $x = 2$, $y = 0$, and $z = -3$.

13. $\frac{(z - 2w) - x}{-y + 1}$
14. $\frac{1}{w}(xy - z)$
15. $(2x + z)^x$
16. Find the prime factorizations of 90 and 756 and then find their GCF.

Factor completely. If the polynomial cannot be factored, write *prime*.

17. $6p^3 - 2p^3r^2 + 8p^2r^3st$
18. $32a^2b - 8b$
19. $4a^2 + 12ab + 9b^2$
20. $x^2 + 15x + 26$
21. $m^2 - 9m + 18$
22. $k^2 - k - 42$
23. $6y^2 + 13y - 5$
24. $x^2 + 4xy + 4y^2 - 16$
25. $a^3 + a^2b - ab^2 - b^3$

Solve. If the equation is an identity or has no solution, say so.

26. $9c - 3 = 24$
27. $|a| - 5 = 3$
28. $\frac{2}{3}m = 18$
29. $7(x - 1) = 4x + 5$
30. $\frac{1}{5}n = -2$
31. $10 - x = -2$
32. $3m - 2 = \frac{1}{2}(8m + 6) - (m + 5)$
33. $2y^2 - 32 = 0$
34. $x^2 - 6x + 15 = 6$
35. $(x + 7)(x + 1) = (x + 2)^2 + 5x$
36. $8b^2 - 10b = 3$
37. $x^3 - 9x^2 + 20x = 0$

38. Marvin has 20 nickels and dimes. He has $\frac{2}{3}$ as many dimes as he does nickels. How many nickels and how many dimes does Marvin have?
39. The 42 km drive from Oakdale to Ridgemont usually takes 28 min. Because highway construction requires a reduced speed limit, the trip now takes 14 min longer. Find the reduced speed limit in km/h.
40. The sum of the squares of two consecutive integers is 9 greater than 8 times the smaller integer. Find the integers.
41. The length of a rectangle is 5 greater than 3 times its width. The area of the rectangle is 22 cm^2. Find the length and width of the rectangle.

Maintaining Skills

Review the five-step problem solving plan described on page 27.

Sample The length of a rectangle is 10 cm less than 4 times the width. If the perimeter is 1.3 m, find the dimensions of the rectangle.

Solution

Step 1 Read the problem carefully. It asks for the length and width of the rectangle. Make a sketch.

Step 2 Choose a variable and use it with the given facts to represent the unknowns described in the problem.

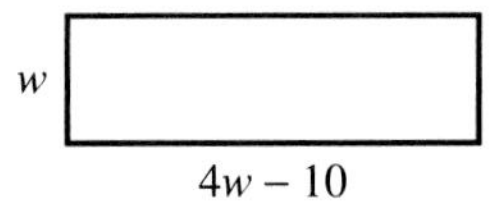

Let w = the width.
Then $4w - 10$ = the length.

Step 3 Write an equation based on the given facts:

$$\underbrace{\text{The perimeter}}_{2w + 2(4w - 10)} \ \underset{\downarrow}{\text{is}} \ \underbrace{1.3 \text{ m}}_{130}$$

$$2w + 2(4w - 10) \stackrel{?}{=} 130 \qquad (1.3 \text{ m} = 130 \text{ cm})$$

Step 4 Solve the equation and find the unknowns asked for:

$$10w - 20 = 130$$
$$10w = 150$$
$$w = 15;\ 4w - 10 = 4(15) - 10 = 50$$

Step 5 Check your results with the words of the problem. Give the answer.
∴ the length is 50 cm and the width is 15 cm. ***Answer***

Use the five-step plan to solve each problem.

1. The length of a rectangle is 2 cm greater than twice its width. The area of the rectangle is 40 cm^2. Find the dimensions of the rectangle.
2. Three consecutive integers are such that the square of the greatest is 32 less than the sum of the squares of the other two. Find the integers.
3. The bottom of a box is a rectangle with length 5 cm more than the width. The height of the box is 4 cm and its volume is 264 cm^3. Find the dimensions of the bottom of the box.
4. A painting is 6 cm longer than it is wide. The painting is to be surrounded by a mat that is 2 cm wide and covered by a piece of glass with area 352 cm^2. Find the dimensions of the painting.
5. A ball is thrown upward with an initial speed of 19.6 m/s. When is the ball opposite a roof top that is 14.7 m high? Use the formula $h = rt - 4.9t^2$ where h is the height. (A calculator may be helpful.)

Mixed Problem Solving

Solve each problem that has a solution. If a problem has no solution, explain why.

A **1.** Paul earns \$4 an hour working at the library and \$8 an hour mowing lawns. This week he worked 25 hours and earned \$164. How many hours did he work at the library?

2. The atomic number of nickel, 28, is $3\frac{1}{2}$ times the atomic number of oxygen. Find the atomic number of oxygen.

3. Maureen jogged 3 km less than her older sister. If each of them had jogged 4 km less, the total of their distances would have been 15 km. How far did each sister jog?

4. The difference between the highest and lowest recorded temperatures in the Yukon is 74.6° C. If the lowest temperature is −44.4° C, find the highest temperature.

5. The sum of two numbers is 5. The sum of their squares is 53. Find the numbers.

6. A can of house paint costs \$4 more than a can of wall paint. If 7 cans of house paint cost the same as 9 cans of wall paint, find the cost of each type of paint.

7. The width of a rectangle is $\frac{2}{3}$ the length. When each dimension is decreased by 2 cm, the area is decreased by 36 cm^2. Find the original dimensions of the rectangle.

8. I have 30 quarters and dimes worth \$5.50. How many dimes do I have?

9. A submarine traveling 64 m below sea level dived 37 m, dived another 28 m, and then rose 70 m. Find its new depth.

10. During July, Ross made deposits of \$837.26, wrote checks for \$709.74, paid a service charge of \$4, and received \$3.70 in interest. If his new balance was \$528.01, what was his balance at the beginning of the month?

B **11.** A doubles tennis court has the same length as a singles court but is 9 ft wider. The length of a singles court is 3 ft less than three times the width. The area of a doubles court is 2808 ft^2. Find the area of a singles court. (A calculator will help you to test possible factors.)

12. At 3:00 P.M. Mark left Pittsburgh and drove toward Cleveland, 208 km away. At 3:30 Carole left Cleveland and headed toward Pittsburgh, driving 2 km/h slower than Mark. If their cars passed each other at 4:30, how fast was each driving?

13. Phil walked to and from school. On his trip home he walked 2 km/h faster and the trip took 5 min less. Find the total distance he walked.

14. Find three consecutive even integers such that half their sum is 7 less than the greatest.

6 Fractions

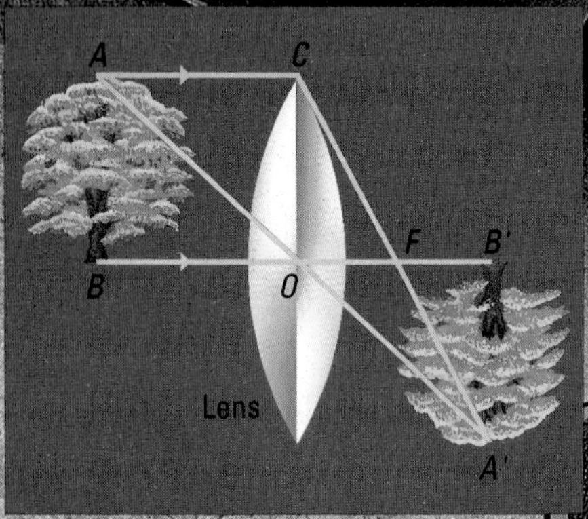

A fractional equation describes the relationships among these distances: between object and lens (OB), lens and film (OB'), and lens and focal point (OF).

$$\frac{1}{OB} + \frac{1}{OB'} = \frac{1}{OF}$$

Algebraic Fractions

6-1 Simplifying Fractions

Objective To simplify algebraic fractions.

When the numerator and denominator of an algebraic fraction have no common factor other than 1 and -1, the fraction is said to be in *simplest form*. To simplify a fraction, first factor the numerator and the denominator.

Example 1 Simplify $\frac{3a + 6}{3a + 3b}$.

Solution $\frac{3a + 6}{3a + 3b} = \frac{\cancel{3}(a + 2)}{\cancel{3}(a + b)}$ {Factor the numerator and denominator and look for common factors.

$= \frac{a + 2}{a + b} \quad (a \neq -b)$ ***Answer***

Remember that you cannot divide by zero. You must *restrict* the variables in a denominator by excluding any values that make the denominator equal to zero. In Example 1, a cannot equal $-b$.

Example 2 Simplify $\frac{x^2 - 9}{(2x + 1)(3 + x)}$.

Solution $\frac{x^2 - 9}{(2x + 1)(3 + x)} = \frac{\cancel{(x + 3)}(x - 3)}{(2x + 1)\cancel{(3 + x)}}$ {$x + 3$ and $3 + x$ are equal.

$= \frac{x - 3}{2x + 1} \quad \left(x \neq -\frac{1}{2}, x \neq -3\right)$ ***Answer***

Note: To see which values of the variable to exclude, look at the denominator of the *original* fraction. Neither $2x + 1$ nor $3 + x$ can equal zero. Since $2x + 1 \neq 0$ and $3 + x \neq 0$, $x \neq -\frac{1}{2}$ and $x \neq -3$.

Example 3 Simplify $\frac{2x^2 + x - 3}{2 - x - x^2}$.

Solution First factor the numerator and the denominator. If you don't see any common factors, look for opposites.

(Solution continues on next page.)

$$\frac{2x^2 + x - 3}{2 - x - x^2} = \frac{(x - 1)(2x + 3)}{(1 - x)(2 + x)} \quad \begin{cases}(x - 1) \text{ and } (1 - x) \text{ are opposites.} \\ (1 - x) = -(x - 1)\end{cases}$$

$$= \frac{\cancel{(x - 1)}(2x + 3)}{-\cancel{(x - 1)}(2 + x)}$$

$$= \frac{2x + 3}{-(2 + x)}, \text{ or } -\frac{2x + 3}{x + 2} \quad (x \neq 1, x \neq -2) \quad \textbf{\textit{Answer}}$$

Example 4 Solve $ax - a^2 = bx - b^2$ for x.

Solution

$$ax - a^2 = bx - b^2$$
$$ax - bx = a^2 - b^2 \quad \begin{cases}\text{Collect all terms with } x \text{ on one side of the} \\ \text{equation and all other terms on the other side.}\end{cases}$$
$$(a - b)x = (a + b)(a - b) \quad \{\text{Factor both sides of the equation.}$$
$$x = \frac{(a + b)(a - b)}{(a - b)} \quad \{\text{Divide both sides by the coefficient of } x.$$
$$x = a + b \quad (a \neq b) \quad \textbf{\textit{Answer}}$$

Oral Exercises

Simplify. State the restrictions on the variable.

1. $\frac{3m + 9}{m + 3}$
2. $\frac{2n + 8}{3n + 12}$
3. $\frac{a^2 - 16}{a - 4}$
4. $\frac{b^2 - 9}{b + 3}$
5. $\frac{x^2 - 2x + 1}{x - 1}$
6. $\frac{x + 6}{36 - x^2}$
7. $\frac{14 - 2c}{7 - c}$
8. $\frac{2c - 2d}{2c + 2d}$
9. $\frac{2t - 1}{1 - 2t}$
10. $\frac{(2y - 8)^2}{(2y - 8)^3}$
11. $\frac{(x + 5)^2}{5 + x}$
12. $\frac{(4 - x)(x^2 - 9)}{(x - 4)(x - 3)}$

Which of the following fractions *cannot* be simplified?

13. $\frac{4x - 6y}{4x + 6y}$
14. $\frac{4x - 7y}{7y + 4x}$
15. $\frac{4x^2 - y^2}{2x - y}$
16. $\frac{4x^2 + y^2}{2x + y}$

Written Exercises

Simplify. Give any restrictions on the variables.

A

1. $\frac{2x + 2y}{4}$
2. $\frac{12m - 15n}{9}$
3. $\frac{5a - 10}{a - 2}$
4. $\frac{4n + 16}{n + 4}$
5. $\frac{3n + 1}{9n + 3}$
6. $\frac{8x - 8y}{8x + 8y}$
7. $\frac{2x - 4}{x^2 - 4}$
8. $\frac{6y + 30}{y^2 - 25}$

9. $\frac{2xy}{x^2y - y^2x}$

10. $\frac{4p^2 - 8p}{4p^3}$

11. $\frac{(x + 4)(2x + 1)}{(1 + 2x)(x - 3)}$

12. $\frac{(x - 5)(2 + 7x)}{(5 - x)(7x + 2)}$

13. $\frac{a^2 + 8a + 16}{16 - a^2}$

14. $\frac{25 - b^2}{b^2 + 12b + 35}$

15. $\frac{2 - y}{y^2 - 4y + 4}$

16. $\frac{(a - 5)^2}{25 - a^2}$

17. $\frac{4n^2 + 144}{6n + 36}$

18. $\frac{25c + 15d}{50c^2 + 30d^2}$

19. $\frac{2n^2 - 5n - 3}{4n^2 - 8n - 5}$

20. $\frac{2w^2 + w - 6}{2w + 4}$

21. $\frac{3x^2 + 6x}{6x^2 + 7x - 10}$

22. $\frac{4b^2 - 5b - 6}{8b^2 + 6b}$

23. $\frac{10 - 3a - a^2}{a^2 - 4}$

24. $\frac{2y^2 - 9y + 4}{8y - 2y^2}$

25. $\frac{x^2 + xy}{x^2 - xy}$

26. $\frac{2ab + 2ac + 4a^2}{4b + 4c + 8a}$

27. $\frac{r^2 - s^2}{4r^2 + rs - 5s^2}$

28. $\frac{3t^2 - 4tv - 7v^2}{t^2 - v^2}$

Solve for x.

B

29. $cx + dx = c^2 - d^2$

30. $ax + bx = a^2 + 2ab + b^2$

31. $abx - b = ax - 1$

32. $3ax + 6 = a^2x + 2a$

33. $5kx - x = 25k^2 - 10k + 1$

34. $4x - 4 = b^2 + 5b - bx$

35. $2cx + 3dx = 4c^2 + 12cd + 9d^2$

36. $2x + 5k = 6k^2 - 3kx - 6$

37. $a(x - a) + 6(x + 6) = 0$

38. $2n(x - n) = x - 5n + 2$

39. Miguel wants to evaluate $\frac{x^2 - 4y^2}{x - 2y}$ when $x = 3$ and $y = 1$. First he simplifies the fraction to $x + 2y$. Then he substitutes $x = 3$ and $y = 1$, getting 5 for his answer. Miguel also uses the simplified form $x + 2y$ to evaluate the given fraction when $x = 4$ and $y = 2$, getting 8 for his answer. Tell which one of these two answers is incorrect and explain why.

40. Donna wants to simplify $\frac{x^2 - 4y^2}{x^2 - 2xy}$.

She gives this solution: $\frac{x^2 - 4y^2}{x^2 - 2xy} = \frac{\cancel{x^2} - 4y^2}{\cancel{x^2} - 2xy} = \frac{-4y^2}{-2xy} = \frac{2y}{x}$

Choose values of x and y to show that her solution is incorrect. Simplify the fraction correctly.

Simplify. Give any restrictions on the variables.

41. $\frac{25x^2 - 36y^2}{10x^2 + 3xy - 18y^2}$

42. $\frac{12x^2 - 5xy - 2y^2}{4y^2 - 4xy - 3x^2}$

43. $\frac{6a^3 + 10a^2}{36a^3 - 100a}$

44. $\frac{8a^2 + 6ab - 5b^2}{16a^2 - 25b^2}$

Simplify. Give any restrictions on the variables.

45. $\dfrac{x(a+b)-2(a+b)}{2-x}$

46. $\dfrac{w^4-1}{w^4(w+1)+(w+1)}$

C 47. $\dfrac{2x^3-13x^2+15x}{15x-7x^2-2x^3}$

48. $\dfrac{x^4-10x^2+9}{3-2x-x^2}$

49. $\dfrac{4a^2-b^2-2a+b}{(2a+b)^2-1}$

50. $\dfrac{x^2+2x+1-y^2}{(x+1)^2+2y(x+1)+y^2}$

For which value(s) of *x* does each fraction equal zero?

51. $\dfrac{x^2-4}{x^2-4x+4}$

52. $\dfrac{3x^2+x}{2x-x^3}$

53. $\dfrac{x^2-2x-15}{x^2+3x-40}$

54. $\dfrac{x^4-x^2}{x^3+x^2-2x}$

Mixed Review Exercises

Simplify. Assume that no denominator equals zero.

1. $12\left(\frac{1}{3}u+\frac{1}{4}v\right)$

2. $(-42n+28p)\left(-\frac{1}{4}\right)$

3. $\dfrac{15a^7b^8}{30a^2b^3}$

4. $\dfrac{(-3y)^5}{(y^2)^5}$

5. $\dfrac{3x^5+6x^3-12x^2}{x^2}$

6. $(-20)(-7)(-4)(-5)$

Solve.

7. $-y+15=9$

8. $68=-\frac{n}{5}$

9. $5p+8=-47$

10. $5(x+2)+2=27$

11. $9y-(7y+5)=11$

12. $(3n-6)-(5-3n)=7$

Computer Exercises

For students with some programming experience.

1. **a.** Write a BASIC program to evaluate each algebraic fraction for $x = 10$, 20, 30, 40, 50.

   (1) $\dfrac{x}{x^2+1}$ (2) $\dfrac{x^2}{x^2+1}$ (3) $\dfrac{x^2}{x+1}$

   b. As the value of x increases, what happens to the value of each of these algebraic fractions? Explain why.

2. **a.** Write a BASIC program that uses READ . . . DATA statements to evaluate the algebraic fraction $\dfrac{x^5+1}{x^4-x^3+x^2-x+1}$ for $x = 2$, 13, 22, 50, 99.

   b. On the basis of your results in part (a), suggest a general formula that evaluates the given fraction for any value of x.

6-2 Multiplying Fractions

Objective To multiply algebraic fractions.

The property of quotients given in Lesson 5-2 states that

$$\frac{ac}{bd} = \frac{a}{b} \cdot \frac{c}{d}.$$

You can rewrite this result to get the multiplication rule for fractions.

Multiplication Rule for Fractions

$$\frac{a}{b} \cdot \frac{c}{d} = \frac{ac}{bd}$$

Example: $\frac{3}{8} \cdot \frac{5}{2} = \frac{3 \cdot 5}{8 \cdot 2} = \frac{15}{16}$

To multiply fractions, you multiply their numerators and multiply their denominators.

Example 1 Multiply: $\frac{8}{9} \cdot \frac{3}{10}$.

Solution 1 $\frac{8}{9} \cdot \frac{3}{10} = \frac{8 \cdot 3}{9 \cdot 10} = \frac{\overset{4}{\cancel{24}}}{\underset{15}{\cancel{90}}} = \frac{4}{15}$ You can multiply first and then simplify.

Solution 2 $\frac{\overset{4}{\cancel{8}}}{\underset{3}{\cancel{9}}} \cdot \frac{\overset{1}{\cancel{3}}}{\underset{5}{\cancel{10}}} = \frac{4}{15}$ You can simplify first and then multiply.

Example 2 Multiply: **a.** $\frac{6x}{y^3} \cdot \frac{y^2}{15}$ **b.** $\frac{x^2 - x - 12}{x^2 - 5x} \cdot \frac{x^2 - 25}{x + 3}$

Solution

a. $\frac{6x}{y^3} \cdot \frac{y^2}{15} = \frac{\cancel{3} \cdot 2x}{\cancel{y^2} \cdot y} \cdot \frac{\cancel{y^2} \cdot 1}{\cancel{3} \cdot 5} = \frac{2x}{5y}$ $(y \neq 0)$

b. $\frac{x^2 - x - 12}{x^2 - 5x} \cdot \frac{x^2 - 25}{x + 3} = \frac{(x - 4)\cancel{(x + 3)}}{x\cancel{(x - 5)}} \cdot \frac{(x + 5)\cancel{(x - 5)}}{\cancel{(x + 3)}}$

$= \frac{(x - 4)(x + 5)}{x}$ $(x \neq 0, x \neq 5, x \neq -3)$ ***Answer***

Another way to write the answer to Example 2(b) is $\frac{x^2 + x - 20}{x}$. The factored form of the answer, as shown in Example 2, is the one we'll show in this book.

In Example 2(b), the denominators of $\frac{x^2 - x - 12}{x^2 - 5x} \cdot \frac{x^2 - 25}{x + 3}$ equal zero when x is 0, 5, or -3, so the product is restricted to values of x other than 0, 5, and -3.

From now on, assume that the domains of the variables do not include values for which any denominator is zero. Therefore, it will not be necessary to show the excluded values of the variables.

In Chapter 4, you learned the rule of exponents for a power of a product:

For every positive integer m, $(ab)^m = a^m b^m$.

The rule below is similar.

Rule of Exponents for a Power of a Quotient

For every positive integer m,

$$\left(\frac{a}{b}\right)^m = \frac{a^m}{b^m}.$$

Example 3 Simplify $\left(\frac{x}{3}\right)^3$.

Solution $\left(\frac{x}{3}\right)^3 = \frac{x^3}{3^3}$

$= \frac{x^3}{27}$ *Answer*

Example 4 Simplify $\left(-\frac{c}{2}\right)^2 \cdot \frac{4}{3c}$.

Solution $\left(-\frac{c}{2}\right)^2 \cdot \frac{4}{3c} = \frac{c^2}{4} \cdot \frac{4}{3c}$

$= \frac{\cancel{c} \cdot c}{\cancel{4}} \cdot \frac{\cancel{4}}{3\cancel{c}}$

$= \frac{c}{3}$ *Answer*

Oral Exercises

Multiply. Express each product in simplest form.

1. $\frac{6}{5} \cdot \frac{10}{3}$ **2.** $\frac{9}{8} \cdot \frac{16}{3}$ **3.** $-\frac{3}{4} \cdot \frac{8}{9}$ **4.** $\frac{a}{b} \cdot \frac{b}{a}$

5. $\frac{2}{x} \cdot \frac{x}{14}$ **6.** $\frac{n}{6} \cdot \frac{16}{n}$ **7.** $\frac{5y^2}{3} \cdot \frac{6}{y^2}$ **8.** $\frac{2a}{3} \cdot \frac{a}{4}$

9. $(3c)^2 \cdot \frac{4}{c}$ **10.** $\frac{b}{(2a)^2} \cdot \frac{a^2}{b}$ **11.** $\frac{(x-1)^2}{8} \cdot \frac{4}{x-1}$ **12.** $\frac{3n-2}{n^2} \cdot \frac{n^4}{2-3n}$

Simplify.

13. $\left(\frac{5a}{b}\right)^2$ **14.** $\left(\frac{x}{2y}\right)^3$ **15.** $\left(-\frac{c^2}{3}\right)^2$ **16.** $\left(-\frac{4}{n^2}\right)^3$

Written Exercises

Multiply. Express each product in simplest form.

A

1. $\frac{4}{7} \cdot \frac{21}{8}$
2. $\frac{4}{9} \cdot \frac{3}{16}$
3. $\frac{15}{4} \cdot \frac{8}{9}$
4. $-\frac{7}{2} \cdot \frac{10}{28}$
5. $\frac{3}{5} \cdot \frac{5}{7} \cdot \frac{7}{9}$
6. $\frac{9}{5} \cdot \frac{2}{3} \cdot \frac{15}{18}$
7. $\left(-\frac{5}{2}\right)^2 \cdot \frac{8}{5}$
8. $(-2)^3 \cdot \frac{35}{16}$
9. $\frac{6}{x^2} \cdot \frac{x^3}{3}$
10. $\frac{5y}{2} \cdot \frac{4}{15y}$
11. $\frac{a}{b} \cdot \frac{b}{c} \cdot \frac{c}{d}$
12. $\frac{4}{x^2} \cdot \frac{7x}{8}$
13. $\frac{4w}{v} \cdot \frac{v^3}{2w^2}$
14. $\frac{6a}{11b^4} \cdot \frac{22b}{3a^3}$
15. $\frac{4d^2e}{9ef} \cdot \frac{f^2}{6d}$
16. $\frac{2rs^2}{3t} \cdot \frac{9t^2}{4rs}$

Simplify.

17. $\left(\frac{a}{6}\right)^2$
18. $\left(\frac{c}{5}\right)^3$
19. $\left(\frac{2n}{7}\right)^2$
20. $\left(\frac{4x}{3}\right)^2$
21. $\left(\frac{2a}{5b^3}\right)^2$
22. $\left(\frac{4m}{7n^2}\right)^2$
23. $\left(\frac{-x^2}{10}\right)^4$
24. $-\left(\frac{5b^4}{6}\right)^2$
25. $\left(\frac{a}{b}\right)^2 \cdot \frac{b}{a}$
26. $\left(\frac{3x}{y}\right)^3 \cdot \frac{y^2}{9}$
27. $\left(-\frac{x}{4y}\right)^2 \cdot \left(-\frac{4y}{x}\right)$
28. $\left(\frac{3z}{y}\right)^3 \cdot \frac{2yz}{15}$
29. Find the area of a square if each side has length $\frac{2x}{7}$ in.
30. Find the volume of a cube if each edge has length $\frac{4n}{5}$ in.
31. A triangle has base $\frac{3x}{4}$ cm and height $\frac{8}{9x}$ cm. What is its area?
32. If you travel for $\frac{7t}{60}$ hours at $\frac{80r}{9}$ mi/h, how far have you gone?

B

33. Find the total dollar cost of $\frac{4y}{3}$ eggs if they cost d dollars per dozen.
34. Find the total dollar cost of n dozen pencils if each pencil costs $\frac{2c}{3}$ cents.

Simplify.

35. $\frac{c+2}{c^2} \cdot \frac{3c}{c^2-4}$
36. $\frac{x^2-1}{16x} \cdot \frac{4x^2}{5x+5}$
37. $\frac{a^2-x^2}{a^2} \cdot \frac{a}{3x-3a}$
38. $\frac{3r-rt}{6r^2t} \cdot \frac{3}{9-t^2}$
39. $(4b^2-3b) \cdot \frac{5b^2}{40b^3-30b^2}$
40. $\frac{2y}{3y^2+15y} \cdot (3y^3-75y)$
41. $\frac{10x^4}{6x-12} \cdot \frac{x^2-x-2}{4x}$
42. $\frac{2x^2+5x-3}{x+2} \cdot \frac{9x+18}{1-2x}$
43. $\frac{n^2-3n+2}{n^2+3n+2} \cdot \frac{8n+8}{4n+8}$
44. $\frac{x^2+4x-21}{x^2-6x-16} \cdot \frac{x^2-8x+15}{x^2+9x+14}$

Simplify.

45. $\dfrac{t^2 - 2t - 8}{4 - t^2} \cdot \dfrac{t^2 - 5t + 6}{t^2 - t - 12}$

46. $\dfrac{a^2 - 7a + 6}{2a^3 - 3a^2} \cdot \dfrac{4a^3 - 9a}{a^2 - 10a + 24}$

47. $\dfrac{3x^2 - 14x - 5}{8x^2 - 12x} \cdot \dfrac{8x^2 - 18}{3x^2 + 4x + 1}$

48. $\dfrac{25 - 16y^2}{6y^3 - 36y^2} \cdot \dfrac{10y + 8y^2}{10 - 3y - 4y^2}$

49. $\dfrac{3d^2 - 9d + 6}{2d^2 - 10d + 12} \cdot \dfrac{6 - 2d}{3 - 3d}$

50. $\dfrac{4c^2 - 8c - 5}{12c^2 + 46c + 40} \cdot \dfrac{20 + 8c}{5 - 2c}$

51. $\left(\dfrac{x - 2}{2}\right)^2 \cdot \left(\dfrac{2}{x - 2}\right)^3$

52. $\left(\dfrac{2n - 1}{3}\right)^4 \cdot \left(\dfrac{9}{2n - 1}\right)^2$

53. $\left(\dfrac{x - y}{x + y}\right)^2 \cdot \dfrac{x^2 + y^2}{x^2 - y^2}$

54. $\dfrac{4a^2 - b^2}{4c^2 - d^2} \cdot \left(\dfrac{2c - d}{2a + b}\right)^2$

C 55. $\dfrac{9x^2 - 1}{6x^2} \cdot \dfrac{12x^2 + 12x}{(1 - 3x)^2} \cdot \dfrac{6 - 18x}{3x^2 + 4x + 1}$

56. $\dfrac{4n^2 - 4}{1 + n^2} \cdot \dfrac{1 - n}{2n} \cdot \dfrac{1 - 2n^2 + n^4}{2 + 2n}$

57. $\dfrac{x^3 + 3x^2 - 4x - 12}{2x^2 - 18} \cdot \dfrac{x^3 - 3x^2 + 3x - 9}{3x^3 - 12x}$

58. $\dfrac{a^2 - (b - c)^2}{2a - 2b + 2c} \cdot \dfrac{6a - 6b + 6c}{b^2 - (a - c)^2}$

59. Find all values of x for which $\dfrac{2x^3 - 2x}{3x^3} \cdot \dfrac{9}{x^2 + 3x + 2}$ is equal to zero.

Mixed Review Exercises

Factor completely.

1. $a^2 + 14a + 45$
2. $x^2 - 7x + 10$
3. $16x^4 - 81$
4. $2x^2 + 5x + 1$
5. $625y^2 - 4z^2$
6. $64 + 16c + c^2$
7. $xy + 3y - 4xz - 12z$
8. $9x^2 - 12x + 4$
9. $3x^2 + 14x - 5$
10. $x^4 + 7x^2 - 8x^3$
11. $n^2 + 5n - 14$
12. $y^2 - 5y - 24$

Challenge

What is wrong with this "proof" that 2 = 1?

$$\begin{aligned} r &= s \\ r^2 &= rs \\ r^2 - s^2 &= rs - s^2 \\ (r + s)(r - s) &= s(r - s) \\ r + s &= s \\ s + s &= s \\ 2s &= s \\ 2 &= 1 \end{aligned}$$

6-3 Dividing Fractions

Objective To divide algebraic fractions.

To divide by a real number, you multiply by its reciprocal. You use the same rule to divide algebraic fractions.

Division Rule for Fractions

$$\frac{a}{b} \div \frac{c}{d} = \frac{a}{b} \cdot \frac{d}{c} \qquad \text{Example: } \frac{5}{8} \div \frac{2}{9} = \frac{5}{8} \cdot \frac{9}{2} = \frac{45}{16}$$

To divide by a fraction, you multiply by its reciprocal.

Example 1 Divide: $\frac{x}{2y} \div \frac{xy}{4}$

Solution

$$\frac{x}{2y} \div \frac{xy}{4} = \frac{x}{2y} \cdot \frac{4}{xy}$$ {Multiply by the reciprocal.

$$= \frac{\cancel{x}}{\cancel{2} \cdot y} \cdot \frac{\cancel{2} \cdot 2}{\cancel{x} \cdot y}$$ {Factor and simplify.

$$= \frac{2}{y^2} \quad \textit{Answer}$$

Example 2 Divide: **a.** $\frac{18}{x^2 - 25} \div \frac{24}{x + 5}$ **b.** $\frac{x^2 + 3x - 10}{2x + 6} \div \frac{x^2 - 4}{x^2 - x - 12}$

Solution

a. $$\frac{18}{x^2 - 25} \div \frac{24}{x + 5} = \frac{18}{x^2 - 25} \cdot \frac{x + 5}{24}$$

$$= \frac{\cancel{6} \cdot 3}{\cancel{(x + 5)}(x - 5)} \cdot \frac{\cancel{x + 5}}{\cancel{6} \cdot 4}$$

$$= \frac{3}{4(x - 5)} \quad \textit{Answer}$$

b. $$\frac{x^2 + 3x - 10}{2x + 6} \div \frac{x^2 - 4}{x^2 - x - 12} = \frac{x^2 + 3x - 10}{2x + 6} \cdot \frac{x^2 - x - 12}{x^2 - 4}$$

$$= \frac{(x + 5)\cancel{(x - 2)}}{2\cancel{(x + 3)}} \cdot \frac{\cancel{(x + 3)}(x - 4)}{(x + 2)\cancel{(x - 2)}}$$

$$= \frac{(x + 5)(x - 4)}{2(x + 2)} \quad \textit{Answer}$$

To simplify an expression that involves more than one operation, follow the order of operations on page 142, as shown in Example 3.

Example 3 Simplify $\left(\frac{2x}{y}\right)^3 \div \frac{x}{y^2} \cdot \frac{x}{4}$.

Solution

$$\left(\frac{2x}{y}\right)^3 \div \frac{x}{y^2} \cdot \frac{x}{4} = \frac{8x^3}{y^3} \cdot \frac{y^2}{x} \cdot \frac{x}{4}$$

$$= \frac{\cancel{4} \cdot 2 \cdot x^3}{y \cdot \cancel{y^2}} \cdot \frac{\cancel{y^2}}{\cancel{x}} \cdot \frac{\cancel{x}}{\cancel{4}}$$

$$= \frac{2x^3}{y} \quad \textit{Answer}$$

Oral Exercises

Simplify.

1. $\frac{5}{7} \div \frac{4}{7}$
2. $\frac{7}{2} \div \frac{4}{5}$
3. $-\frac{1}{4} \div \left(-\frac{2}{3}\right)$
4. $-\frac{4}{7} \div \frac{2}{5}$
5. $\frac{a}{b} \div \frac{c}{d}$
6. $\frac{x}{y} \div \frac{y}{x}$
7. $6a \div \frac{2}{a}$
8. $\frac{c}{2} \div 2c$
9. $\frac{y^2}{4} \div \frac{y^3}{16}$
10. $y \div \frac{1}{3y^2}$
11. $\frac{1}{2} \cdot \frac{1}{3} \div \frac{1}{4}$
12. $\frac{a}{b} \div \frac{c}{d} \cdot \frac{e}{f}$

Written Exercises

Divide. Give your answers in simplest form.

A

1. $\frac{6}{5} \div \frac{9}{10}$
2. $\frac{2}{3} \div \frac{5}{9}$
3. $\frac{a}{6} \div \frac{a}{3}$
4. $\frac{3x}{5} \div \frac{x}{15}$
5. $\frac{x}{y^2} \div \frac{x^2}{y}$
6. $\frac{3n^2}{5} \div \frac{9n}{20}$
7. $\frac{ab}{6} \div \frac{b}{a}$
8. $\frac{c}{2d} \div \frac{d}{8c}$
9. $\frac{3x^2}{4y} \div \frac{xy}{18}$
10. $\frac{2n}{3m^2} \div \frac{1}{12mn}$
11. $\frac{xy^2}{3} \div xy$
12. $\frac{9a^2}{2b} \div 6ab$
13. $1 \div \left(\frac{3x}{5}\right)^2$
14. $4 \div \left(\frac{2}{n}\right)^3$
15. $\frac{2 + 2b}{6} \div \frac{1 + b}{9}$
16. $\frac{6n - 2}{6n} \div \frac{3n - 1}{27}$
17. $\frac{x^2 - 1}{2} \div \frac{x + 1}{16}$
18. $\frac{m^2 - 9}{2m} \div \frac{m - 3}{10}$
19. $\frac{1}{x - y} \div \frac{1}{y - x}$
20. $\frac{1}{8 - 2a} \div \frac{5}{3a - 12}$

Divide. Give your answers in simplest form.

21. $\frac{2x + 2y}{x^2} \div \frac{x^2 - y^2}{4x}$

22. $\frac{3}{n^2 - 9} \div \frac{3n - 9}{n + 3}$

23. $\frac{w^2 - 4}{w^2 - 1} \div \frac{w^2 - w - 2}{w^2 + w - 2}$

24. $\frac{x^2 - x - 20}{5x - 25} \div \frac{x^2 + 4x - 5}{x^2 - 25}$

B **25.** $\frac{4x^2 - 25}{x^2 - 16} \div \frac{12x + 30}{2x^2 + 8x}$

26. $\frac{2x - y}{2y - x} \div \frac{4x^2 - y^2}{4y^2 - x^2}$

27. $\frac{c^4 - d^4}{5c - 5d} \div \frac{c^2 + d^2}{5}$

28. $\frac{8 - 2p^4}{3p^4} \div \frac{2 + p^2}{6p^2}$

29. $\frac{r^2 - t^2}{r^2 + t^2} \div (r + t)$

30. $\frac{3 - 3n}{n^2 + 2n - 3} \div (2n - 2)$

31. $\frac{6 + x - x^2}{x^2 - 13x + 42} \div \frac{2x^2 - 5x - 3}{2x^2 - 13x - 7}$

32. $\frac{2x^2 - 11x + 12}{27 - 18x} \div \frac{x^3 + 4x^2}{6x^3 - 96x}$

Simplify.

33. a. $\frac{3}{8} \cdot \left(\frac{2}{3} \div \frac{1}{4}\right)$

b. $\frac{3}{8} \cdot \frac{2}{3} \div \frac{1}{4}$

34. a. $\frac{1}{2} \div \frac{1}{5} \cdot \frac{3}{4}$

b. $\frac{1}{2} \div \left(\frac{1}{5} \cdot \frac{3}{4}\right)$

35. a. $\frac{r}{5} \div \frac{t}{r} \cdot \frac{5}{t^2}$

b. $\frac{x}{y^2} \cdot \frac{2}{x^2} \div \frac{x}{y}$

36. a. $\left(\frac{n}{2}\right)^2 \div \frac{n}{4} \cdot \frac{n}{3}$

b. $(2c)^3 \cdot \frac{3c}{d} \div \frac{6c^3}{d}$

37. $\frac{c - d}{c + 2d} \cdot \frac{2d + c}{d + c} \div \frac{d - c}{d + c}$

38. $\frac{r^2}{r^2 - s^2} \cdot \frac{r - s}{r + s} \div \left(\frac{r}{r + s}\right)^2$

39. $\frac{2q - 6}{3} \div \left(\frac{3 - q}{6}\right)^2$

40. $\left(\frac{2p - 7}{9}\right)^3 \div \left(\frac{7 - 2p}{3}\right)^4$

41. $\frac{1}{ab} \div \frac{1}{ab^2} \div \frac{1}{a^2b}$

42. $\frac{6y}{6y - 14} \div \frac{21}{9y - 21} \div \frac{y^2}{35}$

C **43.** $\frac{x^2 - 2x}{x^2 - 3x - 4} \cdot \frac{x^2 - 25}{x^2 - 4x - 5} \div \frac{x^2 + 5x}{5x^2 + 10x + 5}$

44. $\frac{b^2 + 6b - 7}{6b^2 - 7b - 20} \cdot \frac{2b^2 + b - 15}{b^2 + 2b - 3} \div \frac{b^2 + 5b - 14}{3b^2 - 2b - 8}$

45. $\frac{2d + 2c - cd - c^2}{2 + d} \div \frac{d^2 - c^2}{2 + c} \cdot \frac{c - d}{c^2 - 4}$

46. $\frac{x^2 + 2xy + y^2 - 16}{16x^4 - 16y^4} \div \frac{x + y - 4}{4x^2 + 4y^2} \cdot \frac{x + y}{x + y + 4}$

Mixed Review Exercises

Solve.

1. $4k = 5k - 13$ **2.** $4p + 20 = 48$ **3.** $(5b - 2) - (3 - 2b) = 9$

4. $\frac{1}{2}(6x - 2) = 5$ **5.** $2n^3 - 8n = 0$ **6.** $3x^2 + x = 4$

Give the prime factorization of each number.

7. 256 **8.** 156 **9.** 120 **10.** 1350

Self-Test 1

Simplify. Give any restrictions on the variable.

1. $\frac{15c - 5c^2}{3c - c^2}$ **2.** $\frac{4a^2 - 9}{6a^2 + 13a + 6}$ **Obj. 6-1, p. 247**

Simplify.

3. $\frac{42a}{6c^3} \cdot \frac{-4c}{3a^2b}$ **4.** $\left(\frac{2x}{3}\right)^3 \cdot \frac{27}{48x}$ **Obj. 6-2, p. 251**

5. $\frac{4x^2}{y} \div \frac{2xy}{7}$ **6.** $\frac{x^2 - 4}{x^2 - x - 6} \div \frac{x - 2}{2x}$ **Obj. 6-3, p. 255**

Check your answers with those at the back of the book.

Calculator Key-In

You can use a calculator to evaluate algebraic fractions for given values of their variables. First evaluate the denominator and store its value in the calculator's memory. (You may want to review the method for evaluating a polynomial given on page 203.) Then evaluate the numerator and divide by what is stored in memory (that is, the value of the denominator).

Evaluate each fraction for the given value of the variable.

1. $\frac{5n - 16}{2n}$; $n = 5$ **2.** $\frac{7a + 20}{3a}$; $a = 4$

3. $\frac{7x^2 + 4x + 12}{x}$; $x = 9$ **4.** $\frac{4m^2 + 11m - 60}{2m + 8}$; $m = -6$

5. $\frac{a^2 + 8a - 10}{2a}$; $a = 0.5$ **6.** $\frac{5y^2 - 22y + 30}{6y - 10}$; $y = -2$

Adding and Subtracting Fractions

6-4 Least Common Denominators

Objective To express two or more fractions with their least common denominator.

You have learned that you can write a fraction in simpler form by *dividing* its numerator and denominator by the same nonzero number.

$$\frac{bc}{bd} = \frac{c}{d} \quad (b \neq 0)$$

You can rewrite this rule as

$$\frac{c}{d} = \frac{bc}{bd} \quad (b \neq 0)$$

Using this form of the rule, you can write a fraction in a different form by *multiplying* its numerator and denominator by the same nonzero number.

Example 1 Complete: $\frac{3}{7} = \frac{?}{35}$

Solution $\frac{3}{7} = \frac{?}{35}$ ⟵ 7 is multiplied by 5 to get 35.

$\frac{3}{7} = \frac{3 \cdot 5}{7 \cdot 5} = \frac{15}{35}$ ⟵ Therefore, multiply 3 by 5 to get 15.

Example 2 Complete: $\frac{8}{3a} = \frac{?}{18a^2}$

Solution $\frac{8}{3a} = \frac{?}{18a^2}$ ⟵ $3a$ is multiplied by $6a$ to get $18a^2$.

$\frac{8}{3a} = \frac{8 \cdot 6a}{3a \cdot 6a} = \frac{48a}{18a^2}$ ⟵ Therefore, multiply 8 by $6a$ to get $48a$.

Example 3 Complete: $\frac{2}{x - 5} = \frac{?}{(x - 5)(x + 1)}$

Solution $\frac{2}{x - 5} = \frac{?}{(x - 5)(x + 1)}$ ⟵ $x - 5$ is multiplied by $x + 1$.

$\frac{2}{x - 5} = \frac{2(x + 1)}{(x - 5)(x + 1)} = \frac{2(x + 1)}{(x - 5)(x + 1)}$ ⟵ Therefore, multiply 2 by $x + 1$.

You can use the method shown in Examples 1, 2, and 3 to rewrite two or more fractions so that they have equal denominators. When you add and subtract fractions in the next lesson, you'll find that it may simplify your work if you use the *least common denominator* (LCD) of the fractions.

Finding the Least Common Denominator

1. Factor each denominator completely. Write any integral factor as a product of primes.
2. Find the product of the greatest power of each factor occurring in the denominators.

Example 4 Find the LCD of the fractions $\frac{3}{4}$, $\frac{11}{30}$, and $\frac{7}{45}$.

Solution

1. Factor each denominator into prime numbers.

   $4 = 2^2 \qquad 30 = 2 \cdot 3 \cdot 5 \qquad 45 = 3^2 \cdot 5$

2. Greatest power of 2: 2^2
   Greatest power of 3: 3^2
   Greatest power of 5: 5

   $2^2 \cdot 3^2 \cdot 5 = 180$

   $\therefore$ the LCD is 180. ***Answer***

Example 5 Find the LCD of $\frac{3}{6x - 30}$ and $\frac{8}{9x - 45}$.

Solution

1. Factor each denominator completely. Factor integers into primes.

   $6x - 30 = 6(x - 5) = 2 \cdot 3(x - 5)$
   $9x - 45 = 9(x - 5) = 3^2(x - 5)$

2. Form the product of the greatest power of each factor.

   $$2 \cdot 3^2(x - 5), \text{ or } 18(x - 5)$$

   $\therefore$ the LCD is $18(x - 5)$ ***Answer***

Example 6 Rewrite $\frac{9}{x^2 - 8x + 16}$ and $\frac{5}{x^2 - 7x + 12}$ with their LCD.

Solution

$x^2 - 8x + 16 = (x - 4)^2$
$x^2 - 7x + 12 = (x - 3)(x - 4)$ $\Big\{$First find the LCD of the fractions.

The LCD is $(x - 3)(x - 4)^2$.

(Solution continues on next page.)

Then rewrite each fraction using the LCD.

$$\frac{9}{x^2 - 8x + 16} = \frac{9}{(x-4)^2} = \frac{9(x-3)}{(x-4)^2(x-3)} = \frac{9(x-3)}{(x-3)(x-4)^2}$$

$$\frac{5}{x^2 - 7x + 12} = \frac{5}{(x-3)(x-4)} = \frac{5(x-4)}{(x-3)(x-4)(x-4)} = \frac{5(x-4)}{(x-3)(x-4)^2}$$

Oral Exercises

Complete.

1. $\frac{2}{5} = \frac{?}{10}$ **2.** $\frac{3}{8} = \frac{?}{40}$ **3.** $\frac{x}{6} = \frac{?}{30}$ **4.** $\frac{a}{3} = \frac{?}{21}$

5. $\frac{2x}{3} = \frac{?}{9}$ **6.** $\frac{a}{b} = \frac{?}{b^2}$ **7.** $\frac{5}{8n} = \frac{?}{16n^2}$ **8.** $\frac{5}{2-x} = \frac{?}{x-2}$

Find the LCD for each group of fractions.

9. $\frac{3}{2}, \frac{7}{10}$ **10.** $\frac{2}{5}, \frac{1}{9}$ **11.** $\frac{5}{18}, \frac{5}{12}$

12. $\frac{7}{90}, \frac{11}{60}$ **13.** $\frac{1}{2}, \frac{1}{3}, \frac{1}{4}$ **14.** $\frac{2}{5}, \frac{5}{6}, \frac{3}{10}$

15. $\frac{6}{5a}, \frac{11}{20a^2}$ **16.** $\frac{8}{x}, \frac{1}{xy}$ **17.** $\frac{12}{x^2}, \frac{10}{xy^2}$

18. $\frac{2}{3a-b}, \frac{5}{6a-2b}$ **19.** $\frac{3}{x^2+x}, \frac{9}{x+1}, \frac{4}{x}$ **20.** $\frac{4}{y^2-1}, \frac{3}{y+1}, \frac{7}{y-1}$

Written Exercises

Complete.

A **1.** $\frac{3}{4} = \frac{?}{28}$ **2.** $\frac{4}{9} = \frac{?}{27}$ **3.** $\frac{5x}{3} = \frac{?}{18}$ **4.** $\frac{2a}{17} = \frac{?}{51}$

5. $\frac{x-3}{4} = \frac{?}{12}$ **6.** $\frac{2n-5}{5} = \frac{?}{25}$ **7.** $\frac{6}{15x} = \frac{?}{30x^2}$ **8.** $\frac{3}{4a} = \frac{?}{16a^3}$

9. $\frac{x}{2y} = \frac{?}{10xy}$ **10.** $\frac{5m}{2n} = \frac{?}{8mn^2}$ **11.** $\frac{7}{n-3} = \frac{?}{(n-3)(n+2)}$

12. $\frac{4}{x+1} = \frac{?}{(x+1)(x-1)}$ **13.** $\frac{5}{2n-3} = \frac{?}{(2n-3)^2}$ **14.** $\frac{2y}{3y-2} = \frac{?}{(3y-2)^2}$

15. $\frac{4}{a-1} = \frac{?}{2a-2}$ **16.** $\frac{2}{3x-1} = \frac{?}{9x-3}$ **17.** $\frac{2}{x+1} = \frac{?}{x^2-1}$

18. $\frac{5}{n-3} = \frac{?}{n^2-9}$ **19.** $\frac{3}{4-y} = \frac{?}{4y-y^2}$ **20.** $\frac{2x}{3-x} = \frac{?}{3x-x^2}$

Find the LCD for each group of fractions.

21. $\frac{1}{6}, \frac{5}{9}$

22. $\frac{3}{8}, \frac{2}{5}$

23. $\frac{5}{2}, \frac{1}{6}, \frac{3}{5}$

24. $\frac{1}{3}, \frac{2}{9}, \frac{3}{4}$

25. $\frac{a + 3b}{8}, \frac{2a - b}{12}$

26. $\frac{n - 3}{20}, \frac{n + 4}{15}$

27. $\frac{1}{4t}, \frac{7}{16rt^2}$

28. $\frac{9}{x^2}, \frac{2}{xy}$

29. $\frac{6}{x + 1}, \frac{x}{x - 2}$

30. $\frac{b}{b + 5}, \frac{2b}{b - 5}$

31. $\frac{7}{m + 2}, \frac{m - 1}{m^2 - 4}$

32. $\frac{3a}{a - 1}, \frac{5}{a^2 - 3a + 2}$

Rewrite each group of fractions with their LCD.

B **33.** $\frac{1}{2xy}, \frac{3}{x^2}$

34. $\frac{1}{3mn^2}, \frac{2}{m^2n}$

35. $\frac{11}{6x^2y^2}, \frac{4}{5xy^3}$

36. $\frac{1}{12a^2b}, \frac{5}{18b^2}$

37. $\frac{5}{x - 3}, \frac{7}{4x - 12}$

38. $\frac{4}{3x - 6y}, \frac{1}{5x - 10y}$

39. $\frac{6}{x - 3}, \frac{4x}{(x - 3)^2}$

40. $\frac{9}{(2n + 1)^2}, \frac{-2n}{2n + 1}$

41. $\frac{3y}{2y - 4}, \frac{1}{y^2 - 4}$

42. $\frac{3}{c^2 - 6c}, \frac{5}{c^2 + 6c}$

43. $\frac{x}{x^2 - x - 6}, \frac{9}{x^2 - 9}$

44. $\frac{2}{a^2 + 3a - 10}, \frac{4a}{a^2 + 10a + 25}$

C **45.** The product of the first n positive integers, denoted by $n!$, is called ***n* factorial.**

a. Find 4!, 5!, and 6!. (*Hint:* $3! = 1 \cdot 2 \cdot 3 = 6$)

b. What is the LCD of the fractions $\frac{1}{4!}, \frac{1}{5!}$, and $\frac{1}{6!}$?

c. What is the LCD of the fractions $\frac{1}{n!}$ and $\frac{1}{(n + 1)!}$?

Mixed Review Exercises

Factor completely.

1. $4n - 8q + 16$

2. $3x^2 - 3$

3. $x^2 - 11x + 18$

4. $x^2 - 5x - 24$

5. $2x^2 - x - 3$

6. $x^2 + 16x + 39$

7. $x^2 + 3x - 28$

8. $x^2 + 22x + 121$

9. $n^2 - 9n$

Write an equation for each sentence.

10. Seven is 4 less than twice the number p.

11. The number n decreased by $\frac{1}{2}$ is $5\frac{1}{4}$.

12. Two thirds of the number k is 16.

Computer Key-In

The following program will find the LCD for two integral denominators.

```
10 PRINT "TO FIND THE LEAST"
20 PRINT "COMMON DENOMINATOR."
30 INPUT "ENTER TWO DENOMINATORS: "; D1, D2
40 LET M=1
50 LET Q=(D2*M)/D1
60 IF Q=INT(Q) THEN 90
70 LET M=M+1
80 GOTO 50
90 PRINT "LCD ("; D1; ", "; D2 ;") = ";
100 PRINT D2 ; " X "; M; " = "; D2*M
110 END
```

Exercises

Run this program for each pair of denominators.

1. D1 = 7, D2 = 21

2. D1 = 21, D2 = 7

3. D1 = 24, D2 = 36

4. D1 = 36, D2 = 24

5. D1 = 13, D2 = 15

6. D1 = 15, D2 = 13

7–12. In order to see how the program works, insert

```
55 PRINT D2*M; "/" ; D1; "=" ; (D2*M)/D1
```

and run the program again for the data in Exercises 1–6.

13. How does each RUN where you enter the smaller denominator first (Exercises 1, 3, and 5) compare with each RUN where you enter the smaller denominator last (Exercises 2, 4, and 6)? That is, which RUN requires fewer steps of computation?

14. Explain how to use the program above to find the least common denominator for the three denominators 27, 36, and 30.

Challenge

Two horses approach each other along the same country road, one walking at 5.5 km/h and the other at 4.5 km/h. When the horses are 10 km apart, a horse-fly leaves one horse and flies at 30 km/h to the other. No sooner does the fly reach that horse than it turns around (losing no time on the turn) and returns to the first horse. If the fly continues to fly back and forth between the approaching horses, how far has the fly flown when the horses meet?

6-5 Adding and Subtracting Fractions

Objective To add and subtract algebraic fractions.

In Lesson 2-9 you learned that

$$\frac{a+b}{c} = \frac{a}{c} + \frac{b}{c} \quad \text{and} \quad \frac{a-b}{c} = \frac{a}{c} - \frac{b}{c}.$$

You can rewrite these results to get the following rules.

Addition Rule for Fractions

$$\frac{a}{c} + \frac{b}{c} = \frac{a+b}{c}$$

Example: $\frac{2}{9} + \frac{5}{9} = \frac{2+5}{9} = \frac{7}{9}$

Subtraction Rule for Fractions

$$\frac{a}{c} - \frac{b}{c} = \frac{a-b}{c}$$

Example: $\frac{4}{5} - \frac{1}{5} = \frac{4-1}{5} = \frac{3}{5}$

To add or subtract fractions with the same denominator, you add or subtract their numerators and write the result over the common denominator.

To simplify an expression involving fractions, you write it as a single fraction in simplest form.

Example 1 Simplify: **a.** $\frac{3c}{16} + \frac{5c}{16}$ **b.** $\frac{5x+4}{10} - \frac{3x-8}{10}$

Solution **a.** $\frac{3c}{16} + \frac{5c}{16} = \frac{3c+5c}{16} = \frac{8c}{16}$

$$= \frac{\cancel{8} \cdot c}{\cancel{8} \cdot 2}$$

$$= \frac{c}{2} \quad \textbf{Answer}$$

b. $\frac{5x+4}{10} - \frac{3x-8}{10} = \frac{5x+4-(3x-8)}{10}$

$$= \frac{5x+4-3x+8}{10}$$

$$= \frac{2x+12}{10}$$

$$= \frac{\cancel{2}(x+6)}{\cancel{2} \cdot 5}$$

$$= \frac{x+6}{5} \quad \textbf{Answer}$$

Example 2 Simplify: **a.** $\dfrac{3}{x+4} + \dfrac{1}{x+4}$ **b.** $\dfrac{2}{x-3} + \dfrac{7}{3-x}$

Solution

a. $\dfrac{3}{x+4} + \dfrac{1}{x+4} = \dfrac{3+1}{x+4} = \dfrac{4}{x+4}$ ***Answer***

b. $\dfrac{2}{x-3} + \dfrac{7}{3-x} = \dfrac{2}{x-3} + \dfrac{7}{-(x-3)}$ $\left\{\begin{array}{l}\text{Since } 3 - x = -(x-3), \\ \text{the LCD is } x - 3.\end{array}\right.$

$= \dfrac{2}{x-3} - \dfrac{7}{x-3}$

$= \dfrac{2-7}{x-3}$

$= \dfrac{-5}{x-3}$, or $-\dfrac{5}{x-3}$ ***Answer***

Example 3 Simplify $\dfrac{a}{4} - \dfrac{5+12a}{18}$.

Solution Since the denominators are different, rewrite the fractions using their least common denominator, 36.

$\dfrac{a}{4} - \dfrac{5+12a}{18} = \dfrac{a \cdot 9}{4 \cdot 9} - \dfrac{(5+12a) \cdot 2}{18 \cdot 2}$

$= \dfrac{9a - 2(5+12a)}{36}$

$= \dfrac{9a - 10 - 24a}{36}$

$= \dfrac{-15a - 10}{36}$, or $-\dfrac{5(3a+2)}{36}$ ***Answer***

Example 4 Find the perimeter of the rectangle shown at the right.

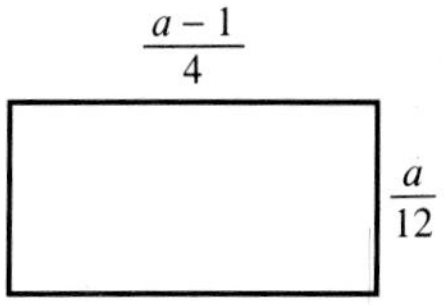

Solution

Perimeter of a rectangle $= (2 \times \text{length}) + (2 \times \text{width})$

$= 2 \cdot \dfrac{a-1}{4} + 2 \cdot \dfrac{a}{12}$

$= \dfrac{a-1}{2} + \dfrac{a}{6}$

$= \dfrac{3(a-1)}{6} + \dfrac{a}{6}$

$= \dfrac{3a - 3 + a}{6}$

$= \dfrac{4a-3}{6}$ ***Answer***

Example 5 Simplify $\frac{3}{2x} - \frac{1}{8x^2}$.

Solution

$$\frac{3}{2x} - \frac{1}{8x^2} = \frac{3 \cdot 4x}{2x \cdot 4x} - \frac{1}{8x^2}$$

$$= \frac{12x}{8x^2} - \frac{1}{8x^2} = \frac{12x - 1}{8x^2} \quad \textit{Answer}$$

Example 6 Simplify $\frac{a-3}{a^2-2a} - \frac{a-4}{a^2-4}$.

Solution

$$\frac{a-3}{a^2-2a} - \frac{a-4}{a^2-4} = \frac{a-3}{a(a-2)} - \frac{a-4}{(a-2)(a+2)}$$

$$= \frac{(a-3)(a+2)}{a(a-2)(a+2)} - \frac{a(a-4)}{a(a-2)(a+2)}$$

$$= \frac{a^2 - a - 6 - (a^2 - 4a)}{a(a-2)(a+2)}$$

$$= \frac{a^2 - a - 6 - a^2 + 4a}{a(a-2)(a+2)}$$

$$= \frac{3a - 6}{a(a-2)(a+2)}$$

$$= \frac{3\cancel{(a-2)}}{a\cancel{(a-2)}(a+2)}$$

$$= \frac{3}{a(a+2)} \quad \textit{Answer}$$

Oral Exercises

Simplify.

1. $\frac{4}{5} + \frac{3}{5}$

2. $\frac{7}{9} - \frac{4}{9}$

3. $\frac{x}{8} + \frac{3x}{8}$

4. $\frac{7a}{12} - \frac{a}{12}$

5. $\frac{4}{x} - \frac{1}{x}$

6. $\frac{7}{2x} + \frac{3}{2x}$

7. $\frac{3}{x+2} + \frac{x}{x+2}$

8. $\frac{n}{n+4} - \frac{5}{n+4}$

9. $\frac{x}{x+7} + \frac{7}{x+7}$

10. $\frac{2x}{2x-1} - \frac{1}{2x-1}$

11. $\frac{4}{a-b} + \frac{1}{b-a}$

12. $\frac{3}{x-5} - \frac{1}{5-x}$

13. $\frac{x}{2} + \frac{x}{8}$

14. $\frac{y}{4} - \frac{y}{6}$

15. $\frac{6}{a} + \frac{3}{2a}$

16. $\frac{5}{n} - \frac{4}{n^2}$

17. $\frac{6y}{5} - \frac{y+3}{5}$

18. $\frac{n^2}{4} - \frac{n^2-4}{4}$

19. $\frac{3c}{2} + \frac{c+1}{4}$

20. $\frac{x+1}{4} - \frac{x}{6}$

Written Exercises

Simplify.

A

1. $\frac{x}{12} + \frac{3x}{12}$
2. $\frac{7x}{15} - \frac{4x}{15}$
3. $\frac{2}{n} - \frac{6}{n}$
4. $\frac{5}{3x} + \frac{9}{3x}$
5. $\frac{2x}{3} - \frac{x - 1}{3}$
6. $\frac{3a}{10} - \frac{5a + 1}{10}$
7. $\frac{y - 3}{4} + \frac{3y + 5}{4}$
8. $\frac{x + 3}{4} - \frac{9x + 11}{4}$
9. $\frac{2}{x + 3} + \frac{5}{x + 3}$
10. $\frac{9}{y - 6} - \frac{3}{y - 6}$
11. $\frac{x}{x - 2} + \frac{1}{x - 2}$
12. $\frac{n}{n - 2} - \frac{3n - 1}{n - 2}$
13. $\frac{3}{x - 5} + \frac{2}{5 - x}$
14. $\frac{5}{4y - 1} - \frac{3}{1 - 4y}$
15. $\frac{5c}{c - d} + \frac{5d}{d - c}$
16. $\frac{6}{3 - 2x} - \frac{4x}{2x - 3}$
17. $\frac{2}{x} + \frac{3}{x^2}$
18. $\frac{8}{ab} - \frac{6}{ab^2}$
19. $\frac{1}{2x^2} - \frac{5}{4x}$
20. $\frac{4}{3xy} + \frac{3}{2x^2}$
21. $\frac{4}{5(x + 1)} + \frac{x}{x + 1}$
22. $\frac{2x}{x - 3} - \frac{3}{2(x - 3)}$
23. $\frac{1 + 2x}{4} + \frac{1 + 2x}{6}$
24. $\frac{5b + 2}{8} + \frac{3b - 4}{10}$
25. $\frac{3y - 2}{6} - \frac{y - 3}{9}$
26. $\frac{a - 6}{15} + \frac{4 - a}{10}$
27. $\frac{5n - 2}{12} - \frac{3(n - 3)}{8}$
28. $\frac{3(a - b)}{20} - \frac{5(a + b)}{12}$
29. $\frac{4x + 3}{3} - \frac{7x}{4} + \frac{x - 3}{6}$
30. $\frac{2m}{5} - \frac{m + 4}{4} + \frac{2 - m}{10}$

Find the perimeter of each figure.

B

31.

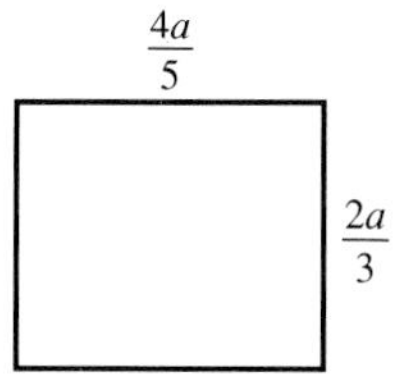

32.

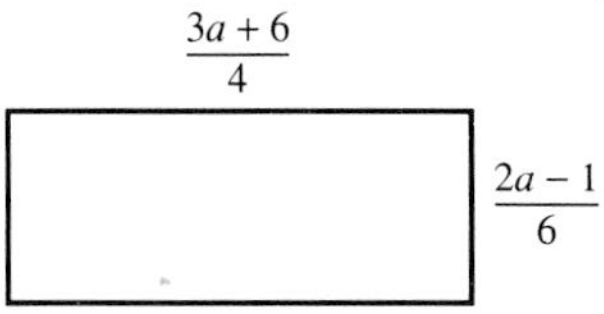

33.

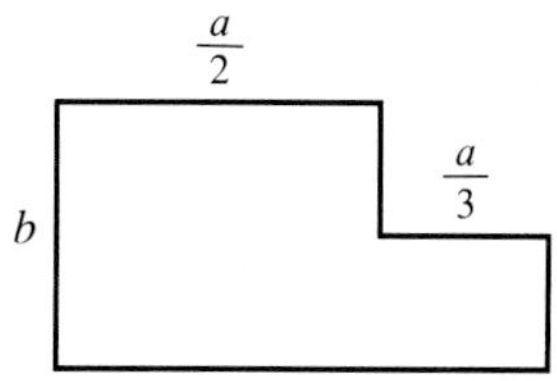

Find the perimeter of the figure.

34.

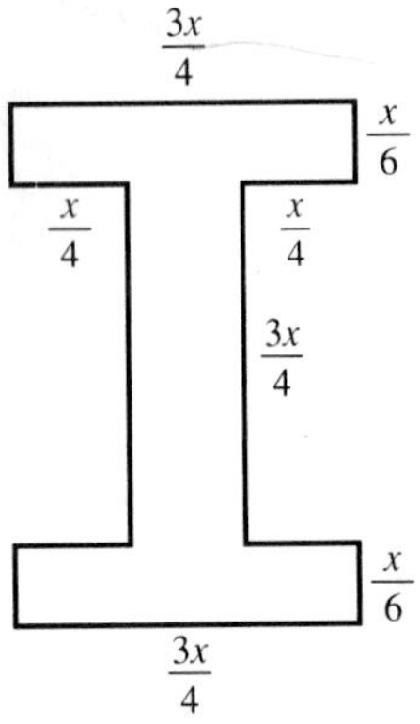

Simplify.

35. $\frac{1}{x-1}+\frac{1}{x}$

36. $\frac{3}{y-6}-\frac{1}{y}$

37. $\frac{2}{x-3}+\frac{4}{x+3}$

38. $\frac{3}{x+4}-\frac{4}{x-2}$

39. $\frac{a+1}{a}-\frac{a}{a+1}$

40. $\frac{x}{x+y}+\frac{y}{x-y}$

41. $\frac{x}{x^2-1}+\frac{4}{x+1}$

42. $\frac{2y}{y^2-25}-\frac{y}{y-5}$

43. $\frac{2m}{2m-1}+\frac{1}{1-2m}$

44. $\frac{3a}{a-2b}+\frac{6b}{2b-a}$

45. $\frac{d+2}{d^2-1}-\frac{3}{2d+2}$

46. $\frac{2n}{n^3-5n^2}+\frac{2}{n^2+5n}$

47. $\frac{a}{ab-b^2}+\frac{b}{ab-a^2}$

48. $\frac{x}{x-x^2}-\frac{1}{x-x^3}$

49. $\frac{n}{n^2+4n}-\frac{n}{(n+4)^2}$

50. $\frac{1}{a^2+4a+4}+\frac{1}{a^2-4}$

51. $\frac{x-11}{x^2-9}-\frac{x-7}{x^2-3x}$

52. $\frac{c-2}{c^2+c-2}-\frac{c+2}{c^2-3c+2}$

C 53. $\frac{x^2+1}{x^2-1}+\frac{1}{x+1}+\frac{1}{x-1}$

54. $\frac{x}{2x-1}+\frac{x-1}{2x+1}-\frac{2x}{4x^2-1}$

55. $\frac{a+2}{a^2+5a+6}-\frac{2+a}{4-a^2}+\frac{2-a}{a^2+a-6}$

56. $\frac{x-3}{2x+6}-\frac{x+3}{3x-9}-\frac{5x^2+27}{6x^2-54}$

57. $\frac{b+1}{(b-1)^2}+\frac{2-2b}{(b-1)^3}+\frac{1}{b-1}$

58. $\frac{4}{c^2-4cd}-\frac{1}{cd-4d^2}-\frac{2}{cd}$

Mixed Review Exercises

Simplify.

1. $-8^2 \cdot 3$

2. $(4 \cdot 6 - 13)^2$

3. $(-4x^2)^3$

4. $5y(y-4)+2y(y+11)$

5. $n^2(n+8)-(2n^2-6)n$

6. $(5x^2y)(3x^3y^2)(6y^3)$

7. $\left(\frac{12x^2y^2}{5}\right)\left(\frac{-10xy^2}{3}\right)$

8. $-\frac{1}{6}(-42x+12y)$

9. $(3n-5p+2)-(-n+6p+1)$

Self-Test 2

Vocabulary least common denominator (LCD) (p. 260)

Find the missing numerators.

1. $\dfrac{3n}{20c} = \dfrac{?}{50c^3}$ **2.** $\dfrac{5}{1 - a} = \dfrac{?}{a - a^2}$ **Obj. 6-4, p. 259**

Find the LCD for each group of fractions.

3. $\dfrac{3}{4x - 8}, \dfrac{-12}{x^2 - 4x + 4}$ **4.** $\dfrac{5}{a}, \dfrac{4}{b}, \dfrac{3}{a - b}$

Simplify.

5. $\dfrac{32c + 3}{6c} - \dfrac{2c + 9}{6c}$ **6.** $\dfrac{4}{3ab} + \dfrac{8}{7ab^2}$ **Obj. 6-5, p. 264**

7. $\dfrac{x}{x - y} + \dfrac{y}{y - x}$ **8.** $\dfrac{1}{n - 1} - \dfrac{n}{5(n - 1)}$

Check your answers with those at the back of the book.

Biographical Note / *Srinivasa Ramanujan*

Srinivasa Ramanujan (1887–1920) was a self-taught mathematician. At 16 he was awarded a scholarship to Government College in India for his proficiency in mathematics. However, he became so absorbed in his mathematical studies that he neglected to study English and lost his scholarship. He continued to study mathematics on his own, discovering over 100 theorems.

Friends convinced Ramanujan to write to G. H. Hardy, one of the leading number theorists at Cambridge University in England. Ramanujan sent about 120 of the theorems he had discovered. Convinced of Ramanujan's exceptional ability, Hardy brought him to England, where he was admitted to Trinity College. Hardy was not always sure how to teach a student with such profound mathematical insight but so little formal training; nevertheless Ramanujan progressed rapidly. While in England he did a great deal of work in number theory.

In 1918 Ramanujan was elected a fellow of the Royal Society and of Trinity College.

6-6 Mixed Expressions

Objective To write mixed expressions as fractions in simplest form.

A mixed number like $2\frac{3}{4}$ represents the sum of an integer and a fraction. You can write a mixed number as a single fraction in simplest form.

Example 1 Write $2\frac{3}{4}$ as a fraction in simplest form.

Solution
$$2\frac{3}{4} = 2 + \frac{3}{4}$$
$$= \frac{2}{1} + \frac{3}{4} \qquad \{\text{Write 2 as } \frac{2}{1}.$$
$$= \frac{8}{4} + \frac{3}{4} \qquad \{\text{LCD} = 4$$
$$= \frac{11}{4} \quad \textit{Answer}$$

The sum or difference of a polynomial and a fraction is called a **mixed expression.**

Example 2 Write each expression as a fraction in simplest form.

a. $c + \frac{5}{c}$ **b.** $5 - \frac{x-3}{x+2}$

Solution

a. $c + \frac{5}{c} = \frac{c}{1} + \frac{5}{c}$ {Write c as $\frac{c}{1}$.
$$= \frac{c^2}{c} + \frac{5}{c} \qquad \{\text{LCD} = c$$
$$= \frac{c^2 + 5}{c} \quad \textit{Answer}$$

b. $5 - \frac{x-3}{x+2} = \frac{5}{1} - \frac{x-3}{x+2}$ {Write 5 as $\frac{5}{1}$.
$$= \frac{5(x+2)}{x+2} - \frac{x-3}{x+2} \qquad \{\text{LCD} = x + 2$$
$$= \frac{5x + 10 - x + 3}{x+2}$$
$$= \frac{4x + 13}{x+2} \quad \textit{Answer}$$

Example 3 Write as a fraction in simplest form: $x + \frac{5x+2}{x-1} - \frac{7}{x-1}$

Solution
$$x + \frac{5x+2}{x-1} - \frac{7}{x-1} = \frac{x(x-1)}{x-1} + \frac{5x+2}{x-1} - \frac{7}{x-1}$$
$$= \frac{x^2 - x + 5x + 2 - 7}{x-1}$$
$$= \frac{x^2 + 4x - 5}{x-1}$$
$$= \frac{\cancel{(x-1)}(x+5)}{\cancel{x-1}}$$
$$= \frac{x+5}{1} = x + 5 \quad \textit{Answer}$$

Oral Exercises

State each expression as a fraction in simplest form.

1. $2\frac{1}{8}$ **2.** $5\frac{2}{3}$ **3.** $-5\frac{2}{9}$ **4.** $-4\frac{4}{7}$

5. $1 + \frac{1}{x}$ **6.** $2 + \frac{4}{a}$ **7.** $n - \frac{3}{n}$ **8.** $\frac{2}{y} + y$

9. $2 - \frac{a}{b}$ **10.** $3 - \frac{1}{x+1}$ **11.** $\frac{5}{x-1} - 2$ **12.** $\frac{b}{b+1} + 1$

13. $2 + \frac{3}{x+1}$ **14.** $4 - \frac{1}{y+3}$ **15.** $\frac{3n}{3n+2} + 2$ **16.** $1 - \frac{2a}{a+1}$

Written Exercises

Write each expression as a fraction in simplest form.

A

1. $4\frac{1}{5}$ **2.** $2\frac{3}{8}$ **3.** $8 + \frac{1}{x}$ **4.** $3 + \frac{7}{a}$

5. $3a - \frac{2}{a}$ **6.** $5x - \frac{3}{x}$ **7.** $\frac{a}{b} - 3$ **8.** $2 - \frac{c}{d}$

9. $5 - \frac{4}{x+2}$ **10.** $8 + \frac{y}{y-1}$ **11.** $\frac{x}{x+2} + 6$ **12.** $\frac{a+3}{a} - 3$

13. $4 + \frac{2n+1}{n+1}$ **14.** $2 - \frac{k-3}{k-4}$ **15.** $6x - \frac{x}{x+1}$ **16.** $4y + \frac{y}{y-5}$

17. $8n - \frac{2}{n+1}$ **18.** $5a + \frac{a-5}{2a+3}$ **19.** $2a^2 - \frac{a-1}{2a+5}$ **20.** $y^2 - \frac{3y+1}{y+2}$

Write each expression as a fraction in simplest form.

B **21.** $x - \frac{8}{x+1} - \frac{6x-2}{x+1}$

22. $y - \frac{4(y+1)}{y+2} - \frac{4}{y+2}$

23. $\frac{b-1}{b} - \frac{3}{b-2} + 1$

24. $\frac{x}{x+1} - \frac{x+1}{x} + 2$

25. $\frac{3a}{a+1} + \frac{2}{a-1} - 1$

26. $2 - \frac{x}{x-3} - \frac{1}{x+3}$

27. $a - 1 - \frac{a^2+a-5}{a+2}$

28. $2a + 3b - \frac{2a^2-b^2}{2a-3b}$

29. $3x - \frac{x^2}{2x+3} - 2$

30. $(x+4)\left(\frac{4}{x} - 1\right)$

31. $\left(a + \frac{2}{a}\right)\left(a - \frac{2}{a}\right)$

32. $\left(2x + \frac{3}{x}\right)\left(x - \frac{2}{x}\right)$

33. $\left(\frac{a+b}{a} - 1\right)\left(\frac{a}{b} + 1\right)$

34. $\left(y - \frac{2}{y+1}\right)\left(1 - \frac{1}{y+2}\right)$

35. $\left(\frac{m}{n} - \frac{n}{m}\right) \div \left(\frac{1}{m} + \frac{1}{n}\right)$

36. $\left(9 - \frac{1}{x^2}\right) \div (3x - 1)$

37. $\left(1 - \frac{2}{a}\right) \div \left(1 - \frac{4}{a^2}\right)$

38. $1 + \frac{2x}{2x-1} - \frac{8x^2}{4x^2-1}$

39. As an algebra exercise, Amy, Don, and Julie were asked to simplify

$$1 - \frac{8x}{x^2 - x} - \frac{2x}{1-x}.$$

Amy used a common denominator of $x(x-1)(1-x)$. Don used $x(x-1)$, and Julie used $x - 1$. Explain why any of these three denominators could be used.

40. It took Jan y hours to drive 200 km. If she had increased her speed by 10 km/h and driven for 2 h less, how far could she have gone? (*Hint:* Make a chart. Answer in terms of y.)

41. Ted bought n rolls of film for a total of \$40. He then sold all but 2 of them for \$1 more per roll than he paid. How much did he receive for the rolls of film that he sold?

Write each expression as a fraction in simplest form.

C **42.** $\left(1 - \frac{b^2+c^2-a^2}{2bc}\right) \div \left(1 - \frac{a^2+b^2-c^2}{2ab}\right)$

43. $\left(2 - \frac{n}{n+1} + \frac{n}{1-n}\right) \div \left(\frac{1}{n-1} - \frac{1}{n+1}\right)$

44. Find the values of A and B if $\frac{A}{x+2} + \frac{B}{x-2} = \frac{4}{x^2-4}$.

45. Find the values of C and D if $\frac{C}{x-2} + \frac{D}{x+1} = \frac{6x}{x^2-x-2}$.

46. Simplify: $\left(1 - \frac{1}{2}\right)\left(1 - \frac{1}{3}\right)\left(1 - \frac{1}{4}\right)\left(1 - \frac{1}{5}\right) \ldots \left(1 - \frac{1}{n}\right)$

Mixed Review Exercises

Simplify.

1. $\frac{5a + 5b}{5a + 10}$

2. $\frac{a^2 - 9a + 14}{49 - a^2}$

3. $\frac{5x^2}{3y^3} \div \frac{10xy}{9}$

4. $\frac{n^2 - 4}{2} \div \frac{n + 2}{8}$

5. $\frac{8}{y^5} \cdot \frac{y^7}{4}$

6. $(-4b^2)^2$

Find the least common denominator.

7. $\frac{1}{2xy}, \frac{3}{x^2}$

8. $\frac{5}{b^2}, \frac{2}{ab}$

9. $\frac{2}{x - 1}, \frac{3}{1 + x}, \frac{1}{1 - x^2}$

Computer Exercises

For students with some programming experience.

In the Computer Exercises on page 145, you wrote a BASIC program to evaluate $n!$ for a value of n entered with an INPUT statement.

1. Write a BASIC program to find the value of each of the following.

$$1 + \frac{1}{1!} + \frac{1}{2!}$$

$$1 + \frac{1}{1!} + \frac{1}{2!} + \frac{1}{3!}$$

$$1 + \frac{1}{1!} + \frac{1}{2!} + \frac{1}{3!} + \frac{1}{4!}$$

$$1 + \frac{1}{1!} + \frac{1}{2!} + \frac{1}{3!} + \frac{1}{4!} + \frac{1}{5!}$$

$$1 + \frac{1}{1!} + \frac{1}{2!} + \frac{1}{3!} + \frac{1}{4!} + \frac{1}{5!} + \frac{1}{6!}$$

$$1 + \frac{1}{1!} + \frac{1}{2!} + \frac{1}{3!} + \frac{1}{4!} + \frac{1}{5!} + \frac{1}{6!} + \frac{1}{7!}$$

2. Based upon your results from Exercise 1, what do you think happens to the sum $1 + \frac{1}{1!} + \frac{1}{2!} + \frac{1}{3!} + \cdots + \frac{1}{n!}$ as n becomes larger?

Challenge

Find at least three numbers that satisfy all three conditions:

(1) there is a remainder of 1 when the number is divided by 2;
(2) there is a remainder of 2 when the number is divided by 3;
(3) there is a remainder of 3 when the number is divided by 4.

6-7 Polynomial Long Division

Objective To divide polynomials.

Dividing polynomials is very much like dividing real numbers. Compare the polynomial division to the numerical long division shown below.

Long Division

Step 1

$$\begin{array}{r} 4 \\ 23\overline{)949} \\ \underline{-92} \\ 29 \end{array}$$

Step 2

$$\begin{array}{r} 41 \\ 23\overline{)949} \\ \underline{-92} \\ 29 \\ \underline{-23} \\ 6 \end{array}$$

Check:

$$949 \stackrel{?}{=} 41 \cdot 23 + 6$$
$$949 \stackrel{?}{=} 943 + 6$$
$$949 = 949 \quad \checkmark$$

$$\therefore \frac{949}{23} = 41\frac{6}{23}$$

Polynomial Division

Step 1

$$\begin{array}{rl} 2x & \\ 4x + 1\overline{)8x^2 + 6x + 3} & \\ \underline{8x^2 + 2x} & \leftarrow \text{Subtract.} \\ 4x + 3 & \end{array}$$

Step 2

$$\begin{array}{rl} 2x + 1 & \\ 4x + 1\overline{)8x^2 + 6x + 3} & \\ \underline{8x^2 + 2x} & \\ 4x + 3 & \\ \underline{4x + 1} & \leftarrow \text{Subtract.} \\ 2 & \end{array}$$

Check:

$$8x^2 + 6x + 3 \stackrel{?}{=} (2x + 1)(4x + 1) + 2$$
$$8x^2 + 6x + 3 \stackrel{?}{=} (8x^2 + 6x + 1) + 2$$
$$8x^2 + 6x + 3 = 8x^2 + 6x + 3 \quad \checkmark$$

$$\therefore \frac{8x^2 + 6x + 3}{4x + 1} = 2x + 1 + \frac{2}{4x + 1}$$

In both divisions above, the answer was written in the following form:

$$\frac{\text{Dividend}}{\text{Divisor}} = \text{Quotient} + \frac{\text{Remainder}}{\text{Divisor}}$$

The following formula was used to check both divisions:

$$\text{Dividend} = \text{Quotient} \times \text{Divisor} + \text{Remainder}$$

When you divide polynomials, always arrange the terms in each polynomial in order of decreasing degree of the variable.

Example 1 Divide: $\dfrac{34x - 16 + 15x^2}{5x - 2}$

Solution First rewrite $34x - 16 + 15x^2$ in order of decreasing degree of x as $15x^2 + 34x - 16$.

$$\begin{array}{r}
3x \;+\; 8 \\
5x - 2\overline{)15x^2 + 34x - 16} \\
\underline{15x^2 - 6x} \\
40x - 16 \\
\underline{40x - 16} \\
0
\end{array}$$

Check: $15x^2 + 34x - 16 \stackrel{?}{=} (3x + 8)(5x - 2) + 0$

$15x^2 + 34x - 16 = 15x^2 + 34x - 16 \quad \checkmark$

$\therefore \dfrac{15x^2 + 34x - 16}{5x - 2} = 3x + 8$ ***Answer***

In Example 1 the remainder is 0. Thus, both $3x + 8$ and $5x - 2$ are *factors* of $15x^2 + 34x - 16$.

Example 2 Divide $\dfrac{2a^3 + 5}{a - 3}$. Write the answer as a mixed expression.

Solution Using zero coefficients, insert missing terms in decreasing degree of a in $2a^3 - 5$. Then divide.

$$\begin{array}{r}
2a^2 + 6a \;+ 18 \\
a - 3\overline{)2a^3 + 0a^2 + 0a + 5} \\
\underline{2a^3 - 6a^2} \\
6a^2 + 0a \\
\underline{6a^2 - 18a} \\
18a + 5 \\
\underline{18a - 54} \\
59
\end{array}$$

Division ends when the remainder is either 0 or of lesser degree than the divisor.

Check: $2a^3 + 5 \stackrel{?}{=} (2a^2 + 6a + 18)(a - 3) + 59$

$2a^3 + 5 \stackrel{?}{=} 2a^3 + 6a^2 + 18a - 6a^2 - 18a - 54 + 59$

$2a^3 + 5 \stackrel{?}{=} 2a^3 + (6a^2 - 6a^2) + (18a - 18a) - 54 + 59$

$2a^3 + 5 = 2a^3 + 5 \quad \checkmark$

$\therefore \dfrac{2a^3 + 5}{a - 3} = 2a^2 + 6a + 18 + \dfrac{59}{a - 3}$ ***Answer***

Oral Exercises

How would you rewrite the terms of the divisor and the dividend before doing the long division? Do not divide.

1. $\frac{x^2 + 3x^3 + 5x - 2}{x + 1}$

2. $\frac{x^3 + 8}{x + 2}$

3. $\frac{2 - 2x^3 + x^2}{3 + 2x}$

Use the given information to find the dividend.

4. divisor = 5
quotient = 11
remainder = 2

5. divisor = $x + 1$
quotient = $x - 1$
remainder = 3

6. divisor = $x^2 + 1$
quotient = $2x$
remainder = $7x + 5$

7. When $x^3 - x - 6$ is divided by $x - 2$, the quotient is $x^2 + 2x + 3$ and the remainder is 0. This means that __?__ and __?__ are factors of __?__.

Written Exercises

Divide. Write the answer as a polynomial or a mixed expression.

A

1. $\frac{x^2 + 5x + 6}{x + 2}$

2. $\frac{x^2 - x - 12}{x - 4}$

3. $\frac{n^2 - 3n - 54}{n - 9}$

4. $\frac{n^2 - 11n - 26}{n + 2}$

5. $\frac{y^2 - 2y + 5}{y + 1}$

6. $\frac{a^2 - 3a + 7}{a - 2}$

7. $\frac{x^2 - 3x - 9}{x - 3}$

8. $\frac{z^2 - 8z - 12}{z + 4}$

9. $\frac{4 + n^2 - 2n}{n - 6}$

10. $\frac{s + s^2 - 8}{s + 4}$

11. $\frac{x^2 + 4}{x + 2}$

12. $\frac{y^2 - 9}{y + 9}$

13. $\frac{3x^2 + 10x - 9}{3x - 2}$

14. $\frac{2a^2 - 5a - 10}{2a + 1}$

15. $\frac{8 + 4x^2}{2x + 1}$

16. $\frac{9y^2 + 6}{3y - 1}$

17. $\frac{n^3 - 2n^2 + n + 2}{n + 2}$

18. $\frac{a^3 + 2a^2 + 3a + 4}{a - 1}$

19. $\frac{a^3 + 8}{a - 2}$

20. $\frac{n^3 - 1}{n - 1}$

21. $\frac{12x^3 - 2x^2 + x - 9}{3x + 1}$

22. $\frac{8n^3 - 6n^2 + 10n + 15}{4n + 1}$

B

23. $\frac{3x^4 - 4x^3 - x^2 - 16x - 12}{3x + 2}$

24. $\frac{6x^4 - x^3 - 11x^2 + 9x - 2}{2x - 1}$

25. $\frac{2n^4 - n^3 - 2n + 1}{2n - 1}$

26. $\frac{8y^4 + 10y^3 + 12y + 15}{4y + 5}$

27. $\frac{z^4 + 16}{z + 2}$

28. $\frac{b^4 + 84}{b - 3}$

29. $\frac{n^4 - n^3 + 3n^2 - 2n + 2}{n^2 + 2}$

30. $\frac{x^3 + 3x^2 - 4x - 12}{x^2 + 5x + 6}$

31. The volume of a rectangular solid is $12n^3 + 8n^2 - 3n - 2$. The length of the solid is $2n + 1$ and the width is $2n - 1$. Find the height.

32. Divide $a^4 + a^2 - 20$ by $a - 2$.
   a. Use long division.
   b. Factor $a^4 + a^2 - 20$ first. Then divide by $a - 2$.
   c. Show that your answers to parts (a) and (b) are the same.

33. Factor $2n^3 - 14n + 12$ completely given that $n + 3$ is a factor.

34. Factor $4x^3 - 12x^2 - 37x - 15$ completely given that $2x + 1$ is a factor.

C 35. Find the value of k if $x - 3$ is a factor of $4x^2 - 15x + k$.

36. Find the value of k if $2x - 1$ is a factor of $4x^3 - 6x^2 - 4x + k$.

37. Find the value of k if $y + 3$ is a factor of $y^3 + y^2 + ky + 3$.

38. When $4x^4 + x^3 - 7x^2 + 3x + k$ is divided by $x - 1$, the remainder is 5. Find the value of k.

Mixed Review Exercises

Simplify.

1. $\frac{x+4}{2} + \frac{2x-1}{2}$
2. $\frac{a^2}{a+3} - \frac{9}{a+3}$
3. $\frac{2}{y} + \frac{1}{3}$
4. $\frac{5c+1}{6c} + \frac{3}{2c}$
5. $\frac{2z+1}{6} - \frac{3z-5}{9}$
6. $\frac{x}{x^2-25} - \frac{1}{2x+10}$
7. $x + \frac{2}{x}$
8. $4 + \frac{n}{n+1}$
9. $y + 3 + \frac{2y-1}{y-2}$

Self-Test 3

Vocabulary mixed expression (p. 270)

Write each expression as a fraction in simplest form.

1. $3 - \frac{8}{y}$
2. $5n + \frac{1}{n}$
3. $a - \frac{a-1}{a+1}$

Obj. 6-6, p. 270

Divide. Write the answer as a polynomial or a mixed expression.

4. $\frac{-2 + 3y^2 + y}{y+1}$
5. $\frac{5b^3 + b^2 + b + 16}{b+2}$

Obj. 6-7, p. 274

Check your answers with those at the back of the book.

Extra / Complex Fractions

A complex fraction is a fraction whose numerator or denominator contains one or more fractions. To express a complex fraction as a simple fraction, use one of the methods below.

Method 1: Simplify the numerator and denominator. Express the fraction as a quotient using the ÷ sign. Multiply by the reciprocal of the divisor.

Method 2: Find the LCD of all the simple fractions. Multiply the numerator and the denominator of the complex fraction by the LCD.

Example Simplify $\dfrac{\frac{1}{a}+\frac{1}{b}}{\frac{b}{2a}-\frac{a}{2b}}$.

Solution *Method 1:*

$$\frac{\frac{1}{a}+\frac{1}{b}}{\frac{b}{2a}-\frac{a}{2b}} = \frac{\frac{b+a}{ab}}{\frac{b^2-a^2}{2ab}}$$

$$= \frac{b+a}{ab} \div \frac{b^2-a^2}{2ab}$$

$$= \frac{\cancel{b+a}}{\cancel{ab}} \cdot \frac{2\cancel{ab}}{\cancel{(b+a)}(b-a)}$$

$$= \frac{2}{b-a}$$

Method 2:

The LCD of all the simple fractions is $2ab$.

$$\frac{\frac{1}{a}+\frac{1}{b}}{\frac{b}{2a}-\frac{a}{2b}} = \frac{\left(\frac{1}{a}+\frac{1}{b}\right)2ab}{\left(\frac{b}{2a}-\frac{a}{2b}\right)2ab}$$

$$= \frac{2b+2a}{b^2-a^2}$$

$$= \frac{2\cancel{(b+a)}}{\cancel{(b+a)}(b-a)}$$

$$= \frac{2}{b-a}$$

Exercises

Simplify. Use either Method 1 or Method 2.

A **1.** $\dfrac{\frac{m}{8}}{\frac{5m}{8}}$ **2.** $\dfrac{\frac{3a}{4}}{\frac{15a}{12}}$ **3.** $\dfrac{\frac{u}{v^2}}{\frac{u}{v}}$ **4.** $\dfrac{\frac{6e}{3}}{7e}$

5. $\dfrac{\frac{1}{4}+\frac{1}{8}}{\frac{1}{4}-\frac{1}{8}}$ **6.** $\dfrac{\frac{1}{6}+\frac{1}{3}}{\frac{1}{2}+\frac{1}{5}}$ **7.** $\dfrac{\frac{5}{6}-\frac{5}{7}}{\frac{5}{6}+\frac{5}{7}}$ **8.** $\dfrac{\frac{3}{x}}{\frac{1}{x}-\frac{1}{3x}}$

9. $\dfrac{\frac{9c^2}{5d^4}}{\frac{3c^2}{10d^3}}$ **10.** $\dfrac{\frac{n^2-25}{n}}{n-5}$ **11.** $\dfrac{\frac{r}{s}+2}{1-\frac{r}{s}}$ **12.** $\dfrac{\frac{2w}{3}+2}{\frac{5w}{3}-\frac{15}{w}}$

Simplify.

B **13.** $\dfrac{z - \dfrac{5z}{z+5}}{z + \dfrac{5z}{z-5}}$

14. $\dfrac{1 - \dfrac{6}{s^2+2}}{\dfrac{4s+2}{s^2+2} + 1}$

15. $\dfrac{k + \dfrac{k-3}{k+1}}{k - \dfrac{2}{k+1}}$

16. $\dfrac{\dfrac{1}{c} - \dfrac{1}{3-3c}}{\dfrac{1}{1-c} - \dfrac{3}{c}}$

17. $\dfrac{\dfrac{e}{e-f} - \dfrac{f}{e+f}}{\dfrac{f}{e-f} + \dfrac{e}{e+f}}$

18. $\dfrac{1-2u}{1+\dfrac{1}{2u}} \div \dfrac{1+2u}{1-\dfrac{1}{2u}}$

19. $\dfrac{\dfrac{2}{z+1} - 2}{\dfrac{2-z}{z^2-1} - 2}$

20. $\dfrac{\dfrac{m-n}{m+n} + \dfrac{n}{m}}{\dfrac{m}{n} - \dfrac{m-n}{m+n}}$

21. If $x = \dfrac{y-1}{y+1}$ and $y = \dfrac{1}{1-z}$, express x in terms of z.

22. If $a = \dfrac{b-c}{1+bc}$ and $b = \dfrac{1}{z-1}$ and $c = \dfrac{1}{z+1}$, find a in terms of z.

23. Sam drives d km at 50 km/h and returns the same distance at 30 km/h. Show that the average speed is 37.5 km/h. (*Hint:* Average speed = total distance divided by total time.)

24. A cyclist travels 12 km on a level road at x km/h and then goes 9 km on a downhill road at $2x$ km/h. Find her average speed in terms of x. (See *Hint* for Exercise 23.)

25. If n items can be purchased for 50 cents, how many items can be purchased for 50 cents after the price per item is decreased by 10 cents?

26. If $a = \dfrac{1-c}{1+c}$ and $c = \dfrac{1+b}{1-b}$, show that $a + b = 0$.

Simplify.

27. $\left(\dfrac{w}{6} - \dfrac{6}{w}\right) \div \left(\dfrac{6}{w} - 4 + \dfrac{w}{2}\right)$

28. $\left(\dfrac{x}{4-x^2} + \dfrac{1}{x-2}\right) \div \left(1 - \dfrac{2}{2+x}\right)$

29. $\left(\dfrac{1}{n-n^2} - \dfrac{1}{n^2+n}\right) \div \left(\dfrac{1}{n^2+1} - \dfrac{1}{n^2-1}\right)$

30. $\left(\dfrac{c^2+d^2}{cd} - 2\right) \div \left(\dfrac{4c^2-4d^2}{2cd}\right)$

31. $\left(\dfrac{9e^2-5}{e-1} - \dfrac{1}{6}\right) \div \left(1 - \dfrac{e-9e^2}{e-1}\right)$

32. $\left(\dfrac{u^2+v^2}{u^2-v^2}\right) \div \left(\dfrac{u-v}{u+v} - \dfrac{u+v}{u-v}\right)$

C **33.** $\dfrac{r}{2}\left(\dfrac{r^2-s^2}{r^2s+rs^2}\right)\left(\dfrac{1}{r-s}\right)\left(\dfrac{1}{r+s}\right) \div \dfrac{1}{r+s}$

34. $\left(\dfrac{4x^2-y^2}{3xy}\right) \div \left(\dfrac{2x^2-y^2}{xy} + 1\right)$

35. $1 - \dfrac{1}{1 - \dfrac{1}{c-2}}$

36. $2 + \dfrac{1}{1 + \dfrac{2}{a + \dfrac{1}{a}}}$

Chapter Summary

1. A fraction can be simplified by factoring its numerator and its denominator and dividing each by their common factors.
2. The *rule of exponents for a power of a quotient* (page 252) is sometimes used when simplifying fractions.
3. The following rules are used with fractions.

Multiplication Rule	Division Rule
$\frac{a}{b} \cdot \frac{c}{d} = \frac{ac}{bd}$	$\frac{a}{b} \div \frac{c}{d} = \frac{a}{b} \cdot \frac{d}{c}$
Addition Rule	**Subtraction Rule**
$\frac{a}{c} + \frac{b}{c} = \frac{a+b}{c}$	$\frac{a}{c} - \frac{b}{c} = \frac{a-b}{c}$

4. When adding or subtracting fractions with different denominators, rewrite the fractions using their *least common denominator (LCD)*. Then apply the appropriate rule. (See page 264.)
5. The sum or difference of a polynomial and a fraction is called a *mixed expression*. A mixed expression can be expressed as a fraction in simplest form.
6. When dividing polynomials, arrange the terms of the *divisor and dividend* in order of decreasing degree of a variable. Wherever the dividend is missing a term, insert one with a zero coefficient.

Chapter Review

Give the letter of the correct answer.

1. Express $\frac{9x^2 - 9}{1 - x^2}$ in simplest form. **6-1**

a. 0 **b.** -9 **c.** $\frac{9(x-1)}{x+1}$ **d.** $\frac{9(x+1)(x-1)}{x^2+1}$

2. Express $\frac{15xy}{10x^2y - y^2x}$ in simplest form.

a. $\frac{3}{2x-y}$ **b.** $\frac{15}{10x-y}$ **c.** $\frac{5}{3x}$ **d.** $\frac{5}{2x-y}$

3. Express $\left(-\frac{2}{5}\right)^3\left(-\frac{25}{4}\right)$ in simplest form. **6-2**

a. $\frac{2}{5}$ **b.** $-\frac{5}{2}$ **c.** $-\frac{2}{5}$ **d.** $\frac{5}{2}$

4. Express $\frac{2ab}{15} \cdot \frac{25}{3ab^2}$ in simplest form.

a. $10b$ **b.** $\frac{10}{9b}$ **c.** $\frac{10}{9b^2}$ **d.** $\frac{10}{3b}$

5. Express $5ab^2 \div \frac{10a}{b}$ in simplest form. 6-3

a. $\frac{b}{2}$ **b.** $\frac{b^3}{2}$ **c.** $\frac{50a^2}{b}$ **d.** $2b^3$

6. Express $\frac{x^2 - 36}{6x + 36} \div (6 - x)$ in simplest form.

a. $-\frac{1}{6}$ **b.** 6 **c.** $\frac{1}{6}$ **d.** -6

7. Complete: $\frac{2}{x - 3} = \frac{?}{x^2 - 6x + 9}$ 6-4

a. 2 **b.** $2(x + 3)$ **c.** $2(9)$ **d.** $2(x - 3)$

8. Find the LCD for $\frac{4n}{9n - 6}$ and $\frac{2n}{15(3n - 2)^2}$.

a. $15(3n - 2)$ **b.** $45(3n - 2)^2$ **c.** $15(3n - 2)^2$ **d.** $5(3n - 2)$

9. Simplify $\frac{3x}{x - 2} + \frac{6}{2 - x}$. 6-5

a. $\frac{3x + 6}{x - 2}$ **b.** -3 **c.** 3 **d.** $\frac{3x - 6}{2 - x}$

10. Simplify $\frac{n - 9}{36} + \frac{n + 35}{108}$.

a. $\frac{n - 2}{27}$ **b.** $\frac{n + 4}{54}$ **c.** $2n + 8$ **d.** $\frac{n - 31}{54}$

11. Write $7 + \frac{x + 2}{x - 2}$ as a fraction in simplest form. 6-6

a. $\frac{6x}{x - 2}$ **b.** $\frac{4(x - 3)}{x - 2}$ **c.** $\frac{8x - 12}{x - 2}$ **d.** $\frac{-6x + 16}{x - 2}$

12. Simplify $y + 3 + \frac{1}{y - 3}$.

a. $\frac{y^2 - 8}{y - 3}$ **b.** $\frac{y + 4}{y - 3}$ **c.** $\frac{y^2 - 8}{y^2 - 9}$ **d.** $\frac{y^2 - 10}{y - 3}$

13. When $x^3 - 3x^2 + 3x + 4$ is divided by $x - 2$, what is the remainder? 6-7

a. 2 **b.** 4 **c.** 6 **d.** 8

14. Divide $\frac{27x^3 + 8}{3x - 2}$. Write the answer as a polynomial or a mixed expression.

a. $9x^2 + 4$ **b.** $9x^2 + 6x + 4 + \frac{16}{3x - 2}$

c. $9x^2 + 6x + 4$ **d.** $9x^2 - 6x + 4$

Chapter Test

Simplify. Give the restrictions on the variable.

1. $\frac{5x + 35}{x^2 - 49}$

2. $\frac{64 - n^2}{n^2 - 4n - 32}$ **6-1**

3. $\frac{3x^2 - 6x - 24}{3x^2 + 2x - 8}$

4. $\frac{15y^2 - 30y - 45}{5y^2 + 10y - 15}$

Express in simplest form.

5. $\left(-\frac{n^3}{7}\right)^2$

6. $\frac{(3b)^2}{5} \cdot \frac{b^3}{5}$

7. $\left(\frac{3a}{b}\right)^2 \cdot \frac{7ab}{54}$ **6-2**

8. $\frac{9}{11} \div \frac{11}{9}$

9. $\frac{4}{7} \div \frac{4}{7}$

10. $\frac{5x^2}{4y^2} \div 20xy$ **6-3**

11. $18 \div \left(\frac{3n}{2}\right)^3$

12. $\frac{6a + 36}{6a} \div \frac{a^2 - 36}{a^2}$

13. $\frac{y}{2x^3} \div \left(\frac{y}{2x}\right)^2$

Complete.

14. $\frac{7n}{16m} = \frac{?}{32m^2n}$

15. $\frac{3}{x + 5} = \frac{?}{x^2 - 25}$ **6-4**

Rewrite each group of fractions with their LCD.

16. $\frac{3}{8x}, \frac{5}{12y^2}, \frac{5}{6x^2y}$

17. $\frac{x - 4}{15}, \frac{x + 2}{10}$

Simplify.

18. $\frac{x}{x - 9} + \frac{1}{x - 9} - \frac{19 - x}{x - 9}$

19. $\frac{x - 1}{3} + \frac{3 - 2x}{6}$ **6-5**

20. $\frac{6n + 3}{n - 5} - \frac{4n + 9}{5 - n}$

21. $\frac{2}{y^2 - 2y} - \frac{3}{y^2 - y - 2}$

Write each expression as a fraction in simplest form.

22. $12 - \frac{n}{5}$

23. $2 + \frac{6}{y - 7}$ **6-6**

24. $4x - \frac{x + 1}{x + 1}$

25. $\frac{x}{x + 2} + \frac{2}{x - 2} + 1$

Divide. Write the answer as a polynomial or a mixed expression.

26. $\frac{45 - 13n + n^2}{n - 5}$

27. $\frac{2x^3 - x^2 - 5x - 2}{2x + 1}$ **6-7**

Cumulative Review *(Chapters 1–6)*

Perform the indicated operations. Express the answers in simplest form. Assume that no denominator is zero.

1. $0.3(-0.5)^2 + 0.7(-0.5)^2$

2. $\dfrac{45x^3y^2z^5}{-30(xyz)^2}$

3. $(4x^3yz^2)^3$

4. $(8a - 9b) + (5a + 6b)$

5. $(5x - 3)(4x + 3)$

6. $-5y(2y^3 - 7y^2 + 1)$

7. $(-13t + 6s) - (4t + 9s)$

8. $(-2b + 7c)^2$

9. $(4t^2s - 9)(4t^2s + 9)$

Evaluate if $a = -1$, $b = 1$, $c = -2$, and $d = 3$.

10. $\dfrac{a + b}{c} - cd$

11. $(a - b)^2 \div (c + d)^2$

12. $(a^2 + b^2) \div c^2 + d$

Factor completely. If the polynomial cannot be factored, write *prime*.

13. $6a^3b + 5a^3b^2 - 3a^2b^2$

14. $49x^2 + 14x + 1$

15. $8t^3 - 56t^2 + 98t$

16. $n^4 + 8n^3 + 15n^2$

17. $m^2 + 12m + 30$

18. $t^2 - 13t + 22$

19. $y^3 + 4y^2 - 32y$

20. $5c^2 + 8c - 4$

21. $4x^2 - 1 + 2x - 1$

Solve. If the equation is an identity or if it has no solution, write *identity* or *no solution*.

22. $6y - 3 = 27$

23. $\dfrac{1}{4}a - 3 = 9$

24. $6 - \dfrac{3}{4}d = -3$

25. $(n + 2)^2 = (n + 4)(n - 2)$

26. $10m^2 - m^3 = 25m$

27. $16c^2 - 9 = 0$

28. $t^2 + 12t + 15 = -5$

29. $x^2 - 6x = 7$

30. $6y^3 + 13y^2 - 5y = 0$

Perform the indicated operations. Express the answers in simplest form.

31. $\dfrac{x^2 + 5x + 4}{2x^2 + 3x + 1} \cdot \dfrac{1 + 2x}{x^2 - 16}$

32. $\dfrac{1}{4x - 8} + \dfrac{x}{x^2 - 3x + 2}$

33. $\dfrac{a^2 - b^2}{(cd)^3} \div \dfrac{a + b}{c^2d}$

34. $\dfrac{3}{a^2 + 6a + 9} - \dfrac{a + 1}{a^2 - 9}$

35. $\dfrac{10y^3 + 7y^2 - 52y + 44}{5y - 4}$

36. $x - \dfrac{x + 1}{x - 5}$

37. Jan worked 38 h last week. She worked four times as many 8-hour shifts as 6-hour shifts. How many 8-hour shifts did she work?

38. Jeremy has 24 quarters and half dollars. If he had twice as many half dollars and half as many quarters, he would have $2 more. How much money does he have?

39. It took Emily 25 min to ride her bicycle to the repair shop and 1 h 15 min to walk back home. If Emily can ride her bicycle 8 km/h faster than she can walk, how far is the repair shop from her house?

40. Find two numbers whose difference is 3 and whose squares total 65.

Maintaining Skills

Express each fraction as a decimal to the nearest hundredth.

Sample 1 $\frac{11}{13}$ **Solution** $13\overline{)11.000}$ with quotient 0.846; $\frac{11}{13} \approx 0.85$

1. $\frac{23}{25}$ **2.** $\frac{35}{20}$ **3.** $\frac{10}{4}$ **4.** $\frac{49}{50}$ **5.** $\frac{81}{25}$ **6.** $\frac{5}{3}$

7. $\frac{51}{30}$ **8.** $\frac{7}{8}$ **9.** $\frac{14}{6}$ **10.** $\frac{41}{24}$ **11.** $\frac{15}{22}$ **12.** $\frac{21}{17}$

Express each percent as a fraction in simplest form.

Sample 2 4.8% **Solution** $\frac{4.8}{100} = \frac{48}{1000} = \frac{6}{125}$

13. 62% **14.** 12% **15.** 85% **16.** 0.5% **17.** 0.03% **18.** 9.2%

Express each decimal as a percent.

Sample 3 0.73 **Solution** **(1)** $0.73 = \frac{73}{100} = 73\%$ **(2)** $0.73 = 73\%$

19. 0.91 **20.** 0.07 **21.** 0.8 **22.** 12 **23.** 0.032 **24.** 1.23

Find each number.

Sample 4 24% of 35 **Solution** $0.24 \times 35 = 8.4$

25. 32% of 85 **26.** 12% of 80 **27.** 0.2% of 40

28. 15.6% of 50 **29.** 130% of 40 **30.** 312% of 20

Find the value of each variable.

Sample 5 35% of $x = 7$ **Solution** $0.35x = 7;\ x = \frac{7}{0.35} = \frac{700}{35} = 20$

Sample 6 $n\%$ of $75 = 33$ **Solution** $\frac{n}{100} \cdot 75 = 33;\ \frac{n}{100} = \frac{33}{75};\ n = 44$

31. 30% of $z = 21$ **32.** 15% of $m = 6$ **33.** 5% of $y = 0.6$

34. 24% of $t = 108$ **35.** $p\%$ of $50 = 30$ **36.** $a\%$ of $45 = 18$

37. $t\%$ of $105 = 21$ **38.** $28 = n\%$ of 112 **39.** $51 = x\%$ of 150

Preparing for College Entrance Exams

Strategy for Success

In some problems, especially those involving length, width, area, perimeter, or relative position, it may help to draw a sketch. Use any available space in the test booklet. Be careful to make no assumptions in drawing the figure. Use only the information specifically given in the problem.

Decide which is the best of the choices given and write the corresponding letter on your answer sheet.

1. How many integral values of k are there for which $x^2 + kx + 24$ is factorable?
(A) 0 **(B)** 2 **(C)** 4 **(D)** 6 **(E)** 8

2. Which of the polynomials is prime?
(A) $35x^2 + 76x + 33$ **(B)** $4x^2 - 26x + 13$
(C) $121y^2 + 176$ **(D)** $21x^2 + 40x - 21$

3. What solutions does the equation $10x^3 - 7x^2 - 12x = 0$ have?
(A) $0, -\frac{5}{4}, \frac{2}{3}$ **(B)** $\frac{5}{4}, -\frac{2}{3}$ **(C)** $\frac{4}{5}, -\frac{3}{2}$ **(D)** $0, -\frac{4}{5}, \frac{3}{2}$

4. A rectangular garden 9 ft by 12 ft includes a uniform border of woodchips around a rectangular bed of flowers. If the flowers take up half the area of the garden, find the perimeter of the flower bed.
(A) 27 ft **(B)** 30 ft **(C)** 33 ft **(D)** 54 ft **(E)** 51 ft

5. Express $\frac{4t + v}{t + v} - \frac{4t^2 - v^2}{t^2 - v^2}$ in simplest form. Assume that no denominator is zero.
(A) $\frac{2tv}{t^2 - v^2}$ **(B)** $\frac{8tv + 2v^2}{v^2 - t^2}$ **(C)** $\frac{5tv}{t^2 - v^2}$ **(D)** $\frac{3tv}{v^2 - t^2}$

6. Which of the following are factors of $6x^3 + 29x^2 - 7x - 10$?
I. $3x - 1$ II. $2x + 2$ III. $x + 5$
(A) I only **(B)** II only **(C)** III only **(D)** I and III only
(E) II and III only

7. Express $\frac{(3n - 5)^4}{(2n + 1)^2} \div \frac{(5 - 3n)^4}{2n^2 + 7n + 3}$ in simplest form.
(A) $\frac{(3n - 5)^4(n + 3)}{(5 - 3n)^4(2n + 1)}$ **(B)** $\frac{n + 3}{2n + 1}$ **(C)** $\frac{2n + 1}{n + 3}$
(D) $\frac{(3n - 5)^4(2n + 1)}{(5 - 3n)^4(n + 3)}$ **(E)** $n + 3$

7 Applying Fractions

This ratio tells how many times the wheels spin for each turn of the pedals:

$$\frac{\textit{Teeth in front gear}}{\textit{Teeth in rear gear}}$$

Ratio and Proportion

7-1 Ratios

Objective To solve problems involving ratios.

The distance from Earth to the moon is about 240,000 mi. The distance from Jupiter to one of its moons, Io, is about 260,000 mi. One way to compare these distances is to write their quotient, or *ratio:*

$$\frac{240{,}000}{260{,}000} = \frac{12}{13}$$

The simplest form of this ratio is $\frac{12}{13}$.

The **ratio** of one number to another is the quotient when the first number is divided by the second number and the second number is not zero. You can write a ratio in three ways:

1. as a quotient using a division sign
2. as a fraction
3. as a ratio using a colon

Example 1 The ratio of 7 to 4 can be written as $7 \div 4$, $\frac{7}{4}$, or 7:4.

You may find it easier to simplify a ratio if you first rewrite it as a fraction.

Example 2 Write each ratio in simplest form.

a. 32:48 **b.** $25x:20x$ **c.** $\frac{9x^2y}{6xy^2}$

Solution **a.** First rewrite the ratio as a fraction. Then simplify.

$$32:48 = \frac{32}{48} = \frac{2}{3}, \text{ or } 2:3$$

b. First rewrite the ratio as a fraction. Then simplify.

$$25x:20x = \frac{25x}{20x} = \frac{5}{4}, \text{ or } 5:4$$

c. $\frac{9x^2y}{6xy^2} = \frac{3x}{2y}$

You can use ratios to compare two quantities *of the same kind,* such as two heights, two masses, or two time periods, as shown below.

To write the ratio of two quantities of the same kind:

1. First express the measures in the same unit.
2. Then write their ratio.

Example 3 Write each ratio in simplest form. **a.** 3 h:15 min **b.** 9 in.:5 ft

Solution **a.** $3\text{ h}:15\text{ min} = \frac{3\text{ h}}{15\text{ min}} = \frac{180\text{ min}}{15\text{ min}} = \frac{12}{1}$, or 12:1

b. $9\text{ in.}:5\text{ ft} = \frac{9\text{ in.}}{5\text{ ft}} = \frac{9\text{ in.}}{60\text{ in.}} = \frac{3}{20}$, or 3:20

Example 4 Write the ratio of the height of a tree 4 m tall to the height of a sapling 50 cm tall in simplest form.

Solution 1 1. Express both heights in *centimeters.*

tree: 4 m = 400 cm
sapling: 50 cm

2. The ratio is the quotient

$$\frac{400\text{ cm}}{50\text{ cm}} = \frac{400}{50} = \frac{8}{1}, \text{ or } 8:1.$$ ***Answer***

Solution 2 1. Express both heights in *meters.*

tree: 4 m
sapling: 50 cm = 0.5 m

2. The ratio is the quotient

$$\frac{4\text{ m}}{0.5\text{ m}} = \frac{4}{0.5} = \frac{8}{1}, \text{ or } 8:1.$$ ***Answer***

When you solve a word problem, you may need to express a ratio in a different form. If two numbers are in the ratio 3:5, you can use $3x$ and $5x$ to represent them, because $\frac{3x}{5x} = \frac{3}{5}$.

Example 5 Jenna plants alfalfa and wheat on 160 acres on her farm. If the ratio of acres of alfalfa to acres of wheat is 3:5, how many acres of each crop are planted?

Solution

Step 1 The problem asks for the number of acres of alfalfa and the number of acres of wheat.

Step 2 Let $3x$ = the number of acres of alfalfa. Let $5x$ = the number of acres of wheat.

Step 3 $3x + 5x = 160$

Step 4 $8x = 160$
$x = 20$

Number of acres of alfalfa = $3x = 3 \cdot 20 = 60$
Number of acres of wheat = $5x = 5 \cdot 20 = 100$

Step 5 *Check:* Are the numbers of acres of alfalfa to acres of wheat in the ratio 3:5?

$$\frac{60}{100} = \frac{3}{5} \quad \checkmark$$

∴ there are 60 acres of alfalfa and 100 acres of wheat. ***Answer***

If three numbers are in the ratio 3:7:11, then the ratio of the first to the second is 3:7 and the ratio of the second to the third is 7:11. Therefore, you can use $3x$, $7x$, and $11x$ to represent the numbers.

Example 6 The lengths of the sides of a triangle are in the ratio 3:4:5. The perimeter of the triangle is 24 in. Find the lengths of each side.

Solution Let the lengths of the sides be $3x$, $4x$, and $5x$.
Then $3x + 4x + 5x = 24$
$12x = 24$
$x = 2$

∴ the lengths of the sides are 6 in., 8 in., and 10 in. ***Answer***

Oral Exercises

State each ratio in simplest form.

1. 5:15 **2.** 18:24 **3.** 49:35 **4.** 9:48

5. $4x:6x$ **6.** $20t:35t$ **7.** $\frac{\pi(3r)^2}{\pi r^2}$ **8.** $\frac{(2s)^3}{s^3}$

9. 4 h to 20 min **10.** 5 m to 25 cm **11.** 1 kg to 50 g

12. Two numbers are in the ratio 10:3. Represent the numbers using a variable.

Written Exercises

Write each ratio in simplest form.

A **1.** 14:21 **2.** 55:33 **3.** $24x:8x$ **4.** $6y:9y$

5. $\frac{s^2}{(3s)^2}$ **6.** $\frac{27m^5}{45m^2}$ **7.** $\frac{64a^3b}{16ab^4}$ **8.** $\frac{72rs^5}{12r^2s^2}$

Write each ratio in simplest form.

9. 20 min:2 h **10.** 4 h:45 min **11.** 6 m:120 cm **12.** 18 cm:1.8 m

13. 6 wk:3 days **14.** 9 days:3 wk **15.** 5 km:450 cm **16.** 200 cm:8 km

17. 1 lb:7 oz **18.** 13 oz:2 lb **19.** 150 g:3 kg **20.** 2 kg:90 g

21. The ratio of school days to nonschool days in a year with 365 days and 180 days of school.

22. The student-teacher ratio in a school with 2592 students and 144 teachers.

23. The ratio of new airplanes to old airplanes in a fleet of 720 planes of which 240 are old.

24. The ratio of raisins to nuts in a mixture containing 3 c raisins and $1\frac{1}{4}$ c nuts.

25. **a.** The ratio of seniors taking a math course to seniors enrolled in a school if 105 out of 270 seniors enrolled are taking a math course.
b. The ratio of seniors taking a math course to seniors not taking a math course in the school in part (a).

26. **a.** The ratio of fiction books to nonfiction books in a library containing 1050 fiction books and 1890 nonfiction books.
b. The ratio of nonfiction to fiction books in the library in part (a).

Find the ratio of (a) the perimeters and (b) the areas of each pair of figures.

27. A rectangle with sides 8 cm and 6 cm and one with sides 10 cm and 9 cm.

28. A rectangle with length 12 cm and perimeter 30 cm and one with length 10 cm and perimeter 30 cm.

29. A square with sides 60 cm and one with sides 1 m.

30. A square with sides 24 in. and one with sides 2 yd.

Find the ratio of x to y determined by each equation. (*Hint:* In Exercises 37–45, collect x-terms on one side and y-terms on the other. Then factor.)

Sample $3x = 7y$

Solution $3x = 7y$ Divide both sides by 3.

$x = \frac{7}{3}y$ Divide both sides by y.

$\frac{x}{y} = \frac{7}{3}$, or 7:3 ***Answer***

B **31.** $8x = 5y$ **32.** $7x = 4y$ **33.** $14x = 12y$

34. $10x = 26y$ **35.** $kx = 2y$ **36.** $3x = ky$

37. $4(x + y) = 8(x - y)$ **38.** $8(2x - 3y) = 6(x + y)$ **39.** $ax + by = ay + bx$

40. $cx - ay = aby - bcx$ **41.** $ax - a^2y = bx - b^2y$ **42.** $r^2x = sy + ry + s^2x$

C **43.** $x^2 + 2y^2 = 2xy + y^2$ **44.** $2(x^2 + y^2) = 5xy$ **45.** $\frac{x}{y} + 1 = \frac{x + y}{x}$

Problems

Solve.

A **1.** Find two numbers in the ratio 4:5 whose sum is 45.

2. Find two numbers in the ratio 3:7 whose sum is 50.

3. Together there are 180 players and coaches in the town soccer league. If the player-coach ratio is 9:1, how many players are there?

4. In a survey of 700 voters, the ratio of men to women taking part was 17:18. How many women took part in the survey?

5. The perimeter of a rectangle is 96 cm. Find the dimensions of the rectangle if the ratio of the length to the width is 7:5.

6. The perimeter of a rectangle is 68 ft. Find the dimensions of the rectangle if the ratio of the length to the width is 9:8.

7. The lengths of the three sides of a triangle are in the ratio 3:5:6. The perimeter of the triangle is 21 cm. Find the length of each side of the triangle.

8. The measures of the angles of a triangle are in the ratio 1:2:3. Find the measures. (*Hint:* The sum of the measures of the angles of a triangle is 180°.)

9. Concrete can be made by mixing cement, sand, and gravel in the ratio 3:6:8. How much gravel is needed to make 850 m^3 of concrete?

10. A new alloy is made by mixing 8 parts of iron, 3 parts of zinc, and 1 part of tungsten. How much of each metal is needed to make 420 m^3 of the alloy?

B **11.** Ling drives her car 18 mi/h faster than Eddie rides his bike. The ratio of the distances they can travel in 1 h 30 min is 5:2. Find their rates of speed. (*Hint:* Make a rate-time-distance chart.)

12. The ratio of Aldo's cycling speed to José's cycling speed is 6:5. José leaves school at 3 P.M. and Aldo leaves at 3:10 P.M. By 3:30, Aldo is only 2 km behind José. How fast is each cycling? (*Hint:* Make a rate-time-distance chart.)

13. A collection of dimes and nickels is worth \$5.60. The ratio of the number of dimes to nickels is 3:2. Find the number of each type of coin. (*Hint:* Make a coin value chart.)

14. In a collection of nickels, dimes, and quarters worth \$6.90, the ratio of the number of nickels to dimes is 3:8. The ratio of the number of dimes to quarters is 4:5. Find the number of each type of coin. (*Hint:* Make a coin value chart.)

15. The Office Mart purchased a supply of mechanical pencils and ball-point pens. The ratio of pencils to pens was 5:9. The pencils cost \$1 each, the pens cost 25¢ each, and the total bill was \$290. How many pencils were purchased? (*Hint:* Make a number-price-cost chart.)

16. The Beach Hut purchased a supply of sunglasses and visors. The ratio of sunglasses to visors was 7:4. Each pair of sunglasses cost \$6.00, each visor cost \$4.50, and the total bill was \$720. How many pairs of sunglasses were purchased? (*Hint:* Make a number-price-cost chart.)

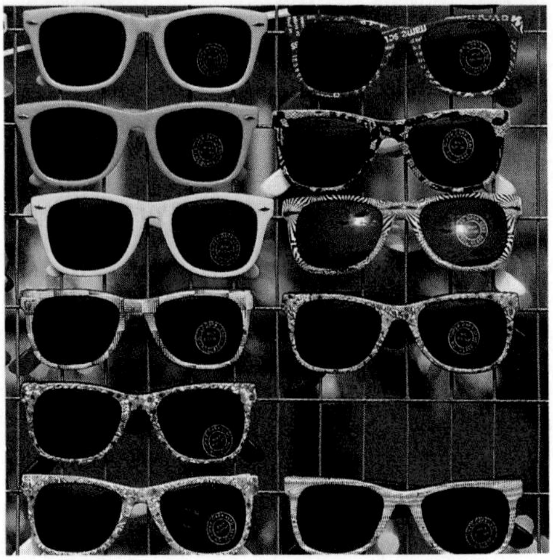

C 17. The ratio of the sum of two positive integers to their difference is 7:5. If the sum of the two numbers is at most 25, find all possible values for the pair of numbers.

18. There are 2820 cars in Farmington. The ratio of medium-size cars to compacts is 7:5, and the ratio of compacts to full-size cars is 8:9. How many full-size cars are there?

19. Find two numbers such that their sum, their difference, and their product have the ratio 3:2:5.

Mixed Review Exercises

Solve.

1. $4x = 24 - 2x$
2. $4(x - 7) + x = 2$
3. $5(4 + n) = 2(9 + 2n)$
4. $\frac{z + 4}{3} = -12$
5. $\frac{16 - 2y}{2} = 3y$
6. $-\frac{c}{9} = 4$
7. $(r + 2)(r - 5) = 0$
8. $3x^2 + 12x - 36 = 0$
9. $3(x - 2) = 4(x - 3)$

Simplify.

10. $\frac{3b + 1}{2c} + \frac{b}{c}$
11. $3x + \frac{5}{x}$
12. $\frac{3a}{4} + \frac{4a + 1}{4}$

Challenge

To conduct an experiment, a scientist needed exactly 2 L of a solution. After searching the storeroom, she could find only 5-liter containers and 8-liter containers. How could the scientist measure exactly 2 L of the solution?

7-2 Proportions

Objective To solve problems using proportions.

An equation that states that two ratios are equal is called a **proportion.** Usually you write a proportion in one of two ways:

$$2:3 = 4:6 \quad \text{or} \quad \frac{2}{3} = \frac{4}{6}$$

Both can be read as "2 is to 3 as 4 is to 6."

In the proportion $a:b = c:d$, a and d are called the **extremes,** and b and c are called the **means.** You can use the multiplication property of equality to show that in any proportion the product of the extremes equals the product of the means (see Oral Exercise 9). That is:

$$\text{If } \frac{a}{b} = \frac{c}{d}, \text{ then } ad = bc.$$

You can use this fact to solve proportions.

Example 1 Solve: **a.** $\frac{3}{x} = \frac{5}{4}$ **b.** $\frac{4}{21} = \frac{-2}{15a}$ **c.** $\frac{3}{n} = 8$

Solution

a.
$$3 \cdot 4 = x \cdot 5$$
$$12 = 5x$$
$$\frac{12}{5} = x$$

$\therefore$ the solution is $\frac{12}{5}$, or 2.4. ***Answer***

b.
$$4(15a) = 21(-2)$$
$$60a = -42$$
$$a = \frac{-42}{60}$$
$$a = \frac{-7}{10}$$

$\therefore$ the solution is $\frac{-7}{10}$, or -0.7. ***Answer***

c.
$$\frac{3}{n} = \frac{8}{1}$$
$$3 \cdot 1 = n \cdot 8$$
$$3 = 8n$$
$$\frac{3}{8} = n$$

$\therefore$ the solution is $\frac{3}{8}$, or 0.375. ***Answer***

Example 2 Solve: **a.** $\frac{x-4}{3} = \frac{2}{15}$ **b.** $\frac{2n-3}{5} = \frac{n+2}{6}$

Solution

a.
$$15(x-4) = 2 \cdot 3$$
$$15x - 60 = 6$$
$$15x = 66$$
$$x = \frac{66}{15}$$
$$x = \frac{22}{5}$$

$\therefore$ the solution is $\frac{22}{5}$, or 4.4. ***Answer***

b.
$$6(2n-3) = 5(n+2)$$
$$12n - 18 = 5n + 10$$
$$7n - 18 = 10$$
$$7n = 28$$
$$n = 4$$

$\therefore$ the solution is 4. ***Answer***

Example 3 With a 5 lb bag of flour the cooking class can make 120 date-nut muffins. How many muffins can they make with a 2 lb bag of flour?

Solution

Step 1 The problem asks for the number of muffins made with 2 lb of flour.

Step 2 Let $x =$ the number of muffins made with 2 lb of flour.

Step 3 5 lb makes 120 muffins.
2 lb makes x muffins. ← Note that since 2 lb is less than half of 5 lb, you can estimate that the answer is less than 60 muffins.

$$\frac{5}{120} = \frac{2}{x}$$

Step 4 Solve.

$$5x = 240$$
$$x = 48$$

Step 5 Since $48 < 60$, the answer is reasonable. The check is left to you.

$\therefore$ 48 muffins can be made with 2 lb of flour. ***Answer***

Example 4 About 8 gal of gas filled the tank after Greg drove 224 mi. How many miles can he expect to drive on a full tank of about 13 gal?

Solution

Step 1 The problem asks for the number of miles he can drive on 13 gal.

Step 2 Let $x =$ the number of miles.

Step 3 224 mi on 8 gal
x mi on 13 gal

$$\frac{224}{8} = \frac{x}{13}$$

Step 4 Solve.

$$224 \cdot 13 = 8x$$
$$2912 = 8x$$
$$364 = x$$

Step 5 The check is left to you. $\therefore$ He can drive 364 mi on a full tank. ***Answer***

Oral Exercises

For each proportion give the equation that states that the product of the extremes equals the product of the means. Do not solve.

1. $\frac{5}{3} = \frac{2}{x}$ **2.** $\frac{3}{y} = \frac{7}{8}$ **3.** $\frac{4x}{5} = \frac{9}{2}$ **4.** $\frac{-1}{n} = \frac{6}{-13}$

5. $\frac{y-3}{4} = \frac{5}{2}$ 6. $\frac{4}{9} = \frac{a-2}{3}$ 7. $\frac{3}{5+d} = \frac{3}{d}$ 8. $\frac{x+1}{8} = \frac{x-1}{7}$

9. If you multiply both sides of the proportion $\frac{a}{b} = \frac{c}{d}$ by bd, what equation do you get?

Written Exercises

Solve.

A

1. $\frac{x}{5} = \frac{3}{4}$
2. $\frac{y}{3} = \frac{4}{7}$
3. $\frac{8}{5} = \frac{4}{3x}$
4. $\frac{6n}{5} = \frac{3}{1}$
5. $\frac{3n}{7} = \frac{4}{5}$
6. $\frac{8}{5k} = \frac{2}{5}$
7. $\frac{7}{6} = \frac{2a}{3}$
8. $\frac{3}{8} = \frac{9}{4k}$
9. $\frac{18x}{13} = \frac{36}{39}$
10. $\frac{15x}{64} = \frac{45}{32}$
11. $\frac{24}{25} = \frac{6y}{7}$
12. $\frac{10}{21} = \frac{5}{16a}$
13. $\frac{15a}{36} = \frac{45}{12}$
14. $\frac{81}{64} = \frac{27n}{40}$
15. $\frac{12t}{-7} = \frac{30}{14}$
16. $\frac{-15}{25} = \frac{4x}{-15}$
17. $\frac{4}{x} = 5$
18. $\frac{5}{2n} = 3$
19. $-4 = \frac{8b}{5}$
20. $4 = \frac{20}{-9w}$
21. $\frac{x-5}{4} = \frac{3}{2}$
22. $\frac{y-3}{8} = \frac{3}{4}$
23. $2 = \frac{6+4n}{7}$
24. $5 = \frac{4-3y}{5}$
25. $\frac{5n-3}{4} = \frac{5n+3}{6}$
26. $\frac{6x-2}{7} = \frac{5x+7}{8}$
27. $\frac{3+2y}{8} = \frac{1-y}{5}$
28. $\frac{2n-9}{7} = \frac{3-n}{4}$
29. $\frac{4x+5}{5} = \frac{2x+7}{7}$
30. $\frac{4x+12}{8} = \frac{x+3}{2}$

B

31. $\frac{4(2x-11)}{13} = -(x+5)$
32. $2x - 2 = \frac{5(x-3)}{11}$
33. $\frac{3+2x}{3-2x} = -3$
34. $-5 = \frac{4-7x}{4+7x}$
35. $\frac{15}{x+7} = \frac{45}{x+21}$
36. $\frac{36}{2x-3} = \frac{72}{2x+3}$

Sample Find the ratio of x to y: $\frac{9x-8y}{2} = \frac{7x-6y}{3}$

Solution

$$3(9x - 8y) = 2(7x - 6y)$$
$$27x - 24y = 14x - 12y$$
$$13x = 12y$$
$$x = \frac{12}{13}y$$
$$\frac{x}{y} = \frac{12}{13}$$

Collect x-terms on one side and y-terms on the other.

Find the ratio of x to y. See the sample on page 295.

37. $\frac{3x + 2y}{5} = \frac{4x - 7y}{6}$

38. $\frac{9x + 3y}{4} = \frac{3x + 9y}{5}$

39. $\frac{x + y}{x - y} = \frac{3}{2}$

40. $\frac{4}{5} = \frac{x - y}{x + y}$

41. $\frac{d}{c} = \frac{x - y}{x + y}$

42. $\frac{x + y}{x - y} = \frac{a}{b}$

43. $\frac{cy}{d - c} = \frac{dx}{d^2 - c^2}$

44. $\frac{b - a}{ay} = \frac{b^2 - a^2}{bx}$

45. Solve $\frac{p}{t} = \frac{P}{T}$ for P. Then solve for T.

46. If $\frac{x}{y} = \frac{z}{w}$, which of the following must also be true? Explain.

(a) $\frac{x}{z} = \frac{y}{w}$ (b) $\frac{x}{w} = \frac{y}{z}$ (c) $\frac{w}{y} = \frac{z}{x}$

When the means of a proportion are equal, each mean is called the *mean proportional* between the two extremes. Find the positive mean proportional between the following extremes.

C **47.** 5 and 125 **48.** 4 and 64 **49.** $\frac{3}{2}$ and $\frac{2}{27}$ **50.** $\frac{4}{5}$ and $\frac{5}{16}$

Problems

Solve. Use estimation to check the reasonableness of your answer.

A **1.** Six oranges cost \$.99. How much do ten oranges cost?

2. Three cans of cat food cost \$.87. How much do eight cans cost?

3. Maria drove 111 mi in 3 h. About how far could she drive in 5 h?

4. A truck uses 8 L of gasoline to go 120 km. How much gasoline will it use to go 300 km?

5. A car that sold for \$11,800 has a sales tax of \$767. How much does a car cost if its sales tax is \$637?

6. A recipe for $2\frac{1}{2}$ dozen whole-wheat muffins requires 600 g of flour. How many muffins can be made with 900 g of flour?

7. At a fixed interest rate, an investment of \$4000 earns \$210. How much do you need to invest at the same rate to earn \$336?

8. An ad claims that in a recent poll, three out of four dentists recommended brushing with a certain brand of toothpaste. If there were 92 dentists polled, how many favored this brand?

B **9.** A consumer survey was taken in a town with 18,000 homes. Of the 360 homes surveyed, 48 had computers. On the basis of this survey, estimate the number of homes in the town that have computers.

10. A 25-acre field yields 550 bushels of wheat each year. How many more acres should be planted so that the yearly yield will be 660 bushels?

11. a. A photograph that measures 20 cm by 15 cm is enlarged so that its length becomes 28 cm. What does the width become?

b. Find these ratios: $\frac{\text{new length}}{\text{old length}}, \frac{\text{new perimeter}}{\text{old perimeter}}, \frac{\text{new area}}{\text{old area}}$

12. On a map, 1 cm represents 10 km, and Wyoming is a rectangle 44.5 cm by 59.1 cm. Find the area of Wyoming in km^2.

C **13.** Mahogany weighs 33.94 lb per ft^3, whereas pine weighs 23.45 lb per ft^3. Which weighs more: a mahogany board that is $5\frac{1}{2}$ in. by 1 in. by 6 ft or a pine board that is $3\frac{1}{2}$ in. by $1\frac{1}{2}$ in. by 8 ft?

Mixed Review Exercises

Find the LCD for each group of fractions.

1. $\frac{1}{4x^2y}, \frac{5}{xy}$ **2.** $\frac{w+4}{4}, \frac{2w-6}{12}$ **3.** $\frac{4}{9}, \frac{7}{12}$

4. $\frac{1}{6}, \frac{1}{5}, \frac{2}{12}$ **5.** $\frac{3}{x-3}, \frac{6}{x+3}$ **6.** $\frac{x}{3y}, \frac{x+1}{2}$

Simplify.

7. $\frac{6}{2(x-1)} + \frac{4}{x-1}$ **8.** $\frac{2r}{3} + \frac{r+1}{12}$ **9.** $\frac{3a}{10} + \frac{4a+1}{8}$

10. $|-7.4| - |2.6|$ **11.** $-|3.2 + 1.1|$ **12.** $9 + 3 \cdot 5$

Self-Test 1

Vocabulary ratio (p. 287) means (p. 293)
proportion (p. 293) extremes (p. 293)

Write each ratio in simplest form.

1. 48 min:1 h **2.** 2 m:5 cm **Obj. 7-1, p. 287**

3. The ratio of trucks to vans at a rental lot was 9:11. If the lot had a total of 80 trucks and vans, how many trucks were on the lot?

Solve.

4. $\frac{17}{25} = \frac{m}{150}$ **5.** $\frac{2}{3n} = 14$ **6.** $\frac{x-5}{3} = \frac{x+2}{4}$ **Obj. 7-2, p. 293**

Check your answers with those at the back of the book.

Fractional Equations

7-3 Equations with Fractional Coefficients

Objective To solve equations with fractional coefficients.

You can solve an equation with fractional coefficients by using the least common denominator of all the fractions in the equation. Multiply both sides of the equation by this LCD and then solve the resulting equation.

Example 1 Solve: **a.** $\frac{x}{7} + \frac{x}{3} = 10$ **b.** $\frac{3a}{5} - \frac{a}{2} = \frac{1}{20}$

Solution **a.** The LCD of the fractions is 21.

$$21\left(\frac{x}{7} + \frac{x}{3}\right) = 21(10)$$
$$21\left(\frac{x}{7}\right) + 21\left(\frac{x}{3}\right) = 210$$
$$3x + 7x = 210$$
$$10x = 210$$
$$x = 21$$

$\therefore$ the solution set is $\{21\}$. ***Answer***

b. The LCD of the fractions is 20.

$$20\left(\frac{3a}{5} - \frac{a}{2}\right) = 20\left(\frac{1}{20}\right)$$
$$20\left(\frac{3a}{5}\right) - 20\left(\frac{a}{2}\right) = 1$$
$$4(3a) - 10a = 1$$
$$12a - 10a = 1$$
$$2a = 1$$
$$a = \frac{1}{2}$$

$\therefore$ the solution set is $\left\{\frac{1}{2}\right\}$. ***Answer***

Example 2 Solve: **a.** $\frac{x}{3} - \frac{x+2}{5} = 2$ **b.** $2n + \frac{n}{3} = \frac{n}{4} + 5$

Solution **a.** The LCD of the fractions is 15.

$$15\left(\frac{x}{3} - \frac{x+2}{5}\right) = 15(2)$$
$$15\left(\frac{x}{3}\right) - 15\left(\frac{x+2}{5}\right) = 30$$
$$5x - 3(x+2) = 30$$
$$5x - 3x - 6 = 30$$
$$2x = 36$$
$$x = 18$$

$\therefore$ the solution set is $\{18\}$. ***Answer***

b. The LCD of the fractions is 12.

$$12\left(2n + \frac{n}{3}\right) = 12\left(\frac{n}{4} + 5\right)$$
$$12(2n) + 12\left(\frac{n}{3}\right) = 12\left(\frac{n}{4}\right) + 12(5)$$
$$24n + 4n = 3n + 60$$
$$28n = 3n + 60$$
$$25n = 60$$
$$n = \frac{60}{25} = \frac{12}{5}$$

$\therefore$ the solution set is $\left\{\frac{12}{5}\right\}$. ***Answer***

Oral Exercises

State the least common denominator of the fractions in each equation. Then state the equation with integral coefficients that results when both sides are multiplied by the LCD.

1. $\frac{x}{3} + \frac{x}{2} = 1$

2. $\frac{3y}{8} + \frac{y}{4} = 10$

3. $\frac{3n}{10} - \frac{n}{5} = \frac{1}{2}$

4. $\frac{2a}{3} - \frac{3a}{2} = -\frac{5}{6}$

5. $\frac{y}{2} - \frac{y+5}{3} = 0$

6. $\frac{x}{3} - \frac{x+2}{7} = 2$

7. $\frac{x+1}{6} + \frac{x+5}{4} = 1$

8. $\frac{y+3}{2} + \frac{y+2}{3} = -2$

9. $\frac{1}{6}(y+4) - \frac{1}{2}(y-2) = \frac{5}{12}$

Written Exercises

A **1–4.** Solve the equations in Oral Exercises 1–4.

Solve.

5. $\frac{w}{3} + \frac{w}{4} = \frac{7}{4}$

6. $\frac{3c}{10} + \frac{c}{5} = \frac{3}{2}$

7. $\frac{3a}{5} - \frac{a}{2} = \frac{1}{20}$

8. $\frac{7m}{8} - \frac{3m}{5} = \frac{11}{2}$

9. $\frac{x}{5} - \frac{x+4}{7} = 0$

10. $\frac{x}{6} - \frac{x+3}{5} = 1$

11. $\frac{4y+1}{3} - \frac{2y+1}{5} = \frac{3}{5}$

12. $\frac{x+2}{15} - \frac{x-3}{5} = \frac{2}{3}$

13. $3u - \frac{u}{5} = 1 + \frac{8u}{10}$

14. $x - \frac{3x}{2} = \frac{3x}{4} - \frac{5}{6}$

15. $0 = 3m - \frac{3m-7}{8}$

16. $0 = 2x + \frac{2x-8}{7}$

B **17.** $\frac{n+3}{3} - \frac{n}{4} = \frac{n-2}{5}$

18. $\frac{x+4}{3} - \frac{x}{7} = \frac{x+7}{5}$

Sample

$$\frac{1}{4}(n+2) - \frac{1}{6}(n-2) = \frac{3}{2}$$

$$12\left[\frac{1}{4}(n+2) - \frac{1}{6}(n-2)\right] = 12\left(\frac{3}{2}\right) \qquad \text{The LCD is 12.}$$

$$3(n+2) - 2(n-2) = 6(3)$$

$$3n + 6 - 2n + 4 = 18$$

$$n + 10 = 18$$

$$n = 8$$

$\therefore$ the solution set is $\{8\}$. ***Answer***

Solve. See the sample on page 299.

19. $\frac{1}{2}(x + 4) - \frac{2}{3}(x - 1) = 3$

20. $\frac{2}{3}(x - 1) - \frac{1}{5}(2x - 3) = 1$

21. $0 = \frac{1}{2}(n + 3) - \frac{1}{4}(n + 4)$

22. $1 = \frac{1}{3}(x + 6) - \frac{1}{6}(9 - x)$

23. $\frac{6b - 4}{3} - 2 = \frac{18 - 4b}{3} + b$

24. $h - \frac{h + 1}{4} = \frac{2h + 3}{5} + 1$

25. $\frac{1}{4}\left(y - \frac{1}{3}\right) - \frac{1}{6}(y - 3) = \frac{2}{3}$

26. $\frac{2}{3}(x - 1) - \frac{1}{5}(x - 2) = \frac{x + 2}{3}$

C 27. $\frac{1}{2}(2x + 5) - x = \frac{3}{4}\left(\frac{6x + 7}{3}\right)$

28. $\frac{2}{5}\left(x + \frac{3}{2}\right) - \frac{5}{6}(2x + 1) = -\frac{44}{15}$

29. $\frac{7}{3}(2x + 3) + \frac{3}{4}\left(\frac{x}{5} - \frac{15}{2}\right) = \frac{11}{8}$

30. $\frac{3}{4}(x - 2) - \frac{2}{3}\left(x - \frac{1}{2}\right) = \frac{x + 1}{2}$

Solve for x in terms of the other variable.

31. $\frac{x + 3a}{10} - \frac{x - a}{2} = \frac{x}{5}$

32. $\frac{x + k}{4} - \frac{2x - 3k}{2} = \frac{k + 5x}{6}$

33. $\frac{m^2 + 10m + 25}{2x} = m^2 + 5m$

34. $\frac{a^2 + 6a + 9}{x} = a^2 + 3a$

Problems

Solve.

A 1. One fourth of a number is two more than one fifth of the number. Find the number.

2. One eighth of a number is ten less than one third of the number. Find the number.

3. Two numbers are in the ratio 5:2. One half of their sum is $10\frac{1}{2}$. Find the numbers.

4. Three numbers are in the ratio 3:5:6. One fourth of their sum is $1\frac{1}{2}$ more than the smallest number. Find the numbers.

5. The width of a poster is $\frac{4}{5}$ of its length. It takes 36 ft of metal framing to frame the poster. Find the dimensions of the poster.

6. The length of a rectangular garden is $\frac{3}{2}$ of its width. It takes 50 m of edging to create a border. Find the dimensions of the garden.

7. Scott spent one ninth of his allowance on a newspaper, and two fifths of his allowance on a snack. If he has $2.20 left, how much does he get for an allowance?

8. Terri spent three eighths of her monthly salary on rent, and one third of her monthly salary on food. If she has $294 left, what is her monthly salary?

9. A rectangle is 9 cm longer than it is wide. The width is one seventh of the perimeter. Find the length and the width.

10. The lengths of the sides of a triangle are consecutive integers. Half of the perimeter is 14 more than the length of the longest side. Find the perimeter.

B 11. Erica hiked up a mountain trail at 3 km/h and returned at 4 km/h. The entire trip took 5 h 10 min, including the half hour she spent at the top. How long was the trail?

12. Consuela walked from her home to the fitness center at 6 km/h. She stayed 45 min, and then got a ride back at 48 km/h. If she returned 1.5 h after starting out, find the distance from home to the fitness center.

13. One eighth of Al's coins are quarters and the rest are nickels. If the total value of the coins is \$3.60, how many of each type of coin does he have?

14. Two thirds of a pile of coins are nickels, one fourth are dimes, and the rest are quarters. If the total value of the coins is \$4.75, how many of each type of coin are there?

C 15. Hannah bought some apples at the price of 3 apples for 95¢. She sold three fourths of them at 45¢ each, making a profit of 75¢. How many apples did Hannah keep?

16. Diophantus was a famous Greek mathematician who lived and worked in Alexandria, Egypt, probably in the third century A.D. After he died, so- one described his life in this puzzle:

He was a boy for $\frac{1}{6}$ of his life.
After $\frac{1}{12}$ more, he acquired a beard.
After another $\frac{1}{7}$, he married.
In the fifth year after his marriage his son was born.
The son lived half as many years as his father.
Diophantus died 4 years after his son.

How old was Diophantus when he died?

Mixed Review Exercises

Write each ratio in simplest form.

1. 8 days:4 wk
2. $15x:90x$
3. 16:12
4. $\frac{16mn^2}{40mn}$
5. $\frac{48x^2y}{36x^3y^2}$
6. $\frac{21a^4}{35ab^2}$

Solve.

7. $\frac{7}{2n} = \frac{3}{6}$
8. $\frac{x+2}{7} = \frac{5}{3}$
9. $\frac{2a+3}{5} = \frac{a+8}{4}$
10. $3x - 2 = 14$
11. $|x| = 5$
12. $8x + 3 = 9x + 1$

Application / *Units of Measurement in Problem Solving*

A *rate* is a ratio that compares the amounts of two different kinds of measurements. For example, suppose a greenhouse is selling four begonia plants for \$1. Then the rate $\frac{4 \text{ plants}}{\$1}$ tells how many plants you get for a certain amount of money. The rate $\frac{\$1}{4 \text{ plants}}$ tells how much you pay for a certain number of plants. The *unit price* is the price of one unit. In this case the unit price is $\frac{\$.25}{1 \text{ plant}}$, which can be written \$.25/plant and read as *\$.25 per plant.*

When you solve a problem involving rates, you can think of multiplying and dividing the units just as you do the numbers to determine the appropriate unit for your answer to the problem.

Example 1 Rosario spent \$8.28 for two bags of dog biscuits. If there are 36 biscuits per bag, find the unit cost per biscuit.

Solution To find the unit cost per biscuit, you divide the total cost by the total number of biscuits.

Total cost: \$8.28

Total number of biscuits: $2 \cancel{\text{bags}} \times \frac{36 \text{ biscuits}}{1 \cancel{\text{bag}}} = 72 \text{ biscuits}$

Unit cost: $\frac{\$8.28}{72 \text{ biscuits}} = \frac{\$.115}{1 \text{ biscuit}}$, or 11.5¢/biscuit. ***Answer***

Example 2 What does it cost to carpet a room 10 ft by 12 ft at \$12 per square foot?

Solution Area: $10 \text{ ft} \times 12 \text{ ft} = 120 \text{ ft}^2$

Cost: $\frac{\$12}{1 \cancel{\text{ft}^2}} \times 120 \cancel{\text{ft}^2} = \$1440$ ***Answer***

Carrying units throughout your computation is also helpful when you want to express a measurement in terms of a larger or smaller unit.

Example 3 An interplanetary probe travels 40,200 km/h. Express this speed in meters per second.

Solution Set up units to "cancel out." Notice that to divide by 60 min/h you multiply by $\frac{1 \text{ h}}{60 \text{ min}}$.

$$\frac{40{,}200 \cancel{\text{km}}}{1 \cancel{\text{h}}} \cdot \frac{1000 \text{ m}}{1 \cancel{\text{km}}} \cdot \frac{1 \cancel{\text{h}}}{60 \cancel{\text{min}}} \cdot \frac{1 \cancel{\text{min}}}{60 \text{ s}} \approx 11{,}167 \text{ m/s}$$ ***Answer***

Exercises

Write the appropriate unit.

1. $\dfrac{39¢}{1 \text{ dozen}} \times 2 \text{ dozen} = 78$ __?__

2. $\dfrac{45 \text{ mi}}{1 \text{ h}} \cdot 2 \text{ h} = 90$ __?__

3. $9 \text{ ft} \times 12 \text{ ft} = 108$ __?__

4. $\dfrac{60 \text{ mi}}{1 \text{ h}} \div \dfrac{60 \text{ min}}{1 \text{ h}} = 1$ __?__

5. $\dfrac{55 \text{ mi}}{1 \text{ h}} \times \dfrac{5280 \text{ ft}}{1 \text{ mi}} \div \dfrac{60 \text{ min}}{1 \text{ h}} = 4840$ __?__

6. The gas tank in an XR-5 car holds up to 15 gal.
   a. If the car averages 36 mi/gal in highway driving, how far can the car be driven on one tank of gas?
   b. If the car is driven at an average speed of 48 mi/h, how many hours can the car be driven on one tank of gas?

7. The Truongs bought a new refrigerator that uses 102 kW · h (kilowatt-hours) of electricity per month. If electricity cost $0.125 per kW · h, find the operating cost of the refrigerator for one day in June.

8. This week the Super-Buy store is selling two 2.5-ounce packages of sliced salami for $1. What is the cost per pound?

Historical Note / *Broken Numbers*

The word "fraction" comes from the Latin verb *frangere,* meaning "to break." A fraction is thus a "broken number," or a part of a number.

The Babylonians used special symbols to represent commonly used fractions such as $\frac{1}{2}$, $\frac{1}{3}$, and $\frac{2}{3}$. However, fractions having denominators of base sixty, called sexagesimals, were used in astronomical calculations and in mathematical texts. Because the denominators of the fractions were restricted to a certain base, a positional notation was used to represent these fractions. Thus, « intended as a fraction meant $\frac{20}{60}$. The many integer divisors of sixty made it easier to simplify fractional computations. Sexagesimal fractions were also used in ancient Greece and then in Europe until the sixteenth century, when they were replaced by decimals.

Like the Babylonians, the Egyptians had special symbols for commonly used fractions. In hieroglyphics the symbol ⬭ was placed over the symbol for a whole number to express its reciprocal. This symbol was replaced by a dot in cursive writing and was later adopted by the English, who wrote $\dot{2}$ for $\frac{1}{2}$.

The Egyptians attempted to avoid computational difficulties by expressing fractions as sums of unit fractions, that is, fractions having a numerator of one. There were numerous rules for forming unit fractions. For example, $\frac{2}{43}$ might have been expressed as

$$\frac{1}{24} + \frac{1}{258} + \frac{1}{1032} \text{ or } \frac{1}{30} + \frac{1}{86} + \frac{1}{645}.$$

7-4 Fractional Equations

Objective To solve fractional equations.

An equation with a variable in the denominator of one or more terms is called a **fractional equation.** To solve a fractional equation you can multiply both sides of the equation by the LCD. You can also solve a fractional equation as you would solve a proportion when the equation consists of one fraction equal to another (see Solution 2 of Example 2).

Example 1 Solve: $\frac{3}{x} - \frac{1}{4} = \frac{1}{12}$

Solution

$$12x\left(\frac{3}{x} - \frac{1}{4}\right) = 12x\left(\frac{1}{12}\right)$$

$$12x\left(\frac{3}{x}\right) - 12x\left(\frac{1}{4}\right) = x$$

$$36 - 3x = x$$

$$36 = 4x$$

$$9 = x$$

Multiply both sides of the equation by the LCD, $12x$. (Notice that x cannot equal 0 because $\frac{3}{0}$ has no meaning.)

Check:

$$\frac{3}{9} - \frac{1}{4} \stackrel{?}{=} \frac{1}{12}$$

$$\frac{1}{3} - \frac{1}{4} \stackrel{?}{=} \frac{1}{12}$$

$$\frac{4}{12} - \frac{3}{12} \stackrel{?}{=} \frac{1}{12}$$

$$\frac{1}{12} = \frac{1}{12} \quad \checkmark$$

$\therefore$ the solution set is $\{9\}$. ***Answer***

Example 2 Solve: $\frac{2 - x}{3 - x} = \frac{4}{9}$

Solution 1 Multiply both sides by the LCD, $9(3 - x)$. (Notice that x cannot equal 3.)

$$9(3 - x)\left(\frac{2 - x}{3 - x}\right) = 9(3 - x)\left(\frac{4}{9}\right)$$

$$9(2 - x) = (3 - x)(4)$$

$$18 - 9x = 12 - 4x$$

$$6 = 5x$$

$$\frac{6}{5} = x$$

$\therefore$ the solution set is $\left\{\frac{6}{5}\right\}$. ***Answer***

Solution 2 Solve as a proportion.

$$\frac{2 - x}{3 - x} = \frac{4}{9}$$

$$9(2 - x) = 4(3 - x)$$

$$18 - 9x = 12 - 4x$$

$$6 = 5x$$

$$\frac{6}{5} = x$$

$\therefore$ the solution set is $\left\{\frac{6}{5}\right\}$. ***Answer***

Example 3 Solve: $\dfrac{2}{b^2 - b} - \dfrac{2}{b - 1} = 1.$

Solution

$$b(b-1)\left(\frac{2}{b(b-1)} - \frac{2}{b-1}\right) = b(b-1)(1)$$
$$b(b-1)\left(\frac{2}{b(b-1)}\right) - b(b-1)\left(\frac{2}{b-1}\right) = b(b-1)$$

Multiply both sides of the equation by the LCD, $b(b-1)$. (Notice that b cannot equal 0 or 1.)

$$2 - 2b = b^2 - b$$
$$0 = b^2 + b - 2$$
$$0 = (b-1)(b+2)$$
$$b = 1 \text{ or } b = -2$$

Check: Since b cannot equal 1 in the original equation, you need to check only -2 in the equation.

$$\frac{2}{(-2)^2 - (-2)} - \frac{2}{-2-1} \stackrel{?}{=} 1$$
$$\frac{2}{6} - \frac{2}{-3} \stackrel{?}{=} 1$$
$$\frac{1}{3} + \frac{2}{3} = 1 \quad \checkmark$$

$\therefore$ the solution set is $\{-2\}$. ***Answer***

Caution: Multiplying both sides of an equation by a variable expression sometimes results in an equation that has an extra root. You must check each root of the transformed equation to see if it satisfies the original equation.

Oral Exercises

State the LCD of the fractions in each equation. Then state the equation that results when both sides are multiplied by the LCD.

1. $\frac{1}{4} + \frac{2}{x} = \frac{3}{4}$

2. $\frac{3}{x} + \frac{1}{2} = 1$

3. $\frac{4}{y} - \frac{1}{4} = \frac{1}{12}$

4. $\frac{9}{2a} - \frac{5}{a} = -\frac{1}{4}$

5. $\frac{n}{n-2} = \frac{6}{5}$

6. $\frac{1+b}{1-b} = \frac{4}{3}$

Written Exercises

A **1–6.** Solve the equations in Oral Exercises 1–6.

Solve and check. If the equation has no solution, write *No solution*.

7. $\frac{6}{n} - \frac{1}{4} = \frac{8}{2n}$

8. $\frac{3}{2a} - \frac{5}{6} = \frac{2}{3a}$

9. $\frac{6-x}{4-x} = \frac{3}{5}$

10. $\frac{5-m}{7-m} = \frac{2}{3}$

11. $1 = \frac{x+5}{x-2}$

12. $2 = \frac{x-4}{x-2}$

Solve and check. If the equation has no solution, write *No solution*.

13. $\frac{3y-6}{y-2}=2$

14. $\frac{2x-4}{x-2}=\frac{1}{3}$

15. $\frac{1}{2}=\frac{3-2m}{4m-6}$

16. $\frac{1}{4}=\frac{2w+1}{2w+4}$

17. $\frac{3y-6}{y-2}=3$

18. $\frac{y-2}{4y-8}=\frac{1}{4}$

19. $\frac{2+c}{3c}=\frac{1}{c}$

20. $\frac{a+1}{6}=\frac{2}{a}$

B 21. $\frac{3}{2a+1}=\frac{3}{2a-1}$

22. $\frac{5}{3+4x}=\frac{4}{4x+3}$

23. $\frac{1}{x}-\frac{2x}{x+1}=0$

24. $\frac{1}{z-3}+\frac{3}{9-3z}=0$

25. $\frac{1}{y-3}=\frac{6}{y^2-9}$

26. $\frac{4}{a^2-4a}=\frac{-1}{4-a}$

27. $\frac{4}{x+1}-\frac{1}{x}=1$

28. $\frac{3}{x-1}+\frac{2}{x}=4$

29. $1=\frac{3}{y+2}+\frac{1}{y-2}$

30. $-2=\frac{1}{1+x}-\frac{3}{1-x}$

31. $\frac{x}{x+1}+\frac{x+1}{x}=\frac{5}{2}$

32. $\frac{y+1}{y-1}-\frac{y-1}{y+1}=\frac{8}{3}$

33. $\frac{n-2}{n}-\frac{n-3}{n-6}=\frac{1}{n}$

34. $\frac{5}{y-5}-\frac{3}{y+5}=\frac{2}{y}$

35. $\frac{3}{x-4}+\frac{2}{x^2-16}=0$

36. $\frac{2}{c^2-2c}+\frac{1}{2-c}=1$

37. $\frac{1}{x-4}+\frac{2}{x^2-16}=\frac{3}{x+4}$

38. $\frac{3a}{a-1}-\frac{4}{a+1}=\frac{4}{a^2-1}$

C 39. $\frac{3}{2x}-\frac{x}{4x^2-1}=\frac{7}{4x+2}$

40. $\frac{x-2}{x^2-x-6}=\frac{1}{x^2-4}+\frac{3}{2x+4}$

Problems

Sample The sum of a number and its reciprocal is $\frac{26}{5}$. Find the number.

Solution Let x be the number. Then $\frac{1}{x}$ is its reciprocal.

$$x+\frac{1}{x}=\frac{26}{5}$$

$$5x\left(x+\frac{1}{x}\right)=5x\left(\frac{26}{5}\right)$$

$$5x^2+5=26x$$

$$5x^2-26x+5=0$$

$$(5x-1)(x-5)=0$$

$$x=\frac{1}{5} \quad \text{or} \quad x=5$$

$\therefore$ the number is $\frac{1}{5}$ or 5. ***Answer***

Solve.

1. The sum of a number and its reciprocal is $\frac{25}{12}$. Find the number.
2. The sum of a number and its reciprocal is $\frac{13}{6}$. Find the number.

3. The sum of the reciprocals of two consecutive odd integers is $\frac{8}{15}$. Find the integers.

4. The sum of the reciprocals of two consecutive even integers is $\frac{11}{60}$. Find the integers.

5. The numerator of a fraction is 1 more than the denominator. If the numerator and the denominator are both increased by 2, the new fraction will be $\frac{1}{4}$ less than the original fraction. Find the original fraction.

6. The numerator of a fraction is 1 less than the denominator. If the numerator and the denominator are both increased by 4, the new fraction will be $\frac{1}{8}$ more than the original fraction. Find the original fraction.

B 7. The sum of two numbers is 10 and the sum of their reciprocals is $\frac{5}{12}$. Find the numbers.

8. Two numbers differ by 11. When the larger number is divided by the smaller, the quotient is 2 and the remainder is 4. Find the numbers.

9. Tina hiked 15 km up a mountain trail. Her return trip along the same trail took 30 min less because she was able to increase her speed by 1 km/h. How long did it take her to climb up and down the mountain?

	Rate	× Time	= Distance
Up	x	$\frac{15}{x}$	15
Down	?	?	?

10. Jacqui commutes 30 mi to her job each day. She finds that if she drives 10 mi/h faster, it takes her 6 min less to get to work. Find her new speed.

	Rate	× Time	= Distance
Slower	x	$\frac{30}{x}$	30
Faster	?	?	?

11. The cost of a bus trip was \$180. The people who signed up for the trip agreed to split the cost equally. However, six people did not show up, so that those who did go each had to pay \$1.50 more. How many people actually went on the trip?

	Number	× Price =	Cost
Planned	?	?	?
Actual	?	?	?

12. The \$75 cost for a party was to be shared equally by all those attending. Since five more people attended than was expected, the price per person dropped by 50¢. How many people attended the party?

	Number	× Price =	Cost
Planned	?	?	?
Actual	?	?	?

Solve.

13. Cindy and Dave left the dock to canoe downstream. Fifteen minutes later Tammy left by motorboat with the supplies. Since the motorboat traveled twice as fast as the canoe, it caught up with the canoe 3 km from the dock. What was the speed of the motorboat?

14. An experienced plumber made \$600 for working on a certain job. His apprentice, who makes \$3 per hour less, also made \$600. However, the apprentice worked 10 h more than the plumber. How much does the plumber make per hour?

Mixed Review Exercises

Solve.

1. $\frac{2a}{5} + \frac{3a}{10} = 14$

2. $\frac{x}{5} - \frac{x}{3} = 4$

3. $\frac{1}{3}(y + 3) + \frac{1}{4}(y + 1) = 3$

4. $\frac{3}{7} = \frac{5a}{14}$

5. $\frac{-9}{7t} = \frac{3}{28}$

6. $\frac{z}{6} = \frac{12}{5}$

Simplify.

7. $(7 - 2)^3$

8. $4x^2(2x^2 - 7 + 3x)$

9. $6 \cdot 2^3$

10. $(4n^2 - n) + (9 + n^2)$

11. $(5z^3)(2y^2z)$

12. $(3pq^2)^3$

Self-Test 2

Vocabulary fractional equation (p. 304)

Solve.

1. $\frac{5k}{48} - \frac{2k}{9} = \frac{17}{18}$

2. $20 = c + \frac{c - 2}{8}$

Obj. 7-3, p. 298

3. $\frac{3x + 4}{5} = \frac{x - 3}{2}$

4. $\frac{m + 6}{10} - \frac{m}{15} = \frac{2}{5}$

Solve and check. If the equation has no solution, write *No solution*.

5. $\frac{3a - 1}{a + 1} = 4$

6. $\frac{2}{n - 3} - \frac{1}{2n - 6} = 0$

Obj. 7-4, p. 304

7. The sum of the reciprocals of two consecutive integers is $\frac{5}{6}$. Find the integers.

Check your answers with those at the back of the book.

Percent Problems

7-5 Percents

Objective To work with percents and decimals.

The word **percent** means "hundredths" or "divided by 100." The symbol % is used to represent percent.

Example 1

a. 29 percent $= 29\% = \frac{29}{100} = 0.29$

b. 2.6 percent $= 2.6\% = \frac{2.6}{100} = \frac{26}{1000} = 0.026$

c. 637 percent $= 637\% = \frac{637}{100} = 6\frac{37}{100} = 6.37$

d. 0.02 percent $= 0.02\% = \frac{0.02}{100} = \frac{2}{10{,}000} = 0.0002$

e. $\frac{1}{4}$ percent $= \frac{1}{4}\% = 0.25\% = \frac{0.25}{100} = \frac{25}{10{,}000} = 0.0025$

f. $33\frac{1}{3}$ percent $= 33\frac{1}{3}\% = \frac{100}{3}\% = \frac{100}{3} \div 100 = \frac{1}{3}$

Example 2 Write each number as a percent: **a.** $\frac{3}{5}$ **b.** $\frac{1}{3}$ **c.** 4.7

Solution

a.
$$\frac{3}{5} = \frac{x}{100}$$
$$5x = 300$$
$$x = 60$$
$$\therefore \frac{3}{5} = \frac{60}{100} = 60\%$$
Answer

b.
$$\frac{1}{3} = \frac{x}{100}$$
$$3x = 100$$
$$x = 33\frac{1}{3}$$
$$\therefore \frac{1}{3} = \frac{33\frac{1}{3}}{100} = 33\frac{1}{3}\%$$
Answer

c.
$$4.7 = \frac{x}{100}$$
$$\frac{4.7}{1} = \frac{x}{100}$$
$$x = 470$$
$$\therefore 4.7 = \frac{470}{100} = 470\%$$
Answer

Most calculators have a key with the % symbol that will help you solve or check percent problems. You can also enter a percent as a decimal or use your calculator and division by 100 to find the decimal form of a percent.

In percent problems the word "of" means "multiply" and the word "is" means "equals."

Example 3 15% of 180 is what number?

Solution 1

$$\frac{15}{100} \cdot 180 = x$$
$$\frac{2700}{100} = x$$
$$27 = x$$

$\therefore$ 15% of 180 is 27. ***Answer***

Solution 2

$$0.15 \cdot 180 = x$$
$$27 = x$$

$\therefore$ 15% of 180 is 27. ***Answer***

Example 4 23 is 25% of what number?

Solution

$$23 = \frac{25}{100} \cdot x$$
$$2300 = 25x$$
$$\frac{2300}{25} = x$$
$$92 = x$$

$\therefore$ 23 is 25% of 92. ***Answer***

Example 5 What percent of 64 is 48?

Solution

$$\frac{x}{100} \cdot 64 = 48$$
$$\frac{64x}{100} = 48$$
$$64x = 4800$$
$$x = 75$$

$\therefore$ 75% of 64 is 48. ***Answer***

When you solve an equation with decimal coefficients, you can multiply both sides of the equation by a power of 10 (10, 100, and so on) to get an equivalent equation with integral coefficients.

Example 6 Solve $1.2x = 36 + 0.4x$.

Solution

$$10(1.2x) = 10(36 + 0.4x)$$ Multiply both sides by 10 when the coefficients are tenths.
$$12x = 360 + 4x$$
$$8x = 360$$
$$x = 45$$

$\therefore$ the solution set is $\{45\}$. ***Answer***

Example 7 Solve $94 = 0.15x + 0.08(1000 - x)$.

Solution

$$100(94) = 100[0.15x + 0.08(1000 - x)]$$ Multiply both sides by 100 when the coefficients are hundredths.
$$9400 = 15x + 8(1000 - x)$$
$$9400 = 15x + 8000 - 8x$$
$$1400 = 7x$$
$$200 = x$$

$\therefore$ the solution set is $\{200\}$. ***Answer***

Example 8 During a sale, a sporting goods store gave a 40% discount on sleeping bags. How much did Ross pay for a sleeping bag with an original price of $75?

Solution 1

1. Find 40% of $75: $0.40 \cdot 75 = 30$
2. Subtract the amount of discount from the original price: $\begin{array}{r} 75 \\ -30 \\ \hline 45 \end{array}$

$\therefore$ Ross paid $45 for the sleeping bag. ***Answer***

Solution 2

1. If the sleeping bag was discounted 40%, it then cost 100% − 40% = 60% of its original price.
2. Find 60% of $75: $0.60 \cdot 75 = 45$

$\therefore$ Ross paid $45. ***Answer***

Oral Exercises

Express each number as a percent.

1. 0.833 **2.** 0.07 **3.** 2.3 **4.** 0.015 **5.** 0.003

6. $\frac{1}{2}$ **7.** 9 **8.** 10 **9.** $\frac{5}{4}$ **10.** $\frac{9}{50}$

Express as a fraction in simplest form.

11. 12% **12.** 70% **13.** 6% **14.** $\frac{1}{2}\%$ **15.** $10\frac{2}{3}\%$

Express as a fraction and then as a mixed number.

16. 105% **17.** 250% **18.** 175% **19.** 420% **20.** 375%

Express as a decimal.

21. 35% **22.** 4% **23.** 0.5% **24.** 125% **25.** $9\frac{1}{2}\%$

Tell whether you would multiply by 10, 100, or 1000 to eliminate the decimal coefficients in each equation. Then state the equation that would result if you did the multiplication.

26. $0.3x = 1.2 + 2.3x$

27. $0.24x = 3.2(10 - x)$

28. $1.2x + 0.95 = 0.02(3 - x)$

29. $15.2(1000 - x) = 2.8$

30. $0.1x - 0.01 = .001$

31. $3.2x = 0.32$

32. $4.06x = 100$

33. $0.03 + 10x = 3.6$

Written Exercises

Write as a fraction in simplest form.

A **1.** 25% **2.** 40% **3.** $37\frac{1}{2}\%$ **4.** 85%

5. 60% **6.** $66\frac{2}{3}\%$ **7.** 72% **8.** 16%

9. 4% **10.** $2\frac{1}{2}\%$ **11.** 360% **12.** 150%

13. 32% of 300 is what number?

14. 6% of 145 is what number?

15. 1% of 3200 is what number?

16. $6\frac{1}{4}\%$ of 500 is what number?

17. $\frac{1}{2}\%$ of 12 is what number?

18. 9.2% of 180 is what number?

19. 8.1% of 250 is what number?

20. 110% of 30 is what number?

21. 8 is 20% of what number?

22. 15 is 25% of what number?

23. 21 is 6% of what number?

24. 99 is 180% of what number?

25. 4.2 is 75% of what number?

26. 32.4 is 45% of what number?

27. What percent of 45 is 7.2?

28. What percent of 7.2 is 45?

29. What percent of 150 is 3?

30. What percent of 3 is 150?

31. What percent of 250 is 50?

32. What percent of 50 is 250?

Complete the tables.

	Original price	% Discount	Price decrease	New price
33.	\$12	25%	?	?
34.	\$18	20%	?	?
35.	\$75	10%	?	?
36.	\$240	15%	?	?

	Original price	% Markup	Price increase	New price
B **37.**	\$44	25%	?	?
38.	\$85	20%	?	?
39.	\$160	30%	?	?
40.	\$25	6%	?	?

Solve.

41. $1.8x = 36$

42. $0.06x = 120$

43. $0.05t = 2.3t - 6.75$

44. $0.21x = 1.2 - 0.15x$

45. $41 = 0.75y + 1.3y$

46. $0.05a + 0.5a = 4.4$

47. $2 + 0.08x = 0.2x + 8$

48. $0.47x - 20 = 0.09x + 3.25$

49. $90 = x + 0.04(180 - x)$

50. $0.4x + 0.24(x - 5) = 0.08$

51. $0.02 = 3.685x - 0.075(100 - x)$

52. $0.05x + 0.065(5000 - x) = 295$

53. $0.06(1000 - x) + 0.05x = 700$

54. $0.1x - 0.01(10 - x) + 0.01(100 - x) = 19$

55. $\frac{0.2x - 0.1}{5} = 3(x - 0.5)$

56. $5(x - 0.4) = \frac{0.5x - 0.5}{2}$

Complete the table below.

	Amount invested	× Annual interest rate	= Annual simple interest
57.	\$400	7.5%	?
58.	\$60,000	9.5%	?
59.	\$1000	?	\$105
60.	\$2500	?	\$275
61.	?	16%	\$136
62.	?	7.25%	\$870

Problems

Solve. You may wish to use a calculator.

A

1. The Chess Club has a goal of 36 new members. So far, they have 30. What percent of the club's goal have they achieved?
2. Laura makes a 10.5% commission on each of her sales. How much does she make when she sells a house for \$85,000?
3. A health research fund drive has raised \$18,700. That is 22% of the goal. What is the goal?

4. Because an item is slightly damaged, a stock clerk reduces the price by \$6. This represents a 15% reduction. What was the original price?

5. Carl makes a 2% commission on each of his sales. When he sold a new car, he made \$190. How much did the car cost?

6. Last year Molly was given a 3% bonus on her regular yearly salary. The bonus amounted to \$720. What is her regular yearly salary?

7. Where Sondra lives, there is a 3% state sales tax, a $1\frac{1}{2}$% county sales tax, and a 1% municipal sales tax. How much tax will Sondra pay if she buys a \$340 bicycle?

8. Mario invests \$4000 in bonds paying $11\frac{1}{2}$% interest and \$5000 in bank accounts paying 9.1% interest. Which investment yields more interest in one year? How much more?

B 9. A \$120 coat goes on sale for \$96. By what percent was the coat discounted?

10. A sporting goods dealer estimates that an \$85 tennis racket will cost 6% more next year. What will be the new price?

11. A dealer buys a new car for \$8400. How much do you have to pay for the car if the dealer makes a 20% profit and there is a 5% sales tax?

12. In a nation of 221 million people, the urban population is 2.25 times the rural population. Find the rural and urban populations.

13. A fertilizer is to be diluted with water so that the fertilizer is just 1% of the solution. How much water should be mixed with 5 cm^3 of fertilizer?

14. Lucinda bought two record albums and a compact disc for a total of \$28.00. The price of each record album was $66\frac{2}{3}$% of the price of the compact disc. How much did Lucinda pay for a record album?

C 15. The price of a share of stock rose 10% on Monday. The price then fell 10% on Tuesday to \$59.40 per share. What was the price of a share of stock before trading began on Monday?

Mixed Review Exercises

Factor completely.

1. $3a^2b + 6a$
2. $3y^3 + 6y^2 + 3y$
3. $m^2 + 5m + 6$
4. $x^2 - 9y^2$
5. $5p^2q^3 + 10p^2q - 15pq^2$
6. $4a^2 + a - 3$
7. $a(a + b) + 4(a + b)$
8. $x^2 + 6x + 9$
9. $t^2 - 2t - 15$

7-6 Percent Problems

Objective To solve problems involving percents.

Whenever a price is changed, you can find the percent of increase or the percent of decrease by using the following formula:

$$\frac{\text{percent of change}}{100} = \frac{\text{change in price}}{\text{original price}}$$

To find the change in price, you calculate the difference between the original price and the new price.

Example 1 Find the change in price.

a. The original price of the car Jasmine wants was \$10,000. It is now on sale for \$8,999.

b. Jerry originally paid \$600 per month to rent his apartment. It now costs him \$650.

Solution

a. The price *decreased* by \$10,000 − \$8999, or \$1001.

b. The price *increased* by \$650 − \$600, or \$50.

Example 2 To attract business, the manager of a musical instruments store decreased the price of an alto saxophone from \$500 to \$440. What was the percent of decrease?

Solution

Step 1 The problem asks for the percent of decrease.

Step 2 Let x = the percent of decrease.

Step 3 $\frac{\text{percent of change}}{100} = \frac{\text{change in price}}{\text{original price}}$

Step 4

$$\frac{x}{100} = \frac{60}{500}$$
$$500x = 6000$$
$$x = 12$$

Step 5 The check is left to you.

$\therefore$ there was a 12% decrease.

Example 3 Ricardo paid \$27 for membership in the Video Club. This was an increase of 8% from last year. What was the price of membership last year?

Solution

Step 1 The problem asks for the original price.

Step 2 Let x = the original price. Then $27 - x$ = the change in price.

Step 3 $$\frac{\text{percent of change}}{100} = \frac{\text{change in price}}{\text{original price}}$$
$$\frac{8}{100} = \frac{27 - x}{x}$$

Step 4 $$8x = 2700 - 100x$$
$$108x = 2700$$
$$x = 25$$

Step 5 The check is left to you.

∴ the membership cost \$25 last year. ***Answer***

Amount invested × Annual interest rate = Annual simple interest

Example 4 Sheila invests part of \$6000 at 6% interest and the rest at 11% interest. Her total annual income from these investments is \$460. How much is invested at 6% and how much at 11%?

Solution

Step 1 The problem asks for the amounts invested at 6% and at 11%.

Step 2 Let x = the amount invested at 6%.
Then $6000 - x$ = the amount invested at 11%.

	Amount invested ×	Rate =	Interest
At 6%	x	0.06	$0.06x$
At 11%	$6000 - x$	0.11	$0.11(6000 - x)$

Step 3 $$0.06x + 0.11(6000 - x) = 460 \longleftarrow \text{Total interest}$$

Step 4 $$100[0.06x + 0.11(6000 - x)] = 100(460) \qquad \text{Multiply both sides by 100.}$$
$$6x + 11(6000 - x) = 46{,}000$$
$$6x + 66{,}000 - 11x = 46{,}000$$
$$-5x = -20{,}000$$
$$x = 4000$$

Step 5 The check is left to you.

∴ \$4000 is invested at 6%; \$2000 at 11%. ***Answer***

Oral Exercises

Complete each table.

	Item	Original price	New price	Price increase	% of increase
1.	Jeans	$25.00	$30.00	?	?
2.	School lunch	$1.60	$2.00	?	?
3.	Haircut	$10.00	$14.00	?	?
4.	Record	$6.00	$7.50	?	?

	Item	Original price	New price	Price decrease	% of decrease
5.	Sweater	$60.00	$45.00	?	?
6.	Fly rod	$20.00	$15.00	?	?
7.	Skis	$240.00	$160.00	?	?
8.	Radio	$45.00	$36.00	?	?

State the equation you would use to find x.

	Original price	New price	% of change
9.	x	$88	10% price increase
10.	x	$75	25% price increase
11.	x	$21	15% price decrease
12.	x	$48	30% price decrease

Written Exercises

Complete the table.

	Item	Original price	New price	% of increase
A 1.	Sneakers	$30.00	$33.00	?
2.	Record album	$12.00	$15.00	?
3.	Bike	$250.00	$300.00	?
4.	Sandwich	$1.80	$2.10	?
5.	Paint	$20.00	$22.50	?

Complete the tables.

	Item	Original price	New price	% of increase
6.	Skis	\$220.00	\$253.00	?
7.	Video tape	\$6.00	\$?	5%
8.	Phone call	\$2.80	\$?	20%
9.	Hammer	\$?	\$8.00	25%
10.	Saw	\$?	\$22.00	10%
11.	Backpack	\$?	\$72.80	12%
12.	Stereo	\$?	\$566.50	3%

	Item	Original price	New price	% of decrease
13.	Shirt	\$25.00	\$20.00	?
14.	Pants	\$36.00	\$27.00	?
15.	Notebook	\$2.00	\$1.65	?
16.	Hiking boots	\$120.00	\$108.00	?
17.	Soccer ball	\$32.00	\$?	20%
18.	Spaghetti sauce	\$2.20	\$?	15%
19.	Shoes	\$?	\$68.25	12.5%
20.	Shampoo	\$?	\$2.09	5%
21.	Skates	\$?	\$59.50	15%

Problems

Solve. You may wish to use a calculator.

A **1.** The population at Dos Pueblos High increased from 1800 students ten years ago to 1926 students last year. What was the percent of increase?

2. The Golds' home was assessed this year at a value of \$162,000. Last year it had been assessed at \$150,000. What was the percent of increase?

3. A \$200 coat is on sale for \$166. What is the percent of discount?

4. Elena bought some shares of stock at \$28 per share and sold them all at \$24.50 per share. What was the percent of her loss?

5. While on vacation, Allison noted that a \$5.50 breakfast actually cost \$5.83 because of the sales tax. What is the sales tax rate?

6. The number of paid subscribers to *The Wildlife Monthly* has declined from 3340 people to 2430 people. What is the percent of decrease?

7. Yvonne paid \$11,448 for a new automobile. This amount included the 6% sales tax. What was the price of the automobile without the tax?

8. Emily Ling is a real estate broker who earns a 12% commission on each house she sells. If she earned \$21,600 on the sale of a house, what was the selling price of the house?

9. At the Runners' Shop anniversary sale, running shoes were on sale at a 15% discount. If Alonzo paid \$35.70 for a pair of running shoes, what was the original price?

10. The number of students at Westwood High School with a driver's license is now 558. This is 24% more than last year. How many students had a driver's license last year?

B 11. Yolanda invests \$6000. Some of the money is invested in stocks paying 6% a year and some in bonds paying 11% year. She receives a total of \$580 each year from these investments. How much money is invested in stocks and how much money in bonds?

12. Craig invested \$4000 in bank certificates and bonds. The certificates pay 5.5% interest and the bonds pay 11% interest. His interest income is \$352 this year. How much money was invested in bank certificates?

13. The Creative Arts Fund must raise \$2500 next year by investing \$30,000 in federal notes paying 9% and in municipal bonds paying 8%. The treasurer wants to invest as much as possible in the bonds, even though they pay less, because the bonds are for projects in the local area. How much should the treasurer invest in bonds?

14. Bruce invested in stock paying a $10\frac{1}{2}$% dividend. Maya invested \$4000 more than Bruce in tax-free bonds paying $7\frac{1}{2}$% annual simple interest. If Maya's income from investment is \$75 more than Bruce's, find how much money each invested.

15. Jesse invested \$2000 more in stocks than in bonds. The bonds paid 7.2% interest and stocks paid 6%. The income from each investment was the same. How much interest did he receive in all?

16. Half of Roberta's money is invested at 12% interest, one third at 11%, and the rest at 9%. Her total annual income from investments is \$1340. How much money has Roberta invested?

Computer Exercises

For students with some programming experience.

1. Suppose that you deposit \$100 in a bank account that pays 6% interest per year. At the end of one year, you will have 100 + 100(0.06) = \$106. At the end of the second year, you will have 106 + 106(0.06) = \$112.36. Write a BASIC program to display in chart form how much money you will have at the end of 1, 2, 3, 4, . . . , 10 years.

2. Write a BASIC program using an array to store data entered with INPUT statements. The program should calculate and print the percent of increase or decrease between each consecutive pair of data. If the percent of change is the same for each consecutive pair, the data are increasing (or decreasing) exponentially. RUN the program for the following sets of data.

a.

Years after 1989	Population of Muddville
1	207
2	200
3	193
4	186
5	179

Is the population of Muddville decreasing exponentially?

b.

Hours after start of experiment	Number of bacteria
1	500
2	705
3	994
4	1402
5	1977

Is the number of bacteria increasing exponentially?

Mixed Review Exercises

Solve.

1. $\frac{3x + 1}{x - 2} = 7$
2. $\frac{a + 3}{4} = \frac{1}{a}$
3. $\frac{5}{n} = \frac{13}{6n}$

4. $1.4x = 28$
5. $m^2 + 3m + 2 = 0$
6. $0.5x + 5.6 = 1.2x$

Simplify.

7. $(z + 3)9$
8. $-4(x - 3y)$
9. $9a + 7 - 2a + b$

10. $16t\left(-\frac{1}{2}\right)$
11. $(-5b)(-6c)$
12. $\frac{1}{7}(-21xz)$

Self-Test 3

Vocabulary percent (p. 309)

Express as a fraction in simplest form.

1. 65%
2. $72\frac{1}{2}\%$
3. 510% **Obj. 7-5, p. 309**

4. Find 16% of 85.
5. 3.75 is 60% of what number?

6. What percent of 70 is 245?
7. What percent of 300 is 225?

8. Last year an accountant earned $28,000. This year she received a 6% raise. How much was the raise?

9. A $162 suit is on sale for $108. What is the percent of discount? **Obj. 7-6, p. 315**

Check your answers with those at the back of the book.

Mixture and Work Problems

7-7 Mixture Problems

Objective To solve mixture problems.

Supermarkets sometimes sell a mixture of two or more items. Similarly, a chemist can make a solution of a certain strength by mixing solutions of different strengths. When you solve a mixture problem, it is helpful to make a chart.

Example 1 A health food store sells a mixture of raisins and roasted nuts. Raisins sell for \$3.50/kg and nuts sell for \$4.75/kg. How many kilograms of each should be mixed to make 20 kg of this snack worth \$4.00/kg?

Solution

Step 1 The problem asks for the number of kilograms of raisins and the number of kilograms of nuts.

Step 2 Let x = the number of kilograms of raisins.
Then $20 - x$ = the number of kilograms of nuts.

	Number of kg ×	Price per kg =	Cost
Raisins	x	3.50	$3.5x$
Nuts	$20 - x$	4.75	$4.75(20 - x)$
Mixture	20	4.00	80

Step 3 Cost of raisins + cost of nuts = total cost of mixture

$$3.5x + 4.75(20 - x) = 80$$

Step 4

$$350x + 475(20 - x) = 8000 \quad \text{Multiply both sides by 100.}$$
$$350x + 9500 - 475x = 8000$$
$$-125x = -1500$$
$$x = 12$$
$$20 - x = 8$$

Step 5 The check is left to you.

$\therefore$ 12 kg of raisins and 8 kg of nuts are needed. ***Answer***

Example 2 An auto mechanic has 300 mL of battery acid solution that is 60% acid. He must add water to this solution to dilute it so that it is only 45% acid. How much water should he add?

Solution

Step 1 The problem asks for the number of milliliters of water to be added.

Step 2 Let x = the number of milliliters of water to be added.

	Total amount ×	% acid =	Amount of acid
Original solution	300	60%	0.60(300)
Water	x	0%	0
New solution	$300 + x$	45%	$0.45(300 + x)$

Step 3 Original amount of acid + added acid = new amount of acid

$$0.60(300) \quad + \quad 0 \quad = \quad 0.45(300 + x)$$

Step 4

$$60(300) = 45(300 + x)$$
$$18{,}000 = 13{,}500 + 45x$$
$$4500 = 45x$$
$$100 = x$$

Step 5 The check is left to you.

∴ 100 mL of water should be added. ***Answer***

Examples 1 and 2 are really very much alike. You can see this in the charts and in Step 3 of each solution. In fact, mixture problems are similar to investment problems, coin problems, and certain distance problems.

Oral Exercises

Read each problem and complete the chart. Use the chart to give an equation to solve the problem. Do not solve.

1. The owner of the Fancy Food Shoppe wants to mix cashews selling at \$8.00/kg and pecans selling at \$7.00/kg. How many kilograms of each kind of nut should be mixed to get 8 kg worth \$7.25/kg?

	Number of kg ×	Price per kg =	Total cost
Cashews	x	?	?
Pecans	?	?	?
Mixture	?	?	?

2. A chemist has 40 mL of a solution that is 50% acid. How much water should he add to make a solution that is 10% acid?

	Total amount ×	% acid	= Amount of acid
Original solution	?	?	?
Water added	x	?	?
New solution	?	?	?

3. If 800 mL of a juice drink is 15% grape juice, how much grape juice should be added to make a drink that is 20% grape juice?

	Total amount ×	% juice	= Amount of juice
Original drink	?	?	?
Juice added	x	?	?
New drink	?	?	?

4. A chemist mixes 12 L of a solution that is 45% acid with 8 L of a solution that is 70% acid. What is the percent of acid of the mixture?

	Total amount ×	% acid	= Amount of acid
1st Solution	?	?	?
2nd Solution	?	?	?
Mixture	?	x	?

5. A grocer mixes 5 lb of egg noodles costing 80¢/lb with 2 lb of spinach noodles costing $1.50/lb. What will the cost per pound of the mixture be?

	Number of lb ×	Cost per lb	= Total cost
Egg noodles	?	?	?
Spinach noodles	?	?	?
Mixture	?	x	?

6. Susan drove for 2 h at 85 km/h and then for 3 h more at 95 km/h. What was her average speed for the entire trip?

	Rate ×	Time	= Distance
1st part of trip	?	?	?
2nd part of trip	?	?	?
Entire trip	x	?	?

7. Sam invested \$2000 at $5\frac{1}{4}\%$ annual interest and \$3000 at $8\frac{1}{2}\%$ annual interest. What percent interest is he earning on his total investment?

	Amount invested × Rate = Interest		
Investment A	?	?	?
Investment B	?	?	?
Total Investments	?	x	?

8. Gina has a pile of 50 dimes and nickels worth \$4.30. How many coins of each type does she have?

	Number of coins × Value per coin = Total value		
Dimes	x	?	?
Nickels	?	?	?
Collection	?	——	?

Problems

A **1–8.** Solve the problems in Oral Exercises 1–8.

Solve.

9. How many liters of water must be added to 50 L of a 30% acid solution in order to produce a 20% acid solution?
10. How many milliliters of water must be added to 60 mL of a 15% iodine solution in order to dilute it to a 10% iodine solution?
11. A spice mixture is 25% thyme. How many grams of thyme must be added to 12 g of the mixture to increase the thyme content to 40%?
12. A grocer mixes two kinds of nuts. One kind costs \$5.00/kg and the other \$5.80/kg. How many kilograms of each type are needed to make 40 kg of a blend worth \$5.50/kg?
13. Joanne makes a mixture of dried fruits by mixing dried apples costing \$6.00/kg with dried apricots costing \$8.00/kg. How many kilograms of each are needed to make 20 kg of a mixture worth \$7.20/kg?
14. A farm stand owner mixes apple juice and cranberry juice. How much should he charge if he mixes 8 L of apple juice selling for 45¢/L with 10 L of cranberry juice selling for \$1.08/L?
15. If you drive for 2 h at 80 km/h, how fast must you drive during the next hour in order to have an average speed of 75 km/h?

16. If Sylvia works overtime, she is paid $1\frac{1}{2}$ times as much per hour as usual. After working her usual 40 h last week, she worked an additional 4 h overtime. If she made $552 last week, find her usual hourly wage.

B 17. A chemist wishes to mix some pure acid with some water to produce 16 L of a solution that is 30% acid. How much pure acid and how much water should be mixed?

18. How many liters of water must be evaporated from 10 L of a 40% salt solution to produce a 50% solution?

19. How many liters of water must be evaporated from 20 L of a 30% salt solution to produce a 50% solution?

20. A wholesaler has 100 kg of mixed nuts that sell for $4.00/kg. In order to make the price more attractive, she plans to mix in some cheaper nuts worth $3.20/kg. If the wholesaler wants to sell the mixture for $3.40/kg, how many kilograms of the cheaper nuts should be used?

21. A securities broker advised a client to invest a total of $21,000 in bonds paying 12% interest and in certificates of deposit paying $5\frac{1}{4}$% interest. The annual income from these investments was $2250. Find out how much was invested at each rate.

22. A collection of 50 coins is worth $5.20. There are 12 more nickels than dimes, and the rest of the coins are quarters. How many coins of each type are in the collection?

23. **(a)** If you bike for 2 h at 30 km/h and for 2 h at 20 km/h, what is your average speed for the whole trip? **(b)** If you bike for 60 km at 30 km/h and return at 20 km/h, what is your average speed for the whole trip?

C 24. The ratio of nickels to dimes to quarters is 3:8:1. If all the coins were dimes, the amount of money would be the same. Show that there are infinitely many solutions to this problem.

25. A grocer wants to make a mixture of three dried fruits. He decides that the ratio of pounds of banana chips to apricots to dates should be 3:1:1. Banana chips cost $1.17/lb, apricots cost $3.00/lb, and dates cost $2.30/lb. What is the cost per pound of the mixture?

Mixed Review Exercises

Evaluate.

1. 9% of 60 + 0.4% of 230
2. What percent of 45 is 18?
3. What percent of 160 is 12?
4. 16 is $12\frac{1}{2}$% of what number?

Evaluate if $a = 2$, $b = 3$, $x = 5$, and $y = 4$.

5. $|-5| + y$
6. $\frac{7 - 2b}{3 + b}$
7. $\frac{1}{7}(9x + y)$
8. xy^2
9. $2a + 5b$
10. $(x - b)^2$

7-8 Work Problems

Objective To solve work problems.

You can use the following formula to solve work problems.

$$\text{work rate} \times \text{time} = \text{work done}$$
$$rt = w$$

"Work rate" means the fractional part of a job done in a given unit of time.

Example 1 Sheri can rake the lawn in 2 h. Her work rate is the part of the job she can do in 1 h. ∴ her work rate is $\frac{1}{2}$ job per hour.

To finish a job, the sum of the fractional parts of the work done must be 1.

Example 2 Josh can split a cord of wood in 4 days. His father can split a cord in 2 days. How long will it take them to split a cord of wood if they work together?

Solution

Step 1 The problem asks for the number of days the job will take them.

Step 2 Let x = the number of days needed to do the job together.

Josh and his father will each work x days.

Since Josh can do the whole job in 4 days, his work rate is $\frac{1}{4}$ job per day.

His father's work rate is $\frac{1}{2}$ job per day.

	Work rate	× Time	= Work done
Josh	$\frac{1}{4}$	x	$\frac{x}{4}$
Father	$\frac{1}{2}$	x	$\frac{x}{2}$

Step 3 Josh's part of the job + Father's part of the job = Whole job

$$\frac{x}{4} + \frac{x}{2} = 1$$

Step 4

$$4\left(\frac{x}{4} + \frac{x}{2}\right) = 4(1) \quad \text{Multiply by the LCD, 4.}$$
$$x + 2x = 4$$
$$3x = 4$$
$$x = \frac{4}{3}, \text{ or } 1\frac{1}{3}$$

Step 5 The check is left to you.

$\therefore$ it would take them $1\frac{1}{3}$ days to do the job together. ***Answer***

Example 3 Robot A takes 6 min to weld a fender. Robot B takes only $5\frac{1}{2}$ min. If they work together for 2 min, how long will it take Robot B to finish welding the fender by itself?

Solution

Step 1 The problem asks for the amount of time it will take Robot B to finish welding the fender.

Step 2 Let x = the number of minutes needed for Robot B to finish.

Robot B's work rate is $\frac{1}{5\frac{1}{2}} = \frac{1}{\frac{11}{2}} = \frac{2}{11}$.

	Work rate	× Time	= Work done
Robot A	$\frac{1}{6}$	2	$\frac{2}{6}$, or $\frac{1}{3}$
Robot B	$\frac{2}{11}$	$2 + x$	$\frac{2}{11}(2 + x)$

Step 3 A's part of job + B's part of job = Whole job

$$\frac{1}{3} + \frac{2}{11}(2 + x) = 1$$

Step 4

$$33\left[\frac{1}{3} + \frac{2}{11}(2 + x)\right] = 33(1) \quad \text{Multiply by the LCD, 33.}$$

$$11 + 6(2 + x) = 33$$

$$11 + 12 + 6x = 33$$

$$6x = 10$$

$$x = \frac{5}{3}, \text{ or } 1\frac{2}{3}$$

Step 5 The check is left to you.

$\therefore$ it will take $1\frac{2}{3}$ min for Robot B to finish welding. ***Answer***

The charts used for work problems look similar to the charts used for other problems. The following formulas show the similarities among some types of problems you have studied.

Work done by A + work done by B = *total* work done

Acid in solution A + acid in solution B = *total* acid in mixture

Interest from banks + interest from bonds = *total* interest

Distance by bike + distance by car = *total* distance traveled

Oral Exercises

State the work rate.

1. Beatrice can wallpaper a room in 8 h.
2. Marty read a novel in 10 h.
3. Annie can wax her car in 45 min.
4. A hose can fill a swimming pool in 3 days.

Complete the charts. Do not solve the problems.

5. Using a new lawn mower, Abby can mow the lawn in 2 h. Her sister Carla uses an older mower and takes 3 h to mow the same lawn. How long will it take them if they work together?

	Work rate	× Time	= Work done
Abby	?	x	?
Carla	?	?	?

6. Phil can paint the garage in 12 h, and Rick can do it in 10 h. They work together for 3 h. How long will it take Rick to finish the job alone?

	Work rate	× Time	= Work done
Phil	?	3	?
Rick	?	$x + 3$	?

7. Chuck can shovel the snow off his driveway in 40 min. He shovels for 20 min and then is joined by Joan. If they shovel the remaining snow in 10 min, how long would it have taken Joan to shovel the driveway alone?

	Work rate	× Time	= Work done
Chuck	?	?	?
Joan	$\frac{1}{x}$	?	?

8. Brett usually takes 50 min to groom the horses. After working 10 min, he was joined by Angela and they finished the grooming in 15 min. How long would it have taken Angela working alone?

	Work rate	× Time	= Work done
Brett	?	?	?
Angela	$\frac{1}{x}$	?	?

Problems

A

1. Rita takes 3 h to type a report. What part of the typing can she do in 2 h? in x h?
2. Franklin can do a job in 6 h and Mike can do it in 4 h. What part of the job can they do by working together for 2 h? for y h?
3. Jake can wallpaper a room in 10 h and Maura can do it in 8 h. What part of the job can they do by working together for 2.5 h? for h h?

4. One drain pipe can empty a swimming pool in 6 h. Another pipe takes 3 h. If both pipes are used at the same time to drain the pool, what part of the job is completed in 2 h? in x h?

5–8. Solve the problems stated in Oral Exercises 5–8.

Solve.

9. It takes Sally 15 min to pick the apples from the tree in her backyard. Lisa can do it in 25 min. How long will it take them working together?

10. It takes Gary 1 h to milk all of the cows, and it takes Dana 1.5 h. How long will it take them to do the job together?

11. A roofing contractor estimates that he can shingle a house in 20 h and that his assistant can do it in 30 h. How long will it take them to shingle the house working together?

12. Stan can load his truck in 24 min. If his brother helps him, it takes them 15 min to load the truck. How long does it take Stan's brother alone?

B **13.** One printing machine works twice as fast as another. When both machines are used, they can print a magazine in 3 h. How many hours would each machine require to do the job alone?

14. Arthur can do a job in 30 min, Bonnie can do it in 40 min, and Claire can do it in 60 min. How long will it take them if they work together?

15. It takes my father 3 h to plow our cornfield with his new tractor. Using the old tractor it takes me 5 h. If we both plow for 1 h before I go to school, how long will it take him to finish the plowing?

16. Phyllis can rake our lawn in 50 min, and I can do it in 40 min. If she rakes for 5 min before I join her, how long will it take us to finish?

17. One pump can fill a water tank in 3 h, and another pump takes 5 h. When the tank was empty, both pumps were turned on for 30 min and then the faster pump was turned off. How much longer did the slower pump have to run before the tank was filled?

18. Pipe A can fill a swimming pool in 12 h. After it has been used for $4\frac{1}{2}$ h, Pipe B is also used, and the pool is filled in another $4\frac{1}{2}$ h. How long would it take for the Pipe B to fill the pool by itself?

19. Ramona can do a job in 12 days. After she has worked for 4 days, she is joined by Carlotta and it takes them 2 days working together to finish the job. How long would it have taken Carlotta to do the whole job herself?

20. The fill pipe for a tank can fill the tank in 4 h, and the drain pipe can drain it in 2 h. If both pipes are accidentally opened, how long will it take to empty a half-filled tank?

21. Nicholas and Marilyn are addressing invitations to the junior class picnic. Nicholas can address one every 30 s and Marilyn can do one every 40 s. How long will it take them to address 140 invitations?

C 22. Jeff can weed the garden in 4 h. His wife Brenda takes the same amount of time. After they worked together for 1 h, their son Rory helped them finish in $\frac{1}{2}$ h. How long would it have taken Rory by himself?

23. If three pipes are all opened, they can fill an empty swimming pool in 3 h. The largest pipe alone takes one third the time that the smallest pipe takes and half the time the other pipe takes. How long would it take each pipe to fill the pool by itself?

Mixed Review Exercises

Complete the table.

	Item	Original price	New price	Percent of increase
1.	Shoes	\$ 34.00	\$40.12	?
2.	Wallpaper	\$130.00	\$?	10%
3.	Tote Bag	\$?	\$26.40	20%

Solve.

4. $\frac{1}{c+3} + \frac{4}{2c+6} = 3$ **5.** $\frac{8}{n} = \frac{16}{7}$ **6.** $\frac{x+3}{7} = \frac{x+5}{14}$

7. $5a - 1 = 3(a + 7)$ **8.** $-0.6 + k = 0.8$ **9.** $-9p = 0$

Self-Test 4

Solve.

1. How many liters of water must be evaporated from 50 L of a 10% salt solution to produce a 20% salt solution? **Obj. 7-7, p. 321**
2. How many kilograms of nuts must be added to 1.8 kg of plain banana bread batter to produce a batter that is 10% nuts?
3. Fran can write a computer program in 9 days. If Doug helps her, they can write the program in 6 days. How long would it take Doug to write the program by himself? **Obj. 7-8, p. 326**
4. The main engine on a rocket can use up the fuel in 60 s. The reserve engine can use it up in 80 s. How long can both run at the same time?

Check your answers with those at the back of the book.

Problems Involving Exponents

7-9 Negative Exponents

Objective To use negative exponents.

You have learned the meaning of a^n when n is a positive number. For example:

$$2^3 = 8 \qquad 2^2 = 4 \qquad 2^1 = 2$$

In this lesson you'll consider the meaning of expressions like 2^0 and 2^{-1} that have zero and negative integers as exponents.

Definition of a^{-n}

If a is a nonzero real number and n is a positive integer,

$$a^{-n} = \frac{1}{a^n}.$$

Example 1 a. $10^{-3} = \frac{1}{10^3} = \frac{1}{1000}$ b. $5^{-4} = \frac{1}{5^4} = \frac{1}{625}$ c. $16^{-1} = \frac{1}{16^1} = \frac{1}{16}$

The rule of exponents for division (page 190) will help you understand why a^{-n} is defined as $\frac{1}{a^n}$. Recall that for $m > n$, $\frac{a^m}{a^n} = a^{m-n}$. For example,

$$\frac{a^7}{a^3} = a^{7-3} = a^4.$$

You can also apply this rule when $m < n$, that is, when $m - n$ is a negative number. For example,

$$\frac{a^3}{a^7} = a^{3-7} = a^{-4}.$$

Since $\frac{a^3}{a^7}$ and $\frac{a^7}{a^3}$ are reciprocals, a^4 and a^{-4} must also be reciprocals. Thus,

$$a^{-4} = \frac{1}{a^4}.$$

If $m = n$, you can still apply $\frac{a^m}{a^n} = a^{m-n}$. For example, $\frac{a^5}{a^5} = a^{5-5} = a^0$. But you already know that $\frac{a^5}{a^5} = 1$. This leads to the following definition.

Definition of a^0

If a is a nonzero real number,

$$a^0 = 1.$$

The expression 0^0 has no meaning.

All the rules for positive exponents also hold for zero and negative exponents.

Summary of Rules for Exponents	Examples
Let m and n be any integers. Let a and b be any nonzero integers.	
1. Products of Powers: $b^m b^n = b^{m+n}$	$2^3 \cdot 2^{-5} = 2^{3+(-5)} = 2^{-2} = \frac{1}{2^2} = \frac{1}{4}$
2. Quotients of Powers: $b^m \div b^n = b^{m-n}$	$6^3 \div 6^7 = 6^{3-7} = 6^{-4} = \frac{1}{6^4} = \frac{1}{1296}$
3. Power of a Power: $(b^m)^n = b^{mn}$	$(2^3)^{-2} = 2^{-6} = \frac{1}{2^6} = \frac{1}{64}$
4. Power of a Product: $(ab)^m = a^m b^m$	$(3x)^{-2} = 3^{-2} \cdot x^{-2} = \frac{1}{3^2} \cdot \frac{1}{x^2} = \frac{1}{9x^2}$
5. Power of a Quotient: $\left(\frac{a}{b}\right)^m = \frac{a^m}{b^m}$	$\left(\frac{3}{5}\right)^{-2} = \frac{3^{-2}}{5^{-2}} = \frac{\frac{1}{3^2}}{\frac{1}{5^2}} = \frac{1}{3^2} \cdot \frac{5^2}{1} = \frac{5^2}{3^2} = \frac{25}{9}$

Example 2 Simplify. Give your answers using positive exponents.

a. $\frac{5}{5^{-3}}$ **b.** $(b^{-1})^{-3}$ **c.** $(3x^{-1})^2$

Solution

a. $\frac{5^1}{5^{-3}} = 5^{1-(-3)}$ Use Rule 2.

$= 5^4$

$= 625$

b. $(b^{-1})^{-3} = b^{(-1)(-3)}$ Use Rule 3.

$= b^3$

c. $(3x^{-1})^2 = 9x^{-2}$ Use Rules 4 and 3.

$= \frac{9}{x^2}$ Use the rule for negative exponents.

Positive and negative exponents are often used in problems involving population growth, interest, or energy consumption.

Example 3 In t years, the population P (in millions) of Centerville will be approximately $P = 2(1.03)^t$. **(a)** What will the population be in two years? **(b)** What is the population now? **(c)** What was the population last year?

Solution

a. Let $t = 2$. $P = 2(1.03)^2 = 2(1.0609) = 2.1218$; 2,121,800

b. Let $t = 0$. $P = 2(1.03)^0 = 2(1) = 2$; 2,000,000

c. Let $t = -1$. $P = 2(1.03)^{-1} = \frac{2}{1.03} \approx 1.941748$; 1,941,748

Oral Exercises

Simplify. In Exercises 17–24, give answers using positive exponents.

1. 10^{-1} **2.** 6^{-1} **3.** 5^{-1} **4.** 1^{-1}

5. 10^{-2} **6.** 6^{-2} **7.** 5^{-2} **8.** 1^{-2}

9. 2^{-3} **10.** 4^{-3} **11.** $7^{-4} \cdot 7^3$ **12.** $3^6 \cdot 3^{-8}$

13. $(3^{-1})^2$ **14.** $(3^{-1})^{-2}$ **15.** $\frac{10}{10^{-2}}$ **16.** $\frac{10^{-3}}{10^{-5}}$

17. $(5x)^{-2}$ **18.** $(3^{-1} \cdot 4^{-1})^{-1}$ **19.** $\left(\frac{1}{2} \cdot \frac{1}{4}\right)^{-1}$ **20.** $\left(\frac{3}{2}\right)^{-2}$

21. $a^{-1}b^2$ **22.** $\frac{c^{-2}}{d^{-3}}$ **23.** $(5x^2)^{-1}$ **24.** $(2y^{-2})^3$

25. The electrical energy consumption in a city has been increasing. In n years the annual electrical consumption will be approximately $C = 1.3(1.07)^n$ billion kilowatt-hours. What value of n should be substituted to find the value of C **(a)** now? **(b)** 10 years from now? **(c)** 10 years ago?

Written Exercises

Simplify.

A

1. 5^{-1} **2.** 4^{-1} **3.** 3^{-2} **4.** 2^{-2}

5. 9^{-2} **6.** 8^{-2} **7.** 3^{-3} **8.** 2^{-3}

9. 2^{-4} **10.** 3^{-4} **11.** 1^{-6} **12.** 6^{-1}

13. 4^{-2} **14.** $3^7 \cdot 3^{-9}$ **15.** $(2^{-3})^{-1}$ **16.** $(4^{-1})^{-3}$

17. $\frac{3}{3^{-2}}$ **18.** $\frac{6^{-2}}{6^{-3}}$ **19.** $\frac{7^{-2} \cdot 7}{7^{-1}}$ **20.** $\frac{3^{-5} \cdot 3^3}{3^{-4}}$

21. $\left(\frac{3^{-1}}{3}\right)^2$ **22.** $\left(\frac{8^4}{8^{-4}}\right)^0$ **23.** $\frac{(2^{-3} \cdot 4^2)^{-1}}{2^{-1}}$ **24.** $\left(\frac{3^0 \cdot 2}{2^{-2}}\right)^{-3}$

25. $\left(\frac{2}{3}\right)^{-4}$ **26.** $\left(\frac{5}{4}\right)^{-2}$ **27.** $\left(\frac{4}{5}\right)^{-3}$ **28.** $\left(\frac{7}{6}\right)^{-1}$

Simplify.

29. **a.** $(2 \cdot 3)^{-3}$ **b.** $2 \cdot 3^{-3}$

30. **a.** $(4 \cdot 5)^{-2}$ **b.** $4 \cdot 5^{-2}$

31. **a.** $(2^{-1} + 2^{-2})^{-1}$ **b.** $(2^{-1} \cdot 2^{-2})^{-1}$

32. **a.** $(2 + 3^{-1})^{-2}$ **b.** $(2 \cdot 3^{-1})^{-2}$

33. Why is b^{-1} not defined when $b = 0$?

34. Suppose that you did not know that $b^0 = 1$. Explain how you could arrive at this fact by using the laws of exponents to simplify $b^2 \cdot b^0 = b^2$.

Simplify. Give your answers using positive exponents.

B

35. $3x^{-2}$ **36.** $2n^{-3}$ **37.** $(3x)^{-2}$ **38.** $(5m)^{-2}$

39. $x^{-1}y^2$ **40.** $a^{-2}b^{-3}$ **41.** $(m^{-3})^4$ **42.** $(x^{-2})^3$

43. $m^{-3} \cdot m^4$ **44.** $a^5 \cdot a^{-2}$ **45.** $(3x^{-2})^3$ **46.** $(4n^{-1})^2$

47. $2x^5 \cdot x^{-5}$ **48.** $3x^{-2} \cdot (3x^2)^{-1}$ **49.** $(a^2 \cdot a^{-5})^2$ **50.** $(b^5 \cdot b^{-7})^3$

51. $\frac{y^3}{y^{-5}}$ **52.** $\frac{u^{-4}}{u^{10}}$ **53.** $\frac{c^{-5}}{c^2}$ **54.** $\frac{d^{-3}}{d^{-5}}$

55. $\left(\frac{a^{-6}}{a^{-2}}\right)^{-1}$ **56.** $\left(\frac{b^{-3}}{b^{-6}}\right)^4$ **57.** $\left(\frac{n^{-3}}{n}\right)^{-2}$ **58.** $\left(\frac{y^5}{y^{-2}}\right)^{-3}$

Simplify. Use the table of powers of 5.

Sample

$$\frac{3125}{0.008} = \frac{5^5}{5^{-3}} = 5^8 = 390{,}625$$

Answer

$5^1 = 5$	$5^{-1} = 0.2$
$5^2 = 25$	$5^{-2} = 0.04$
$5^3 = 125$	$5^{-3} = 0.008$
$5^4 = 625$	$5^{-4} = 0.0016$
$5^5 = 3125$	$5^{-5} = 0.00032$
$5^6 = 15{,}625$	$5^{-6} = 0.000064$
$5^7 = 78{,}125$	$5^{-7} = 0.0000128$
$5^8 = 390{,}625$	$5^{-8} = 0.00000256$

59. 3125×0.008 **60.** $0.0000128 \times 78{,}125$ **61.** $(78{,}125)^{-1}$

62. $(0.0016)^{-2}$ **63.** $\frac{0.2}{0.00000256}$ **64.** $\frac{0.000064}{25}$

65. $\frac{(3125)^2}{15{,}625}$ **66.** $\frac{(625)^4}{78{,}125}$ **67.** $(0.0000128)^3(390{,}625)^2$

Exponents can be fractions as well as integers. Exercises 68–71 will help you see how fractional exponents can be defined.

C

68. If Rule 1 for integral exponents were to hold for fractional exponents, then $9^{\frac{1}{2}} \cdot 9^{\frac{1}{2}} = 9^{\frac{1}{2}+\frac{1}{2}} = 9^1$. Therefore, $9^{\frac{1}{2}}$ ought to be defined as the number __?__.

69. If Rule 1 for integral exponents were to hold for fractional exponents, then $16^{\frac{1}{2}} \cdot 16^{\frac{1}{2}} = 16^1$. Therefore, $16^{\frac{1}{2}}$ ought to be defined as the number __?__.

70. If Rule 3 for integral exponents were to hold for fractional exponents, then $(8^{\frac{1}{3}})^3 = 8^{\frac{1}{3} \cdot 3} = 8^1$. Therefore, $8^{\frac{1}{3}}$ ought to be defined as the number __?__.

71. How could you define $(x^2)^{\frac{1}{2}}$ and $(x^3)^{\frac{1}{3}}$? (*Hint:* See Exercises 68–70.)

Problems

Solve. A calculator may be helpful.

A 1. If you have 1 kg of radioactive iodine, it will gradually decay so that d days later you will have 1.09^{-d} kg. Find how many kilograms you will have 4 days later and 8 days later.

2. The value V of a new \$12,000 automobile y years after it is purchased is given by the formula $V = 12{,}000(1.4)^{-y}$. Copy and complete the table at the right.

Years	0	1	2	3	5	10
Value (V)	?	?	?	?	?	?

3. The population of a certain state t years from now will be about $P = 12(1.03)^t$ million. Estimate to the nearest million the population **(a)** now, **(b)** 10 years from now, and **(c)** 10 years ago.

4. The cost of living in a certain city has been increasing so that an item costing one dollar today may cost $(1.08)^t$ dollars in t years. **(a)** How much may today's one-dollar item cost in 3 years? **(b)** How much in 9 years? **(c)** How much did today's one-dollar item cost 9 years ago?

5. A microbiologist has a bacteria culture whose growth rate can be described by $N = n(2.72)^{2t}$, where n is the original number of bacteria and N is the number after t hours. At noon the culture has 100 bacteria. Find, to the nearest whole number, the number on the same day at:
(a) 2 P.M. **(b)** 10 A.M. **(c)** 6 P.M. **(d)** 6 A.M.

Mixed Review Exercises

Simplify. Give restrictions on the variables.

1. $\dfrac{30x^2z^2}{18x^3z}$

2. $\dfrac{y^2 + 10y + 25}{y^2 + 7y + 10}$

3. $\left(\dfrac{-3p}{q}\right)^2$

4. $\dfrac{8}{5mn} - \dfrac{2}{m}$

5. $4 - \dfrac{2a}{a - 2}$

6. $\dfrac{x^2 - 9}{x^2 + 5x + 6}$

Divide. Write your answer as a polynomial or as a mixed expression.

7. $\dfrac{4x^2 + 2x + 36}{x + 4}$

8. $\dfrac{16}{x^2 - 9} \div \dfrac{24}{x^2 + 8x + 15}$

9. $\dfrac{a^3 + 27}{a - 3}$

7-10 Scientific Notation

Objective To use scientific notation.

Some numbers are so large or so small that they are difficult to read or to write. For example, consider the following measurements:

diameter of the solar system: 118,000,000,000 km

diameter of a silver atom: 0.00000000000025 km

Scientific notation makes it easier to work with such numbers. To write a positive number in **scientific notation,** you express it as the product of a number greater than or equal to 1 but less than 10 and an integral power of 10. Study the following examples.

Number	Number Written in Scientific Notation	Movement of the Decimal Point
118,000,000,000 (11)	1.18×10^{11}	11 places
4,709,000,000 (9)	4.709×10^{9}	9 places
0.000152 (4)	1.52×10^{-4}	4 places
0.00000000000025 (13)	2.5×10^{-13}	13 places

Notice that when a positive number greater than or equal to 10 is written in scientific notation, the power of 10 used is positive. When the number is less than 1, the power of 10 used is negative.

Example 1 Write each number in scientific notation.

a. 58,120,000,000
b. 0.00000072

Solution **a.** Move the decimal point *left* 10 places to get a number between 1 and 10.

$$58{,}120{,}000{,}000 = 5.812 \times 10^{10}$$

10

b. Move the decimal point *right* 7 places to get a number between 1 and 10.

$$0.00000072 = 7.2 \times 10^{-7}$$

7

Example 2 Write each number in decimal form.

a. 4.95×10^8 **b.** 7.63×10^{-5}

Solution **a.** Move the decimal point 8 places.

$4.95 \times 10^8 = 495{,}000{,}000$

b. Move the decimal point 5 places.

$7.63 \times 10^{-5} = 0.0000763$

Numbers written in scientific notation can be multiplied and divided easily by using the rules of exponents.

Example 3 Simplify. Write your answers in scientific notation.

a. $\dfrac{3.2 \times 10^7}{2.0 \times 10^4}$ **b.** $(2.5 \times 10^3)(6.0 \times 10^2)$ **c.** 0.4×10^6

Solution **a.**

$$\frac{3.2 \times 10^7}{2.0 \times 10^4} = \frac{3.2}{2.0} \times \frac{10^7}{10^4} \quad \left\{\text{Subtract exponents when you divide.}\right.$$
$$= 1.6 \times 10^{7-4}$$
$$= 1.6 \times 10^3 \quad \textit{Answer}$$

b.

$$(2.5 \times 10^3)(6.0 \times 10^2) = (2.5 \times 6.0)(10^3 \times 10^2) \quad \left\{\text{Add exponents when you multiply.}\right.$$
$$= (15)(10^{3+2})$$
$$= (15)(10^5)$$
$$= 1.5 \times 10^6 \quad \textit{Answer}$$

c.

$$0.4 \times 10^6 = (4 \times 10^{-1})(10^6)$$
$$= 4 \times 10^5 \quad \textit{Answer}$$

Example 4 The distance from the sun to Mercury is approximately 6×10^8 km. The distance from the sun to Pluto is approximately 5.9×10^9 km. Find the ratio of the first distance to the second.

Solution

$$\frac{\text{Distance from sun to Mercury}}{\text{Distance from sun to Pluto}} = \frac{6 \times 10^8}{5.9 \times 10^9}$$
$$= \frac{6}{5.9} \times \frac{10^8}{10^9}$$
$$= \frac{6}{5.9} \times 10^{8-9}$$
$$= \frac{6}{5.9} \times 10^{-1}$$
$$= \frac{6}{5.9} \times \frac{1}{10}$$
$$= \frac{6}{59} \quad \textit{Answer}$$

To see how your calculator handles very large numbers, see the Calculator Key-In on page 341.

Our decimal number system is based on powers of 10.

Example 5 Write each number in *expanded notation* using powers of 10.

Solution

a. $8572 = 8000 + 500 + 70 + 2$
$= 8 \cdot 10^3 + 5 \cdot 10^2 + 7 \cdot 10^1 + 2 \cdot 10^0$ ***Answer***

b. $0.3946 = 0.3 + 0.09 + 0.004 + 0.0006$
$= 3 \cdot 10^{-1} + 9 \cdot 10^{-2} + 4 \cdot 10^{-3} + 6 \cdot 10^{-4}$ ***Answer***

c. $25.03 = 20 + 5 + 0.0 + 0.03$
$= 2 \cdot 10^1 + 5 \cdot 10^0 + 0 \cdot 10^{-1} + 3 \cdot 1^{-2}$ ***Answer***

The metric system is also based upon powers of 10. To change from one metric unit to another, you simply multiply by a power of 10.

Example 6 Complete each statement by writing a power of 10.

a. 1 km = _?_ m **b.** 1 mL = _?_ L

Solution

a. To change from kilometers to meters, multiply by 10^3.
$1 \text{ km} = 10^3 \text{ m}$

b. To change from milliliters to liters, multiply by 10^{-3}.
$1 \text{ mL} = 10^{-3} \text{ L}$

Oral Exercises

Express each number in scientific notation.

1. 38,500 **2.** 4,070,000 **3.** 36,040,000

4. 0.000409 **5.** 0.000028 **6.** 0.0000000902

7–12. Express each number in Exercises 1–6 in expanded notation.

State each number as a single power of 10.

13. $10^5 \cdot 10^{-2} \cdot 10^4$ **14.** $\frac{10^9 \cdot 10^8}{10}$ **15.** $\frac{10^8}{10^6 \cdot 10^6}$

16. $\frac{10^5}{10^{-2}}$ **17.** $\frac{10^{-9}}{10^{-2}}$ **18.** $\frac{10^{-1} \cdot 10^{-4}}{10^{-3}}$

Simplify. Express your answers in scientific notation.

19. $(2 \times 10^5)(4 \times 10^6)$ **20.** $\frac{6 \times 10^7}{2 \times 10^2}$ **21.** $(3 \times 10^8)(6 \times 10^{-4})$

22. $\frac{6 \times 10^5}{12 \times 10^{-4}}$ **23.** $\frac{9 \times 10^{-5}}{3 \times 10^{-3}}$ **24.** $\frac{(4 \times 10^4)(9 \times 10^{-2})}{2 \times 10^5}$

Written Exercises

Rewrite each number in decimal form.

A **1.** The speed of light is 3.0×10^8 m/s.

2. The diameter of the sun is about 1.39×10^9 m.

3. The mass of the sun is about 2.0×10^{30} kg.

4. The frequency of an AM radio wave is 1.4×10^6 hertz (cycles per second).

5. The wavelength of ultraviolet light is 1.36×10^{-6} cm.

6. The wavelength of gamma rays is 3.0×10^{-10} cm.

7. The diameter of the nucleus of a hydrogen atom is 5.0×10^{-17} cm.

8. The mass of an atom of helium is 6.65×10^{-24} g.

Complete each statement by writing a power of 10.

9. a. 1 kg = _?_ g
b. 1 g = _?_ kg

10. a. 1 m = _?_ cm
b. 1 cm = _?_ m

11. a. 1 kg = _?_ mg
b. 1 mg = _?_ kg

12. a. 1 mm = _?_ cm
b. 1 cm = _?_ mm

13. a. 1 km = _?_ mm
b. 1 mm = _?_ km

14. a. 1 g = _?_ mg
b. 1 mg = _?_ g

Write each number in (a) scientific notation and (b) expanded notation.

15. 2500 **16.** .0123 **17.** 0.0000000024 **18.** 26,870,000

19. 3,030,000 **20.** 0.0000485 **21.** 0.0000909 **22.** 798,100,000

B **23.** 98.6% **24.** 2.3 million **25.** 12 billion **26.** 200 trillion

Simplify. Express your answers in scientific notation.

27. $(3 \times 10^{-8})(1.2 \times 10^4)$

28. $\dfrac{2.5 \times 10^{-5}}{5 \times 10^4}$

29. $\dfrac{1.08 \times 10^8}{3 \times 10^{-10}}$

30. $\dfrac{(5 \times 10^7)(9 \times 10^{-3})}{3 \times 10^{-2}}$

31. $\dfrac{(2 \times 10^5)^2}{(8 \times 10^{-3})(5 \times 10^{12})}$

32. $\dfrac{(4 \times 10^{-5})^3}{(2 \times 10^{-7})^2}$

Problems

Solve. Write your answers in scientific notation.

A **1. a.** Find the number of kilometers in a light year. A light year is the distance that light travels in one year. Light travels at the rate of 3.0×10^5 km/s. Assume a year is 365 days.

b. The Andromeda galaxy is approximately 1.5×10^6 light years from Earth. Find the distance in kilometers.

c. The distance from Earth to the star Alpha Centauri is about 4.07×10^{13} km. Use the result of Problem 1 to find how long it takes light from this star to reach Earth.

d. How long does it take light from the sun to reach Earth? The sun is 1.5×10^{8} km from Earth.

2. A sheet of paper is 0.015 cm thick. Suppose that you rip it in half, place the two halves together and rip them in half. Then you place the four pieces you now have in a stack and then rip the stack in half. If it were possible to continue this process of stacking the cut pieces and ripping the stacks apart for 50 times, the stack would have 2^{50} pieces.
(*Hint:* $2^{50} \approx 1.13 \times 10^{15}$)

a. How high would the stack reach?
b. Would it be higher than your room?
c. Higher than the tallest redwood tree (83 m)?
d. Higher than the world's tallest building (443.18 m)?
e. Higher than the moon (384,432 m)?
f. Higher than the sun (1.5×10^{8} km)?

3. The diagram shows the repetitive pattern of an electromagnetic wave. The frequency of such a wave is the number of repetitions, or cycles, per second. A typical television wave could have a frequency of 1.3×10^{8} cycles per second. The wavelength, L, is the distance from the peak of one wave to the peak of the next. The frequency, F, and wavelength, L, in centimeters, are related by the following formula:

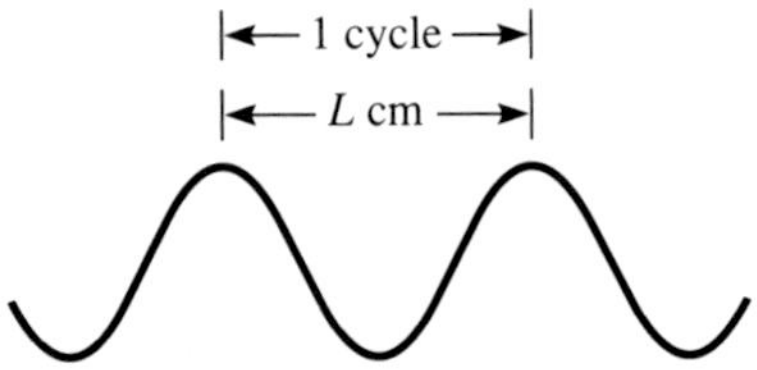

$$F \cdot L = 3.0 \times 10^{10} = \text{speed of light in cm/s}$$

Use this formula to complete the table below.

	a. Television	**b.** Red light	**c.** Violet light	**d.** x rays
Frequency F	1.3×10^{8}	4.0×10^{14}	?	?
Wavelength L	?	?	1.3×10^{-8}	1×10^{-11}

Mixed Review Exercises

Simplify. Give your answers using positive exponents.

1. $-[y + (-21)] + 2y + 3$
2. $(x^{-2}y^{5})^{3}$
3. $(13 - 25) - (8 - 28)$
4. $55:22$
5. $[4 + (-6)] + 7$
6. $3t + [(-6) + (-2) + 9]$
7. $\left(\frac{c^{-3}}{c^{3}}\right)^{2}$
8. $-\frac{5}{2} + 5 + \left(-\frac{1}{2}\right)$
9. $\frac{14b^{3}c^{2}}{12c^{3}b}$

Self-Test 5

Vocabulary scientific notation (p. 336) expanded notation (p. 338)

Simplify. Give your answers using positive exponents.

1. $(3^{-2})^{-5}$ **2.** $\frac{2^{-3}}{2^0}$ **3.** $-\frac{2^0}{2^{-3}}$ **Obj. 7-9, p. 331**

4. x^{-5} **5.** $4a^{-2}$ **6.** $(3a^2)^{-4}$

7. $x^3 \cdot x^{-3}$ **8.** $b^{-7} \cdot b^5$ **9.** $(a^3 \cdot a^{-6})^2$

Express each number in (a) scientific notation and (b) expanded notation.

10. 47 million **11.** 0.00000006 **12.** 12.34 **Obj. 7-10, p. 336**

Check your answers with those at the back of the book.

Calculator Key-In

To display very large numbers, most calculators use a form of exponential notation similar to scientific notation. Try this on a calculator:

Press the 9 key until the display is filled with 9's. Next, estimate what the answer would be if you were to multiply this number by 2. Write your estimate. Now multiply by 2 on the calculator. Compare the displayed answer with your estimate. They should be two different forms of the same number.

Enter 9's again. Predict what the calculator will display when you multiply by 20. Try it. Were you right? What will be displayed if you multiply by 400 instead of 20?

Career Note / *Electrical Engineer*

Electrical engineers work with physicists, chemists, metallurgists, mathematicians, and statisticians to design the parts that go into electronic products such as computers, stereos, televisions, and telephones. They may work in research, in development, or in quality control.

A bachelor's degree or a master's degree is usually needed since most engineers specialize in highly technical areas. Electrical engineers must always stay informed of new developments in their field of engineering.

Chapter Summary

1. A *ratio* of two numbers is their quotient. The ratio 6 to 8 can be written as 6:8 or more simply as $3 \div 4$, $\frac{3}{4}$, or 3:4. If the ratio of two numbers is 5:7, you can express the numbers as $5x$ and $7x$.
2. A *proportion* is an equation stating that two ratios are equal. In a proportion the product of the extremes is equal to the product of the means. Thus,

$$\text{if } \frac{a}{b} = \frac{c}{d}, \text{ then } ad = bc.$$

3. You can eliminate fractions from *equations with fractional coefficients* and from *fractional equations* by multiplying both sides of the equation by the LCD. Similarly, you can eliminate decimals from equations by multiplying each side by a suitable power of 10.
4. *Percent* means "hundredths" or "divided by 100." Percent problems usually involve finding a percent of a number, finding what percent one number is of another, or finding a number when a percent of the number is known. (See the example on pages 309–311.) When solving word problems, it is often convenient to express the percent as a decimal. For example,

$$7\frac{1}{2}\% = 7.5\% = 0.075.$$

5. The similarities among mixture, coin, investment, work, and distance problems can be seen in the charts and equations used to solve them.
6. Exponents can be positive, negative, or zero. The rules for positive exponents continue to hold for zero and negative exponents.
7. Expressing very large or very small numbers in *scientific notation* makes these numbers easier to use in calculations.

Chapter Review

1. State the ratio of 5 h:35 min in simplest form. **7-1**

a. $\frac{7}{1}$ **b.** $\frac{60}{7}$ **c.** $\frac{7}{60}$ **d.** $\frac{53}{60}$

2. In a ceramics class the ratio of students making projects they intend to keep to students making projects they intend to give as gifts is 3:5. If there are 24 students in the class, how many of the students intend to keep the projects they are making?

a. 3 **b.** 12 **c.** 9 **d.** 15

3. Solve $\frac{x+3}{44} = \frac{42}{24}$. **7-2**

a. $\frac{11}{42}$ **b.** $\frac{77}{3}$ **c.** 77 **d.** 74

4. Chanda is drawing a map. If she lets 1.5 cm represent 175 km, how long should she draw a segment that represents 875 km?
a. 20 cm **b.** 5 cm **c.** 7.5 cm **d.** 2.0 cm

5. Solve $\frac{x}{4} - \frac{x+4}{5} = 1$. 7-3
a. 4 **b.** 16 **c.** 36 **d.** 14

6. Solve $\frac{1}{a-1} + \frac{3}{3a-1} = 0$. 7-4
a. $\frac{2}{3}$ **b.** 0 **c.** $\frac{3}{2}$ **d.** no solution

7. Express $16\frac{2}{3}\%$ as a fraction in simplest form. 7-5
a. $\frac{50}{3}$ **b.** $\frac{5}{3}$ **c.** $\frac{1}{6}$ **d.** $\frac{1}{60}$

8. 72% of 72 is what number?
a. 100 **b.** 1 **c.** $\frac{18}{25}$ **d.** 51.84

9. 18 is 6% of what number?
a. 3 **b.** 300 **c.** 1.08 **d.** $\frac{3}{50}$

10. What percent of 36 is 27?
a. $\frac{4}{3}\%$ **b.** $\frac{3}{4}\%$ **c.** 75% **d.** 7.5%

11. A team won 57 games and lost 18. What percent did the team win?
a. 24% **b.** 76% **c.** 3.16% **d.** 31%

12. Monty saves 20% by buying a record on sale for \$6.36. What was the original price of the record? 7-6
a. \$7.95 **b.** \$9.54 **c.** \$7.99 **d.** \$8.48

13. A chemist has 10 cm^3 of a 20% salt solution. How many cubic centimeters of water should she add to produce a 5% salt solution? 7-7
a. 13 cm^3 **b.** 18 cm^3 **c.** 22 cm^3 **d.** 30 cm^3

14. Anita can paint the shed in 5 h. If Kris helps her, they can paint the shed in 3 h. How long would it take Kris to paint the shed alone? 7-8
a. $7\frac{1}{2}$ h **b.** $3\frac{3}{5}$ h **c.** $5\frac{1}{3}$ h **d.** 6 h

15. Simplify $(2x^3)^{-2}$. 7-9
a. $\frac{1}{4x}$ **b.** $\frac{1}{2x^6}$ **c.** $\frac{1}{4x^3}$ **d.** $\frac{1}{4x^6}$

16. Express 234 million in scientific notation. 7-10
a. 234×10^6 **b.** 2.34×10^8 **c.** 2.34×10^{-8} **d.** 2.34×10^6

Chapter Test

Express each ratio in simplest form.

1. 21 days:35 wk　　**2.** 63 cm:0.9 cm　　7-1

Solve.

3. The ratio of time Sean spent writing an essay to the time he spent revising it was 4:1. If he spent a total of $2\frac{1}{2}$ h writing and revising the essay, how long did it take him to write it?

4. $\frac{104}{x} = \frac{13}{2}$　　**5.** $\frac{16}{3y} = \frac{12}{5}$　　7-2

6. $\frac{3x}{10} = \frac{5x}{6}$　　**7.** $\frac{4a + 1}{7} = \frac{3a - 4}{3}$

8. $2n + \frac{3n}{5} = 5 - \frac{n}{10}$　　**9.** $\frac{3y + 5}{2} - \frac{3y + 2}{5} = \frac{3}{10}$　　7-3

10. $\frac{1}{b} + \frac{3b}{5b - 2} = 0$　　**11.** $\frac{2c + 3}{2c + 6} = \frac{1}{c}$　　7-4

Express as a fraction in simplest form.

12. 49%　　**13.** $73\frac{1}{2}\%$　　**14.** 540%　　7-5

15. 22% of 78 is what number?

16. 48 is 32% of what number?

17. What percent of 945 is 315?

Solve.

18. The number of people at this year's walkathon was 12% higher than last year. If 1344 people walked this year, how many people walked last year?　　7-6

19. How many liters of grape juice must be added to 14 L of cranberry juice to make a drink that is 16% grape juice?　　7-7

20. Working alone, Mandi can complete a project in 7 h. It would take Colin 3 h to complete the same project. If they work together, how long will it take them to complete the project?　　7-8

Simplify. Give answers using positive exponents.

21. $3^{-5} \cdot 3^4$　　**22.** $\frac{5^0}{5^{-2}}$　　**23.** $(4m^2)^{-3}$　　7-9

24. $12x^{-5}$　　**25.** $(a^{-3})^2$　　**26.** $n^2 \cdot n^{-6}$

27. Express 0.000128 in scientific notation.　　7-10

Cumulative Review *(Chapters 1–7)*

Simplify. Give your answers using positive exponents.

1. $24 \div 2 + 2^2 - 4^3 \div 2^4$

2. $\left(\frac{18}{36}\right)\left(\frac{3}{17}\right) + \left(\frac{1}{2}\right)\left(\frac{3}{17}\right)$

3. $(-2m^3n^4)(8m^5n^3)$

4. $x^2y^2(-3xy^3 + 4x^3y + 14)$

5. $(-4a^2b^3c)^2$

6. $(10b + 9)^2$

7. $(5t^2v - 6)^2$

8. $(3bc - 4)(5bc + 6)$

9. $(2x - y)(x^2 - 5xy + 3y^2)$

10. $\frac{x^2 - 12x + 36}{x - 3} \cdot \frac{x^2 - 9}{x^2 - x - 30}$

11. $\frac{3z - 1}{xyz^3} \div \frac{9xz^2 - x}{yz^2}$

12. $\frac{t}{t + 5} + \frac{t + 4}{t^2 + 2t - 15}$

13. $\frac{12b^2 + b - 6}{3b - 2}$

14. $\left(\frac{y^3}{y - 4}\right)^3$

15. $\left(\frac{x^{-7}}{x - 4}\right)^{-2}$

16. What percent of 400 is 336?

17. 56 is what percent of 600?

Factor completely. If the polynomial cannot be factored, write *prime*.

18. $-18s^3t^2 + 24s^2t^3 + 36st^3$

19. $49z^2 - 28z + 4$

20. $-64x^2 + 100t^2$

21. $6b^2 + 27b + 27$

22. $18t^2 + 27t + 12$

23. $12x^2 + 47x - 4$

Solve. If the equation is an identity or has no solution, state that fact.

24. $-7x + 2 = -33$

25. $\frac{2}{3}t - 8 = 12$

26. $(n + 4)^2 = (n + 2)^2 + 4(n + 3)$

27. $4y^2 + 28y + 49 = 0$

28. $m^2 + 14 + 9m = 0$

29. $y^3 - 12y^2 + 11y = 0$

30. $0.02(700 - x) + 0.5x = 20$

31. $\frac{n - 3}{n + 3} + \frac{1}{n - 3} = \frac{18}{n^2 - 9}$

Express in scientific notation.

32. 67 billion

33. 0.0000043

34. $(7.3 \times 10^5)(2.0 \times 10^{-2})$

35. The product of two consecutive odd integers is 22 less than the square of the greater integer. Find the integers.

36. Three numbers are in the ratio 3:4:5 and their sum is 144. Find the numbers.

37. A stereo receiver that normally costs \$425 at Berman's would cost an employee \$340. What is the percent of the employee's discount?

38. How many liters of water should be added to 20 L of a 30% acid solution to make a solution that is 10% acid?

39. One pipe can fill a tank in 2 h. A second pipe can fill it in $1\frac{3}{4}$ h. How long will it take to fill the tank with both pipes open?

Maintaining Skills

Simplify.

Sample 1 $-5(a + 3b) - 4(-2a + b) = -5a - 15b + 8a - 4b$
$= 3a - 19b$ ***Answer***

1. $7a^2 + 2 - 5a + 2a^2 + 6$
2. $-4c + 2d - 3 - 5d + 3c - 6$
3. $(12 - 2x) + (-8x + 5x)$
4. $(3m - 2n) - (-4m + 3n)$
5. $4(x - 3z) - 8(-x + z)$
6. $-2(5y^2 - 2y) + 3(-3y + 1)$
7. $-2(5x + 3) + 4(3x - 2y)$
8. $-3(5x - y) + 5x(2y + 2)$
9. $\frac{3}{4}(8a - 2b) - \frac{2}{3}(9a + b)$
10. $\frac{2}{3}(-12j - k) + \frac{1}{6}(18j + 8k)$

Sample 2 $(-4x^2yz)(-5xy^4z^3) = [(-4)(-5)](x^2 \cdot x)(y \cdot y^4)(z \cdot z^3)$
$= 20x^3y^5z^4$ ***Answer***

11. $(-2a^2b^2)(3ab^2c)$
12. $(4st^2)(-s^3t)(-2s^2t^2)$
13. $(4m^2np)\left(-\frac{1}{4}m^3np^2\right)$
14. $(-5a^2b^3)(2a^3b^2) + (a^4b)(6ab^4)$

Sample 3 $(-9a^3b^2)^3 = (-9)^3(a^3)^3(b^2)^3 = -729a^9b^6$ ***Answer***

15. $(2x^2y^3)^4$
16. $(-11m^4n^3)^2$
17. $(r^3s^2t)^4(rst)^3$
18. $-9(fg^3)^2(-2f^3g)^2$
19. $(2c^2d^2e)^6 + (-2c^4d^4e^2)^3$
20. $-ab(a^3b^2)^4 + a^3b^4(-a^2b)^5$

Multiply.

Sample 4 $5x^2y(3x^2 - 4xy + 2y^2) = 15x^4y - 20x^3y^2 + 10x^2y^3$ ***Answer***

21. $3ab^2(a^2 - ab + b^2)$
22. $-4m^2n(3mn^2 - 2m + n^3)$
23. $c^2d^3(d^4 - 2d^2c + c^3)$
24. $-xy(5x^3y^2 - 2x^2y + 7y^5)$

Sample 5 $(2r - 5s)(-3r + 2s) = 2r(-3r + 2s) - 5s(-3r + 2s)$
$= -6r^2 + 4rs + 15rs - 10s^2$
$= -6r^2 + 19rs - 10s^2$ ***Answer***

25. $(z - 3)(z + 8)$
26. $(2d + 7)(7d - 2)$
27. $(y - 2)(y + 10)$
28. $(2y - 5)(5y - 3)$
29. $(4z + 1)(3z - 3)$
30. $(3c + 4)(5c + 3)$
31. $(9d - 3)(9d + 3)$
32. $(4y + 5)^2$
33. $(x^2 - 6)(x^2 + 6)$
34. $(3a - 4)(7a + 2)$
35. $(y - 3)(3y^2 - 4y + 1)$
36. $(b - 7)(-2b^2 + 5b - 2)$

Mixed Problem Solving

Solve each problem that has a solution. If a problem has no solution, explain why.

A

1. The home team scored 50 points more than half the number scored by the visitors. Their scores totaled 194 points. Which team won? By how many points?
2. How many kilograms of salt must be added to 12 kg of an 8% salt solution to make a solution that is 20% salt?
3. An apple is 85% water. If an apple contains 187 mg of water, find the weight of the apple.
4. The ratio of the lengths of two pieces of ribbon is 1:3. If 4 ft were cut from each piece, the sum of the new lengths would be 4 ft. How long would each piece be?
5. Mia went downtown by bus, traveling at 60 km/h. She walked home at 6 km/h. Her total traveling time was 2.75 h. How far did she travel?
6. A wholesaler mixed coffee beans worth \$6/kg with another kind worth \$8.80/kg. The 16 kg mixture was worth \$6.70/kg. How many kilograms of each type were used?
7. I can weed the garden in 90 min. My friend needs 20 min more. How long will it take us to do the job together?
8. A \$24 jigsaw is on sale for \$18.60. Find the percent of discount.
9. A child's movie ticket costs \$3 and an adult's ticket cost \$5. If \$236 was collected for one show, how many of each type of ticket were sold?

B

10. The sum of two numbers is 40. When the greater number is divided by the smaller, the quotient is 4 and the remainder is 5. Find the numbers.
11. Miriam drove x km at 80 km/h. On her return trip, a detour added 10 km and reduced her speed to 60 km/h. Find her total traveling time in simplified form, in terms of x.
12. The sum of the squares of two consecutive odd integers is 2 more than 6 times their sum. Find the numbers.
13. I invested \$2000 more in stocks paying 11% than in an account paying 6%. If my average interest rate was $9\frac{1}{2}$%, how much did I invest in all?
14. A photograph is 2 cm longer than it is wide. It is in a frame that is 2 cm wide. Including the frame, the area is 255 cm^2. Find the dimensions of the photograph.

8 Introduction to Functions

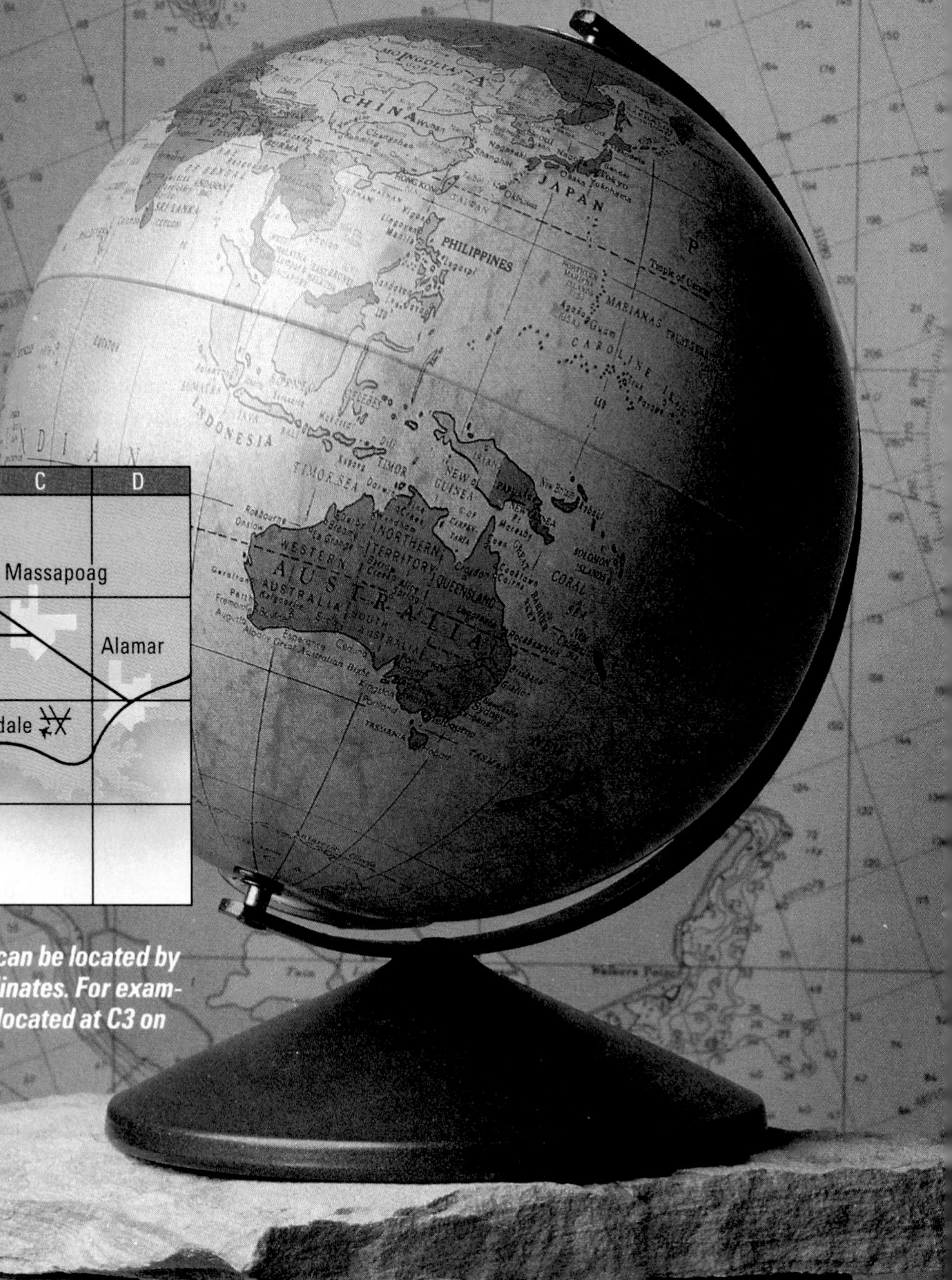

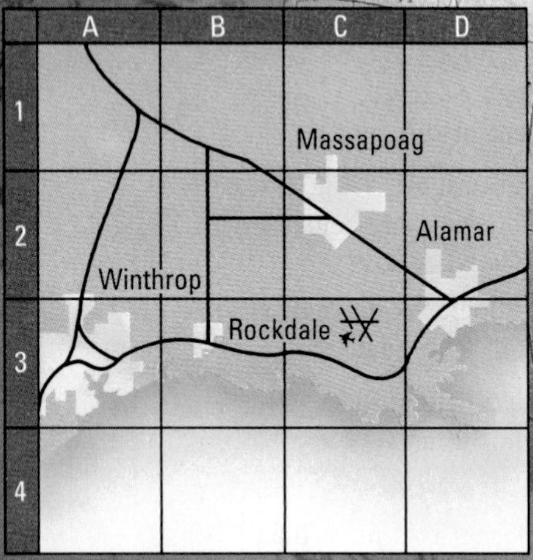

Places on a map can be located by giving two coordinates. For example, an airport is located at C3 on this map.

Using Two Variables

8-1 Equations in Two Variables

Objective To solve equations in two variables over given domains of the variables.

In earlier chapters, you worked with equations that contained only one variable. In this chapter, you will work with equations that contain two variables.

One-variable equations	**Two-variable equations**
$2x - 3 = 7$	$4x + 3y = 10$
$1 - y = 9$	$xy = 6$
$x^2 + 5x + 4 = 0$	$x^2 + y^2 = 4$

The solutions to equations in one variable are numbers. The solutions to equations in two variables are *pairs* of numbers. For example, the pair of numbers $x = 1$ and $y = 2$ is a **solution** of the equation

$$4x + 3y = 10 \text{ because } 4 \cdot 1 + 3 \cdot 2 = 10.$$

The solution $x = 1$ and $y = 2$ can be written as $(1, 2)$, with the x-value written first. A pair of numbers, such as $(1, 2)$, for which the order of the numbers is important, is called an **ordered pair.**

Example 1 State whether each ordered pair of numbers is a solution of $4x + 3y = 10$.

a. $(4, -2)$ **b.** $(-2, 6)$

c. $\left(\frac{3}{2}, \frac{4}{3}\right)$ **d.** $(3, -1)$

Solution Substitute each ordered pair in the equation $4x + 3y = 10$.

a. $(4, -2)$ is a solution because $4(4) + 3(-2) = 10$.

b. $(-2, 6)$ is a solution because $4(-2) + 3(6) = 10$.

c. $\left(\frac{3}{2}, \frac{4}{3}\right)$ is a solution because $4\left(\frac{3}{2}\right) + 3\left(\frac{4}{3}\right) = 10$.

d. $(3, -1)$ is *not* a solution because $4(3) + 3(-1) \neq 10$.

The equation $4x + 3y = 10$ has many solutions. However, if both x and y are required to be whole numbers, then $(1, 2)$ is the only solution. When you find the set of all solutions of an equation, whether it is a one- or two-variable equation, you have **solved** the equation.

Example 2 Solve $(x + 1)y = 3$ if x and y are whole numbers.

Solution

1. Solve the equation for y in terms of x.

$$y = \frac{3}{x + 1}$$

2. Replace x with successive whole numbers and find the corresponding values of y. If y is a whole number, you have found a solution pair.

$\therefore$ the solutions are $(0, 3)$ and $(2, 1)$. ***Answer***

x	$y = \frac{3}{x + 1}$	Solution
0	$\frac{3}{0 + 1} = 3$	(0, 3)
1	$\frac{3}{1 + 1} = \frac{3}{2}$	No
2	$\frac{3}{2 + 1} = 1$	(2, 1)
Values of x greater than 2 give fractional values of y.		

Example 3 Dawn spent \$13 on pens and notebooks. The pens cost \$2 each and the notebooks cost \$3 each. How many of each did she buy?

Solution

Step 1 The problem asks for the number of pens and the number of notebooks Dawn bought.

Step 2 Let p = number of pens, and n = the number of notebooks.

	Number	× Price	= Cost
Pens	p	2	$2p$
Notebooks	n	3	$3n$

Step 3 Since the total cost is \$13, you have: $2p + 3n = 13$.

Step 4 Solve for p: $2p = 13 - 3n$

$$p = \frac{13 - 3n}{2}$$

Both n and p must be whole numbers because Dawn cannot buy a negative or fractional number of pens or notebooks.

Step 5 Check that $(1, 5)$ and $(3, 2)$ are solutions of the problem:

$$2(5) + 3(1) = 13 \quad \checkmark$$
$$2(2) + 3(3) = 13 \quad \checkmark$$

$\therefore$ Dawn bought either 1 notebook and 5 pens or 3 notebooks and 2 pens. ***Answer***

n	$p = \frac{13 - 3n}{2}$	Solution
1	$\frac{13 - 3}{2} = 5$	(1, 5)
2	$\frac{13 - 6}{2} = \frac{7}{2}$	No
3	$\frac{13 - 9}{2} = 2$	(3, 2)
4	$\frac{13 - 12}{2} = \frac{1}{2}$	No
Values of n greater than 4 give negative values of p.		

When solving equations in two variables, we will give the numbers in a solution pair in the alphabetical order of the variables. Therefore, in Example 3 the solutions were given as (n, p) instead of (p, n).

Oral Exercises

State whether each ordered pair is a solution of the given equation.

1. $x - y = 5$
   $(9, 4), (7, 3)$
2. $x + 2y = 8$
   $(3, 3), (0, 4)$
3. $3x + y = 6$
   $(2, 0), (3, -1)$
4. $12 - y = 3x$
   $(5, -3), \left(\frac{1}{3}, 11\right)$
5. $y = x^2$
   $(-3, 9), (4, 2)$
6. $x^2 + y^2 = 10$
   $(1, 3), (-3, -1)$
7. $st = 6$
   $(3, -2), \left(\frac{9}{2}, \frac{4}{3}\right)$
8. $a^2 - 4b^2 = 0$
   $(-2, 1), (1, 2)$

Solve each equation for y in terms of x.

9. $2x + y = 4$
10. $3x - y = 7$
11. $x = 4 + 3y$
12. $2x + 5y = 9$

Solve each equation if x and y are whole numbers.

13. $x + y = 3$
14. $x + 2y = 7$
15. $2xy = 8$
16. $x^2 = -y^2$

Written Exercises

State whether each ordered pair is a solution of the given equation.

A

1. $5x + 2y = 23$
   $(3, 4), (7, -6)$
2. $4m - 5n = 9$
   $(6, 7), (6, 3)$
3. $3a - 2b = 13$
   $(3, -2), (5, -1)$
4. $3a - 5b = 21$
   $(7, 0), (-2, -3)$
5. $2x + 3y = 13$
   $(5, 1), (11, -3)$
6. $5x - 4y = 9$
   $(7, 6), (-3, -6)$
7. $3a - 4b = 11$
   $\left(\frac{1}{3}, -\frac{5}{2}\right), \left(-\frac{5}{3}, -4\right)$
8. $3m - 2n = 6$
   $(0, 3), \left(\frac{5}{3}, -\frac{1}{2}\right)$
9. $x^2 - 3y^2 = 15$
   $(4, -1), (-4, 1)$
10. $2x^2 + 3y^2 = 57$
    $(-3, 5), (4, -5)$
11. $4st = t$
    $\left(-\frac{1}{4}, -3\right), \left(\frac{1}{4}, 0\right)$
12. $s^3 = 4s^2t$
    $\left(-2, -\frac{1}{2}\right), \left(0, \frac{2}{3}\right)$

Solve each equation if x and y are whole numbers.

13. $2x + y = 6$
14. $5x + y = 7$
15. $3x + 2y = 8$
16. $2x + 5y = 10$
17. $3x + 7y = 7$
18. $x + 3y = 9$
19. $x + 2y = 9$
20. $3x + y = 7$

B

21. $xy = 4$
22. $xy = 12$
23. $3xy = 9$
24. $5xy = 30$
25. $xy + 7 = 23$
26. $xy + 6 = 12$
27. $2xy + 5 = 15$
28. $4xy + 8 = 36$
29. $(x + 2)y = 5$
30. $(x + 6)y = 7$
31. $y(4 - x) = 4$
32. $y(3 - x) = 6$
33. $xy = 4 - x$
34. $xy = 6 - x$
35. $xy + x = 9$
36. $xy + x = 12$

37. Lisa bought some small posters costing \$2 each and some large posters costing \$8 each. If she spent \$34, how many of each kind of poster did she buy? (There is more than one solution.)

38. Linda and Bill Gomez spent \$100 for some spruce trees. Some were blue spruce priced at \$20 each, and the rest were green spruce priced at \$10 each. How many of each kind of spruce did the Gomezs buy? (There is more than one solution.)

39. Ed McDonald spent \$280 for some baby pigs and some chickens. The pigs cost \$40 each and the chickens \$3 each. If Ed bought more than one pig, how many pigs and how many chickens did he buy?

40. The perimeter of the figure at the right is 60. Find x and y if they represent positive integers.

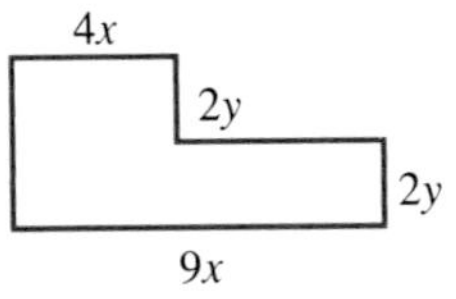

Solve for y.

C **41.** $\frac{2x - y}{2} = \frac{1 - y}{3}$ **42.** $\frac{5y + x}{4} = \frac{3x - 2y}{3}$ **43.** $\frac{1}{x} + \frac{1}{y} = \frac{1}{2}$

44. Let c and d be positive integers with $c < d$. What is the greatest value for c if $5c + 4d = 79$?

45. If a and b are positive two-digit integers, how many solutions are there of the equation $2a + 3b = 100$?

Mixed Review Exercises

Write each number in scientific notation.

1. 308,000,000 **2.** 0.000437 **3.** 119 million
4. 0.0000216 **5.** 49,000 **6.** 56,201,000

Simplify. Give answers in terms of positive exponents.

7. $\frac{3n^3}{6n}$ **8.** $(5x)^{-3}$ **9.** $\frac{48x^4y^3}{16x^3y^2}$ **10.** $\frac{b^{-4}}{b^3}$

Computer Exercises

For students with some programming experience

Write a BASIC program that determines whether an ordered pair entered with an INPUT statement is a solution to a given equation. Run the program for the following equations with the given ordered pairs.

1. $3x - 2y = 1$; (3, 4), (4, 6) **2.** $4x + y = 10$; (−3, 2), (5, −10)
3. $xy + y^2 = 6$; (1, 2), (6, 0) **4.** $x^2 + y^2 = 25$; (−4, −3), (0, 5)
5. $x^2y + xy^2 = 0$; (−1, −1), (1, −1) **6.** $x^2 + (xy)^2 = 45$; (3, −2), (3, 2)

8-2 Points, Lines, and Their Graphs

Objective To graph ordered pairs and linear equations in two variables.

You know how to graph a number as a point on a number line. You can graph, or **plot,** an ordered pair as a point in a "number plane." You can make a "number plane" as follows:

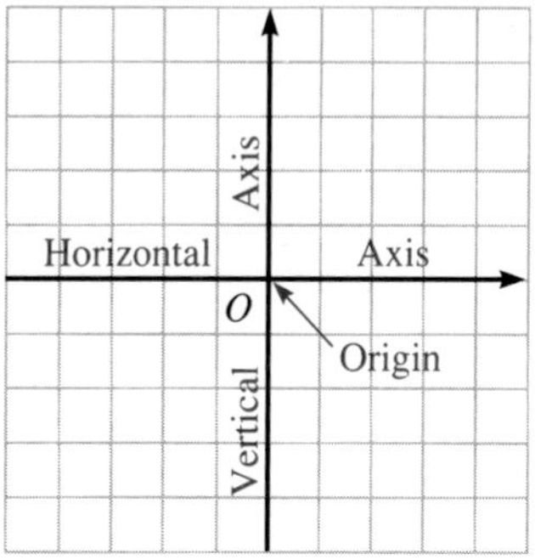

1. Draw a horizontal number line. This number line is called the **horizontal axis.**
2. Draw a second number line intersecting the first at right angles so that both number lines have the same zero point, or **origin** (*O*). The second number line is called the **vertical axis.**
3. Indicate the positive direction on each axis by an arrowhead. The positive direction is to the right on the horizontal axis and upward on the vertical axis.

The horizontal axis is often labeled with an *x* and referred to as the ***x*-axis.** The vertical axis is often labeled with a *y* and referred to as the ***y*-axis.**

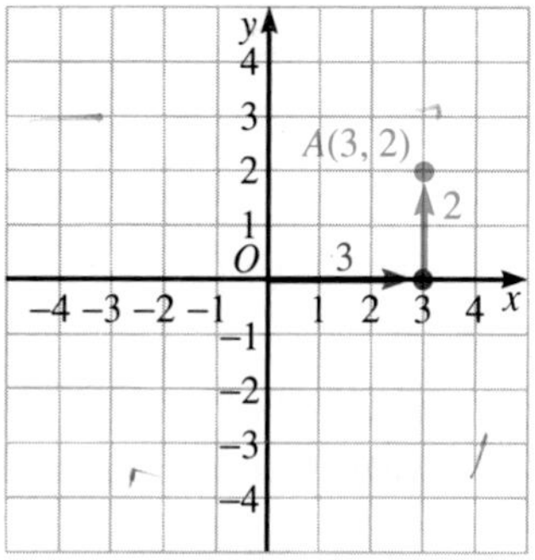

The diagram at the right shows a point *A* that is the **graph of the ordered pair** (3, 2). Point *A* is located by moving 3 units to the right of the origin and 2 units up. The numbers 3 and 2 are called the **coordinates** of point *A*; 3 is the ***x*-coordinate,** or **abscissa,** of *A*, and 2 is the ***y*-coordinate,** or **ordinate,** of *A*. Although there is a difference between the ordered pair of numbers (3, 2) and the point *A*, it is customary to stress their association by referring to the point as *A*(3, 2).

Example 1 Plot each point in a number plane.

a. $B(-2, 4)$ **b.** $C(4, -2)$ **c.** $D(-3, -2)$

Solution

a.

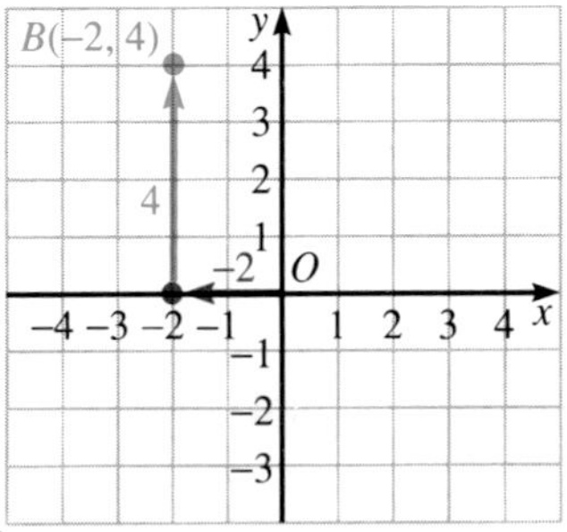

b.

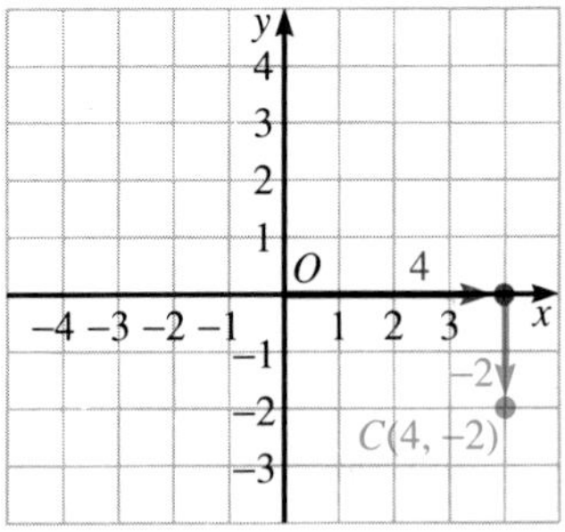

c.

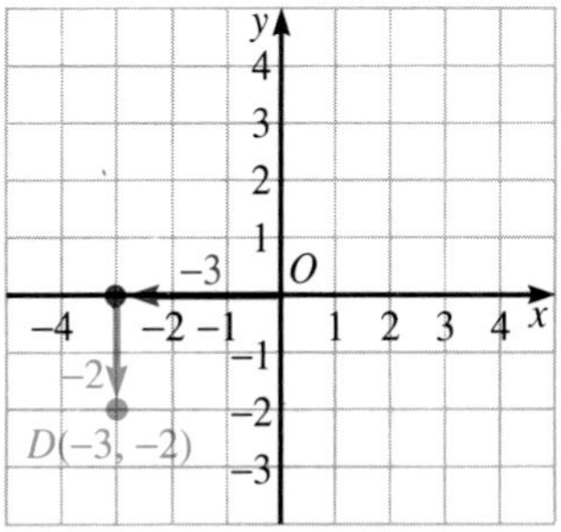

The x- and y-axes are also called **coordinate axes** and the number plane is often called a **coordinate plane.** The coordinate axes separate a coordinate plane into four **quadrants** as shown in the figure at the right. Points *on* the coordinate axes are not considered to be in any quadrant.

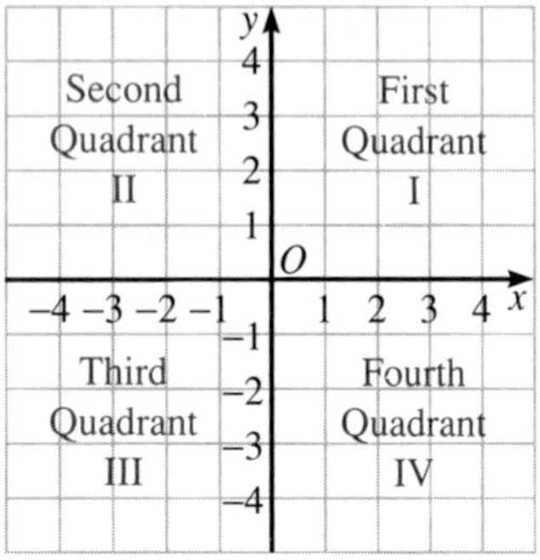

The **graph of an equation** in two variables consists of all the points that are the graphs of the solutions of the equation. For example, the equation $x + 2y = 6$ has the ordered pairs (0, 3), (2, 2), (4, 1), (6, 0), and (−2, 4) as some of its solutions. These solutions are graphed at the left below. There are many other solutions, such as $(1, 2\frac{1}{2})$ and (6.2, −0.1). The graphs of all the solutions lie on the straight line shown at the right below. This line is the graph of the equation $x + 2y = 6$.

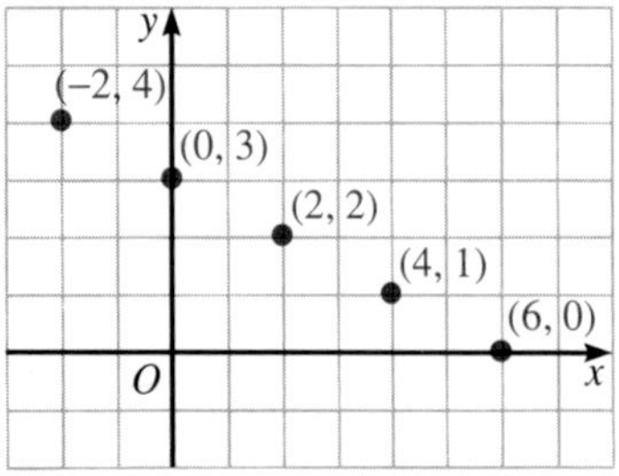

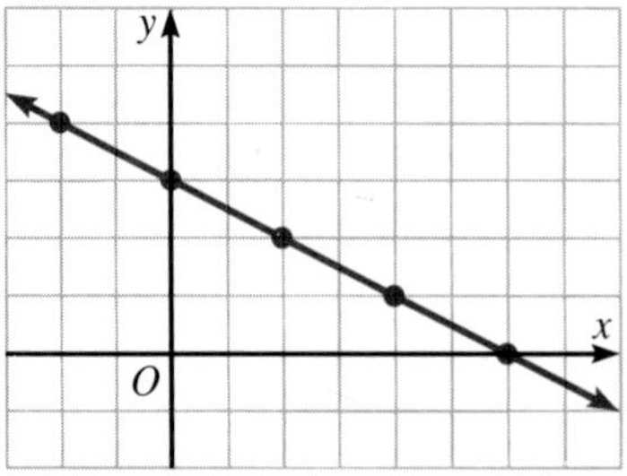

The equation $x + 2y = 6$ is called a **linear equation** because its graph is a line.

If you have a computer or a graphing calculator, you may wish to investigate the graphs of other equations of the form $ax + by = c$ described below.

All linear equations in the variables x and y can be written in the form

$$ax + by = c$$

where a, b, and c are real numbers with a and b not both zero. If a, b, and c are integers, the equation is said to be in **standard form.**

Linear equations in standard form	**Linear equations not in standard form**	**Nonlinear equations**
$2x - 5y = 7$	$\frac{1}{2}x + 4y = 12$	$x^2y + 3y = 4$
$4x + 9y = 0$	$y = 3x - 2$	$xy = 6$
$y = 3$	$x + y - 1 = x - y + 1$	$\frac{1}{x} + 3y = 1$

Since two points determine a line, you need to find only two solutions of a linear equation in order to graph it. However, it is a good idea to find a third solution as a check. The easiest solutions to find are those where the line crosses the x-axis ($y = 0$) and the y-axis ($x = 0$).

Example 2 Graph $2x - 3y = 6$ in a coordinate plane.

Solution

Let $y = 0$:

$2x - 3(0) = 6$

$2x = 6$

$x = 3$: *Solution* $(3, 0)$

Let $x = 0$:

$2(0) - 3y = 6$

$-3y = 6$

$y = -2$: *Solution* $(0, -2)$

A third solution, such as $(6, 2)$, can be used as a check.

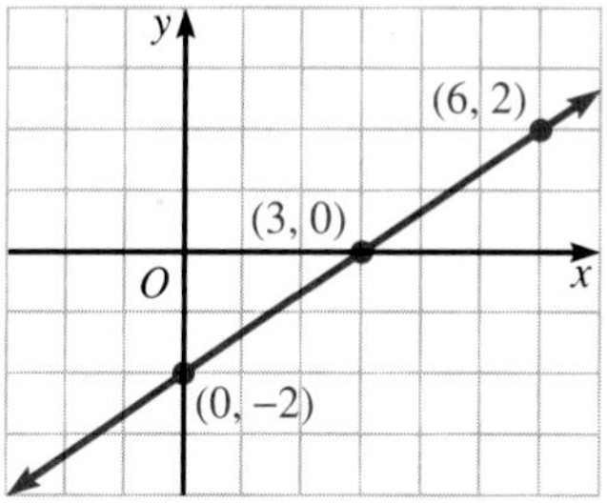

Example 3 **a.** Graph $x = -2$ in a coordinate plane.

b. Graph $y = 3$ in a coordinate plane.

Solution **a.** The equation $x = -2$ places no restriction on y.
All points with x-coordinate -2 are graphs of solutions.
The graph of $x = -2$ is a vertical line.

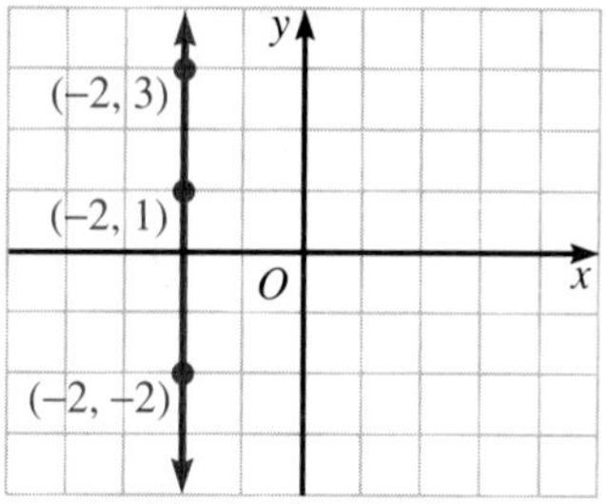

b. The equation $y = 3$ places no restriction on x.
All points with y-coordinate 3 are graphs of solutions.
The graph of $y = 3$ is a horizontal line.

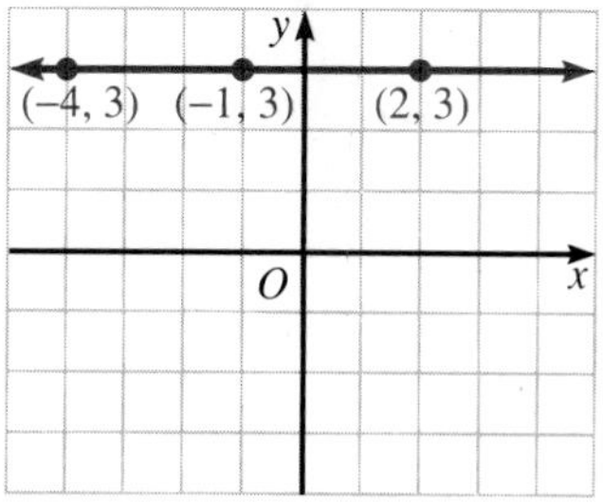

Oral Exercises

Exercises 1–20 refer to the diagram below.

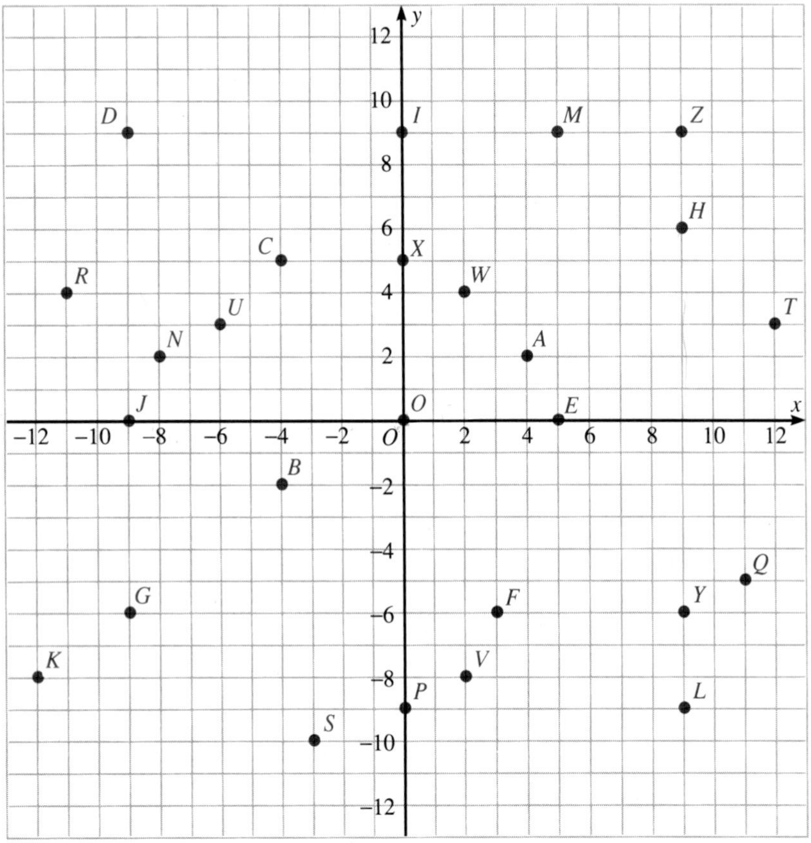

Name the point that is the graph of each ordered pair.

1. (2, 4) **2.** (4, 2) **3.** (−6, 3) **4.** (3, −6)

5. (9, 6) **6.** (9, −6) **7.** (0, −9) **8.** (−9, 0)

9. (0, 9) **10.** (11, −5) **11.** (−11, 4) **12.** (−3, −10)

Give the coordinates and the quadrant (if any) of each point.

13. M **14.** L **15.** D **16.** B

17. E **18.** V **19.** G **20.** X

Describe the graphs of the following equations.

21. $x = 2$ **22.** $x = -1$ **23.** $x = 0$

24. $y = -3$ **25.** $y = 4$ **26.** $y = 0$

Give the coordinates of the points where the graph of each equation crosses the *x*-axis and the *y*-axis.

27. $2x + y = 10$ **28.** $5x - y = 25$ **29.** $6x + 4y = 24$

Classify each equation as a linear equation in standard form, a linear equation not in standard form, or a nonlinear equation.

30. $2x + 5y = 2$ **31.** $\frac{2}{x} + \frac{3}{y} = 3$ **32.** $\frac{x}{4} + \frac{y}{7} = 1$

33. $x^2 + y^2 = 16$ **34.** $x + y = x - y$ **35.** $xy = 9$

Written Exercises

Plot each of the given points in a coordinate plane.

A **1.** $A(5, 3)$ **2.** $B(7, 2)$ **3.** $C(-5, -3)$ **4.** $D(-7, -2)$

5. $E(-8, 0)$ **6.** $F(0, -8)$ **7.** $G(-6, 4)$ **8.** $H(4, -6)$

9. $O(0, 0)$ **10.** $P(-3, 5)$ **11.** $R(7, -2)$ **12.** $S(-4, -6)$

Refer to the diagram on page 356. Name the point(s) described.

13. The point on the positive *x*-axis

14. The point on the negative *y*-axis

15. The points on the vertical line through point *Z*

16. The points on the horizontal line through point *Y*

17. The *x*-coordinate is zero.

18. The *y*-coordinate is zero.

19. The points on the axes 9 units from the origin

20. The points on the axes 5 units from the origin

21. The points having equal *x*- and *y*-coordinates

22. The points having opposite *x*- and *y*-coordinates

23. The point in Quadrant IV nearest the *y*-axis

24. The point in Quadrant III nearest the *x*-axis

Graph each equation. You may wish to verify your graphs on a computer or a graphing calculator.

25. $x - y = 10$ **26.** $x + y = 6$ **27.** $y = 2x + 5$ **28.** $y = -2x + 4$

29. $2x + y = 6$ **30.** $x - 3y = 9$ **31.** $4x - 3y = 12$ **32.** $2x + 5y = 10$

33. $x = 4$ **34.** $y = 2$ **35.** $y = -3$ **36.** $x = -6$

B **37.** $\frac{x}{2} = \frac{y}{3}$ **38.** $\frac{x}{4} + y = 0$ **39.** $\frac{1}{3}x + \frac{1}{6}y = 3$ **40.** $\frac{y}{4} - \frac{x}{3} = \frac{1}{2}$

41. $\frac{x}{3} + \frac{y}{2} = 6$ **42.** $\frac{x}{2} + \frac{y}{2} = 12$ **43.** $\frac{1}{5}x + \frac{1}{4}y = 2$ **44.** $\frac{x - y}{2} = \frac{x + y}{4}$

Plot the points A, B, C, and D. Then connect A to B, B to C, C to D, and D to A. Is the resulting figure best described as a square, a rectangle, a parallelogram, or a trapezoid?

45. $A(-3, -4), B(5, -2), C(6, 4), D(-2, 2)$

46. $A(-2, 0), B(0, -4), C(4, -2), D(2, 2)$

47. $A(-4, -1), B(-6, 5), C(3, 8), D(5, 2)$

48. $A(-1, 4), B(0, 1), C(4, -1), D(7, 0)$

Mixed Review Exercises

State whether each ordered pair is a solution of the given equation.

1. $2x + y = 5$
$(5, -5), (2, -1)$

2. $3a + 2b = 9$
$(3, 0), \left(2, \frac{3}{2}\right)$

3. $x + 4y = 13$
$(3, 2), (-3, 4)$

4. $5m + 3n = 9$
$(4, -3), (3, -2)$

Solve.

5. $x^2 + 3x + 2 = 0$

6. $-z + 13 = 2$

7. $4t^2 - 20t + 24 = 0$

8. $\frac{14 - 3y}{2} = 2$

9. $6x + 12 = 3x - 15$

10. $12 = \frac{4}{5}(n)$

Self-Test 1

Vocabulary

solution (p. 349)
ordered pair (p. 349)
plot (p. 353)
horizontal axis (p. 353)
origin (p. 353)
vertical axis (p. 353)
x-axis (p. 353)
y-axis (p. 353)
graph of an ordered pair (p. 353)
coordinates (p. 353)
x-coordinate (p. 353)
abscissa (p. 353)
y-coordinate (p. 353)
ordinate (p. 353)
coordinate axes (p. 354)
coordinate plane (p. 354)
quadrants (p. 354)
graph of an equation (p. 354)
linear equation (p. 354)
standard form (p. 354)

State whether each ordered pair is a solution of the given equation.

Obj. 8-1, p. 349

1. $2x + 4y = 12$
$(2, 2), \left(7, \frac{1}{2}\right)$

2. $3x + 5y = 30$
$(3, 5), (10, 0)$

Solve each equation if x and y are whole numbers.

3. $2x + 3y = 12$

4. $5y + 2x = 20$

(Self-Test continues on next page.)

Plot each of the given points in a coordinate plane.

5. (3, 7) **6.** (−2, 4) **7.** (−5, −2) **Obj. 8-2, p. 353**

Graph the equation.

8. $y = -3$ **9.** $x + y = 8$ **10.** $2x + 3y = 6$

Check your answers with those at the back of the book.

Computer Key-In

The following program will find the intercepts where a linear equation $Px + Qy = R$ crosses the x-axis and the y-axis when P, Q, and R are entered with an INPUT statement. The program will report if the graph does not cross either the x-axis or the y-axis.

```
10 PRINT "INPUT P, Q, R";
20 INPUT P, Q, R
30 PRINT
40 IF P< >0 THEN 70
50 PRINT "THE GRAPH DOES NOT CROSS THE X-AXIS."
60 GOTO 120
70 IF Q< >0 THEN 110
80 PRINT "THE GRAPH DOES NOT CROSS THE Y-AXIS."
90 PRINT "THE GRAPH CROSSES THE X-AXIS AT" ; R/P
100 GOTO 130
110 PRINT "THE GRAPH CROSSES THE X-AXIS AT" ; R/P
120 PRINT "THE GRAPH CROSSES THE Y-AXIS AT" ; R/Q
130 END
```

Exercises

RUN the program for the following linear equations.

1. $2x - 3y = 6$

2. $8x + y = 12$

3. $7x + 0y = -14$

4. $0x - 5y = 2$

5. $3x + 3y = 8$

6. $6x - 4y = 9$

Historical Note / *Coordinates*

The ancient Egyptians and Romans used the idea of coordinates in land surveying. The Egyptian hieroglyphic for a surveyed district was a grid.

In the seventeenth century two French mathematicians, Pierre de Fermat and René Descartes, used a version of coordinates in their work. In fact, the coordinate plane described on pages 353 and 354 is sometimes called a rectangular Cartesian coordinate plane in honor of Descartes.

8-3 Slope of a Line

Objective To find the slope of a line.

You can describe the steepness, or *slope*, of an airplane's flight path shortly after takeoff by giving the ratio of its vertical *rise* to its horizontal *run*, as shown below.

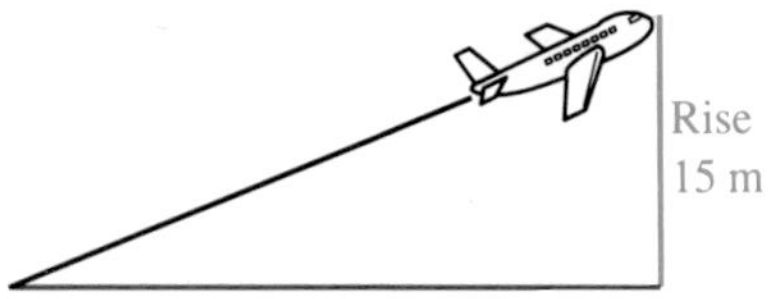

$$\frac{\text{rise}}{\text{run}} = \frac{15}{100} = \frac{3}{20}$$

To describe the slope of a straight line, first choose any two points on the line. Then count the units in the rise and the units in the run from one point to the other. The ratio of the rise to the run is the slope of the line.

Example 1

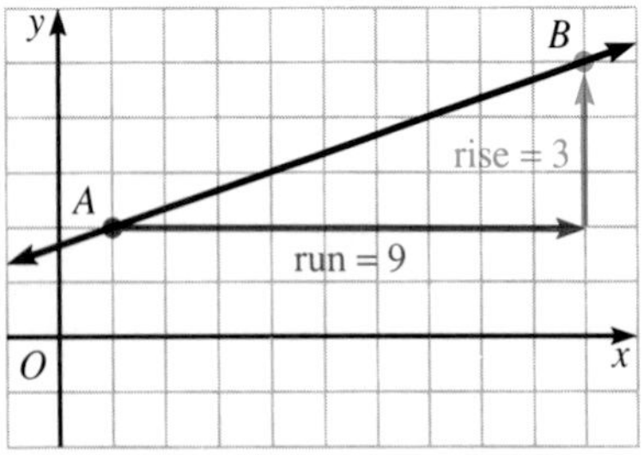

$$\text{slope} = \frac{\text{rise}}{\text{run}} = \frac{3}{9} = \frac{1}{3}$$

Example 2

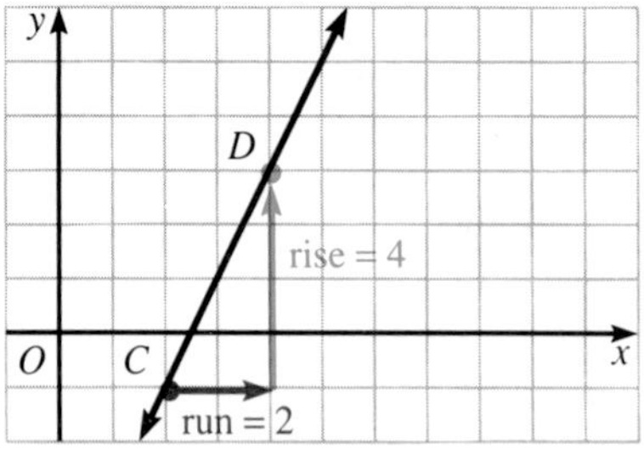

$$\text{slope} = \frac{\text{rise}}{\text{run}} = \frac{4}{2} = 2$$

Example 1 and Example 2 show lines that have a *positive* slope. Lines that rise more steeply as you move from left to right have a greater slope. Example 3 and Example 4 on the next page show lines that fall as you move from left to right. The rise of these lines is *negative,* and so is their slope.

Example 3

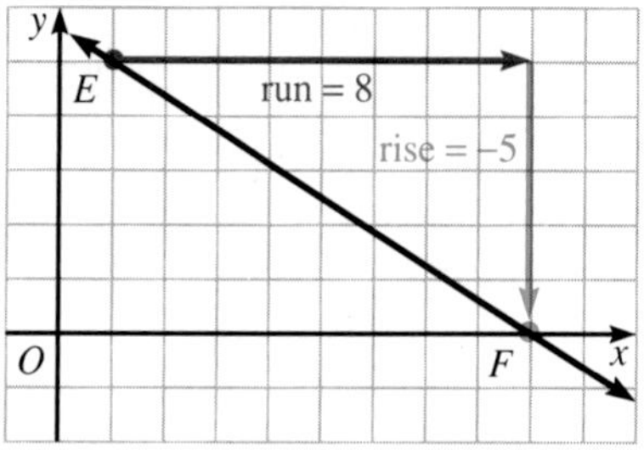

$$\text{slope} = \frac{\text{rise}}{\text{run}} = \frac{-5}{8} = -\frac{5}{8}$$

Example 4

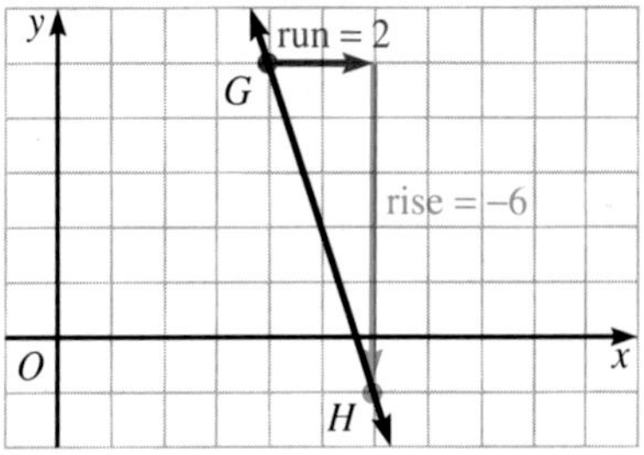

$$\text{slope} = \frac{\text{rise}}{\text{run}} = \frac{-6}{2} = -3$$

The slope of a line can be defined by using the coordinates of a pair of points on the line.

$$\textbf{slope} = \frac{\text{rise}}{\text{run}} = \frac{\text{vertical change}}{\text{horizontal change}} = \frac{\text{difference between } y\text{-coordinates}}{\text{difference between } x\text{-coordinates}}$$

Suppose that

(x_1, y_1), read "x sub 1, y sub 1," and

(x_2, y_2), read "x sub 2, y sub 2,"

are any two different points on a line. We have the following *slope formula.*

$$\textbf{slope} = \frac{y_2 - y_1}{x_2 - x_1} \quad (x_1 \neq x_2)$$

Example 5 Find the slope of the line through the points $(-2, 3)$ and $(4, 8)$.

Solution 1 $\text{slope} = \dfrac{8 - 3}{4 - (-2)} = \dfrac{5}{6}$

Solution 2 $\text{slope} = \dfrac{3 - 8}{-2 - 4} = \dfrac{-5}{-6} = \dfrac{5}{6}$

Example 5 shows that when you find the slope of a line, the order in which you consider the points is not important. However, you *must use the same order* for finding both the difference between the y-coordinates and the difference between the x-coordinates. If you don't, your result will be the opposite of the slope.

Example 6 Find the slope of the line with equation $2x + 4y = 12$.

Solution

1. Find any two points on the line.
   If $x = 0$: $4y = 12$, so $y = 3$.
   If $y = 0$: $2x = 12$, so $x = 6$.
   Two points: (0, 3) and (6, 0)

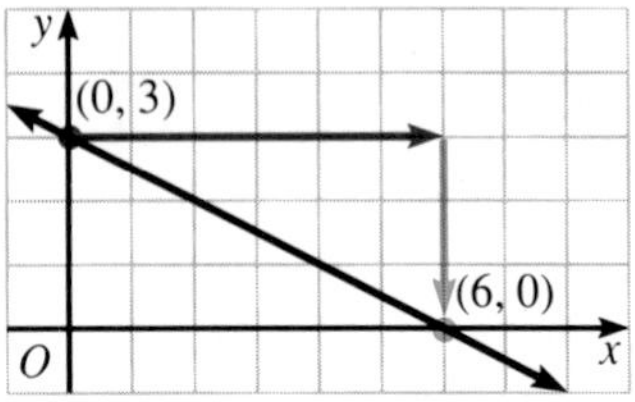

2. $\text{slope} = \dfrac{y_2 - y_1}{x_2 - x_1}$

   $= \dfrac{0 - 3}{6 - 0} = -\dfrac{1}{2}$ ***Answer***

Note that *any* two points of a line can be used to calculate its slope. For instance, in Example 6 we could have used the points (2, 2) and (4, 1), and the slope would still be $-\frac{1}{2}$.

A basic property of a straight line is that its slope is constant.

Example 7 Find the slope of each line.

a. $y = 3$

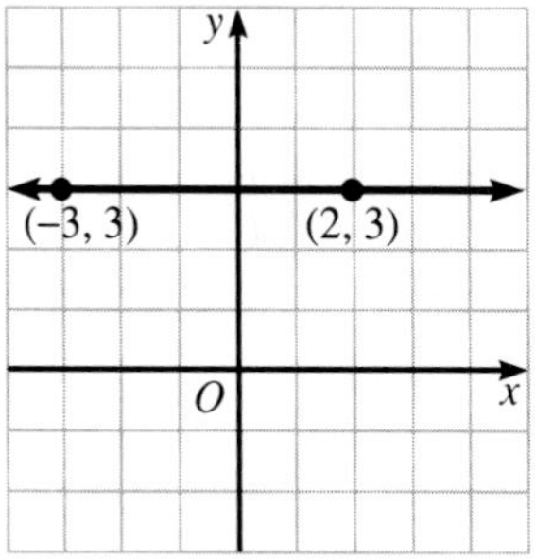

b. $x = 4$

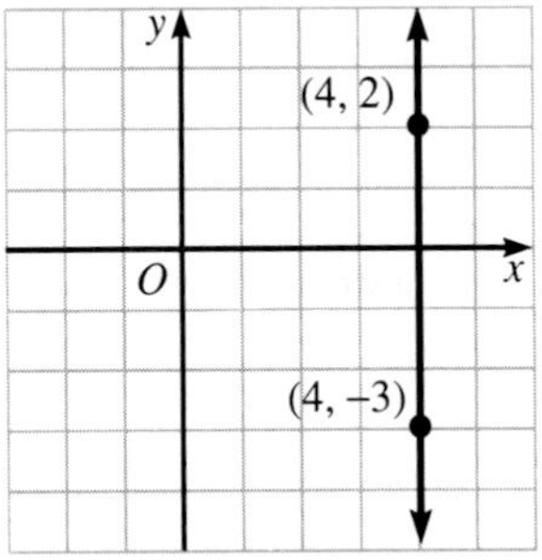

Solution

a. $\text{slope} = \dfrac{3 - 3}{-3 - 2} = \dfrac{0}{-5} = 0$

$\therefore$ the slope is 0. ***Answer***

b. $\text{slope} = \dfrac{-3 - 2}{4 - 4} = \dfrac{-5}{0}$ (undefined)

$\therefore$ the line has no slope. ***Answer***

Example 7 shows the following properties about slopes.

The slope of every horizontal line is 0.
A vertical line has no slope.

Oral Exercises

Use the figure at the right.

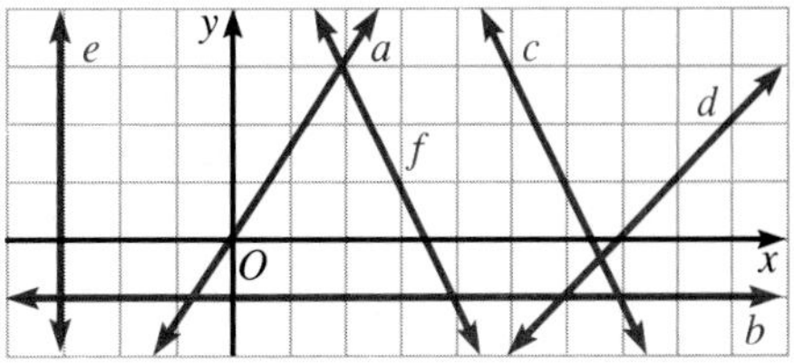

1. Which lines have positive slope?
2. Which lines have negative slope?
3. Which line has zero slope?
4. Which line has no slope?

Find the slope of each line.

5.

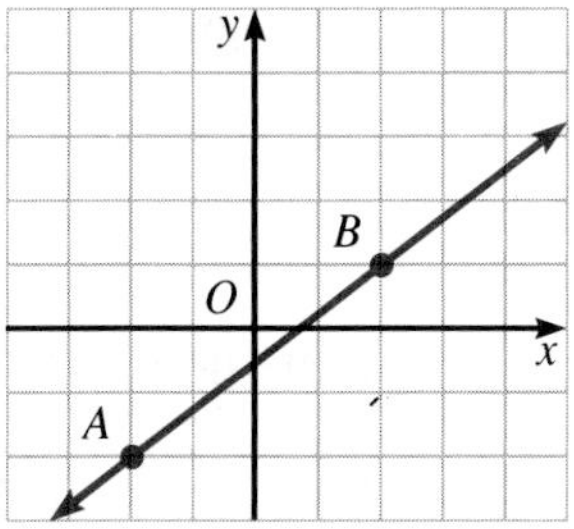

6.

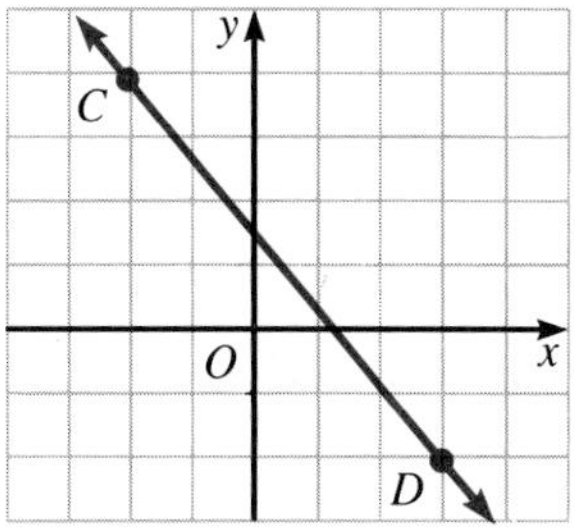

7.

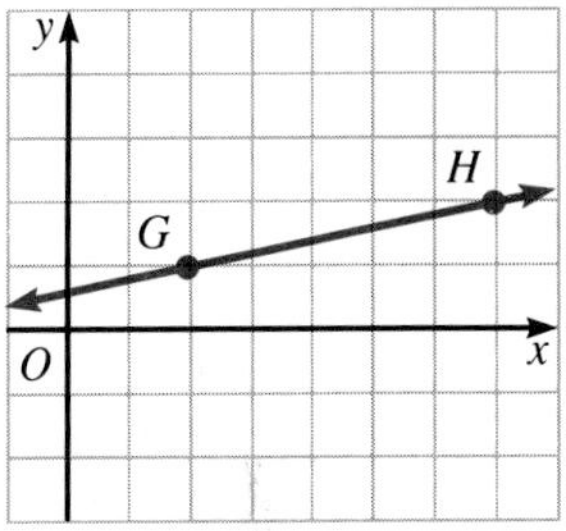

8.

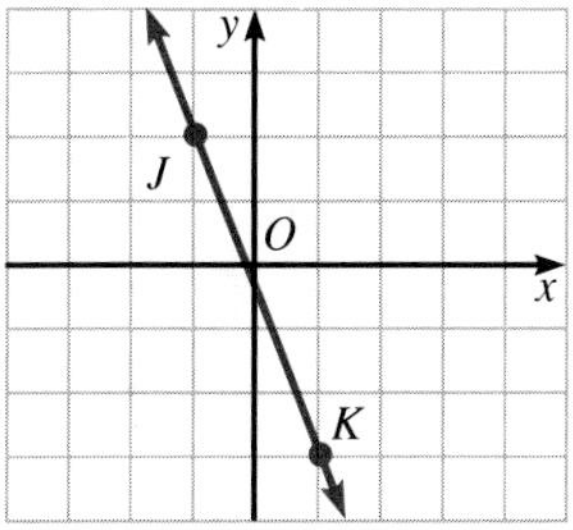

9.

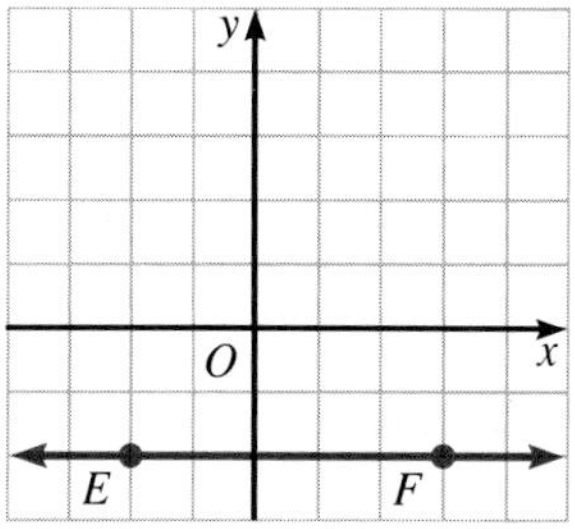

10.

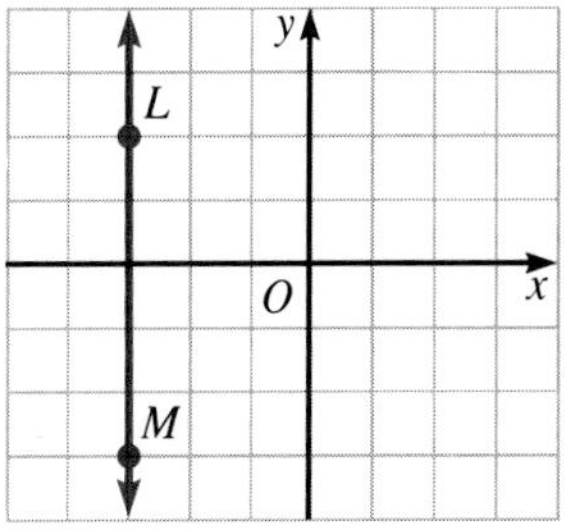

Written Exercises

Find the slope of the line through the given points.

A

1. (8, 4), (6, 5) **2.** (−4, 2), (−6, 5) **3.** (−6, 3), (−4, 5)

4. (0, 7), (2, 3) **5.** (−5, 3), (6, 5) **6.** (−4, 3), (4, 9)

7. (−2, −3), (0, −1) **8.** (6, 3), (2, 0) **9.** (4, 8), (1, 3)

10. (−8, −7), (−6, −4) **11.** (0, −3), (3, −1) **12.** (−2, 7), (−5, −7)

Find the slope of each line. If the line has no slope, say so.

13. $y = 2x + 1$ **14.** $y = 3x - 2$ **15.** $y = 8 - 2x$ **16.** $y = 12 - 4x$

17. $3x + 2y = 6$ **18.** $2x + 5y = 10$ **19.** $3x - 5y = 10$ **20.** $x - 3y = 9$

21. $y = 3$ **22.** $y + 4 = 0$ **23.** $x = 2$ **24.** $3x - 5 = 0$

Through the given point, draw a line with the given slope.

Sample $P(-2, 1)$; slope -3

Solution

1. Plot point P.
2. Write the slope as $\frac{-3}{1}$.

   From P, measure 1 unit to the right and 3 units down to locate a second point, T.

   Draw the line through P and T.

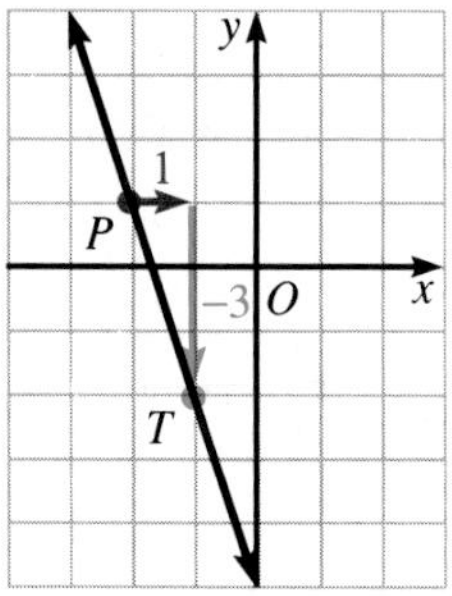

25. $A(3, 2)$; slope 4

26. $B(-3, 4)$; slope -2

27. $R(2, -7)$; slope 0

28. $N(-2, -1)$; slope $\frac{2}{7}$

29. $K(-5, 1)$; slope $-\frac{1}{2}$

30. $H(4, -3)$; slope $-\frac{3}{5}$

Points that lie on the same line are said to be *collinear*. Determine whether the given points are collinear.

Sample

a. (3, 5), (4, 7), and (7, 13)

b. (8, 9), (5, 3), and (2, −2)

Solution

1. Make a table of the coordinates in order of increasing x-coordinates.
2. Find the changes in the x-coordinates and y-coordinates as you move from one point to the next.
3. If the ratio $\frac{\text{vertical change}}{\text{horizontal change}}$ is constant, the points are collinear. Otherwise, they are not.

a.

change in x	x	y	change in y
	3	5	
1			2
	4	7	
3			6
	7	13	

$$\frac{2}{1} = \frac{6}{3}$$

∴ the points are collinear.

b.

change in x	x	y	change in y
	2	−2	
3			5
	5	3	
3			6
	8	9	

$$\frac{5}{3} \neq \frac{6}{3}$$

∴ the points are not collinear.

B **31.** (1, 4), (3, 0), (5, −4)

32. (8, 1), (6, 5), (4, 8)

33. (−5, 9), (−1, 1), (1, −4)

34. (−3, 7), (0, 5), (6, 1)

35. (0, −1), (1, −2), (2, −4), (−1, 0)

36. (1, −1), (−1, 2), (−3, 5), (−5, 8)

37. The vertices of a triangle are $A(-4, 6)$, $B(5, 6)$, and $C(-4, -2)$. Find the slope of each side of the triangle.

38. The vertices of a rectangle are $M(-2, -3)$, $N(3, 2)$, $P(10, -5)$, and $Q(5, -10)$. Find the slope of each side of the rectangle.

39. Determine the slope of the line through the points (4, 6) and (0, 4). Find the value of y if $(8, y)$ lies on this line.

40. The slope of a line through the point (1, 3) is 1.5. If the point $(-3, y)$ lies on the line, find the value of y.

C 41. The vertices of a square are $A(3, 5)$, $B(11, 3)$, $C(9, -5)$, and $D(1, -3)$. Use the idea of slope to show that the point $M(6, 0)$ lies on the diagonal joining A and C, and on the diagonal joining B and D.

42. The vertices of a right triangle are $P(-4, 2)$, $Q(-4, -6)$, and $R(6, -6)$. Use the idea of slope to show that $S(1, -2)$ lies on one of the sides of the triangle.

Mixed Review Exercises

Solve.

1. $\frac{x+3}{3} + \frac{x}{2} = 0$
2. $-5 = \frac{9b}{4}$
3. $\frac{3+z}{2z} = \frac{3}{z}$
4. $-5(y+3) = 30$
5. $|z| = 1.7$
6. $3m(m-5) = 0$

Evaluate if $x = 2$, $y = 1$, $a = -3$, and $b = 4$.

7. $\frac{a+4b}{2a-b}$
8. $5(x+2y)$
9. $\frac{1}{3}(4x+y)$
10. $(xy^2)^2$
11. $(3a-2b)+7$
12. $(2y^3)^3$

Calculator Key-In

You can use a calculator to find the slope of a straight line through two given points (x_1, y_1) and (x_2, y_2).

1. First enter $x_2 - x_1$ and store the result in memory.
2. Then enter $y_2 - y_1$ and divide the result by the value stored in memory.

The result of the division in Step 2 is the slope.

Find the slope of the line through the given points.

1. (2, 0), (3, 7)
2. (3, 2.8), (2.22, −5)
3. (−0.8, 5.7), (3.2, −2)
4. (3, 2.5), (6.2, 7)
5. (−1, −2), (−5, −6)
6. (3, 4.4), (−1.5, 7.1)

8-4 The Slope-Intercept Form of a Linear Equation

Objective To use the slope-intercept form of a linear equation.

The points with coordinates $(-2, -4)$, $(-1, -2)$, $(0, 0)$, $(1, 2)$, and $(2, 4)$ are on the graph of the linear equation

$$y = 2x.$$

The graph, shown at the right, is the straight line that has slope $\frac{2}{1}$, or 2, and that passes through the origin.

The graph

$$y = -\frac{1}{3}x,$$

also shown at the right, is a line that has slope $-\frac{1}{3}$ and that passes through the origin.

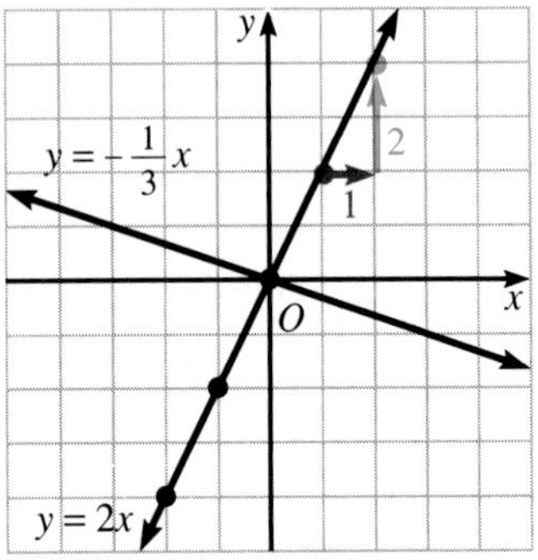

For every real number m, the graph of the equation

$$\boldsymbol{y = mx}$$

is the line that has slope m and passes through the origin.

The graphs of the linear equations $y = 2x$ and $y = 2x + 4$ are shown at the right. The lines have the same slope, but they cross the y-axis at different points. The y-coordinate of a point where a graph crosses the y-axis is called the **y-intercept** of the graph.

To determine the y-intercept of a line, replace x with 0 in the equation of the line:

$y = 2x$	$y = 2x + 4$
$y = 2(0) = 0$	$y = 2(0) + 4 = 4$
y-intercept: 0	y-intercept: 4

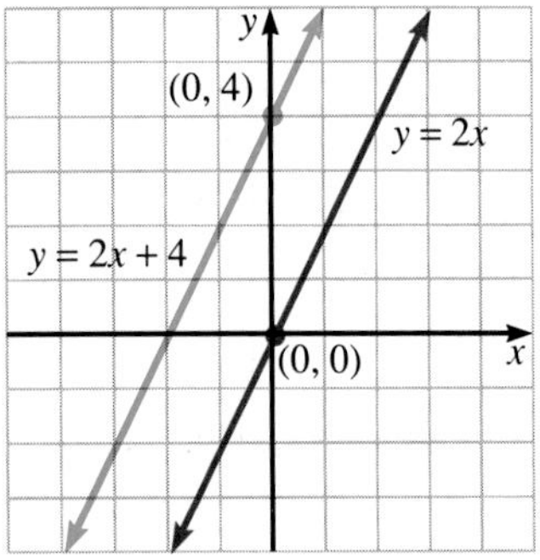

If you write $y = 2x$ as $y = 2x + 0$, you can see that the constant term of each equation is the y-intercept of each graph:

$y = 2x + 0$ $\qquad\qquad$ $y = 2x + 4$

For all real numbers m and b, the graph of the equation

$$\boldsymbol{y = mx + b}$$

is the line whose slope is m and whose y-intercept is b.

This is called the **slope-intercept form** of an equation of a line.

Example 1 Find the slope and y-intercept of $y = \frac{3}{5}x + 2$.

Solution For $y = \frac{3}{5}x + 2$, we have $m = \frac{3}{5}$ and $b = 2$.

$\therefore$ the slope is $\frac{3}{5}$ and the y-intercept is 2. ***Answer***

Example 2 Use only the slope and y-intercept to graph $y = -\frac{3}{4}x + 6$.

Solution The slope is $-\frac{3}{4}$. The y-intercept is 6.

Since the y-intercept is 6, plot (0, 6).

Since the slope is $-\frac{3}{4}$, move 4 units to the right of (0, 6) and 3 units down to locate a second point.

Draw the line through the two points.

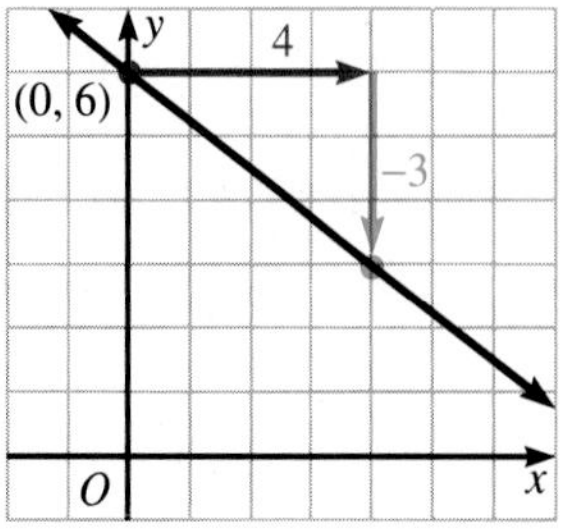

Example 3 Use only the slope and y-intercept to graph $2x - 5y = 10$.

Solution Solve for y to transform the equation into the form $y = mx + b$.

$$
\begin{aligned}
2x - 5y &= 10 \\
-5y &= -2x + 10 \\
y &= \frac{2}{5}x - 2
\end{aligned}
$$

The slope is $\frac{2}{5}$. The y-intercept is -2.

Since the y-intercept is -2, plot $(0, -2)$.

Since the slope is $\frac{2}{5}$, move 5 units to the right of $(0, -2)$ and 2 units up to locate a second point.

Draw the line through the two points.

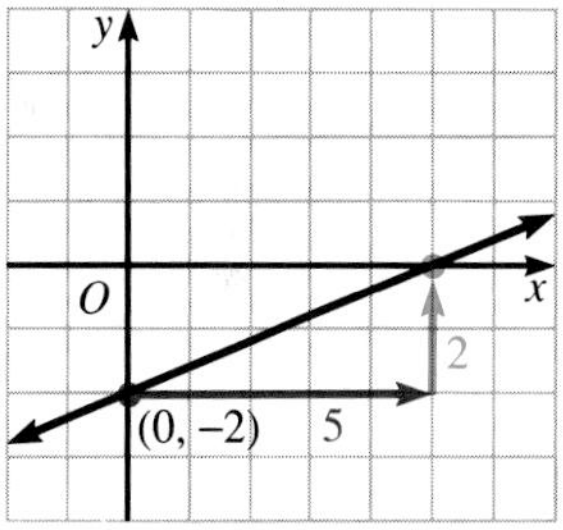

If you have a computer or a graphing calculator, you can use it to investigate the relationships among the graphs of equations that have the same slope, but different y-intercepts.

Lines in the same plane that do not intersect are **parallel.** The following relationships exist between parallel lines and their slopes.

1. Different lines with the same slope are parallel.
2. Parallel lines that are not vertical have the same slope.

Example 4 Show that the lines whose equations are $2x + y = 8$ and $2x + y = 6$ are parallel.

Solution
1. Write each equation in slope-intercept form:

   $y = -2x + 8$ $\qquad$ $y = -2x + 6$

2. Find the slope and y-intercept of each line.

   For $y = -2x + 8$: slope $= -2$, y-intercept $= 8$

   For $y = -2x + 6$: slope $= -2$, y-intercept $= 6$

Since both lines have the *same* slope and *different* y-intercepts, they're parallel.

Oral Exercises

State the slope and y-intercept of each line.

1. $y = 3x + 7$ **2.** $y = -2x - 1$ **3.** $y = \frac{1}{2}x + 4$ **4.** $y = \frac{2}{3}x - 5$

5. $y = 5x$ **6.** $y = -3x$ **7.** $y - 6x = 4$ **8.** $y - 2x = 7$

9. $3x + y = 8$ **10.** $4x + y = 10$ **11.** $-2x + y = 7$ **12.** $-3x + y = 8$

Written Exercises

Find the slope and y-intercept of each line.

A **1.** $y = 2x + 1$ **2.** $y = 3x - 4$ **3.** $y = \frac{1}{2}x - 3$

4. $y = \frac{2}{3}x + 3$ **5.** $y = -\frac{1}{2}x + 6$ **6.** $y = -\frac{1}{3}x - 2$

7. $y = 8 - 2x$ **8.** $y = 9 - 3x$ **9.** $y = x$

10. $y = -x$ **11.** $y = -4$ **12.** $y = 4$

Use only the slope and y-intercept to graph each equation. You may wish to verify your graphs on a computer or a graphing calculator.

13. $y = -x + 5$ **14.** $y = 2x - 3$ **15.** $y = \frac{2}{3}x + 4$

16. $y = \frac{4}{5}x - 3$ **17.** $y = -\frac{1}{2}x + 4$ **18.** $y = -\frac{3}{4}x - 5$

19. $x + y = 8$ **20.** $2x + y = 6$ **21.** $3x - y = 6$

22. $2x - y = -4$ **23.** $3x + y = 9$ **24.** $2x + y = -4$

B **25.** $3x - 5y = 10$ **26.** $4x - 3y = 9$ **27.** $x + 5y = 5$

28. $6x + 4y = 8$ **29.** $3x = 2y$ **30.** $4y = 3$

Show that the lines whose equations are given are parallel.

31. $2x - 3y = 7$
$-2x + 3y = 4$

32. $x - 2y = 1$
$-2x + 4y = 9$

33. $x - y = 4$
$y - x = 4$

34. $4x - y = 1$
$-8x + 2y = 2$

35. $\frac{1}{2}x + \frac{1}{2}y = 5$
$2x + 2y = 3$

36. $\frac{1}{3}x - \frac{1}{3}y = 2$
$3x - 3y = 1$

37. Write an equation of the line that has y-intercept 7 and is parallel to the graph of $y = 5x - 3$.

38. Write an equation of the line that is parallel to the graph of $y - 3x = 4$ and has the same y-intercept as the graph of $4y + x = 36$.

39. In the equation $2y + px = 5$, for what value of p is the graph of the equation parallel to the graph of $x + y = 5$? the graph of $x - y = 5$?

40. In the equation $dy + 3x = 2$, for what value of d is the graph of the equation parallel to the graph of $x - 3y = 0$? the y-axis?

In Exercises 41–43, use the points $A(5, 3)$, $B(2, 6)$, and $C(-2, 0)$.

41. Find r if the line joining A to $(r, 2r)$ is parallel to the line joining B and C.

42. Find s if the line joining B to $(s + 4, s)$ is parallel to the line joining A and C.

43. Find t if the line joining C to $(-3t, 2t + 1)$ is parallel to the line joining A and B.

C **44.** A radio beacon is located at $(-1, 0)$ and another at $(2, -1)$. A navigator's equipment tells her that the line joining her position to the first beacon has slope -5 and the line joining her position to the second beacon has slope 3. What is the navigator's approximate location?

45. Using the standard form of a linear equation, $ax + by = c$, find a formula for the slope and a formula for the y-intercept in terms of the coefficients, assuming that $b \neq 0$.

Mixed Review Exercises

Find the slope of the line through each pair of given points.

1. $(-3, 1), (-2, 3)$ **2.** $(1, 2), (4, 3)$ **3.** $(-2, 5), (-1, 2)$ **4.** $(1, 5), (3, 13)$

Factor.

5. $3s^2 + 7s + 4$

6. $20x^2 + 15x$

7. $3p^2 - 24p + 48$

8. $81y^2 - 16z^2$

9. $-3x(x + y) + 4(x + y)$

10. $m^2 - 9mn - 36n^2$

Extra / Perpendicular Lines

In a coordinate plane, the x-axis and the y-axis intersect to form right angles. Any two lines that intersect to form right angles are **perpendicular.** The graphs of $y = 2x + 1$ and $y = -\frac{1}{2}x - 2$ shown are perpendicular. The following relationships exist between perpendicular lines and their slopes.

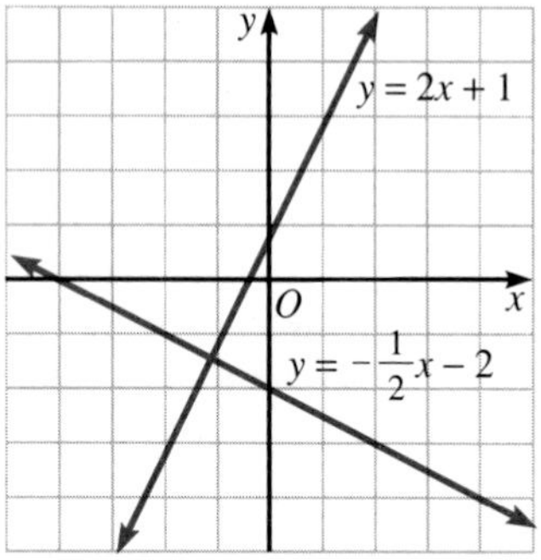

1. If the product of the slopes of two lines is -1, the lines are perpendicular.
2. Perpendicular lines that are not horizontal and vertical have slopes whose product is -1.

Example Show that the graphs of $y = \frac{3}{4}x - 1$ and $6y + 8x = 7$ are perpendicular.

Solution

1. Write $6y + 8x = 7$ in slope-intercept form: $y = -\frac{4}{3}x + \frac{7}{6}$
2. The slope of $y = \frac{3}{4}x - 1$ is $\frac{3}{4}$. The slope of $y = -\frac{4}{3}x + \frac{7}{6}$ is $-\frac{4}{3}$.
3. $\frac{3}{4}\left(-\frac{4}{3}\right) = -1$ $\quad\therefore$ the lines are perpendicular. ***Answer***

Exercises

Find the slope of the line perpendicular to the graph of each line.

1. $y = \frac{3}{2}x + 7$ **2.** $y = \frac{4}{5}x - 2$ **3.** $y = -\frac{3}{8}x + 5$

4. $2x + y = 3$ **5.** $3x - 5y = 110$ **6.** $y = -x$

7. $y = 1$ **8.** $x = 3$ **9.** $x - 3y - 8 = 0$

Tell whether the graphs of each pair of equations are parallel, perpendicular, or neither.

10. $3x + 6y = 8$, $y = 2x - 8$ **11.** $3x + y = 7$, $y = -3x + 2$ **12.** $2x + 5y = 7$, $2x + 5y = 9$

13. $2x - 8y = 9$, $12x + 3y = 7$ **14.** $y = x + 5$, $y = 8 - x$ **15.** $4x + 6y = 9$, $2x + 3y = 5$

16. Show that the graphs of $y = 4 - 3x$ and $3y - x = 12$ have the same y-intercept and are perpendicular.

17. The graph of $y = \frac{2}{3}x - 12$ intersects the y-axis at $Q(0, -12)$ and is perpendicular to a line joining Q to the point $P(x, 0)$. Find x.

8-5 Determining an Equation of a Line

Objective To find an equation of a line given the slope and one point on the line, or given two points on the line.

You have learned to graph a line when given its equation. Now you will learn to find an equation of a line when given information about its graph.

Example 1 Write an equation of a line that has slope 2 and y-intercept 3.

Solution Substitute 2 for m and 3 for b in $y = mx + b$.
The equation is $y = 2x + 3$. ***Answer***

Example 2 Write an equation of a line that has slope -4 and x-intercept 3.

Solution The *x-intercept* is the x-coordinate of the point where a line crosses the x-axis. In this example, this point is (3, 0).

1. Substitute -4 for m in $y = mx + b$.
$$y = -4x + b$$
2. To find b, substitute 3 for x and 0 for y in $y = -4x + b$.
$$\begin{aligned} y &= -4x + b \\ 0 &= -4(3) + b \\ 0 &= -12 + b \\ 12 &= b \end{aligned}$$

$\therefore$ the equation is $y = -4x + 12$. ***Answer***

Example 3 Write an equation of the line passing through the points $(-2, 5)$ and $(4, 8)$.

Solution

1. Find the slope: $\dfrac{y_2 - y_1}{x_2 - x_1} = \dfrac{8 - 5}{4 - (-2)} = \dfrac{3}{6} = \dfrac{1}{2}$
Substitute $\frac{1}{2}$ for m in $y = mx + b$.
$$y = \frac{1}{2}x + b$$
2. Choose one of the points, say (4, 8). Substitute 4 for x and 8 for y.
$$\begin{aligned} y &= \frac{1}{2}x + b \\ 8 &= \frac{1}{2}(4) + b \\ 8 &= 2 + b \\ 6 &= b \end{aligned}$$

$\therefore$ the equation is $y = \frac{1}{2}x + 6$. ***Answer***

Note that in the second step of Example 3 we could have used the point $(-2, 5)$. The resulting equation would have been the same.

Oral Exercises

Give the equation in slope-intercept form of each line described.

1. slope -5, y-intercept 8
2. slope $\frac{2}{3}$, y-intercept -7
3. slope 3, passes through $(0, 4)$
4. y-intercept 2, x-intercept 2
5. slope $\frac{1}{2}$, passes through $(0, 0)$
6. passes through $(1, 4)$ and $(2, 5)$

Written Exercises

Write an equation in slope-intercept form of each line described.

A

1. slope 2; y-intercept 5
2. slope -3; y-intercept 4
3. slope $-\frac{1}{2}$; y-intercept 7
4. slope $\frac{2}{3}$; y-intercept 9
5. slope $\frac{1}{2}$; x-intercept 4
6. slope $-\frac{1}{3}$; x-intercept 3
7. slope 2; passes through $(-5, 1)$
8. slope 3; passes through $(4, 1)$
9. slope -2; passes through $(3, 5)$
10. slope -1; passes through $(8, 5)$
11. slope $\frac{1}{2}$; passes through $(4, -1)$
12. slope $\frac{1}{3}$; passes through $(6, 0)$
13. slope $-\frac{3}{4}$; passes through $(8, -3)$
14. slope $-\frac{2}{5}$; passes through $(5, 7)$
15. slope 0; passes through $(1, 3)$
16. slope 0; passes through $(-5, 4)$

Write an equation in slope-intercept form of the line passing through the given points.

17. $(0, 7), (1, 9)$
18. $(0, 3), (2, -1)$
19. $(5, 2), (7, 0)$
20. $(-3, 4), (3, -4)$
21. $(8, 1), (1, 8)$
22. $(-2, 4), (4, 2)$
23. $(3, -1), (6, 7)$
24. $(-3, -1), (1, -4)$
25. $(0, -1), (1, 4)$
26. $(-1, -2), (0, 3)$
27. $(-2, 0), (2, -3)$
28. $(3, 0), (-2, 5)$

Write an equation in slope-intercept form for each line described.

B

29. y-intercept -2; x-intercept 5
30. y-intercept -5; x-intercept 3
31. x-intercept 6; y-intercept -3
32. x-intercept -4; y-intercept -2
33. horizontal line through $(3, 5)$
34. horizontal line through $(-2, -1)$

Write an equation in standard form for each line described.

35. The line that passes through $(-1, 3)$ and is parallel to $3x - y = 4$.
36. The line that is parallel to $x - 2y + 7 = 0$ and contains $(-4, 0)$.
37. The line that passes through $(-4, -5)$ and has the same y-intercept as $x + 3y + 9 = 0$.
38. The line that contains $(7, 1)$, $(p, 0)$, and $(0, p)$ for $p \neq 0$.
39. **a.** Can the equation of the line through $(2, 5)$ and $(2, 8)$ be written in slope-intercept form? Why or why not?
    b. Write the equation of the line in standard form.
40. A horizontal line intersects a vertical line at $(-3, 7)$. Give the equation of each line in standard form.

C 41. A line passes through $(-2, 3)$, $(2, 5)$, and $(6, k)$. Find k.

42. A line with x-intercept -4 passes through $(2, 6)$ and $(p, 10)$. Find p.

Mixed Review Exercises

Simplify.

1. $\left(\frac{4}{3}t^3\right)(12t^2)$	**2.** $\frac{1}{2}(4s^2 - 8st)$	**3.** $(7pq^2)^2$	**4.** $(-3m^2n^4)^3$
5. $3 \cdot 4 - 3^2$	**6.** $(3a^3b)(-6ab^2)$	**7.** $2 \cdot (8 - 4)^3$	**8.** $(8x + 3y) - (3x + y)$

Self-Test 2

Vocabulary slope (p. 361)
collinear (p. 364)
y-intercept (p. 366)
slope-intercept form of an equation (p. 366)
parallel (p. 367)
x-intercept (p. 371)

1. Find the slope of the line that passes through $(4, 7)$ and $(1, 3)$. **Obj. 8-3, p. 360**
2. Find the slope of the line whose equation is $y = 4$.
3. Find the slope and y-intercept of the line $3x - 7y = 28$. **Obj. 8-4, p. 366**
4. Use only the slope and y-intercept to graph $2x + 3y = -6$.
5. Write an equation in slope-intercept form of the line with slope 3 that passes through the point $(-2, -1)$. **Obj. 8-5, p. 371**
6. Write an equation in slope-intercept form of the line through the points $(5, 0)$ and $(0, -5)$.

Check your answers with those at the back of the book.

8-6 Functions Defined by Tables and Graphs

Objective To understand what a function is and to define a function by using tables and graphs.

A **function** is a correspondence between two sets, the **domain** and the **range,** that assigns to each member of the domain *exactly one* member of the range. Each member of the range must be assigned to *at least one* member of the domain.

You can represent a function either as a correspondence, as stated in the definition, or as a set of ordered pairs, as shown in Example 1.

Example 1 The birthday function matches each person with his or her birthday. Some of these pairings are shown below.

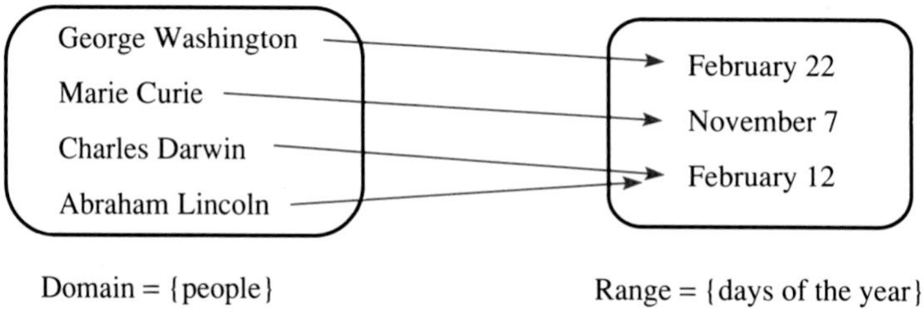

Write each pairing as an ordered pair.

Solution (George Washington, February 22)
(Marie Curie, November 7)
(Charles Darwin, February 12)
(Abraham Lincoln, February 12)

The table at the right shows the average height in feet associated with each of several types of trees. This association is a function. The table provides a rule by assigning one height to each tree. The domain of the function is the set of first coordinates:

{Douglas fir, Juniper, Oak, Poplar, Yew}

The range of the function is the set of second coordinates:

{10, 12, 25, 30, 40}

Tree	Height (feet)
Douglas fir	40
Juniper	10
Oak	25
Poplar	30
Yew	12

It is easier to compare the heights if the facts are displayed in a *bar graph*.

Example 2 Draw a bar graph for the function in the table on page 374.

Solution Choose one axis for the members of the domain, say the horizontal axis. List the members of the range on the left along the vertical axis. For each member of the domain draw a vertical bar to represent the corresponding value in the range of the function. Start the scale of the bars at zero, so that their relative lengths are correct.

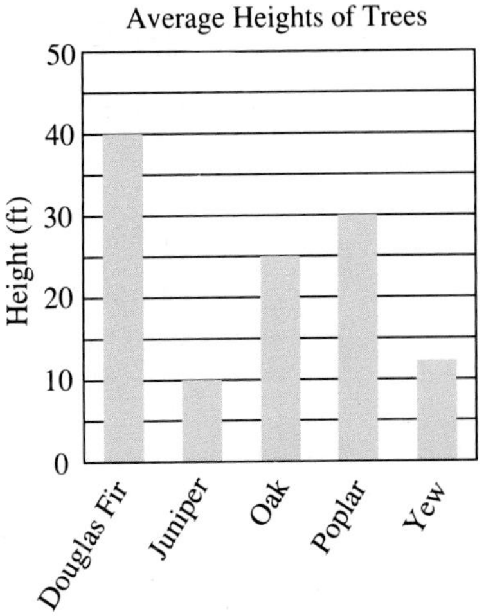

When a measurement varies over time we say that it is a function of time. For functions of this type it is better to use a *broken-line* graph to display the facts.

Example 3 Draw a broken-line graph for the function in the table below.

Year	1900	1920	1940	1960	1980
United States population (in millions)	76	106	132	179	227

Solution List the members of the domain along the horizontal axis. For each member of the domain plot a point to represent the corresponding value in the range of the function. Then connect the points by line segments.

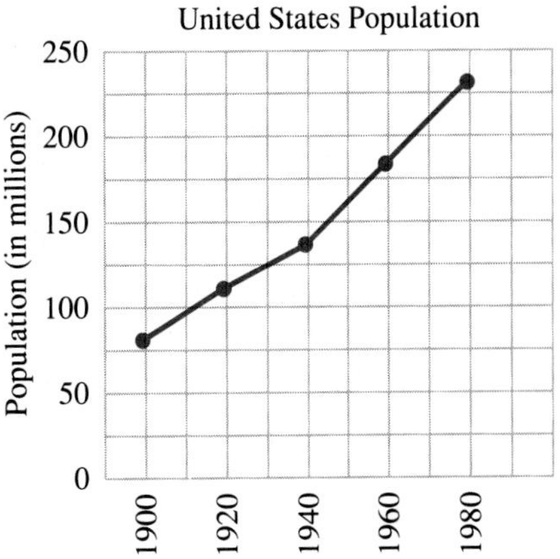

Note that the line segments in the graph of Example 3 do not necessarily show the actual population. However, they do help you to estimate the population and to see the trend over time.

Oral Exercises

State the domain and range of the function shown by each table. Then give each correspondence as a set of ordered pairs.

1.

Activity	Calories burned
Jogging	210
Swimming	270
Tennis	210
Walking	120
Bicycling	330

2.

Species	Chromosomes
Human	46
Horse	64
Mouse	40
Tomato	24
Corn	40

3.

Tuesday night television	Nielsen rating
Situation comedy	10.8
Basketball game	6.2
Drama	12.0
News	16.3
Documentary	14.2
Hockey game	4.1
Movie	6.9

4.

Appliance	Percent of total electrical energy used in the house
Air conditioner	8
Clothes dryer	5
Electric range	15
Refrigerator	20
TV	9
Water heater	38
All others	5

5.

Cost of seeing a movie at the Bijou Theater						
Year	1940	1950	1960	1970	1980	1990
Cost	$.30	$.60	$1.25	$2.00	$3.25	$5.00

6.

Consumer Price Index (CPI)							
Year	1967	1970	1973	1976	1979	1982	1985
CPI	100	116.3	133.1	170.5	217.4	289.1	317.4

Written Exercises

A **1–4.** Draw a bar graph for the function shown in each table in Oral Exercises 1–4.

5–6. Draw a broken-line graph for each function shown in Oral Exercises 5 and 6.

B **7.** Use the broken-line graph you drew in Exercise 5 to estimate the cost of seeing a movie in 1955 and in 1975.

8. Use the broken-line graph you drew in Exercise 6 to estimate the CPI in 1980 and in 1984.

Exercises 9 and 10 require you to find data. Sources that you may use are results of experiments in your science classes, surveys that you conduct in your class or neighborhood, or reference materials in your library.

9. Find data suitable for presentation as a bar graph, and then draw the graph.

10. Find data suitable for presentation on a broken-line graph, and then draw the graph.

Mixed Review Exercises

Write an equation in slope-intercept form of each line described.

1. passes through (2, 4) and (4, 6)

2. slope 5; passes through (1, 7)

3. slope $\frac{1}{3}$; y-intercept -4

4. passes through $(-4, 3)$ and $(0, -3)$

Graph each equation.

5. $y = -3x + 1$

6. $x + y = 9$

7. $y = \frac{1}{2}x - 5$

8. $x = -3$

Career Note / *Statistician*

Statisticians plan surveys and analyze data. To plan a survey, statisticians decide how many people to contact and what types of questions to ask them. Statisticians then analyze the data and present it in reports. They often use tables and graphs to give a clear picture of the results.

Statisticians need a strong mathematics background. A degree in mathematics or statistics, or in some field using statistics with a minor in statistics, is usually the minimum educational background.

Application / *Line of Best Fit*

Can your adult height be predicted from that of your father or mother? Will your future income be related to the number of years you attend school? When there is a clear relationship between two measurements, researchers can base predictions on data gathered about many, many people. For each person, there must be a pair of measurements.

For example, to predict a person's height at age 24 from that person's height at age 14, researchers begin by collecting data such as that shown in the chart below for a group of adults. Each pair of heights can be plotted as a point (x, y) on a graph.

Height at 14	Height at 24
62 in.	73 in.
59 in.	67 in.
58 in.	67 in.
61 in.	70 in.
64 in.	76 in.
60 in.	69 in.

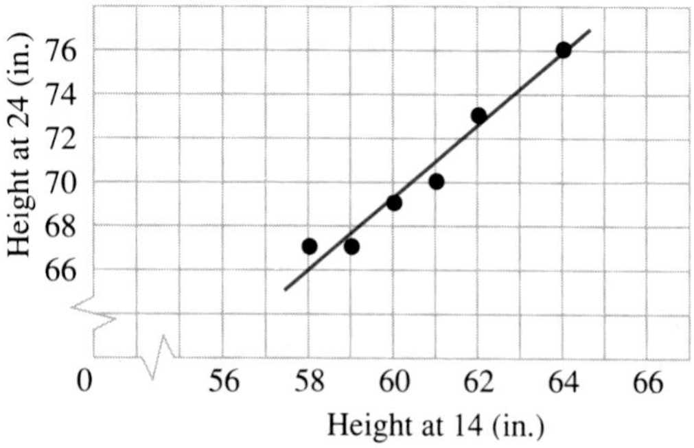

If the data were plotted for many more people, the graph would contain many more points. These points tend to cluster around a line (shown in red) called the line of best fit, since it fits closer to the points than any other line. Mathematicians have derived exact formulas for determining the line of best fit, but you can fit a line quite well "by eye." From graphs based on extensive data gathered over a period of several years, predictions are made.

Projects

1. **a.** Gather the following data from your classmates: the height of each girl and her mother; the height of each boy and his father.

   b. For each girl, plot (x, y) on a graph such that the x-coordinate is the girl's height and the y-coordinate is her mother's height. Make a second graph in the same way using the boy's data.

   c. On each graph, draw the line that seems to fit the points of the graph most closely. (You may wish to use a computer program to draw the line.)

   d. Determine the heights of other students in the same age group as your class. Predict the heights of their mothers or fathers from your graphs. Find out how good your estimates are. (*Note:* Your estimates may be inaccurate, but if you based your graph on more data and estimated heights for a larger group of people, your estimates would be better.)

2. Using Project 1 as a model, design a statistical experiment to study a problem of your own choice.

8-7 Functions Defined by Equations

Objective To define a function by using equations.

Tickets to the senior class play cost \$5. Production expenses are \$500. The class's profit, p will depend on n, the number of tickets sold.

$$\text{profit} = \$5 \cdot (\text{number of tickets}) - \$500 \quad \text{or} \quad p = 5n - 500$$

The equation $p = 5n - 500$ describes a correspondence between the number of tickets sold and the profit. This correspondence is a function whose domain is the set of tickets that could possibly be sold.

$$\text{domain } D = \{0, 1, 2, \ldots\}.$$

The range is the set of profits that are possible, including "negative profits," or losses, if too few tickets are sold.

$$\text{range } R = \{-500, -495, -490, \ldots\}.$$

If we call this profit function P, we can use **arrow notation** and write the rule

$$P\colon n \rightarrow 5n - 500,$$

which is read "the function P that assigns $5n - 500$ to n" or "the function P that pairs n with $5n - 500$." We could also use **functional notation:**

$$P(n) = 5n - 500$$

which is read "P of n equals $5n - 500$" or "the value of P at n is $5n - 500$."

To specify a function completely, you must describe the domain of the function as well as give the rule. The numbers assigned by the rule then form the range of the function.

Example 1 List the range of

$$g\colon x \rightarrow 4 + 3x - x^2$$

if the domain $D = \{-1, 0, 1, 2\}$.

Solution In $4 + 3x - x^2$ replace x with each member of D to find the members of the range R.

$\therefore R = \{0, 4, 6\}$ ***Answer***

x	$4 + 3x - x^2$
-1	$4 + 3(-1) - (-1)^2 = 0$
0	$4 + 3(0) - 0^2 = 4$
1	$4 + 3(1) - 1^2 = 6$
2	$4 + 3(2) - 2^2 = 6$

Note that the function g in Example 1 assigns the number 6 to both 1 and 2. In listing the range of g, however, you name 6 only once.

Members of the range of a function are called **values of the function.** In Example 1, the values of the function g are 0, 4, and 6. To indicate that the function g assigns to 2 the value 6, you write

$$g(2) = 6,$$

which is read "g of 2 equals 6" or "the value of g at 2 is 6." Note that $g(2)$ is *not* the product of g and 2. It names the number that g assigns to 2.

Example 2 Given f: $x \to x^2 - 2x$ with the set of real numbers as the domain.
Find: **a.** $f(4)$ **b.** $f(-3)$ **c.** $f(2)$

Solution First write the equation: $f(x) = x^2 - 2x$
Then substitute: **a.** $f(4) = 4^2 - 2 \cdot 4 = 16 - 8 = 8$
b. $f(-3) = (-3)^2 - 2(-3) = 9 - (-6) = 15$
c. $f(2) = 2^2 - 2 \cdot 2 = 4 - 4 = 0$

You may use whatever variable you wish to define a function. For example, G: $t \to t^2 - 2t$ with the set of real numbers as the domain is the same function as f in Example 2.

Oral Exercises

State the range of each function.

1. F: $x \to x + 5$, $D = \{0, 1, 2\}$
2. H: $y \to y - 3$, $D = \{-2, 0, 2\}$
3. $p(w) = w^2 + 3$, $D = \{-3, 0, 3\}$
4. $g(r) = 2r^3$, $D = \{-2, 0, 2\}$
5. $M(x) = 3x^2 - 7$, $D = \{-2, 0, 2\}$
6. $Q(n) = 3n^3 + 2$, $D = \{-1, 0, 1\}$

Given the functions g: $x \to 3x - 6$ and h: $t \to t^2$, find the following values.

7. $g(5)$ 8. $g(7)$ 9. $g(-7)$ 10. $g(0)$ 11. $g(2)$
12. $h(0)$ 13. $h(-3)$ 14. $h(5)$ 15. $h(8)$ 16. $h(-8)$

Complete each statement about the function P: $n \to 5n - 500$.

17. The value of P at 200 is _?_.
18. The value of P at 500 is _?_.
19. The value of P at _?_ is 0.
20. The value of P at _?_ is -250.

Written Exercises

Find the range of each function.

A

1. g: $x \to 5x + 1$, $D = \{-1, 0, 1\}$
2. f: $x \to 3x - 4$, $D = \{1, 2, 3\}$
3. $s(z) = 5 - 4z$, $D = \{-2, 0, 2\}$
4. $h(y) = 1 - 2y$, $D = \{-3, 0, 1\}$
5. G: $a \to 4a^2 - 1$, $D = \{-1, 0, 1\}$
6. H: $b \to b^2 + 3$, $D = \{0, 2, 4\}$
7. $F(x) = x^2 + 4x - 3$, $D = P\{1, 2, 4\}$
8. $M(x) = x^2 + 5x + 2$, $D = \{-1, -2, -4\}$
9. $P(z) = z^2 - 5z + 6$, $D = \{2, 3, 4\}$
10. $N(a) = a^2 - 3a - 2$, $D = \{-2, -1, 0\}$
11. q: $c \to c^3 + c^2 + 3c$, $D = \{0, 1, 3\}$
12. K: $x \to x^3 - 5x^2 + 6x$, $D = \{0, 2, 3\}$

Find the values for each given function with the set of real numbers as the domain.

13. $f(x) = 5x - 9$	**a.** $f(3)$	**b.** $f(-3)$	**c.** $f(-8)$
14. $p(x) = 8 - 4x$	**a.** $p(2)$	**b.** $p(0)$	**c.** $p(-2)$
15. $R: t \rightarrow t + 1$	**a.** $R(3)$	**b.** $R(-2)$	**c.** $R(-5)$
16. $G: n \rightarrow n - 2$	**a.** $G(0)$	**b.** $G(2)$	**c.** $G(-3)$
17. $h(a) = 3a^2 - 2$	**a.** $h(4)$	**b.** $h(-5)$	**c.** $h(0)$
18. $k(t) = 3t^2 + 9$	**a.** $k(5)$	**b.** $k(-2)$	**c.** $k(-3)$
19. $g(x) = x^2 - 2$	**a.** $g(5)$	**b.** $g(-5)$	**c.** $g(0)$
20. $h(y) = 3y^2 + 2$	**a.** $h(2)$	**b.** $h(-2)$	**c.** $h(-4)$
21. $R: y \rightarrow y^3 + 8$	**a.** $R(0)$	**b.** $R(-2)$	**c.** $R(2)$
22. $N: t \rightarrow t^3 - 27$	**a.** $N(3)$	**b.** $N(-3)$	**c.** $N(0)$

B

23. $f: x \rightarrow x^2 + 3x$	**a.** $f(7)$	**b.** $f(-7)$	**c.** $f(-3)$
24. $g: t \rightarrow 5t^2 - 7t$	**a.** $g(3)$	**b.** $g(-3)$	**c.** $g(0)$
25. $P(y) = y - y^3$	**a.** $P(3)$	**b.** $P(1)$	**c.** $P(-1)$
26. $m(y) = y(1 - 2y)$	**a.** $m\left(-\frac{1}{2}\right)$	**b.** $m\left(\frac{1}{2}\right)$	**c.** $m(0)$
27. $Z: x \rightarrow \lvert 3x - 1 \rvert$	**a.** $Z\left(\frac{1}{3}\right)$	**b.** $Z(0)$	**c.** $Z\left(\frac{2}{3}\right)$
28. $Q: m \rightarrow \lvert 3 - 6m \rvert$	**a.** $Q(-2)$	**b.** $Q\left(\frac{1}{2}\right)$	**c.** $Q\left(-\frac{1}{2}\right)$

For each function, (a) find $f(0)$, (b) solve $f(x) = 0$.

29. $f(x) = 3x - 12$ **30.** $f(x) = 4x + 7$ **31.** $f(x) = 5x - 1$

32. $f(x) = 2 - 3x$ **33.** $f(x) = -\frac{1}{2}x + 7$ **34.** $f(x) = 3 - \frac{1}{2}x$

35. $f(x) = x^2 - 2x - 3$ **36.** $f(x) = x^2 - 13x + 40$ **37.** $f(x) = x^4 - x^2$

38. $f(x) = \frac{x + 1}{x - 2}$ **39.** $f(x) = \frac{x^2 - 1}{x^2 + 1}$ **40.** $f(x) = \frac{x^2 - 3x + 2}{x + 1}$

Given that $f(x) = 3x + 4$ and $g(x) = -x^2$, find each of the following.

41. $\frac{1}{2}g(6)$ **42.** $2f(5)$ **43.** $f(1) + g(1)$ **44.** $f(2) \cdot g(2)$

In Exercises 45–47, let $f(x) = x^2$ and $g(x) = 2x$. Find each of the following. (*Hint:* To find $g[f(2)]$, first find $f(2)$.)

C

45. a. $g(1)$ **b.** $f(1)$ **c.** $g[f(1)]$ **d.** $f[g(1)]$

46. a. $g(-2)$ **b.** $f(-2)$ **c.** $g[f(-2)]$ **d.** $f[g(-2)]$

47. Is there any real number x for which $f[g(x)] = g[f(x)]$? If there is such a number, find it. If there is no such number, explain why not.

48. If $f(x) = x + 1$, and $g[f(x)] = x$, what is $g(x)$?

Mixed Review Exercises

Simplify.

1. $\frac{4n-1}{3n^3}+\frac{3}{n}$

2. $7\frac{1}{4}+3\frac{2}{3}+2\frac{3}{4}+5\frac{1}{3}$

3. $(-15)\left(\frac{y}{5}\right)$

4. $(-3)(3a-2b+c)$

5. $-[9+(-2)]+(-x)+8$

6. $3(4m-7)$

7. $-120\left(\frac{1}{2}\right)\left(\frac{1}{5}\right)$

8. $\frac{3ef^2}{2e^3}\cdot\frac{4de^2}{6ef}$

9. $\frac{x^2-y^2}{x^2+2xy+y^2}$

Computer Exercises

For students with some programming experience

Write a BASIC program to calculate the value of a function for values of x entered with READ . . . DATA statements. (Recall that the BASIC statement that corresponds to $f(x)=x^2$ is DEF FNA(X) = X*X.) Run the program for the functions and values of x given below.

1. $f(x)=3x-7;\ x=-2, 0, 1, 10$

2. $f(x)=x^2+3x+2;\ x=0, 1, -1, -2$

3. $f(x)=\frac{1}{x^2+1};\ x=-10, -2, 0, 2, 10$

4. $f(x)=4x-x^3;\ x=-3, -2, -1, 0, 1, 2, 3$

Challenge

1. a. Find each sum.

$\frac{1}{1\cdot 2}+\frac{1}{2\cdot 3}=\underline{\ ?\ }$

$\frac{1}{1\cdot 2}+\frac{1}{2\cdot 3}+\frac{1}{3\cdot 4}=\underline{\ ?\ }$

$\frac{1}{1\cdot 2}+\frac{1}{2\cdot 3}+\frac{1}{3\cdot 4}+\frac{1}{4\cdot 5}=\underline{\ ?\ }$

b. If this pattern were continued for 100 fractions, what would the sum be?

c. If this pattern were continued for n fractions, what would the sum be?

2. a. Find each sum.

$\frac{1}{1\cdot 3}+\frac{1}{3\cdot 5}=\underline{\ ?\ }$

$\frac{1}{1\cdot 3}+\frac{1}{3\cdot 5}+\frac{1}{5\cdot 7}=\underline{\ ?\ }$

$\frac{1}{1\cdot 3}+\frac{1}{3\cdot 5}+\frac{1}{5\cdot 7}+\frac{1}{7\cdot 9}=\underline{\ ?\ }$

b. If this pattern were continued for 50 fractions, what would the sum be?

c. If this pattern were continued for n fractions, what would the sum be?

8-8 Linear and Quadratic Functions

Objective To graph linear and quadratic functions.

The function g defined by

$$g(x) = 2x - 3$$

is called a *linear function*. If its domain is the set of all real numbers, then the straight line that is the graph of

$$y = g(x) = 2x - 3$$

is the **graph** of g. The slope of the graph is 2. The y-intercept is -3.

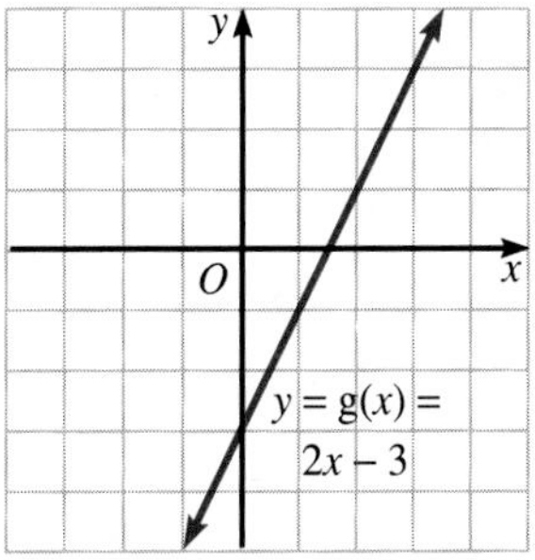

A function f defined by $f(x) = mx + b$ is a **linear function.**

If the domain of f is the set of real numbers, then its graph is the straight line with slope m and y-intercept b.

Now consider the function h defined by

$$h(x) = x^2 - 2x - 2.$$

If the domain of h is the set of all real numbers, then the graph of h is the graph of

$$y = h(x) = x^2 - 2x - 2.$$

Example 1 Graph the function h defined by the equation $y = h(x) = x^2 - 2x - 2$.

Solution Find the coordinates of selected points as shown in the table below. Plot the points and connect them with a smooth curve.

x	$x^2 - 2x - 2 = y$
-2	$(-2)^2 - 2(-2) - 2 = 6$
-1	$(-1)^2 - 2(-1) - 2 = 1$
0	$0^2 - 2(0) - 2 = -2$
1	$1^2 - 2(1) - 2 = -3$
2	$2^2 - 2(2) - 2 = -2$
3	$3^2 - 2(3) - 2 = 1$
4	$4^2 - 2(4) - 2 = 6$

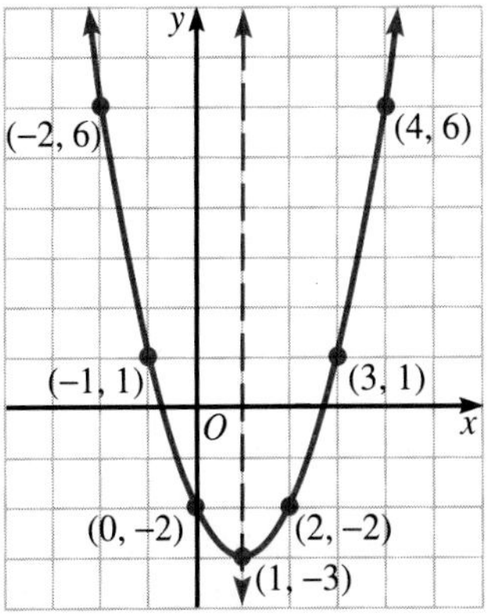

The curve shown in Example 1 is a **parabola.** This parabola opens upward and has a **minimum point,** or lowest point, at $(1, -3)$. The y-coordinate of this point is the **least value** of the function.

The vertical line $x = 1$, containing the minimum point, is called the **axis of symmetry** of the parabola. If you fold the graph along the axis of symmetry, the two halves of the parabola coincide.

Example 2 Graph the function k defined by the equation $y = k(x) = -x^2 + 2x + 2$.

Solution

x	$-x^2 + 2x + 2 = y$
-2	$-(-2)^2 + 2(-2) + 2 = -6$
-1	$-(-1)^2 + 2(-1) + 2 = -1$
0	$-0^2 + 2(0) + 2 = 2$
1	$-1^2 + 2(1) + 2 = 3$
2	$-2^2 + 2(2) + 2 = 2$
3	$-3^2 + 2(3) + 2 = -1$
4	$-4^2 + 2(4) + 2 = -6$

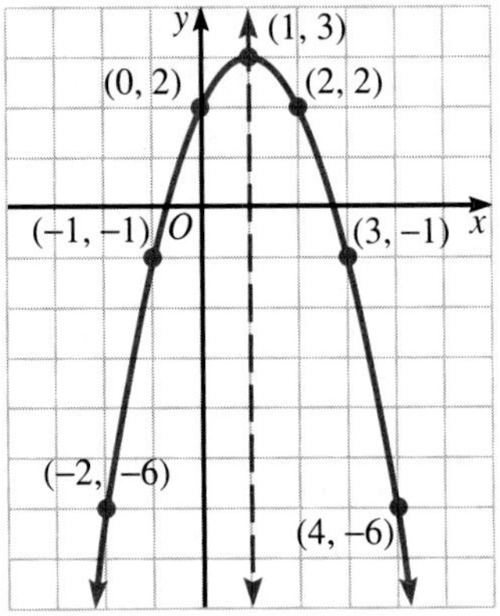

The graph in Example 2 is a parabola that opens downward and has a **maximum point,** or highest point, at $(1, 3)$. The y-coordinate of this point is the **greatest value** of the function. Notice that the maximum point $(1, 3)$ lies on the axis of symmetry.

A function f defined by $f(x) = ax^2 + bx + c \quad (a \neq 0)$ is a **quadratic function.**
If the domain of f is the set of real numbers, then the graph of f is a parabola.
If a is positive, the parabola opens upward.
If a is negative, the parabola opens downward.

The minimum or maximum point of a parabola is called the **vertex.** Notice that in Examples 1 and 2 the points, except the vertex, occur in *pairs that have the same y-coordinate.* The average of the x-coordinates of any such pair of points is the x-coordinate of the vertex.

If you have a computer or a graphing calculator, you can compare the graphs of $y = x^2 - 4x$ and $y = x^2 - 4x + 3$. For quadratic equations, such as $y = x^2 - 4x$ and $y = x^2 - 4x + 3$, that differ only in the constant term, the x-coordinates of the vertices are the same. You can find a formula for the x-coordinate of the vertex of $y = ax^2 + bx + c$, as shown on the next page, by using the two points where the graph of $y = ax^2 + bx$ crosses the x-axis, that is, the points where $y = 0$.

$$\begin{aligned} & y = ax^2 + bx \\ \text{Let } y = 0: \quad & 0 = ax^2 + bx \\ & 0 = x(ax + b) \\ & x = 0 \text{ or } ax + b = 0 \\ \therefore\ & x = 0 \text{ or } x = -\frac{b}{a} \end{aligned}$$

The average of these x-coordinates is $-\frac{b}{2a}$.

The x-coordinate of the vertex of the parabola $y = ax^2 + bx + c$ ($a \neq 0$) is $-\frac{b}{2a}$. The axis of symmetry is the line $x = -\frac{b}{2a}$.

Unless otherwise stated, you may assume that the domain of each linear or quadratic function is the set of real numbers.

Example 3 Find the vertex of the graph of $H: x \to 2x^2 + 4x - 3$.
Use the vertex and four other points to graph H.
Identify and draw the axis of symmetry.

Solution

1. x-coordinate of vertex $= -\frac{b}{2a} = -\frac{4}{2 \cdot 2} = -\frac{4}{4} = -1$
2. To find the y-coordinate of the vertex, substitute -1 for x.

   $y = 2x^2 + 4x - 3$
   $y = 2(-1)^2 + 4(-1) - 3$
   $\quad = 2 - 4 - 3 = -5$
   $\therefore$ the vertex is $(-1, -5)$.
3. For values of x, select two numbers greater than -1 and two numbers less than -1 to obtain paired points with the same y-coordinate.

	x	$2x^2 + 4x - 3 = y$
	-3	$2(-3)^2 + 4(-3) - 3 = 3$
	-2	$2(-2)^2 + 4(-2) - 3 = -3$
Vertex	-1	$2(-1)^2 + 4(-1) - 3 = -5$
	0	$2(0)^2 + 4(0) - 3 = -3$
	1	$2(1)^2 + 4(1) - 3 = 3$

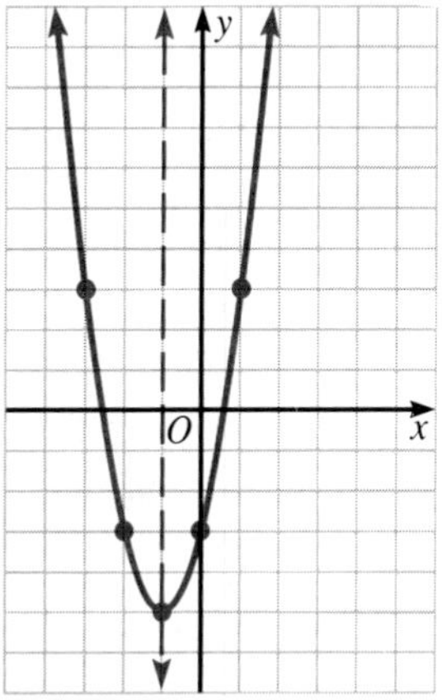

4. Plot the points. Connect them with a smooth curve.
5. The axis of symmetry is the line $x = -1$ (shown as a dashed line on the graph).

Oral Exercises

State the slope and *y*-intercept of the graph of each linear function.

1. $f: x \rightarrow -3x + 9$
2. $g: x \rightarrow 4x - 8$
3. $p(x) = 4 + \frac{3}{2}x$
4. $t(x) = -\frac{2}{3}x$
5. $t(x) = 0$
6. $f(x) = 5$

State whether the graph of each quadratic function opens upward or downward.

7. $y = x^2 - 3x + 4$
8. $y = -2x^2 + x + 1$
9. $y = 9 - x^2$
10. $x^2 - 9 = y$
11. $3x^2 - 3x = y$
12. $y = -\frac{1}{3}x^2$

State whether the graph of each quadratic function has a minimum or a maximum point.

13. $f: x \rightarrow x^2 - 2x + 1$
14. $g: x \rightarrow 3 - 2x - x^2$
15. $h: x \rightarrow 3x^2 - x$
16. $P: x \rightarrow 1 - x^2$
17. $T: x \rightarrow 8x^2 + x - 6$
18. $f: x \rightarrow \frac{2}{5}x^2$

Written Exercises

Draw the graph of each linear function. You may wish to verify your graphs on a computer or a graphing calculator.

A

1. $g: x \rightarrow x - 3$
2. $f: x \rightarrow -x + 1$
3. $q(x) = 2 - \frac{1}{3}x$
4. $d(x) = -\frac{3}{4}x$
5. $r(x) = -7$
6. $n(x) = 0$

Find the coordinates of the vertex. Then give the equation of the axis of symmetry and the least value of the function.

7. $f(x) = x^2 - 5$
8. $g(x) = x^2 + 4$
9. $h(x) = x^2 - x - 6$
10. $t(x) = 4 - 10x + 5x^2$
11. $G(x) = 9x^2 - 4$
12. $F(x) = \frac{1}{4}x^2$

Find the coordinates of the vertex. Then give the equation of the axis of symmetry and the greatest value of the function.

13. $g(x) = -x^2 - 3x$
14. $f(x) = 4x - x^2$
15. $H(x) = -x^2 - 8x - 15$
16. $K(x) = 1 - 3x - 6x^2$
17. $f(x) = x - 2x^2$
18. $h(x) = 1 - \frac{1}{3}x^2$

Find the vertex and the axis of symmetry of the graph of each equation. Use the vertex and at least four other points to graph the equation. You may wish to verify your graphs on a computer or a graphing calculator.

19. $y = 2x^2$ **20.** $y = 3 - x^2$ **21.** $y = 3x^2$

22. $y = -3x^2$ **23.** $y = \frac{1}{2}x^2$ **24.** $y = -\frac{1}{2}x^2$

25. $y = x^2 - 4x$ **26.** $y = -x^2 + 2x$ **27.** $y = -x^2 - 5x + 6$

28. $y = x^2 - 3x - 10$ **29.** $y = 4 - \frac{1}{3}x^2$ **30.** $y = 6 + 6x - \frac{1}{3}x^2$

You may wish to use a computer or a graphing calculator to do Ex. 31–32.

B **31. a.** On the same set of axes draw the graphs of $y = x^2$, $y = x^2 + 1$, and $y = x^2 - 2$.

b. Use your results in part (a) to describe the changes in the graph of $y = x^2 + c$ as the value of c increases; as c decreases.

32. a. On the same set of axes draw the graphs of $y = \frac{1}{2}x^2$, $y = x^2$, and $y = 2x^2$.

b. On the same set of axes draw the graphs of $y = -\frac{1}{2}x^2$, $y = -x^2$, and $y = -2x^2$.

c. Use your results in parts (a) and (b) to describe the change in the graph of $y = ax^2$ as $|a|$ increases.

The *zeros* of a function f are the values of x for which $f(x) = 0$. In Exercises 33–40, find (a) $f(0)$; (b) the zeros of f.

33. $f(x) = 2x + 10$ **34.** $f(x) = 3x - 9$

35. $f(x) = 4x - 11$ **36.** $f(x) = 5x + 8$

37. $f(x) = x^2 - 6x + 8$ **38.** $f(x) = x^2 - 8x + 15$

39. $f(x) = x^2 + 8x + 12$ **40.** $f(x) = x^2 + 9x + 20$

41. Interpret the zeros of the function f in terms of the graph of f.

42. Interpret $f(0)$ in terms of the graph of f.

Mixed Review Exercises

Find the range of each function.

1. $H: x \rightarrow 3x^2 + 2$, $D = \{0, 1, 2\}$ **2.** $f(a) = 2a - 4$, $D = \{-2, 0, 2\}$

3. $M(b) = b^3 + 7$, $D = \{-1, 1, 3\}$ **4.** $K: z \rightarrow z^2 - z$, $D = \{1, 2, 3\}$

Translate each phrase into a variable expression.

5. 7 times the sum of a number and 4 **6.** The difference between a number and 3

7. The product of a number and 9 **8.** 5 less than one third of a number

Computer Exercises

For students with some programming experience

Write a BASIC program that determines the vertex of the graph of a quadratic equation $y = Ax^2 + Bx + C$ when A, B, and C are entered with an INPUT statement. The program should also give three points on each side of the vertex that can be used to graph the quadratic equation. Run the program for the following quadratic equations.

1. $y = x^2$

2. $y = -x^2 + 2x + 2$

3. $y = x^2 - 4x + 3$

4. $y = x^2 - 4x$

5. $y = 2x^2 + 4x - 3$

6. $y = -x^2 - 5x + 6$

Self-Test 3

Vocabulary

function (p. 374)
domain of a function (p. 374)
range of a function (p. 374)
bar graph (p. 375)
broken-line graph (p. 375)
arrow notation (p. 379)
functional notation (p. 379)
value of function (p. 379)
graph (p. 383)
linear function (p. 383)
parabola (p. 384)
minimum point (p. 384)
least value (p. 384)
axis of symmetry (p. 384)
maximum point (p. 384)
greatest value (p. 384)
quadratic function (p. 384)
vertex (p. 384)

1. The table below defines a function. **Obj. 8-6, p. 374**

a. State the domain and range of the function.

b. Graph the function by means of a bar graph or a broken-line graph, whichever is more suitable.

Earnings per share of Common Foods Corp.						
Year	1985	1986	1987	1988	1989	1990
Earnings per share ($)	0.75	0.90	1.12	1.43	1.65	2.05

2. Find the range of g if $g: n \rightarrow n^2 + 2n + 3$ and $D = \{-1, 0, 1, 2, 3\}$. **Obj. 8-7, p. 379**

3. Given $f(x) = 7x - 3$, find: **a.** $f(2)$ **b.** $f(-1)$ **c.** $f(0)$

4. Find the coordinates of the vertex of $f(x) = x^2 + 8x + 10$. Then give the least value of the function. **Obj. 8-8, p. 383**

5. Find the coordinates of the vertex and the equation of the axis of symmetry of the graph of $y = 2x^2 - 4x + 1$. Use the vertex and at least four other points to graph the equation.

Check your answers with those at the back of the book.

Extra / Relations

The diagram at the right shows how each number in the set

$$D = \{0, 1, 2, 3\}$$

is paired with one or more numbers in the set

$$R = \{-1, 1, 2, 3\}.$$

The same pairing is shown in the table next to the diagram and in the list of ordered pairs shown below.

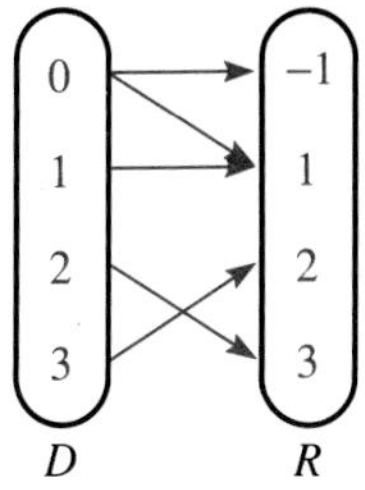

D	R
0	−1
0	1
1	1
2	3
3	2

$$\{(0, -1), (0, 1), (1, 1), (2, 3), (3, 2)\}$$

Notice that this pairing assigns to the number 0 in D two different numbers, -1 and 1, in R. Therefore, the pairing is *not* a function with domain D and range R, since in a function each member of the domain is assigned *exactly one* member of the range. The pairing described above is an example of a *relation*.

A **relation** is any set of ordered pairs.
The set of first coordinates of the ordered pairs is the **domain** of the relation.
The set of second coordinates is the **range.**

The figure at the right shows the graphs of all the ordered pairs that form the relation described above. We call this set the **graph of the relation.**

A function is a special kind of relation.

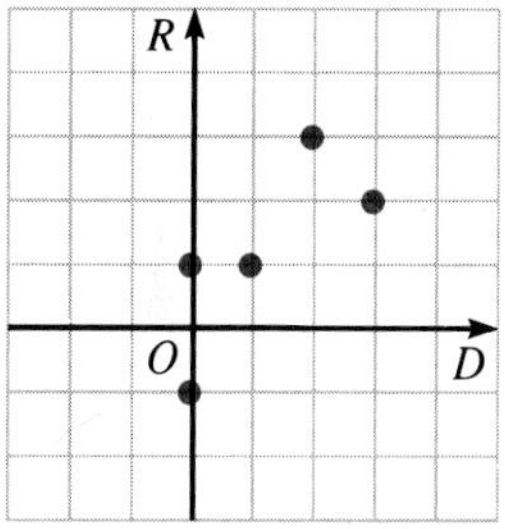

A function is a relation in which different ordered pairs have different first coordinates.

Therefore, in the graph of a function, there is only one point plotted for each value in the domain.

Exercises

State the domain and range of each relation. Is the relation a function?

1. $\{(3, 4), (2, 3), (3, 6), (2, 0)\}$

2. $\{(1, -1), (2, 3), (3, 5), (4, 8)\}$

3. $\{(2, -1), (3, 0), (4, 6), (1, -3)\}$

4. $\{(5, 0), (5, 1), (5, 2), (0, 4)\}$

5. $\{(-1, 1), (1, 1), (2, 4), (-2, 4)\}$

6. $\{(4, 2), (4, -2), (9, 3), (9, -3)\}$

Give the domain and range of the relation graphed in each diagram. Is the relation a function?

7.

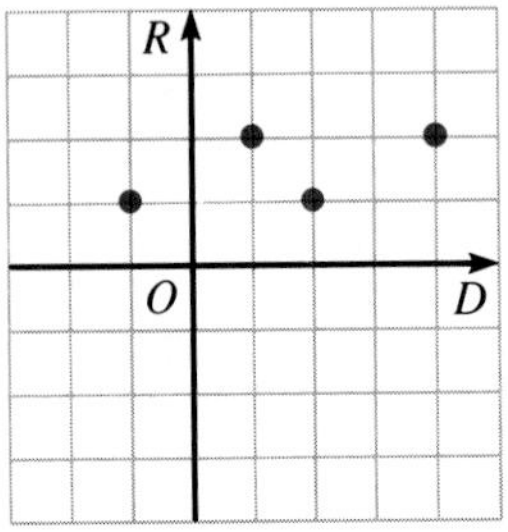

8.

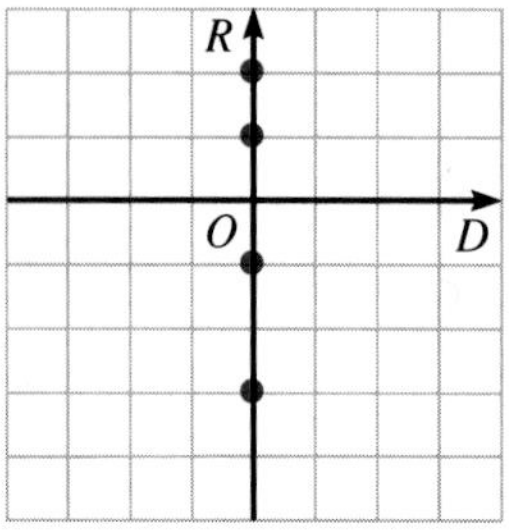

9.

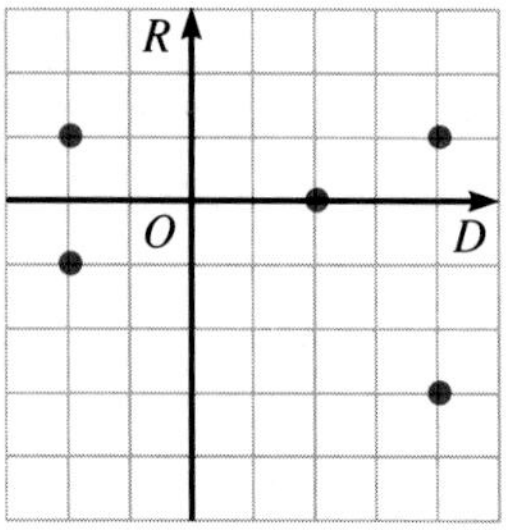

10.

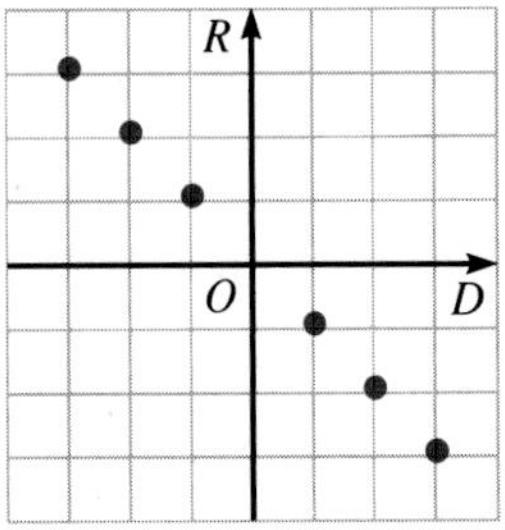

11.

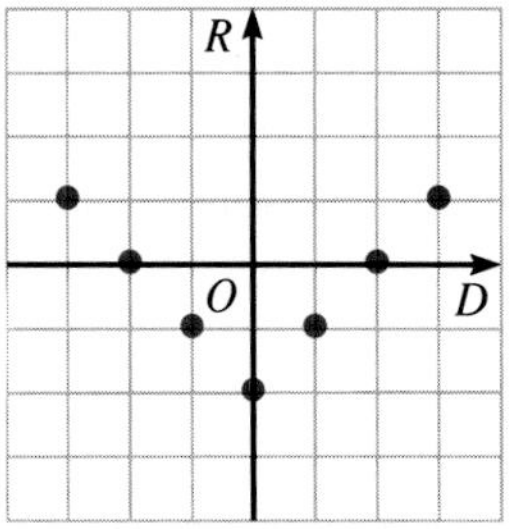

12.

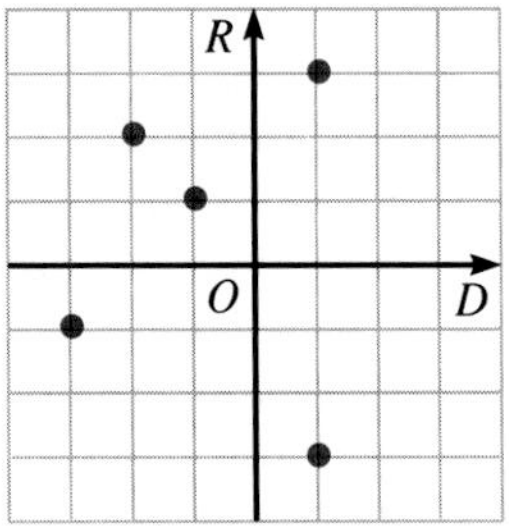

In Exercises 13–18, graph each relation and determine whether it is a function. If it is not a function, explain how that fact shows up on the graph.

13. $\{(-4, 2), (-1, 3), (4, 4), (4, -3)\}$

14. $\{(0, -1), (1, -2), (2, -3), (-1, 2)\}$

15. $\{(-3, 2), (0, 1), (3, -2), (-3, 0)\}$

16. $\{(-1, 1), (0, 0), (1, 1), (2, 4)\}$

17. $\{(0, 0), (1, 2), (2, 9), (-2, -7)\}$

18. $\{(1, 0), (2, 3), (3, -1), (1, 5)\}$

19. Consider the set of all ordered pairs of real numbers (x, y) that satisfy the equation $|y| = |x|$. Is this set of ordered pairs a relation? Is it a function? Justify your answers.

20. The circle shown at the right is the graph of the equation $x^2 + y^2 = 4$. Do the coordinates of the points of the circle form a relation? a function? Why or why not? If the points form a relation or a function, what are the domain and range?

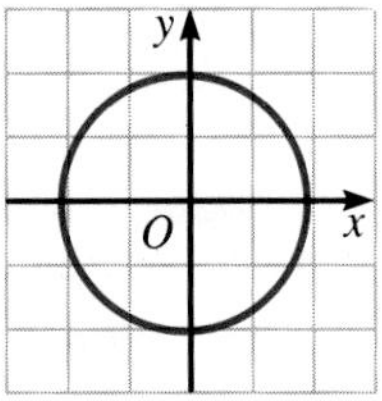

In Exercises 21–24, consider the set of all ordered pairs (x, y) as described. Is the set a relation? Is it a function?

21. (x, y), where x is the name of a telephone subscriber in your town and y is the subscriber's telephone number.

22. (x, y), where x is the name of each mother in your town and y is the name of her child.

23. (x, y), where x is each man in London, England, and y is his right thumbprint.

24. (x, y), where x is any nonvertical line in the coordinate plane and y is its slope.

Variation

8-9 Direct Variation

Objective To use direct variation to solve problems.

The table below shows the mass m of a gold bar whose volume is V cubic centimeters.

Volume in cubic centimeters: V	Mass in grams: m
1	19.3
2	38.6
3	57.9
4	77.2
5	96.5

You can see that $m = 19.3V$. This equation defines a linear function. Note that if the volume of the bar is doubled, the mass is doubled; if the volume is tripled, the mass is tripled, and so on. You can say that the mass *varies directly* as the volume. This function is an example of a *direct variation*.

A **direct variation** is a function defined by an equation of the form

$$y = kx, \text{ where } k \text{ is a nonzero constant.}$$

You can say that y *varies directly as* x.
The constant k is called the **constant of variation.**

When the domain is the set of real numbers, the graph of a direct variation is a straight line with slope k that passes through the origin.

Example 1 Given that m varies directly as n and that $m = 42$ when $n = 2$, find the following.

a. the constant of variation **b.** the value of m when $n = 3$

Solution Let $m = kn$.

a. Substitute $m = 42$ and $n = 2$: $42 = k \cdot 2$

$21 = k$ ***Answer***

b. Substitute $k = 21$ and $n = 3$: $m = 21 \cdot 3 = 63$ ***Answer***

Suppose (x_1, y_1) and (x_2, y_2) are two ordered pairs of a direct variation defined by $y = kx$ and that neither x_1 nor x_2 is zero. Since (x_1, y_1) and (x_2, y_2) must satisfy $y = kx$, you know that

$$y_1 = kx_1 \text{ and } y_2 = kx_2.$$

From these equations you can write the ratios

$$\frac{y_1}{x_1} = k \text{ and } \frac{y_2}{x_2} = k.$$

Since each ratio equals k, the ratios are equal.

$$\frac{y_1}{x_1} = \frac{y_2}{x_2}, \text{ read ``} y_1 \text{ is to } x_1 \text{ as } y_2 \text{ is to } x_2\text{.''}$$

This equation, which states that two ratios are equal, is a proportion (page 293). For this reason, k is sometimes called the **constant of proportionality,** and y is said to be *directly proportional to x.*

When you use a proportion to solve a problem, you will find it helpful to recall that the product of the extremes equals the product of the means.

Example 2 The amount of interest earned on savings is directly proportional to the amount of money saved. If \$104 interest is earned on \$1300, how much interest will be earned on \$1800 in the same period of time?

Solution 1

Step 1 The problem asks for the interest on \$1800 if the interest on \$1300 is \$104.

Step 2 Let i, in dollars, be the interest on d dollars.

$$i_1 = 104 \qquad i_2 = \underline{\ ?\ }$$
$$d_1 = 1300 \qquad d_2 = 1800$$

Step 3 An equation can be written in the form $\frac{i_1}{d_1} = \frac{i_2}{d_2}$.

$$\frac{104}{1300} = \frac{i_2}{1800}$$

Step 4

$$104(1800) = 1300i_2$$
$$187{,}200 = 1300i_2$$
$$144 = i_2$$

Step 5 The check is left to you.

$\therefore$ the interest earned on \$1800 will be \$144. ***Answer***

Solution 2 To solve Example 2 by the method shown in Example 1, first write the equation $i = kd$. Then solve for the constant of variation, k, by using the fact that $i = 104$ when $d = 1300$. Use the value of k to find the value of i when $d = 1800$. You may wish to complete the problem this way.

You will find the exercises and problems of this lesson easier if you understand *both* methods.

Oral Exercises

State whether or not each equation defines a direct variation. For each direct variation, state the constant of variation.

1. $y = 3x$ **2.** $p = 9s$ **3.** $xy = 4$ **4.** $d = 3.3t$

5. $\frac{1}{2}x = 7$ **6.** $\frac{y}{x} = -5$ **7.** $p = \frac{4}{q}$ **8.** $C = \pi d$

9. $A = \pi r^2$ **10.** $\frac{c}{d} = 1$ **11.** $y = 3x^2$ **12.** $\frac{x}{y} = \frac{5}{2}$

State whether or not the given ordered pairs are in the same direct variation.

Sample (6, 8), (9, 12), (18, 24)

Solution $\frac{8}{6} = \frac{4}{3}, \frac{12}{9} = \frac{4}{3}, \frac{24}{18} = \frac{4}{3}$. Since the ratios are equal, the ordered pairs are in the direct variation $y = \frac{4}{3}x$.

13. (2, 4), (6, 12), (10, 20)

14. (1, 3), (−6, −18), (5, 15)

15. (1, 1), (2, 1), (3, 3)

16. (−1, 2), (2, −4), (4, −8)

State whether or not the statement is true. If it is not true, explain why.

17. Every linear function is a direct variation.

18. All direct variations are linear functions.

19. Some linear functions are direct variations.

20. No function is both a linear function and a direct variation.

State whether or not each formula shows a direct variation.

21. $\frac{x_1}{y_1} = \frac{x_2}{y_2}$ **22.** $\frac{x_1}{x_2} = \frac{y_1}{y_2}$ **23.** $\frac{y_1}{x_2} = \frac{y_2}{x_1}$ **24.** $\frac{y_2}{x_2} = \frac{y_1}{x_1}$

Written Exercises

In Exercises 1–6, find the constant of variation.

A **1.** y varies directly as x, and $y = 9$ when $x = 54$.

2. y varies directly as x, and $y = 6$ when $x = 72$.

3. t varies directly as s, and $t = -16$ when $s = -2$.

4. h varies directly as m, and $h = 112$ when $m = -16$.

5. W is directly proportional to m, and $W = 150$ when $m = 6$.

6. P is directly proportional to t, and $P = 210$ when $t = 14$.

7. y varies directly as x, and $y = 450$ when $x = 6$. Find y when $x = 10$.

8. d varies directly as z, and $d = 6$ when $z = 48$. Find d when $z = 20$.

9. h is directly proportional to a, and $h = 425$ when $a = 8.5$. Find h when $a = 12$.

10. r is directly proportional to A, and $r = 14$ when $A = 87.5$. Find r when $A = 25$.

(x_1, y_1) and (x_2, y_2) are ordered pairs of the same direct variation. Find each missing value.

11. $x_1 = 15, y_1 = 9$
$x_2 = 40, y_2 = \underline{?}$

12. $x_1 = 45, y_1 = \underline{?}$
$x_2 = 60, y_2 = 100$

13. $x_1 = 3.6, y_1 = 3$
$x_2 = \underline{?}, y_2 = 1$

14. $x_1 = \underline{?}, y_1 = 7$
$x_2 = 7.65, y_2 = 9$

15. $x_1 = \frac{1}{10}, y_1 = \frac{1}{6}$
$x_2 = \frac{2}{5}, y_2 = \underline{?}$

16. $x_1 = \frac{6}{5}, y_1 = \underline{?}$
$x_2 = \frac{2}{3}, y_2 = \frac{1}{9}$

For each direct variation described, write (a) a formula and (b) a proportion.

Sample The speed, v, of a skydiver in free fall is directly proportional to the number, t, of seconds of fall. After 2 s, the speed is 19.6 m/s.

Solution **a.** $v = kt$; $v = 19.6$ when $t = 2$.

$19.6 = k(2)$, so $k = \frac{19.6}{2} = 9.8$

$\therefore v = 9.8t$

b. Let $v_1 = 19.6$ and $t_1 = 2$.

$\frac{19.6}{2} = \frac{v_2}{t_2}$

B 17. The length, L, of the shadow of a tree at any moment varies directly with the height, h, of the tree. At a certain moment, a tree 20 ft tall casts a shadow 14 ft long.

18. The heat, H, required to melt a substance varies directly with its mass, m. Forty-nine calories of heat are needed to melt one gram of copper.

19. The weight, M, of an object on the moon is directly proportional to the weight, E, on Earth. An object weighing 168 lb on Earth weighs 28 lb on the moon.

20. Distance, m, on a map varies directly with the actual distance, d. On a certain map, 1 in. represents 10 mi.

21. At any given temperature, the electrical resistance of a wire is directly proportional to the length. At 20° C, 500 m of No. 18 gauge copper wire has a resistance of 10.295 ohms.

22. Under constant pressure, the volume, V, of a dry gas is directly proportional to its temperature, T, in Kelvin. A sample of oxygen occupies a volume of 5 L at 300 K.

Let (x_1, y_1) and (x_2, y_2) be ordered pairs of direct variation. Suppose that no coordinate is 0. Show that each given statement is true.

C 23. $\frac{y_1}{x_1} = \frac{y_2}{x_2}$

24. $\frac{y_1}{y_2} = \frac{x_1}{x_2}$

Problems

Solve.

A 1. An employee's wages are directly proportional to the time worked. If an employee earns \$100 for 5 h, how much will the employee earn for 18 h?

2. A certain car uses 15 gal of gasoline in 3 h. If the rate of gasoline consumption is constant, how much gasoline will the car use on a 35-hour trip?

3. The amount of money that a magazine pays for an article varies directly as the number of words in the article. If the magazine pays \$720 for a 1200-word article, how much will be paid for an article of 1500 words?

4. The distance traveled by a truck at a constant speed varies directly with the length of time it travels. If the truck travels 168 mi in 4 h, how far will it travel in 7 h?

5. The number of words typed is directly proportional to the time spent typing. If a typist can type 275 words in 5 min, how long will it take the typist to type a 935-word essay?

6. When an electric current is 32 A (amperes), the electromotive force is 288 V (volts). Find the force when the current is 65 A if the force varies directly as the current.

7. The area covered by a painter is directly proportional to the number of hours worked. A painter covered 52 m^2 in the first 8 h on the job. How large an area will the painter cover in 24 h?

8. A restaurant buys 20 lb of ground beef to prepare 110 servings of chili. At this rate, how many servings can be made with 30 lb of ground beef?

9. A mass of 25 g stretches a spring 10 cm. If the distance a spring is stretched is directly proportional to the mass, what mass will stretch the spring 22 cm?

10. The amount of chlorine needed for a pool varies directly as the size of the pool. If 5 units of chlorine is the amount needed for 2500 L of water, how much chlorine is needed for 3750 L of water?

B 11. Thermometer F is marked off into 180 equal units. Thermometer C is marked off into 100 equal units. A reading of 66.6 degrees on thermometer F is equal to a reading of how many degrees on thermometer C?

12. The odometer on the Goldmans' car was not measuring distance correctly. For a 220-mi trip the odometer registered only 216.7 mi. On the return trip, the Goldmans had to detour due to road repairs. If the odometer registered 453.1 mi for the round trip, how many actual miles was the detour?

13. On a map, 1 cm represents an actual distance of 75 m. Find the area of a piece of land that is represented on the map by a rectangle measuring 11.5 cm by 18.5 cm.

14. In a scale model of a sailboat, an object that is 6 ft tall is represented by a figure 8 in. high. How many feet tall should the mast of the sailboat be in the model if the actual mast of the sailboat is 38 ft tall?

C 15. If the circumference of a circle varies directly as the diameter, and the diameter varies directly as the radius, show that the circumference varies directly as the radius.

Mixed Review Exercises

Multiply.

1. $(2p + 3)(3p + 1)$
2. $(4x - 2)(x^2 + 3x - 6)$
3. $-3s(5 - 4s)$
4. $(3c + 2)(3c - 2)$
5. $(t + 2)(3t - 5)$
6. $(7y - 3)(2y + 4)$

Draw the graph of each function.

7. $h(x) = 6$
8. $f\colon x \rightarrow -3x + 4$
9. $g(x) = \frac{5}{2}x + 1$
10. $K\colon x \rightarrow 2x - 7$
11. $t(x) = \frac{1}{3}x$
12. $d\colon x \rightarrow -4$

Biographical Note / *Hsien Wu*

Hsien Wu attended school in China and came to the United States to attend the Massachusetts Institute of Technology. He received his Ph.D. in biochemistry from Harvard University in 1917.

Wu developed methods to analyze small samples of blood. This was a major breakthrough as previous methods required large samples, a procedure that was not advantageous for the patient.

In 1924 Wu was appointed to head the biochemistry department at Peking Union Medical College. He conducted studies in eating habits and health, nutrition, and food composition. His many research papers made Wu the foremost nutritionist in China. He was appointed to a number of international committees and was made director of the Nutrition Institute of China.

8-10 Inverse Variation

Objective To use inverse variation to solve problems.

The table shows the time, t, that it takes a car to travel a distance of 40 mi at the speed of r mi/h. You can see that

$$rt = 40.$$

Notice that if the speed is increased, the time is decreased, so that the product is always 40. You can say that the time *varies inversely* as the rate. This example illustrates an *inverse variation*.

Rate in mi/h: r	Time in hours: t
20	2
30	$\frac{4}{3}$
40	1
50	$\frac{4}{5}$

An **inverse variation** is a function defined by an equation of the form

$$xy = k, \text{ where } k \text{ is a nonzero constant,}$$

or

$$y = \frac{k}{x}, \text{ where } x \neq 0.$$

You say that y *varies inversely as* x or that y *is inversely proportional to* x. The constant k is the **constant of variation.**

The graph of an inverse function is not a straight line, since the equation

$$xy = k$$

is not linear. The term xy is of degree 2.

Example 1 Graph the equation $xy = 1$.

Solution

x	y
-4	$-\frac{1}{4}$
-2	$-\frac{1}{2}$
-1	-1
$-\frac{1}{2}$	-2
$-\frac{1}{4}$	-4

x	y
$\frac{1}{4}$	4
$\frac{1}{2}$	2
1	1
2	$\frac{1}{2}$
4	$\frac{1}{4}$

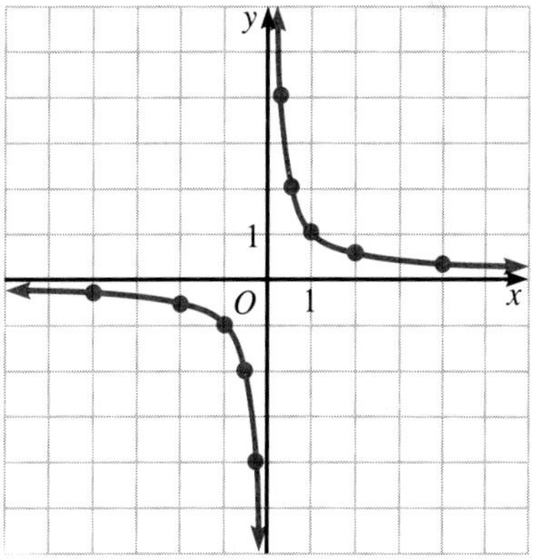

The graph of $xy = 1$ shown in Example 1 is called a *hyperbola*. Since neither x nor y can have the value 0, the graph does not intersect either the x-axis or the y-axis.

For every nonzero value of k, the graph of $xy = k$ is a **hyperbola.**
When k is positive, the branches of the graph are in Quadrants I and III.
When k is negative, the branches of the graph are in Quadrants II and IV.

Let (x_1, y_1) and (x_2, y_2) be two ordered pairs of the same inverse variation. Since the coordinates must satisfy the equation $xy = k$, you know that

$$x_1y_1 = k \text{ and } x_2y_2 = k,$$

or

$$x_1y_1 = x_2y_2.$$

You can compare the equations for direct variation and inverse variation.

Direct Variation	**Inverse Variation**
$y = kx$	$xy = k$, or $y = \frac{k}{x}$
$\frac{y_1}{x_1} = \frac{y_2}{x_2}$	$x_1y_1 = x_2y_2$

The equations above show that *for direct variation the quotients of the coordinates are constant and for inverse variation the products of the coordinates are constant.*

One example of an inverse variation is the law of the lever. A *lever* is a bar pivoted at a point called the *fulcrum*. If masses m_1 and m_2 are placed at distances d_1 and d_2 from the fulcrum, and the bar is balanced, then

$$m_1d_1 = m_2d_2.$$

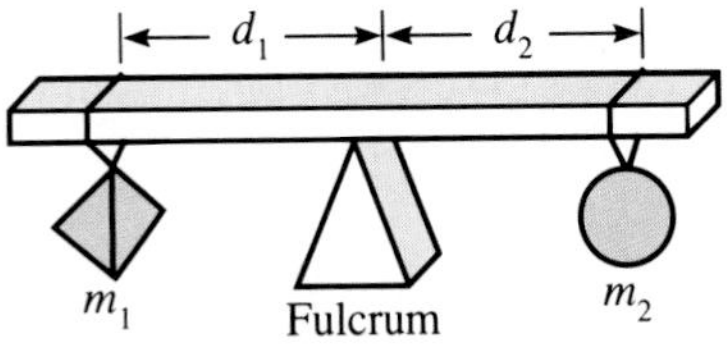

Example 2 If a 24 g mass is 30 cm from the fulcrum of a lever, how far from the fulcrum is a 45 g mass that balances the 24 g mass?

Solution Let $m_1 = 24$, $d_1 = 30$, and $m_2 = 45$, $d_2 = \underline{\ ?\ }$.

Use $m_1d_1 = m_2d_2$.

$$24 \cdot 30 = 45d_2$$

$$\frac{720}{45} = d_2$$

$$16 = d_2$$

$\therefore$ the distance of the 45 g mass from the fulcrum is 16 cm. ***Answer***

Oral Exercises

State whether each equation defines an inverse variation or a direct variation. k is a nonzero constant.

1. $\frac{y}{x} = k$
2. $y = \frac{k}{x}$
3. $p = \frac{k}{z}$
4. $xy = 25$
5. $d = 40t$
6. $m = \frac{1}{d}$
7. $\frac{c_1}{d_1} = \frac{c_2}{d_2}$
8. $a_1b_1 = a_2b_2$
9. $\frac{1}{4} = rt$
10. $\frac{m}{n} = \frac{5}{8}$
11. $\frac{x}{y} = \frac{1}{k}$
12. $kxy = 5$

Complete the ordered pairs so they satisfy the given inverse variation.

13. $xy = 12$ and $(x, y) = (2, \underline{\ ?\ })$ $(\underline{\ ?\ }, 4)$ $(-6, \underline{\ ?\ })$
14. $mn = 60$ and $(m, n) = (10, \underline{\ ?\ })$ $(\underline{\ ?\ }, 5)$ $(-2, \underline{\ ?\ })$
15. $144 = pq$ and $(p, q) = (8, \underline{\ ?\ })$ $(-3, \underline{\ ?\ })$ $(\underline{\ ?\ }, 12)$
16. $xy = -1$ and $(x, y) = (-1, \underline{\ ?\ })$ $\left(\frac{1}{4}, \underline{\ ?\ }\right)$ $(\underline{\ ?\ }, 2)$
17. If $rs = k$, and r is tripled while k remains the same, how does s change?
18. If $d = rt$, and t is halved while d remains constant, how does r change?

Written Exercises

Graph each equation if both the domain and the range are the set of nonzero real numbers. You may wish to verify your graphs on a computer or a graphing calculator.

A

1. $xy = 6$
2. $xy = 4$
3. $xy = -1$
4. $xy = -16$
5. $x = \frac{9}{y}$
6. $y = \frac{2}{x}$
7. $\frac{x}{2} = \frac{-2}{y}$
8. $\frac{x}{3} = \frac{4}{y}$

Exercises 9 and 10 refer to the lever at balance shown on page 398. Find the missing value.

9. $m_1 = 12, m_2 = 9, d_1 = 30, d_2 = \underline{\ ?\ }$
10. $m_1 = \underline{\ ?\ }, m_2 = 60, d_1 = 5, d_2 = 9$

(x_1, y_1) and (x_2, y_2) are ordered pairs of the same inverse variation. Find the missing value.

11. $x_1 = 4, y_1 = 54, x_2 = 8, y_2 = \underline{\ ?\ }$
12. $x_1 = 32, y_1 = 9, x_2 = \underline{\ ?\ }, y_2 = 12$
13. $x_1 = \underline{\ ?\ }, y_1 = 19.5, x_2 = 11.7, y_2 = 10.5$
14. $x_1 = 10, y_1 = \underline{\ ?\ }, x_2 = 8, y_2 = \frac{1}{4}$

For each inverse variation described, state (a) a formula and (b) a proportion.

Sample The height, h, of a right circular cylinder of fixed volume varies inversely as the area, A, of the base. A cylinder 6 in. high has a base of 20 in^2.

Solution **a.** $Ah = k$; $h = 6$ when $A = 20$.
$20(6) = k$, so $k = 120$

$\therefore Ah = 120, \quad \text{or} \quad h = \frac{120}{A}$

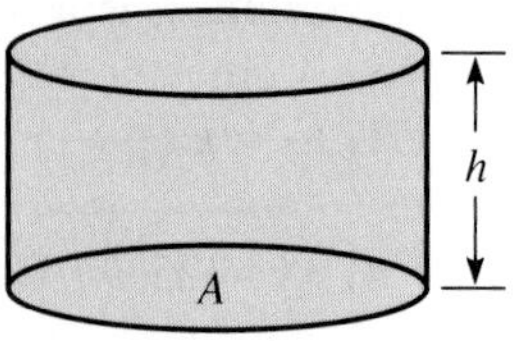

b. $A_1h_1 = A_2h_2$
Divide by h_1h_2 to obtain the proportion:

$$\frac{A_1}{h_2} = \frac{A_2}{h_1}$$

Let $A_1 = 20$ and $h_1 = 6$. $\frac{20}{h_2} = \frac{A_2}{6}$

B **15.** Length l and width w of a rectangle of given area vary inversely. When the length is 18, the width is 5.

16. The force, f, needed to move a rock varies inversely as the length, l, of the crowbar used. When the length is 2 m, the force needed is 1.5 N (newtons).

17. The frequency, f, of a periodic wave is inversely proportional to the length, l, of the wave. The frequency is 2.5 Hz (hertz) when the wavelength is 0.60 m.

18. The time, t, required to drive between two cities is inversely proportional to the average speed, r. The trip took 3 h at an average speed of 52 mi/h.

19. At a fixed temperature, the volume, V, of a gas varies inversely as the pressure, P. A volume of 465 cm^3 of a gas is at a pressure of 725 mm.

20. The amount of current, I, flowing through a circuit is inversely proportional to the amount of resistance, R, of the circuit. In a circuit with a resistance of 18 ohms, the current is 0.25 amperes.

Problems

Solve.

A **1.** The number of days needed to remodel a house varies inversely as the number of people working on the job. It takes 18 weeks for 4 people to complete the project. If the job has to be finished in 8 weeks, how many people are needed?

2. Three friends on a fishing trip pay $100 each to share the rent of a cottage. The cost per person varies inversely as the number of people sharing the rent. How many people would have to share the rent of the cottage to make the cost $60 per person?

3. A rectangle has length 36 cm and width 28 cm. Find the length of another rectangle of equal area whose width is 21 cm.

4. The winner of a race ran the distance in 45 s at an average speed of 9.6 m/s. The runner who came in last finished in 48 s. What was the last runner's average speed?

5. A fifteen-centimeter pulley runs at 250 r/min (revolutions per minute). How fast does the five-centimeter pulley it drives revolve, if the number of revolutions per minute varies inversely as the diameter?

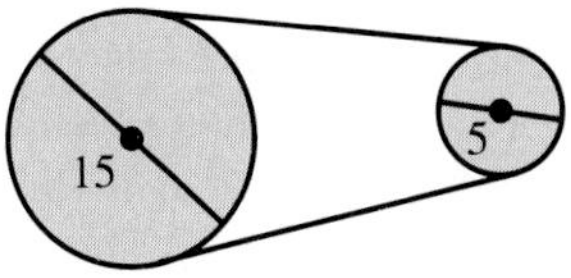

6. A gear with 42 teeth revolves at 1200 r/min and meshes with a gear having 72 teeth. What is the speed of the second gear if the rotational speed of a gear varies inversely with the number of teeth?

7. The number of chairs on a ski lift varies inversely as the distance between them. When they are 10 m apart, the ski lift can accommodate 32 chairs. If 40 evenly spaced chairs are used on the lift, what is the space between them?

8. The number of plants used to fill a row of given length in a garden varies inversely as the distance between the plants. If 75 plants are used to fill the row when planted 20 cm apart, how many plants are used to fill the row when planted 15 cm apart?

9. A string on a violin is 25.8 cm long and produces a tone whose frequency is 440 Hz. What is the length of a string needed to produce a tone of frequency 516 Hz, if the frequency of a vibrating string is inversely proportional to its length?

10. The frequency of a vibrating string is inversely proportional to its diameter. A violin string with diameter 0.50 mm produces a tone of frequency 440 Hz. What is the frequency of the tone produced by a similar string whose diameter is 0.55 mm?

In Exercises 11–14, apply the law of the lever.

11. Sara weighs 106 lb and Levon weighs 156 lb. If Levon sits 6 ft from the seesaw support, how far from the support must Sara sit to balance the seesaw?

12. One end of a pry bar is under a 350 kg boulder. The fulcrum of the bar is 15 cm from the boulder and 175 cm from the other end of the bar. What mass at that end of the bar will balance the boulder?

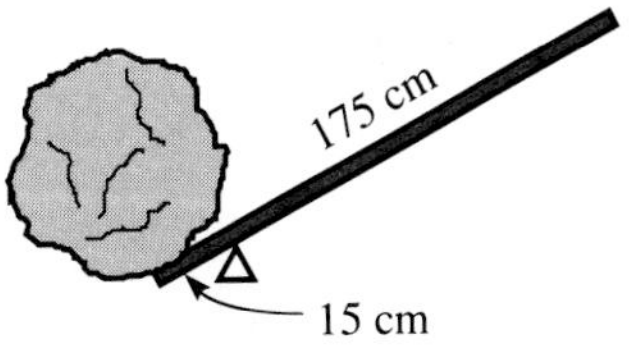

B 13. An 18 kg mass is placed at one end of a steel bar that is 1 m long. A 35 kg mass is placed at the other end. Where should the fulcrum be placed to balance the bar?

14. A lever has a 500 kg steel ball on one end and a 300 kg log on the other end. The lever is balanced. The steel ball is 1 m closer to the fulcrum than the log. How far from the fulcrum is the log?

The following formula holds for the wave motion of sound:

$$fl = v.$$

f is the frequency (number of cycles per second), l is the wavelength (in meters), and v is the speed of sound (about 335 m/s in air). Use this information in the following problems.

15. The frequency of a note an octave above a given note is twice that of the given note. How does the wavelength of the higher note compare with that of the lower note?

16. If the wavelength of a note is $\frac{3}{2}$ that of a given note, how do the frequencies compare?

17. An open organ pipe produces a sound wave that has a length that is twice the length of the pipe. Find the length of an open pipe that will produce the note A with the frequency 440. Give the answer to the nearest tenth of a meter.

18. A stopped organ pipe produces a sound wave that has a length that is four times the length of the pipe. What is the frequency of the sound produced by a stopped organ pipe that is 2 m long?

Mixed Review Exercises

Show that the lines whose equations are given are parallel.

1. $2x + 3y = 3$ $2x + 3y = 6$	**2.** $2x + 10y = 3$ $x + 5y = 2$	**3.** $x - y = 5$ $y - x = 5$	**4.** $-4x + 6y = 1$ $2x - 3y = 2$

Find the constant of variation.

5. t varies directly as s, and $t = 24$ when $s = -4$.

6. y varies directly as x, and $y = 14$ when $x = 70$.

7. m is proportional to n, and $m = 63$ when $n = 7$.

Computer Exercises

For students with some programming experience

Write a BASIC program to determine whether a set of ordered pairs represents a direct variation, an inverse variation, or neither. At least three ordered pairs should be entered with INPUT statements. Run the program for the data below.

1. (2, 3), (8, 12), (10, 15), (−24, −36)

2. (12, −4), (−16, 3), (−15, 3.2)

3. (0, 0), (3, 4), (9, 8), (−2, −3)

4. (2, 1.6), (12, 9.6), (5, 4), (9, 7.2)

Calculator Key-In

You can use a calculator to solve a direct variation or an inverse variation.

For a direct variation, first set up the equation

$$\frac{y_1}{x_1} = \frac{y_2}{x_2}$$

and then use your calculator to multiply and divide to find the missing value.

For an inverse variation, first set up the equation

$$x_1 y_1 = x_2 y_2$$

and then use your calculator to multiply and divide to find the missing value.

Find the missing value.

1. $\frac{y_1}{12} = \frac{14}{8}$
2. $\frac{13}{x_1} = \frac{6}{9}$
3. $\frac{93}{21} = \frac{y_2}{35}$
4. $\frac{y_1}{4.2} = \frac{5.6}{3.2}$
5. $\frac{1.2}{x_1} = \frac{5}{1.5}$
6. $\frac{2.6}{6.5} = \frac{y_2}{4.5}$
7. $12(24) = 15y_2$
8. $15y_1 = (16)36$
9. $4(65) = 50y_2$
10. $1.2(0.8) = 1.6y$
11. $(10.8)12 = 14.4y_2$
12. $(4.8)(600) = 400y_2$

Self-Test 4

Vocabulary direct variation (p. 391)
constant of variation (p. 391)
constant of proportionality (p. 392)
inverse variation (p. 397)
hyperbola (p. 398)

(x_1, y_1) and (x_2, y_2) are ordered pairs of the same direct variation. Find each missing value.

Obj. 8-9, p. 391

1. $x_1 = 10$, $y_1 = 25$
   $x_2 = 2$, $y_2 = \underline{\ ?\ }$
2. $x_1 = 24$, $y_1 = 64$
   $x_2 = \underline{\ ?\ }$, $y_2 = 8$
3. A worker's earnings are directly proportional to the number of hours worked. If \$60 is earned for 4 h of work, how much is earned for 35 h?

(x_1, y_1) and (x_2, y_2) are ordered pairs of the same inverse variation. Find each missing value.

Obj. 8-10, p. 397

4. $x_1 = 20$, $y_1 = \underline{\ ?\ }$
   $x_2 = 5$, $y_2 = 12$
5. $x_1 = 8$, $y_1 = 16$
   $x_2 = 4$, $y_2 = \underline{\ ?\ }$
6. Four friends on a ski trip pay \$210 each to share the rent of a cabin. The cost per person varies inversely as the number of persons. How many people sharing the rent would make the cost \$120 per person?

Check your answers with those at the back of the book.

Reading Algebra / Problem-Solving Strategies

To be a successful problem solver, you must first master the art of reading word problems. Read each problem slowly and carefully. Here are some questions you can ask yourself as you begin to work a problem.

- Will it help to organize the information in a chart?
- Is there a standard formula to use?
- Will drawing a sketch or making a model help to visualize the problem?
- Is it reasonable to use a trial-and-error (guess-and-check) approach?

If you are having trouble understanding a word problem or figuring out how to begin solving it, there are a number of things you can do. The first is rereading. Perhaps you overlooked something when you first read the problem. Then, attempt to break the problem down. You may be able to use the parts that you understand to make sense of the parts that you do not. Sometimes, substituting simpler data and solving a simpler, related problem may help you see how to solve the given problem.

When you have chosen a strategy and found an answer, check your answer to be sure it makes sense. For example, the length of a room cannot be negative. Estimate before solving and use your estimate to check that your answer is within a reasonable range. Then check your answer in the words of the problem for accuracy. The time you spend on planning and checking will be well worthwhile.

Exercises

1. A coin box contains \$26.50 in dimes and quarters. There are 157 coins altogether. How many of each type of coin are in the box?

2. The length of a rectangle is 4 cm more than twice the width. The perimeter is 56 cm. Find the length and the width.

3. Two planes leave an airport at the same time flying in opposite directions. The first plane is traveling at a speed of 1100 km/h. After 4 h, the planes are 7600 km apart. Find the speed of the second plane.

4. The trip from Winston to Carver takes 8 min longer during rush hour, when the average speed is 75 km/h, than in off-peak hours, when the average speed is 90 km/h. Find the distance between the two towns.

5. A rectangle is 5 cm longer than it is wide. If the length is doubled and the width is tripled, the area is increased by 420 cm^2. Find the original dimensions.

6. The sum of two numbers is 11 and the sum of their squares is 65. Find the numbers.

7. The edges of one cube are 2 cm longer than the edges of another. The volume of the smaller cube is 152 cm^3 less than the volume of the larger cube. Find the lengths of the edges of each cube.

8. A soccer league signed up 440 players. The ratio of returning players to new players was 4:7. How many players were new?

Chapter Summary

1. The solution set of a linear equation in two variables is the set of all ordered pairs of numbers that make the equation into a true statement.
2. Ordered pairs of real numbers can be graphed as points in a coordinate plane. The graph of a linear equation in two variables is a line.
3. The slope of a line can be found by using any two points on the line. Different lines with the same slope are parallel.
4. An equation of a line can be found from: (a) the slope and the y-intercept; (b) the slope and any point on the line; (c) two points on the line.
5. A function can be defined by a correspondence, a table, an equation, or a set of ordered pairs.
6. The value of a function F at 2 is denoted by $F(2)$. Any value of a function can be found by replacing the variable in the defining equation of the function by the given number.
7. A linear function is defined by a linear equation. Its graph is a line.
8. A quadratic function is defined by an equation of the form $y = ax^2 + bx + c$, $a \neq 0$. Its graph is a parabola that opens upward if a is positive or downward if a is negative.
9. A direct variation is a linear function defined by an equation of the form $y = kx$, $k \neq 0$.
10. An inverse variation is a function defined by an equation of the form $xy = k$, $k \neq 0$, or $y = \frac{k}{x}$, $k \neq 0$.

Chapter Review

Give the letter of the correct answer.

1. Which ordered pair is a solution of $3x - 2y = 5$? **8-1**

a. $(1, -1)$ **b.** $(2, 1)$ **c.** $(-1, 1)$ **d.** $(-2, 1)$

2. Solve $2x + 3y = 9$ if x and y are whole numbers.

a. $(0, 3), (1, 3)$ **b.** $(0, 3), (3, 1)$ **c.** $(3, 0), (1, 3)$ **d.** $(3, 0), (3, 1)$

3. In which quadrant is the graph of $(-3, 5)$? **8-2**

a. I **b.** II **c.** III **d.** IV

4. Where is the graph of $(-3, 0)$ in the coordinate plane?

a. in Quadrant II **b.** in Quadrant III **c.** on the x-axis **d.** on the y-axis

5. Find the slope of the line that passes through (4, 4) and (−4, 6). **8-3**

a. −4 b. 0 c. $-\frac{1}{4}$ d. no slope

6. Find the slope of the line whose equation is $y + 3 = 0$.

a. 3 b. 0 c. −3 d. no slope

7. Find the slope and y-intercept of the line whose equation is $y = \frac{3}{2}x - 2$. **8-4**

a. $m = -2,\ b = \frac{3}{2}$ b. $m = 2,\ b = \frac{3}{2}$ c. $m = \frac{3}{2},\ b = 2$ d. $m = \frac{3}{2},\ b = -2$

8. Write an equation in slope-intercept form of the line that is parallel to $y = -\frac{1}{3}x$ and that has y-intercept 5.

a. $y = -\frac{1}{3}x + 5$ b. $y = 5x - \frac{1}{3}$ c. $y = -\frac{1}{3}x - 5$ d. $5y = -\frac{1}{3}x$

9. Find the equation of a line with slope $-\frac{4}{3}$ that passes through (12, −3). **8-5**

a. $y = -\frac{4}{3}x - 19$ b. $y = -\frac{4}{3}x + 19$ c. $y = -\frac{4}{3}x + 13$ d. $y = -\frac{4}{3}x - 13$

10. Write an equation in standard form of the line that passes through the points (0, −7) and (−7, 0).

a. $-x + y = 7$ b. $-x + y = -7$ c. $x + y = -7$ d. $y = -7$

11. Write the range of the function {(−1, 1), (0, 0), (1, 0), (2, 6)}. **8-6**

a. {0, 1, 2, 3, 4, 5, 6} b. {−1, 0, 1, 2}
c. {(−1, 1), (1, 1)} d. {0, 1, 6}

12. Find $G(0)$ given $G(x) = 4 - 8x$. **8-7**

a. 0 b. 2 c. 8 d. 4

13. Find $F(-1)$ given $F\colon x \rightarrow 5 - x^2$.

a. 25 b. 7 c. 4 d. 5

14. Find the vertex and give the least value of $f(x) = x^2 + 8x + 3$. **8-8**

a. (−4, −13); −13 b. (4, 13); 13 c. (−4, 13); 13 d. (4, −13); −13

15. Find the vertex and give the greatest value of $f(x) = 2x - x^2$.

a. (2, 1); 1 b. (1, 2); 2 c. (1, 1); 1 d. (1, 0); 0

16. Find the constant of variation if y varies directly as x, and $y = 95$ when $x = 19$. **8-9**

a. 5 b. $\frac{1}{5}$ c. 19 d. 95

17. Find the missing value if (75, 30) and (__?__, 18) are ordered pairs of the same inverse variation. **8-10**

a. 125 b. 75 c. 45 d. 7.2

Chapter Test

State whether each ordered pair is a solution of the given equation.

1. $3x - 2y = 12$
$(-2, 3)$, $(4, 0)$

2. $7x + 5y = -3$
$(-1, -2)$, $(-4, -5)$ 8-1

Solve each equation if x and y are whole numbers.

3. $2x + 5y = 12$

4. $2x + 3y = 15$

Plot each of the given points in a coordinate plane.

5. $(5, 3)$ **6.** $(0, 6)$ **7.** $(3, -4)$ **8.** $(-2, 5)$ 8-2

Graph each equation.

9. $y = 3x - 4$

10. $y = \frac{1}{2}x + 2$

Find the slope of the line passing through the two given points.

11. $(-6, 0)$, $(8, -7)$

12. $(-5, 7)$, $(8, 7)$ 8-3

13. $(9, 5)$, $(9, -5)$

14. $(-2, 4)$, $(3, -1)$

Find the slope of each line whose equation is given.

15. $y = -3x + 2$

16. $x + y = 0$

17. $3x - 5y = 15$

18. $2x + 4y = 1$

Give the slope and y-intercept of each line. Are any of the lines parallel? If so, which?

19. $y = 3x + 2$

20. $y = -\frac{2}{3}x + 4$ 8-4

21. $y = -\frac{2}{3}x - 3$

22. $y = \frac{9}{4}x + 6$

Change each equation to slope-intercept form. Then draw the graph using only the slope and y-intercept.

23. $5x - y = 1$

24. $-x + 3y + 6 = 0$

25. $2y = 7$

26. $x + 2y - 6 = 0$

Write an equation in slope-intercept form of the line that has the given slope and passes through the given point.

27. slope -3; $(0, -1)$

28. slope $\frac{5}{2}$; $(-6, 7)$ 8-5

29. slope 0; $\left(2, -\frac{1}{4}\right)$

30. slope $\frac{3}{4}$; $(-3, -4)$

31. Write an equation in slope-intercept form of the line passing through the points $(-4, -6)$ and $(4, 10)$.

32. The table below shows a function. 8-6

a. State the domain and range of the function.

b. Graph the function by means of a bar graph or a broken-line graph, whichever is more suitable.

Value of U.S. Exports in Billions of Dollars	
Year	Value
1960	\$29
1965	\$41
1970	\$66
1975	\$156
1980	\$345
1985	\$359

Find the range of each function.

33. $F(t) = 2t - 2,\ D = \{-1, 0, 2\}$

34. $g: x \rightarrow x^2 - 1,\ D = \{-1, 0, 1\}$ 8-7

35. If $f: x \rightarrow \frac{2x}{3} - 1$, find: **a.** $f(3)$ **b.** $f(-3)$

36. If $f(x) = \frac{2x - 1}{3}$, find: **a.** $f(3)$ **b.** $f(-3)$

Draw the graph of each function.

37. $g: x \rightarrow 3x + 1$

38. $t(x) = -\frac{3}{4}x - 2$ 8-8

39. Find the coordinates of the vertex and the equation of the axis of symmetry of the graph of the equation $y = 2x - x^2$. Use the vertex and at least four other points to graph the equation.

(x_1, y_1) and (x_2, y_2) are ordered pairs of the same direct variation. Find the missing value.

40. $x_1 = 72,\ y_1 = 3$
$x_2 = \underline{\ ?\ },\ y_2 = 2$

41. $x_1 = \underline{\ ?\ },\ y_1 = 70$
$x_2 = 2,\ y_2 = 25$ 8-9

(x_1, y_1) and (x_2, y_2) are ordered pairs of the same inverse variation. Find the missing value.

42. $x_1 = 20,\ y_1 = 5$
$x_2 = \underline{\ ?\ },\ y_2 = 50$

43. $x_1 = 10,\ y_1 = 75$
$x_2 = 30,\ y_2 = \underline{\ ?\ }$ 8-10

Cumulative Review *(Chapters 1–8)*

Simplify.

1. $(7p - 2r) - (-3p + 4r)$
2. $(8b - 4c)(2b + 3c)$
3. $3y^3z(10y^2 + 4yz - 7z^3)$
4. $(2x^3y^2z^4)^4 \div (4x^2yz^3)^2$
5. $(3m - 5n)^2$
6. $(3.2 \times 10^{-8})(1.5 \times 10^{12})$

Factor completely.

7. $20x^2 + 13x - 15$
8. $4y^2 - 12y + 9$
9. $3z^2 - 21z - 24$

Express in simplest form. Assume that no denominator is zero.

10. $\dfrac{b^2 + 2b + 1}{b^2 - 2b - 3}$
11. $\dfrac{x^2 + 4x + 3}{x + 1} \cdot \dfrac{(x^2 - 1)}{2x^2 + x - 1}$
12. $\dfrac{3z^2 + 8z - 3}{3z^2 + 5z - 2} \div \dfrac{z^2 + 6z + 9}{z^3 - 4z}$
13. $\dfrac{r}{r - 4} - \dfrac{r}{r + 4} - 5$

Write an equation in slope-intercept form for each line described.

14. The line with slope -3 that passes through $(2, -2)$.
15. The line that passes through $(5, 2)$ and $(2, 5)$.
16. The line that contains $(1, 3)$ and is parallel to $2x + y = 4$.
17. Find the range of the function $f\colon x \to x^2 + 2x + 1$ with domain $\{-3, -2, -1, 0, 1, 2, 3\}$.

Graph each equation.

18. $3x + 5y = 10$
19. $y = x^2 - x + 1$
20. Find the coordinates of the vertex and the equation of the axis of symmetry of the graph of $y = 2x^2 + 3x + 4$.

Solve each equation. Assume that no denominator is zero.

21. $4(x + 3) = 3(3x - 7)$
22. $2|x| + 1 = 5$
23. $y\%$ of $50 = 27$
24. $9a^2 - 12a + 4 = 0$
25. $49t^2 - 36 = 0$
26. $10t^2 + t = 3$
27. $\dfrac{1}{x + 1} + 1 = x + 2$
28. $\dfrac{a + 2}{a - 1} = \dfrac{a + 1}{a + 4}$
29. $\dfrac{2z}{z - 3} - \dfrac{1}{z + 1} = -1$
30. $m\%$ of $60 = 48$
31. $2(x + 7) = 5(3x - 5)$
32. $\frac{1}{3}(m + 2) = m - 4$
33. The number of units manufactured varies directly with the number of hours worked. If 10 units are manufactured in 4 h, how many units are manufactured in 14 h?
34. For a given distance, the speed at which a car travels varies inversely as the time it travels. If it takes 1.5 h to travel a distance at 84 km/h, how long would it take to travel the same distance at 90 km/h?

Maintaining Skills

Factor completely. If the polynomial cannot be factored, write "prime."

Sample 1 $24x^2y - 60xy^4$ **Solution** $24x^2y - 60xy^4 = 12xy(2x - 5y^3)$

1. $25b^2c^3 + 15b^5c^4$
2. $12m^3 - 15mn^2 - 8n^2$
3. $9u^5v + 36u^4v^2 - 15u^4v^3$
4. $-vx^3 + 40x^2v^3 - v^6$
5. $-24x^7y^5 + 32x^6y^3 - 8x^2y^4$
6. $20m^6n^6 - 4m^6n^5 + 24m^5n^7$

Sample 2 $81y^4 - 16$

Solution $81y^4 - 16 = (9y^2 + 4)(9y^2 - 4) = (9y^2 + 4)(3y + 2)(3y - 2)$

Sample 3 $9y^2 + 30y + 25$

Solution $9y^2 + 30y + 25 = (3y)^2 + 2(3y \cdot 5) + 5^2 = (3y + 5)^2$

7. $z^3 - 121z$
8. $27bc^2 - 12b$
9. $-x^6 + 49$
10. $9x^2 - 12x + 4$
11. $25m^4 + 9$
12. $1 - 16y^8$
13. $16a^2 - 40a + 25$
14. $4n^2 - 16n + 16$
15. $25x^2 + 30x + 9$

Sample 4 $g^2 - 2g - 35$ **Solution** $g^2 - 2g - 35 = (g + 5)(g - 7)$

16. $z^2 + 8z - 16$
17. $n^2 + 11n + 18$
18. $y^2 - 9y + 18$
19. $-c^2 + 5cd + 14d^2$
20. $2d^2 + 18d - 72$
21. $x^2 + 10x + 21$
22. $4c^2 - 36c + 32$
23. $n^2 - 5np + 6p^2$
24. $7f + f^2 - 30$

Sample 5 $3cd + 21d - 2c - 14$

Solution $3cd + 21d - 2c - 14 = 3d(c + 7) - 2(c + 7) = (3d - 2)(c + 7)$

25. $ry - 2sy + 3r - 6s$
26. $2xy - y^2 + 6x - 3y$
27. $s^2 - 4t^2 - 12t - 9$
28. $x^2 - 10x + 25 - y^2$
29. $16a^2 - 9b^2 + 30b - 25$
30. $m^2t - 5m^2 + 5t - 25$

Sample 6 $10p^2 - 19p - 15$

Solution Test the possibilities for the first terms: $10p$ and p; $5p$ and $2p$
Test the possibilities for the second terms: -15 and 1; 15 and -1; -5 and 3; 5 and -3.
$10p^2 - 19p - 15 = (5p + 3)(2p - 5)$

31. $3b^2 + 2b - 5$
32. $10n^2 + 3n - 1$
33. $6m^2 - 8m - 8$
34. $6a^2 + 7a - 3$
35. $25z^3 + 15z^2 + 2z$
36. $14 + 15y - 9y^2$
37. $-7y^2 - 20y + 3$
38. $22n + 8n^2 - 6$
39. $12b^2 - 14b - 10$

Preparing for College Entrance Exams

Strategy for Success

Depending upon how a multiple-choice test is scored, it may not be wise to guess. However, if you can eliminate several of the possible answers, guessing may be worthwhile. For example, suppose you do not know the answer to a problem, but your knowledge of algebra tells you the answer must be a positive integer. This may help you improve your chances of guessing correctly.

Decide which is the best of the choices given and write the corresponding letter on your answer sheet.

1. A total of \$15,000 was invested in accounts earning 6% annual simple interest and in bonds earning 10% annual simple interest. If twice as much of the \$15,000 had been invested in bonds, the earnings would have been \$160 higher. How much was invested in bonds?

(A) \$4000 **(B)** \$7000 **(C)** \$8000 **(D)** \$11,000

2. Identify the point(s) on the line that contains $(-4, 3)$ and has slope $-\frac{1}{4}$.

I. $(8, 0)$ II. $(-1, -3)$ III. $(-12, -13)$

(A) I only **(B)** II only **(C)** III only
(D) I, II, and III **(E)** None of the above

3. A rectangle has area 24. The graph of the length as a function of the width

(A) is a parabola that opens upward. **(B)** is a parabola that opens downward.
(C) is a hyperbola. **(D)** is one branch of a hyperbola.
(E) cannot be determined from the given information.

4. The inlet pipe on a water tank can fill the tank in 8 hours. When the tank was full, both the inlet pipe and the drain pipe were accidentally opened. Twenty-four hours later, the tank was empty. How many hours would it take to empty a full tank if only the drain were open?

(A) 6 hours **(B)** 9 hours **(C)** 10 hours **(D)** 12 hours

5. A runner won a 5 km road race with a time of exactly 15 min. An observer, using a watch that was running fast, clocked the winning time as 15 min 24 s. To the nearest tenth of a minute, how many minutes does the observer's watch gain in a day?

(A) 24.0 min **(B)** 38.4 min **(C)** 58.4 min **(D)** 61.0 min **(E)** 61.6 min

6. Find an equation of the line that intersects the y-axis at the same point as the line containing $(2, 2)$ and $(-4, -1)$ and that is parallel to the line containing $(6, 6)$ and $(-3, 3)$.

(A) $x - 3y = -3$ **(B)** $x - 2y = -8$ **(C)** $x + 2y = 8$ **(D)** $2x + y = 4$

9 Systems of Linear Equations

Wherever the legal paths of chess pieces cross, conflict can occur and a piece may be taken. This chapter will show you how to find the intersection of two such paths or lines.

Solving Systems of Linear Equations

9-1 The Graphing Method

Objective To use graphs to solve systems of linear equations.

Two or more equations in the same variables form a **system of equations.** The examples below give systems that consist of two equations in the variables x and y. To **solve a system** like these, you must find all ordered pairs (x, y) that make *both* equations true. Since a **solution** of a system satisfies both equations at the same time, the system is often called a **system of simultaneous equations.**

Example 1 Solve the system by graphing:

$$2x - y = 8$$
$$x + y = 1$$

Solution Graph $2x - y = 8$ and $x + y = 1$ in the same coordinate plane. The only point on *both* lines is the *intersection point* $(3, -2)$ The only solution of *both* equations is $(3, -2)$ You can check that $(3, -2)$ is a solution of the system by substituting $x = 3$ and $y = -2$ in *both* equations.

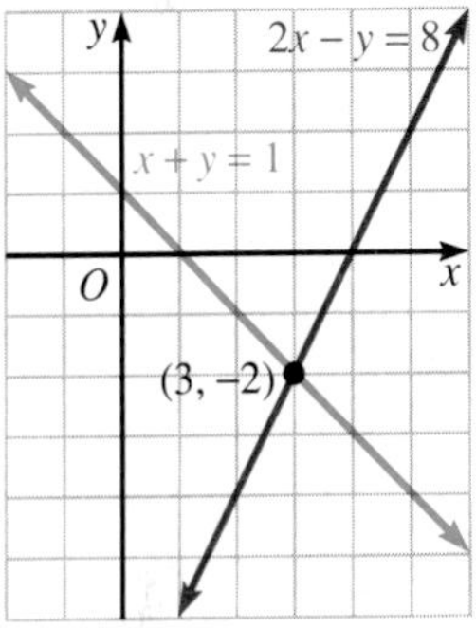

$$2x - y = 8 \qquad\qquad x + y = 1$$
$$2(3) - (-2) = 8 \ \checkmark \qquad 3 + (-2) = 1 \ \checkmark$$

$\therefore$ the system has the solution $(3, -2)$. ***Answer***

Example 2 Solve the system by graphing:

$$x - 2y = -6$$
$$x - 2y = 2$$

Solution When you graph the equations in the same coordinate plane, you see that the lines have the same slope but different y-intercepts. The graphs are *parallel lines*. Since the lines do not intersect, there is no point that represents a solution of both equations.

$\therefore$ the system has no solution. ***Answer***

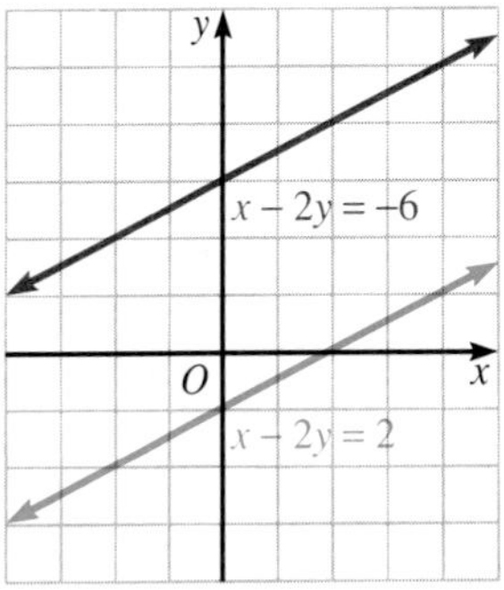

Example 3 Solve the system by graphing: $2x + 3y = 6$
$4x + 6y = 12$

Solution When you graph the equations in the same coordinate plane, you see that the graphs *coincide*. The equations are equivalent. Every point on the line represents a solution of both equations.

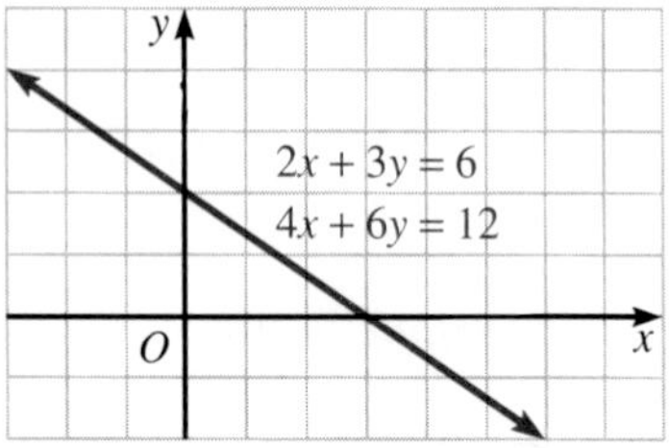

$\therefore$ the system has infinitely many solutions. ***Answer***

All the examples show how to solve a system of linear equations by the *graphing method*. If you have a computer or a graphing calculator, you can easily solve or estimate the solution to a system of equations by this method.

The Graphing Method

To solve a system of linear equations in two variables, draw the graph of each linear equation in the same coordinate plane.

1. If the lines intersect, there is only one solution, namely, the intersection point.
2. If the lines are parallel, there is no solution.
3. If the lines coincide, there are infinitely many solutions.

Oral Exercises

State whether the given ordered pair is a solution of the system.

1. (5, 3)
$2x - y = 7$
$x + y = 2$

2. (−1, 4)
$4x + 3y = 8$
$3x + y = 0$

3. (2, −2)
$9x = 10 - 4y$
$y = 3x - 8$

State the solution of each system.

4.
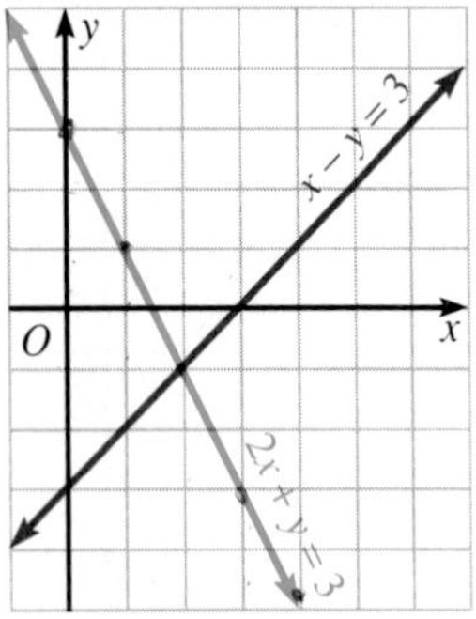

5.
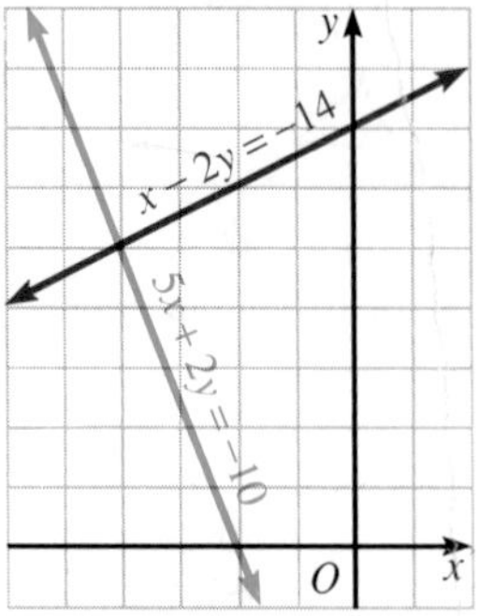

6.
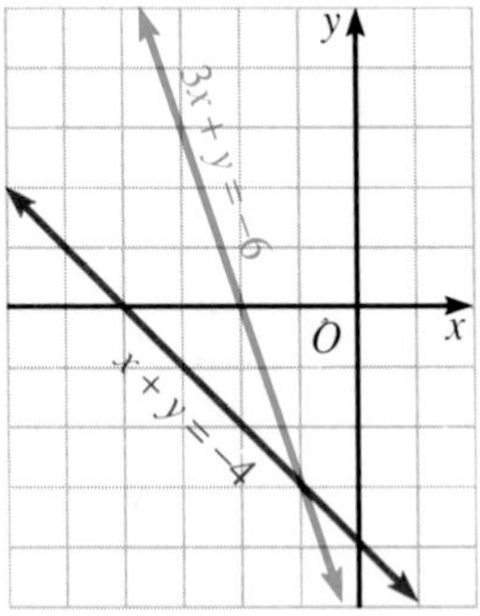

7. Suppose the graphs of a pair of linear equations appear to intersect at the point $(-1, 4)$. How can you check whether $(-1, 4)$ really is a solution of the system?

8. If a system of linear equations has no solution, what do you know about the graphs of the equations?

9. Suppose $(1, 5)$ and $(3, 7)$ are known to be solutions of a system of two linear equations. Are there any other solutions?

Written Exercises

Solve each system by the graphing method.

A

1. $y = x$; $y = 6 - x$
2. $y = -x$; $y = x + 9$
3. $y = -x + 2$; $y = 2x + 5$
4. $y = 3x + 1$; $y = 3x - 8$
5. $x - y = 6$; $2x + y = 0$
6. $4x + y = -3$; $5x - y = -6$
7. $3x - 9y = 0$; $-x + 3y = -3$
8. $-2x + y = -1$; $x + y = 5$
9. $y = \frac{1}{2}x + 1$; $4x - 8y = -8$
10. $2y - x = 2$; $x - 2y = 8$
11. $y - 2x = -5$; $y - x = -3$
12. $6x + 4y = 2$; $3x + 2y = 1$

Solve each system by the graphing method. Estimate the coordinates of the intersection point to the nearest half unit. You may wish to check your graphs using a computer or a graphing calculator.

B

13. $x + y = 3$; $x - y = 4$
14. $x + y = -2$; $2x - y = 10$
15. $3x + 5y = 15$; $x - y = 4$
16. $2y - 3x = 9$; $4y + 3x = 12$

The graphing method of solving a system of equations is particularly useful when the equations are not linear. Estimate the solutions of each nonlinear system below by studying the graphs. Check whether your estimate satisfies both equations.

17. $y = x^2$ and $y = 8 - x^2$

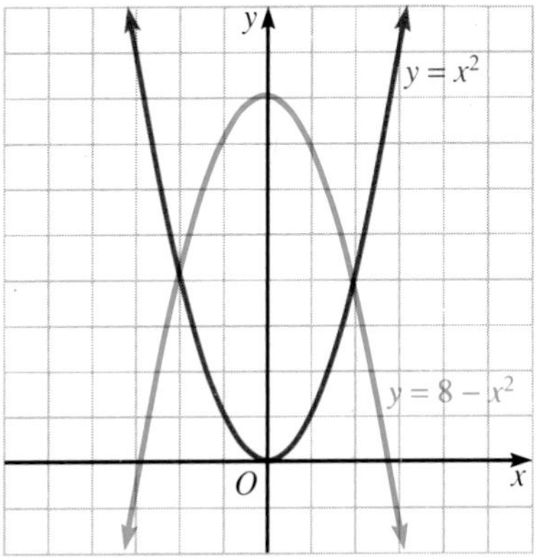

18. $y = x^2 - 2x$ and $y = -x^2 + 6x - 6$

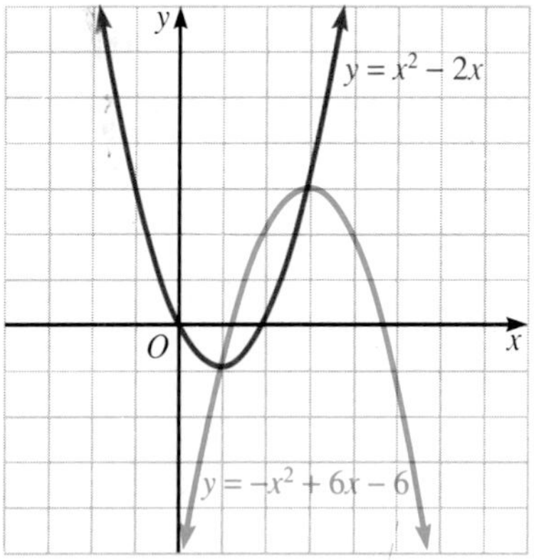

19. Where on the graph of $5x - 2y = 15$ is the x-coordinate equal to the y-coordinate?

20. Where on the graph of $3x - y = 12$ are the x- and y-coordinates opposites of each other?

21. Where on the graph of $4x + y + 12 = 0$ is the y-coordinate twice the x-coordinate?

22. The triangular region shown is enclosed by the x-axis and by the graphs of $x + 2y = 8$ and $y = \frac{3}{2}x$. Find the area of this region. (*Hint:* Area of a triangle $= \frac{1}{2} \times$ base $\times$ height.)

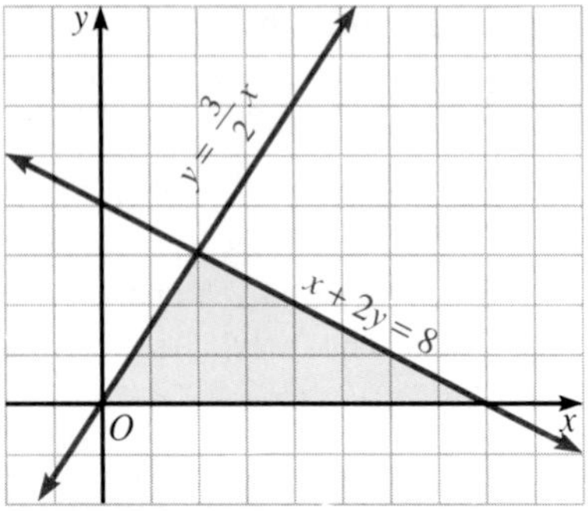

Ex. 22

C 23. Find the area of the triangular region enclosed by the y-axis and the graphs of $6x + 5y = 30$ and $2x - y = 2$.

24. Find the area of the region whose vertices are the points of intersection of the graphs of $2x + y = 5$, $y = x - 4$, and $y = 5$.

Mixed Review Exercises

Simplify. Give answers using positive exponents.

1. $\dfrac{15s^3t}{3s^2t^3}$

2. $(a^{-3}b^2)^4$

3. $\dfrac{14m^6n}{35m^4n^3}$

4. $(x^2y)^{-2}$

5. p^5p^{-2}

6. $\dfrac{x^4y^3}{x^{-3}y}$

Computer Exercises

For students with some programming experience

Write a BASIC program to print out a table of ordered pairs for each of two linear equations $Ax + By = C$ and $Dx + Ey = F$, where A, B, C, D, E, and F are entered with INPUT statements. If the two equations have an ordered pair in common, the program should report that the ordered pair is a solution of the system of equations. Run the program for the following pairs of equations with the given values of x.

1. $2x - 7y = 9$, $x + y = 0$ $\quad x \in \{0, 1, 2, 3, 4, 5\}$

2. $x + 3y = 1$, $\frac{1}{2}x - 4y = -5$ $\quad x \in \{-3, -2, -1, 0, 1\}$

3. $4x - 3y = 0$, $2x + y = 2$ $\quad x \in \{0, 1, 2, 3, 4\}$

4. $3x - 4y = -6$, $3x - 2y = 0$ $\quad x \in \{-2, -1, 0, 1, 2\}$

9-2 The Substitution Method

Objective To use the substitution method to solve systems of linear equations.

There are several ways to solve a system without using graphs. One of these is the *substitution method* shown in the examples below.

Example 1 Solve: $x + y = 15$
$4x + 3y = 38$

Solution Solve the first equation for y.

$$x + y = 15$$
$$y = 15 - x$$

Substitute this expression for y in the other equation, and solve for x.

$$4x + 3y = 38$$
$$4x + 3(15 - x) = 38$$
$$4x + 45 - 3x = 38$$
$$x + 45 = 38$$
$$x = -7$$

Substitute the value of x in the equation in Step 1, and solve for y.

$$y = 15 - x$$
$$y = 15 - (-7)$$
$$y = 22$$

Check $x = -7$ and $y = 22$ in *both* equations.

$$x + y = 15 \qquad 4x + 3y = 38$$
$$-7 + 22 \stackrel{?}{=} 15 \qquad 4(-7) + 3(22) \stackrel{?}{=} 38$$
$$15 = 15 \ \checkmark \qquad 38 = 38 \ \checkmark$$

$\therefore$ the solution is $(-7, 22)$. ***Answer***

Example 2 Solve: $2x - 3y = 4$
$x + 4y = -9$

Solution Solve the second equation for x since x has a coefficient of 1.

$$x + 4y = -9$$
$$x = -9 - 4y$$

Substitute this expression for x in the other equation, and solve for y.

$$2x - 3y = 4$$
$$2(-9 - 4y) - 3y = 4$$
$$-18 - 8y - 3y = 4$$
$$-11y = 22$$
$$y = -2$$

Substitute the value of y in the equation in Step 1, and solve for x.

$$x = -9 - 4y$$
$$x = -9 - 4(-2)$$
$$x = -1$$

The check in *both* equations is left to you.

$\therefore$ the solution is $(-1, -2)$. ***Answer***

The substitution method is most convenient to use when the coefficient of one of the variables is 1 or -1 as in Examples 1 and 2.

The Substitution Method

To solve a system of linear equations in two variables:

1. Solve one equation for one of the variables.
2. Substitute this expression in the other equation and solve for the other variable.
3. Substitute this value in the equation in Step 1 and solve.
4. Check the values in both equations.

Example 3 Solve by the substitution method: $2x - 8y = 6$
$x - 4y = 8$

Solution

$$x - 4y = 8$$
$$x = 8 + 4y$$

$$2x - 8y = 6$$
$$2(8 + 4y) - 8y = 6$$
$$16 + 8y - 8y = 6$$
$$16 = 6 \leftarrow \text{False}$$

The false statement indicates that there is *no* ordered pair (x, y) that satisfies both equations. (If you graph the equations, you'll see that the lines are parallel.)

$\therefore$ the system has no solution. ***Answer***

Example 4 Solve by the substitution method: $\frac{y}{2} = 2 - x$
$6x + 3y = 12$

Solution

$$\frac{y}{2} = 2 - x$$
$$y = 4 - 2x$$

{Multiply both sides by 2 to solve for y.

$$6x + 3y = 12$$
$$6x + 3(4 - 2x) = 12$$
$$6x + 12 - 6x = 12$$
$$12 = 12 \leftarrow \text{True}$$

Every ordered pair (x, y) that satisfies one of the equations also satisfies the other. (If you graph the equations, you'll see that the lines coincide.)

$\therefore$ the system has infinitely many solutions. ***Answer***

Oral Exercises

For each system, solve one of the equations for one of the variables.

1. $x - 2y = 0$
   $x + y = 6$
2. $3x + 2y = 10$
   $x + y = 10$
3. $5a + 3b = 1$
   $3a - b = 4$
4. $8m - n = 12$
   $2m - 3n = 18$
5. $2s + 5t = 14$
   $\frac{s}{2} = \frac{t}{4}$
6. $3p - 10 = 4q$
   $\frac{p}{6} + \frac{q}{3} = 0$

Solve by the substitution method.

7. $x = 6$
   $y = x - 5$
8. $b = a - 2$
   $b = 1$
9. $m = -2$
   $2n = m$
10. $y = 3x$
    $x + y = 8$
11. $d = 4c$
    $c + d = 20$
12. $y = x - 2$
    $x + y = 12$

Written Exercises

Solve by the substitution method.

A

1. $y = 6x$
   $x + y = 28$
2. $y = 2x$
   $5x - y = 30$
3. $a = 3b$
   $a - b = 12$
4. $m = 4n$
   $3m - 2n = 20$
5. $s = t + 2$
   $2t + s = 17$
6. $c = 3d - 4$
   $c + d = 16$
7. $3x + 1 = y$
   $2x + 3y = 25$
8. $3a = 2b - 6$
   $a = b - 1$
9. $4f - 3h = 0$
   $f + 4h = 19$
10. $3n + 5m = 7$
    $m - 4n = 6$
11. $2a - b = 17$
    $3a + 4b = -13$
12. $3y - x = -9$
    $2y + 5x = 11$
13. $2r + 3s = 0$
    $r + 5 = 6s$
14. $3x + 2y = 11$
    $x - 2 = -4y$
15. $2a - b = 1$
    $a = \frac{3}{5}b$
16. $3x + 2y = 550$
    $x = \frac{4}{5}y$
17. $c - d = 8$
    $\frac{c}{5} = d + 4$
18. $\frac{y}{2} - x = 1$
    $x + y + 7 = 0$
19. $2u + v = 9$
    $\frac{u}{2} - \frac{1}{2} = -v$
20. $\frac{m}{3} + \frac{n}{3} = 2$
    $2m + 3n = 10$
21. $\frac{y}{2} + \frac{x}{2} = 7$
    $3y + 2x = 48$
22. $3b - 2a = 4$
    $\frac{b}{2} - \frac{2a}{3} = 1$
23. $\frac{r}{2} + \frac{s}{3} = 1$
    $\frac{r}{4} + \frac{2s}{3} = -1$
24. $\frac{c}{2} - \frac{d}{5} = -4$
    $\frac{2c}{3} - \frac{3d}{5} = -7$

Solve by the substitution method.

B **25.** $x + y = 1000$
$0.05x + 0.06y = 57$

26. $a + b = 5000$
$0.08a = 0.06b - 20$

27. $\frac{x + y}{2} = 10$
$2x = 3y$

28. $\frac{3d + e}{4} = \frac{d + 1}{2}$
$\frac{d - e}{4} = 1$

29. $\frac{3p - q}{4} = p + 1$
$\frac{5p + q}{2} = p$

30. $2x - \frac{y + 2}{2} = 22$
$3x + \frac{y + 2}{3} = 7$

Determine whether each of the following systems has no solution or infinitely many solutions. If there are infinitely many solutions, give three of them.

31. $5y - 2x = 3$
$6x = 15y - 1$

32. $3y - 6x = 24$
$8 + 2x = y$

33. $2x = 14y$
$\frac{x - y}{3} = \frac{x + y}{4}$

Solve each system by (a) the graphing method; (b) the substitution method.

34. $y = 3x - 7$
$6x - 2y = 12$

35. $y = \frac{2}{3}x - 5$
$4x - 6y = 30$

36. $4x + y = 20$
$\frac{1}{2}y = -2x + 10$

37. The graphs of the equations $ax + 4y = 6$ and $x + by = -8$ intersect at $(-2, 3)$. Find a and b.

38. The graphs of $ax + by = 13$ and $ax - by = -3$ intersect at $(1, 4)$. Find a and b.

Use the substitution method to solve each system.

C **39.** $x + y + z = 180$
$y = 3x$
$z = 5x$

40. $a + b + c = 62$
$a = 2c - 5$
$b = 3c - 5$

41. $x + y + 2z = 1$
$x - y = 1$
$x - z = 2$

Mixed Review Exercises

Solve each system by the graphing method.

1. $3x + 2y = 5$
$y = x - 5$

2. $x + y = 9$
$2y - x = 6$

3. $y = 4x$
$x - y = 3$

4. $y = \frac{1}{2}x$
$x + 2y = 8$

5. $3x + 4y = 0$
$3x - y = 15$

6. $5x + y = -12$
$4x - y = 3$

Write an equation in slope-intercept form for each line described.

7. slope -4, passes through $(2, -7)$

8. slope $\frac{2}{3}$, passes through $(6, 6)$

9. slope $-\frac{1}{2}$, y-intercept -6

10. passes through $(3, 8)$ and $(0, -1)$

11. passes through $(2, -4)$ and $(5, -7)$

12. slope 0, y-intercept 2

9-3 Solving Problems with Two Variables

Objective To use systems of linear equations in two variables to solve problems.

You have learned to solve problems using equations in one variable. Now you can solve problems with equations in two variables. Example 1 compares these two methods.

Example 1 John has 15 coins, all dimes and quarters, worth \$2.55. How many dimes and how many quarters does John have?

Solution 1 (Using one variable)

Step 1 The problem asks for the number of dimes and the number of quarters.

Step 2 Let x = the number of dimes. Then $15 - x$ = the number of quarters. Make a chart.

	Number ×	Value per coin =	Total Value
Dimes	x	10	$10x$
Quarters	$15 - x$	25	$25(15 - x)$

Step 3 The only fact not recorded in this chart is the total value of the coins, \$2.55 (or 255 cents). Use this fact to write an equation.

$$10x + 25(15 - x) = 255$$

Step 4

$$\begin{aligned} 10x + 375 - 25x &= 255 \\ -15x &= -120 \\ x &= 8 \\ 15 - x &= 7 \end{aligned}$$

Step 5 The check is left to you.

∴ John has 8 dimes and 7 quarters. ***Answer***

Solution 2 (Using two variables)

Step 1 The problem asks for the number of dimes and the number of quarters.

Step 2 Let d = the number of dimes and q = the number of quarters. Make a chart.

	Number ×	Value per coin =	Total Value
Dimes	d	10	$10d$
Quarters	q	25	$25q$

(Solution continues on the next page.)

Step 3 The two facts not recorded in the chart are the total number of coins, 15, and the total value, \$2.55. Use these facts to write a system of equations.

$$d + q = 15$$
$$10d + 25q = 255$$

Step 4

$$q = 15 - d \qquad \{\text{Find } q \text{ in terms of } d.$$

$$10d + 25(15 - d) = 255 \qquad \{\text{Substitute.}$$
$$10d + 375 - 25d = 255$$
$$-15d = -120$$
$$d = 8$$

$$q = 15 - d$$
$$q = 15 - 8$$
$$q = 7$$

Step 5 The check is left to you.

∴ John has 8 dimes and 7 quarters. ***Answer***

Example 2 Ann and Betty together have \$60. Ann has \$9 more than twice Betty's amount. How much money does each have?

Solution Let a = the amount of Ann's money and b = the amount of Betty's money.

Ann and Betty together have \$60. → $a + b = 60$
Ann has \$9 more than twice Betty's amount. → $a = 2b + 9$

The system of the two equations above can be used to solve the problem. The rest of the solution is left to you (see Oral Exercise 1).

Example 3 Joan Wu has \$8000 invested in stocks and bonds. The stocks pay 4% interest, and the bonds pay 7% interest. If her annual income from the stocks and bonds is \$500, how much is invested in bonds?

Solution Let s = the amount invested in stocks and b = the amount invested in bonds. Make a chart.

	Principal ×	Rate =	Interest
Stocks	s	0.04	$0.04s$
Bonds	b	0.07	$0.07b$
Total	8000		500

The total amount invested is \$8000. → $s + b = 8000$
The total amount of interest earned is \$500 → $0.04s + 0.07b = 500$

The rest of the solution is left to you (see Oral Exercise 2).

You can use either one variable or two variables to solve problems like those in the examples. The advantage of using two variables is that it is sometimes easier to write the equations that will solve the problem.

Oral Exercises

1. Complete the solution to Example 2.
2. Complete the solution to Example 3.

Give a system of equations that can be used to solve each problem.

In Exercises 3–6 use n, d, and q for the number of nickels, the number of dimes, and the number of quarters, respectively.

3. Sam has 30 nickels and dimes worth \$2.40. How many nickels does he have?
4. Kelley has 24 dimes and quarters worth \$3.60. How many quarters does she have?
5. Bruce has \$5.50 in dimes and quarters. He has 8 more quarters than dimes. How many quarters does he have?
6. Luis and Julia have the same number of coins. Luis has only dimes and Julia has only quarters. If Julia has \$1.80 more than Luis does, how many coins does each have?

In Exercises 7–12, use whatever variables seem appropriate.

7. Dick and Connie purchased a radio for \$128. Dick paid \$36 more than Connie. How much did each pay?
8. Annette and June bowled together and had a combined score of 425. June's score was 25 less than Annette's score. Find their scores.
9. Steve has \$3 more than twice as much as Tracy. Together they have \$57. How much does each have?
10. The length of a rectangle is 5 cm less than three times its width. If the perimeter is 70 cm, find the dimensions.
11. A radio station broadcasts programs and commercials 20 hours everyday. The ratio of the time spent on commercials to the programming time is 1:4. How much time each day does the station spend broadcasting commercials?

12. A person invests \$5000 in treasury notes and bonds. The notes pay 8% annual interest and the bonds pay 10% annual interest. If the annual income is \$480, how much is invested in treasury notes?

Problems

A **1–10.** Solve the problems given in Oral Exercises 3–12.

Solve, using two equations in two variables.

B **11.** The sum of two numbers is 100. Five times the smaller is 8 more than the larger. Find the numbers.

12. One number is 12 more than half another number. The two numbers total 60. Find the numbers.

13. Lisa and Beverly had just $5 to spend for an after-school snack. They could have bought 2 hamburgers and 1 carton of milk with no change back or 1 hamburger and 2 cartons of milk with 40 cents change back. How much does a carton of milk cost?

14. If you buy six pens and one mechanical pencil, you'll get only $1 change from your $10 bill. But if you buy four pens and two mechanical pencils, you'll get $2 change. How much does each pen and each pencil cost?

15. Marty Lister invested $9000 in stocks and bonds. The stocks paid 5% and the bonds 8%, giving an annual income of $525. How much did he invest in bonds?

16. Melinda Bowen receives an annual income of $234.50 from investing one amount of money at 6% and another amount at 5%. If the investments were interchanged, her income would increase by $5.10. Find the amounts she invested.

17. A car and a bike set out at noon from the same point headed in the same direction. At 1:00 P.M., the car is 60 km ahead of the bike. Find how fast each travels, given that the car travels four times as fast as the bike.

18. A grocer mixes together some cashews costing $8 per kilogram with some Brazil nuts costing $10 per kilogram. The grocer sold 12 kg of the mixture for $8.50 per kilogram. How many kilograms of cashews were in the mixture the grocer sold?

19. One number is 16 more than another. If the smaller number is subtracted from two thirds of the larger number, the result is one fourth of the sum of the two numbers. Find the numbers.

20. If Bill rides his bike 3 mi to Fred's house and then walks with Fred the remaining 1 mi to school, it will take him 30 min. But if he rides the entire distance, it will take him only 20 min. Find his biking speed and walking speed.

Solve each problem by using a system of three equations in three variables.

C **21.** I have 30 coins, all nickels, dimes, and quarters, worth $4.60. There are two more dimes than quarters. How many of each kind of coin do I have?

22. Carl, Diane, and Ed together have $46. Carl has half as much as Diane, and Ed has $2 less than Diane. How much does each have?

Mixed Review Exercises

Solve.

1. $\frac{1}{2}s + 8 = 3$
2. $\frac{1}{4}y = 2\frac{1}{4}$
3. $\frac{x+2}{3} = 11$
4. $4(a + 3) = 12 - 2(a - 18)$
5. $-12 + n = 5$
6. $3x + 14 = x + 4$

Solve by the substitution method.

7. $y = \frac{1}{2}x - \frac{5}{2}$
   $2x + 10 = 4y$
8. $b - 2a = -1$
   $3b + a = 18$
9. $y = 3x - 2$
   $\frac{y-1}{3} = x$
10. $y = x - 3$
    $x + y = 5$
11. $3c - 4d = 6$
    $2c + d = -7$
12. $q = 3p$
    $2p + q = 15$

Career Note / *Nutritionist*

Schools, hospitals, and other large institutions rely on nutritionists to plan appealing meals that supply the nutrients necessary for good health. Special meals are often needed for individuals on a salt-free, a low-cholesterol, or a high-protein diet.

Nutritionists may need to teach others about good nutrition habits, and so they should be able to work well with people. They also rely on their mathematical skills to measure ingredients and to make conversions in recipes for changing the size of the portions or the number of servings.

A nutritionist must have a bachelor's degree with course work in physiology, food and nutrition, bacteriology, and chemistry. Training often continues after graduation with an internship in a hospital.

Challenge

The numbers 21 and 22 can be written using five 4's and mathematical symbols as shown below.

$$21 = 4 \cdot 4 + 4 + 4 \div 4 \qquad 22 = 44 \div \sqrt{4} \div (4 \div 4)$$

Which of the numbers 23 through 29 can you write using five 4's and mathematical symbols?

9-4 The Addition-or-Subtraction Method

Objective To use addition or subtraction to solve systems of linear equations in two variables.

When solving a system of two equations, you can sometimes add or subtract the equations to obtain a new equation with just one variable. This method is called the *addition-or-subtraction method*.

Example 1 (The Addition Method) Solve: $5x - y = 12$
$3x + y = 4$

Solution

1. Add similar terms of the two equations.

$$\begin{aligned} 5x - y &= 12 \\ 3x + y &= 4 \\ \hline 8x \qquad &= 16 \end{aligned}$$

{The y-terms are eliminated.

2. Solve the resulting equation. $x = 2$

3. Substitute 2 for x in either of the original equations to find y.

$$\begin{aligned} 3x + y &= 4 \\ 3(2) + y &= 4 \\ y &= -2 \end{aligned}$$

4. Check $x = 2$ and $y = -2$ in *both* original equations.

$$\begin{aligned} 3x + y &= 4 \\ 3(2) + (-2) &\stackrel{?}{=} 4 \\ 4 &= 4 \quad \surd \end{aligned} \qquad \begin{aligned} 5x - y &= 12 \\ 5(2) - (-2) &\stackrel{?}{=} 12 \\ 12 &= 12 \quad \surd \end{aligned}$$

$\therefore$ the solution is $(2, -2)$. ***Answer***

Example 2 (The Subtraction Method) Solve: $6c + 7d = -15$
$6c - 2d = 12$

Solution

1. Subtract similar terms of the two equations.

$$\begin{aligned} 6c + 7d &= -15 \\ 6c - 2d &= 12 \\ \hline 9d &= -27 \end{aligned}$$

{The c-terms are eliminated.

2. Solve the resulting equation. $d = -3$

3. Substitute -3 for d in either of the original equations to find c.

$$\begin{aligned} 6c + 7d &= -15 \\ 6c + 7(-3) &= -15 \\ 6c &= 6 \\ c &= 1 \end{aligned}$$

4. The check in both original equations is left to you.

$\therefore$ the solution is $(1, -3)$. ***Answer***

Notice that in Example 2 the coefficients of c are the *same,* and in Example 1 the coefficients of y are *opposites*. Whenever two equations have the same or opposite coefficients for one of their terms, the addition-or-subtraction method can be used.

The Addition-or-Subtraction Method

To solve a system of linear equations in two variables:

1. Add or subtract the equations to eliminate one variable.
2. Solve the resulting equation for the other variable.
3. Substitute in either original equation to find the value of the first variable.
4. Check in both original equations.

Oral Exercises

Use the addition method to solve for x.

1. $3x + 2y = 7$
$5x - 2y = 1$

2. $x - 5y = 1$
$2x + 5y = 17$

3. $4y + 3x = 9$
$-4y - x = 7$

Use the subtraction method to solve for s.

4. $3t + 5s = 10$
$3t + s = 2$

5. $4s - 5t = 7$
$2s - 5t = 3$

6. $3s + 4t = 18$
$-2s + 4t = 8$

Use the addition-or-subtraction method to solve for one of the variables.

7. $3a + 2b = 11$
$2a - 2b = 4$

8. $3p + 2q = 19$
$3p - 5q = 5$

9. $-4s + 7t = 10$
$4s - 2t = 5$

Written Exercises

Solve by the addition-or-subtraction method.

A

1. $x + y = 7$
$x - y = 3$

2. $a + b = 5$
$a - b = 7$

3. $3n - 2t = 16$
$5n + 2t = 8$

4. $3c + 5d = 17$
$3c + 8d = 5$

5. $12n + 3m = 18$
$5n + 3m = 4$

6. $3a - 5b = 31$
$7a - 5b = 59$

7. $6p - 7q = 28$
$-6p + 3q = -12$

8. $4a - 7b = 13$
$2a - 7b = 3$

9. $2c + 3d = 0$
$5c - 3d = 21$

10. $-3x + 5y = 45$
$3x + 13y = 9$

11. $12p - 18q = 14$
$-15p - 18q = -4$

12. $9y + 5z = 1$
$-9y - 10z = 2$

Solve by the addition-or-subtraction method.

13. $21x - 16y = -1$
$33x + 16y = 19$

14. $-28g + 15h = -18$
$-28g - 40h = -29$

15. $0.02x + 0.03y = 9$
$0.02x + 0.05y = 13$

16. $0.07a - 0.03b = 12$
$0.01a + 0.03b = 12$

17. $\frac{1}{2}x + \frac{1}{3}y = 4$
$\frac{5}{2}x - \frac{1}{3}y = 8$

18. $\frac{3}{4}x - \frac{1}{6}y = -12$
$\frac{5}{4}x - \frac{1}{6}y = -22$

Solve by either the substitution method or the addition-or-subtraction method.

B 19. $a = 6b + 3$
$a + 2b = 5$

20. $x - 5y = 2$
$2x + y = 4$

21. $4(x - 2y) = 8$
$x + 6y = 2$

22. $4(a - 2b) = 8$
$2(a + 4b) = -8$

23. $n = 2 - 6m$
$\frac{1}{2}n - m = 1$

24. $\frac{1}{3}a - \frac{2}{3}b = 1$
$a + b + 7 = 0$

25. $y = \frac{2}{3}x$
$x + 6y = 30$

26. $\frac{5a}{6} - \frac{b}{3} = 6$
$a + 2b = 0$

27. $3n + 1 = \frac{p}{4}$
$n = \frac{p + 1}{15}$

28. **a.** Use the graph shown at the right to estimate the solution of the system
$$7x + 5y = 25$$
$$2x - 5y = 15$$
to the nearest half unit.

b. Use algebra to find the exact solution of this system.

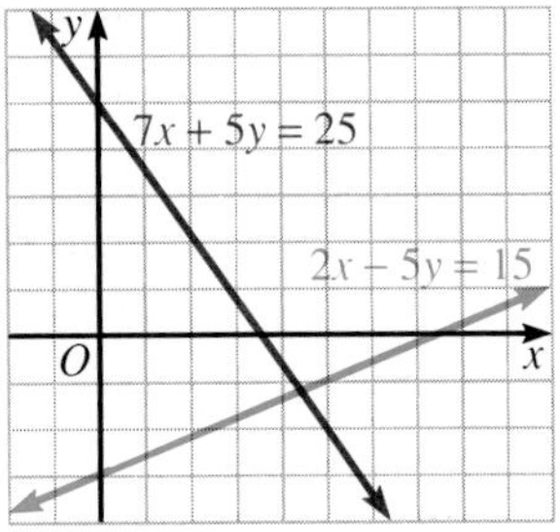

29. The graphs of $ax + by = 18$ and $ax - by = 6$ intersect at $(3, -2)$. Find a and b.

C 30. The graphs of $5x - 3y = 35$, $7x - 3y = 43$, and $4x - ay = 61$ all intersect in the same point. Find a.

31. Show that the graphs of $\frac{x - 2y}{x + 2y} = \frac{1}{3}$ and $\frac{x - y}{x + y} = \frac{3}{5}$ coincide.

Problems

Solve using two equations in two variables. Use either the substitution method or the addition-or-subtraction method.

A 1. The sum of two numbers is 21 and their difference is 5. What are the numbers?

2. The sum of two numbers is 64. Twice the smaller number is 10 less than the larger number. Find the numbers.

3. There are 812 students in a school. There are 36 more girls than boys. How many girls are there?

4. Three pizzas and four sandwiches cost \$34. Three pizzas and seven sandwiches cost \$41.50. How much does a pizza cost?

B 5. There are 26 times as many students in Lincoln High School as teachers. When all the teachers and students are seated in the 900-seat school auditorium, only 9 seats are unoccupied. How many students are at Lincoln High?

6. At an amusement park you get 5 points for each bull's eye you hit, but you lose 10 points for every miss. After 30 tries, Yolanda lost 90 points. How many bull's eyes did she have?

7. Since my uncle's farmyard appeared to be overrun with chickens and dogs, I asked him how many of each he had. Being a puzzler as well as a farmer, my uncle replied that his dogs and chickens had a total of 148 legs and 60 heads. How many dogs and how many chickens does my uncle have?

8. A shipment of 18 cars, some weighing 3000 lb apiece and the others 5000 lb each, has a total weight of 30 tons. Find the number of each kind of car.

C 9. If Tom gives Maria 30 cents, they will have equal amounts of money. But if Maria then gives Tom 50 cents, he will have twice as much money as she does. How much money does each have now?

10. In a running and swimming race, the athletes must run 2 mi and swim 1 mi. It took Peggy 42 min to do this, but if she were able to run the total 3 mi, it would have taken only 18 min. At what rate did she swim the mile?

Mixed Review Exercises

Simplify.

1. $7x^3 + 5x^2 - 3x + 6x^2$
2. $3 \cdot 4^2$
3. $(1 \cdot 10^3) + (3 \cdot 10^2) + (4 \cdot 10)$
4. $-2[3n - 2(n - 1)]$
5. $(6x^4y^3)\left(\frac{3}{2}xy^2\right)$
6. $(3a^3)^2$
7. $(-2p^2q)^3$
8. $3x[4x + 3(2 - x)]$
9. $(6ab)(-3a^2b)(2a^3b^2)$
10. $\left(-\frac{1}{15}\right)(105)\left(\frac{1}{7}\right)$
11. $\frac{-8}{\frac{1}{3}}$
12. $\frac{1}{6}(-54m + 36n)$

9-5 Multiplication with the Addition-or-Subtraction Method

Objective To use multiplication with the addition-or-subtraction method to solve systems of linear equations.

The two equations in a system don't always have the same or opposite coefficients for one of their terms. Before you can use the addition-or-subtraction method to solve the system you need a step that gives an equivalent system that has the same or opposite coefficients for one of the terms.

Example 1 Solve: $4x - 5y = 23$
$3x + 10y = 31$

Solution

1. Multiply both sides of the first equation by 2 so that the y-terms are opposites. $2(4x - 5y) = 2(23) \rightarrow 8x - 10y = 46$; $3x + 10y = 31 \rightarrow 3x + 10y = 31$
2. Add similar terms. $11x = 77$
3. Solve the resulting equation. $x = 7$
4. Substitute 7 for x in either original equation to find the value of y.
$$4x - 5y = 23$$
$$4(7) - 5y = 23$$
$$-5y = -5$$
$$y = 1$$
5. The check in both original equations is left to you.

$\therefore$ the solution is (7, 1). ***Answer***

Example 2 Solve: $3a + 4b = 2$
$5a + 9b = 1$

Solution

1. Transform *both* equations by multiplication so that a-terms are the same. $5(3a + 4b) = 5(2) \rightarrow 15a + 20b = 10$; $3(5a + 9b) = 3(1) \rightarrow 15a + 27b = 3$
2. Subtract similar terms. $-7b = 7$
3. Solve the resulting equation. $b = -1$
4. Substitute -1 for b in either original equation to find the value of a.
$$3a + 4b = 2$$
$$3a + 4(-1) = 2$$
$$3a = 6$$
$$a = 2$$
5. The check is left to you.

$\therefore$ the solution is $(2, -1)$. ***Answer***

Example 3 Solve: $\frac{5x}{3} + y = 7$

$$x + \frac{y}{4} = \frac{7}{2}$$

Solution When a system has fractions, it is usually convenient to eliminate the fractions first.

1. Multiply each equation by the LCD of its denominators.

$$3\left(\frac{5x}{3} + y\right) = 3(7) \rightarrow 5x + 3y = 21$$

$$4\left(x + \frac{y}{4}\right) = 4\left(\frac{7}{2}\right) \rightarrow 4x + y = 14$$

2. Multiply the second equation by 3 so that the y-terms are the same.

$$\begin{aligned} 5x + 3y = 21 &\rightarrow 5x + 3y = 21 \\ 3(4x + y) = 3(14) &\rightarrow 12x + 3y = 42 \end{aligned}$$

3. Subtract similar terms. $\quad -7x = -21$
4. Solve the resulting equation. $\quad x = 3$
5. Substitute 3 for x in either original equation to find the value of y.

$$\begin{aligned} \frac{5x}{3} + y &= 7 \\ \frac{5(3)}{3} + y &= 7 \\ 5 + y &= 7 \\ y &= 2 \end{aligned}$$

6. The check is left to you.

$\therefore$ the solution is (3, 2). ***Answer***

Oral Exercises

Explain how to use multiplication with the addition-or-subtraction method to solve each system by answering these questions:

a. Which variable will you eliminate?
b. Which equation(s) will you transform by multiplication?
c. By what number(s) will you multiply?
d. Will you then add or subtract similar terms?

1. $2x + y = 8$
$3x - 2y = 5$

2. $3a + 5b = 3$
$a + 2b = 13$

3. $3x - 2t = 4$
$2x + t = 5$

4. $4x - 3y = 7$
$5x - y = 6$

5. $4p - q = 6$
$2p - 3q = 8$

6. $4x - 3y = 8$
$2x + y = 14$

7. $5p - 2q = 1$
$4p + 5q = 47$

8. $2c - 3d = -1$
$3c - 4d = -3$

9. $3r - 2s = 15$
$7r - 3s = 15$

Written Exercises

Solve each system by using multiplication with the addition-or-subtraction method.

A **1–9.** Solve the systems given in Oral Exercises 1–9.

10. $3c - 8d = 7$
$c + 2d = -7$

11. $3a + b = 4$
$a - 2b = 6$

12. $x + y = 7$
$3x - 2y = 11$

13. $4x + 5t = 22$
$5x - t = 13$

14. $2n + 5a = 14$
$6n + 7a = 10$

15. $3p + 4q = 4$
$5p + 2q = 16$

16. $3t - 8z = 34$
$7t + 4z = -34$

17. $2c - 7d = 41$
$6c + 5d = -7$

18. $4r + 9s = 23$
$-7r + 3s = -34$

19. $4b + 13c = -24$
$12b - 5c = 16$

20. $18a - 5b = 17$
$6a + 10b = -6$

21. $3p + 8q = 8$
$5p - 2q = 21$

22. $4x + 15t = 10$
$3x + 10t = 5$

23. $6n + 8c - 4 = 0$
$9n + 10c - 7 = 0$

24. $6z - 5t + 10 = 0$
$4z - 7t + 25 = 0$

B **25.** Show that the equations $6n + 4c = 5$ and $9n + 6c = 8$ have no common solution.

26. Show that the equations $8a - 10b = \frac{1}{3}$ and $20a - 25b = \frac{5}{6}$ have many solutions.

Solve each system by using multiplication with the addition-or-subtraction method.

27. $0.4x + 1.5y = -5.7$
$-0.2x + 0.8y = -1.8$

28. $0.9x - 2.1y = 12.3$
$4.6x - 6.3y = 40.7$

29. $0.3x + 0.5y = 31$
$0.2x - 0.1y = -1$

30. $0.05x + 0.06y = 215$
$x + y = 400$

31. $\frac{a}{4} + \frac{b}{3} = 2$
$\frac{a}{2} - b = -1$

32. $\frac{x}{2} - y = 9$
$x + \frac{y}{2} = 8$

33. $\frac{a}{6} + \frac{b}{4} = \frac{3}{2}$
$\frac{2a}{3} = \frac{b}{2}$

34. $\frac{p}{8} + \frac{q}{6} = 1$
$\frac{p}{q} = -\frac{2}{3}$

35. $\frac{x}{2} + \frac{y}{3} = -4$
$\frac{x}{5} + \frac{y}{5} = -2$

C **36.** Determine whether the graphs of $3x - 4y = 3$, $6x + 6y = 13$, and $9x + 2y = 16$ intersect in a single point.

37. The point $(8, -3)$ is the intersection of the graphs of $ax + by = 25$ and $3ax - 5by = 3$. Find a and b.

Solve for x and y by the method you prefer. $\left(\textit{Hint:}\ \text{Let } \frac{1}{x} = a \text{ and } \frac{1}{y} = b.\right)$

38. $\frac{1}{x} + \frac{1}{y} = 1$
$\frac{3}{x} - \frac{2}{y} = 8$

39. $\frac{1}{x} + \frac{1}{y} = 5$
$\frac{3}{x} - \frac{5}{y} = -9$

40. $\frac{8}{x} + \frac{15}{y} = 33$
$\frac{4}{x} - \frac{35}{y} = -43$

Solve for x and y in terms of a and b.

41. $ax + y = 5$
$3ax - 2y = 0$

42. $ax + by = 1$
$3ax - 2by = 4$

43. $ax - by = 1$
$bx + ay = 1$

Solve for x, y, and z. (*Hint:* Eliminate one variable from the first two equations and then eliminate the same variable from the second two equations. This will give two new equations in two variables. Your answer will be an ordered triple of the form (x, y, z).)

44. $x + y + z = 7$
$2x - y + z = 4$
$3x + 2y + z = 11$

45. $x + y + z = 4$
$2x - y + z = 0$
$x - y + 2z = -3$

46. $6x + 4y - z = -7$
$-5x + 6y + 2z = 14$
$3x - 2y - 3z = -13$

Mixed Practice

Solve by the graphing method.

A

1. $y - x = 4$
$y = 3x + 2$

2. $x + y = 1$
$5x + y = -7$

3. $4x + 2y = 6$
$x - y = 3$

Solve by the substitution method.

4. $a = 3b$
$a - 5b = 16$

5. $8c - d = -3$
$4c + 5d = 15$

6. $9p = 2q - 6$
$3p - q = 12$

Solve by the addition-or-subtraction method.

7. $2a + 3b = -1$
$a - 3b = 4$

8. $5x - 9y = -3$
$4x - 3y = 6$

9. $2p + 3q + 1 = 0$
$3p + 5q + 2 = 0$

Solve by whatever method you prefer.

B

10. $y = x + 2$
$2x + y = 11$

11. $x + y = 9$
$x - 3y = -3$

12. $3x - 2y = 1$
$4y = 7 + 3x$

13. $3x + 5y = 14$
$2x - y = -1$

14. $2a - 4b = 6$
$7 + a = -3b$

15. $r - s = 4$
$r - 6 = 2(s - 6)$

16. $a - 2b = 10$
$a + b = 2(b + 6)$

17. $t + u = 11$
$(10t + u) - (10u + t) = 27$

18. $u - t = 5$
$10t + u = 3(t + u)$

19. $4x + 3y = 1$
$6x - 2y = 21$

20. $3a + 4b = -25$
$2a - 3b = 6$

21. $5n - 2m = 1$
$4n + 5m = 47$

22. $0.04x - 0.06y = 40$
$x + y = 6000$

23. $2.4 = 0.3x + 0.4y$
$5x = 2 + 6y$

24. $3a + 2b = 4$
$\frac{1}{3}(2a + b) = 1$

25. $\frac{1}{3}(3a - 2b) = -3$
$3(a - b) = -9$

26. $\frac{5c}{4} + d = \frac{11}{2}$
$c + \frac{d}{3} = 3$

27. $2x - \frac{5}{2}y = 13$
$\frac{x}{3} + \frac{y}{3} = \frac{14}{15}$

Problems

Solve by whatever method you prefer, using one or two variables.

A **1.** The sum of two numbers is 25 and their difference is 7. Find the numbers.

2. One number is 4 less than eleven times another. The sum of the two numbers is 92. Find the numbers.

3. Cory has \$24 more than twice as much as Stan. Together they have \$150. How much money does each have?

4. Marcia has \$84 less than three times as much as Sue. Together they have \$132. How much money does Marcia have?

5. The length of a rectangle is 5 more than twice the width. The perimeter is 130. What is the area?

6. A rectangle is five times as long as it is wide. If it were 24 cm shorter and 24 cm wider, it would be a square. What are its dimensions?

7. Phil has 50 nickels and dimes worth \$4.15. How many dimes does he have?

8. Sally has \$21.40 in dimes and quarters, for a total of 100 coins. How many of each kind of coin does Sally have?

9. The bill for five glasses of apple juice and four salads is \$9.50, but the bill for four glasses of apple juice and five salads is \$10.30. What would be the bill for a glass of juice and a salad?

10. Three pens and two notebooks cost \$8.25. Two pens and three notebooks cost \$8.00. How much would two pens and two notebooks cost?

11. A movie theater charges \$5 for an adult's ticket and \$2 for a child's ticket. One Saturday the theater sold 785 tickets for \$3280. How many child's tickets were sold for the movie that Saturday?

12. Six grapefruit cost as much as a dozen oranges. The cost of a dozen grapefruit and two dozen oranges is \$12. How much does one grapefruit cost?

13. A chemist has 1000 g of a solution that is 40% acid. How many grams of water must be added to reduce the acidity to 25%?

14. A chemist has 800 g of a dye solution that is 20% of its original strength. How much dye must be added to increase the strength to 50%?

15. Edna Britten's income from two stocks each year totals \$280. Stock A pays dividends at the rate of 5% and stock B at the rate of 6%. If she has invested a total of \$5000, how much is invested in each stock?

16. Beatrice Roberts receives \$375 per year from a \$6000 investment in stocks and bonds. The bonds pay 10% interest and the stocks pay 5% in dividends. How much is invested in stocks?

B **17.** Ted's bill for 6 cans of grape juice and 4 cans of orange juice was \$13.20. When he got home, he found that he should have bought 4 cans of grape juice and 6 cans of orange juice. Although he mixed up the order, Ted did save 60 cents. How much does each can cost?

18. Joe Tyson is the place kicker for his college football team. Last season he kicked 38 times and never missed. Each field goal scored 3 points and each point after touchdown scored 1 point for a total of 70 points. How many field goals did Joe kick last season?

19. A store received $823 from the sale of 5 tape decks and 7 radios. The receipts from the tape decks exceeded the receipts from the radios by $137. What is the cost of a radio?

20. Rebecca has 45 coins, all nickels and dimes. The total value of the coins is $3.60. How many of each type of coin does Rebecca have?

21. Before last weekend's hiking trip, Juanita mixed 3 kg of peanuts and raisins as an energy snack. The peanuts cost $4.25 per kilogram and the raisins cost $3.50 per kilogram. The whole mix cost $12. How many kilograms of peanuts did Juanita have?

22. A grocer prepares a mixture of 30 lb of dried fruit to sell for $4.10 per pound. For the mixture he uses two types of dried fruit, one selling at $4.30 per pound, the other at $3.90 per pound. How much of each type should he use for the mixture?

23. A car traveled at a steady speed for 120 km. Due to a mechanical problem, it returned at half that speed. If the total time for the round trip was 4 h 30 min, find the two speeds.

24. Larry can paint the walls of his apartment in 8 h. After he has worked for 3 h, Patrick joins him, and together they finish the job in 2 h. How long would it take Patrick to do the entire painting job without Larry?

25. Todd has 48 words to spell for a puzzle. As an incentive, his mother offers to pay him 10 cents for each word he spells correctly, if Todd will pay her 6 cents for each word he spells incorrectly. If Todd makes $1.92, how many words does he spell correctly?

26. Elsa works at the China Emporium on Saturdays packing dishes for shipment. She receives 12 cents for each piece she packs successfully and is fined 18 cents for each piece she breaks. If she handles 188 pieces and is paid $20.16, how many pieces does she break?

27. Does the equation $2x + 6y = 35$ have any whole-number solutions? Why or why not?

28. Find the area enclosed between the x-axis and the graphs of $x + y = 20$ and $3x - 2y = 0$.

C 29. On a simple pan balance, 3 apples and 1 banana exactly balance 10 plums. Also, 1 apple and 6 plums balance 1 banana. How many plums will balance one banana?

30. Roger, Sue, and Tim have \$155 among them. Roger has \$5 more than Sue and Tim together. If Sue gives Tim \$5, he will have twice as much as she does. How much does each have?

31. If the length of a rectangle is increased by 12 and the width is decreased by 8, the area is unchanged. The area is also unchanged if the original length is increased by 5 and the original width is decreased by 4. Find the original dimensions of the rectangle.

32. If Alexandra increases her usual driving speed by 15 km/h, it will take her 2 h less to make a trip to her grandparents' house. If she decreases her usual speed by 15 km/h, it will take her 3 h more than usual to make the trip. How long is the trip?

Mixed Review Exercises

Factor completely.

1. $6 - 36t + 54t^2$ **2.** $12m^2n - 24mn^3$ **3.** $25c^2 - 36d^2$

4. $x^2 + 7x + 12$ **5.** $2y^2 + 11y + 15$ **6.** $p^2 - 3p - 10$

Find the constant of variation.

7. y varies directly as x, and $y = 68$ when $x = 17$.

8. t varies directly as s, and $t = -24$ when $s = 72$.

9. p is directly proportional to n, and $p = 36$ when $n = 54$.

10. h is directly proportional to b, and $h = 35$ when $b = 5$.

Computer Exercises

For students with some programming experience

1. Use multiplication with the addition-or-subtraction method to verify that the solution of the system

$$\begin{aligned} Ax + By &= C \\ Dx + Ey &= F \end{aligned} \quad \text{is} \quad \left(\frac{CE - BF}{AE - BD}, \frac{AF - CD}{AE - BD}\right).$$

2. Using the result in Exercise 1, write a BASIC program to solve a system of linear equations in two variables. Provide for the case $AE - BD = 0$.

3. Run the program for each of the following.

a. $3x + 4y = -25$
$2x - 3y = 6$

b. $5x + 4y = 22$
$3x + y = 9$

c. $2x + 4y = 11$
$3x + 6y = 17$

d. $2x + y = 8$
$3x - 2y = 5$

Self-Test 1

Vocabulary system of equations (p. 413)
solution of a system (p. 413)
intersection point (p. 413)
system of simultaneous equations (p. 413)

Solve by the graphing method.

1. $y - 3x = -1$
$y = x + 3$

2. $x - 3y = -10$
$2x + y = 1$

Obj. 9-1, p. 413

Solve by the substitution method.

3. $m - 4n = -5$
$m = 2n - 4$

4. $a - 2b = 1$
$3a - b = -4$

Obj. 9-2, p. 417

5. Solve by using two equations in two variables: The talent show ticket committee sold a total of 805 tickets in advance. The student tickets cost \$3 each and the adult tickets cost \$4 each. If the total receipts were \$1740, how many of each type of ticket were sold?

Obj. 9-3, p. 421

Solve by the addition-or-subtraction method.

6. $a - 3b = 0$
$a + 3b = 0$

7. $3c + 5d = 20$
$-2c + 5d = 20$

Obj. 9-4, p. 426

Solve by using multiplication with the addition-or-subtraction method.

8. $s + 2t = -7$
$3s - 8t = 7$

9. $2x + 3y = 12$
$3x + 2y = 13$

Obj. 9-5, p. 430

Check your answers with those at the back of the book.

Challenge

The diagrams show some equalities of mass among spheres, cubes, cylinders, and cones. What is the least number of objects that will balance the final scale?

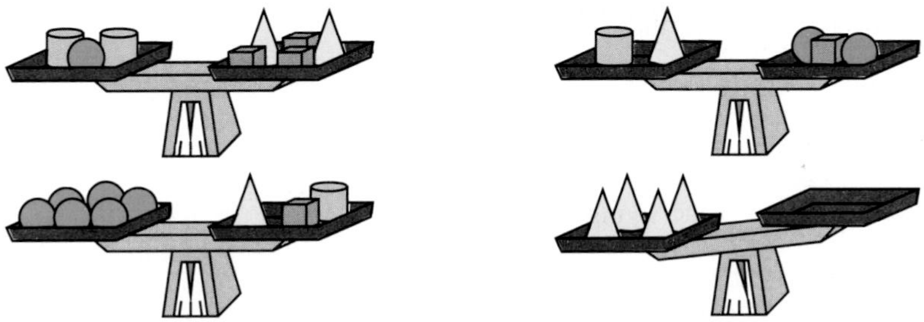

9-6 Wind and Water Current Problems

Objective To use systems of equations to solve wind and water current problems.

Suppose that you can paddle a canoe at the rate, or speed, of 3 mi/h in still water. If you paddle downstream on a river with a current of 1 mi/h, your speed is increased to 3 + 1, or 4 mi/h. If you paddle upstream against the current, your speed is reduced to 3 − 1, or 2 mi/h. Since the current increases your speed downstream by as much as it decreases your speed upstream, you might think that the current has no effect on the total travel time. However, the calculations below show that the current actually increases the total time for the round trip and decreases the average speed for the round trip.

Suppose that you travel 12 mi downstream and 12 mi back upstream. The time for each trip can be found by using the relationship

$$\text{Time} = \text{Distance} \div \text{Rate},$$

which is another form for the basic relationship

$$\text{Distance} = \text{Rate} \times \text{Time}.$$

	No current			1 mi/h current		
	Rate ×	Time =	Distance	Rate ×	Time	= Distance
Downstream	3	4	12	3 + 1 = 4	12 ÷ 4 = 3	12
Upstream	3	4	12	3 − 1 = 2	12 ÷ 2 = 6	12

Total distance = 12 + 12 = 24 (miles)
Total time = 4 + 4 = 8 (hours)
Average speed = $\frac{\text{Total distance}}{\text{Total time}} = \frac{24 \text{ mi}}{8 \text{ h}} = 3$ mi/h

Total distance = 12 + 12 = 24 (miles)
Total time = 3 + 6 = 9 (hours)
Average speed = $\frac{24 \text{ mi}}{9 \text{ h}} = 2\frac{2}{3}$ mi/h

The principles illustrated above apply to wind currents as well as water currents. Thus, if

r = the rate of a plane when there is no wind

and

w = the rate of the wind,

then

$r + w$ = the rate of the plane flying with the wind

and

$r - w$ = the rate of the plane flying against the wind.

Example A jet can travel the 6800 km distance between New York and Paris in 6 h 48 min with the wind. The return trip against the same wind takes 8 h. Find the rate of the jet in still air and the rate of the wind.

Solution

Step 1 The problem asks for the rate of the jet in still air and the rate of the wind.

Step 2 Let r = the rate in km/h of the jet in still air and let w = the rate in km/h of the wind. The time 6 h 48 min is $6\frac{48}{60}$ h, or 6.8 h.

	Rate	× Time	= Distance
With the wind	$r + w$	6.8	6800
Against the wind	$r - w$	8	6800

Step 3 Use the information in the chart to write two equations:

$$6.8(r + w) = 6800, \quad \text{or} \quad r + w = 1000$$
$$8(r - w) = 6800, \quad \text{or} \quad r - w = 850$$

Step 4

$$\begin{aligned} r + w &= 1000 \\ r - w &= 850 \\ \hline 2r &= 1850 \\ r &= 925 \end{aligned}$$

$$\begin{aligned} 925 + w &= 1000 \\ w &= 75 \end{aligned}$$

Step 5 The check is left to you.

∴ the rate of the jet is 925 km/h and the rate of the wind is 75 km/h. ***Answer***

Oral Exercises

Complete the table. All rates are in km/h.

	Rate of plane in still air	Rate of wind	Rate of plane with wind	Rate of plane against wind
1.	700	50	?	?
2.	825	100	?	?
3.	900	w	?	?
4.	p	w	?	?

The following rates are given in km/h.

r = rate of a rowboat in still water
s = rate of a swimmer in still water
c = rate of the current of Silver River

Explain what rate each expression represents.

5. $r + c$ **6.** $r - c$ **7.** $s + c$ **8.** $s - c$

Each equation below states some fact about a rowboat or swimmer. What is this fact?

9. $r + c = 12$ **10.** $r - c = 8$ **11.** $s + c = 3$ **12.** $s - c = 1$

Match each equation with its corresponding statement on the right.
(*Hint:* $\frac{\text{Distance}}{\text{Rate}} = \text{Time}$)

13. $\frac{30}{r + c} = 2$

14. $\frac{30}{r - c} = 2$

15. $\frac{30}{r + c} = \frac{20}{r - c}$

16. $\frac{30}{r + c} + \frac{20}{r - c} = 2$

a. A rowboat traveled 20 km upstream and 30 km downstream in 2 h.

b. A rowboat traveled 30 km upstream in 2 h.

c. A rowboat traveled 30 km downstream in 2 h.

d. A rowboat traveled 30 km downstream and 20 km upstream in the same amount of time.

Problems

Let r = rate in km/h of the rowboat in still water and c = rate in km/h of the current. Write an equation that expresses each fact.

A

1. The rate of the rowboat going downstream is 15 km/h.
2. The rate of the rowboat going upstream is 10 km/h.
3. The rowboat takes 3 hours to go 24 km upstream.
4. The rowboat takes 2 hours to go 20 km upstream.

Solve.

5. Jim's motorboat travels downstream at the rate of 15 km/h. Going upstream it travels at 7 km/h. Write an equation that expresses each fact. What is the rate of the current?
6. Camille can swim against the current at 1.5 m/s and with the current at 3.5 m/s. Write an equation that expresses each fact. How fast can she swim in still water?

Complete each table.

7. A motorboat travels at 10 km/h in still water. The boat makes a trip 30 km downstream and 30 km back.

	No current			5 km/h current		
	Rate ×	Time =	Distance	Rate ×	Time =	Distance
Downstream	?	?	30	?	?	30
Upstream	?	?	30	?	?	30

No current:

Total distance = ?
Total time = ?
Average speed = ?

5 km/h current:

Total distance = ?
Total time = ?
Average speed = ?

8. In a canoe race Norma travels 300 m upstream and then returns. Norma can paddle at a rate of 5 m/s in still water, and the rate of the current is 1 m/s.

	Rate ×	Time =	Distance
Upstream	?	?	?
Downstream	?	?	?

Total distance = ?
Total time = ?
Average speed = ?

9. Flying with no wind, a plane makes a 600 km trip in 3 h. On the return trip, the plane flies with a 50 km/h wind.

	Rate ×	Time =	Distance
No wind	?	?	?
With wind	?	?	?

Total distance = ?
Total time = ?
Average speed = ?

10. Flying with no wind, a plane makes an 840 mi trip in 6 h. On the return trip, the plane flies with a 70 mi/h wind.

	Rate ×	Time =	Distance
No wind	?	?	?
With wind	?	?	?

Total distance = ?
Total time = ?
Average speed = ?

Solve.

11. A plane travels 8400 km against the wind in 7 h. With the wind, the plane makes the return trip in 6 h. Find the speed of the plane in still air and the speed of the wind.

12. In a canoe race, a team paddles downstream 480 m in 60 s. The same team makes the trip upstream in 80 s. Find the team's rate in still water and the rate of the current.

13. A sailboat travels 12 mi downstream in only 2 h. The return trip upstream takes 3 h. Find the speed of the sailboat in still water and the rate of the current.

14. It takes an airplane 1 h 30 min to fly 600 km against the wind. The return trip with the wind takes only 1 h. Find the total flying time for the round trip if there was no wind.

15. The 4200 km trip from New York to San Francisco takes 6 h flying against the wind but only 5 h returning. Find the speed of the plane in still air and the speed of the wind.

16. The 1080 km trip from Madrid to Paris takes 2 h flying against the wind and 1.5 h flying with the wind. Find the speed of the plane in still air and the speed of the wind.

B 17. Len is planning a three-hour trip down the Allenem River and back to his starting point. He knows that he can paddle in still water at 3 mi/h and that the rate of the current is 2 mi/h. How much time can he spend going downstream? How far downstream can he travel?

18. A motorboat has a four-hour supply of gasoline. How far from the marina can it travel if the rate going out against the current is 20 mi/h and the rate coming back with the current is 30 mi/h?

19. A motorboat goes 36 km downstream in the same amount of time that it takes to go 24 km upstream. If the current is flowing at 3 km/h, what is the rate of the boat in still water?

20. The rate of the current in the Susanna River is 4 km/h. If a canoeist can paddle 5 km downstream in the same amount of time that she can paddle 1 km upstream, how fast can she paddle in still water?

21. The steamboat River Queen travels at the rate of 30 km/h in still water. If it can travel 45 km upstream in the same amount of time that it takes to go 63 km downstream, what is the rate of the current?

22. An airplane whose speed in still air is 760 km/h can travel 2000 km with the wind in the same amount of time that it takes to fly 1800 km against the wind. What is the speed of the wind?

C 23. A plane has a speed of p km/h in still air. It makes a round trip, flying with and against a wind of w km/h. Show that its average speed is $\frac{p^2 - w^2}{p}$ km/h.

Mixed Review Exercises

Solve each system using multiplication with the addition-or-subtraction method.

1. $3x + 2y = 11$
$x - y = 7$

2. $5a + 4b = 3$
$2a + 3b = 3$

3. $7p + 2q = 10$
$p + 3q = -4$

Simplify.

4. $\frac{9b^2 + b - 2}{12b + 4}$

5. $\frac{4}{x - 2} + \frac{5}{2 - x}$

6. $(-2t^2)^2 \cdot \frac{4s}{t}$

7. $\frac{4r^2 - t^2}{r^2 - t^2} \div \frac{2r - t}{5}$

8. $\frac{3p + 2}{8} - \frac{2p + 1}{6}$

9. $2a - 1 - \frac{a - 2}{a + 3}$

Biographical Note / *Emily Warren Roebling*

Emily Warren Roebling (1843–1903) helped supervise the completion of the Brooklyn Bridge. She was married to Washington Roebling, an engineer whose father, John Roebling, was commissioned to build the bridge. Emily and Washington Roebling went to Europe, where Washington studied the experimental method of using watertight chambers of compressed air to sink underwater foundations. Soon after their return to the United States, John Roebling died and Washington Roebling became the chief engineer. He was disabled with caisson disease (the bends) ten years before the bridge was completed.

To continue the project, Emily Roebling studied calculus and cable construction. She learned to read bridge specifications, to determine the stress various materials could tolerate, and to calculate catenary curves. As acting chief engineer, she negotiated with representatives of construction supply firms, inspected the work, and delivered instructions to the assistant engineers.

Nine months before the completion of the bridge, the board of trustees tried to dismiss Washington Roebling as chief engineer. As a result of the presentation Emily Roebling made before the American Society of Civil Engineers, Washington Roebling retained his position.

The Brooklyn Bridge is a tribute to Emily Roebling's intense involvement in its construction. A plaque in her honor was placed on the bridge in 1950 by the Brooklyn Engineers Club.

9-7 Puzzle Problems

Objective To use systems of equations to solve digit, age, and fraction problems.

Digit problems are based on our decimal system of numeration. Note the value of 537, 604, and a number with digits h, t, and u shown below.

Hundreds digit	Tens digit	Units digit	Value
5	3	7	$5 \cdot 100 + 3 \cdot 10 + 7 \cdot 1$
6	0	4	$6 \cdot 100 + 0 \cdot 10 + 4 \cdot 1$
h	t	u	$h \cdot 100 + t \cdot 10 + u \cdot 1$

Example 1 (Digit Problem)
The sum of the digits in a two-digit number is 12. The new number obtained when the digits are reversed is 36 more than the original number. Find the original number.

Solution

Step 1 The problem asks for the original number.

Step 2 Let t = the tens digit of the original number.
Let u = the units digit of the original number.

	Tens	Units	Value
Original number	t	u	$10t + u$
Number with digits reversed	u	t	$10u + t$

Step 3 Use the facts of the problem to write two equations.

$$t + u = 12 \quad \{\text{Sum of the digits of the original number is 12.}$$

$$\begin{aligned} (10u + t) - (10t + u) &= 36 \\ 10u + t - 10t - u &= 36 \\ 9u - 9t &= 36 \\ 9(u - t) &= 36 \\ u - t &= 4 \end{aligned} \quad \left\{\begin{array}{l}\text{Difference between new number and original} \\ \text{number is 36.}\end{array}\right.$$

Step 4

$$\begin{aligned} u + t &= 12 \\ u - t &= 4 \\ \hline 2u &= 16 \\ u &= 8 \end{aligned}$$

$$\begin{aligned} u - t &= 4 \\ 8 - t &= 4 \\ t &= 4 \end{aligned} \quad \left\{\begin{array}{l}\text{Substitute 8 for } u \text{ in} \\ \text{the second equation.}\end{array}\right.$$

Step 5 The check is left to you.

∴ the original number is 48. ***Answer***

The technique of using more than one variable and organizing the given facts in a chart is also useful when solving age and fraction problems.

Example 2 (Age problem)
Mimi is four years older than Ronald. Five years ago she was twice as old as he was. Find their ages now.

Solution

Step 1 The problem asks for Mimi's age and Ronald's age now.

Step 2 Let m = Mimi's age now, and let r = Ronald's age now. Make a chart.

Age	Now	5 years ago
Mimi	m	$m - 5$
Ronald	r	$r - 5$

Step 3 Use the facts of the problem to write two equations.

$$m = 4 + r \qquad \{\text{now}$$
$$m - 5 = 2(r - 5) \qquad \{\text{five years ago}$$

Step 4 Simplify the equations and solve.

$$m = 4 + r \rightarrow m - r = 4$$
$$m - 5 = 2(r - 5) \rightarrow m - 2r = -5$$
$$r = 9$$

$$m - r = 4$$
$$m - 9 = 4$$
$$m = 13$$

Step 5 The check is left to you.

∴ Mimi is 13 years old and Ronald is 9. ***Answer***

Example 3 (Fraction problem)
The numerator of a fraction is 3 less than the denominator. If the numerator and denominator are each increased by 1, the value of the resulting fraction is $\frac{3}{4}$. Find the original fraction.

Solution

Step 1 The problem asks for the original fraction.

Step 2 Let n = the numerator of the original fraction and d = the denominator of the original fraction. Then $\frac{n}{d}$ = the original fraction.

(Solution continues on next page.)

Step 3 Use the facts of the problem to write two equations.

$$n = d - 3$$

$$\frac{n+1}{d+1} = \frac{3}{4}, \quad \text{or} \quad 4(n+1) = 3(d+1)$$

Step 4 Simplify the equations and solve.

$$\begin{array}{rcrcr} n = d - 3 & \rightarrow & n - d = -3 & \rightarrow & 4n - 4d = -12 \\ 4(n+1) = 3(d+1) & \rightarrow & 4n - 3d = -1 & \rightarrow & 4n - 3d = -1 \\ & & & & -d = -11 \\ & & & & d = 11 \end{array}$$

$$n = d - 3$$
$$n = 11 - 3$$
$$n = 8$$

Step 5 The check is left to you.

$\therefore$ the original fraction is $\frac{8}{11}$. ***Answer***

Oral Exercises

A two-digit number has tens digit *t* and units digit *u*. Express the following in terms of *t* and *u*.

1. The value of the two-digit number.

2. The value of the two-digit number obtained by reversing the digits.

3. The tens digit exceeds the units digit by 5.

4. The units digit exceeds the tens digit by 8.

5. The tens digit is one half the units digit.

A three-digit number has hundreds digit *h*, tens digit *t*, and units digit *u*. Express the following as equations.

6. The sum of the digits is 20.

7. The tens digit is three times the sum of the other two digits.

8. The number obtained by reversing the order of the digits exceeds the original number by 99.

Let b = Bob's age now and c = Claire's age now. Express the following in terms of *b* and *c*.

9. Bob's age in 4 years

10. Claire's age in 4 years

11. Bob's age 2 years ago

12. Claire's age 2 years ago

13. The sum of their ages in 4 years

14. The sum of their ages 2 years ago

15. Bob is half as old as Claire.

16. Claire is twice as old as Bob.

17. Four years ago, Bob was one-third as old as Claire was.

18. Next year, the sum of Bob's age and Claire's age will be 26.

A fraction is represented by $\frac{n}{d}$. Express in terms of n and d the new fraction obtained by doing each of the following.

19. Increase both the numerator and the denominator by 4.

20. Decrease both the numerator and the denominator by 7.

21. Interchange the numerator and the denominator.

22. Increase the numerator by 5 and decrease the denominator by 3.

Problems

Write an equation expressing each fact.

A

1. The sum of the digits of a two-digit number is 15.
2. The sum of the digits of a three-digit number is 10.
3. A two-digit number is four times the sum of its digits.
4. A three-digit number is sixteen times the sum of its digits.
5. When the digits of a two-digit number are reversed, the new number is 18 more than the original number.
6. When the digits of a three-digit number are reversed, the new number is 198 less than the original number.

Solve each of the following problems about two-digit numbers.

7. A two-digit number is four times the sum of its digits. The tens digit is 3 less than the units digit. What is the number?
8. The sum of the digits of a two-digit number is one third of the number. The units digit is 5 more than the tens digit. What is the number?
9. When the digits of a two-digit number are reversed, the new number is 36 more than the original number. The units digit is twice the tens digit. What is the original number?
10. When the digits of a two-digit number are reversed, the new number is 54 less than the original number. If the sum of its digits is 8, what is the original number?

Solve by using a system of two equations in two variables.

11. Nicole is 5 years older than Pierre. Last year she was twice as old as he was. How old is each now?
12. Cecilia is 24 years younger than Joe. Six years ago she was half as old as he was. How old is each now?
13. Steve is three times as old as Theresa. In four years he will be twice as old as she will be. How old is each now?

14. Four years ago, Marion was $\frac{2}{3}$ as old as Les was. Now she is $\frac{3}{4}$ as old as he is. How old is each now?

15. The denominator of a fraction is 8 more than the numerator. If 3 is added to both the numerator and the denominator, the value of the resulting fraction is $\frac{1}{2}$. What is the original fraction?

16. The denominator of a fraction is 9 more than the numerator. If the numerator is decreased by 3 and the denominator is increased by 3, the value of the resulting fraction is $\frac{1}{4}$. What is the original fraction?

17. If 1 is subtracted from the numerator of a fraction, the value of the resulting fraction is $\frac{1}{2}$. However, if 7 is added to the denominator of the original fraction, the value of the resulting fraction is $\frac{1}{3}$. Find the original fraction.

18. If the numerator of a fraction is increased by 4, the value of the resulting fraction is $\frac{3}{4}$. If the denominator of the original fraction is increased by 2, the value of the resulting fraction is $\frac{1}{2}$. Find the original fraction.

B 19. Next year, Lyle will be twice as old as Sean will be. Four years ago, he was three times as old as Sean was. How old is each now?

20. Mary is three years older than her twin brothers. Next year, the sum of the ages of the three will be exactly 102. How old are they now?

21. The Golden Gate Bridge was completed 54 years after the Brooklyn Bridge was. In 1983, the Golden Gate Bridge was $\frac{23}{50}$ as old as the Brooklyn Bridge. When was each bridge completed?

22. In 1985, the Lincoln Memorial was $1\frac{1}{2}$ times as old as the Jefferson Memorial. If the Lincoln Memorial was built 21 years before the Jefferson Memorial, give the year when each was built.

Solve each of the following problems about three-digit numbers.

23. A number between 300 and 400 is forty times the sum of its digits. The tens digit is 6 more than the units digit. Find the number.

24. A three-digit number, which is divisible by 10, has a hundreds digit that is one less than its tens digit. The number also is 52 times the sum of its digits. Find the number.

25. The sum of the three digits is 12. The tens digit exceeds the hundreds digit by the same amount that the units digit exceeds the tens digit. If the digits are reversed, the new number exceeds the original number by 198. Find the original number.

26. The sum of the three digits is 9. The tens digit is 1 more than the hundreds digit. When the digits are reversed, the new number is 99 less than the original number. Find the original number.

Solve by using a system of two equations in two variables.

27. A father, being asked his age and that of his son, said, "If you add 4 to my age and divide the sum by 4, you will have my son's age. But 6 years ago I was $7\frac{1}{2}$ times as old as my son." Find their ages.

28. The two digits in the numerator of a fraction whose value is $\frac{4}{7}$ are reversed in its denominator. The reciprocal of the fraction is the value obtained when 16 is added to the original numerator and 5 is subtracted from the original denominator. Find the original fraction.

29. The numerator equals the sum of the two digits in the denominator. The value of the fraction is $\frac{1}{4}$. When both numerator and denominator are increased by 3, the resulting fraction has the value $\frac{1}{3}$. Find the original fraction.

30. The two digits in the numerator of a fraction are reversed in its denominator. If 1 is subtracted from both the numerator and the denominator, the value of the resulting fraction is $\frac{1}{2}$. The fraction whose numerator is the difference and whose denominator is the sum of the units and tens digits equals $\frac{2}{5}$. Find the original fraction.

C 31. Laura is 3 times as old as Maria was when Laura was as old as Maria is now. In 2 years, Laura will be twice as old as Maria was 2 years ago. Find their present ages.

32. Find a two-decimal-place number between 0 and 1 such that the sum of its digits is 9 and such that if the digits are reversed the number is increased by 0.27.

33. Cindy's age equals the sum of Paul's age and Sue's age. Two years ago, Cindy was 4 times as old as Sue was, and two years from now, Cindy will be 1.4 times as old as Paul will be. How old is each now? (*Hint:* Use a system of three equations in three variables.)

34. A man is three times as old as his son was at the time when the father was twice as old as his son will be two years from now. Find the present age of each person if the sum of their ages is 55 years.

Mixed Review Exercises

Simplify.

1. $(27 - 12) - (4 - 7)$ **2.** $4 + 6 \div 3$ **3.** $|10| + 3 - |2|$

4. $7 - (18 \div 6)$ **5.** $[40 + (-4)] + [1 + (-3)]$ **6.** $4 \cdot (15 - 3)$

Solve.

7. $\frac{x + 4}{3} - \frac{x}{4} = \frac{2}{3}$ **8.** $\frac{3n + 5}{2} = \frac{n - 1}{5}$ **9.** $\frac{4 + c}{2 + c} = \frac{1}{2}$

10. $|x| = 7.7$ **11.** $3.3 = 70t - 0.2$ **12.** $-\frac{1}{6}p = 14$

Self-Test 2

Solve by using a system of two equations in two variables.

1. A jet travels at a rate of 798 mi/h with the wind. Going against the same wind, the jet travels at a rate of 762 mi/h. What is the rate of the jet in still air? What is the rate of the wind? **Obj. 9-6, p. 438**
2. The sum of the digits in a two-digit number is 15. If the digits are reversed, the number is decreased by 27. What is the number? **Obj. 9-7, p. 444**
3. Five years ago, Jerry was $\frac{2}{3}$ as old as Jeff. Ten years from now, he will be $\frac{5}{6}$ as old as Jeff will be. How old is each now?
4. The numerator of a fraction is 3 less than the denominator. If 5 is added to each, the value of the resulting fraction is $\frac{3}{4}$. Find the original fraction.

Check your answers with those at the back of the book.

Historical Note / *The Equality Symbol*

The Englishman Robert Recorde is credited with the invention of the equals sign. He wrote a mathematics book called *Whetstone of Witte,* which was published in 1557. In that book he used the symbol ═══ "to avoid the tedious repetition of the words 'is equal to.'" He said that he chose a pair of line segments of the same length because "no two things could be more equal." Eventually, the segments shortened until the symbol became =.

Another English mathematician, Thomas Harriot, who served as Sir Walter Raleigh's tutor in mathematics, later helped popularize the equality symbol by persuading other mathematicians of the day to adopt this notation. It was Harriot who invented two of the most useful mathematical symbols, the symbols $>$ and $<$.

Chapter Summary

1. The solution of systems of linear equations in two variables can be estimated by using the graphing method. Solutions can be computed algebraically by using the following methods:

   substitution method
   addition-or-subtraction method
   multiplication with the addition-or-subtraction method

2. Systems of linear equations in two variables may be used to solve word problems involving wind, water current, age, fractions, and digits, as well as other types.

Chapter Review

Give the letter of the correct answer.

1. The solution of the system $\begin{aligned} 2x + y &= 13 \\ 5x - 2y &= 19 \end{aligned}$ is (5, 3). **9-1**

How are the graphs of the two equations related?

a. The graphs are parallel.
b. The graphs coincide.
c. The graphs intersect at (5, 3).
d. The graphs intersect at (5, 0) and (0, 3).

2. Solve by the substitution method: $\begin{aligned} 2x + y &= 6 \\ 3x - 2y &= 2 \end{aligned}$ **9-2**

a. (2, 2) **b.** (−2, −2) **c.** (3, 0) **d.** (0, −2)

3. Solve by using two equations in two variables: One positive integer is 17 more than a second positive integer. If the sum of the first integer and twice the second integer is 152, find each integer. **9-3**

a. 54, 37 **b.** 45, 28 **c.** 55, 28 **d.** 62, 45

4. Solve by the addition-or-subtraction method: $\begin{aligned} a + 3b &= 9 \\ 2a + 3b &= 15 \end{aligned}$ **9-4**

a. (−6, 5) **b.** (1, 6) **c.** $\left(8, \frac{1}{3}\right)$ **d.** (6, 1)

5. Solve by using multiplication with the addition-or-subtraction method: **9-5**

$$\begin{aligned} 3s - 5t &= 27 \\ s + 4t &= -8 \end{aligned}$$

a. (14, 3) **b.** (4, 3) **c.** (3, 14) **d.** (4, −3)

6. A boat travels downstream at 37 mi/h. The same boat travels upstream at 17 mi/h. Find the rate of the current. **9-6**

a. 20 mi/h **b.** 10 mi/h **c.** 27 mi/h **d.** 54 mi/h

7. The sum of the digits of a two-digit number is 8. If the digits are reversed, the number is increased by 54. Find the original number. **9-7**

a. 71 **b.** 17 **c.** 26 **d.** 62

8. Two years ago, Rick's age was 1 year less than twice Barbara's age. Four years from now, Rick will be 8 years more than half Barbara's age. How old is Rick?

a. 1 **b.** 3 **c.** 7 **d.** 9

9. The denominator of a fraction is 7 more than the numerator. If 5 is added to each, the value of the resulting fraction is $\frac{1}{2}$. Find the original fraction.

a. $\frac{7}{14}$ **b.** $\frac{9}{2}$ **c.** $\frac{5}{12}$ **d.** $\frac{2}{9}$

Chapter Test

Solve by the graphing method. 9-1

1. $x - 2y = 9$
$3x - y = 7$

2. $y = 2x - 1$
$2x - 4y = 10$

Solve by the substitution method. 9-2

3. $8m + n = 3$
$5m + 2n = -27$

4. $3a - 4b = 17$
$a + 2b = 1$

5. Show that the following system has infinitely many solutions:

$y = 3x - 4$
$6x - 2y = 8$

6. Show that the following system has no solution:

$y = 4x - 3$
$2y - 8x = -8$

7. Solve using two equations in two variables: Jason bought a total of 7 post-cards for $1.80. If the small postcards cost 20¢ each and the large ones cost 30¢ each, how many postcards of each size did he buy? 9-3

Solve by the addition-or-subtraction method. 9-4

8. $4x - 5y = 0$
$8x + 5y = -60$

9. $10p + 4q = 2$
$10p - 8q = 26$

Solve by using multiplication with the addition-or-subtraction method. 9-5

10. $-8r + s = -17$
$5r - 3s = -6$

11. $2x + 5y = 16$
$5x - 3y = -22$

Solve by using a system of two equations in two variables.

12. Gretchen paddles a canoe upstream at 3 mi/h. Traveling downstream, she travels at 8 mi/h. What is Gretchen's paddling rate in still water and what is the rate of the current? 9-6

13. Six years ago, Joe Foster was two years more than five times as old as his daughter. Six years from now, he will be 11 years more than twice as old as she will be. How old is Joe? 9-7

14. The numerator of a fraction is 4 less than the denominator. If 17 is added to each, the value of the fraction is $\frac{5}{6}$. Find the original fraction.

Cumulative Review *(Chapters 1–9)*

Perform the indicated operations. Express the answers in simplest form. Assume that no denominator is zero.

1. $(28p^4q^3 + 16p^3q^2 - 84p^2q^5) \div (2pq)^2$
2. $(-2x^3yz^2)^4(x^2y^2)^3$
3. $4j^4(jk^3 - 6j^2k + 7k^4)$
4. $(5c - 3)(2c^2 + 4c + 1)$
5. $(21z - 3)(2z + 4)$
6. $(7x^2 + 3b)(7x - 3b)$
7. $\dfrac{15t^2 - 11t - 12}{3t - 4}$
8. $\dfrac{3}{2b - 1} + \dfrac{b^2 + 2}{1 - 4b^2} + b$
9. $\dfrac{x^2 - 7x + 10}{x^2 - 4} \div \dfrac{x + 3}{x^2 - x - 6}$
10. $(10y^2 + 27y - 15) \div (2y + 7)$
11. $(1.7 \times 10^5)(0.4 \times 10^6)$
12. $\left(\dfrac{m^{-4}}{m^{-5}}\right)^{-3}$

Factor completely. If the polynomial cannot be factored, write "prime."

13. $49x^2 + 98xy + 81y^2$
14. $64x^4 - 81y^4$
15. $30x^2 + 15x + 1$
16. $28y^2 + 37y + 12$
17. $8y^2 - 26y + 5$
18. $16y^2 - 25x^2 + 10x - 1$

Solve. Assume that no denominator is zero. If the equation is an identity or has no solution, say so.

19. $16 - \frac{1}{2}|m| = 5$
20. $\frac{1}{5}(x - 6) = 34 - 3x$
21. $196x^2 - 16 = 0$
22. $18t^2 + 53t - 3 = 0$
23. $\dfrac{2x + 1}{x - 3} + \dfrac{x + 3}{2x + 1} = \dfrac{2x}{3 - x}$

Write an equation in standard form for each line described.

24. slope $\frac{1}{4}$, passes through $(12, 2)$
25. passes through $(1, 0)$ and $(2, -3)$

Solve algebraically.

26. $4x + 3y = 12$
    $3y - 8x = -12$
27. $5x = y + 3$
    $3x + 2y = 20$
28. $2x + 5y = 9$
    $3x - 2y = 4$
29. The sum of the digits of a two-digit number is 6. When the digits are reversed, the resulting number is 6 greater than 3 times the original number. Find the original number.
30. It took a cyclist 6 h to travel 48 mi going against the wind. The next day on the return trip, it took the cyclist 3 h, traveling with the wind. What was the speed of the cyclist?
31. How many kilograms of nuts worth \$5/kg should be mixed with 6 kg of nuts worth \$9/kg to produce a mix worth \$6.50/kg?

Maintaining Skills

Simplify. Assume that no denominator is zero.

Sample 1 $\frac{5x + 15}{2x} \cdot \frac{4x^3}{x^2 + 6x + 9} = \frac{5(x + 3)}{2x} \cdot \frac{4x^3}{(x + 3)^2} = \frac{20x^3(x + 3)}{2x(x + 3)^2} = \frac{10x^2}{x + 3}$

1. $\frac{ab}{4a - 4b} \cdot \frac{a^2 - ab}{ab}$
2. $\frac{2x - 14}{-5x} \cdot \frac{5x^3}{3x - 21}$
3. $\frac{8f + 24g}{2f - 4g} \cdot \frac{4f - 8g}{2f + 6g}$
4. $\frac{m + 2}{2m - 6} \cdot \frac{m^2 - 5m + 6}{2m + 4}$
5. $\frac{3z - 6}{5z} \cdot \frac{z^2 - z - 6}{z^2 - 4}$
6. $\frac{x^2 - 4}{x^2 - 9} \cdot \frac{2x^2 + 6x}{x - 2}$
7. $\frac{3n^2 + 2n - 1}{5n^2 - 9n - 2} \cdot \frac{10n^2 - 13n - 3}{2n^2 - n - 3}$
8. $\frac{y^2 + 12y + 36}{36 - y^2} \cdot \frac{y^2 - 5y - 6}{2y^2 - 2y - 84}$

Sample 2 $\frac{2m^2 + 5m + 2}{m^2 + 4m + 3} \div \frac{m + 2}{2m^2 + 7m + 3}$

Solution $\frac{(2m + 1)(m + 2)}{(m + 3)(m + 1)} \cdot \frac{(2m + 1)(m + 3)}{m + 2} = \frac{(2m + 1)^2}{m + 1}$

9. $\frac{10a - 10b}{ab} \div \frac{2a - 2b}{a^2b^2}$
10. $\frac{16m^2 - n^2}{6m + 3n} \div \frac{4mn - n^2}{2mn + n^2}$
11. $\frac{2b^2 + 17b + 21}{b + 1} \div (b + 7)$
12. $\frac{x^2 + x}{-x^2 - 2x - 1} \div \frac{x^2 - 3x}{2x^2 - 2}$
13. $\frac{c^2 - c - 6}{c^2 + 2c - 15} \div \frac{c^2 - 4c - 5}{c^2 - 25}$
14. $\frac{6y^2 - y - 2}{12y^2 + 5y - 2} \div \frac{8y^2 - 6y + 1}{4y^2 - 1}$
15. $\frac{r^2 - r - 20}{r^2 - 6r + 5} \cdot \frac{r^2 - 36}{r^2 - 9} \div \frac{r^2 + 7r + 12}{r^2 + 5r - 6}$

Sample 3 $\frac{b}{b - 2} - \frac{2}{b^2 - 4} + 1$

Solution $\frac{b(b + 2) - 2 + (b + 2)(b - 2)}{(b + 2)(b - 2)} = \frac{b^2 + 2b - 2 + b^2 - 4}{(b + 2)(b - 2)} = \frac{2(b^2 + b - 3)}{(b + 2)(b - 2)}$

16. $\frac{2t - 3}{r^2t} + \frac{r - t}{r^2t}$
17. $\frac{x + 2y}{x - y} + \frac{x + y}{x - y}$
18. $\frac{3b + 2}{b^3} - \frac{2b + 2}{b^3}$
19. $\frac{w - 2}{w - 3} - \frac{w^2 + w}{w - 3}$
20. $z + \frac{z - 1}{z + 1} + 1$
21. $\frac{8}{v^2 - 1} + \frac{v}{v + 1}$
22. $\frac{s}{s - t} - \frac{s}{s + t}$
23. $\frac{3b}{2b - 1} - b$
24. $\frac{x + 3}{x - 1} + \frac{x}{x + 2}$
25. $\frac{d - 3}{2d + 1} + \frac{1}{d + 1}$
26. $\frac{v + 4}{v + 2} - \frac{v + 2}{v + 4}$
27. $\frac{t}{t^2 - 4} - \frac{5t}{4 - t^2}$
28. $\frac{2b}{b + 2} + \frac{b + 1}{b} - 1$
29. $\frac{x + 4}{x - 4} - \frac{x - 4}{x + 3} + 2$
30. $\frac{3a + b}{a^2 - b^2} - \frac{1}{a + b}$

Mixed Problem Solving

Solve each problem that has a solution. If a problem has no solution, explain why.

A

1. As the altitude increases from sea level to 6000 m, the air pressure decreases from 101.3 kilopascals to 47.2 kilopascals. Find the approximate percent decrease in air pressure.

2. The ratio of boys to girls in a sophomore class of 460 students is 11 : 12. How many girls are there?

3. The sum of the squares of two consecutive even integers is 34. Find the integers.

4. Eight ears of corn and a cantaloupe cost \$2.37. Six ears of corn and 3 cantaloupes cost \$3.51. What does a cantaloupe cost?

5. An airplane travels 1800 km in 6 h flying with the wind. It travels only two thirds as far in the same time against the wind. Find the speed of the wind.

6. At 9:00 A.M. two boys began hiking at 6 km/h. At 10:30 A.M. their mother started after them in her car at 60 km/h, bringing a friend to join them. At what time did she catch up with them?

7. The amount of tax is directly proportional to the cost of an item. If the tax on a \$12,300 car is \$738, find the tax on a \$9450 car.

8. The tens digit of a two-digit number is 1 more than 3 times the units digit. Subtracting 45 from the number reverses it. Find the original number.

B

9. Ramon can do the weekly billing in 2 h. Luann needs 3 h. If Ramon works for 30 min and is then joined by Luann, how long will it take them to finish?

10. The rectangular base of a radio receiver is twice as long as it is wide. A design engineer finds that in order to fit the receiver into the space available on an airplane, she must decrease the length by 7 in. and increase the width by 2 in. If this change decreases the area of the base by 32 in.^{2}, what were the original dimensions of the receiver?

11. How many kilograms of water must be evaporated from 8 kg of a 25% salt solution to produce a 40% salt solution?

12. The value of a fraction is $\frac{3}{4}$. When 7 is added to its numerator, the resulting fraction is equal to the reciprocal of the original fraction. Find the original fraction.

13. The Kwons invested \$6000, part at $7\frac{1}{4}\%$ and part at 10%, and earned \$567 in interest. How much did they invest at each rate?

14. I have dimes and quarters worth \$1.15. How many of each could I have? (*Hint:* There is more than one solution.)

10 Inequalities

Above the boiling point** ($t > 212°F$) **water is steam. Below the freezing point** ($t < 32°F$) **it's ice. In between** ($32°F < t < 212°F$), **it's liquid.

Inequalities in One Variable

10-1 Order of Real Numbers

Objective To review the concept of order and to graph inequalities in one variable.

A number line shows order relationships among real numbers.

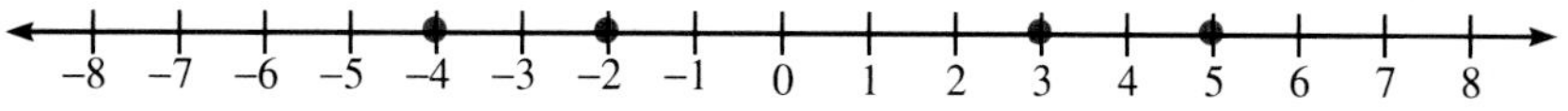

−4 is to the left of 3.	5 is to the right of −2.
−4 is less than 3.	5 is greater than −2.
$-4 < 3$	$5 > -2$

The value of a variable may be unknown, but you may know that it's greater than or equal to another number. For example,

$x \geq 5$ is read "x is greater than or equal to 5."

$x \geq 5$ is another way of writing "$x > 5$ or $x = 5$."

Example 1 Translate the statement into symbols.

a. −3 is greater than −5. **b.** x is less than or equal to 8.

Solution **a.** $-3 > -5$ **b.** $x \leq 8$

To show that x is *between* −4 and 2, you write

$$-4 < x < 2,$$

which is read

"−4 is less than x and x is less than 2,"

or

"x is greater than −4 and less than 2."

The same comparisons are stated in the sentence $2 > x > -4$.

When all the numbers are known, you can determine whether the statements are true or false.

Example 2 Classify each statement as true or false.

a. $-4 < 1 < 2$ **b.** $-4 < 8 < 2$

c. $7 \geq 6$ **d.** $6 \geq 6$

(Solution is on next page.)

Solution **a.** $-4 < 1 < 2$ is true since *both* $-4 < 1$ *and* $1 < 2$ are true.

b. $-4 < 8 < 2$ is false since $-4 < 8$ is true but $8 < 2$ is false.

c. For $7 \geq 6$ to be true, *either* $7 > 6$ *or* $7 = 6$ must be true. $7 \geq 6$ is true since $7 > 6$ is true.

d. $6 \geq 6$ is true since $6 = 6$ is true.

The statements given in Examples 1 and 2 are *inequalities*. An **inequality** is formed by placing an inequality symbol ($>$, $<$, $\geq$, $\leq$) between numerical or variable expressions, called the **sides** of the inequality.

$-2 < 0$ (sides: -2 and 0) $\qquad 3x - 5 > 1$ (sides: $3x - 5$ and 1) $\qquad y \leq 9x + 4$ (sides: y and $9x + 4$)

As with equations, an inequality containing a variable is called an *open sentence* (page 10). You solve an inequality by finding the values from the *domain* of the variable for which the inequality is a true statement. Such values are called **solutions of the inequality.** All the solutions make up the **solution set of the inequality.**

Example 3 Solve $y + 5 \leq 7$ if $y \in \{-1, 0, 1, 2, 3, 4\}$.

Solution Replace y with each of its values in turn:

$$y + 5 \leq 7$$

$-1 + 5 \leq 7$ True	$2 + 5 \leq 7$ True
$0 + 5 \leq 7$ True	$3 + 5 \leq 7$ False
$1 + 5 \leq 7$ True	$4 + 5 \leq 7$ False

$\therefore$ the solution set is $\{-1, 0, 1, 2\}$. ***Answer***

When you graph the numbers in the solution set of an inequality on a number line, you are drawing the **graph of the inequality.** The graph of the inequality $y + 5 \leq 7$ in Example 3 is shown below.

Example 4 Graph $-3 \leq x < 2$ over the domain {the real numbers}.

Solution For the inequality to be a true statement, x must represent any number between -3 and 2, including -3 but not 2.

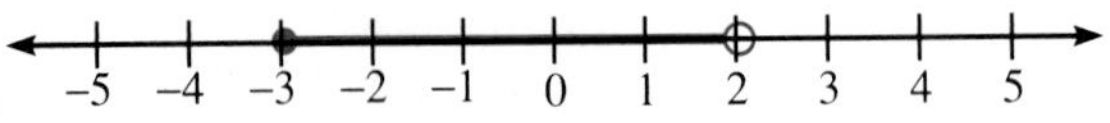

Answer

Notice that the graph in Example 4 includes all the points on the number line from the graph of -3 up to, but not including, the graph of 2. The open circle shows that 2 is not a solution.

Oral Exercises

Classify each statement as true or false.

1. $6 \geq 3$

2. $17 \leq 23$

3. $-10 \leq -15$

4. $-1 > -2$

5. $4 > -4 > -1$

6. $-5 < 5 < 9$

7. $3 > 0 > -5$

8. $-1.5 < 0.5 < 2.5$

9. $|-4| \geq 0$

10. $|-2| > |-8|$

11. $2^4 < 4^2$

12. $\frac{1}{2} \leq \left(\frac{1}{2}\right)^2$

Match each graph with its description.

13.

14.

15.
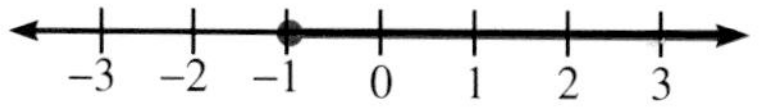

16.
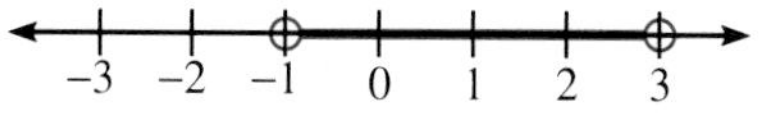

17.
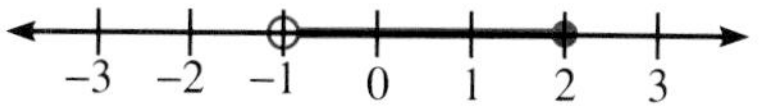

18.

19.
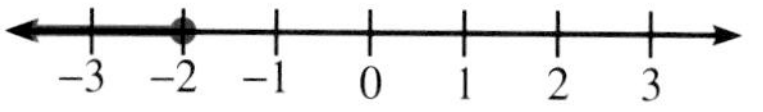

20.
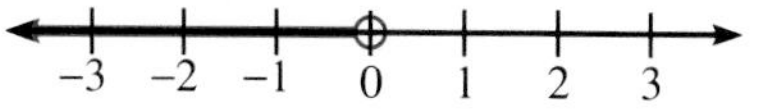

a. The real numbers greater than or equal to 0.

b. $\{-2, 0, 2\}$

c. The real numbers between -1 and 3.

d. $\{-3, -1, 0, 2\}$

e. The real numbers less than 0.

f. The real numbers greater than -1 and less than or equal to 2.

g. The real numbers greater than or equal to -1.

h. The real numbers less than or equal to -2.

Written Exercises

Translate each statement into symbols.

A

1. 4 is greater than -7.

2. -5 is less than -3.

3. -12 is less than or equal to -9.

4. 6 is greater than or equal to 2.

5. 3 is greater than 2 and less than 3.5.

6. 0 is greater than $-\frac{1}{2}$ and less than 1.

Translate each statement into symbols.

7. -8 is between 0 and -10.
8. 5 is between -9 and 9.
9. 4.6 is greater than 4 and 4 is greater than 0.
10. -1.5 is less than -1 and -1 is less than 2.
11. The number n is greater than 10.
12. The number n is less than 20.
13. The absolute value of -2 is greater than 1.
14. The absolute value of n is less than or equal to n.

Classify each statement as true or false.

15. $|-3| > -3$
16. $0 \le |-2|$
17. $|-25| < |-10|$
18. $|-0.5| \le -0.5$
19. $\left|-\frac{1}{2}\right| \ge 0$
20. $-6 < 1 < 7$
21. $6 > 0 > 2$
22. $-5 < -4 < 4$

Solve each inequality if $x \in \{-4, -3, -2, -1, 0, 1, 2, 3, 4\}$.

23. $4x < 8$
24. $3x \ge 6$
25. $-3x \le 9$
26. $x + 2 < 3$
27. $-5 - x \le 1$
28. $1 - x \ge 0$
29. $x^2 \ge 10$
30. $x^2 \le 4$

Graph each inequality over the given domain.

B 31. $1 \le x \le 6$; {the positive integers}
32. $2 < h < 8$; {the positive integers}
33. $-5 \le x < 1$; {the integers}
34. $3 \ge t \ge -1$; {the integers}
35. $6 > u > 0$; {the real numbers}
36. $-2 < m < 2$; {the real numbers}
37. $-5 \le h < 1$; {the negative integers}
38. $4 \ge n > -5$; {the negative integers}

For each statement in Exercises 39–42:

a. Find a pair of values of x and y for which the statement is true.
b. Find a pair of values of x and y for which the statement is false.

C 39. If $x \ge y$, then $|x| \le |y|$.
40. If $x \le 0$ and $y > 0$, then $xy \ge 0$.
41. If $x > y$, then $xy > y^2$.
42. $|x + y| > x + y$

Computer Exercises

For students with some programming experience

Write a BASIC program to find the solution set of an inequality for a specified domain of the variable. Run the program to find the solution set of each of the following inequalities for the given domain.

1. $2x - 5 < 7$; $x \in \{0, 1, 2, \ldots, 10\}$
2. $x^2 - x < 6$; $x \in \{-4, -3, -2, \ldots, 1, 2, 3, 4\}$
3. $|4 - 5x| > 13$; $x \in \{0, 1, 2, 3, 4, 5\}$
4. $x^2 + 3x + 4 < 10$; $x \in \{-3, -2, -1, 0, 1, 2, 3\}$
5. $x^2 - 4x + 1 > 6$; $x \in \{0, 1, 2, 3, \ldots, 8, 9, 10\}$

Mixed Review Exercises

Solve.

1. $x - 5 = 13$ **2.** $14 = 2(c + 1)$ **3.** $5 - 2a = 17$

4. $\frac{s}{5} = -10$ **5.** $\frac{21}{y} = \frac{7}{9}$ **6.** $\frac{3x + 1}{5} = \frac{x + 12}{4}$

7. $5(2 + n) = 4(n - 6)$ **8.** $(x + 4)(x + 7) = (x + 5)^2$ **9.** $\frac{b}{5} + 8 = b$

10. $\frac{x}{4} = \frac{x - 3}{5}$ **11.** $\frac{3p}{10} + \frac{p}{5} = \frac{1}{2}$ **12.** $\frac{1}{3}(x + 9) = 3$

Biographical Note / *Daniel Hale Williams*

Daniel Hale Williams (1856–1931) was a pioneer in heart surgery. After serving as a surgeon's apprentice for almost two years, Williams attended Chicago Medical College, and received his diploma in 1883. Dr. Williams opened a medical practice in Chicago's South Side, where he often performed surgery in his office or in patients' homes. Realizing a need for a hospital that would admit and give quality care to all, as well as provide training for doctors and nurses, Williams helped found Provident Hospital, the first interracial hospital in the United States. Williams's colleagues, impressed by his extraordinary techniques and skill, often observed him as he performed surgery.

Dr. Williams's most famous case occurred on July 9, 1893. A young man who had been stabbed in the chest was admitted to the hospital. Risking both his career and his reputation, Williams opened the patient's chest cavity, something no doctor had done before. He cleansed the wound, rejoined an artery, and stitched the membrane surrounding the heart. The operation saved the patient's life and won Williams the praise of the medical world.

The following year Williams was appointed chief surgeon of Freedmen's Hospital in Washington, D.C. Williams completely reorganized and modernized the hospital, adding departments in bacteriology and pathology, and instituting training programs for nurses and interns. In addition to the many honors he received, Williams was elected vice president of the National Medical Association, which he had actively helped to organize.

10-2 Solving Inequalities

Objective To transform inequalities in order to solve them.

Only the first of the following statements is true:

$-7 < 4$	$-7 = 4$	$-7 > 4$
True	False	False

When you compare real numbers, you take the *property of comparison* for granted.

Property of Comparison

For all real numbers a and b, one and only one of the following statements is true:

$$a < b, \quad a = b, \quad \text{or} \quad a > b.$$

Suppose you know two facts about the graphs of three numbers a, b, and c.

1. The graph of a is to the left of the graph of b: $a < b$
2. The graph of b is to the left of the graph of c: $b < c$

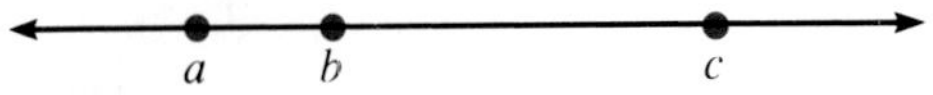

From the graphs above, you can see that the graph of a is to the left of the graph of c: $a < c$.

The facts above illustrate the following property:

Transitive Property of Order

For all real numbers a, b, and c:

1. If $a < b$ and $b < c$, then $a < c$;
2. If $c > b$ and $b > a$, then $c > a$.

What happens when the same number is added to or subtracted from each side of an inequality?

$3 < 6$	$3 < 6$
$3 + 4 \underline{\ ?\ } 6 + 4$	$3 - 4 \underline{\ ?\ } 6 - 4$
$7 < 10$	$-1 < 2$

These numerical examples suggest the property of order stated on the next page. (Remember that subtracting a number is the same as adding the opposite of that number.)

Addition Property of Order

For all real numbers, a, b, and c:

1. If $a < b$, then $a + c < b + c$;
2. If $a > b$, then $a + c > b + c$.

What happens when each side of the inequality $-4 < 3$ is multiplied by a nonzero real number?

Multiply by 2:	Multiply by -2:
Is $2(-4) < 2(3)$?	Is $-2(-4) < -2(3)$?
Yes, $-8 < 6$.	No, $8 > -6$.

These examples suggest that multiplying each side of an inequality by a *negative* number *reverses the direction,* or order, of the inequality.

Multiplication Property of Order

For all real numbers, a, b, and c such that

$c > 0$ (c is positive):

1. If $a < b$, then $ac < bc$;
2. If $a > b$, then $ac > bc$.

$c < 0$ (c is negative):

1. If $a < b$, then $ac > bc$;
2. If $a > b$, then $ac < bc$.

Multiplying both sides of an inequality by zero does not produce an inequality; the result is the identity $0 = 0$.

The properties that have been stated guarantee that the following transformations of a given inequality always produce an **equivalent inequality,** that is, one with the same solution set.

Transformations That Produce an Equivalent Inequality

1. Substituting for either side of the inequality an expression equivalent to that side.
2. Adding to (or subtracting from) each side of the inequality the same real number.
3. Multiplying (or dividing) each side of the inequality by the same positive number.
4. Multiplying (or dividing) each side of the inequality by the same negative number *and reversing the direction of the inequality.*

To solve an inequality, you usually try to transform it into a simple equivalent inequality whose solution set can be easily seen.

Example 1 Tell how to transform the first inequality into the second one.

a. $m - 9 < 2$
$m < 11$

b. $-8k \geq 16$
$k \leq -2$

Solution **a.** Add 9 to each side. **b.** Divide each side by -8 and reverse the direction of the inequality.

You may assume that the domain of all variables is the set of real numbers unless otherwise stated.

Example 2 Solve $6x - 3 < 7 + 4x$ and graph its solution set.

Solution

$$6x - 3 < 7 + 4x$$

$$6x - 3 + 3 < 7 + 4x + 3 \qquad \text{Add 3 to each side.}$$

$$6x < 10 + 4x$$

$$6x - 4x < 10 + 4x - 4x \qquad \text{Subtract } 4x \text{ from each side.}$$

$$2x < 10$$

$$\frac{2x}{2} < \frac{10}{2} \qquad \text{Divide each side by 2.}$$

$$x < 5$$

$\therefore$ the solution set is {the real numbers less than 5}.

The graph is:

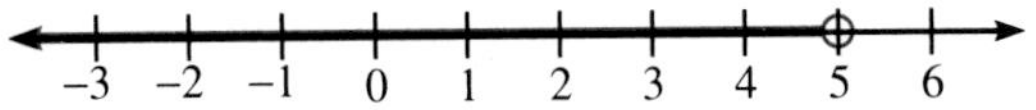

Answer

To solve an inequality, you take the same steps used to solve equations:

1. Simplify each side of the inequality as needed.
2. Use the inverse operations to undo any additions or subtractions.
3. Use the inverse operations to undo any multiplications or divisions.

Example 3 Solve $2(w - 8) + 9 \geq 3(4 - w) - 4$ and graph its solution set.

Solution

$$2(w - 8) + 9 \geq 3(4 - w) - 4$$

$$2w - 16 + 9 \geq 12 - 3w - 4$$

$$2w - 7 \geq 8 - 3w$$

$$5w \geq 15$$

$$w \geq 3$$

$\therefore$ the solution set is {the real numbers greater than or equal to 3}.

The graph is:

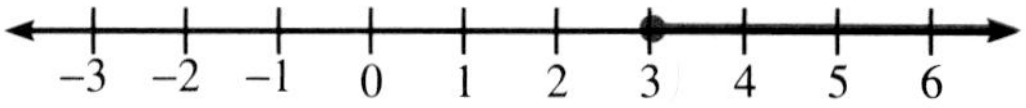

Answer

Some inequalities have no solution, and some inequalities are true for all real numbers.

Example 4 Solve $4x > 4(x + 2)$ and graph its solution set.

Solution

$4x > 4(x + 2)$

$4x > 4x + 8$

$0 > 8$

Since $0 > 8$ is false, the original inequality has no solution. There is no graph. ***Answer***

Example 5 Solve $y + 5 < 7y - 6(y - 1)$ and graph its solution set.

Solution

$y + 5 < 7y - 6(y - 1)$

$y + 5 < 7y - 6y + 6$

$y + 5 < y + 6$

$5 < 6$

Since $5 < 6$ is true, the original inequality is true for every real number.

∴ the solution set is {the real numbers}, and the graph is the entire number line.

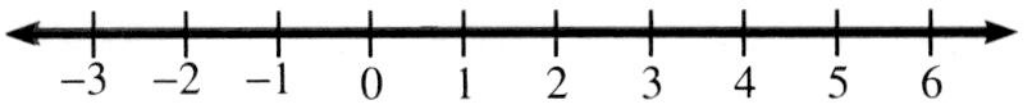

Answer

Oral Exercises

Tell how to transform the first inequality to obtain the second one.

1. $t + 3 < 7$; $t < 4$

2. $r - 5 > 7$; $r > 12$

3. $-1 < x - 2$; $1 < x$

4. $y + 6 < 0$; $y < -6$

5. $4p < 20$; $p < 5$

6. $3m < -18$; $m < -6$

7. $-6a < 18$; $a > -3$

8. $\frac{x}{2} > 4$; $x > 8$

9. $2 > \frac{v}{7}$; $14 > v$

10. $\frac{r}{-3} \le -5$; $r \ge 15$

11. $3y \le \frac{1}{2}$; $y \le \frac{1}{6}$

12. $-\frac{t}{2} \ge 0$; $t \le 0$

Explain how to transform each inequality in order to solve it. Then state the transformed inequality.

13. $y - 5 < 8$

14. $6 < x + 1$

15. $10p > 100$

16. $-8 > -2c$

17. $\frac{w}{2} \geq 12$

18. $2 \leq -\frac{r}{3}$

Written Exercises

Solve each inequality in Exercises 1–10 and write the letter of its graph.

A

1. $y - 2 \geq 7$

2. $10 < z + 8$

3. $6p < 24$

4. $18 \leq 6v$

5. $-28 > -7m$

6. $\frac{d}{2} > -10$

7. $2 - g > 0$

8. $3 \leq \frac{x}{-2}$

9. $b - 1 < b - 2$

10. $t + 2 > t + 1$

a.
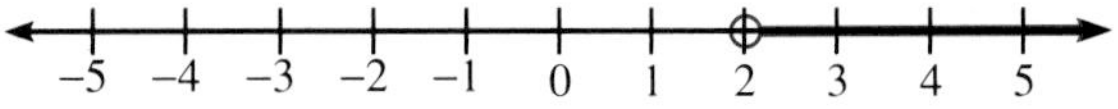

b.
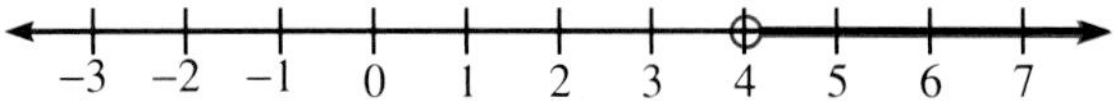

c.

d.
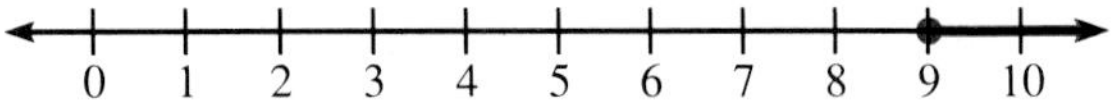

e.
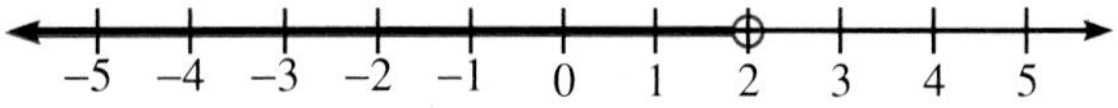

f.
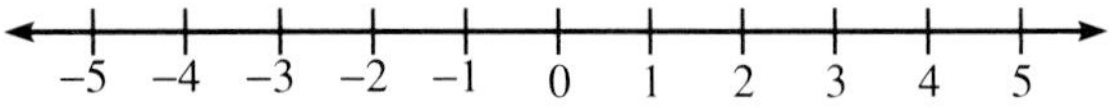

g.
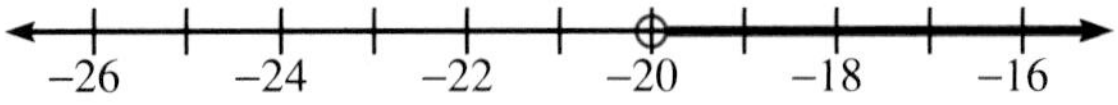

h.
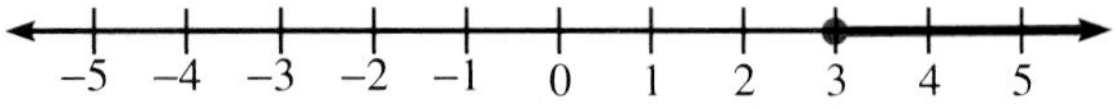

i.

j.
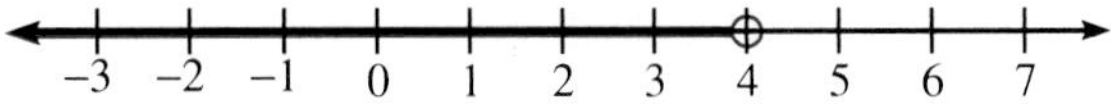

Solve each inequality. Graph the solution set, if there is one.

11. $n - 4 > 11$

12. $a + 3 < 11$

13. $-\frac{y}{2} > 4$

14. $4q < 12$

15. $36 < \frac{x}{-9}$

16. $-6 > \frac{s}{3}$

17. $-6m \geq 6$

18. $-5w \leq 15$

19. $\frac{x}{2} - 4 > -6$

20. $2v + 1 > 7$

21. $-\frac{d}{3} \geq 0$

22. $7 \geq 2k - 7$

23. $\frac{3}{2}t - 7 < 2$

24. $-4 \geq 4 - \frac{u}{2}$

25. $-1 < 9 + \frac{2}{3}g$

26. $5 + \frac{x}{3} \leq 6$

27. $12 - \frac{3}{2}c > 0$

28. $0 > 6 - \frac{2}{3}d$

29. $5y < 4y + 6$

30. $3f - 4 < 2f + 5$

31. $4r - 5 < 5r + 7$

32. $8 - 2b > 4 - b$

33. $2(x - 4) \leq 6$

34. $8 < 2(4 - m)$

35. $-5(x + 3) < -5x + 1$

36. $7a < 3 + 7(a - 1)$

37. $5(1 - t) > 4(3 - t)$

38. $4(2 - v) \geq -(v - 5)$

39. $\frac{5}{6}r + 1 \geq \frac{4}{3}$

40. $\frac{3}{4} < 6 - \frac{1}{2}a$

B 41. $5(x - 1) > \frac{5}{4}x$

42. $\frac{1}{2}y \geq 2(y - 3)$

43. $n - \frac{5}{2} > \frac{3}{4}(n - 6)$

44. $3w - \frac{1}{2}(2w + 8) > 0$

45. $5(5 - k) - 7(7 + k) < 0$

46. $5(v - 1) > 3(v + 4) - 5$

47. $4\left(r - \frac{1}{2}\right) - 3 \leq 5(r - 1) + 4$

48. $4(t + 1) - 2(t - 1) \leq 3 - t$

49. $5 - a + 6(a - 2) \geq 5(a + 1)$

50. $5(2b + 1) - 3(b + 1) < 7b + 5$

Given that a and b are real numbers such that $a > b$, describe the real numbers c, if any, for which each statement is true.

C 51. $a + c > b + c$

52. $a - c < b - c$

53. $ac > bc$

54. $ac < bc$

55. $ac = bc$

56. $\frac{a}{c} > \frac{b}{c}$

57. $\frac{a}{c} < \frac{b}{c}$

58. $ac^2 < bc^2$

Given that a and b are real numbers such that $a > b > 0$, classify each of the following statements as true or false. If you classify a statement as false, give an example of values for which it is false.

59. $a > 0$

60. $a^2 > a$

61. $\frac{a}{b} > 0$

62. $a + b > b$

63. $a^2 > b$

64. $a - b > 0$

65. $\frac{a}{b} > \frac{b}{a}$

66. $a^2 > b^2$

Mixed Review Exercises

Classify each statement as true or false.

1. $-(-2) < |-3|$

2. $|-3| \geq |3|$

3. $|-13| < |-12|$

4. $5(4 + 3 \cdot 2) = 70$

5. $2x + 10 = 2(x + 5)$

6. $(x + 3)(x + 7) = x^2 + 10x$

Solve.

7. $3f - 4 = 2f + 5$

8. $0 = 2x + 5$

9. $a(a + 5) = (a - 9)(a - 7)$

10. $4y - 2(y + 1) = -6$

11. $p - 2(6 - p) = -p$

12. $3b + 2(b + 1) = b + 6$

Reading Algebra / Inequalities

When working with inequalities, it is important to read both the symbols and the words slowly and carefully. Unlike equations, which involve only one sign, $=$, inequalities can contain any of the four inequality symbols, $<$, $>$, $\leq$, or $\geq$. Whichever symbol is used determines what your answer will be. For example, the equation $2x + 6 = 14$ is equivalent to $x = 4$, and the solution set is simply $\{4\}$. However, the inequalities

$$2x + 6 < 14, \quad 2x + 6 > 14, \quad 2x + 6 \leq 14, \quad \text{and } 2x + 6 \geq 14$$

all have different solution sets.

$2x + 6 < 14$ is equivalent to $x < 4$. The solution set is {the real numbers less than 4}.

$2x + 6 > 14$ is equivalent to $x > 4$. The solution set is {the real numbers greater than 4}.

$2x + 6 \leq 14$ is equivalent to $x \leq 4$. The solution set is {the real numbers less than or equal to 4}.

$2x + 6 \geq 14$ is equivalent to $x \geq 4$. The solution set is {the real numbers greater than or equal to 4}.

Word problems involving inequalities also require very careful reading. An important step in solving this type of problem is determining which inequality symbol to use. Is the problem asking for a number that is less than, greater than, less than or equal to, or greater than or equal to a particular number or expression? Before you write your inequality you should be certain that you will use the correct symbol.

Exercises

For each of the following:

a. Determine whether the inequality symbol means less than, greater than, less than or equal to, or greater than or equal to.

b. Determine whether the graph has a closed circle or an open circle and whether the graph goes to the right or the left of that circle.

c. Solve and graph the solution.

1. $x - 3 > 12$

2. $3y + 1 > 7$

3. $5 \geq 2y - 3$

4. $12 + y \leq 24$

5. $-9 < 21 + 2m$

6. $-6 \leq 6 - k$

7. $18 - 3y > 0$

8. $1 + 3r \geq 5 - r$

9. $2x - 3 < 4x + 5$

10. $21 - 15x < -8x - 7$

11. $4(t - 2) > 5(t - 3)$

12. $6(z - 5) \leq 15 + 5(7 - 2z)$

10-3 Solving Problems Involving Inequalities

Objective To solve problems that involve inequalities.

Example 1 Molly set her car's trip odometer at zero at the start of her trip home. When the odometer showed that she had driven 16 mi, a highway sign showed her that she was still more than 25 mi from her home. What is the minimum total distance, to the nearest mile, that she will have traveled when she arrives home?

Solution

Step 1 The problem asks for the minimum total distance Molly will have traveled.

Step 2 Choose a variable to represent the total distance.
Let $d =$ the total distance in miles.
Then $d - 16 =$ the distance from the sign to home.

Step 3 Use the variable to write an inequality based on the given information.

$$\underbrace{\text{The distance from the sign to home}}_{d-16}\ \underbrace{\text{is more than}}_{>}\ \underbrace{25\text{ mi.}}_{25}$$

Step 4 Solve the open sentence:

$$d - 16 > 25$$
$$d > 41$$

The smallest integer that is greater than 41 is 42.
Thus the minimum distance traveled is 42 mi.

Step 5 *Check:* Is the distance from the sign to home more than 25 mi?

$$42 - 16 \stackrel{?}{>} 25$$
$$26 > 25 \quad \checkmark$$

Is the distance the least possible?
Suppose the distance is the next smaller integer, 41.

$$41 - 16 \stackrel{?}{>} 25$$
$$25 > 25 \quad \text{False}$$

$\therefore$ the minimum total distance Molly will have traveled is 42 mi. ***Answer***

To translate phrases such as "is at least" and "is no less than" or "is at most" and "is no more than" into mathematical terms, you use the symbols $\geq$ or $\leq$. For example:

The age of the tree is at least 70 years:	$a \geq 70$
The rent is no less than \$400 per month:	$r \geq 400$
The price of the paperback book is at most \$5.95:	$p \leq 5.95$
Her time in the 10 km race was no more than 40 min:	$t \leq 40$

Example 2 Mike wants to rent a car for his vacation. The rental costs \$125 a week plus \$.15 a mile. How far to the nearest mile can Mike travel if he wants to spend at most \$200?

Solution

Step 1 The problem asks for the number of miles Mike can travel.

Step 2 Let m = the number of miles Mike can travel.

Step 3 $\underbrace{\text{Cost of car rental}}_{125 + 0.15m} \quad \underbrace{\text{is at most}}_{\leq} \quad \underbrace{\$200.}_{200}$

Step 4
$$125 + 0.15m \leq 200$$
$$0.15m \leq 75$$
$$m \leq 500$$

$\therefore$ Mike can travel 500 mi or less and still spend no more than \$200.

Step 5 *Check:* Is the number of miles the most possible?
Suppose Mike traveled 501 mi.

$$125 + 0.15(501) \stackrel{?}{\leq} 200$$
$$200.15 \leq 200 \quad \text{False}$$

$\therefore$ Mike can travel at most 500 mi. ***Answer***

Example 3 The width of a rectangular computer screen is 20 cm less than twice the length. The perimeter is at least 53 cm. Find the minimum dimensions, in centimeters, of the screen if each dimension is an integer.

Solution

Step 1 The problems asks for the minimum length and width in centimeters.

You are told that:
a. the length and width are integers;
b. the width is 20 cm less than twice the length;
c. the perimeter is at least 53 cm.

Step 2 Let l = the length in centimeters.
Then $2l - 20$ = the width in centimeters.

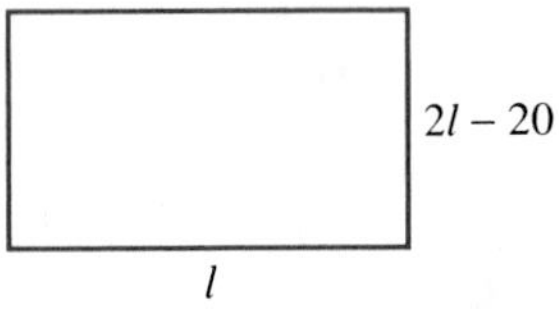

Step 3 $\underbrace{\text{The perimeter}}_{2l + 2(2l - 20)} \quad \underbrace{\text{is at least}}_{\geq} \quad \underbrace{\text{53 cm.}}_{53}$

Step 4 $2l + 2(2l - 20) \geq 53$

$$2l + 4l - 40 \geq 53$$
$$6l - 40 \geq 53$$
$$6l \geq 93$$
$$l \geq 15.5$$

$\therefore$ the minimum integral length is 16 cm.
The minimum width is $2(16) - 20$, or 12 cm.

Step 5 *Check:* Is the perimeter at least 56 cm?

$$2(16) + 2(12) \stackrel{?}{\geq} 56$$
$$56 \geq 56 \quad \checkmark$$

Are the dimensions the least possible?
Suppose the length is the next smaller integer, 15.
Then the width would be $2(15) - 20$, or 10 cm.
Is the perimeter at least 56 cm?

$$2(15) + 2(10) \stackrel{?}{\geq} 56$$
$$50 \geq 56 \quad \text{False}$$

$\therefore$ the dimensions are 16 cm and 12 cm. ***Answer***

Written Exercises

For each of the following:
a. Choose a variable to represent the number indicated in color.
b. Use the variable to write an inequality based on the given information. (Do not solve.)

A

1. Ilene, who is not yet 21 years old, is two years older than Ida.
(Ida's age)
2. After addressing 75 envelopes, a political volunteer has fewer than 26 envelopes left to address.
(the total number of envelopes the volunteer needs to address)
3. A sales executive traveled a certain number of kilometers by airplane and then one tenth as far by automobile. Her total trip was more than 3000 km.
4. Clark and John cut the grass of a neighbor's lawn. Clark started the job and then John finished the job, working $\frac{1}{2}$ hour longer than Clark. The job took at least 2 hours.
(the number of hours Clark worked)
5. Beth's balance in her checking account is \$75. She must deposit enough money in her account to be able to pay the telephone bill, which is \$110.
(the amount of deposit)

For each of the following:
a. Choose a variable to represent the number indicated in color.
b. Use the variable to write an inequality based on the given information. (Do not solve.)

6. The length of a rectangle is 4 cm longer than the width. The perimeter is no more than 28 cm.

7. In a marathon Peter ran 15 more kilometers than half the number Juan ran. Peter ran at most 36 km.

8. The cost for Rhoda to operate her car for one month was at least \$190. The cost for gas and repairs was one half the amount of the monthly payment on the car loan.

9. The sum of three consecutive odd integers is no less than 51. (the middle integer)

10. The product of two consecutive odd integers is at most 255. (the greater integer)

B **11.** Two trucks start from the same point at the same time, but travel in opposite directions. One truck travels at 86 km/h, the other at 78 km/h. After some hours of traveling, the trucks are at least 650 km apart.

12. If a motorist drove 10 mi/h faster, then he would travel farther in 3 h than he does in 4 h at his present speed.

13. A coin bank containing only nickels, dimes, and quarters has twice as many nickels as dimes and one third as many quarters as nickels. The total value of the coins does not exceed \$2.80. (the number of dimes)

14. At a school cafeteria, a student paid \$1.25 for a whole-wheat muffin and a glass of milk. The milk cost less than two thirds of the cost of the muffin.

15. A dowel 25 cm long is cut into two pieces. One piece is at least 1 cm longer than twice the length of the shorter piece.

16. The greater of two consecutive even integers is at most 50 less than five times the smaller.

17. The sum of two consecutive even integers is no more than 100 less than one eighth of the smaller integer.

18. The sum of three consecutive odd integers is more than 60 decreased by twice the smallest of the three integers. (the greatest integer)

In Exercises 19–20, express in symbols the property that is stated in words.

C **19.** The absolute value of the sum of two real numbers is no greater than the sum of the absolute values of the numbers.

20. The sum of the squares of two integers is no less than twice the product of the integers.

Problems

Solve.

A

1. After selling a dozen copies of the *Daily Bulletin,* a newsdealer had fewer than 75 copies left. How many copies did the newsdealer have originally?
2. A house and lot together cost more than \$89,000. The house costs \$1000 more than seven times the cost of the lot. How much does the lot cost?
3. Martha wants to rent a car for a week and to pay no more than \$130. How far can she drive if the car rental costs \$94 a week plus \$.12 a mile?
4. Jordan's salary is \$1250 a month plus a 5% commission on all his sales. What must the amount of his sales be to earn at least \$1500 each month?
5. The sum of two consecutive integers is less than 55. Find the pair of integers with the greatest sum.
6. The sum of two consecutive even integers is at most 400. Find the pair of integers with the greatest sum.
7. Two trucks start from the same point at the same time and go in opposite directions. One truck travels at 88 km/h and the other travels at 72 km/h. How long must they travel to be at least 672 km apart?
8. Between them, Terry and Shelley have 50 cassettes. If Shelley has more than two thirds as many cassettes as Terry, at least how many cassettes does Shelley have? At most how many does Terry have?
9. A bag contains 100 marbles, some red, the rest blue. If there are no more than $1\frac{1}{2}$ times as many red marbles as blue ones in the bag, at most how many red marbles are in the bag? At least how many blue ones are in the bag?

10. Ken has 22 coins, some of which are dimes and the rest are quarters. Altogether, the coins are worth more than \$3.40. At least how many of the coins are quarters? At most how many are dimes?
11. The length of a rectangle is 4 cm longer than the width, and the perimeter is at least 48 cm. What are the smallest possible dimensions for the rectangle?
12. A pair of consecutive integers has the property that 7 times the smaller is less than 6 times the greater. What are the greatest such integers?

B

13. At 1 P.M. two trains, traveling toward each other, leave from towns that are 312 km apart. One train averages at most 82 km/h, and the other at most 74 km/h. What is the earliest possible time for them to meet?

14. If Maura were able to increase her average cycling speed by 3.5 km/h, she would be able to cover in 2 h a distance at least as great as that which now takes 3 h. What is her best average speed at present?

15. There are three exams in a marking period. A student received grades of 75 and 81 on the first two exams. What grade must the student earn on the last exam to get an average of no less than 80 for the marking period?

16. Betty earns a salary of $14,000 per year plus an 8% commission on all her sales. How much must her sales be if her annual income is to be no less than $15,600?

17. A mechanic earns $20 an hour, but 25% of his earnings are deducted for taxes and various types of insurance. What is the least number of hours the mechanic must work in order to have no less than $450 in after-tax income?

18. At least how many grams of copper must be alloyed with 387 g of pure silver to produce an alloy that is no more than 90% pure silver?

19. Randy walked at the rate of 5.2 km/h in a straight path from his campsite to a ranch. He returned immediately on horseback at the rate of 7.8 km/h. Upon his return, he found that he had been gone no more than 3.5 h. At most how far is it from his campsite to the ranch?

20. The length of a rectangle exceeds the width by 10 cm. If each dimension were increased by 3 cm, the area would be no less than 111 cm^2 more. What are the least possible dimensions of the rectangle?

C **21.** During the first week of their vacation trip, the Gomez family spent $200 more than three fifths of their vacation money and had more than $400 less than half of it left. If they started their trip with a whole number of dollars, what was the greatest amount of vacation money they could have had?

22. Three consecutive integers have the property that the difference of the squares of the middle integer and the least integer exceeds the largest integer by more than 3. Find the three smallest consecutive integers having this property.

23. Verna decided to sell her collection of paperback books. To Fred, she sold 2 books, and one fifth of what was left. Later to Joan she sold 6 books, and one fifth of what then remained. If she sold more books to Fred than to Joan, what was the least possible number of books in her original collection?

Mixed Review Exercises

Solve.

1. $|s| = 7$ **2.** $|2 - 5| = k$ **3.** $|y| - 2 = 10$

4. $3|b| = 12$ **5.** $x = |-2 - (-6)|$ **6.** $p = -|7 - 10|$

Factor completely.

7. $x^2 + 15x + 36$ **8.** $x^3 - 5x^2 - 24x$ **9.** $49x^2 - 25$

10. $2y^2 + y - 3$ **11.** $x^2 + 6xy + 9y^2$ **12.** $16x^3 - 4x$

Self-Test 1

Vocabulary inequality (p. 458)
sides of an inequality (p. 458)
solutions of an inequality (p. 458)
solution set of an inequality (p. 458)
graph of an inequality (p. 458)
equivalent inequalities (p. 463)

1. Translate "-3 is between -7 and -2" into symbols. **Obj. 10-1, p. 457**

2. Solve $4x + 7 \leq 15$ if the domain of x is $\{-3, -2, -1, 0, 1, 2, 3\}$.

Solve and graph.

3. $r - 4 < -3$ **4.** $5 - 3t \leq 20$ **Obj. 10-2, p. 462**

Solve.

5. A purse contains 26 coins, some of which are dimes and the rest nickels. Altogether, the coins are worth more than \$2.10. At least how many dimes are in the purse? **Obj. 10-3, p. 469**

Check your answers with those at the back of the book.

Challenge

What is wrong with the following "proof" that $0 > 3$?

$$a > 3$$
$$3a > 3(3)$$
$$3a - a^2 > 9 - a^2$$
$$a(3 - a) > (3 - a)(3 + a)$$
$$a > 3 + a$$
$$\therefore 0 > 3$$

Extra / *Intersection and Union of Sets*

The diagrams below, called *Venn diagrams,* show how shading can be used to represent the relationships among the sets:

$$A = \{1, 2, 3, 4, 5\}$$
$$B = \{2, 4, 6\}$$
$$C = \{7, 8\}$$

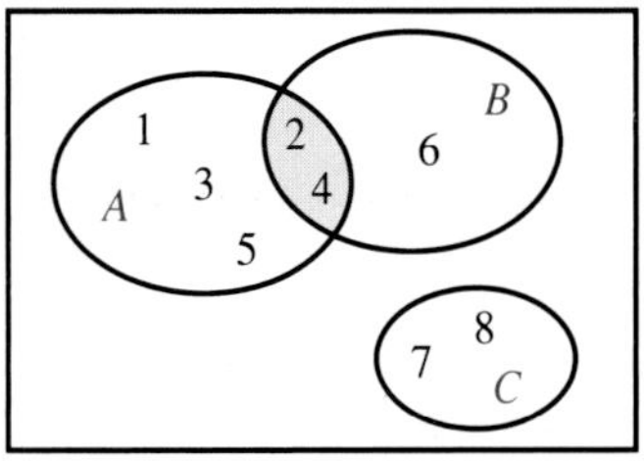

$A \cap B = \{2, 4\}$

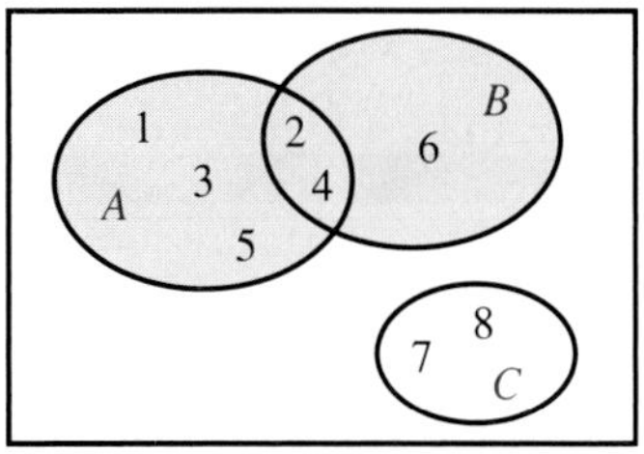

$A \cup B = \{1, 2, 3, 4, 5, 6\}$

To find the *intersection* of A and B, we shade the region consisting of those members and only those members *common to both* set A and set B. From the diagram at the left above, you can see that the intersection of $\{1, 2, 3, 4, 5\}$ and $\{2, 4, 6\}$ is $\{2, 4\}$. This is written

$$\{1, 2, 3, 4, 5\} \cap \{2, 4, 6\} = \{2, 4\}.$$

Notice in the diagrams that the regions A and C do not overlap. Two sets, such as A and C, that have no members in common are called *disjoint sets*. Their intersection is the empty set: $A \cap C = \emptyset$.

In the diagram at the right above, we shade the region consisting of the members that belong to *at least one* of the sets A and B, in order to find the *union* of A and B. This diagram shows that the union of $\{1, 2, 3, 4, 5\}$ and $\{2, 4, 6\}$ is $\{1, 2, 3, 4, 5, 6\}$. This is written

$$\{1, 2, 3, 4, 5\} \cup \{2, 4, 6\} = \{1, 2, 3, 4, 5, 6\}.$$

Exercises

Refer to the diagram and list the members of each of the following sets.

1. $D \cap E$

2. $D \cup E$

3. $E \cup F$

4. $E \cap F$

5. $(D \cap E) \cap F$

6. $D \cup (E \cap F)$

7. $D \cap (E \cup F)$

8. $(D \cup E) \cup F$

9. $(D \cap F) \cup (E \cap F)$

10. Express $\{6, 7, 8, 9\}$ in terms of D, E, and F.

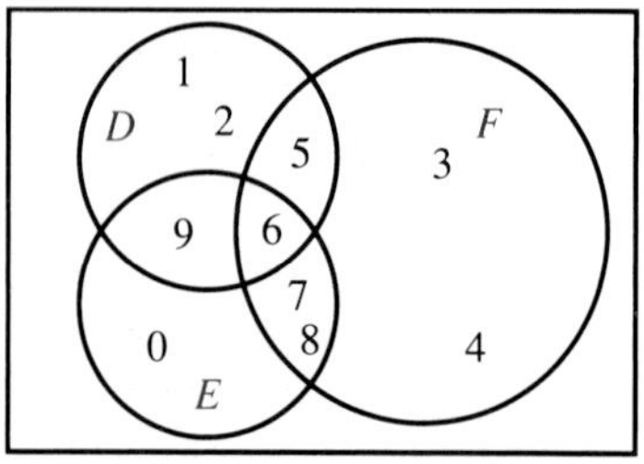

Specify the union and the intersection of the given sets. If the sets are disjoint, say so.

11. $\{-2, -3, -4\}, \{-3, -2, -1, 0\}$

12. $\{-1, 0, 1\}, \{0, 1, 2, 3\}$

13. $\{3, 5, 7\}, \{4, 6, 8\}$

14. $\{6, 8\}, \{5, 6, 7, 8, 9\}$

15. $\{3, 4, 6, 8, 12\}, \{2, 4, 6, 8, 10\}$

16. $\{-5, -4, -3\}, \{-2, -1, 0\}$

In Exercises 17–24, refer to the number lines shown and describe each set.

P = {the real numbers greater than -1}
Q = {the real numbers between -3 and 3}
R = {the real numbers less than 2}

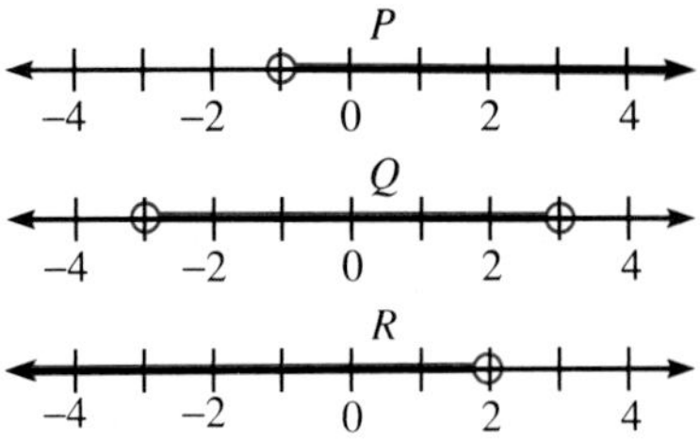

17. $P \cap R$ **18.** $P \cap Q$ **19.** $P \cup Q$

20. $P \cup R$ **21.** $Q \cap R$ **22.** $Q \cup R$

23. $P \cap (Q \cap R)$ **24.** $P \cup (Q \cap R)$

For each of Exercises 25 and 26, make two enlarged copies of the diagram shown at the right. Shade the regions representing the sets named.

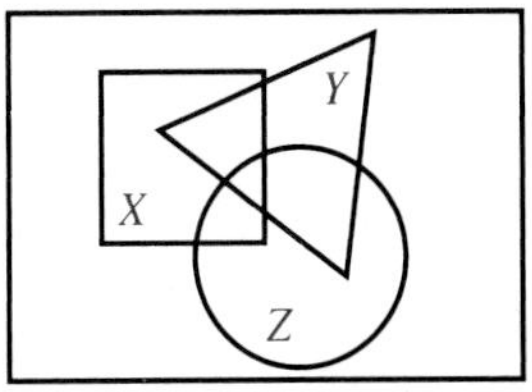

25. $X \cap (Y \cup Z)$; $(X \cap Y) \cup (X \cap Z)$

26. $X \cup (Y \cap Z)$; $(X \cup Y) \cap (X \cup Z)$

27. State a "distributive axiom" that appears to be true on the basis of Exercise 25.

28. State a "distributive axiom" that appears to be true on the basis of Exercise 26.

29. Copy the diagram at the right and write in the remaining members of these sets:

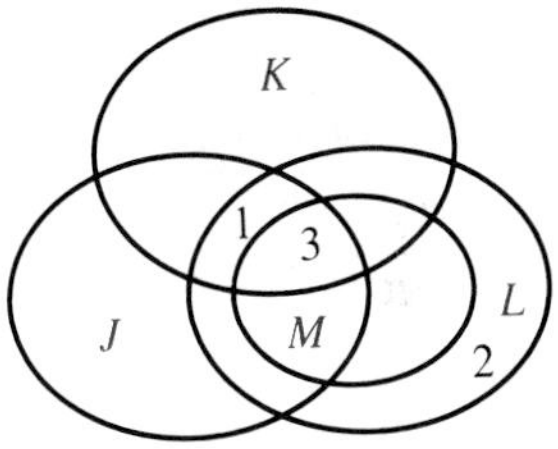

$$J = \{1, 3, 5, 7, 9\}$$
$$K = \{-3, -1, 1, 3, 4\}$$
$$L = \{1, 2, 3, 4, 5, 6, 7\}$$
$$M = \{3, 4, 5, 6, 7\}$$

Historical Note / *The Seqt of a Pyramid*

To check the uniform slope of the faces of a pyramid, the ancient Egyptians determined the pyramid's seqt. "Seqt" was the ratio of rise to run. (Modern architects use the same ratio to describe slope.) The units of measurement were fingers, hands, and cubits. There were four fingers in a hand and seven hands in a cubit.

Problems 56 and 57 of the Rhind mathematical papyrus, a collection of practical problems copied from an earlier document by the scribe Ahmes about 1550 B.C., deal with the seqt of a pyramid. Problem 56 asks for the seqt of a pyramid 250 cubits high having a square base of 360 cubits on a side. Problem 57 asks for the height of a pyramid having a square base 140 cubits on a side and a seqt of 5 hands and 1 finger per cubit.

Combining Open Sentences

10-4 Solving Combined Inequalities

Objective To find the solution sets of combined inequalities.

Each of the four sentences below involves one or two inequalities.

Sentences **Graph**

(a) $-2 < x$

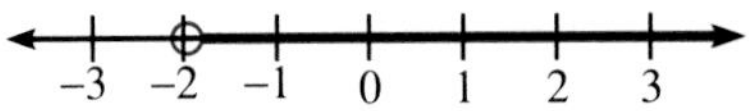

(b) $x < 3$

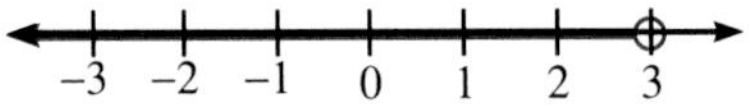

(c) $-2 < x$ and $x < 3$

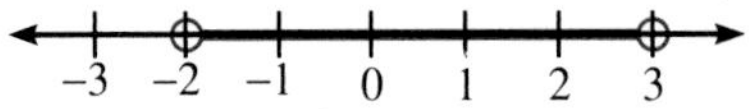

(d) $-2 < x$ or $x < 3$

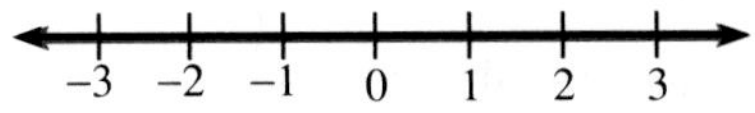

The sentence in (c) is formed by joining the sentences in (a) and (b) by the word and. Such a sentence is called a **conjunction.** To **solve a conjunction** of two open sentences in a given variable, you find the values of the variable for which *both* sentences are true. Note that the conjunction $-2 < x$ and $x < 3$ can be written as

$$-2 < x < 3.$$

The graph of the conjunction consists of the points common to *both* the graph of $-2 < x$ and the graph of $x < 3$. (Notice where the graphs in (a) and (b) overlap.)

In (d) above, the inequalities in (a) and (b) have been joined by the word or. Such a sentence is called a **disjunction.** To **solve a disjunction** of two open sentences, you find the values of the variable for which *at least one* of the sentences is true (that is, one or the other or both are true). The graph consists of all points that are in the graph of (a), the graph of (b), or both.

Remember (page 457) that the disjunction

$$y > 2 \text{ or } y = 2$$

is usually written "$y \geq 2$." Similarly, "$y \leq 2$" means

$$y < 2 \text{ or } y = 2.$$

Example 1 Draw the graph of each open sentence.

a. conjunction: $t < 5$ and $t \geq 5$ **b.** disjunction: $t < 5$ or $t \geq 5$

Solution **a.** No real number can be less than 5 and also greater than or equal to 5.

∴ the solution set is the empty set, and it has no graph. ***Answer***

b. Every real number is either less than 5 or greater than or equal to 5.

∴ the solution set is {the real numbers}, and its graph contains every point.

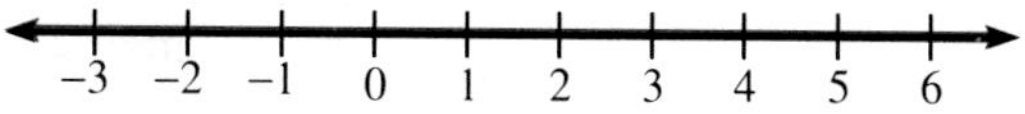

Answer

To solve conjunctions and disjunctions of inequalities, you use the transformations listed on page 463.

Example 2 Solve the conjunction $-3 \le x - 2 < 4$ and graph its solution set.

Solution To solve the inequality $-3 \le x - 2 < 4$, you solve the conjunction:

$$\begin{array}{rcr} -3 \le x - 2 & \text{and} & x - 2 < 4 \\ -3 + 2 \le x - 2 + 2 & | & x - 2 + 2 < 4 + 2 \\ -1 \le x & \text{and} & x < 6 \end{array}$$

$$-1 \le x < 6$$

∴ the solution set is {−1, and all the real numbers between −1 and 6}.

The graph is:

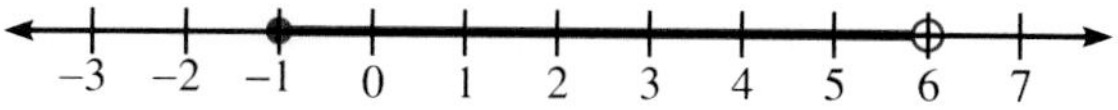

Answer

Below is a more compact way of solving the conjunction in Example 2:

$$\begin{aligned} -3 &\le x - 2 < 4 \\ -3 + 2 &\le x - 2 + 2 < 4 + 2 \\ -1 &\le x < 6 \end{aligned}$$

Example 3 Solve the disjunction $2w - 1 < 3$ or $3w \ge w + 10$ and graph its solution set.

Solution

$$\begin{array}{rcr} 2w - 1 < 3 & \text{or} & 3w \ge w + 10 \\ 2w - 1 + 1 < 3 + 1 & | & 3w - w \ge w + 10 - w \\ 2w < 4 & & 2w \ge 10 \\ w < 2 & \text{or} & w \ge 5 \end{array}$$

∴ the solution set is {5, and the real numbers greater than 5 or less than 2}.

The graph is:

Answer

Oral Exercises

Match each graph with one of the open sentences in a–g.

1. 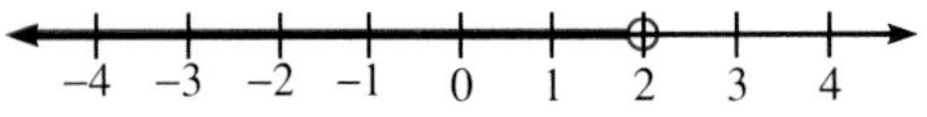

2. 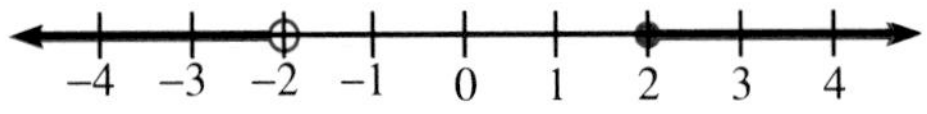

3. 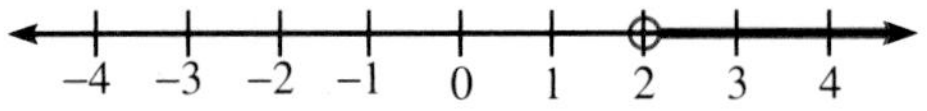

4. 

5. 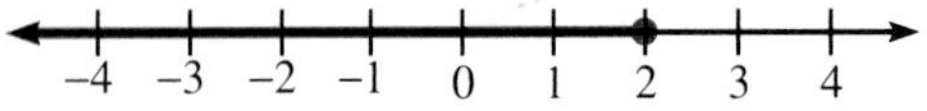

6. 

7. 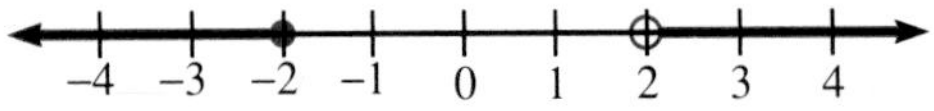

a. $t > 2$

b. $-2 < t < 2$

c. $-2 \le t \le 2$

d. $t \le 2$

e. $t \le -2$ or $t > 2$

f. $t < 2$

g. $t \ge 2$ or $t < -2$

Match each open sentence with an equivalent inequality in a–e.

8. $x = 3$ or $x < 3$

9. $x < 3$ and $x > -1$

10. $x \le 3$ and $x > -1$

11. $x = 3$ or $x > 3$

12. $x \le 3$ and $x \ge -1$

a. $-1 \le x \le 3$

b. $-1 < x \le 3$

c. $x \le 3$

d. $-1 < x < 3$

e. $x \ge 3$

Written Exercises

Draw the graph of each open sentence.

A **1.** $-3 < t \le 2$ **2.** $r > 3$ or $r \le -2$ **3.** $1 \le n \le 5$ **4.** $s < -2$ or $s \ge 0$

Solve each open sentence. Graph the solution set, if there is one.

5. $-2 < a + 1 < 3$

6. $-2 < y - 2 \le 1$

7. $-4 < -3 + d \le 2$

8. $-6 \le 3 + r < 4$

9. $-2 \le 2a + 4 < 8$

10. $-2 < 2b - 1 \le 5$

11. $-5 \le 3m + 1 < 4$

12. $-8 < 3n + 7 \le 1$

13. $y - 2 < -5$ or $y - 2 > 5$

14. $h + 5 \le -2$ or $h + 5 \ge 2$

15. $2x + 1 \le -3$ or $2x + 1 \ge 3$

16. $1 + 2y < -9$ or $1 + 2y > 9$

17. $3n - 1 \le -5$ or $5 \le 3n - 1$

18. $2d - 5 < -7$ or $7 < 2d - 5$

B

19. $-6 \le -x \le 2$

20. $-8 \le -2x \le 6$

21. $-4 \le 2 - t < 3$

22. $-2 < 3 - y \le 1$

23. $-5 < 1 - 2x \le 7$

24. $-7 < -1 - 3x \le 8$

25. $-2m < 4$ and $12 + 2m < 0$

26. $-6r > 18$ or $12 + 3r \ge 0$

27. $-8 \le -1 - s < -3$

28. $-9 < -10 - p \le -4$

29. $5 - v > 7$ or $v - 5 > 7$

30. $t - 5 \ge 2$ or $5 - t \ge 2$

31. $5 - 2p \ge 11$ or $5 - 2p < -1$

32. $7 - 3q \ge 10$ and $3q - 7 \ge 2$

33. $2d - 5 \ge -8$ and $-2d - 5 < d - 3$

34. $9 - y \le 3 - 2y$ and $-1 - 2y \ge -5$

C

35. $6 - c < 2c + 3 \le 8 + c$

36. $5 - d \le 3 - 2d$ or $d + 2 > 3d - 2$

37. $2(1 - w) \ge 6$ or $4w - 5 \le 3w - 1$

38. $1 - 4m \le 3 - 5m \le m - 3$

39. Find an example of real values of a, b, c, and d for which the following statement is **(a)** true and **(b)** false.

If $a > b$ and $c > d$, then $ac > bd$.

40. Find a value of k so that the solution set of

$$k - 5 \le x - 6 \le 3$$

will be the same as the solution set of

$$3x - 7 \le 2(1 + x) \text{ and } 5x - 7 \ge 23.$$

Computer Exercises

For students with some programming experience

The sum of two positive integers must be no more than 10, but their product must be at least 9. Write a BASIC program to list all the ordered pairs (x, y) that satisfy these requirements.

Mixed Review Exercises

Choose a variable and use the variable to write an inequality.

1. The net is at least 10 yd away.

2. The temperature cannot exceed 78°F.

3. The weight is at most 150 lb.

4. The trip takes at least 3 h.

5. The cost is not less than $17.

6. The gap is smaller than 2 cm.

7. Her score was at most 340 points.

8. Jane owns at least 5 pairs of shoes.

Evaluate each expression if $k = -4$, $m = 7$, and $x = 4$.

9. $|k - m|$

10. $|m - k|$

11. $|m - x|$

12. $|x - m|$

13. $|k - x|$

14. $|x - k|$

10-5 Absolute Value in Open Sentences

Objective To solve equations and inequalities involving absolute value.

You learned in Lesson 1-9 (page 37) that $|a|$ is the distance between the graph of a number a and the origin on a number line.

$|x| = 3$ means x is 3 units from 0: $x = -3$ or $x = 3$.

$|x| < 3$ means x is less than 3 units from 0: $-3 < x < 3$.

$|x| > 3$ means x is more than 3 units from 0: $x < -3$ or $x > 3$.

On a number line, the distance between the graphs of two numbers a and b is the absolute value of the difference of a and b. Notice that $|a - b| = |b - a|$.

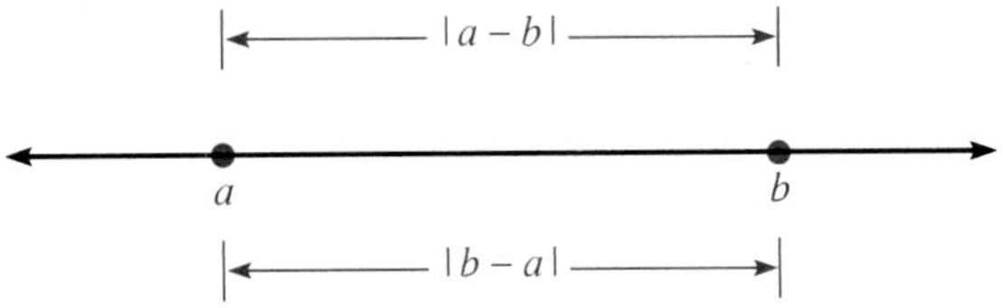

The following examples show how to solve equations and inequalities by two methods: (1) by graphing and (2) by writing the open sentence as a conjunction or a disjunction.

Example 1 Solve $|y - 2| = 4$.

Solution 1 To satisfy the equation $|y - 2| = 4$, y must be a number whose distance from 2 is 4. Thus, to arrive at y, start at 2 and move 4 units in either direction on the number line.

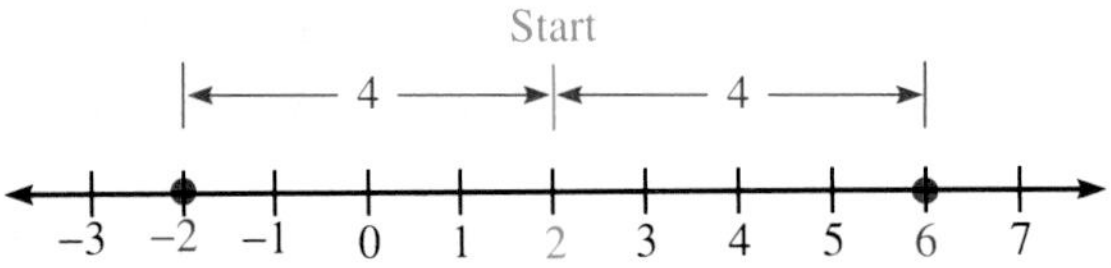

You arrive at 6 and -2 as the values of y.

$\therefore$ the solution set is $\{-2, 6\}$. ***Answer***

Solution 2 Note that $|y - 2| = 4$ is equivalent to the disjunction

$$y - 2 = -4 \quad \text{or} \quad y - 2 = 4$$
$$y = -2 \quad \text{or} \quad y = 6$$

$\therefore$ the solution set is $\{-2, 6\}$. ***Answer***

Example 2 Solve $|x + 1| \leq 3$ and graph its solution set.

Solution 1 Because $x + 1 = x - (-1)$, $|x + 1| \leq 3$ is equivalent to

$$|x - (-1)| \leq 3.$$

Therefore, the distance between x and -1 must be no more than 3.

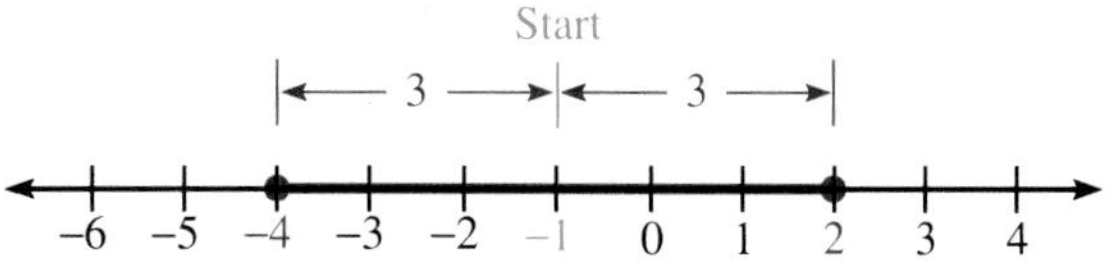

So, starting at -1, the numbers up to and including 2 will satisfy the given inequality, along with the numbers down to and including -4. Thus, the given inequality is equivalent to

$$-4 \leq x \leq 2.$$

$\therefore$ the solution set is $\{-4, 2$, and the real numbers between -4 and $2\}$. The graph is shown above. ***Answer***

Solution 2 $|x + 1| \leq 3$ is equivalent to the conjunction:

$$-3 \leq x + 1 \leq 3$$
$$-3 - 1 \leq x + 1 - 1 \leq 3 - 1$$
$$-4 \leq x \leq 2$$

$\therefore$ the solution set and graph are as in Solution 1. ***Answer***

Example 3 Solve $|t - 3| > 2$ and graph its solution set.

Solution 1 The distance between t and 3 must be greater than 2, as shown in the graph below.

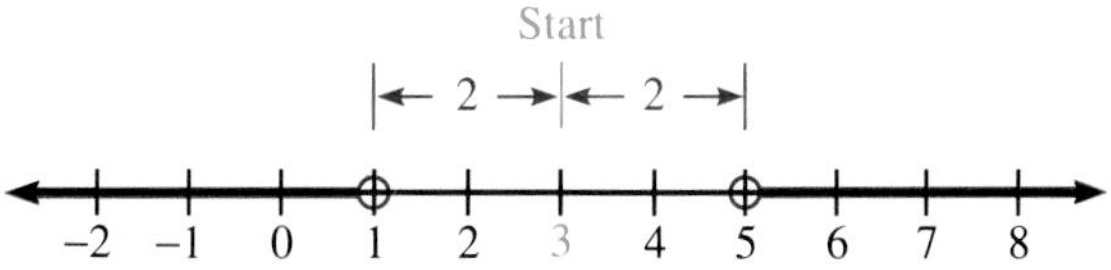

Therefore, the given inequality is equivalent to the disjunction

$$t < 1 \quad \text{or} \quad t > 5.$$

$\therefore$ the solution set is {the real numbers less than 1 or greater than 5}. The graph is shown above. ***Answer***

Solution 2 $|t - 3| > 2$ is equivalent to the disjunction:

$$t - 3 < -2 \quad \text{or} \quad t - 3 > 2$$
$$t < 1 \quad \text{or} \quad t > 5$$

$\therefore$ the solution set and graph are as in Solution 1. ***Answer***

Oral Exercises

In Exercises 1–12:
a. Translate the equation or inequality into a word sentence about the distance between numbers.
b. State a conjunction or disjunction equivalent to the given sentence.

Sample $|r + 2| > 7$

Solution **a.** The distance between r and -2 is greater than 7.
b. $r + 2 > 7$ or $r + 2 < -7$

1. $|x| = 4$
2. $|y| = 3$
3. $|r| > 5$
4. $|p| < 6$
5. $|n - 1| \leq 3$
6. $|n - 2| > 3$
7. $|v + 5| > 2$
8. $|v + 5| < 2$
9. $4 \leq |1 - s|$
10. $3 > |2 - q|$
11. $1 > |2 + m|$
12. $8 \leq |3 + w|$

In Exercises 13–18, match each open sentence with its graph.

13. $|x| \leq 3$
14. $|x| \geq 3$
15. $|x - 3| = 2$
16. $|x + 1| > 1$
17. $|x - 1| = 2$
18. $|3 - x| < 2$

a.
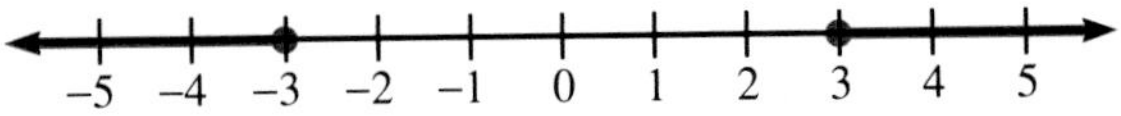

b.
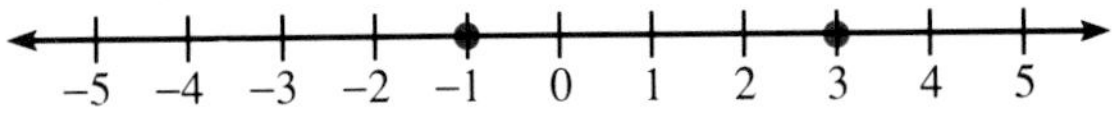

c.
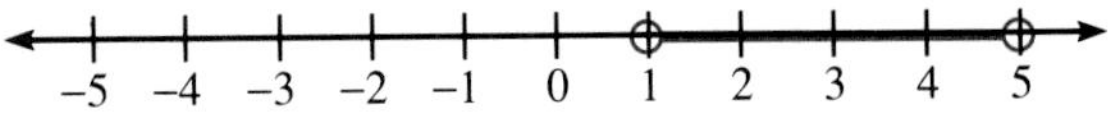

d.

e.
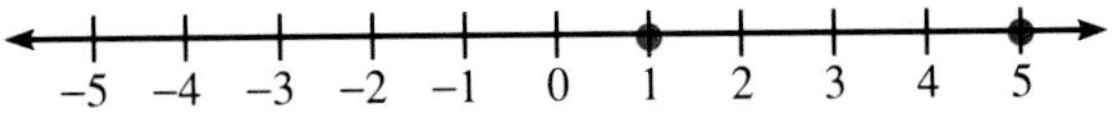

f.

Written Exercises

In Exercises 1–6:
a. Translate the equation or inequality into a word sentence about the distance between numbers.
b. State a conjunction or disjunction equivalent to the given sentence.

A
1. $|x - 5| = 1$
2. $|y + 2| = 2$
3. $|r + 3| > 5$
4. $|p - 7| < 4$
5. $|n - 4| \leq 1$
6. $|n + 6| \geq 3$

Write an equation or an inequality involving absolute value to describe each graph. Use x as the variable.

Sample

Solution The center point of the graph is 1. Since 1 is 2 units from 3 and 2 units from -1, and x represents a number *between* -1 and 3, the distance between x and 1 must be less than 2.

$\therefore |x - 1| < 2$ ***Answer***

7. 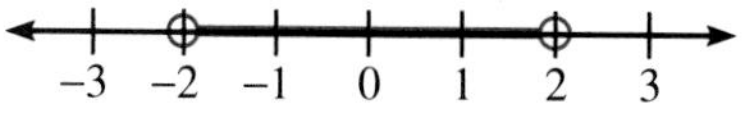

8. 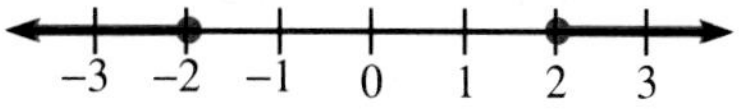

9. 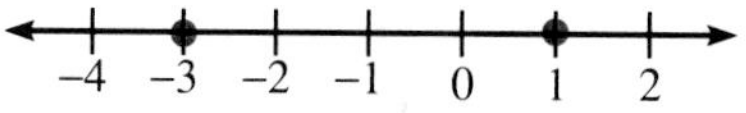

10. 

11. 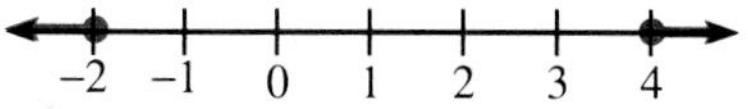

12. 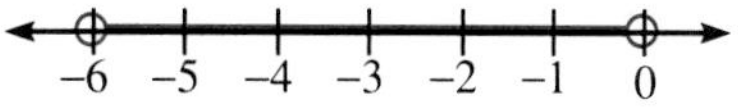

Solve each open sentence and graph its solution set.

13. $|m - 6| = 8$ **14.** $|k + 7| = 3$ **15.** $|3 + x| = 5$

16. $|7 - y| = 4$ **17.** $|r| < 2.5$ **18.** $|s| \geq 1.5$

19. $|y + 5| > 8$ **20.** $|t + 4| < 10$ **21.** $|6 - p| \leq 2$

22. $|4 - v| \geq 5$ **23.** $|-2 - a| \geq 4$ **24.** $|-1 - b| \leq 6$

B **25.** $3|s| - 2 \geq 7$ **26.** $4|p| - 1 < 15$ **27.** $|2 - z| + 3 > 8$

28. $|2 - q| - 3 < 1$ **29.** $4 - 3|r| \geq -7$ **30.** $4 - 3|y| < 1$

31. $6 - |2 - p| \leq 4$ **32.** $8 - |1 - x| > 7$ **33.** $2(3|a| - 1) \leq 10$

C **34.** $|x - 2| = \frac{x}{3}$ **35.** $|y + 1| = \frac{y}{2}$ **36.** $|y - 4| = y - 4$

37. $|t - 4| > t - 4$ **38.** $|n + 5| < n + 5$ **39.** $|n + 5| \geq n + 5$

Mixed Review Exercises

Solve each inequality and graph its solution set.

1. $x - 5 < 4$ **2.** $\frac{x}{2} + 5 < 1$ **3.** $10 < 5(2 + m)$

4. $-1 < x + 5 < 2$ **5.** $h + 1 \leq 10$ or $h - 5 > 7$ **6.** $3 \leq -x \leq 10$

Simplify. Assume that no denominator is zero.

7. $\frac{20x}{3y^2} \div 5xy$ **8.** $\left(\frac{2a}{b}\right)^3 \cdot \left(\frac{4b^2}{3a}\right)$ **9.** $\frac{x + 4}{3} - \frac{2x}{9}$ **10.** $3x + \frac{x}{7}$

10-6 Absolute Values of Products in Open Sentences

Objective To extend your skill in solving open sentences that involve absolute value.

Example 1 Solve $|2p - 3| = 7$.

Solution $|2p - 3| = 7$ is equivalent to the disjunction:

$$
\begin{array}{rcl}
2p - 3 = -7 & \text{or} & 2p - 3 = 7 \\
2p - 3 + 3 = -7 + 3 & & 2p - 3 + 3 = 7 + 3 \\
2p = -4 & & 2p = 10 \\
\frac{2p}{2} = \frac{-4}{2} & & \frac{2p}{2} = \frac{10}{2} \\
p = -2 & \text{or} & p = 5
\end{array}
$$

$\therefore$ the solution set is $\{-2, 5\}$. ***Answer***

You can use a number line to solve the open sentence in Example 1. First consider the following statements about the absolute value of a product of two numbers.

$$|-7 \cdot 4| = |-28| = 28 = 7 \cdot 4 = |-7| \cdot |4|$$
$$|(-5) \cdot (-3)| = |15| = 15 = 5 \cdot 3 = |-5| \cdot |-3|$$

The statements above suggest that the absolute value of a product of numbers equals the products of their absolute values: $|ab| = |a| \cdot |b|$. Using this property, you see that:

$$|2p - 3| = 7$$
$$\left|2\left(p - \frac{3}{2}\right)\right| = 7$$
$$|2| \cdot \left|p - \frac{3}{2}\right| = 7$$
$$2\left|p - \frac{3}{2}\right| = 7$$
$$\left|p - \frac{3}{2}\right| = \frac{7}{2}$$

Therefore, the distance between p and $\frac{3}{2}$ is $\frac{7}{2}$.

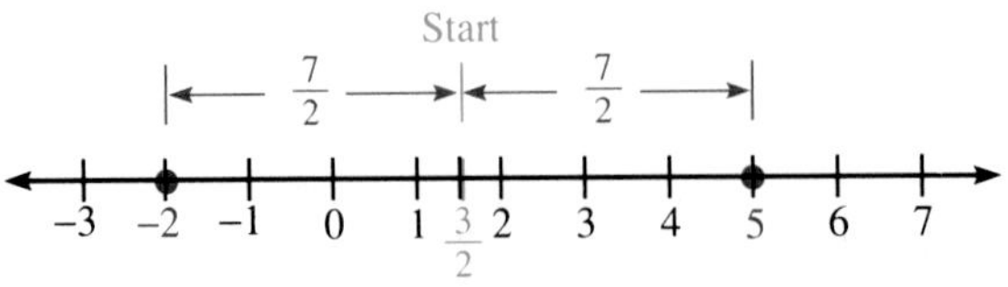

Starting at $\frac{3}{2}$ the numbers -2 and 5 are exactly $\frac{7}{2}$ units away in either direction. Therefore, the solution set is $\{-2, 5\}$.

Example 2 Solve $|10 - 2k| \geq 6$ and graph its solution set.

Solution 1

$$|10 - 2k| \geq 6$$
$$|(-2)(k - 5)| \geq 6$$
$$|-2| \cdot |k - 5| \geq 6$$
$$2|k - 5| \geq 6$$
$$\therefore \quad |k - 5| \geq 3$$

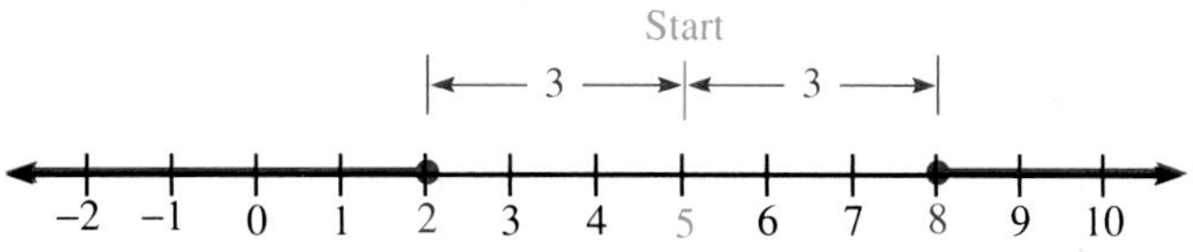

The distance between k and 5 must be 3 or more, as shown above. Thus the given inequality is equivalent to the disjunction

$$k \leq 2 \text{ or } k \geq 8.$$

$\therefore$ the solution set is {2, 8, and the real numbers less than 2 or greater than 8}. The graph is shown above.

Answer

Solution 2 $|10 - 2k| \geq 6$ is equivalent to the disjunction

$10 - 2k \leq -6$	or	$10 - 2k \geq 6$
$-2k \leq -16$		$-2k \geq -4$
$k \geq 8$	or	$k \leq 2$

$\therefore$ the solution set and graph are as given in Solution 1. ***Answer***

Oral Exercises

Express each given absolute value as the product of a number and the absolute value of a difference.

Sample $|16 - 8y|$

Solution $|16 - 8y| = |(-8)(y - 2)| = 8|y - 2|$

1. $|3x - 27|$ **2.** $|5m - 20|$ **3.** $|22 - 11p|$ **4.** $|12 - 4c|$

5. $|2k + 10|$ **6.** $|7n + 42|$ **7.** $|5r - 4|$ **8.** $|2b - 9|$

Written Exercises

Solve each open sentence and graph its solution set.

A

1. $|3x| = 12$
2. $|5y| = 35$
3. $\left|\frac{y}{4}\right| \geq 1$
4. $\left|\frac{t}{3}\right| \leq 2$
5. $|2a - 1| = 9$
6. $|3b - 2| = 7$
7. $|4d - 11| \leq 3$
8. $|5h - 2| \geq 8$
9. $|3 + 4n| \leq 15$
10. $|1 + 8c| > 23$
11. $\left|\frac{y}{5} - 2\right| \geq 4$
12. $\left|\frac{x}{2} - 3\right| \leq 2$

B

13. $|1 - (3 - 2x)| < 18$
14. $|6 - (2y - 3)| \leq 9$
15. $4 + 3|5n + 1| = 13$
16. $2|3k - 7| + 11 = 19$
17. $5 - 4|2 - 3t| > 21$
18. $21 - 4|2 - 5w| > 13$

Classify each of the following sentences as true for all real values of the variable or false for some real value. If you classify a sentence as false, give at least one value of the variable for which it is false.

C

19. $|a^2| = a^2$
20. $|-a^2| = a^2$
21. $\left|\frac{a}{3}\right| = \frac{a}{3}$
22. $|a - 3| < |a + 3|$
23. $|a + 1| \leq |a| + 1$
24. $|a| - 1 \leq |a - 1|$
25. During January in Colton the absolute value of the temperature in degrees Celsius never exceeded 10°. In degrees Fahrenheit, what were the greatest and least possible temperatures in Colton that month? (*Hint:* $C = \frac{5}{9}(F - 32)$, where C and F are the temperatures in degrees Celsius and Fahrenheit, respectively.)

Mixed Review Exercises

Give the slope and *y*-intercept of each line.

1. $y = 4x + 2$
2. $4y = 20x - 8$
3. $2x + 3y + 9 = 0$
4. $y = 9$
5. $3x - y - 11 = 0$
6. $x = -2y + 8$

Graph each equation.

7. $y = -2x + 1$
8. $y = 3x - 2$
9. $x = -6$
10. $y = 5$
11. $y = \frac{3}{2}x + 5$
12. $y = -\frac{1}{3}x - 4$

Self-Test 2

Vocabulary conjunction (p. 478) disjunction (p. 478) solve a conjunction (p. 478) solve a disjunction (p. 478)

Solve each open sentence and graph its solution set.

1. $3x - 1 > 8$ or $2 - x > 0$
2. $-2 \le y + 4 < 5$ **Obj. 10-4, p. 478**
3. $3m + 1 \le -5$ or $3m - 1 \ge 5$
4. $-5 \le 3x + 1 < 4$
5. $|p - 2| = 3$
6. $|3 - n| \ge 7$ **Obj. 10-5, p. 482**
7. $|1 - x| = 6$
8. $|x + 4| < 2$
9. $|4s - 13| \le 7$
10. $|2p - 4| = 10$ **Obj. 10-6, p. 486**
11. $|4m - 7| = 1$
12. $|1 - 6a| < 13$

Check your answers with those at the back of the book.

Career Note / *Pharmacist*

The primary responsibility of a pharmacist is to prepare and dispense medicine prescribed by doctors. Pharmacists are experts in the use, composition, and effect of drugs. Occasionally, it is necessary for pharmacists to "compound" or mix ingredients for a prescription. However, the vast majority of medicines are now prepared by manufacturers rather than by pharmacists.

Many pharmacies offer more than medical and health supplies. An individual owning or managing such a pharmacy orders and sells merchandise, supervises personnel, and handles the finances of the business.

At least five years of study beyond high school are required to receive a degree from a college of pharmacy. During the first few years of study, mathematics and basic science courses are emphasized.

Inequalities in Two Variables

10-7 Graphing Linear Inequalities

Objective To graph linear inequalities in two variables.

The graph of the linear equation

$$y = x + 3$$

separates the coordinate plane into three sets of points:

the points *on* the line,
the points *above* the line,
the points *below* the line.

The regions above and below the line are called **open half-planes,** and the line is the **boundary** of each half-plane.

If you start at any point on the line, say $P(2, 5)$, and move upward from P, the y-coordinate increases. If you move downward from P, the y-coordinate decreases.

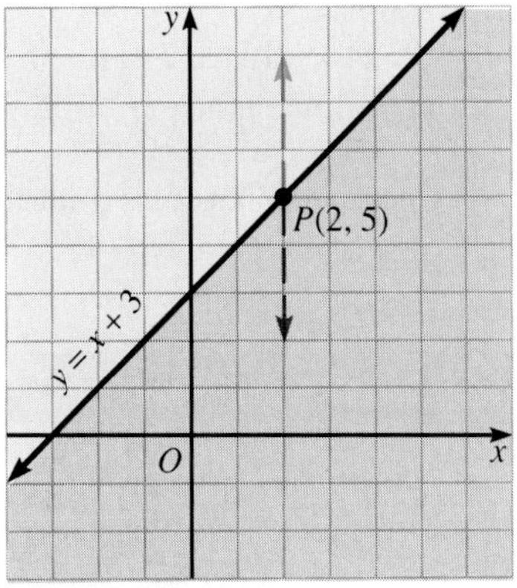

Thus, the upper open half-plane is the graph of the inequality

$$y > x + 3,$$

and the lower open half-plane is the graph of the inequality

$$y < x + 3.$$

The graphs of

$$y > x + 3, \qquad y = x + 3, \qquad \text{and} \qquad y < x + 3$$

completely cover the coordinate plane. The upper half-plane and the boundary line together form the graph of

$$y \geq x + 3.$$

The lower half-plane and the boundary line together form the graph of

$$y \leq x + 3.$$

The graph of an open half-plane and its boundary is called a **closed half-plane.**

The graphs of inequalities are shown by shading. If the boundary line is part of a graph, it is drawn as a solid line. If the boundary line is *not* part of the graph, it is drawn as a dashed line. This is shown by the diagrams at the top of the next page.

(a) $y > x + 3$ (b) $y \geq x + 3$ (c) $y < x + 3$ (d) $y \leq x + 3$

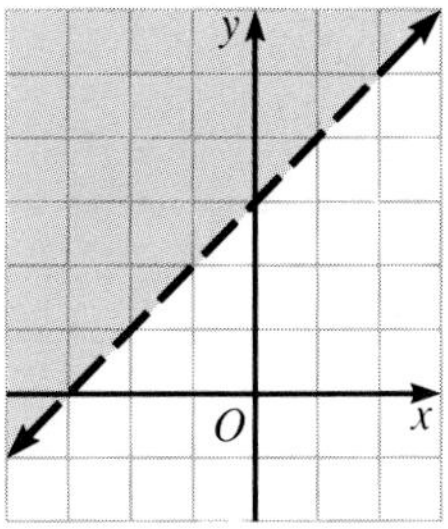

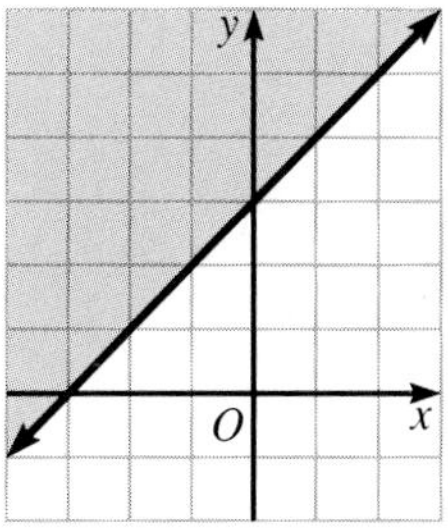

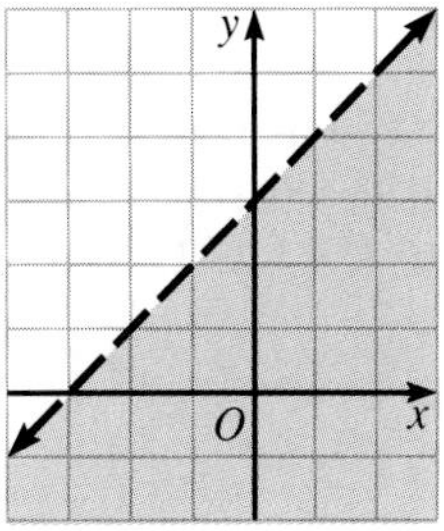

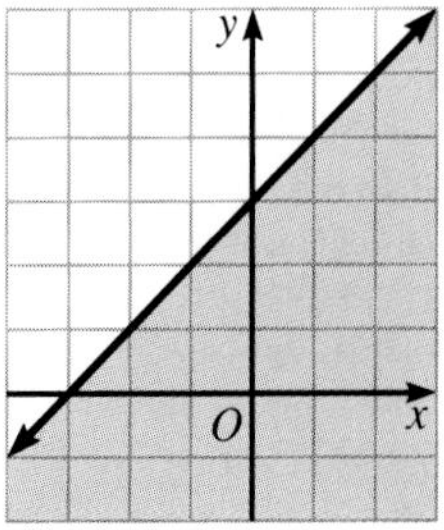

In general, you follow these steps.

To graph a linear inequality in the variables x and y, when the coefficient of y is not zero:

1. Transform the given inequality into an equivalent inequality that has y alone as one side.
2. Graph the equation of the boundary. Use a solid line if the symbol $\geq$ or $\leq$ is used; use a dashed line if $>$ or $<$ is used.
3. Shade the appropriate region.

Example 1 Graph $3x - 2y \geq -4$.

Solution

1. Transform the inequality:

$$3x - 2y \geq -4$$
$$-2y \geq -4 - 3x$$
$$y \leq 2 + \frac{3}{2}x$$

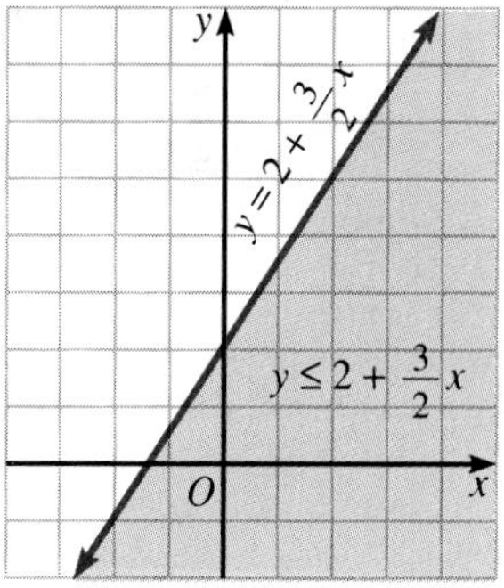

2. Draw the boundary line $y = 2 + \frac{3}{2}x$ as a *solid* line, since the symbol $\leq$ includes the equals sign.

3. Shade the region *below* the line since the symbol $\leq$ includes the less than sign.

Check: Choose a point of the graph not on the boundary, say (0, 0). See whether its coordinates satisfy the given inequality:

$$3x - 2y \geq -4$$
$$3(0) - 2(0) \overset{?}{\geq} -4$$
$$0 \geq -4 \quad \checkmark$$

Thus, (0, 0) is in the solution set, and the correct region has been shaded.

Example 2 Graph $y > 2$.

Solution Graph $y = 2$ as a dashed horizontal line. Any point above that horizontal line has a y-coordinate that satisfies $y > 2$. Therefore, the graph of $y > 2$ is the open half-plane above the graph of $y = 2$.

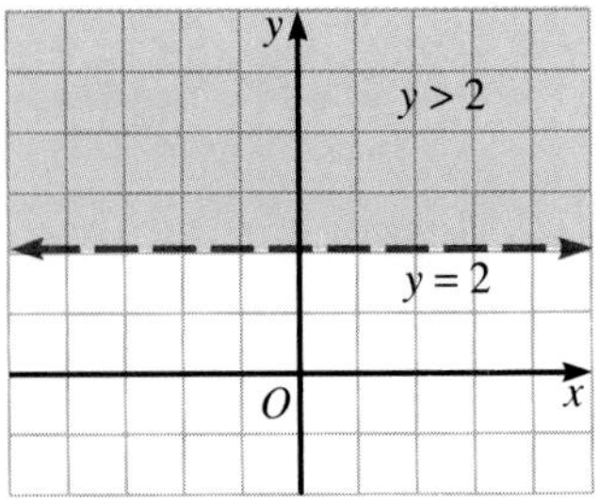

Example 3 Graph $x < -3$.

Solution Graph $x = -3$ as a dashed vertical line. Any point to the left of that vertical line has an x-coordinate that satisfies $x < -3$. Therefore, the graph of $x < -3$ is the open half-plane to the left of the graph of $x = -3$.

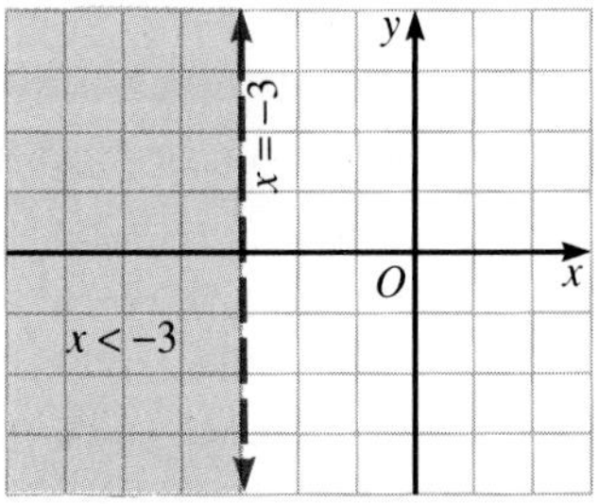

Oral Exercises

State whether the given points belong to the graph of the given inequality.

1. $x \geq 2$; $(2, 3)$, $(-2, 3)$, $(0, 0)$
2. $y < -3$; $(2, -3)$, $(4, -4)$, $(0, 0)$
3. $y < x + 4$; $(4, 2)$, $(-1, 4)$, $(0, 0)$
4. $y \leq 2x - 1$; $(2, 0)$, $(1, 1)$, $(0, 0)$
5. $2x + y < 0$; $(-1, -1)$, $(1, 1)$, $(0, 0)$
6. $x - 3y \geq -2$; $(1, -1)$, $(-1, 1)$, $(0, 0)$

Transform each inequality into an equivalent inequality having y alone as one side. Then state the equation of the boundary of the graph.

7. $x + y < 5$
8. $-x + y > 1$
9. $4x + y \geq 7$
10. $2x + y \leq -2$
11. $2x + 3y > 0$
12. $15x + 5y < 0$
13. $5y < x$
14. $2x > -3y$
15. $x - y \geq 1$
16. $12x - 6y \leq 0$
17. $x - 6y > 24$
18. $6 > x - y$

Written Exercises

Graph each inequality.

A

1. $y \geq 4$
2. $y > 4$
3. $x < 1$
4. $x \leq 1$
5. $x > 0$
6. $y < 0$
7. $y \geq -1$
8. $x \leq -4$
9. $y < x + 5$
10. $y > -x + 1$
11. $y \leq 3 - x$
12. $y \geq 1 - 3x$

Transform each inequality into an equivalent inequality with y as one side. Then graph the inequality.

13. $x + y < 1$
14. $x - y \geq 3$
15. $x - 3y \leq -6$
16. $2x + y > -4$
17. $4x - y > 6$
18. $y - 2x \leq -3$
19. $3x - 2y \geq 8$
20. $3y - 2x < 0$
21. $7x + 4y \leq x - 8$
22. $3y - 1 > 2x - 7$
23. $4(x - y) \geq 3x + 2$
24. $5y - 8 < 2(x + 2y)$

In each of Exercises 25–33, write an inequality whose graph is shown.

B 25.

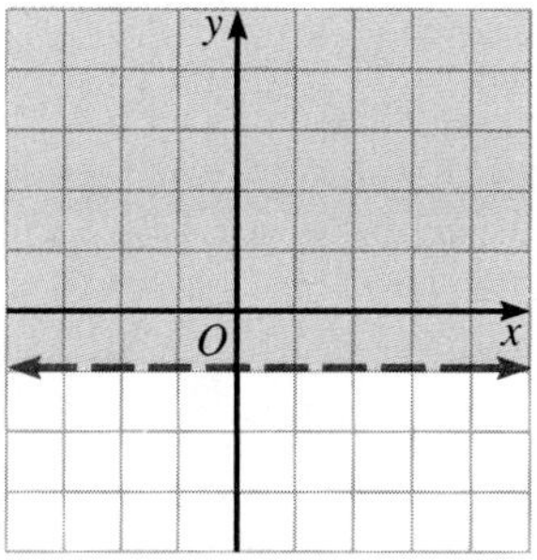

26.

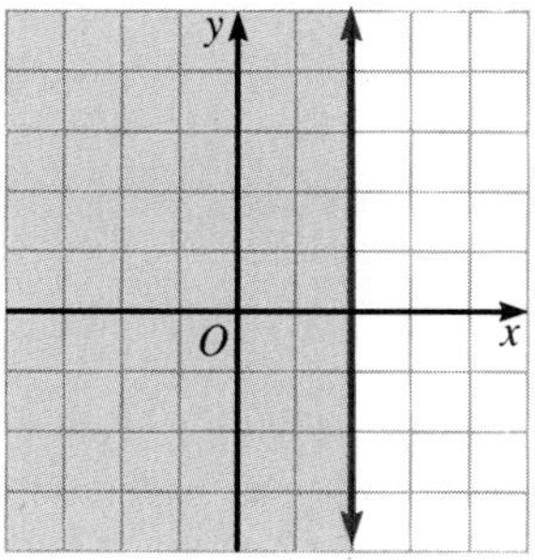

27.

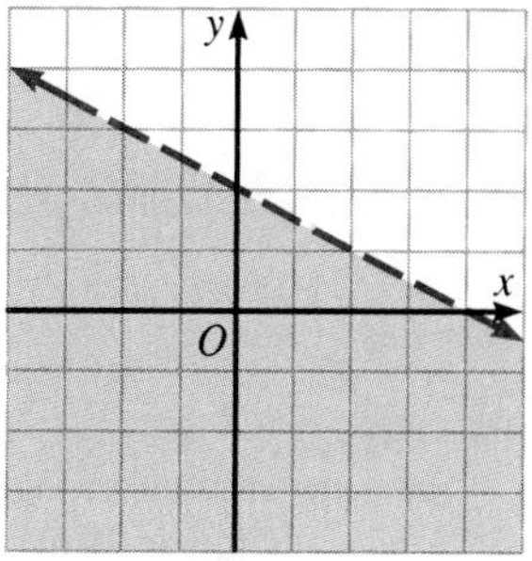

28.

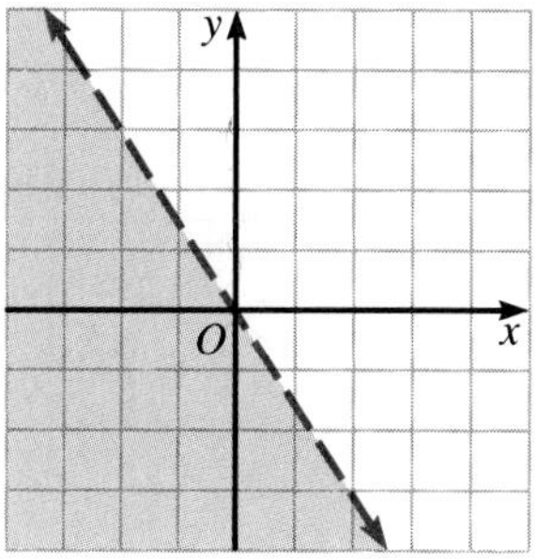

29.

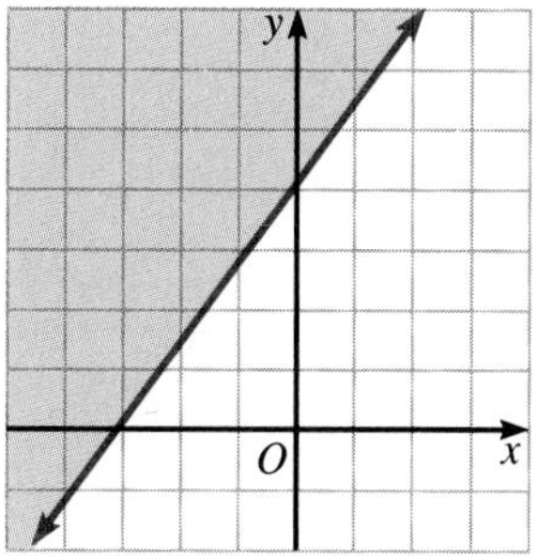

30.

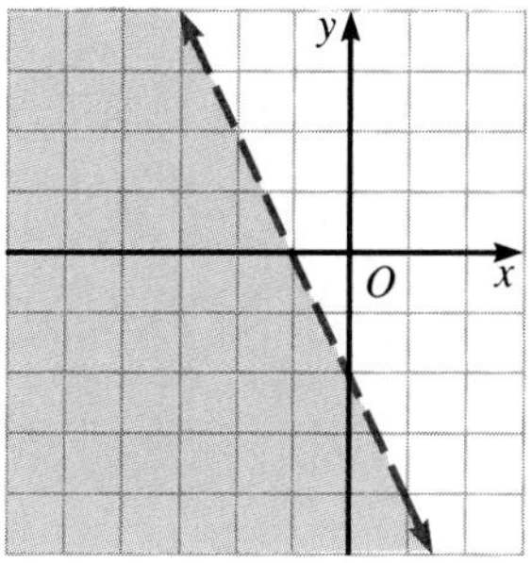

31.

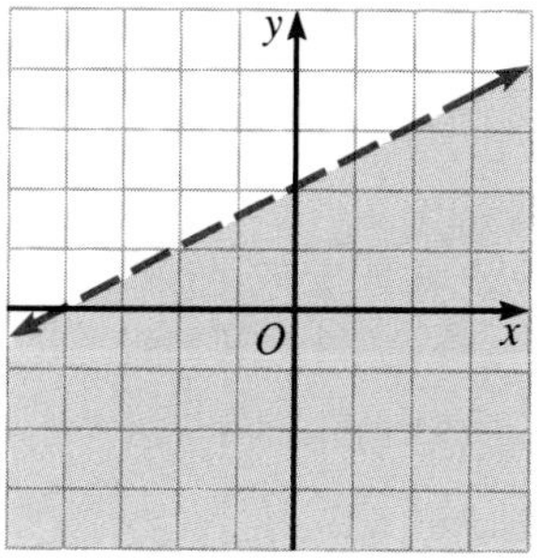

32.

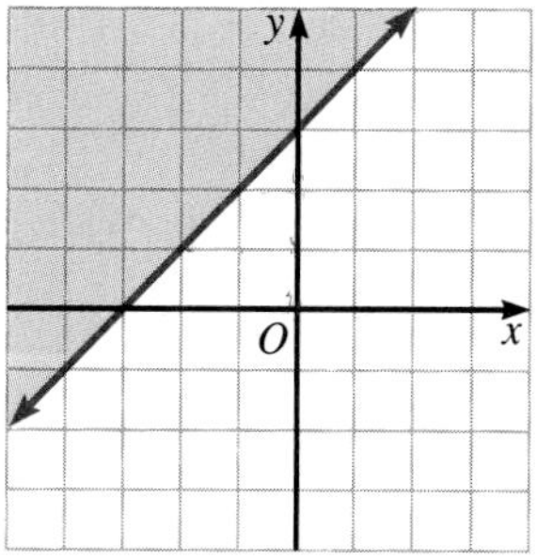

33.

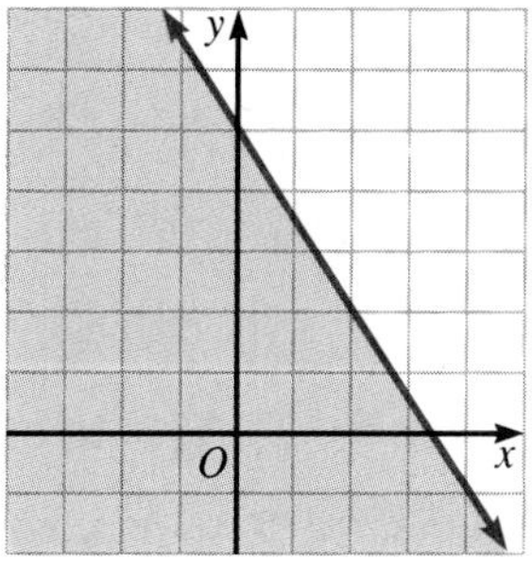

Graph each of the following in a coordinate plane.

C 34. $y = |x|$
35. $y = -|x|$
36. $y > |x|$
37. $y \leq |x|$
38. $|y| > 2$
39. $|y| < 2$

Mixed Review Exercises

Solve each system by whatever method you prefer.

1. $y = 3x$
$x - y = 4$

2. $m + n = 9$
$m - n = 5$

3. $10p + 4q = 2$
$10p - 12q = 34$

Solve each open sentence and graph its solution set.

4. $|4p| = 20$

5. $|3p + 3| = 15$

6. $|3x| < 21$

7. $|2y + 5| \geq 6$

8. $-6 \leq x + 1 < 5$

9. $2x + 5 > 7$ or $2 - x \geq 2$

Extra / The Graph of $y = |ax + b| + c$

The graph of $y = |x|$ is the V-shape shown in black in the drawings below. You can verify this by making a table of values and plotting the corresponding points. Study the different graphs shown in color below. Compare each graph with the graph of $y = |x|$.

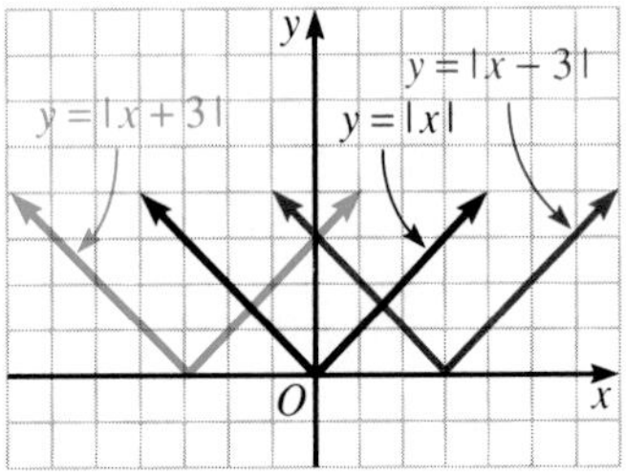

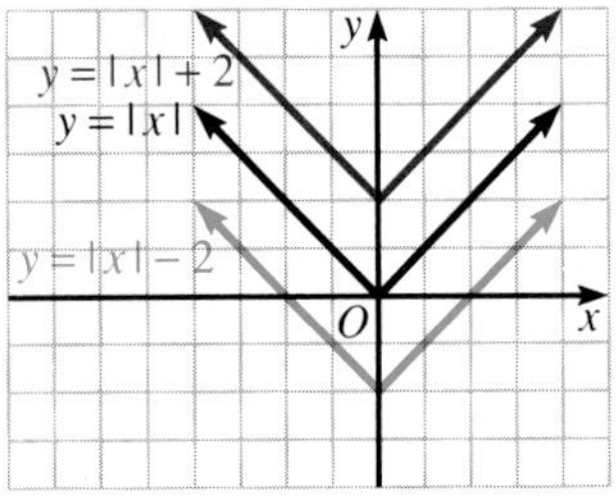

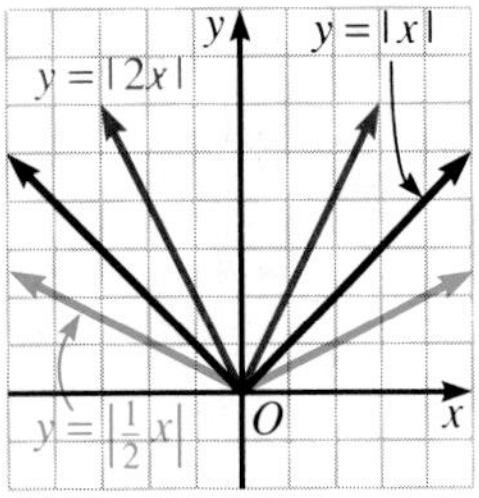

You can see that if you move the graph of $y = |x|$ *to the left* or *to the right* b units, you get the graph of $y = |x + b|$ or of $y = |x - b|$. If you move the graph of $y = |x|$ *up* or *down* c units, you get the graph of $y = |x| + c$ or of $y = |x| - c$. Also, you can see that the graph of $y = |ax|$ is narrower or wider than the graph of $y = |x|$, depending on the factor a.

If you have a computer or a graphing calculator, you may wish to explore what effect the changes in the values of a, b, and c have on the graph of $y = |ax + b| + c$.

Exercises

Graph each set of equations in the same coordinate plane. You may wish to check your graphs using a computer or a graphing calculator.

1. a. $y = |x - 3| + 2$ **b.** $y = |2x - 3| + 2$ **c.** $y = |-2x - 3| + 2$

2. a. $y = |2x + 1|$ **b.** $y = -|2x + 1|$ **c.** $y = \left|\frac{1}{2}x + 1\right| - 3$

10-8 Systems of Linear Inequalities

Objective To graph the solution set of a system of two linear inequalities in two variables.

You can use graphs to find the solution set of a system of linear inequalities.

Example Graph the solution set of the system: $y - x - 3 \leq 0$
$2x + 3y > -6$

Solution

1. Transform each inequality into an equivalent one with y as one side.

$$y - x - 3 \leq 0 \rightarrow y \leq x + 3$$

$$2x + 3y > -6 \rightarrow y > -\frac{2}{3}x - 2$$

2. Draw the graph of $y = x + 3$, the boundary for the first inequality. Use a solid line and shade the region below this line to show the graph of $y \leq x + 3$ (red shading).

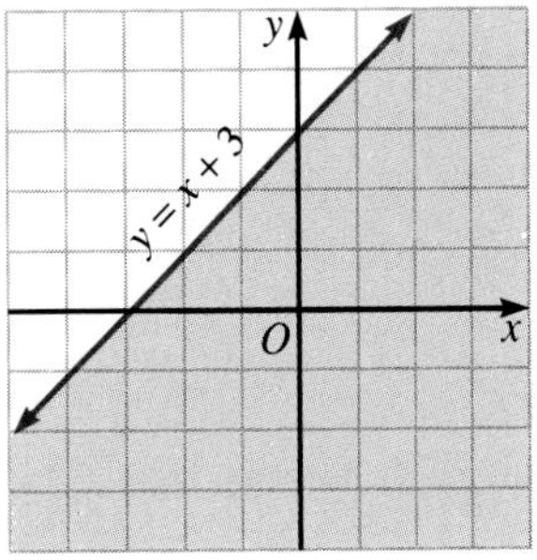

3. In the same coordinate system, draw the graph of $y = -\frac{2}{3}x - 2$, the boundary for the second inequality. Use a dashed line, and shade the region above this line to show the graph of $y > -\frac{2}{3}x - 2$ (blue shading).

4. The doubly shaded region (the intersection of the red and blue shadings) is the graph of the solution set of the given system.

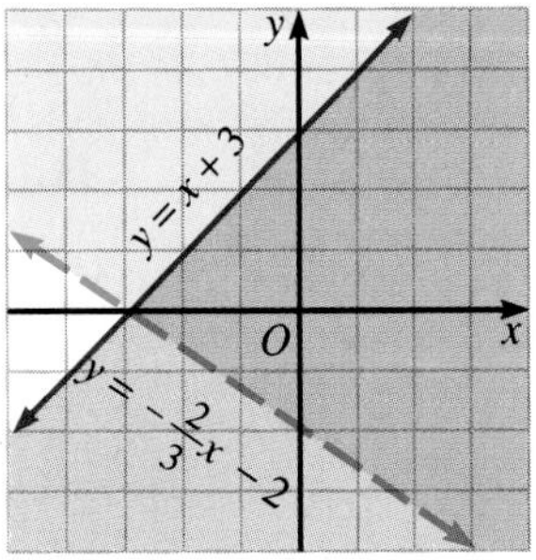

Oral Exercises

Give a system of two linear inequalities whose solution set is shown by the shaded region in each graph.

1.

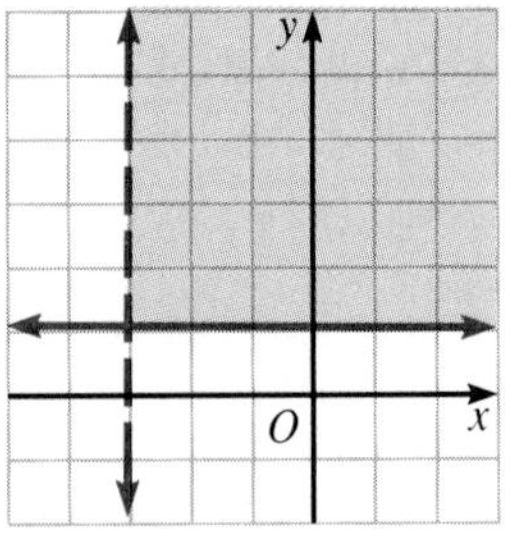

2.

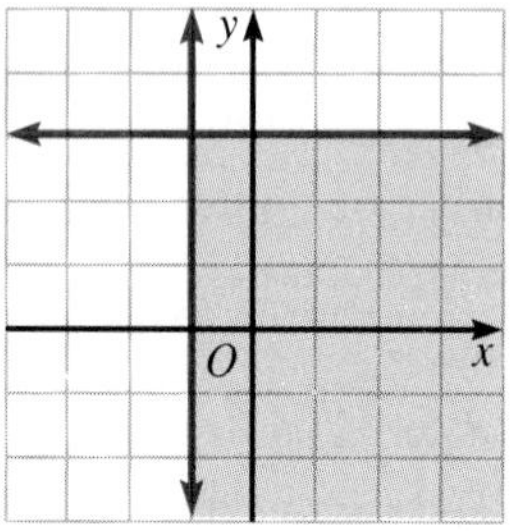

3.

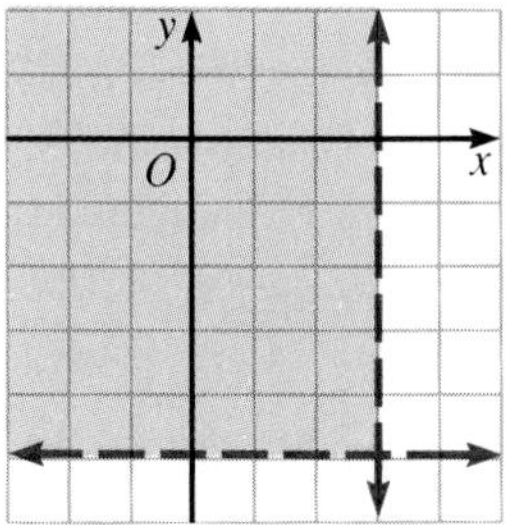

State whether or not each ordered pair is a solution of the system: $y \geq 4$ and $x < 5$.

4. (0, 0) **5.** (5, 4) **6.** (4, 4) **7.** (−2, 4) **8.** (−2, −4)

9. (4, 5) **10.** (5, 9) **11.** (4, 3) **12.** (0, 8) **13.** (0, 4)

State whether each point belongs to the graph of the solution set of the system: $y \leq 2$ and $x - y \leq 5$.

14. (0, −5) **15.** (8, 2) **16.** (−8, 2) **17.** (−8, 3) **18.** (0, 2)

19. (0, 0) **20.** (7, 2) **21.** (0, −6) **22.** (−4, −5) **23.** (−9, 2)

Written Exercises

Graph each pair of inequalities and indicate the solution set of the system with crosshatching or shading.

A

1. $y < 0$, $x \leq 0$

2. $y \leq 5$, $x \geq 1$

3. $y > 3$, $x < -2$

4. $y < -4$, $x > 4$

5. $x < y$, $y > 2$

6. $y > 3x$, $x < 1$

7. $x \leq 3$, $y > 5 - x$

8. $x > -2$, $y \leq 2x + 7$

9. $y \leq x + 1$, $y \geq 2 - x$

10. $y < 4x + 4$, $y > -4x + 4$

11. $y > 2x - 3$, $y < 2x + 6$

12. $y < 5x + 3$, $y > 5 - 5x$

B

13. $x - y \geq 4$, $x + y \leq 6$

14. $x + y \geq 5$, $x - 2y > 8$

15. $3x - y > -1$, $x - y > -4$

16. $x - y < 7$, $x - 3y > 15$

17. $3x - 4y < -12$, $3x + 4y > 0$

18. $2x - 5y > 0$, $x - 4y \leq -8$

Write a system of linear inequalities whose solution set is shown by the shaded region in each graph.

19.

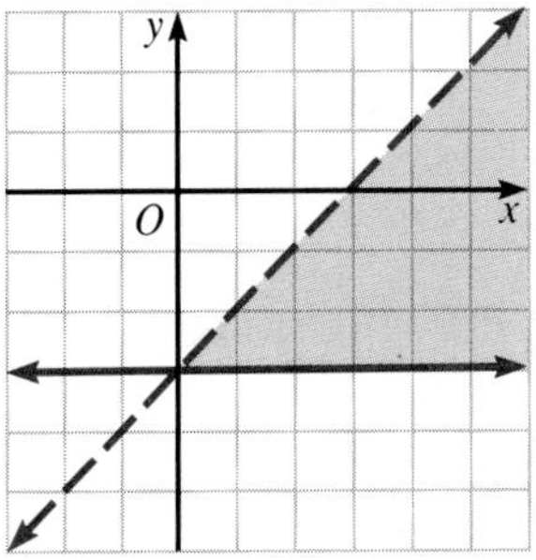

20.

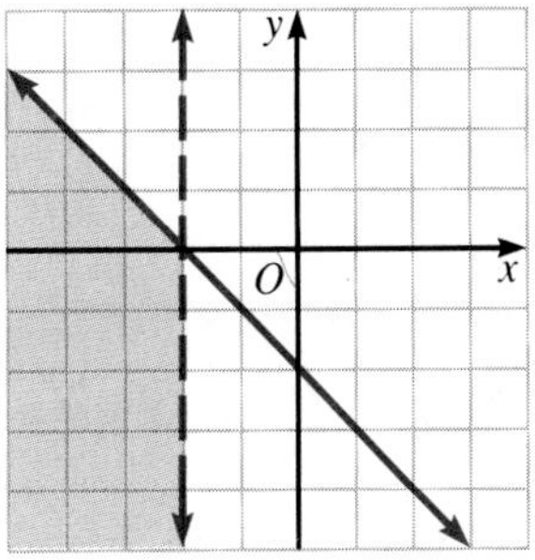

21.

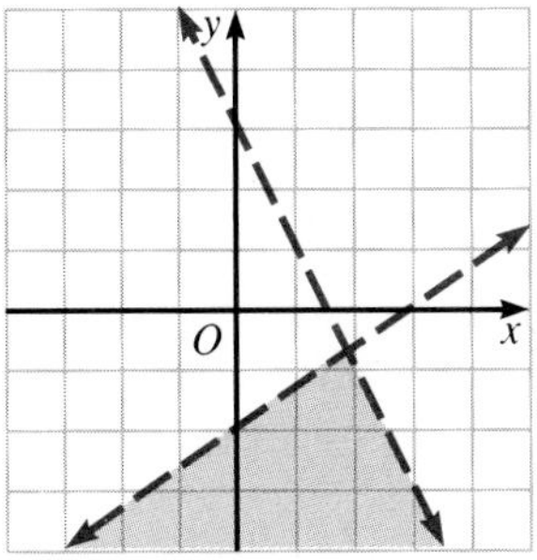

22.

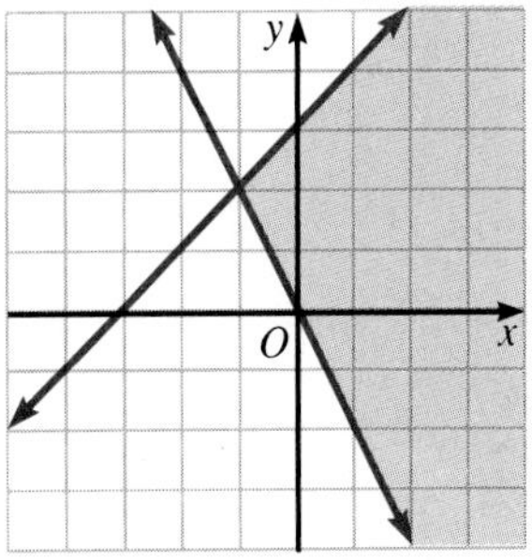

Sample

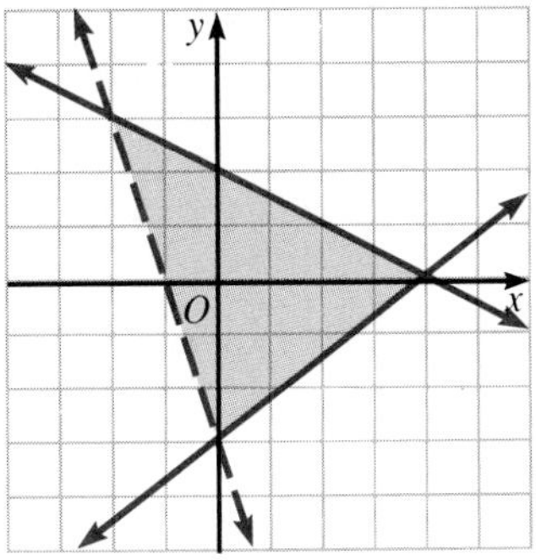

Solution

$y \geq \frac{3}{4}x - 3$

$y > -3x - 3$

$y \leq -\frac{1}{2}x + 2$

C **23.**

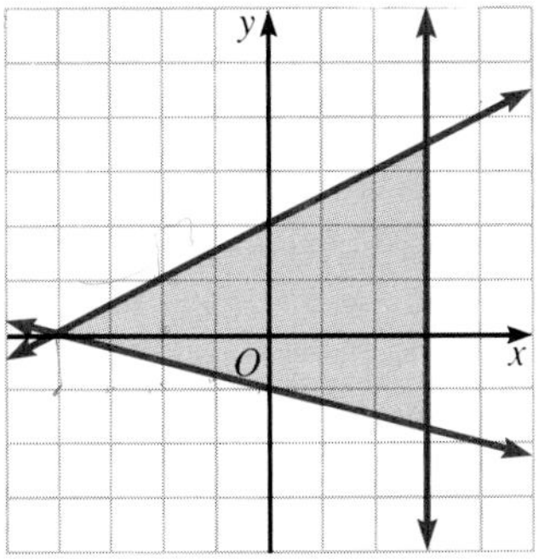

24.

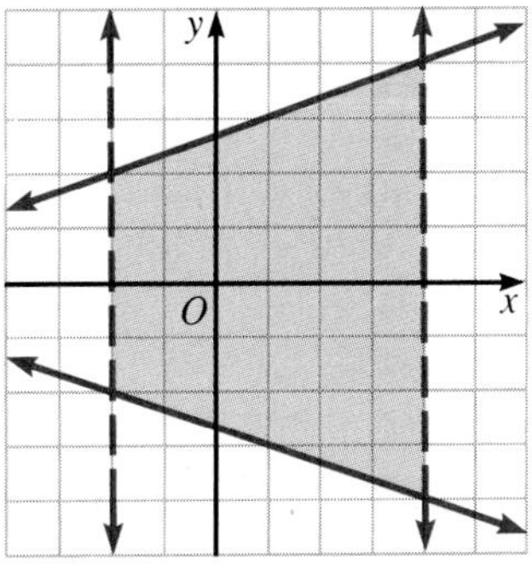

Graph each system of inequalities. Determine exactly the *corner points* of the graph of the solution set of the system, that is, the points where boundary lines intersect.

25. $y \le x$
$y \ge -x$
$x \le 4$

26. $y \ge 2x$
$3y < x$
$y \ge -3$

27. $2x - y \ge 4$
$x \le -1$
$|y| \le 2$

28. $x + 3y \le 6$
$y \ge -1$
$|x| \le 3$

Mixed Review Exercises

Rewrite each group of fractions with their LCD.

1. $\frac{1}{6}, \frac{4}{15}, \frac{3}{5}$

2. $\frac{a}{3}, \frac{2}{9}, \frac{a+1}{12}$

3. $\frac{k}{k+5}, \frac{3k}{k^2+10k+25}$

4. $\frac{2y+3}{y-6}, \frac{4}{y}, \frac{y}{5}$

5. $\frac{8}{x+2}, \frac{x}{x-2}$

6. $\frac{1}{x^2-16}, \frac{5}{4-x}, \frac{x}{4+x}$

Evaluate each expression if $a = \frac{3}{5}$, $b = \frac{1}{2}$, and $c = \frac{5}{12}$.

7. $a + b \div c$

8. $b(c - a)$

9. $a - (b + c)$

10. $\frac{1}{2}(a + b + c)$

11. $c + \frac{1}{2}(b - c)$

12. $b - \frac{1}{2}(a - b)$

Self-Test 3

Vocabulary open half-plane (p. 490) closed half-plane (p. 490)
boundary (p. 490)

Graph each inequality in a coordinate plane.

1. $x > -2$ **2.** $x + 3y \le 9$ **Obj. 10-7, p. 490**

3. Graph the solution set of the system: $x - y > 5$
$3x + y \ge -1$ **Obj. 10-8, p. 495**

Check your answers with those at the back of the book.

Calculator Key-In

You can compare two fractions with the aid of a calculator. First change each fraction to a decimal by dividing the numerator by the denominator. Then compare the decimals.

True or false?

1. $\frac{5}{8} > \frac{9}{20} > \frac{6}{13}$

2. $\frac{17}{23} < \frac{18}{24} < \frac{19}{25}$

3. $\frac{90}{101} > \frac{91}{102} > \frac{92}{103}$

Application / *Linear Programming*

Business decisions aim at making some quantities, such as profit, as large as possible, and other quantities, such as cost, as small as possible. A decision to maximize or minimize a quantity is usually subject to conditions *(constraints)*. If the quantity can be represented by a linear equation, and the constraints can be represented by a system of linear inequalities, the decision problem can be solved by using a branch of mathematics called *linear programming*.

Example A machine shop makes two parts, I and II, each requiring the use of three machines, A, B, and C. Each Part I requires 4 min on Machine A, 4 min on Machine B, and 5 min on Machine C. Each Part II requires 5 min on Machine A, 1 min on Machine B, and 6 min on Machine C. The shop makes a profit of $8 on each Part I and $5 on each Part II. However, the number of units of Part II produced must not be less than half the number of Part I. Also, each day, the shop has only 120 min of Machine A, 72 min of Machine B, and 180 min of Machine C available for the production of Parts I and II. What should the daily production be to maximize the shop's profit?

Solution Let x = the number of units of Part I.
Let y = the number of units of Part II.
Let P = the total profit on Parts I and II.

The data in the problem are summarized in the following chart.

		Minutes on Machine			Profit per Unit
Part	Number	A	B	C	
I	x	4	4	5	$8
II	y	5	1	6	$5
Available Time		120	72	180	

The information in the chart can be expressed by these inequalities:

$4x + 5y \leq 120$ (Total time on Machine A must not exceed 120 min.)

$4x + y \leq 72$ (Total time on Machine B must not exceed 72 min.)

$5x + 6y \leq 180$ (Total time on Machine C must not exceed 180 min.)

$y \geq \frac{1}{2}x$ (Number of units of Part II must not be less than half the number of Part I.)

$\left.\begin{array}{l} x \geq 0 \\ y \geq 0 \end{array}\right\}$ (A negative number of parts cannot be produced.)

You want to find values of x and y that are subject to these inequalities (constraints) and that maximize the total profit, P, where $P = 8x + 5y$.

(Solution continues on the next page.)

Step 1 Graph the solution set of this system of inequalities. The solution set, which is shaded, is called the *feasible region.*

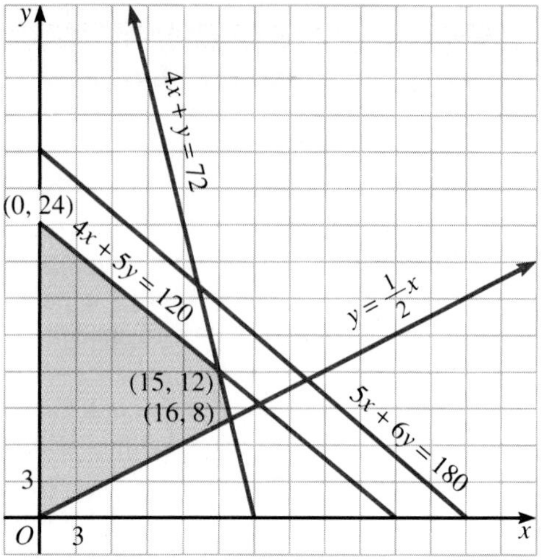

Step 2 Find the points of the feasible region where the boundary lines intersect. These points, called *corner points,* are (0, 0), (16, 8), (15, 12), and (0, 24).

A remarkable fact, proved in more advanced mathematics courses, is that if a maximum or minimum value of a *linear expression* $ax + by$ exists, it must occur at a corner point of the feasible region. You use this fact in the next step.

Step 3 Evaluate $P = 8x + 5y$ at each corner point.

(0, 0): $P = 8(0) + 5(0) = 0$ (15, 12): $P = 8(15) + 5(12) = 180$

(16, 8): $P = 8(16) + 5(8) = 168$ (0, 24): $P = 8(0) + 5(24) = 120$

The maximum value of P, \$180, occurs at (15, 12). The shop should produce 15 units of Part I and 12 units of Part II each day. ***Answer***

Exercises

1. a. Draw the graph of the solution set of the system:

$$x \geq 2y + 4$$
$$x + y \geq -2$$
$$4x + y \leq 4$$

b. Find the corner points of the solution set.

c. Find the maximum and minimum values of $4x + 7y$ subject to the inequalities in part (a).

2. Find x and y to maximize $R = x + 3y$ subject to the constraints $x \geq 2$, $y \geq 1$, $x + 2y \leq 8$, and $x + y \leq 6$.

3. a. A farmer plants two crops, corn and soybeans. The expenses are \$6 for each acre of corn and \$12 for each acre of soybeans. Each acre of corn requires 12 bushels of storage, and each acre of soybeans requires 16 bushels of storage. The farmer has at most 3600 bushels of storage available and \$2400 to spend on expenses. Choose variables for the number of acres of corn and soybeans planted. Write four inequalities that express the conditions of the problem.

b. Graph the solution set of the system of inequalities described in part (a). State the coordinates of the corner points for this feasible region.

c. Suppose that the farmer earns a profit of \$24 for each acre of corn and \$48 for each acre of soybeans. Find two ways the farmer can satisfy the conditions while maximizing the profits. (Notice that a linear programming problem can have more than one solution.)

Chapter Summary

1. The symbols $>$, $<$, $\geq$, and $\leq$ are used to express inequalities. $-2 < 4 < 9$ (or $9 > 4 > -2$) means that 4 is between -2 and 9.
2. Open inequalities can be solved by transformations to obtain simpler equivalent inequalities whose solution sets can be seen at a glance. The graph of the solution set of an inequality in one variable can be shown on a number line.
3. Sentences joined by "and" are conjunctions. A conjunction of two statements is true if and only if both statements are true. Sentences joined by "or" are disjunctions. A disjunction of two statements is true if at least one of the statements is true.
4. The distance between the graphs of two numbers a and b on a number line is the absolute value of the difference between a and b. This concept can be used to solve open sentences involving the absolute value of a variable. These open sentences also may be written as equivalent conjunctions or disjunctions.
5. The solution set of a linear inequality in two variables is an open or closed half-plane.
6. The graph of the solution set of a system of inequalities consists of the points common to the graphs of all the inequalities in the system.

Chapter Review

Give the letter of the correct answer.

1. Which statement is true? 10-1
   a. $-3 < -5 < -7$ **b.** $6 > -4 > 2$
   c. $-9 < -4 < 0$ **d.** $-5 > 2 > 1$
2. Find the solution set of $1 - x \leq 0$ if $x \in \{-4, -2, 0, 2, 4\}$.
   a. $\{-4, -2, 0, 2, 4\}$ **b.** $\{-4, -2\}$ **c.** $\{2, 4\}$ **d.** $\{0\}$
3. Find an inequality equivalent to $-4x < 12$. 10-2
   a. $x > -48$ **b.** $x < -16$ **c.** $x > -3$ **d.** $x < -3$
4. Find an inequality equivalent to $3(3 + y) < 5(5 + y)$.
   a. $y < -8$ **b.** $y > -8$ **c.** $y < 8$ **d.** $y > 8$
5. Write as an inequality: "The sum of two consecutive odd integers is at most 35." 10-3
   a. $n + (n + 1) > 35$ **b.** $n + (n + 1) < 35$
   c. $n + (n + 2) \geq 35$ **d.** $n + (n + 2) \leq 35$

6. Which is the graph of the disjunction $x < -2$ or $x > 4$? **10-4**

a. 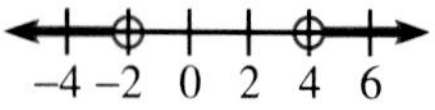

b. 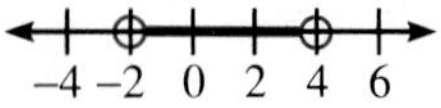

c. 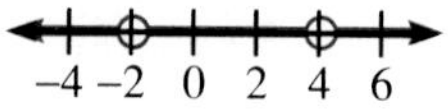

7. Which is the graph of the conjunction $-6 \leq x$ and $x < 4$?

a. 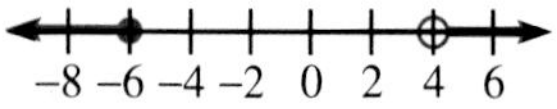

b. 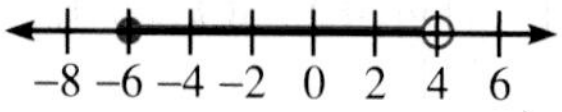

c. 

d. 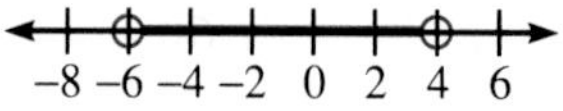

8. Which open sentence states that the distance from r to 3 is greater than 4? **10-5**
   a. $r - 3 > 4$ **b.** $r - 3 \geq 4$ **c.** $|r - 3| > 4$ **d.** $|r - 3| \geq 4$

9. Which inequality is equivalent to $|8n - 4| < 12$? **10-6**
   a. $|2n - 1| < 12$ **b.** $|2n - 1| < 3$
   c. $|4n - 2| < 12$ **d.** $|2n - 1| > -3$

10. What is the equation of the boundary of the graph of $x - 2y > 4$? **10-7**
    a. $y = 2x - 4$ **b.** $y = \frac{1}{2}x - 2$ **c.** $y \leq \frac{1}{2}x - 2$ **d.** $y \geq 2x - 4$

11. Which point belongs to the graph of the solution set of the system: **10-8**
    $x < 2$
    $y \leq 2x + 3$
    a. $(0, 5)$ **b.** $(0, -5)$ **c.** $(-5, 0)$ **d.** $(-3, 5)$

Chapter Test

1. Classify the statement as true or false: $4 > -\frac{1}{2} > -2$. **10-1**
2. Find the solution set of $y + 1 < 3$ if $y \in \{-2, -1, 0, 1, 2\}$.
3. Solve the inequality $5 \geq 2x - 3$ and graph the solution set on a number line. **10-2**
4. Of all pairs of consecutive odd integers whose sum is greater than 75, find the pair whose sum is the least. **10-3**

Solve each open sentence and graph its solution set.

5. $-1 \leq 2c + 1 < 5$ 6. $k + 5 \leq -3$ or $k + 5 \geq 3$ **10-4**
7. $|2 - y| = 3$ 8. $|y + 1| < 12$ **10-5**
9. $|6 - 2x| = 8$ 10. $|2m - 1| \leq 7$ **10-6**

Graph each inequality in a coordinate plane.

11. $x \geq -3$ 12. $y \geq 3 - x$ **10-7**
13. Graph the solution set of the system: $y < 2x + 2$, $y > 2 - 2x$ **10-8**

Cumulative Review *(Chapters 1–10)*

Simplify. Assume that no denominator is zero.

1. $(-7b + 2) + (8b - 5)$

2. $-3x^2(4x^3 - 2x^2 - 11x)$

3. $(3x^3y^4)^5 \div (9xy^8)$

4. $(3x + 5y)(7x - 4y)$

5. $(3c^2 - 4cd + 8d^2)(c - 2d)$

6. $(5t - 7v)^2$

7. $\dfrac{3x^2 - 8x - 3}{9x^2 + 9x + 2}$

8. $(12m^3n^2 - 11r^3)(12m^3n^2 + 11r^3)$

9. $\dfrac{4.8 \times 10^{25}}{2.0 \times 10^{11}}$

10. $\dfrac{z^2 + 8z + 16}{z^2 + 7z + 12} \cdot \dfrac{z^2 - 9}{z^2 + z - 12}$

11. $\dfrac{y^3 + 4y^2 + 3y}{y^2 + 7y + 10} \div \dfrac{y^2 + 3y}{y^3 + 2y^2}$

12. $2 + \dfrac{4}{b - 1} - \dfrac{3b}{b^2 - 1}$

Factor completely.

13. $30z^2 + 240z + 96$

14. $81r^4 - 1$

15. $16z^2 - y^2 - 10y - 25$

Write an equation in standard form for each line described.

16. The line that contains $(-1, 10)$ and $(4, -5)$.

17. The line that has slope $\frac{1}{2}$ and contains $(5, 6)$.

Graph each inequality.

18. $|x - 3| \le 7$

19. $4y + 5 < -7$ or $2y - 1 > 3$

20. Graph the solution set of the system: $\begin{array}{r} x + y < 2 \\ 2x - y \le 0 \end{array}$

Solve each equation, inequality, or system. Assume that no denominator is zero.

21. $|z| - 3 = 4$

22. $5q - 8 = 22$

23. $|z + 1| = 10$

24. $b^2 - 8 = 1$

25. $5(d - 3) = 3(2d - 5)$

26. $(x - 2)(x - 1) = 0$

27. $x^2 + 11x + 10 = 0$

28. $2b^2 + 9b - 5 = 0$

29. $z^3 + 3z^2 - 10z = 0$

30. $\dfrac{18}{x} = \dfrac{3 + 3x}{x}$

31. $\dfrac{b + 1}{b + 2} - \dfrac{b + 2}{b + 1} = \dfrac{1}{b + 2}$

32. $\dfrac{1}{a^2 - a} = \dfrac{3}{a} - 1$

33. $\begin{array}{l} y = 5x - 1 \\ 2x + 3y = 14 \end{array}$

34. $\begin{array}{l} 3r + 2s = -4 \\ 4r - 2s = -10 \end{array}$

35. $\begin{array}{l} 6m + 5n = 4 \\ 4m + 3n = 2 \end{array}$

36. $1 + 3t \le 10$

37. $2 - b > 7$

38. $2|3x - 1| + 1 < 5$

39. Marcy can do a job alone in 5 h. If Mark helps her, they can do the job together in 3 h. How long would Mark take working alone?

40. The units' digit of a two-digit number is 1 less than the tens' digit. Nine times the tens' digit is less than the number with the digits reversed. Find the least such number.

Maintaining Skills

Solve. If the equation is an identity or has no solution, say so. Assume that no denominator is zero.

Sample 1 $12t^2 - 3 = 5t$

Solution

$$12t^2 - 5t - 3 = 0$$
$$(4t - 3)(3t + 1) = 0$$
$$4t - 3 = 0 \quad \text{or} \quad 3t + 1 = 0$$
$$4t = 3 \quad \quad 3t = -1$$
$$t = \frac{3}{4} \quad \text{or} \quad t = -\frac{1}{3}$$

The check is left to you. ∴ the solution set is $\left\{\frac{3}{4}, -\frac{1}{3}\right\}$.

1. $t^2 - 6t - 40 = 0$
2. $x^2 = 15x - 56$
3. $y^2 + 12y + 36 = 0$
4. $n^2 + 400 = 40n$
5. $5z^2 + 4z = 1$
6. $10m^2 + 29m + 10 = 0$
7. $8 + 14z = 15z^2$
8. $21b^2 + 25b + 6 = 0$
9. $9d^2 + 7d = 16$

Sample 2 $\frac{z+3}{z+1} + \frac{z}{z-2} = \frac{2}{z-2}$

Solution Note that $z \neq -1$ and $z \neq 2$.

$$(z+1)(z-2)\left[\frac{z+3}{z+1} + \frac{z}{z-2}\right] = (z+1)(z-2)\left(\frac{2}{z-2}\right)$$
$$(z-2)(z+3) + z(z+1) = 2(z+1)$$
$$z^2 + z - 6 + z^2 + z = 2z + 2$$
$$2z^2 = 8$$
$$z^2 = 4$$
$$z = 2 \text{ or } z = -2$$

The check is left to you. ∴ the solution set is $\{-2\}$.

10. $\frac{1}{x} + \frac{3}{x} = 4$
11. $\frac{2}{3} + \frac{2}{t} = \frac{10}{3t}$
12. $\frac{5}{y} - \frac{4}{y} = \frac{1}{y}$
13. $\frac{a+5}{a} + \frac{2}{a^2} = 1$
14. $y - \frac{y}{y+1} = \frac{1}{y+1}$
15. $\frac{3}{4b-6} - \frac{1}{2b-3} = 0$
16. $\frac{3x}{x+1} - \frac{1}{x} = \frac{x+1}{x}$
17. $\frac{b-2}{b+2} + \frac{b}{b-2} = 2$
18. $\frac{1}{t} - \frac{1}{t+1} = \frac{t+2}{t^2+t}$
19. $\frac{x^2+12}{x^2-4} - \frac{1}{x-2} = \frac{3}{x-2}$
20. $\frac{5}{d-1} - \frac{10}{d^2-1} = 3$
21. $\frac{b^2+1}{b^2-1} = \frac{b}{b-1} + \frac{2}{b+1}$

Preparing for College Entrance Exams

Strategy for Success

Remember that you are asked to determine the *best* answer. More than one answer may be "right" to some degree. Do not choose the first answer that seems reasonable. Be sure to check all possible choices before determining which is the best answer.

Decide which is the best of the choices given and write the corresponding letter on your answer sheet.

1. Which method(s) could be used to solve: $\begin{aligned} 3x - y &= 6 \\ x + y &= 6 \end{aligned}$

I. Graphing II. Multiplication with Addition-or-Subtraction III. Substitution

(A) I only **(B)** II only **(C)** III only
(D) I, II, and III **(E)** I and III only

2. The length of a rectangle is 3 cm less than twice its width. A second rectangle is such that each of its dimensions is the reciprocal of the corresponding dimension of the first rectangle. The perimeter of the second rectangle is $\frac{1}{5}$ the perimeter of the first. Find the perimeter of the first rectangle.

(A) 6 cm **(B)** 9 cm **(C)** 12 cm **(D)** 18 cm

3. How many sets of three consecutive positive even integers are there such that three times the sum of the first two integers is less than five times the third integer?

(A) none **(B)** two **(C)** four **(D)** six **(E)** eight

4. Two notebooks and three packages of pencils cost \$7. It would cost \$3 more to buy three notebooks and four packages of pencils. How much would it cost to buy one notebook and one package of pencils?

(A) \$1 **(B)** \$2 **(C)** \$3 **(D)** \$4

5. The sum of a positive integer and the square of the next consecutive integer is 131. Find the sum of the two integers.

(A) 19 **(B)** 20 **(C)** 21 **(D)** 22 **(E)** 23

6. Identify the inequality whose graph is shown at the right.

(A) $x + 3y \leq 6$ **(B)** $x + 3y \geq 6$
(C) $3x - y \leq 3$ **(D)** $3x - y \geq 3$

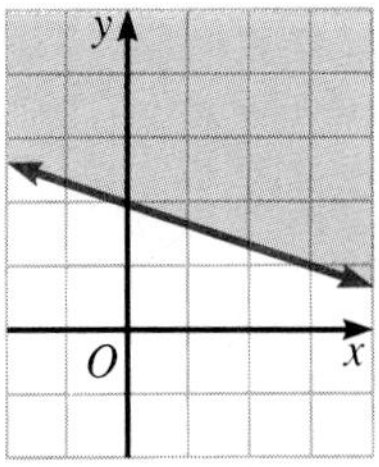

11 Rational and Irrational Numbers

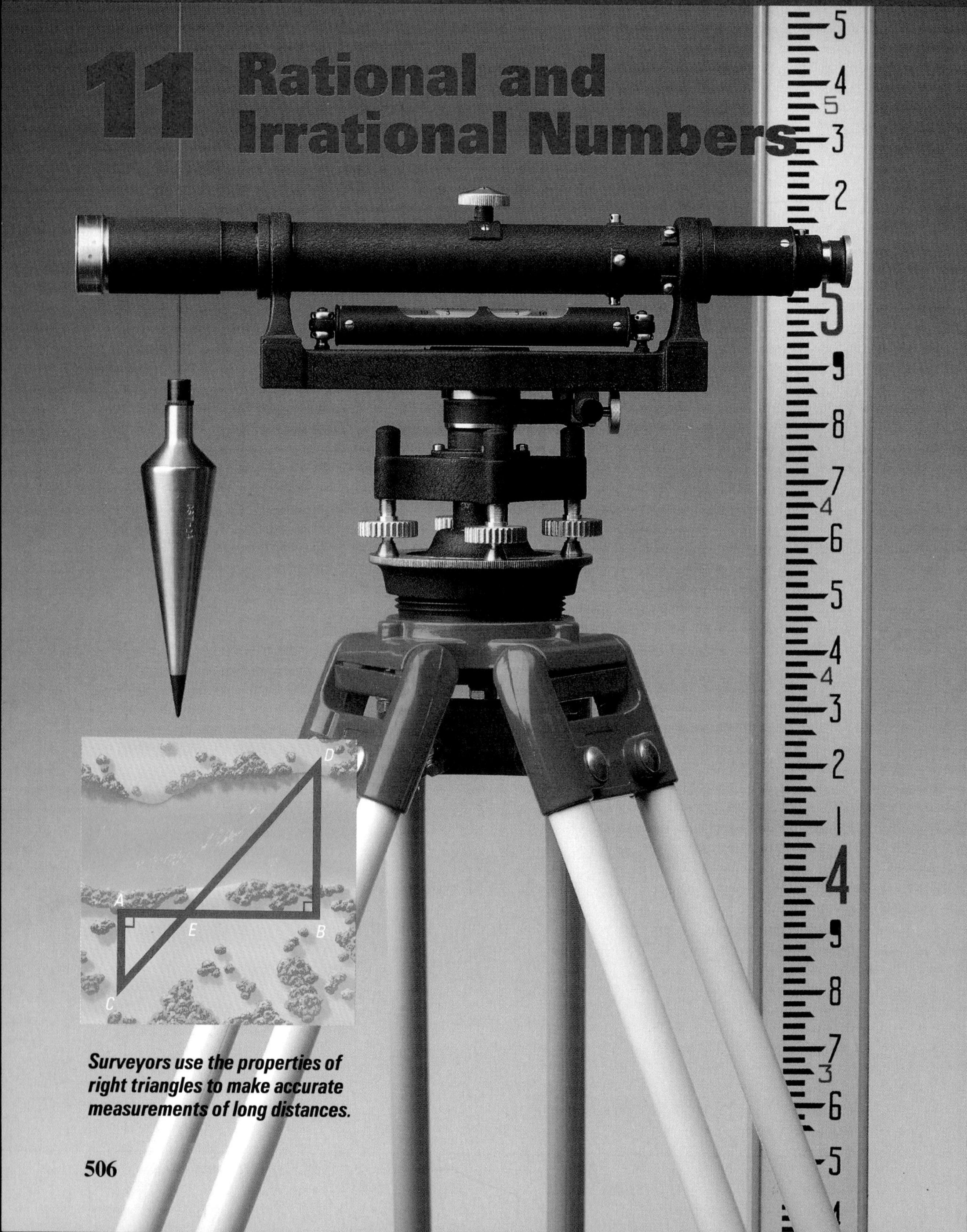

Surveyors use the properties of right triangles to make accurate measurements of long distances.

Rational Numbers

11-1 Properties of Rational Numbers

Objective To learn and apply some properties of rational numbers.

In Chapter 1, you learned that the positive numbers, the negative numbers, and zero are called real numbers.

A real number that can be expressed as the quotient of two integers is called a **rational number.**

Each number below is a rational number.

$$0 = \frac{0}{1} \qquad 7 = \frac{7}{1} \qquad 5\frac{2}{3} = \frac{17}{3} \qquad 0.43 = \frac{43}{100} \qquad -\frac{4}{9} = \frac{-4}{9}$$

A rational number can be written as a quotient of integers in an unlimited number of ways.

Example 1 Write as a quotient of integers: **a.** 3 **b.** $-1\frac{4}{5}$ **c.** 48% **d.** 0.6

Solution **a.** $3 = \frac{6}{2} = \frac{12}{4} = \frac{-15}{-5} = \ldots$ **b.** $-1\frac{4}{5} = \frac{-9}{5} = \frac{18}{-10} = \ldots$

c. $48\% = \frac{48}{100} = \frac{24}{50} = \ldots$ **d.** $0.6 = \frac{6}{10} = \frac{12}{20} = \ldots$

To determine which of two rational numbers is greater, you can write them with the same positive denominator and compare their numerators.

Example 2 Which rational number is greater, $\frac{8}{3}$ or $\frac{17}{7}$?

Solution The LCD is 21.

$\frac{8}{3} = \frac{56}{21}$ and $\frac{17}{7} = \frac{51}{21}$.

Compare $\frac{56}{21}$ and $\frac{51}{21}$.

Since $56 > 51$, $\frac{56}{21} > \frac{51}{21}$.

$\therefore \frac{8}{3} > \frac{17}{7}$ ***Answer***

For all integers a and b and all positive integers c and d:

1. $\frac{a}{c} > \frac{b}{d}$ if and only if $ad > bc$.
2. $\frac{a}{c} < \frac{b}{d}$ if and only if $ad < bc$.

(See Exercise 36 on page 511 for a proof of the second statement.)

Thus, $\frac{4}{7} > \frac{3}{8}$ because $(4)(8) > (3)(7)$;

$\frac{7}{9} < \frac{4}{5}$ because $(7)(5) < (4)(9)$.

Example 3 Replace the _?_ with <, =, or > to make a true statement.

a. $-\frac{5}{8}$ _?_ $-\frac{7}{13}$.

b. $6\frac{4}{7}$ _?_ $\frac{53}{9}$.

Solution

a. $-\frac{5}{8} = \frac{-5}{8}$ and $-\frac{7}{13} = \frac{-7}{13}$.

$\frac{-5}{8}$ _?_ $\frac{-7}{13}$

$(-5)(13)$ _?_ $(-7)(8)$

$-65 < -56$

$\therefore -\frac{5}{8} < -\frac{7}{13}$ ***Answer***

b. Write $6\frac{4}{7}$ as $\frac{46}{7}$.

$\frac{46}{7}$ _?_ $\frac{53}{9}$

$(46)(9)$ _?_ $(53)(7)$

$414 > 371$

$\therefore 6\frac{4}{7} > \frac{53}{9}$ ***Answer***

Rational numbers differ from integers in several ways. For example, given any integer, there is a next greater integer: -8 follows -9, 1 follows 0, 24 follows 23, and so on. However, there is no "next greater" rational number after a given rational number. This property of rational numbers is called the *density property*.

The Density Property for Rational Numbers

Between every pair of different rational numbers there is another rational number.

The density property implies that it is possible to find an unlimited or endless number of rational numbers between two given rational numbers. For example, if a and b are rational numbers and $a < b$, then the number halfway from a to b is $a + \frac{1}{2}(b - a)$; the number one third of the way from a to b is $a + \frac{1}{3}(b - a)$; and so on.

Example 4 Find a rational number between $\frac{3}{4}$ and $\frac{5}{6}$.

Solution Choose, for example, the number halfway between $\frac{3}{4}$ and $\frac{5}{6}$. This number can be expressed as:

$$\begin{aligned}\frac{3}{4} + \frac{1}{2}\left(\frac{5}{6} - \frac{3}{4}\right) &= \frac{3}{4} + \frac{1}{2}\left(\frac{10}{12} - \frac{9}{12}\right)\\ &= \frac{3}{4} + \frac{1}{2}\left(\frac{1}{12}\right)\\ &= \frac{3}{4} + \frac{1}{24}\\ &= \frac{18}{24} + \frac{1}{24}\\ &= \frac{19}{24}\end{aligned}$$

Check:

Is $\frac{3}{4} < \frac{19}{24}$?
Is $(3)(24) < (19)(4)$?
$72 < 76$ ✓

Is $\frac{19}{24} < \frac{5}{6}$?
Is $(19)(6) < (5)(24)$?
$114 < 120$ ✓

$\therefore \frac{19}{24}$ is a rational number between $\frac{3}{4}$ and $\frac{5}{6}$. ***Answer***

The number halfway between two numbers is also their average since

$$a + \frac{1}{2}(b - a) = \frac{2a}{2} + \frac{b - a}{2} = \frac{a + b}{2}.$$

Oral Exercises

Express each number as a quotient of two integers.

Sample 5.34 **Solution** $\frac{534}{100}$

1. 4.6 **2.** -3.5 **3.** $-2\frac{3}{4}$ **4.** 61%

5. -7 **6.** 32 **7.** 0 **8.** $\frac{3}{11} + \left(-\frac{7}{11}\right)$

Which rational number in each pair is the greater?

9. $\frac{7}{13}, \frac{9}{13}$ **10.** $-\frac{4}{7}, -\frac{5}{7}$ **11.** $-5, \frac{1}{2}$

12. $\frac{1}{4}, \frac{1}{5}$ **13.** $\frac{5}{8}, \frac{3}{4}$ **14.** $-\frac{9}{2}, -\frac{13}{3}$

15. How many integers are between -4 and -2? How many rational numbers?

16. How many integers are between 100 and 101? How many rational numbers?

17. Is -7 a real number? an integer? a rational number?

Written Exercises

Replace the $\underline{\ ?\ }$ with <, =, or > to make a true statement.

A

1. $\frac{1}{9} \underline{\ ?\ } \frac{4}{27}$
2. $\frac{11}{15} \underline{\ ?\ } \frac{2}{3}$
3. $-\frac{3}{4} \underline{\ ?\ } -\frac{9}{13}$
4. $-\frac{7}{8} \underline{\ ?\ } -\frac{5}{6}$
5. $\frac{3}{4} \underline{\ ?\ } \frac{24}{32}$
6. $\frac{12}{19} \underline{\ ?\ } \frac{17}{24}$
7. $-18\frac{2}{5} \underline{\ ?\ } -\frac{131}{7}$
8. $-\frac{214}{14} \underline{\ ?\ } -15\frac{2}{3}$

Arrange each group of numbers in order from least to greatest.

9. $\frac{4}{7}, \frac{3}{8}, \frac{5}{9}$
10. $\frac{3}{5}, \frac{5}{7}, \frac{2}{9}$
11. $5.6, \frac{107}{18}, -5$
12. $-3.8, -\frac{35}{8}, -3$
13. $\frac{7}{24}, \frac{4}{15}, \frac{5}{16}, \frac{1}{2}$
14. $-\frac{3}{7}, -\frac{5}{6}, -\frac{3}{5}, -\frac{7}{9}$

Find the number halfway between the given numbers.

15. $\frac{5}{9}$ and $\frac{4}{7}$
16. $\frac{7}{11}$ and $\frac{3}{4}$
17. $-\frac{4}{25}$ and $-\frac{9}{50}$
18. $-\frac{5}{39}$ and $-\frac{6}{117}$
19. $2\frac{3}{4}$ and $-3\frac{3}{4}$
20. $-5\frac{1}{5}$ and $8\frac{2}{3}$

If $x \in \{0, 1, 2, 3\}$, state whether each fraction increases or decreases in value as x takes on its values in increasing order.

Sample $\frac{x}{4}$ becomes $\frac{0}{4}, \frac{1}{4}, \frac{2}{4}, \frac{3}{4}$. $\therefore$ the fraction increases.

B

21. $\frac{x}{3}$
22. $\frac{x}{5}$
23. $\frac{7}{x+1}$
24. $\frac{x+1}{6}$
25. $\frac{9-2x}{5}$
26. $\frac{14}{12-3x}$
27. Find the number one-third of the way from $\frac{1}{6}$ to $\frac{4}{5}$.
28. Find the number one-fourth of the way from $\frac{5}{8}$ to $1\frac{1}{4}$.
29. Find the number one-fifth of the way from $-\frac{2}{3}$ to $\frac{3}{5}$.
30. Find the number three-fourths of the way from $\frac{1}{2}$ to $\frac{8}{9}$.
31. Find a rational number between $\frac{1}{3}$ and $\frac{3}{4}$.
32. Find a rational number between $-\frac{1}{6}$ and $-\frac{1}{4}$.
33. Write an expression in simplest form for the number halfway between $\frac{3a}{7}$ and $-\frac{a}{12}$.
34. Write an expression in simplest form for the number two-thirds of the way from $-\frac{7b}{5}$ to $-\frac{2b}{3}$.

35. a. Brian and Lou agreed to share equally the profits from their lawn mowing business. At the end of one week, Brian had earned \$27.50 and Lou had earned \$35.50. Brian said, "You owe me half the difference, which is \$4.00." Was he right?

b. In general, suppose Brian received a dollars and Lou received b dollars, where $b > a$. Show that if Lou gives Brian $\frac{1}{2}(b - a)$ dollars, then each will have exactly the same amount of money.

C **36.** Supply the missing reasons in the proof of the following theorem:

For all integers a and b and all positive integers c and d, $\frac{a}{c} < \frac{b}{d}$ if and only if $ad < bc$.

Proof: If $\frac{a}{c} < \frac{b}{d}$, then $ad < bc$.

1. $\frac{a}{c} < \frac{b}{d}$	1. Given
2. $\frac{ad}{cd} < \frac{bc}{cd}$ $\left(\text{since } \frac{d}{d} = \frac{c}{c} = 1\right)$	2. ___?___
3. $ad < bc$	3. ___?___

$\therefore$ if $\frac{a}{c} < \frac{b}{d}$, then $ad < bc$.

Proof: If $ad < bc$, $\frac{a}{c} < \frac{b}{d}$.

1. $ad < bc$	1. Given
2. $\frac{ad}{cd} < \frac{bc}{cd}$ (since $cd > 0$)	2. ___?___
3. $\frac{a}{c} < \frac{b}{d}$	3. ___?___

$\therefore$ if $ad < bc$, then $\frac{a}{c} < \frac{b}{d}$.

$\therefore$ $\frac{a}{c} < \frac{b}{d}$ if and only if $ad < bc$.

State conditions for w and z that make the following true.

37. $\frac{x}{w} > \frac{x}{z}$; $x > 0$

38. $\frac{x}{w - z} < \frac{x}{z - w}$; $x > 0$

Mixed Review Exercises

Solve each inequality and graph its solution.

1. $3y + 4 \le 10$

2. $|0.5 + x| < 10$

3. $10 + 6|2 - k| \ge 22$

4. $|3 + z| \ge 5$

5. $4 \le 2x + 4 < 6$

6. $6 \le 2 - 4m$

Write as a fraction in simplest form.

7. 35%

8. 0.6

9. 4.4

10. $3 \cdot 10^{-4}$

11. $62\frac{1}{2}\%$

12. $\frac{1}{4}\%$

11-2 Decimal Forms of Rational Numbers

Objective To express rational numbers as decimals or fractions.

Any common fraction can be written as a decimal by dividing the numerator by the denominator. If the remainder is zero, the decimal is called a **terminating, ending,** or **finite decimal.**

Example 1 Express $\frac{3}{8}$ as a decimal.

Solution

$$\begin{array}{r} 0.375 \\ 8\overline{)3.000} \\ \underline{2\,4} \\ 60 \\ \underline{56} \\ 40 \\ \underline{40} \\ 0 \end{array}$$

The division at the left shows that $\frac{3}{8}$ can be expressed as the terminating decimal 0.375. ***Answer***

If you don't reach a remainder of zero when dividing the numerator by the denominator, continue to divide until the remainders begin to repeat.

Example 2 Express each rational number as a decimal: **a.** $\frac{5}{6}$ **b.** $\frac{7}{11}$ **c.** $3\frac{2}{7}$

Solution

a. $\frac{5}{6} \rightarrow$

$$\begin{array}{r} 0.833 \\ 6\overline{)5.000} \\ \underline{4\,8} \\ 20 \\ \underline{18} \\ 20 \\ \underline{18} \\ 2 \end{array}$$

$\therefore \frac{5}{6} = 0.833\ldots$

b. $\frac{7}{11} \rightarrow$

$$\begin{array}{r} 0.6363 \\ 11\overline{)7.0000} \\ \underline{6\,6} \\ 40 \\ \underline{33} \\ 70 \\ \underline{66} \\ 40 \\ \underline{33} \\ 7 \end{array}$$

$\therefore \frac{7}{11} = 0.6363\ldots$

c. $3\frac{2}{7} = \frac{23}{7} \rightarrow$

$$\begin{array}{r} 3.2857142 \\ 7\overline{)23.0000000} \\ \underline{21} \\ 2\,0 \\ \underline{1\,4} \\ 60 \\ \underline{56} \\ 40 \\ \underline{35} \\ 50 \\ \underline{49} \\ 10 \\ \underline{7} \\ 30 \\ \underline{28} \\ 20 \\ \underline{14} \\ 6 \end{array}$$

$\therefore 3\frac{2}{7} = 3.285714285714\ldots$

The decimal quotients shown in Example 2 are **nonterminating, unending,** or **infinite.** The dots indicate that the decimals continue without end. We write:

$$\frac{5}{6} = 0.833\ldots \qquad \frac{7}{11} = 0.6363\ldots \qquad 3\frac{2}{7} = 3.285714285714\ldots$$

They are also called **repeating** or **periodic** because the same digit or block of digits repeats unendingly. A bar is used to indicate the block of digits that repeat, as shown below.

$$\frac{5}{6} = 0.8\overline{3} \qquad \frac{7}{11} = 0.\overline{63} \qquad 3\frac{2}{7} = 3.\overline{285714}$$

When you divide a positive integer n by a positive integer d, the remainder r at each step must be zero or a positive integer less than d. For example, if the divisor is 6, the remainders will be 0, 1, 2, 3, 4, or 5, and the division will terminate or begin repeating within 5 steps after only zeros remain to be brought down. In general:

For every integer n and every positive integer d, the decimal form of the rational number $\frac{n}{d}$ either terminates or eventually repeats in a block of fewer than d digits.

To express a terminating decimal as a common fraction, express the decimal as a common fraction with a power of ten as the denominator. This fraction is then usually expressed in simplest form.

Example 3 Express each terminating decimal as a fraction in simplest form.

a. 0.38 **b.** 0.425

Solution **a.** $0.38 = \frac{38}{100} = \frac{19}{50}$ **b.** $0.425 = \frac{425}{1000} = \frac{17}{40}$

The following examples show how to express a repeating decimal as a common fraction.

Example 4 Express $0.5\overline{42}$ as a fraction in simplest form.

Solution Let $N =$ the number $0.5\overline{42}$.
Let $n =$ the number of digits in the block of repeating digits.

Multiply N by 10^n.
Since $0.5\overline{42}$ has 2 digits in the repeating block, $n = 2$.
Therefore, multiply both sides of the equation $N = 0.5\overline{42}$ by 10^2, or 100.

$$100N = 100(0.5\overline{42})$$

(Solution continues on the next page.)

Since $0.5\overline{42} = 0.54242\ldots$, $0.5\overline{42}$ can also be written as $0.542\overline{42}$

Then
$$100(0.5\overline{42}) = 100(0.542\overline{42}) = 54.2\overline{42}$$

Subtract N from $100N$.
$$\begin{aligned} 100N &= 54.2\overline{42} \\ N &= 0.5\overline{42} \\ \hline 99N &= 53.7 \end{aligned}$$

Solve for N.
$$N = \frac{53.7}{99} = \frac{537}{990} = \frac{179}{330}$$

$\therefore 0.5\overline{42} = \frac{179}{330}$ ***Answer***

Example 5 Express $-0.\overline{375}$ as a fraction in simplest form.

Solution First, express $0.\overline{375}$ as a common fraction.

Let $N =$ the number.

$$\begin{aligned} 1000N &= 375.\overline{375} \\ N &= 0.\overline{375} \\ \hline 999N &= 375 \end{aligned}$$

{ Since there are 3 digits in the repeating block, multiply N by 10^3, or 1000. Then subtract.

$$N = \frac{375}{999} = \frac{125}{333}$$

Since $0.\overline{375} = \frac{125}{333}$, $-0.\overline{375} = -\frac{125}{333}$. ***Answer***

All terminating decimals and all repeating decimals represent rational numbers that can be written in the form $\frac{n}{d}$, where n is an integer and d is a positive integer.

It is often convenient to use an approximation of a lengthy decimal. For example, you may approximate $\frac{7}{13}$ as 0.53846, 0.538, or 0.54.

To round a decimal:

1. If the first digit dropped is greater than or equal to 5, add 1 to the last digit retained.
2. If the first digit dropped is less than 5, don't change the last digit retained.

Example 6 shows decimals being rounded to various decimal places. The symbol $\approx$ means "is approximately equal to."

Example 6

a. $0.41\overline{6} \approx 0.417$ (to the nearest thousandth)
≈ 0.42 (to the nearest hundredth)

b. $0.\overline{416} \approx 0.416$ (to the nearest thousandth)
≈ 0.42 (to the nearest hundredth)

c. $0.\overline{53} \approx 0.54$ (to the nearest hundredth)
≈ 0.5 (to the nearest tenth)

d. $3.\overline{481} \approx 3.5$ (to the nearest tenth)
≈ 3 (to the nearest unit)

e. $0.\overline{681} \approx 0.7$ (to the nearest tenth)
≈ 1 (to the nearest unit)

Oral Exercises

Round each number to the nearest tenth.

1. 5.358 **2.** -0.729 **3.** $4.\overline{6}$ **4.** $3.48\overline{2}$ **5.** $-0.2\overline{7}$

6–10. Round the numbers in Exercises 1–5 to the nearest hundredth.

Tell whether the decimal form terminates or repeats.

11. $\frac{1}{2}$ **12.** $-\frac{5}{6}$ **13.** $\frac{7}{4}$ **14.** $\frac{59}{2000}$ **15.** $\frac{18}{7}$ **16.** $-\frac{8}{13}$

Written Exercises

Express each rational number as a terminating or repeating decimal.

A

1. a. $\frac{2}{3}$ **b.** $\frac{2}{30}$

2. a. $\frac{9}{2}$ **b.** $\frac{9}{200}$

3. a. $-\frac{4}{9}$ **b.** $-\frac{4}{9000}$

4. a. $-\frac{3}{5}$ **b.** $-\frac{3}{50}$

5. $\frac{11}{8}$ **6.** $\frac{11}{12}$ **7.** $\frac{15}{11}$ **8.** $\frac{4}{7}$

9. $-\frac{7}{18}$ **10.** $-\frac{15}{32}$ **11.** $3\frac{9}{20}$ **12.** $2\frac{5}{11}$

13. $\frac{3}{11}$ **14.** $-6\frac{3}{4}$ **15.** $-\frac{18}{37}$ **16.** $\frac{22}{37}$

Express each rational number as a fraction in simplest form.

17. 0.2 **18.** 0.66 **19.** 0.325 **20.** 3.8

21. $0.\overline{4}$ **22.** $1.\overline{15}$ **23.** $-0.28\overline{3}$ **24.** $2.3\overline{9}$

25. $0.\overline{07}$ **26.** $-1.\overline{36}$ **27.** $-2.\overline{3}$ **28.** $0.\overline{857142}$

Find the number halfway between the given numbers.

Sample $\frac{3}{4}$ and 0.756 **Solution** $\frac{3}{4} = \frac{75}{100} = 0.75$

$$0.75 + \frac{1}{2}(0.756 - 0.75) = 0.75 + \frac{1}{2}(0.006)$$
$$= 0.75 + 0.003$$
$$= 0.753 \quad \textit{Answer}$$

B **29.** $\frac{1}{4}$ and 0.259 **30.** $\frac{5}{8}$ and 0.634 **31.** 0.44 and $0.\overline{4}$

32. 0.77 and $0.\overline{7}$ **33.** 0.83 and $\frac{5}{6}$ **34.** 0.121 and $\frac{1}{8}$

Express both numbers as fractions. Then find their product.

35. $\frac{3}{5}$ and 0.75 **36.** 0.875 and $\frac{5}{7}$ **37.** $0.\overline{6}$ and $\frac{7}{12}$

38. $\frac{9}{20}$ and $0.\overline{5}$ **39.** $0.\overline{407}$ and $0.2\overline{7}$ **40.** $0.3\overline{5}$ and $1.\overline{336}$

C **41. a.** Express $\frac{1}{9}$, $\frac{5}{9}$, and $\frac{8}{9}$ as repeating decimals.

b. Express $\frac{1}{27}$, $\frac{5}{27}$, and $\frac{8}{27}$ as repeating decimals.

c. What is the relationship between the numbers in (a) and (b)?

42. a. Express $\frac{1}{7}$ and $\frac{6}{7}$ as repeating decimals.

b. What is the relationship between the blocks of digits that repeat in (a)?

c. Express $\frac{3}{7}$, $\frac{4}{7}$, and $\frac{5}{7}$ as decimals.

43. Since $\frac{1}{99} = 0.\overline{01}$, $\frac{n}{99} = n(0.\overline{01})$ for $1 \le n < 100$.

a. Confirm the fact above by expressing $\frac{8}{99}$, $\frac{32}{99}$, and $\frac{87}{99}$ as decimals.

b. Express 1 as $\frac{99}{99}$ to show that $0.\overline{9} = 1$.

c. Use the method of Example 4 to show that $0.\overline{9} = 1$.

Mixed Review Exercises

Find the prime factorization of each number.

1. 200 **2.** 98 **3.** 1089 **4.** 2250 **5.** 392 **6.** 576

Solve.

7. $(y + 3)(y - 4) = 0$ **8.** $(a + 5)^2 = 9$ **9.** $y^2 = -36$

10. $k^3 - 16k = 0$ **11.** $|x + 2| = 10$ **12.** $k + 4 < 16$

11-3 Rational Square Roots

Objective To find the square roots of numbers that have rational square roots.

On page 107, you learned that subtraction "undoes" addition, and that division by a nonzero number "undoes" multiplication. Similarly, squaring a number can be undone by finding a square root.

If $a^2 = b$, then a is a **square root** of b.

Because $7^2 = 49$ and $(-7)^2 = 49$, both 7 and -7 are square roots of 49.

The symbol $\sqrt{}$ is used to write the **principal,** or positive, square root of a positive number.

$\sqrt{49} = 7$ is read "The *positive* square root of 49 equals 7."

A negative square root is associated with the symbol $-\sqrt{}$.

$-\sqrt{49} = -7$ is read "The *negative* square root of 49 equals -7."

It is often convenient to use *plus-or-minus* notation:

$\pm\sqrt{49}$ means the positive *or* negative square root of 49.

In the expression $\sqrt{49}$, the number written beneath the radical sign, such as 49, is called the **radicand.** On scientific calculators you press the key labeled $\sqrt{}$ to find the square root of a number.

For all positive real numbers a:
Every positive real number a has two square roots: $\sqrt{a}$ and $-\sqrt{a}$.
The symbol $\sqrt{a}$ denotes the principal square root of a.
Zero has only one square root, namely zero itself; that is, $\sqrt{0} = 0$.

It follows from the definition of square root that $(\sqrt{a})^2 = a$.

Because the square of every real number is either positive or zero, *negative numbers do not have square roots in the set of real numbers.* If you try to take the square root of a negative number on a calculator, the display will indicate an error.

Notice that $\sqrt{4 \cdot 25} = \sqrt{100} = 10$ and $\sqrt{4} \cdot \sqrt{25} = 2 \cdot 5 = 10$. Therefore $\sqrt{4 \cdot 25} = \sqrt{4} \cdot \sqrt{25}$.

Product Property of Square Roots

For any nonnegative real numbers a and b:

$$\sqrt{ab} = \sqrt{a} \cdot \sqrt{b}$$

Example 1 Find $\sqrt{225}$.

Solution

$$\begin{aligned}\sqrt{225} &= \sqrt{9 \cdot 25}\\ &= \sqrt{9} \cdot \sqrt{25}\\ &= 3 \cdot 5\\ &= 15 \quad \textit{Answer}\end{aligned}$$

If you cannot see any squares that divide the radicand, begin by factoring the radicand (page 185).

Example 2 Find $\sqrt{2304}$.

Solution

$$\begin{aligned}\sqrt{2304} &= \sqrt{2^2 \cdot 3^2 \cdot 8^2}\\ &= \sqrt{2^2} \cdot \sqrt{3^2} \cdot \sqrt{8^2}\\ &= 2 \cdot 3 \cdot 8\\ &= 48 \quad \textit{Answer}\end{aligned}$$

Notice that $\sqrt{\frac{100}{25}} = \sqrt{4} = 2$ and $\frac{\sqrt{100}}{\sqrt{25}} = \frac{10}{5} = 2$. Therefore $\sqrt{\frac{100}{25}} = \frac{\sqrt{100}}{\sqrt{25}}$.
This result suggests another property of square roots.

Quotient Property of Square Roots

For any nonnegative real number a and any positive real number b:

$$\sqrt{\frac{a}{b}} = \frac{\sqrt{a}}{\sqrt{b}}$$

Example 3 Find the indicated square root: **a.** $\sqrt{\frac{36}{121}}$ **b.** $\pm\sqrt{\frac{144}{3025}}$

Solution

a. $\sqrt{\frac{36}{121}} = \frac{\sqrt{36}}{\sqrt{121}} = \frac{6}{11}$

b. $\pm\sqrt{\frac{144}{3025}} = \pm\frac{\sqrt{144}}{\sqrt{3025}} = \pm\frac{12}{\sqrt{5^2 \cdot 11^2}} = \pm\frac{12}{55}$

Oral Exercises

Find the indicated square roots.

1. $\sqrt{16}$ **2.** $-\sqrt{81}$ **3.** $\sqrt{25}$ **4.** $-\sqrt{144}$ **5.** $\pm\sqrt{169}$

6. $\sqrt{15^2}$ **7.** $\sqrt{84^2}$ **8.** $-\sqrt{52^2}$ **9.** $(\sqrt{6})^2$ **10.** $(\sqrt{43})^2$

11. $-\sqrt{\frac{1}{25}}$ **12.** $\sqrt{\frac{1}{64}}$ **13.** $-\sqrt{\frac{100}{49}}$ **14.** $\sqrt{\frac{81}{16}}$ **15.** $-\sqrt{\frac{121}{36}}$

16. $\sqrt{5^2 - 4^2}$ **17.** $\sqrt{5^2} - \sqrt{4^2}$ **18.** $\sqrt{13^2 - 5^2}$ **19.** $\sqrt{13^2} - \sqrt{5^2}$ **20.** $\sqrt{10^2 - 6^2}$

Sample $\sqrt{\left(\frac{3}{7}\right)^2} = \sqrt{\frac{3^2}{7^2}} = \frac{\sqrt{3^2}}{\sqrt{7^2}} = \frac{3}{7}$

21. $\sqrt{\left(\frac{2}{5}\right)^2}$ **22.** $\sqrt{\left(\frac{12}{29}\right)^2}$ **23.** $\left(\sqrt{\frac{7}{11}}\right)^2$ **24.** $\left(\sqrt{\frac{5}{23}}\right)^2$

Written Exercises

Find the indicated square root.

A

1. $\sqrt{36}$ **2.** $\sqrt{64}$ **3.** $\sqrt{100}$ **4.** $\sqrt{121}$

5. $-\sqrt{400}$ **6.** $-\sqrt{196}$ **7.** $\sqrt{625}$ **8.** $\sqrt{576}$

9. $\pm\sqrt{2500}$ **10.** $\pm\sqrt{1225}$ **11.** $-\sqrt{\frac{81}{1600}}$ **12.** $-\sqrt{\frac{225}{49}}$

13. $\pm\sqrt{\frac{121}{25}}$ **14.** $\pm\sqrt{\frac{1}{256}}$ **15.** $\sqrt{\frac{144}{441}}$ **16.** $\sqrt{\frac{529}{576}}$

17. $-\sqrt{\frac{484}{100}}$ **18.** $-\sqrt{\frac{324}{729}}$ **19.** $\sqrt{\frac{361}{2304}}$ **20.** $\sqrt{\frac{1156}{289}}$

Sample 1 $\sqrt{\frac{18}{32}} = \sqrt{\frac{2 \cdot 9}{2 \cdot 16}} = \sqrt{\frac{9}{16}} = \frac{3}{4}$

B

21. $-\sqrt{\frac{28}{63}}$ **22.** $-\sqrt{\frac{12}{75}}$ **23.** $\sqrt{\frac{99}{44}}$ **24.** $\sqrt{\frac{20}{45}}$

25. $\pm\sqrt{\frac{175}{28}}$ **26.** $\pm\sqrt{\frac{92}{207}}$ **27.** $\sqrt{\frac{7}{175}}$ **28.** $\sqrt{\frac{5}{180}}$

29. $\pm\sqrt{\frac{33}{132}}$ **30.** $\pm\sqrt{\frac{180}{845}}$ **31.** $-\sqrt{\frac{3200}{648}}$ **32.** $-\sqrt{\frac{1682}{20{,}000}}$

Find the indicated square root. Express as a decimal. You may wish to use a calculator to check your answers.

Sample 2 $\sqrt{0.64} = \sqrt{\frac{64}{100}} = \frac{\sqrt{64}}{\sqrt{100}} = \frac{8}{10} = 0.8$

33. $\sqrt{0.04}$ **34.** $\sqrt{0.09}$ **35.** $-\sqrt{0.81}$ **36.** $-\sqrt{0.64}$

37. $\sqrt{1.21}$ **38.** $\sqrt{2.25}$ **39.** $\pm\sqrt{7.84}$ **40.** $\pm\sqrt{12.25}$

41. $\sqrt{0.0196}$ **42.** $\sqrt{0.0289}$ **43.** $\sqrt{0.0009}$ **44.** $\sqrt{0.000049}$

Evaluate the expression $\sqrt{x^2 - y^2} - (\sqrt{x})^2$ for the given values of x and y.

45. $x = 5,\ y = 3$ **46.** $x = 17,\ y = 15$

47. $x = 20,\ y = 16$ **48.** $x = 37,\ y = 12$

Mixed Review Exercises

Express as a fraction in simplest form.

1. 0.125 **2.** -6.4 **3.** $0.\overline{3}$ **4.** $2.\overline{16}$ **5.** $\frac{1}{2}\left(\frac{4}{5} - \frac{2}{3}\right)$ **6.** $\frac{2}{3}\left(\frac{x}{4} - \frac{2x}{7}\right)$

Factor completely.

7. $4b^2 - 12b - 72$ **8.** $16t^2 - 8t - 9v^2 + 1$ **9.** $64k^3 - k$

10. $9w^2 - 24wy + 16y^2$ **11.** $2x^2 - 9xy - 5y^2$ **12.** $3 - 2ab - 5a^2b^2$

Challenge

Solve the systems if a, b, and c are positive integers:

$$4a - 11b + 12c = 22$$
$$a + 5b - 4c = 17$$

Self-Test 1

Vocabulary

rational number (p. 507)
terminating decimal (p. 512)
repeating decimal (p. 513)
square root (p. 517)
principal square root (p. 517)
radical sign (p. 517)
radical (p. 517)
radicand (p. 517)

Find the number halfway between the given numbers.

1. $\frac{5}{8}$ and $\frac{4}{9}$ **2.** $\frac{5}{4}$ and $\frac{4}{3}$ **3.** $4\frac{1}{6}$ and $5\frac{1}{8}$ **Obj. 11-1, p. 507**

Replace the __?__ with <, =, or > to make a true statement.

4. $\frac{11}{3}$ __?__ $\frac{7}{5}$ **5.** $-\frac{13}{7}$ __?__ $-\frac{9}{5}$ **6.** $\frac{32}{20}$ __?__ $\frac{37}{22}$

Express each rational number as a decimal.

7. $\frac{12}{25}$ **8.** $\frac{13}{4}$ **9.** $\frac{7}{30}$ **10.** $\frac{24}{35}$ **Obj. 11-2, p. 512**

11. Express $0.2\overline{02}$ as a fraction in simplest form.

Find the indicated square root.

12. $\sqrt{1089}$ **13.** $\sqrt{\frac{64}{2025}}$ **14.** $\sqrt{2.56}$ **Obj. 11-3, p. 517**

Check your answers with those at the back of the book.

Irrational Numbers

11-4 Irrational Square Roots

Objective To simplify radicals and to find decimal approximations of irrational square roots.

You can use the product property of square roots to simplify radicals when the radicand has a factor that is the square of an integer other than 1.

Example 1 Simplify: **a.** $\sqrt{324}$ **b.** $\sqrt{75}$ **c.** $2\sqrt{112}$ **d.** $\sqrt{891}$

Solution

a. $\sqrt{324} = \sqrt{9 \cdot 36} = \sqrt{9} \cdot \sqrt{36} = 3 \cdot 6 = 18$

b. $\sqrt{75} = \sqrt{25 \cdot 3} = \sqrt{25} \cdot \sqrt{3} = 5\sqrt{3}$

c. $2\sqrt{112} = 2\sqrt{16 \cdot 7} = 2 \cdot 4\sqrt{7} = 8\sqrt{7}$

d. $\sqrt{891} = \sqrt{81 \cdot 11} = 9\sqrt{11}$

Since integers such as 3, 7, and 11 are not squares of integers, numbers such as $\sqrt{3}$, $\sqrt{7}$, and $\sqrt{11}$ are not in the set of rational numbers. These numbers are in another major subset of the real numbers called the set of *irrational numbers*. Their exact values cannot be expressed as either terminating or repeating decimals. However, you can use a calculator or the table of square roots at the back of the book to find the decimal approximation of an irrational square root. For example, $\sqrt{3} \approx 1.732$, $\sqrt{7} \approx 2.646$, and $\sqrt{11} \approx 3.317$.

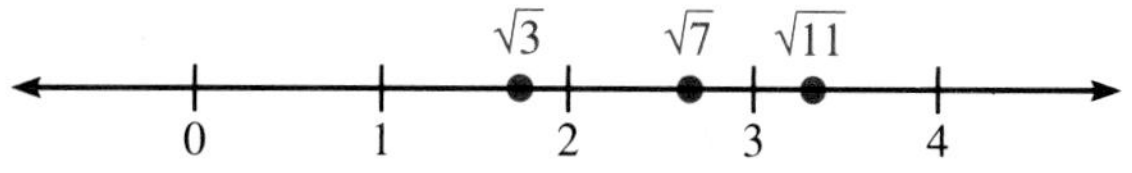

Irrational numbers are real numbers that cannot be expressed in the form $\frac{a}{b}$, where a and b are integers.

Irrational square roots are not the only irrational numbers. For example, π is an irrational number, as is 0.13579111315. . . .

The set of real numbers is made up of the rational numbers and the irrational numbers. The real numbers have all the properties that you have studied so far in this course. In addition, the set of real numbers has the *property of completeness*.

Property of Completeness

Every decimal number represents a real number, and every real number can be represented as a decimal.

The product and quotient properties of square roots can be used with a table of square roots to approximate irrational square roots if you don't have a calculator.

Example 2 Approximate each square root to the nearest hundredth.

a. $\sqrt{684}$ **b.** $\sqrt{0.8}$

Solution

a. $\sqrt{684} = \sqrt{2^2 \cdot 3^2 \cdot 19}$

$= \sqrt{2^2 \cdot 3^2} \cdot \sqrt{19}$

$= 6\sqrt{19}$

From the table: $\sqrt{19} \approx 4.359$

$6\sqrt{19} \approx 6(4.359) = 26.154$

$\therefore \sqrt{684} \approx 26.15$ ***Answer***

b. $\sqrt{0.8} = \dfrac{\sqrt{80}}{\sqrt{100}}$

$\approx \dfrac{8.944}{10} = 0.8944$

$\therefore \sqrt{0.8} \approx 0.89$ ***Answer***

Oral Exercises

State whether each number represents a rational or an irrational number.

1. $\sqrt{17}$ **2.** $\sqrt{49}$ **3.** $\sqrt{11}$ **4.** $\sqrt{1.21}$ **5.** $5 + \sqrt{2}$

6. $(\sqrt{2})^4$ **7.** $\sqrt{3} - \sqrt{3}$ **8.** 7π **9.** $2.\overline{91}$ **10.** 1.23456789. . .

Simplify.

11. $\sqrt{50}$ **12.** $\sqrt{150}$ **13.** $\sqrt{98}$ **14.** $\sqrt{128}$ **15.** $\sqrt{220}$

Approximate each square root to the nearest tenth. Use your calculator or the table at the back of the book.

16. $\sqrt{500}$ **17.** $\sqrt{1200}$ **18.** $\sqrt{2800}$ **19.** $\sqrt{4300}$ **20.** $\sqrt{6300}$

Written Exercises

Simplify.

A **1.** $\sqrt{63}$ **2.** $\sqrt{28}$ **3.** $\sqrt{98}$ **4.** $\sqrt{50}$ **5.** $\sqrt{75}$

6. $\sqrt{24}$ **7.** $\sqrt{256}$ **8.** $\sqrt{120}$ **9.** $2\sqrt{48}$ **10.** $6\sqrt{108}$

11. $5\sqrt{72}$ **12.** $9\sqrt{90}$ **13.** $\sqrt{529}$ **14.** $\sqrt{324}$ **15.** $6\sqrt{45}$

16. $14\sqrt{75}$ 17. $\sqrt{361}$ 18. $\sqrt{864}$ 19. $10\sqrt{125}$ 20. $3\sqrt{160}$

21. $\sqrt{192}$ 22. $\sqrt{432}$ 23. $5\sqrt{600}$ 24. $4\sqrt{363}$ 25. $6\sqrt{245}$

26. $5\sqrt{567}$ 27. $\sqrt{5625}$ 28. $\sqrt{9200}$ 29. $7\sqrt{1200}$ 30. $5\sqrt{2050}$

In Exercises 31–50, use your calculator or the table at the back of the book.

Approximate each square root to the nearest tenth.

B 31. $\sqrt{800}$ 32. $\sqrt{500}$ 33. $-\sqrt{700}$ 34. $-\sqrt{600}$

35. $-\sqrt{5900}$ 36. $-\sqrt{4800}$ 37. $\pm\sqrt{7800}$ 38. $\pm\sqrt{5600}$

Approximate each square root to the nearest hundredth.

39. $\sqrt{68}$ 40. $\sqrt{42}$ 41. $-\sqrt{0.5}$ 42. $-\sqrt{0.3}$

43. $\pm\sqrt{0.87}$ 44. $\pm\sqrt{0.73}$ 45. $-\sqrt{0.07}$ 46. $-\sqrt{0.08}$

Approximate each square root to the nearest whole number.

47. $\sqrt{150{,}000}$ 48. $\sqrt{240{,}000}$ 49. $\sqrt{420{,}000}$ 50. $\sqrt{580{,}000}$

Mixed Review Exercises

Find the indicated square roots.

1. $\sqrt{400}$ 2. $-\sqrt{169}$ 3. $\sqrt{\frac{25}{81}}$

4. $-\sqrt{\frac{49}{225}}$ 5. $\sqrt{176^2}$ 6. $\sqrt{\left(\frac{3}{8}\right)^2}$

Simplify.

7. $(17x)^2$ 8. $(3y^4z^9)^2$ 9. $(2x + 3y)^2$

10. $[15(a + 2)]^2$ 11. $(11a^4b^{11}c)^2$ 12. $(6z^3 + 5y^4)(6z^3 - 5y^4)$

Historical Note / π

The number π occurs naturally as the ratio of the circumference of a circle to its diameter. It is not possible to get an exact value for π since it is an irrational number.

The first known approximation (other than just using 3) was given in the Rhind mathematical papyrus as $(\frac{4}{3})^4$, or 3.1604 . . . . This was used until 240 B.C. when Archimedes calculated π to be between $\frac{223}{71}$ and $\frac{22}{7}$, or 3.14, to two decimal places. Four hundred years later this approximation was improved slightly to $\frac{377}{120}$, or 3.1416. In China, Tsu Ch'ung-chih gave a value for π of $\frac{355}{113}$, or 3.1415929 . . . , which is correct to six decimal places. Indian mathematicians used $\frac{62{,}832}{20{,}000}$, although this was later refined to $\frac{754}{240}$.

Following the Middle Ages, European mathematicians once again tried to get better approximations for π. In 1706, the calculation had reached 100 decimal places. William Jones became the first person to use the symbol π to represent the number. By 1737, π was in general use.

In 1767 π was shown to be an irrational number. This did not stop people from calculating more decimal places. In 1948 the last calculation by hand was done to 808 places. Since 1949 computers have been used to approximate π. The first attempt in 1949 produced 2037 decimal places (after 70 hours of computer time). By 1967 the value had been calculated to over 500,000 places.

Extra / Irrationality of $\sqrt{2}$

The following proof shows that 2 does not have a rational square root. You begin by assuming that 2 has a rational square root and then show that this assumption leads to a contradiction. Hence, the original assumption that 2 has a rational square root must be false.

1. Assume that 2 has a rational square root.
2. Then, $\sqrt{2} = \frac{a}{b}$, where a and b are positive integers that have no common prime factor; that is, $\frac{a}{b}$ is in simplest form.
3. If $\sqrt{2} = \frac{a}{b}$, then $2 = \frac{a^2}{b^2}$. Since a^2 has the same prime factors as a, and b^2 has the same prime factors as b, a^2 and b^2 have no common prime factors. Thus, $\frac{a^2}{b^2}$ is in simplest form.
4. Multiplying both sides of the equation $\frac{a^2}{b^2} = 2$ by b^2, you have $a^2 = 2b^2$. Thus, a must be even because its square is even. (Recall that the square of an even integer is even and that the square of an odd integer is odd.)
5. Since a is even, you can write $a = 2n$ for some integer n. Then, substituting $2n$ for a in $a^2 = 2b^2$, you have $(2n)^2 = 2b^2$, $4n^2 = 2b^2$, or $2n^2 = b^2$.
6. Since $2n^2 = b^2$, b must be even because its square is even. Therefore, you may write $b = 2m$ for some integer m.
7. Therefore, both a and b have 2 as a factor. This contradicts the fact that a and b have no common prime factor.
8. Hence the assumption that 2 has a rational root is false since it leads to a contradiction.

Exercise

Prove that $\sqrt{3}$ is irrational.

11-5 Square Roots of Variable Expressions

Objective To find square roots of variable expressions and to use them to solve equations and problems.

Is it always true that $\sqrt{x^2} = x$? Recall that the symbol $\sqrt{}$ names the principal, or positive, square root of a positive number. Thus, when $x = -9$, you have

$$\sqrt{(-9)^2} = \sqrt{81} = 9.$$

Therefore, it is not always true that $\sqrt{x^2} = x$. If x is positive, $\sqrt{x^2} = x$, but if x is negative, then $\sqrt{x^2} = -x$. In either case, it *is* true that

$$\sqrt{x^2} = |x|.$$

When you are finding square roots of variable expressions, you must be careful to use absolute value signs when needed to ensure that your answer is positive.

Example 1 Simplify:

a. $\sqrt{196y^2}$ **b.** $\sqrt{36x^8}$ **c.** $\sqrt{m^2 - 6m + 9}$ **d.** $\sqrt{18a^3}$

Solution

a. $\sqrt{196y^2} = \sqrt{196} \cdot \sqrt{y^2} = 14|y|$

b. $\sqrt{36x^8} = \sqrt{36} \cdot \sqrt{(x^4)^2} = 6x^4$ (x^4 is always nonnegative.)

c. $\sqrt{m^2 - 6m + 9} = \sqrt{(m-3)^2} = |m - 3|$

d. $\sqrt{18a^3} = \sqrt{9 \cdot 2 \cdot a^2 \cdot a} = \sqrt{9} \cdot \sqrt{a^2} \cdot \sqrt{2a} = 3a\sqrt{2a}$

Example 2 Solve $9x^2 = 64$.

Solution 1

$$9x^2 = 64$$
$$9x^2 - 64 = 0$$
$$(3x + 8)(3x - 8) = 0$$
$$3x = -8 \quad \text{or} \quad 3x = 8$$
$$x = -\frac{8}{3} \quad \text{or} \quad x = \frac{8}{3}$$

Solution 2

$$9x^2 = 64$$
$$x^2 = \frac{64}{9}$$
$$x = \pm\sqrt{\frac{64}{9}}$$
$$x = \pm\frac{8}{3}$$

Check: $9\left(\frac{8}{3}\right)^2 \stackrel{?}{=} 64$ and $9\left(-\frac{8}{3}\right)^2 \stackrel{?}{=} 64$

$64 = 64$ ✓ and $64 = 64$ ✓

$\therefore$ the solution set is $\left\{\frac{8}{3}, -\frac{8}{3}\right\}$. ***Answer***

The second solution of Example 2 is based upon the following property.

Property of Square Roots of Equal Numbers

For any real numbers r and s:

$$r^2 = s^2 \text{ if and only if } r = s \text{ or } r = -s.$$

Oral Exercises

Simplify.

1. $\sqrt{25x^2}$
2. $\sqrt{144y^2}$
3. $\sqrt{81a^4}$
4. $\sqrt{64x^2y^2}$
5. $\sqrt{0.09c^2}$
6. $\sqrt{\frac{x^2}{49}}$
7. $\sqrt{\frac{16}{a^4}}$
8. $\sqrt{\frac{x^4y^4}{64}}$
9. $\sqrt{\frac{r^6s^6}{36}}$
10. $\sqrt{\frac{m^{16}}{100n^8}}$

Written Exercises

Simplify.

A

1. $\sqrt{121a^2}$
2. $\sqrt{100z^2}$
3. $\sqrt{28x^2}$
4. $\sqrt{32b^4}$
5. $-\sqrt{9c^4}$
6. $-\sqrt{64x^2}$
7. $-\sqrt{25d^6}$
8. $-\sqrt{16d^8}$
9. $\sqrt{80a^2b^2}$
10. $\sqrt{49a^2b^2}$
11. $\sqrt{75r^3}$
12. $\sqrt{80n^6}$
13. $\pm\sqrt{54x^2y^3}$
14. $\pm\sqrt{56r^6s^4}$
15. $-\sqrt{144x^2z^2}$
16. $-\sqrt{400a^6b^4}$
17. $\pm\sqrt{\frac{100f^{10}}{121}}$
18. $\pm\sqrt{\frac{256}{400s^{12}}}$
19. $\sqrt{\frac{x^4y^6}{4r^2}}$
20. $\sqrt{\frac{45m^3n^2}{5mn^4}}$
21. $\sqrt{\frac{64g^{18}}{8100h^{20}}}$
22. $\sqrt{\frac{324r^{50}}{49}}$
23. $-\sqrt{3.24x^4}$
24. $\sqrt{1.96k^6}$
25. $\sqrt{y^2 - 8y + 16}$
26. $\sqrt{m^2 - 12m + 36}$

Solve.

27. $x^2 = 25$
28. $n^2 = 64$
29. $x^2 - 4 = 0$
30. $d^2 - 49 = 0$
31. $0 = a^2 - 100$
32. $0 = m^2 - 81$
33. $2m^2 - 50 = 0$
34. $50b^2 - 450 = 0$
35. $81y^2 - 16 = 0$
36. $9c^2 - 64 = 0$
37. $0 = 81z^2 - 49$
38. $0 = 80p^2 - 125$

Find both roots of each equation to the nearest tenth.

B

39. $x^2 = 618$
40. $a^2 = 154$
41. $0.38 = r^2$
42. $0.29 = k^2$
43. $c^2 - 212 = 0$
44. $w^2 - 204 = 0$
45. $y^2 - 10.25 = 0$
46. $n^2 - 13.08 = 0$
47. $9z^2 = 513$
48. $7z^2 = 133$
49. $0 = 4b^2 - 0.48$
50. $0 = 6n^2 - 0.42$

C

51. $0.13m^2 = 9.36$
52. $9k^2 = 168$
53. $(x + 1)^2 + (x - 1)^2 = 176$
54. $(a + 3)^2 + (a - 3)^2 = 256$

Problems

Solve. Find each answer to the nearest tenth. Use 3.14 for π. A calculator may be helpful.

A

1. Find the length of a side of a square whose area is 300 cm^2.
2. Find the length of a side of a square whose area is the same as that of a rectangle 24 cm by 30 cm.
3. The length of the base of a triangle is 3 times the length of its altitude. Find the length of the base if the area of the triangle is 54 m^2.
4. Find the length of a side of a square if its area is the same as the area of a triangle with an altitude of 18 cm and a base of 11 cm.
5. The search for a missing boat covered a circular region with an area of 164 km^2. What was the radius of the search region?

6. If the area of the figure at the right below is 600 mm^2, find s.

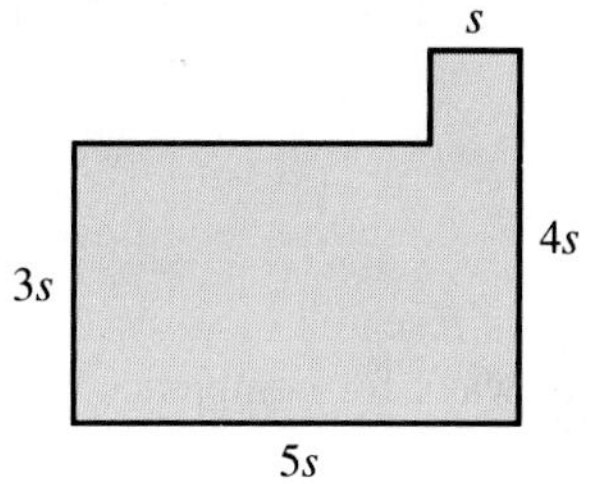

Ex. 6

B

7. The formula $s = 4.9t^2$ gives the approximate distance traveled in t seconds by an object falling from rest. How long does it take a rock falling from rest to travel 1587.6 m?
8. A circle inside a square just touches its sides. If the area of the circle is 341.9 cm^2, what is the length of a side of the square?
9. An old water pipe is to be replaced by a new one so that twice as much water can flow through the pipe. What is the ratio of the radius of the new pipe to that of the old pipe?

Let a, b, and c be the lengths of the sides of a triangle. Let $s = \frac{1}{2}(a + b + c)$. Then the area, A, of the triangle is $A = \sqrt{s(s - a)(s - b)(s - c)}$. Find the area, to the nearest tenth, of a triangle with sides of the given lengths.

C

10. 8 cm, 10 cm, and 14 cm
11. 14 m, 19 m, and 25 m
12. 6 cm, 6 cm, and 6 cm

Mixed Review Exercises

Simplify.

1. $\pm\sqrt{250}$
2. $-6\sqrt{76}$
3. $5\sqrt{396}$
4. $2^{-2} - 3^{-2}$
5. $6^2 \cdot 3^{-3}$
6. $(4x^3)^2(-2x^5)^{-3}$

Evaluate if $x = 9$, $y = 4$, and $n = 1$.

7. $x^2 + y^2$
8. x^2y^2
9. $x^2 - n^2$
10. $\sqrt{\frac{n}{x}}$
11. $\sqrt{\frac{x}{y}}$
12. $(\sqrt{y})^4$

Calculator Key-In

Use a calculator and the formula $A = \sqrt{s(s - a)(s - b)(s - c)}$ where $s = \frac{1}{2}(a + b + c)$ to find the approximate area of each triangle whose sides are given. Give your answers to the nearest hundredth.

1. 7 cm, 11 cm, and 14 cm
2. 13 mm, 18 mm, and 27 mm
3. 12 m, 12 m, and 16 m
4. 48 mm, 64 mm, and 84 mm
5. 2.8 m, 3.9 m, and 5.7 m
6. 15.8 cm, 16.9 cm, and 23.4 cm
7. 9.2 cm, 11.8 cm, and 17.1 cm
8. 37.1 m, 46.4 m, and 69.7 m

Career Note / *Operations Research Analyst*

Operations research analysts find more efficient ways for companies to control inventory, schedule personnel, predict future needs, and allocate resources. An operations research analyst may be asked to find the ideal number of parts for a manufacturing company to have on hand. When working on such problems mathematicians often use a method called linear programming (see the Extra on pages 499–500).

Operations research analysts approach a problem by breaking it down and learning everything they can about each part of the problem. They then use computers and statistics to examine possible solutions. When their analysis is complete, they make recommendations to the decision-making managers of the company.

11-6 The Pythagorean Theorem

Objective To use the Pythagorean theorem and its converse to solve geometric problems.

The Pythagorean theorem can be used to find the lengths of sides of right triangles. The hypotenuse of a right triangle is the side opposite the right angle. It is the longest side. The other two sides of a right triangle are called the legs of the triangle.

The Pythagorean Theorem

In any right triangle, the square of the length of the hypotenuse equals the sum of the squares of the lengths of the legs. For the triangle shown,

$$a^2 + b^2 = c^2.$$

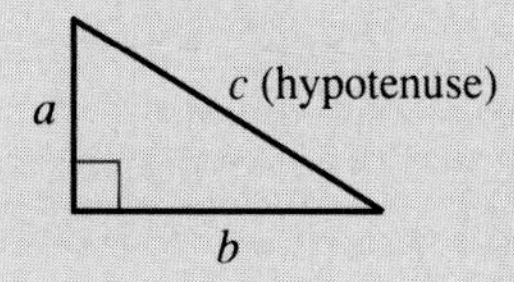

The diagrams below suggest a proof of the Pythagorean theorem. Each diagram shows a square, $(a + b)$ units on a side, divided into other figures. The diagrams suggest different expressions for the area of the square. Equating these expressions leads to the equation $a^2 + b^2 = c^2$.

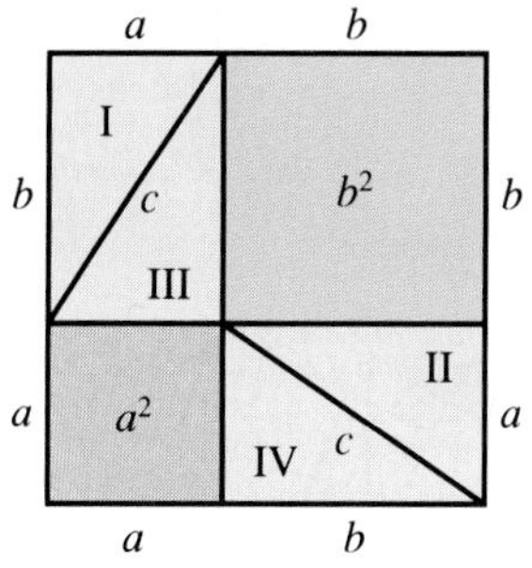

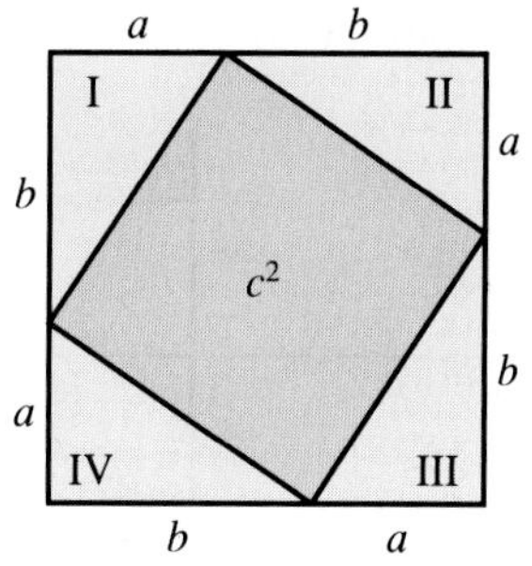

$$(a + b)^2 = a^2 + b^2 + 4\left(\frac{1}{2}ab\right) \qquad (a + b)^2 = c^2 + 4\left(\frac{1}{2}ab\right)$$

$$a^2 + b^2 + 4\left(\frac{1}{2}ab\right) = c^2 + 4\left(\frac{1}{2}ab\right)$$

$$\therefore a^2 + b^2 = c^2$$

Example 1 The length of one side of a right triangle is 28 cm. The length of the hypotenuse is 53 cm. Write and solve an equation for the length of the unknown side.

Solution

$$a^2 + b^2 = c^2 \qquad a = \sqrt{c^2 - b^2}$$

$$a^2 = c^2 - b^2 \qquad = \sqrt{53^2 - 28^2}$$

$$= \sqrt{2809 - 784} = \sqrt{2025} = 45$$ *(Check on next page.)*

(Check on next page.)

Check: $28^2 + 45^2 \stackrel{?}{=} 53^2$
$2809 = 2809$ ✓

$\therefore$ the length of the third side of the right triangle is 45 cm. ***Answer***

To draw a line segment with a length of $\sqrt{2}$ units, draw a right triangle whose legs are each 1 unit long, as shown in the following diagram.

Then:

$$a^2 + b^2 = c^2$$
$$1^2 + 1^2 = c^2$$
$$1 + 1 = c^2$$
$$2 = c^2$$
$$\pm\sqrt{2} = c$$

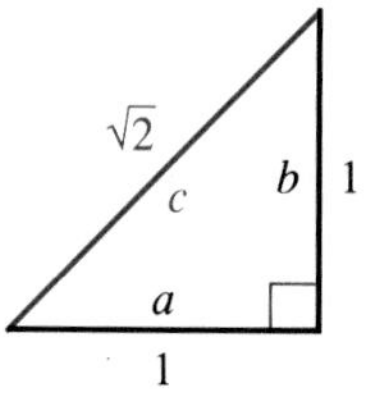

$\therefore$ the length of the hypotenuse is $\sqrt{2}$ units.

The following diagrams show that a segment $\sqrt{2}$ units long can be used to construct a segment $\sqrt{3}$ units long, that a segment $\sqrt{3}$ units long can be used to construct a segment $\sqrt{4}$ units long, and so on.

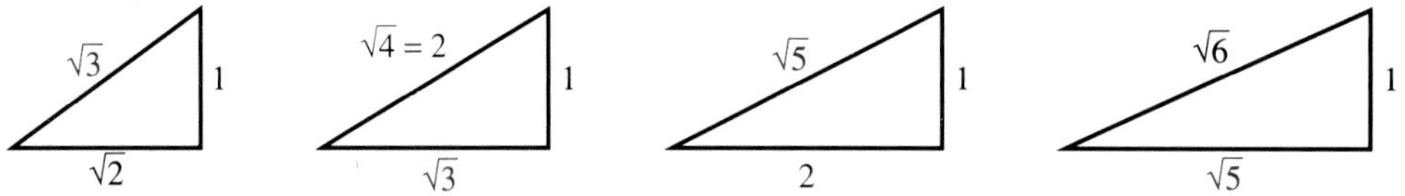

A series of such triangles can be used to locate irrational square roots such as $\sqrt{2}$, $\sqrt{3}$, and $\sqrt{5}$ on the number line. The arcs are drawn to transfer the length of the hypotenuse of each triangle to the x-axis. Note that $-\sqrt{2}$ is located $\sqrt{2}$ units to the left of O.

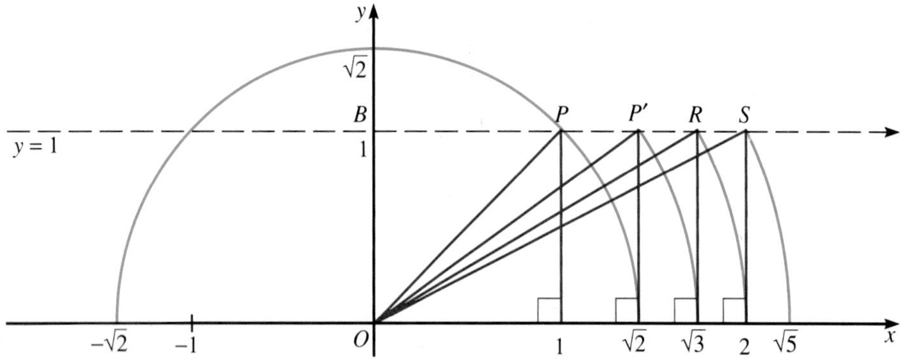

The converse of the Pythagorean theorem is also true. It can be used to see if a given triangle is a right triangle.

Converse of the Pythagorean Theorem

If the sum of the squares of the lengths of the two shorter sides of a triangle is equal to the square of the length of the longest, then the triangle is a right triangle. The right angle is opposite the longest side.

Example 2 State whether or not the three given numbers could represent the lengths of the sides of a right triangle.

a. 8, 15, 17 **b.** 16, 24, 30

Solution

a.
$$a^2 + b^2 = c^2$$
$$8^2 + 15^2 \stackrel{?}{=} 17^2$$
$$64 + 225 \stackrel{?}{=} 289$$
$$289 = 289 \quad \checkmark$$

$\therefore$ 8, 15, and 17 could form a right triangle. ***Answer***

b.
$$a^2 + b^2 = c^2$$
$$16^2 + 24^2 \stackrel{?}{=} 30^2$$
$$256 + 576 \stackrel{?}{=} 900$$
$$832 \neq 900$$

$\therefore$ 16, 24, and 30 could not form a right triangle. ***Answer***

Example 3 To the nearest hundredth, what is the length of a diagonal of a rectangle whose width is 18 cm and whose length is 30 cm?

Solution

$$a^2 + b^2 = c^2$$
$$\sqrt{a^2 + b^2} = c$$
$$\sqrt{18^2 + 30^2} = c$$
$$\sqrt{1224} = c$$
$$\sqrt{2^2 \cdot 3^2 \cdot 34} = c$$
$$6\sqrt{34} = c$$
$$6(5.831) \approx c$$
$$34.99 \approx c$$

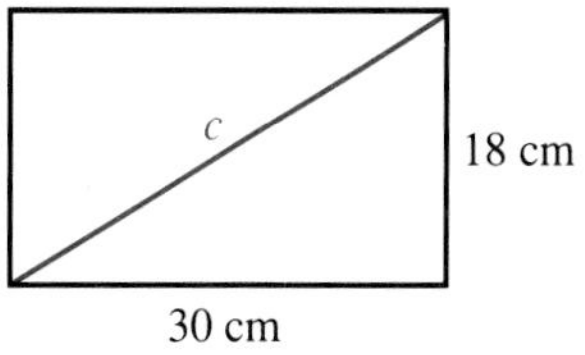

Check: $18^2 + 30^2 \stackrel{?}{\approx} (34.99)^2$

$1224 \approx 1224.3 \quad \checkmark$

$\therefore$ the length of a diagonal of the rectangle is 34.99 cm. ***Answer***

Oral Exercises

Evaluate.

1. $\sqrt{6^2 + 8^2}$
2. $\sqrt{5^2 - 3^2}$
3. $\sqrt{13^2 - 5^2}$

State and solve an equation for the length of the unknown side.

4.

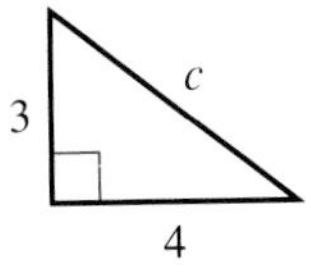

$$a^2 + b^2 = c^2$$
$$(\underline{\ ?\ })^2 + (\underline{\ ?\ })^2 = c^2$$
$$\underline{\ ?\ } = c^2$$
$$\underline{\ ?\ } = c$$

5.

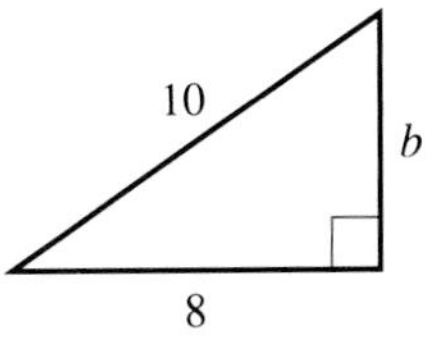

$$a^2 + b^2 = c^2$$
$$(\underline{\ ?\ })^2 + b^2 = (\underline{\ ?\ })^2$$
$$b^2 = \underline{\ ?\ }$$
$$b = \underline{\ ?\ }$$

Written Exercises

In Exercises 1–10, refer to the triangle at the right. Find the missing length correct to the nearest hundredth. A calculator may be helpful.

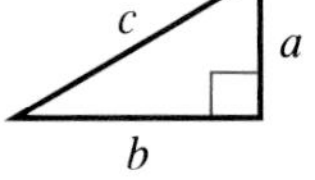

A

1. $a = 10$, $b = 24$, $c = \underline{\ ?\ }$

2. $a = 5$, $b = 12$, $c = \underline{\ ?\ }$

3. $a = 8$, $b = 5$, $c = \underline{\ ?\ }$

4. $a = 13$, $b = 9$, $c = \underline{\ ?\ }$

5. $a = 8$, $b = 8$, $c = \underline{\ ?\ }$

6. $a = 16$, $b = 8$, $c = \underline{\ ?\ }$

7. $a = \underline{\ ?\ }$, $b = 21$, $c = 29$

8. $a = \underline{\ ?\ }$, $b = 11$, $c = 17$

9. $a = 6$, $b = \underline{\ ?\ }$, $c = 40$

10. $a = 5$, $b = \underline{\ ?\ }$, $c = 8$

State whether or not the three given numbers could represent the lengths of the sides of a right triangle.

11. 20, 21, 29

12. 3, 9, 11

13. 12, 16, 20

14. 16, 32, 36

15. 15, 20, 25

16. 17, 34, 39

B

17. $2a$, $3a$, $4a$

18. $3a$, $4a$, $5a$

19. $8a$, $15a$, $17a$

20. $6a$, $7a$, $8a$

In Exercises 21–26, refer to the diagram for Exercises 1–10. Find the missing length correct to the nearest hundredth.

21. $a = b = 12$, $c = \underline{\ ?\ }$

22. $a = 15$, $b = \frac{1}{5}a$, $c = \underline{\ ?\ }$

23. $a = 18$, $b = \frac{1}{3}a$, $c = \underline{\ ?\ }$

24. $a = \frac{1}{2}b$, $b = 14$, $c = \underline{\ ?\ }$

25. $a = \frac{4}{5}b$, $b = 20$, $c = \underline{\ ?\ }$

26. $a = \frac{5}{7}b$, $b = 28$, $c = \underline{\ ?\ }$

In Exercises 27–30, refer to the diagram for Exercises 1–10. Find *a* and *b* correct to the nearest hundredth.

C

27. $a = b$, $c = 60$

28. $a = 3b$, $c = 20$

29. $a = \frac{1}{3}b$, $c = 30$

30. $a = \frac{2}{3}b$, $c = 52$

Computer Exercises

Write a BASIC program that will report whether three positive numbers entered with INPUT statements could represent the lengths of the sides of a right triangle. RUN the program for the following series of numbers.

1. 14, 48, 50

2. 0.8, 1.5, 1.7

3. 27, 36, 45

Problems

Make a sketch for each problem. Approximate each square root to the nearest hundredth. A calculator may be helpful.

A

1. Find the length of each diagonal of a rectangle whose dimensions are 33 cm by 56 cm.
2. A guywire 20 m long is attached to the top of a telephone pole. The guywire is just able to reach a point on the ground 12 m from the base of the telephone pole. Find the height of the telephone pole.
3. A baseball diamond is a square 90 ft on a side. What is the length from first base to third base?
4. The dimensions of a rectangular doorway are 200 cm by 90 cm. Can a table top with a diameter of 210 cm be carried through the doorway?
5. The base of an isosceles triangle is 18 cm long. The equal sides are each 24 cm long. Find the altitude.

B

6. A right triangle has sides whose lengths in feet are consecutive even integers. Determine the length of each side.
7. The longer leg of a right triangle is 6 cm longer than 6 times the shorter leg and also 1 cm shorter than the hypotenuse. Find the perimeter of the triangle.
8. Find the area of a triangle with three sides of length 4 cm. (*Hint:* Find the height first.)

C

9. What is the length of each diagonal of a cube that is 45 cm on each side?

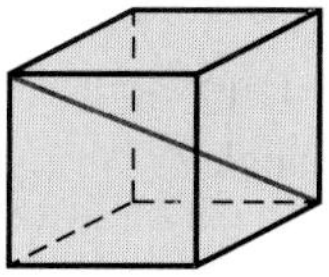

10. Show that a triangle with sides of lengths $x^2 + y^2$, $2xy$, and $x^2 - y^2$ is a right triangle. Assume that $x > y$.
11. What is the length of each diagonal of a rectangular box with length 55 cm, width 48 cm, and height 70 cm? Would a meter stick fit in the box?
12. Gary is standing on a dock 2.0 m above the water. He is pulling in a boat that is attached to the end of a 5.2 m rope. If he pulls in 2.3 m of rope, how far did he move the boat?

Mixed Review Exercises

Simplify.

1. $\sqrt{16x^{16}y^2}$

2. $\sqrt{c^2 - 10c + 25}$

3. $\sqrt{50a^5(b + 4)^2}$

Write as a fraction in simplest form.

4. $(3 \cdot 10^{-4})^2$

5. $(2x^{-3}y^{-5})^2$

6. $\frac{7}{8} \div \frac{8}{7}$

7. $\frac{a - 1}{6} + \frac{3 - 2a}{9}$

8. $5y + \frac{3 - y}{y - 3}$

9. $\frac{3r^2}{8x} \div 24rx$

10. $\left(-\frac{k^2}{6}\right)^3$

11. $\frac{2r^3 - 10r^2 - 28r}{2r - 14}$

12. $\frac{2s^2 + 9s - 5}{5 + s}$

Self-Test 2

Vocabulary irrational numbers (p. 521) Pythagorean theorem (p. 529)

Approximate each square root to the nearest tenth. Use a calculator or the table at the back of the book as necessary.

1. $\sqrt{0.81}$

2. $\sqrt{1700}$

3. $-\sqrt{0.88}$

Obj. 11-4, p. 521

Simplify.

4. $\sqrt{144m^2n^2}$

5. $-\sqrt{81x^8y^6}$

6. $\sqrt{0.25a^4}$

Obj. 11-5, p. 525

Solve.

7. $w^2 = 64$

8. $n^2 - 49 = 0$

9. $36y^2 - 25 = 0$

10. Find c correct to the nearest hundredth if $a = 14$ and $b = 17$.

11. Is a triangle with sides 9, 12, and 14 units long a right triangle?

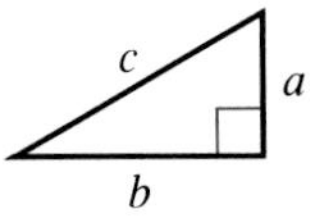

Obj. 11-6, p. 529

Check your answers with those at the back of the book.

Challenge

The following "Problem of the Hundred Fowl" dates to sixth-century China: If a rooster is worth 5 yuan, a hen is worth 3 yuan, and 3 chicks are worth 1 yuan, how many of each, 100 in all, would be worth 100 yuan? Assume that at least 5 roosters are required.

Extra / The Distance Formula

The distance between two points on the x-axis or on a line parallel to that axis is the absolute value of the difference between their x-coordinates. Using the notation $A'B'$ to denote the distance from A' to B', you can write the following:

$$A'B' = |3 - 7| = |7 - 3| = 4$$

$$AB = |3 - 7| = |7 - 3| = 4$$

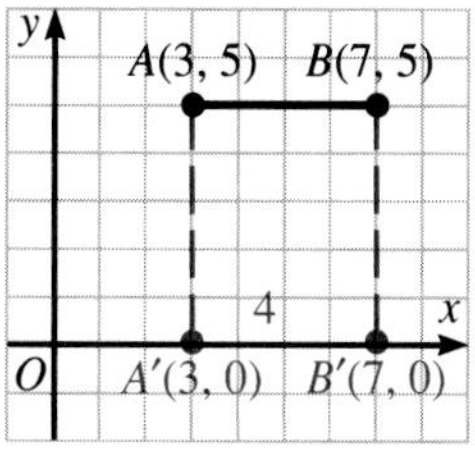

The distance between two points on the y-axis or on a line parallel to that axis is the absolute value of the difference between their y-coordinates.

$$A'C' = |2 - 8| = |8 - 2| = 6$$

$$AC = |2 - 8| = |8 - 2| = 6$$

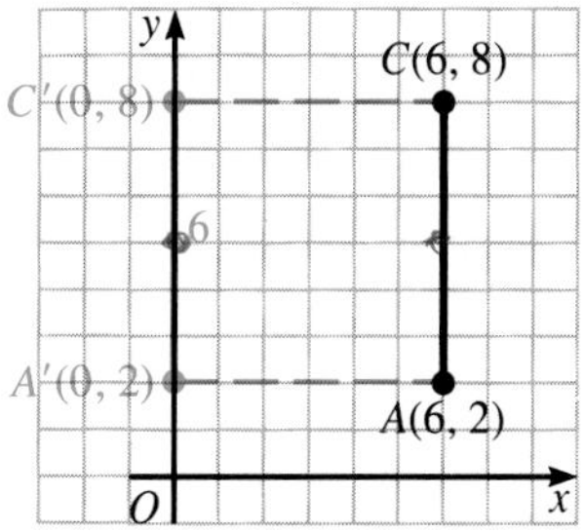

To find the distance between two points not on an axis or a line parallel to an axis, use the Pythagorean theorem:

$$\begin{aligned} AC &= \sqrt{(AB)^2 + (BC)^2} \\ &= \sqrt{(9 - 3)^2 + (6 - 4)^2} \\ &= \sqrt{6^2 + 2^2} \\ &= \sqrt{36 + 4} \\ &= \sqrt{40} \\ &= 2\sqrt{10} \end{aligned}$$

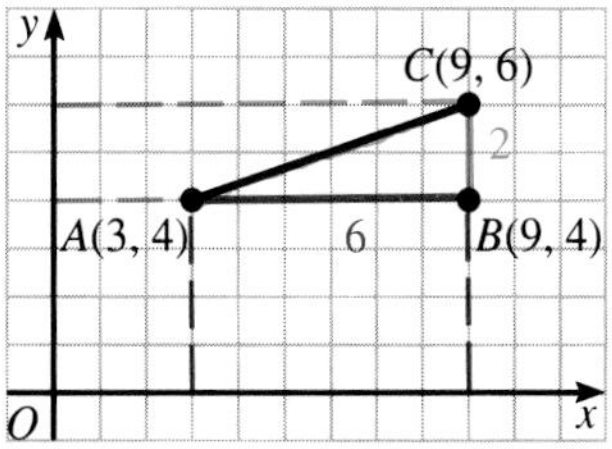

This method for finding the distance between any two points can be generalized in the distance formula.

The Distance Formula

For any points $P_1(x_1, y_1)$ and $P_2(x_2, y_2)$.

$$P_1P_2 = \sqrt{(x_2 - x_1)^2 + (y_2 - y_1)^2}$$

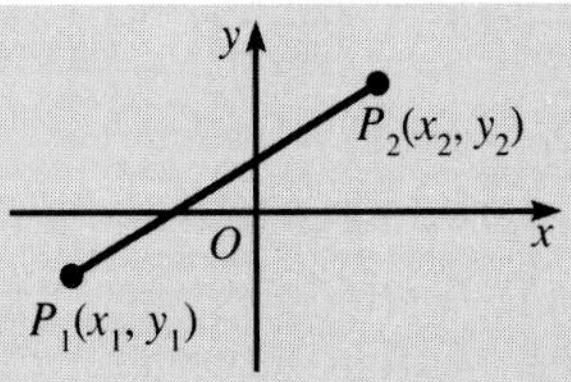

Example Find the distance between points $P(-5, 4)$ and $Q(3, -2)$.

Solution 1

$$PQ = \sqrt{(3 - (-5))^2 + (-2 - 4)^2} = \sqrt{8^2 + (-6)^2} = \sqrt{64 + 36} = \sqrt{100} = 10 \quad \textbf{Answer}$$

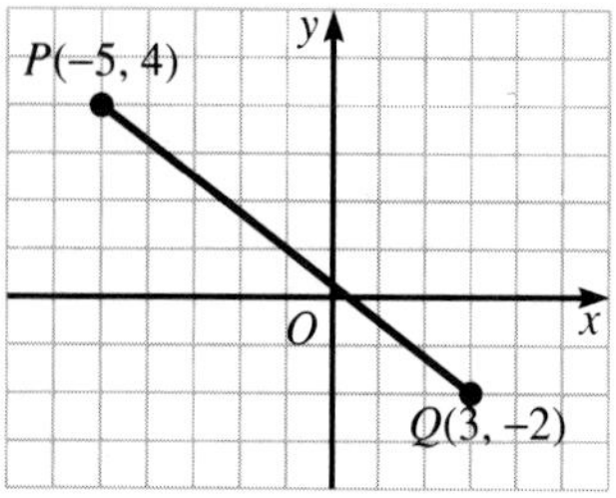

Solution 2

$$QP = \sqrt{(-5 - 3)^2 + (4 - (-2))^2} = \sqrt{(-8)^2 + (6)^2} = \sqrt{64 + 36} = \sqrt{100} = 10 \quad \textbf{Answer}$$

Exercises

Use the distance formula to find the distance between the given points to the nearest tenth.

1. $(-6, 0), (4, 0)$

2. $(0, -9), (0, 7)$

3. $(3, 4), (9, 7)$

4. $(10, 3), (-4, 9)$

5. $(-5, -3), (-9, -6)$

6. $(7, -2), (4, -6)$

7. $(-4, 6), (5, 2)$

8. $(-4, 7), (-9, -5)$

9. $(4, -4), (9, -8)$

10. $(3, -7), (12, -8)$

11. $(-2, 1), (-8, -5)$

12. $(10, -11), (-9, 3)$

13. Use the distance formula to show that the point $M(-2, -3)$ is equidistant from points $A(3, 9)$ and $B(-7, -15)$.

14. Show that the points $R(-4, -1)$, $S(3, 6)$, and $T(2, 7)$ are the vertices of a right triangle.

Challenge

1. On the same set of axes, graph the following line segments to draw a picture.

$x = 0,\ 2 \le y \le 7$

$x = 6,\ 0 \le y \le 5$

$x = 18,\ 4 \le y \le 9$

$x + 3y = 6,\ 0 \le x \le 6$

$x + 3y = 21,\ 0 \le x \le 6$

$x - y = -7,\ 0 \le x \le 3$

$x - 3y = 6,\ 6 \le x \le 18$

$x - 3y = -9,\ 6 \le x \le 18$

$x - 3y = -27,\ 3 \le x \le 15$

$5x + 3y = 45,\ 3 \le x \le 6$

$5x + 3y = 117,\ 15 \le x \le 18$

2. Draw a picture on graph paper using line segments. Write a set of equations and inequalities to describe your picture as in Exercise 1.

Radical Expressions

11-7 Multiplying, Dividing, and Simplifying Radicals

Objective To simplify products and quotients of radicals.

You can use the product and quotient properties of square roots together with the commutative, associative, and distributive properties to multiply, divide, and simplify square-root radicals.

Example 1 Simplify $3\sqrt{2} \cdot 4\sqrt{18}$.

Solution

$$\begin{aligned} 3\sqrt{2} \cdot 4\sqrt{18} &= (3 \cdot 4)(\sqrt{2} \cdot \sqrt{18}) \\ &= 12\sqrt{36} \\ &= 12 \cdot 6 \\ &= 72 \quad \textbf{\textit{Answer}} \end{aligned}$$

Example 2 Simplify $\sqrt{\frac{3}{7}} \cdot \sqrt{\frac{14}{27}}$.

Solution

$$\sqrt{\frac{3}{7}} \cdot \sqrt{\frac{14}{27}} = \sqrt{\frac{3}{7} \cdot \frac{14}{27}} = \sqrt{\frac{3 \cdot 14}{7 \cdot 27}} = \sqrt{\frac{2}{9}} = \frac{\sqrt{2}}{\sqrt{9}} = \frac{\sqrt{2}}{3}$$

You can eliminate the radical from the denominator by multiplying a radical expression by an appropriate value of 1. For example:

$$\frac{\sqrt{5}}{\sqrt{7}} = \frac{\sqrt{5} \cdot \sqrt{7}}{\sqrt{7} \cdot \sqrt{7}} = \frac{\sqrt{5 \cdot 7}}{(\sqrt{7})^2} = \frac{\sqrt{35}}{7} \quad \leftarrow \text{no radical in denominator}$$

The process of expressing $\frac{\sqrt{5}}{\sqrt{7}}$ as $\frac{\sqrt{35}}{7}$ is called **rationalizing the denominator.** As you can see, it is easier to name the decimal value of $\frac{\sqrt{35}}{7}$ than of $\frac{\sqrt{5}}{\sqrt{7}}$. Of course with a calculator it may not matter. In general:

An expression having a square-root radical is in **simplest form** when:

1. no integral radicand has a perfect-square factor other than 1,
2. no fractions are under a radical sign, and
3. no radicals are in a denominator.

Example 3 Simplify: **a.** $\frac{3}{\sqrt{5}}$ **b.** $\sqrt{\frac{7}{8}}$ **c.** $\frac{9\sqrt{3}}{\sqrt{24}}$ **d.** $\sqrt{3\frac{3}{7}} \cdot \sqrt{2\frac{1}{3}}$

Solution

a. $\frac{3}{\sqrt{5}} = \frac{3}{\sqrt{5}} \cdot \frac{\sqrt{5}}{\sqrt{5}} = \frac{3\sqrt{5}}{(\sqrt{5})^2} = \frac{3\sqrt{5}}{5}$

b. $\sqrt{\frac{7}{8}} = \frac{\sqrt{7}}{\sqrt{8}} = \frac{\sqrt{7}}{2\sqrt{2}} = \frac{\sqrt{7}}{2\sqrt{2}} \cdot \frac{\sqrt{2}}{\sqrt{2}} = \frac{\sqrt{7 \cdot 2}}{2(\sqrt{2})^2} = \frac{\sqrt{14}}{4}$

c. $\frac{9\sqrt{3}}{\sqrt{24}} = \frac{9\sqrt{3}}{2\sqrt{6}} = \frac{9\sqrt{3}}{2\sqrt{6}} \cdot \frac{\sqrt{6}}{\sqrt{6}} = \frac{9\sqrt{18}}{2(\sqrt{6})^2} = \frac{9\sqrt{9 \cdot 2}}{2 \cdot 6} = \frac{9 \cdot 3\sqrt{2}}{2 \cdot 6} = \frac{9\sqrt{2}}{4}$

d. $\sqrt{3\frac{3}{7}} \cdot \sqrt{2\frac{1}{3}} = \sqrt{\frac{24}{7}} \cdot \sqrt{\frac{7}{3}} = \sqrt{\frac{24}{7} \cdot \frac{7}{3}} = \sqrt{8} = 2\sqrt{2}$

Example 4 Multiply. Assume that all variables represent positive real numbers.

a. $3\sqrt{ab^2}(-2\sqrt{a})$ **b.** $\sqrt{r}(5 - \sqrt{r})$

Solution

a. $3\sqrt{ab^2}(-2\sqrt{a}) = 3(-2)\sqrt{ab^2 \cdot a} = -6\sqrt{a^2b^2} = -6ab$

b. $\sqrt{r}(5 - \sqrt{r}) = 5\sqrt{r} - (\sqrt{r})^2 = 5\sqrt{r} - r$

Oral Exercises

Simplify.

1. $\sqrt{2} \cdot \sqrt{5}$ **2.** $\frac{\sqrt{32}}{\sqrt{2}}$ **3.** $\frac{\sqrt{45}}{\sqrt{5}}$ **4.** $4\sqrt{2} \cdot \sqrt{3}$ **5.** $\sqrt{3} \cdot \sqrt{6}$

6. $\sqrt{3} \cdot \sqrt{12}$ **7.** $\frac{\sqrt{18}}{\sqrt{3}}$ **8.** $\frac{\sqrt{48}}{\sqrt{2}}$ **9.** $\frac{\sqrt{5}}{\sqrt{15}}$ **10.** $\sqrt{\frac{2}{7}}$

Written Exercises

Simplify. Assume that all variables represent positive real numbers.

A **1.** $5\sqrt{3} \cdot 2\sqrt{3}$ **2.** $4\sqrt{7} \cdot 2\sqrt{7}$ **3.** $\sqrt{3} \cdot \sqrt{3} \cdot \sqrt{4}$ **4.** $\sqrt{5} \cdot \sqrt{5} \cdot \sqrt{9}$

5. $2\sqrt{5} \cdot \sqrt{7}$ **6.** $6\sqrt{2} \cdot \sqrt{5}$ **7.** $\sqrt{3} \cdot \sqrt{27}$ **8.** $\sqrt{5} \cdot \sqrt{20}$

9. $\sqrt{11} \cdot \sqrt{44}$ **10.** $\sqrt{7} \cdot \sqrt{35}$ **11.** $6\sqrt{72}$ **12.** $9\sqrt{242}$

13. $\sqrt{\frac{3}{8}} \cdot \sqrt{\frac{8}{3}}$ **14.** $\sqrt{\frac{4}{9}} \cdot \sqrt{\frac{18}{4}}$ **15.** $\sqrt{\frac{8}{11}} \cdot \sqrt{\frac{22}{32}}$ **16.** $\sqrt{\frac{7}{3}} \cdot \sqrt{\frac{3}{28}}$

17. $\sqrt{\frac{3}{4}} \cdot \sqrt{\frac{8}{9}}$ **18.** $\sqrt{\frac{4}{5}} \cdot \sqrt{\frac{10}{36}}$ **19.** $\sqrt{3\frac{3}{5}} \cdot \sqrt{2\frac{1}{2}}$ **20.** $\sqrt{2\frac{2}{5}} \cdot \sqrt{1\frac{2}{3}}$

21. $\sqrt{\frac{10}{13}} \cdot \sqrt{\frac{1}{2}}$

22. $\sqrt{\frac{15}{11}} \cdot \sqrt{\frac{1}{3}}$

23. $\frac{6\sqrt{7}}{\sqrt{35}}$

24. $\frac{5\sqrt{48}}{\sqrt{39}}$

25. $3\sqrt{\frac{48}{9}}$

26. $7\sqrt{\frac{40}{49}}$

27. $\frac{14\sqrt{320}}{2\sqrt{5}}$

28. $\frac{15\sqrt{6}}{\sqrt{90}}$

29. $\sqrt{5}(\sqrt{5} - 2)$

30. $\sqrt{7}(6 - \sqrt{2})$

31. $(3\sqrt{2})(-2\sqrt{8})(3\sqrt{27})$

32. $(3\sqrt{5})(-\sqrt{10})(\sqrt{27})$

B 33. $(4\sqrt{a^2b})(3\sqrt{b})$

34. $(5\sqrt{mn^2})(-2\sqrt{m})$

35. $(-x\sqrt{x^2y})(y\sqrt{xy^2})$

36. $(-r\sqrt{r^2s})(-s\sqrt{r^2s})$

37. $\sqrt{m}(\sqrt{m^3} + 6)$

38. $\sqrt{x}(\sqrt{x^5} + 7)$

39. $(\sqrt{5x})(\sqrt{2x})(3\sqrt{10x^2})$

40. $(\sqrt{3a})(\sqrt{2a})(2\sqrt{6a^2})$

41. $\sqrt{32} \cdot \sqrt{2x} \cdot \sqrt{3x}$

42. $\sqrt{27} \cdot \sqrt{3n} \cdot \sqrt{5n}$

43. $(2\sqrt{5x})^2$

44. $2n(\sqrt{7n})^2$

45. $3x\sqrt{\frac{x}{y}} \cdot \sqrt{\frac{9x}{y}}$

46. $3q\sqrt{\frac{3q}{2r}} \cdot \sqrt{\frac{q}{r}}$

C 47. $\sqrt{3a}(\sqrt{12a} - 2\sqrt{8a^2})$

48. $\sqrt{6x}(\sqrt{3x} - 4\sqrt{8x^2})$

49. $3\sqrt{8m^3}(2\sqrt{2m} - 5\sqrt{8m^4})$

50. $2\sqrt{6x^3}(3\sqrt{8x} - 5\sqrt{3x^4})$

51. $(2\sqrt{3y^3})^3$

52. $(5\sqrt{2x^3})^3$

53. $(\sqrt{10xy})^3(x\sqrt{5x^3y} - y\sqrt{10xy^3})$

54. $(\sqrt{18ab})^3(a\sqrt{3a^2b} + b\sqrt{5ab^2})$

Rationalize the numerator.

Sample $\frac{\sqrt{5}}{\sqrt{7}} = \frac{\sqrt{5} \cdot \sqrt{5}}{\sqrt{7} \cdot \sqrt{5}} = \frac{(\sqrt{5})^2}{\sqrt{7 \cdot 5}} = \frac{5}{\sqrt{35}}$ ← no radical in numerator

55. $\frac{\sqrt{11}}{\sqrt{3}}$

56. $\frac{\sqrt{2}}{\sqrt{5}}$

57. $\frac{\sqrt{6}}{\sqrt{13}}$

58. $\frac{\sqrt{7}}{\sqrt{15}}$

59. $\frac{\sqrt{19}}{\sqrt{8}}$

Mixed Review Exercises

Solve.

1. $x^2 = 169$

2. $2s^2 - 200 = 0$

3. $25z^2 - 1 = 15$

4. $\frac{1}{c} + \frac{1}{3} = \frac{1}{2}$

5. $\frac{5}{9} = \frac{25}{y}$

6. $\frac{8b - 5}{5b - 4} = \frac{13}{8}$

Simplify.

7. $19x + 2(3x - 4) + 5$

8. $12a + 7 - (8a - 17)$

9. $4(2b - 6) - 5(b - 4)$

10. $(-5c^2d)(-4cd^4)$

11. $-4m + 3 + 11m - 4$

12. $x(x + 2) + (x - 4)(2x + 1)$

11-8 Adding and Subtracting Radicals

Objective To simplify sums and differences of radicals.

You can use the distributive property to simplify the sum of $4\sqrt{7}$ and $5\sqrt{7}$ because each term has $\sqrt{7}$ as a common factor.

Example 1 Simplify $4\sqrt{7} + 5\sqrt{7}$.

Solution $4\sqrt{7} + 5\sqrt{7} = (4 + 5)\sqrt{7} = 9\sqrt{7}$

On the other hand, terms that have unlike radicands *cannot* be combined.

Example 2 Simplify $3\sqrt{6} - 2\sqrt{13} + 5\sqrt{6}$.

Solution $3\sqrt{6} - 2\sqrt{13} + 5\sqrt{6} = (3 + 5)\sqrt{6} - 2\sqrt{13} = 8\sqrt{6} - 2\sqrt{13}$

By expressing each radical in simplest form, you can sometimes combine terms in sums and differences of radicals.

Example 3 Simplify $7\sqrt{3} - 4\sqrt{6} + 2\sqrt{48} - 6\sqrt{54}$.

Solution
$$\begin{aligned} 7\sqrt{3} - 4\sqrt{6} + 2\sqrt{48} - 6\sqrt{54} &= 7\sqrt{3} - 4\sqrt{6} + 2\sqrt{16 \cdot 3} - 6\sqrt{9 \cdot 6} \\ &= 7\sqrt{3} - 4\sqrt{6} + 2(4\sqrt{3}) - 6(3 \cdot \sqrt{6}) \\ &= 7\sqrt{3} - 4\sqrt{6} + 8\sqrt{3} - 18\sqrt{6} \\ &= 15\sqrt{3} - 22\sqrt{6} \quad \textit{Answer} \end{aligned}$$

To simplify sums or differences of square-root radicals:
1. Express each radical in simplest form.
2. Use the distributive property to add or subtract radicals with like radicands.

Oral Exercises

State the terms in each expression that can be expressed with the same radicand. Simplify the expression if possible.

1. $3\sqrt{5} + 2\sqrt{5}$
2. $8\sqrt{3} - 5\sqrt{3}$
3. $4\sqrt{11} - 8\sqrt{11}$
4. $6\sqrt{7} + 9\sqrt{7} + 2\sqrt{7}$
5. $8\sqrt{14} - 5\sqrt{14} + \sqrt{3}$
6. $3\sqrt{17} - 3\sqrt{13} + 5\sqrt{11}$
7. $12\sqrt{3} - 7\sqrt{3}$
8. $8\sqrt{15} - 5\sqrt{15} + 7\sqrt{15}$
9. $6\sqrt{17} - 5\sqrt{17} + 3\sqrt{17}$
10. $\sqrt{27} - \sqrt{3}$
11. $\sqrt{48} + \sqrt{3}$
12. $\sqrt{24} + \sqrt{6}$

Written Exercises

Simplify.

A

1. $8\sqrt{3} - 6\sqrt{3}$
2. $9\sqrt{5} + 4\sqrt{5}$
3. $-13\sqrt{17} - 7\sqrt{17}$
4. $5\sqrt{80} - 12\sqrt{5}$
5. $5\sqrt{3} + 2\sqrt{75}$
6. $-2\sqrt{24} - 3\sqrt{6}$
7. $3\sqrt{32} - 4\sqrt{63}$
8. $3\sqrt{45} + 7\sqrt{36}$
9. $5\sqrt{28} - 2\sqrt{45}$
10. $-4\sqrt{75} + 3\sqrt{147}$
11. $-11\sqrt{8} - 7\sqrt{12}$
12. $\sqrt{150} - 5\sqrt{96}$
13. $9\sqrt{13} - 6\sqrt{11} + \sqrt{13}$
14. $-4\sqrt{2} + 6\sqrt{72} - 8\sqrt{32}$
15. $5\sqrt{28} + 2\sqrt{7} - \sqrt{14}$
16. $-3\sqrt{72} + 6\sqrt{52} - 7\sqrt{128}$
17. $-\sqrt{338} - \sqrt{200} + \sqrt{162}$
18. $4\sqrt{112} + 5\sqrt{56} - 9\sqrt{126}$

Sample

$$\sqrt{15} - \sqrt{\frac{3}{5}} = \sqrt{15} - \frac{\sqrt{3}}{\sqrt{5}}$$
$$= \sqrt{15} - \frac{\sqrt{3}}{\sqrt{5}} \cdot \frac{\sqrt{5}}{\sqrt{5}}$$
$$= \sqrt{15} - \frac{\sqrt{15}}{5}$$
$$= \frac{5\sqrt{15} - \sqrt{15}}{5}$$
$$= \frac{4\sqrt{15}}{5} \quad \textit{Answer}$$

B

19. $\sqrt{55} - 7\sqrt{\frac{5}{11}}$
20. $\sqrt{3} - \sqrt{\frac{1}{3}}$
21. $3\sqrt{18} + \sqrt{\frac{2}{25}}$
22. $2\sqrt{75} + \sqrt{\frac{3}{16}}$
23. $\sqrt{\frac{5}{11}} - \sqrt{\frac{11}{5}}$
24. $\sqrt{\frac{2}{7}} - \sqrt{\frac{7}{2}}$
25. $4\sqrt{\frac{5}{6}} - \sqrt{\frac{3}{10}}$
26. $5\sqrt{\frac{16}{3}} - \sqrt{\frac{9}{2}}$
27. $3\sqrt{3} - 2\sqrt{12} + 4\sqrt{\frac{1}{3}}$
28. $8\sqrt{10} - 3\sqrt{40} + 5\sqrt{\frac{1}{10}}$
29. $2\sqrt{\frac{7}{2}} + 4\sqrt{\frac{7}{8}} - \frac{1}{2}\sqrt{98}$
30. $3\sqrt{\frac{5}{12}} + \sqrt{\frac{12}{5}} - \frac{1}{3}\sqrt{60}$
31. $5\sqrt{3}(\sqrt{6} + 2\sqrt{8})$
32. $5\sqrt{2}(4\sqrt{8} - 2\sqrt{12})$

Simplify. Assume that all variables represent positive real numbers.

C

33. $2\sqrt{49x^3} - 3\sqrt{16x^5}$
34. $4\sqrt{72s^4} - 2s\sqrt{200s^2}$
35. $\sqrt{\frac{x^2}{16} + \frac{x^2}{25}}$
36. $\sqrt{\frac{x^2}{49} - \frac{x^2}{121}}$
37. $\sqrt{\frac{x^2}{a^2} + \frac{x^2}{b^2}}$
38. $\sqrt{\frac{x}{a}} - \sqrt{\frac{a}{x}}$

Mixed Review Exercises

Write each equation in slope-intercept form.

1. $2y = 6x + 10$
2. $5y - x + 10 = 0$
3. $3x - y = 3$
4. $5x + 5y = 4$
5. $x = 2y + 6$
6. $2x - 7y = 0$
7. $x = -y + 11$
8. $7 - x + 11y = 0$
9. $12x - 4 = -2y$

For each parabola whose equation is given, find the coordinates of the vertex and the equation of the axis of symmetry.

10. $y = -4x^2$
11. $y = x^2 - 6x + 9$
12. $y = 5 - 2x^2$

Solve. Assume that no denominator is zero.

13. $\frac{4x}{5} = \frac{10x}{9}$
14. $\frac{4}{b + 6} = \frac{-1}{2b + 3}$
15. $11 - \frac{10}{x} = x$
16. $\frac{3}{t} = \frac{-7}{2t^2 - 1}$
17. $\frac{1}{y} + \frac{2 - y}{y + 3} = \frac{1}{y + 3}$
18. $\frac{p + 2}{4p - 1} = \frac{p}{4p + 3}$

Biographical Note / *Juan de la Cierva*

Juan de la Cierva was born in Murcia, Spain, in 1895. He attended school there and later graduated from the Special Technical College in Madrid.

Juan de la Cierva was interested in aircraft design. At age 17, de la Cierva and two friends assembled a biplane using the wreckage from a French aircraft. This airplane became the first Spanish-built plane to fly. De la Cierva later designed and built a monoplane and the world's second trimotor, a plane powered by three engines.

After the crash of the trimotor, de la Cierva designed a new type of aircraft, the autogiro. This aircraft resembled a cross between a helicopter and an airplane. The large rotor at the top of the plane was not powered, but moved when air passed over the blades. De la Cierva hoped that this design would eliminate crashes caused by engines stalling at low speeds. In 1923, one of his autogiros flew successfully.

In 1928 de la Cierva was able to fly an autogiro across the English Channel. The concept of the autogiro reached its high point in 1933 with a model that could take off in a space of six yards and was capable of a speed of 100 mi/h.

Extra / Proving Divisibility Tests

You may have learned the following divisibility tests in an earlier course.

Divisibility by	Test
2	Number must end in 0, 2, 4, 6, or 8
3	Sum of digits must be divisible by 3
4	Last two digits must be divisible by 4 (81,736 is divisible by 4 because 36 is.)
5	Number must end in 0 or 5
6	Number must pass tests for both 2 and 3
8	Last 3 digits must be divisible by 8 (145,320 is divisible by 8 because 320 is.)
9	Sum of digits must be divisible by 9

These tests rely on our decimal system of numeration. They can be proved by writing expressions for the values of the numbers involved.

Example Prove the divisibility test for 9 for a three-digit number.

Solution A three-digit number with digits h, t, and u has a value of

$$100h + 10t + u = (99h + 9t) + (h + t + u).$$

Since $99h + 9t$ is divisible by 9, the entire right-hand side of the equation is divisible by 9 if and only if the sum of the digits, $h + t + u$, is divisible by 9.

Exercises

1. Prove the test for divisibility by 3 for a three-digit number.

2. The number 87,154,316 can be written as $(871{,}543) \cdot 100 + 16$. Explain why you need look only at the last two digits to see if the original number is divisible by 4.

3. Prove the test for divisibility by 4 for a six-digit number.

4. Prove the test for divisibility by 8 for a six-digit number. (*Hint:* See Exercise 3.)

5. Prove that a six-digit number is divisible by 11 if and only if the sum of the first, third, and fifth digits minus the sum of the second, fourth, and sixth digits is divisible by 11.

6. Devise a test to check whether eleven-digit numbers are divisible by 11.

11-9 Multiplication of Binomials Containing Radicals

Objective To multiply binomials containing square-root radicals and to rationalize binomial denominators that contain square-root radicals.

In Chapter 5, you learned some special methods of multiplying binomials. We can use these methods when multiplying binomials containing square-root radicals.

Example 1 Simplify $(6 + \sqrt{11})(6 - \sqrt{11})$.

Solution The pattern is $(a + b)(a - b) = a^2 - b^2$.

$$\begin{aligned}(6 + \sqrt{11})(6 - \sqrt{11}) &= 6^2 - (\sqrt{11})^2 \\ &= 36 - 11 \\ &= 25 \quad \textit{Answer}\end{aligned}$$

Example 2 Simplify $(3 + \sqrt{5})^2$.

Solution The pattern is $(a + b)^2 = a^2 + 2ab + b^2$.

$$\begin{aligned}(3 + \sqrt{5})^2 &= 3^2 + 2[(3)(\sqrt{5})] + (\sqrt{5})^2 \\ &= 9 + 6\sqrt{5} + 5 \\ &= 14 + 6\sqrt{5} \quad \textit{Answer}\end{aligned}$$

Example 3 Simplify $(2\sqrt{3} - 5\sqrt{7})^2$.

Solution The pattern is $(a - b)^2 = a^2 - 2ab + b^2$.

$$\begin{aligned}(2\sqrt{3} - 5\sqrt{7})^2 &= (2\sqrt{3})^2 - 2[(2\sqrt{3})(5\sqrt{7})] + (5\sqrt{7})^2 \\ &= (2\sqrt{3})^2 - 2[(2)(5)(\sqrt{3})(\sqrt{7})] + (5\sqrt{7})^2 \\ &= 4(3) - 20\sqrt{21} + 25(7) \\ &= 12 - 20\sqrt{21} + 175 \\ &= 187 - 20\sqrt{21} \quad \textit{Answer}\end{aligned}$$

If b and d are both nonnegative, then the binomials

$$a\sqrt{b} + c\sqrt{d} \quad \text{and} \quad a\sqrt{b} - c\sqrt{d}$$

are called **conjugates** of one another. Conjugates differ only in the sign of one term. If a, b, c, and d are all integers, then the product

$$(a\sqrt{b} + c\sqrt{d})(a\sqrt{b} - c\sqrt{d})$$

will be an integer (see Example 1). Conjugates can be used to rationalize binomial denominators that contain radicals.

Example 4 Rationalize the denominator of $\frac{3}{5 - 2\sqrt{7}}$.

Solution
$$\frac{3}{5 - 2\sqrt{7}} = \frac{3}{5 - 2\sqrt{7}} \cdot \frac{5 + 2\sqrt{7}}{5 + 2\sqrt{7}}$$
$$= \frac{3(5 + 2\sqrt{7})}{25 - (2\sqrt{7})^2}$$
$$= \frac{15 + 6\sqrt{7}}{25 - 28}$$
$$= \frac{15 + 6\sqrt{7}}{-3}$$
$$= \frac{15}{-3} + \frac{6\sqrt{7}}{-3}$$
$$= -5 - 2\sqrt{7}$$ ***Answer***

Oral Exercises

Complete. Express in simplest form.

1. $(\sqrt{5} + 3)(\sqrt{5} - 3) = 5 - \underline{\ ?\ } = \underline{\ ?\ }$

2. $(8 - \sqrt{6})(8 + \sqrt{6}) = 64 - \underline{\ ?\ } = \underline{\ ?\ }$

3. $(\sqrt{2} + 3)^2 = 2 + \underline{\ ?\ } + 9 = 11 + \underline{\ ?\ }$

4. $(6 - \sqrt{11})^2 = 36 - \underline{\ ?\ } + \underline{\ ?\ } = \underline{\ ?\ }$

State the conjugate of each binomial.

5. $8 + 4\sqrt{5}$

6. $-7 - 3\sqrt{11}$

7. $-4 + 6\sqrt{7}$

8. $5 - 8\sqrt{13}$

Written Exercises

Simplify.

A

1. $(2 + \sqrt{3})(2 - \sqrt{3})$

2. $(4 + \sqrt{11})(4 - \sqrt{11})$

3. $(\sqrt{15} + 6)(\sqrt{15} - 6)$

4. $(\sqrt{19} - 9)(\sqrt{19} + 9)$

5. $(\sqrt{3} - \sqrt{2})(\sqrt{3} + \sqrt{2})$

6. $(\sqrt{15} - \sqrt{3})(\sqrt{15} + \sqrt{3})$

7. $(2 + \sqrt{7})^2$

8. $(8 - \sqrt{6})^2$

9. $(2\sqrt{2} - 3)^2$

10. $(4\sqrt{10} + 3)^2$

11. $(\sqrt{13} - 2\sqrt{5})^2$

12. $(3\sqrt{7} - \sqrt{3})^2$

13. $(2\sqrt{7} + \sqrt{3})(2\sqrt{7} - \sqrt{3})$

14. $(3\sqrt{5} - \sqrt{2})(3\sqrt{5} + \sqrt{2})$

15. $(6\sqrt{5} - \sqrt{7})(6\sqrt{5} + \sqrt{7})$

16. $(8\sqrt{11} + 2\sqrt{6})(8\sqrt{11} - 2\sqrt{6})$

17. $(4\sqrt{3} - 5)(2\sqrt{3} + 3)$

18. $(6\sqrt{2} + 4)(3\sqrt{2} - 5)$

B

19. $(2\sqrt{5} - 6\sqrt{7})(3\sqrt{5} + \sqrt{7})$

20. $(7\sqrt{13} + 2\sqrt{6})(2\sqrt{13} + 3\sqrt{6})$

21. $(4\sqrt{11} - 2\sqrt{2})(6\sqrt{11} + 8\sqrt{2})$

22. $(8\sqrt{6} - 2\sqrt{3})(2\sqrt{6} - 3\sqrt{3})$

Rationalize the denominator of each fraction.

23. $\frac{1}{1+\sqrt{5}}$
24. $\frac{1}{2+\sqrt{3}}$
25. $\frac{3}{\sqrt{5}-2}$
26. $\frac{1}{\sqrt{7}-3}$
27. $\frac{1+\sqrt{7}}{2-\sqrt{7}}$
28. $\frac{4+\sqrt{5}}{3-\sqrt{5}}$
29. $\frac{\sqrt{3}-4}{\sqrt{7}+2}$
30. $\frac{\sqrt{5}-2}{\sqrt{3}+1}$
31. $\frac{7}{2\sqrt{5}+1}$
32. $\frac{5}{3\sqrt{7}-5}$
33. $\frac{4+2\sqrt{2}}{2\sqrt{5}-3}$
34. $\frac{6-2\sqrt{3}}{3\sqrt{2}+3}$

If $f(x) = x^2 - 5x - 7$, find the value of each function.

Sample $f(\sqrt{7}) = (\sqrt{7})^2 - 5(\sqrt{7}) - 7$
$= 7 - 5\sqrt{7} - 7$
$= -5\sqrt{7}$ ***Answer***

35. $f(\sqrt{6})$
36. $f(\sqrt{10})$
37. $f(\sqrt{2}+1)$
38. $f(\sqrt{3}+2)$
39. $f(-2+\sqrt{11})$
40. $f(\sqrt{7}-2)$

41. Show that $(4+\sqrt{7})$ and $(4-\sqrt{7})$ are roots of the equation $x^2 - 8x + 9 = 0$.
42. Show that $(5+\sqrt{3})$ and $(5-\sqrt{3})$ are roots of the equation $y^2 - 10y + 22 = 0$.
43. Show that $\left(\frac{2}{3}+\frac{\sqrt{7}}{3}\right)$ and $\left(\frac{2}{3}-\frac{\sqrt{7}}{3}\right)$ are roots of the equation $3x^2 - 4x - 1 = 0$.

C 44. Write an expression in simplest form for the area of a triangle whose base is $\frac{4\sqrt{5}-2}{5}$ units and whose height is $\frac{\sqrt{5}+6}{2}$ units.

Simplify each expression, assuming that the value of each variable is nonnegative.

45. $(x+\sqrt{y})(x-\sqrt{y})$
46. $(x-3\sqrt{2})^2$
47. $(3a\sqrt{b}-c)(5a\sqrt{b}+3c)$

Mixed Review Exercises

Simplify. Assume the radicands are nonnegative real numbers.

1. $\sqrt{18x^8}$
2. $4\sqrt{15x} \cdot 3\sqrt{5}$
3. $6\sqrt{8} - 4\sqrt{2}$
4. $4\sqrt{63} + 5\sqrt{28}$
5. $\sqrt{\frac{3}{5}} \cdot \sqrt{\frac{5}{9}}$
6. $\sqrt{1\frac{5}{6}} \cdot \sqrt{4\frac{1}{6}}$
7. $(3-5k^2)^2$
8. $(2p+7z)^2$
9. $(6ab+x)(6ab-x)$

Solve.

10. $7p - 3 = 6(p+2)$
11. $x^2 - 14x + 45 = 0$
12. $36g^2 = 16$

11-10 Simple Radical Equations

Objective To solve simple radical equations.

Skydivers must plan carefully before free-falling from an airplane. The formula they use to determine the velocity of their free falling is $v = \sqrt{2gd}$, where v is the velocity in m/s, $g = 9.8$ m/s^2, and d is the distance in meters.

An equation like $v = \sqrt{2gd}$ that has a variable in the radicand is called a **radical equation.** Simple radical equations are solved by isolating the radical on one side of the equals sign and then squaring both sides of the equation.

Example 1 Solve $140 = \sqrt{2(9.8)d}$.

Solution

$$140 = \sqrt{2(9.8)d}$$
$$140 = \sqrt{19.6d}$$
$$(140)^2 = (\sqrt{19.6d})^2$$
$$19{,}600 = 19.6d$$
$$1000 = d$$

Check:

$$140 \stackrel{?}{=} \sqrt{2(9.8)(1000)}$$
$$140 \stackrel{?}{=} \sqrt{19{,}600}$$
$$140 = 140 \quad \checkmark$$

$\therefore$ the solution set is $\{1000\}$. ***Answer***

Example 2 Solve $\sqrt{5x + 1} + 2 = 6$.

Solution

$$\sqrt{5x + 1} + 2 = 6$$
$$\sqrt{5x + 1} = 4$$
$$5x + 1 = 16$$
$$5x = 15$$
$$x = 3$$

Check:

$$\sqrt{5(3) + 1} + 2 \stackrel{?}{=} 6$$
$$\sqrt{15 + 1} + 2 \stackrel{?}{=} 6$$
$$\sqrt{16} + 2 \stackrel{?}{=} 6$$
$$4 + 2 \stackrel{?}{=} 6$$
$$6 = 6 \quad \checkmark$$

$\therefore$ the solution set is $\{3\}$. ***Answer***

When you square both sides of an equation, the new equation may not be equivalent to the original equation. Therefore, you must *check every possible root in the original equation* to see whether it is indeed a root. By the multiplication property of equality, any root of the original equation is also a root of the squared equation. Thus, you are sure to find all the roots of the original equation among the roots of the squared equation.

Example 3 Solve $\sqrt{11x^2 - 63} - 2x = 0$.

Solution $\sqrt{11x^2 - 63} - 2x = 0$

$\sqrt{11x^2 - 63} = 2x$ {Set apart the radical on one side of the equation.

$11x^2 - 63 = 4x^2$ {Square both sides.

$7x^2 = 63$

$x^2 = 9$

$x = 3$ or $x = -3$

Check: $\sqrt{11(3)^2 - 63} - 2(3) \stackrel{?}{=} 0$ | $\sqrt{11(-3)^2 - 63} - 2(-3) \stackrel{?}{=} 0$

$\sqrt{99 - 63} - 6 \stackrel{?}{=} 0$ | $\sqrt{99 - 63} + 6 \stackrel{?}{=} 0$

$\sqrt{36} - 6 \stackrel{?}{=} 0$ | $\sqrt{36} + 6 \stackrel{?}{=} 0$

$6 - 6 = 0$ ✓ | $6 + 6 \neq 0$

-3 is not a solution.

$\therefore$ the solution set is $\{3\}$. ***Answer***

Oral Exercises

Solve.

1. $\sqrt{x} = 7$
2. $\sqrt{y} = 8$
3. $\sqrt{d} = 10$
4. $\sqrt{y} = 5$
5. $\sqrt{4a} = 10$
6. $\sqrt{4m} = 8$
7. $\sqrt{m} = -1$
8. $\sqrt{k} = 0$
9. $\sqrt{z^2} = 6$

State the first step in the solution of each equation.

10. $\sqrt{3x} = 9$
11. $\sqrt{5a + 9} = 12$
12. $\sqrt{5z - 1} = 7$
13. $\sqrt{x - 5} + 1 = 8$
14. $2\sqrt{5b} = 6$
15. $\sqrt{9x} - 5 = 13$

Written Exercises

Solve.

A

1. $\sqrt{x} = 3$
2. $\sqrt{y} = 14$
3. $4 = \sqrt{2x}$
4. $9 = \sqrt{3a}$
5. $\sqrt{8x} = \frac{2}{5}$
6. $\sqrt{4n} = \frac{1}{3}$
7. $1 = \sqrt{m} - 3$
8. $7 = \sqrt{z} - 2$
9. $\frac{2}{3} + \sqrt{b} = 1$
10. $\sqrt{y} - \frac{1}{2} = 2$
11. $3 = \sqrt{\frac{x}{2}}$
12. $8 = \sqrt{\frac{s}{5}}$
13. $\sqrt{x + 1} = 3$
14. $\sqrt{m + 5} = 1$
15. $20 = 5\sqrt{2x}$
16. $5 = 2\sqrt{3x}$
17. $\sqrt{4x} + 2 = 6$
18. $\sqrt{3x} + 4 = 7$

19. $4 = \sqrt{8a} + 3$

20. $3 = \sqrt{4x + 1}$

21. $\sqrt{5y - 2} + 3 = 9$

22. $\sqrt{5m - 5} + 6 = 7$

23. $\sqrt{x} = 3\sqrt{7}$

24. $\sqrt{r} = 5\sqrt{2}$

B 25. $8 = \sqrt{\frac{5a}{4}} - 2$

26. $14 = \sqrt{\frac{7x}{3}} + 2$

27. $\sqrt{\frac{2x + 9}{5}} = 3$

28. $\sqrt{\frac{2n - 4}{8}} = 2$

29. $4 = \sqrt{\frac{7k - 10}{9}}$

30. $3 = \sqrt{\frac{4x - 5}{7}}$

31. $15\sqrt{2} = 5\sqrt{t}$

32. $5\sqrt{10} = 6\sqrt{m}$

33. $\sqrt{2a^2 - 5} = 11$

34. $\sqrt{2m^2 - 10} = 4$

35. $10 = 2\sqrt{3c^2 - 2}$

36. $36 = 4\sqrt{4m^2 + 5}$

37. $\sqrt{5b^2 - 36} = 2b$

38. $\sqrt{19x^2 - 51} = 4x$

39. $\sqrt{x^2 + 1} = 1 - x$

40. $\sqrt{x^2 + 9} = 3 - x$

41. $\sqrt{3a^2 - 32} = a$

42. $\sqrt{13b^2 + 33} = 4b$

C 43. $\sqrt{x^2 + 6x} = 4$

44. $\sqrt{a^2 + 3a} = 2$

45. $\sqrt{15x^2 - 12x} = 9x$

46. $\sqrt{20y^2 - 13y} = 5y$

47. $\sqrt{x} + 6 = \sqrt{16x}$

48. $3\sqrt{a} + 7 = \sqrt{16a}$

Solve each system of equations.

49. $3\sqrt{a} + 5\sqrt{b} = 31$
$5\sqrt{a} - 5\sqrt{b} = -15$

50. $5\sqrt{x} - 2\sqrt{y} = 4\sqrt{2}$
$2\sqrt{x} + 3\sqrt{y} = 13\sqrt{2}$

Problems

Solve.

A 1. The square root of three times a number is 15. Find the number.

2. Twice the square root of a number is 22. Find the number.

3. One eighth of the square root of a number is 3. Find the number.

4. The square root of one eighth of a number is 3. Find the number.

5. When 4 times a number is increased by 5, the square root of the result is 11. Find the number.

6. When 23 is subtracted from the square root of three times a number, the result is 16. Find the number.

B 7. The radius (r) of a cylinder is related to its volume (V) and its height (h) by the formula $r = \sqrt{\frac{V}{\pi h}}$. Find the volume of a cylinder whose radius is 15 cm and whose height is 36 cm. Express your answer in terms of π.

8. The time it takes a free-falling object to fall can be found by using the formula $t = \sqrt{\frac{2s}{g}}$, where t is in seconds, $g = 9.8\ \text{m/s}^2$, and s is the distance in meters. Find the distance an object falls in 15 s.

9. The current I that flows through an electrical appliance is determined by $I = \sqrt{\frac{P}{R}}$, where P is the power required and R is the resistance of the appliance. The current is measured in amperes (A), the power in watts (W), and the resistance in ohms (Ω). An electric hair dryer has a resistance of 60 Ω and draws 4.5 A of current. How much power does it use?

C 10. The geometric mean of two positive numbers is the positive square root of their product. Find two consecutive positive even integers whose geometric mean is $4\sqrt{39}$.

11. The period of a pendulum (T) is the amount of time (in seconds) it takes the pendulum to make a complete swing back and forth. The period is determined by the formula $T = 2\pi\sqrt{\frac{l}{9.8}}$ where l is the length of the pendulum in meters. Find the length of a pendulum with a period of 8 seconds. Give your answer to the nearest tenth. (Use 3.14 for π.)

Mixed Review Exercises

Express in simplest form.

1. $(5 + \sqrt{6})(5 - \sqrt{6})$
2. $(2 + \sqrt{5})^2$
3. $\frac{2}{3 + \sqrt{11}}$
4. $\frac{2 + \sqrt{5}}{1 - \sqrt{5}}$
5. $3\sqrt{5}(\sqrt{15} - 2\sqrt{5})$
6. $(2\sqrt{3} + 1)(\sqrt{3} - 4)$

Factor completely.

7. $7c^2 - 14a + 7$
8. $t^3 - 4t^2 - 45t$
9. $6x(x + 2) + 4(x + 2)$
10. $y^3 + y^2 - 6y - 6$
11. $4g^5 - 100g$
12. $36x^2 + 24xy + 4y^2$

Self-Test 3

Vocabulary simplest form of a radical (p. 537) conjugate (p. 544) rationalizing the denominator (p. 537) radical equation (p. 547)

Simplify.

1. $2\sqrt{3} \cdot 5\sqrt{3}$
2. $\sqrt{\frac{5}{4}} \cdot \sqrt{\frac{12}{15}}$

Obj. 11-7, p. 537

3. $6\sqrt{7} + \sqrt{13} - 4\sqrt{13} + \sqrt{7}$
4. $5\sqrt{48} - 8\sqrt{27}$

Obj. 11-8, p. 540

5. $(3 - \sqrt{6})^2$
6. $(\sqrt{2} + \sqrt{3})(\sqrt{2} - \sqrt{3})$

Obj. 11-9, p. 544

Rationalize the denominator.

7. $\dfrac{2}{\sqrt{7} - 3}$

8. $\dfrac{\sqrt{5}}{\sqrt{5} + 4}$

Solve.

9. $4 + \sqrt{m} = 9$

10. $\sqrt{5x - 2} + 3 = 6$

Obj. 11-10, p. 547

Check your answers with those at the back of the book.

Extra / Fractional Exponents

In Chapter 4, you learned the rule of exponents for products of powers:

$$\text{For all positive integers } m \text{ and } n,\ a^m \cdot a^n = a^{m+n}.$$

Thus, you can simplify $2^4 \cdot 2^5$ as follows:

$$2^4 \cdot 2^5 = 2^{4+5} = 2^9.$$

If the rule of exponents for products of powers were to hold for all positive numbers, and not just for positive integers, what would be the value of n in the equation $2^n \cdot 2^n = 2$? Of course, $n = \frac{1}{2}$, as the following shows.

Since $$2^n \cdot 2^n = 2^{n+n} = 2^{2n}$$

you have $$2^{2n} = 2^1.$$

The bases are equal (and not -1, 0, or 1). Therefore, the exponents must be equal. Thus, $2n = 1$, or $n = \frac{1}{2}$, and you have $2^{1/2} \cdot 2^{1/2} = 2$.

Because $\sqrt{2} \cdot \sqrt{2} = 2$ and $(-\sqrt{2})(-\sqrt{2}) = 2$, it makes sense to define $2^{1/2}$ as either the positive or negative square root of 2. Selecting the positive, or principal, square root, we define

$$2^{1/2} = \sqrt{2}.$$

Radicals are not restricted to square roots. The symbol $\sqrt[n]{a}$ is used to indicate the principal nth root of a, where n is a positive integer. Thus, you can have third (or cube) roots, fourth roots, fifth roots, and so on. As you have seen, the *root index, n,* is omitted when $n = 2$.

Just as the inverse of squaring a number is finding the square root of that number, the inverse of cubing a number is finding the cube root. For example, since $2^3 = 8$, $\sqrt[3]{8}$, read "the cube root of 8," is 2. Likewise, since $(-2)^3 = -8$, $\sqrt[3]{-8} = -2$.

While $\sqrt[3]{-8}$ is a real number, $\sqrt{-8}$ is not. In general, you can find *odd* roots of negative numbers but not even roots.

If n is an odd positive integer, $\sqrt[n]{a^n} = a$.
If n is an even positive integer, $\sqrt[n]{a^n} = |a|$.

Example 1 Solve $4^n \cdot 4^n \cdot 4^n = 4$

Solution

$$4^n \cdot 4^n \cdot 4^n = 4$$
$$4^{3n} = 4^1 \qquad \text{Since the bases are equal, the exponents are equal.}$$
$$3n = 1$$
$$n = \frac{1}{3}$$

Is it always possible to find the nth root of a? Think of a^n. Since a^n is always positive when n is an even integer, $\sqrt[n]{a}$, and hence $a^{1/n}$, its exponential form, do not name a real number if n is even and $a < 0$. For example, since $2^4 = (-2)^4 = 16$, $\sqrt[4]{-16}$, or $(-16)^{1/4}$, does not name a real number. Thus, we have the following definition.

For all integers $n > 1$,

$$a^{1/n} = \sqrt[n]{a}.$$

When $a < 0$ and n is even, neither $a^{1/n}$ nor $\sqrt[n]{a}$ names a real number.

Example 2 Write each of the following radicals in exponential form.

a. $\sqrt{5}$ **b.** $\sqrt[3]{7}$ **c.** $\sqrt[5]{2}$ **d.** $\sqrt[7]{-12}$

Solution

a. $\sqrt{5} = \sqrt[2]{5^1} = 5^{1/2}$ **b.** $\sqrt[3]{7} = \sqrt[3]{7^1} = 7^{1/3}$

c. $\sqrt[5]{2} = \sqrt[5]{2^1} = 2^{1/5}$ **d.** $\sqrt[7]{-12} = \sqrt[7]{(-12)^1} = (-12)^{1/7}$

Example 3 Simplify: **a.** $49^{1/2}$ **b.** $64^{1/3}$ **c.** $(-32)^{1/5}$ **d.** $(-81)^{1/4}$

Solution

a. $49^{1/2} = \sqrt{49} = 7$

b. $64^{1/3} = \sqrt[3]{64} = \sqrt[3]{4^3} = 4$

c. $(-32)^{1/5} = \sqrt[5]{-32} = \sqrt[5]{(-2)^5} = -2$

d. $(-81)^{1/4} = \sqrt[4]{-81}$, which does not name a real number.

You know that $\sqrt[3]{7} = 7^{1/3}$. How would you write $(\sqrt[3]{7})^2$ in exponential form? If the rule of exponents for a power of a power is to be true for all positive exponents, then

$$(\sqrt[3]{7})^2 = (7^{1/3})^2 = 7^{(1/3)2} = 7^{2/3}.$$

If $\sqrt[n]{a}$ is a real number and m and n are positive integers, then $(\sqrt[n]{a})^m = a^{m/n}$.

Example 4 Write each of the following radicals in exponential form.

a. $(\sqrt[3]{5})^2$ **b.** $(\sqrt{6})^5$ **c.** $(\sqrt[5]{2})^3$ **d.** $(\sqrt[5]{10})^4$

Solution **a.** $(\sqrt[3]{5})^2 = (5^{1/3})^2 = 5^{2/3}$ **b.** $(\sqrt{6})^5 = (6^{1/2})^5 = 6^{5/2}$

c. $(\sqrt[5]{2})^3 = (2^{1/5})^3 = 2^{3/5}$ **d.** $(\sqrt[5]{10})^4 = (10^{1/5})^4 = 10^{4/5}$

Example 5 Simplify.

a. $4^{3/2}$ **b.** $32^{4/5}$ **c.** $(-27)^{2/3}$ **d.** $(-16)^{5/2}$

Solution **a.** $4^{3/2} = (4^{1/2})^3 = (\sqrt{4})^3 = 2^3 = 8$

b. $32^{4/5} = (32^{1/5})^4 = (\sqrt[5]{32})^4 = (\sqrt[5]{2^5})^4 = 2^4 = 16$

c. $(-27)^{2/3} = [(-27)^{1/3}]^2 = (\sqrt[3]{-27})^2 = (\sqrt[3]{(-3)^3})^2 = (-3)^2 = 9$

d. $(-16)^{5/2} = [(-16)^{1/2}]^5 = (\sqrt{-16})^5$, which does not name a real number.

Exercises

Write each of the following radicals in exponential form.

A
1. $\sqrt{6}$ **2.** $\sqrt{10}$ **3.** $\sqrt[3]{11}$ **4.** $\sqrt[7]{5}$
5. $\sqrt[4]{2}$ **6.** $\sqrt[5]{3}$ **7.** $\sqrt[3]{-15}$ **8.** $\sqrt[4]{14}$
9. $\sqrt[6]{10}$ **10.** $\sqrt[5]{-12}$ **11.** $(\sqrt[3]{4})^2$ **12.** $(\sqrt[6]{8})^5$
13. $(\sqrt{2})^3$ **14.** $(\sqrt{7})^5$ **15.** $(\sqrt[4]{3})^5$ **16.** $(\sqrt[7]{5})^3$

Simplify. If the expression does not name a real number, say so.

B
17. $64^{1/2}$ **18.** $8^{1/3}$ **19.** $27^{1/3}$
20. $100^{1/2}$ **21.** $(-64)^{1/3}$ **22.** $(-625)^{1/4}$
23. $(-1296)^{1/4}$ **24.** $(-343)^{1/3}$ **25.** $32^{3/5}$
26. $16^{3/4}$ **27.** $9^{5/2}$ **28.** $81^{3/4}$
29. $(-9)^{3/2}$ **30.** $(-1000)^{2/3}$ **31.** $36^{3/2}$
32. $25^{3/2}$ **33.** $125^{4/3}$ **34.** $243^{4/5}$

Solve.

C
35. $5^n \cdot 5^n = 5$ **36.** $3^n \cdot 3^n \cdot 3^n \cdot 3^n = 3$ **37.** $2^n \cdot 2^n \cdot 2^n = 2$
38. $6^{(1/2)n} \cdot 6^{(1/2)n} = 36$ **39.** $4^{(1/3)n} \cdot 4^{(1/3)n} = 16$ **40.** $7^{(7/5)n} \cdot 7^{(3/5)n} = 343$

Calculator Key-In

Many calculators have a square-root key. It is possible to use this key to find the fourth root, eighth root, sixteenth root, and so on, of a number. You do this by working with powers of 2. If you have a scientific calculator you may be able to use a special key to find $\sqrt[n]{a}$ for other values of n that are not powers of two.

Find the indicated roots of each number.

Sample Eighth root of 32

Solution Express 8 as a power of 2: $8 = 2^3$

This tells you that you need to press the $\sqrt{}$ key three times.

1.5422108 ***Answer***

1. Fourth root of 48

2. Fourth root of 196

3. Eighth root of 150

4. Eighth root of 38

5. Sixteenth root of 164

6. Thirty-second root of 200

Chapter Summary

1. A rational number can be expressed as a fraction in simplest form, $\frac{a}{b}$, where a and b are integers and $b > 0$. Rational numbers in fractional form can be expressed as either terminating or repeating decimals by dividing.
2. Irrational numbers are represented by nonterminating, nonrepeating decimals which may be rounded to a convenient number of places for use in computation. These numbers cannot be represented in fractional form.
3. Square roots may be rational or irrational. Irrational square roots may be approximated using a calculator or a table of square roots.
4. Some quadratic equations can be solved using the property of square roots of equal numbers (page 526).
5. Many problems involving right triangles can be solved using the Pythagorean theorem:

$$a^2 + b^2 = c^2.$$

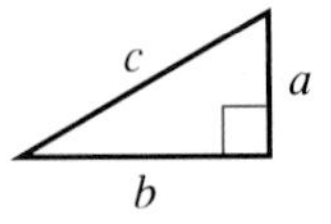

6. Radical expressions can be added, subtracted, multiplied, and divided. The product and quotient properties of square roots (pages 517–518) are useful in simplifying expressions involving radicals. Divisions can often be simplified by rationalizing the denominator.

Chapter Review

Give the letter of the correct answer.

1. Find the rational number halfway between $\frac{1}{2}$ and $\frac{5}{8}$. **11-1**

a. $\frac{7}{16}$ **b.** $\frac{9}{16}$ **c.** $\frac{4}{7}$ **d.** $\frac{3}{8}$

2. Compare $\frac{3}{4}$ and $\frac{11}{15}$.

a. $\frac{3}{4} > \frac{11}{15}$ **b.** $\frac{11}{15} > \frac{3}{4}$ **c.** $\frac{3}{4} = \frac{11}{15}$

3. Express $\frac{5}{11}$ as a decimal. **11-2**

a. 0.45 **b.** $0.\overline{454}$ **c.** $0.\overline{45}$ **d.** $0.0\overline{45}$

4. Express $0.\overline{57}$ as a fraction in simplest form.

a. $\frac{57}{100}$ **b.** $\frac{57}{99}$ **c.** $\frac{575}{1000}$ **d.** $\frac{19}{33}$

5. Find $\sqrt{1764}$. **11-3**

a. 420 **b.** 42 **c.** 4.2 **d.** 0.42

6. Find $\sqrt{\frac{576}{400}}$.

a. $\frac{12}{5}$ **b.** $\frac{3}{4}$ **c.** $\frac{6}{5}$ **d.** $\frac{8}{5}$

7. Approximate $\sqrt{2700}$ to the nearest hundredth. Use a calculator or the table of square roots at the back of the book. **11-4**

a. 5.196 **b.** 51.96 **c.** 519.6 **d.** 51.9

8. Simplify $\sqrt{96}$.

a. $6\sqrt{4}$ **b.** $16\sqrt{6}$ **c.** $4\sqrt{6}$ **d.** $8\sqrt{6}$

9. Simplify $\sqrt{2.25a^4b^2c^6}$. **11-5**

a. $1.5a^2|bc^3|$ **b.** $1.5\sqrt{a^4b^2c^6}$ **c.** $1.5a^2bc^3$

10. Solve $5n^2 - 405 = 0$.

a. $\{9\}$ **b.** $\{9, -9\}$ **c.** $\{3, -3\}$ **d.** $\{81, -81\}$

11. The shorter sides of a right triangle are 16 cm and 30 cm long. Find the length of the hypotenuse. **11-6**

a. 14 cm **b.** 46 cm **c.** 34 cm **d.** 1156 cm

12. Can a right triangle have sides 15 m, 36 m, and 20 m long?

a. yes **b.** no

13. Simplify $\sqrt{15} \cdot \sqrt{12}$. **11-7**

a. $6\sqrt{5}$ **b.** $9\sqrt{20}$ **c.** $12\sqrt{5}$ **d.** $5\sqrt{6}$

14. Simplify $\sqrt{16} + 3\sqrt{8} - 2\sqrt{2}$. **11-8**

a. $4 + 3\sqrt{8} - 2\sqrt{2}$ **b.** $4 + 5\sqrt{2}$ **c.** $4 + 4\sqrt{2}$ **d.** $8\sqrt{2}$

15. Multiply $(4 + \sqrt{7})(4 - \sqrt{7})$. 11-9

a. 16 b. 23 c. $16 - 2\sqrt{7}$ d. 9

16. Rationalize the denominator of $\frac{\sqrt{3}}{\sqrt{3} - 2}$.

a. $\frac{\sqrt{3}}{5}$ b. $-3 - 2\sqrt{3}$ c. $\frac{3 + 2\sqrt{3}}{5}$ d. $3 + 2\sqrt{3}$

17. Solve $\sqrt{5x + 1} - 6 = 8$. 11-10

a. 39 b. 3 c. 51 d. $\frac{13}{5}$

Chapter Test

1. Find the rational number halfway between $\frac{5}{16}$ and $\frac{7}{8}$. 11-1

2. Arrange $\frac{4}{21}$, $\frac{2}{15}$, and $\frac{5}{27}$ in order from least to greatest.

3. Express $\frac{7}{12}$ as a decimal. 11-2

4. Express $0.1\overline{6}$ as a fraction in simplest form.

5. Find $\sqrt{\frac{225}{900}}$.

6. Find $\sqrt{0.0049}$. 11-3

7. Approximate $\sqrt{3400}$ to the nearest tenth. Use a calculator or the table of square roots at the back of the book. 11-4

8. Simplify $\sqrt{150}$.

9. Simplify $4\sqrt{216}$.

10. Simplify $\sqrt{121a^4b^{10}}$.

11. Solve $3a^2 - 108 = 0$. 11-5

12. In a right triangle, the hypotenuse is 19 m long, and one of the shorter sides is 8 m long. Find the length of the other side to the nearest hundredth. 11-6

13. Is a triangle with sides 14 units, 40 units, and 50 units long a right triangle?

Simplify.

14. $\sqrt{\frac{4}{5}} \cdot \sqrt{\frac{35}{4}}$

15. $\frac{6\sqrt{18}}{18\sqrt{6}}$ 11-7

16. $4\sqrt{2} + \sqrt{72}$

17. $3\sqrt{24} - 4\sqrt{54}$ 11-8

18. $(\sqrt{5} + 3)^2$

19. $(\sqrt{7} - \sqrt{2})(\sqrt{7} + \sqrt{2})$ 11-9

20. Rationalize the denominator of $\frac{3}{5 - 2\sqrt{3}}$.

21. Solve $\sqrt{3x + 2} = 4$. 11-10

Cumulative Review *(Chapters 1–11)*

Simplify. Assume that no denominator is zero.

1. $-21 - 2 \cdot 6 \div 3$

2. $(2ab^2)^2(3a^2 + 5ab + b^2)$

3. $(4a^3b + 9c^2)^2$

4. $(-3p + 2q)(12p - q)$

5. $(3.2 \times 10^{-4})^2$

6. $(6x^2 - 13x - 28) \div (2x - 7)$

7. $\frac{96 - 40x + 4x^2}{x^2 - 8x + 16} \cdot \frac{x^2 + 5x - 6}{2x^2 - 72}$

8. $\frac{3x^2 - 14x + 15}{x^2 + 10x + 25} \div \frac{3x^2 + 10x - 25}{x^2 - 25}$

9. $\frac{t - 3}{t + 2} + \frac{1}{t} - 5$

10. $\sqrt{720}$

11. $\sqrt{112} - \sqrt{63}$

12. $2\sqrt{3}(5\sqrt{6} + 4\sqrt{2})$

13. $\frac{5\sqrt{75}}{\sqrt{90}}$

14. $\frac{5}{\sqrt{6} + 1}$

15. $\sqrt{\frac{2}{3}} + \sqrt{\frac{5}{6}}$

Factor completely.

16. $16y^4 - 8y^2 + 1$

17. $4c^2 - 4cd + d^2 - 9$

18. $12c^2 - 17c - 5$

Graph the solution set. (In Exercise 19, use a number line.)

19. $|2 - x| \le 4$

20. $2x - 3y = 3$

21. $2x + y < 6$

22. Write an equation in standard form of the line that contains (0, 2) and (−1, 8).

23. Find the least value of the function f: $x \rightarrow x^2 - 4x + 4$.

24. Express $0.\overline{5}$ and $0.\overline{15}$ as fractions. Then find their sum.

25. Graph the solution set of the system: $x + y < 4$
$y - 2x \ge 0$

Solve each equation, inequality, or system. Assume that no denominator is zero. If there is no solution, say so.

26. $2y - 3 = |-15|$

27. $y\%$ of $75 = 12$

28. $\frac{1}{3}y - 2 = \frac{1}{2}$

29. $4d^2 - 12d + 9 = 0$

30. $2n^2 + 5n - 3 = 0$

31. $\frac{1}{x} + \frac{3 - x}{x + 6} = \frac{x - 1}{2x + 12}$

32. $x - 2y = 8$
$3x + 2y = 9$

33. $2x - 5y = -1$
$3x - 10y = -1$

34. $2x + 11y = 3$
$5x + 28y = 7$

35. $5 \le 2x - 1 \le 9$

36. $4|y - 2| > 12$

37. $7 - 3b < 9$

38. $2\sqrt{t} = 3\sqrt{2}$

39. $\sqrt{2p - 1} = p$

40. $\sqrt{z^2 + 7} = z - 1$

41. The hypotenuse of a right triangle is 9 cm long and another side is 5 cm long. Find the length of the third side to the nearest hundredth. Use a calculator or the table of square roots at the back of the book.

42. Two groups entering a museum each paid \$70. One group included ten adults and four children. The other included five adults and sixteen children. Find the admission price for children and for adults.

Maintaining Skills

Solve each system. Use either method shown below.

Sample 1
$$\begin{aligned} x - 2y &= 1 \\ 3x - 5y &= 6 \end{aligned}$$

Solution (Substitution Method) Solve one equation for one of the variables (in this case, x), and substitute in the other equation.

$$\begin{aligned} x - 2y &= 1 \quad \rightarrow \quad & x &= 2y + 1 \\ 3x - 5y &= 6 & 3(2y + 1) - 5y &= 6 \\ & & 6y + 3 - 5y &= 6 \\ & & y + 3 &= 6 \\ & & y &= 3 \end{aligned}$$

$$x = 2(3) + 1 = 7$$

The check is left to you. ∴ the solution is (7, 3).

Sample 2
$$\begin{aligned} 7x - 2y &= 4 \\ 3x + y &= 11 \end{aligned}$$

Solution (Multiplication with the Addition-or-Subtraction Method)

$$\begin{aligned} 7x - 2y &= 4 & 7x - 2y &= 4 & 7(2) - 2y &= 4 \\ 3x + y &= 11 \xrightarrow{\times 2} & 6x + 2y &= 22 & 14 - 2y &= 4 \\ & & 13x \quad &= 26 & -2y &= -10 \\ & & x &= 2 & y &= 5 \end{aligned}$$

The check is left to you. ∴ the solution is (2, 5).

1. $x + y = 1$
   $2x + y = 0$
2. $x + y = 3$
   $2x - y = 6$
3. $2x + y = 15$
   $x + 2y = 15$
4. $3x + 4y = -2$
   $4x + 3y = -12$
5. $2x + 3y = 2$
   $8x + 9y = 7$
6. $9x + 4y = 5$
   $y = 4x$
7. $4x + 5 = y$
   $2x + y = 1$
8. $y - x = 20$
   $2x + 3y = 10$
9. $3x - 4y = 9$
   $x + 2y = 13$
10. $5x - 6y = 2$
    $4y - 5x = 12$
11. $x + 10y = 2$
    $\frac{1}{3}x + y = 3$
12. $\frac{4}{5}x - \frac{1}{2}y = 18$
    $\frac{1}{2}x - \frac{3}{4}y = 20$
13. $y = 7x$
    $5x - 8y = 0$
14. $x - 2y = 5$
    $-2x + 3y = -5$
15. $2x + 3y = 11$
    $3x + 14y = 7$
16. $5x + 6y = 4$
    $3x + 6y = 3$
17. $4x + 3y = 8$
    $5x + 4y = 13$
18. $5x - 6y = 1$
    $2x - 3y = 7$
19. $6x - 5y = 0$
    $5x - 3y = 7$
20. $2x - 7y = 9$
    $x + 8y = 16$
21. $3x - 5y = 7$
    $-2x + 7y = 10$

Mixed Problem Solving

Solve each problem that has a solution. If a problem has no solution, explain why.

A

1. A boat travels 4 km in 20 min with the current. The return trip takes 24 min. Find the speed of the current and the speed of the boat in still water.

2. Half the square root of twice a number is 5. Find the number.

3. The base of a triangle of a given area varies inversely as the height. A triangle has a base of 18 cm and a height of 10 cm. Find the height of a triangle of equal area and with base 15 cm.

4. Two trains leave a station at noon traveling in opposite directions. The speeds of the trains are 80 km/h and 100 km/h. At what time will the trains be 225 km apart?

5. The average orbital speed of Saturn is 14 km/s slower than the speed of Mars. The speed of Saturn is also $\frac{5}{12}$ the speed of Mars. Find each speed.

6. A fraction's value is $\frac{3}{5}$. If its numerator and denominator are both increased by 3, the resulting fraction equals $\frac{5}{8}$. Find the original fraction.

7. The Robinsons bought a computer at 25% off the usual price. The total cost, including a 4% tax on the sale price, was \$1170. Find the usual price excluding taxes.

8. How many liters of water should be added to 24 L of an 18% acid solution to form a 15% solution?

B

9. Sandy can complete her paper route in 45 min. When her sister Kris helps her, it takes them 18 min to complete the route. How long would it take Kris alone to complete the route?

10. Isabel invested \$8000, part in an account paying 6% interest and part in bonds paying 8%. If she had reversed the amounts invested, she would have received \$100 less. How much did she invest in each?

11. The numbers of nickels and quarters in a bank are in the ratio 23:25. If the coins are worth \$7, how many of each type are there?

12. The length of a rectangle is 1 cm shorter than a diagonal. The length is 2 cm longer than twice the width. Find the perimeter of the rectangle.

13. Find the price per kilogram when 8 kg of almonds worth x dollars per kilogram are mixed with 4 kg of raisins worth $x + 2$ dollars per kilogram. Give your simplified answer in terms of x.

12 Quadratic Functions

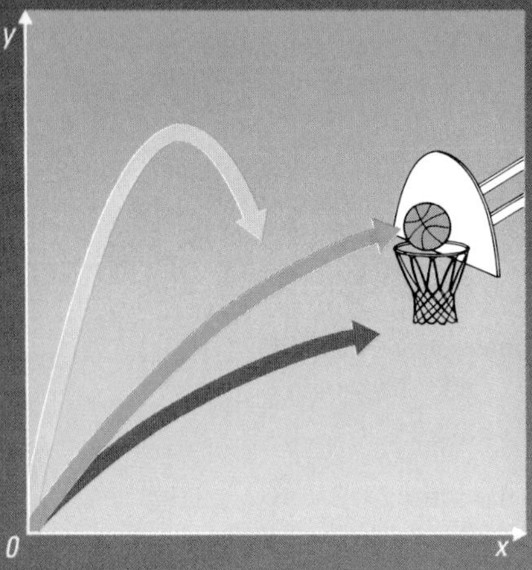

The path of a ball thrown upward is a parabola. The height of the ball at a time t is given by the quadratic equation $h = -4.9t^2 + at$, ***where the coefficient a depends on the initial angle and speed of the ball.***

Quadratic Equations

12-1 Quadratic Equations with Perfect Squares

Objective To solve quadratic equations involving perfect squares.

In Chapter 5 you learned how to solve certain quadratic equations by factoring. In Chapter 11 you learned how to solve quadratic equations of the form $x^2 = k$. This lesson extends what you learned in Chapter 11 to any quadratic equation involving a *perfect square*. Later in this chapter you'll learn more general methods that can be used to solve any quadratic equation and to determine its number of roots.

The property of square roots of equal numbers (page 526) leads you to the following information about the roots of $x^2 = k$.

If $k > 0$, then $x^2 = k$ has two real-number roots: $x = \pm\sqrt{k}$.

If $k = 0$, then $x^2 = k$ has one real-number root: $x = 0$.

If $k < 0$, then $x^2 = k$ has no real-number roots.

Examples 1 and 2 show you how to use this information about roots to solve some quadratic equations.

Example 1 Solve: **a.** $m^2 = 49$ **b.** $5r^2 = 45$

Solution

a. $m^2 = 49$

$m = \pm\sqrt{49}$

$m = \pm 7$

$\therefore$ the solution set is $\{7, -7\}$.

b. $5r^2 = 45$

$r^2 = 9$

$r = \pm\sqrt{9} = \pm 3$

$\therefore$ the solution set is $\{3, -3\}$.

Example 2 Solve $(x + 6)^2 = 64$.

Solution

$(x + 6)^2 = 64$

$x + 6 = \pm 8$

$x = -6 \pm 8$

$x = 2$ or $x = -14$

Check: $(2 + 6)^2 \stackrel{?}{=} 64$ $(-14 + 6)^2 \stackrel{?}{=} 64$

$(8)^2 \stackrel{?}{=} 64$ $(-8)^2 \stackrel{?}{=} 64$

$64 = 64$ ✓ $64 = 64$ ✓

$\therefore$ the solution set is $\{2, -14\}$. ***Answer***

An expression such as $(x + 1)^2$, x^2, or $(5x - 3)^2$ is called a **perfect square.** Whenever an equation can be expressed in the form

$$\text{perfect square} = k \qquad (k \geq 0),$$

you can solve the equation by the method shown in Examples 1 and 2. (You may find it helpful to review Lesson 5-6 about squares of binomials.)

Example 3 Solve: **a.** $5(x - 4)^2 = 40$ **b.** $y^2 + 6y + 9 = 49$

Solution

a.
$$5(x - 4)^2 = 40$$
$$(x - 4)^2 = 8$$
$$x - 4 = \pm\sqrt{8}$$
$$x = 4 \pm \sqrt{8}$$
$$x = 4 \pm 2\sqrt{2}$$

The check is left to you.
∴ the solution set is $\{4 + 2\sqrt{2}, 4 - 2\sqrt{2}\}$. ***Answer***

b.
$$y^2 + 6y + 9 = 49$$
$$(y + 3)^2 = 49$$
$$y + 3 = \pm 7$$
$$y = -3 \pm 7$$
$$y = 4 \quad \text{or} \quad y = -10$$

The check is left to you.
∴ the solution set is $\{4, -10\}$. ***Answer***

The perfect squares occurring in Example 3 are $(x - 4)^2$ and $(y + 3)^2$. Note that Example 3(b) could also have been solved by factoring.

An equation that has a negative number as one side and a perfect square as the other side has no real-number solutions. This is so because *the square of any real number is always a nonnegative real number.*

Example 4 Solve $2(3x - 5)^2 + 15 = 7$.

Solution
$$2(3x - 5)^2 + 15 = 7$$
$$2(3x - 5)^2 = -8$$
$$(3x - 5)^2 = -4$$

∴ there is no real-number solution. ***Answer***

Oral Exercises

Express each trinomial as the square of a binomial.

Sample $y^2 + 8y + 16 = (y + 4)^2$

1. $x^2 + 6x + 9$ **2.** $x^2 - 4x + 4$ **3.** $x^2 + 10x + 25$

4. $x^2 + 16x + 64$ **5.** $x^2 - 14x + 49$ **6.** $x^2 - 20x + 100$

Solve.

7. $5r^2 = 180$ **8.** $y^2 = \frac{1}{121}$ **9.** $4x^2 = 32$

Written Exercises

Solve. Express irrational solutions in simplest radical form. If the equation has no real-number solution, write "no real-number solution."

A

1. $x^2 = 64$ **2.** $(y - 7)^2 = 0$ **3.** $t^2 = \frac{100}{169}$

4. $a^2 = -9$ **5.** $3x^2 = 108$ **6.** $6t^2 = 156$

7. $14t^2 = 126$ **8.** $x^2 - 48 = 0$ **9.** $x^2 + 32 = 0$

10. $m^2 - 54 = 0$ **11.** $6x^2 - 18 = 0$ **12.** $7m^2 - 42 = 0$

13. $4y^2 + 7 = 19$ **14.** $4r^2 - 7 = 29$ **15.** $3z^2 - 18 = 3$

16. $(x + 6)^2 = 16$ **17.** $(y - 6)^2 = 13$ **18.** $(y + 2)^2 = 12$

19. $(s - 7)^2 = 28$ **20.** $(z - 3)^2 = 32$ **21.** $2(x - 5)^2 = 18$

22. $5(m - 8)^2 = 25$ **23.** $8(x + 3)^2 = 56$ **24.** $6(z + 5)^2 = 42$

B

25. $x^2 + 6x + 9 = 16$ **26.** $x^2 - 14x + 49 = 64$ **27.** $r^2 - 22r + 121 = 4$

28. $y^2 - 18y + 81 = 144$ **29.** $\frac{1}{5}x^2 - \frac{5}{49} = 0$ **30.** $\frac{1}{4}t^2 - \frac{9}{64} = 0$

31. $\frac{1}{5}r^2 - 2 = \frac{5}{6}$ **32.** $\frac{1}{6}x^2 - 4 = \frac{5}{6}$ **33.** $t^2 + 18t + 81 = 225$

34. $0.49x^2 + 2 = 3.96$ **35.** $1.44z^2 - 1.36 = -0.64$ **36.** $5(t + 2)^2 = \frac{3}{5}$

37. $4(x - 2)^2 = \frac{1}{49}$ **38.** $\left(y - \frac{3}{7}\right)^2 = -\frac{8}{9}$ **39.** $\left(z - \frac{3}{5}\right)^2 = \frac{7}{16}$

Solve each equation by factoring.

40. $7y^3 - 28y = 0$ **41.** $7a^3 - 175a = 0$ **42.** $\frac{1}{4}t^3 - 16t = 0$

43. $4b^3 - \frac{1}{4}b = 0$ **44.** $8x^3 = 392x$ **45.** $8x^3 = 512x$

Solve.

C

46. $3(5x - 2)^2 = 27$ **47.** $5(6x - 1)^2 = 5$ **48.** $2(7x - 2)^2 + 5 = 11$

49. How many different real-number solutions does $a(x + b)^2 = c$ have if:

a. $a > 0$ and $c > 0$? **b.** $a < 0$ and $c < 0$?

c. $a < 0$ and $c > 0$? **d.** $a > 0$ and $c = 0$?

Mixed Review Exercises

Express each square as a trinomial.

1. $(x - 11)^2$ **2.** $(2x + 5)^2$ **3.** $(6x - 7)^2$ **4.** $(-3c + 4)^2$

5. $\left(x + \frac{1}{2}\right)^2$ **6.** $\left(x + \frac{1}{3}\right)^2$ **7.** $\left(\frac{1}{2}x + \frac{2}{3}\right)^2$ **8.** $\left(\frac{1}{3}x + \frac{3}{4}\right)^2$

12-2 Completing the Square

Objective To solve quadratic equations by completing the square.

In Lesson 12-1 you learned that it is always possible to solve a quadratic equation that has the form

$$\text{perfect square} = k \quad (k \geq 0).$$

If a quadratic equation does not have this form, it may be possible to transform it into one that does by a method called **completing the square.**

Study the perfect squares below. The main idea behind completing the square is shown.

$$(x + 4)^2 = x^2 \underbrace{+ 8x}_{\left(\frac{8}{2}\right)^2 = 16} + 16$$

$$(x - 5)^2 = x^2 \underbrace{- 10x}_{\left(-\frac{10}{2}\right)^2 = 25} + 25$$

$$(x + a)^2 = x^2 \underbrace{+ 2ax}_{\left(\frac{2a}{2}\right)^2 = a^2} + a^2$$

In each case, notice that the coefficient of x^2 is 1 and that the constant term is *the square of half the coefficient of x.*

Method of Completing the Square

For $x^2 + bx + \underline{\ ?\ }$:

1. Find half the coefficient of x: $\frac{b}{2}$
2. Square the result of Step 1: $\left(\frac{b}{2}\right)^2$
3. Add the result of Step 2 to $x^2 + bx$: $x^2 + bx + \left(\frac{b}{2}\right)^2$
4. You have completed the square: $x^2 + bx + \left(\frac{b}{2}\right)^2 = \left(x + \frac{b}{2}\right)^2$

Example 1 Complete the square.

a. $x^2 + 14x + \underline{\ ?\ }$

b. $x^2 - 9x + \underline{\ ?\ }$

Solution

a. $x^2 \underbrace{+ 14x}_{\left(\frac{14}{2}\right)^2 = 49} + 49 = (x + 7)^2$

b. $x^2 \underbrace{- 9x}_{\left(-\frac{9}{2}\right)^2 = \frac{81}{4}} + \frac{81}{4} = \left(x - \frac{9}{2}\right)^2$

Example 2 Solve $x^2 - 3x - 18 = 0$ by completing the square.

Solution

$$x^2 - 3x - 18 = 0$$

$$x^2 - 3x = 18$$

$$x^2 - 3x + \left(-\frac{3}{2}\right)^2 = 18 + \left(-\frac{3}{2}\right)^2$$

Half the coefficient of x is $-\frac{3}{2}$. Square it and add the result to *both* sides.

$$x^2 - 3x + \frac{9}{4} = 18 + \frac{9}{4}$$

$$\text{perfect square} \longrightarrow \left(x - \frac{3}{2}\right)^2 = \frac{81}{4} \longleftarrow \text{constant}$$

$$x - \frac{3}{2} = \pm\frac{9}{2}$$

$$x = \frac{3}{2} \pm \frac{9}{2} = \frac{3 \pm 9}{2}$$

$$x = 6 \quad \text{or} \quad x = -3$$

The check is left to you.

$\therefore$ the solution set is $\{6, -3\}$. ***Answer***

Example 3 Solve $5x^2 + 8x + 1 = 0$ by completing the square. Give irrational roots in simplest form.

Solution

$$5x^2 + 8x + 1 = 0$$

$$5x^2 + 8x = -1$$

Divide both sides by 5 so that the coefficient of x^2 will be 1.

$$x^2 + \frac{8}{5}x = -\frac{1}{5}$$

$$x^2 + \frac{8}{5}x + \left(\frac{4}{5}\right)^2 = -\frac{1}{5} + \left(\frac{4}{5}\right)^2$$

$$x^2 + \frac{8}{5}x + \frac{16}{25} = -\frac{1}{5} + \frac{16}{25}$$

$$\left(x + \frac{4}{5}\right)^2 = \frac{11}{25}$$

$$x + \frac{4}{5} = \pm\sqrt{\frac{11}{25}}$$

$$x = -\frac{4}{5} \pm \frac{\sqrt{11}}{5} = \frac{-4 \pm \sqrt{11}}{5}$$

$$x = \frac{-4 + \sqrt{11}}{5} \quad \text{or} \quad x = \frac{-4 - \sqrt{11}}{5}$$

The check is left to you.

$\therefore$ the solution set is $\left\{\frac{-4 + \sqrt{11}}{5}, \frac{-4 - \sqrt{11}}{5}\right\}$. ***Answer***

You can use a calculator or the table of square roots on page 682 to find decimal approximations of the irrational roots in Example 3.

$$\frac{-4 + \sqrt{11}}{5} \approx \frac{-4 + 3.32}{5} = \frac{-0.68}{5} = -0.136 \approx -0.1$$

$$\frac{-4 - \sqrt{11}}{5} \approx \frac{-4 - 3.32}{5} = \frac{-7.32}{5} = -1.464 \approx -1.5$$

Oral Exercises

Complete the square.

1. $z^2 + 18z + \underline{\ ?\ } = (z + \underline{\ ?\ })^2$
2. $k^2 - 12k + \underline{\ ?\ } = (k - \underline{\ ?\ })^2$
3. $m^2 + 5m + \underline{\ ?\ } = (m + \underline{\ ?\ })^2$
4. $r^2 - 11r + \underline{\ ?\ } = (r - \underline{\ ?\ })^2$
5. $t^2 + 1.6t + \underline{\ ?\ } = (t + \underline{\ ?\ })^2$
6. $q^2 - \frac{2}{3}q + \underline{\ ?\ } = (q - \underline{\ ?\ })^2$

Written Exercises

Solve by completing the square. Give irrational roots in simplest radical form and then approximate them to the nearest tenth. You may wish to use a calculator.

A

1. $x^2 - 4x = 17$
2. $y^2 + 8y = 10$
3. $w^2 + 6w = -3$
4. $c^2 + 18c - 175 = 0$
5. $v^2 - 20v + 19 = 0$
6. $z^2 - 6z - 307 = 8$
7. $y^2 + 18y + 32 = 226$
8. $2b^2 + 16b = 4$
9. $5x^2 - 20x = 10$
10. $w^2 + w = 3$
11. $x^2 - 5x = 2$
12. $c^2 - 7c - 2 = 4$

Solve the equations by (a) completing the square and (b) factoring.

13. $x^2 - 12x + 35 = 0$
14. $y^2 + 15y + 56 = 0$
15. $z^2 - 2z - 35 = 0$
16. $3c^2 - 7c = 6$
17. $2y^2 = 9y - 9$
18. $4n^2 + 12n + 5 = 0$

Solve. Write irrational roots in simplest radical form.

B

19. $\frac{x^2}{4} - x = 3$
20. $\frac{2y^2}{3} - y - 3 = 0$
21. $m^2 - 3 = \frac{11m}{2}$
22. $a^2 + \frac{a}{3} = 3$
23. $\frac{3m^2}{4} - 3 = \frac{m}{2}$
24. $\frac{y^2}{2} - \frac{y}{4} = 3$
25. $x + 1 = \frac{2 + x}{4x}$
26. $y - 2 = \frac{3y - 2}{2y}$
27. $9t = \frac{6t - 1}{t + 2}$

Solve for x in terms of a, b, and c.

C

28. $x^2 + bx + 1 = 0$
29. $x^2 - bx + c = 0$
30. $ax^2 + bx + c = 0$

Mixed Review Exercises

Simplify.

1. $\sqrt{188}$
2. $\sqrt{2400}$
3. $\sqrt{10x^4y^9}$
4. $\sqrt{120a^6b^7c^5}$
5. $\frac{z}{4 - z} + \frac{6}{z + 4}$
6. $1 + \frac{b^2}{2b + 1}$
7. $3(2x - 1) + (3x + 5)(5x + 3)$

12-3 The Quadratic Formula

Objective To learn the quadratic formula and use it to solve equations.

In Lesson 5-12, you learned that the standard form of a quadratic equation is given by

$$ax^2 + bx + c = 0,$$

where $a \neq 0$. Solving this equation by completing the square gives a formula for finding all real-number solutions of any quadratic equation.

$$ax^2 + bx + c = 0$$

$$ax^2 + bx = -c$$

$$x^2 + \frac{b}{a}x = -\frac{c}{a}$$

$$x^2 + \frac{b}{a}x + \left(\frac{b}{2a}\right)^2 = -\frac{c}{a} + \left(\frac{b}{2a}\right)^2 \qquad \text{Complete the square.}$$

$$\left(x + \frac{b}{2a}\right)^2 = -\frac{c}{a} + \frac{b^2}{4a^2}$$

$$\left(x + \frac{b}{2a}\right)^2 = \frac{b^2 - 4ac}{4a^2}$$

$$x + \frac{b}{2a} = \pm\sqrt{\frac{b^2 - 4ac}{4a^2}} \qquad \text{If } b^2 - 4ac \geq 0.$$

$$x = -\frac{b}{2a} \pm \sqrt{\frac{b^2 - 4ac}{4a^2}}$$

$$x = -\frac{b}{2a} \pm \frac{\sqrt{b^2 - 4ac}}{2a}$$

$$x = \frac{-b \pm \sqrt{b^2 - 4ac}}{2a}$$

The last equation in the solution above is called the **quadratic formula.** It gives the roots of the quadratic equation $ax^2 + bx + c = 0$ in terms of the coefficients a, b, and c. In this solution, notice the assumptions that $a \neq 0$ and that $b^2 - 4ac \geq 0$.

The Quadratic Formula

If $ax^2 + bx + c = 0$, $a \neq 0$, and $b^2 - 4ac \geq 0$,

then $$x = \frac{-b \pm \sqrt{b^2 - 4ac}}{2a}.$$

Example 1 Use the quadratic formula to solve $9x^2 + 12x - 1 = 0$. Give irrational roots in simplest radical form and then approximate them to the nearest tenth.

Solution

$$9x^2 + 12x - 1 = 0$$

$$x = \frac{-b \pm \sqrt{b^2 - 4ac}}{2a}, \text{ where } a = 9,\ b = 12, \text{ and } c = -1.$$

$$x = \frac{-(12) \pm \sqrt{(12)^2 - 4(9)(-1)}}{2(9)} = \frac{-12 \pm \sqrt{144 + 36}}{18}$$

$$= \frac{-12 \pm \sqrt{180}}{18} = \frac{-12 \pm \sqrt{36 \cdot 5}}{18} = \frac{-12 \pm 6\sqrt{5}}{18}$$

$$= \frac{6(-2 \pm \sqrt{5})}{18} = \frac{-2 \pm \sqrt{5}}{3}$$

Since $\sqrt{5} \approx 2.24$, $x \approx \frac{-2 + 2.24}{3} = \frac{0.24}{3} \approx 0.1$

or $x \approx \frac{-2 - 2.24}{3} = \frac{-4.24}{3} \approx -1.4$

The check is left to you.

$\therefore$ the solution set is $\left\{\frac{-2 + \sqrt{5}}{3}, \frac{-2 - \sqrt{5}}{3}\right\}$, or $\{0.1, -1.4\}$. ***Answer***

Remember to write a quadratic equation in the form

$$ax^2 + bx + c = 0$$

before using the quadratic formula. For example, to solve

$$4x^2 = 9x - 1,$$

first rewrite the equation as

$$4x^2 - 9x + 1 = 0$$

so that you can easily identify the values of a, b, and c.

Example 2 Use the quadratic formula to solve $x^2 = x - 8$.

Solution

$$x^2 = x - 8$$

$$x^2 - x + 8 = 0 \quad \left\{\text{Rewrite the equation in standard form.}\right.$$

$$x = \frac{-b \pm \sqrt{b^2 - 4ac}}{2a}, \text{ where } a = 1,\ b = -1, \text{ and } c = 8.$$

$$x = \frac{-(-1) \pm \sqrt{(-1)^2 - 4(1)(8)}}{2(1)} = \frac{1 \pm \sqrt{1 - 32}}{2} = \frac{1 \pm \sqrt{-31}}{2}$$

Since $\sqrt{b^2 - 4ac} = \sqrt{-31}$, and $\sqrt{-31}$ does not represent a real number, the equation has *no real-number solution*. ***Answer***

Oral Exercises

Read each equation in standard form. Then tell what the values of *a*, *b*, and *c* are for each equation.

1. $3x^2 + 5x - 2 = 0$
2. $3a^2 - 9a + 5 = 0$
3. $2p^2 + 7p - 3 = 0$
4. $5d^2 + 9d = 2$
5. $x^2 - 7x = 4$
6. $y^2 = 6y - 7$
7. $8m^2 = m + 5$
8. $6 - q^2 = 4q$
9. $5x^2 = 7x$
10. $z = 10z^2$
11. $8x^2 = 3$
12. $12t^2 = 0$

Written Exercises

Use the quadratic formula to solve each equation. Give irrational roots in simplest radical form and then approximate them to the nearest tenth. You may wish to use a calculator.

A

1. $x^2 - 3x - 10 = 0$
2. $2s^2 - 3s - 2 = 0$
3. $5z^2 - 11z + 2 = 0$
4. $2y^2 - 6y - 8 = 0$
5. $z^2 - 5z - 6 = 0$
6. $m^2 + 8m + 7 = 0$
7. $x^2 - 6x - 11 = 0$
8. $k^2 - 3k - 1 = 0$
9. $r^2 + 8r + 5 = 0$
10. $n^2 - 6n - 1 = 0$
11. $7x^2 + 2x - 2 = 0$
12. $-2z^2 + 8z + 5 = 0$
13. $-4x^2 + 2x + 3 = 0$
14. $j^2 - 6j = 13$
15. $4y^2 - 12y = -7$
16. $4v^2 = 10v - 5$
17. $3x^2 + 8x = 2$
18. $2r = 5 - 4r^2$

Solve.

B

19. $a^2 + 0.7a - 0.1 = 0$
20. $3x^2 - 1.8x + 0.03 = 0$
21. $4r^2 = 0.6r + 0.5$
22. $t^2 + \frac{3}{2}t + \frac{2}{3} = 0$
23. $2c^2 + \frac{1}{2}c + \frac{2}{3} = 0$
24. $x + \frac{1}{x} = \frac{3}{x} + 3$
25. $\frac{3}{2}x^2 + \frac{1}{3}x + \frac{2}{3} = 0$
26. $\frac{1}{3} - \frac{2}{2y + 1} = \frac{3}{y}$
27. $\frac{3x}{x + 2} - \frac{x + 1}{x - 1} = 0$
28. $\frac{w + 3}{w - 1} - \frac{7}{w + 5} = 3$

The roots of a quadratic equation $ax^2 + bx + c = 0$ are

$$\frac{-b + \sqrt{b^2 - 4ac}}{2a} \quad \text{and} \quad \frac{-b - \sqrt{b^2 - 4ac}}{2a}.$$

C

29. Find the sum of the roots of $ax^2 + bx + c = 0$.
30. Find the product of the roots of $ax^2 + bx + c = 0$.
31. Write a quadratic equation whose roots are $2 \pm \sqrt{5}$. (*Hint:* Find the sum and the product of the roots. Then use the results of Exercises 29 and 30 to find values for *a*, *b*, and *c*.)

Mixed Review Exercises

Solve each open sentence and graph its solution set.

1. $|x - 4| \leq 7$
2. $2|y + 7| = 10$
3. $|3p + 5| < 7$
4. $0 < 2z + 1 \leq 9$
5. $\sqrt{x} = 9$
6. $\sqrt{6n + 1} = 5$
7. $3\sqrt{3p} = 18$
8. $|9 + 2k| = 15$
9. $4|4 - m| = 20$

Solve by completing the squares.

10. $y^2 - 10y + 16 = 0$
11. $2p^2 + 12p = 0$
12. $c^2 - c = 6$

Computer Exercises

For students with some programming experience

1. Write a program that will solve quadratic equations by using the quadratic formula. Provide an output if $b^2 - 4ac$ is negative.

Use your program to solve the following equations.

2. $2x^2 + 7x + 3 = 0$
3. $4x^2 - 7x + 3 = 0$
4. $3x^2 - 8x + 2 = 0$
5. $x^2 - 4x + 2 = 0$
6. $x^2 - 6x + 9 = 0$
7. $x^2 - 2x + 3 = 0$

Extra / Imaginary Numbers

You know that there are no real-number solutions to the equation $x^2 = -16$. If you take another course in algebra, you'll learn that equations like this have solutions that are *imaginary numbers*. The imaginary number i is defined to be the square root of -1. All imaginary numbers involve i. Some examples are $3i$, $-\frac{5i}{2}$, and $2i\sqrt{3}$.

$$i = \sqrt{-1}, \quad \text{and} \quad i^2 = -1$$

The definition of i allows us to solve $x^2 = -16$ over the set of imaginary numbers.

Example Solve $x^2 = -16$.

Solution $x = \pm\sqrt{-16} = \pm\sqrt{16} \cdot \sqrt{-1} = \pm 4\sqrt{-1} = \pm 4i$

In general:

> If $r > 0$, then $\sqrt{-r} = i\sqrt{r}$.

We write $i\sqrt{r}$ rather than $\sqrt{r}\, i$ to avoid confusion with $\sqrt{ri}$.

An interesting pattern occurs when you find i^n for increasing powers of n:

$i^1 = \sqrt{-1} = i$	i	$i^5 = i^2 \cdot i^3 = (-1)(-i) = i$	i
$i^2 = -1$	-1	$i^6 = i^3 \cdot i^3 = (-i)(-i) = i^2 = -1$	-1
$i^3 = i \cdot i^2 = i(-1) = -i$	$-i$	$i^7 = i^3 \cdot i^4 = (-i)(1) = -i$	$-i$
$i^4 = i^2 \cdot i^2 = (-1)(-1) = 1$	1	$i^8 = i^4 \cdot i^4 = 1(1) = 1$	1

Likewise, it can be shown that $i^9 = i$, $i^{10} = -1$, $i^{11} = -i$, $i^{12} = 1$, and so on.

Exercises

Simplify each expression to i, -1, $-i$, or 1.

1. i^{14} **2.** i^{23} **3.** i^{17} **4.** i^{36} **5.** i^{19} **6.** i^{27}

Simplify.

Sample **a.** $-\sqrt{-12}$ **b.** $\sqrt{96} \cdot \sqrt{-54}$ **c.** $\sqrt{\frac{-16}{25}}$

Solution

a. $-\sqrt{-12} = -\sqrt{-1 \cdot 2^2 \cdot 3} = -2i\sqrt{3}$

b. $\sqrt{96} \cdot \sqrt{-54} = \sqrt{4^2 \cdot 6} \cdot \sqrt{-1 \cdot 3^2 \cdot 6}$
$= 4\sqrt{6} \cdot 3i\sqrt{6} = 12i \cdot 6 = 72i$

c. $\sqrt{\frac{-16}{25}} = \frac{\sqrt{-16}}{\sqrt{25}} = \frac{\sqrt{-1 \cdot 4^2}}{\sqrt{5^2}} = \frac{4i}{5}$

7. $\sqrt{-49}$ **8.** $-\sqrt{-500}$ **9.** $\sqrt{96}$ **10.** $-\sqrt{-144}$

11. $\sqrt{12} \cdot \sqrt{-75}$ **12.** $\sqrt{-3} \cdot \sqrt{48}$ **13.** $\sqrt{18} \cdot \sqrt{-108}$ **14.** $(\sqrt{-4} \cdot \sqrt{9})^2$

15. $\sqrt{\frac{16}{-81}}$ **16.** $-\sqrt{\frac{-25}{64}}$ **17.** $-\sqrt{\frac{-49}{121}}$ **18.** $\frac{\sqrt{-150}}{-\sqrt{54}}$

Solve.

19. $x^2 = -100$ **20.** $x^2 + 63 = 0$ **21.** $x^2 = -98$ **22.** $x^2 + 272 = 0$

12-4 Graphs of Quadratic Equations: The Discriminant

Objective To use the discriminant to find the number of roots of the equation $ax^2 + bx + c = 0$ and the number of x-intercepts of the graph of the related equation $y = ax^2 + bx + c$.

You learned in Lesson 8-8 that the graph of the function defined by the quadratic equation

$$y = x^2 - 2x - 3$$

is the parabola shown at the right. The x-coordinate of a point where the curve intersects the x-axis is called an ***x*-intercept** of the curve. This parabola has two x-intercepts, -1 and 3, because $y = 0$ for both of these values of x. You can also see that the equation

$$x^2 - 2x - 3 = 0, \quad \text{or} \quad (x + 1)(x - 3) = 0,$$

has -1 and 3 as roots.

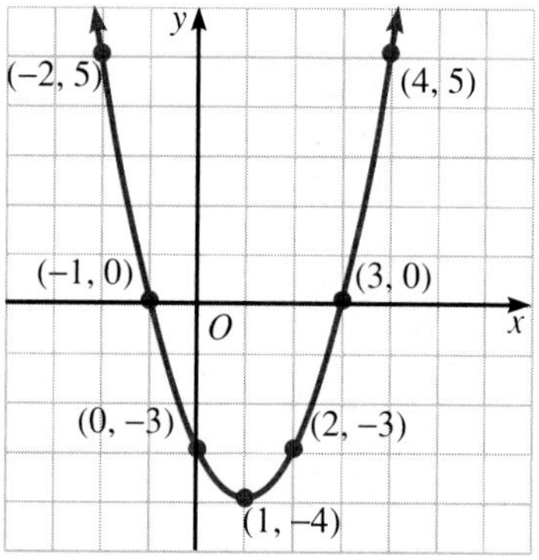

The roots of any quadratic equation of the form

$$ax^2 + bx + c = 0$$

are the x-intercepts of the graph of the related equation

$$y = ax^2 + bx + c.$$

The algebraic fact that a quadratic equation can have two, one, or no real-number roots corresponds to the geometric fact that a parabola can have two, one, or no x-intercepts, as illustrated in the following examples.

Example 1

Equation: $x^2 + 4x + 1 = 0$

Solution:

$$x = \frac{-(4) \pm \sqrt{(4)^2 - 4(1)(1)}}{2(1)}$$

$$= \frac{-4 \pm \sqrt{12}}{2} = \frac{-4 \pm 2\sqrt{3}}{2}$$

$$= -2 \pm \sqrt{3}$$

$\therefore$ the solution set is $\{-2 + \sqrt{3}, -2 - \sqrt{3}\}$.

Number of roots: two real-number roots

Related equation: $y = x^2 + 4x + 1$

Graph:

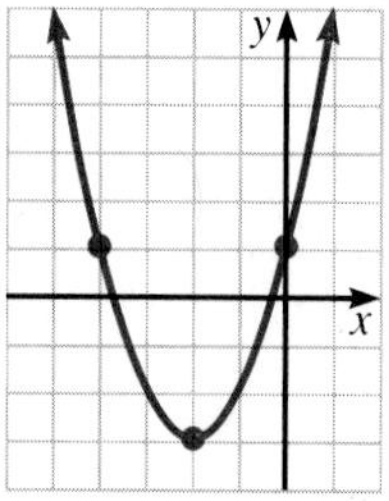

Number of x-intercepts: two

Example 2

Equation: $x^2 + 2x + 1 = 0$

Solution:

$$x = \frac{-(2) \pm \sqrt{(2)^2 - 4(1)(1)}}{2(1)}$$

$$= \frac{-2 \pm \sqrt{0}}{2}$$

$$= -1$$

$\therefore$ the solution set is $\{-1\}$.

Number of roots: one real-number root

Related equation: $y = x^2 + 2x + 1$

Graph:

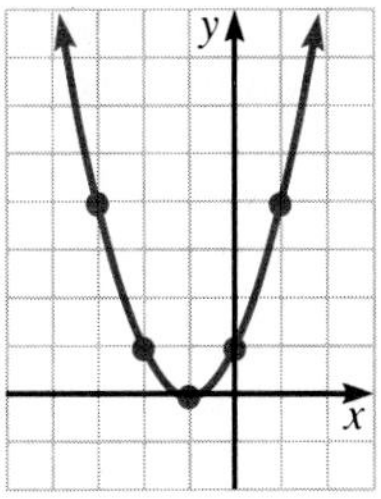

Number of x-intercepts: one

Example 3

Equation: $x^2 - 4x + 7 = 0$

Solution:

$$x = \frac{-(-4) \pm \sqrt{(-4)^2 - 4(1)(7)}}{2(1)}$$

$$= \frac{4 \pm \sqrt{-12}}{2}$$

There is no real-number root since $\sqrt{-12}$ does not represent a real number.

Number of roots: no real-number roots

Related equation: $y = x^2 - 4x + 7$

Graph:

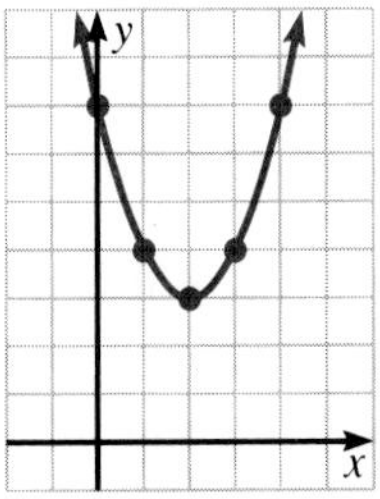

Number of x-intercepts: none

In Examples 1, 2, and 3, the value of $b^2 - 4ac$ in the quadratic formula is shown in color. This value is the key to the number of real roots, as shown in the following chart.

	Value of $b^2 - 4ac$	Number of different real roots of $ax^2 + bx + c = 0$	Number of x-intercepts of the graph of $y = ax^2 + bx + c$
Case 1	positive	2	2
Case 2	zero	1 (a double root)	1
Case 3	negative	0	0

Note that when $b^2 - 4ac$ is negative, there is no real-number root of the equation $ax^2 + bx + c = 0$ because square roots of negative numbers do not exist in the set of real numbers.

Because the value of $b^2 - 4ac$ discriminates, or points out differences, among the three cases shown in the box, it is called the **discriminant** of the quadratic equation.

Oral Exercises

The value of the discriminant of an equation is given. Tell how many different real-number roots the equation has.

1. 31 **2.** −8 **3.** 0 **4.** 1 **5.** 49

State the value of the discriminant.

6. $x^2 - 5x + 7 = 0$ **7.** $-2x^2 + 3x + 2 = 0$ **8.** $6x^2 - 7x - 4 = 0$

Written Exercises

Write the value of the discriminant of each equation. Then use it to decide how many different real-number roots the equation has. (Do not solve.)

A

1. $x^2 - 5x + 4 = 0$ **2.** $r^2 - 3r + 9 = 0$ **3.** $n^2 - 16n + 64 = 0$

4. $2z^2 + 5z - 3 = 0$ **5.** $9y^2 - 12y + 4 = 0$ **6.** $3t^2 - 4t + 3 = 0$

7. $4m^2 + 20m + 25 = 0$ **8.** $3a^2 - 2a - 6 = 0$ **9.** $-5b^2 + b + 1 = 0$

10. $-4q^2 + 3q - 2 = 0$ **11.** $2c^2 - 1.4c + 0.1 = 0$ **12.** $\frac{1}{2}d^2 - 2d + 2 = 0$

Without drawing the graph of the given equation, determine (a) how many *x*-intercepts the parabola has and (b) whether its vertex lies above, below, or on the *x*-axis.

Sample $y = 5x - x^2 + 6$

Solution **a.** The *x*-intercepts of the graph are the roots of the equation

$$5x - x^2 + 6 = 0, \quad \text{or} \quad -x^2 + 5x + 6 = 0.$$

Its discriminant is $(5)^2 - 4(-1)(6)$, or 49.
The equation has two real-number roots.
The parabola has two *x*-intercepts.

b. Since the coefficient of x^2 is negative, the parabola opens downward (see page 384). Its vertex must be above the *x*-axis (otherwise the parabola would not intersect the *x*-axis in two points).

B

13. $y = x^2 - 5x + 5$ **14.** $y = -x^2 + 3x + 6$ **15.** $y = x^2 + 16 - 8x$

16. $y = 2x^2 + 4x + 3$ **17.** $y = 7x + 2 - 3x^2$ **18.** $y = 4x^2 + 2x - 1$

C

19. Find k so that the equation $9x^2 + 12x + k = 0$ has one real-number (double) root.

20. Find k so that the equation $4x^2 + 12kx + 9 = 0$ has one real-number (double) root.

Mixed Review Exercises

Simplify. Assume no denominator equals zero.

1. $\frac{\sqrt{3} - 3}{\sqrt{6}}$

2. $\sqrt{\frac{12c^3}{5}} \cdot \sqrt{\frac{3c^5}{20}}$

3. $6\sqrt{8} - 15\sqrt{2} + \sqrt{18}$

4. $\frac{2x + 14}{x^3 + 8x^2 + 7x}$

5. $\frac{b}{b + 1} + \frac{5}{4b + 4}$

6. $(6.2 \cdot 10^4)(8.1 \cdot 10^3)$

Find the vertex and the axis of symmetry of the graph of each equation.

7. $y = 4x^2$

8. $y = x^2 + 10x + 25$

9. $y = 2x^2 + 3$

10. $y = -x^2 + 9x - 3$

11. $y = 6 - 5x + \frac{1}{3}x^2$

12. $y = -2x^2 + 3x$

Computer Exercises

For students with some programming experience

Write a BASIC program that computes the value of the discriminant of a quadratic equation $AX^2 + BX + C = 0$, where the values of A, B, and C are entered with INPUT statements. The program should then report the number of real roots of the equation. Run the program for the following equations.

1. $2x^2 - 3x - 1 = 0$

2. $4x^2 + 28x + 49 = 0$

3. $x^2 - x + 1 = 0$

Self-Test 1

Vocabulary perfect square (p. 562)
completing the square (p. 564)
quadratic formula (p. 567)
x-intercept (p. 572)
discriminant (p. 573)

Solve.

1. $6x^2 = 54$

2. $(x - 3)^2 = 7$

Obj. 12-1, p. 561

Solve by completing the square.

3. $a^2 - 12a + 35 = 0$

4. $x^2 - 6x - 16 = 0$

Obj. 12-2, p. 564

Solve by using the quadratic formula.

5. $2x^2 - 3x - 2 = 0$

6. $t^2 - 3t - 6 = 0$

Obj. 12-3, p. 567

Give the number of real roots.

7. $2y^2 - 2y + 8 = 0$

8. $c^2 - c + 3 = 0$

Obj. 12-4, p. 572

Check your answers with those at the back of the book.

Using Quadratic Equations

12-5 Methods of Solution

Objective To choose the best method for solving a quadratic equation.

You have learned four methods for solving quadratic equations. Although the quadratic formula can be used to solve any quadratic equation in the form $ax^2 + bx + c = 0$, one of the other methods may be easier. Here are some guidelines to help you decide which method to use.

Methods for Solving a Quadratic Equation

Method	When to Use the Method
1. Using the quadratic formula	1. If an equation is in the form $ax^2 + bx + c = 0$, especially if you use a calculator.
2. Factoring	2. If an equation is in the form $ax^2 + bx = 0$, or if the factors are easily seen.
3. Using the property of square roots of equal numbers	3. If an equation is in the form $ax^2 + c = 0$.
4. Completing the square	4. If an equation is in the form $x^2 + bx + c = 0$ and b is an even number.

Example Solve each quadratic equation using the most appropriate method.

a. $12x^2 - 108 = 0$ **b.** $4x^2 - 12x + 7 = 0$

c. $4t^2 - 56t = 0$ **d.** $n^2 + 8n - 2 = 0$

Solution **a.** $12x^2 - 108 = 0$

$$12x^2 = 108$$
$$x^2 = 9$$
$$x = \pm 3$$

$\therefore$ the solution set is $\{3, -3\}$. ***Answer***

Use the property of square roots of equal numbers, since the equation has the form $ax^2 + c = 0$.

b. $4x^2 - 12x + 7 = 0$

$$x = \frac{-(-12) \pm \sqrt{(-12)^2 - 4(4)(7)}}{2(4)}$$
$$= \frac{12 \pm \sqrt{32}}{8} = \frac{12 \pm 4\sqrt{2}}{8} = \frac{3 \pm \sqrt{2}}{2}$$

$\therefore$ the solution set is $\left\{\frac{3 + \sqrt{2}}{2}, \frac{3 - \sqrt{2}}{2}\right\}$. ***Answer***

Use the quadratic formula, since the equation has the form $ax^2 + bx + c = 0$.

c. $4t^2 - 56t = 0$ Form: $ax^2 + bx = 0$

$4t(t - 14) = 0$ Factor.

$4t = 0$ or $t - 14 = 0$

$t = 0$ or $t = 14$

$\therefore$ the solution set is $\{0, 14\}$. ***Answer***

d. $n^2 + 8n - 2 = 0$ Form: $x^2 + bx + c = 0$

$n^2 + 8n = 2$ Complete the square.

$n^2 + 8n + 16 = 2 + 16$

$(n + 4)^2 = 18$

$n + 4 = \pm\sqrt{18}$

$n = -4 \pm 3\sqrt{2}$

$\therefore$ the solution set is $\{-4 + 3\sqrt{2}, -4 - 3\sqrt{2}\}$. ***Answer***

Oral Exercises

State which method you would use to solve each quadratic equation.

1. $x^2 + 5x - 6 = 0$
2. $x^2 - 2x = 1$
3. $11x^2 = 44$
4. $8x^2 + 11x = 0$
5. $x^2 + 7x + 2 = 0$
6. $3x^2 - 5x = 4$
7. $x^2 + 6x = 5$
8. $2x^2 + 7x + 3 = 0$
9. $5x^2 - 20x = 0$
10. $(x - 2)^2 = 7$
11. $x^2 - 8x + 1 = 3$
12. $4x^2 - 2x - 3 = 0$
13. Explain why the quadratic formula can be used to solve all quadratic equations.

Written Exercises

A **1–12.** Solve the quadratic equations given in Oral Exercises 1–12. Write the answers in simplest radical form.

Solve each quadratic equation by using the most appropriate method. Write irrational answers in simplest radical form.

13. $5x^2 + 19x = 4$
14. $x^2 - 8x = 11$
15. $3x^2 = 2x + 7$
16. $\frac{2x^2}{3} + \frac{3x}{4} = 1$
17. $\frac{(y + 3)^2}{4} = 5$
18. $0.75x^2 - 0.3x + 0.03 = 0$
19. $1.4x^2 - 0.7x = 0.2$
20. $\frac{1}{3x} = \frac{2x - 3}{2}$
21. $\frac{4x - 3}{2x - 3} = \frac{5x - 3}{x + 1}$

B **22.** $5x(x - 3) + 4(x + 4) = 31 - 7x^2$
23. $2x(x - 3) + 7(x^2 - 1) = 2$
24. $(x + 3)^2 + 6(x + 3) = 16$
25. $9(x - 4)^2 + 4(x - 4) = 0$
26. $(3x + 2)(x - 1) - 13 = 2x(2 - x)$
27. $(3x - 5)^2 = (8x + 3)^2$

Solve. Be sure that you have found all real roots of each equation. Write irrational answers in simplest form. (*Hint:* Substitute y for x^2.)

C **28.** $9x^4 - 14x^2 + 5 = 0$

29. $4x^4 + 21x^2 - 18 = 0$

30. $3x^4 - 7x^2 = 0$

31. $9x^4 - 64 = 0$

Mixed Review Exercises

Evaluate if $x = 1$, $y = 8$, and $z = -9$. Write irrational expressions in simplest radical form.

1. $\pm\sqrt{y^2 - 4xz}$

2. $-\sqrt{y^2 + 4zx}$

3. $\sqrt{z^2 - 4xy}$

4. $\sqrt{z^2 + 4xy}$

5. $\pm\sqrt{x^2 - 4yz}$

6. $\sqrt{x^2 + 4yz}$

Solve. Write irrational roots in simplest radical form.

7. $4x^2 - 4x - 15 = 0$

8. $2d^2 + 3d - 77 = 0$

9. $2(x + 4)(x + 7) = (2x + 1)(x - 9) - 3$

10. $c^2 - 4c - 2 = 0$

11. $3p^2 - 4p + 1 = 0$

12. $12y^2 + 24y = 5$

Biographical Note / *Albert Einstein*

Albert Einstein was born in Ulm, Germany in 1879. He attended school in Munich and went to college in Switzerland. As he excelled only in mathematics and science, Einstein was unable to secure a teaching position after his graduation in 1901 and ended up working as a minor official in the Swiss patent office. The job, however, left him time to work on his scientific studies.

In 1905 Einstein published three important papers that were to have a far-reaching effect on science. One paper helped to establish the quantum, or particle, theory of light, and for this research Einstein was awarded the 1921 Nobel Prize in physics. A second paper contained equations that described molecular motion and that could be used to determine the size of molecules.

However, it was Einstein's paper on the special theory of relativity that made him famous. This theory replaced Isaac Newton's theories of the universe when dealing with objects whose speeds approached that of light.

Einstein became a professor at the University of Zurich. He eventually took a position with the Institute of Advanced Studies in Princeton, New Jersey. At the time of his death in 1955, Einstein, like Newton, left science greatly different from the way it was before his work.

12-6 Solving Problems Involving Quadratic Equations

Objective To use quadratic equations to solve problems.

Example The parks commission wants a new rectangular sign with an area of 25 m^2 for the visitor center. The length of the sign is to be 4 m longer than the width. To the nearest tenth of a meter, what will be the length and the width of the sign?

Solution

Step 1 The problem asks for the length and width of the sign.

Step 2 Let x = the width in meters.
Then $x + 4$ = the length in meters.

Step 3 Use the formula for the area of a rectangle to write an equation.

$$x(x + 4) = 25$$

Step 4 Solve $x(x + 4) = 25$.

$$x^2 + 4x = 25$$
$$x^2 + 4x + 4 = 25 + 4 \qquad \text{Complete the square.}$$
$$(x + 2)^2 = 29$$
$$x + 2 = \pm\sqrt{29}$$
$$x = -2 \pm \sqrt{29}$$

Use your calculator or the table of square roots on page 682 to approximate the roots to the nearest tenth:

$$-2 + \sqrt{29} \approx -2 + 5.39 = 3.39 \approx 3.4$$
$$-2 - \sqrt{29} \approx -2 - 5.39 = -7.39 \approx -7.4$$

Step 5 Discard the negative root since a negative length has no meaning.

Check 3.4:

$$3.4(3.4 + 4) \stackrel{?}{=} 25$$
$$3.4(7.4) \stackrel{?}{=} 25$$
$$25.16 \approx 25 \quad \checkmark$$

The numbers are approximately equal, so the approximate solution is correct.

$\therefore$ the width of the sign is 3.4 m and the length is 7.4 m. ***Answer***

Problems

Solve. Give irrational roots to the nearest tenth. Use your calculator or the table of square roots on page 682 as necessary.

A **1.** The width of a rectangular park is 5 m shorter than its length. If the area of the park is 300 m^2, find the length and the width.

2. The length of a rectangle is 3 times the width. The area of the rectangle is 75 cm^2. Find the length and the width.

3. The sum of a number and its square is 56. Find the number.

4. The difference of a number and its square is 182. Find the number.

5. The length of the base of a triangle is 4 times its altitude. If the area of the triangle is 162 cm^2, find the altitude.

(*Hint:* Area of a triangle $= \frac{1}{2} \times$ base $\times$ height.)

6. The altitude of a triangle is 5 m less than its base. The area of the triangle is 42 m^2. Find the base.

7. If the sides of a square are increased by 3 cm, its area becomes 100 cm^2. Find the length of the sides of the original square.

8. Holly has a rectangular garden that measures 12 m by 14 m. She wants to increase the area to 255 m^2 by increasing the width and length by the same amount. What will be the dimensions of the new garden?

9. Cindy and Olaf leave the same point at the same time. Cindy is bicycling west at a rate of 2 mi/h faster than Olaf, who is traveling south. After one hour, they are 10 mi apart. How fast is each person traveling? (*Hint:* Use the Pythagorean theorem.)

B **10.** Working alone, Colleen can paint a house in 2 h less than James. Working together, they can paint the house in 10 h. How long would it take James to paint the house by himself?

11. Together Maria and Johannes can pick a bushel of apples in 16 min. Maria takes 4 min more to pick a bushel than Johannes does. Find the time it takes each person to pick a bushel of apples alone.

12. The Computer Club went on a field trip to a computer museum. The trip cost $240 to be paid for equally by each club member. The day before the trip, 4 students decided not to go. This increased the cost by $2 per student. How many students went to the computer museum?

13. The Math Club bought a $72 calculator for club use. If there had been 2 more students in the club, each would have had to contribute 50 cents less. How many students were in the club?

14. Judith can ride her bike 2 mi/h faster than Kelly. Judith takes 48 min less to travel 50 mi than Kelly does. What is each person's speed in miles per hour?

C **15.** Pipe A can fill a tank in 4 h. Pipe B can fill the tank in 9 h less than the time it takes pipe C, a drain pipe, to empty the tank. When all 3 pipes are open, it takes 2 h to fill the tank. How much time is required for pipe C to empty the tank if pipes A and B are closed?

Mixed Review Exercises

Solve.

1. $\frac{\sqrt{n}}{3} = \frac{\sqrt{5}}{1}$ **2.** $\frac{\sqrt{x-3}}{6} = \frac{3}{2}$ **3.** $\frac{\sqrt{5t}}{8} = \frac{1}{4}$

4. $\frac{13}{7} = \frac{20}{m}$ **5.** $m^2 = 14m - 45$ **6.** $y - \frac{7}{y+2} - \frac{3y-1}{y+2} = 5$

In Exercises 7–9, (x_1, y_1) and (x_2, y_2) are ordered pairs of the same direct variation. Find the missing value.

7. $x_1 = 1,\ y_1 = 3$; $x_2 = 4,\ y_2 =$ _?_

8. $x_1 = 10,\ y_1 =$ _?_; $x_2 = 2,\ y_2 = 5$

9. $x_1 = 24,\ y_1 = 64$; $x_2 =$ _?_, $y_2 = 8$

Extra / Quadratic Inequalities

The graph of the quadratic function $y = x^2 - 6x + 8$ can be used to illustrate the solutions of the following:

(1) $x^2 - 6x + 8 = 0$
(2) $x^2 - 6x + 8 > 0$
(3) $x^2 - 6x + 8 < 0$

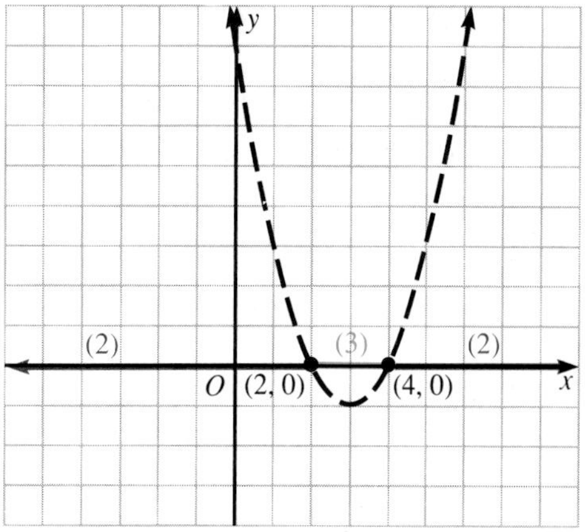

The solution set of quadratic equation **(1)** is **{2, 4}**. These two values of x are called the *zeros* of the quadratic function.

To solve quadratic inequality (2), you reason as follows:

a. If (x, y) is on the graph, then $y = x^2 - 6x + 8$.

b. If (x, y) is above the x-axis, then $y > 0$.

c. Therefore, if (x, y) is on the graph *and* above the x-axis, then $y = x^2 - 6x + 8 > 0$.

d. Therefore, the solution set for **(2)** is $\{x < 2 \text{ or } x > 4\}$ because these values of x give points that are on the graph above the x-axis.

Similar reasoning shows that the solution set for (3) is $\{2 < x < 4\}$ because these values of x give points on the graph below the x-axis.

Example Solve for x.

(1) $x^2 + 2x + 1 = 0$
(2) $x^2 + 2x + 1 > 0$
(3) $x^2 + 2x + 1 < 0$

Solution Use the graph of $y = x^2 + 2x + 1$.

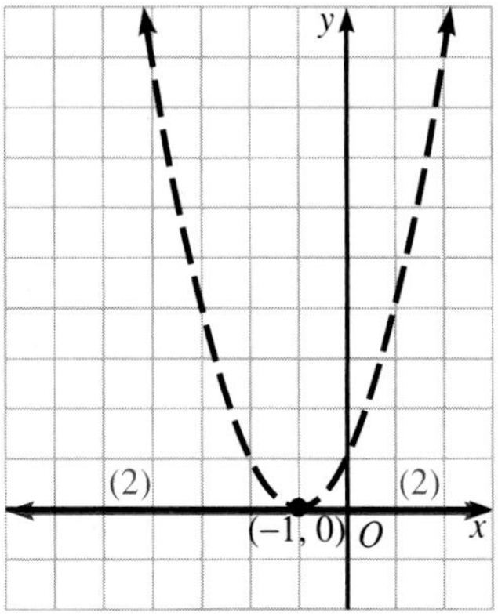

(1) Factor the quadratic equation $x^2 + 2x + 1 = 0$.
Since $(x + 1)(x + 1) = 0$,
$x = -1$.

(2) Since the graph lies above the x-axis for all x except -1,
$x^2 + 2x + 1 > 0$ for all $x \neq -1$.

(3) There are no values of x for which $x^2 + 2x + 1 < 0$, since the graph does not go below the x-axis.

Exercises

Graph each quadratic equation. Solve for x when (1) $y = 0$, (2) $y > 0$, and (3) $y < 0$.

1. $y = x^2 - 36$
2. $y = 3x + x^2$
3. $y = 16 - x^2$
4. $y = x^2 + 2x - 15$
5. $y = x^2 - 8x + 12$
6. $y = 3x^2 - 5x - 2$

Find the values of x for which each expression represents a real number.

7. $\sqrt{x^2 - 3x}$
8. $\sqrt{x^2 + 4x + 3}$
9. $\sqrt{x^2 - 10x + 21}$

Self-Test 2

Solve the following quadratic equations using the most convenient method.

Obj. 12-5, p. 576

1. $3(x + 2)^2 = 12$
2. $2x^2 + 6x + 3 = 0$
3. $x^2 - 10x = 20$
4. $3x^2 + 9x = 0$

Solve.

Obj. 12-6, p. 579

5. The length of a rectangle is twice the width. The area of the rectangle is 200 cm^2. Find the length and the width.

6. The perimeter of a rectangular wading pool is 172 m and its area is 1800 m^2. Find the length and width of the pool.

Check your answers with those at the back of the book.

Application / *Boyle's Gas Law*

Air and other gases have characteristics of temperature, pressure, and volume much the same as do liquids, such as water. Air temperature is measured in degrees, volume in cubic centimeters or liters, and pressure in millimeters.

Robert Boyle, a seventeenth-century English scientist, investigated many properties of air and gases. He conducted experiments to see how the pressure of a gas in an enclosed space is related to its volume. His discovery is used today in the modern internal combustion engine and in a simple pump for inflating basketballs or tires.

Boyle observed that pressure on a confined gas reduces its volume. In fact, he found that with a constant temperature, the volume of a gas varies inversely with the pressure exerted on it. This statement, known as Boyle's Law, can be written in these two ways.

$pV = k$, where k is a constant, V is the volume, and p is the pressure

or $pV = p'V'$, where p' and V' are the new pressure and the new volume, respectively.

Example A gas has a volume of 600 mL at a pressure of 760 mm. What is the volume of the gas at a pressure of 800 mm?

Solution

$$pV = p'V'$$
$$760 \times 600 = 800V'$$
$$\frac{760 \times 600}{800} = V'$$
$$570 = V'$$

$\therefore$ the volume is 570 mL.

Exercises

1. A certain gas has a volume of 420 cm^3 at a pressure of 720 mm. What will its volume be if the pressure is increased to 840 mm?
2. A gas kept at 760 mm of pressure occupies 2 L. What pressure must be exerted for the volume to decrease to 1.9 L?
3. A certain gas has a volume of 500 cm^3 at a pressure of 750 mm. If the pressure is decreased to 625 mm, what is the resulting volume?
4. A gas occupies 2 m^3 of space at 760 mm of pressure. It is compressed to 1 m^3 of space. What is the new pressure?
5. An underinflated balloon contains 9 m^3 of helium when the pressure is 760 mm. What is the volume of the balloon when it reaches an altitude where the pressure is 304 mm?

12-7 Direct and Inverse Variation Involving Squares

Objective To use quadratic direct variation and inverse variation as a square in problem solving.

In Lessons 8-9 and 8-10 you learned about direct and inverse variation. In the world around us, there are many examples in which a quantity varies either directly or inversely *as the square* of another quantity. For example, the surface area of a sphere varies directly as the square of the radius: $S = 4\pi r^2$. This is an example of a *quadratic direct variation.*

A **quadratic direct variation** is a function defined by an equation of the form

$$y = kx^2, \text{ where } k \text{ is a nonzero constant.}$$

You say that y *varies directly as* x^2 or that y *is directly proportional to* x^2.

If (x_1, y_1) and (x_2, y_2) are ordered pairs of the same quadratic variation, and neither x_1 nor x_2 is zero, then

$$\frac{y_1}{x_1^2} = \frac{y_2}{x_2^2}.$$

Example 1 Given that a varies directly as the square of d, and $a = 45$ when $d = 3$, find the value of d when $a = 60$.

Solution 1 Use $a = kd^2$.

$$45 = k(3)^2$$
$$45 = 9k$$
$$5 = k$$
$$\therefore \quad a = 5d^2$$

For $a = 60$:

$$60 = 5d^2$$
$$12 = d^2$$
$$\pm\sqrt{12} = d$$
$$\pm 2\sqrt{3} = d \quad \textit{Answer}$$

Solution 2 Use $\dfrac{a_1}{d_1^2} = \dfrac{a_2}{d_2^2}$.

$$\frac{45}{3^2} = \frac{60}{d_2^2}$$
$$\frac{45}{9} = \frac{60}{d_2^2}$$
$$45d_2^2 = 540$$
$$d_2^2 = 12$$
$$d_2 = \pm\sqrt{12}$$
$$d_2 = \pm 2\sqrt{3} \quad \textit{Answer}$$

Remember to examine your solution to see if each one makes sense. For example, if d represents a length, you can discard the negative solution since a negative length has no meaning.

The intensity of sound *varies inversely as the square* of the distance of a listener from the source of sound. Therefore, if you halve the distance between yourself and a trumpeter, the intensity of the sound that reaches your ears will be quadrupled.

An **inverse variation as the square** is a function defined by an equation of the form

$$x^2y = k, \text{ where } k \text{ is a nonzero constant,}$$

or

$$y = \frac{k}{x^2}, \text{ where } x \neq 0.$$

You say that *y varies inversely as* x^2 or *y is inversely proportional to* x^2.

If (x_1, y_1) and (x_2, y_2) are ordered pairs of the function defined by $x^2y = k$, then

$$x_1{}^2y_1 = x_2{}^2y_2.$$

Example 2 Given that h varies inversely as the square of r, and that $h = 2$ when $r = 3$, find the value of r when $h = \frac{3}{10}$.

Solution 1 Use $h = \frac{k}{r^2}$.

$$2 = \frac{k}{3^2}$$
$$18 = k$$
$$\therefore \quad h = \frac{18}{r^2}$$

For $h = \frac{3}{10}$:

$$\frac{3}{10} = \frac{18}{r^2}$$
$$3r^2 = 180$$
$$r^2 = 60$$
$$r = \pm\sqrt{60}$$
$$= \pm 2\sqrt{15}$$ ***Answer***

Solution 2 Use $r_1{}^2h_1 = r_2{}^2h_2$.

$$3^2(2) = r_2{}^2\left(\frac{3}{10}\right)$$
$$18 = \frac{3r_2{}^2}{10}$$
$$3r_2{}^2 = 180$$
$$r_2{}^2 = 60$$
$$r_2 = \pm\sqrt{60}$$
$$= \pm 2\sqrt{15}$$ ***Answer***

Remember that in a particular situation you must examine each root to see if it makes sense.

Oral Exercises

Translate each statement into a formula. Use k as the constant of variation where needed.

1. The kinetic energy, e, of a moving body varies directly as the square of its velocity, v.
2. The force, F, between two point charges of static electricity is inversely proportional to the square of the distance, d, between them.
3. The weight, w, of an object is inversely proportional to the square of its distance, d, from the center of Earth.
4. The area, A, of the surface of a steel ball is directly proportional to the square of the diameter, d, of the ball.
5. The time, t, required to fill a pool varies inversely as the square of the radius, r, of the hose.
6. The quantity, Q, of heat energy in an electrical circuit is directly proportional to the square of the current, I.

Problems

Solve. Give irrational roots to the nearest tenth. You may wish to use a calculator.

A

1. The amount of material needed to cover a ball is directly proportional to the square of its diameter. A ball with a diameter of 12 cm needs 452 cm^2 of material to cover it. If 1017 cm^2 of material is to be used, what is the diameter of the ball?
2. The price of a diamond varies directly as the square of its mass in carats. If a 1.5 carat diamond costs $2700, find the mass in carats of a diamond that costs $4800.
3. The distance it takes an automobile to stop varies directly as the square of its speed. If the stopping distance for a car traveling at 80 km/h is 175 m, what is the stopping distance for a car traveling at 64 km/h?
4. The height that a person is above the water is directly proportional to the square of the distance the person can see across the ocean. If the captain of a ship is 4 m above the water, he can see about 30 km across the ocean. How far can the captain see if he is 10 m above the water?
5. The height of a cylinder of a given volume is inversely proportional to the square of the radius. A cylinder of radius 6 cm has a height of 24 cm. What is the radius of a cylinder of equal volume whose height is 96 cm?

6. The brightness of the light on an object varies inversely as the square of the distance from the object to the light source. At a distance of 1.2 m from a light source, the brightness on a book page was measured at 25 lm/m^2 (lumens per square meter). If the page were moved 0.4 m closer to the light source, what would the brightness measure?

7. The length of a pendulum varies directly as the square of the time in seconds that it takes to swing from one side to the other. If it takes a 100 cm pendulum 1 s to swing from one side to the other, how many seconds does it take a 150 cm pendulum to swing?

8. The exposure time needed for a photograph is inversely proportional to the square of the radius of the camera lens. If the lens radius is 1 cm, the exposure time needed is 0.01 s. Find the radius of the lens for an exposure time of 0.0025 s.

B 9. The height of a circular cylinder of given volume varies inversely as the square of the radius of the base. How many times greater is the radius of a cylinder 3 m high than the radius of a cylinder 6 m high with the same volume?

10. The strength of a radio signal is inversely proportional to the square of the distance from the source of the signal. An observer is 200 m away from a source. She then moves to a position closer to the source. The strength of the signal at the second position is 16 times as strong as at the first position. How far is she from the source of the signal?

C 11. The volume of a sphere varies directly as the cube of the radius. If the ratio of the radii of two spheres is 4:3, what is the ratio of the volumes of the spheres?

12. The heat emitted from a star is directly proportional to the fourth power of the surface temperature of the star. If the ratio of the amount of heat emitted from two stars is 16:81, what is the ratio of their surface temperatures?

Mixed Review Exercises

Solve for the indicated variable. State any restrictions.

1. $3x^2 - 2y = 1;\ y$
2. $A = \dfrac{h(b + c)}{2};\ h$
3. $A = \dfrac{h(b + c)}{2};\ b$
4. $1 - x = ax;\ x$
5. $t = \dfrac{V - k^2}{g};\ V$
6. $Er^2 = k;\ r$

Write an equation, in standard form, of the line passing through the given points.

7. (4, 1), (0, −7)
8. (3, 2), (−6, −4)
9. (4, 3), (−4, 7)
10. (−1, −1), (7, 23)
11. (0, −4), (−12, −6)
12. (0, −10), (13, −5)

12-8 Joint and Combined Variation

Objective To solve problems involving joint variation and combined variation.

If Danalee earns \$750 next summer and puts her earnings into a savings account, the amount of simple interest, I, she will receive depends on her bank's interest rate, r, and on the length of time, t, that she leaves the money in the account. That is:

$$I = 750rt$$

The interest is directly proportional to the product of the rate and the time. This is an example of a *joint variation*.

If a variable varies directly as the product of two or more other variables, the resulting relationship is called a **joint variation.** You can express the relationship in the forms

$$z = kxy, \text{ where } k \text{ is a nonzero constant,}$$

and $$\frac{z_1}{x_1y_1} = \frac{z_2}{x_2y_2}.$$

You say that *z varies jointly as x and y.*

Example 1 The volume of a right circular cone varies jointly as the height, h, and the square of the radius, r. If $V_1 = 320\pi$, $h_1 = 15$, $r_1 = 8$, $h_2 = 12$, and $r_2 = 16$, find V_2.

Solution

$$\frac{V_1}{h_1{r_1}^2} = \frac{V_2}{h_2{r_2}^2}$$

$$\frac{320\pi}{15(8)^2} = \frac{V_2}{12(16)^2}$$

$$15(64)V_2 = 12(256)(320\pi)$$

$$V_2 = 1024\pi \quad \textit{Answer}$$

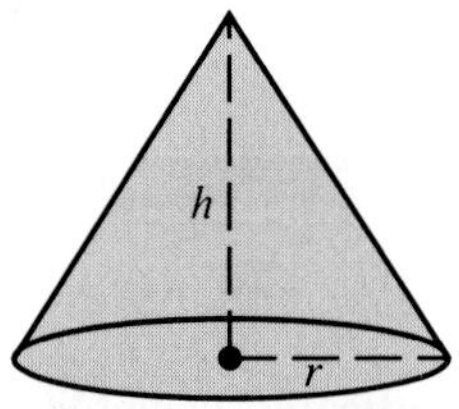

If a variable varies *directly* as one variable and *inversely* as another, the resulting relationship is called a **combined variation.** You can express the relationship in the forms

$$zy = kx \left(\text{or } z = \frac{kx}{y}\right), \text{ where } k \text{ is a nonzero constant,}$$

and $$\frac{z_1y_1}{x_1} = \frac{z_2y_2}{x_2}.$$

Example 2 The power, P, of an electric current varies directly as the square of the voltage, V, and inversely as the resistance, R. If 6 volts applied across a resistance of 3 ohms produces 12 watts of power, how much voltage applied across a resistance of 6 ohms will produce 13.5 watts of power?

Solution Let $P_1 = 12$, $V_1 = 6$, $R_1 = 3$, $P_2 = 13.5$, and $R_2 = 6$. $V_2 = \underline{\ ?\ }$

$$\frac{P_1R_1}{V_1^2} = \frac{P_2R_2}{V_2^2}$$

$$\frac{12(3)}{6^2} = \frac{(13.5)(6)}{V_2^2}$$

$$12(3)V_2^2 = 36(13.5)(6)$$

$$V_2^2 = 81$$

$$V_2 = \pm\sqrt{81} = \pm 9$$

Discard the negative root since a negative voltage has no meaning.

$\therefore$ the amount of voltage is 9 volts. ***Answer***

Oral Exercises

Translate each statement into a formula. Use k as the constant of variation where needed.

1. T varies jointly as s and p.
2. V varies directly as d and inversely as t.
3. a varies directly as the square of b and inversely as c.
4. Q varies directly as m and inversely as the square of t.
5. y varies directly as the square of x and inversely as the square of z.
6. V varies jointly with l, w, and h.
7. The total force, F, of a liquid varies jointly as the area of the surface, A, the depth of liquid, h, and the density, d.
8. The volume, V, of a cylinder varies jointly as its height, h, and the square of its radius, r.
9. The heat, H, produced by an electric lamp varies jointly as the resistance, R, and the square of the current, C.
10. The pressure, P, of a gas varies directly as its temperature, T, and inversely as its volume, V.
11. The centrifugal force, F, of an object moving in a circular path is directly proportional to the square of its velocity, v, and inversely proportional to the diameter, d, of its path.
12. The acceleration, a, of a moving object is directly proportional to the distance, d, it travels and inversely proportional to the square of the time, t, it travels.

Translate each statement into a formula. Use k as the constant of variation where needed.

13. The kinetic energy, e, of a moving object varies jointly as the mass, m, of the object and the square of the velocity, v.

14. The wind resistance, R, of an object varies jointly as the area, A, of its surface facing the wind and the square of the speed, s, of the wind.

Written Exercises

Solve. Give irrational roots to the nearest tenth. You may wish to use a calculator.

A

1. c varies directly as a and inversely as b. If $c = 15$ when $a = 18$ and $b = 40$, find c when $a = 36$ and $b = 25$.

2. d varies jointly as r and t. If $d = 45$ when $r = 15$ and $t = 14$, find d when $r = 21$ and $t = 8$.

3. m varies jointly as v and the square of u. If $m = 9$ when $v = 15$ and $u = 6$, find u when $m = 60$ and $v = 25$.

4. c varies inversely as the square of h and directly as n. If $c = 1$ when $h = 11$ and $n = 50$, find h when $c = 3.63$ and $n = 6$.

5. The square of y varies inversely as x and directly as z. If $y = 3$ when $x = 12$ and $z = 21$, find y when $x = 8$ and $z = 28$.

6. a varies directly as r and inversely as the square of v. If $a = 15$ when $r = 27$ and $v = 8$, find v when $r = 4.5$ and $a = 10$.

B

7. x varies jointly as u and v. How does x change when both u and v are doubled? when u is doubled and v is halved?

8. m varies directly as the square of r and inversely as s. How does m change when both r and s are doubled? when both r and s are tripled?

9. In the formula $h^2 = \frac{3r^2}{\pi d}$, how does h change when r is doubled and d is halved?

10. In the formula $t^2 = \frac{Fs}{r}$, how does t change when F remains constant, s is tripled, and r is halved?

Problems

Solve. Give irrational roots to the nearest tenth. You may wish to use a calculator.

A

1. The volume of a pyramid varies jointly as the height and the area of the base. A pyramid 20 cm high has base area of 63 cm^2 and a volume of 420 cm^3. What is the volume if the height is 8 cm and the area of the base is 39 cm^2?

2. The lateral surface area of a cylindrical jar varies jointly as the diameter and the height of the jar. For a diameter of 10.4 cm and a height of 18 cm, the lateral surface area is 588 cm^2. What is the height if the lateral surface area is 294 cm^2 and the diameter is 7.8 cm?

In Exercises 3 and 4, apply the statement: The number of persons needed to do a job varies directly as the amount of work to be done and inversely as the time in which the job must be done.

3. If 5 students in a typing pool can type 280 pages in 2 days, how many students will be needed to type 2100 pages in 3 days?

4. If 3 people can mow 300 m^2 of grass in 0.5 h, how long will it take 7 people to mow 7000 m^2?

5. The cost of running an appliance varies jointly as the number of watts used, the hours of operation, and the cost per kilowatt-hour. A 6000 watt convection oven operates for 10 min for 15¢ at a cost of 7.5¢ per kilowatt-hour. What is the cost of cooking two meals if each meal takes 70 min to cook?

6. The volume of a cone varies jointly as its height and the square of its radius. A certain cone has a volume of 702π cm^3, a height of 15 cm, and a radius of 12 cm. Find the radius of another cone that has a height of 27 cm and a volume of 576π cm^3.

7. The distance a car travels from rest varies jointly as its acceleration and the square of the time of motion. A car travels 250 m from rest in 5 s at an acceleration of 20 m/s^2. How many seconds will it take the car to travel 1800 m at acceleration of 25 m/s^2?

8. The resistance of a wire to the transmission of electricity varies directly as the length of the wire and inversely as the square of the radius of a cross section of the wire. An 800 m wire has a radius of 0.48 cm and a resistance of 0.3125 ohms. If another wire made from the same metal has a length of 500 m and a resistance of 0.5 ohms, what is its radius?

B 9. Using the mass of the sun as the unit of mass, and measuring distance in astronomical units (AU) and time in years, the total mass of a double star is directly proportional to the cube of the maximum distance between the stars and inversely proportional to the square of the period (the time it takes each star to revolve about the other). The double star Sirius has a period of 50.0 years, a maximum distance of 41.0 AU, and a total mass of 3.45. What is the total mass of Capella if its period is 0.285 years and the maximum distance is 1.51 AU?

10. For a two-year period, the growth factor of an investment varies directly as the square root of the final value and inversely as the square root of the original investment. A $2000 investment with a growth factor of 1.5 yields $4500 in 2 years. Find the growth factor of a $1600 investment that yields $4900 in 2 years.

11. The heat lost through a windowpane varies jointly as the difference of the inside and outside temperatures and the window area, and inversely as the thickness of the pane. In one hour, 49.5 joules of heat are lost through a pane 40 cm by 28 cm that is 0.8 cm thick, when the temperature difference is 44° C. How many joules are lost in one hour through a pane 0.5 cm thick having an area that is 0.25 times the area of the other pane, when the temperature difference is 40° C?

12. The wind pressure on a plane varies jointly as the surface area and the square of the speed of the wind. With a wind speed of 12 mi/h, the pressure on a 4 ft by 1.5 ft rectangle is 20 lb. What is the speed of the wind when the pressure on a 2 ft by 2 ft square is 30 lb?

C 13. The heat generated by a stove element varies jointly as the resistance and the square of the current. What is the effect on the heat generated in the following cases?

a. The current is unchanged but the resistance is doubled.

b. The resistance is unchanged but the current is doubled.

c. The current is tripled and the resistance is doubled.

14. The power in an electric circuit varies directly as the square of the voltage and inversely as the resistance. What is the effect on the power in the following cases?

a. The resistance is constant and the voltage is halved.

b. The voltage is constant and the resistance is halved.

c. The voltage is tripled and the resistance is quadrupled.

Mixed Review Exercises

Solve each system.

1. $3x - 2y = 1$; $x - y = 0$
2. $x + y = 10$; $x - 2y = 16$
3. $2x - 5y = 3$; $-x + 5y = 6$
4. $5x + 3y = 5$; $4x + 3y = 10$
5. $x - y = 0$; $x + y = 4$
6. $x + y = 3$; $2x + 3y = -2$

Multiply.

7. $(2x + 1)(4x + 2)$
8. $(8s + 4)(5 + 6s)$
9. $(7t - 2y)(7t + 2y)$
10. $(3p - 4k)^2$
11. $(r - 2)^2$
12. $(xy - 2)(3xy + 4)$

Application / *Illumination*

Suppose you had to use a flashlight to help you see an object at a very close range. You would need to hold the light close to the object to make it clearer and brighter. To see a larger area, you would put more distance between the light and the object.

Scientists have measured how illumination is related to distance and brightness. The brightness, or intensity (I), of a light source is measured in units called candelas (cd). A 100-watt bulb gives about 130 cd. Illumination is the amount of light energy per second that falls on a unit area. Illumination is measured in luxes (lx).

Illumination is directly proportional to the intensity of the source. If the intensity is doubled, the illumination is doubled. Illumination on a surface is also dependent on its distance from the source. The farther the light source is from the surface, the lower the illumination.

Specifically, illumination (E) on a surface perpendicular to a light source varies inversely as the square of the distance (r) from the light source:

$$E = \frac{I}{r^2}$$

Thus, if the distance from the light source is doubled, the illumination is one fourth of what it was originally. If the distance is tripled, the illumination is one ninth. This equation is called the *law of illumination.*

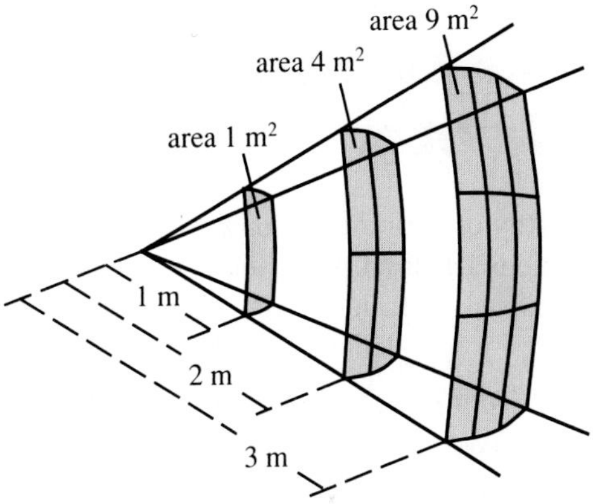

Example What illumination is provided on the surface of a table 3 m directly below a 99 cd lamp?

Solution Use the formula to solve for E: $E = \frac{99}{3^2} = \frac{99}{9} = 11$

$\therefore$ the illumination is 11 lx.

Exercises

1. What illumination is provided on a surface 4 m from a 160 cd lamp?
2. If a light is giving 315 cd from 3 m above a desk top, what illumination is provided?
3. If a lamp gives 216 cd, how far must it be placed from a table surface to provide 24 lx of illumination?
4. What illumination does a 120 cd lamp provide at a distance of 2 m?
5. What illumination is provided on the surface of a desk 2.5 m directly below a 125 cd lamp?

Self-Test 3

Vocabulary quadratic direct variation (p. 584) joint variation (p. 588) inverse variation as the square (p. 585) combined variation (p. 588)

1. The distance that the signal from a radio station travels varies directly as the square of the number of kilowatts (kW) it produces. A 40 kW station can broadcast a distance of 64 km. How far could the station broadcast if it produced 70 kW? **Obj. 12-7, p. 584**

2. The mass of a circular coin varies jointly as the thickness and the square of the radius of the coin. A silver coin 2 cm in radius and 0.2 cm thick has a mass of 26.4 g. What is the mass of a silver coin 4 cm in radius and 0.3 cm thick? **Obj. 12-8, p. 588**

Check your answers with those at the back of the book.

Chapter Summary

1. Any quadratic equation can be solved using the quadratic formula (see item 2 below). Some quadratic equations, however, may be more easily solved by factoring, applying the property of square roots of equal numbers, or by completing the square.
2. When $ax^2 + bx + c = 0$ and $a \neq 0$, the quadratic formula is expressed as:

$$x = \frac{-b \pm \sqrt{b^2 - 4ac}}{2a}$$

3. The graph of a quadratic equation of the form $y = ax^2 + bx + c$ is a parabola. The x-intercepts of the parabola correspond to the roots of the related quadratic equation $ax^2 + bx + c = 0$.
4. The discriminant, $b^2 - 4ac$, is used to determine the number of roots of a quadratic equation.

   If $b^2 - 4ac > 0$, there are two real-number roots.
   If $b^2 - 4ac = 0$, there is one (double) real-number root.
   If $b^2 - 4ac < 0$, there are no real-number roots.
5. Several kinds of variation have been described (k is a nonzero constant):
   a. A quadratic direct variation is a quadratic function defined by an equation of the form $y = kx^2$.
   b. An inverse variation as the square is a function defined by an equation of the form $x^2y = k \left(\text{or } y = \frac{k}{x^2}\right)$.
   c. A joint variation is defined by an equation of the form $z = kxy$.
   d. A combined variation is defined by an equation of the form $zy = kx$ or $z = \frac{kx}{y}$.

Chapter Review

Write the letter of the correct answer.

Solve.

1. $2x^2 - 128 = 0$ **12-1**

a. $\{64\}$ **b.** $\{64, -64\}$ **c.** $\{8\}$ **d.** $\{8, -8\}$

2. $(a - 25)^2 = 9$

a. $\{22, 28\}$ **b.** $\{2, -8\}$ **c.** $\{2, -2\}$ **d.** $\{2, 8\}$

Solve by completing the square.

3. $x^2 - 4x - 77 = 0$ **12-2**

a. $\{11, 7\}$ **b.** $\{-11, -7\}$ **c.** $\{11, -7\}$ **d.** $\{-11, 7\}$

4. $c^2 - 10c - 20 = 0$

a. $\{-5 + 3\sqrt{5}, -5 - 3\sqrt{5}\}$ **b.** $\{3\sqrt{5} + 5, 3\sqrt{5} - 5\}$

c. $\{5 + 3\sqrt{5}, 5 - 3\sqrt{5}\}$ **d.** $\{-3\sqrt{5} + 5, -3\sqrt{5} - 5\}$

Solve by using the quadratic formula.

5. $5z^2 + 11z + 2 = 0$ **12-3**

a. $\left\{-2, -\frac{1}{5}\right\}$ **b.** $\left\{2, \frac{1}{5}\right\}$ **c.** $\left\{2, -\frac{1}{5}\right\}$ **d.** $\left\{-2, \frac{1}{5}\right\}$

6. $10y^2 - y - 3 = 0$

a. $\left\{-\frac{3}{5}, -\frac{1}{2}\right\}$ **b.** $\left\{\frac{3}{5}, \frac{1}{2}\right\}$ **c.** $\left\{-\frac{3}{5}, \frac{1}{2}\right\}$ **d.** $\left\{\frac{3}{5}, -\frac{1}{2}\right\}$

7. Give the discriminant of $2x^2 - 3x - 2 = 0$. **12-4**

a. -25 **b.** 25 **c.** -5 **d.** 5

8. How many real roots does $x^2 + 2x + 5 = 0$ have?

a. 0 **b.** 1 **c.** 2 **d.** 3

9. Give the best method for solving $2y^2 + 8y = 0$. **12-5**

a. Factoring **b.** Property of square roots of equal numbers

c. Completing the square **d.** Quadratic formula

Solve.

10. The dimensions of a sheet of paper can be represented by consecutive odd integers. If the area of the paper is 143 cm^2, find the dimensions. **12-6**

a. $l = 9$ cm, $w = 7$ cm **b.** $l = 11$ cm, $w = 9$ cm **c.** $l = 15$ cm, $w = 13$ cm **d.** $l = 13$ cm, $w = 11$ cm

11. If y varies inversely as x^2, and x is halved, then y is __?__. 12-7

a. doubled **b.** quadrupled **c.** divided by 4 **d.** halved

12. If r varies directly as the cube of t and inversely as the square of s, and $r = \frac{1}{2}$ when $s = 6$ and $t = 2$, find r when $s = 12$ and $t = 4$. 12-8

a. $\frac{1}{4}$ **b.** 0 **c.** $\frac{1}{2}$ **d.** 1

Chapter Test

Solve.

1. $36x^2 = 49$ **2.** $3(a - 5)^2 = 21$ 12-1

Solve by completing the square.

3. $c^2 + 2c - 15 = 0$ **4.** $b^2 - 4b - 10 = 0$ 12-2

Solve by using the quadratic formula.

5. $3z^2 - 6z - 9 = 0$ **6.** $y^2 + 6y - 23 = 0$ 12-3

Give the number of real roots.

7. $2x^2 + 3x + 2 = 0$ **8.** $x^2 + 4x - 4 = 0$ 12-4

Solve by using the most appropriate method.

9. $7x^2 - 3x = 0$ **10.** $3x^2 - 10x - 4 = 0$ 12-5

Solve. Approximate irrational roots to the nearest tenth.

11. A garden is currently 4 m wide and 7 m long. If the area of the garden is to be doubled by increasing the width and the length by the same number of meters, find the new dimensions of the garden. 12-6

12. The area of a square is directly proportional to the square of its diagonal. If the area of a square having a diagonal 16 cm long is 128 cm^2, what is the area of a square having a diagonal 24 cm long? 12-7

13. If v varies jointly as b and h, and $v = 50$ when $b = 25$ and $h = 6$, find h when $b = 36$ and $v = 108$. 12-8

Cumulative Review *(Chapters 1–12)*

Evaluate if $a = -1$, $b = 1$, $c = 0$, $d = 3$, and $e = -\frac{5}{2}$.

1. $a(b - e)$

2. $(b \div d + e)^a$

3. $c \div e$

4. $(ad)^2 - (ad)^3$

5. $(de + ab)^c$

6. $d \div e^a$

Simplify. Assume that no denominator is zero. Each variable represents a positive real number.

7. $5 \cdot 58 - 7 \cdot 58 - (-58)$

8. $6^2 \div 3^2 + 4 \div 3$

9. $(6 - 13)(6 + 13)$

10. $3x - (0.4x + 1.2y)$

11. $15(3x - 4) + 5 - 9c$

12. $\left(-\frac{1}{8}x^5y^3z\right)(-24x^2y)$

13. $-\frac{3}{5}a^3b(-20ab^2 - 15b^3)$

14. $(5x^3y^2)^2(3x^4y^3)^2$

15. $\dfrac{-72wx^4y^5z}{-96x^3y^7z}$

16. $\dfrac{(3r^3s^4)^3}{(-9r^5s^6)^2}$

17. $(4u^2 - 2u + 1)(2u + 1)$

18. $a - 2(3a - 2)$

19. $(9z - 3)(5z + 4)$

20. $(3a^3 - 2)^2$

21. $(8r^3t - 3v)(8r^3t + 3v)$

22. $(3.4 \times 10^{12})(0.2 \times 10^{-3})$

23. $\dfrac{12c^2 - 26cd + 12d^2}{12c^2 - 44cd + 24d^2}$

24. $(18x^2 - x - 4) \div (9x + 4)$

25. $(27x^3 + 64) \div (3x + 4)$

26. $\dfrac{b^2 + b - 12}{b + 2} \cdot \dfrac{b^2 - 4}{b^2 - 5b - 6}$

27. $\dfrac{3z^2 - 8z - 16}{z^2 + 6z + 9} \div \dfrac{z^2 - 3z - 4}{z + 3}$

28. $\dfrac{85k^8 + 51k^4 - 17k^2}{-17k^4}$

29. $\dfrac{4a - 4}{3} - \dfrac{5 - 2a}{3}$

30. $\dfrac{n + 1}{2n - 3} - \dfrac{4}{n + 1} + 3$

31. $\dfrac{3}{m + 3} - \dfrac{1}{2m - 6}$

32. $-\sqrt{2.25x^6z^3}$

33. $3\sqrt{5}(\sqrt{180} - \sqrt{81})$

34. $(3\sqrt{2} + 1)^2$

35. $\sqrt{\dfrac{18a^7}{7}} \cdot \sqrt{\dfrac{112}{2a^5}}$

36. $\sqrt{108} - \sqrt{24} + \sqrt{6}$

37. $3\sqrt{80} + \dfrac{2\sqrt{35}}{\sqrt{7}}$

38. $\dfrac{3\sqrt{5} - 4}{\sqrt{2} - 3}$

39. $(2\sqrt{5} + 4\sqrt{2})(6\sqrt{5} + 4\sqrt{2})$

Factor completely. If the polynomial cannot be factored, write "prime."

40. $49r^2 + 56rs + 16s^2$

41. $4t^5 + 9t^3$

42. $30x^2 + 91x - 30$

43. $-16z^4 - 48z^3 - 64z^2$

44. $125a^4 - 45a^2$

45. $12a^2 - 5a - 12$

46. $2a^3 - a^2b - 8a + 4b$

47. $c^2 - 8c + 16$

48. $-10p^2 + 27p + 28$

Solve each equation, inequality, or system. Assume that no denominator is zero. If there is no real-number solution, write "no real-number solution."

49. $\frac{1}{5}x - 2 = \frac{2}{3}$

50. $15 - 3(y + 1) = 14 - 5y$

51. $7w + 4 = |-39|$

52. $16 = 4.8x - 2.48$

53. 35% of $t = 105$

54. $3|x| + 5 = 9$

55. $z^2 - 9z + 18 = 0$

56. $9t^2 - 24t + 16 = 0$

57. $12b^2 + 5b = 2$

58. $(3a - 2)(4a + 1) = 5$

59. $\begin{aligned} 3x + 4y &= 2 \\ -5x + 4y &= -2 \end{aligned}$

60. $\begin{aligned} 2x + y &= 7 \\ x - 2y &= 11 \end{aligned}$

61. $\frac{x - 2}{8} - \frac{2x + 1}{12} = \frac{1}{3}$

62. $\frac{3x + 2}{x - 1} = \frac{3x + 4}{x + 1}$

63. $|t - 3| \geq 5$

64. $-4 < 3t - 5 < 13$

65. $0 \leq 4 - 2t \leq 7$

66. $\frac{1}{3} - \frac{7}{2}t < -\frac{5}{6}$

67. $-2\sqrt{t - 1} = 6$

68. $\sqrt{x^2 + 1} = x - 1$

69. $\sqrt{3r + 1} = 2r - 6$

70. $\frac{1}{2}m^2 + 2m + 2 = 0$

71. $3t^2 - 5t + 1 = 0$

72. $3t^2 + 2t - 7 = 0$

Graph the solution set. (In Exercise 73, use a number line.)

73. $|x + 1| > 3$

74. $2x - y = 5$

75. $3x - y < 4$

76. Write an equation in standard form of the line containing $(-1, 1)$ and $(6, -1)$.

77. Graph the function $f(x) = 4 - 2x - x^2$.

78. Write $0.4\overline{25}$ as a fraction in simplest form.

79. Graph the solution set of the system:

$$\begin{aligned} y &\geq 2x - 3 \\ 2x - 2y &\leq 1 \end{aligned}$$

80. Find the length, to the nearest hundredth of a meter, of the diagonal of a rectangle that is 10 m by 9 m. (Use a calculator or the table of square roots on page 682.)

81. A plumber and an assistant finished a job in 4 h. The job would have taken the plumber 6 h working alone. How long would the job have taken the assistant working alone?

82. a varies directly as b and inversely as the square of c, and $a = 10$ when $b = 8$ and $c = 2$. Find a when $b = 20$ and $c = 5$.

83. During a canoe trip, Roberto paddled twice as many hours as Edward, and Jim paddled for one hour. If the three of them paddled less than a total of ten hours, what is the number of hours that Roberto could have paddled?

84. During a 3000 mi flight, a plane encountered a strong tail wind that increased its speed by 100 mi/h. This increase in speed shortened the flying time by one hour. Find the speed of the plane relative to the ground.

Preparing for College Entrance Exams

Strategy for Success

Take your time and be sure to read each question and all the possible answers carefully. Although it is important to work quickly, you must be sure not to work so quickly that you lose accuracy. Remember that no partial credit is given.

Decide which is the best of the choices given and write the corresponding letter on your answer sheet.

1. Which number is $\frac{3}{5}$ of the way from $-\frac{4}{7}$ to $1\frac{1}{8}$?

(A) $\frac{31}{56}$ **(B)** $\frac{95}{56}$ **(C)** $\frac{93}{280}$ **(D)** $\frac{25}{56}$ **(E)** $\frac{57}{56}$

2. The length of a rectangle is four times the width. The area is 184.96 m^2. Find the width of the rectangle to the nearest tenth of a meter.

(A) 6.4 m **(B)** 6.6 m **(C)** 6.8 m **(D)** 7.2 m **(E)** 7.4 m

3. Two sides of a right triangle are 8 cm and 15 cm long. Find the length of the hypotenuse to the nearest tenth of a centimeter.

(A) 12.9 cm **(B)** 17.0 cm **(C)** 13.0 cm

(D) No such triangle is possible.

(E) Cannot be determined from the given information.

4. Evaluate $\frac{x(x+1)}{x+2}$ if $x = \sqrt{3}$.

(A) $3 - \sqrt{3}$ **(B)** $\sqrt{3} - 3$ **(C)** $-3 - \sqrt{3}$ **(D)** $\frac{1 + \sqrt{3}}{2}$

5. The sum of a positive integer and the square of the next consecutive integer is 131. Find the sum of the two integers.

(A) 19 **(B)** 20 **(C)** 21 **(D)** 22 **(E)** 23

6. The graph of an equation of the form $y = ax^2 + bx + c$ is shown at the right. Identify the true statement(s).

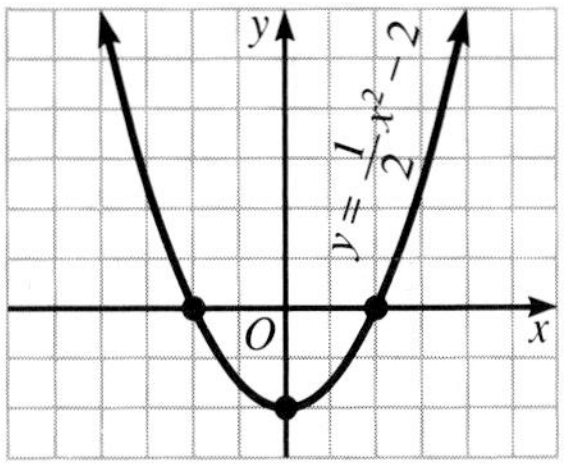

I. $0 < a < 1$

II. $b^2 > 4c$

III. $c > 0$

(A) I only **(B)** II only **(C)** III only

(D) I and II only **(E)** I, II, and III

7. The equation $ax^2 + 3x + c = 0$ has two distinct roots. Which of the following is (are) possible?

I. $a = 1, c = 2$ II. $a = -1, c = -2$ III. $a = -1, c = 2$

(A) I only **(B)** II only **(C)** III only

(D) I and II only **(E)** I, II, and III

Looking Ahead

Probability

Sample Spaces and Events

Objective To specify the sample space and events for a random experiment.

So far you have been solving mathematical problems that deal with definite situations. You'll now consider the branch of mathematics called *probability,* which deals with the possibility, or likelihood, that an event will happen. For example, a food company can use the data from a survey to determine the probability that a new cereal will be successful in the marketplace.

Suppose you toss a coin many times in exactly the same way. On each toss it will land with either a head or a tail up. However, you can't predict with certainty which it will be. An activity repeated under essentially the same conditions is called a **random experiment** when the outcome can't be predicted.

Although you don't know before a toss whether the result will be a head or a tail, you do know that only these two outcomes are possible. The set of all possible outcomes of a random experiment is called the **sample space** of the experiment. For the coin-tossing experiment, if the outcomes are denoted by H and T, then the sample space is $\{H, T\}$.

Any possible subset of the sample space of an experiment is called an **event.** When an event involves a single member of the sample space, it is called a **simple event.** In the coin-tossing experiment, there are two simple events: $\{H\}$ and $\{T\}$.

Example 1 For the experiment of spinning the pointer of the green spinner at the right, give:

a. the sample space for the experiment.

b. the event that an even number results.

c. the event that a number greater than 6 results.

Solution a. {1, 2, 3, 4, 5, 6, 7, 8}

b. {2, 4, 6, 8}

c. {7, 8}

Suppose you now have two spinners, one blue and one red. A simple event in this experiment can be represented by the ordered pair (b, r), where b is the number from the blue spinner and r is the number from the red spinner. The ordered pair (4, 2) represents the simple event, "blue spinner shows 4 and red spinner shows 2."

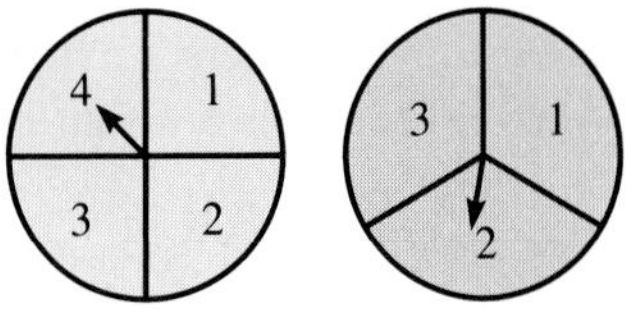

Example 2 For the two-spinner experiment, give:

a. the sample space for the experiment.

b. the event that the sum of the numbers on the two spinners equals 4.

c. the event that the sum of the numbers on the two spinners is less than 4.

Solution a. {(1, 1), (1, 2), (1, 3), (2, 1), (2, 2), (2, 3), (3, 1), (3, 2), (3, 3), (4, 1), (4, 2), (4, 3)}

b. {(1, 3), (2, 2), (3, 1)}

c. {(1, 1), (1, 2), (2, 1)}

Oral Exercises

A penny and a nickel are tossed. The sample space is {(H, H), (H, T), (T, H), (T, T)}. State each event.

1. Two tails up
2. One head up and one tail up
3. Exactly one tail up
4. At least one head up

Each letter of the word FLOWER is written on a separate card. The cards are shuffled. Then one card is drawn at random.

5. What is the sample space for this experiment?
6. What is the event that the letter on the card is a vowel?
7. What is the event that the letter on the card is neither L nor W?

Each of the numbers from 1 to 8 is written on a separate card. The cards are shuffled. Then one card is drawn at random.

8. What is the sample space for this experiment?
9. What is the event that the number on the card is even?
10. What is the event that the number on the card is not less than 5?

Written Exercises

For the experiments described in Exercises 1–7, first give the sample space and then give each event.

A **1.** Each of the letters A, B, C, D, E, F, G, H, I, J, and K is written on a card. The cards are shuffled, and then one card is drawn at random.

a. The letter is a vowel. **b.** The letter is not a vowel. **c.** The letter is C, F, or H.

2. A bowl contains a yellow marble and a red marble. A second bowl contains a yellow, a green, and a blue marble. One marble is taken at random from each bowl.

a. One marble is green. **b.** At least one marble is yellow. **c.** Neither marble is blue.

3. A hat contains cards numbered 2, 4, 8, and 15. A second hat contains cards numbered 1, 4, and 9. One card is drawn at random from each hat.

a. Both numbers are the same.

b. Both numbers are odd.

c. The sum of the numbers is greater than 12.

d. The sum of the numbers is less than 6.

4. A spinner is divided into three equal sections numbered 3, 6, and 9. A second spinner is divided into five equal sections numbered 1, 5, 10, 15, and 20. Each pointer is spun.

a. Both numbers are odd.

b. Exactly one number is odd.

c. The sum of the numbers is between 12 and 21.

d. The product of the numbers is greater than 60.

B **5.** There are three on-off switches on a light panel. Each switch controls one light.

a. All three lights are on. **b.** At least two lights are off. **c.** At least one light is off.

6. Refer to the two-spinner experiment of Example 2. As before, the ordered pair (b, r) represents a simple event.

a. $b + r > 4$ **b.** $b < r$

c. $b + r$ is a multiple of 3 **d.** $b \cdot r > b + r$

C **7.** A coin collection consists of a penny, a nickel, and a dime. Either 1, 2, or 3 coins are randomly selected.

a. The total amount is even.

b. The total amount is odd.

c. The total amount is greater than 2¢ and less than 16¢.

d. The total amount is less than 6¢ or greater than 15¢.

Probability

Objective To find the probability that an event will happen.

Suppose you toss a coin repeatedly. The sample space is $\{H, T\}$. Assuming that the coin is fair, the two simple events $\{H\}$ and $\{T\}$ are *equally likely* to happen. That is, for a large number of tosses, you would expect the number of heads, or the number of tails, to be about one half the number of tosses.

The **probability** of an event is the ratio of the number of outcomes favoring the event to the total number of possible outcomes. We write the ratio as a fraction. In the case of a tossed coin, if the probability of $\{H\}$ is written as $P(H)$ and the probability of $\{T\}$ as $P(T)$, then

$$P(H) = P(T) = \frac{1}{2}.$$

The probability of an impossible event is 0. For example, the probability that the result of the toss of a coin is both heads and tails is 0.

$$P(H \text{ and } T) = 0$$

The probability of an event that is certain is 1. For example, the probability that the result of the toss of a coin is either heads or tails is 1.

$$P(H \text{ or } T) = 1$$

Thus, for any probability P,

$$0 \le P \le 1.$$

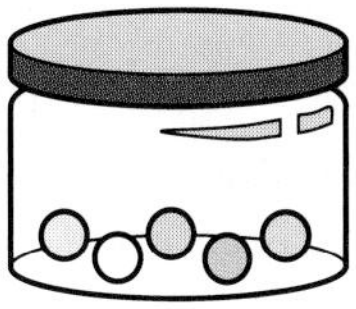

The jar shown at the right contains 5 differently colored marbles. The sample space is $\{B, G, Y, R, W\}$. If you randomly pick a marble, the five simple events are equally likely to occur. Thus,

$$P(B) = P(G) = P(Y) = P(R) = P(W) = \frac{1}{5}.$$

In general, if $\{a_1, a_2, a_3, \ldots, a_n\}$ is a sample space with n equally likely simple events, then

$$P(a_1) = P(a_2) = P(a_3) = \cdots = P(a_n) = \frac{1}{n}.$$

The sum of the probabilities assigned to all simple events in a sample space of a random experiment is 1. For example, in the experiment of randomly picking a marble,

$$P(B) + P(G) + P(Y) + P(R) + P(W) = \frac{1}{5} + \frac{1}{5} + \frac{1}{5} + \frac{1}{5} + \frac{1}{5} = 1.$$

Thus, for the general sample space $\{a_1, a_2, a_3, \ldots, a_n\}$,

$$P(a_1) + P(a_2) + P(a_3) + \cdots + P(a_n) = 1.$$

Example A glass bowl contains 3 red marbles, 2 blue marbles, and 1 green marble. A marble is drawn at random from the bowl. Find the probability of each event.

a. *Event A:* The marble drawn is blue.

b. *Event B:* The marble drawn is either blue or green.

c. *Event C:* The marble drawn is not green.

Solution The sample space is {red 1, red 2, red 3, blue 1, blue 2, green}.

a. Since there are 2 blue marbles, *Event A* has 2 equally likely outcomes. So $P(A) = \frac{2}{6} = \frac{1}{3}$.

b. Since there are 2 blue marbles and 1 green marble, *Event B* has 3 equally likely outcomes. So $P(B) = \frac{3}{6} = \frac{1}{2}$.

c. If the marble is not green, then it must be either red or blue. Since there are 3 red marbles and 2 blue marbles, *Event C* has 5 equally likely outcomes. So $P(C) = \frac{5}{6}$.

Oral Exercises

A letter is selected randomly from the word PARABOLA. Name the probability of each event.

1. The letter is a vowel.

2. The letter is a consonant.

3. The letter is an A.

4. The letter is a B.

A cube whose sides are numbered 1, 2, 3, 4, 5, and 6 is tossed. Name the probability of each event.

5. The number is odd.

6. The number is prime.

7. The number is less than 7.

8. The number is greater than 0.

9. The number is not an integer.

10. The number is 3 or 5.

11. Explain why the probability of an event cannot be greater than 1.

Written Exercises

Solve.

A **1.** A box contains 4 opals, 5 garnets, and 6 pearls. A jewel is selected at random from the box. Find the probability of the event that the jewel is:

a. an opal **b.** either an opal or a pearl

c. a garnet **d.** not a garnet

2. One card is drawn at random from a deck of 13 hearts, 13 diamonds, 13 clubs, and 13 spades. Find the probability of the event that the card is:

a. a 5 **b.** a red 7

c. a club **d.** the king of hearts

e. a 3 or 7 **f.** an 8, 9, or 10

3. There are 24 students in your algebra class. The students are to explain a problem at the board. Each student determines his or her turn by taking a number at random from a jar. The jar contains the numbers 1–24. Find the probability of the event that:

a. you are the first person to explain a problem.

b. you are one of the first 9 people to explain a problem.

c. your number is between 8 and 16 (not including 8 or 16).

d. your number is divisible by 5.

4. The results of rolling two numbered cubes are shown in the table at the right. Copy and complete the table. Then use it to find the probability of each event listed below. *P*(5) means "the probability of getting a sum of 5."

6	(6, 1)	(6, 2)	(?)	(?)	(?)	(?)
5	(5, 1)	(5, 2)	(?)	(?)	(?)	(?)
4	(4, 1)	(4, 2)	(?)	(?)	(?)	(?)
3	(3, 1)	(3, 2)	(?)	(?)	(?)	(?)
2	(2, 1)	(2, 2)	(2, 3)	(2, 4)	(?)	(?)
1	(1, 1)	(1, 2)	(1, 3)	(1, 4)	(1, 5)	(?)
	1	2	3	4	5	6

a. *P*(5) **b.** *P*(not 5) **c.** *P*(4 or 7)

d. *P*(12) **e.** *P*(13) **f.** *P*(2 or 8)

g. *P*(not 6) **h.** *P*(even number) **i.** *P*(odd number)

B 5. A penny, a nickel, and a dime are tossed. Find the probability of the event that the coins give:

a. 3 heads **b.** exactly two tails

c. at least 2 heads **d.** one or two heads

6. A spinner is divided into three equal sections numbered 1, 2, and 3. A second spinner is divided into four equal sections numbered 2, 4, 6, and 7. Each pointer is spun. Find the probability of each event.

a. *P*(1, 4) **b.** *P*(2, not 2)

c. *P*(3, 6) **d.** *P*(even number, even number)

e. *P*(sum is 7) **f.** *P*(sum is less than 8)

C 7. A bag contains 1 red marble, 2 green marbles, and 3 white marbles. Two marbles are randomly selected. Find the probability of the event that the marbles are:

a. 1 red and 1 green **b.** 1 green and 1 white

c. neither red nor green **d.** neither red nor white

e. two of the same color **f.** 1 red and a green or a white

Statistics

Frequency Distributions

Objective To recognize and analyze frequency distributions.

Thirty-one students received the following scores on a test.

77 67 91 63 81 89 100 73 67 85 89 89 95 83 79 89
66 83 88 97 74 77 88 89 95 79 83 95 83 98 94

A collection of data is more meaningful when you have organized the data. The table at the right arranges the scores in decreasing order and also tells how many students received each score. The information given in this table is called a **frequency distribution.**

Score	Number of Students
100	1
98	1
97	1
95	3
94	1
91	1
89	5
88	2
85	1
83	4
81	1
79	2
77	2
74	1
73	1
67	2
66	1
63	1

Another way to describe a frequency distribution is to draw a graph called a **histogram,** as shown below. In a histogram, data are grouped into convenient intervals. The intervals in this histogram of test scores are 60–65, 65–70, and so on. A test score of 75 is considered to be in the interval 70–75, while a score of 80 is in the interval 75–80. A "boundary" score in a histogram like the one below is usually included in the interval to its left.

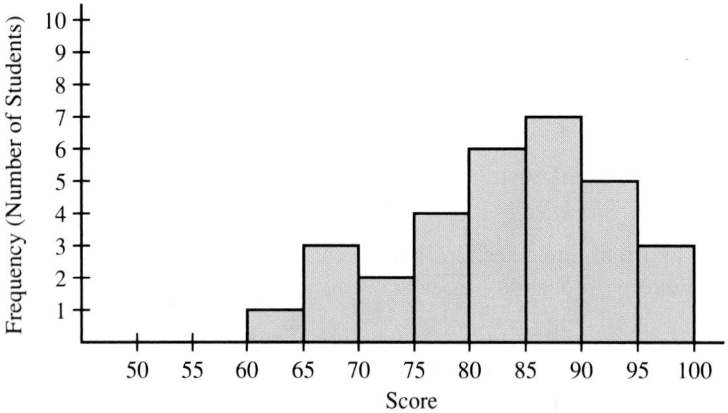

Frequency distributions are often analyzed using numbers called *statistics*. The *mean, median,* and *mode* are statistics used in analyzing a distribution. The **mean** of a collection of data is the sum of the data divided by the number of items of data. The sum of the test scores given for the 31 students is 2606. Then the mean (M) of the test scores is

$$M = \frac{\text{sum of data}}{\text{number of items}} = \frac{2606}{31} = 84.06 \approx 84.$$

The **median** of a frequency distribution is the middle number when the data are arranged in order. If the number of data is even, the average of the two numbers closest to the middle is the median. Arranging the test scores in increasing order gives:

63	66	67	67	73	74	77	77	79	79	81	83	83	83	83	85
88	88	89	89	89	89	89	91	94	95	95	95	97	98	100	

The median is 85, which is the sixteenth score.

The **mode** is the most frequently occurring number in a frequency distribution. A set of data may have one or more modes or none at all. From the frequency table, the mode of the test scores is 89. The mode is most useful in analyzing nonnumerical data, such as color or taste preferences.

Another important statistic is the *range,* which is used to indicate the spread of the data in a distribution. The **range** of a frequency distribution is the difference between the highest and the lowest values. For example, the range of the data in the table is $100 - 63$, or 37.

Example Two numbered cubes are rolled 10 times. The product of the numbers after each roll are, in increasing order, 2, 6, 8, 12, 18, 20, 24, 24, 30, and 36. Find the mean, the median, the mode, and the range of the data.

Solution $M = \frac{2 + 6 + 8 + 12 + 18 + 20 + 24 + 24 + 30 + 36}{10} = \frac{180}{10} = 18$

Since there is an even number of data, the median is the average of the two middle scores.

$$\text{median} = \frac{18 + 20}{2} = \frac{38}{2} = 19$$

Since 24 is the score that occurs most frequently, it is the mode.

The range is the difference between 36 and 2, or 34.

Computers and calculators, especially graphing calculators, are very useful when doing a statistical analysis of data.

Oral Exercises

1. The histogram at the right shows the frequency distribution for the number of points scored in a game by a high school basketball team for a season of 18 games.

   State the number of games in which the team scored:

   a. between 50 and 60 points

   b. between 90 and 100 points

   c. between 60 and 80 points

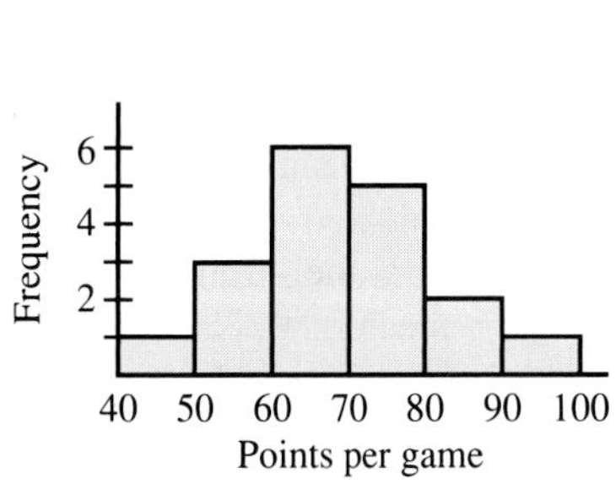

2. In four days Michelle earned \$5, \$3, \$9, and \$3. For her earnings, find:
   a. the mean **b.** the mode **c.** the median **d.** the range

3. In five successive baseball games, the Apex Cougars scored 3, 2, 0, 6, and 4 runs. For this distribution, find:
   a. the mean **b.** the mode **c.** the median **d.** the range

4. If the range for a given set of data is 0, explain why the mean, median, and mode are all equal.

Written Exercises

For the data in Exercises 1–6, find (a) the mean, (b) the median, (c) the mode, and (d) the range. Wherever appropriate, give answers to the nearest tenth.

A

1. 53, 32, 49, 24, 62
2. 8, 15, 41, 31, 15
3. 32, 29, 40, 17, 32, 22
4. 11, 9, 19, 9, 19, 9, 13
5. 61, 53, 52, 56, 61, 53, 56
6. 72, 78, 63, 49, 81, 50, 66
7. In six debate matches David scored 81, 92, 85, 81, 84, and 92. Find the mean, the median, the mode, and the range of his scores.
8. Find the mean and range for the average monthly temperatures given in degrees Celsius: $-1.5°$, $-2°$, $5°$, $16.5°$, $20°$, $24.5°$, $28°$, $33.5°$, $29.5°$, $18.5°$, $6°$, $2.5°$.
9. For ten consecutive days, Lara ran 8, 10, 7, 9, 10, 11, 12, 11, 12, and 12 laps around the track. To the nearest tenth of a lap, find the mean, the median, the mode, and the range.
10. In a class of 25 students, the test scores were 78, 90, 95, 76, 65, 80, 90, 96, 100, 98, 84, 88, 81, 76, 100, 94, 90, 83, 73, 85, 90, 81, 79, 81, and 88. First make a frequency table. Then group the data into the intervals 60–65, 65–70, and so on. Draw a histogram for the data.

B

11. Vin needs an average of 90% in 6 classes in order to participate in a Scholastic Fair this summer. He knows his percentages in 5 classes: 85, 98, 87, 85, and 89. What percentage must he have in the sixth class?
12. If each score on an algebra test is increased by 10 points, how does this affect the:
    a. mean? **b.** mode? **c.** median? **d.** range?
13. If each number in a set of data is multiplied by three, how does this affect the:
    a. mean? **b.** mode? **c.** median? **d.** range?
14. The mean of 8 numbers is 17. What is the sum of the numbers?

C

15. Find the mean of 12 numbers if the mean of the first three is 32 and the mean of the last nine numbers is 40.
16. Felicia has a score of 89 for each of her first eight geometry tests. Her score on the ninth test is 96. What does her score for the tenth test have to be for a final mean score of 90?

Extra / Measures of Variation

Objective To calculate measures of variation for a given distribution.

You learned previously (pages 606–607) that the mean, median, and mode are important numbers for analyzing a set of data. Statisticians are also interested in how the data are dispersed, or spread, throughout the distribution. The statistics used to measure this dispersion are called measures of variation.

The range (page 607) is a *weak* measure of variation because it uses only two values of the distribution. For example, compare the range values for the following two groups of data.

Group A:	11, 12, 14, 14, 14, 14, 19	Range = 19 − 11 = 8
Group B:	11, 12, 14, 16, 17, 17, 18	Range = 18 − 11 = 7

Groups A and B have almost the same range, but the data in Group A are more clustered together than in Group B. Although the range is easy to calculate, it can be a misleading measure of variation.

Strong measures of variation use the distance of each value of the distribution from the mean, M. The **variance,** denoted by σ^2 (σ is the Greek letter sigma), is the mean of the squares of the distance of each data item (x_i) from the mean. For a distribution of n data items,

$$\sigma^2 = \frac{(x_1 - M)^2 + (x_2 - M)^2 + \cdots + (x_n - M)^2}{n}.$$

The **standard deviation,** denoted by σ, is the principal square root of the variance.

Example 1 Calculate, to the nearest tenth, the variance and standard deviation for the data 6, 7, 9, 10, and 13.

Solution First find the mean: $M = \frac{6 + 7 + 9 + 10 + 13}{5} = 9$

Make a table to find the square of the distance of each data item from the mean ($M = 9$).

x_i	$x_i - M$	$(x_i - M)^2$
6	−3	9
7	−2	4
9	0	0
10	1	1
13	4	16

Since $n = 5$, the variance is:

$$\sigma^2 = \frac{9 + 4 + 0 + 1 + 16}{5} = 6$$

Answer

Then the standard deviation is:

$\sigma = \sqrt{\sigma^2} = \sqrt{6} \approx 2.4$ ***Answer***

A useful statistic for identifying the relative position of an individual value within a distribution is the distance that a data item is from the mean *in terms of the standard deviation*. This distance is called the *standard score*, or *z-score*. For a distribution with mean M and standard deviation σ, a data item x_i has a standard score given by

$$z = \frac{x_i - M}{\sigma}.$$

Example 2 Find to the nearest tenth the standard score for each data item in the distribution in Example 1.

Solution In Example 1, $M = 9$ and $\sigma = 2.4$. The standard scores are computed at the right. Notice the data item 13 has 1.7 as its standard score. This means that 13 is 1.7 standard deviations from the mean 9.

x_i	$\frac{x_i - M}{\sigma}$ = standard score
6	$\frac{6-9}{2.4} \approx -1.3$
7	$\frac{7-9}{2.4} \approx -0.8$
9	$\frac{9-9}{2.4} = 0$
10	$\frac{10-9}{2.4} \approx 0.4$
13	$\frac{13-9}{2.4} \approx 1.7$

Exercises

1. Explain why the standard deviation for 7, 7, 7, 7, 7, and 7 is 0.
2. Groups A and B on page 609 have almost the same range. Explain why Group B must have a higher variance than Group A. Verify this by finding the variance for each group.
3. Golf scores for a 9-hole course for six players were 38, 41, 48, 45, 38, and 36.
   a. Find the mean golf score.
   b. Find the standard deviation to the nearest tenth.
   c. Find the standard score to the nearest tenth for each score.
4. A set of test scores had a mean of 26 and a standard deviation of 5. Find the standard score for each of the following scores from the distribution.
   a. 31 b. 22 c. 17 d. 29 e. 26 f. 40
5. Two factories compared the number of items their workers could produce in an hour:

   Factory I: $M = 235$, $\sigma = 14$
   Factory II: $M = 235$, $\sigma = 6$

   In which factory were the production rates of the workers more nearly alike? How do you know?
6. On a chapter test, you received a standard score of 3.4. If the mean score was 76 and the standard deviation was 5, what was your actual score?

Presenting Statistical Data

Objective To construct stem-and-leaf plots and box-and-whisker plots.

Statisticians organize data they have collected in order to present it in a useful form. You have learned that bar graphs, broken-line graphs (page 375), and histograms (page 606) can be used to summarize data.

Another way to organize data is by a **stem-and-leaf plot.** In this type of display the raw data values themselves are incorporated into a frequency distribution. This method is illustrated for the following set of thirty scores.

83	71	92	79	74	80	63	86	84	74
100	81	94	98	79	62	50	82	56	67
75	86	83	96	57	100	87	67	98	44

First the *stems* (in black), derived by dropping the unit's digit from each score, are written in order to the left of a vertical line. For each score the *leaf,* or unit's digit (in red), is then recorded to the right of the corresponding stem. For the score of 84, for example, the leaf 4 is recorded to the right of the stem 8. The leaves are separated by commas, using equal space for each leaf. Then the plot can be rotated to become a histogram, displaying the shape of the frequency distribution. Unlike a standard histogram, the stem-and-leaf plot still retains every individual score in coded form.

4	4
5	0, 6, 7
6	3, 2, 7, 7
7	1, 9, 4, 4, 9, 5
8	3, 0, 6, 4, 1, 2, 6, 3, 7
9	2, 4, 8, 6, 8
10	0, 0

Researchers often wish to compare pairs of data, such as these semester mathematics (M) and history (H) averages collected from twenty students.

M	83	90	64	49	73	81	71	60	79	62	85	72	78	66	93	81	74	85	66	76
H	76	85	75	67	88	90	88	78	90	57	93	71	96	71	91	54	81	78	81	82

Scatter graphs or *diagrams* often are used to show researchers whether a relationship exists between two measurements. Researchers can then base predictions on the patterns they observe in these relationships. The diagram shown in the Application on page 378 is a scatter graph. Each pair of points in the table above can be plotted on a scatter graph to investigate the relationship between the mathematics and history averages.

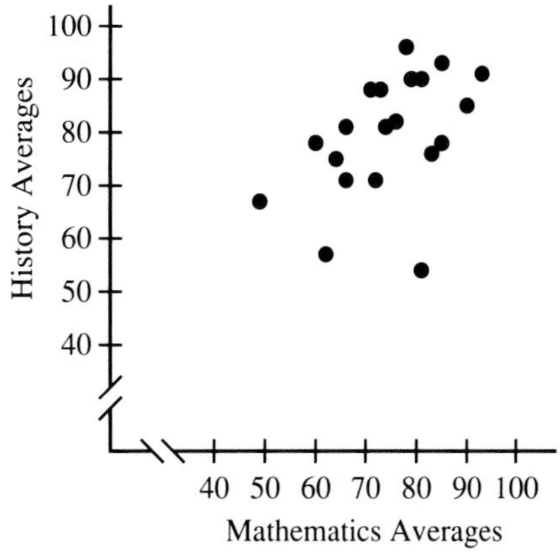

The averages can also be compared by using **box-and-whisker plots.** To construct a box-and-whisker plot, the following values must be identified for each set of data: highest score, lowest score, median score, and first and third quartile scores.

Recall that the median of a set of scores is the middle score when the data are arranged in order. The first quartile score is the median of the bottom half of the data, and the third quartile score is the median of the upper half of the data. In the example on the previous page, the mathematics averages, in order, are:

bottom half of data: 49 60 62 64 66 66 71 72 73 74

top half of data: 76 78 79 81 81 83 85 85 90 93

lowest score	first quartile score	median score	third quartile score	highest score
49	66	75	82	93

Identify these five special values with dots below a number line.

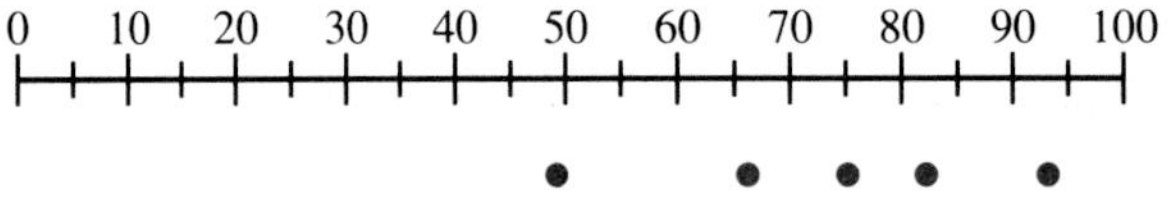

Next, make a box with the two quartile scores on the outer sides. Draw a line inside the box, through the median dot. Finally, draw "whiskers" from the sides of the box to the dots of the lowest and highest scores.

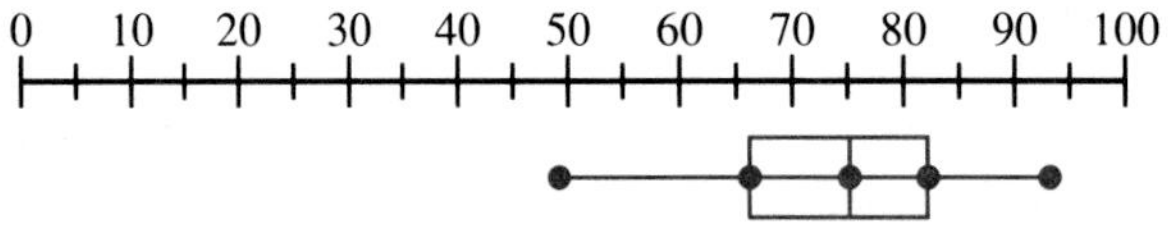

Verify the given box-and-whisker plot for the set of history averages (median: 81; lowest score: 54; highest score: 96; first quartile: 73; third quartile: 89).

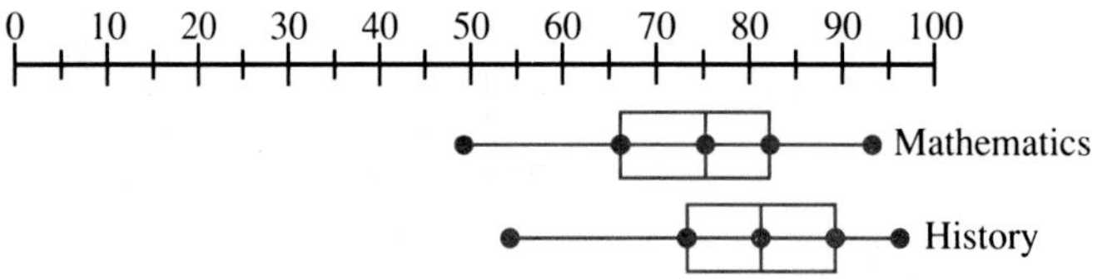

Notice that the box encloses the middle half of the data while the whiskers show the range. By studying the box-and-whisker plot for each set of data, you can easily compare the ranges and the locations of the middle halves of the distributions.

Oral Exercises

1. Use the distribution of scores given by the stem-and-leaf plot at the left below to list the original scores in order.

1	5
2	2, 8, 2
3	5, 2, 1, 8, 0
4	5, 3, 4
5	6, 3

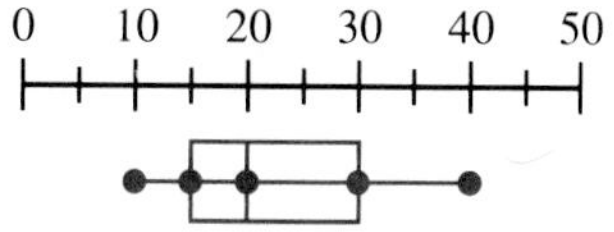

2. Use the box-and-whisker plot at the right above to state the value of the:
   a. first quartile **b.** median **c.** third quartile **d.** range

Written Exercises

A

1. Use the distribution of scores given by the stem-and-leaf plot shown at the right.
   a. List the original scores of the distribution in order.
   b. What are the median, the mode, and the range of the scores?

5	3, 1, 4
6	8, 2, 3, 5
7	7, 3, 6, 9, 0, 1
8	4, 8, 4
9	5, 0

2. Twenty students reported the amount of money they earned last week in part-time jobs. They earned (in dollars) 102, 115, 87, 91, 80, 73, 114, 145, 137, 135, 127, 120, 86, 100, 134, 129, 133, 88, 75, and 109. Construct a stem-and-leaf plot for their earnings.

3. Eleven students were asked to rate a presentation given by a speaker on a scale from 1 to 10, with 10 as the highest score. The results were 7, 9, 8, 5, 8, 10, 9, 7, 8, 6, and 4. Find the:
   a. median **b.** first quartile score **c.** third quartile score
   d. highest score **e.** lowest score **f.** range

4. Make a box-and-whisker plot for the data in Exercise 3.

Use the following data for Exercises 5–7: Fifteen cars were road tested on both city streets and highways. The resulting fuel economy data were recorded.

City (mi/gal)	22	21	28	19	28	30	21	20	19	28	22	24	21	24	28
Highway (mi/gal)	24	27	32	23	29	38	24	25	24	30	23	26	26	26	31

B

5. For the city driving test, find the median, first quartile score, third quartile score, highest score, and lowest score.

6. For the highway driving test, find the median, first quartile score, third quartile score, highest score, and lowest score.

7. Using the same number-line scale, construct box-and-whisker plots to compare the mi/gal figures for city and highway driving.

Application / *Misuse of Statistics*

In today's world statistics plays an increasingly important role in decision making. Decisions are usually based on conclusions drawn from a study of a particular fact about a large population. If people do not use statistics correctly, either by accident or on purpose, faulty conclusions can be drawn.

Data are often collected by a survey. Since it is not practical to survey an entire group, statisticians must select a small part of the population, a sample, that is representative of the total population. Misleading statistics can be produced if the data collection for a given population is faulty. There are two important things to consider when a sample is used: the way in which the sample is selected and the size of the sample.

Example 1 Study each advertisement. Do you agree with the conclusion of the ad?

a.

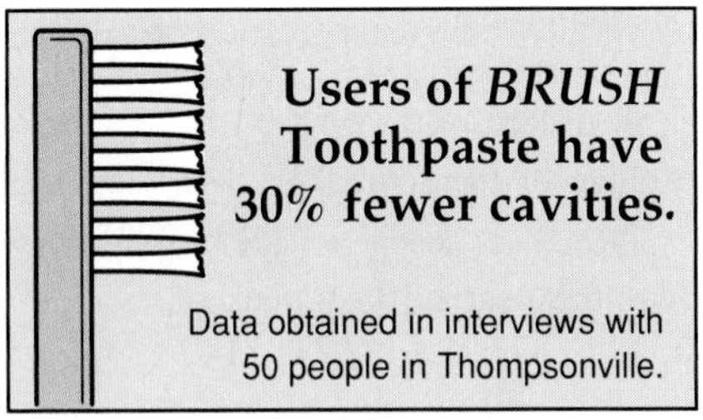

b.

Solution

a. In this advertisement, only 50 people were surveyed. This is a very small number of people on which to base the conclusion that BRUSH toothpaste reduces cavities for everyone.

b. The sample of 936 people used in this advertisement is large, but the way in which this sample was selected is not correct. This sample is probably not representative of the entire population because it does not indicate which music students in other high schools or adults prefer. Surveys must be conducted so that they represent the entire population.

Graphs are often used to summarize data in a form that is easy to read. Choices must be made about how to draw a particular graph. Sometimes graphs of the same data can be made to tell different stories.

Example 2 Study and compare the two different broken-line graphs of the same data shown on the next page. Do you think profits are growing during the years 1982 to 1988?

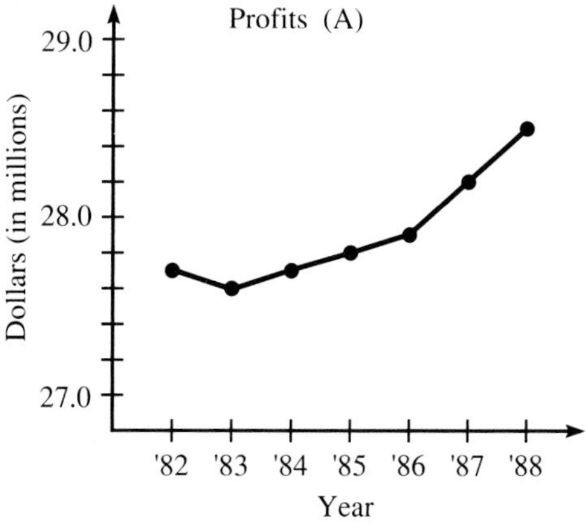

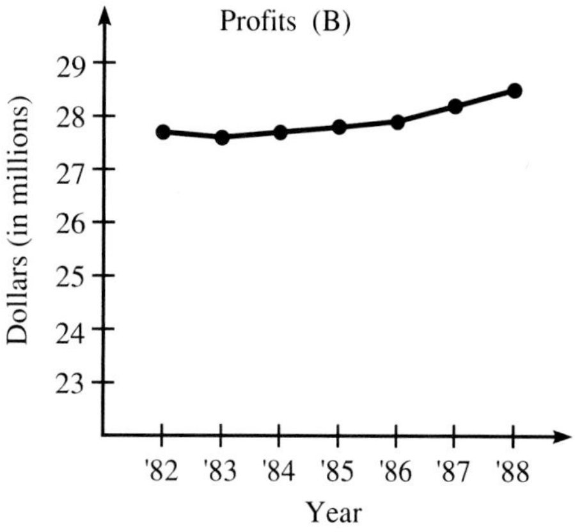

Solution Each of these graphs shows the same data, yet they tell very different stories. Graph A makes it seem that the profits are definitely growing. Graph B makes it seem that the profits are not changing much. The different stories come from using two different scales on the vertical axes. (Notice that the range of the values for the vertical axis of Graph A is 2 whereas the range of the values for the vertical axis of Graph B is 6.) While nothing in either graph is untrue, the graph you might use to describe the data would depend on which story you wanted to tell.

Exercises

Analyze each advertisement. Do you think that the use of statistics is misleading? Give a reason for your answer.

1.

2.

3. The table shows the salaries of a company's employees.

Yearly Salaries	
\$21,500	\$22,000
\$21,750	\$22,000
\$21,750	\$22,350
\$21,800	\$47,500
\$22,000	\$53,000

a. Find the median salary for these ten employees.

b. Find the mean salary for these ten employees.

c. Do you think the mean or the median is the better description of what most people earn at this company? Give a reason for your answer.

d. If you want to tell the story that all ten employees earn similar salaries, what scale would you use on the vertical axis of your graph? Draw the broken-line graph.

e. If you want to tell the story that there is a large difference between some of the salaries, what scale would you use on the vertical axis of your graph? Draw the broken-line graph.

Geometry

Points, Lines, and Angles

Objective To represent points, lines, and angles and to measure angles.

You have shown relationships among numbers by representing them as points on a number line. Likewise, you have shown relationships among ordered pairs of numbers by representing them as points in a coordinate plane. The study of *points, lines,* and *planes* is the subject of the branch of mathematics called *geometry*.

Geometric points and *lines* are abstract ideas, not actual objects. A point has no size; a line has no thickness. To illustrate these abstract ideas, however, you draw figures that do have size and thickness. To represent the idea of a geometric point, you draw a dot. To represent the idea of a geometric line, you draw a straight line.

A line consists of infinitely many points. Any two points determine a line. A line determined by points A and B is denoted by $\overleftrightarrow{AB}$ or $\overleftrightarrow{BA}$. The arrowheads indicate that the line extends in both directions without end.

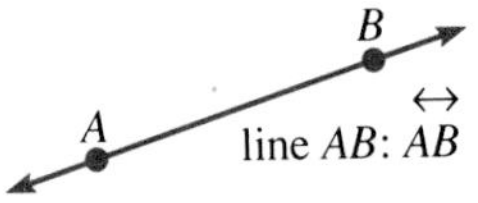

The part of $\overleftrightarrow{AB}$ that consists of points A and B and all points of $\overleftrightarrow{AB}$ between A and B is called a **line segment,** or a **segment.** The segment is denoted by $\overline{AB}$ or $\overline{BA}$. The length of $\overline{AB}$ is denoted by AB.

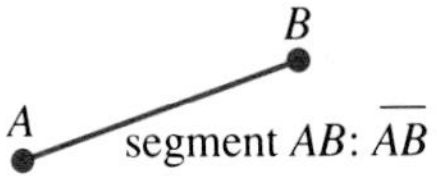

The part of $\overleftrightarrow{AB}$ that starts at point A and extends without ending through point B is a **ray,** denoted by $\overrightarrow{AB}$. A is called the **endpoint** of $\overrightarrow{AB}$.

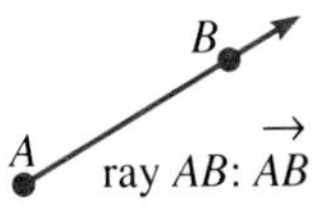

An **angle** is a figure formed by two different rays that have the same endpoint. The rays are called the **sides** of the angle and the common endpoint is called the **vertex** of the angle. The angle shown at the right is formed by $\overrightarrow{AB}$ and $\overrightarrow{AC}$. It is denoted by $\angle A$, $\angle BAC$, or $\angle CAB$. When three letters are used to name an angle, the middle letter is always the vertex.

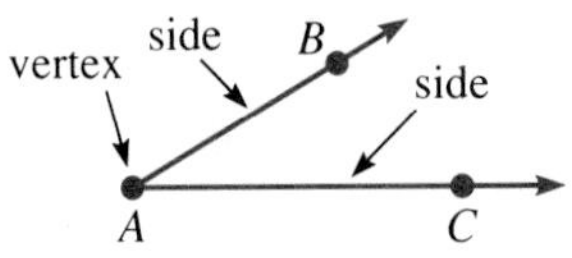

To find the **degree measure** of an angle, you use a protractor. Using the outer scale, you can see that the degree measure of $\angle POQ$ is 60. You will see this fact written as $m\angle POQ = 60$, $m\angle POQ = 60°$, or $\angle POQ = 60°$. For simplicity, we will use $\angle POQ = 60°$. Also, $\angle POR = 90°$ and $\angle POS = 150°$.

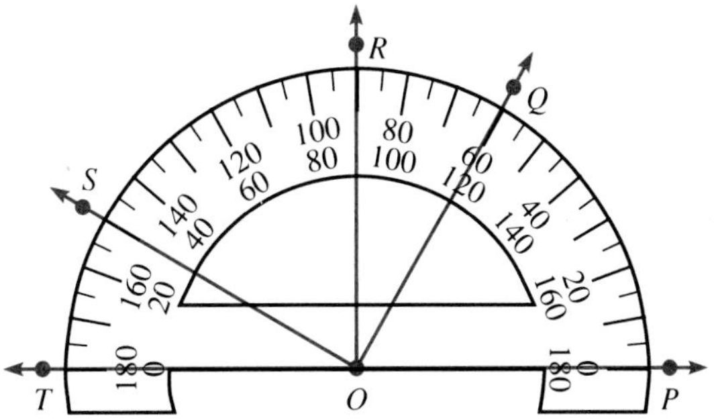

Angles are classified according to their measures.

An **acute angle** has measure between 0° and 90°.
A **right angle** has measure 90°.
An **obtuse angle** has measure between 90° and 180°.
A **straight angle** has measure 180°.

The degree measure of $\angle QOR$ in the diagram above is found by subtracting 60 from 90: $\angle QOR = 30°$. Do you see that $\angle ROS = 60°$ and $\angle QOS$ is a right angle? To state that $\angle POQ$ and $\angle ROS$ have equal measures, write $\angle POQ = \angle ROS$.

Oral Exercises

Exercises 1–8 refer to the diagram below.

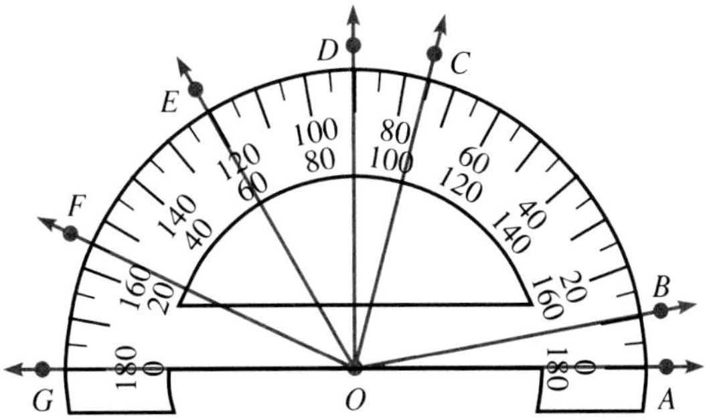

State the measure of the angle.

1. $\angle AOC$ **2.** $\angle EOF$ **3.** $\angle BOE$ **4.** $\angle BOF$

Name an angle whose measure is given.

5. 15° **6.** 65° **7.** 90° **8.** 80°

Written Exercises

In Exercises 1–4, name five different line segments in each diagram.

A 1.

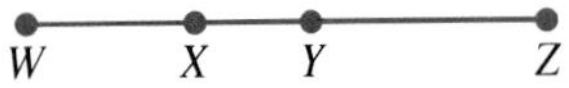

2.

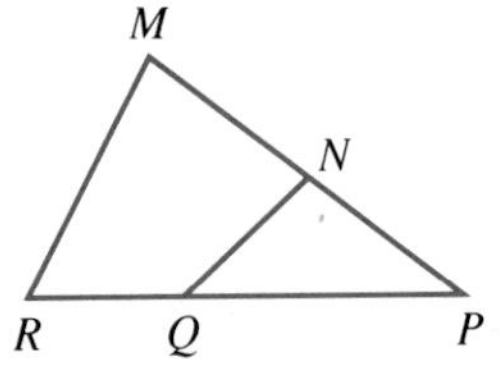

3.

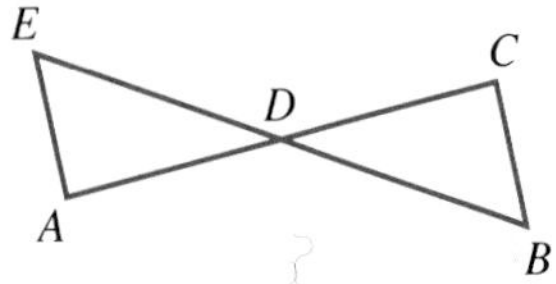

4.

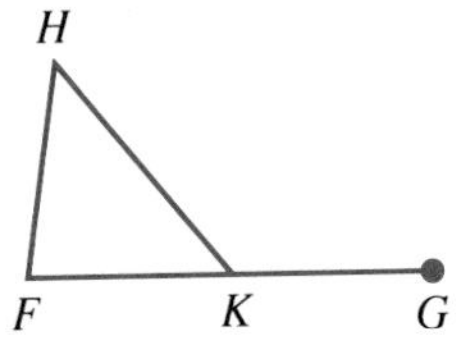

Measure the given angle and classify it as acute, obtuse, right, or straight.

5. $\angle DOE$
6. $\angle AOC$
7. $\angle EOG$
8. $\angle BOH$
9. $\angle EOH$
10. $\angle AOE$
11. $\angle DOF$
12. $\angle FOH$

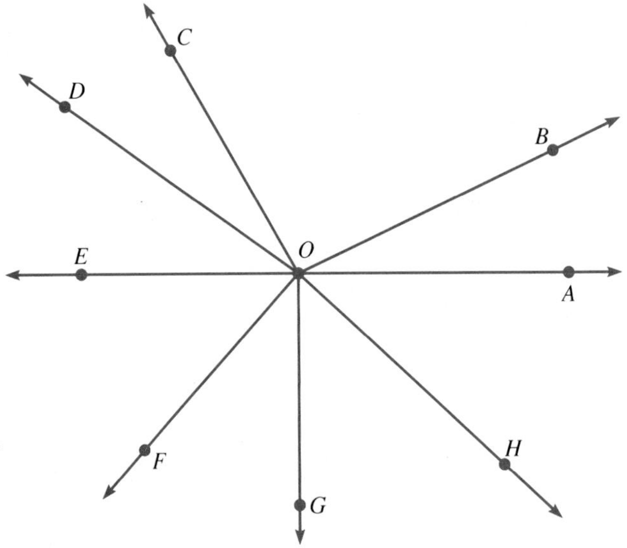

Graph the solution set of each sentence. Identify the graph as a point, a line, a line segment, or a ray.

B 13. $x \le 2$
14. $-5 \le x \le -1$
15. $x = -4$
16. $-7 \le x + 2 \le 11$
17. $3x - 4 = 1$
18. $x + 5 = x - 2 + 7$

C 19. $x - 3 \ge 1$ and $x + 2 \le 10$
20. $1 + x \ge 5$ or $x - 3 \le 9$
21. $2x \ge 8$ or $-3x \ge -9$
22. $3x + 7 \ge 1$ and $4x - 3 \ge 17$

Pairs of Angles

Objective To learn the names and properties of special pairs of angles.

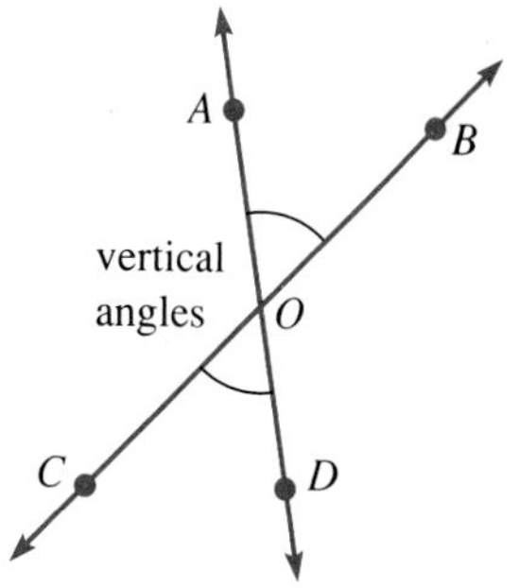

The diagram at the right shows two lines intersecting at O and forming $\angle AOB$, $\angle AOC$, $\angle COD$, and $\angle DOB$. Two angles such as $\angle AOB$ and $\angle COD$ whose sides are rays in the same lines but in opposite directions are called **vertical angles.** Another pair of vertical angles is $\angle AOC$ and $\angle DOB$. Vertical angles have equal measures. You can use a protractor to see that $\angle AOB$ has the same measure as $\angle COD$ and $\angle AOC$ has the same measure as $\angle DOB$.

Two angles are **complementary angles** if the sum of their measures is 90°. Each angle is called a **complement** of the other. The diagram at the left below shows a pair of complementary angles.

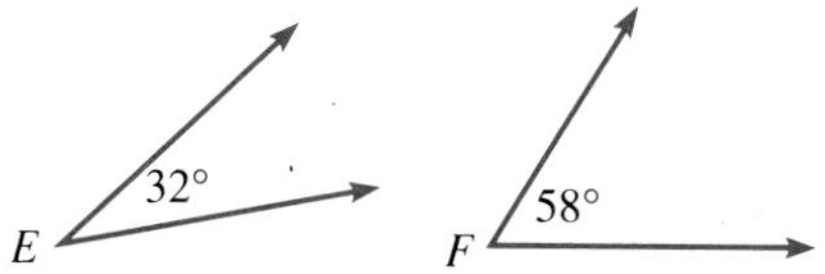

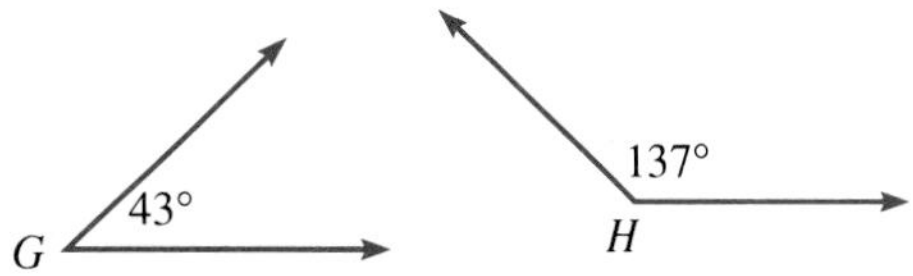

$\angle E$ and $\angle F$ are complementary.
$\angle E$ is a complement of $\angle F$.
$\angle F$ is a complement of $\angle E$.

$\angle G$ and $\angle H$ are supplementary.
$\angle G$ is a supplement of $\angle H$.
$\angle H$ is a supplement of $\angle G$.

Two angles are **supplementary angles** if the sum of their measures is 180°. Each angle is called a **supplement** of the other. The diagram at the right above shows a pair of supplementary angles.

Example The measure of a supplement of an angle is 10° more than five times the measure of its complement. Find the measure of the angle.

Solution Let n = the measure of the angle in degrees.
Then $90 - n$ = the measure of its complement,
and $180 - n$ = the measure of its supplement.

$$\begin{aligned} 180 - n &= 5(90 - n) + 10 \\ 180 - n &= 450 - 5n + 10 \\ 4n &= 280 \\ n &= 70 \end{aligned}$$

The measure of the complement is $(90 - 70)°$, or 20°.
The measure of the supplement is $(180 - 70)°$, or 110°.

Check: $110 \stackrel{?}{=} 5(20) + 10$
$110 = 110$ ✓

$\therefore$ the measure of the angle is 70°. ***Answer***

Oral Exercises

State the measure of a complement of an angle with the given measure.

1. 20° **2.** 87° **3.** 45° **4.** 33° **5.** $x°$ **6.** $7x°$

State the measure of a supplement of an angle with the given measure.

7. 40° **8.** 90° **9.** 153° **10.** 12° **11.** $y°$ **12.** $21t°$

Classify each statement as true or false.

13. The measures of two complementary angles are never equal.

14. If the measures of the supplements of two angles are equal, then the measures of the angles are equal.

15. The complement of an acute angle is obtuse.

16. The supplement of an acute angle is an obtuse angle.

17. A supplement of a right angle is a right angle.

18. If two supplementary angles are vertical, then the angles are both right angles.

Written Exercises

In Exercises 1–4, use the diagram at the right. Assume that the measures of $\angle EAB$ and $\angle ABF$ are equal.

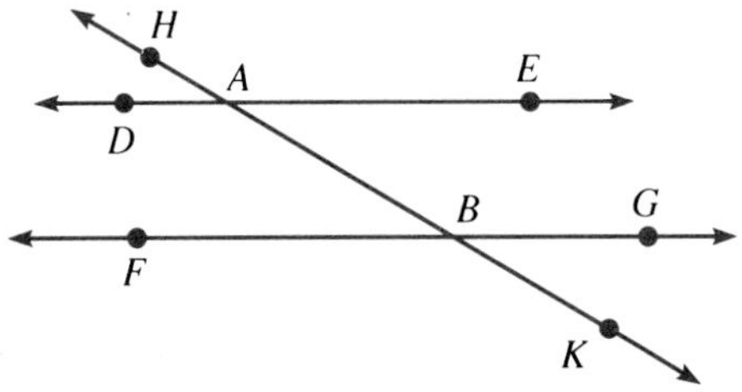

A **1.** List all the angles with measures equal to the measure of $\angle ABF$.

2. List all the angles supplementary to $\angle DAH$.

3. If $\angle ABG = 150°$, then $\angle GBK =$ __?__ °

4. If $\angle EAH = 135°$, then $\angle ABG =$ __?__ °

5. The smaller of two complementary angles measures 50° less than the larger. Find the measures of the two angles.

6. The larger of two supplementary angles measures 8 times the smaller. Find the measures of the two angles.

7. Find the measure of an angle that is 74° more than the measure of its supplement.

8. Find the measure of an angle that is $\frac{1}{4}$ of the measure of its complement.

B **9.** The sum of the measures of a complement and a supplement of an angle is 144°. Find the measure of the angle.

10. The measure of a supplement of an angle exceeds 10 times the measure of its complement by 9°. Find the measure of the angle.

Triangles

Objective To learn some properties of triangles.

A **triangle** is the figure formed by three segments joining three points not on the same line. Each segment is a **side** of the triangle. Each of the three points is a **vertex** (vertices) of the triangle.

"Triangle *ABC*" can be written $\triangle ABC$.

Sides of $\triangle ABC$: $\overline{AB}$, $\overline{BC}$, $\overline{CA}$
Vertices of $\triangle ABC$: A, B, C
Angles of $\triangle ABC$: $\angle A$, $\angle B$, $\angle C$

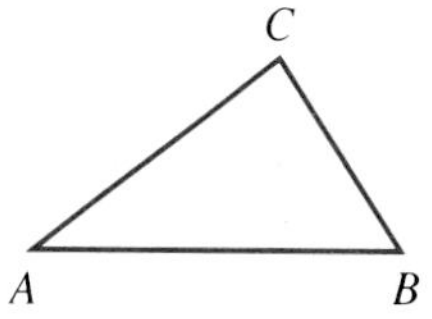

In any triangle, the sum of the measures of the angles is 180°. To check this statement for a particular triangle, measure each angle with a protractor and then find the sum of the measures. You can also show this by tearing off the corners of a paper triangle and fitting them together so that they form a straight angle, as shown below.

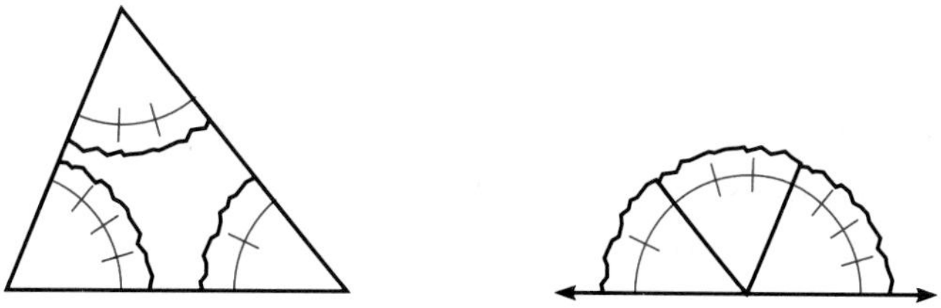

Here are some special triangles:

Right triangle
The small square in the right triangle indicates the right angle: $\angle C = 90°$

$(AC)^2 + (BC)^2 = (AB)^2$

(Recall the Pythagorean theorem and its converse on pages 529 and 530.)

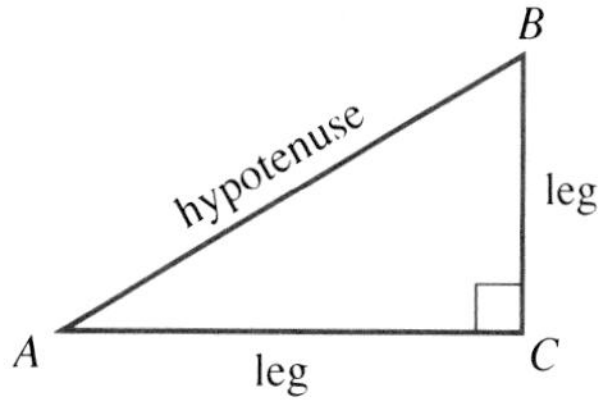

Isosceles triangle
$MN = NP$; $\angle M = \angle P$
Base: $\overline{MP}$
Base angles: $\angle M$ and $\angle P$

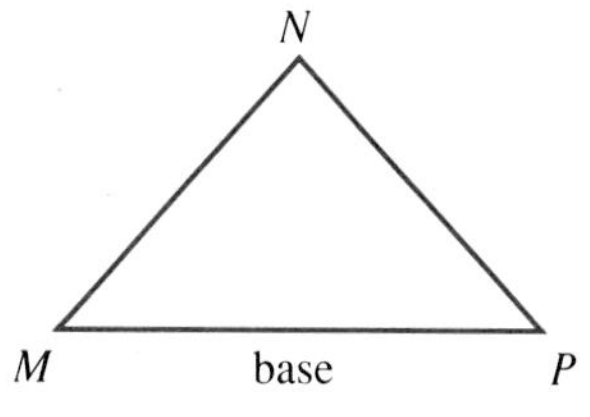

Equilateral triangle
$RS = ST = TR$
$\angle R = \angle S = \angle T = 60°$

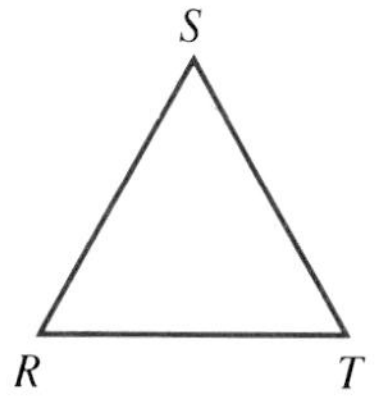

Oral Exercises

Identify $\triangle ABC$ as right, isosceles, or equilateral.

1. $\angle A = 90°$
2. $AB = BC = CA$
3. $AB = 12$, $AC = 12$, $BC = 9$
4. $AB = 3$, $BC = 4$, $CA = 5$
5. $\angle B = 38°$, $\angle C = 38°$
6. $\angle C = 16°$, $\angle A = 74°$
7. $\angle A = 60°$, $\angle B = 60°$
8. $\angle A = 40°$, $\angle B = 100°$

Written Exercises

The measures of two angles of a triangle are given. Find the measure of the third angle.

A

1. 28°, 59°
2. 122°, 41°
3. 38°, 52°
4. 15°, 27°
5. 90°, 24°
6. 138°, 21°

In Exercises 7–12, use the converse of the Pythagorean theorem to determine whether or not the triangle is a right triangle.

7. $\triangle ABC$: $AB = 9$, $BC = 8$, $AC = 13$
8. $\triangle DEF$: $EF = 8$, $FD = 10$, $DE = 6$
9. $\triangle GHI$: $GH = HI = 12$, $GI = 16$
10. $\triangle JKL$: $JK = 15$, $KL = 17$, $JL = 8$
11. $\triangle MNO$: $MN = 24$, $MO = 10$, $NO = 26$
12. $\triangle PQR$: $PQ = 10$, $QR = 12$, $PR = 8$

13. If $\triangle STU$ is a right triangle with $\angle T = 90°$, $TU = 12$, and $ST = 9$, find SU.
14. If $\triangle XYZ$ is a right triangle with $\angle Z = 90°$, $XZ = 12$, and $YZ = 5$, find XY.
15. If $\triangle ABC$ is a right triangle with $\angle A = 90°$, $AB = 24$, and $BC = 30$, find AC.
16. If $\triangle DEF$ is isosceles, $DE = DF$, and $\angle D = 50°$, find $\angle E$.
17. If $\triangle GHI$ is isosceles, $GH = GI$, and $\angle H = 20°$, find $\angle G$.
18. If $\triangle MNO$ is a right isosceles triangle and $\angle M = 90°$, find the measures of $\angle N$ and $\angle O$.

In Exercises 19–26, $\angle C = 90°$ in $\triangle ABC$. Given the lengths of the other two sides, find the length of the third side in simplest radical form.

B

19. $AC = 4$, $BC = 12$
20. $AC = 3$, $BC = 6$
21. $AC = 6$, $AB = 10$
22. $BC = 9$, $AB = 41$
23. $BC = 16$, $AB = 24$
24. $AC = 11$, $AB = 25$

C

25. $AC = BC = x$
26. $AC = y$, $AB = 2y$

Problems

Solve.

A **1.** In a right triangle, the measure of one acute angle is four times the measure of the other. Find the measures of the two acute angles.

2. Find the measure of each angle of an isosceles triangle if the measure of the third angle is 10 times the measure of each base angle.

3. In a triangle, the measure of the second angle is 7 times the measure of the first angle, and the measure of the third angle is 10 times the measure of the first angle. Find the measure of each angle.

4. The measures of the angles of a triangle are in the ratio 4:5:6. Find the measure of each angle.

5. The measure of the second angle of a triangle is three times the measure of the first angle, and the measure of the third angle is twice the measure of the second angle. Find the measure of each angle.

6. The measure of the second angle of a triangle is 4 times the measure of the first angle, and the measure of the third angle is 63° less than the measure of the second angle. Find the measure of each angle.

7. The measures of two angles of a triangle are equal. The measure of the third angle is $\frac{1}{2}$ of the sum of the measures of the first two angles. Find the measure of each angle.

8. The measure of the second angle of a triangle is twice the measure of the first angle, and the measure of the third angle is 5° more than 4 times the measure of the first angle. Find the measure of each angle.

B **9.** The measure of the second angle of a triangle is 5° more than four times that of the first, and the measure of the third angle is 27° less than three times that of the second angle. Find the measure of each angle.

10. In a triangle, the measure of the third angle is 3° more than twice the measure of the second angle. The measure of the first angle is 24° more than twice the measure of the third angle. Find the measure of each angle.

11. The measure of the first angle of a triangle is 2° less than twice the measure of the second angle. The measure of the third angle is 35° more than half the measure of the first angle. Find the measure of each angle.

C **12.** In a triangle, the measure of the second angle is six times the measure of the first angle. The measure of the third angle is 18° less than the sum of the measures of the second angle and the square of the first angle. Find the measure of each angle.

13. The measure of the second angle of a triangle is 22° more than the measure of the complement of the first angle, and the measure of the third angle is 49° less than the measure of the supplement of the first angle. Find the measure of each angle.

Similar Triangles

Objective To solve problems involving similar triangles.

An object viewed under a magnifying lens appears larger than it is, but its shape is not changed. Two figures that have the same shape are called *similar*.

Two triangles are **similar triangles** when the measures of two angles of one triangle equal the measures of two angles of the other triangle. (Since the sum of the measures of the angles of a triangle is 180°, you can see that the remaining angles also have equal measures.) The triangles shown below are similar.

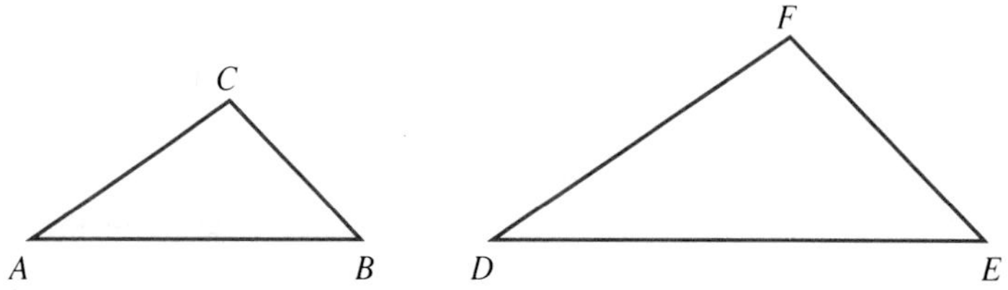

$$\angle A = \angle D = 35°, \quad \angle B = \angle E = 45°, \quad \angle C = \angle F = 100°$$

You show that the triangles ABC and DEF are similar by writing

$$\triangle ABC \sim \triangle DEF.$$

Notice that the vertices of angles with equal measures are written in corresponding positions in the names of the triangles. Angles with equal measures in similar triangles are called **corresponding angles.** The sides opposite corresponding angles are called **corresponding sides.** $\overline{AB}$ corresponds to $\overline{DE}$, and so on. *It is a geometric fact that the lengths of corresponding sides of similar triangles are proportional.* For the triangles shown above,

$$\frac{AB}{DE} = \frac{BC}{EF} = \frac{CA}{FD}.$$

Example 1 In the diagram $\triangle ABC \sim \triangle DEF$. Find AC and BC.

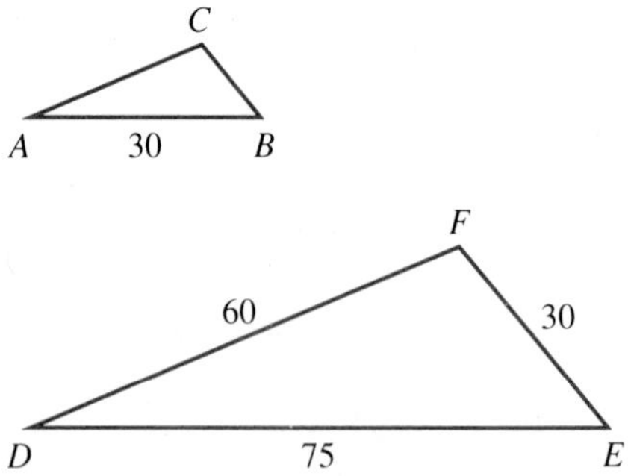

Solution Corresponding sides are proportional:

$$\frac{AB}{DE} = \frac{AC}{DF} \quad \text{and} \quad \frac{AB}{DE} = \frac{BC}{EF}$$

$$\frac{30}{75} = \frac{AC}{60} \quad \text{and} \quad \frac{30}{75} = \frac{BC}{30}$$

$$75(AC) = 1800 \quad \text{and} \quad 75(BC) = 900$$

$$AC = 24 \quad \text{and} \quad BC = 12$$ ***Answer***

Example 2 In the diagram, $\triangle ABC \sim \triangle AEF$. Find EF and AF.

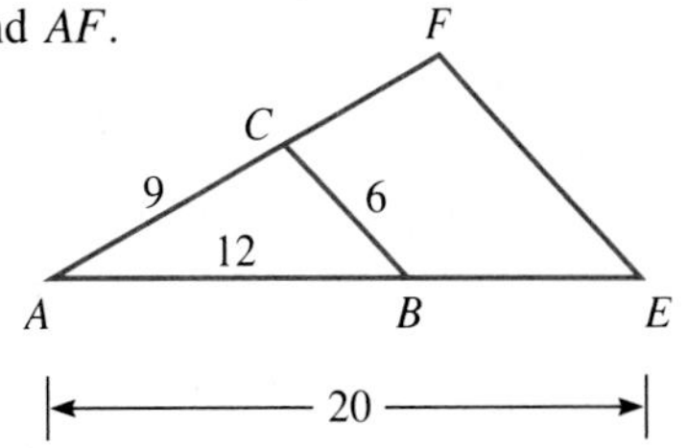

Solution Corresponding sides are proportional:

$$\frac{BC}{EF} = \frac{AB}{AE} \quad \text{and} \quad \frac{AC}{AF} = \frac{AB}{AE}$$

$$\frac{6}{EF} = \frac{12}{20} \quad \text{and} \quad \frac{9}{AF} = \frac{12}{20}$$

$$12(EF) = 120 \quad \text{and} \quad 12(AF) = 180$$

$$EF = 10 \quad \text{and} \quad AF = 15$$ ***Answer***

Oral Exercises

In the diagram for Exercises 1–3, $\triangle ABC \sim \triangle ADE$.

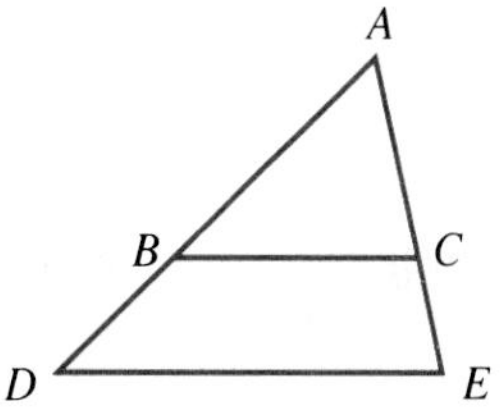

1. Name the corresponding angles.
2. Name the corresponding sides.
3. Name three equal ratios.

Written Exercises

A 1. In $\triangle RST$, $\angle R = 50°$ and $\angle S = 70°$. In $\triangle XYZ$, $\angle Y = 50°$ and $\angle Z = 70°$.
   a. Write the corresponding angles.
   b. Write the corresponding sides.
   c. Complete: $\triangle RST \sim \triangle$ __?__

2. In $\triangle JKL$ and $\triangle MNP$, $\angle K = \angle M = 35°$, and $\angle L = \angle N = 88°$. Write three equal ratios.

Classify each statement as true or false.

3. All right triangles are similar.
4. All isosceles triangles are similar.
5. All equilateral triangles are similar.
6. All isosceles right triangles are similar.
7. If $\triangle ABC \sim \triangle BCA$, then $\triangle ABC$ is equilateral.

In Exercises 8–11, $\triangle ABC \sim \triangle DEF$. Find the lengths of the sides not given.

8. $AB = 3$, $BC = 5$, $AC = 6$, $DE = 9$
9. $DE = 15$, $EF = 21$, $DF = 12$, $AC = 8$
10. $AB = 24$, $BC = 16$, $AC = 32$, $EF = 12$
11. $AB = BC = 10$, $AC = 15$, $DE = 14$

In Exercises 12–15, $\triangle ABC \sim \triangle DEF$. Find the lengths of the sides not given.

B **12.** $AB = 4$, $BC = 6$, $DE = 6$, $DF = 12$

13. $AB = 16$, $AC = 20$, $DF = 15$, $EF = 18$

14. $BC = 21$, $AC = 28$, $DE = 25$, $DF = 20$

15. $AC = 32$, $BC = 18$, DE $= 39$, $DF = 48$

C **16.** In $\triangle RST$ at the right, $\angle RTS = 90°$ and $\angle TUR = 90°$. Complete the following statement:
$\triangle RTS \sim \triangle \underline{\ ?\ } \sim \triangle \underline{\ ?\ }$

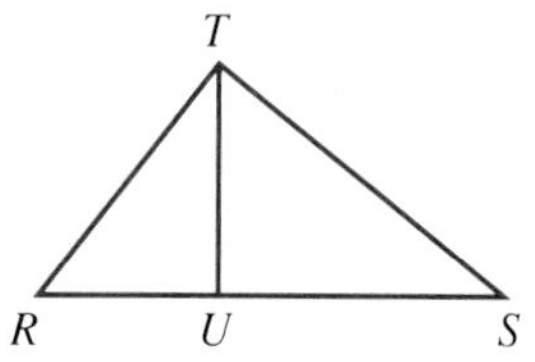

Problems

Solve.

A **1.** The sides of a triangle have lengths of 6 cm, 10 cm, and 12 cm. If the longest side of a similar triangle is 18 cm, find its shortest side.

2. Leigh is 5 ft tall and casts a shadow 2 ft long at the same time a tree casts a shadow 26 ft long. How tall is the tree?

3. A sign 4 m high casts a shadow 3 m long at the same time a building casts a shadow 27 m long. How tall is the building?

4. An isosceles triangle has two sides of length 28 cm and a base of 35 cm. The base of a similar triangle is 15 cm. Find the perimeter of the smaller triangle.

5. To find the length of a swamp, two similar triangles were roped off. The measurements are shown on the diagram. How long is the swamp?

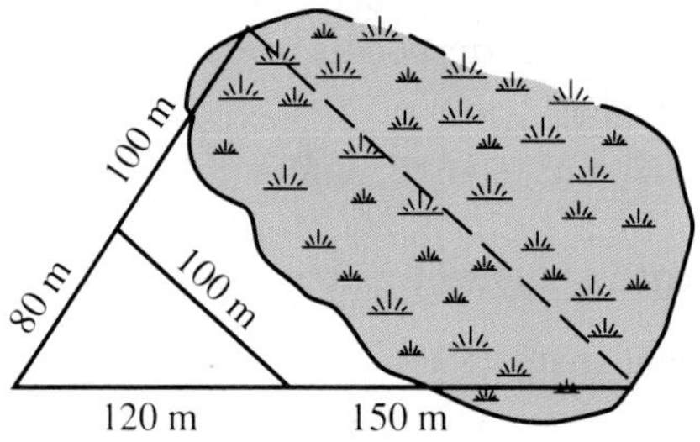

B **6.** $\overline{AC}$ and $\overline{DE}$ intersect at point B and $\triangle ABE \sim \triangle CBD$. If $AB = x$, $BC = 4x$, $BD = 20$, and $DC = 32$, find EB.

7. Chen walks 5 m up a ramp and is 2 m above the ground. If he were to walk 10 m farther, how far above the ground would he be?

8. From a point on the ground 7 m from the base of a tree 8 m tall, it is possible to see the top of a building 400 m tall just over the top of the tree. How far is the point from the base of the building?

C **9.** A boy whose eye level at A is 1.5 m above the ground wants to find the height ED of a tree. He places a mirror flat on the ground 15 m from the tree. If he stands at a point B, which is 2 m from the mirror at C, he can see the reflection of the top of the tree. Find the height of the tree.

Trigonometry

Trigonometric Ratios

Objective To find the sine, cosine, and tangent of an acute angle.

In the branch of mathematics called *trigonometry* you study the measurement of triangles. Any acute angle, such as $\angle A$ in the diagram, can be made an angle of a right triangle ABC. The legs opposite and adjacent to this angle are labeled. Ratios of the lengths of the sides of $\triangle ABC$ are called **trigonometric ratios** of $\angle A$. These ratios have special names and symbols.

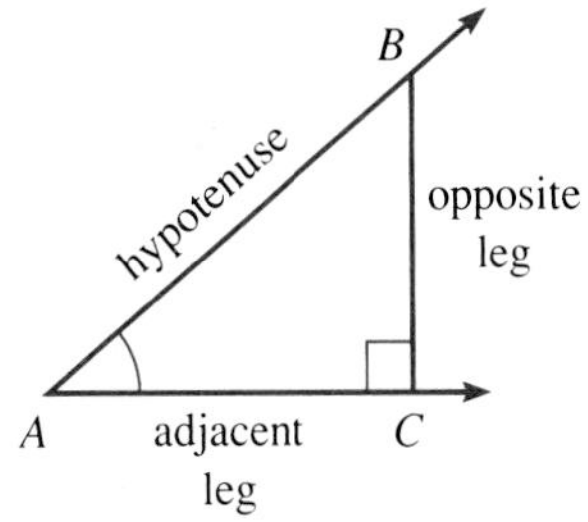

sine of $\angle A$ (symbol: $\sin A$) $= \dfrac{\text{length of leg opposite } \angle A}{\text{length of hypotenuse}} = \dfrac{BC}{AB}$

cosine of $\angle A$ (symbol: $\cos A$) $= \dfrac{\text{length of leg adjacent to } \angle A}{\text{length of hypotenuse}} = \dfrac{AC}{AB}$

tangent of $\angle A$ (symbol: $\tan A$) $= \dfrac{\text{length of leg opposite } \angle A}{\text{length of leg adjacent to } \angle A} = \dfrac{BC}{AC}$

Example 1 Find the sine, cosine, and tangent of $\angle A$ and of $\angle B$.

Solution

$\sin A = \dfrac{8}{17}$ $\quad$ $\sin B = \dfrac{15}{17}$

$\cos A = \dfrac{15}{17}$ $\quad$ $\cos B = \dfrac{8}{17}$

$\tan A = \dfrac{8}{15}$ $\quad$ $\tan B = \dfrac{15}{8}$

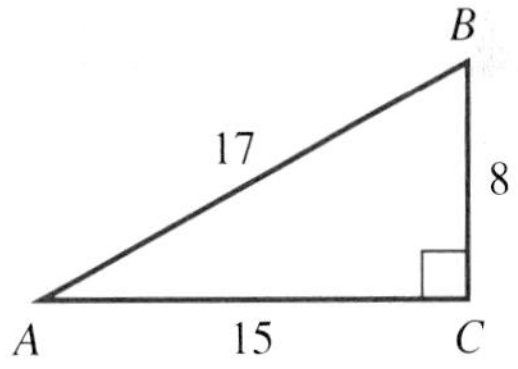

Example 2 Find the sine, cosine, and tangent of $\angle Q$.

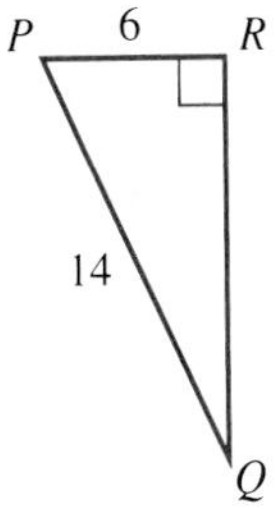

Solution

$$a^2 + 6^2 = 14^2$$
$$a^2 + 36 = 196$$
$$a^2 = 160$$
$$a = 4\sqrt{10}$$

{Use the Pythagorean theorem to find RQ.

$\sin Q = \dfrac{6}{14} = \dfrac{3}{7}$ $\quad$ $\cos Q = \dfrac{4\sqrt{10}}{14} = \dfrac{2\sqrt{10}}{7}$ $\quad$ $\tan Q = \dfrac{6}{4\sqrt{10}} = \dfrac{3\sqrt{10}}{20}$

The values of the trigonometric ratios of an angle depend only on the measure of the angle and not on the particular right triangle that contains the angle. For example, in the two right triangles below, $\angle A$ and $\angle D$ have equal measures. It can be shown that the trigonometric ratios of $\angle A$ and $\angle D$ are also equal.

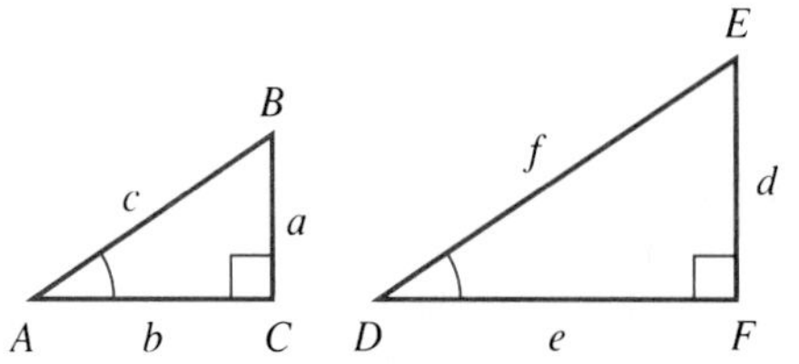

Since $\angle A = \angle D = 30°$ and $\angle C = \angle F = 90°$, the triangles are similar and their corresponding sides are proportional:

$$\frac{a}{d} = \frac{c}{f}$$

Multiplying both ratios by $\frac{d}{c}$, you obtain the equivalent proportion

$$\frac{a}{c} = \frac{d}{f}, \text{ or } \sin A = \sin D.$$

You can show similarly that $\cos A = \cos D$ and $\tan A = \tan D$.

Because the values of $\sin A$, $\cos A$, and $\tan A$ depend only on the measure of $\angle A$ and not on the triangle containing $\angle A$, you can think of these trigonometric ratios as the values of three functions each having the set of acute angles as its domain. These functions are called **trigonometric functions.**

Oral Exercises

State the value of each trigonometric ratio for the triangle shown.

1. $\sin A$
2. $\cos A$
3. $\tan A$
4. $\sin B$
5. $\cos B$
6. $\tan B$

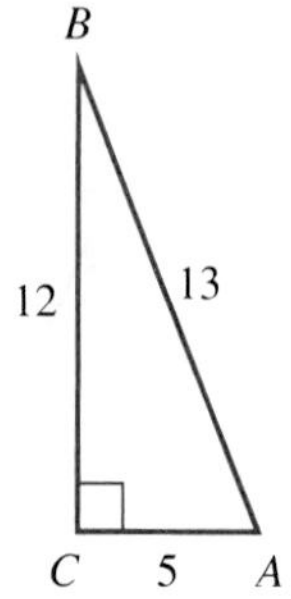

7. $\sin X$
8. $\cos X$
9. $\tan X$
10. $\sin Y$
11. $\cos Y$
12. $\tan Y$

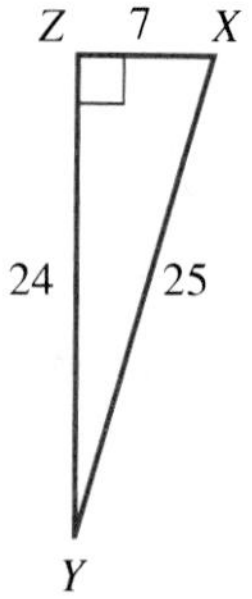

13. Explain why the sine and the cosine of an acute angle are always less than 1.

Written Exercises

For each right triangle shown, find sin A, cos A, tan A, sin B, cos B, and tan B. Write irrational answers in simplest radical form.

A

1.

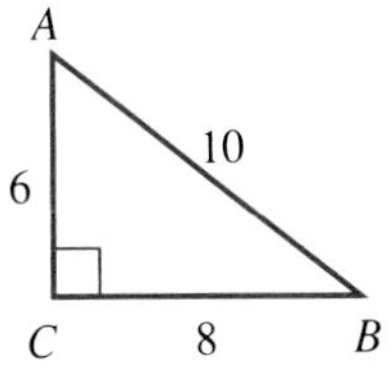

2.

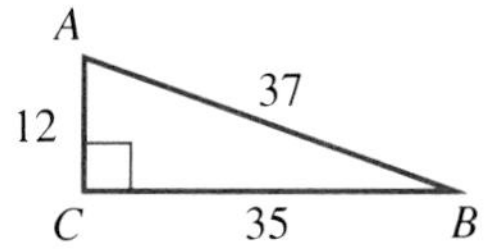

3.

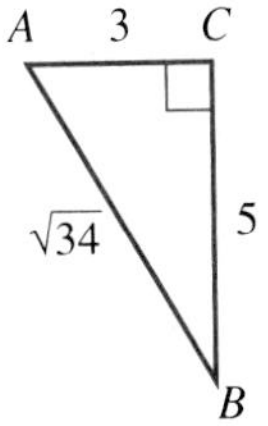

4.

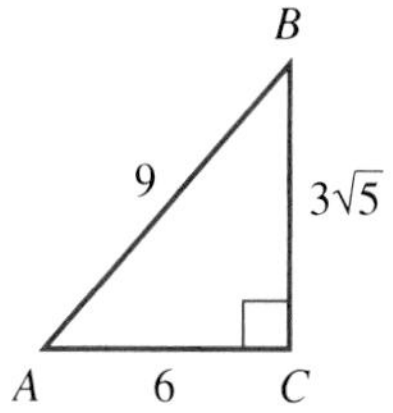

5.

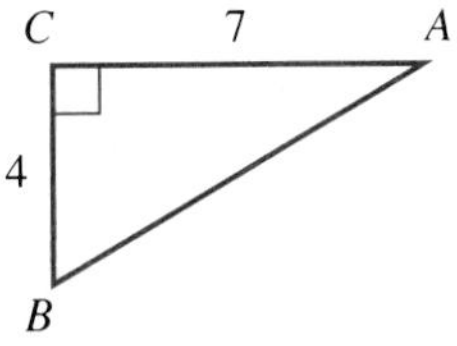

6.

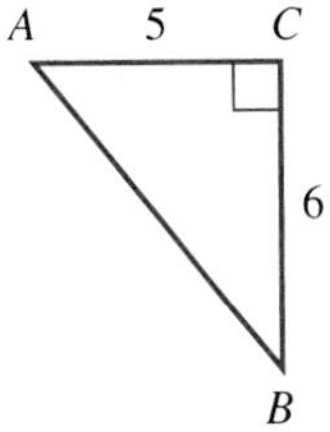

7.

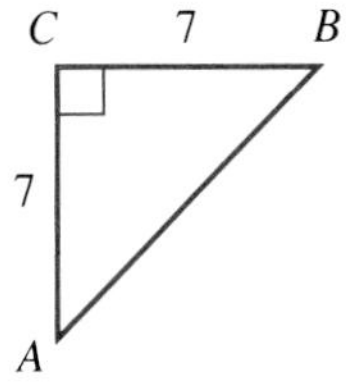

8.

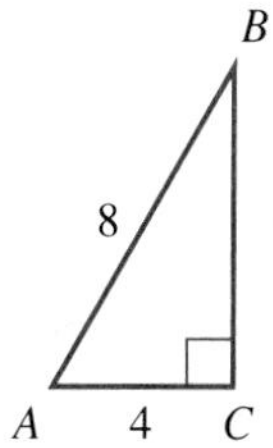

9.

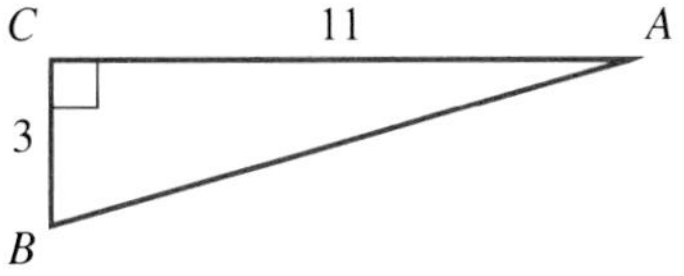

In Exercises 10–13, $\triangle ABC$ is a right triangle with $\angle C$ as the right angle. Show that the following statements are true.

B

10. $\sin A = \cos B$

11. $\cos A = \sin B$

12. $(\sin A)^2 + (\cos A)^2 = 1$

13. $\tan A = \dfrac{\sin A}{\cos A}$

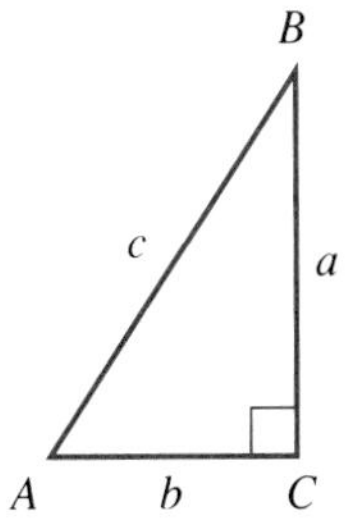

C

14. If $\sin R = \frac{3}{5}$, find $\cos R$.

15. If $\sin Z = \frac{3}{8}$, find the sine of the complement of $\angle Z$.

16. If $\tan X = \frac{11}{60}$, find $\sin X$ and $\cos X$.

Values of Trigonometric Ratios

Objective To find values of trigonometric ratios for given angles, and measures of angles for given trigonometric ratios.

Values of the trigonometric ratios are needed to solve practical problems involving right triangles. A few values can be easily computed using the properties of special triangles and the Pythagorean theorem. For an isosceles right triangle:

$$\sin 45° = \frac{1}{\sqrt{2}} = \frac{\sqrt{2}}{2} \approx 0.707$$

$$\cos 45° = \frac{1}{\sqrt{2}} = \frac{\sqrt{2}}{2} \approx 0.707$$

$$\tan 45° = \frac{1}{1} = 1$$

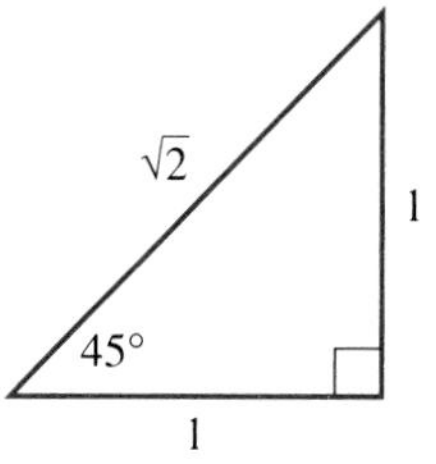

It is not possible to give *exact* values of the trigonometric ratios for most angles. You can use a scientific calculator or the table on page 683 to find approximate values of sin A, cos A, and tan A for any angle A with a whole-number measure from 1° to 89°.

Example 1 Find the values of sin 58°, cos 58°, and tan 58°.

Solution 1 Using a Table

Locate 58° in the left-hand column of the portion of the table shown at the right, then read across the row to find:

sin 58° ≈ 0.8480
cos 58° ≈ 0.5299
tan 58° ≈ 1.6003 ***Answer***

Angle	*Sine*	*Cosine*	*Tangent*
1°	.0175	.9998	.0175
56°	.8290	.5592	1.4826
57°	.8387	.5446	1.5399
58°	.8480	.5299	1.6003
59°	.8572	.5150	1.6643
60°	.8660	.5000	1.7321

For convenience, you may write = instead of ≈ in statements such as these.

Solution 2 Using a Calculator

To find the value for sin 58°, you enter 58 and then press the sin key to get 0.8480481.

∴ to the nearest ten-thousandth, sin 58° = 0.8480. Likewise, you enter 58 and then press the cos key or the tan key to get:

cos 58° ≈ 0.5299193, or cos 58° = 0.5299
tan 58° ≈ 1.6003345, or tan 58° = 1.6003 ***Answer***

A trigonometric table or a calculator can also be used to approximate the measure of an angle if one of its trigonometric ratios is given.

Example 2 Find the measure of $\angle A$ to the nearest degree.

a. $\cos A = 0.5150$ **b.** $\sin A = 0.8368$

Solution 1 Using a Table

a. Locate the value 0.5150 in the cosine column, if possible. Since it is there, read across the row to the left-hand column to find that the angle has a measure of 59°. ***Answer***

b. Since 0.8368 is not listed in the sine column, locate the entries between which 0.8368 lies:

$\sin 56° = 0.8290$ and $\sin 57° = 0.8387$, so the measure of $\angle A$ must be between 56° and 57°.

Since 0.8368 is closer to 0.8387 than it is to 0.8290, $\angle A = 57°$, to the nearest degree. ***Answer***

Solution 2 Using a Calculator

Most calculators have the inverse keys ($\sin^{-1}$, $\cos^{-1}$, $\tan^{-1}$, or inv sin, inv cos, inv tan) that give the measure of an acute angle.

a. Enter 0.5150, then press the $\cos^{-1}$ key to get 59.002545°.

$\therefore$ to the nearest degree, $\angle A = 59°$. ***Answer***

b. Enter 0.8368, then press the $\sin^{-1}$ key to get 56.803734°.

$\therefore$ to the nearest degree, $\angle A = 57°$. ***Answer***

Oral Exercises

For Exercises 1–12, use a calculator or the portion of the table of trigonometric ratios shown on the previous page.

State the value of each trigonometric ratio.

1. sin 59° **2.** cos 56° **3.** tan 1°

4. tan 60° **5.** sin 57° **6.** cos 59°

Find the measure of angle A to the nearest degree.

7. $\sin A = 0.8290$ **8.** $\cos A = 0.9998$ **9.** $\tan A = 1.5399$

10. $\cos A = 0.5100$ **11.** $\tan A = 1.6832$ **12.** $\sin A = 0.8475$

13. Explain why $\sin 10° = \cos 80°$ by referring to the diagram and the definitions on page 627.

Written Exercises

Use a calculator or the table on page 683 to find sin *A*, cos *A*, and tan *A* for the given measure of angle *A*.

A **1.** 20° **2.** 40° **3.** 15°

4. 39° **5.** 68° **6.** 83°

7. 24° **8.** 59° **9.** 4°

10. 71° **11.** 45° **12.** 35°

Use a calculator or the table on page 683 to find the measure of angle *A* to the nearest degree.

13. $\sin A = 0.9781$ **14.** $\cos A = 0.6561$

15. $\tan A = 0.1584$ **16.** $\tan A = 0.9431$

17. $\sin A = 0.8431$ **18.** $\cos A = 0.4128$

19. $\cos A = 0.9243$ **20.** $\tan A = 8.2198$

21. $\sin A = 0.5801$ **22.** $\sin A = 0.2340$

23. $\tan A = 0.8724$ **24.** $\cos A = 0.9913$

25. $\tan A = 0.3712$ **26.** $\sin A = 0.9299$

27. $\cos A = 0.8300$ **28.** $\tan A = 3.2276$

Complete with >, <, or = to make a true statement.

B **29.** If $\angle A > \angle B$, then $\sin A$ _?_ $\sin B$.

30. If $\angle A > \angle B$, then $\cos A$ _?_ $\cos B$.

31. If $\angle A$ is a complement of $\angle B$, then $\sin A$ _?_ $\cos B$.

C **32.** If $\angle A = 23°$, show that $\sin (2A) = 2 \cdot \sin A \cdot \cos A$.

33. If $\angle B = 36°$, show that $\cos (2B) = (\cos B)^2 - (\sin B)^2$.

Challenge

Is the reasoning logical in each case?

1. The sum of the measures of the angles of a triangle is 180°. The sum of the measures of $\angle A$, $\angle R$, and $\angle Z$ is 180°. Therefore, $\angle A$, $\angle R$, and $\angle Z$ are the angles of a triangle.
2. A square is a rectangle with four sides of equal length. A rectangle has four right angles. Therefore, a square has four right angles.
3. A parallelogram is a figure in geometry. Geometry is a branch of mathematics. Therefore, a parallelogram is a figure in mathematics.

Problem Solving Using Trigonometry

Objective To use trigonometric ratios to solve problems.

Trigonometric ratios can be used to solve practical problems involving right triangles. You can find values for these ratios by using the table on page 683 or a scientific calculator.

Example 1 A radio transmission tower is 83 m high. A support wire is attached to the tower 25 m from the top. If the support wire and the ground form an angle of 42°, what is the length of the support wire?

Solution Draw a triangle and label the different values. First, find how high on the tower the support wire is attached:

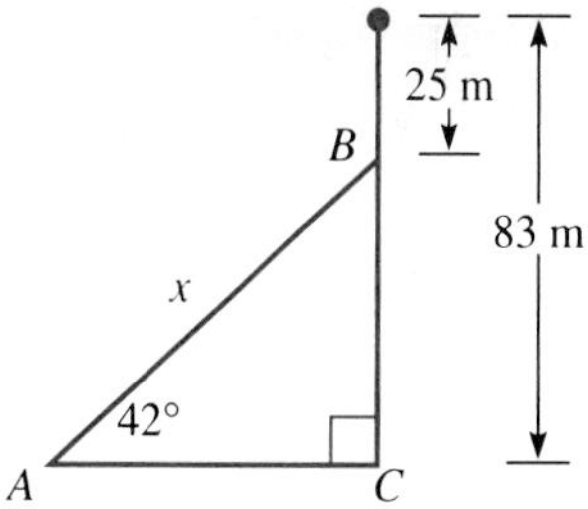

$$83 - 25 = 58$$

Since $\triangle ABC$ is a right triangle,

$\sin 42° = \frac{58}{x}$, or $x = \frac{58}{\sin 42°}$.

From the table on page 683 or a calculator, $\sin 42° = 0.6691$.

Then $x = \frac{58}{0.6691} \approx 86.7$.

$\therefore$ to the nearest tenth of a meter, the support wire is 86.7 m long.

In surveying and navigation problems involving right triangles, the terms *angle of elevation* and *angle of depression* are used. In the diagram below, $\angle CBA$ is an angle of elevation, since the point A is elevated with respect to an observer at B. $\angle DAB$ is an angle of depression, since the point B is depressed with respect to an observer at A.

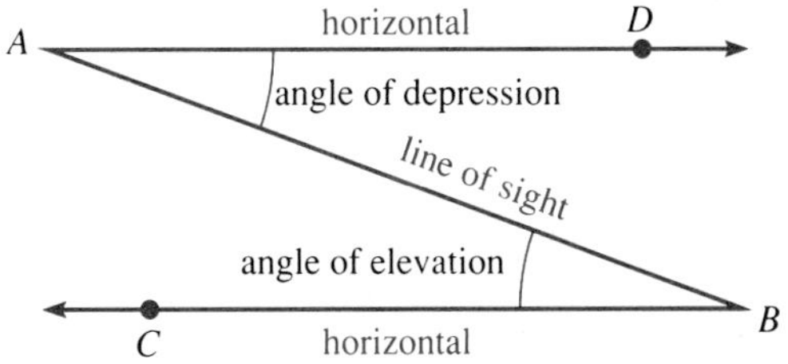

Example 2 At a point 166 m from the base of the World Trade Center in New York City, the angle of elevation to the top is 68°. To the nearest meter, what is the height of the World Trade Center?

Solution Draw a triangle and label the different values. You want to find x, the height of the World Trade Center. Since $\triangle ABC$ is a right triangle,

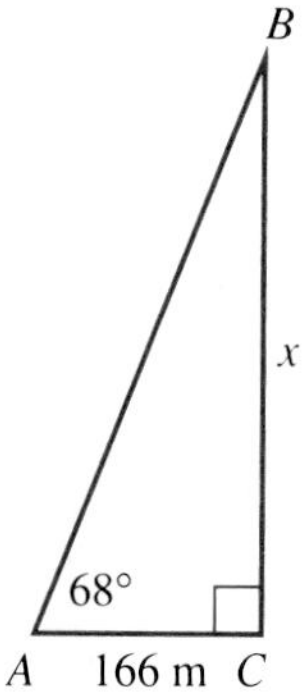

$$\tan 68° = \frac{x}{166}, \text{ or}$$

$$x = 166(\tan 68°).$$

From the table on page 683 or a calculator, $\tan 68° = 2.4751$.

Then $x = 166(2.4751)$
$= 410.8666$.

∴ to the nearest meter, the World Trade Center is 411 m high. ***Answer***

Oral Exercises

State whether you would use the sine, the cosine, or the tangent ratio to find x for each figure.

1.

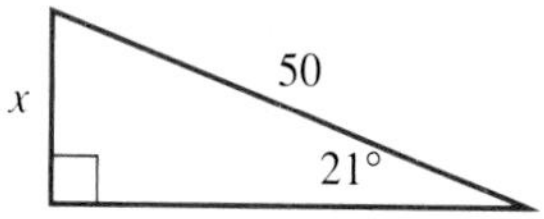

2.

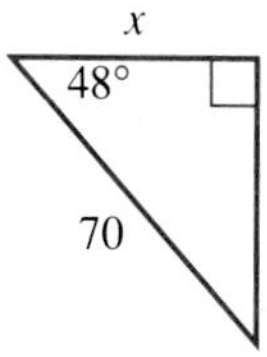

3.

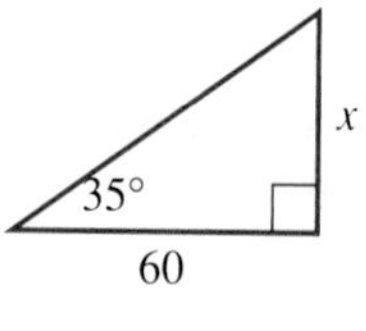

4.

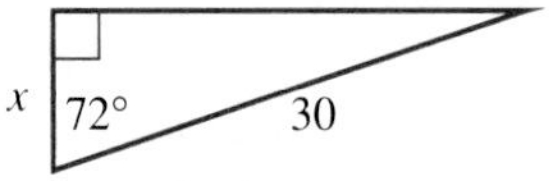

5.

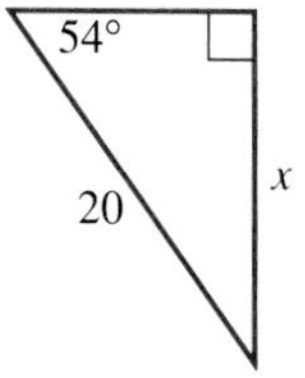

6.

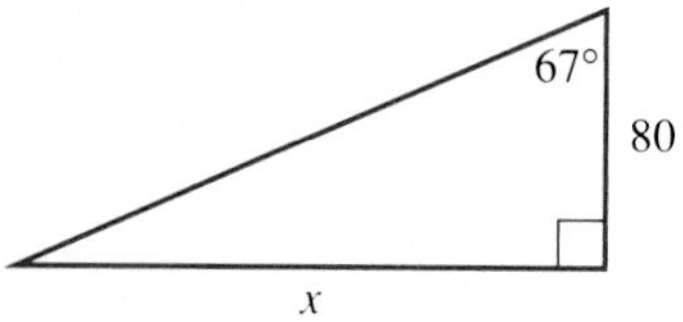

Written Exercises

Use the table on page 683 or a calculator as needed.

A **1–6.** In Oral Exercises 1–6, find the value of x to the nearest whole number.

In a right $\triangle ABC$, $\angle C = 90°$. Find the lengths of the other sides of the triangle to the nearest whole number.

7. $\angle A = 39°$, $AB = 53$

8. $\angle B = 21°$, $AB = 12$

9. $\angle B = 80°$, $AC = 48$

10. $\angle A = 65°$, $BC = 28$

In a right $\triangle DEF$, $\angle E = 90°$. Find the measures of $\angle D$ and $\angle F$ to the nearest degree.

Sample $DE = 16$, $DF = 25$

Solution

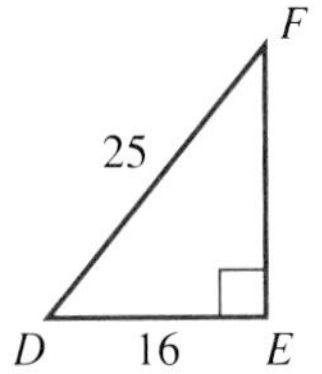

$$\cos \angle D = \frac{DE}{DF}$$

$$\cos \angle D = \frac{16}{25}$$

$$\cos \angle D = 0.6400$$

$$\angle D = 50°$$

Since the sum of the measures of the angles of a triangle is 180°, $\angle F = 180° - (90° + 50°)$. $\angle F = 40°$

B **11.** $DE = 48$, $EF = 36$

12. $DF = 30$, $EF = 25$

13. $EF = 42$, $DF = 54$

14. $DE = 63$, $EF = 81$

15. In the right $\triangle XYZ$, $\angle Y = 90°$, $\angle X = 41°$, and $XZ = 95$. Find XY and ZY to the nearest whole number.

16. In the right $\triangle RST$, $\angle S = 90°$, $RT = 120$, $\angle T = 30°$. Find RS and TS to the nearest whole number.

Problems

Solve each problem, drawing a sketch for each. Express distances to the nearest unit and angle measures to the nearest degree. Use the table on page 683 or a calculator as needed.

A **1.** How far is the ladder from the foot of the building?

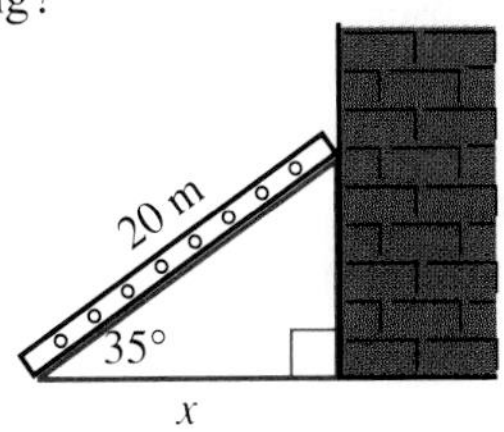

2. How long is the cable that supports the pole?

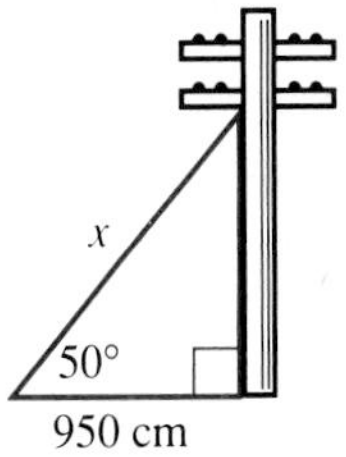

3. How high is the cliff?

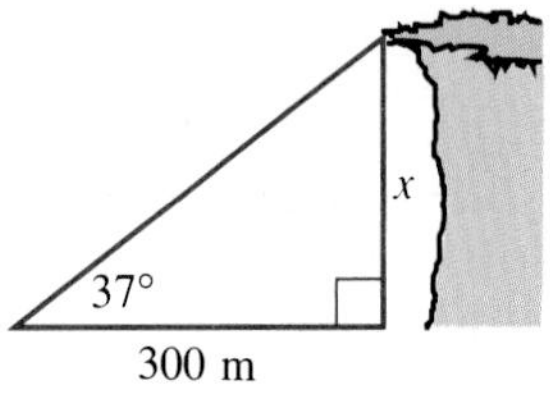

4. How far is the boy from the monument?

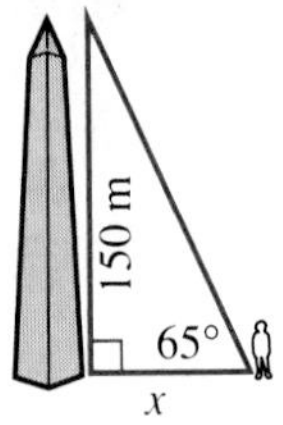

5. How far below sea level will a porpoise be if it swims 250 m at a 12° angle of depression?

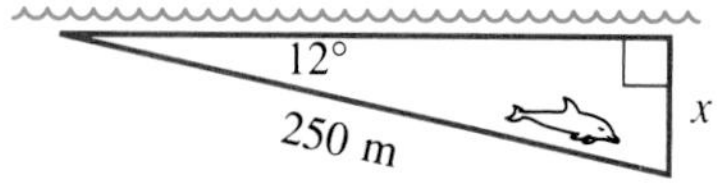

6. The length of a water ski jump is 720 cm and the angle of elevation is 35°. Find the height of the ski jump.

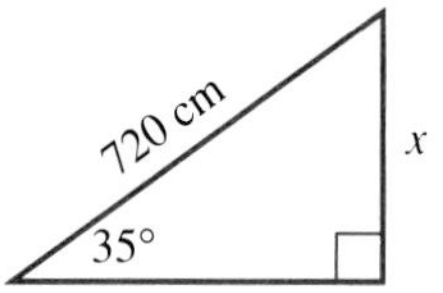

7. A bird rises 20 m vertically over a horizontal distance of 80 m. What is the angle of elevation?

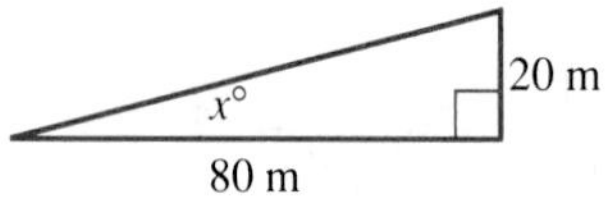

8. If a plane flies 1° off course for 6000 km, how far away will the plane be from the correct path?

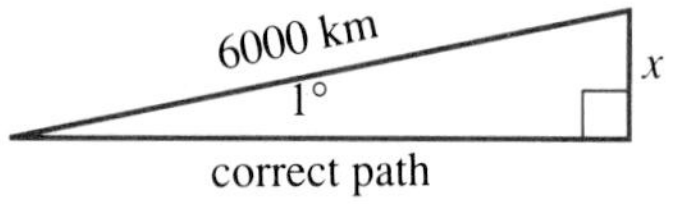

B **9.** An escalator is 15 m in length with a 37° incline. How high is the escalator?

10. From the top of a 20 m lighthouse, the angle of depression of the nearest point on the beach is 8°. Find the distance from the bottom of the lighthouse to the beach.

11. A hot air balloon with an altitude of 120 m is directly over a bridge that is 313 m from the balloon's landing point. The navigator finds the angle of depression to the landing point. What will be the angle of depression she finds?

12. A submarine travels through the water at a steady rate of 360 m/min on a diving path that forms a 4° angle of depression with the surface of the water. After 5 min, how far below the surface is the submarine?

C **13.** From the top of a 65 m lighthouse, an airplane was observed directly over a whale in the water. The angle of elevation of the airplane was 16° and the angle of depression of the whale was 46°. How far was the whale from the base of the lighthouse? How high was the plane flying?

14. A car is traveling on a level road toward a mountain 2 km high. The angle of elevation from the car to the top of the mountain changes from 6° to 15°. How far has the car traveled?

Summary

1. Probability is the branch of mathematics that is concerned with the possibility that an event will happen. For any event with probability P, $0 \le P \le 1$.
2. Data can be summarized and analyzed using statistics. This can be done by using histograms, frequency distributions, stem-and-leaf plots, and box-and-whisker plots.
3. Geometry is the branch of mathematics that is concerned with the properties of sets of points such as lines, rays, angles, and triangles.
4. Two angles whose sides are rays in the same lines but in opposite directions are called vertical angles. Two angles are complementary if the sum of their measures is 90°. Two angles are supplementary if the sum of their measures is 180°.
5. The sum of the measures of the angles of a triangle is 180°. Some special triangles are right triangles, isosceles triangles, and equilateral triangles.
6. Similar triangles have the same shape but not necessarily the same size. Their corresponding angles have the same measure and corresponding sides are proportional.
7. Trigonometry is the branch of mathematics that includes the measurement of triangles.

   Three trigonometric ratios are $\sin A = \frac{a}{c}$, $\cos A = \frac{b}{c}$, and $\tan A = \frac{a}{b}$. Approximate values for these ratios are given in the table on page 683. Trigonometric ratios can be used to solve problems involving right triangles.

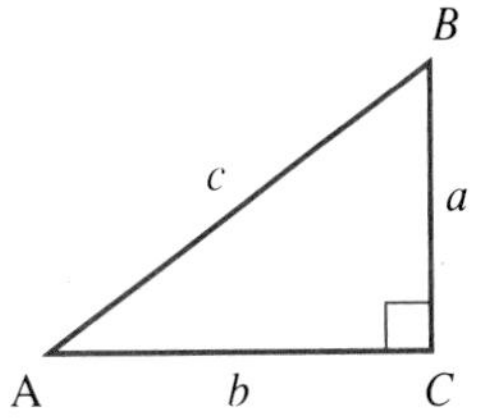

Review

Give the letter of the correct answer.

1. A cube with letters A, B, C, D, E, and F is rolled. Specify the event that the letter turned up is a vowel.

a. $\{A, B, C, D, E, F\}$ **b.** $\{A, E, I, O, U\}$
c. $\{A, E\}$ **d.** $\{B, C, D, F\}$

2. A spinner is divided into five equal sections, numbered 1, 2, 3, 4, and 5. The pointer is spun. Find the probability that the number on which the pointer stops is odd.

a. 0 **b.** 1 **c.** $\frac{1}{5}$ **d.** $\frac{3}{5}$

3. Find the mean for the data 42, 44, 46, 53, 55:

a. 48 **b.** 46 **c.** 42 **d.** 55

4. Find the range for the data 33, 43, 57, 61, 76:

a. 54 **b.** 57 **c.** 43 **d.** 76

5. The histogram at the right shows the frequency distribution for the height in centimeters of all the students in the Drama Club. How many of these students are between 150 and 170 cm?

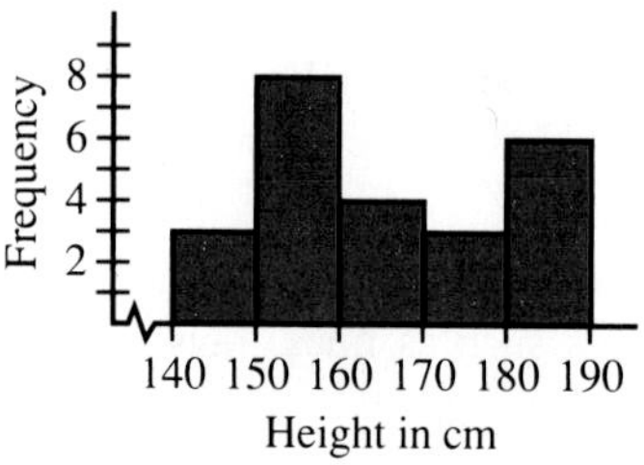

a. 11 **b.** 7

c. 12 **d.** 6

6. Find the first quartile score for the data:

2, 4, 4, 5, 7, 8, 8

a. 5.4 **b.** $\frac{10}{3}$ **c.** $\frac{15}{2}$ **d.** 4

7. Which angle is a right angle?

a. $\angle A = 99°$ **b.** $\angle B = 60°$ **c.** $\angle C = 90°$ **d.** $\angle D = 45°$

8. Find the measure of the supplement of an angle with measure 63°.

a. 17° **b.** 127° **c.** 117° **d.** 27°

9. Find the complement of an angle with measure $x°$.

a. $(90 - x)°$ **b.** $(90 + x)°$ **c.** $(180 - x)°$ **d.** $(180 + x)°$

10. What is the sum of the measures of the angles of a right triangle?

a. 45° **b.** 90° **c.** 180° **d.** 360°

11. If $\triangle ABC \sim \triangle DEF$, $\frac{AB}{DE} = \frac{12}{5}$, and $CA = 8$, find FD.

a. $\frac{3}{5}$ **b.** $\frac{3}{10}$ **c.** 1 **d.** $\frac{10}{3}$

12. Use the diagram to find cos A.

a. $\frac{3}{4}$ **b.** $\frac{4}{5}$

c. $\frac{3}{5}$ **d.** $\frac{4}{3}$

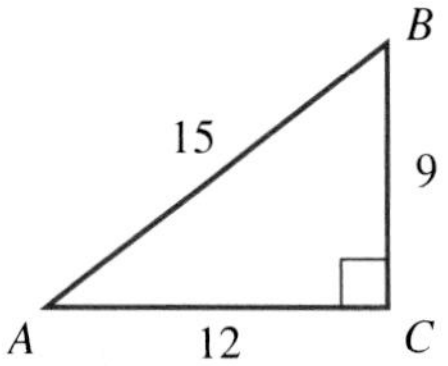

13. Use the table on page 683 to find sin 54°.

a. 1.3764 **b.** 0.5878 **c.** 0.8090 **d.** 0.1584

14. The angle of elevation to the top of a tree from a point on the ground 800 cm from the base of the tree is 47°. Find the height of the tree to the nearest centimeter.

a. 600 cm **b.** 858 cm **c.** 585 cm **d.** 546 cm

Extra Practice: Skills

Chapter 1

Simplify each expression. (1-1, 1-2)

1. $5 + (4 \times 8)$
2. $(3 + 7) \times 2$
3. $(30 \times 3) + (5 \times 2)$
4. $(40 \div 4) - (9 - 5)$
5. $(30 + 3) \times (4 + 2)$
6. $(40 - 4) \div (9 - 5)$
7. $9 + 7 - 2 \times 8 \div 4$
8. $32 \div 8 + 3 \times 7 - 6$
9. $4 \times 6 - 16 \div 2 + 7$

Evaluate each expression if $e = 2$, $f = 3$, $g = 4$, $u = 0$, $v = 5$, and $w = 1$. (1-1, 1-2)

10. $ev - f$
11. $5g + 4w$
12. $(uv) + (fg)$
13. $w(v - f) + g$
14. $(3g) \cdot (e + u)$
15. $(v - u)w + g$
16. $(e + f)(g + v)$
17. $e(u + v - w)$
18. $(4e - 2f)(v + w)$
19. $\frac{e + g}{v - f}$
20. $\frac{gv - 5e}{5 - 3u}$
21. $f(we + v) + \frac{g}{e}$

Solve each equation if $x \in \{0, 1, 2, 3, 4, 5, 6\}$. (1-3)

22. $7 + x = 12$
23. $x - 4 = 2$
24. $8 - x = 3$
25. $x - x = 0$
26. $6x = 18$
27. $0 = 5x$
28. $8x = 32$
29. $x \cdot x = 36$
30. $x \cdot x = 1$
31. $\frac{1}{2}x = 2$
32. $\frac{1}{3}x = 2$
33. $x \cdot x = 5x$
34. $3x + 9 = 26$
35. $15 = 9x - 3$
36. $4x = x \cdot 4$
37. $x(9 - x) = 0$

Translate each phrase into a variable expression. (1-4)

38. Three more than twice the number m
39. Four less than half the number z
40. Two more than eight times the number k
41. The difference of five times a number w and one
42. Three times the sum of a number h and six

Complete each statement with a variable expression. (1-4)

43. In x weeks there are _?_ days.
44. In y yards there are _?_ feet.
45. A house is x years old. Four years ago it was _?_ years old.
46. Tony weighs w lb. Ray is 7 lb heavier than Tony. Ray weighs _?_ lb.
47. My car is 5 years older than my sister's car. If my car is n years old, then her car is _?_ years old.

In Exercises 48–50, **(1-5)**
a. Choose a variable to represent the number described by the words in parentheses.
b. Write an equation that represents the given information.

48. A package of a dozen pencils costs \$1.39. (Cost of one pencil in cents)

49. The perimeter of a square is 52 m. (Length of a side in meters)

50. All but 5 of the 34 invited guests came to the party. (Number of guests at the party)

Translate each problem into an equation. Drawing a sketch may help you. **(1-6)**

51. Henry is 4 years older than Celia. If the product of their ages is 140, find each person's age.

52. The length of a rectangle is 5 cm more than its width. If the area of the rectangle is 176 cm^2, find the dimensions of the rectangle.

Solve using the five-step plan. Write out each step. A choice of possible numbers for one unknown is given. **(1-7)**

53. The number of tickets Cynthia sold is 12 less than half the number Holly sold. Together they sold 114 tickets. How many tickets did each sell? Choices for the number Holly sold: 68, 72, 84

54. Jim weighs 40 lb more than Stephanie. Stephanie weighs three fourths as much as Jim. How much does each weigh? Choices for Stephanie's weight: 100 lb, 118 lb, 120 lb

Write a number to represent each situation. Then write the opposite of that situation and write a number to represent it. **(1-8)**

55. 400 ft above sea level

56. A bank withdrawal of \$50

57. Ten losses

58. Seven floors up

Graph the given numbers on a number line. **(1-8)**

59. $5, -2, \frac{1}{2}, 3, -4$

60. $-3, 0, 1, -2.5, 2$

Simplify. **(1-9)**

61. $-(7 - 4)$

62. $[-(-8)] + 10$

63. $3 + [-(-6)]$

64. $2 + |-9|$

65. $|-3| + |0|$

66. $|6| - |6|$

67. $|-3.2| + |-0.8|$

68. $|-4.7| + |4.7|$

Replace each __?__ with one of the symbols < or > to make a true statement. **(1-9)**

69. $9 - 8$ __?__ -1

70. 7 __?__ $6 + 5$

71. $|0|$ __?__ 1

72. -4.3 __?__ -4.4

73. $-(7 + 3)$ __?__ $|-14|$

74. $-\frac{3}{7}$ __?__ $-\frac{2}{7}$

Chapter 2

Simplify. (2-1)

1. $237 + 75 + 13 + 25$
2. $456 + 29 + 44 + 21$
3. $0.2 + 16.4 + 2.8 + 0.6$
4. $3.75 + 4.85 + 1.25 + 3.15$
5. $6\frac{3}{8} + 1\frac{2}{7} + 4\frac{5}{8} + 3\frac{5}{7}$
6. $25\frac{3}{4} + \frac{4}{5} + \frac{1}{4} + 2\frac{1}{5}$
7. $8 + 3m + 4$
8. $15 + 5f + 7$
9. $9 + 6w + 3$
10. $5(7u)$
11. $(8n)(11)$
12. $(4b)9$
13. $(3p)(4q)(5r)$
14. $(2x)(5k)(7l)$
15. $(10w)(3h)(2m)$

Simplify. If necessary, draw a number line to help you. (2-2)

16. $(-4 + 8) + 9$
17. $(-7 + 10) + (-3)$
18. $[16 + (-21)] + 4$
19. $[-5 + (-13)] + 6$
20. $[0 + (-7)] + [-8 + (-22)]$
21. $[27 + (-7)] + [1 + (-1)]$
22. $-3 + (-4) + (-9)$
23. $(-5) + (-8) + (-6)$
24. $-7.2 + (-3.5) + 10.7$
25. $5.4 + (-3.1) + (-7.9)$

Add. (2-3)

26. $9 + 8 + (-3) + 4$
27. $-6 + (-7) + 10 + 2$
28. $112 + (-32) + (-40) + (-25)$
29. $-265 + (-88) + 105 + 95$
30. $-[24 + (-8)] + [-(-4 + 6)]$
31. $[-9 + (-2)] + [-(-9 + 2)]$

Evaluate each expression if $x = 2$, $y = -5$, and $z = 3$. (2-3)

32. $-8 + x + (-y)$
33. $-z + y + (-4)$
34. $1 + (-x) + z$
35. $|x + y + z|$
36. $x + (-z) + (-12)$
37. $-|z + (-y) + x|$

Simplify. (2-4, 2-5)

38. $48 - 218$
39. $53 - (-47)$
40. $-18 - (-5)$
41. $-27 - 56$
42. $133 - (62 - 59)$
43. $186 - (40 - 69)$
44. $(33 - 44) - (66 - 77)$
45. $(54 - 32) - (-8 + 13)$
46. $[14 - (-8) - [6 - (-3)]$
47. $-18 - 7 - [-6 - (-11)]$
48. $6 + x - (6 - x) - x$
49. $y - (-4) - [y + (-4)] - 4$
50. $30\left(\frac{1}{6} + \frac{1}{3}\right)$
51. $\frac{1}{5}(24) + \frac{1}{5}(16)$
52. $\frac{1}{4}(16 + 12)$
53. $(0.25)(34) + (0.75)(34)$
54. $(37 \times 22) - (7 \times 22)$
55. $(16 \times 58) - (6 \times 58)$
56. $14m + 7m$
57. $15q + (-8)q$
58. $53n - 110n$
59. $79a - 37a$
60. $3u + 7u + 8$
61. $7(c + 3) + 6$

Simplify. (2-5, 2-6)

62. $26 + 4(h + 3)$
63. $8(j - 4) + 17$
64. $23 + 6(t - 2)$
65. $5x + 9 + 3x + 11$
66. $(-5)m + 3 + 13m + 17$
67. $14u - 8 - 12u + 13$
68. $4h + 8k + (-2)h + 12k$
69. $9f + 3g - 7f + 7g$
70. $10x + 14y - 6x - 3y$
71. $(-27)(-5)$
72. $38(-2)$
73. $(-4)45$
74. $(-8)(-6)(30)$
75. $(-5)(-9)(-3)$
76. $(-13)(-14)(0)$
77. $5(-4)(-12)(-2)$
78. $-3(-2 - 9)$
79. $(-17 + 6)(-1)$
80. $(-6 \times 13) + (-6 \times 15)$
81. $[27 \times (-5)] - (27 \times 5)$
82. $-16 \times (-1) - [-16 \times (-11)]$
83. $7(-m + 6p)$
84. $-5(2u - h)$
85. $-4(6n - 9v)$
86. $-x + 7 + 6x - 5$
87. $4 - t - 8 - 7t$
88. $-l + 9 + 6l - 4$
89. $3(x + 4y) + (-4)(8x - y)$
90. $-4(2u + v) + 5(u - v)$
91. $-2(3c + d) - 3(5d - c)$
92. $7(e - f) - 3(2e - 3f)$

Write an equation to represent the given relationship among integers. (2-7)

93. The sum of three consecutive integers is 75.
94. The sum of three consecutive odd integers is 87.
95. The sum of three consecutive even integers is 138.
96. The product of two consecutive integers is 156.
97. The greater of two consecutive odd integers is eight more than three times the lesser.
98. The smaller of two consecutive even integers is one less than half of the greater.

Simplify each expression. (2-8, 2-9)

99. $-\frac{1}{11}(55)$
100. $-5000\left(\frac{1}{50}\right)$
101. $-\frac{1}{9}(-63)$
102. $112\left(-\frac{1}{7}\right)\left(-\frac{1}{2}\right)$
103. $-\frac{1}{5}(80)\frac{1}{4}$
104. $6uv\left(-\frac{1}{6}\right)$
105. $44xy\left(\frac{1}{4}\right)$
106. $\frac{1}{m}(3mn),\ m \neq 0$
107. $(8fg)\left(\frac{1}{f}\right),\ f \neq 0$
108. $\frac{1}{5}(-35a + 15)$
109. $(27h - 18)\frac{1}{3}$
110. $-\frac{1}{4}(-32e + 40f)$
111. $(42x - 63y)\left(-\frac{1}{7}\right)$
112. $\frac{1}{12}(-480 - 144m)$
113. $(-50p - 100q)\left(-\frac{1}{10}\right)$
114. $-392 \div 56$
115. $216 \div (-27)$
116. $55 \div \left(-\frac{1}{5}\right)$
117. $0 \div (-29)$
118. $\dfrac{-36}{-\frac{1}{6}}$
119. $\dfrac{8}{-\frac{1}{5}}$
120. $\dfrac{-12}{\frac{1}{4}}$
121. $\dfrac{0}{-\frac{1}{3}}$

122. $\frac{168m}{-12}$

123. $\frac{252a}{-8}$

124. $\frac{-756x}{7x}$, $x \neq 0$

125. $\frac{-253u}{-23u}$, $u \neq 0$

126. $-\frac{c}{17}(-17)$

127. $-9 \cdot \frac{x}{9}$

128. $\frac{8w}{7} \cdot 7$

129. $-\frac{5h}{3}(-3)$

Chapter 3

Solve. Check your answers. **(3-1, 3-2, 3-3)**

1. $a - 13 = 17$
2. $c + 8 = 22$
3. $s - 20 = -12$
4. $y + 14 = -33$
5. $15 + h = 0$
6. $0 = k - 13$
7. $f - 4 = |16|$
8. $g + 7 = |-2|$
9. $-x + 6 = 9$
10. $23 - y = 47$
11. $-5 - m = 7$
12. $13 = -q + 8$
13. $(e + 4) + 3 = 9$
14. $6 = 10 + (n + 3)$
15. $-5 + (1 + z) = 8$
16. $13u = 338$
17. $-396 = 22a$
18. $-12x = -444$
19. $126 = -9w$
20. $\frac{1}{7}t = 13$
21. $\frac{1}{8}h = -8$
22. $11 = -\frac{1}{4}v$
23. $-10 = -\frac{1}{5}m$
24. $-42 = \frac{n}{7}$
25. $-\frac{c}{4} = 32$
26. $-\frac{m}{27} = 0$
27. $-\frac{m}{3} = -40$
28. $4x = -\frac{2}{7}$
29. $-\frac{3}{2} = -9z$
30. $\frac{1}{4}v = 2\frac{3}{4}$
31. $3\frac{1}{2} = \frac{1}{2}u$
32. $5k + 8 = 43$
33. $7h - 6 = 36$
34. $-3 + 3m = -45$
35. $2n + 8n = 80$
36. $9v - 5v = 44$
37. $3c - 8c = 65$
38. $\frac{n}{5} + 9 = -11$
39. $-\frac{x}{3} - 2 = 7$
40. $\frac{5}{6}u + 15 = 0$
41. $x - 5 - 6x = -25$
42. $0 = y - 14 - 3y$
43. $e + 3e + 4e = 48$
44. $5(k + 3) = -10$
45. $-\frac{4}{3}(n - 6) = 12$
46. $2(v + 7) - 9 = 19$

Solve each problem using the five-step plan to help you. **(3-4)**

47. The sum of 37 and three times a number is 67. Find the number.
48. Four times a number, decreased by 24, is −20. Find the number.
49. The perimeter of a rectangle is 108. If the length is 33, find the width.
50. A large bucket holds 3 L more than twice as much as a small bucket. It took 2 small buckets and 5 large buckets to fill a 63 L tank. How much does a large bucket hold?
51. The lengths, in meters, of the sides of a triangle are consecutive even integers. The perimeter is 18 m. How long are the sides?
52. Bruce's savings account contains $122 more than his younger brother's account. Together, they have $354. Find the amount in each account.

Solve each equation. If the equation is an identity or if it has no solution, write *identity* or *no solution*. (3-5)

53. $10w = 8w + 14$

54. $x = 45 - 4x$

55. $48 - 6k = -12k$

56. $9m + 3 = 6m + 21$

57. $27 + u = 3 - 3u$

58. $4n + 1 = -1 + 4n$

59. $2(v - 8) = 6v$

60. $3x = 5(x - 6)$

61. $7y - 3 = 6(y + 2)$

62. $\frac{1}{3}(18 - 9c) = 6 - 3c$

63. $m - 5 = \frac{1}{2}(12 - 14m)$

64. $\frac{4}{5}(25x - 15) = 50x + 38$

65. $5(3 + h) = 4(h + 2)$

66. $(6x - 3)2 = (4x + 7)3$

67. $7(n - 3) = 5(n - 3)$

Solve. Use a chart to help you solve the problem. (3-6, 3-7)

68. Jay's salary is $\frac{2}{3}$ of his wife's salary. In January, when they both get \$2000 raises, their combined income will be \$49,000. What are their current salaries?

69. Erin's three test scores were consecutive odd integers. If her next test score is 18 points more than the highest score of the three tests, her total number of points will be 328. Find Erin's test scores.

70. Julius weighs twice as much as each of his twin brothers. If each of the twins gains 5 lb and Julius gains twice that amount, the sum of the three brothers' weights will be 240 lb. How much does each weigh now?

71. The width of a rectangle is 6 cm less than the length. A second rectangle, with a perimeter of 54 cm, is 3 cm wider and 2 cm shorter than the first. What are the dimensions of each rectangle?

72. Martha has some nickels and dimes worth \$6.25. She has three times as many nickels as dimes. How many nickels does she have?

73. Elliot paid \$1.50 a dozen for some flowers. He sold all but 5 dozen of them for \$2 a dozen, making a profit of \$18. How many dozen flowers did he buy?

74. Rachel spent \$16.18 for some cans of dog food costing 79 cents each and some cans of cat food costing 69 cents each. She bought two more cans of cat food than of dog food. How many cans of each did she buy?

75. Victor earns \$3 an hour working after school and \$4 an hour working on Saturdays. Last week he earned \$43, working a total of 13 h. How many hours did he work on Saturday?

State a reason for each step in Exercises 76–78. (3-8)

76. $6 + (15 + 4) = 6 + (4 + 15)$ _?_
$= (6 + 4) + 15$ _?_
$= 10 + 15 = 25$ _?_

77. $20 + (-4) = (16 + 4) + (-4)$ _?_
$= 16 + [4 + (-4)]$ _?_
$= 16 + 0$ _?_
$= 16$ _?_

78. $-7 + 19 = 19 + (-7)$ __?__
$= 12 + 7 + (-7)$ __?__
$= 12 + 0$ __?__
$= 12$ __?__

Chapter 4

Simplify. **(4-1)**

1. 7^3 **2.** $(-5)^4$ **3.** $-3 \cdot 2^4$ **4.** $(-2 \cdot 5)^3$

5. $7 + 5^2$ **6.** $(8 - 4)^3$ **7.** $6 - 2^5$ **8.** $(4 + 7)^2$

9. $5^3 \div (3^2 + 4^2)$ **10.** $(8^2 - 6^2) \div 7$ **11.** $4(9^2 - 4^3)$

Evaluate if $a = -3$ and $b = 2$. **(4-1)**

12. $3a + b^2$ **13.** $(3a + b)^2$ **14.** $4a - b^3$ **15.** $(4a - b)^3$

16. $7 + ab^2$ **17.** $(7 + ab)^2$ **18.** $-\frac{3a}{b^2}$ **19.** $\left(-\frac{3a}{b}\right)^2$

Add. **(4-2)**

20. $\begin{array}{r} 4x - 3 \\ \underline{7x + 8} \end{array}$ **21.** $\begin{array}{r} 3b + 4 \\ \underline{-2b - 6} \end{array}$ **22.** $\begin{array}{r} 5m + 8 \\ \underline{4m + 3} \end{array}$ **23.** $\begin{array}{r} -2t - 7 \\ \underline{6t - 3} \end{array}$

24. $\begin{array}{r} 5k - 6l + 4 \\ \underline{-5k + 8l + 2} \end{array}$ **25.** $\begin{array}{r} 6x^2 - 2xy + 3y^2 \\ \underline{4x^2 - xy - y^2} \end{array}$

26. $\begin{array}{r} 2m^2 - 3mn - 5n \\ \underline{-8m^2 \qquad\quad - n} \end{array}$ **27.** $\begin{array}{r} 5a^2 - 6ab \\ \underline{-2a^2 + 9ab - b^2} \end{array}$

28–35. In Exercises 20–27, subtract the lower polynomial from the upper one.

Simplify. **(4-3, 4-4)**

36. $e^6 \cdot e^3 \cdot e$ **37.** $(4f^3)(2f^4)$ **38.** $(-3c^2d)(-4cd^2)$

39. $(-2gh^2)(5g^3h)$ **40.** $(3mn)(6m^2n)(2n^2)$ **41.** $(-5j^4k^2)(4jl^3)(-3kl^2)$

42. $\left(\frac{8}{3}x^5y\right)\left(\frac{9}{2}xy^6\right)$ **43.** $(-6a^3)\left(\frac{1}{6}a^3\right)$ **44.** $(3u^2v)(-7v^3)\left(\frac{4}{9}u^2\right)$

45. $3^w \cdot 3^{5-w} \cdot 3$ **46.** $4^2 \cdot 4^{a+1} \cdot 4^a$ **47.** $2^5 \cdot 2^{b+3} \cdot 2^{3-b}$

48. $(3p^5)(5p^2) + (7p^3)(2p^4)$ **49.** $(8d^3)(2d^7) - (3d^6)(4d^4)$

50. $(w^5)^2$ **51.** $(x^2)^5$ **52.** $y^2 \cdot y^5$ **53.** $z^n \cdot z^n$

54. $(a^n)^3$ **55.** $(b^3)^n$ **56.** $c^3 \cdot c^n$ **57.** $d^n \cdot d^n \cdot d^n$

58. $(5f)^2$ **59.** $(gh)^4$ **60.** $(6m^3)^2$ **61.** $(4mn^5)^3$

62. $(2u^3v)^5$ **63.** $(3a^5b^4)^2$ **64.** $(-7x^4)^2$ **65.** $-(8x^5)^3$

66. $(3k)^2(3k)^4$ **67.** $(-2x^3)^3 \cdot (5x^2)^2$ **68.** $-(4t^2)^2(3t)^3$ **69.** $(5x^2y)^3 \cdot 3xy^2$

Multiply. (4-5, 4-6)

70. $7(x + 3)$ **71.** $5(y - 4)$ **72.** $-3(n - 2)$ **73.** $-8(1 + 4m)$

74. $3n(n + 5)$ **75.** $-4t(3 - 2t)$ **76.** $6k(2k - 7)$ **77.** $-5h(8h + 3)$

78. $9a(a^2 - 3a - 4)$ **79.** $-5b^2(3b^2 - 2b + 6)$

80. $\frac{1}{3}c(6c^2 - 3cd + 9d^2)$ **81.** $\frac{1}{2}uv^2(10u^2 - 4uv + 8v^2)$

82. $(m + 4)(m + 2)$ **83.** $(n - 3)(n + 5)$ **84.** $(a - 6)(a - 7)$

85. $(5x - 2)(x + 7)$ **86.** $(4y - 2)(3y - 1)$ **87.** $(6m + 4)(5m + 3)$

88. $(u + 3)(u^2 + 2u + 5)$ **89.** $(v - 1)(3v^2 + 4v + 7)$ **90.** $(3c - 5)(2c^2 - c + 8)$

91. $\begin{array}{r} 7x - 4y \\ \underline{3x - 2y} \end{array}$ **92.** $\begin{array}{r} 5a - 8b \\ \underline{4a + b} \end{array}$ **93.** $\begin{array}{l} e^2 + ef + f^2 \\ \underline{e + f } \end{array}$ **94.** $\begin{array}{l} 3m^2 - 4mn + n^2 \\ \underline{5m + n } \end{array}$

Solve the given formula for the variable shown in color. State the restrictions, if any, for the formula obtained to be meaningful. (4-7)

95. $A = \frac{1}{2}ap$; a **96.** $V = \frac{1}{3}Bh$; h **97.** $A = \frac{1}{2}h(b_1 + b_2)$; b_1

98. $y = mx + b$; b **99.** $A = \pi r^2$; r **100.** $S = (n - 2)180$; n

101. $F = \frac{9}{5}C + 32$; C **102.** $P = \frac{A}{1 + rt}$; A **103.** $r = \frac{I}{Pt}$; t

Solve. Use a chart to help you solve the problem. (4-8)

104. Two buses leave a depot at the same time, one traveling north and the other south. The speed of the northbound bus is 15 mi/h greater than the speed of the southbound bus. After 3 h on the road, the buses are 255 mi apart. What are their speeds?

105. Exactly 10 min after Alex left his grandparents' house, his cousin Alison set out from there to overtake him. Alex drives at 36 mi/h. Alison drives at 40 mi/h. How long did it take Alison to overtake Alex?

106. A plane flew from the Sky City airport to the Plainsville airport at 800 km/h and then returned to Sky City at 900 km/h. The return trip took 30 min less than the flight to Plainsville. How far apart are the airports and how long did the trip to Plainsville take?

107. A poster is three times as long as it is wide. It is framed by a mat such that there is a 4 in. border around the poster. Find the dimensions of the poster if the area of the mat is 488 in^2. (4-9)

108. A square piece of remnant material is on sale. A rectangular piece of the same material, whose length is 1 yd longer than a side of the square and whose width is $\frac{5}{9}$ yd shorter than a side of the square, is also on sale. If the square and the rectangle have the same area and you purchase both remnants, how much material will you get?

Chapter 5

List all pairs of factors of each integer. (5-1)

1. 42 **2.** 80 **3.** 91 **4.** 72 **5.** 52

6–10. Find the prime factorization of each integer in Exercises 1–5.

Give the GCF of each group of numbers. (5-1)

11. 126, 168 **12.** 144, 84 **13.** 65, 52 **14.** 90, 330

Simplify. Assume that no denominator equals 0. (5-2)

15. $\frac{12x^5}{4x}$ **16.** $\frac{25m^4n}{-15mn^6}$ **17.** $\frac{-7ab}{21ab^5}$ **18.** $\frac{-8(uv)^7}{-10(uv)^5}$

19. $\frac{(w^4)^2}{(w^5)^4}$ **20.** $\frac{(5k)^2}{5k^2}$ **21.** $\frac{(-3y)^3}{(y^3)^2}$ **22.** $\frac{(2c^5)(4c^3)}{(8c^2)^3}$

Divide. (5-3)

23. $\frac{12e + 8}{4}$ **24.** $\frac{6x - 9y + 12}{3}$ **25.** $\frac{2x^3 + 6x^2 + x}{x}$

26. $\frac{18ab - 24a^2}{-6a}$ **27.** $\frac{15m - 25m^2 - 5m^3}{5m}$ **28.** $\frac{28h^5k^3 - 35hk^2}{7hk^2}$

Factor each polynomial as the product of its greatest monomial factor and another polynomial. (5-3)

29. $15w^2 - 10w + 5$ **30.** $9x^2 + 18x$ **31.** $7u^3 + 14u^2$

32. $12a^3 - 6a^2 + 18a$ **33.** $15c^2 + 3cd$ **34.** $8m^2n - 24mn^2$

Write each product as a trinomial. (5-4)

35. $(x + 5)(x + 3)$ **36.** $(b - 2)(b - 4)$ **37.** $(n - 3)(n + 7)$

38. $(e - 8)(e + 6)$ **39.** $(3 + m)(2 + m)$ **40.** $(3f + 2)(f + 5)$

41. $(4y - 3)(2y - 1)$ **42.** $(8z + 7)(z - 2)$ **43.** $(5n - 3)(4n - 2)$

44. $a(6a - 4)(5a - 3)$ **45.** $h(3h + 7)(4h + 9)$ **46.** $2x(9x - 1)(2x + 3)$

Write each product as a binomial. (5-5)

47. $(k - 5)(k + 5)$ **48.** $(3 - y)(3 + y)$ **49.** $(4d - 8)(4d + 8)$

50. $(w^2 - 6)(w^2 + 6)$ **51.** $(5m^2 + n)(5m^2 - n)$ **52.** $(ab + c^2)(ab - c^2)$

Factor. You may use a calculator or the table of squares. (5-5)

53. $16e^2 - 9$ **54.** $36u^2 - 25$ **55.** $81 - f^2$ **56.** $144a^2 - 64b^2$

57. $49 - 100y^2$ **58.** $v^4 - w^4$ **59.** $s^6 - 4$ **60.** $16x^8 - 625$

Express each square as a trinomial. (5-6)

61. $(g + 7)^2$
62. $(k - 3)^2$
63. $(2x + 6)^2$
64. $(5y - 3)^2$
65. $(2m + 3n)^2$
66. $(7a - 5b)^2$
67. $(ef - 8)^2$
68. $(-4 + 9f)^2$

Factor. (5-6)

69. $x^2 - 6x + 9$
70. $e^2 + 18e + 81$
71. $4 - 28h + 49h^2$
72. $64x^2 + 80xy + 25y^2$
73. $4m^2 - 36mn + 81n^2$
74. $16w^2 + 24wz + 9z^2$

Factor. Check by multiplying the factors. If the polynomial is not factorable, write *prime*. (5-7, 5-8, 5-9)

75. $k^2 + 8k + 7$
76. $v^2 - 9v + 20$
77. $a^2 - 2a + 1$
78. $35 + 12u + u^2$
79. $n^2 - 16n + 48$
80. $w^2 + 18w + 80$
81. $x^2 + 13xy + 42y^2$
82. $m^2 - 10mn + 21n^2$
83. $e^2 - 15ef + 44f^2$
84. $c^2 + 3c - 18$
85. $x^2 - 2x - 35$
86. $k^2 + 8k - 32$
87. $h^2 - 7h - 18$
88. $b^2 + 7b - 30$
89. $y^2 - 4y - 45$
90. $a^2 - 2ab - 3b^2$
91. $u^2 + 3uv - 4v^2$
92. $m^2 - mn - 20n^2$
93. $2x^2 + 11x + 12$
94. $10e^2 - 12e + 3$
95. $10d^2 + d - 3$
96. $-10 - 26y - 12y^2$
97. $-7 - 39z - 18z^2$
98. $-10 + 24z - 8z^2$
99. $15x^2 + 13xy + 2y^2$
100. $8a^2 - 22ab + 12b^2$
101. $14m^2 - mn - 3n^2$

Factor. Check by multiplying. (5-10)

102. $8(m - 3) - 5m(3 - m)$
103. $6a(a + 2) + 4(a + 2)$
104. $u(u - 2v) - (2v - u)$
105. $b(b - 2)(b + 1) - 3 - 3b$
106. $a^2 + 2a + ab + 2b$
107. $7cw + 3c - 7w^2 - 3w$
108. $n^3 + n^2 - 6n - 6$
109. $64 - 64m^2 + m^4 - m^6$

Factor completely. Check by multiplying. (5-11)

110. $42x^3 + 68x^2 + 16x$
111. $60y^3 - 18y^2 - 6y$
112. $12x^5 - 20x^4 + 3x^3$
113. $16a^4 - 144a^2$
114. $4n^5 - 100n$
115. $28w^7 - 102w^5$
116. $36m^2 + 24mn + 4n^2$
117. $24cd - 12c^2 - 12d^2$
118. $-7x^3 + 14x^2y - 7xy^2$

Solve and check. (5-12)

119. $(a + 13)(a + 8) = 0$
120. $(f - 16)(f - 27) = 0$
121. $(2x - 4)(3x - 5) = 0$
122. $(6h - 5)(6h + 5) = 0$
123. $7w(4w + 3) = 0$
124. $m(2m + 7)(3m - 4) = 0$
125. $a^2 + 7a + 6 = 0$
126. $q^2 - 21q = -20$
127. $d^2 = 14d - 45$
128. $y^2 - 7y - 18 = 0$
129. $c^2 - 36 = -5c$
130. $h^2 = -3h + 54$
131. $6 - 23z - 4z^2 = 0$
132. $3m^2 + 1 = 4m$
133. $2n^2 = 10 + n$
134. $e^2 - 49 = 0$
135. $36g^2 = 16$
136. $w^3 - 9w = 0$

137. The sum of a number and its square is 56. Find the number. **(5-13)**

138. Find two consecutive negative odd integers whose product is 143.

139. The length of a rectangle is 5 cm less than twice the width. If the area of the rectangle is 88 cm^2, find the dimensions of the rectangle.

140. Find two numbers that total 12 and whose squares total 74.

Chapter 6

Simplify. Give the restrictions on the variable. **(6-1)**

1. $\frac{5m - 15}{m - 3}$ **2.** $\frac{2a + 1}{6a + 3}$ **3.** $\frac{7c - 7d}{7c + 7d}$ **4.** $\frac{6k - k^2}{36 - k^2}$

5. $\frac{3uv}{u^2v - v^2u}$ **6.** $\frac{8w^3}{8w^2 - 12w}$ **7.** $\frac{x^2 - 64}{x^2 - x - 56}$ **8.** $\frac{(e - 7)^2}{49 - e^2}$

9. $\frac{15m + 6n}{25m^2 - 4n^2}$ **10.** $\frac{a^2 + ab}{a^2 - ab}$

11. $\frac{(k - 3)(7k - 2)}{(2 - 7k)(k - 3)}$ **12.** $\frac{3x^2 + 17xy + 20y^2}{3x^2 - xy - 10y^2}$

13. $\frac{14 - 9t + t^2}{t^2 - 4}$ **14.** $\frac{u^2 - v^2}{u^2 + 2uv + v^2}$

15. $\frac{(5w - x)^5}{(x - 5w)^7}$ **16.** $\frac{(4s - 6)^2(3s - 2)}{(2 - 3s)(6 - 4s)}$

Multiply. Express each product in simplest form. **(6-2)**

17. $\frac{5}{8} \cdot \frac{32}{15}$ **18.** $\frac{4}{3} \cdot \frac{3}{5} \cdot \frac{5}{7}$ **19.** $\left(\frac{-2}{5}\right)^2 \cdot \frac{15}{16}$ **20.** $\left(-\frac{3}{2}\right)^3 \cdot \frac{24}{9}$

21. $\frac{e}{f} \cdot \frac{f}{g} \cdot \frac{g}{h}$ **22.** $\frac{5}{w} \cdot \frac{w^2}{10}$ **23.** $\frac{8m}{3} \cdot \frac{9}{12m}$ **24.** $\frac{a^2}{3b} \cdot \frac{b^2}{4a}$

25. $\frac{14v}{12v^2} \cdot \frac{4uw^2}{7v^2}$ **26.** $\frac{a + 5}{a} \cdot \frac{a^2}{a^2 - 25}$

27. $\frac{4x - xy}{8x^2y} \cdot \frac{2}{16 - y^2}$ **28.** $\frac{m + n}{m - n} \cdot \frac{m^2 - n^2}{3m + 3n}$

Simplify. Use the rules of exponents for a power of a product and a power of a quotient. **(6-2)**

29. $(5k^3)^2$ **30.** $\left(\frac{x}{7}\right)^2$ **31.** $\left(\frac{3x}{4}\right)^2$ **32.** $\left(\frac{2m}{3n^2}\right)^3$

33. $\left(-\frac{x^2}{5}\right)^3$ **34.** $\left(\frac{e}{f}\right)^3 \cdot \frac{e}{f}$ **35.** $\left(\frac{4c}{d}\right)^3 \cdot \frac{c^2}{8}$ **36.** $\left(\frac{7a}{b}\right)^2 \cdot \frac{3ab}{14}$

Divide. Express the answers in simplest form. (6-3)

37. $\frac{4}{9} \div \frac{16}{3}$

38. $\frac{a^2}{4} \div \frac{a}{12}$

39. $\frac{m}{3n} \div \frac{mn}{6}$

40. $\frac{8x^2}{5y} \div 4xy$

41. $\frac{e+f}{5} \div \frac{3e+3f}{15}$

42. $\frac{u^2 - v^2}{u^2 + v^2} \div (u + v)$

43. $\frac{5}{n^2 - 25} \div \frac{5n - 15}{n + 5}$

44. $\frac{4n - 12}{4} \div \frac{5n - 15}{8}$

45. $\frac{x^4 - y^4}{2x^2 + 8x} \div \frac{x^2 + y^2}{x^2 - 16}$

46. $\frac{4a^2 - 25}{6a^2} \div \frac{12a - 30}{3a^4}$

47. $\frac{m^2 + n^2}{8s - 10t} \div \frac{7m + 7n}{4t - 6s}$

Simplify. (6-3)

48. $\frac{1}{3} \div \frac{2}{6} \cdot \frac{5}{7}$

49. $\frac{x}{7} \div \frac{y^2}{x} \cdot \frac{7}{y}$

50. $\frac{e^2}{3} \cdot \frac{f^2}{e} \div \frac{e}{f}$

51. $\left(\frac{c}{3}\right)^2 \div \frac{c}{9} \cdot \frac{c}{3}$

52. $\left(\frac{w}{4}\right)^2 \div \left(\frac{w}{8} \cdot \frac{w}{2}\right)$

53. $\frac{a - b}{a + 3b} \cdot \frac{3b + a}{b + a} \div \frac{b - a}{b + a}$

Complete. (6-4)

54. $\frac{5x}{11} = \frac{?}{33}$

55. $\frac{h - 4}{7} = \frac{?}{14}$

56. $\frac{3k - 5}{2} = \frac{?}{8}$

57. $\frac{6m - n}{7} = \frac{?}{35}$

58. $\frac{c}{d} = \frac{?}{c^3d}$

59. $\frac{4s}{5t} = \frac{?}{15st^2}$

60. $\frac{8}{7d + 2} = \frac{?}{(7d + 2)^2}$

61. $\frac{5}{e - 1} = \frac{?}{e^2 - 1}$

62. $\frac{3}{h - 2} = \frac{?}{2 - h}$

63. $\frac{5}{z - 3} = \frac{?}{z^2 - 3z}$

64. $\frac{w}{w + 4} = \frac{?}{w^2 + 4w}$

65. $\frac{3}{a^2b} = \frac{?}{a^3b^2}$

Write each group of fractions with their LCD. (6-4)

66. $\frac{2}{3}, \frac{4}{5}, \frac{3}{7}$

67. $\frac{x - 2}{16}, \frac{x + 3}{12}$

68. $\frac{3m - n}{10}, \frac{3m + n}{15}$

69. $\frac{1}{3cd}, \frac{4}{cd^2}$

70. $\frac{7}{e + f}, \frac{5}{e}, \frac{6}{f}$

71. $\frac{2w}{3x - 9}, \frac{1}{x^2 - 9}$

Simplify. (6-5)

72. $\frac{3}{a} + \frac{5}{a} - \frac{4}{a}$

73. $\frac{7}{2x} + \frac{6}{2x} - \frac{5}{2x}$

74. $\frac{u}{7} - \frac{3u + 5}{7}$

75. $\frac{k + 3}{5} - \frac{2k + 7}{5}$

76. $\frac{c}{c - 3} + \frac{1}{c - 3} - \frac{8 - c}{c - 3}$

77. $\frac{4}{g - 3} - \frac{3}{3 - g}$

78. $\frac{3m}{m - n} + \frac{3n}{n - m}$

79. $\frac{5}{y^2} + \frac{3}{y}$

80. $\frac{4}{5x} - \frac{1}{15x^2}$

81. $\frac{1}{5wx} - \frac{3}{10w}$

82. $\frac{3k - 2}{2k^3} + \frac{6}{k^2}$

83. $\frac{2}{3(x + 2)} + \frac{x}{x + 2}$

84. $\frac{5a-4}{6}+\frac{a-2}{9}$ **85.** $\frac{2h+4}{8}-\frac{h}{4}+\frac{3h-2}{10}$ **86.** $\frac{4(m-n)}{16}-\frac{3(m+n)}{12}$

87. $\frac{3}{x+2}-\frac{1}{x+3}$ **88.** $\frac{3z}{z^2-16}+\frac{z}{z-4}$ **89.** $\frac{u}{u-4}+\frac{3}{4-u}$

Write each expression as a fraction in simplest form. **(6-6)**

90. $7\frac{1}{3}$ **91.** $5+\frac{1}{n}$ **92.** $4m-\frac{3}{m}$ **93.** $\frac{x}{y}+3$

94. $6-\frac{5}{k+3}$ **95.** $\frac{n}{n-2}+7$ **96.** $\frac{x+3}{x}-2$ **97.** $8h-\frac{h}{h+3}$

98. $3y+\frac{y}{2y+7}$ **99.** $5-\frac{e+3}{e^2-1}$ **100.** $a+\frac{5a+3}{a+3}$ **101.** $2w-\frac{w+3}{w-3}$

102. $n-\frac{7}{n+2}-\frac{3n-1}{n+2}$ **103.** $\frac{v}{u+v}+\frac{u}{v-u}+1$ **104.** $\frac{x}{x-4}+\frac{x}{x+4}-3$

Divide. Write the answer as a polynomial or mixed expression. **(6-7)**

105. $\frac{x^2+7x+10}{x+2}$ **106.** $\frac{y^2-2y-35}{y-7}$ **107.** $\frac{a^2-5a-3}{a+2}$ **108.** $\frac{n^2-16}{n+4}$

109. $\frac{7+k^2-4k}{k-5}$ **110.** $\frac{8y^2+6}{2y-1}$ **111.** $\frac{b^3-1}{b+1}$ **112.** $\frac{x^3+5}{x+3}$

113. $\frac{w^3+w^2+2w-4}{w-1}$ **114.** $\frac{u^3+2u^2-16}{u-2}$ **115.** $\frac{2n^2-13n+20}{2n-5}$

116. $\frac{2-9h+7h^2}{7h-2}$ **117.** $\frac{v^3+v^2+v+1}{v-2}$ **118.** $\frac{5n^2+6n^3+9}{3+2n}$

Chapter 7

Write each ratio in simplest form. **(7-1)**

1. 40 s:2 min **2.** 4 m:250 cm **3.** 3 kg:45 g

4. $6y:15y$ **5.** $36d^2:10d$ **6.** $(4a)^2:6a$

7. The ratio of old cars to new cars if there are 180 cars and 55 are new.

8. The ratio of wins to losses for a baseball team that played 84 games and won 48 of them.

Solve each proportion. **(7-2)**

9. $\frac{3}{5}=\frac{x}{15}$ **10.** $\frac{5}{7}=\frac{25}{a}$ **11.** $\frac{24}{7}=\frac{4}{c}$

12. $\frac{3x}{2}=\frac{2}{5}$ **13.** $\frac{15a}{64}=\frac{45}{32}$ **14.** $\frac{17d}{25}=\frac{51}{125}$

15. $\frac{x-4}{x}=\frac{7}{9}$ **16.** $\frac{3w}{10w+2}=\frac{2}{7}$ **17.** $\frac{8a-5}{5a-4}=\frac{13}{8}$

Solve and check. If the equation has no solution, write *No Solution*. (7-3, 7-4)

18. $\frac{a}{3} - \frac{a}{9} = 2$

19. $\frac{2x}{3} - \frac{x}{2} = 12$

20. $\frac{6}{7}x - \frac{1}{2}x = 5$

21. $\frac{2}{3}x - \frac{5}{9}x = -1$

22. $\frac{y+2}{2} = \frac{2y}{3}$

23. $\frac{x+1}{5} - \frac{3}{2} = \frac{3x-6}{10}$

24. $\frac{12}{z} = \frac{4+4z}{z}$

25. $\frac{1}{x} + \frac{1}{3} = \frac{1}{2}$

26. $\frac{4}{5y} + \frac{y-2}{y} = -\frac{1}{5}$

27. $\frac{c}{c+3} = \frac{2}{5}$

28. $\frac{3m+5}{6} - \frac{10}{m} = \frac{m}{2}$

29. $\frac{h}{2h+4} - \frac{1}{h+2} = 1$

Evaluate. (7-5)

30. 80% of 700

31. 45% of 450

32. 3.25% of 48

33. 18 is 60% of what number?

34. 63 is 150% of what number?

35. What percent of 180 is 45?

36. What percent of 36 is 54?

Solve. (7-5, 7-6, 7-7, 7-8)

37. $1.2x = 48$

38. $0.6z = 180$

39. $0.08y = 64$

40. $0.4a - 0.7 = 2.9$

41. $0.3b + 0.03b = 99$

42. $0.05c = 6.6 - 0.06c$

43. How many kilograms of zinc are contained in 30 kg of an alloy containing 28% zinc?

44. Ed Jefferson bought a new suit that cost \$140. If he also paid \$6.30 in sales tax, find the sales tax rate.

45. A camera that originally cost \$150 is on sale at 15% off the original price. Find the sale price.

46. How many kilograms of water must be added to 12 kg of a 30% salt solution to produce a 20% solution?

47. How many kilograms of water must be evaporated from 40 kg of a 10% salt solution to produce a 25% solution?

48. A coin-sorting machine can sort a certain number of coins in 15 min. A second machine can sort the same number of coins in 30 min. How long would it take both machines working together to do the job?

49. An air conditioner takes 20 min to cool a room. If a second air conditioner is used together with the first, it takes only 12 min to cool the room. How long would it take the second air conditioner alone to cool the room?

Evaluate. (7-9)

50. 6^{-2}

51. 5^{-3}

52. 7^{-2}

53. 9^{-3}

54. $2^{-4} \cdot 2^{-3}$

55. $(6^{-2})^{-1}$

56. $\frac{3^{-4}}{3^{-3}}$

57. $\frac{8^{-2}}{8^{-4}}$

Simplify. Give answers in terms of positive exponents. (7-9)

58. $5y^{-2}$ **59.** $(9y)^{-3}$ **60.** x^2y^{-5} **61.** $a^{-2}b^{-3}$

62. $uv^{-2}w^{-1}$ **63.** $d^{-4}e^2f^{-2}$ **64.** $(a^{-2}b^3)^2$ **65.** $(x^{-4}y^{-5}z^3)^{-3}$

Write each of the following numbers in scientific notation. (7-10)

66. 64,800,000 **67.** 147,000,000 **68.** 643 billion

69. 0.0000098 **70.** 0.000000006 **71.** 0.00000000001

Chapter 8

State whether each ordered pair of numbers is a solution of the given equation. (8-1)

1. $x - 2y = 6$
$(3, 0), (0, -3)$

2. $x + 3y = 9$
$(3, 2), (-3, 4)$

3. $2x - y = 5$
$(4, -1), (1, -7)$

4. $2x + 3y = 7$
$(1, 2), (5, -1)$

5. $4x + 2y = 6$
$\left(\frac{3}{2}, 0\right), (1, 1)$

6. $-3x + 4y = -7$
$(1, -1), \left(2, \frac{1}{4}\right)$

Solve each equation if *x* and *y* are whole numbers. (8-1)

7. $x + 2y = 8$ **8.** $3x + y = 5$ **9.** $4x + 3y = 12$

10. $xy = 5$ **11.** $x + 4y = 10$ **12.** $2xy + 12 = 14$

Graph each equation. (8-2)

13. $y = -7$ **14.** $x = 4$ **15.** $y = 3x + 2$

16. $y = 2x - 5$ **17.** $5x = 3y$ **18.** $8x - 2y = 0$

19. $3x + y = -6$ **20.** $4x + 3y = 12$ **21.** $2x + 3y = 7$

Find the slope of the line through the given points. (8-3)

22. $(1, 2), (4, 6)$ **23.** $(-7, 1), (-1, 2)$ **24.** $(-1, 6), (0, 0)$

25. $(-4, -3), (2, -3)$ **26.** $(2, 1), (8, -2)$ **27.** $(-7, -7), (6, -4)$

Find the slope of each line. If the line has no slope, say so.

28. $y = 7x - 3$ **29.** $x = 5$ **30.** $3x - 2y = 8$

31. $y - 9 = 0$ **32.** $5x + 4y = 16$ **33.** $y = 1 - x$

Determine whether the given points are collinear. (8-3)

34. $(2, 1), (0, -3), (4, 5), (-2, -7)$ **35.** $(0, 4), (9, -2), (-3, 6), (6, 0)$

36. $(-3, -2), (2, -4), (6, -5), (-5, 2)$ **37.** $(-5, 3), (0, 3), (5, 3), (-2, 3)$

Through the given point, draw a line with the given slope. (8-3)

38. $P(3, 1)$; slope 2
39. $P(-4, 5)$; slope 0
40. $P(0, -6)$; slope 5
41. $P(7, 0)$; slope -3
42. $P(-2, -3)$; slope $\frac{1}{4}$
43. $P(3, 4)$; slope $-\frac{2}{3}$

Change each equation to the slope-intercept form. Use only the slope and *y*-intercept to draw the graph of each equation. (8-4)

44. $x + y = -3$
45. $7x = 2y$
46. $4x - y = 3$
47. $2x + 2y = 6$
48. $-x + 5y = 10$
49. $3x - 4y - 5 = 0$

Use the slope-intercept form to show that the lines whose equations are given are parallel. (8-4)

50. $x - y = 2$
$y - x = -3$

51. $3x - 2y = 6$
$-2y = 12 - 3x$

52. $-x - 5y = 1$
$2x + 10y = 2$

Write an equation in slope-intercept form of the line that has the given slope and *y*-intercept. (8-5)

53. $m = 3, b = \frac{1}{2}$
54. $m = -4, b = \frac{3}{5}$
55. $m = \frac{1}{3}, b = 6$
56. $m = 0, b = -3.5$
57. $m = -\frac{3}{7}, b = \frac{3}{8}$
58. $m = -1.5, b = 2.7$

Write an equation in slope-intercept form of the line that has the given slope and passes through the given point. (8-5)

59. $m = 3$; $(-3, -5)$
60. $m = -2$; $(3, -4)$
61. $m = \frac{3}{4}$; $(0, -2)$
62. $m = 0$; $\left(\frac{1}{2}, 3\right)$
63. $m = -\frac{1}{5}$; $(-5, 0)$
64. $m = \frac{7}{3}$; $(3, 7)$

Write an equation in slope-intercept form of the line passing through the points. (8-5)

65. $(2, 1), (6, 4)$
66. $(2, -1), (1, -7)$
67. $(0, 0), (6, -1)$
68. $(-3, 2), (-3, -4)$
69. $(-2, 8), (1, 2)$
70. $(6, -4), (-7, -7)$

State the domain and range of the function shown by each table. (8-6)

71.

Longest Suspension Bridges	
Mackinac Straits	3800 ft
Humber Estuary	4626 ft
Golden Gate	4200 ft
Ataturk	3524 ft
Verrazano Narrows	4260 ft

72.

Airports in U.S.	
1930	1782
1940	2331
1950	6403
1960	6881
1970	11,261

73. Make a bar graph for the function shown in Exercise 71.

74. Make a broken-line graph for the function shown in Exercise 72.

Given $f: x \to 5 - 3x$, find the following values of f. (8-7)

75. $f(4)$ **76.** $f\left(-\frac{1}{3}\right)$ **77.** $f(0)$ **78.** $f(-5)$

Given $G(n) = n^3 + 2n$, find the following values of G. (8-7)

79. $G(0)$ **80.** $G(-2)$ **81.** $G\left(\frac{1}{2}\right)$ **82.** $G(3)$

Find all the values of each function. (8-7)

83. $h(x) = 5 - 2x - x^2$, $D = \{1, 2, 3\}$

84. $M(u) = \frac{6}{4u + 2}$, $D = \{-1, 0, 1\}$

Find the range of each function. (8-7)

85. $r: z \to -3 - 4z$, $D = \{-2, -1, 0\}$

86. $N: s \to \frac{10}{s - 3}$, $D = \{2, 4, 8\}$

87. $G: w \to (w - 1)(w + 1)$, $D = \{-2, 0, 2\}$

88. $k: v \to v^2 - 4v + 2$, $D = \{3, 4, 5\}$

Find the vertex and the axis of symmetry of the graph of each equation. Use the vertex and at least four other points to graph the equation. (8-8)

89. $y = 4x^2$ **90.** $y = -2x^2$ **91.** $y = \frac{1}{5}x^2$

92. $y = -x^2 + 3x$ **93.** $y = x^2 - 2x + 5$ **94.** $y = 4 - \frac{1}{2}x^2$

Find the vertex. Then give the least value of the function. (8-8)

95. $f: x \to x^2 + 7x$ **96.** $g: x \to x^2 - 3x - 4$ **97.** $h: x \to \frac{1}{2}x^2$

Find the vertex. Then give the greatest value of the function. (8-8)

98. $f(x) = x - 3x^2$ **99.** $g(x) = 2 - \frac{1}{3}x^2$ **100.** $h(x) = -x^2 - x - 1$

In Exercises 101 and 102, find the constant of variation. (8-9)

101. y varies directly as x, and $y = 12$ when $x = 60$.

102. q is directly proportional to p, and $q = 144$ when $p = 24$.

103. If n varies directly as m, and $n = 300$ when $m = 5$, find n when $m = 15$.

104. If b is directly proportional to a, and $b = 28.7$ when $a = 4.1$, find b when $a = 13$.

(x_1, y_1) and (x_2, y_2) are ordered pairs of the same direct variation. Find each missing value. (8-9)

105. $x_1 = 35$, $y_1 = 7$
$x_2 = 105$, $y_2 = \underline{\ ?\ }$

106. $x_1 = 5.2$, $y_1 = 5$
$x_2 = \underline{\ ?\ }$, $y_2 = 1$

107. $x_1 = \frac{3}{8}$, $y_1 = \underline{\ ?\ }$
$x_2 = \frac{2}{5}$, $y_2 = \frac{1}{10}$

For each variation described, state (a) a formula and (b) a proportion. (8-9, 8-10)

108. The circumference, C, of a circle is directly proportional to the diameter, d, of the circle.

109. The elongation, e, of a coil spring varies directly as the mass, m, suspended from it.

110. The length, l, of the shadow of a vertical object at a given time and location varies directly with the height, h, of the object.

111. The monthly rent, r, for each roommate in an apartment is inversely proportional to the number, n, of roommates.

112. The height, h, of a triangle of constant area varies inversely as the base length, b.

113. The number of tickets remaining to be sold, n, varies inversely as the number of tickets sold, s.

Graph each equation if the domain and the range are both the set of non-zero real numbers. (8-10)

114. $xy = 4$ **115.** $3xy = 1$ **116.** $x = \frac{10}{y}$ **117.** $\frac{x}{2} = \frac{4}{y}$

(x_1, y_1) and (x_2, y_2) are ordered pairs of the same inverse variation. Find each missing value. (8-10)

118. $x_1 = 5,\ y_1 = 8$
$x_2 = 4,\ y_2 = \underline{\ ?\ }$

119. $x_1 = 0.6,\ y_1 = 1.2$
$x_2 = \underline{\ ?\ },\ y_2 = 0.4$

120. $x_1 = \frac{1}{4},\ y_1 = \underline{\ ?\ }$
$x_2 = \frac{1}{6},\ y_2 = \frac{1}{2}$

Chapter 9

Solve each system by the graphic method. (9-1)

1. $x + y = 6$
$x - y = 2$

2. $x + y = 9$
$y = 2x$

3. $x + y = 0$
$x + 2y = 2$

4. $y = 3 - x$
$x + y = 5$

5. $y = \frac{2}{3}x + 1$
$y = -\frac{2}{3}x + 5$

6. $y = \frac{1}{2}x + 1$
$x + 2 = 2y$

Solve by the substitution method. (9-2)

7. $3x + y = 5$
$y = 2x$

8. $m - 3n = -4$
$2m + 6n = 5$

9. $2a + b = 4$
$b = 1 - a$

10. $4c - 3d = 9$
$2c - d = 5$

11. $x + 3y = 2$
$2x + 3y = 7$

12. $3x - 2y = 5$
$x + 2y = 15$

Solve by using a system of two equations in two variables. **(9-3)**

13. On a jury there are 3 fewer men than twice the number of women. If there were 2 more women on the jury, the numbers of men and women would be equal. How many men are on the jury?

14. Janet and Lynn live 8 mi apart in opposite directions from their office. If Lynn lives 1 mi less than twice as far from the office as Janet does, how far does each live from the office?

Solve by the addition-or-subtraction method. **(9-4)**

15. $r - s = -3$
$r + s = 9$

16. $c + 2n = -20$
$c - 2n = 30$

17. $x - 3y = 2$
$x + 4y = 16$

18. $6r + 5y = -8$
$2r - 5y = -16$

19. $12m + 3n = 51$
$7m - 3n = 44$

20. $8g + 7h = 26$
$8g - 10h = 60$

Solve by using multiplication with the addition-or-subtraction method. **(9-5)**

21. $v + w = 3$
$3v - 5w = 17$

22. $4a - 3b = -1$
$a - b = -1$

23. $3x - y = 3$
$x + 3y = 11$

24. $3x + 4y = -25$
$2x - 3y = 6$

25. $2w - 3z = -1$
$3w + 4z = 24$

26. $5a - 2b = 0$
$2a - 3b = -11$

Solve by using a system of two equations in two variables. **(9-6, 9-7)**

27. A plane can fly 1120 km in 80 min with the wind. Flying against the same wind, the plane travels the same distance in 84 min. Find the speed of the wind and the speed of the plane in still air.

28. The sum of the digits of a two-digit number is 7. With the digits reversed the number is 5 times the tens digit of the original number. Find the original number.

29. In five years Jenny will be two thirds as old as her aunt. Three years ago she was half as old as her aunt is now. How old are Jenny and her aunt now?

30. The numerator of a fraction is 1 less than the denominator. If 1 is subtracted from the numerator, and the denominator is unchanged, the resulting fraction has a value of $\frac{3}{4}$. Find the original fraction.

Chapter 10

Classify each statement as true or false. **(10-1)**

1. $-8 > 7 > 6$

2. $-5 < -4 < 5$

3. $-1.5 < -1 < -0.05$

4. $-\frac{1}{2} < 0 < 1$

5. $7 > 0 > 2$

6. $-10 < -15 < -20$

7. $|-0.6| < 0.4$

8. $\left|-\frac{1}{3}\right| \geq 0$

9. $|5 - 3| \leq |3 - 5|$

Solve each inequality if $x \in \{-4, -3, -2, -1, 0, 1, 2, 3, 4\}$. (10-1)

10. $5x \le 15$ **11.** $-7x > 14$ **12.** $-4 - x \ge 0$ **13.** $x^2 < 10$

Graph each inequality over the given domain. (10-1)

14. $4 < x$; {the positive numbers}

15. $-6 \le k < 2$; {the negative integers}

16. $3 > t \ge -4$; {the integers}

17. $-2 < n < 2$; {the real numbers}

Solve each inequality and graph its solution set. (10-2)

18. $e - 8 > 12$ **19.** $13 > n + 9$ **20.** $4q < -20$

21. $-\frac{x}{7} < 14$ **22.** $\frac{m}{3} - 5 > -2$ **23.** $-3 > 7 + \frac{4}{5}k$

24. $5v + 3 > 18$ **25.** $48 - 6y < 0$ **26.** $7n < 6n + 8$

27. $8f - 5 > 4f + 11$ **28.** $-6(v - 3) \le 42$ **29.** $5(m + 2) > 4(m - 1)$

30. $\frac{4}{9}h + 3 \le \frac{1}{3}$ **31.** $2(w - 1) < \frac{3}{2}w$ **32.** $2x - \frac{1}{4}(3x + 8) > 0$

In Exercises 33–37: (10-3)

a. Choose a variable to represent the number indicated in color.

b. Use the variable to write an inequality based on the given information. (Do not solve.)

33. Marquita sold 9 fewer magazine subscriptions than twice the number Juanita sold. Marquita sold at most 43 subscriptions.

34. Rick, who is not yet 16 years old, is 3 years older than Sam. (Sam's age)

35. Andrea lives 10 mi less than half as far as Roger lives from the beach. Andrea lives at least 25 mi from the beach.

36. The number of San Marcos High School students who ride the bus is one third the number who walk or ride their bikes. The total number of students is at least 1800.

37. Six years ago, Buford was less than half as old as he is now. (His present age)

Solve each open sentence and graph its solution set. (10-4)

38. $-3 < n + 5 < 7$ **39.** $-6 < -6 + w \le 2$

40. $-4 \le 3a - 1 < 5$ **41.** $-1 \le 8m + 7 \le 23$

42. $u - 2 < -5$ or $u - 2 \ge 4$ **43.** $k + 6 \le -3$ or $k + 6 > 2$

44. $4n + 3 < -1$ or $4n + 3 > 7$ **45.** $2x - 2 \le -8$ or $8 < 2x - 2$

46. $-5e < 15$ and $6 + 3e < 0$ **47.** $h - 4 \ge 2$ or $4 - h \ge 2$

Solve each open sentence and graph its solution set. (10-5, 10-6)

48. $|v - 6| = 3$
49. $|8 - k| = 5$
50. $|m| > 2\frac{1}{2}$
51. $|x| \leq 1.5$
52. $|y + 5| > 2$
53. $|3 + z| \leq 4$
54. $|7 - f| < 6$
55. $|-4 - g| > 7$
56. $|-a - 2| \geq 1$
57. $4|s| + 2 \leq 8$
58. $5 - 3|z| < 14$
59. $9 - |3 - b| > 2$
60. $|8k| = 16$
61. $\left|\frac{a}{2}\right| \geq 3$
62. $\left|\frac{c}{4}\right| \leq 1$
63. $|5x - 3| = 17$
64. $|7 + 6n| < 19$
65. $|2w - 3| > 5$
66. $\left|\frac{u}{3} + 4\right| = 1$
67. $\left|\frac{v}{2} - 1\right| \leq 3$
68. $\left|\frac{a}{4} + 2\right| \geq 1$
69. $|5 - (3 - 2x)| < 6$
70. $7 + 3|2m + 1| = 13$
71. $10 - 6|2 - k| \geq 22$

Graph each inequality. (10-7)

72. $x < 3$
73. $x \geq -4$
74. $y > 0$
75. $y \leq -2$
76. $y > x - 1$
77. $y \leq -x + 2$
78. $y < 3 + 4x$
79. $y \geq -5x - 1$

Transform each inequality into an equivalent inequality with y as one side. Then graph the inequality. (10-7)

80. $x - y \geq 5$
81. $4x + y \leq -2$
82. $x - 3y > 6$
83. $6x - y < 2$
84. $y - 5x \geq 3$
85. $4y - 5x < 0$
86. $7x + 6y \geq x - 3$
87. $3y - 2 > 6x - 4$
88. $8y - 7 \leq 3(x + 2y)$

Graph each pair of inequalities and indicate the solution set of the system with crosshatching or shading. (10-8)

89. $y \leq 0$, $x > 0$
90. $y \geq -3$, $x \leq 2$
91. $y > 4x$, $x < 3$
92. $x \geq -1$, $y < 2x - 5$
93. $y < x + 3$, $y > 3 - x$
94. $y \leq 5x - 4$, $y \geq 2x + 1$
95. $x + y > 2$, $x - y < 6$
96. $3x - 4y \leq 0$, $x - 2y \geq -6$

Chapter 11

Replace the __?__ with <, =, or > to make a true statement. (11-1)

1. $\frac{17}{23}$ __?__ $\frac{15}{19}$
2. $-\frac{87}{29}$ __?__ $-\frac{39}{13}$
3. $\frac{197}{6}$ __?__ $33\frac{2}{7}$

Arrange each group of numbers in order from least to greatest. (11-1)

4. $-\frac{39}{8}, -4.7, -\frac{41}{9}$
5. $\frac{5}{7}, \frac{2}{3}, \frac{11}{15}, \frac{12}{17}$
6. $-\frac{4}{9}, -\frac{5}{8}, -\frac{6}{11}, -\frac{5}{7}$

Find the number halfway between the given numbers. (11-1)

7. $\frac{27}{41}, \frac{31}{37}$ 8. $-\frac{17}{140}, -\frac{11}{32}$ 9. $-5\frac{2}{7}, 9\frac{1}{4}$

If $x \in \{0, 1, 2, 3\}$ state whether each fraction increases or decreases in value as x takes on its values in increasing order. (11-1)

10. $\frac{5}{x+1}$ 11. $\frac{x-3}{7}$ 12. $\frac{8}{x+2}$ 13. $\frac{6-x}{4}$ 14. $\frac{10}{5+2x}$

Express each rational number as a terminating or repeating decimal. (11-2)

15. $\frac{4}{9}$ 16. $-\frac{29}{24}$ 17. $3\frac{11}{20}$ 18. $-7\frac{5}{11}$ 19. $\frac{41}{55}$

Express each rational number as a fraction in simplest form. (11-2)

20. 0.77 21. $0.\overline{6}$ 22. $-0.31\overline{8}$ 23. $2.\overline{37}$ 24. $0.\overline{4135}$

Find the number halfway between the given numbers. (11-2)

25. $\frac{5}{8}$ and 0.63 26. 0.66 and $0.\overline{6}$ 27. $\frac{7}{11}$ and $0.6\overline{28}$

Express both numbers as fractions. Then find their product. (11-2)

28. $\frac{2}{5}$ and 0.85 29. $0.\overline{4}$ and $\frac{2}{3}$ 30. -2.2 and $0.\overline{3}$

Find the indicated square roots. (11-3)

31. $\sqrt{441}$ 32. $\sqrt{784}$ 33. $\sqrt{2704}$ 34. $\sqrt{5184}$ 35. $\sqrt{10816}$
36. $\sqrt{0.04}$ 37. $\sqrt{0.64}$ 38. $\sqrt{1.96}$ 39. $\sqrt{0.0144}$ 40. $\sqrt{0.0036}$
41. $\sqrt{\frac{81}{225}}$ 42. $\sqrt{\frac{1}{289}}$ 43. $\sqrt{\frac{324}{1936}}$ 44. $\sqrt{\frac{32}{50}}$ 45. $\sqrt{\frac{320}{405}}$

Simplify. (11-4)

46. $\sqrt{63}$ 47. $\sqrt{176}$ 48. $2\sqrt{52}$ 49. $4\sqrt{99}$ 50. $5\sqrt{175}$
51. $10\sqrt{162}$ 52. $\sqrt{192}$ 53. $\sqrt{672}$ 54. $\sqrt{224}$ 55. $\sqrt{2646}$

Approximate to the nearest tenth by using a calculator or the square root table at the back of the book. (11-4)

56. $\sqrt{720}$ 57. $-\sqrt{800}$ 58. $\sqrt{440}$ 59. $\sqrt{8400}$ 60. $-\sqrt{5400}$

Simplify. (11-5)

61. $\sqrt{169m^2}$ 62. $\sqrt{48a^2}$ 63. $\sqrt{125x^4}$ 64. $\sqrt{54e^3}$ 65. $-\sqrt{36t^6}$
66. $\sqrt{98u^2v^2}$ 67. $-2\sqrt{72x^3y^2}$ 68. $\sqrt{324r^4s^6}$ 69. $-\sqrt{4.84w^4}$ 70. $\sqrt{5.76c^6}$

71. $\sqrt{\frac{a^4b^6}{12c^2}}$ 72. $\sqrt{\frac{48u^5v^2}{4uv^4}}$ 73. $\sqrt{\frac{144k^8}{256}}$ 74. $\sqrt{\frac{3600}{81m^{36}}}$ 75. $\sqrt{\frac{225x^{40}}{16}}$

76. $\sqrt{x^2 + 8x + 16}$ 77. $\sqrt{a^2 - 4a + 4}$ 78. $\sqrt{81 + 18k + k^2}$

Solve. **(11-5)**

79. $g^2 = 49$ 80. $h^2 - 64 = 0$ 81. $25m^2 = 16$

82. $9x^2 - 4 = 0$ 83. $6y^2 - 54 = 0$ 84. $32t^2 - 27 = 0$

Find both roots of each equation to the nearest tenth. **(11-5)**

85. $a^2 = 132$ 86. $b^2 - 208 = 0$ 87. $11c^2 = 473$

In Exercises 88–95, refer to the right triangle shown at the right. Find the missing length correct to the nearest hundredth. **(11-6)**

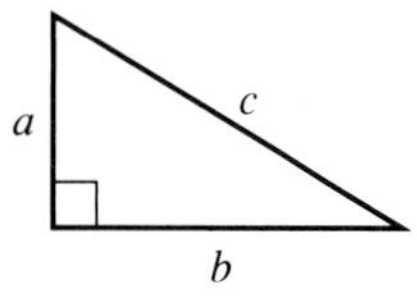

88. $a = 3,\ b = 4,\ c =$ __?__ 89. $a = 5,\ b = 8,\ c =$ __?__

90. $a =$ __?__, $b = 9,\ c = 13$ 91. $a =$ __?__, $b = 10,\ c = 15$

92. $a = 8,\ b =$ __?__, $c = 16$ 93. $a = 20,\ b =$ __?__, $c = 30$

94. $a = 12,\ b = \frac{3}{4}a,\ c =$ __?__ 95. $a = \frac{2}{3}b,\ b = 15,\ c =$ __?__

State whether or not the three numbers given could represent the lengths of the sides of a right triangle. **(11-6)**

96. 21, 28, 35 97. 9, 9, 12 98. 45, 60, 75

99. 31, 41, 51 100. $6a,\ 8a,\ 10a,\ a > 0$ 101. $5a,\ 7a,\ 9a,\ a > 0$

Simplify. **(11-7)**

102. $\sqrt{3} \cdot 4\sqrt{3}$ 103. $2\sqrt{5} \cdot 3\sqrt{5}$ 104. $\sqrt{7} \cdot \sqrt{6} \cdot \sqrt{2}$

105. $\sqrt{7} \cdot \sqrt{7} \cdot \sqrt{4}$ 106. $5\sqrt{2} \cdot \sqrt{3}$ 107. $8\sqrt{162}$

108. $\sqrt{\frac{5}{9}} \cdot \sqrt{\frac{9}{5}}$ 109. $\sqrt{\frac{7}{5}} \cdot \sqrt{\frac{45}{14}}$ 110. $\sqrt{5\frac{5}{6}} \cdot \sqrt{2\frac{4}{7}}$

111. $\frac{1}{4}\sqrt{\frac{16}{3}} \cdot \frac{1}{2}\sqrt{\frac{3}{2}}$ 112. $\frac{12\sqrt{20}}{4\sqrt{3}}$ 113. $\frac{11\sqrt{6}}{\sqrt{98}}$

Simplify. Assume all variables represent positive real numbers. **(11-7)**

114. $(3\sqrt{y})(-5\sqrt{x^2y})$ 115. $\sqrt{n}(\sqrt{n^3} + 3)$ 116. $(7\sqrt{3})(-4\sqrt{6})(5\sqrt{22})$

Simplify. **(11-8)**

117. $9\sqrt{3} - 5\sqrt{3}$ 118. $7\sqrt{2} + 6\sqrt{2}$ 119. $3\sqrt{54} - 2\sqrt{6}$

120. $4\sqrt{28} + 6\sqrt{112}$ 121. $-10\sqrt{18} - 5\sqrt{32}$ 122. $\sqrt{242} - 3\sqrt{363}$

Simplify. (11-8)

123. $\sqrt{8} - \sqrt{\frac{5}{6}}$

124. $\sqrt{\frac{2}{3}} - \sqrt{\frac{3}{2}}$

125. $5\sqrt{\frac{16}{7}} + \sqrt{\frac{9}{8}}$

126. $3\sqrt{63} + 2\sqrt{28} - \sqrt{35}$

127. $\sqrt{120} - \sqrt{270} + \sqrt{300}$

128. $2\sqrt{\frac{5}{3}} + 4\sqrt{\frac{3}{8}} - \frac{1}{2}\sqrt{68}$

129. $3\sqrt{5}(\sqrt{75} - 2\sqrt{12})$

Simplify. (11-9)

130. $(5 - \sqrt{3})(5 + \sqrt{3})$

131. $(\sqrt{7} + 6)(\sqrt{7} - 6)$

132. $(\sqrt{6} - \sqrt{5})(\sqrt{6} + \sqrt{5})$

133. $(4 + \sqrt{2})^2$

134. $(5 - \sqrt{5})^2$

135. $(3\sqrt{2} - 4)^2$

136. $(\sqrt{11} + 3\sqrt{7})^2$

137. $2\sqrt{6}(5\sqrt{2} - 4\sqrt{3})$

138. $(4\sqrt{5} - 6)(2\sqrt{7} + 7)$

139. $(3\sqrt{14} + 2\sqrt{7})(5\sqrt{14} + 3\sqrt{7})$

Rationalize the denominator of each fraction. (11-9)

140. $\frac{5}{3 + \sqrt{7}}$

141. $\frac{2 + \sqrt{3}}{1 - \sqrt{5}}$

Solve. (11-10)

142. $\sqrt{m} = 7$

143. $\sqrt{6x} = \frac{3}{2}$

144. $\sqrt{a} - 5 = 4$

145. $\frac{1}{5} + \sqrt{y} = 1$

146. $\sqrt{\frac{x}{3}} = 6$

147. $\sqrt{n - 2} = 9$

148. $4\sqrt{5t} = 8$

149. $\sqrt{3z} + 2 = 5$

150. $\sqrt{4k - 5} + 1 = 8$

151. $\sqrt{\frac{5u}{2}} - 3 = -2$

152. $\sqrt{\frac{4c - 3}{7}} = 3$

153. $8\sqrt{n} = 24\sqrt{5}$

Chapter 12

Solve. Express irrational solutions in simplest radical form. If the equation has no real-number solution, write "no real-number solution." (12-1)

1. $m^2 = \frac{25}{49}$

2. $5a^2 = 60$

3. $w^2 + 52 = 0$

4. $x^2 - 108 = 0$

5. $7u^2 - 112 = 0$

6. $4c^2 + 7 = 23$

7. $3t^2 - 12 = -3$

8. $2n^2 + 9 = 4$

9. $(v + 5)^2 = 16$

10. $(z - 5)^2 = 6$

11. $3(k + 4)^2 = 81$

12. $4(f - 1)^2 = 60$

13. $2(h + 7)^2 = 42$

14. $(2x + 3)^2 = 100$

15. $7(3y - 1)^2 = 168$

16. $e^2 + 6e + 9 = 64$

17. $a^2 - 12a + 36 = 49$

18. $m^2 + 18m + 81 = 36$

Solve by completing the square. Give irrational roots in simplest form and then approximate them to the nearest tenth. (12-2)

19. $x^2 + 16x = -15$ **20.** $y^2 - 8y + 7 = 0$ **21.** $n^2 - 12n - 202 = 8$

22. $4a^2 + 10a = 12$ **23.** $b^2 - 3b = 5$ **24.** $3c^2 + 6c - 1233 = 0$

Solve the equations by (a) completing the square and (b) factoring. (12-2)

25. $e^2 - 10e + 21 = 0$ **26.** $4f^2 - 18f = 10$ **27.** $6h^2 + 9h - 42 = 0$

Solve. Write irrational roots in simplest radical form. (12-2)

28. $\frac{m^2}{3} - 2m = 7$ **29.** $n^2 + \frac{n}{2} = 5$ **30.** $\frac{x^2}{2} - \frac{x}{4} = 2$

Use the quadratic formula to solve each equation. Give irrational roots in simplest radical form and then approximate them to the nearest tenth. (12-3)

31. $z^2 + 7z + 3 = 0$ **32.** $w^2 + 8w - 4 = 0$ **33.** $2u^2 - 10u - 6 = 0$

34. $5y^2 = -9y - 1$ **35.** $3k^2 + 2 = 5k$ **36.** $6m = 3 - 2m^2$

37. $x^2 + 0.3x - 0.2 = 0$ **38.** $n^2 + \frac{2}{3}n - \frac{1}{2} = 0$ **39.** $\frac{1}{2}y^2 - \frac{7}{2}y = 1$

Write the value of the discriminant of each equation. Then use it to decide how many different real-number roots the equation has. (Do not solve the equations.) (12-4)

40. $x^2 - 6x + 2 = 0$ **41.** $5n^2 + 3n + 7 = 0$ **42.** $-2t^2 + 4t - 2 = 0$

43. $3k^2 - 1.2k + 1.1 = 0$ **44.** $3s^2 + 6s + 3 = 0$ **45.** $\frac{1}{3}b^2 - b - 3 = 0$

Without drawing the graph of the given equation, determine (a) how many *x*-intercepts the parabola has, and (b) whether its vertex lies above, below, or on the *x*-axis. (12-4)

46. $y = 3x^2 + 2x - 5$ **47.** $y = -6 + 3x - 2x^2$ **48.** $y = x^2 - 4x + 16$

Solve each equation by the most appropriate method. Write irrational answers in simplest radical form. (12-5)

49. $x^2 + 7x + 12 = 0$ **50.** $13x^2 = 52$

51. $5x^2 - 9x = 0$ **52.** $3x^2 - 11x = 2$

53. $x^2 + 8x + 3 = 0$ **54.** $(x - 3)^2 = 6$

55. $6x^2 + 4x = 1$ **56.** $\frac{(x + 4)^2}{3} = 8$

57. $\frac{3}{4}x^2 - \frac{2}{3}x = 1$ **58.** $\frac{1}{2x} = \frac{3x - 2}{3}$

59. $1.2x^2 - 0.4x = 0.2$ **60.** $\frac{2x - 1}{4x + 3} = \frac{x + 1}{3x - 2}$

61. $4x(x - 2) + 3(x + 8) = 27 + 5x^2$ **62.** $(x + 6)^2 + 2(x - 1) = 13$

Solve. Give irrational roots to the nearest tenth. Use your calculator or the Table of Square Roots at the back of the book as necessary. **(12-6)**

63. The length of a rectangle is 6 times the width. The area of the rectangle is 84 cm^2. Find the length and width.

64. The difference of a number and its square is 56. Find the number.

65. The altitude of a triangle is 2 m less than the base. The area of the triangle is 84 m^2. Find the base.

66. Theresa is crocheting an afghan that is already 30 in. wide by 40 in. long. If she continues to crochet by increasing the width and the length by the same number of inches until the afghan's area is doubled, what will be the new dimensions?

Translate each statement into a formula. Use *k* as the constant of variation where needed. **(12-7, 12-8)**

67. The height, h, of a right circular cylinder of a given volume is inversely proportional to the square of the radius, r.

68. Wind pressure, p, on a flat surface varies directly as the square of the wind velocity, v.

69. The lateral area, L, of a cylinder varies jointly as the radius, r, of the base, and the height, h.

70. The volume, V, of a cone varies jointly as the height, h, and the square of the radius, r, of the base.

71. The rate of speed, r, of a moving body varies inversely as the time traveled, t, and directly as the distance traveled, d.

72. Centrifugal force, F, varies inversely as the radius, r, of the circular path, and directly as the square of the velocity, v, of a moving body.

Extra Practice: Problem Solving

Chapter 1

Use the five-step plan to solve each problem. **(1-7)**

1. A train is traveling at an average speed of 90 km/h. How far will it travel in 2.5 h?
2. If a number is decreased by 27, the result is 36. Find the number.
3. A football team finished its 12-game season with no ties. The team won twice as many games as it lost. How many games did the team win?
4. A store sold 102 record albums during a two-day sale. Twice as many albums were sold the second day as the first. How many albums were sold the first day?
5. If three times a number is increased by 11, the result is 68. Find the number.
6. A bank contains 57 nickels, dimes, and quarters. There are 8 more dimes than quarters and 5 more nickels than dimes. How much money is in the bank?

Chapter 2

Solve. **(2-3)**

1. A football team gained 23 yd on one play. However, the ball was brought back to the line of scrimmage and then the team was given a 15 yd penalty. How far was the ball from where it would have been had no penalty been assessed?
2. An elevator left the twenty-sixth floor of a building and went up eight floors, then down twelve, and back up four. On what floor was the elevator then?
3. At the beginning of the month the Cranes had $250 in their vacation fund. They were able to add $10 per week for four weeks. Then they had to take out $85 for emergency household repairs. How much was in the fund at the end of the month?
4. A neighborhood association collected $85 in dues, earned $280 at a garage sale, and got $124 in donations. The association needs $500 to build a playground. How much more must it collect?
5. An 8:00 A.M. flight from Boston to Minneapolis took three hours. The time in Minneapolis is one hour earlier than Boston. What time was it in Minneapolis when the flight arrived?

6. A train is traveling at the rate of 100 km/h. A conductor is walking toward the back of the train at 5 km/h. What is the conductor's speed relative to the ground?

Solve. (2-4)

1. Neon freezes at $-248.61°$ C and boils at $-246.09°$ C. Find the difference between the boiling point and the freezing point.
2. The highest point in California is Mount Whitney at 4418 m above sea level. The lowest point is Death Valley at 86 m below sea level. Find the difference in altitude.
3. A candidate goes door to door along Main Street from a point 16 blocks west of campaign headquarters to a point 12 blocks east of headquarters. How many blocks has she gone?
4. Find the difference in degrees of longitude between Chicago at about 88° W and Rome at about 12° E.
5. Mount Everest at 8848 m above sea level is 9245 m higher than the Dead Sea. Find the altitude of the Dead Sea.
6. One winter day the temperature in Marshview reached a record high of 18.3° C. That was 22.7° C higher than the average temperature for that day. Find the average temperature.

Chapter 3

Solve. (3-1)

1. A number increased by 13 is -5. Find the number.
2. A glass of milk costs 70¢. If a glass of milk and a sandwich cost $2.50, how much does the sandwich cost?
3. Fifteen less than a number is 43. Find the number.
4. A plane flew 145 km/h faster when it was flying with the wind than it would have flown in still air. If its speed with the wind was 970 km/h, find the speed of the plane in still air.
5. The Booster Club had $425 in its treasury. The members earned $642 selling refreshments. They donated $320 to the football team for bus rentals. How much money did they have left?
6. Seventy-six tickets were sold in advance for a museum field trip. Thirteen tickets were sold the day of the trip. Seven people had to return their tickets and did not go. How many people went altogether?

Solve. (3-2)

1. The opposite of seven times a number is 238. Find the number.
2. One fourth of a number is 73. Find the number.
3. A 2.5 kg bag of apples costs $1.40. Find the cost per kilogram of the apples.

4. Frank works the same number of hours each week at a part-time job. In the last 8 weeks he worked 68 h. How many hours does Frank work each week?
5. A rectangle is 24 cm long and has a perimeter of 72 cm. Find the width.
6. A restaurant cuts its large pizza into 8 slices and sells each slice for 90¢. If the pizzas were cut into 6 slices, how much would the restaurant have to charge for each slice to make the same amount?

Solve. (3-4)

1. If you subtract 34 from the product of 15 and a number, you get 146. Find the number.
2. The perimeter of a rectangle is 152 cm. The width is 35 cm. Find the length.
3. Charlene paid $131.44, including tax, for a desk. The tax was 31 cents less than $\frac{1}{16}$ the cost of the desk. Find the cost of the desk.
4. Twin Cinema I seats 150 more people than Twin Cinema II. If the cinemas seat 1250 people altogether, find the number of seats in Twin Cinema II.
5. A bank contains 36 nickels, dimes, and quarters. There are 4 more dimes than quarters and twice as many nickels as quarters. How many of each coin are in the bank?
6. The longest side of a triangle is 8 cm longer than the shortest side and 5 cm longer than the third side. If the perimeter of the triangle is 56 cm, find the lengths of the three sides.

Solve. (3-5)

1. The larger of two consecutive integers is 10 more than twice the smaller. Find the integers.
2. Find a number whose product with 6 is the same as its sum with 45.
3. Five times a number, increased by 3, is the same as three times the number, increased by 27. Find the number.
4. The sum of two numbers is 20. Twice one number is 4 more than four times the other. Find the numbers.
5. The lengths of the sides of a triangle are consecutive odd integers. If the perimeter is 1 less than four times the shortest side, find the length of each side.
6. A sandwich costs 20¢ more than a salad plate. Six sandwiches cost as much as seven salad plates. Find the cost of each.

Solve. (3-6)

1. Kevin works 3 times as many hours in a week as Karen does. If each were to work 6 h more per week, Kevin would be working twice as many hours as Karen does. How many hours does each work now?

2. Aaron, Betsy, and Charita work part-time at the public library. Betsy works 4 h more each week than Aaron, and together they work half as many hours as Charita. How long does each person work if their total time is 45 h?
3. Zach's last quiz score was 30 points less than twice his first score. What was his first quiz score if the sum of his two scores is 150?
4. The length of a rectangle is 18 cm more than the width. A second rectangle is 6 cm shorter and 3 cm wider than the first and has a perimeter of 126 cm. Find the dimensions of each rectangle.
5. Becky has as many dimes as Ryan and Amy have together. Ryan has 2 more dimes than Amy, and Amy has one third as many dimes as Becky has. How many dimes does each have?
6. A cup of skim milk has 10 more than half the calories of a cup of whole milk. A cup of whole milk has 40 more calories than a glass of apple juice. If the total number of calories in one cup of each is 370, find the number of calories in each.

Solve. (3-7)

1. A collection of quarters and dimes is worth \$6.75. The number of dimes is 4 less than three times the number of quarters. How many of each are there?
2. A total of 720 people attended the school basketball game. Adult tickets cost \$2.50 each and student tickets cost \$1.50 each. If \$1220 worth of tickets were sold, how many students and how many adults attended?
3. A worker earns \$9 per hour for a regular workday and \$13.50 per hour for additional hours. If the worker was paid \$114.75 for an 11-hour workday, what is the length of a regular workday?
4. Carrots cost 75¢ per kilogram and potatoes cost 70¢ per kilogram. A shopper bought 9 kg of the vegetables for \$6.60. How many kilograms of each did the shopper buy?
5. A collection of 102 nickels, dimes, and quarters is worth \$13.60. There are 14 more nickels than dimes. How many quarters are there?

Chapter 4

Solve. (4-8)

1. Two trains leave a station at the same time, heading in opposite directions. One train is traveling at 80 km/h, the other at 90 km/h. How long will it take for the trains to be 425 km apart?
2. Grace leaves home at 8:00 A.M. Ten minutes later, Will notices Grace's lunch and begins bicycling after her. If Grace walks at 5 km/h and Will cycles at 15 km/h, how long will it take him to catch up with her?

3. A jet took one hour longer flying to Lincoln from Adams at 800 km/h than to return at 1200 km/h. Find the distance from Lincoln to Adams.
4. Gene spent 10 min riding his bicycle to a friend's house. He left his bike there and, with his friend, walked for 15 min to the gym. Gene rides his bicycle 10 km/h faster than he walks. If the entire trip covered a distance of 2.75 km, how far is it from his friend's house to the gym?
5. At noon, Sheila left a boat landing and paddled her canoe 20 km downstream and 20 km back. If she traveled 10 km/h downstream and 4 km/h upstream, what time did she arrive back at the landing?

Solve. **(4-9)**

1. A rectangle is 4 m longer than it is wide. If the length and width are both increased by 5 m, the area is increased by 115 m^2. Find the original dimensions.
2. A rectangle is 3 cm longer and 2 cm narrower than a square with the same area. Find the dimensions of each figure.
3. A rectangular swimming pool is 4 m longer than it is wide. It is surrounded by a cement walk 1 m wide. The area of the walk is 32 m^2. Find the dimensions of the pool.
4. When the length of a square is increased by 6 and the width is decreased by 4, the area remains unchanged. Find the dimensions of the square.
5. A print is 10 cm longer than it is wide. It is mounted in a frame 1.5 cm wide. The area of the frame is 399 cm^2. Find the dimensions of the print.

Solve. **(4-10)**

1. Find two consecutive integers whose sum is 104.
2. A plane averaged 1000 km/h on the first half of a round trip, but heavy winds slowed its speed on the return trip to 600 km/h. If the entire trip took 6 h, find the total distance.
3. Jill earned 12 more points on her quiz than Jack. If they both get 8 bonus points, Jill will have three times as many points as Jack does. How many points does each have?
4. The side of a square is 2 cm longer than the side of a second square. The area of the first square exceeds that of the second by 220 cm^2. Find the side of each square.
5. Find three consecutive integers whose sum is four times the greatest integer.

Chapter 5

Solve. **(5-13)**

1. The sum of a number and its square is 132. Find the number.
2. The sum of the squares of two consecutive positive odd integers is 202. Find the numbers.

3. A rectangle is 8 cm longer than it is wide. The area is 240 cm^2. Find the dimensions.
4. The sum of two numbers is 12 and the sum of their squares is 74. Find the numbers.
5. A rectangular flower garden is planted in a rectangular yard that is 16 m by 12 m. The garden occupies $\frac{1}{6}$ of the area of the yard and leaves a uniform strip of grass around the edges. Find the dimensions of the garden.
6. The edge of one cube is 4 cm longer than the edge of a second cube. The volumes of the cubes differ by 316 cm^3. Find the length of the edge of each cube.

Chapter 7

Solve. **(7-1)**

1. Two numbers are in the ratio 2:3 and their sum is 125. Find the numbers.
2. The measures of the angles of a triangle are in the ratio 2:3:5. Recall that the sum of the measures of the angles of a triangle is 180°. Find the measure of each angle.
3. Three numbers are in the ratio 2:3:5 and their sum is 200. Find the numbers.
4. The ratio of teachers to assistants to children at a day care center is 2:1:9. Of the 96 people at the center, how many are children?
5. A collection of quarters, dimes, and nickels is worth $22.80. If the ratio of quarters to dimes to nickels is 5:3:7, how many coins are there?
6. Two trains leave a station at the same time heading in opposite directions. After 2 h, the trains are 376 km apart. If the ratio of their speeds is 22:25, find the speed of each train.

Solve. **(7-2)**

1. A 1.5-lb steak costs $5.80. Find the cost of a 2-lb steak.
2. A poll showed that 400 voters out of 625 favor Question 1 in the town election. If there are 7500 voters altogether, how many can be expected to vote in favor of the question?
3. Group-rate admissions to a museum cost $140.70 for a group of 42. How much would it cost for a group of 50?
4. The tax on a restaurant meal that costs $24 is $1.44. Find the tax on a meal that costs $35.
5. The Sommers' scale is inaccurate. If it registers 120 lb for Karen, who actually weighs 116 lb, how much will it register for Neil, who actually weighs 174 lb?

6. On a wall map, 1 cm represents 25 km. Colorado is represented by a rectangle 25.8 cm long and 18.4 cm wide. Find the approximate area of Colorado in square kilometers.

Solve. (7-3)

1. Juan spent \$2 more on books than Sylvia did. If they each spent \$4 less, Sylvia would have spent exactly $\frac{5}{6}$ of what Juan spent. How much did each spend?
2. Three fifths of a number added to one fourth of the number is 51. Find the number.
3. Bart's age is one third of his mother's age. Seven years ago, his age was one fifth of hers. How old are both now?
4. A rectangle is 11 cm narrower than it is long. The length is two sevenths of the perimeter. Find the length and the width.
5. Two thirds of the coins in a collection of quarters and dimes are quarters. The collection is worth \$12. How many dimes are there?
6. A bus, traveling at 90 km/h, takes 15.2 h longer to get from Ardmore to Zepher than a plane flying at 850 km/h. How far is it from Ardmore to Zepher?

Solve. (7-4)

1. The sum of a number and its reciprocal is $\frac{25}{12}$. Find the number.
2. The sum of a number and its reciprocal is $\frac{29}{10}$. Find the number.
3. The denominator of a fraction is 2 more than the numerator. If the numerator and denominator are increased by 2, the new fraction is $\frac{4}{15}$ greater than the original fraction. Find the original fraction.
4. The denominator of a fraction is 2 more than the numerator. The sum of the fraction and its reciprocal is $\frac{34}{15}$. Find the fraction.
5. If the speed limit is decreased by 10 km/h on a 100 km stretch of a highway, the trip will take a half hour longer than usual. What is the usual speed limit?
6. Sue can ride her bike 14 km/h faster than she can walk. It takes 17.5 min longer to walk 2.5 km than to ride. Find Sue's walking speed.

Solve. (7-5)

1. If there is a 6% tax on clothing, find the tax on a suit that costs \$175.
2. A real estate agent makes a 7% commission on all sales. How much does the agent make on a sale of \$182,500?
3. A discount store sold a sweater for \$32. If the discount was 20%, find the original price.
4. If the Gannons' \$84 monthly gas bill goes up 8%, what will be their new monthly payment?

5. An \$840 personal computer is discounted 25%. What is the final cost?
6. How much greater is the income on \$3600 invested at 12% than on \$4200 invested at 8%?

Solve. (7-6)

1. Last season, when a football team was doing poorly, weekly attendance averaged 42,000. This season weekly attendance averages 56,700. What is the percent of increase?
2. A single monthly issue of *Sports Spotlight* costs \$2.25 at the newsstand. A yearly subscription of 12 issues costs \$21.60. Find the percent of discount from the newsstand price.
3. Enrollment in the summer recreation program this year increased by 16% to 1711 people. How many people enrolled last year?
4. The Katchners invested \$7500 at 8% and \$3500 at 5%. Find the total annual income from the two investments.
5. The Ozakas invested a sum of money at 10%. They could have earned the same interest by investing \$1600 less at 12%. How much did they invest?
6. The Sanjurjos invested three fourths of their money at 12% and the rest at 8%. If their annual income from the investment is \$1320, how much have they invested?

Chemistry

Solve. (7-7)

1. How many liters of water must be added to 20 L of a 75% acid solution to produce a solution that is 15% acid?
2. How many liters of acid should be added to 4 L of a 10% acid solution to make a solution that is 80% acid?
3. A chemist mixes 16 L of a 40% acid solution and 24 L of a 16% acid solution. What is the percent of acid of the mixture?
4. How many kilograms of water must be evaporated from 84 kg of a 5% salt solution to produce a solution that is 35% salt?

Grocery

Solve. (7-7)

1. Students working at a refreshment stand mixed cranberry juice at 50¢ per liter and apple juice at 35¢ per liter to make 120 L of a fruit drink worth 40¢ per liter. How many liters of each did they use?

2. A grocer mixes a premium blend worth \$17 per kilogram with a blend worth \$7 per kilogram to make 36 kg of a blend worth \$11 per kilogram. How many kilograms of each type are included?

3. A butcher mixes 12 lb of ground pork at \$1.25 per pound with 24 lb of ground beef at \$2 per pound to sell as meat loaf mix. What should be the cost per pound of the mixture?

4. How many kilograms of cranberries at \$2.10 per kilogram should a grocer mix with 10 kg of pineapple chunks at \$1.20 per kilogram to make a relish worth \$1.35 per kilogram?

Investment and Wages

Solve. (7-7)

1. A worker earns $1\frac{1}{2}$ times the regular wage for overtime. In one week the worker's total income was \$625 for 35 h of regular work plus 10 h of overtime. What is the regular hourly wage?

2. The Esperanzas invested part of their \$8000 at 12% and part at 8%. If their annual investment income is \$825, how much is invested at each rate?

3. The Lees invested two thirds of their money at 12.5%, one fourth at 8%, and the rest at 6%. If their annual investment income is \$1625, how much did they invest altogether?

4. An investor has \$10,000 invested in two stocks. If one stock pays 15% and the other 16%, and the total annual income is \$1520, how much is invested in each?

Solve. (7-8)

1. Joe can do a job in 6 h and Charlie can do the same job in 5 h. What part of the job can they finish by working together for 2 h?

2. Charlotte can finish her paper route in 2 h. When Ralph helps, they finish in 45 min. How long would it take Ralph working alone?

3. A crew of 2 could put siding on a house in 30 h. Another crew of 3 could do the same job in 24 h. How long would it take all 5 people working together?

4. Flora can finish her chores in 4 h. One week, after Flora worked alone for 1 h, she was joined by her younger sister Fiona and they finished the job in 2 h. How long would it have taken Fiona working alone?

5. One pipe can fill a tank in 50 min and a second pipe can fill it in 90 min. When the tank was empty, the first pipe was opened for 20 min, then shut. How long will it take the second pipe to finish the job?

6. One machine can produce an order of Wonder Widgets in 45 min. A second machine takes 60 min, and a third takes 90 min. How long would it take all three working together?

Solve. (7-9)

1. The population of a certain area in t years is expected to be $10(1.03)^t$ thousand people. Find the population (a) now, (b) last year, and (c) next year.
2. A certain isotope has a half-life of 100 years. Starting with 100 g of the isotope, in t years there will be $100(0.5)^{t/100}$ g left. (a) How much will be left in 1000 years? (b) How much was there 1000 years ago?
3. A certain bacteria culture quadruples every 2 days. The number present t days from now will be $1{,}000{,}000(4)^{t/2}$. How many bacteria were there 2 weeks ago?
4. A \$10,000 investment earning 8%, compounded annually, will be worth $\$10{,}000(1.08)^t$ in t years. What was the amount 4 years ago?
5. The growth rate of a certain city is such that its population t years from now is given by the formula $12{,}000(1.06)^t$. What was the population 10 years ago?
6. In one country the cost of living has been increasing so that an item costing one dollar now will cost $(1.05)^t$ dollars t years from now. How much did today's one-dollar item cost 5 years ago?

Solve. (7-10)

1. The speed of light is about 3.00×10^5 km/s. The average distance from Earth to the moon is about 3.84×10^5 km. How long does it take light reflected from Earth to reach the moon?
2. At its farthest, the moon is about 4.07×10^5 km from Earth. At its closest, it is about 3.56×10^5 km from Earth. Find the difference between the two distances.
3. The average distance from the sun to Pluto is about 6.10×10^9 km. About how long does it take light from the sun to reach Pluto? (See Exercise 1 above.)
4. **a.** A parsec is about 3.3×10^3 light years. The star Deneb is about 5.0×10^2 parsecs from the sun. How many light years is that?
   b. A light year is about 9.5×10^{12} km. Find the distance from Deneb to the sun in kilometers.
5. The approximate wavelength of visible light is 6.0×10^3 Angstrom units. An Angstrom unit is equal to 1.0×10^{-8} cm. Find the wavelength of visible light in centimeters.

Chapter 8

Solve. (8-9)

1. A beam bends 1.6 cm with a mass of 32 kg on it. If the amount of bending is directly proportional to the mass, find the amount of bending caused by a mass of 62 kg.

2. A baker uses 18 cups of flour to make 48 sandwich rolls. How many cups of flour are needed to make 104 sandwich rolls?

3. A grocer uses 22 kg of premium nuts in making 54 kg of a mixture. How much of the premium nuts is needed for 81 kg of the mixture?

4. On a scale drawing, a child 4 ft tall is represented by a figure 6 in. tall. How tall a figure should be used to represent an 11 ft elephant?

5. On a map, 1 cm represents 60 km. Find the actual area of a region represented on the map by a rectangle 7.5 cm by 8.4 cm.

6. A factory is to be built in the shape of a rectangular solid. The actual building will be 62 m long, 30 m wide, and 12 m high. A scale model is built with a scale of 1 cm to 5 m. Find the volume of the model.

Solve. **(8-10)**

1. The time required to drive a given distance is inversely proportional to the speed. If it takes 7.5 h to cover a distance at 84 km/h, how long will it take at 90 km/h?

2. A gear with 36 teeth revolves at 800 r/min and meshes with a gear with 24 teeth. Find the speed of the second gear if the speed varies inversely as the number of teeth.

3. How much would you have to invest at 8% to earn as much interest as $1250 invested at 12%?

4. A room is to be partitioned into a row of carrels. If each carrel is 1.8 m wide, there will be room for 16 carrels. How many carrels will fit if each is 1.92 m wide?

5. A mass of 18 g and a mass of 22 g are on the ends of a meter stick. Where should a fulcrum be placed to balance the meter stick?

6. A lever has a mass of 400 g on one end and a mass of 250 g on the other. The lever is balanced when the mass of 400 g is 0.75 m closer to the fulcrum than the other mass. How far from the fulcrum is the mass of 250 g?

Chapter 9

Solve. **(9-3)**

1. A collection of 77 quarters and dimes is worth $12.50. How many quarters are there?

2. The sum of two numbers is 32. One number is 4 more than the other. Find the numbers.

3. The length of a rectangle is 3 less than twice the width. The perimeter is 54. Find the dimensions.

4. The sum of two numbers is 66. If the smaller number is subtracted from two thirds of the larger number, the result is one third the positive difference of the original numbers. Find the numbers.

5. If 1 is subtracted from the numerator of a fraction, the resulting fraction is $\frac{1}{3}$. If 2 is subtracted from the denominator, the resulting fraction is $\frac{1}{2}$. Find the original fraction.
6. If 2 is added to the numerator of a fraction, the resulting fraction is $\frac{2}{3}$. If 1 is subtracted from the denominator, the resulting fraction is $\frac{1}{2}$. Find the original fraction.

Solve. **(9-4)**

1. The sum of two numbers is 36 and their difference is 6. Find the numbers.
2. The sum of two numbers is 73. When the smaller number is subtracted from twice the greater number, the result is 50. Find the numbers.
3. There are 158 members in the soccer program. There are 16 more boys than girls. How many boys are there?
4. If Cathy walks for 2 h and rides her bicycle for 1 h, she can travel 36 km. If she walks for 2 h and rides her bicycle for 2 h, she can travel 56 km. How fast can she walk? How fast can she ride her bicycle?
5. Craig has 38 quarters and dimes. If he had twice as many quarters, he would have $11. How many of each coin does he have?
6. Olivia has $30 more than Carl. If they each had $7 less, the sum of their funds would equal the amount that Olivia has now. How much money does each have now?

Solve. **(9-5)**

1. The sum of two numbers is 51 and their difference is 13. Find the numbers.
2. A collection of 27 nickels and dimes is worth $1.95. How many of each coin are there?
3. The side of a square house is 24 ft long, and the house is located on a lot which is 50 ft longer than it is wide. The perimeter of the lot is 20 ft more than 5 times the perimeter of the house. Find the length of the lot.
4. Museum passes cost $5 for adults and $2 for children. One day the museum sold 1820 passes for $6100. How many of each type were sold?
5. In a math contest, each team is asked 50 questions. The teams earn 15 points for each correct answer and lose 8 for each incorrect answer. One team finished with a score of 566. How many questions did this team answer correctly?
6. A grocer mixes two types of nuts, Brand A and Brand B. If the mix includes 4 kg of Brand A and 6 kg of Brand B, the mix will cost $6.20 per kilogram. If it includes 2 kg of Brand A and 8 kg of Brand B, it will cost $5.60 per kilogram. Find the cost per kilogram of each brand.

Solve. **(9-6)**

1. A boat can travel 16 km/h against the current. The same boat can travel 30 km/h with the current. Find the rate of the boat in still water and the rate of the current.

2. A jet flies with the wind at 1100 km/h and against the same wind at 750 km/h. Find the rate of the wind and the speed of the jet in still air.
3. A swimmer can swim 4 km with the current in 24 min. The same distance would take 40 min against the current. Find the rate of the current and the speed of the swimmer.
4. A plane flies the first half of a 5600 km flight into the wind in 3.5 h. The return trip, with the same wind, takes 2.5 h. Find the speed of the wind and the speed of the plane in still air.
5. A plane has a speed of 840 km/h in still air. It can travel 3120 km with the wind in the same time it would take to travel 1920 km against the wind. Find the speed of the wind.
6. A rowboat can travel a distance of 66 km in 3 h with the current. The rowboat can travel 33 km in 3 h against the current. Find the rate of the current and the rate of the rowboat in still water.

Chapter 10

Solve. (10-3)

1. The sum of two consecutive integers is less than 83. Find the pair of such integers with the greatest sum.
2. A collection of quarters and dimes is worth more than $20. There are twice as many quarters as dimes. At least how many dimes are there?
3. Four members of a bowling team had scores of 240, 180, 220, and 200. Find the lowest score a fifth person must get to maintain an average for the group of at least 220.
4. The sum of three consecutive even integers is less than 80. Find the greatest such integers.
5. When road repairs begin, the current speed limit will be cut by 40 km/h. It will then take at least 3.6 h to cover the same distance that can be covered in 2 h now. What is the speed limit now?
6. The length of a rectangle is 1 cm greater than twice the width. If each dimension were increased by 5 cm, the area would be at least 150 cm^2 greater. Find the least possible dimensions.

Chapter 11

Solve. (11-5)

1. A square has an area of 184 cm^2. Find the length of a side to the nearest tenth of a centimeter.
2. A square has the same area as a rectangle that is 25 m by 18 m. Find the length of a side of the square to the nearest tenth of a meter.

3. A square has the same area as a triangle that has a base of 8 cm and a height of 5 cm. Find the length of a side of the square to the nearest tenth of a centimeter.
4. A circle inside a square just touches its sides. The area of the circle is 226.08 m^2. Find the length of a side of the square to the nearest tenth of a meter. Use 3.14 as an approximation for π.
5. A circular wading pool covers an area of 34.54 m^2. Find the radius of the pool to the nearest tenth of a meter. Use 3.14 as an approximation for π.
6. A circular flower bed is surrounded by a crushed-stone walk that is 1 m wide. If the area of the whole region is 21.98 m^2, find the radius of the flower bed to the nearest tenth of a meter. Use 3.14 as an approximation for π.

Solve. Approximate each square root to the nearest hundredth. **(11-6)**

1. A small park in the shape of a rectangle has dimensions 50 m by 20 m. A road through the park follows the diagonal of the rectangle. Find the length of the road.
2. A rope from the top of a mast of a sailboat is attached to a point 2 m from the mast. If the rope is 6 m long, how tall is the mast?
3. The length of one leg of a right triangle is one centimeter less than twice the length of the second leg. The hypotenuse is one centimeter more than twice the length of the second leg. Find the length of each leg.
4. The bottom of a 7 m ramp is 5 m from the base of a loading platform. Find the height of the platform.
5. The length of the longer leg of a right triangle is 3 cm more than the length of the shorter leg. The length of the hypotenuse is 3 cm more than the length of the longer leg. Find the length of each leg.

Solve. **(11-10)**

1. One fourth the square root of a number is 7. Find the number.
2. When 8 is subtracted from 3 times a number, the square root of the result is 10. Find the number.
3. Four times the square root of a number is 28. Find the number.
4. When 5 is subtracted from the square root of twice a number, the result is 9. Find the number.
5. The geometric mean of two positive numbers is the positive square root of their product. Find two consecutive even integers whose geometric mean is $8\sqrt{15}$.
6. Find two consecutive positive odd integers whose geometric mean is $15\sqrt{3}$.

Chapter 12

Solve. (12-6)

1. The sum of a number and its square is 30. Find the number.
2. The foundation of a house is 13 m by 7 m. If the builder increases each dimension by the same amount, the area of the foundation will increase to 135 m^2. Find the new dimensions.
3. The perimeter of a rectangular yard is 138 m and the area is 540 m^2. Find the dimensions of the yard.
4. The sum of the squares of two consecutive even integers is 340. Find the integers.
5. One work crew can finish a job in 18 h less than a second crew. Working together, they can finish the job in 40 h. How long would each crew take working alone?
6. One number is 2 more than 3 times another. The sum of their squares is 212. Find the numbers.

Solve. (12-7)

1. The stopping distance of a car varies directly as the square of its speed. If the stopping distance is 112 m at 64 km/h, find the stopping distance at 56 km/h.
2. The price of a diamond varies directly as the square of its mass. If a 1.4 carat diamond costs $1764, find the cost of a similar stone with a mass of 1.7 carats.
3. The height of a cone of given volume is inversely proportional to the square of the radius of the base. If a cone that is 4 units high has a base with radius 3 units, find the height of a cone of equal volume with a base of radius 6 units.
4. The time needed to fill a tank varies inversely as the square of the radius of the hose. If a hose of radius 3.5 cm takes 8 min to fill a tank, how long will it take using a hose of radius 2 cm?
5. The force between two magnets varies inversely as the square of the distance between them. Two magnets are initially 4 cm apart. They are moved 8 cm farther apart. What is the effect on the force?
6. The distance an object falls varies directly as the square of the time it falls. If an object falls 175.5 m in 6 s, how long would it take to fall 487.5 m?

Solve. (12-8)

1. The cost of operating an appliance varies jointly as the number of watts, hours of operation, and the cost per kilowatt-hour. It costs 45¢ to operate a 3000-watt air conditioner for 2 h at a cost of 7.5¢ per kilowatt-hour. Find the cost of operating a 1200-watt dishwasher for 40 min.

2. The number of persons needed to do a job varies directly as the amount of work to be done and inversely as the time in which the job is to be done. If 8 factory workers can produce 520 items in 4 days, how many workers will be needed to produce 585 items in 3 days?

3. If 2 painters can cover 320 ft^2 in 3 h, how long will it take 3 painters to cover 840 ft^2? (See Exercise 2 above.)

4. The mass of a metal disc varies directly as the thickness and the square of the radius. A disc 2 cm thick with radius 5 cm has a mass of 840 g. Find the mass of a disc of the same metal that has radius 3 cm and is 0.5 cm thick.

Table 1 / *Squares of Integers from 1 to 100*

Number	Square	Number	Square	Number	Square	Number	Square
1	1	**26**	676	**51**	2601	**76**	5776
2	4	**27**	729	**52**	2704	**77**	5929
3	9	**28**	784	**53**	2809	**78**	6084
4	16	**29**	841	**54**	2916	**79**	6241
5	25	**30**	900	**55**	3025	**80**	6400
6	36	**31**	961	**56**	3136	**81**	6561
7	49	**32**	1024	**57**	3249	**82**	6724
8	64	**33**	1089	**58**	3364	**83**	6889
9	81	**34**	1156	**59**	3481	**84**	7056
10	100	**35**	1225	**60**	3600	**85**	7225
11	121	**36**	1296	**61**	3721	**86**	7396
12	144	**37**	1369	**62**	3844	**87**	7569
13	169	**38**	1444	**63**	3969	**88**	7744
14	196	**39**	1521	**64**	4096	**89**	7921
15	225	**40**	1600	**65**	4225	**90**	8100
16	256	**41**	1681	**66**	4356	**91**	8281
17	289	**42**	1764	**67**	4489	**92**	8464
18	324	**43**	1849	**68**	4624	**93**	8649
19	361	**44**	1936	**69**	4761	**94**	8836
20	400	**45**	2025	**70**	4900	**95**	9025
21	441	**46**	2116	**71**	5041	**96**	9216
22	484	**47**	2209	**72**	5184	**97**	9409
23	529	**48**	2304	**73**	5329	**98**	9604
24	576	**49**	2401	**74**	5476	**99**	9801
25	625	**50**	2500	**75**	5625	**100**	10,000

Table 2 / Square Roots of Integers from 1 to 100

Exact square roots are shown in red. For the others, rational approximations are given correct to three decimal places.

Number N	Positive Square Root $\sqrt{N}$	Number N	Positive Square Root $\sqrt{N}$	Number N	Positive Square Root $\sqrt{N}$	Number N	Positive Square Root $\sqrt{N}$
1	1	**26**	5.099	**51**	7.141	**76**	8.718
2	1.414	**27**	5.196	**52**	7.211	**77**	8.775
3	1.732	**28**	5.292	**53**	7.280	**78**	8.832
4	2	**29**	5.385	**54**	7.348	**79**	8.888
5	2.236	**30**	5.477	**55**	7.416	**80**	8.944
6	2.449	**31**	5.568	**56**	7.483	**81**	9
7	2.646	**32**	5.657	**57**	7.550	**82**	9.055
8	2.828	**33**	5.745	**58**	7.616	**83**	9.110
9	3	**34**	5.831	**59**	7.681	**84**	9.165
10	3.162	**35**	5.916	**60**	7.746	**85**	9.220
11	3.317	**36**	6	**61**	7.810	**86**	9.274
12	3.464	**37**	6.083	**62**	7.874	**87**	9.327
13	3.606	**38**	6.164	**63**	7.937	**88**	9.381
14	3.742	**39**	6.245	**64**	8	**89**	9.434
15	3.873	**40**	6.325	**65**	8.062	**90**	9.487
16	4	**41**	6.403	**66**	8.124	**91**	9.539
17	4.123	**42**	6.481	**67**	8.185	**92**	9.592
18	4.243	**43**	6.557	**68**	8.246	**93**	9.644
19	4.359	**44**	6.633	**69**	8.307	**94**	9.695
20	4.472	**45**	6.708	**70**	8.367	**95**	9.747
21	4.583	**46**	6.782	**71**	8.426	**96**	9.798
22	4.690	**47**	6.856	**72**	8.485	**97**	9.849
23	4.796	**48**	6.928	**73**	8.544	**98**	9.899
24	4.899	**49**	7	**74**	8.602	**99**	9.950
25	5	**50**	7.071	**75**	8.660	**100**	10

Table 3 / *Trigonometric Ratios*

Angle	Sine	Cosine	Tangent	Angle	Sine	Cosine	Tangent
1°	.0175	.9998	.0175	46°	.7193	.6947	1.0355
2°	.0349	.9994	.0349	47°	.7314	.6820	1.0724
3°	.0523	.9986	.0524	48°	.7431	.6691	1.1106
4°	.0698	.9976	.0699	49°	.7547	.6561	1.1504
5°	.0872	.9962	.0875	50°	.7660	.6428	1.1918
6°	.1045	.9945	.1051	51°	.7771	.6293	1.2349
7°	.1219	.9925	.1228	52°	.7880	.6157	1.2799
8°	.1392	.9903	.1405	53°	.7986	.6018	1.3270
9°	.1564	.9877	.1584	54°	.8090	.5878	1.3764
10°	.1736	.9848	.1763	55°	.8192	.5736	1.4281
11°	.1908	.9816	.1944	56°	.8290	.5592	1.4826
12°	.2079	.9781	.2126	57°	.8387	.5446	1.5399
13°	.2250	.9744	.2309	58°	.8480	.5299	1.6003
14°	.2419	.9703	.2493	59°	.8572	.5150	1.6643
15°	.2588	.9659	.2679	60°	.8660	.5000	1.7321
16°	.2756	.9613	.2867	61°	.8746	.4848	1.8040
17°	.2924	.9563	.3057	62°	.8829	.4695	1.8807
18°	.3090	.9511	.3249	63°	.8910	.4540	1.9626
19°	.3256	.9455	.3443	64°	.8988	.4384	2.0503
20°	.3420	.9397	.3640	65°	.9063	.4226	2.1445
21°	.3584	.9336	.3839	66°	.9135	.4067	2.2460
22°	.3746	.9272	.4040	67°	.9205	.3907	2.3559
23°	.3907	.9205	.4245	68°	.9272	.3746	2.4751
24°	.4067	.9135	.4452	69°	.9336	.3584	2.6051
25°	.4226	.9063	.4663	70°	.9397	.3420	2.7475
26°	.4384	.8988	.4877	71°	.9455	.3256	2.9042
27°	.4540	.8910	.5095	72°	.9511	.3090	3.0777
28°	.4695	.8829	.5317	73°	.9563	.2924	3.2709
29°	.4848	.8746	.5543	74°	.9613	.2756	3.4874
30°	.5000	.8660	.5774	75°	.9659	.2588	3.7321
31°	.5150	.8572	.6009	76°	.9703	.2419	4.0108
32°	.5299	.8480	.6249	77°	.9744	.2250	4.3315
33°	.5446	.8387	.6494	78°	.9781	.2079	4.7046
34°	.5592	.8290	.6745	79°	.9816	.1908	5.1446
35°	.5736	.8192	.7002	80°	.9848	.1736	5.6713
36°	.5878	.8090	.7265	81°	.9877	.1564	6.3138
37°	.6018	.7986	.7536	82°	.9903	.1392	7.1154
38°	.6157	.7880	.7813	83°	.9925	.1219	8.1443
39°	.6293	.7771	.8098	84°	.9945	.1045	9.5144
40°	.6428	.7660	.8391	85°	.9962	.0872	11.4301
41°	.6561	.7547	.8693	86°	.9976	.0698	14.3007
42°	.6691	.7431	.9004	87°	.9986	.0523	19.0811
43°	.6820	.7314	.9325	88°	.9994	.0349	28.6363
44°	.6947	.7193	.9657	89°	.9998	.0175	57.2900
45°	.7071	.7071	1.0000				

Introducing Explorations

The following sixteen pages provide you with activities for exploring various concepts of algebra. The activities give you a chance to discover for yourself some of the ideas presented in this textbook. They carefully lead you to interesting conclusions and applications; they will make some of the abstract concepts of algebra easier to understand.

Some of the questions in these activities are open-ended. They ask you to describe, explain, analyze, design, summarize, write, predict, check, generalize, and recognize patterns. Often there is more than one correct way to answer a question. You can work on these activities by yourself or in small groups. You will need to use the materials listed below.

With these explorations we hope you enjoy exploring algebra!

Explorations

Exploring Density of Real Numbers

Use with Lesson 1-8

In this activity, you will use a calculator in finding a number between two given numbers.

Explore by Multiplying

1. a. Choose a positive integer less than 10 and use your calculator to multiply it by $\frac{1}{2}$. Graph the number you chose and the product on a number line.
b. Multiply the product by $\frac{1}{2}$, and graph it on the same number line.
c. Continue the process three more times.
d. Describe what would happen if you continued this process. Will you reach zero? If so, when? If not, why not?

2. Repeat Exercise **1,** but choose a negative integer greater than $^{-}10$.

3. What can you conclude from these explorations?

Explore by Finding Averages

4. a. Choose two integers between 5 and 15, and find their average. Graph the numbers you chose and their average on a number line.
b. Find the average of the larger number and the average you found in part **a.** Graph the result.
c. Find the average of the larger number and the average you found in part **b.** Graph the result.
d. Describe what you observe.

5. a. Choose two numbers between 5 and 15, different from those you chose in Exercise **4a.** Find their average. Graph the numbers and their average.
b. Repeat steps **4b–4c,** but this time use the smaller number and the resulting average each time. Describe what you observe.

Use What You Have Observed

6. a. How can you find a number between 0 and any other number x?
b. How can you find a number between any two given numbers?

7. A set of numbers is said to be **dense** if, for any two numbers in the set, we can find another number that is between those two numbers and is also a member of that set. Are these sets of numbers dense? Explain your answer.
a. All proper fractions **b.** All integers

Exploring Addition of Integers

Use before Lesson 2-3

In this activity, you will use two different colors of plastic chips to help you develop rules for adding different combinations of positive and negative numbers. Each chip will have an absolute value of 1. Choose one color for positive integers and one color for negative integers. Here, one blue chip represents +1 and one red chip represents −1.

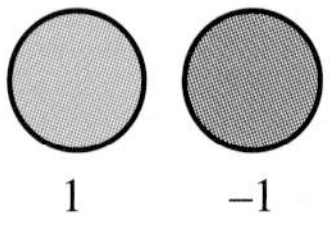

Explore the Property of Opposites

1. **a.** Use the chips to represent 1 + (−1).
   b. Use the chips to represent (−2) + 2.
   c. What integer is represented by the sum of the chips in each part above?
   d. Use three pairs of chips to represent zero.
   e. Describe a general way to show that the sum of an integer and its opposite is zero, using the chips.

Explore the Identity Property of Addition

2. **a.** What sum is represented by the chips shown at the right?
   b. What integer is represented by the sum of the chips in part **a**?
   c. Use both red and blue chips to represent the number −2.

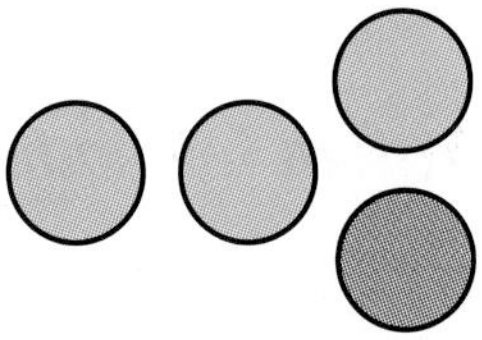

Explore Addition

3. **a.** Use chips to represent the sums 2 + 1 and −2 + (−1).
   b. Think about the signs of the addends and also the signs of their sums. What do you notice?
   c. Can you think of an example in which adding two numbers having the same sign yields a sum with the opposite sign?

4. In both cases in Exercise **3,** the signs of the addends were the same. What happens when the signs of the addends are different?
   a. Use chips to represent 1 + (−2) and 2 + (−1), and find the sums.
   b. What is the sign of the sum in each case?
   c. How do the absolute values and signs of the addends affect the sign of the sum?

Use What You Have Observed

5. Use your observations to find each sum. Then check by using colored chips.
   a. 3 + 5 **b.** −3 + (−5) **c.** −3 + 5 **d.** 3 + (−5)

Exploring Subtraction of Integers

Use before Lesson 2-4

On the previous page, you used colored chips to model addition of integers. This activity builds on what you have learned to explore subtraction.

Explore Subtraction

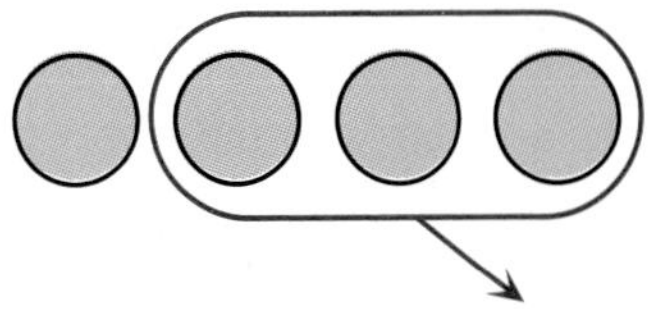

1. Use the chips to find the difference 4 – 3.
 a. Start with 4 blue chips.
 b. Take away 3 blue chips.
 c. Count the remaining chips. How many are left?
 d. Write a number sentence that expresses your result.

2. Use the chips to find the difference –4 – (–3). Follow steps similar to those in Exercise **1.**

3. Use the chips to find the difference 4 – (–3).
 a. In terms of chips, how can you represent 4 – (–3)?
 b. Start with 4 blue chips.
 c. There are no red chips to remove. Add zero by using a combination of 3 blue chips and 3 red chips.
 d. Take away 3 red chips. Name the chips that remain.
 e. Write a number sentence that expresses the result.

4. Use the chips to find the difference –4 – 3.
 a. What chips will you start with?
 b. What chips must you take away?
 c. What combination of red and blue chips will you add in order to take away the chips you need to?
 d. Take away the necessary chips. Name the chips that remain.
 e. Write a number sentence that expresses the result.

Use What You Have Observed

5. Use chips to compute and compare –5 – (–3) with –3 –(–5).

6. Use chips to find each sum and difference.
 a. 4 – 3 and 4 + (–3)
 b. 4 – (–2) and 4 + 2
 c. 4 – 5 and 4 + (–5)
 d. –5 – 3 and –5 + (–3)

7. Analyze your answers in Exercise **6,** and look for a pattern. Is the following statement true or false? "Subtracting one number, b, from another, a, gives the same result as adding the opposite of b to a."

Exploring Ways to Solve Equations

Use before Lesson 3-1

In this activity, you will use a double pan balance to explore properties of equality and to solve equations. Each pan of the balance represents one side of the equation.

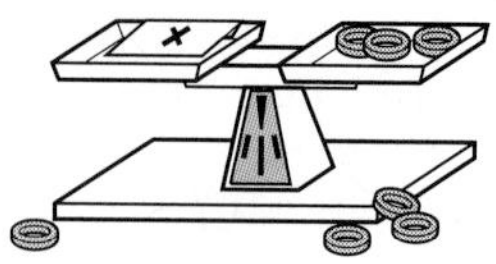

Explore Properties of Equality

1. a. Start with the empty pans in balance. Place 6 metal washers on each pan. What do you notice? Write an equation represented by the balance.

b. Add 2 more washers to each pan. What happens? How many washers are on each side? Write an equation represented by the balance.

c. Remove 3 washers from each pan. What happens? How many washers are on each side? Write an equation represented by the balance.

d. Remove 1 washer from the left pan and 2 washers from the right pan. What happens? Write an inequality represented by the balance.

e. What conclusion can you draw from these results?

Explore by Subtracting

2. For this activity your teacher will give you an envelope marked X, which contains some washers, and an empty envelope.

a. Start with the empty pans in balance. Place envelope X, together with 3 washers, on one pan. Place the empty envelope, together with 10 washers, on the other pan. What happens? Write an equation.

b. Remove 1 washer from each pan until only envelope X is left on one pan. How many washers did you remove from each side of the balance? Describe the results.

c. How many washers are on the side with the empty envelope? How many washers must be in envelope X? Write an equation.

Explore by Adding

3. For this activity your teacher will give you an envelope marked Y, which contains some washers, and an empty envelope.

a. Start with the empty pans in balance. Without looking inside, remove 4 washers from envelope Y, and place it on one pan. Place 7 washers and the empty envelope on the other pan. What happens? Write an equation.

b. Replace the 4 washers you removed from envelope Y. Add an equal number of washers to the other side. Write an equation.

Use What You Have Observed

4. Explain how you can solve each equation.

a. $x + 6 = 10$ **b.** $y - 6 = 7$ **c.** $x + 75 = 203$ **d.** $y - 173 = 511$

Exploring Monomial and Binomial Products

Use before Lessons 4-5 and 4-6

In this activity, you will use square and rectangular tiles like those shown below to represent products of monomials and binomials.

x-by-x tile: 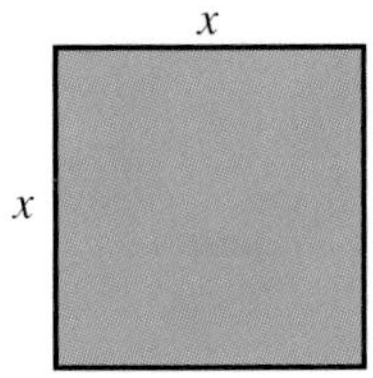

1-by-x tile: 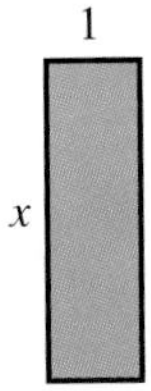

1-by-1 tile: 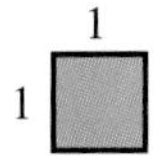

Explore the Product of a Monomial and a Binomial

1. Build a rectangle by placing one 1-by-x tile next to one x-by-x tile as shown.

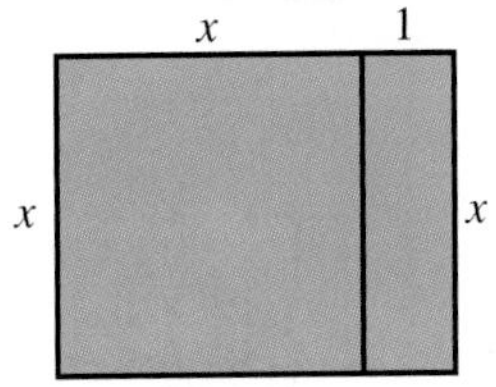

- **a.** What *monomial* represents the length of one side of the rectangle?
  What *binomial* represents the length of one side of the rectangle?
- **b.** Express the area of the rectangle as the product of a monomial and a binomial.
- **c.** What is the area of the x-by-x tile?
  What is the area of the 1-by-x tile?
- **d.** How is the area of the rectangle related to the areas of the tiles?
- **e.** Write an expression that shows the relationship described in part **d.**

2. Use tiles as described below to find the product $2x(x + 2)$.

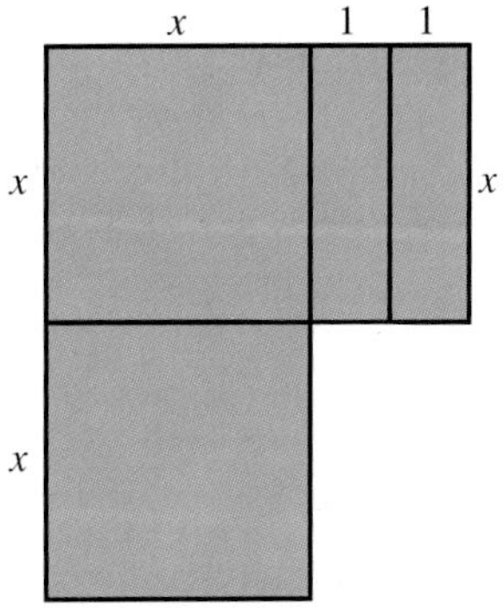

- **a.** Place two x-by-x tiles and two 1-by-x tiles together as shown.
- **b.** Complete the rectangle by including two more 1-by-x tiles.
- **c.** What are the lengths of the sides of the rectangle?
- **d.** Use the expressions from part **c** to express the area of the rectangle.
- **e.** Find the sum of the areas of the tiles that form the rectangle.
- **f.** What is the product $2x(x + 2)$?

(Continued on next page.)

Exploring Monomial and Binomial Products

Use before Lessons 4-5 and 4-6 (continued)

Explore the Product of Two Binomials

3. Use tiles as described below to find the product of $x + 1$ and $x + 3$.

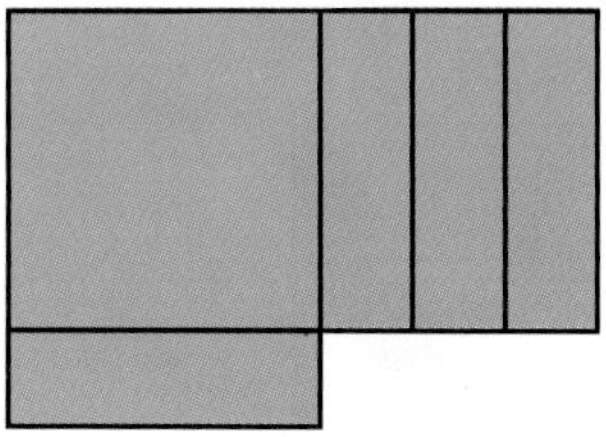

a. Place one x-by-x tile and four 1-by-x tiles as shown.
b. What tiles must you include to complete the rectangle?
c. What are the lengths of the sides of the rectangle?
d. What is the sum of the areas of the tiles?
e. What is the product $(x + 1)(x + 3)$?

Use What You Have Observed

4. Write the product represented by each tile model. Then find the product.

a.

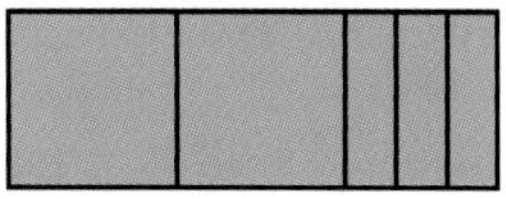

b.

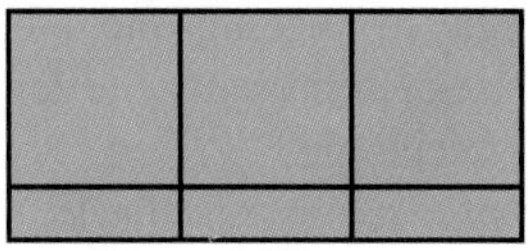

c.

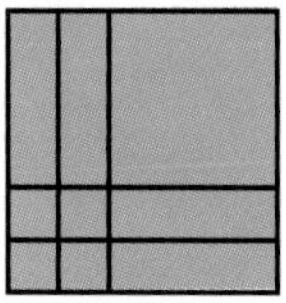

d.

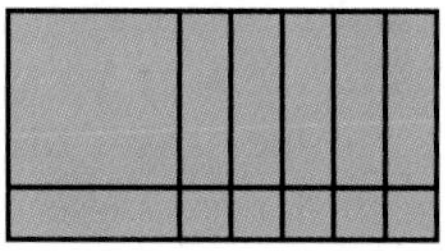

5. Find each product by using tiles. Refer to Exercises **1** and **2** as a guide.
a. $x(2x + 3)$ **b.** $3x(2x + 1)$ **c.** $(x + 5)3x$

6. Find each product by using tiles. Refer to Exercise **3** as a guide.
a. $(x + 2)(2x + 1)$ **b.** $(2x + 3)(3x + 1)$ **c.** $(x + 3)^2$

Exploring Polynomial Factors

Use before Lesson 5-7

In this activity, you will use the square and rectangular tiles from the previous exploration to find the factors of polynomials.

Explore Monomial Factors

1. Represent $x^2 + 3x$ with one x-by-x tile and three 1-by-x tiles as shown.

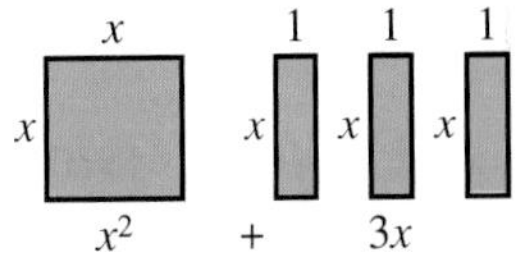

a. Arrange the tiles to form a rectangle. What is the area of this rectangle in terms of the areas of the tiles?

b. What is the length of the rectangle? What is the width of the rectangle?

c. Express the area of the rectangle as the product of its length and width.

d. Write an expression that shows the factors of $x^2 + 3x$.

2. Use tiles to find the factors of $2x^2 + 4x$.

a. What tiles can you use to represent the given expression?

b. Arrange the tiles to form a rectangle that has a width of x. What is the length of the rectangle?

c. Write an expression that shows these factors of the given expression.

d. Rearrange the tiles to form a different rectangle. What are the lengths of the sides of this rectangle?

e. Write an expression that shows another way to factor the given expression.

Explore Binomial Factors

3. Use tiles to factor $x^2 + 7x + 12$.

a. What tiles will you start with?

b. Arrange the tiles to form a rectangle.

c. What are the lengths of the sides of the rectangle?

d. What are the factors of $x^2 + 7x + 12$?

Use What You Have Observed

4. Write the polynomial and its factors represented by the tiles.

a.

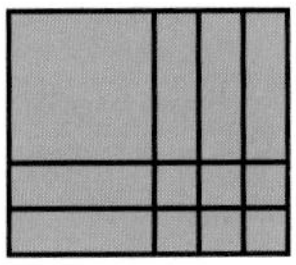

b.

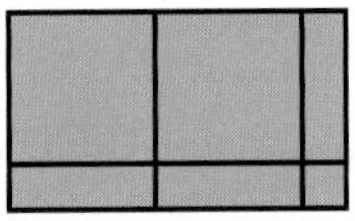

c.

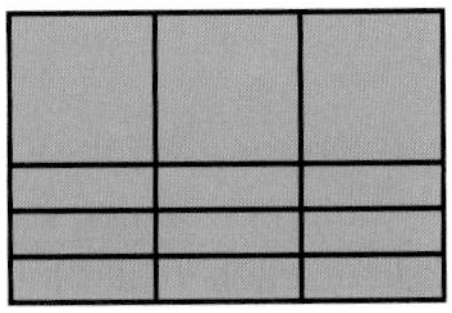

5. Use tiles to find the factors of each polynomial.

a. $2x^2 + x$ **b.** $x^2 + 2x + 1$ **c.** $3x^2 + 7x + 2$

Exploring GCF and LCM

Use before Lesson 6-4

In this activity, you will explore the connection between the factored forms of the greatest common factor (GCF) and the least common multiple (LCM) of two numbers. You will need to use the following definitions:

To find the GCF and LCM of two numbers, first find the prime factorization of each number.
The **GCF** is the product of the *smaller* powers of each *common* prime factor.
The **LCM** is the product of the *larger* powers of each prime factor.

Explore Using Whole Numbers

1. a. Find the factored form of the GCF of 18 and 24 as described above.
b. What prime factors of 18 and 24 are *not* included in the GCF?
c. Find the factored form of the LCM of 18 and 24 as described above.
d. What prime factors of 18 and 24 are *not* included in the LCM?
e. What do you observe about your answers to parts **a–d**?

2. a. Find the factored form of the product of 18 and 24.
b. How is the product related to the GCF and LCM?

Explore Using Algebraic Expressions

3. a. Using the following two expressions $N = ab^2c^3$ and $P = a^2bc^2d$, find the GCF of N and P.
b. What factors of N and P are not included in the GCF?
c. Find the factored form of the LCM of N and P.
d. What factors of N and P are not included in the LCM?
e. What do you observe about your answers to parts **a–d**?

4. a. Find the factored form of the product of N and P.
b. How is the product related to the GCF and LCM?

Use What You Have Observed

5. Find the GCF of 48 and 60. Then use the GCF and the product of 48 and 60 to find the LCM of these two numbers.

6. For fractions, the least common denominator (LCD) is the LCM of the denominators of the fractions. Use the method of Exercise **5** to find the LCD for each pair of fractions.

a. $\frac{1}{4}, \frac{1}{6}$ **b.** $\frac{7}{12}, \frac{5}{18}$ **c.** $\frac{3}{25}, \frac{4}{15}$

Exploring Applications of Proportions

Use with Lesson 7-2

In this activity, you will use real data or randomly generated data along with proportions to make estimates in real-life situations.

Explore Using Real Data

1. Use a local phone book for the data in this exercise.

a. Use the number of listings in one column to write and solve a proportion to estimate the number of listings in the entire book.

b. Count the listings on one page that use only initials for first names.

c. Find a ratio that represents the following: $\frac{\text{number of listings with initials}}{\text{number of listings}}$

d. Use a proportion to estimate the number of listings in the entire phone book that use initials.

Explore Using Randomly-Generated Data

2. Since it is impractical to identify every member of a given wildlife population, population samples are frequently used to make estimates of entire populations. Follow the example below.

a. Use a computer to generate 200 random numbers from 1 to 1000.

b. Generate a second set of 200 random numbers from 1 to 1000.

c. Assume the first set of numbers represents the initial portion of a wildlife population that was captured, tagged, and released. Assume the second set of numbers represents a second captured portion. Based on the two sets of numbers, how many animals were captured both times?

d. Parts **a–c** are a model of a capture-recapture method used to estimate wildlife populations. This method uses the following proportion:

$$\frac{\text{number of animals initially tagged and released}}{\text{total population of animals}} = \frac{\text{number of tagged animals in second sample}}{\text{total number of animals in second sample}}$$

Use this proportion to find how many animals you should have expected to capture both times in part **c.**

Use What You Have Observed

3. To estimate how many fish are in Lake Rainbow, fish-and-wildlife rangers captured, tagged, and released 100 fish. Later, they captured a second sample of 100 fish and found that 8 of them had been previously tagged. What is the fish population of Lake Rainbow?

4. Design a method for determining how many students in your school participate in a certain extracurricular activity.

Exploring Linear Equations

Use before Lesson 8-4

In this activity, you will use a graphing calculator or a computer with graphing software to graph linear equations. You will be able to watch the lines change as you change values of different parts of the equation.

For $y = mx + b$, choose a value for m and choose a value for b.

Explore Changes in the Value of m

1. **a.** Use the software to graph the equation you selected above.
b. Increase the value of m by 1, and graph this equation.
c. Increase the value of m by 1 several more times. Graph each equation.
d. How are the graphs alike? How are they different? How are the equations alike? How are they different?

2. **a.** Use the software to graph the original equation you selected above.
b. Decrease the value of m by 1 several times. Graph each equation.
c. How are the graphs alike? How are they different? How are the equations alike? How are they different?

3. Write a statement that summarizes your results in Exercises **1** and **2.**

Explore Changes in the Value of b

4. **a.** Use the software to graph the original equation you selected above.
b. Increase the value of b by 1 several times. Graph each equation.
c. How are the graphs alike? different? How are the equations alike? different?

5. **a.** Use the software to graph the original equation you selected above.
b. Decrease the value of b by 1 several times. Graph each equation.
c. How are the graphs alike? different? How are the equations alike? different?

6. Write a statement that summarizes your results in Exercises **4** and **5.**

Use What You Have Observed

7. How are the graphs of $y = 2x + 5$ and $y = 3x + 5$ related? First make a prediction; then graph the lines to check.

8. How are the graphs of $y = 2x + 5$ and $y = 2x + 1$ related? First make a prediction; then graph the lines to check.

Exploring Systems of Linear Equations

Use before Lesson 9-1

In this activity, you will use a graphing calculator or a computer with graphing software to graph more than one linear equation on the same pair of axes. You will be able to see how the graphs are related to each other as you form new equations by changing values of different parts of the equations.

For $ax + by = c$, choose a value for a, for b, and for c. For example, you might let $a = 1$, $b = -2$, and $c = \frac{1}{2}$.

Explore Changes in the Value of c

1. a. Use the software to graph the equation you selected above.

b. Choose a different value for c, and graph this equation on the same set of axes. How are the two graphs related?

c. Repeat step **b** four more times. Summarize the results of changing the value of c.

Explore Multiplying by a Constant

2. a. Use the software to graph the original equation you selected above.

b. Choose any number and multiply each term of the original equation by this number; then graph this equation on the same set of axes. How are the two graphs related?

c. Repeat step **b** four more times. Summarize the results of multiplying each term of the original equation by a different constant each time.

Explore Changes in the Value of a or b

3. a. Use the software to graph the original equation you selected above.

b. Choose a different value for a only or for b only, and graph this equation on the same set of axes. How are the graphs related?

c. Is the point of intersection a solution of the original equation? Is it a solution of the new equation?

d. Repeat step **b** four more times. Summarize the results of changing the value of a or b.

Use What You Have Observed

4. Explain how the graphs of $2x - 3y = -\frac{1}{2}$ and $2x - 3y = 0$ are related.

5. Explain how the graphs of $-3x + y = -2$ and $6x - 2y = 4$ are related.

6. Explain how the graphs of $3x + 2y = 5$ and $3x + 4y = 5$ are related.

Exploring Properties of Equality and Order

Use before Lesson 10-2

In Lesson 2-1, you used three important properties of the equals relationship.

For all real numbers a, b, and c:

Reflexive Property	$a = a$
Symmetric Property	If $a = b$, then $b = a$.
Transitive Property	If $a = b$ and $b = c$, then $a = c$.

Do you think these properties hold true for other relationships? Let's see.

Explore Relationships in Real Situations

1. Think of the relationship "is next door to." Let a, b, and c represent houses. Write how each property would be stated.
a. reflexive property
b. symmetric property
c. transitive property

2. Which of the properties in Exercise **1** hold true in real life? Use the diagram to help you decide.

3. Determine which of the properties, if any, hold true for each relationship. Let a, b, and c represent people. Use diagrams to help you decide.
a. is shorter than
b. is the sibling (brother or sister) of
c. is the classmate of
d. is older than

Explore Relationships in Mathematics

4. Think of the relationship "is a factor of." Let a, b, and c represent numbers. Write how each property would be stated.
a. reflexive property **b.** symmetric property **c.** transitive property

5. Which of the properties in Exercise **4** hold true?

6. Determine which properties, if any, hold true for each relationship.
a. is a multiple of **b.** is *not* equal to **c.** is less than **d.** is greater than

Use What You Have Observed

7. Suppose you want to list 4 people (all of different ages) in increasing order of age. They will not tell you their ages but they will answer "yes" or "no" when asked if each is older than another. What is the fewest possible number of questions needed to list them properly?

8. Which property was helpful in solving Exercise **7**?

Exploring Decimals

Use with Lesson 11-2

In this activity you will use a calculator to explore which fractions can be expressed as terminating decimals and which can be expressed as repeating decimals.

Explore Decimal Forms of Unit Fractions

1. a. Use a calculator to find the decimal form of $\frac{1}{2}$ by dividing 1 by 2.

b. Find the decimal form of the next ten unit fractions: $\frac{1}{3}, \frac{1}{4}, \frac{1}{5}, \frac{1}{6}, \ldots, \frac{1}{12}$. Make a table of your results.

c. Which fractions have decimal forms that terminate?

d. Which fractions have decimal forms that repeat?

e. Find the prime factors of the denominator for each fraction in parts **c** and **d**. Compare the two sets of results.

f. What seems to be true of the fractions with denominators having prime factors of only 2 and/or 5?

g. What seems to be true of the fractions with denominators having prime factors other than 2 or 5?

2. Predict whether the decimal form of each fraction will terminate or repeat. Then check with a calculator.

a. $\frac{1}{13}$ **b.** $\frac{1}{20}$ **c.** $\frac{1}{27}$ **d.** $\frac{1}{200}$

Explore the Fraction Forms of Decimals

3. a. Write each of the following decimals in fraction form: 0.4, 0.29, 0.325, 0.4791

b. Write the prime factorization of each denominator from part **a.**

c. What do you observe about the factored forms of all the denominators? Does this agree or disagree with your results in Exercise **1**?

Use What You Have Observed

4. What generalization can you make about the denominators of fractions in simplest form that represent terminating decimals?

5. What generalization can you make about the denominators of fractions in simplest form that represent repeating decimals?

Exploring Irrational Numbers

Use after Lesson 11-6

In this activity you will explore relationships between sides of a right triangle and then explore two methods of creating segments having irrational lengths.

Explore the Sides of a Right Triangle

1. a. Find the length of the hypotenuse of a right triangle with both legs having a length of 1.

b. Using your answer to part **a** as the length of one leg and 1 as the length of the other leg, find the length of the hypotenuse of this new triangle.

c. Using your answer to part **b** as the length of one leg and 1 as the length of the other leg, find the length of the hypotenuse of this new triangle.

d. Continue this process, finding the length of the hypotenuse of the next five new triangles formed by the procedure above.

e. What pattern do you notice?

2. a. Find the length of the hypotenuse of a right triangle with both legs having a length of 2.

b. Using your answer to part **a** as the length of one leg and 2 as the length of the other leg, find the length of the hypotenuse of this new triangle.

c. Using your answer to part **b** as the length of one leg and 2 as the length of the other leg, find the length of the hypotenuse of this new triangle.

d. Continue this process, finding the length of the hypotenuse of the next five new triangles formed.

e. What pattern do you notice?

Generalize What You Have Observed

3. If the lengths of the legs of a right triangle are x and $x\sqrt{y}$, what will be the length of the hypotenuse?

Explore Using Diagrams

4. a. Use a ruler and a protractor to draw a right triangle with legs of length 1 in. each, as shown at the right.

b. At point A, draw a 1-in. segment that is perpendicular to $\overline{AB}$ and connect the end of this segment to point B to form a new right triangle. Label the new vertex C.

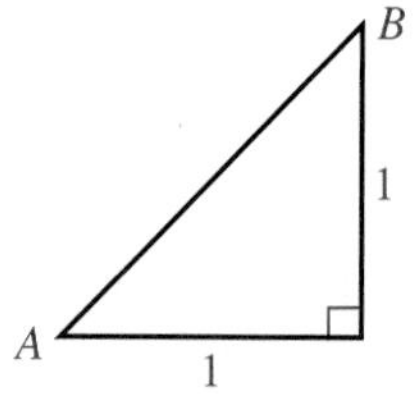

(Continued on next page.)

Exploring Irrational Numbers

Use after Lesson 11-6 (continued)

4. c. What are the lengths of the sides of triangle *ABC?*

d. At point *C*, draw a 1-in. segment that is perpendicular to $\overline{CB}$ and connect the end of this segment to point *B* to form a new right triangle. Label the new vertex *D*.

e. What are the lengths of the sides of triangle *CBD?*

f. Continue drawing new right triangles until your diagram will overlap your first triangle. The diagram you have generated is called the *Wheel of Theodorus*.

g. What lengths of irrational measure have you constructed?

Explore Using a Geoboard or Dot Paper

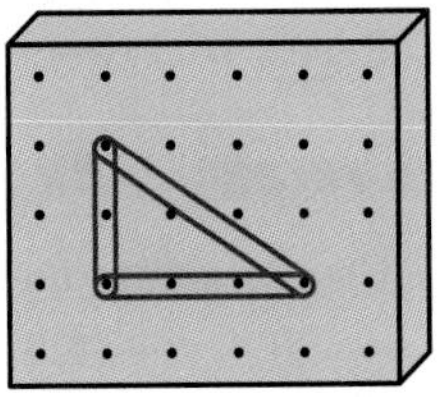

5. a. The right triangle built on the geoboard at the right has legs of length 2 and 3. What is the length of the hypotenuse?

b. Use a geoboard or dot paper to build a triangle with legs of length 1 and 2. What is the length of the hypotenuse? Is it irrational?

c. Build another triangle with a hypotenuse of irrational length. Give the lengths of the legs and hypotenuse.

d. Build a square with sides of length 2. Then build the diagonal and find its length.

e. Build a rectangle with width of 2 and length of 5. Then build the diagonal and find its length.

Use What You Have Observed

6. Describe two ways to construct a segment with length $\sqrt{17}$.

7. Can you construct a segment with length $\sqrt{21}$ using a Wheel of Theodorus? using a geoboard?

8. How can you construct a segment with length $5\sqrt{7}$ in.?

Exploring Quadratic Equations

Use with Lesson 12-4

In this activity, you will use a computer with graphing software or a graphing calculator to graph quadratic equations. You will then change the scale of the graph, if necessary, to find the number of real roots and to estimate these roots.

Explore $ax^2 + bx + c = 0$, where $b^2 - 4ac = 0$

1. **a.** Choose values for a, b, and c such that $b^2 - 4ac = 0$. For example, let $a = 2$, $b = 4$, and $c = 2$. Graph the resulting equation $y = ax^2 + bx + c$.
   b. In how many points does the graph intersect the x-axis?
   c. Enlarge the scale on the x-axis, if necessary, until you can estimate the root(s) to the nearest tenth.
   d. Repeat steps **a–c** for a different set of values.

Explore $ax^2 + bx + c = 0$, where $b^2 - 4ac > 0$

2. **a.** Choose values for a, b, and c, such that $b^2 - 4ac > 0$, and graph the resulting equation $y = ax^2 + bx + c$.
   b. In how many points does the graph intersect the x-axis?
   c. Enlarge the scale on the x-axis, if necessary, until you can estimate these root(s) to the nearest tenth.
   d. Repeat steps **a–c** for a different set of values.

Explore $ax^2 + bx + c = 0$, where $b^2 - 4ac < 0$

3. **a.** Choose values for a, b, and c, such that $b^2 - 4ac < 0$, and graph the resulting equation $y = ax^2 + bx + c$.
   b. In how many points does the graph intersect the x-axis?
   c. What can you conclude about the real roots for this equation?
   d. Repeat steps **a–c** for a different set of values.

Use What You Have Observed

4. How many real roots does $3x^2 - 8x + 9 = 0$ have? How do you know?

5. How many real roots does $x^2 - \sqrt{12}x + 3 = 0$ have? How do you know? Graph the related equation and estimate the root(s) to the nearest tenth.

6. How many real roots does $3x^2 - 6x + 1 = 0$ have? How do you know? Graph the related equation and estimate the root(s) to the nearest tenth.

7. Make up quadratic equations that have no roots, one root, and two roots. Graph your equations to verify the number of roots.

Portfolio Projects

To make a portfolio, an artist selects a variety of original work to represent the range of his or her skills. Each of the following projects will give you a chance to create a finished product that you will be proud to add to your algebra portfolio.

The projects will help you develop your ability to present and communicate your ideas. They will also help you develop your problem-solving and reasoning abilities as you make connections between what you know and what is new. Your individual insight and creativity will help shape the mathematics you discover.

Let these projects be springboards for further exploration. Feel free to expand them to include new questions or areas of interest that arise. Most of all, have fun!

Hailstone Sequences (Chapter 1)

A *sequence* is an ordered list of numbers. The rules given below generate some interesting sequences, called *hailstone sequences*. Begin with any positive integer n.

Step 1 If the integer is even, then the next number is $\frac{1}{2}n$.

If the integer is odd, then the next number is $3n + 1$.

Step 2 For each number you obtain, repeat step (1) to find the next number.

Here is an example:

Start with $n = 10$.

10 is even, so the next number is $\frac{1}{2}(10) = 5$.

5 is odd, so the next number is $3 \cdot 5 + 1 = 16$.

1. Continue listing numbers of the sequence above until a pattern becomes clear.
2. The diagram at the right represents the sequence in Exercise 1. Draw a similar diagram of the sequence that begins with **(a)** $n = 6$ and **(b)** $n = 18$.

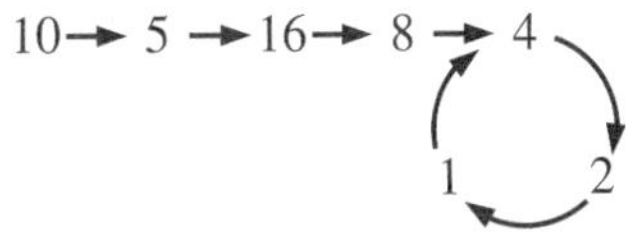

3. Draw diagrams of at least five more hailstone sequences.
4. Investigate the following questions: Does every hailstone sequence end in a loop? If so, do they all end in the same loop? What is the longest stretch of numbers before a hailstone sequence enters a loop? What is the highest value reached by a hailstone sequence?
5. Investigate the consequences of changing the rules for generating a hailstone sequence. Again, begin with any positive integer n. Then:

   Divide the integer by 3.

   If the remainder is 0, then the next number is $\frac{1}{3}n$.

   If the remainder is 1, then the next number is $4n - 1$.

   If the remainder is 2, then the next number is $4n + 1$.

Diagramming Operations (Chapter 2)

The diagram at the right represents the arithmetic operation "add 2." Notice, for example, that an arrow joins -1 on the upper number line to $-1 + 2$, or 1, on the lower number line. Similarly, an arrow joins each number n on the upper number line to $n + 2$ on the lower number line.

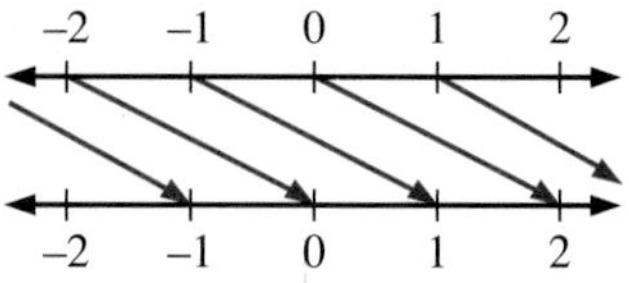

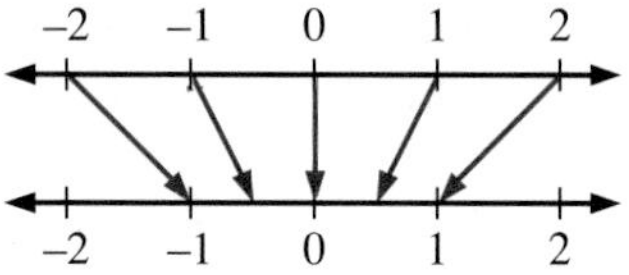

1. Describe the operation represented by the diagram at the right in words and with an algebraic expression.

2. Draw a diagram to represent each operation, and write an algebraic expression to describe the operation.
a. Subtract 1 **b.** Multiply by 3 **c.** Take the reciprocal

The diagram at the left below represents two operations applied one after the other. The upper and middle number lines represent the first operation, and the middle and lower number lines represent the second operation. The combined operations are represented by the diagram at the right below, in which the middle number line has been eliminated and each pair of arrows has been replaced by one arrow.

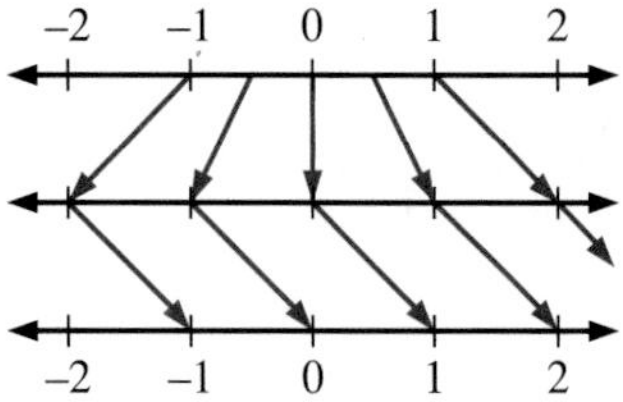

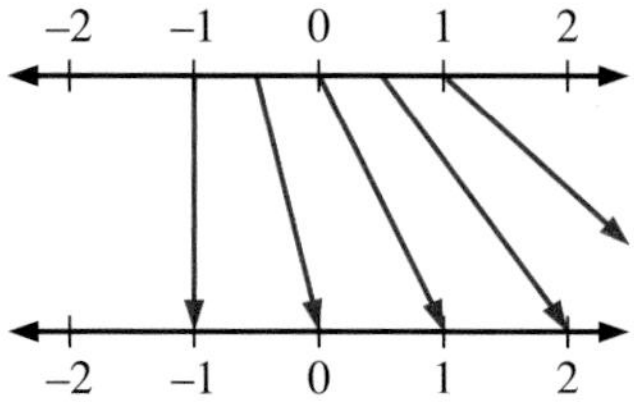

3. a. Describe in words the two operations represented by the diagram at the left above. Write an algebraic expression to describe the combined operations represented by the diagram at the right above.

b. What two operations would you use to *reverse the directions* of the arrows, that is, to move from the lower to the middle and upper number lines? Write an algebraic expression to describe the combined operations represented by the diagram at the right with the arrows reversed.

ISBNs and Check Digits (Chapter 3)

Every book published after 1968 has a 10-digit ISBN, or *International Standard Book Number.* The diagram at the right shows how to interpret the first 9 digits of an ISBN. The last digit of an ISBN is a *check digit,* which allows a person or a computer to tell if a mistake was made in one of the other nine digits.

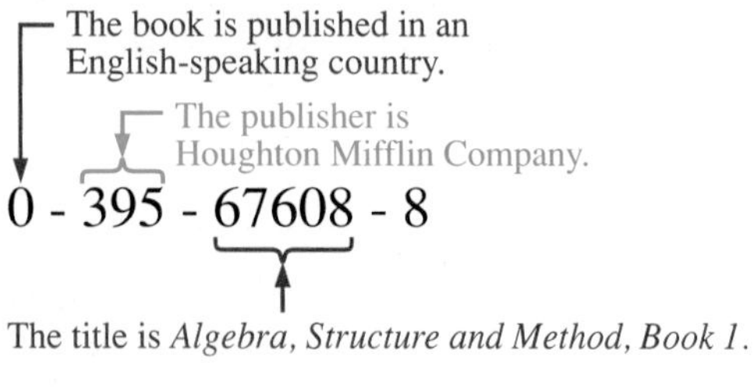

The check digit is chosen so that when the digits of the ISBN are inserted in order into the blanks of the expression shown below, the result of the calculation is divisible by 11.

1 • __ + 2 • __ + 3 • __ + 4 • __ + 5 • __ + 6 • __ + 7 • __ + 8 • __ + 9 • __ + 10 • __

For example, the "check calculation" for the ISBN 0-395-67608-8 is:

$1 \cdot 0 + 2 \cdot 3 + 3 \cdot 9 + 4 \cdot 5 + 5 \cdot 6 + 6 \cdot 7 + 7 \cdot 6 + 8 \cdot 0 + 9 \cdot 8 + 10 \cdot 8 = 319 = 11 \cdot 29$

1. Find the ISBNs of two books (they usually appear on the copyright page). Do the check calculation for each book. Verify that the result is divisible by 11.
2. Find the correct check digit n for **(a)** 0-231-10245-n and **(b)** 0-101-10200-n.
3. A typist enters ISBNs into a computer, which checks them to see if they are valid. Show by example that the typist could type two wrong digits without the computer detecting the errors. Is it possible for the typist to enter only a single wrong digit without the error being detected? Explain.
4. Why do you think that 11 was chosen as the number that must divide evenly into the result of the check calculation? Would some other number, such as 7 or 8 or 12, work just as well? Explain.
5. Devise your own code that uses a check digit and give the check calculation formula for your code.

Bumper-to-Bumper *(Chapter 4)*

Traffic volume and *traffic density* are two measures of the number of cars on a highway at any given time. The average speed maintained by cars on a highway depends in part on both the traffic volume and the traffic density.

Traffic volume is the number of cars per hour (cars/h) that pass a given point.
Traffic density is the average number of cars per mile (cars/mi).

1. Suppose that there are 2 cars in every mile of highway, and that they are traveling at an average speed of 50 mi/h. What is the traffic volume? Draw a picture and explain your method.
2. Find the traffic volume for a highway on which cars are traveling at an average speed of 40 mi/h with a density of 15 cars/mi.
3. For a given stretch of highway, let s = the average speed in mi/h of cars on the highway, let v = the traffic volume in cars/h, and let d = the traffic density in cars/mi. Write a formula relating these three variables.
4. For any fixed average speed, what happens to the traffic volume as traffic density increases? Will this always happen? Explain.
5. Two lanes of bumper-to-bumper traffic merge into one lane. The cars are moving at an average speed of 10 mi/h before the merge. If the traffic volume is the same before and after the merge, then what is the average speed of the cars immediately after the merge? Explain your reasoning.

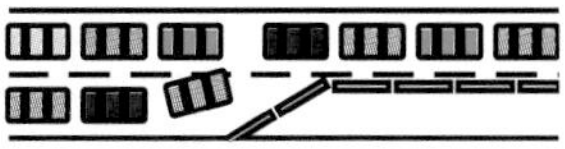

Pursuing Primes (Chapter 5)

For centuries, people have tried to find formulas that generate prime numbers. Formulas have been found that work in some cases, but never in *all*. In Exercises 2 and 3, you will investigate two of these formulas. First, though, you should establish an efficient method of testing a number for primeness, which is the purpose of Exercise 1. Exercise 4 involves a little research. Exercise 5 is a game you can play that relies on knowing prime numbers and factors of numbers.

1. Which of the following numbers are prime: 79, 157, 253, and 679? Describe an efficient method of testing whether a number is prime.
2. A polynomial formula that has been tried as a prime-number generator is $x^2 + x + 17$. Show that the formula gives a prime number for $x = 0, 1, 2,$ and 3. Find a positive integer for which the formula does not produce a prime.
3. In the seventeenth century, the French abbot Marin Mersenne looked for primes that can be written in the form $2^p - 1$, where p is a prime number. (In 1975, the postmark pictured at the right commemorated the discovery of the *Mersenne prime* $2^{11213} - 1$.) Find a prime number p less than 20 for which $2^p - 1$ is *not* prime.

4. In a book on mathematics, find Goldbach's Conjecture and then demonstrate that it is true for at least the first 10 even numbers greater than 4.
5. In this solitaire game, your goal is to get the highest score you can by taking numbers according to the rules given below. Play the game several times and then describe your strategy for choosing the numbers you take.

   Begin with a list of the first 20 positive integers. Take a number that has at least one of the remaining numbers as a factor. Then eliminate from the list all factors of the number you took. Continue to take numbers in this way for as long as you can. Your score is the sum of all the numbers you take.

Continued Fractions (Chapter 6)

$$1 + \cfrac{1}{2 + \cfrac{1}{1 + \cfrac{1}{4}}}$$

The expression shown at the right could be described as the sum of an integer and a fraction that has within it two other fractions. The numerators of all the fractions are 1. Such an expression is called a *continued fraction.* To evaluate the continued fraction, start at the bottom and work your way up:

$$1 + \cfrac{1}{2 + \cfrac{1}{1 + \frac{1}{4}}} = 1 + \cfrac{1}{2 + \cfrac{1}{\frac{5}{4}}} = 1 + \cfrac{1}{2 + \frac{4}{5}} = 1 + \cfrac{1}{\frac{14}{5}} = 1 + \frac{5}{14} = \frac{19}{14}$$

To write a fraction in continued-fraction form, follow the steps illustrated by the example at the top of the next page.

$$\frac{37}{10} = 3 + \frac{7}{10} = 3 + \cfrac{1}{\frac{10}{7}} = 3 + \cfrac{1}{1 + \frac{3}{7}} = 3 + \cfrac{1}{1 + \cfrac{1}{\frac{7}{3}}} = 3 + \cfrac{1}{1 + \cfrac{1}{2 + \frac{1}{3}}}$$

Split off the integer part of $\frac{37}{10}$.

Write $\frac{7}{10}$ as $1 \div \frac{10}{7}$.

Split off the integer part of $\frac{10}{7}$.

Write $\frac{3}{7}$ as $1 \div \frac{7}{3}$.

Split off the integer part of $\frac{7}{3}$.

Stop when all the numerators are 1.

1. Evaluate each continued fraction: **a.** $2 + \cfrac{1}{1 + \frac{1}{3}}$ **b.** $\cfrac{1}{4 + \cfrac{1}{2 + \frac{1}{5}}}$

2. Write each fraction in continued-fraction form: **a.** $\frac{17}{12}$ **b.** $\frac{5}{16}$

3. By trying several examples, discover and describe how to find the continued-fraction form of any fraction of the type $\frac{n}{n+1}$, where n is a positive integer.

4. By trying several examples, discover and describe the relationship between the continued-fraction forms of a fraction and its reciprocal.

A Transportation Problem (Chapter 7)

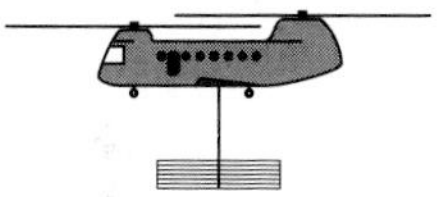

A certain construction company often moves lumber to construction sites by helicopter. The lumber can be loaded inside the helicopter or it can be carried below the helicopter, attached by a cable. Packing the lumber inside the helicopter takes more time than simply attaching the lumber with a cable, but the helicopter can fly faster if it carries the lumber inside rather than underneath. Here are the facts:

Loading the lumber into the helicopter takes 30 minutes and unloading it takes 20 minutes. Carrying the lumber inside, the helicopter travels 144 mi/h.

Attaching the lumber by cable takes 15 minutes, and detaching it takes only 10 minutes. Carrying its load underneath, the helicopter travels 120 mi/h.

It costs \$300 per hour to fly the helicopter and \$40 per hour to load and unload the lumber (whether loading it inside or attaching it by cable).

The company management asks you to answer two questions:

1. For what distances is each method of transporting lumber most economical?

2. Sometimes the company has a rush job that requires them to transport the lumber as quickly as possible, regardless of cost. For what distances does it make sense for them to take the time to load the lumber inside the helicopter?

Prepare a written report for the company management giving your solutions.

Slopes of Staircases (Chapter 8)

Materials: *Ruler or tape measure*

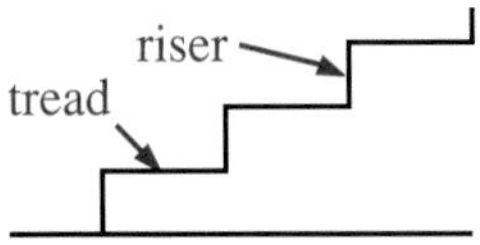

The horizontal parts of a staircase are called *treads* and the vertical parts are called *risers*.

1. How would you use the height of the risers and the depth of the treads to measure the slope of a staircase?
2. Many communities have building-code requirements that place restrictions on the slope of a staircase. Why do you think this is so? (How will the slope of a staircase affect your sense of comfort and safety when you use the stairs?) By drawing pictures, estimate a good range of slopes for staircases.
3. Measure the riser height and tread depth of staircases in a number of buildings, both public (such as your school) and private (such as your home). Include different types of stairs, such as front stairs, back stairs, attic stairs, and basement stairs. Find the average slope, and the smallest and largest slopes of the staircases you measure. For each staircase, rate or otherwise describe the sense of comfort and safety you feel walking up and down the stairs.
4. Find a set of recommended specifications for the design of stairs. (You could find this in a reference book or you could call a local building inspector to find out what the building-code requirements are in your community.) How closely do the staircases you measured conform to these recommendations?

Breaking Even (Chapter 9)

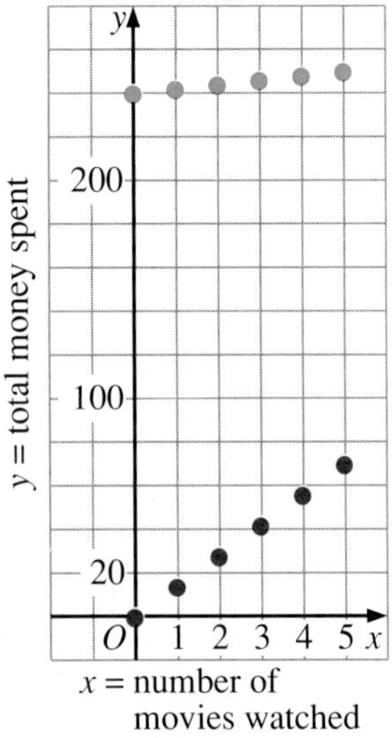

Zack and Zoe spend \$14 every time they go to the local cinema. They're thinking about buying a VCR for \$240 and renting tapes for \$2 each. The graph shows the couple's total expenses if they continue to go to the cinema (red dots) and if they buy a VCR and rent tapes (blue dots). Each set of colored dots is linear.

1. **a.** The red dots lie on the line with equation $y = 14x$. What is an equation for the set of blue dots?
   b. Graph the two equations in part (a) and find the intersection point of the two lines. You may want to use a graphing calculator or a computer with graphing software.
   c. The point you found in part (b) is called a *break-even* point. Explain what this means for Zack and Zoe.
2. Find other situations in which making some investment, such as buying a VCR, lowers a regularly-occurring expense, such as the cost of watching a movie. Use graphs, equations, and words to analyze the situations, especially with regard to break-even points and what they mean.

The Classified Ads (Chapter 10)

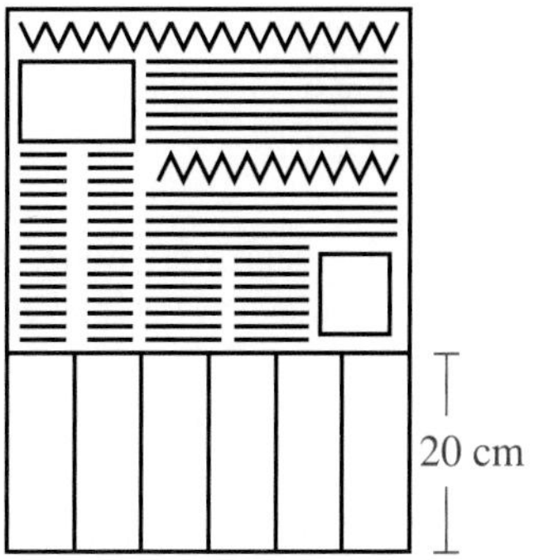

Suppose you have been hired to lay out the classified ads for a newspaper. Classified ads may appear only in the bottom 20 cm of any given page, and each page of the newspaper is divided into 6 columns. Ads are one column wide, and no ad can begin at the bottom of one column and then end at the top of another column. You want to do the job efficiently, keeping wasted space to a minimum, but you don't want to spend too much time "tinkering" with the placement of the ads. Instead, you need a general procedure that you can use day after day to position the ads using as few columns as possible.

For today's paper, the ads are of the following lengths:

5 cm, 8 cm, 4 cm, 6 cm, 4 cm, 2.5 cm, 3.5 cm, 5 cm, 7 cm, 7.5 cm, 6 cm, 6.5 cm, 3.5 cm, 2 cm, 6 cm, 4 cm, 7 cm, 5 cm, 5 cm, 5.5 cm, 4.5 cm, 6 cm, 5 cm

Using the lengths given above as an example, devise a systematic approach to the problem of positioning the ads. Can you fit all of today's ads in the 20 cm at the bottom of one page or must you use part of a second page? Describe your procedure in detail so that someone else could use it and get the same results. Make up another set of lengths of ads and use your procedure to position the ads.

A Swimming Race (Chapter 11)

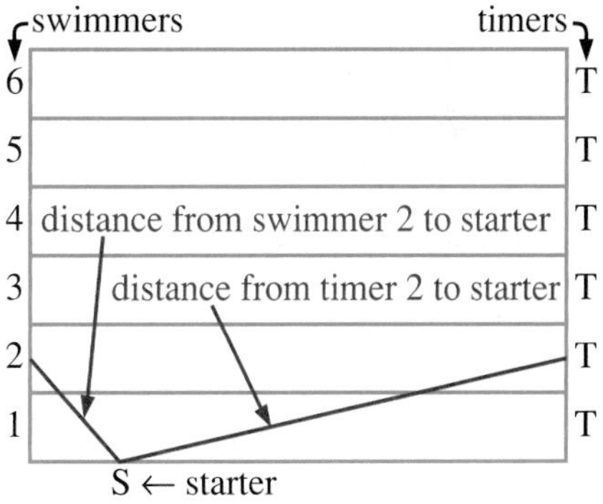

Six swimmers are about to begin a 50 m race, which will cover one length of the pool. Each swimmer stands in the middle of his or her lane, which is 2.75 m wide. The race will begin when the starter, standing at the side of the pool 3 m from the starting end, fires the starting pistol. The moment they hear the starting signal, the swimmers will dive into the pool and the timers (one for each lane) will start their stop-watches. As each swimmer finishes the race, the timer for that swimmer's lane will stop his or her watch.

Because the swimmers and timers are different distances from the starter, each one will hear the sound of the gun at a slightly different time. As a result, there may be a discrepancy between a given swimmer's actual and recorded times.

Suppose that the swimmer in lane 2 wins the race with a recorded time of 30.87 s. The swimmer in lane 6 comes in second with a recorded time of 30.88 s. Assuming that under the conditions of this race the speed of sound is 343 m/s, show that the swimmer in lane 6 may actually have won. Write up your solution in detail.

Solving Equations by Iteration (Chapter 12)

Have you ever tried to solve a quadratic equation by getting the x^2 term alone on one side of the equation and then dividing both sides by x? For example:

$$x^2 + 3x - 4 = 0$$
$$x^2 = -3x + 4$$

Although x is "alone," you still don't know a value of x that makes the equation true. → $x = -3 + \frac{4}{x}$

With the equation $x^2 + 3x - 4 = 0$ written in the form $x = -3 + \frac{4}{x}$, you can, however, use a method called *solving by iteration* to the find a solution. The steps of the process are illustrated below.

(1) Start by *guessing* a solution.	Guess $x = 2$.
(2) Substitute the guess into the expression on the right side of the equation.	$-3 + \frac{4}{x} = -3 + \frac{4}{2} = -1$
(3) Use the result as a new guess for a solution.	Guess $x = -1$.
(4) Repeat step 2 with the new guess.	$-3 + \frac{4}{x} = -3 + \frac{4}{-1} = -7$
(5) Use the result as a new guess for a solution.	Guess $x = -7$.
(6) With each guess, repeat steps 2 and 3 until the value of the new guess is the same as the value of the old guess.	$\textit{new guess} = -3 + \frac{4}{\textit{old guess}}$

1. Continue the process shown above from $x = -7$, until the values of the guesses settle down to one number. By substituting this number for x, show that the number is a solution of the equation $x = -3 + \frac{4}{x}$, and also of the equation $x^2 + 3x - 4 = 0$.

2. Show that another way to get x "alone" in the equation $x^2 + 3x - 4 = 0$ is to write the equation in the form $x = \frac{4 - x^2}{3}$. Then try solving by iteration. What is the result?

3. Use the quadratic formula or solve by factoring to confirm that the values of x you found in Exercises 1 and 2 are the solutions of the equation $x^2 + 3x - 4 = 0$.

4. Solve by iteration. Find as many solutions as you can. Use the quadratic formula or solving by factoring to confirm your solutions.

a. $x^2 - 4x + 3 = 0$ **b.** $4x^2 + 2x - 1 = 0$

5. Write a quadratic equation that has no real solutions and then try to solve it by iteration. Describe what happens.

Appendix

Preparing for College Entrance Exams

If you plan to attend college, you will most likely be required to take college entrance examinations. Some of these exams attempt to measure the extent to which your verbal and mathematical reasoning skills have been developed. Others test your knowledge of specific subject areas. Usually the best preparation for college entrance examinations is to follow a strong academic program in high school, to study, and to read as extensively as possible. The following test-taking strategies may prove useful:

- Familiarize yourself with the type of test you will be taking well in advance of the test date. Sample tests, with accompanying explanatory material, are available for many standardized tests. By working through this sample material, you become comfortable with the types of questions and directions that will appear on the test and you develop a feeling for the pace at which you must work in order to complete the test.
- Find out how the test is scored so that you know whether it is advantageous to guess.
- Skim sections of the test before starting to answer the questions, to get an overview of the questions. You may wish to answer the easiest questions first. In any case, do not waste time on questions you do not understand; go on to those that you do.
- Mark your answer sheet carefully, checking the numbering on the answer sheet about every five questions to avoid errors caused by misplaced answer markings.
- Write in the test booklet if it is helpful; for example, cross out incorrect alternatives and do mathematical calculations.
- Work carefully, but do not take time to double-check your answers unless you finish before the deadline and have extra time.
- Arrive at the test center early and come well prepared with any necessary supplies such as sharpened pencils and a watch.

College entrance examinations that test general reasoning abilities, such as the Scholastic Aptitude Test, usually include questions dealing with basic algebraic concepts and skills. The College Board Achievement Tests in mathematics (Level I and Level II) include many questions on algebra. The following first-year algebra topics often appear on these exams. For each of the topics listed on pages 710 – 711, a page reference to the place in your textbook where this topic is discussed has been provided. As you prepare for college entrance exams, you may wish to review the topics on these pages.

Types of Numbers (pages 31–32, 75, 185)

Positive integers	$\{1, 2, 3, 4, \ldots\}$
Negative integers	$\{-1, -2, -3, -4, \ldots\}$
Integers	$\{\ldots, -4, -3, -2, -1, 0, 1, 2, 3, 4, \ldots\}$
Odd numbers	$\{1, 3, 5, 7, 9, \ldots\}$
Even numbers	$\{0, 2, 4, 6, 8, \ldots\}$
Consecutive integers	$\{n, n + 1, n + 2, \ldots\}$ (n = an integer)
Consecutive even integers	$\{n, n + 2, n + 4, \ldots\}$ (n = even integer)
Consecutive odd integers	$\{n, n + 2, n + 4, \ldots\}$ (n = odd integer)
Prime numbers	$\{2, 3, 5, 7, 11, 13, \ldots\}$

Properties (See the Glossary of Properties on pages 721-722.)

Rules for Operations on Positive and Negative Numbers
(pages 54, 71)

Rules for Addition

1. If a and b are both positive, then
$$a + b = |a| + |b|.$$
2. If a and b are both negative, then
$$a + b = -(|a| + |b|).$$
3. If a is positive and b is negative and a has the greater absolute value, then
$$a + b = |a| - |b|.$$
4. If a is positive and b is negative and b has the greater absolute value, then
$$a + b = -(|b| - |a|).$$
5. If a and b are opposites, then
$$a + b = 0.$$

Rules for Multiplication

1. If two numbers have the *same* sign, their product is *positive*.
   If two numbers have *opposite* signs, their product is *negative*.
2. The product of an *even* number of negative numbers is *positive*.
   The product of an *odd* number of negative numbers is *negative*.

Factoring (pages 185–186, 194–195, 204–227)

Integers	$a^2 + 2ab + b^2$
$a^2 - b^2$	$a^2 - 2ab + b^2$
$ax^2 + bx$	$ax^2 + bx + c$

Algebraic Fractions (pages 247–279)

Simplification	Multiplication
Addition	Division

Graphing (pages 31–32, 353–355, 366–368, 383–385, 457–458, 478–479, 490–492, 495, 572–573)

Points on a number line
Inequalities on a number line
Points and lines in a number plane
Inequalities in a number plane
Quadratic functions

Percents (pages 309–311, 315–316)

Converting decimals and fractions to percents
Percents greater than 100
Percents less than 1
Percent problems

Solving Equations (pages 95–96, 102–103, 230–232, 561–562, 567–568, 573)

Transformation by substitution (p. 96)
Transformation by addition (p. 96)
Transformation by subtraction (p. 96)
Transformation by multiplication (p. 102)
Transformation by division (p. 102)

Factoring (pp. 230–232)
$x^2 = k$ (p. 561)
Quadratic formula (p. 567)
Discriminant (p. 573)

Simultaneous Equations (pages 413–414, 417–418, 426–427, 430–431)

The graphic method
The substitution method
The addition-or-subtraction method
Multiplication with the addition-or-subtraction method

Variation (pages 391–392, 397–398, 584–585, 588–589)

Direct variation
Inverse variation
Direct variation involving powers
Inverse variation involving powers
Joint variation
Combined variation

Word Problems (pages 23–24, 26, 27–28, 75–76, 112–113, 121–122, 126, 165, 167–169, 172, 175–176, 234–235, 287–289, 293–294, 302, 315–316, 321–322, 326–327, 350, 421–423, 438–439, 444–446, 469–471, 579, 588–589)

Age
Area
Consecutive integers
Cost and value
Digit
Fraction
Investment
Mixture
Percent
Proportion
Ratio
Uniform motion
Wind and water current
Without solutions
Work

Types of Questions

The types of questions you can expect may include five-choice *Multiple–Choice* questions, four-choice *Quantitative Comparison* questions, or *Grid–in* questions. Here is an example of a **Multiple–Choice** question:

If $4x + 4x + 4x = 72$, what is the value of $x + 3$?
(A) 6
(B) 7
(C) 8
(D) 9 *the correct answer*
(E) 10

Quantitative Comparison questions give you two quantities and ask you to compare them. Here is an example of a Quantitative Comparison question:

Column A	Column B
7^2	$4^2 + 3^2$

You must choose whether the quantity in Column A is greater, the quantity in column B is greater, the two quantities are equal, or if you cannot determine which is greater from the information given. For this example, the quantity in Column A is greater.

Grid–in questions emphasize active problem solving and critical thinking by asking you to grid the answer directly on the answer sheet rather than recognize it from among the choices. Using the same example as the Multiple–Choice question, the answer is still 9, but you would have to grid 9 on the answer sheet rather than choose (D).

Calculator Use

Some college entrance exams allow students to use calculators. If calculator use is permitted, bring a familiar calculator with you to the test center, but don't plan to use it for every problem. First decide how to solve the problem, and then decide if a calculator will help with the computation. For example, suppose you are given the numbers 1, 4, 82, 93, 45, 232, and 19. If you are asked to find the median, the middle value listed, using a calculator will not help. You should list the numbers in order and choose 45. If you are asked to find the mean, the average of the numbers, using a calculator may help. You should add $1 + 4 + 82 + 93 + 45 + 232 + 19$ and then divide by 7 to get 68. In general, calculators help solve problems involving data, number patterns, or guess-and-check problem solving strategies.

A-2 Point-Slope Form

Objective To derive linear equations using the point-slope formula.

Use after Chapter 8

A shipping company charges \$10 to ship a package weighing 3 lb or less. For every pound over 3 lb, it charges an additional \$.50 per pound. The graph of this pricing scheme consists of pieces of two lines. The lines can be described algebraically.

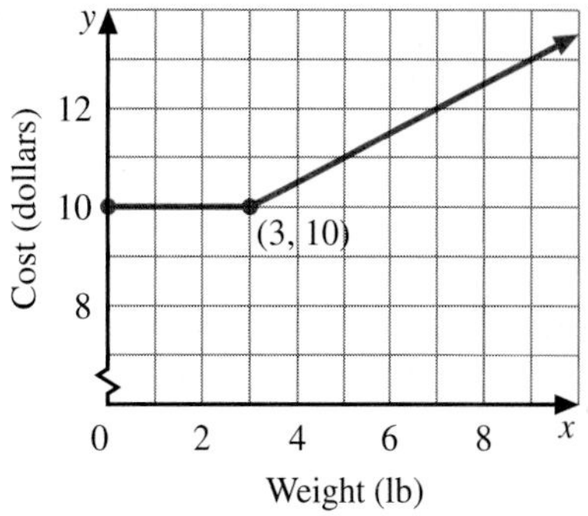

For weights ≤ 3 lb: $y = 10$

For weights > 3 lb: $y = 10 + 0.50(x - 3)$

number of pounds over 3

The second equation features the coordinates of a point on the line, (3, 10), as well as the slope of the line, 0.50. When you know the coordinates of a point on a line, (x_0, y_0), and the slope of the line, m, you can use the *point-slope* formula to write an equation of the line:

Point-slope formula	**Example**
$y - y_0 = m(x - x_0)$	$y - 10 = 0.50(x - 3)$

Example 1 Write an equation in point-slope form of the line through the point (7, 8) with slope 4.

Solution

$$y - y_0 = m(x - x_0)$$
$$y - 8 = 4(x - 7)$$

Equations of Perpendicular Lines

When two lines are perpendicular, their slopes have a product of –1. In other words, if the slope of one line is m, then the slope of a line perpendicular to it is $-\frac{1}{m}$. You can use this fact to write an equation.

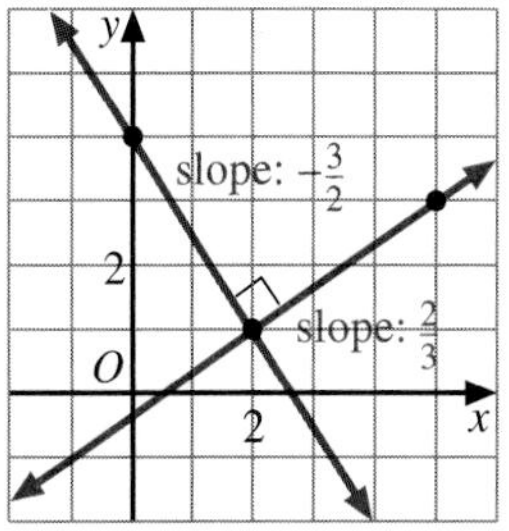

Example 2 Line A has equation $y = 3x - 7$ and passes through the point $(-2, 6)$. Line B passes through the same point and is perpendicular to Line A. Write an equation of Line B in slope-intercept form .

Solution First write an equation in point-slope form. Then rewrite it in slope-intercept form.

$$y - y_0 = m(x - x_0)$$

$$y - 6 = -\frac{1}{3}(x - (-2)) \quad \left\{\begin{array}{l}\text{The slope of Line } A \text{ is } 3,\\ \text{so the slope of Line } B \text{ is } -\frac{1}{3}.\end{array}\right.$$

$$y - 6 = -\frac{1}{3}(x + 2)$$

$$y = 6 - \frac{1}{3}x - \frac{2}{3}$$

$$y = -\frac{1}{3}x + \frac{16}{3}$$

Written Exercises

For Exercises 1–8, a point and the slope of a line are given. Write an equation in point-slope form.

1. $(1, 2); 3$ **2.** $(5, 9); 2$ **3.** $(3, 4); -\frac{1}{2}$ **4.** $(-2, 4); 5$

5. $(-3, -8); 5$ **6.** $(1, -7); -\frac{2}{3}$ **7.** $(0, 3); \frac{4}{7}$ **8.** $(0, b); m$

9. An equation of a line is $y - 2 = \frac{3}{4}(x - 5)$. Write an equation in slope-intercept form. Then write an equation in standard form.

For Exercises 10 and 11, write an equation in slope-intercept form for the line described.

10. **a.** The line through $(2, 5)$ that is parallel to the line $y = \frac{4}{3}x + 1$

b. The line through $(2, 5)$ that is perpendicular to the line $y = \frac{4}{3}x + 1$

11. **a.** The line through $(-7, 6)$ that is parallel to the line $4x + 2y = 9$

b. The line through $(-7, 6)$ that is perpendicular to the line $4x + 2y = 9$

12. Read the first three paragraphs on page 378. Notice that the red line passes approximately through the point $(62, 73)$.

a. Estimate the slope of the line and write an equation for the line in point-slope form.

b. A boy is 70 in. tall at age 14. Use your equation from part (a) to predict his height at age 24.

A-3 Inductive and Deductive Reasoning

Objective To identify and use inductive and deductive reasoning.

Use after Chapter 12

Suppose you observe the following pattern:

$1 = 1$	
$1 + 3 = 4$	The sum of the first 2 odd integers is 2^2.
$1 + 3 + 5 = 9$	The sum of the first 3 odd integers is 3^2.
$1 + 3 + 5 + 7 = 16$	The sum of the first 4 odd integers is 4^2.

Based on the pattern, you could use inductive reasoning to make the following generalization:

The sum of the first n positive odd integers is n^2.

Inductive reasoning involves making a general statement based on a number of observations.

You can test the statement above for many different values of n. Observing that the statement is true for many values of n is not the same as *proving* that it is true for all values of n, however. You can use *deductive reasoning* to *prove* that the statement is true for all values of n. **Deductive reasoning** uses known facts, definitions, and accepted properties in a logical order to reach a conclusion or to show that a statement is true.

Example Prove that the sum of the first n positive odd integers is n^2.

Solution Let S = the sum of the first n odd integers. First write an equation.

$$S = 1 + 3 + 5 + \dots + (2n - 3) + (2n - 1)$$

The nth even integer is $2n$, so the nth odd integer is 1 less than $2n$.

$$\begin{array}{rrcrcrcrcr} & S = & 1 & + & 3 & + \dots + & (2n-3) & + & (2n-1) \\ + & S = & (2n-1) & + & (2n-3) & + \dots + & 3 & + & 1 \\ \hline & 2S = & 2n & + & 2n & + \dots + & 2n & + & 2n \end{array}$$

Now write S as a "forward sum" and a "backward sum." Add the two equations, term by term.

$2S = n(2n)$ The term $2n$ occurs n times.

$2S = 2n^2$

$S = n^2$

Using Counterexamples

You may wonder why it is important to prove a statement like the one in the Example. After all, the statement appears to be true for all values of n. To see why a deductive proof is important, consider the following statement:

For every positive integer n, $n^2 + n + 41$ is a prime number.

If you test the statement for different values of n, it appears to be true.

When $n = 1$,	$1^2 + 1 + 41 = 43$	prime
When $n = 2$,	$2^2 + 2 + 41 = 47$	prime
When $n = 3$,	$3^2 + 3 + 41 = 53$	prime

Testing many numbers may lead you to believe that the statement above is true, but you would be wrong! For example:

When $n = 41$, $41^2 + 41 + 41 = 1763$ not prime because $1763 = 43 \cdot 41$

In fact, $n^2 + n + 41$ is prime when $n = 1, 2, 3, \ldots, 39$, but it is not prime when $n = 40$ or 41. These values of n are called *counterexamples*.

Proving that a statement is false requires just one counterexample. Proving that a statement is true requires a deductive proof.

Written Exercises

For Exercises 1–3, tell whether each argument uses *inductive* or *deductive* reasoning.

1. Tim is Veronica's cousin. Since David is Veronica's twin brother, Tim is also David's cousin.
2. The school librarian notices that many students are requesting books about different countries in Africa. The librarian concludes that one of the social studies classes must be studying about Africa.
3. Julie notices that each term in the sequence 1, 3, 9, 27, … is found by multiplying the previous term by 3. She concludes that the next two terms are 81 and 243.
4. Study the equations and algebraic reasoning shown below the two colored figures on page 529. Is the final equation $a^2 + b^2 = c^2$ reached by using *inductive* or *deductive* reasoning?
5. Give an example of inductive reasoning. Then give an example of deductive reasoning. How are the two types of reasoning different?

6. Look for a pattern in the statements below:

$$2 = 1 \cdot 2$$
$$2 + 4 = 2 \cdot 3$$
$$2 + 4 + 6 = 3 \cdot 4$$

a. Write the next two statements in the pattern.

b. Use inductive reasoning to write a general statement.

c. Use deductive reasoning to prove your statement. *Hint:* Start by letting S = the sum of the first n positive even integers. Then write two equations and add them vertically, term by term:

$$\begin{array}{rl} & S = 2 + 4 + \ldots + (2n-2) + (2n) \\ + & S = (2n) + (2n-2) + \ldots + 4 + 2 \\ \hline \end{array}$$

7. Consider the equation $(x + 3)(x + 4) = x^2 + 7x + 12$.

a. How are the numbers 7 and 12 related to the numbers 3 and 4?

b. Does this relationship work when you multiply $(x + 5)(x + 8)$?

c. Use inductive reasoning to multiply $(x + a)(x + b)$.

d. Use deductive reasoning and the FOIL method to show that your generalization in part (c) is true for all values of a and b.

Provide a counterexample for each statement to show that it is false.

8. $(n + 2)^3 = n^3 + 2^3$

9. $|a + b| = |a| + |b|$

10. $x^2 > x$ for all values of x.

11. If $a > 0$, then $a^3 > a$.

Tell whether each statement is *True* or *False*. If it is false, give a counterexample.

12. For every positive integer n, $n^2 + n + 11$ is a prime number.

13. Perfect square numbers always end in 1, 4, 5, 6, or 9.

14. The result of multiplying the sum of the first n positive even integers by 4 and then adding 1 is always a perfect square.

15. Use deductive reasoning to prove that the statement in Exercise 14 is always true. (*Hint:* Look back at Exercise 6(c).)

A-4 Hypothesis and Conclusion

Objective To identify the hypothesis and the conclusion of a statement.

Use after Appendix A-3

Logical arguments are based on statements that can be expressed in this form:

"If statement p is true, then statement q is true."

Statement p is called the *hypothesis*. Statement q is called the *conclusion*.

	Hypothesis	Conclusion
(1)	If a and b are even integers,	then $a + b$ is an even integer.
(2)	If $x \neq 0$,	then $x^2 > 0$.

Example 1 Peggy says that $n^2 > n^3$ for all negative numbers n. Write Peggy's statement as an if-then statement. Identify the hypothesis and the conclusion.

Solution If n is a negative number, then $n^2 > n^3$.
Hypothesis: n is a negative number. Conclusion: $n^2 > n^3$

Whenever you try to prove that an "If p, then q" statement is true, you use the hypothesis as the starting point, assuming it is true. Then you can use deductive reasoning to prove that the conclusion is true.

Example 2 Prove that this statement is true: If $2(x + 3) = -8$, then $x = -7$.

Solution Use properties of real numbers to prove the statement.

$$2(x + 3) = -8$$
$$2x + 6 = -8 \quad \text{Distributive property}$$
$$2x = -14 \quad \text{Addition property of equality}$$
$$x = -7 \quad \text{Multiplication property of equality}$$

The Converse of a Statement

A statement that contains a hypothesis and a conclusion has a *converse*. In the **converse** of a statement, the hypothesis and the conclusion are reversed. Even though a statement may be true, its converse is not necessarily true.

	Statement	Converse
(1)	If a and b are even integers, then $a + b$ is an even integer	If $a + b$ is an even integer, then a and b are even integers.
(2)	If $x \neq 0$, then $x^2 > 0$.	If $x^2 > 0$, then $x \neq 0$.

Example 3 Tell whether the converse of each statement at the bottom of page 718 is true or false. Justify your reasoning.

Solution

(1) Let $a = 3$ and $b = 5$. Then $a + b = 3 + 5 = 8$, an even integer. But 3 and 5 are not even, so the converse of statement (1) is false.

(2) If $x^2 > 0$, then $x \neq 0$ because $0^2 = 0$. The converse of statement (2) is true.

Written Exercises

For Exercises 1–4, write the hypothesis and the conclusion of each statement. Tell whether the statement is *true* or *false*. Justify your reasoning.

1. If the current month is September, then there are 30 days in the month.
2. If a and b are negative, then ab is positive.
3. Joe lives in New England if he lives in Vermont.
4. $|a + b| = |a| + |b|$ if a and b are both positive.
5. Give the converse of each statement in Exercises 1–4. Tell whether the converse is *true* or *false*. Justify your reasoning.
6. After trying many different pairs of numbers, Jim stated that the sum of any two odd integers is always even.
   a. Identify the hypothesis and the conclusion of Jim's statement. Then write an if-then statement.
   b. Write the converse of your statement from part (a). Tell whether the converse is *true* or *false*. Justify your reasoning.
7. Write the converse of the statement in Example 1. Then try different values of n to see whether the converse is *true* or *false*. Explain your reasoning.
8. Consider the inequality $|x| - 1 \geq 0$. For what values of x is the inequality true? For what values is it not true? Based on your observations, write an if-then statement about the inequality $|x| - 1 \geq 0$. Identify the hypothesis and the conclusion of your statement.

Tell whether each statement is *sometimes true*, *always true*, or *never true*. Explain your reasoning.

9. For real numbers a and b, $|a \cdot b| = |a| \cdot |b|$.
10. If a and b are nonzero real numbers and $a > b$, then $\frac{1}{a} > \frac{1}{b}$.
11. If a and b are real numbers and $a > b$, then $ax > bx$.
12. If $2x^2 - 12x + 18 = 0$, then $x = 3$.
13. If m and n are prime numbers, then mn is also prime.
14. If m and n are prime numbers, then $m + n$ is also prime.

A-5 Indirect Reasoning

Objective To use indirect reasoning in a logical argument.

Use after Appendix A-4

Sharon King returns home to find that a large slice of freshly baked rhubarb pie has been eaten. The only people with access to the house are her husband, son, and daughter. Since her husband is out of town and her daughter hates rhubarb, she concludes that her son must have eaten the pie.

Sharon does not reason directly that her son ate the pie. Instead, she uses *indirect reasoning*. In other words, she shows that all other alternatives are impossible. **Indirect reasoning** is used in mathematics as well.

Example Use indirect reasoning to prove the following statement:
If n^2 is odd, then n is odd.

Solution Start by identifying the hypothesis and the conclusion of the statement. Then try to show that the alternative conclusion leads to a contradiction in the statement.

Hypothesis and known fact: n^2 is odd.
Desired conclusion: n is odd.
Alternative Conclusion: n is even.

Assume temporarily that the alternative conclusion is true. If n is even, then n can be described as the product of 2 and some integer k. Then n^2 is as follows:

$$n^2 = (2k)^2 = 4k^2 = 2(2k^2)$$

Notice that n^2 has a factor of 2. This implies that n^2 is even, which contradicts the known fact that n^2 is odd. The desired conclusion must be accepted, and the original statement is true.

Written Exercises

Use indirect reasoning to prove each statement.

1. If n^3 is negative, then n is negative.
2. If n^2 is even, then n is even.
3. If $x > 3$, then $|x| - 3 > 0$.
4. If an equation in the form $ax^2 + bx + c = 0$ has no real-number solutions, then the graph of the related equation $y = ax^2 + bx + c = 0$ has no x-intercepts.
5. If n^2 is a multiple of 3, then n is a multiple of 3. (*Hint:* The desired conclusion is that n is 3 times some integer k. There are two alternative conclusions you must consider: $n = 3k + 1$ or $n = 3k + 2$.)

Glossary of Properties

addition property of equality (p. 95): If a, b, and c are any real numbers, and $a = b$, then $a + c = b + c$ and $c + a = c + b$.

addition property of order (p. 463): For all real numbers a, b, and c:
1. If $a < b$, then $a + c < b + c$;
2. If $a > b$, then $a + c > b + c$.

associative properties (p. 45): For all real numbers a, b, and c:

$$(a + b) + c = a + (b + c)$$
$$(ab)c = a(bc)$$

closure properties (p. 45): For all real numbers a and b:

$a + b$ is a unique real number.
ab is a unique real number.

commutative properties (p. 45): For all real numbers a and b:

$$a + b = b + a$$
$$ab = ba$$

density property for rational numbers (p. 508): Between every pair of different rational numbers there is another rational number.

distributive property (of multiplication with respect to addition) (p. 65): For all real numbers a, b, and c,

$$a(b + c) = ab + ac \text{ and}$$
$$(b + c)a = ba + ca.$$

distributive property (of multiplication with respect to subtraction) (p. 66): For all real numbers a, b, and c,

$$a(b - c) = ab - ac \text{ and}$$
$$(b - c)a = ba - ca.$$

division property of equality (p. 102): If a and b are any real numbers, c is any nonzero real number, and $a = b$, then $\frac{a}{c} = \frac{b}{c}$.

identity property of addition (p. 50): There is a unique real number 0 such that for every real number a, $a + 0 = a$ and $0 + a = a$.

identity property of multiplication (p. 70): There is a unique real number 1 such that for every real number a, $a \cdot 1 = a$ and $1 \cdot a = a$.

multiplication property of equality (p. 102): If a, b, and c are any real numbers, and $a = b$, then $ca = cb$ and $ac = bc$.

multiplication property of order (p. 463): For all real numbers a, b, and c such that $c > 0$:
1. If $a < b$, then $ac < bc$;
2. If $a > b$, then $ac > bc$.

For all real numbers a, b, and c such that $c < 0$:
1. If $a < b$, then $ac > bc$;
2. If $a > b$, then $ac < bc$.

multiplicative property of −1 (p. 70): For every real number a, $a(-1) = -a$ and $(-1)a = -a$.

multiplicative property of zero (p. 70): For every real number a, $a \cdot 0 = 0$ and $0 \cdot a = 0$.

product property of square roots (p. 517): For any nonnegative real numbers a and b, $\sqrt{ab} = \sqrt{a} \cdot \sqrt{b}$.

property of comparison (p. 462): For all real numbers a and b, one and only one of the following statements is true: $a < b$, $a = b$, $a > b$.

property of completeness (p. 522): Every decimal represents a real number, and every real number can be represented by a decimal.

property of the opposite of a sum (p. 51): For all real numbers a and b: $-(a + b) = (-a) + (-b)$.

property of opposites (p. 50): For every real number a, there is a unique real number $-a$ such that $a + (-a) = 0$ and $(-a) + a = 0$.

property of opposites in products (p. 71): For all real numbers a and b, $(-a)(b) = -ab$, $a(-b) = -ab$, and $(-a)(-b) = ab$.

property of quotients (p. 189): If a, b, c, and d are real numbers with $b \neq 0$ and $d \neq 0$, then $\frac{ac}{bd} = \frac{a}{b} \cdot \frac{c}{d}$.

property of the reciprocal of the opposite of a number (p. 79): For every nonzero number a, $\frac{1}{-a} = -\frac{1}{a}$.

property of the reciprocal of a product (p. 80): For all nonzero numbers a and b, $\frac{1}{ab} = \frac{1}{a} \cdot \frac{1}{b}$.

property of reciprocals (p. 79): For every nonzero real number a, there is a unique real number $\frac{1}{a}$ such that $a \cdot \frac{1}{a} = 1$ and $\frac{1}{a} \cdot a = 1$.

property of square roots of equal numbers (p. 526): For any real numbers r and s: $r^2 = s^2$ if and only if $r = s$ or $r = -s$.

quotient property of square roots (p. 518): For any nonnegative real number a and any positive real number b, $\sqrt{\frac{a}{b}} = \frac{\sqrt{a}}{\sqrt{b}}$.

reflexive property of equality (p. 46): If a is a real number, then $a = a$.

substitution principle (p. 2): An expression may be replaced by another expression that has the same value.

subtraction property of equality (p. 95): If a, b, and c are any real numbers, and $a = b$, then $a - c = b - c$.

symmetric property of equality (p. 46): If a and b are real numbers, and $a = b$, then $b = a$.

transitive property of equality (p. 46): For all real numbers, a, b, and c, if $a = b$ and $b = c$, then $a = c$.

transitive property of order (p. 462): For all real numbers a, b, and c,
1. If $a < b$ and $b < c$, then $a < c$;
2. If $c > b$ and $b > a$, then $c > a$.

zero-product property (p. 230): For all real numbers a and b, $ab = 0$ if and only if $a = 0$ or $b = 0$.

Glossary of Terms

abscissa (p. 353): The first coordinate in an ordered pair of numbers associated with a point in a coordinate plane. Also called *x-coordinate*.

absolute value (pp. 37, 482): The positive number of any pair of opposite nonzero real numbers is the absolute value of each number. The absolute value of 0 is 0. The absolute value of a number a is denoted by $|a|$.

acute angle (p. 617): An angle with measure between 0° and 90°.

addition-or-subtraction method (pp. 426–427): A method of solving a system of two equations; one variable is eliminated by adding or subtracting the equations.

additive inverses (p. 50): A number and its opposite.

angle (p. 616): A figure formed by two different rays that have the same endpoint.

area: The area of a region is the number of square units it contains.

arrow notation (p. 379): A notation used in defining a function; for example, $P\colon n \rightarrow 5n - 500$.

average (p. 85): The average of a set of numbers is the sum of the numbers divided by the number of numbers.

axes (p. 354): *See* coordinate axes.

axis of symmetry of a parabola (p. 384): The line containing the maximum or minimum point of the parabola.

base of a power (p. 141): The number that is used as a factor a given number of times; in 2^5, 2 is the base.

BASIC (p. 111): A programming language.

binomial (p. 146): A polynomial of only two terms.

boundary (p. 490): A line that separates the coordinate plane into three sets of points: the points *on* the line; the points *above* the line; the points *below* the line.

box-and-whisker plot (p. 612): A display of data useful for comparing two distributions.

closed half-plane (p. 490): The graph of an open half-plane and its boundary.

coefficient (p. 146): In the monomial $15a^2b^2$, 15 is the coefficient, or *numerical coefficient*.

collinear points (p. 364): Points that lie on the same line.

combined variation (p. 588): If a variable varies directly as one variable and inversely as another, the resulting relationship is a combined variation (expressed by $zy = kx$, k a nonzero constant).

common factor (p. 186): A factor of two or more integers is called a common factor of the integers.

complementary angles (p. 619): Two angles are complementary if the sum of their measures is 90°. Each angle is a *complement* of the other.

completing the square (p. 564): A method of transforming a quadratic equation so that it is in the form "perfect square = k" ($k \geq 0$).

complex fraction (p. 278): A fraction whose numerator or denominator contains one or more fractions.

conjugates (p. 544): If b and d are both nonnegative, then the binomials $a\sqrt{b} + c\sqrt{d}$ and $a\sqrt{b} - c\sqrt{d}$ are conjugates of one another.

conjunction (p. 478): A sentence formed by joining two open sentences by the word *and*.

consecutive even integers (p. 75): Integers obtained by counting by twos, beginning with any even integer.

consecutive integers (p. 75): Numbers obtained by counting by ones from any number in the set of integers.

consecutive odd integers (p. 75): Integers obtained by counting by twos, beginning with any odd integer.

constant (monomial) (pp. 146, 201): A monomial consisting of a numeral only; a term with no variable factor.

constant of variation (pp. 391, 397): The nonzero constant k in a direct variation defined by $y = kx$ or in an inverse variation defined by $xy = k$. Also called *constant of proportionality*.

converse (p. 230): The converse of a statement in "if-then" form is obtained by interchanging the "if" and "then" parts of the statement.

coordinate axes (p. 354): The x- and y-axes in the coordinate plane.

coordinate plane (p. 354): A plane in which an ordered pair can be located by reference to two intersecting number lines.

coordinate of a point (p. 31): The number paired with that point on a number line.

coordinates of a point (p. 353): The abscissa and ordinate of the point, written as an ordered pair of numbers.

cosine (p. 627): The cosine of an acute angle A in a right triangle = $\dfrac{\text{length of leg adjacent to } \angle A}{\text{length of hypotenuse}}$.

cubic equation (p. 231): A polynomial equation with a term of degree 3 as its term of highest degree.

degree (p. 617): A unit of angle measurement.

degree of a monomial (p. 146): The sum of the degrees of the variables in the monomial.

degree of a polynomial (p. 147): The greatest of the degrees of its terms after it has been simplified.

degree of a variable in a monomial (p. 146): The number of times that the variable occurs as a factor in the monomial.

difference (p. 59): *See* subtraction.

direct variation (p. 391): A function defined by an equation of the form $y = kx$, where k is a nonzero constant. We say that y is directly proportional to x. (*See also* quadratic direct variation.)

discriminant (p. 573): For a quadratic equation in the form $ax^2 + bx + c = 0$, the value of $b^2 - 4ac$ is called the discriminant.

disjoint sets (p. 476): Two sets that have no members in common.

disjunction (p. 478): A sentence formed by joining two open sentences by the word *or*.

distance formula (p. 535): For any points $P_1(x_1, y_1)$ and $P_2(x_2, y_2)$, $P_1P_2 = \sqrt{(x_2 - x_1)^2 + (y_2 - y_1)^2}$.

divisible (p. 195): One polynomial is (evenly) divisible by another polynomial if the quotient is also a polynomial.

division (p. 83): For every real number a and every nonzero real number b, the quotient $a \div b$, or $\frac{a}{b}$, is defined by $a \div b = a \cdot \frac{1}{b}$.

domain of a function (p. 374): *See under* function.

domain of a variable (p. 10): The given set of numbers that the variable may represent.

double root (p. 231): *See* multiple root.

empty set (p. 117): The set with no members; the null set.

endpoint (p. 616): The starting point of a ray.

equation (p. 10): A statement formed by placing an equals sign between two numerical or variable expressions.

equilateral triangle (p. 621): A triangle with all sides of equal length.

equivalent equations (p. 96): Equations that have the same solution set over a given domain.

equivalent expressions (p. 67): Expressions that represent the same number for all values of the variable that they contain.

equivalent inequality (p. 463): An inequality that has the same solution set as a given inequality.

equivalent system (p. 430): A system of equations having the same solution set as another system.

evaluating a variable expression (p. 2): Replacing each variable in the expression by a given value and simplifying the result.

even integer (p. 75): An integer that is the product of 2 and any integer.

event (p. 600): Any possible subset of the sample space resulting from an experiment.

expanded notation (p. 338): A way of writing numbers that uses powers of 10 to express place values.

exponent (p. 141): In a power, the number that indicates how many times the base is used as a factor; in 6^5, 5 is the exponent.

exponential form of a power (p. 141): The expression n^4 is the exponential form of $n \cdot n \cdot n \cdot n$.

extremes (p. 293): In the proportion $a:b = c:d$, a and d are the extremes.

factor (p. 46): When two or more numbers are multiplied, each of the numbers is a factor of the product.

factor set (p. 185): The name given to the set over which a number is factored.

factored completely (p. 227): A polynomial is factored completely when it is expressed as the product of a monomial and one or more prime polynomials.

factoring (p. 185): Factoring a number over a given set is writing the number as a product of numbers in that set.

factors (p. 46): Numbers that are multiplied together to produce a product.

finite decimal (p. 512): *See* terminating decimal.

formula (p. 15): An equation that states a rule about a relationship.

fraction (pp. 83, 247): An expression in the form $\frac{a}{b}$, $b \neq 0$.

fractional equation (p. 304): An equation with a variable in the denominator of one or more terms.

frequency distribution (p. 606): A summary of data that displays the items according to frequency of occurrence.

function (p. 374): A correspondence between two sets, the *domain* and the *range,* that assigns to each member of the domain *exactly one* member of the range.

functional notation (p. 379): A notation used in defining a function; for example, $P(n) = 5n - 500$.

graph of an equation in two variables (p. 354): All the points that are the graphs of the solutions of the equation.

graph of a function (p. 383): The graph of the equation that defines the function.

graph of an inequality (p. 458): The graph representing all the numbers in the solution set of the sentence.

graph of a number (p. 31): The point on a number line that is paired with the number.

graph of an ordered pair (p. 353): The point in a coordinate plane associated with an ordered pair of real numbers.

graph of a relation (p. 389): The graphs of all the ordered pairs that form the relation.

graphing method (p. 414): A method of solving a system of equations in two variables.

greatest common factor (GCF) of integers (p. 186): The greatest integer that is a factor of two or more given integers.

greatest common factor (GCF) of two or more monomials (p. 190): The common factor with the greatest coefficient and the greatest degree in each variable.
greatest monomial factor of a polynomial (p. 195): The GCF of the terms of the polynomial.
greatest value of a function (p. 384): The y-coordinate of the highest point of the graph of the function.
grouping symbol (p. 6): A device used to enclose an expression that should be simplified before other operations are performed. Examples: parentheses, brackets, fraction bar.

half-plane (p. 490): *See* closed half-plane *and* open half-plane.
histogram (p. 606): A graph that describes a frequency distribution.
horizontal axis (p. 353): The horizontal number line in a coordinate plane. Also called the *x-axis*.
hyperbola (pp. 397–398): The graph of $xy = k$ for any nonzero value of k.
hypotenuse (p. 529): In a right triangle, the side opposite the right angle.

identity (p. 117): An equation that is true for every value of the variable(s).
identity element for addition (p. 50): Zero (0).
identity element for multiplication (p. 70): One (1).
imaginary numbers (p. 570): Numbers that involve the imaginary unit i, defined as $\sqrt{-1}$.
inequality (p. 458): A statement formed by placing an inequality symbol between numerical or variable expressions.
inequality symbols (pp. 32, 457): Symbols used to show the order of two real numbers. The symbol $\neq$ means "is not equal to."
infinite decimal (p. 513): *See* nonterminating decimal.
integers (p. 31): The set consisting of the positive integers, the negative integers, and zero.
intersection of sets (p. 476): For any two sets A and B, the set consisting of those members and only those members common to A and B.
inverse operations (p. 107): Operations that "undo" each other – for example, multiplication and division.
inverse variation (p. 397): A function defined by an equation of the form $xy = k$, where k is a nonzero constant.
inverse variation as the square (p. 585): A function defined by an equation of the form $x^2y = k$, where k is a nonzero constant.
irrational numbers (p. 521): Real numbers that cannot be expressed in the form $\frac{a}{b}$, where a and b are integers.
irreducible polynomial (p. 214): A polynomial that cannot be expressed as a product of polynomials of lower degree.
isosceles triangle (p. 621): A triangle having two sides of equal length. The third side is called the *base*. The angles opposite the equal sides are the *base angles*.

joint variation (p. 588): If a variable varies directly as the product of two or more other variables, the resulting relationship is a joint variation (expressed by $z = kxy$, k a nonzero constant).

least common denominator (LCD) (p. 260): The least positive common multiple of the denominators of two or more given fractions.
least value of a function (p. 384): The y-coordinate of the lowest point of the graph of the function.
legs of a right triangle (p. 529): The sides that form the right angle.
like terms (p. 146): *See* similar terms.

line segment (p. 616): The part of a line that consists of two points and all points between them. Also called *segment*.

linear equation (pp. 231, 354): A polynomial equation of degree one.

linear equation in two variables (p. 354): Any equation equivalent to one of the form $ax + by = c$, where a, b, and c are real numbers with a and b not both zero. Its graph is a line.

linear function (p. 383): A function defined by $f(x) = mx + b$.

linear programming (p. 499): A branch of mathematics concerned with problems that involve maximizing or minimizing a quantity.

linear term (p. 201): A term of degree one.

maximum point of a parabola (p. 384): The highest point; the point whose y-coordinate is the greatest value of the corresponding function.

mean (p. 606): The sum of the data in a collection divided by the number of items.

mean proportional (p. 296): When the means of a proportion are equal, each mean is called the mean proportional between the two extremes.

means (p. 293): In the proportion $a:b = c:d$, b and c are the means.

median (p. 607): In a frequency distribution, the middle number or the average of the two middle numbers when the data are arranged in order.

minimum point of a parabola (p. 384): The lowest point; the point whose y-coordinate is the least value of the corresponding function.

mixed expression (p. 270): The sum or difference of a polynomial and a fraction.

mixed number (p. 270): The sum of an integer and a fraction.

mode (p. 607): The most frequently occurring number in a frequency distribution.

monomial (p. 146): An expression that is either a numeral, a variable, or the product of a numeral and one or more variables.

multiple (p. 78): The product of any real number and an integer is a multiple of the real number.

multiple root (p. 231): A solution of an equation that occurs more than once.

multiplicative inverses (p. 79): *See* reciprocals.

natural order of integers (p. 75): Order from least to greatest.

negative integers (p. 31): The numbers -1, -2, -3, -4, and so on.

negative number (p. 31): A number paired with a point on the negative side of a number line.

negative side (p. 31): On a horizontal number line, the side to the left of the origin.

nonterminating decimal (p. 513): When a common fraction is written as a decimal by dividing the numerator by the denominator, the result is a nonterminating decimal if a digit or block of digits repeats endlessly as the remainder. Also called *unending, infinite, repeating,* or *periodic decimal.*

null set (p. 117): The set with no members; the empty set.

numeral (p. 1): An expression that names a particular number; a numerical expression.

numerical coefficient (p. 146): *See* coefficient.

numerical expression (p. 1): An expression that names a particular number; a numeral.

obtuse angle (p. 617): An angle with measure between 90° and 180°.

odd integer (p. 75): An integer that is not even.

open half-plane (p. 490): Either of the two regions into which a boundary line separates the coordinate plane.

open sentence (p. 10): A sentence containing one or more variables.

opposite of a number (p. 36): Each of the numbers in a pair such as 6 and -6 or -2.5 and 2.5. Also called *additive inverse*.

ordered pair (p. 349): A pair of numbers for which the order of the numbers is important; $(2, -3)$ is an ordered pair.

ordinate (p. 353): The second coordinate in an ordered pair of numbers associated with a point in a coordinate plane. Also called *y-coordinate*.

origin (pp. 31, 353): The zero point on a number line. The intersection of the axes on a coordinate plane.

parabola (p. 384): The graph of $f(x) = ax^2 + bx + c$, where the domain is the set of real numbers and $a \neq 0$.

parallel lines (p. 367): Lines in the same plane that do not intersect; nonvertical lines that have the same slope.

percent (p. 309): Another way of saying *hundredths*, or *divided by 100*. Usually denoted by the symbol %.

perfect square (p. 562): An expression such as x^2, $(x + 1)^2$, or $(5x - 3)^2$.

perfect square trinomial (p. 209): An expression with three terms that is the square of a binomial.

perimeter: The perimeter of a plane figure is the distance around it.

periodic decimal (p. 513): *See* nonterminating decimal.

perpendicular lines (p. 370): Any two lines that intersect to form right angles.

plot a point (p. 353): Locate the graph of an ordered pair of real numbers in a coordinate plane.

polynomial (p. 146): A sum of monomials.

polynomial equation (p. 231): An equation whose sides are both polynomials.

positive integers (p. 31): The numbers 1, 2, 3, 4, and so on.

positive number (p. 31): A number paired with a point on the positive side of a number line.

positive side (p. 31): On a horizontal number line, the side to the right of the origin.

power of a number (p. 141): The product when a number is multiplied by itself a given number of times; $4 \times 4 \times 4$, or 4^3, is the third power of 4.

prime factorization (p. 185): Expressing a positive integer as a product of primes.

prime number (prime) (p. 185): An integer greater than 1 that has no positive integral factor other than itself and 1.

prime polynomial (p. 214): An irreducible polynomial with integral coefficients whose greatest monomial factor is 1.

principal square root (p. 517): The positive square root of a positive number; denoted by the symbol $\sqrt{\ }$.

probability (p. 600): The branch of mathematics that deals with the possibility that an event will happen.

probability of an event (p. 603): The ratio of the number of outcomes favoring the event to the total number of outcomes.

proof (p. 130): Logical reasoning that uses given facts, definitions, properties, and previously proved theorems to show that a theorem is true.

proportion (p. 293): An equation that states that two ratios are equal.

Pythagorean theorem (p. 529): In any right triangle, the square of the length of the hypotenuse equals the sum of the squares of the lengths of the legs. (The converse is also true.)

quadrant (p. 354): One of the four regions into which the coordinate axes separate the plane.

quadratic direct variation (p. 584): A function defined by an equation of the form $y = kx^2$, where k is a nonzero constant.

quadratic equation (p. 231): A polynomial equation whose term of highest degree is quadratic.

quadratic formula (p. 567): The solutions of a quadratic equation in the form $ax^2 + bx + c = 0$, $a \neq 0$ and $b^2 - 4ac \geq 0$, are given by the formula

$$x = \frac{-b \pm \sqrt{b^2 - 4ac}}{2a}.$$

quadratic function (p. 384): A function defined by $f(x) = ax^2 + bx + c$ $(a \neq 0)$.

quadratic polynomial (p. 201): A trinomial whose term of greatest degree is quadratic.

quadratic term (p. 201): A term of degree two.

quotient (p. 83): *See* division.

radical (p. 517): An expression in the form $\sqrt{a}$.

radical equation (p. 547): An equation containing a radical with a variable in the radicand.

radical sign (p. 517): The symbol $\sqrt{}$.

radicand (p. 517): The symbol written beneath a radical sign.

random experiment (p. 600): An activity whose outcome can't be predicted when the activity is repeated under essentially the same conditions.

range of a frequency distribution (p. 607): The difference between the highest and the lowest values.

range of a function (p. 374): *See under* function.

rate (p. 302): A ratio that compares the amounts of two different kinds of measurements, for example, meters per second.

ratio (p. 287): The ratio of one number to another is the quotient when the first number is divided by the second number (not zero).

rational expression (p. 507): An expression for a rational number.

rational number (p. 507): A real number that can be expressed as the quotient of two integers.

rationalizing the denominator (p. 537): The process of eliminating a radical from the denominator of a fraction.

ray (p. 616): The part of a line that consists of a point A and all points of the line on one side of A.

real number (p. 32): Any number that is either positive, negative, or zero.

reciprocals (p. 79): Two numbers whose product is 1; also called *multiplicative inverses*.

relation (p. 389): Any set of ordered pairs. The set of first coordinates of the ordered pairs is the *domain* of the relation; the set of second coordinates is the *range*.

repeating decimal (p. 513): *See* nonterminating decimal.

right angle (p. 617): An angle with measure 90°.

right triangle (p. 621): A triangle having one right angle.

root of a sentence: *See* solution of a sentence.

sample space (p. 600): The set of all possible outcomes of a random experiment.

satisfy an open sentence (p. 10): Any solution of the sentence satisfies the sentence.

scientific notation (p. 336): A positive number in scientific notation is expressed as the product of a number greater than or equal to 1 but less than 10, and an integral power of 10.

sides of an angle (p. 616): The two rays that form the angle.

sides of an equation (p. 10): The two expressions joined by the equals sign.

sides of an inequality (p. 458): The expressions joined by an inequality symbol.

sides of a triangle (p. 621): The three segments that form the triangle.

similar terms (p. 146): Two monomials that are exactly alike or are the same except for their numerical coefficients. Also called *like terms*.

similar triangles (p. 624): Two triangles are similar if the measures of two angles of one triangle equal the measures of two angles of the other. Angles with equal measures are called *corresponding angles*. Sides opposite corresponding angles are called *corresponding sides*.

simple event (p. 600): An event that involves a single member of a sample space.

simplest form of an algebraic fraction (p. 247): A form of the fraction in which the numerator and denominator have no common factor other than 1 and -1.

simplest form of an expression having a square-root radical (p. 537): The form of the expression in which no integral radicand has a square factor other than 1; no fractions are under a radical sign; no radicals are in a denominator.

simplest form of a polynomial (p. 146): A polynomial is in simplest form when no two of its terms are similar.

simplifying an expression (p. 67): Replacing an expression containing variables by an equivalent expression with as few terms as possible.

simplifying a numerical expression (p. 2): Replacing the expression by the simplest name for its value.

simultaneous equations (p. 413): *See under* system of (simultaneous) equations.

sine (p. 627): The sine of an acute angle A in a right triangle $= \frac{\text{length of leg opposite } \angle A}{\text{length of hypotenuse}}$.

slope of a line (p. 361): If (x_1, y_1) and (x_2, y_2) are two different points on a line, the slope of the line is given by $\frac{y_2 - y_1}{x_2 - x_1}$. A horizontal line has slope 0; a vertical line has no slope.

slope-intercept form of an equation (p. 366): The equation of a line in the form $y = mx + b$, where m is the slope and b is the y-intercept.

solution of an equation in two variables (p. 349): An ordered pair of numbers that make the sentence true.

solution of a sentence (pp. 10, 458): Any value of a variable that turns an open sentence into a true statement.

solution of a system of two equations in two variables (p. 413): An ordered pair that satisfies both equations at the same time.

solution set of an open sentence (pp. 10, 458): The set of all solutions of the sentence.

solve a conjunction (p. 478): To find the values of the variable for which both open sentences in the conjunction are true.

solve a disjunction (p. 478): To find the values of the variable for which at least one of the open sentences in the disjunction is true.

solve an equation (p. 349): To find the set of all solutions of the equation.

solve an open sentence (p. 10): To find the solution set of the sentence.

solve a system of two equations in x and y (p. 413): To find all ordered pairs (x, y) that make both equations true.

square root (p. 517): If $a^2 = b$, then a is a square root of b.

standard deviation (p. 609): In a frequency distribution, the principal square root of the variance.

standard form of a linear equation (p. 354): $ax + by = c$, where a, b, and c are integers and a and b are not both zero.

standard form of a polynomial equation (p. 231): A form of the equation in which one side is zero and the other is a simplified polynomial arranged in order of decreasing degree of the variable.

stem-and-leaf plot (p. 611): A way of displaying a frequency distribution.

straight angle (p. 617): An angle with measure 180°.

substitution method (p. 418): A method of solving a system of linear equations in two variables.

subtraction (p. 59): For all real numbers a and b, the difference $a - b$ is defined by $a - b = a + (-b)$.

supplementary angles (p. 619): Two angles are supplementary if the sum of their measures is 180°. Each angle is a *supplement* of the other.

system of (simultaneous) equations (p. 413): Two or more equations in the same variables.

tangent (p. 627): The tangent of an acute angle A in a right triangle $= \dfrac{\text{length of leg opposite } \angle A}{\text{length of leg adjacent to } \angle A}$.

terminating decimal (p. 512): When a common fraction is written as a decimal by dividing the numerator by the denominator, the result is a terminating decimal if the remainder is zero. Also called *ending decimal* or *finite decimal*.

terms (p. 46): In the sum $a + b$, a and b are called terms.

theorem (p. 130): A statement that is shown to be true by use of a logically developed argument.

transformations (pp. 96, 102, 463): Operations on an equation or an inequality that produce a simpler equivalent statement.

triangle (p. 621): A figure formed by three segments joining three points not on the same line. Each segment is a *side,* and each point is a *vertex,* of the triangle.

trigonometric functions (p. 628): The functions sine, cosine, and tangent, each having the set of acute angles as domain.

trigonometric ratios (p. 627): Ratios of the lengths of the sides of a right triangle.

trinomial (p. 146): A polynomial of only three terms.

uniform motion (p. 167): Motion without change in speed, or rate.

union of sets (p. 476): For any two sets A and B, the set whose members belong to at least one of the sets A and B.

unit price (p. 302): The price of one unit of a given item.

value of a numerical expression (p. 1): The number named by the expression.

values of a function (p. 379): Members of the range of the function.

values of a variable (p. 1): The numbers that can be represented by the variable.

variable (p. 1): A symbol used to represent one or more numbers.

variable expression (p. 1): An expression that contains a variable.

variance (p. 609): In a frequency distribution, the mean of the squares of the distance of each score from the mean.

vertex of an angle (p. 616): The common endpoint of the rays forming the angle.

vertex of a parabola (p. 384): The maximum or minimum point of the graph.

vertical angles (p. 619): Two angles whose sides are rays in the same line, but in opposite directions.

vertical axis (p. 353): The vertical number line in a coordinate plane.

vertices of a triangle (p. 621): *See under* triangle.

whole numbers (p. 31): The set consisting of zero and all the positive integers.

work rate (p. 326): The fractional part of a job done in a given unit of time.

***x*-axis** (p. 353): The horizontal axis in the coordinate plane.

***x*-coordinate** (p. 353): *See* abscissa.

***x*-intercept** (pp. 371, 572): The x-coordinate of a point where a graph intersects the x-axis.

***y*-axis** (p. 353): *See* vertical axis.

***y*-coordinate** (p. 353): *See* ordinate.

***y*-intercept** (p. 366): The y-coordinate of a point where a graph crosses the y-axis.

zeros of a quadratic function (p. 581): The members of the solution set of the related quadratic equation.

Index

Acknowledgments

Book designed by Ligature, Inc.
Technical Art by Precision Graphics
Illustrations by Gary Torrisi
Cover design by Ligature, Inc.
Cover and chapter opener photos by John Payne Photo, Ltd.;
Luis Casteneda/Image Bank/Chicago (background photo)

Photos

xiv Peter Chapman
xv Peter Chapman
5 Ray Pfortner/Peter Arnold, Inc.
15 Joe Outland/FPG
15 Tad Goodale
25 Arthur Grace/Stock Boston
29 Warren Morgan/Focus on Sports
32 Tad Goodale
40 Kevin Galvin/Bruce Coleman
57 Lou Jones
63 NASA
65 Hanson Carroll/Peter Arnold, Inc.
74 Cody/FPG
75 Elliot Smith
101 James Ballard
102 Gabe Palmer/Stock Market
105 Frank Fisher/After Image
112 D.P. Hershkowitz/Bruce Coleman
115 Edward L. Miller/Light Images
125 National Optical Astronomy Observatory
128 Stuart Cohen/Stock Market
165 Cy Furlan/Berg and Associates
170 Robert C. Dawson/After Image
171 Vince Streano/Click/Chicago
172 Alan C. Ross/Photo Researchers, Inc.
176 Gabe Palmer/Stock Market
198 R.L. Goddard/Berg and Associates
223 Ed Lettau/Photo Researchers, Inc.
229 Jeff Zaruba/After Image
234 E.A. McGee/FPG
236 MacDonald Photography/Picture Cube
267 Alese and Mort Pechter/Stock Market
268 Michael Radigan/Stock Market
272 Rui Coutinho/Nawrocki
291 Sal Maimone/Shostal Associates
292 Bob Daemmrich/Uniphoto
294 Charles Ronear/Nawrocki
303 George Meinzinger/After Image
311 Peter Chapman
314 Renaud W. Granel/Index Stock
315 Ken Sexton/Nawrocki
321 Index Stock
326 Runk/Schoenberg/Grant Heilman
329 Frank Rossotto/Stock Market
341 Brownie Harris/Stock Market
360 Reed Chestner/Nawrocki
369 Gus Schonefeld/Berg and Associates
377 Caroline Brown/Fran Heyl Associates
391 Tom Tracy/FPG
394 Cynthia Matthews/Stock Market
402 Alan Goldsmith/Stock Market
422 Ken O'Donoghue
425 Gabe Palmer/Stock Market
428 Julie Habel/Westlight
435 Howard Zyrb/FPG
442 Wendell Metzen/Bruce Coleman
448 Henley and Savage/Stock Market

Photos *(continued)*

473 Coco McCoy/Rainbow
474 Michael Hayman/After Image
488 Sylvia Schlender/Nawrocki
489 Bob Daemmrich/Image Works
527 H. Armstrong Roberts
528 Camerique/H. Armstrong Roberts
533 Index Stock
547 Keith Kent/Peter Arnold, Inc.
550 Mark Antman/Image Works
579 Steve Raye/Taurus Photos
585 Tibor Bognar/Stock Market
586 Bob Daemmrich
592 Michael Amberger/Stock Market
600 Caroline Brown/Fran Heyl Associates
663 Mark and Chris Beattie/After Image

Answers to Selected Exercises

Chapter 1 Variables and Equations

Written Exercises, pages 3–4 **1.** 8 **3.** 60 **5.** 6 **7.** 29 **9.** 340 **11.** 2 **13.** 10 **15.** 6 **17.** 15 **19.** 13 **21.** 10 **23.** 56 **25.** 1 **27.** 5 **29.** 0 **31.** 58 **33.** 300 **35.** 60 **37.** 98.6 **39.** 1250 **41.** 3 **43.** any number **45.** $\frac{1}{2}$ **47.** 0, 2 **49.** 1, 3

Mixed Review Exercises, page 5 **1.** 0.36 **2.** 29.32 **3.** 4 **4.** 3.4 **5.** 219 **6.** 1.62 **7.** 151.914 **8.** 16 **9.** $\frac{29}{30}$ **10.** $\frac{5}{8}$ **11.** $\frac{4}{3}$ **12.** $\frac{1}{8}$ **13.** $\frac{4}{15}$ **14.** $\frac{7}{20}$ **15.** $\frac{26}{21}$ **16.** $\frac{8}{3}$

Application, page 5 **1.** 2.016 kW · h

Written Exercises, pages 8–9 **1. a.** 20 **b.** 44 **3. a.** 5 **b.** 1 **5.** 3 **7.** 2 **9. a.** 13 **b.** 20 **11. a.** 6 **b.** 42 **13. a.** 17 **b.** 27 **15. a.** 72 **b.** 108 **17.** 0 **19.** 40 **21.** 4 **23.** $\frac{11}{2}$ **25.** 78 **27.** 8 **29.** 54 **31.** 384 **33.** 16.28 **35.** $12 \neq 6$ **37.** $30 = 30$ **39.** $5 \cdot (8 - 6) \div 2$ **41.** $5 \cdot (8 - 6 \div 2)$ **43.** $5 \cdot (2 + 8 - 4) \div 2$ **45.** $[(5 \cdot 2) + 8 - 4] \div 2$

Mixed Review Exercises, page 9 **1.** 3 **2.** 436 **3.** 144 **4.** 12 **5.** 4 **6.** 55 **7.** 23 **8.** 10 **9.** 5 **10.** 5 **11.** 60 **12.** 32

Challenge, page 9 **a.** 110 **b.** 5050

Written Exercises, pages 11–12 **1.** {4} **3.** {5} **5.** {5} **7.** {4} **9.** {2} **11.** {0} **13.** {3} **15.** {4} **17.** {1} **19.** {0, 1, 2, 3, 4, 5} **21.** 4 **23.** 8 **25.** 2 **27.** {4} **29.** {2} **31.** {8} **33.** {7} **35.** {0, 2} **37.** {0, 6} **39. a.** More than one **b.** None **c.** One; {4} **41. a.** One; {2} **b.** More than one **c.** None For Exs. 43–45, answers may vary. Examples are given. **43.** $1 \cdot x = 3, x + 1 = 4$ **45.** $x - x = 0, 4x \div 2 = x + x$

Mixed Review Exercises, page 12 **1.** 132 **2.** 10 **3.** 3 **4.** $\frac{7}{8}$ **5.** 6 **6.** 2 **7.** 22 **8.** 12 **9.** 88 **10.** 55 **11.** 2.4 **12.** 6

Calculator Key-In, page 13 **1.** 0 **3.** 0.1 **5.** 333,333 **7. a.** 100 **b.** 0 **c.** 37

Self-Test 1, page 13 **1.** 22 **2.** 84 **3.** 23 **4.** 6 **5.** {5} **6.** {3}

Written Exercises, pages 16–18 **1.** $8 + n$ **3.** $n - 11$ **5.** $\frac{1}{2}n$ **7.** $\frac{17}{d}$ **9.** $11x$ **11.** $7 + 2y$ **13.** $\frac{1}{2}n - 8$ **15.** $5 + \frac{n}{8}$ **17.** i **19.** g **21.** h **23.** b **25.** c **27.** $f + 3$ **29.** $m - 10$ **31.** $17 - x$ **33. a.** $s - 3$ **b.** $d + 3$ **35. a.** $g - 12$ **b.** $b + 12$ **37.** $(3r)$ mi **39.** $(5p)$ cents **41.** $5l$ **43.** $(3p + 2n)$ cents **45.** 180 min; $60h$ min **47.** 3 years; $\frac{m}{12}$ years **49.** $10c$; $10(c - 5)$ **51.** $n - 5$ **53.** $(p + 29) + 2p + (p + 42)$

Mixed Review Exercises, page 18 **1.** 13 **2.** 64 **3.** 12 **4.** 27 **5.** 26 **6.** 16 **7.** {4} **8.** {4} **9.** {1} **10.** {0} **11.** {3} **12.** {2} **13.** {4} **14.** {3}

Written Exercises, pages 20–22 **1.** a **3.** a **5.** b **7.** b **9.** e **11.** b **13.** d **15.** h **17.** $24 = x + 17$ **19.** $12 = 7 + x$ **21.** $40 = 8x$ **23.** s; $4s = 116$ **25.** c; $c + 7 = 50$ **27.** d; $d + 12 = 120$ **29.** p; $\frac{1}{8}p = 0.95$ **31.** t; $462 = 132t$ **33.** l; $\frac{1}{100}l = 8.5$ **35.** r; $24 - r = 3 + 2r$

Mixed Review Exercises, page 22 **1.** {4} **2.** {6} **3.** {5} **4.** {6} **5.** {3} **6.** {2} **7.** {5} **8.** {0, 1, 2, 3, 4, 5, 6} **9.** $n - 5$ **10.** $5 + n$ **11.** $\frac{5}{n}$ **12.** $2(5 + n)$

Problems, pages 24–26 **1.** $s + (s + 5) = 73$ **3.** $w + (4 + w) = 12$ **5.** $w + (3 + w) = 25$ **7.** $t + 8 = 2t$ **9.** $c + (5 + c) = 33$ **11.** $b + (2 + b) = 34$ **13.** $x + (x + 1) = 9$ **15.** $2(2w) + 2w = 60$ **17.** $30 = 7 + x + (x + 1)$ **19.** $x + (x + 1) + [(x + 1) + 2] = 12$ **21.** $x + (x + 1) + [2 + (1 + x)] = 10$

Mixed Review Exercises, page 26 **1.** {1} **2.** {2} **3.** {4} **4.** {4} **5.** {5} **6.** {5} **7.** {2} **8.** {4} **9.** $\frac{1}{3}x$ **10.** $4x - 2$ **11.** $5 + 2x$ **12.** $\frac{1}{4}x - 4$

Reading Algebra, page 26 **1.** Twice as much milk as apple juice and three times as much milk as fruit punch was served; a total of 660 cartons was served. **3.** No; the amount of apple juice served was $\frac{1}{2}x$, not $2x$, and the amount of punch served was $\frac{1}{3}x$, not $3x$.

Problems, pages 28–29 **1.** water color, 8; oil painting, 24 **3.** smaller, 64; larger, 121 **5.** car, 159 km; bus, 477 km **7.** 44 Republicans; 56 Democrats **9.** Ramon, \$90; Elena, \$135 **11.** school, 18 m **13.** width, 11 m; length, 23 m **15.** width, 12 ft; length, 27 ft **17.** Luis, 115 lb; Carla, 110 lb; Rita, 108 lb

Mixed Review Exercises, page 29 **1.** 10 **2.** 4 **3.** 24 **4.** 153 **5.** $6x = 36$ **6.** $6 = x - 2$ **7.** $2 + 2x = 10$ **8.** $\frac{1}{3}x = 6$

Self-Test 2, page 30 **1.** $8(n + 4)$ **2.** $2x = 2 + x$ **3.** $x + (2 + 2x) = 11$ **4.** length, 11 ft; width, 5 ft

Written Exercises, pages 33–35 **1.** $^-5$, 5; five steps up **3.** 190, $^-190$; 190 m below sea level **5.** 18, $^-18$; a loss of \$18 **7.** $^-15$, 15; 15 km east **9.** 85, $^-85$; payments of \$85 **11.** $^-1$, 1; one foot above ground **13.** $^-50$, 50; a profit of \$50 **15.** $6 > {}^-9$ **17.** $^-8 > {}^-10$ **19.** $6 < 6.5$ **21.** $^-13 < 0$ **23.** *S, F* **25.** *N, R* **27.** *Q, A, U* **29.** *M, T, P* **31.** $^-1 < 3$, $3 > {}^-1$ **33.** $0 < 2$, $2 > 0$ **35.** $^-6 < {}^-2$, $^-2 > {}^-6$ **37.** $0 < 5$, $5 > 0$ **39.** < **41.** < **43.** > **45.** > **47.** $^-2$, $^-1$, 1, 2

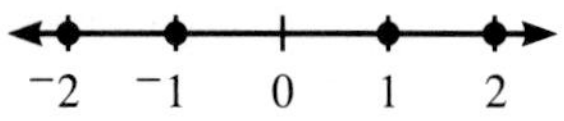

49. $^-1$, $^-0.5$, 0, 1.5

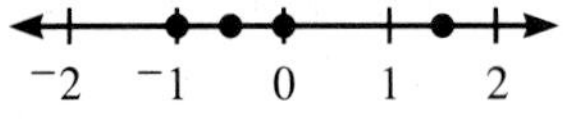

51. $^-3$, $^-1\frac{2}{3}$, $^-\frac{1}{3}$, 0

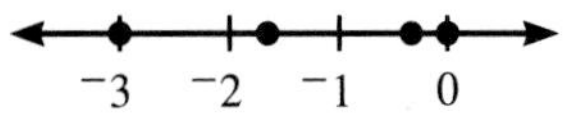

53. $^-1\frac{1}{4}$, $^-\frac{1}{4}$, $\frac{3}{4}$, $2\frac{1}{4}$

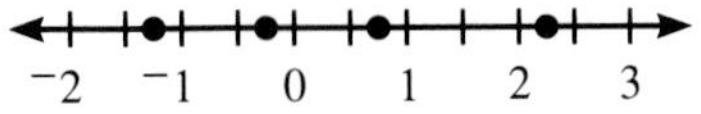

55. Cora, Freida, Stu, Janelle **57.** 3

Mixed Review Exercises, page 35 **1.** 24 **2.** 24 **3.** 6 **4.** 3 **5.** 15 **6.** 14 **7.** $30 - x = 12$ **8.** $x + 4 = 2$ **9.** $6x = 2$ **10.** $\frac{1}{4}x = 1$

Challenge, page 35 **1.** 21, 28, 36, 45, 55

Written Exercises, pages 38–39 **1.** -12 **3.** 0 **5.** 19 **7.** 8 **9.** 11 **11.** 14 **13.** $\frac{3}{2}$ **15.** 4 **17.** 1 **19.** 0 **21.** > **23.** < **25.** = **27.** $|-5| > 2$ **29.** $-(-2) > -(-1)$ **31.** {0} **33.** $\left\{\frac{1}{2}, -\frac{1}{2}\right\}$ **35.** No sol. because the absolute value of a number cannot be negative. **37.** $\{1, -1\}$ **39.** 3.5 **41.** 2.3 **43.** 6.3 **45.** (a) is false. 0 is a real number and $|0| = 0$, which is not a positive number.

Mixed Review Exercises, page 39 **1.** 1 **2.** 7 **3.** 2 **4.** 8 **5.** 1 **6.** 13 **7.** -3, 3 **8.** -50, 50 **9.** 1000, -1000 **10.** 0.5, -0.5

Self-Test 3, page 39
1.

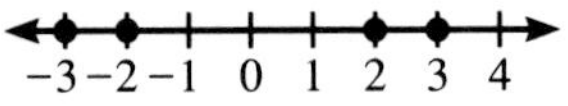

2. -7 **3.** 14 **4.** -3 **5.** $\frac{2}{3}$

Chapter Review, page 41 **1.** d **3.** b **5.** c **7.** c **9.** b **11.** d

Maintaining Skills, page 43 **1.** 29.9476 **3.** 377.7 **5.** 1653.6 **7.** 16.522 **9.** 989.04 **11.** 45.79 **13.** $\frac{5}{8}, \frac{6}{8}$ **15.** $\frac{6}{21}, \frac{14}{21}$ **17.** $\frac{47}{45}$ **19.** $\frac{67}{72}$ **21.** $\frac{15}{52}$ **23.** $\frac{5}{6}$ **25.** $\frac{23}{21}$ **27.** $\frac{49}{64}$

Chapter 2 Working with Real Numbers

Written Exercises, pages 47–48 **1.** 360 **3.** 630 **5.** 7400 **7.** 13 **9.** 8 **11.** $7y + 7$ **13.** $2x + 6$ **15.** $10a$ **17.** $35yz$ **19.** $48xyz$ **21.** $a + b + 7$ **23.** $4a + 3n + 6$ **25.** $7x + 4y + z + 8$ **27.** $10{,}000bcde$

29. Comm. prop. of mult. **31.** Comm. prop. of add. **33.** Assoc. prop. of mult.
35. a. Comm. prop. of add. **b.** Assoc. prop. of add. **c.** Subst. prop. **d.** Subst. prop.
37. a. 1; 5 **b.** no **39.** No; for example, $10 \div 2 = 5$ but $2 \div 10 = \frac{1}{5}$.

Mixed Review Exercises, page 48 **1.** 2 **2.** 90 **3.** $\frac{2}{3}$ **4.** 5 **5.** 29 **6.** 8 **7.** 24 **8.** 16 **9.** 1

Challenge, page 48 5 pennies, 1 nickel, and 9 dimes

Written Exercises, pages 52–53 **1.** 11 **3.** 0 **5.** −1 **7.** −8 **9.** 17 **11.** −36 **13.** 30 **15.** −38 **17.** −13 **19.** −11 **21.** −2.4 **23.** 0 **25.** $x + (-5)$ **27.** $2n$ **29.** $5n + (-8)$ **31.** $3a + 4b + (-13)$ **33.** $7x + (-y) + (-10)$ **35.** a **37.** 0
39. a. $(a + b) + [(-a) + (-b)] = [a + (-a)] + [b + (-b)] = 0 + 0 = 0$
b. Prop. of opposites **c.** Since the opp. of a number is unique and $-(a + b)$ and $[(-a) + (-b)]$ both have the sum of zero when added to $(a + b)$, $-(a + b) = (-a) + (-b)$.

Mixed Review Exercises, page 53 **1.** 10 **2.** 9 **3.** 4 **4.** 5 **5.** $\frac{2}{3}$ **6.** $\frac{1}{3}$ **7.** 120 **8.** 2500 **9.** $24abc$ **10.** 18 **11.** 9.4 **12.** 170

Challenge, page 53
1. 36, 49 **3.**
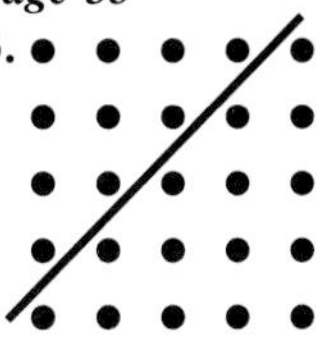
25 = 10 + 15

Written Exercises, pages 55–56 **1.** −1 **3.** 41 **5.** −28 **7.** 10 **9.** −12 **11.** −23 **13.** 24.8 **15.** −46 **17.** 0 **19.** $\frac{1}{2}$ **21.** $-\frac{9}{4}$ **23.** $x + (-4)$ **25.** 0 **27.** $-c$ **29.** −9 **31.** 2 **33.** −6 **35.** −9 **37.** 1 **39.** −15 **41.** x **43.** $-b$

Problems, pages 56–58 **1.** 20th floor **3.** \$818 **5.** \$1148 **7.** 13 fewer guests on the 4th day **9.** 3 blocks east and 9 blocks south **11.** 54 m below sea level **13.** 12:30 P.M. **15.** \$121.75

Mixed Review Exercises, page 58 **1.** 2 **2.** 1200 **3.** 13 **4.** 1 **5.** 2.4 **6.** 9 **7.** 9 **8.** $20\frac{2}{3}$ **9.** 9 **10.** 16 **11.** −10 **12.** −11

Calculator Key-In, page 58 **1.** −19 **3.** −391 **5.** −8.1

Written Exercises, pages 61–62 **1.** −188 **3.** 71 **5.** −16 **7.** −7.2 **9.** 198 **11.** 2.94 **13.** −27 **15.** −25 **17.** 121 **19.** 265 **21.** 0 **23.** −9 **25.** 390 **27.** 12 **29.** 21 **31.** −9 **33.** 116 **35.** −84 **37.** $-x + 7$ **39.** −5 **41.** $-b + 12$ **43.** $z - y - 8$ **45.** $-z + 2$ **47.** y **49.** 17 **51.** −19 **53.** −10 **55.** −2 **57.** −4 **59.** −14 **61. a.** Def. of subtraction; Comm. prop. of add.; Assoc. prop. of add.; Prop. of opposites; Ident. prop. of add. **b.** a

Problems, pages 62–63 **1.** 92.9 millions of miles **3.** 28 years old **5.** 3.8°C **7.** 91 blocks **9.** 4478 m **11.** 79 lb

Mixed Review Exercises, page 63 **1.** 16 **2.** 540 **3.** $7x + 3y + 9$ **4.** $\frac{1}{5}$ **5.** −3 **6.** $-2\frac{1}{3}$ **7.** 3 **8.** 0.5 **9.** −18 **10.** 68 **11.** 12 **12.** $-x - 16$

Self-Test 1, pages 63–64 **1.** 6300 **2.** $x + 131$ **3.** −1 **4.** 5 **5.** $2x - 1$ **6.** −20 **7.** −20 **8.** −14 **9.** $-y + 18$

Reading Algebra, page 64 **1.** Add and subtract polynomials, multiply monomials **3.** A monomial is an expression that is either a numeral, a variable, or the product of a numeral and one or more variables. A polynomial is a sum of monomials. **5.** Index and/or Table of Contents

Written Exercises, pages 67–69 **1.** 248 **3.** 340 **5.** 188 **7.** 208 **9.** 38 **11.** 16 **13.** 1800 **15.** 0 **17.** 32 **19.** $7a$ **21.** $9y$ **23.** $4p$ **25.** $3x + 6$ **27.** $4n - 8$ **29.** $18n + 12$ **31.** $3j - 3k$ **33.** $6n + 14$ **35.** $10x + 15y$ **37.** $8a + 7$ **39.** $12n - 5$ **41.** $y + 4$ **43.** $7a + 4b$ **45.** $s + 4t$ **47.** $6x$ **49.** $4x + 15$ **51.** $3a - 25$ **53.** $-2x + 17$ **55.** $5x + 17$ **57.** $12y + 15$ **59.** $6x + 3y + 3$ **61.** $21a + 17b$ **63.** $11r + 12$ **65.** $34c + 14d + 50$ **67.** $5(c + d) + 2(3c + d)$; $11c + 7d$ **69.** $8 + (-5 + 15y) + \frac{1}{2}(12y - 8)$; $21y - 1$ **71.** 3 **73.** $248x + 160$ **75.** $113n - 9p - 99$ **77.** $-6x + 9y - 12$

Mixed Review Exercises, page 69 **1.** 28 **2.** 4 **3.** 2 **4.** 3 **5.** 9 **6.** 7 **7.** -1 **8.** 1 **9.** -4 **10.** 5 **11.** 10 **12.** 0

Challenge, page 69 **3. a.** 714,285 **b.** 857,142

Written Exercises, pages 72–73 **1.** 74 **3.** 480 **5.** -84 **7.** 0 **9.** -300 **11.** 420 **13.** $6ab$ **15.** $-14pq$ **17.** $140ac$ **19.** $-2x + 6y$ **21.** $-21m - 28n$ **23.** $-35x + 21$ **25.** $-a - b + 3$ **27.** $-a + b + c$ **29.** $2a + 2b$ **31.** 8 **33.** $-16c + 25p$ **35.** $-2s + 5.3y$ **37.** $-20x$ **39.** 380 **41.** -5700 **43.** $-\frac{1}{3}m + 2n$ **45.** $-3r - 3s + 7$ **47.** $-19x + 13y$ **49.** $3q - 9w$ **51.** $e + 3f$ **53.** $-22r - 31s$ **55.** $-12g + 33$ **57.** $(500p + 500)$ points down **59. a.** Ident. prop. of mult. **b.** Dist. prop. (of mult. with respect to add.) **c.** Prop. of opposites **d.** Mult. prop. of 0

Mixed Review Exercises, page 73 **1.** $4x = 44$ **2.** $n + 2 = 32$ **3.** $\frac{1}{2}x = 12$ **4.** $2x + 7 = 11$ **5.** 112 **6.** 194 **7.** $-y + 12$ **8.** 128 **9.** $-4n$ **10.** $4n + 16$

Application, page 74 **1.** \$5.00 per liter **3.** \$3.30 per liter

Written Exercises, pages 77–78
1. $x + (x + 1) = 43$
3. $x + (x + 1) + (x + 2) + (x + 3) = -106$
5. $x + (x + 2) + (x + 4) = 75$
7. $x(x + 2) = 168$
9. $x + (x + 2) + (x + 4) + (x + 6) = -100$
11. $x + (x + 2) + (x + 4) + (x + 6) = 36$
13. 17, 19, 21 **15.** 0, 1; 9, 10
17. $(x - 4) + [(x + 3) - 4] + [(x + 6) - 4] = 42$

Mixed Review Exercises, page 78 **1.** -2 **2.** -4.9 **3.** $2c + 3$ **4.** $-\frac{3}{5}$ **5.** 18 **6.** 1 **7.** 2 **8.** $19a$ **9.** $5y + 16$ **10.** $-x - y + z$ **11.** $6a - 6b$ **12.** $3y - 15$

Self-Test 2, page 78 **1.** $4x + 6y$ **2.** $4y - 7$ **3.** $2a$ **4.** $2x + 4$ **5.** -180 **6.** $56xy$ **7.** $-3a - 3b + 3c$ **8.** 396 **9.** $29 = x - 1$, $31 = x + 1$ **10.** $x + 2 = 2x - 1$

Written Exercises, pages 81–82 **1.** -4 **3.** -10 **5.** 1 **7.** -3 **9.** $-r$ **11.** 5 **13.** $4xy$ **15.** $-2ab$ **17.** $2pg$ **19.** $-8a + 10$ **21.** $9c - 2d$ **23.** $6m + 13k$ **25.** $-u + 6v$ **27.** $-4x - 17y$ **29.** $-27m$ **31.** $-r$ **33.** n **35.** $\frac{2}{3}, \frac{3}{2}$

Mixed Review Exercises, page 82
1. $5x + 4 = 24$ **2.** $x - 15 = 250$
3. $x + (x + 1) = 67$ **4.** $x(x + 1) = 42$
5. -120 **6.** 1800 **7.** 42 **8.** $-35a + 14d$
9. $-7x - 2$ **10.** $3x + 2$

Calculator Key-In, page 82 **1.** 16 **3.** 0.00032 **5.** the number

Written Exercises, pages 85–86 **1.** -8 **3.** 4 **5.** -16 **7.** 0 **9.** 36 **11.** -35 **13.** x **15.** $2y$ **17.** $13a$ **19.** $-9x$ **21.** $-\frac{13}{2}$ **23.** -1 **25.** -3 **27.** -1 **29.** -3 **31.** 0 **33.** -1 **35.** $\frac{a - b}{c} = (a - b) \cdot \frac{1}{c} = \left(a \cdot \frac{1}{c}\right) - \left(b \cdot \frac{1}{c}\right) = \frac{a}{c} - \frac{b}{c}$

Mixed Review Exercises, page 86 **1.** {5} **2.** {6} **3.** {3} **4.** {2} **5.** {2} **6.** {4} **7.** {5} **8.** {3} **9.** {3} **10.** {2} **11.** {1} **12.** {0, 1, 2, 3, 4, 5}

Self-Test 3, page 86 **1.** $\frac{1}{3y}$ **2.** -2 **3.** -10 **4.** -48 **5.** -27 **6.** 18 **7.** 8 **8.** $-4x$

Computer Key-In, page 87 **1.** -6 **3.** 17.62 **5.** -1 **7.** 3.524

Chapter Review, page 89 **1.** d **3.** b **5.** b **7.** b **9.** c **11.** d **13.** c **15.** d

Cumulative Review, page 91 **1.** 6 **3.** 6 **5.** 51 **7.** 32 **9.** -103 **11.** $13x + 11y$ **13.** -28 **15.** 0 **17.** -2 **19.** $-3, -2, -\frac{1}{2}, 0, \frac{1}{2}, 4$

21.

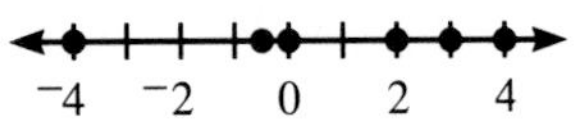

23. $\{10, -10\}$ **25.** $\{-12\}$ **27.** {0} **29.** $\{-3\}$ **31.** $7y + 5$ **33.** $-x = 8 - 4$ **35.** the third floor

Maintaining Skills, page 92 **1.** 11.32 **3.** 291.82 **5.** 2.5996 **7.** 0.757 **9.** 55 **11.** 662 **13.** 0.0025 **15.** 192 **17.** $\frac{2}{7}$ **19.** $\frac{3}{4}$

21. $\frac{7}{9}$ **23.** $\frac{1}{2}$ **25.** $\frac{1}{28}$ **27.** $\frac{34}{55}$ **29.** $\frac{1}{3}$ **31.** $\frac{28}{15}$ **33.** $\frac{144}{125}$

Preparing for College Entrance Exams, page 93 **1.** D **3.** A **5.** C **7.** C

Chapter 3 Transforming Equations

Written Exercises, pages 97–98 **1.** {20} **3.** {23} **5.** {136} **7.** {7} **9.** {−50} **11.** {−38} **13.** {42} **15.** {−4} **17.** {0} **19.** {−10} **21.** {−1} **23.** {2.9} **25.** {2} **27.** {−7} **29.** {10} **31.** {−17} **33.** {−5} **35.** {−5} **37.** {−7} **39.** {11} **41.** {92} **43.** {−7} **45.** {5} **47.** {18, −18} **49.** {8, −8} **51.** {2, −2} **53.** no solution **55.** {4, −4} **57.** {4, −4} **59.** {0}

Problems, pages 98–100 **1.** −63 **3.** −21 **5.** 76 **7.** 32 mi/h **9.** −7°C **11.** $2.45 **13.** 454 employees **15.** 111° **17.** $.35 **19.** 14 km

Mixed Review Exercises, pages 100–101 **1.** 3 **2.** 1 **3.** 12 **4.** 2 **5.** $\frac{1}{12}$ **6.** 36 **7.** 420 **8.** −270 **9.** $-4a$ **10.** 1 **11.** $12b$ **12.** $5a - 5b$

Application, page 101 **1. a.** $3240 **b.** $240 **3. a.** $5058 **b.** $558

Written Exercises, page 104 **1.** {11} **3.** {−3} **5.** {−9} **7.** {3} **9.** {24} **11.** {−35} **13.** {−64} **15.** {18} **17.** {−80} **19.** {−33} **21.** {−24} **23.** {0} **25.** {−45} **27.** {−18} **29.** {7} **31.** {−0.4} **33.** {16} **35.** {−11} **37.** {−3} **39.** {0} **41.** {9, −9} **43.** no solution **45.** {10, −10} **47.** {21, −21} **49.** {6, −6} **51.** {4, −4}

Problems, pages 105–106 **1.** −75 **3.** −21 **5.** 360 seniors **7.** 196 m **9.** $7.20 **11.** 7 games **13.** 250 apples **15.** 9 hard-cover books **17.** $21,250 **19.** $\frac{1}{72}$ mi/s; 50 mi/h

Mixed Review Exercises, page 106 **1.** 20 **2.** 48 **3.** 11 **4.** 1 **5.** $\frac{15}{4}$ **6.** 1 **7.** $16a + 6$ **8.** $5n$ **9.** $9p + 2$ **10.** $-4m - 8$ **11.** $8x + 56$ **12.** $6y - 15$

Calculator Key-In, page 106 **1.** 0.75 **3.** −0.2 **5.** 0.025 **7.** −0.24 **9.** 0.96875 **11–20.** yes

Written Exercises, pages 109–110 **1.** {6} **3.** {−3} **5.** {−7} **7.** {−2} **9.** {12} **11.** {16} **13.** {−13} **15.** {18} **17.** {0} **19.** {4} **21.** {−5} **23.** {15} **25.** {5} **27.** {5} **29.** {2} **31.** {−36} **33.** {−12} **35.** {−2} **37.** {−4} **39.** {−4} **41.** {8} **43.** {4} **45.** {6} **47.** {2} **49.** {−34} **51.** {4} **53.** {0} **55.** {−18} **57.** {5} **59.** {7, −7}

Mixed Review Exercises, page 110 **1.** {−161} **2.** {6} **3.** {16} **4.** {4} **5.** {3} **6.** {34} **7.** {−8} **8.** {−4} **9.** {−4} **10.** {1.3} **11.** {0} **12.** {20}

Computer Exercises, page 111 **1. a.** 8 **b.** −2 **c.** −10 **d.** 6 **e.** 36 **f.** 11 **3. a.** {2, −2} **b.** no solution **c.** {0.5, −0.5}

Self-Test 1, page 111 **1.** {38} **2.** {42} **3.** {125} **4.** {−11} **5.** 6 cm by 18 cm **6.** {7} **7.** {24}

Calculator Key-In, page 111 **1.** no **3.** no

Problems, pages 113–115 **1.** 43 **3.** 42 **5.** 27 **7.** 56, 57, 58 **9.** 58, 60, 62, 64 **11.** with cheese, 165; without cheese, 330 **13.** 32 weeks **15.** 90 cm **17.** 130 cm **19.** 17 cm by 32 cm **21.** width, 14 cm; length, 50 cm **23.** $m\angle A = 84$, $m\angle B = 28$, $m\angle C = 68$ **25.** $AB = 9$; $AC = 18$; $BC = 21$ **27.** Theo, $22; Rudy, $6; Denise, $17 **29.** Mach. A, 15,800 bottles; Mach. B, 7900 bottles; Mach. C, 16,300 bottles **31.** $21,800 **33.** 15 or −8

Mixed Review Exercises, page 115 **1.** {6} **2.** {−1.5} **3.** {13} **4.** {5} **5.** {−63} **6.** {−100} **7.** {30} **8.** {57} **9.** {0} **10.** {2} **11.** {10} **12.** $\left\{-\frac{3}{2}\right\}$

Written Exercises, page 118 **1.** {2} **3.** {6} **5.** {2} **7.** {−11} **9.** {8} **11.** {−14} **13.** {−1} **15.** {3} **17.** {6} **19.** {−12} **21.** {4} **23.** {10} **25.** {1} **27.** {1} **29.** {−14} **31.** identity **33.** {4} **35.** {−3} **37.** identity **39.** {−1} **41.** identity **43.** {−1} **45.** {−2} **47.** {1}

Problems, pages 118–119 **1.** 48 **3.** 7 **5.** 23 **7.** −14, −13 **9.** Cliff, 6; Kyle and Lyle, 18 **11.** 7, 8 **13.** 14 units **15.** 6 years

17. Marcia, \$87.50; Eric, \$175; Laurel, \$262.50 **19.** If $n + (n + 1) + (n + 2) = n + 200$, then $n = 98.5$, which is not an integer. $\therefore$ it is impossible.

Mixed Review Exercises, page 120 **1.** 2 **2.** $-1\frac{2}{5}$ **3.** -199 **4.** $14x - 5$ **5.** $15y + 18$ **6.** -420 **7.** $\{-12\}$ **8.** $\{1\}$ **9.** $\{-98\}$ **10.** $\{9\}$ **11.** $\{42\}$ **12.** $\{38\}$

Computer Exercises, page 120 **1.** $\{-3\}$ **3.** no solution **5.** $\{5\}$

Self-Test 2, page 120 **1.** \$21 **2.** $\{5\}$ **3.** $\{7\}$ **4.** Paul, \$4.50; Jeff, \$9.50; Hilary, \$13.50

Problems, pages 122–125 **1.** 14 shifts **3.** 306 lb **5.** orange, 65 Calories; peach, 35 Calories **7.** red, 9 cm by 24 cm; blue, 14 cm by 22 cm **9.** \$120 **11.** 15 ft by 45 ft; 9 ft by 75 ft **13.** Greg, 8; Rodney, 16 **15.** 420 Calories **17.** Angel Falls, 807 m; Niagara Falls, 57 m **19.** 65 Calories

Mixed Review Exercises, page 125 **1.** $\{24\}$ **2.** $\{15\}$ **3.** $\{0\}$ **4.** $\{65\}$ **5.** $\{3\}$ **6.** $\{-8\}$ **7.** $\{7\}$ **8.** $\{4\}$ **9.** $\{11\}$ **10.** $\{-7\}$ **11.** $\{18\}$ **12.** $\{-20\}$

Problems, pages 127–129 **1.** 12 students **3.** 22 nickels **5.** 50 programs **7.** 14 quarters **9.** \$44 **11.** plumber, \$25.50; apprentice, \$21 **13.** 7 quarters **15.** Solution involves a fractional number of coins. **17.** \$3.80

Mixed Review Exercises, page 129 **1.** 1 **2.** 216 **3.** $13y + 1$ **4.** 35 **5.** $3x + 28$ **6.** $15x + 23y$ **7.** 5 **8.** $\frac{5}{8}$ **9.** 23

Written Exercises, pages 131–133
1. (1) Reflex. prop. of =; (3) Substitution principle **3.** (2) Mult. prop. of =; (3) Assoc. prop. of mult.; (4) Prop. of reciprocals; (5) Identity prop. of mult. **5.** (1) Prop. of opposites; (2) Prop. of opposites; (3) Substitution principle or Trans. prop. of equality; (4) Comm. prop. of add. **7.** (1) Subtraction; (3) 5; (4) Comm. prop. of add.; (5) Def. of subtr.

9. (1) $a = b$ (Given)

(2) $a \cdot \frac{1}{c} = b \cdot \frac{1}{c}$ (Mult. prop. of =)

(3) $\frac{a}{c} = \frac{b}{c}$ (Def. of div.)

11. (1) $\frac{a}{b} \cdot \frac{b}{a} = \left(a \cdot \frac{1}{b}\right)\left(b \cdot \frac{1}{a}\right)$ (Def. of division)

(2) $\frac{a}{b} \cdot \frac{b}{a} = \left(a \cdot \frac{1}{a}\right)\left(b \cdot \frac{1}{b}\right)$ (Commutative and associative props. of mult.)

(3) $\frac{a}{b} \cdot \frac{b}{a} = 1 \cdot 1$ (Prop. of reciprocals)

(4) $\frac{a}{b} \cdot \frac{b}{a} = 1$ (Identity prop. of mult.)

(5) $\frac{a}{b} \cdot \left(\frac{1}{\frac{a}{b}}\right) = 1$ (Prop. of reciprocals)

(6) $\frac{a}{b} \cdot \frac{1}{\frac{a}{b}} = \frac{a}{b} \cdot \left(\frac{b}{a}\right)$ (Substitution)

(7) $\frac{1}{\frac{a}{b}} = \frac{b}{a}$ (Div. prop. of =)

Mixed Review Exercises, page 133 **1.** 14 **2.** 32 **3.** $3x$ **4.** $-4 - a$ **5.** $b + 1$ **6.** 20 **7.** 50 **8.** 3 **9.** 3 **10.** $\frac{7}{6}$ **11.** 5 **12.** 5

Self-Test 3, page 134 **1.** 51 cm by 59 cm; 56 cm by 65 cm **2.** nickels, 22; quarters, 12 **3.** (1) Assoc. prop. of add.; (2) Prop. of opposites; (3) Identity prop. of add.

Chapter Review, page 135 **1.** c **3.** d **5.** a **7.** b **9.** a **11.** b

Cumulative Review, page 137 **1.** 25 **3.** 4 **5.** 24 **7.** -20 **9.** $3\frac{3}{4}$ **11.** $2x - 2$ **13.** -28 **15.** $17x$ **17.** 1 **19.** -6 **21.** $-4\frac{1}{2}$ **23.** no solution **25.** $\{-4\}$ **27.** $\{16\}$ **29.** $\{18\}$ **31.** $\{2\}$ **33.** $\{11\}$ **35.** $\left\{\frac{9}{5}\right\}$ **37.** peach, \$.30; melon, \$1.20 **39.** 95 employees

Maintaining Skills, page 138 **1.** $2\frac{1}{12}$ **3.** $5\frac{1}{5}$ **5.** $7\frac{7}{12}$ **7.** $9\frac{1}{4}$ **9.** $\frac{25}{6}$ **11.** $\frac{25}{9}$ **13.** $\frac{47}{13}$ **15.** $\frac{119}{12}$ **17.** $18\frac{1}{5}$ **19.** $-1\frac{1}{21}$ **21.** $25\frac{1}{2}$ **23.** $3\frac{9}{40}$ **25.** $4\frac{3}{10}$ **27.** $21\frac{27}{35}$ **29.** $-2\frac{13}{22}$ **31.** $1\frac{11}{36}$ **33.** $-1\frac{13}{21}$ **35.** $26\frac{1}{12}$

Mixed Problem Solving Review, page 139 **1.** 5 **3.** 75 km/h **5.** 7 oranges, 5 apples **7.** −5°C **9.** 3, 4, 5 **11.** 7 \$10 bills, 11 \$5 bills **13.** \$480,000 **15.** 7 h **17.** no solution

Chapter 4 Addition and Subtraction

Written Exercises, pages 143–144 **1.** $6y$ **3.** $8z^2$ **5.** m^3 **7.** $3c^3$ **9.** $-5y^2$ **11.** $-14n^2$ **13.** c^3d **15.** $9u^3v$ **17.** $-4rs^2$ **19.** p^2q^2rs **21.** d **23.** c **25. a.** 4 **b.** -4 **27. a.** -48 **b.** 144 **29. a.** 34 **b.** 1000 **31. a.** 3 **b.** -13 **33.** 1776 **35.** 2 **37.** 13 **39.** 3 **41. a.** 16 **b.** 4 **43. a.** -1 **b.** 11 **45.** -11 **47.** -6 **49.** 0

Mixed Review Exercises, page 144 **1.** $\{-8\}$ **2.** $\{16\}$ **3.** $\{-12\}$ **4.** $\{2\}$ **5.** $\{10\}$ **6.** $\{4\}$ **7.** $\{-8\}$ **8.** $\{50\}$ **9.** $\left\{-\frac{2}{7}\right\}$

Calculator Key-In, page 145 **1.** 0.01 **3.** 0.25 **5.** 0.0121 **7.** 0.027

Written Exercises, pages 148–149 **1.** $3x - 2y - x - 3y$; $2x - 5y$ **3.** $3x^2 - 2x - 2x^2 - 4x - 3$; $x^2 - 6x - 3$ **5.** $a^2 + 3ab - 4ab + 3a^2$; $4a^2 - ab$ **7.** $r^2s - 3rs^2 + 4s^3 - 2r^2s - 3s^2$; $-r^2s - 3rs^2 - 3s^2 + 4s^3$ **9.** $7y + 6$ **11.** $5y + 3$ **13.** $r + 3$ **15.** $5x^2 + x - 10$ **17.** $6x^2 - 2xy - 8y^2$ **19.** $4a - 3b - c$ **21.** $3y - 12$ **23.** $y + 13$ **25.** $3r - 6x + 7$ **27.** $-x^2 - 7x + 2$ **29.** $2x^2 - 4xy - 2y^2$ **31.** $7x + y - 5$ **33.** $x - 3$ **35.** $4x - t - 4$ **37.** $2n^2 + 2n - 3$ **39.** $4x^2 - 9$ **41.** $u^3 - v^3$ **43.** $2a^3 + 2ab^2 + b^3$ **45.** $\{2\}$ **47.** $\{-2\}$ **49.** $\{8\}$ **51.** $\{8\}$ **53.** $\{3\}$ **55.** no sol.

Problems, page 150 **1.** $2x^2 + 5x + 2$ **3.** $3x^2 + 4x + 1$ **5.** 24, 25 **7.** 61, 62, 63, 64 **9.** 11, 12 **11.** 7, 9, 11 **13.** 4, 6, 8, 10

Mixed Review Exercises, pages 150–151 **1.** -25 **2.** 25 **3.** 17 **4.** 4 **5.** $\left\{\frac{13}{5}\right\}$ **6.** $\left\{\frac{9}{2}\right\}$ **7.** $\left\{-\frac{41}{9}\right\}$ **8.** $\left\{-\frac{25}{2}\right\}$ **9.** $\{10\}$ **10.** $\{17\}$

Self-Test 1, page 151 **1.** mn^3 **2.** $-15x^2$ **3.** $-8y^2$ **4.** 16 **5.** -16 **6.** -27 **7.** -213 **8.** -16 **9.** 2 **10. a.** $10x + 4$ **b.** $4x + 6$ **11. a.** $6x^2 - 12$ **b.** $4x^2 + 12x - 4$ **12. a.** 3 **b.** $2x^2y - 6xy^2 + 11$ **13.** 12, 14, 16

Written Exercises, pages 153–154 **1.** n^8 **3.** x^9 **5.** $10x^7$ **7.** m^3n^5 **9.** $6a^2b^6$ **11.** $-12x^7$ **13.** $6x^4y^4$ **15.** $10a^3b^7c^3$ **17.** $24p^3q^3$ **19.** $6x^6y^6$ **21.** t^6 **23.** $6a^4b^3$ **25.** $4x^6$ **27.** $\frac{5}{2}p^7q^4$ **29.** $-16x^2y^6$ **31.** $22x^5$ **33.** $9a^8$ **35.** $P = 10ab$; $A = 6a^2b^2$ **37.** $P = 18a$; $A = 10a^2$ **39.** $46x^2$ **41.** a^{2m} **43.** 3^{p+q} **45.** 4^x **47.** a^{x+3} **49.** 2^{2x+3} **51.** $5nx^{10}$

Mixed Review Exercises, page 154 **1.** 8 **2.** 36 **3.** $3p^2 + 3q^2 - 2p^2q$ **4.** 147 **5.** 441 **6.** $7x^2 + 2x + 5$ **7.** $\{-12\}$ **8.** $\{6\}$ **9.** $\{1\}$ **10.** $\{15\}$ **11.** $\{7\}$ **12.** $\{8\}$

Written Exercises, pages 156–157 **1. a.** 81 **b.** 729 **c.** 729 **3. a.** 12 **b.** 36 **c.** 36 **5. a.** c^7 **b.** c^{10} **c.** c^{10} **7. a.** $-125a^{12}$ **b.** $-125a^{12}$ **c.** $-5a^{12}$ **9.** $49a^2$ **11.** $-64c^3$ **13.** $64k^6$ **15.** $-27y^9$ **17.** $27a^6b^3$ **19.** $16r^{12}s^{16}$ **21.** $64x^6$ **23.** $1{,}000{,}000b^6$ **25.** $54a^9b^4$ **27.** $2p^{10}q^{11}$ **29.** $16x^8$ **31.** $54x^7y^4$ **33. a.** $17x^6$ **b.** $72x^{12}$ **35. a.** $2a^4b^6$ **b.** a^8b^{12} **37. a.** $3a^4b^6$ **b.** $-4a^8b^{12}$ **39.** x^{2n} **41.** a^{x+3} **43.** x^{2n} **45.** z^{3x} **47.** $72r^{5n}$ **49.** $9x^{4n}$ **51. a.** $8x^3$; $64x^3$ **b.** right **c.** 8 times **53.** $16^x \cdot (4^x)^2 = 16^x \cdot 4^{2x} = (2^4)^x \cdot (2^2)^{2x} = 2^{4x} \cdot 2^{4x} = 2^{8x} = (2^x)^8$

Mixed Review Exercises, page 157 **1.** $24a^3b^3$ **2.** $8x^3y^3$ **3.** $16x^8y^{12}$ **4.** $\frac{1}{3}t^5$ **5.** $4c - 2a$ **6.** $5x + 5y + 2$ **7.** 60 **8.** -75 **9.** 4

Written Exercises, pages 159–160 **1.** $4x - 12$ **3.** $c^2 - 2c$ **5.** $3y^2 + 15y$ **7.** $-14r + 6r^2$ **9.** $6y^3 - 2y^2 - 10y$ **11.** $-2a^3b^2 + 6a^2b^3 - 10ab^4$ **13.** $3x^3 - 6x^2 + 12x$ **15.** $p^3q^2 - 3p^2q^3 - 4pq^4$ **17.** $2x^4 - 3x^3y - x^2y^2$ **19.** $x^2 - x$ **21.** $9r^2$ **23.** $9y - 12$ **25.** $2a$ **27.** $\{4\}$ **29.** $\{10\}$ **31.** $\{6\}$ **33.** $\{2\}$ **35.** $\{9\}$ **37.** $\{2\}$ **39. a.** $2x^2 + xy$ **b.** $2x^2 + xy$ **c.** Distributive prop. **41.** $3x^2 + 23x$ **43.** S.A. $= 48x^2$; $V = 20x^3$

Mixed Review Exercises, page 160 **1.** $27x^6y^3$ **2.** $25r^6y^8$ **3.** $-27n^3$ **4.** $72a^{13}y^7$ **5.** $10x^5$ **6.** $3n^6$ **7.** $10p + 5$ **8.** $x + 4$ **9.** $675x^6y^9$

Written Exercises, pages 162–164 **1.** $6x^2 - 7x - 5$ **3.** $2a^3 - 3a^2 - a + 12$ **5.** $6x^2 + 11xy - 10y^2$ **7.** $c^3 - 7cd^2 + 6d^3$ **9.** $y^2 + 5y + 6$ **11.** $a^2 + 3a - 4$ **13.** $2x^2 - 11x + 5$ **15.** $6z^2 + 5z - 6$ **17.** $16s^2 - 25$ **19.** $a^3 + 5a^2 + 11a + 10$ **21.** $m^3 + m^2 + 4m - 6$ **23.** $2x^3 - 3x^2 + 7x - 3$

25. $9z^3 - 9z^2 + 14z - 8$ **27. a.** $x^2 + 10x + 21$ **b.** $x^2 + 10x + 21$ **c.** equal **29.** $y^3 - y + 6$
31. $2y^3 + y^2 - 14y + 12$
33. $-3x^3 + 8x^2 - 19x + 10$
35. $8r^3 - 12r^2s + 6rs^2 - s^3$
37. $\{13\}$ **39.** $\left\{\frac{20}{11}\right\}$ **41.** $\{6\}$
43. $x^4 - 6x^3 + 19x^2 - 30x + 25$
45. $x^3 + 15x^2 + 75x + 125$
47. $16 - 32y + 24y^2 - 8y^3 + y^4$
49. $x^3 - 2x^2 - 5x + 6$

Mixed Review Exercises, page 164 **1.** $\{3\}$ **2.** $\{4\}$ **3.** $\{2\}$ **4.** 0 **5.** 5 **6.** -2 **7.** 49 **8.** -1 **9.** -27

Self-Test 2, page 164 **1.** $3x^6$ **2.** $18a^9$ **3.** $-2a^5$ **4.** a^5b^5 **5.** $125x^3y^6$ **6.** $-8x^6y^3$ **7.** $-8x^6y^3$ **8.** $9x^6$ **9.** $-10n + 2n^2$
10. $8x^3y^2 - 7x^2y^3 + \frac{1}{7}xy^4$ **11.** $\{13\}$
12. $12x^2 - 7x - 10$ **13.** $5a^3 + 11a^2 - 2a - 8$
14. $6a^2 - 59a + 45$
15. $63 - 103y + 114y^2 - 56y^3$

Written Exercises, page 166 **1.** $r = \frac{c}{2\pi}$
3. $r = \frac{v}{s}$; $s \neq 0$ **5.** $P = \frac{I}{rt}$; $r \neq 0, t \neq 0$
7. $h = \frac{A - 2a^2}{4a}$; $a \neq 0$ **9.** $h = \frac{2A}{a + b}$; $a + b \neq 0$ **11.** $w = \frac{P - 2l}{2}$ **13.** $y = 2m - x$
15. $a = \frac{2S - nl}{n}$; $n \neq 0$ **17.** $t = \frac{v - u}{a}$; $a \neq 0$
19. $s = \frac{v^2 - u^2}{2a}$; $a \neq 0$ **21.** $r = \frac{Sa - a}{S}$; $S \neq 0$
23. $d = \frac{Ff + Fg - fg}{F}$; $F \neq 0$ **25.** $n = \frac{360}{180 - a}$; $a \neq 180$ **27.** $a = \frac{br}{b - r}$; $b \neq r$
29. $R = \frac{Cr}{C - Kr}$; $C \neq Kr$

Mixed Review Exercises, page 166
1. $y^2 - 2y - 15$ **2.** $6n^2 - 16n + 8$
3. $-2a^2 - 8a$ **4.** $2x^2y + 3xy^2$
5. $4x^3 - 12x^2 + 8x$ **6.** $-27x^9$ **7.** n^6 **8.** $36a^7b$

Problems, pages 170–171 **1.** 2:20 P.M. **3.** 1 h 48 min **5.** east, 650 km/h; west, 600 km/h **7.** 10:30 A.M. **9.** 43 km/h **11.** 22.5 km **13.** 165 km **15.** 26 knots **17.** when $t = \frac{P}{s - r}$ **19.** when $t = \frac{d}{r + s}$

Mixed Review Exercises, page 171 **1.** $\{-8\}$ **2.** $\{6\}$ **3.** $\{-42\}$ **4.** $\left\{\frac{1}{9}\right\}$ **5.** $\{15\}$ **6.** $\{-12\}$
7. $x = \frac{12}{b}$ **8.** $x = \frac{a - 5}{3}$

Problems, pages 173–174 **1.** 15 cm by 5 cm **3.** 36 m by 12 m **5.** 10 m by 5 m **7.** 924 m^2 **9.** $A = 2\pi rw + \pi w^2$ **11.** 9 m **13. a.** $(2\pi r + 8r + \pi)$ m **b.** 6π m

Mixed Review Exercises, page 174 **1.** -4 **2.** $3c - 7$ **3.** $64x^3y^9$ **4.** 14 **5.** 500 **6.** 8
7. 0 **8.** $\frac{1}{5}x^7$ **9.** $13x$ **10.** 0 **11.** $\frac{1}{5}y^4$
12. $81y^8z^4$

Problems, pages 176–177 **1.** No sol.; insufficient info. **3.** No sol.; insufficient info. **5.** No sol.; contradiction **7.** 85 km/h **9.** 11, 13, 15 **11.** No. sol.; insufficient info. **13.** 52 mi/h **15.** No sol.; unrealistic result

Self-Test 3, page 177 **1.** $V = \frac{kT}{P}$; $P \neq 0$
2. 25 km/h **3.** 17 ft by 10 ft **4.** No sol.; unrealistic result

Chapter Review, pages 178–179 **1.** b **2.** c **3.** b **4.** a **5.** d **6.** d **7.** d **8.** c **9.** d **10.** a **11.** d **12.** c **13.** a **14.** c **15.** b **16.** b **17.** a **18.** d

Cumulative Review, page 181 **1.** $2x - 5$ **3.** 0 **5.** 3 **7.** 45 **9.** -18 **11.** $100a^5$ **13.** $-12x^4 + 8x^3 + 20x^2$ **15.** $15 - 2x - 8x^2$ **17.** 1 **19.** 10 **21.** no sol. **23.** $\{-12\}$ **25.** $\{-1\}$ **27.** $\{-3\}$ **29.** $\{2\}$ **31.** $\{4\}$ **33.** $\{5\}$
35. $m = \frac{c + bn}{a}$; $a \neq 0$ **37.** 17, 19
39. Jessica: 10 dimes, 6 quarters; Whitney: 20 dimes, 2 quarters

Maintaining Skills, page 182 **1.** 1045
3. -44 **5.** -23 **7.** -85 **9.** $\frac{5}{8}$ **11.** 19.15
13. 72 **15.** -92 **17.** -21.275 **19.** 3.282
21. -28.96 **23.** $-\frac{7}{15}$ **25.** $\frac{19}{17}$ **27.** 13
29. -0.45 **31.** $\frac{1}{2}$

Preparing for College Entrance Exams, page 183 **1.** B **3.** B **5.** A **7.** C

Chapter 5 Quotients and Factoring

Written Exercises, pages 186–187 **1.** (1)(13), (−1)(−13) **3.** (1)(24), (2)(12), (3)(8), (4)(6), (−1)(−24), (−2)(−12), (−3)(−8), (−4)(−6) **5.** (1)(29), (−1)(−29) **7.** (1)(40), (2)(20), (4)(10), (5)(8), (−1)(−40), (−2)(−20), (−4)(−10), (−5)(−8) **9.** (1)(−121), (−1)(121), (11)(−11) **11.** (1)(−33), (−1)(33), (3)(−11), (−3)(11) **13.** (1)(53), (−1)(−53) **15.** (1)(26), (2)(13), (−1)(−26), (−2)(−13) **17.** (1)(68), (2)(34), (4)(17), (−1)(−68), (−2)(−34), (−4)(−17) **19.** (1)(38), (2)(19), (−1)(−38), (−2)(−19) **21.** 2^4 **23.** $3 \cdot 23$ **25.** $3 \cdot 5^2$ **27.** 3^3 **29.** $3^2 \cdot 11$ **31.** $2^3 \cdot 13$ **33.** 5^3 **35.** $2 \cdot 3^2 \cdot 5^2$ **37.** $3^2 \cdot 11^2$ **39.** $2 \cdot 17 \cdot 23$ **41.** 6 **43.** 14 **45.** 15 **47.** 147 **49.** 14 **51.** 1

Mixed Review Exercises, page 187 **1.** $3x - 1$ **2.** 81 **3.** 18 **4.** $x - 10$ **5.** $18a^4b$ **6.** $24x^3y^2$ **7.** $27x^4$ **8.** $6n^3$ **9.** $-32x^5$ **10.** $2x^2 + 3x$ **11.** $2y^2 + 11y + 15$ **12.** $3x^2 - 8x - 16$

Challenge, page 188 7^5 hekats of grain

Written Exercises, pages 192–193 **1.** $\frac{2}{3}$ **3.** $\frac{1}{100}$ **5.** 4 **7.** 200 **9.** $\frac{x^4}{2}$ **11.** $\frac{3y^2}{x}$ **13.** $-\frac{3xy}{4}$ **15.** $\frac{4cd}{3b}$ **17.** $\frac{z^2}{x^2}$ **19.** $\frac{8ac^2}{5}$ **21.** 8 **23.** 3 **25.** $2a$ **27.** $-z^3$ **29.** $-x^8$ **31.** $3t^3$ **33.** $3ab^2$ **35.** $-5xy^4$ **37.** $-16c^2d^2$ **39.** $3a^3b^2$ **41.** x^2y^4 **43.** $3r^2s^2$ **45.** $6x$ **47.** $24abc^2$ **49.** $5pq^2$ **51.** $x + y$ **53.** $a + b$ **55.** $\frac{x-y}{x+y}$ **57.** $\frac{8x}{11}$ **59.** $\frac{x^{n+1}}{y^{n-1}}$ **61. a.** Def. of division **b.** Prop. of the reciprocal of a product **c.** Comm. prop. of mult.; Assoc. prop. of mult. **d.** Def. of division

Mixed Review Exercises, page 193 **1.** −5 **2.** 37 **3.** 47 **4.** n^8 **5.** −45 **6.** $6y^3$ **7.** 1 **8.** $\frac{8}{5}$ **9.** 64

Calculator Key-In, page 193 **1.** 3; $\frac{3}{13}$ **3.** 5; $\frac{5}{11}$ **5.** 26; $\frac{13}{18}$

Written Exercises, pages 196–197 **1.** $2a + 3$ **3.** $4t - 2$ **5.** $m - 2n$ **7.** $4x + 9$ **9.** $2z^2 - 3z - 4$ **11.** $3y^3 + y^2 - 4y$ **13.** $-4r^2 + 2r + 3$ **15.** $q^2 - p^2$ **17.** $x - y - 1$ **19.** $-4r - 6s + 8rs$ **21.** 650 **23.** 190 **25.** 8300 **27.** 130 **29.** 140 **31.** $5(3a - 5b + 4)$ **33.** $2x(3x + 5)$ **35.** $3pq(2p - 3)$ **37.** $7y(y^2 - 3y - 2)$ **39.** $2ab(3b - 4a)$ **41.** $-3xy^2(5x + 2)$ **43.** $5a(x^2 + 2ax - 3a^2)$ **45.** $24a^2b^2(2a + 3b)$ **47.** $48wxy^2z^2(2x^2 - 3w^2)$ **49.** $3a - 1$ **51.** p **53.** $3x$

Problems, pages 197–199 **1.** $r^2(4 - \pi)$ **3.** $r^2(4 + \pi)$ **5.** $4r^2(4 - \pi)$ **7.** $2r^2(2\pi - 1)$ **9.** $r\left(2n + \frac{3}{2}\pi r\right)$ **11.** $r^2(4 + 3\pi)$

Mixed Review Exercises, page 199 **1.** n^6 **2.** $6x^5$ **3.** $6a^2 - 7a^2c - 3ac^2$ **4.** $\frac{x^2}{2y}$ **5.** −112 **6.** $8a^5$ **7.** $256a^4$ **8.** 69 **9.** $x^3 + x - 10$

Self-Test 1, page 199 **1.** (1)(45), (−1)(−45), (3)(15), (−3)(−15), (5)(9), (−5)(−9) **2.** $2 \cdot 3^3$ **3.** 9 **4.** $-3x$ **5.** $\frac{2n^6}{15m^2}$ **6.** $9x^2$ **7.** $-5ab^4$ **8.** $7t^2 + 5t - 3$ **9.** $5m(m^2 - 4m + 5)$

Written Exercises, pages 201–202 **1.** $x^2 + 13x + 40$ **3.** $y^2 - 7y + 12$ **5.** $z^2 - 3z - 28$ **7.** $n^2 + 4n - 21$ **9.** $6 + 5z + z^2$ **11.** $2y^2 + 9y + 10$ **13.** $7x^2 + 48x - 7$ **15.** $6y^2 + 7y + 2$ **17.** $2 - 7s + 6s^2$ **19.** $6h^2 - 7h - 5$ **21.** $20n^2 - 9n - 20$ **23.** $3x^2 - 7xy + 2y^2$ **25.** $8h^2 + 10hk - 3k^2$ **27.** $35a^2 - 31ab + 6b^2$ **29.** $3a^4 + 8a^2b - 3b^2$ **31.** $p^6 - p^3q^3 - 12q^6$ **33.** $4x^6 + 3x^4y^2 - x^2y^4$ **35.** $4y^3 - 5y^2 - 6y$ **37.** $3x^4 - 14x^3 + 8x^2$ **39.** {−1} **41.** {11} **43.** {9} **45.** $p = 3$, $q = -2$, $r = -10$ **47.** $2x^{2n} + x^ny^n - 3y^{2n}$ **49.** $(2n + 1)^2 = 4n^2 + 4n + 1 = 2(2n^2 + 2n) + 1$

Mixed Review Exercises, page 203 **1.** $-8x^4y^4$ **2.** $125x^6y^{15}$ **3.** $12n^3 + 24n^2 + 3n - 3$ **4.** $2r^2 + 5r - 6$ **5.** $125y^3$ **6.** $5 - 3x - x^2$ **7.** {14} **8.** {5} **9.** {3} **10.** {10} **11.** {5} **12.** {4}

Computer Exercises, page 203 **1.** $x^2 + 8x + 15$ **3.** $8x^2 - 14x - 15$ **5.** $9x^2 - 4$ **7.** $50x^2 + 40x + 8$ **9.** $144x^2 - 100$

Calculator Key-In, page 203 **1.** 44 **3.** 11 **5.** 600 **7.** 728 **9.** 17.5

Written Exercises, pages 206–207 **1.** $y^2 - 49$ **3.** $16 - x^2$ **5.** $25y^2 - 4$ **7.** $1 - 9a^2$ **9.** $9x^2 - 4y^2$ **11.** $16s^2 - 25t^2$ **13.** $x^4 - 81y^2$ **15.** $4r^4 - 49s^4$ **17.** $a^2b^2 - c^4$ **19.** 1596 **21.** 8091 **23.** 8099 **25.** 4884 **27.** $(b + 6)(b - 6)$ **29.** $(2c + 9)(2c - 9)$ **31.** $(5z + 1)(5z - 1)$ **33.** $(13u + 15)(13u - 15)$ **35.** $(1 + 3a)(1 - 3a)$ **37.** $(7a + 3b)(7a - 3b)$ **39.** $(4 + c^2)(2 + c)(2 - c)$ **41.** $(u^2 + 9v^2)(u + 3v)(u - 3v)$ **43.** $(x^4 + y^4)(x^2 + y^2)(x + y)(x - y)$ **45.** $5x(x + 2)(x - 2)$ **47.** $4a^2(3 + 2a)(3 - 2a)$ **49.** $uv(v + u)(v - u)$ **51.** $2a(a^2 + 9)(a + 3)(a - 3)$ **53.** $8(x + 2)$ **55.** $8s$ **57.** $(a^n + b^n)(a^n - b^n)$ **59.** $(u^{2n} + 2v^n)(u^{2n} - 2v^n)$ **61.** $(x^{2n} + y^{2n})(x^n + y^n)(x^n - y^n)$ **63.** $r(t^{2n} + 4)(t^n + 2)(t^n - 2)$ **65.** $(a + b)^2 - (a - b)^2 =$ $[(a + b) + (a - b)][(a + b) - (a - b)] =$ $(2a)(2b) = 4ab$

Mixed Review Exercises, page 207 **1.** $7z^2 + 8z$ **2.** $x^2 - 2x - 35$ **3.** $-5m^2 + 8m - 6$ **4.** $5a^2b$ **5.** $7a + 1$ **6.** $4n$ **7.** $2a^2 - a - 3$ **8.** $15b^3 - 25b^2 - 10b$ **9.** x^3 **10.** $2y^2 + 6y - 1$ **11.** $2x^2 + 3x - 1$ **12.** $18y$

Written Exercises, pages 210–212 **1.** $n^2 + 10n + 25$ **3.** $a^2 - 18a + 81$ **5.** $16u^2 - 8u + 1$ **7.** $25n^2 - 40n + 16$ **9.** $4r^2 + 36rs + 81s^2$ **11.** $25p^2 - 60pq + 36q^2$ **13.** $m^2n^2 + 4mn + 4$ **15.** $4a^2b^2 + 4abc^2 + c^4$ **17.** $16m^4 + 24m^2n + 9n^2$ **19.** $81p^6 + 180p^3 + 100$ **21.** $(y + 3)^2$ **23.** $(p - 7)^2$ **25.** $(11 - u)^2$ **27.** $(2x + 3)^2$ **29.** not a perfect square trinomial **31.** $(2s - 9t)^2$ **33.** $2(2x + 1)^2$ **35.** $9(1 - 4m)^2$ **37.** $x^3(x + 1)^2$ **39.** $b(a + 3b)^2$ **41.** $4p^2(3p - 2)^2$ **43.** $(u - 1 + v)(u - 1 - v)$ **45.** $(a + b - 3)(a - b + 3)$ **47.** $(x^3 + 5)^2$ **49.** $(pq - 6)^2$ **51.** not a perfect square trinomial **53.** x^2 **55.** $x^4 - 8x^2 + 16 =$ $(x^2 - 4)^2 = [(x + 2)(x - 2)]^2 =$ $(x + 2)^2(x - 2)^2$ **57.** $4x^2 - 12xy + 9y^2$; $9y^2 - 12xy + 4x^2$ **59.** $\{-2\}$ **61.** $\{-2\}$ **65.** 19 m × 19 m

Mixed Review Exercises, page 212 **1.** -2 **2.** -1 **3.** 25 **4.** 289 **5.** 512 **6.** 4096 **7.** $16s^2 - 9$ **8.** $x^2 + 12x + 27$ **9.** 8 **10.** -22 **11.** $\frac{1}{a^3}$ **12.** x

Self-Test 2, page 212 **1.** $n^2 + 11n + 24$ **2.** $m^2 - 11m + 30$ **3.** $6y^2 + 13y - 28$ **4.** $6x^3 - 28x^2 + 16x$ **5.** $x^2 - 81$ **6.** $81a^2 - 4b^2$ **7.** $(2n + 9)(2n - 9)$ **8.** $4(3x^2 + 2)(3x^2 - 2)$ **9.** $4n^2 + 16n + 16$ **10.** $9z^2 - 30kz + 25k^2$ **11.** $(3a + 2)^2$ **12.** $(4m - 3n)^2$

Written Exercises, pages 215–216 **1.** $(x + 4)(x + 1)$ **3.** $(r - 4)(r - 2)$ **5.** $(y - 7)(y - 2)$ **7.** $(q + 15)(q + 1)$ **9.** $(a - 13)(a - 2)$ **11.** $(x + 18)(x + 2)$ **13.** prime **15.** $(21 - k)(2 - k)$ **17.** $(5 + r)(15 + r)$ **19.** $(p + 17q)(p + 2q)$ **21.** $(c - 12d)(c - 4d)$ **23.** $(u - 49v)(u - v)$ **25.** prime **27.** $(a + 13b)(a + 4b)$ **29.** $(r - 9s)(r - 6s)$ **31.** $(y + 7z)(y + 13z)$ **33.** $(4 - y)(31 - y)$ **35.** $(8a - b)(14a - b)$ **37.** $\pm 15, \pm 9$ **39.** $\pm 13, \pm 8, \pm 7$ **41.** $\pm 10, \pm 6$ **43.** 5, 8, 9 **45.** 7, 12, 15, 16 **47.** $(y - 3)(y + 1)$ **49.** $(y + 6)^2$ **51.** $(x + 2)(x - 2)(x + 1)(x - 1)$ **53.** $t(t + 4)(t - 4)(t + 2)(t - 2)$ **55.** $(a^n - 11b^{2n})(a^n - 19b^{2n})$

Mixed Review Exercises, page 216 **1.** $\{4\}$ **2.** $\{-1\}$ **3.** $\{23\}$ **4.** $\{1\}$ **5.** $\{4\}$ **6.** $\{-30\}$ **7.** $\{-24\}$ **8.** $\{27\}$ **9.** $\{-12\}$ **10.** $25y^2 - 49$ **11.** $8x^3y^9$ **12.** $64x^{12}$

Written Exercises, pages 218–219 **1.** $(y + 6)(y - 1)$ **3.** $(x - 8)(x + 2)$ **5.** $(c - 6)(c + 2)$ **7.** prime **9.** $(b - 15)(b + 2)$ **11.** prime **13.** $(x - 27)(x + 2)$ **15.** $(y - 24)(y + 3)$ **17.** $(a - 7b)(a + 6b)$ **19.** $(u + 14v)(u - 5v)$ **21.** $(h - 27k)(h + 2k)$ **23.** $(p - 18q)(p + 2q)$ **25.** $(1 - 8n)(1 + 6n)$ **27.** $(x - 15y)(x + 5y)$ **29.** $(1 + 16pq)(1 - 5pq)$ **31.** $(p + 20)(p - 18)$ **33.** $(-19 + x)(20 + x)$ **35.** $\pm 27, \pm 12, \pm 3$ **37.** $\pm 34, \pm 2$ **39.** $-3, -8$ **41.** $-6, -14$ **43.** $-5, -12$ **45.** $(x + 2)(x - 2)(x^2 + 1)$ **47.** $(x + 4y)(x - 4y)(x^2 + y^2)$ **49.** $y(y + 11)$ **51.** $(a + b - 2)(a + b + 1)$ **53.** $(a + b - 2c)(a + b + c)$ **55.** $(x^n + 13y^{2n})(x^n - 17y^{2n})$

Mixed Review Exercises, page 219 **1.** $54x^5y^3$ **2.** $6x^2 + x - 12$ **3.** $-21x^3 + 14x^2 - 28x$ **4.** $9x^2 - 24x + 16$ **5.** $343x^{15}y^6$

6. $10y^3 + 15y^2 + 25y$ **7.** $\frac{x^3y^3}{2}$ **8.** $\frac{1}{3b^2}$
9. $-\frac{1}{n^4}$ **10.** $n^2 + 6np + 9p^2$
11. $5a^2 - 28a - 12$ **12.** $4y^2 + 28y + 49$
13. $3(5m - 7n + 3)$ **14.** $(11k + 9)(11k - 9)$
15. $(a + 9)^2$ **16.** $(a - 7b)(a - 6b)$
17. $8x(2x + 3)$ **18.** $(8 + n)(8 - n)$
19. $(u - 5)^2$ **20.** $(11 + y)(4 + y)$
21. $7ab(ab^2 - 2)$ **22.** $(7w^2 + 4x)(7w^2 - 4x)$
23. $4(m + 2)(m + 3)$ **24.** $(c - 13)(c + 2)$
25. $(3x - 4y)^2$ **26.** $(7 - z)(8 - z)$
27. $(x + 1)(x - 1)$ **28.** $(a + 17)(a - 4)$
29. $(5w^3 + 12x^3)(5w^3 - 12x^3)$ **30.** $(5a + 2b)^2$

Written Exercises, pages 222–223
1. $(3x + 1)(x + 2)$ **3.** $(3c - 5)(c - 1)$
5. $(5y - 1)(y + 1)$ **7.** prime
9. $(7x + 1)(x + 1)$ **11.** $(5x - 2)(x - 3)$
13. $(3p - 2)(p + 3)$ **15.** $(y - 1)(4y + 3)$
17. $(5 - 3x)(1 + 2x)$ **19.** prime
21. $(3m + 2n)(m + 3n)$ **23.** $(2x + 3y)(x - y)$
25. $(9m + 2n)(m - 3n)$ **27.** $(6r - 5p)(r - p)$
29. $(7c + 6)(3c - 2)$ **31.** $(2 + 5a)(3 - 4a)$
33. $(4n - 3)(8n + 5)$ **35.** $(3c - 2)(7c + 12)$
37. $(2a + 3)(a + 5)$
39. $(2a + 4b - c)(a + 2b + 3c)$
41. $(2x + 1)(2x - 1)(x + 2)(x - 2)$
43. $(y + 2)(y + 1)(y + 4)(y - 1)$
45. $(30x^3 + 77x^2 - 92x + 21)^2$

Mixed Review Exercises, page 223
1. $(x + 15)(x - 15)$ **2.** $(x - 4)(x - 5)$
3. $(r - 7)(r + 2)$ **4.** $(c - 3)^2$
5. $(3y + 17x)(3y - 17x)$ **6.** $(2a^2 + 7)(2a^2 - 7)$
7. $(y + 7)(y + 8)$ **8.** $(p + 6)^2$ **9.** $(4y + 3)^2$
10. $(m - 9)(m + 8)$ **11.** $(n + 12)(n + 3)$
12. $(b - 6)(b + 4)$

Self-Test 3, page 223 **1.** $(a + 5)(a + 7)$
2. $(x - 8)(x - 2)$ **3.** $(n + 4)(n - 7)$
4. $(c + 8d)(c - 5d)$ **5.** $(2r - 3)(r - 2)$
6. $(3x - 2y)(x + 4y)$

Challenge, page 223 **1.** 6
2. $(2^{32} + 1)(2^{16} + 1)(2^8 + 1)(2^4 + 1)(2^2 + 1) \cdot (2 + 1)(2 - 1)$; $2^4 + 1 = 17$, $2^2 + 1 = 5$, $2 + 1 = 3$

Written Exercises, pages 225–226
1. $(3 + z)(x + y)$ **3.** $(e - 4)(f - g)$
5. $(7 - t)(r - s)$ **7.** $(2a - 1)(a + 3)$
9. $(2x - y)(x - y)$ **11.** $(2u + v + 1)(u - 2v)$
13. $(x - 1)(2w - 3v + u)$
15. $(s - 2)(s - 2p + 2)$ **17.** $(3t - r)(1 - s)$
19. $(4x - 5z)(3x - 2y)$ **21.** $(a + c)(3 + b)$
23. $(x + y)(x - 2)$ **25.** $(h + r)(h - k)$
27. $(p^2 + 4)(p - 2)$ **29.** $(p + r)(p - 2q)$
31. $(k - 4)(3h - 2)$ **33.** $(2z^2 - 3)(2z - 3)$
35. $k(k + 1)(h^2 + 4)$
37. $(x + 1)(x - 1)(x - 3)$
39. $(x + y - z)(x - y + z)$
41. $(u - 2v + 2w)(u - 2v - 2w)$
43. $(a + 4b + c)(a - c)$
45. $(a + 2 + b)(a + 2 - b)$
47. $(u + v - 1)(u - v + 1)$
49. $(h - 2 + 2k)(h - 2 - 2k)$
51. $(p - r + q)(p - r - q)$
53. $(x - 2z + 2y)(x - 2z - 2y)$
55. $(a + b + 2)(a + b)$
57. $(x^2 - 2 + y^2)(x^2 - 2 - y^2)$
59. $(p - q + r - 1)(p - q - r + 1)$
61. $(x^2 + 2x + 2)(x^2 - 2x + 2)$
63. $(a + b^{2n})(a^{2n} + b)$

Mixed Review Exercises, page 226 **1.** $\{-17\}$
2. $\{8\}$ **3.** $\{14\}$ **4.** $\{5\}$ **5.** $\{9\}$ **6.** $\left\{\frac{1}{3}\right\}$
7. $\{50\}$ **8.** $\{-12\}$ **9.** $\{12\}$ **10.** $\{-3\}$
11. $\{11\}$ **12.** $\{5\}$

Written Exercises, pages 228–229
1. $3(2a - 5b)(a + b)$ **3.** $5r(3r - 2s)(r + 2s)$
5. $4(z - 2)(z - 6)$ **7.** $5(a + b)^2$
9. $m(2m + 1)(2m - 1)$ **11.** $y^2(y - 2)(y + 1)$
13. $(x - 1)(x - y)$ **15.** $(7a - 2)(3a - 5)$
17. $a(a + 3)(a - 2b)$ **19.** $u^2v(2 - 5v)(3 + 2v)$
21. $k(k + 1)(k - 1)$
23. $u(2u^2 + 1)(u + 2)(u - 2)$
25. $(r - 3 + 3s)(r - 3 - 3s)$
27. $(u + 2v + 3)(u - 2v)$
29. $(p + 2q + 1)(p - 2q - 1)$
31. $4(x - 5 + 2y)(x - 5 - 2y)$
33. $(a^2 + b^2)(a + b)(a - b)$
35. $(2p + q - r)(q + r)$
37. $(2a + b - c)(b + c)$
39. $(x + y)(x - y)^2$
41. $(a - 3)(a - 2)(a + 4)$
43. $16(c^8 + 1)(c^4 + 1)(c^2 + 1)(c + 1)(c - 1)$
45. $(a + 3)(a - 6)(a + 1)$
47. $9(u + v - 2w)(u - v + 2w)$
49. $(x + 2)(x + 3)(x - 4)$
51. $(t + 3)(t - 3)(t + 1)(t - 1)$
53. $(a - b + c - d)(a - b - c + d)$
55. $(x^2 + x + 1)(x^2 - x + 1)$
57. $(a + b)(a^2 - ab + b^2)$

Mixed Review Exercises, page 229 **1.** -2 **2.** 7 **3.** 1 **4.** $20b$ **5.** 676 **6.** -125 **7.** $(x-7)(x-5)$ **8.** $(x+7)(x-4)$ **9.** $(x-2)(x+1)$ **10.** $(2n+1)(n+9)$ **11.** $(3x+5)(x+2)$ **12.** $(3+2n)(x-4)$

Written Exercises, pages 232–233 **1.** $\{-5, 7\}$ **3.** $\{0, -15\}$ **5.** $\left\{\frac{3}{2}, \frac{2}{3}\right\}$ **7.** $\left\{0, -\frac{1}{2}, -\frac{5}{2}\right\}$ **9.** $\{2, 1\}$ **11.** $\{-6, -8\}$ **13.** $\{18, -2\}$ **15.** $\{8, -4\}$ **17.** $\{0, 16\}$ **19.** $\left\{-\frac{3}{2}, \frac{3}{2}\right\}$ **21.** $\left\{-\frac{2}{3}, \frac{1}{2}\right\}$ **23.** $\left\{\frac{1}{2}\right\}$ **25.** $\left\{\frac{11}{7}, 1\right\}$ **27.** $\left\{0, \frac{1}{4}\right\}$ **29.** $\left\{0, \frac{1}{2}\right\}$ **31.** $\left\{\frac{1}{8}, 1\right\}$ **33.** $\left\{-\frac{7}{5}, \frac{7}{3}\right\}$ **35.** $\left\{\frac{11}{2}\right\}$ **37.** $\{0, 1, 2\}$ **39.** $\left\{0, \frac{1}{3}, 3\right\}$ **41.** $\{\pm 3, \pm 1\}$ **43.** $\{7, -3\}$ **45.** $\{-4, 3\}$ **47.** $\{2, 8\}$ **49.** $x^2 + x - 6 = 0$ **51.** $2x^2 - x - 10 = 0$ **53.** $6x^2 - 11x + 3 = 0$ **55. a.** Given **b.** Prop. of reciprocals **c.** Mult. prop. of equality **d.** Mult. prop. of 0 **e.** Assoc. prop. of mult. **f.** Prop. of reciprocals **g.** Identity prop. of mult.

Mixed Review Exercises, page 233 **1.** 16 **2.** 256 **3.** 40 **4.** 1000 **5.** 24 **6.** 20 **7.** 144 **8.** 64 **9.** 64 **10.** $-6x^4y^6$ **11.** $729a^3$ **12.** $-5x - 10$

Problems, pages 235–238 **1.** -8 or 7 **3.** 6 **5.** $-10, -9$ **7.** 12, 14 **9.** 7 cm × 15 cm **11.** 9 m × 14 m **13.** 12, 13 **15.** 17 cm × 20 cm **17.** at 1 s and 4 s **19.** 7.5 s **21.** 30 s **23. a.** 5 s **b.** There is only one time. **25.** 4 m × 12 m or 6 m × 8 m **27.** 180 cm^3 **29.** 30 m × 100 m **31.** 3 cm, 5 cm

Mixed Review Exercises, page 238 **1.** $16a^3b^3$ **2.** $125a^6$ **3.** $12a - 6ab$ **4.** $2r^2s^2$ **5.** $2n - 3p$ **6.** $4x + 2y$ **7.** $6a^3 - 17a^2 + a + 10$ **8.** $9b^4y^2$ **9.** $6x^3 - 48x$ **10.** $2(5m-7)(m+2)$ **11.** $9a(2a+b)(2a-b)$ **12.** $(7n-2)(3n+4)$ **13.** $y^2(y-4)(y+3)$ **14.** $(5m+2n)(3m+4n)$ **15.** $(5x-1)(2x-3)$

Self-Test 4, page 238 **1.** $(r+s)(7-3t)$ **2.** $(n-1+10t^2)(n-1-10t^2)$ **3.** $2a(3a-1)^2$ **4.** $-3(3x-2y)(2x-y)$ **5.** $\{8, -4\}$ **6.** $\{-2\}$ **7.** $\{0, 13, -13\}$ **8.** $\{0, 6, -5\}$ **9.** 6 cm × 15 cm

Extra, page 239 **1.** $(x+y)(x^2 - xy + y^2) = x^3 - x^2y + xy^2 + x^2y - xy^2 + y^3 = x^3 + y^3$ **3.** $(m+2)(m^2 - 2m + 4)$ **5.** $(n+5)(n^2 - 5n + 25)$ **7. a.** $w^6 - 1 = (w^2)^3 - (1)^3 = (w^2 - 1)(w^4 + w^2 + 1) = (w-1)(w+1)(w^4 + w^2 + 1)$ **b.** $w^6 - 1 = (w^3)^2 - (1)^2 = (w^3 - 1)(w^3 + 1) = (w-1)(w^2 + w + 1)(w+1)(w^2 - w + 1) = (w-1)(w+1)(w^2 + w + 1)(w^2 - w + 1)$ **c.** $w^4 + w^2 + 1 = (w^4 + 2w^2 + 1) - w^2 = (w^2 + 1)^2 - w^2 = (w^2 + 1 + w)(w^2 + 1 - w) = (w^2 + w + 1)(w^2 - w + 1)$

Chapter Review, pages 240–241 **1.** c **3.** c **5.** c **7.** d **9.** d **11.** b **13.** b **15.** c **17.** b **19.** b **21.** c **23.** a

Cumulative Review (Chapters 1–5), page 243 **1.** -20 **3.** $-7a$ **5.** $5z - 7$ **7.** $216a^{12}b^6$ **9.** $3x^2y - x + \frac{8}{9}$ **11.** $49a^2 + 56a + 16$ **13.** -4 **15.** 1 **17.** $2p^2(3p - pr^2 + 4r^3st)$ **19.** $(2a + 3b)^2$ **21.** $(m-6)(m-3)$ **23.** $(3y-1)(2y+5)$ **25.** $(a+b)^2(a-b)$ **27.** $\{8, -8\}$ **29.** $\{4\}$ **31.** $\{12\}$ **33.** $\{4, -4\}$ **35.** $\{3\}$ **37.** $\{0, 4, 5\}$ **39.** 60 km/h **41.** 2 cm × 11 cm

Maintaining Skills, page 244 **1.** 4 cm × 10 cm **3.** 6 cm × 11 cm **5.** 1 s, 3 s

Mixed Problem Solving, page 245 **1.** 9 h **3.** Maureen, 10 km; sister, 13 km **5.** 7, -2 **7.** 8 cm × 12 cm **9.** 59 m below sea level **11.** 2106 ft^2 **13.** No sol.; insufficient info.

Chapter 6 Fractions

Written Exercises, pages 248–250 **1.** $\frac{x+y}{2}$ **3.** 5; $a \neq 2$ **5.** $\frac{1}{3}$; $n \neq -\frac{1}{3}$ **7.** $\frac{2}{x+2}$; $x \neq 2$, $x \neq -2$ **9.** $\frac{2}{x-y}$; $x \neq 0$, $x \neq y$, $y \neq 0$ **11.** $\frac{x+4}{x-3}$; $x \neq 3$, $x \neq -\frac{1}{2}$ **13.** $\frac{a+4}{4-a}$; $a \neq 4$, $a \neq -4$ **15.** $-\frac{1}{y-2}$; $y \neq 2$ **17.** $\frac{2(n^2+36)}{3(n+6)}$; $n \neq -6$ **19.** $\frac{n-3}{2n-5}$; $n \neq -\frac{1}{2}$, $n \neq \frac{5}{2}$ **21.** $\frac{3x}{6x-5}$; $x \neq -2$, $x \neq \frac{5}{6}$ **23.** $-\frac{5+a}{a+2}$; $a \neq 2$, $a \neq -2$ **25.** $\frac{x+y}{x-y}$; $x \neq 0$, $x \neq y$

27. $\frac{r+s}{4r+5s}$; $r \neq s$, $r \neq -\frac{5s}{4}$ 29. $c - d$; $c \neq -d$ 31. $\frac{1}{a}$; $a \neq 0$, $b \neq 1$ 33. $5k - 1$; $k \neq \frac{1}{5}$ 35. $2c + 3d$; $c \neq -\frac{3d}{2}$ 37. $a - 6$; $a \neq -6$ 39. 2nd case; variable restriction $x \neq 2y$; in case 2, $x = 2y$, so results are invalid. 41. $\frac{5x+6y}{2x+3y}$; $x \neq \frac{6y}{5}$, $x \neq -\frac{3y}{2}$ 43. $\frac{a}{2(3a-5)}$; $a \neq 0$, $a \neq \frac{5}{3}$, $a \neq -\frac{5}{3}$ 45. $-a - b$; $x \neq 2$ 47. $\frac{5-x}{5+x}$; $x \neq 0$, $x \neq \frac{3}{2}$, $x \neq -5$ 49. $\frac{2a-b}{2a+b+1}$; $b \neq 1 - 2a$, $b \neq -(2a+1)$ 51. $x = -2$ 53. $x = -3$

Mixed Review Exercises, page 250
1. $4u + 3v$ 2. $\frac{21n}{2} - 7p$ 3. $\frac{a^5b^5}{2}$ 4. $\frac{-243}{y^5}$ 5. $3x^3 + 6x - 12$ 6. 2800 7. {6} 8. {−340} 9. {−11} 10. {3} 11. {8} 12. {3}

Written Exercises, pages 253–254 1. $\frac{3}{2}$ 3. $\frac{10}{3}$ 5. $\frac{1}{3}$ 7. 10 9. $2x$ 11. $\frac{a}{d}$ 13. $\frac{2v^2}{w}$ 15. $\frac{2df}{27}$ 17. $\frac{a^2}{36}$ 19. $\frac{4n^2}{49}$ 21. $\frac{4a^2}{25b^6}$ 23. $\frac{x^8}{10{,}000}$ 25. $\frac{a}{b}$ 27. $-\frac{x}{4y}$ 29. $\frac{4x^2}{49}$ in.^{2} 31. $\frac{1}{3}$ cm^2 33. $\frac{dy}{9}$ dollars 35. $\frac{3}{c(c-2)}$ 37. $-\frac{a+x}{3a}$ 39. $\frac{b}{2}$ 41. $\frac{5x^3(x+1)}{12}$ 43. $\frac{2(n-1)(n-2)}{(n+2)^2}$ 45. $\frac{3-t}{t+3}$ 47. $\frac{(x-5)(2x+3)}{2x(x+1)}$ 49. 1 51. $\frac{2}{x-2}$ 53. $\frac{(x-y)(x^2+y^2)}{(x+y)^3}$ 55. $-\frac{12}{x}$ 57. $\frac{x^2+3}{6x}$ 59. $x = 1$

Mixed Review Exercises, page 254
1. $(a+9)(a+5)$ 2. $(x-5)(x-2)$ 3. $(2x-3)(2x+3)(4x^2+9)$ 4. prime 5. $(25y-2z)(25y+2z)$ 6. $(8+c)^2$ 7. $(y-4z)(x+3)$ 8. $(3x-2)^2$ 9. $(3x-1)(x+5)$ 10. $x^2(x-7)(x-1)$ 11. $(n-2)(n+7)$ 12. $(y-8)(y+3)$

Challenge, page 254 The proof requires division of both sides by $(r - s)$. But it is given that $r = s$, so $r - s = 0$, and division by 0 is undefined.

Written Exercises, pages 256–257 1. $\frac{4}{3}$ 3. $\frac{1}{2}$ 5. $\frac{1}{xy}$ 7. $\frac{a^2}{6}$ 9. $\frac{27x}{2y^2}$ 11. $\frac{y}{3}$ 13. $\frac{25}{9x^2}$ 15. 3 17. $8(x-1)$ 19. −1 21. $\frac{8}{x(x-y)}$ 23. $\frac{(w+2)^2}{(w+1)^2}$ 25. $\frac{x(2x-5)}{3(x-4)}$ 27. $c + d$ 29. $\frac{r-t}{r^2+t^2}$ 31. $-\frac{2+x}{x-6}$ 33. a. 1 b. 1 35. a. $\frac{r^2}{t^3}$ b. $\frac{2}{x^2y}$ 37. −1 39. $-\frac{24}{3-q}$ 41. a^2b^2 43. $\frac{5(x-2)}{x-4}$ 45. $\frac{1}{2+d}$

Mixed Review Exercises, page 258 1. {13} 2. {7} 3. {2} 4. {2} 5. {0, 2, −2} 6. $\left\{1, -\frac{4}{3}\right\}$ 7. 2^8 8. $2^2 \cdot 3 \cdot 13$ 9. $2^3 \cdot 3 \cdot 5$ 10. $2 \cdot 3^3 \cdot 5^2$

Self-Test 1, page 258 1. 5; $c \neq 0$, $c \neq 3$ 2. $\frac{2a-3}{3a+2}$; $a \neq -\frac{2}{3}$, $a \neq -\frac{3}{2}$ 3. $\frac{-28}{3abc^2}$ 4. $\frac{x^2}{6}$ 5. $\frac{14x}{y^2}$ 6. $\frac{2x}{x-3}$

Calculator Key-In, page 258 1. 0.9 3. $68.\overline{33}$ 5. −5.75

Written Exercises, pages 261–262 1. 21 3. $30x$ 5. $3(x-3)$ 7. $12x$ 9. $5x^2$ 11. $7(n+2)$ 13. $5(2n-3)$ 15. 8 17. $2(x-1)$ 19. $3y$ 21. 18 23. 30 25. 24 27. $16rt^2$ 29. $(x+1)(x-2)$ 31. $(m+2)(m-2)$ 33. $\frac{x}{2x^2y}, \frac{6y}{2x^2y}$ 35. $\frac{55y}{30x^2y^3}, \frac{24x}{30x^2y^3}$ 37. $\frac{20}{4(x-3)}, \frac{7}{4(x-3)}$ 39. $\frac{6(x-3)}{(x-3)^2}, \frac{4x}{(x-3)^2}$ 41. $\frac{3y(y+2)}{2(y-2)(y+2)}, \frac{2}{2(y-2)(y+2)}$ 43. $\frac{x(x+3)}{(x+2)(x-3)(x+3)}, \frac{9(x+2)}{(x+2)(x-3)(x+3)}$ 45. a. 24, 120, 720 b. 720 c. $(n+1)!$

Mixed Review Exercises, page 262
1. $4(n-2q+4)$ 2. $3(x-1)(x+1)$ 3. $(x-9)(x-2)$ 4. $(x-8)(x+3)$ 5. $(2x-3)(x+1)$ 6. $(x+13)(x+3)$ 7. $(x+7)(x-4)$ 8. $(x+11)^2$ 9. $n(n-9)$ 10. $7 = 2p - 4$ 11. $n - \frac{1}{2} = 5\frac{1}{4}$ 12. $\frac{2}{3}k = 16$

Computer Key-In, page 263 **1.** 21 **3.** 72 **5.** 195 **7.** 21 **9.** 72 **11.** 195 **13.** smaller denominator first

Challenge, page 263 30 km

Written Exercises, pages 267–268 **1.** $\frac{x}{3}$ **3.** $\frac{-4}{n}$ **5.** $\frac{x+1}{3}$ **7.** $\frac{1-y}{2}$ **9.** $\frac{7}{x+3}$ **11.** $\frac{x+1}{x-2}$ **13.** $\frac{1}{x-5}$ **15.** 5 **17.** $\frac{2x+3}{x^2}$ **19.** $\frac{2-5x}{4x^2}$ **21.** $\frac{4+5x}{5(x+1)}$ **23.** $\frac{10x+5}{12}$ **25.** $\frac{7y}{18}$ **27.** $\frac{n+23}{24}$ **29.** $\frac{-x+2}{4}$ **31.** $\frac{44a}{15}$ **33.** $\frac{5a+6b}{3}$ **35.** $\frac{2x-1}{x(x-1)}$ **37.** $\frac{6x-6}{(x-3)(x+3)}$ **39.** $\frac{2a+1}{a(a+1)}$ **41.** $\frac{5x-4}{x^2-1}$ **43.** 1 **45.** $\frac{7-d}{2(d^2-1)}$ **47.** $\frac{a+b}{ab}$ **49.** $\frac{4}{(n+4)^2}$ **51.** $-\frac{7}{x(x+3)}$ **53.** $\frac{x+1}{x-1}$ **55.** $\frac{1}{a-2}$ **57.** $\frac{2}{b-1}$

Mixed Review Exercises, page 268 **1.** -192 **2.** 121 **3.** $-64x^6$ **4.** $7y^2+2y$ **5.** $-n^3+8n^2+6n$ **6.** $90x^5y^6$ **7.** $-8x^3y^4$ **8.** $7x-2y$ **9.** $4n-11p+1$

Self-Test 2, page 269 **1.** $\frac{15c^2n}{2}$ **2.** $5a$ **3.** $4(x-2)^2$ **4.** $ab(a-b)$ **5.** $\frac{5c-1}{c}$ **6.** $\frac{28b+24}{21ab^2}$ **7.** 1 **8.** $\frac{5-n}{5(n-1)}$

Written Exercises, pages 271–272 **1.** $\frac{21}{5}$ **3.** $\frac{8x+1}{x}$ **5.** $\frac{3a^2-2}{a}$ **7.** $\frac{a-3b}{b}$ **9.** $\frac{5x+6}{x+2}$ **11.** $\frac{7x+12}{x+2}$ **13.** $\frac{6n+5}{n+1}$ **15.** $\frac{6x^2+5x}{x+1}$ **17.** $\frac{8n^2+8n-2}{n+1}$ **19.** $\frac{4a^3+10a^2-a+1}{2a+5}$ **21.** $x-6$ **23.** $\frac{2b^2-8b+2}{b(b-2)}$ **25.** $\frac{2a^2-a+3}{a^2-1}$ **27.** $\frac{3}{a+2}$ **29.** $\frac{5x^2+5x-6}{2x+3}$ **31.** $\frac{a^4-4}{a^2}$ **33.** $\frac{a+b}{a}$ **35.** $m-n$ **37.** $\frac{a}{a+2}$ **39.** $\frac{8x}{x^2-x}$ can be reduced to $\frac{8}{x-1}$. Thus, $x-1$ is the LCD. Any multiple is a common denominator, so $x(x-1)(1-x)$ and $x(x-1)$ will also work. **41.** $\$\left(\frac{n^2+38n-80}{n}\right)$ **43.** -1 **45.** $C=4$, $D=2$

Mixed Review Exercises, page 273 **1.** $\frac{a+b}{a+2}$ **2.** $-\frac{a-2}{7+a}$ **3.** $\frac{3x}{2y^4}$ **4.** $4(n-2)$ **5.** $2y^2$ **6.** $16b^4$ **7.** $2x^2y$ **8.** ab^2 **9.** $1-x^2$

Challenge, page 273 Answers may vary; for example, 11, 23, and 35.

Written Exercises, pages 276–277 **1.** $x+3$ **3.** $n+6$ **5.** $y-3+\frac{8}{y+1}$ **7.** $x-\frac{9}{x-3}$ **9.** $n+4+\frac{28}{n-6}$ **11.** $x-2+\frac{8}{x+2}$ **13.** $x+4-\frac{1}{3x-2}$ **15.** $2x-1+\frac{9}{2x+1}$ **17.** $n^2-4n+9-\frac{16}{n+2}$ **19.** $a^2+2a+4+\frac{16}{a-2}$ **21.** $4x^2-2x+1-\frac{10}{3x+1}$ **23.** x^3-2x^2+x-6 **25.** n^3-1 **27.** $z^3-2z^2+4z-8+\frac{32}{z+2}$ **29.** n^2-n+1 **31.** $3n+2$ **33.** $2(n+3)(n-1)(n-2)$ **35.** 9 **37.** -5

Mixed Review Exercises, page 277 **1.** $\frac{3x+3}{2}$ **2.** $a-3$ **3.** $\frac{6+y}{3y}$ **4.** $\frac{5c+10}{6c}$ **5.** $\frac{13}{18}$ **6.** $\frac{1}{2(x-5)}$ **7.** $\frac{x^2+2}{x}$ **8.** $\frac{5n+4}{n+1}$ **9.** $\frac{y^2+3y-7}{y-2}$

Self-Test 3, page 277 **1.** $\frac{3y-8}{y}$ **2.** $\frac{5n^2+1}{n}$ **3.** $\frac{a^2+1}{a+1}$ **4.** $3y-2$ **5.** $5b^2-9b+19-\frac{22}{b+2}$

Extra, pages 278–279 **1.** $\frac{1}{5}$ **3.** $\frac{1}{v}$ **5.** 3 **7.** $\frac{1}{13}$ **9.** $\frac{6}{d}$ **11.** $\frac{r+2s}{s-r}$ **13.** $\frac{z-5}{z+5}$ **15.** $\frac{k+3}{k+2}$ **17.** 1 **19.** $\frac{2z(z-1)}{2z^2+z-4}$ **21.** $\frac{z}{2-z}$

23. $s_{avg} = \frac{d_{total}}{t_{total}}$; $t_{total} = t_1 + t_2$, $t_1 = \frac{d}{50}$, $t_2 = \frac{d}{30}$

$t_{total} = \frac{4d}{75}$; $d_{total} = 2d$; $s_{avg} = \frac{2d}{\left(\frac{4d}{75}\right)} = 37.5$

25. $\frac{5n}{5-n}$ items **27.** $\frac{w+6}{3(w-2)}$ **29.** $n^2 + 1$

31. $\frac{54e^2 - e - 29}{6(3e+1)(3e-1)}$ **33.** $\frac{1}{2s}$ **35.** $\frac{1}{3-c}$

Chapter Review, pages 280–281 **1.** b **2.** b **3.** a **4.** b **5.** b **6.** a **7.** d **8.** c **9.** c **10.** b **11.** c **12.** a **13.** c **14.** b

Cumulative Review, page 283 **1.** 0.25 **3.** $64x^9y^3z^6$ **5.** $20x^2 + 3x - 9$ **7.** $-17t - 3s$ **9.** $16t^4s^2 - 81$ **11.** 4 **13.** $a^2b(6a + 5ab - 3b)$ **15.** $2t(2t - 7)^2$ **17.** prime **19.** $y(y + 8)(y - 4)$ **21.** $2(2x - 1)(x + 1)$ **23.** $\{48\}$ **25.** $\{-6\}$ **27.** $\left\{-\frac{3}{4}, \frac{3}{4}\right\}$ **29.** $\{7, -1\}$ **31.** $\frac{1}{x-4}$ **33.** $\frac{a-b}{cd^2}$ **35.** $2y^2 + 3y - 8 + \frac{12}{5y-4}$ **37.** four 8-hour shifts **39.** 5 km

Maintaining Skills, page 284 **1.** 0.92 **3.** 2.50 **5.** 3.24 **7.** 1.70 **9.** 2.33 **11.** 0.68 **13.** $\frac{31}{50}$ **15.** $\frac{17}{20}$ **17.** $\frac{3}{10{,}000}$ **19.** 91% **21.** 80% **23.** 3.2% **25.** 27.2 **27.** 0.08 **29.** 52 **31.** 70 **33.** 12 **35.** 60 **37.** 20 **39.** 34

Preparing for College Entrance Exams, page 285 **1.** E **3.** D **5.** D **7.** B

Chapter 7 Applying Fractions

Written Exercises, pages 289–290 **1.** 2:3 **3.** 3:1 **5.** $\frac{1}{9}$ **7.** $\frac{4a^2}{b^3}$ **9.** 1:6 **11.** 5:1 **13.** 14:1 **15.** 10,000:9 **17.** 16:7 **19.** 1:20 **21.** 36:37 **23.** 2:1 **25. a.** 7:18 **b.** 7:11 **27. a.** 14:19 **b.** 8:15 **29. a.** 3:5 **b.** 9:25 **31.** 5:8 **33.** 6:7 **35.** 2:k **37.** 3:1 **39.** 1:1 **41.** $(a + b)$:1 **43.** 1:1 **45.** 1:1, −1:1, or 1:−1

Problems, pages 291–292 **1.** 20 and 25 **3.** 162 players **5.** 28 cm by 20 cm **7.** $4\frac{1}{2}$ cm, $7\frac{1}{2}$ cm, and 9 cm **9.** 400 m^3 **11.** Eddie, 12 mi/h; Ling, 30 mi/h **13.** 42 dimes and 28 nickels **15.** 200 pencils **17.** 1 and 6; 2 and 12; 3 and 18 **19.** 10 and 2

Mixed Review Exercises, page 292 **1.** $\{4\}$ **2.** $\{6\}$ **3.** $\{-2\}$ **4.** $\{-40\}$ **5.** $\{2\}$ **6.** $\{-36\}$ **7.** $\{-2, 5\}$ **8.** $\{-6, 2\}$ **9.** $\{6\}$ **10.** $\frac{5b+1}{2c}$ **11.** $\frac{3x^2+5}{x}$ **12.** $\frac{7a+1}{4}$

Challenge, page 292 Fill 2 5-liter containers and pour both into an 8-liter container. What will not fit equals 2 L of the solution.

Written Exercises, pages 295–296 **1.** $\left\{\frac{15}{4}\right\}$ **3.** $\left\{\frac{5}{6}\right\}$ **5.** $\left\{\frac{28}{15}\right\}$ **7.** $\left\{\frac{7}{4}\right\}$ **9.** $\left\{\frac{2}{3}\right\}$ **11.** $\left\{\frac{28}{25}\right\}$ **13.** $\{9\}$ **15.** $\left\{-\frac{5}{4}\right\}$ **17.** $\left\{\frac{4}{5}\right\}$ **19.** $\left\{-\frac{5}{2}\right\}$ **21.** $\{11\}$ **23.** $\{2\}$ **25.** $\{3\}$ **27.** $\left\{-\frac{7}{18}\right\}$ **29.** $\{0\}$ **31.** $\{-1\}$ **33.** $\{3\}$ **35.** $\{0\}$ **37.** $\frac{47}{2}$ **39.** $\frac{5}{1}$ **41.** $\frac{d+c}{c-d}$ **43.** $\frac{c(d+c)}{d}$ **45.** $P = \frac{pT}{t}$; $T = \frac{Pt}{p}$ **47.** 25 **49.** $\frac{1}{3}$

Problems, pages 296–297 **1.** \$1.65 **3.** 185 mi **5.** \$9800 **7.** \$6400 **9.** 2400 homes **11. a.** 21 cm **b.** $\frac{7}{5}, \frac{7}{5}, \frac{49}{25}$ **13.** mahogany board

Mixed Review Exercises, page 297 **1.** $4x^2y$ **2.** 12 **3.** 36 **4.** 60 **5.** $x^2 - 9$ **6.** $6y$ **7.** $\frac{7}{x-1}$ **8.** $\frac{9r+1}{12}$ **9.** $\frac{32a+5}{40}$ **10.** 4.8 **11.** −4.3 **12.** 24

Self-Test 1, page 297 **1.** 4:5 **2.** 40:1 **3.** 36 trucks **4.** $\{102\}$ **5.** $\left\{\frac{1}{21}\right\}$ **6.** $\{26\}$

Written Exercises, pages 299–300 **1.** $\left\{\frac{6}{5}\right\}$ **3.** $\{5\}$ **5.** $\{3\}$ **7.** $\left\{\frac{1}{2}\right\}$ **9.** $\{10\}$ **11.** $\left\{\frac{1}{2}\right\}$ **13.** $\left\{\frac{1}{2}\right\}$ **15.** $\left\{-\frac{1}{3}\right\}$ **17.** $\{12\}$ **19.** $\{-2\}$ **21.** $\{-2\}$ **23.** $\{4\}$ **25.** $\{3\}$ **27.** $\left\{\frac{1}{2}\right\}$ **29.** $\{0\}$ **31.** $\left\{\frac{4a}{3}\right\}$ **33.** $\left\{\frac{m+5}{2m}\right\}$

Problems, pages 300–301 **1.** 40 **3.** 15 and 6 **5.** 8 ft by 10 ft **7.** \$4.50 **9.** 15 cm by 6 cm **11.** 8 km (one way) **13.** 6 quarters and 42 nickels **15.** 9 apples

Mixed Review Exercises, page 301 **1.** 2:7 **2.** 1:6 **3.** 4:3 **4.** $\frac{2n}{5}$ **5.** $\frac{4}{3xy}$ **6.** $\frac{3a^3}{5b^2}$ **7.** {7} **8.** $\left\{\frac{29}{3}\right\}$ **9.** $\left\{\frac{28}{3}\right\}$ **10.** $\left\{\frac{16}{3}\right\}$ **11.** {5, −5} **12.** {2}

Application, page 303 **1.** ¢ **3.** ft^2 **5.** ft/min **7.** 42.5¢/day

Written Exercises, pages 305–306 **1.** {4} **3.** {12} **5.** {12} **7.** {8} **9.** {9} **11.** No sol. **13.** No sol. **15.** No sol. **17.** {All real numbers except 2} **19.** {1} **21.** No sol. **23.** $\left\{-\frac{1}{2}, 1\right\}$ **25.** No sol. **27.** {1} **29.** {0, 4} **31.** {−2, 1} **33.** {3} **35.** $\left\{-\frac{14}{3}\right\}$ **37.** {9} **39.** $\left\{1, \frac{3}{4}\right\}$

Problems, pages 306–308 **1.** $\frac{4}{3}$ or $\frac{3}{4}$ **3.** 3 and 5 **5.** $\frac{3}{2}$ **7.** 4 and 6 **9.** 5.5 h **11.** 24 people **13.** 12 km/h

Mixed Review Exercises, page 308 **1.** {20} **2.** {−30} **3.** {3} **4.** $\left\{\frac{6}{5}\right\}$ **5.** {−12} **6.** $\left\{\frac{72}{5}\right\}$ **7.** 125 **8.** $8x^4 + 12x^3 - 28x^2$ **9.** 48 **10.** $5n^2 - n + 9$ **11.** $10y^2z^4$ **12.** $27p^3q^6$

Self-Test 2, page 308 **1.** {−8} **2.** {18} **3.** {−23} **4.** {−6} **5.** {−5} **6.** No sol. **7.** 2 and 3

Written Exercises, pages 312–313 **1.** $\frac{1}{4}$ **3.** $\frac{3}{8}$ **5.** $\frac{3}{5}$ **7.** $\frac{18}{25}$ **9.** $\frac{1}{25}$ **11.** $\frac{18}{5}$ **13.** 96 **15.** 32 **17.** 0.06 **19.** 20.25 **21.** 40 **23.** 350 **25.** 5.6 **27.** 16% **29.** 2% **31.** 20% **33.** \$3; \$9 **35.** \$7.50; \$67.50 **37.** \$11; \$55 **39.** \$48; \$208 **41.** {20} **43.** {3} **45.** {20} **47.** {−50} **49.** {86.25} **51.** {2} **53.** {−64,000} **55.** {0.5} **57.** \$30 **59.** 10.5% **61.** \$850

Problems, pages 313–314 **1.** $83\frac{1}{3}\%$ **3.** \$85,000 **5.** \$9500 **7.** \$18.70 **9.** 20% **11.** \$10,584 **13.** 495 cm^3 of water **15.** \$60

Mixed Review Exercises, page 314 **1.** $3a(ab + 2)$ **2.** $3y(y + 1)^2$ **3.** $(m + 2)(m + 3)$ **4.** $(x - 3y)(x + 3y)$ **5.** $5pq(pq^2 + 2p - 3q)$ **6.** $(4a - 3)(a + 1)$ **7.** $(a + b)(a + 4)$ **8.** $(x + 3)^2$ **9.** $(t + 3)(t - 5)$

Written Exercises, pages 317–318 **1.** 10% **3.** 20% **5.** 12.5% **7.** \$6.30 **9.** \$6.40 **11.** \$65 **13.** 20% **15.** 17.5% **17.** \$25.60 **19.** \$78 **21.** \$70

Problems, pages 318–319 **1.** 7% **3.** 17% **5.** 6% **7.** \$10,800 **9.** \$42 **11.** \$1600 in stocks, \$4400 in bonds **13.** \$20,000 **15.** \$1440

Computer Exercises, pages 319–320

1.

Years	\$
1	106
2	112.36
3	119.10
4	126.25
5	133.82
6	141.85
7	150.36
8	159.38
9	168.95
10	179.08

Mixed Review Exercises, page 320 **1.** $\left\{\frac{15}{4}\right\}$ **2.** {−4, 1} **3.** No sol. **4.** {20} **5.** {−1, −2} **6.** {8} **7.** $9z + 27$ **8.** $-4x + 12y$ **9.** $7a + b + 7$ **10.** $-8t$ **11.** $30bc$ **12.** $-3xz$

Self-Test 3, page 320 **1.** $\frac{13}{20}$ **2.** $\frac{29}{40}$ **3.** $\frac{51}{10}$ **4.** 13.6 **5.** 6.25 **6.** 350% **7.** 75% **8.** \$1680 **9.** $33\frac{1}{3}\%$

Problems, pages 324–325 **1.** 2 kg cashews, 6 kg pecans **3.** 50 mL juice **5.** \$1.00/lb **7.** 7.2% **9.** 25 L **11.** 3 g **13.** 8 kg apples, 12 kg apricots **15.** 65 km/h **17.** 4.8 L acid, 11.2 L water **19.** 8 L **21.** \$17,000 at 12%, \$4000 at $5\frac{1}{4}\%$ **23.** **(a)** 25 km/h **(b)** 24 km/h **25.** about \$1.76

Mixed Review Exercises, page 325 **1.** 6.32 **2.** 40% **3.** 7.5% **4.** 128 **5.** 9 **6.** $\frac{1}{6}$ **7.** 7 **8.** 80 **9.** 19 **10.** 4

Problems, pages 328–330 **1.** $\frac{2}{3}; \frac{x}{3}$ **3.** $\frac{9}{16}; \frac{9h}{40}$ **5.** $1\frac{1}{5}$ h **7.** 40 min **9.** $9\frac{3}{8}$ min **11.** 12 h **13.** 4.5 h; 9 h **15.** $1\frac{2}{5}$ h **17.** $3\frac{2}{3}$ h **19.** 4 days **21.** 40 min or 2400 s **23.** largest, $5\frac{1}{2}$ h; medium, 11 h; smallest, $16\frac{1}{2}$ h

Mixed Review Exercises, page 330 **1.** 18% **2.** $143 **3.** $22 **4.** {−2} **5.** {3.5} **6.** {−1} **7.** {11} **8.** {1.4} **9.** {0}

Self-Test 4, page 330 **1.** 25 L **2.** 0.2 kg **3.** 18 days **4.** $34\frac{2}{7}$ s

Written Exercises, pages 333–335 **1.** $\frac{1}{5}$ **3.** $\frac{1}{9}$ **5.** $\frac{1}{81}$ **7.** $\frac{1}{27}$ **9.** $\frac{1}{16}$ **11.** 1 **13.** $\frac{1}{16}$ **15.** 8 **17.** 27 **19.** 1 **21.** $\frac{1}{81}$ **23.** 1 **25.** $\frac{81}{16}$ **27.** $\frac{125}{64}$ **29. a.** $\frac{1}{216}$ **b.** $\frac{2}{27}$ **31. a.** $\frac{4}{3}$ **b.** 8 **33.** 0 has no reciprocal. **35.** $\frac{3}{x^2}$ **37.** $\frac{1}{9x^2}$ **39.** $\frac{y^2}{x}$ **41.** $\frac{1}{m^{12}}$ **43.** m **45.** $\frac{27}{x^6}$ **47.** 2 **49.** $\frac{1}{a^6}$ **51.** y^8 **53.** $\frac{1}{c^7}$ **55.** a^4 **57.** n^8 **59.** 25 **61.** 0.0000128 **63.** 78,125 **65.** 625 **67.** 0.00032 **69.** 4 **71.** x^1

Problems, page 335 **1.** 0.7084252 kg; 0.5018663 kg **3. (a)** 12 million **(b)** 16 million **(c)** 9 million **5. (a)** 5474 **(b)** 2 **(c)** 16,399,358 **(d)** 0

Mixed Review Exercises, page 335 **1.** $\frac{5z}{3x}$; $x \neq 0$, $z \neq 0$ **2.** $\frac{y+5}{y+2}$; $y \neq -5$, $y \neq -2$ **3.** $\frac{9p^2}{q^2}$; $q \neq 0$ **4.** $\frac{2(4-5n)}{5mn}$; $m \neq 0$, $n \neq 0$ **5.** $\frac{2(a-4)}{a-2}$; $a \neq 2$ **6.** $\frac{x-3}{x+2}$; $x \neq -3$, $x \neq -2$ **7.** $4x - 14 + \frac{92}{x+4}$ **8.** $\frac{2(x+5)}{3(x-3)}$ **9.** $a^2 + 3a + 9 + \frac{54}{a-3}$

Written Exercises, page 339 **1.** 300,000,000 **3.** 2,000,000,000,000,000,000,000,000,000,000 **5.** 0.00000136 **7.** 0.0000000000000005 **9. a.** 10^3 **b.** 10^{-3} **11. a.** 10^6 **b.** 10^{-6} **13. a.** 10^6 **b.** 10^{-6} **15. a.** 2.5×10^3 **b.** $2 \cdot 10^3 + 5 \cdot 10^2$ **17. a.** 2.4×10^{-9} **b.** $2 \cdot 10^{-9} + 4 \cdot 10^{-10}$ **19. a.** 3.03×10^6 **b.** $3 \cdot 10^6 + 0 \cdot 10^5 + 3 \cdot 10^4$ **21. a.** 9.09×10^{-5} **b.** $9 \cdot 10^{-5} + 0 \cdot 10^{-6} + 9 \cdot 10^{-7}$ **23. a.** 9.86×10^{-1} **b.** $9 \cdot 10^{-1} + 8 \cdot 10^{-2} + 6 \cdot 10^{-3}$ **25. a.** 1.2×10^{10} **b.** $1 \cdot 10^{10} + 2 \cdot 10^9$ **27.** 3.6×10^{-4} **29.** 3.6×10^{17} **31.** 1×10^0

Problems, pages 339–340 **1. a.** about 9.5×10^{12} km **b.** about 1.4×10^{19} km **c.** about 4.3 years **d.** about 500 s or $8\frac{1}{3}$ min **3. a.** 2.3×10^2 **b.** 7.5×10^{-5} **c.** 2.3×10^{18} **d.** 3.0×10^{21}

Mixed Review Exercises, page 340 **1.** $y + 24$ **2.** $\frac{y^{15}}{x^6}$ **3.** 8 **4.** 5:2 **5.** 5 **6.** $3t + 1$ **7.** $\frac{1}{c^{12}}$ **8.** 2 **9.** $\frac{7b^2}{6c}$

Self-Test 5, page 341 **1.** 3^{10} **2.** $\frac{1}{2^3}$ or $\frac{1}{8}$ **3.** $-(2^3)$ or -8 **4.** $\frac{1}{x^5}$ **5.** $\frac{4}{a^2}$ **6.** $\frac{1}{81a^8}$ **7.** 1 **8.** $\frac{1}{b^2}$ **9.** $\frac{1}{a^6}$ **10. a.** 4.7×10^7 **b.** $4 \cdot 10^7 + 7 \cdot 10^6$ **11. a.** 6×10^{-8} **b.** $6 \cdot 10^{-8}$ **12. a.** 1.234×10^1 **b.** $1 \cdot 10^1 + 2 \cdot 10^0 + 3 \cdot 10^{-1} + 4 \cdot 10^{-2}$

Chapter Review, pages 342–343 **1.** b **3.** d **5.** c **7.** c **9.** b **11.** b **13.** d **15.** d

Cumulative Review, page 345 **1.** 12 **3.** $-16m^8n^7$ **5.** $16a^4b^6c^2$ **7.** $25t^4v^2 - 60t^2v + 36$ **9.** $2x^3 - 11x^2y + 11xy^2 - 3y^3$ **11.** $\frac{1}{x^2z(3z+1)}$ **13.** $4b + 3$ **15.** $x^{14}(x-4)^2$ **17.** $9\frac{1}{3}$% **19.** $(7z-2)^2$ **21.** $3(2b+3)(b+3)$ **23.** $(12x-1)(x+4)$ **25.** {30} **27.** $\left\{-\frac{7}{2}\right\}$ **29.** {0, 1, 11} **31.** {−1, 6} **33.** 4.3×10^{-6} **35.** 9 and 11 **37.** 20% **39.** 56 min or $\frac{14}{15}$ h

Maintaining Skills, page 346 **1.** $9a^2 - 5a + 8$ **3.** $12 - 5x$ **5.** $12x - 20z$ **7.** $2x - 8y - 6$ **9.** $-\frac{13}{6}b$ **11.** $-6a^3b^4c$ **13.** $-m^5n^2p^3$ **15.** $16x^8y^{12}$ **17.** $r^{15}s^{11}t^7$ **19.** $56c^{12}d^{12}e^6$

21. $3a^3b^2 - 3a^2b^3 + 3ab^4$
23. $c^2d^7 - 2c^3d^5 + c^5d^3$ **25.** $z^2 + 5z - 24$
27. $y^2 + 8y - 20$ **29.** $12z^2 - 9z - 3$
31. $81d^2 - 9$ **33.** $x^4 - 36$
35. $3y^3 - 13y^2 + 13y - 3$

Mixed Problem Solving, page 347 **1.** home; 2 points **3.** 220 mg **5.** 30 km **7.** 49.5 min **9.** No sol.; insufficient info. **11.** $\frac{7x + 40}{240}$ h **13.** \$5,000

Chapter 8 Introduction to Functions

Written Exercises, pages 351–352 **1.** yes; yes **3.** yes; no **5.** yes; yes **7.** yes; yes **9.** no; no **11.** no; yes **13.** (0, 6), (1, 4), (2, 2), and (3, 0) **15.** (0, 4) and (2, 1) **17.** (0, 1) **19.** (1, 4), (3, 3), (5, 2), (7, 1), and (9, 0) **21.** (1, 4), (2, 2), and (4, 1) **23.** (1, 3) and (3, 1) **25.** (1, 16), (2, 8), (4, 4), (8, 2), and (16, 1) **27.** (1, 5) and (5, 1) **29.** (3, 1) **31.** (0, 1), (2, 2), and (3, 4) **33.** (1, 3), (2, 1), and (4, 0) **35.** (9, 0), (3, 2), and (1, 8) **37.** 5 small and 3 large or 9 small and 2 large **39.** 4 pigs and 40 chickens **41.** $y = 6x - 2$ **43.** $y = \frac{2x}{x - 2}$ **45.** 9

Mixed Review Exercises, page 352
1. 3.08×10^8 **2.** 4.37×10^{-4} **3.** 1.19×10^8 **4.** 2.16×10^{-5} **5.** 4.9×10^4 **6.** 5.6201×10^7 **7.** $\frac{n^2}{2}$ **8.** $\frac{1}{125x^3}$ **9.** $3xy$ **10.** $\frac{1}{b^7}$

Computer Exercises, page 352 **1.** yes; no **2.** no; yes **3.** yes; no **4.** yes; yes **5.** no; yes **6.** yes; yes

Written Exercises, pages 357–358
1–11.

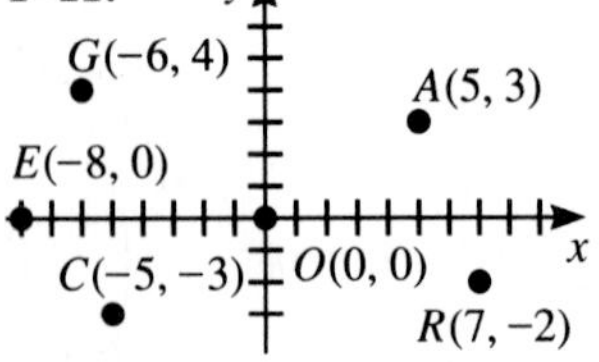

13. *E* **15.** *Z, H, Y, L* **17.** *I, X, O, P* **19.** *J, I, P* **21.** *Z, O* **23.** *V*

25.

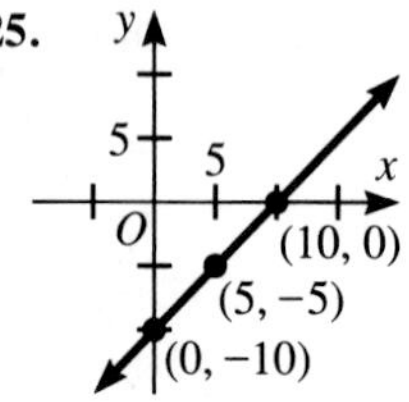

27.

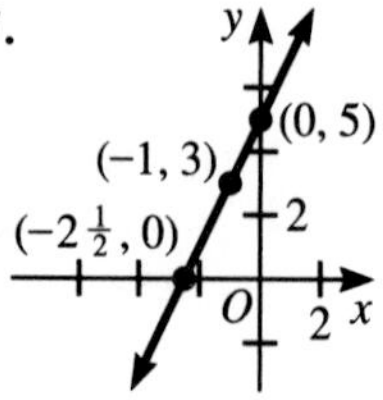

29.

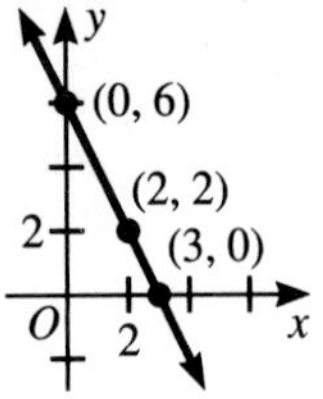

31.

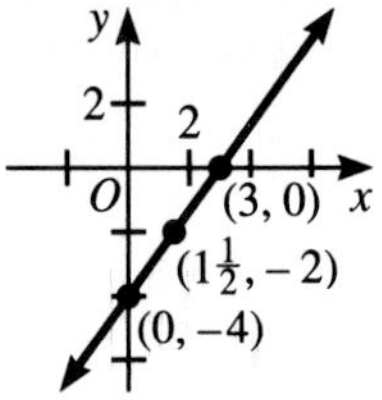

33.

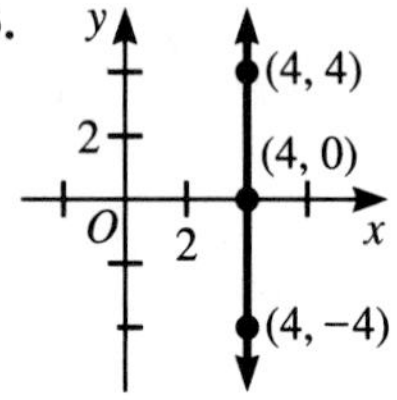

35.

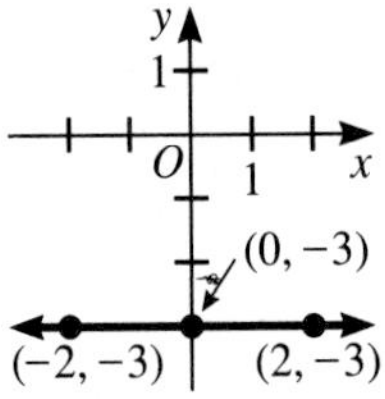

37.

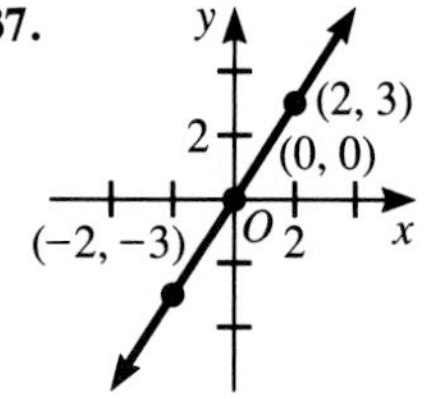

39.

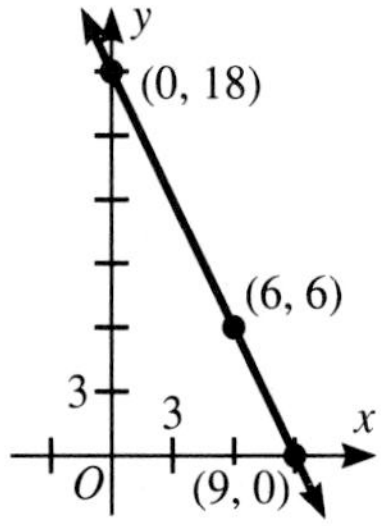

41.

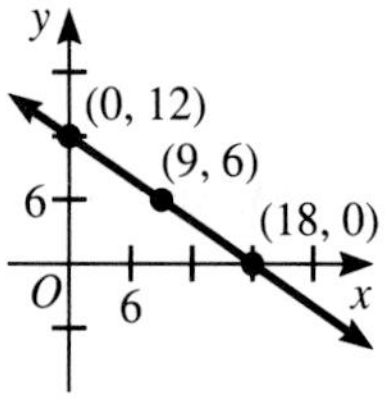

43.

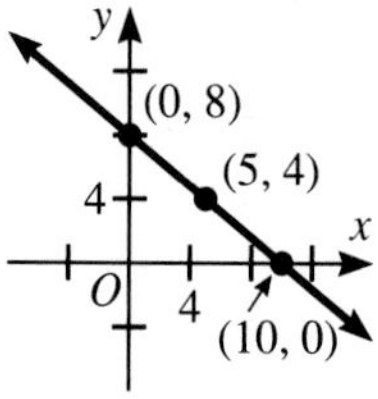

45.

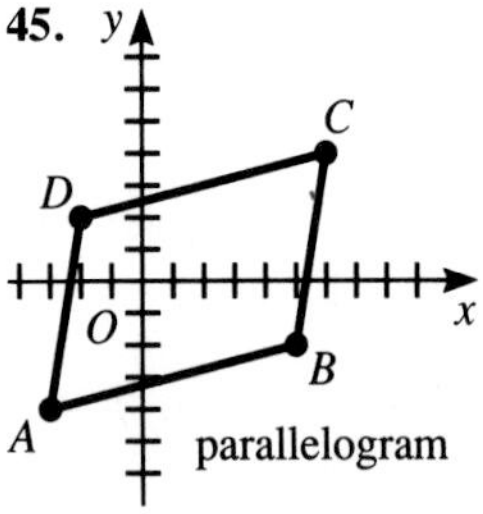

47.

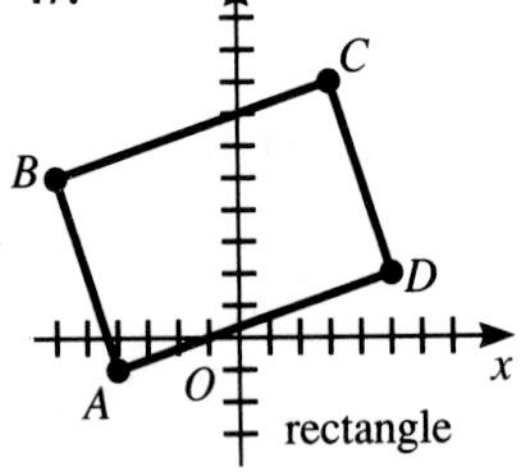

Mixed Review Exercises, page 358 **1.** yes; no **2.** yes; yes **3.** no; yes **4.** no; yes **5.** $\{-1, -2\}$ **6.** $\{11\}$ **7.** $\{2, 3\}$ **8.** $\left\{\frac{10}{3}\right\}$ **9.** $\{-9\}$ **10.** $\{15\}$

Self-Test 1, page 358 **1.** yes; no **2.** no; yes **3.** (0, 4), (3, 2), (6, 0) **4.** (0, 4), (5, 2), (10, 0)

5–7.

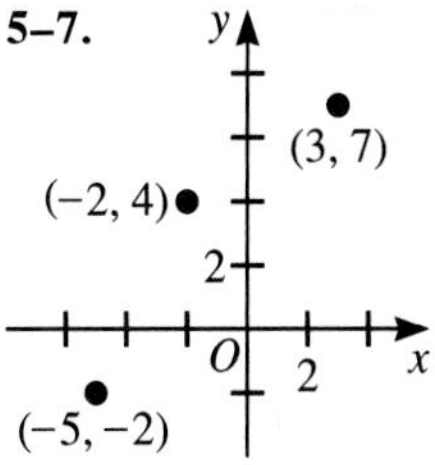

8.

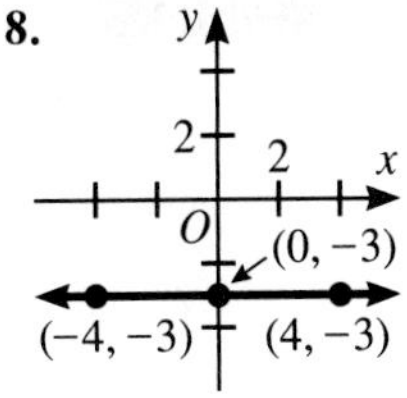

9.

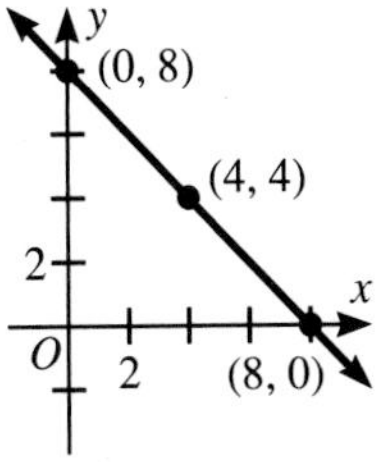

10.

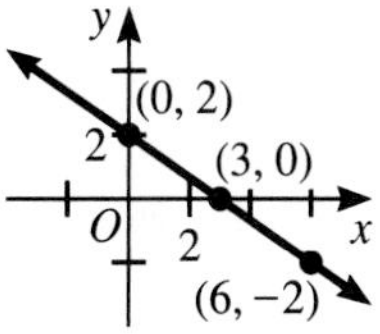

Computer Key-In, page 359 **1.** x-axis at 3, y-axis at -2 **3.** x-axis at -2, does not cross the y-axis **5.** x-axis at 2.6666667, y-axis at 2.6666667

Written Exercises, pages 363–365 **1.** $-\frac{1}{2}$

3. 1 **5.** $\frac{2}{11}$ **7.** 1 **9.** $\frac{5}{3}$ **11.** $\frac{2}{3}$ **13.** 2

15. -2 **17.** $-\frac{3}{2}$ **19.** $\frac{3}{5}$ **21.** 0 **23.** no slope

25.

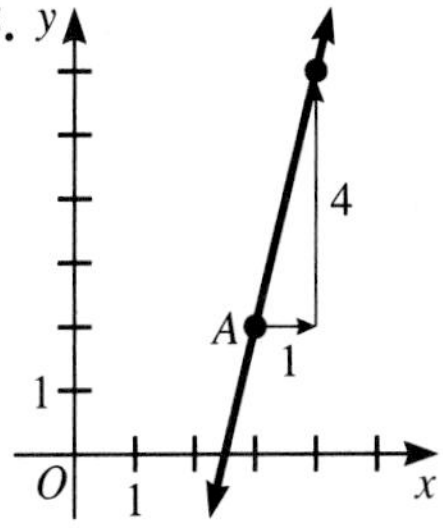

27.

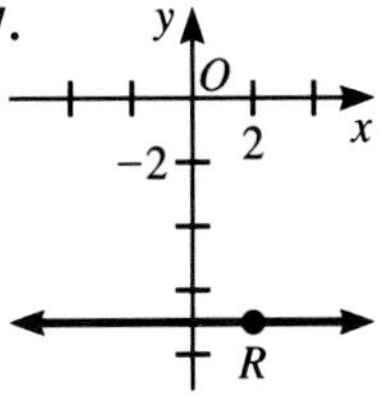

29.

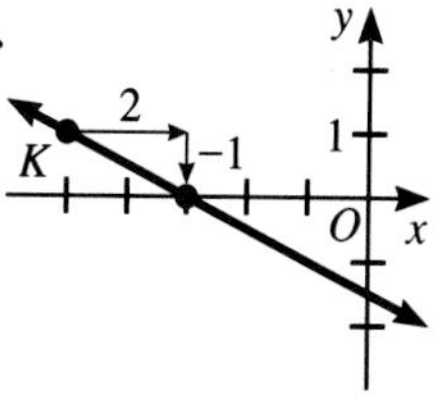

31. collinear **33.** not collinear **35.** not collinear **37.** $\overline{AB}$, 0; $\overline{AC}$, no slope; $\overline{BC}$, $\frac{8}{9}$ **39.** $\frac{1}{2}$; 8

41. The slopes of $\overline{AC}$ and $\overline{AM}$ are both $-\frac{5}{3}$; thus M lies on $\overline{AC}$. The slopes of $\overline{DB}$ and $\overline{DM}$ are both $\frac{3}{5}$; thus M lies on $\overline{DB}$.

Mixed Review Exercises, page 365 **1.** $\left\{-\frac{6}{5}\right\}$

2. $\left\{-\frac{20}{9}\right\}$ **3.** {3} **4.** {−9} **5.** {1.7, −1.7}

6. {0, 5} **7.** $-\frac{13}{10}$ **8.** 20 **9.** 3 **10.** 4

11. −10 **12.** 8

Calculator Key-In, page 365 **1.** 7 **3.** −1.925 **5.** 1

Written Exercises, pages 368–369 **1.** 2; 1

3. $\frac{1}{2}$; −3 **5.** $-\frac{1}{2}$; 6 **7.** −2; 8 **9.** 1; 0

11. 0; −4 **13.**

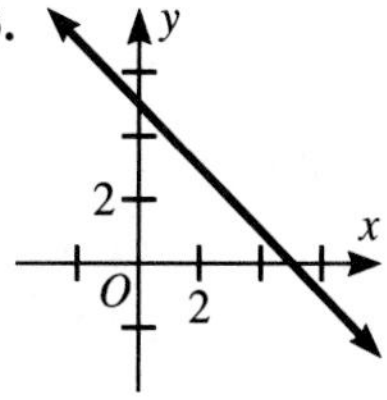

15.

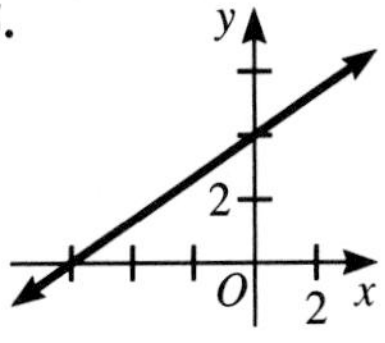

17.

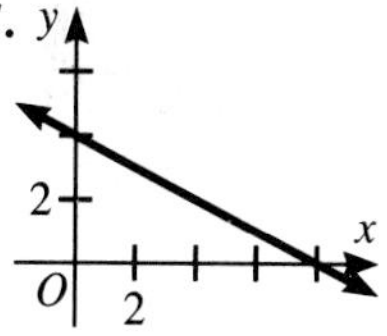

19.

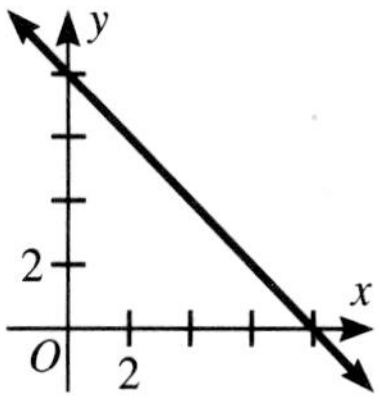

21.

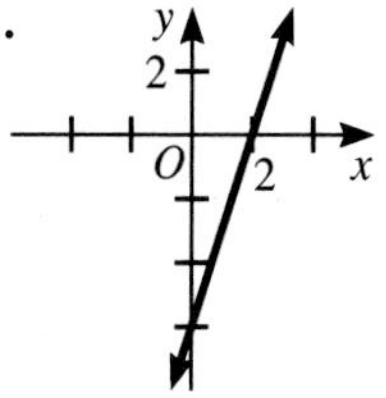

23.

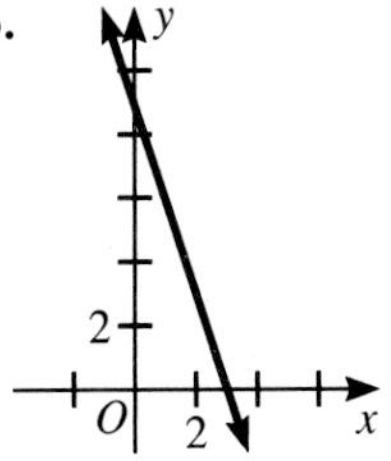

25.

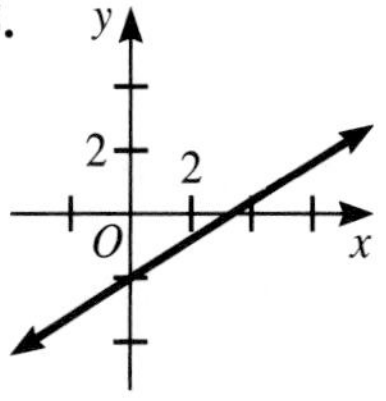

27.

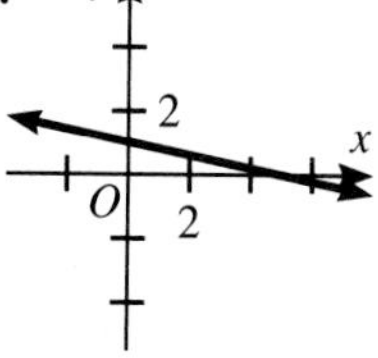

29.

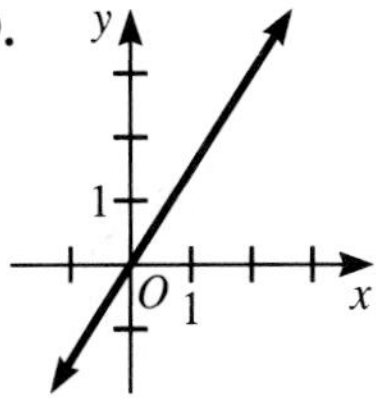

31. both lines have slope of $\frac{2}{3}$ and different y-intercepts **33.** both lines have slope of 1 and different y-intercepts **35.** both lines have slope of -1 and different y-intercepts **37.** $y = 5x + 7$

39. 2; -2 **41.** -9 **43.** 3 **45.** $m = -\frac{a}{b}$ and $b = \frac{c}{b}$

Mixed Review Exercises, page 369 **1.** 2 **2.** $\frac{1}{3}$ **3.** -3 **4.** 4 **5.** $(3s + 4)(s + 1)$ **6.** $5x(4x + 3)$ **7.** $3(p - 4)^2$ **8.** $(9y - 4z)(9y + 4z)$ **9.** $(x + y)(-3x + 4)$ **10.** $(m - 12n)(m + 3n)$

Extra, page 370 **1.** $-\frac{2}{3}$ **3.** $\frac{8}{3}$ **5.** $-\frac{5}{3}$ **7.** no slope **9.** -3 **11.** parallel **13.** perpendicular **15.** parallel **17.** -8

Written Exercises, pages 372–373

1. $y = 2x + 5$ **3.** $y = -\frac{1}{2}x + 7$ **5.** $y = \frac{1}{2}x - 2$ **7.** $y = 2x + 11$ **9.** $y = -2x + 11$ **11.** $y = \frac{1}{2}x - 3$ **13.** $y = -\frac{3}{4}x + 3$ **15.** $y = 3$ **17.** $y = 2x + 7$ **19.** $y = -x + 7$ **21.** $y = -x + 9$ **23.** $y = \frac{8}{3}x - 9$ **25.** $y = 5x - 1$ **27.** $y = -\frac{3}{4}x - \frac{3}{2}$ **29.** $y = \frac{2}{5}x - 2$ **31.** $y = \frac{1}{2}x - 3$ **33.** $y = 5$ **35.** $3x - y = -6$ **37.** $x - 2y = 6$ **39. a.** No; there is no slope or y-intercept. **b.** $x = 2$ **41.** 7

Mixed Review Exercises, page 373 **1.** $16t^5$ **2.** $2s^2 - 4st$ **3.** $49p^2q^4$ **4.** $-27m^6n^{12}$ **5.** 3 **6.** $-18a^4b^3$ **7.** 128 **8.** $5x + 2y$

Self-Test 2, page 373 **1.** $\frac{4}{3}$ **2.** 0 **3.** $\frac{3}{7}$; -4

4.

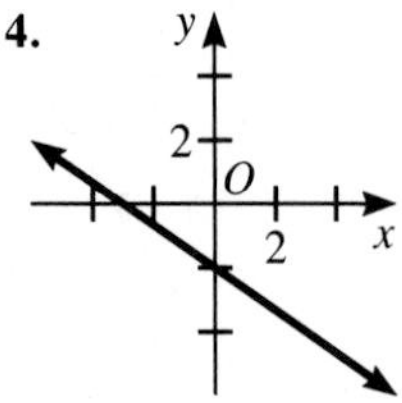

5. $y = 3x + 5$
6. $y = x - 5$

Written Exercises, page 377

1.

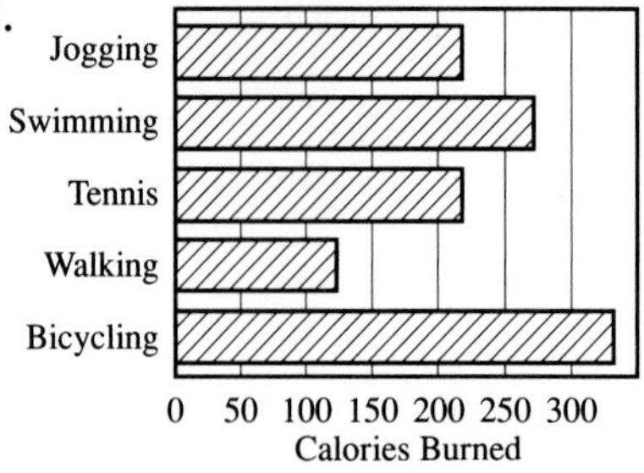

3.

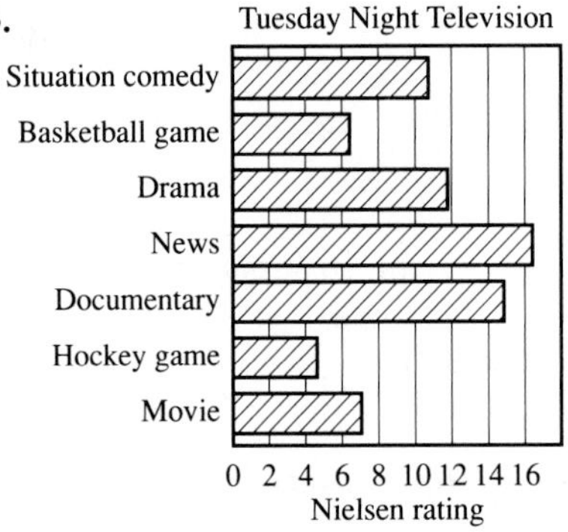

5.

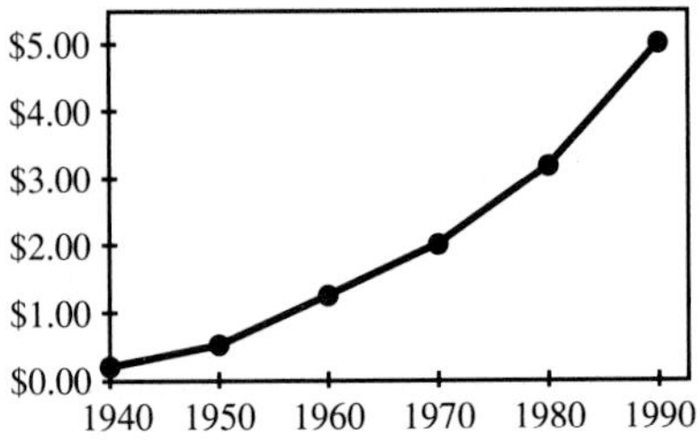

7. \$.90; \$2.50 **9.** Answers will vary.

Mixed Review Exercises, page 377

1. $y = x + 2$ **2.** $y = 5x + 2$ **3.** $y = \frac{1}{3}x - 4$ **4.** $y = -\frac{3}{2}x - 3$

5.

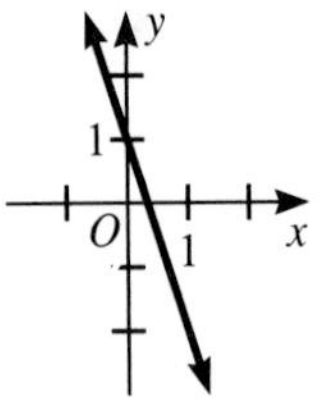

6.

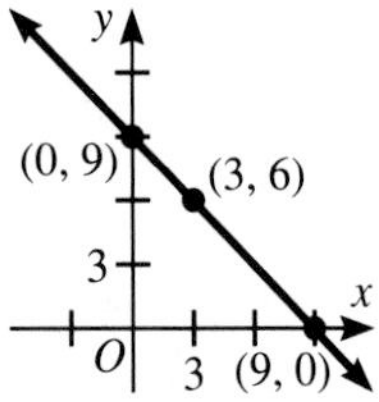

7. 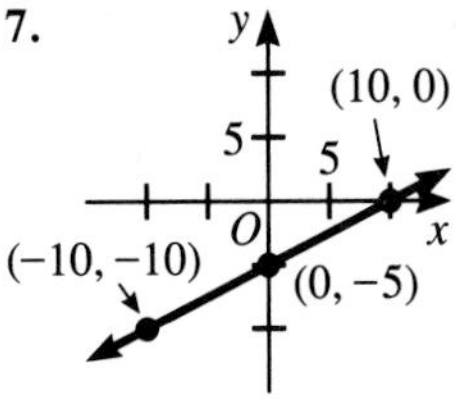

8. 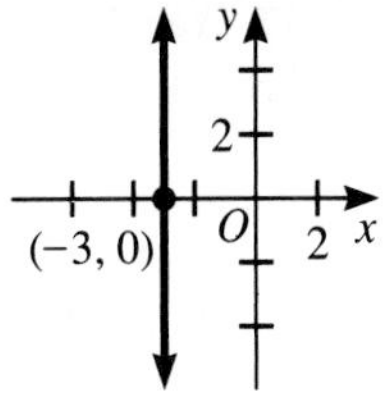

Written Exercises, pages 380–381
1. {−4, 1, 6} **3.** {−3, 5, 13} **5.** {−1, 3} **7.** {2, 9, 29} **9.** {0, 2} **11.** {0, 5, 45} **13. a.** 6 **b.** −24 **c.** −49 **15. a.** 4 **b.** −1 **c.** −4 **17. a.** 46 **b.** 73 **c.** −2 **19. a.** 23 **b.** 23 **c.** −2 **21. a.** 8 **b.** 0 **c.** 16 **23. a.** 70 **b.** 28 **c.** 0 **25. a.** −24 **b.** 0 **c.** 0 **27. a.** 0 **b.** 1 **c.** 1 **29.** −12; {4} **31.** −1; $\left\{\frac{1}{5}\right\}$ **33.** 7; {14} **35.** −3; {−1, 3} **37.** 0; {−1, 0, 1} **39.** −1; {1, −1} **41.** −18 **43.** 6 **45. a.** 2 **b.** 1 **c.** 2 **d.** 4 **47.** 0

Mixed Review Exercises, page 382
1. $\frac{9n^2 + 4n - 1}{3n^3}$ **2.** 19 **3.** $-3y$ **4.** $-9a + 6b - 3c$ **5.** $1 - x$ **6.** $12m - 21$ **7.** −12 **8.** $\frac{df}{e}$ **9.** $\frac{x - y}{x + y}$

Computer Exercises, page 382 **1.** −13, −7, −4, 23 **3.** 0.0099, 0.2, 1, 0.2, 0.0099

Challenge, page 382 **1. a.** $\frac{2}{3}; \frac{3}{4}; \frac{4}{5}$ **b.** $\frac{100}{101}$ **c.** $\frac{n}{n + 1}$

Written Exercises, pages 386–387

1. 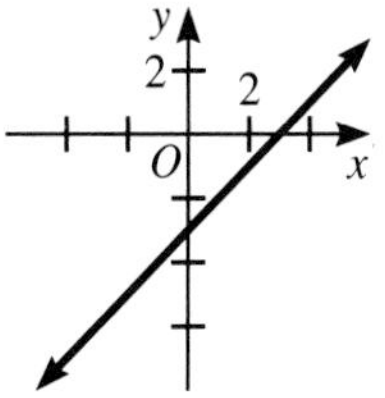

3. 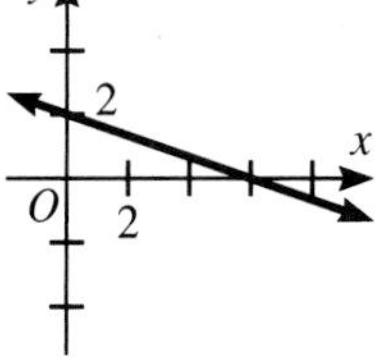

5. 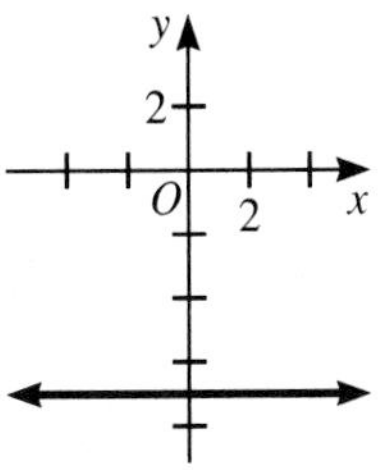

7. (0, −5); $x = 0$; −5

9. $\left(\frac{1}{2}, -6\frac{1}{4}\right)$; $x = \frac{1}{2}$; $-6\frac{1}{4}$ **11.** (0, −4); $x = 0$; −4 **13.** $\left(-1\frac{1}{2}, 2\frac{1}{4}\right)$; $x = -1\frac{1}{2}$; $2\frac{1}{4}$ **15.** (−4, 1); $x = -4$; 1 **17.** $\left(\frac{1}{4}, \frac{1}{8}\right)$; $x = \frac{1}{4}$; $\frac{1}{8}$

19. (0, 0); $x = 0$;

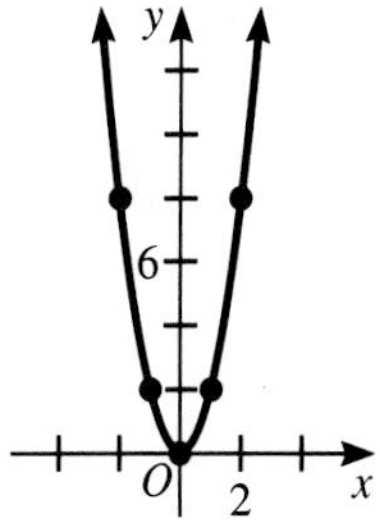

21. (0, 0); $x = 0$;

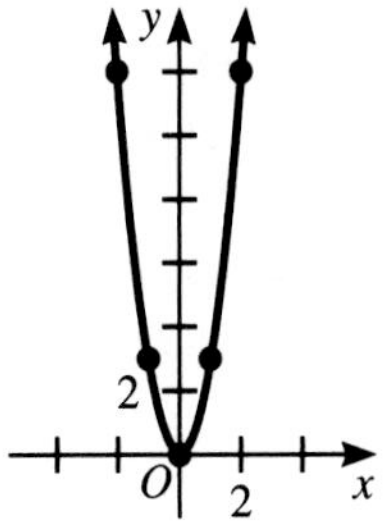

23. (0, 0); $x = 0$;

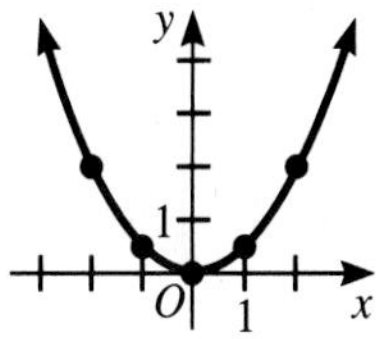

25. (2, −4); $x = 2$;

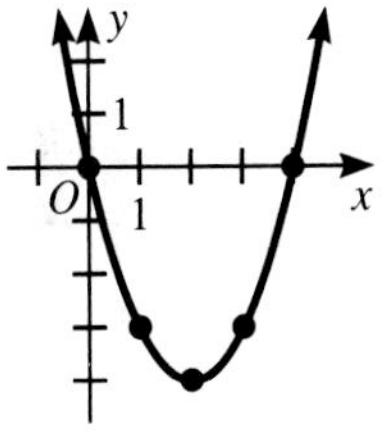

27. $\left(-2\frac{1}{2}, 12\frac{1}{4}\right)$; $x = -2\frac{1}{2}$;

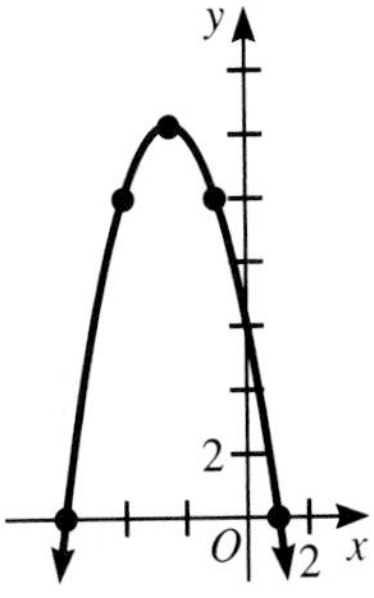

29. (0, 4); $x = 0$;

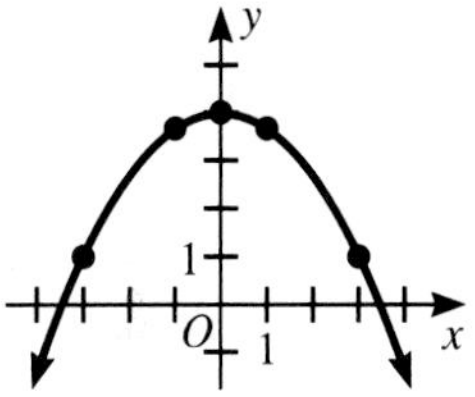

31. a. 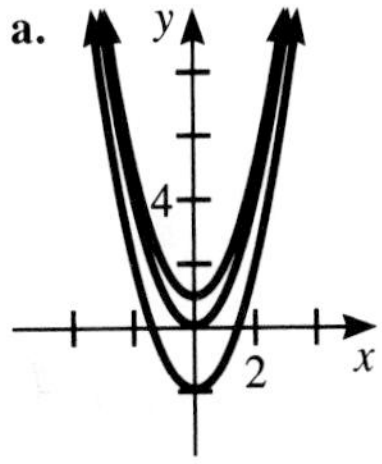

b. graph rises; graph lowers

33. 10; {−5} **35.** −11; $\left\{2\frac{3}{4}\right\}$ **37.** 8; {2, 4} **39.** 12; {−6, −2} **41.** x-intercepts

Mixed Review Exercises, page 387
1. {2, 5, 14} **2.** {−8, −4, 0} **3.** {6, 8, 34} **4.** {0, 2, 6} **5.** $7(x + 4)$ **6.** $x - 3$ **7.** $9x$ **8.** $\frac{1}{3}x - 5$

Computer Exercises, page 388 **1.** (0, 0); (−3, 9), (−2, 4), (−1, 1); (1, 1)(2, 4)(3, 9) **3.** (2, −1); (−1, 8), (0, 3), (1, 0); (3, 0)(4, 3)(5, 8) **5.** (−1, −5); (−4, 13), (−3, 3), (−2, −3); (0, −3), (1, 3), (2, 13)

Self-Test 3, page 388
1. a. $D = \{1985, 1986, 1987, 1988, 1989, 1990\}$; $R = \{0.75, 0.90, 1.12, 1.43, 1.65, 2.05\}$

b. Earnings Per Share
Common Foods Corp.

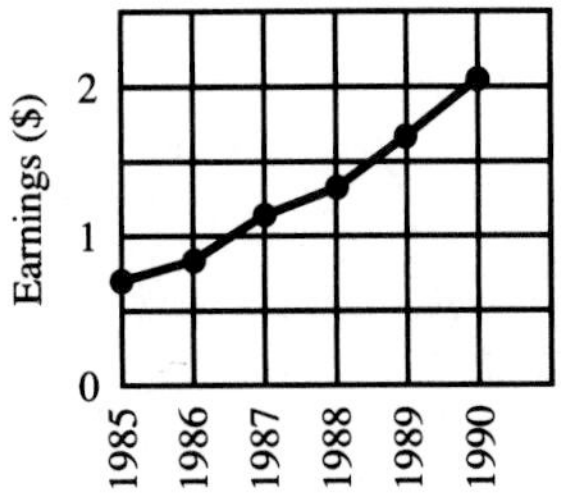

2. $R = \{2, 3, 6, 11, 18\}$
3. a. 11 **b.** −10 **c.** −3
4. (−4, −6); −6
5. (1, −1); $x = 1$; see graph at right.

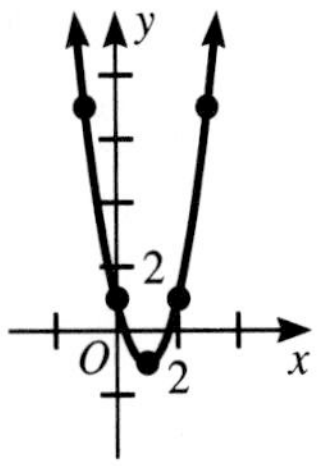

Ex. 5

Extra, pages 389–390 **1.** $D = \{2, 3\}$; $R = \{0, 3, 4, 6\}$; no **3.** $D = \{1, 2, 3, 4\}$; $R = \{-3, -1, 0, 6\}$; yes
5. $D = \{-2, -1, 1, 2\}$; $R = \{1, 4\}$; yes
7. $D = \{-1, 1, 2, 4\}$; $R = \{1, 2\}$; yes
9. $D = \{-2, 2, 4\}$; $R = \{-3, -1, 0, 1\}$; no
11. $D = \{-3, -2, -1, 0, 1, 2, 3\}$; $R = \{-2, -1, 0, 1\}$; yes

13. Not a function; (4, 4) and (4, −3) have the same first coordinate.

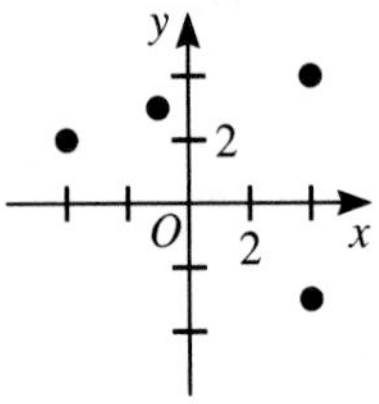

15. Not a function; (−3, 0) and (−3, 2) have the same first coordinate.

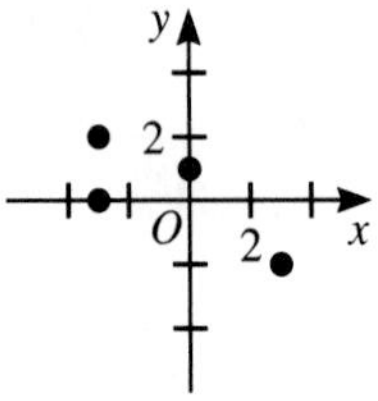

17. Yes, it is a function. See graph at right. **19.** Yes; no; it is not a function because all nonzero x's are paired with 2 y's. **21.** yes; no **23.** yes; yes

Ex. 17

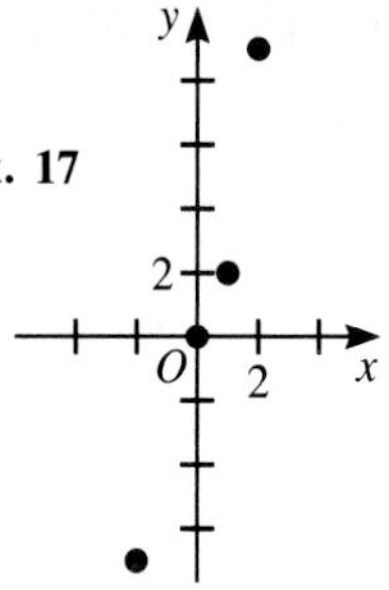

Written Exercises, pages 393–395 **1.** $\frac{1}{6}$ **3.** 8 **5.** 25 **7.** 750 **9.** 600 **11.** 24 **13.** 1.2 **15.** $\frac{2}{3}$ **17. a.** $L = \frac{7}{10}h$ **b.** $\frac{14}{20} = \frac{L_2}{h_2}$ **19. a.** $M = \frac{1}{6}E$ **b.** $\frac{28}{168} = \frac{M_2}{E_2}$ **21. a.** $R = 0.02059\ l$ **b.** $\frac{10.295}{500} = \frac{R_2}{l_2}$ **23.** Since (x_1, y_1) and (x_2, y_2) are ordered pairs of a direct variation and neither is (0, 0), $\frac{x_1}{y_1}$ and $\frac{x_2}{y_2}$ are equivalent fractions, so $\frac{x_1}{y_1} = \frac{x_2}{y_2}$; $x_1y_2 = x_2y_1$; $y_2 = \frac{x_2y_1}{x_1}$; $\frac{y_2}{x_2} = \frac{y_1}{x_1}$, or $\frac{y_1}{x_1} = \frac{y_2}{x_2}$.

Problems, pages 395–396 **1.** \$360 **3.** \$900 **5.** 17 min **7.** 156 m^2 **9.** 55 g **11.** 37 degrees **13.** 1,196,718.75 m^2 **15.** If $C = k_1d$ and $d = k_2r$, then $C = k_1(k_2r)$ or $C = (k_1 \cdot k_2)r$ and C varies directly with r.

Mixed Review Exercises, page 396
1. $6p^2 + 11p + 3$ **2.** $4x^3 + 10x^2 - 30x + 12$ **3.** $-15s + 12s^2$ **4.** $9c^2 - 4$ **5.** $3t^2 + t - 10$ **6.** $14y^2 + 22y - 12$

7.

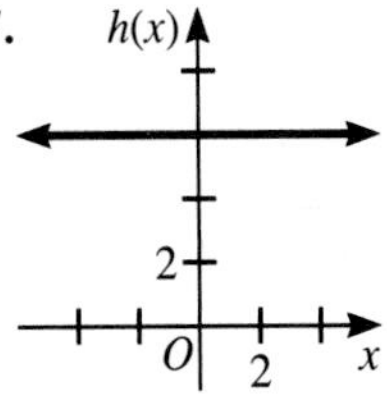

8.

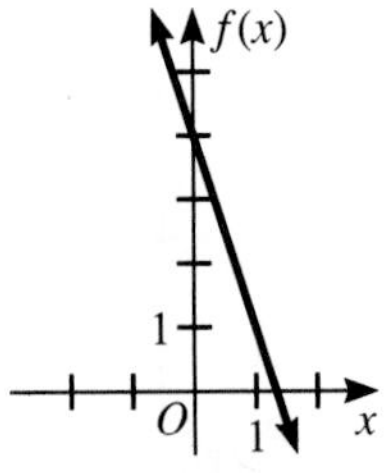

9.

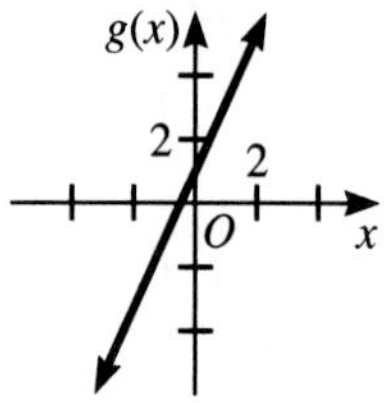

10.

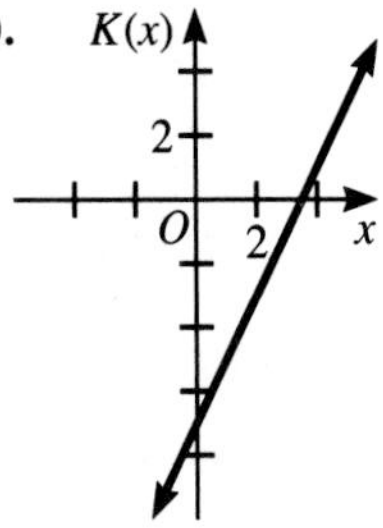

11. 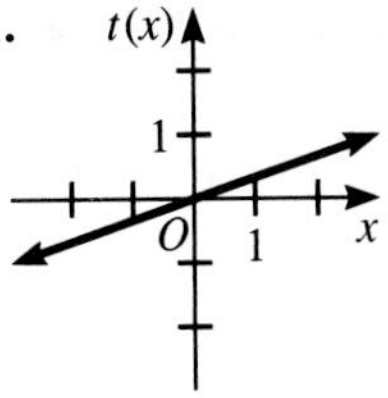

12. 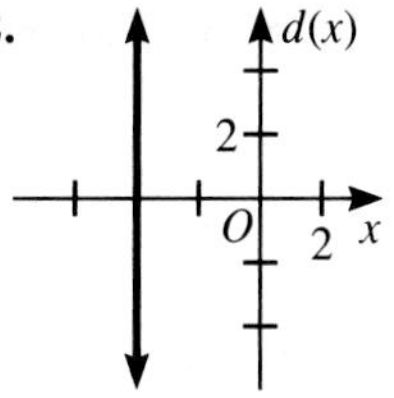

Written Exercises, pages 399–400

1. 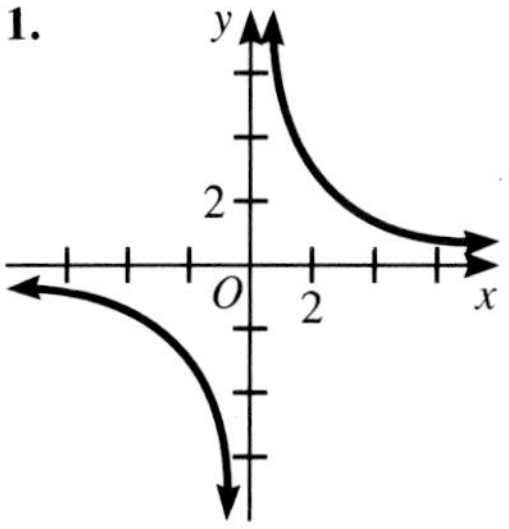

3. 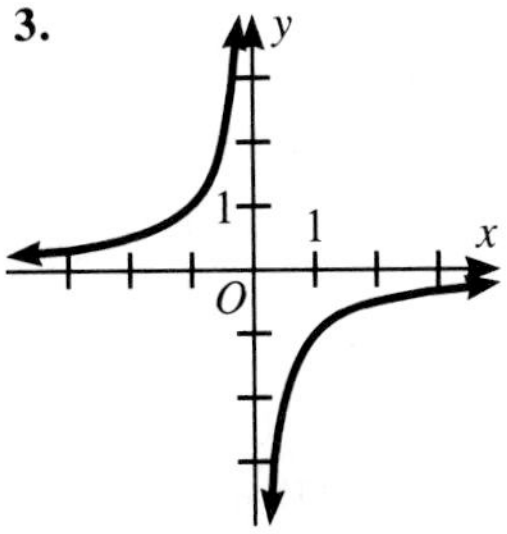

5. 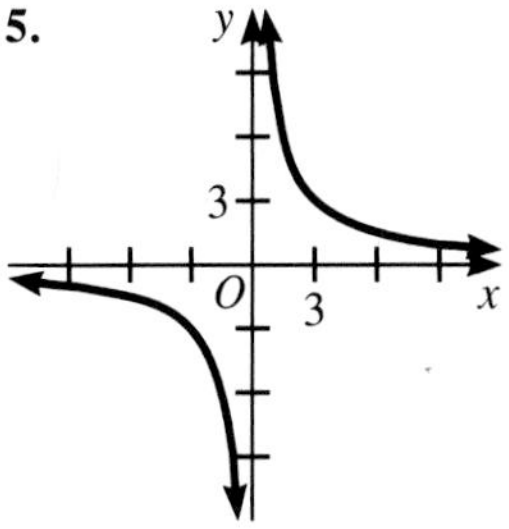

7. 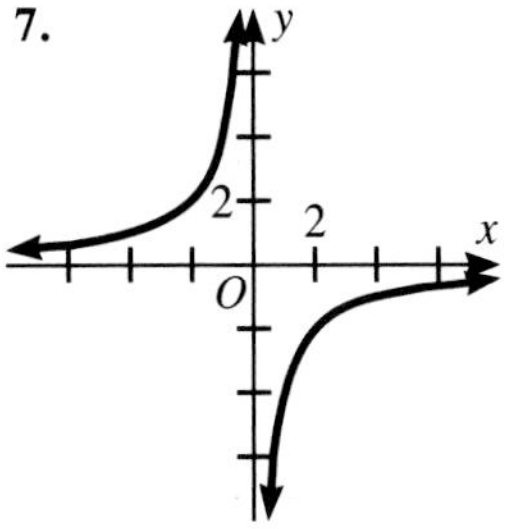

9. 40 **11.** 27 **13.** 6.3 **15. a.** $lw = 90$ **b.** $\frac{5}{l_2} = \frac{w_2}{18}$ **17. a.** $fl = 1.5$ **b.** $\frac{0.6}{f_2} = \frac{l_2}{2.5}$ **19. a.** $PV = 337{,}125$ **b.** $\frac{725}{V_2} = \frac{P_2}{465}$

Problems, pages 400–401 **1.** 9 people **3.** 48 cm **5.** 750 r/min **7.** 8 m **9.** 22 cm **11.** about 8.8 ft **13.** about 66 cm from the 18 kg mass **15.** $\frac{1}{2}$ the wavelength of the lower note **17.** 0.4 m

Mixed Review Exercises, page 402 **1.** Both lines have a slope of $-\frac{2}{3}$ and different y-intercepts. **2.** Both lines have a slope of $-\frac{1}{5}$ and different y-intercepts. **3.** Both lines have a slope of 1 and different y-intercepts. **4.** Both lines have a slope of $\frac{2}{3}$ and different y-intercepts. **5.** -6 **6.** $\frac{1}{5}$ **7.** 9

Computer Exercises, page 402 **1.** direct **3.** neither

Calculator Key-In, page 403 **1.** 21 **3.** 155 **5.** 0.36 **7.** 19.2 **9.** 5.2 **11.** 9

Self-Test 4, page 403 **1.** 5 **2.** 3 **3.** \$525 **4.** 3 **5.** 32 **6.** 7 people

Reading Algebra, page 404 **1.** 85 dimes, 72 quarters **3.** 800 km/h **5.** 7 cm by 12 cm **7.** 4 cm; 6 cm

Chapter Review, pages 405–406 **1.** a **3.** b **5.** c **7.** d **9.** c **11.** d **13.** c **15.** c **17.** a

Cumulative Review, page 409 **1.** $10p - 6r$ **3.** $30y^5z + 12y^4z^2 - 21y^3z^4$ **5.** $9m^2 - 30mn + 25n^2$ **7.** $(4x + 5)(5x - 3)$ **9.** $3(z + 1)(z - 8)$ **11.** $\frac{(x + 3)(x - 1)}{2x - 1}$ **13.** $\frac{-5r^2 + 8r + 80}{(r - 4)(r + 4)}$ **15.** $y = -x + 7$ **17.** $\{0, 1, 4, 9, 16\}$

19. 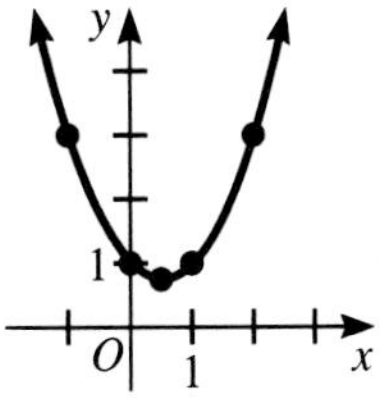

21. $\left\{\frac{33}{5}\right\}$ **23.** $\{54\}$ **25.** $\left\{-\frac{6}{7}, \frac{6}{7}\right\}$ **27.** $\{0, -2\}$ **29.** $\left\{0, \frac{1}{3}\right\}$ **31.** $\{3\}$ **33.** 35 units

Maintaining Skills, page 410
1. $5b^2c^3(5 + 3b^3c)$ **3.** $3u^4v(3u + 12v - 5v^2)$ **5.** $8x^2y^3(-3x^5y^2 + 4x^4 - y)$ **7.** $z(z + 11)(z - 11)$ **9.** $(7 - x^3)(7 + x^3)$ **11.** prime **13.** $(4a - 5)^2$ **15.** $(5x + 3)^2$ **17.** $(n + 2)(n + 9)$ **19.** $(7d - c)(2d + c)$ **21.** $(x + 3)(x + 7)$ **23.** $(n - 3p)(n - 2p)$ **25.** $(r - 2s)(y + 3)$ **27.** $(s + 2t + 3)(s - 2t - 3)$ **29.** $(4a + 3b - 5)(4a - 3b + 5)$ **31.** $(3b + 5)(b - 1)$ **33.** $2(3m + 2)(m - 2)$ **35.** $z(5z + 2)(5z + 1)$ **37.** $(3 + y)(1 - 7y)$ **39.** $2(3b - 5)(2b + 1)$

Preparing for College Entrance Exams, page 411 **1.** A **3.** D **5.** B

Chapter 9 Solving Systems of Linear Equations

Written Exercises, pages 415–416

1.

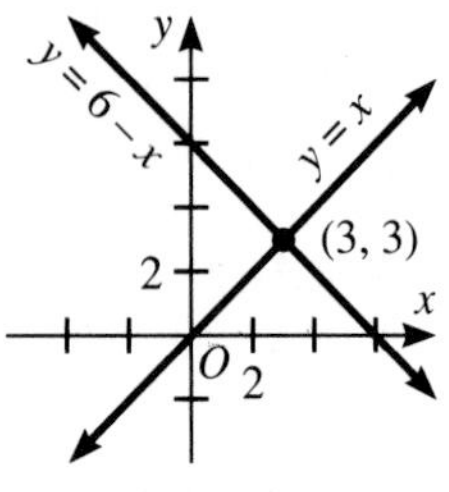

3.

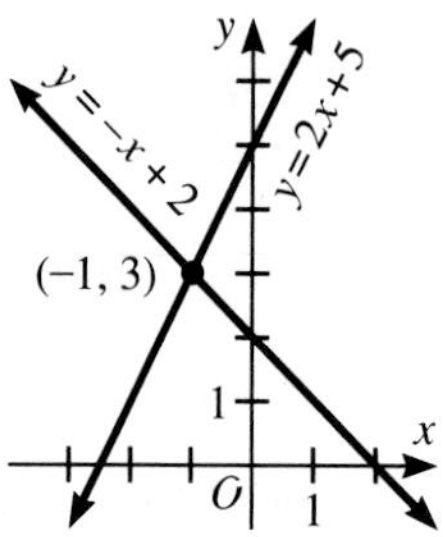

5.

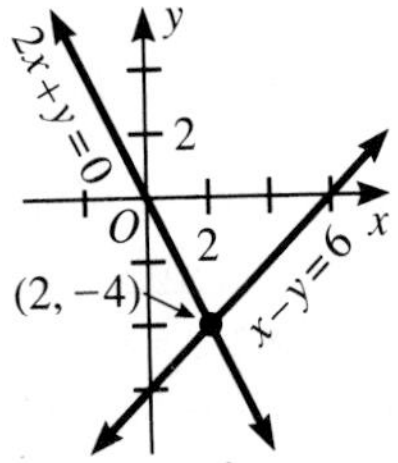

7.

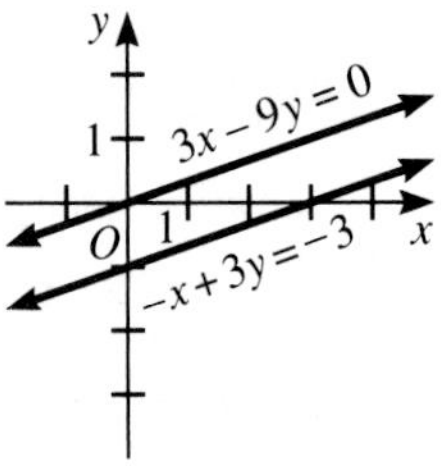

9.

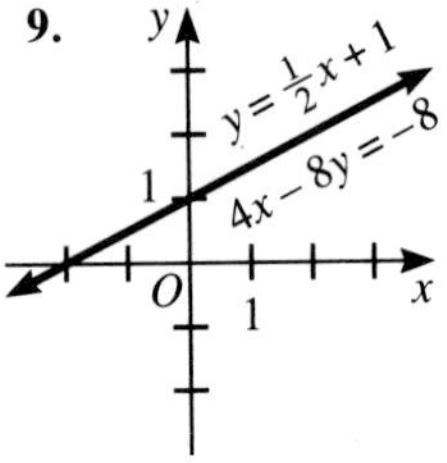

11.

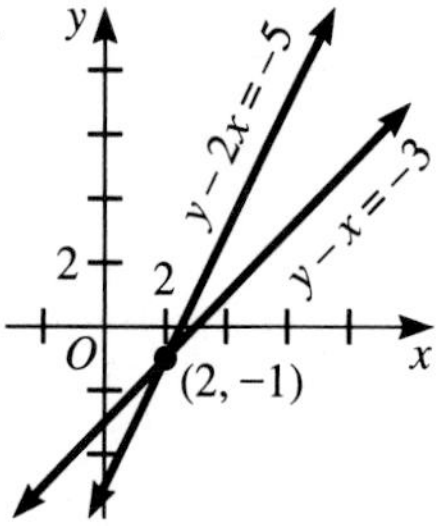

13.

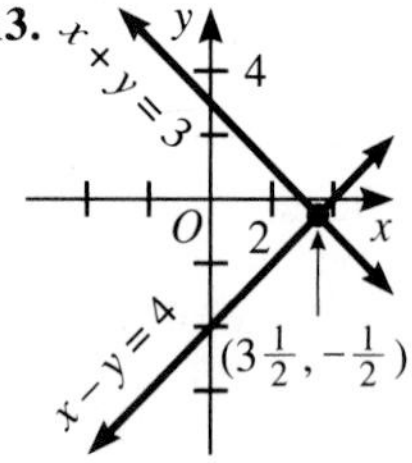

15.

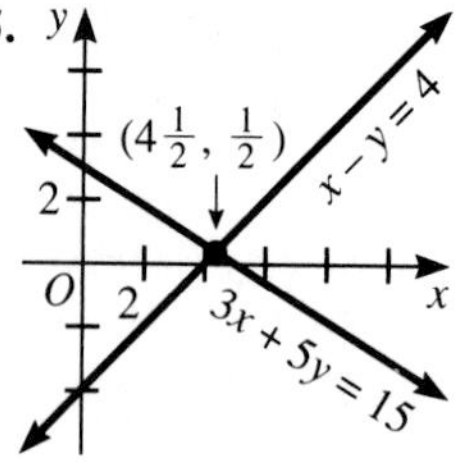

17. $(-2, 4)$ and $(2, 4)$ **19.** $(5, 5)$
21. $(-2, -4)$ **23.** 10 sq. units

Mixed Review Exercises, page 416 **1.** $\frac{5s}{t^2}$
2. $\frac{b^8}{a^{12}}$ **3.** $\frac{2m^2}{5n^2}$ **4.** $\frac{1}{x^4y^2}$ **5.** p^3 **6.** x^7y^2

Computer Exercises, page 416 **1.** $(1, -1)$
3. No pairs in common.

Written Exercises, pages 419–420 **1.** $(4, 24)$
3. $(18, 6)$ **5.** $(7, 5)$ **7.** $(2, 7)$ **9.** $(3, 4)$
11. $(5, -7)$ **13.** $\left(-1, \frac{2}{3}\right)$ **15.** $(3, 5)$
17. $(5, -3)$ **19.** $\left(\frac{17}{3}, -\frac{7}{3}\right)$ **21.** $(-6, 20)$
23. $(4, -3)$ **25.** $(300, 700)$ **27.** $(12, 8)$
29. $(2, -6)$ **31.** no sol. **33.** infinitely many; $(7, 1)$, $(14, 2)$, $(0, 0)$

35. infinitely many

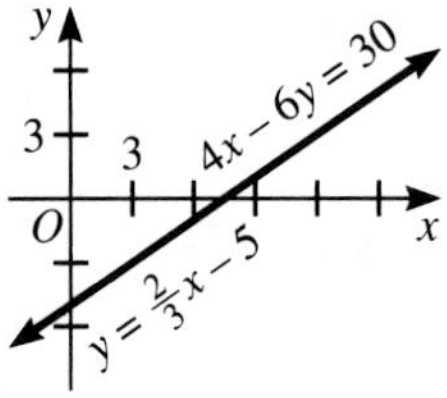

37. $a = 3$, $b = -2$ **39.** $x = 20$, $y = 60$, $z = 100$ **41.** $x = \frac{3}{2}$, $y = \frac{1}{2}$, $z = -\frac{1}{2}$

Mixed Review Exercises, page 420

1.

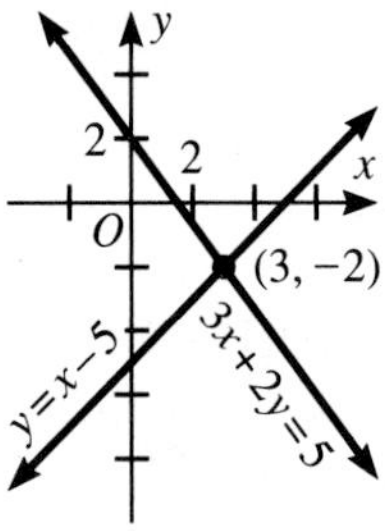

2.

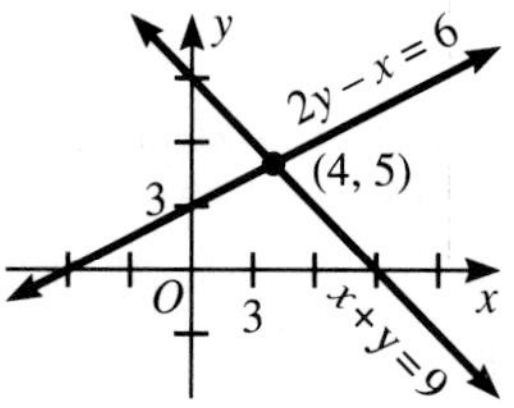

3.

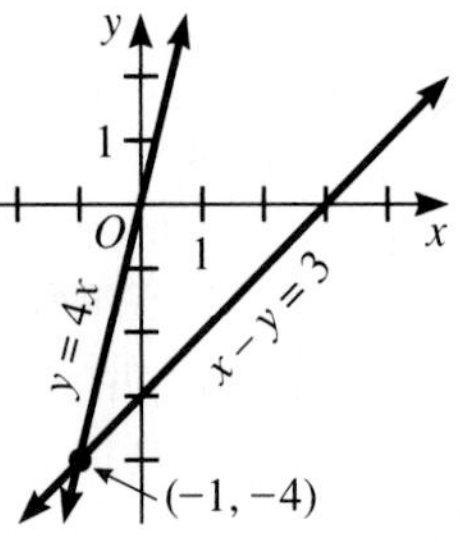

4.

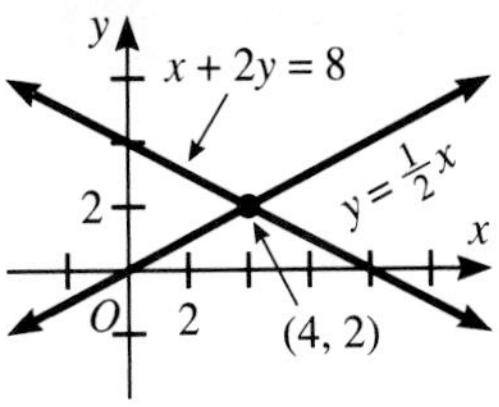

5.

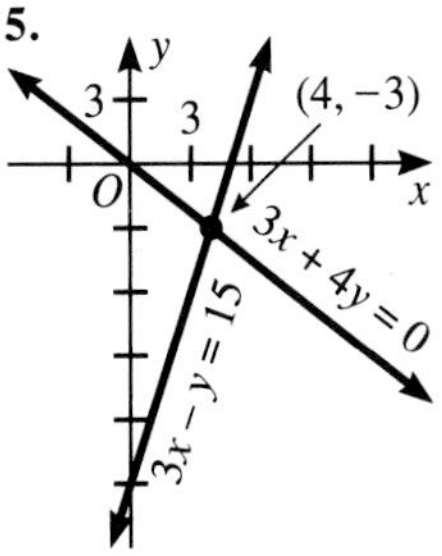

6.

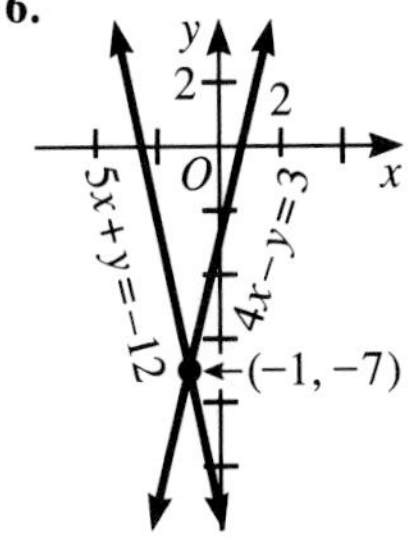

7. $y = -4x + 1$ **8.** $y = \frac{2}{3}x + 2$

9. $y = -\frac{1}{2}x - 6$ **10.** $y = 3x - 1$

11. $y = -x - 2$ **12.** $y = 2$

Problems, page 424 **1.** 12 nickels **3.** 18 quarters **5.** Dick, \$82; Connie, \$46 **7.** Tracy, \$18; Steve, \$39 **9.** 4 hours **11.** 18 and 82 **13.** \$1.40 **15.** \$2500 **17.** bike, 20 km/h; car, 80 km/h **19.** 8 and 24 **21.** 4 nickels, 14 dimes, 12 quarters

Mixed Review Exercises, page 425 **1.** $\{-10\}$ **2.** $\{9\}$ **3.** $\{31\}$ **4.** $\{6\}$ **5.** $\{17\}$ **6.** $\{-5\}$ **7.** no sol. **8.** (3, 5) **9.** no sol. **10.** (4, 1) **11.** (−2, −3) **12.** (3, 9)

Challenge, page 425 All; Answers may vary;
$23 = 44 \div \sqrt{4} + 4 \div 4$,
$24 = \sqrt{4} \cdot 4 \cdot 4 - 4 - 4$,
$25 = (\sqrt{4} + \sqrt{4} + 4 \div 4)^{\sqrt{4}}$,
$26 = 44 \div \sqrt{4} + \sqrt{4} + \sqrt{4}$,
$27 = 44 \div 4 + 4 \cdot 4$, $28 = 4 \cdot 4 + 4 \cdot 4 - 4$,
$29 = (4 + 4 \div 4)^{\sqrt{4}} + 4$

Written Exercises, pages 427–428 **1.** (5, 2) **3.** $\left(3, -\frac{7}{2}\right)$ **5.** (−2, 2) **7.** (0, −4) **9.** (3, −2) **11.** $\left(\frac{2}{3}, -\frac{1}{3}\right)$ **13.** $\left(\frac{1}{3}, \frac{1}{2}\right)$ **15.** (150, 200) **17.** (4, 6) **19.** $\left(\frac{9}{2}, \frac{1}{4}\right)$ **21.** (2, 0) **23.** (0, 2) **25.** (6, 4) **27.** $\left(\frac{5}{3}, 24\right)$ **29.** $a = 4$, $b = -3$ **31.** They both reduce to the same equation: $y = \frac{1}{4}x$

Problems, pages 428–429 **1.** 13 and 8 **3.** 424 girls **5.** 858 students **7.** 14 dogs, 46 chickens **9.** Maria, \$1.20; Tom, \$1.80

Mixed Review Exercises, page 429
1. $7x^3 + 11x^2 - 3x$ **2.** 48 **3.** 1340 **4.** $-2n - 4$ **5.** $9x^5y^5$ **6.** $9a^6$ **7.** $-8p^6q^3$ **8.** $3x^2 + 18x$ **9.** $-36a^6b^4$ **10.** −1 **11.** −24 **12.** $-9m + 6n$

Written Exercises, pages 432–433 **1.** (3, 2) **3.** (1, 2) **5.** (1, −2) **7.** (3, 7) **9.** (−3, −12) **11.** (2, −2) **13.** (2, 3) **15.** (4, −2) **17.** (3, −5) **19.** $\left(\frac{1}{2}, -2\right)$ **21.** $\left(4, -\frac{1}{2}\right)$ **23.** $\left(-\frac{1}{2}, \frac{4}{3}\right)$ **25.** Solving the system by using multiplication with the addition-or-subtraction method gives a false statement. Thus, there is no ordered pair that is a solution of both equations. **27.** (−3, −3) **29.** (20, 50) **31.** (4, 3) **33.** (3, 4) **35.** (−4, −6) **37.** $a = 2$, $b = -3$ **39.** $\left(\frac{1}{2}, \frac{1}{3}\right)$ **41.** $\left(\frac{2}{a}, 3\right)$ **43.** $\left(\frac{a+b}{a^2+b^2}, \frac{a-b}{a^2+b^2}\right)$ **45.** (2, 3, −1)

Mixed Practice, page 433

1.

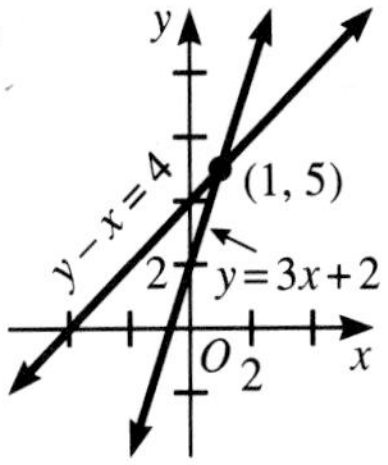

3.

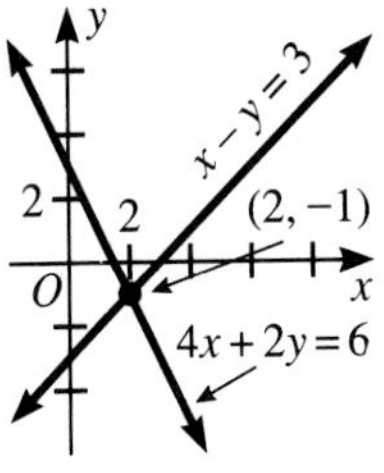

5. (0, 3) **7.** (1, −1) **9.** (1, −1) **11.** (6, 3) **13.** $\left(\frac{9}{13}, \frac{31}{13}\right)$ **15.** (14, 10) **17.** (7, 4) **19.** $\left(\frac{5}{2}, -3\right)$ **21.** (7, 3) **23.** (4, 3) **25.** (−3, 0) **27.** $\left(\frac{40}{9}, -\frac{74}{45}\right)$

Problems, pages 434–436 **1.** 16 and 9 **3.** Stan, \$42; Cory, \$108 **5.** 900 sq. units **7.** 33 **9.** \$2.20 **11.** 215 tickets **13.** 600 g **15.** A, \$2000; B, \$3000 **17.** grape, \$1.20; orange, \$1.50 **19.** \$49 **21.** 2 kg **23.** 80 km/h, 40 km/h **25.** 30 **27.** If x and y are both whole numbers, then $2x + 6y$ is even. Since 35 is odd, x and y cannot both be whole numbers. **29.** 7 plums **31.** 28 by 30

Mixed Review Exercises, page 436
1. $6(1 - 3t)^2$ **2.** $12mn(m - 2n^2)$
3. $(5c + 6d)(5c - 6d)$ **4.** $(x + 3)(x + 4)$
5. $(2y + 5)(y + 3)$ **6.** $(p + 2)(p - 5)$ **7.** 4
8. $-\frac{1}{3}$ **9.** $\frac{2}{3}$ **10.** 7

Computer Exercises, page 436 **3. a.** $(-3, -4)$ **b.** $(2, 3)$ **c.** no sol. **d.** $(3, 2)$

Self-Test 1, page 437 **1.** $(2, 5)$ **2.** $(-1, 3)$
3. $\left(-3, \frac{1}{2}\right)$ **4.** $\left(-\frac{9}{5}, -\frac{7}{5}\right)$ **5.** no sol.
6. $(0, 0)$ **7.** $(0, 4)$ **8.** $(-3, -2)$ **9.** $(3, 2)$

Problems, pages 440–442 **1.** $r + c = 15$
3. $\frac{24}{r - c} = 3$ **5.** 4 km/h

7. No current

	Rate × Time = Distance		
Downstream	10	3	30
Upstream	10	3	30

Total distance = 60 km
Total time = 6 h
Average speed = 10 km/h

5 km/h current

Rate × Time = Distance		
15	2	30
5	6	30

Total distance = 60 km
Total time = 8 h
Average speed = 7.5 km/h

9.

	Rate × Time = Distance		
No wind	200	3	600
With wind	250	2.4	600

Total distance = 1200 km
Total time = 5.4 h
Average speed = 222.2 km/h

11. 1300 km/h; 100 km/h **13.** 5 mi/h; 1 mi/h **15.** 770 km/h; 70 km/h **17.** 0.5 h; 2.5 mi **19.** 15 km/h **21.** 5 km/h **23.** total distance is $2d$; total time is $\frac{d}{p + w} + \frac{d}{p - w} = \frac{2pd}{p^2 - w^2}$;
Average speed is $\frac{2d}{\frac{2pd}{p^2 - w^2}} = \frac{p^2 - w^2}{p}$

Mixed Review Exercises, page 443 **1.** $(5, -2)$
2. $\left(-\frac{3}{7}, \frac{9}{7}\right)$ **3.** $(2, -2)$ **4.** $\frac{9b^2 + b - 2}{4(3b + 1)}$
5. $\frac{1}{2 - x}$ **6.** $16st^3$ **7.** $\frac{5(2r + t)}{(r + t)(r - t)}$ **8.** $\frac{p + 2}{24}$
9. $\frac{2a^2 + 4a - 1}{a + 3}$

Problems, pages 447–449 **1.** $t + u = 15$
3. $4(t + u) = 10t + u$
5. $10t + u + 18 = 10u + t$ **7.** 36 **9.** 48
11. Nicole, 11 years old; Pierre, 6 years old
13. Steve, 12 years old; Theresa, 4 years old
15. $\frac{5}{13}$ **17.** $\frac{5}{8}$ **19.** Lyle, 19 years old; Sean, 9 years old **21.** Golden Gate, 1937; Brooklyn, 1883 **23.** 360 **25.** 345 **27.** son, 10 years old; father, 36 years old **29.** $\frac{6}{24}$ **31.** Laura, 18 years old; Maria, 12 years old **33.** Cindy, 26 years old; Paul, 18 years old; Sue, 8 years old

Mixed Review Exercises, page 449 **1.** 18
2. 6 **3.** 11 **4.** 4 **5.** 34 **6.** 48 **7.** $\{-8\}$
8. $\left\{-\frac{27}{13}\right\}$ **9.** $\{-6\}$ **10.** $\{-7.7, 7.7\}$
11. $\{0.05\}$ **12.** $\{-84\}$

Self-Test 2, page 450 **1.** 780 mi/h; 18 mi/h
2. 96 **3.** Jerry, 15 years old; Jeff, 20 years old
4. $\frac{4}{7}$

Chapter Review, page 451 **1.** c **3.** d **5.** d
7. b **9.** d

Cumulative Review, page 453
1. $7p^2q + 4p - 21q^3$ **3.** $4j^5k^3 - 24j^6k + 28j^4k^4$
5. $42z^2 + 78z - 12$ **7.** $5t + 3$
9. $\frac{(x - 5)(x - 3)}{(x + 3)}$ **11.** 6.8×10^{10} **13.** prime
15. prime **17.** prime **19.** $\{22, -22\}$
21. $\left\{-\frac{2}{7}, \frac{2}{7}\right\}$ **23.** $\left\{-\frac{4}{3}, \frac{2}{3}\right\}$ **25.** $3x + y = 3$
27. $(2, 7)$ **29.** 15 **31.** 10 kg

Maintaining Skills, page 454 **1.** $\frac{a}{4}$ **3.** 8
5. $\frac{3(z - 3)}{5z}$ **7.** $\frac{3n - 1}{n - 2}$ **9.** $5ab$ **11.** $\frac{2b + 3}{b + 1}$

13. $\frac{c+2}{c+1}$ 15. $\frac{(r-6)(r+6)^2}{(r-3)(r+3)^2}$ 17. $\frac{2x+3y}{x-y}$
19. $\frac{2+w^2}{3-w}$ 21. $\frac{v^2-v+8}{(v+1)(v-1)}$ 23. $\frac{2b(2-b)}{2b-1}$
25. $\frac{d^2-2}{(2d+1)(d+1)}$ 27. $\frac{6t}{t^2-4}$
29. $\frac{2x^2+13x-28}{(x-4)(x+3)}$

Mixed Problem Solving, page 455 **1.** 53.4% **3.** No sol.; contradictory facts **5.** 50 km/h **7.** \$567 **9.** 54 min **11.** 3 kg **13.** \$1200 at $7\frac{1}{4}$%, \$4800 at 10%

Chapter 10 Inequalities

Written Exercises, pages 459–460 **1.** $4 > -7$
3. $-12 \le -9$ **5.** $2 < 3 < 3.5$
7. $-10 < -8 < 0$ **9.** $0 < 4 < 4.6$ **11.** $n > 10$
13. $|-2| > 1$ **15.** T **17.** F **19.** T **21.** F
23. {−4, −3, −2, −1, 0, 1}
25. {−3, −2, −1, 0, 1, 2, 3, 4}
27. {−4, −3, −2, −1, 0, 1, 2, 3, 4}
29. {−4, 4}
31.

33.

35.
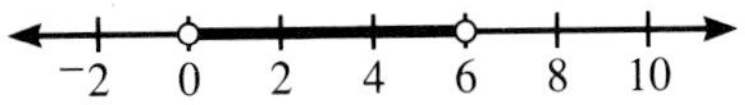

37.

39–41. Answers may vary. **39. a.** (−2, −3) **b.** (3, 2) **41. a.** (2, 1) **b.** (2, −1)

Computer Exercises, page 460
1. {0, 1, 2, 3, 4, 5} **3.** {4, 5}
5. {6, 7, 8, 9, 10}

Mixed Review Exercises, page 461 **1.** {18}
2. {6} **3.** {−6} **4.** {−50} **5.** {27} **6.** {8}
7. {−34} **8.** {−3} **9.** {10} **10.** {−12}
11. {1} **12.** {0}

Written Exercises, pages 466–467 **1.** d **3.** j
5. b **7.** e **9.** f
11. {the real numbers greater than 15}
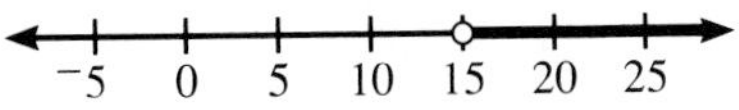

13. {the real numbers less than −8}
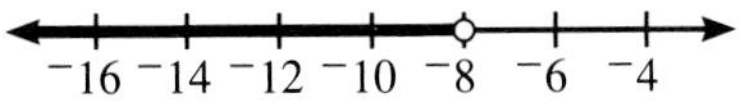

15. {the real numbers less than −324}
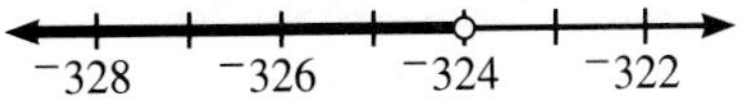

17. {the real numbers less than or equal to −1}
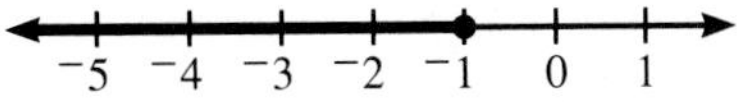

19. {the real numbers greater than −4}
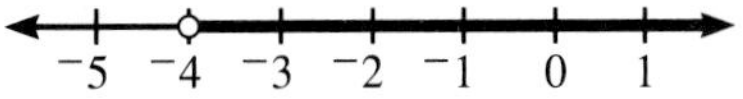

21. {the real numbers less than or equal to 0}
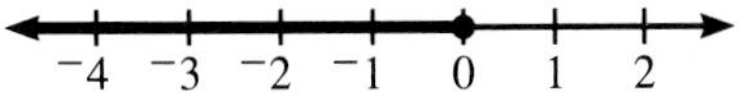

23. {the real numbers less than 6}
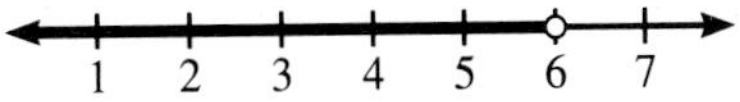

25. {the real numbers greater than −15}
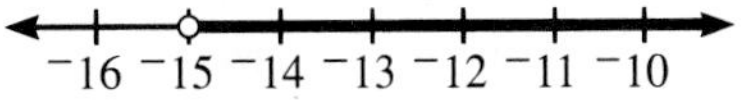

27. {the real numbers less than 8}
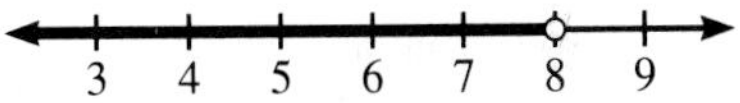

29. {the real numbers less than 6}
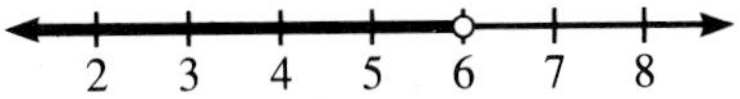

31. {the real numbers greater than −12}
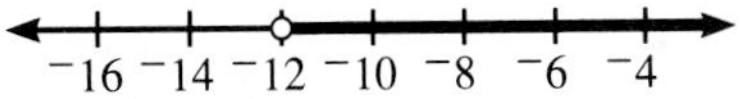

33. {the real numbers less than or equal to 7}

35. {the real numbers}

37. {the real numbers less than −7}
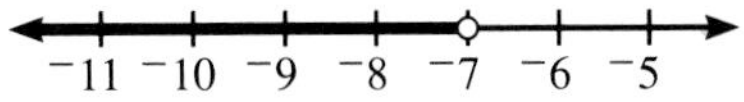

39. {the real numbers greater than or equal to $\frac{2}{5}$}
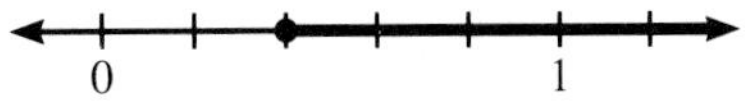

41. {the real numbers greater than $\frac{4}{3}$}

43. {the real numbers greater than −8}
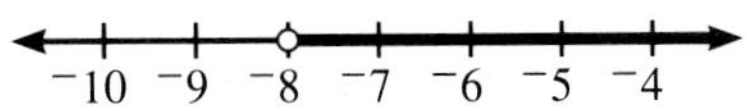

45. {the real numbers greater than -2}

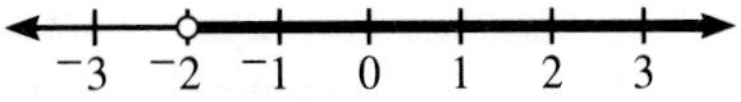

47. {the real numbers greater than or equal to -4}

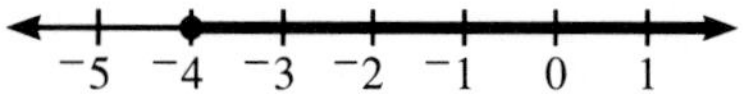

49. no solution **51.** all real numbers **53.** all pos. real numbers **55.** 0 **57.** all neg. real numbers **59.** T **61.** T **63.** F; $a = \frac{1}{2}$, $b = \frac{1}{3}$ **65.** T

Mixed Review Exercises, page 467 **1.** T **2.** T **3.** F **4.** F **5.** T **6.** F **7.** {9} **8.** $\left\{-\frac{5}{2}\right\}$ **9.** {3} **10.** {−2} **11.** {3} **12.** {1}

Reading Algebra, page 468

1. a. greater than **b.** open; right **c.** {the real numbers greater than 15}

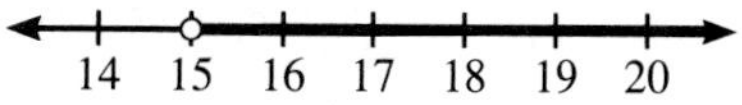

3. a. greater than or equal to **b.** closed; left **c.** {the real numbers less than or equal to 4}

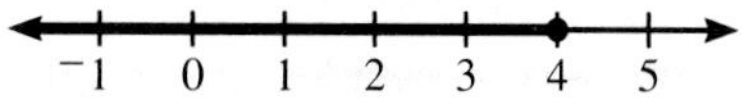

5. a. less than **b.** open; right **c.** {the real numbers greater than −15}

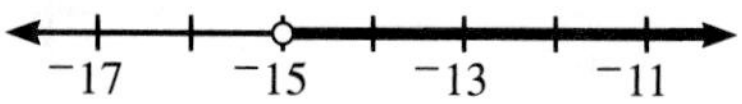

7. a. greater than **b.** open; left **c.** {the real numbers less than 6}

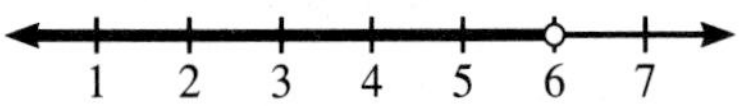

9. a. less than **b.** open; right **c.** {the real numbers greater than −4}

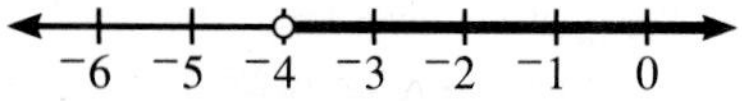

11. a. greater than **b.** open; left **c.** {the real numbers less than 7}

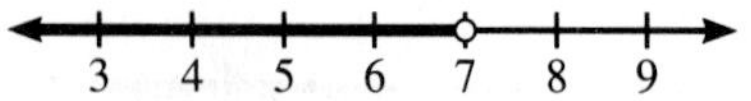

Written Exercises, pages 471–472 **1. a.** i **b.** $i + 2 < 21$ **3. a.** x **b.** $x + 0.1x > 3000$ **5. a.** d **b.** $75 + d \geq 110$ **7. a.** j **b.** $\frac{j}{2} + 15 \leq 36$ **9. a.** m **b.** $(m - 2) + m + (m + 2) \geq 51$ **11. a.** t **b.** $86t + 78t \geq 650$ **13. a.** d **b.** $10d + 5(2d) + 25\left(\frac{2d}{3}\right) \leq 280$ **15. a.** s **b.** $25 - s \geq 2s + 1$ **17. a.** s **b.** $s + (s + 2) \leq \frac{s}{8} - 100$ **19.** $|a + b| \leq |a| + |b|$

Problems, pages 473–474 **1.** less than 87 copies **3.** 300 mi or less **5.** 26 and 27 **7.** at least 4.2 h **9.** 60 red marbles; 40 blue marbles **11.** 10 cm by 14 cm **13.** 3 P.M. **15.** 84 **17.** 30 h **19.** 10.92 km **21.** \$1999 **23.** 97 books

Mixed Review Exercises, page 475 **1.** {−7, 7} **2.** {3} **3.** {−12, 12} **4.** {−4, 4} **5.** {4} **6.** $\{-\frac{3}{2}\}$ **7.** $(x + 3)(x + 12)$ **8.** $x(x + 3)(x - 8)$ **9.** $(7x - 5)(7x + 5)$ **10.** $(2y + 3)(y - 1)$ **11.** $(x + 3y)^2$ **12.** $4x(2x - 1)(2x + 1)$

Self-Test 1, page 475 **1.** $-7 < -3 < -2$ **2.** {−3, −2, −1, 0, 1, 2}

3. {the real numbers less than 1}

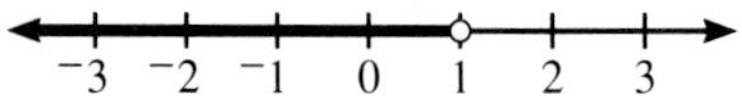

4. {the real numbers greater than or equal to −5}

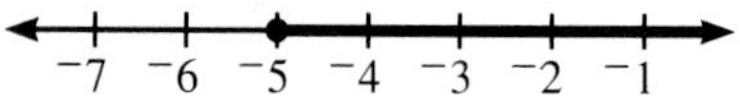

5. at least 17 dimes

Challenge, page 475 Step 4: If you divide by $3 - a$, which is negative (because $a > 3$), the inequality must be reversed so that Step 5 is $a < 3 + a$.

Extra, pages 476–477 **1.** {6, 9} **3.** {0, 3, 4, 5, 6, 7, 8, 9} **5.** {6} **7.** {5, 6, 9} **9.** {5, 6, 7, 8} **11.** {−4, −3, −2, −1, 0}; {−3, −2} **13.** {3, 4, 5, 6, 7, 8}; disjoint sets **15.** {2, 3, 4, 6, 8, 10, 12}; {4, 6, 8} **17.** {the real numbers between −1 and 2} **19.** {the real numbers greater than −3} **21.** {the real numbers between −3 and 2} **23.** {the real numbers between −1 and 2}

25.

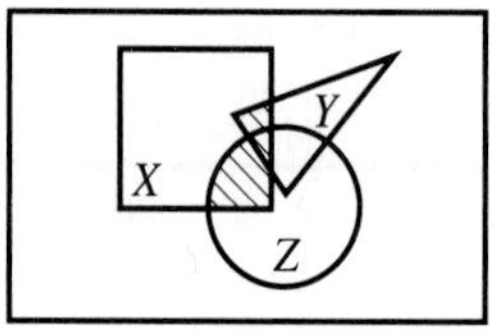

27. $X \cap (Y \cup Z) = (X \cap Y) \cup (X \cap Z)$

29.

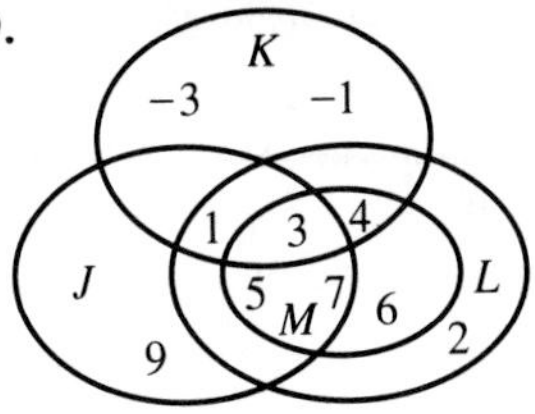

Written Exercises, pages 480–481

1.

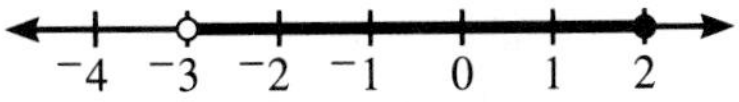

3.

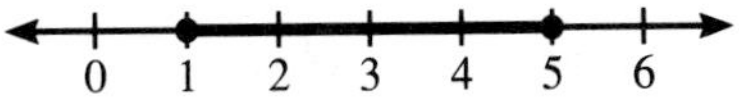

5. {the real numbers between −3 and 2}

7. {5 and the real numbers between −1 and 5}

9. {−3 and the real numbers between −3 and 2}

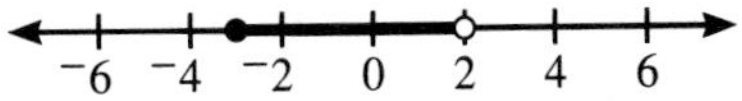

11. {−2 and the real numbers between −2 and 1}

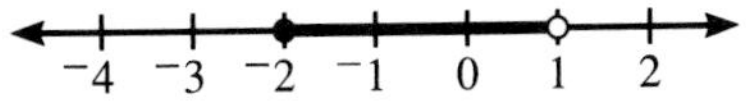

13. {the real numbers less than −3 or greater than 7}

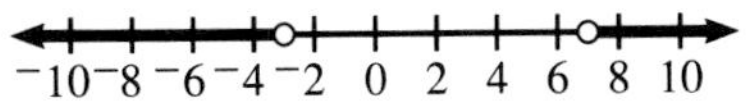

15. {−2, 1, and the real numbers less than −2 or greater than 1}

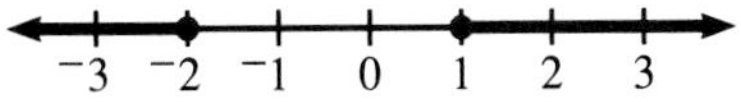

17. $\left\{-\frac{4}{3}\right.$, 2, and the real numbers less than $-\frac{4}{3}$ or greater than $\left.2\right\}$

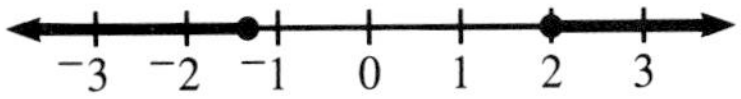

19. {−2, 6, and the real numbers between −2 and 6}

21. {6 and the real numbers between −1 and 6}

23. {−3 and the real numbers between −3 and 3}

25. no solution

27. {7 and the real numbers between 2 and 7}

29. {the real numbers less than −2 or greater than 12}

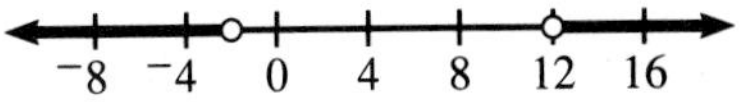

31. {−3 and the real numbers less than −3 or greater than 3}

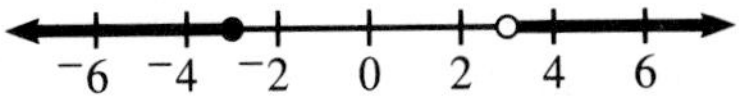

33. $\left\{\text{the real numbers greater than } -\frac{2}{3}\right\}$

35. {5 and the real numbers between 1 and 5}

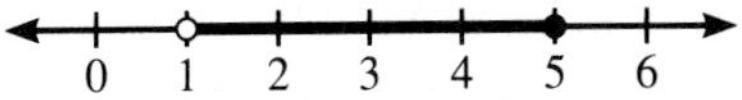

37. {the real numbers less than or equal to 4}

39. a. $a = 2$, $b = 1$, $c = 4$, $d = 3$ **b.** $a = 1$, $b = -2$, $c = 2$, $d = -3$

Computer Exercises, page 481 (1, 9), (2, 5), (2, 6), (2, 7), (2, 8), (3, 3), (3, 4), (3, 5), (3, 6), (3, 7), (4, 3), (4, 4), (4, 5), (4, 6), (5, 2), (5, 3), (5, 4), (5, 5), (6, 2), (6, 3), (6, 4), (7, 2), (7, 3), (8, 2), and (9, 1)

Mixed Review Exercises, page 481 **1.** $n \geq 10$ **2.** $t \leq 78$ **3.** $w \leq 150$ **4.** $t \geq 3$ **5.** $c \geq 17$ **6.** $g < 2$ **7.** $s \leq 340$ **8.** $s \geq 5$ **9.** 11 **10.** 11 **11.** 3 **12.** 3 **13.** 8 **14.** 8

Written Exercises, pages 484–485 **1. a.** The distance between x and 5 is 1. **b.** $x - 5 = 1$ or $x - 5 = -1$ **3. a.** The distance between r and −3 is greater than 5. **b.** $r + 3 > 5$ or $r + 3 < -5$ **5. a.** The distance between n and 4 is less than or equal to 1. **b.** $-1 \leq n - 4 \leq 1$ **7.** $|x| < 2$ **9.** $|x + 1| = 2$ **11.** $|x - 1| \geq 3$ **13.** {14, −2}

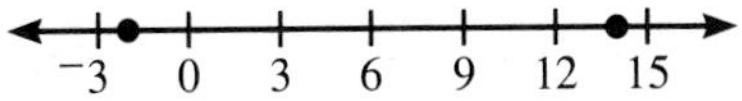

15. $\{-8, 2\}$

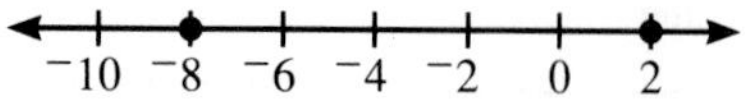

17. {the real numbers between -2.5 and 2.5}

19. {the real numbers less than -13 or greater than 3}

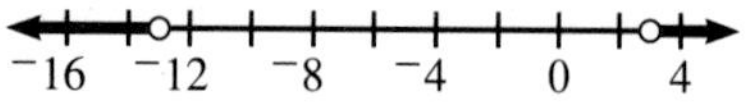

21. {4, 8, and the real numbers between 4 and 8}

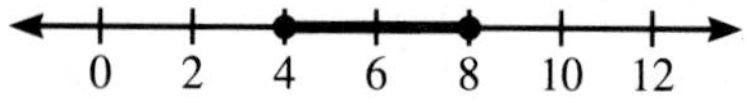

23. {-6, 2, and the real numbers less than -6 or greater than 2}

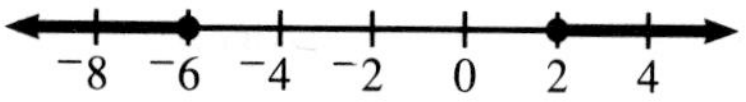

25. {-3, 3, and the real numbers less than -3 or greater than 3}

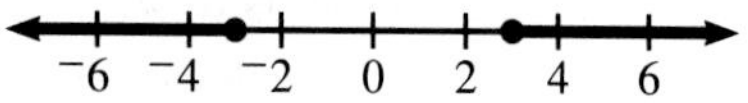

27. {the real numbers less than -3 or greater than 7}

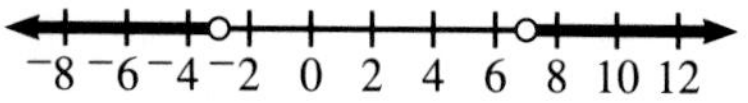

29. $\left\{-\frac{11}{3}, \frac{11}{3}\right.$, and the real numbers between $\left.-\frac{11}{3} \text{ and } \frac{11}{3}\right\}$

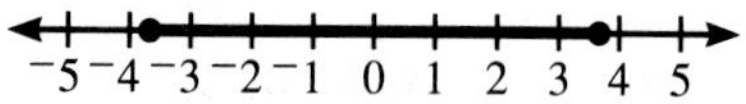

31. {0, 4, and the real numbers less than 0 or greater than 4}

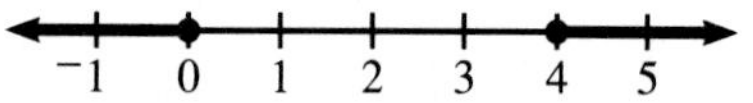

33. {-2, 2, and the real numbers between -2 and 2}

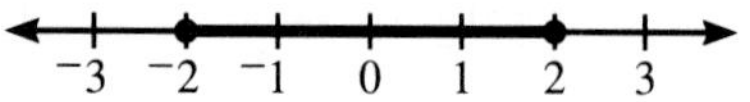

35. no solution

37. {the real numbers less than 4}

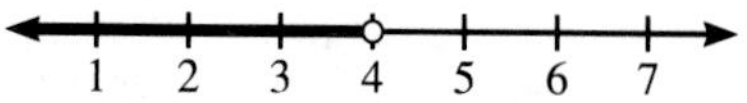

39. {the real numbers}

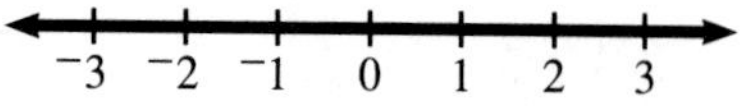

Mixed Review Exercises, page 485

1. {the real numbers less than 9}

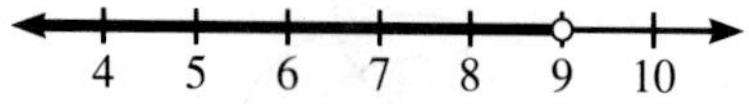

2. {the real numbers less than -8}

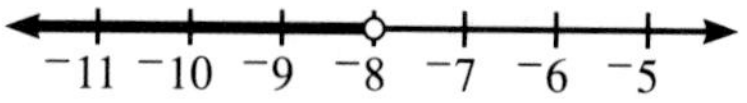

3. {the real numbers greater than 0}

4. {the real numbers between -6 and -3}

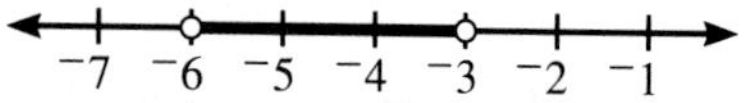

5. {9, and the real numbers less than 9 or greater than 12}

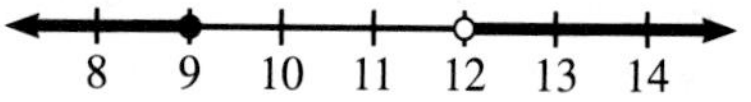

6. {-10, -3, and the real numbers between -10 and -3}

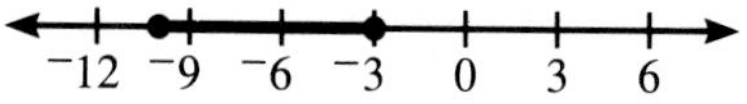

7. $\frac{4}{3y^3}$ 8. $\frac{32a^2}{3b}$ 9. $\frac{x+12}{9}$ 10. $\frac{22x}{7}$

Written Exercises, page 488

1. $\{-4, 4\}$

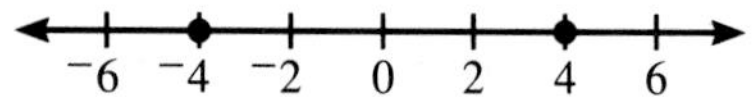

3. {-4, 4, and the real numbers less than -4 or greater than 4}

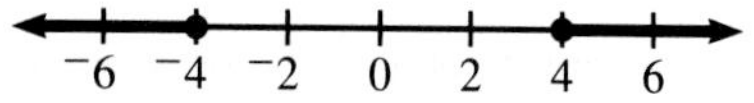

5. $\{-4, 5\}$

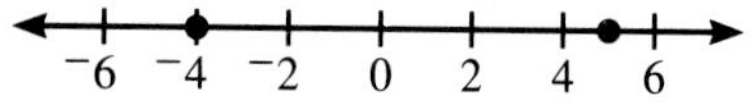

7. $\left\{2, \frac{7}{2}\right.$, and the real numbers between 2 and $\left.\frac{7}{2}\right\}$

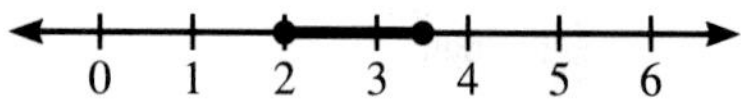

9. $\left\{-\frac{9}{2}\right.$, 3, and the real numbers between $-\frac{9}{2}$ and $\left.3\right\}$

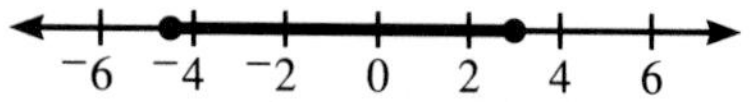

11. {-10, 30, and the real numbers less than -10 or greater than 30}

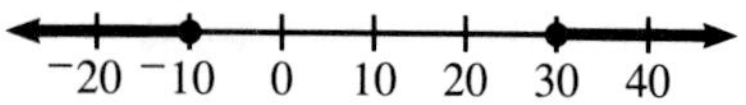

13. {the real numbers between −8 and 10}

15. $\left\{-\frac{4}{5}, \frac{2}{5}\right\}$

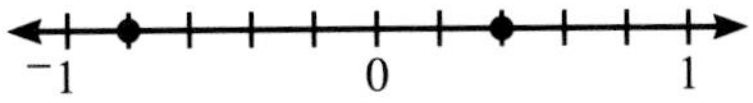

17. no solution **19.** T **21.** F; $a = -1$ **23.** T
25. 50°F; 14°F

Mixed Review Exercises, page 488 **1.** 4; 2
2. 5; −2 **3.** $-\frac{2}{3}$; −3 **4.** 0; 9 **5.** 3; −11
6. $-\frac{1}{2}$; 4

7.

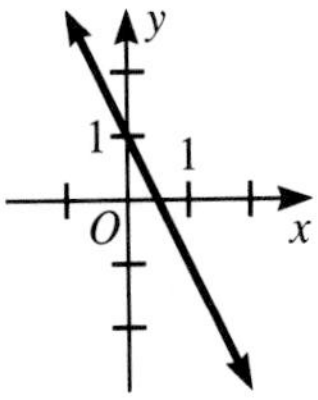

8.

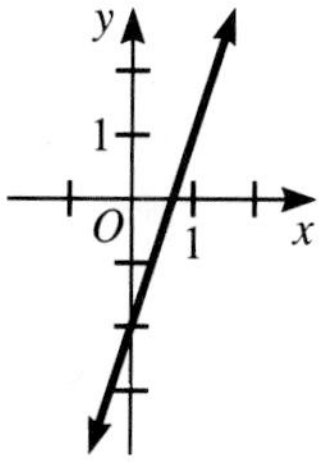

9.

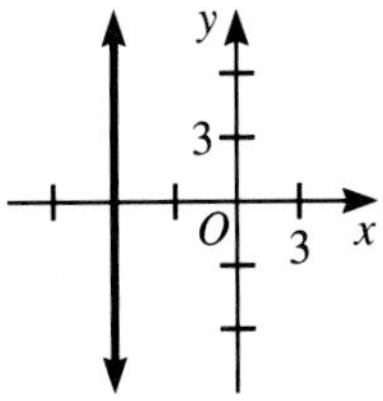

10.

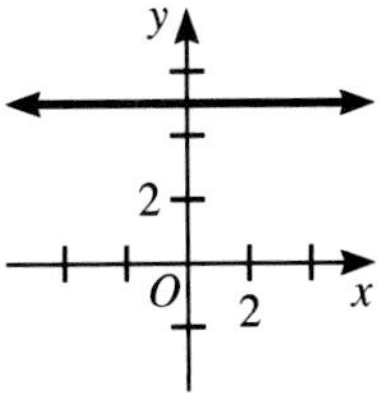

11.

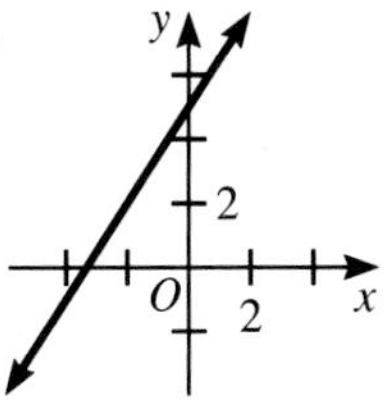

12.

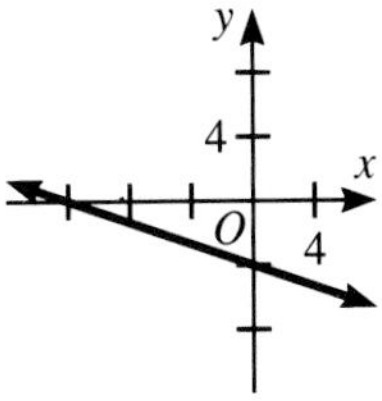

Self-Test 2, page 489

1. {the real numbers less than 2 or greater than 3}

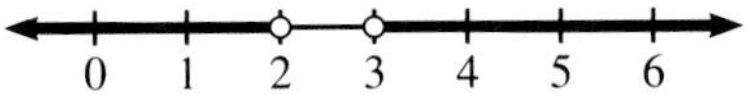

2. {−6 and the real numbers between −6 and 1}

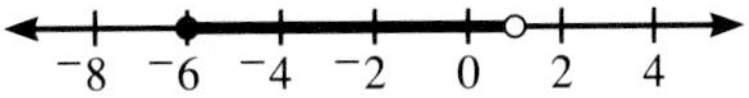

3. {−2, 2, and the real numbers less than −2 or greater than 2}

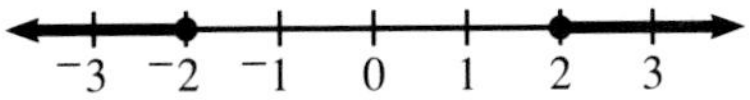

4. {−2 and the real numbers between −2 and 1}

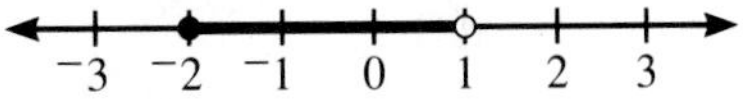

5. {−1, 5}

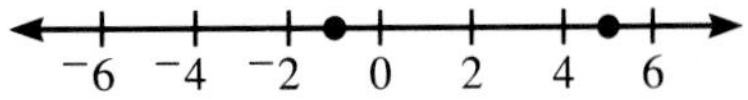

6. {−4, 10, and the real numbers less than −4 or greater than 10}

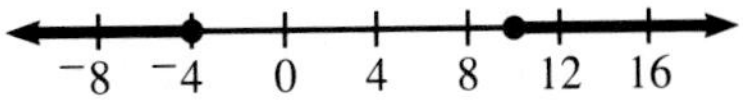

7. {−5, 7}

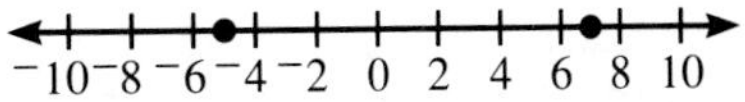

8. {the real numbers between −6 and −2}

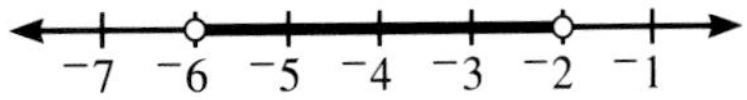

9. $\left\{\frac{3}{2}\right.$, 5, and the real numbers between $\frac{3}{2}$ and $\left.5\right\}$

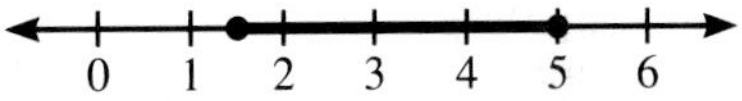

10. {−3, 7}

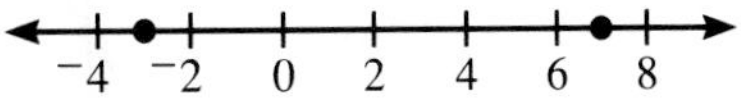

11. $\left\{\frac{3}{2}, 2\right\}$

12. $\left\{\text{the real numbers between } -2 \text{ and } \frac{7}{3}\right\}$

Written Exercises, pages 492–493

1.

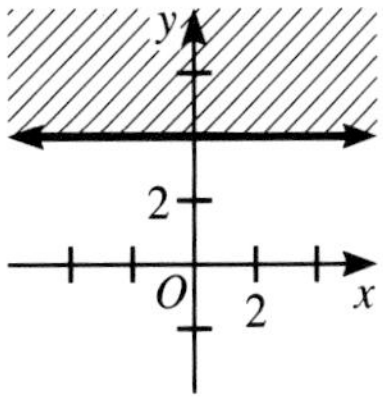

3.

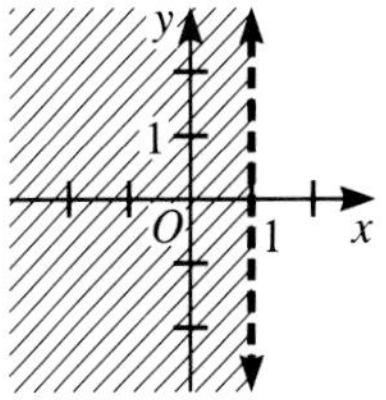

5.

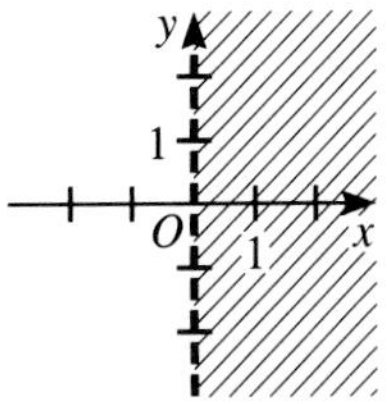

7.

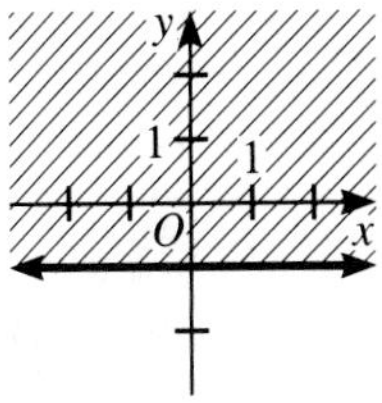

9. 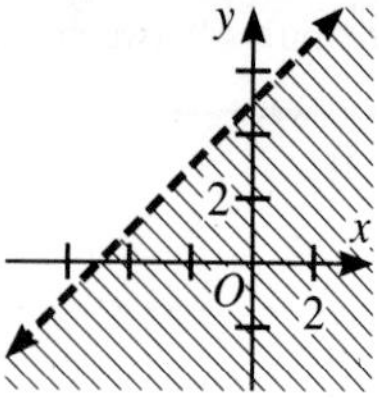 11. 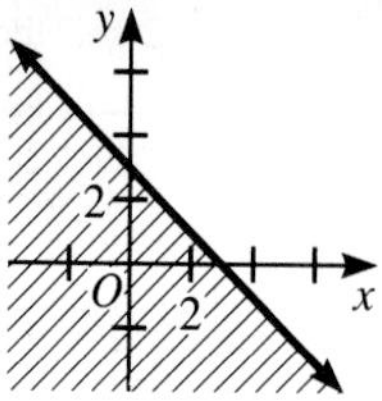

39. 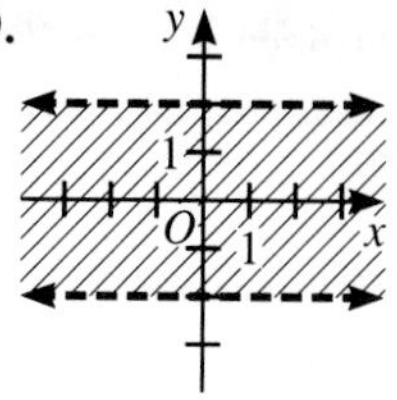

13. $y < -x + 1$

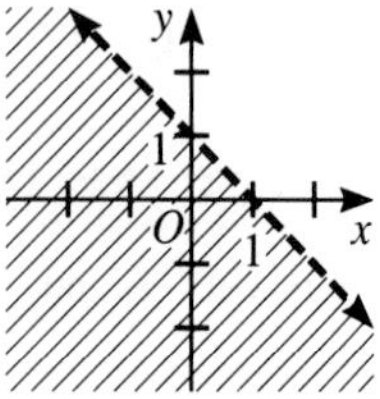

15. $y \geq \frac{1}{3}x + 2$

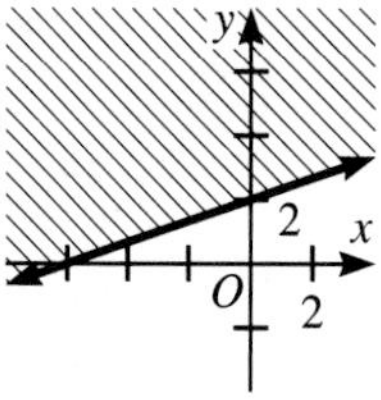

17. $y < 4x - 6$

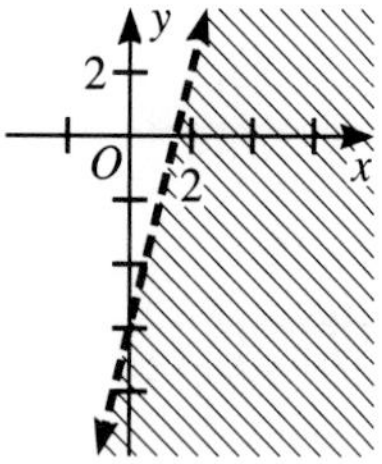

19. $y \leq \frac{3}{2}x - 4$

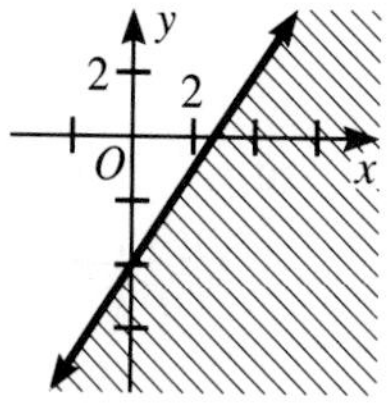

21. $y \leq -\frac{3}{2}x - 2$

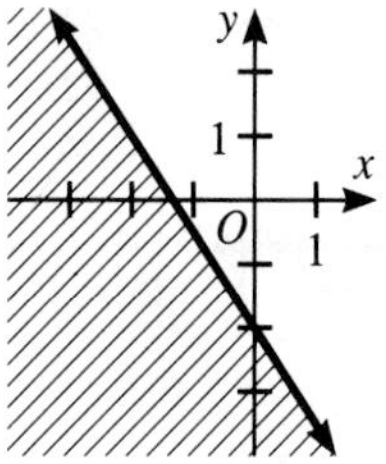

23. $y \leq \frac{1}{4}x - \frac{1}{2}$

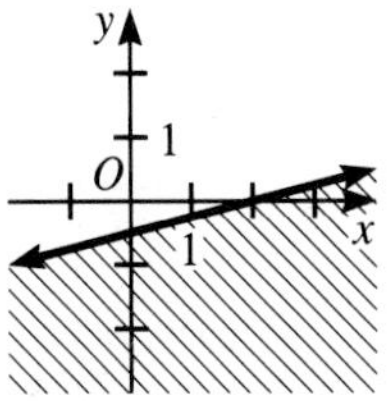

25. $y > -1$ **27.** $y < -\frac{1}{2}x + 2$

29. $y \geq \frac{4}{3}x + 4$ **31.** $y < \frac{1}{2}x + 2$

33. $y \leq -\frac{3}{2}x + 5$

35. 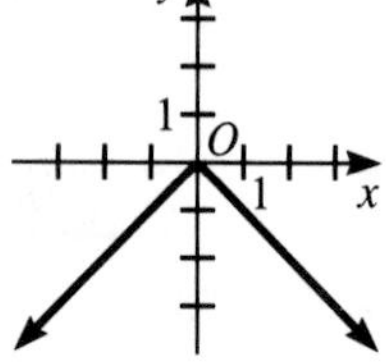 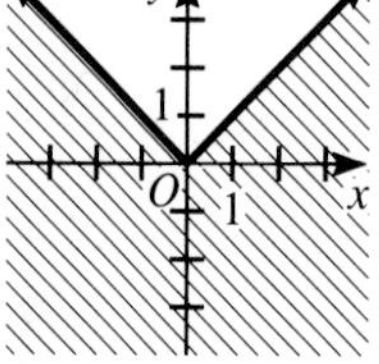

Mixed Review Exercises, page 494

1. (−2, −6) **2.** (7, 2) **3.** (1, −2)

4. {5, −5}

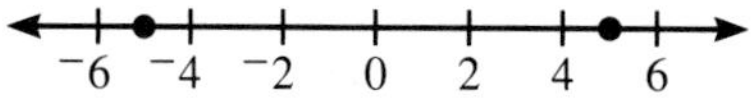

5. {−6, 4}

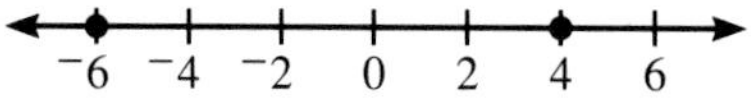

6. {the real numbers between −7 and 7}

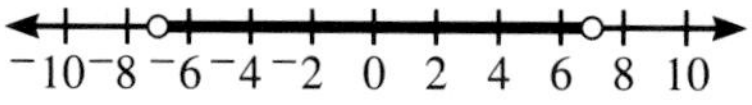

7. $\left\{-\frac{11}{2}, \frac{1}{2}\right.$, and the real numbers less than $-\frac{11}{2}$ or greater than $\left.\frac{1}{2}\right\}$

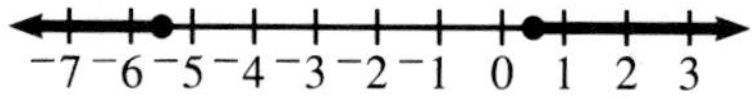

8. {−7 and the real numbers between −7 and 4}

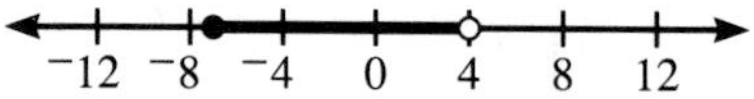

9. {0 and the real numbers less than 0 or greater than 1}

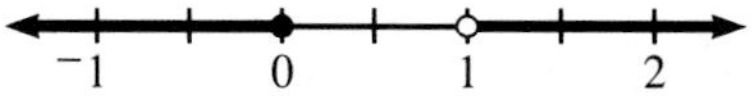

Extra, page 494

1. 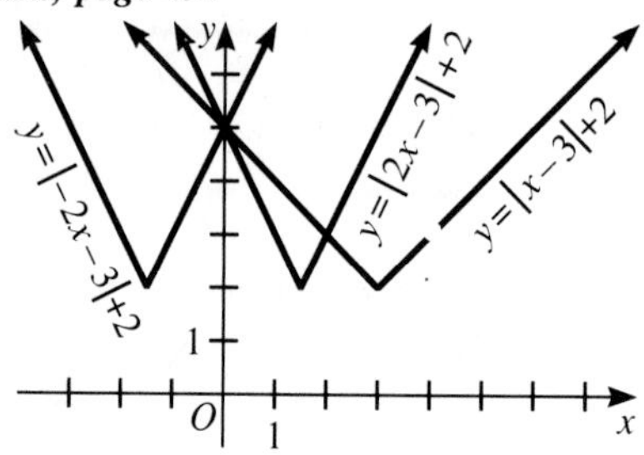

Written Exercises, pages 496–498

1.

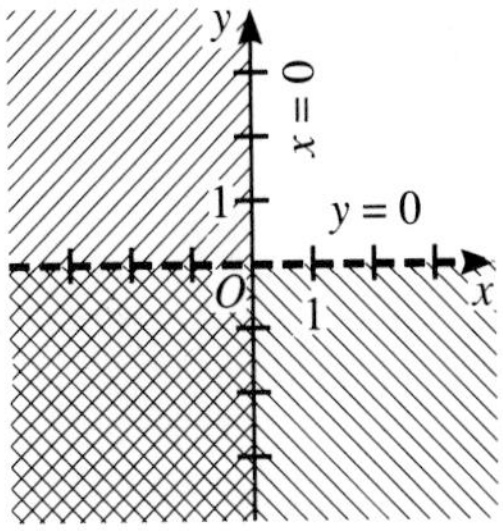

3.

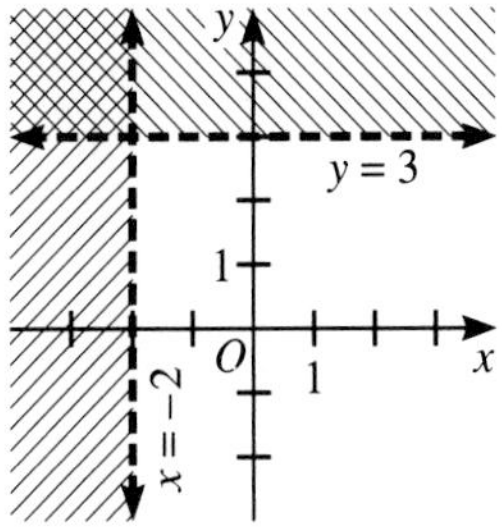

5.

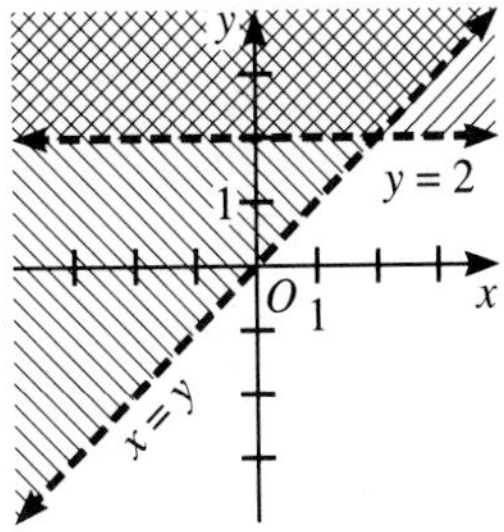

7.

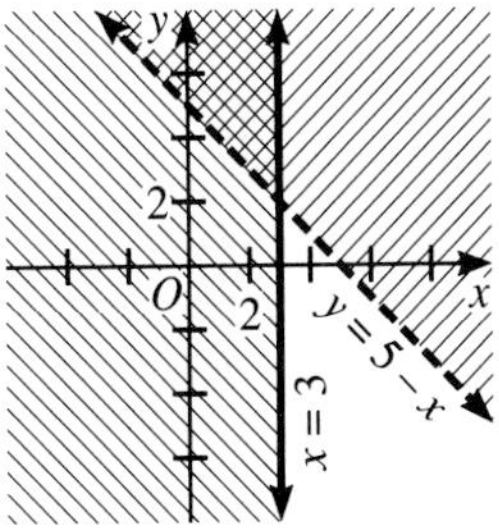

9.

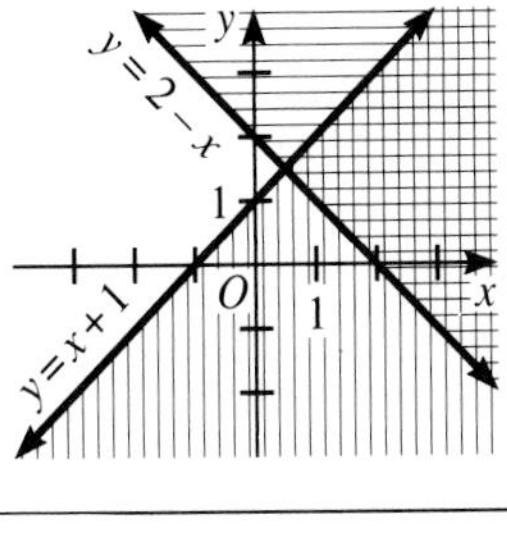

11.

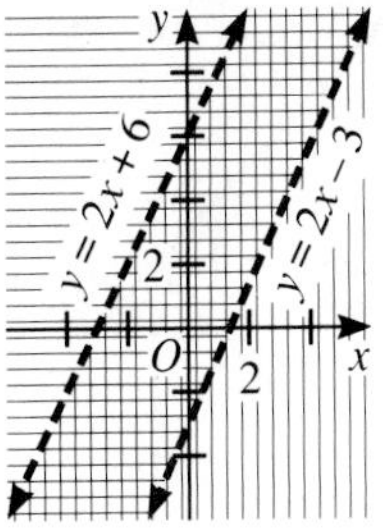

13.

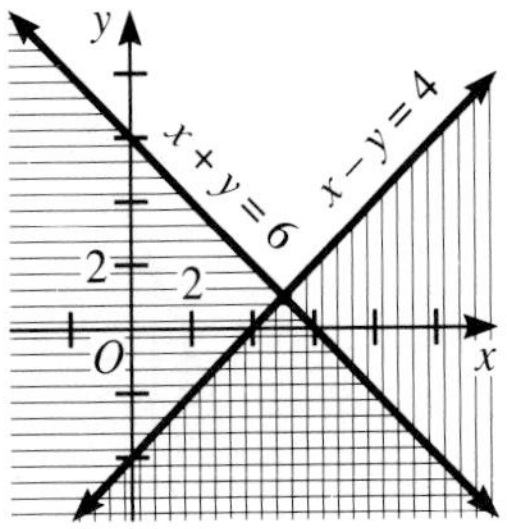

15.

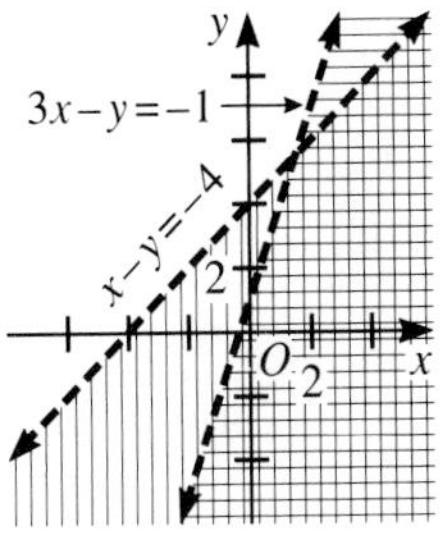

17.

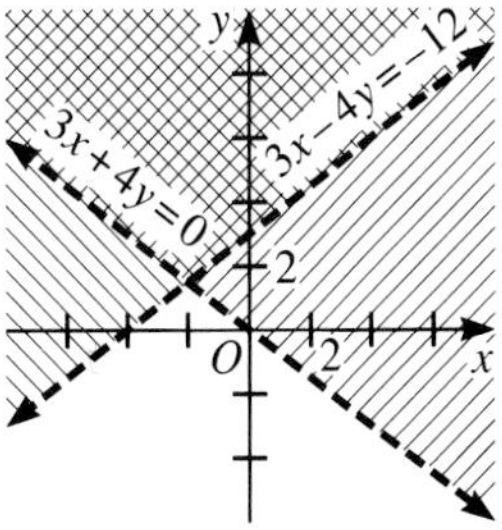

19. $y \geq -3$
$y < x - 3$

21. $y < \frac{2}{3}x - 2$
$y < -2x + 3$

23. $x \leq 3$

$y \leq \frac{1}{2}x + 2$

$y \geq -\frac{1}{4}x - 1$

25. (0, 0), (4, 4), (4, −4)

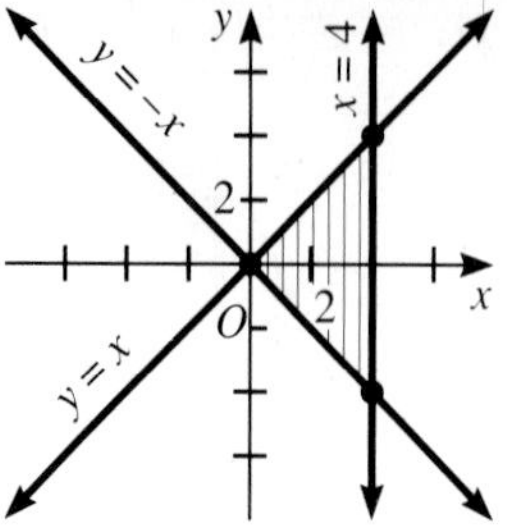

27. no solution

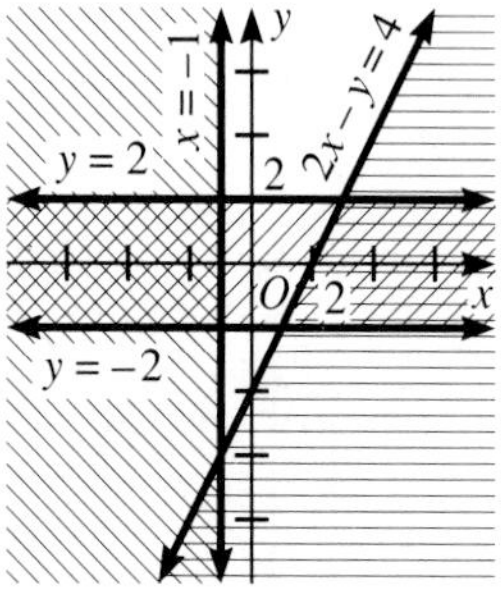

Mixed Review Exercises, page 498 **1.** $\frac{5}{30}$, $\frac{8}{30}$, $\frac{18}{30}$ **2.** $\frac{12a}{36}$, $\frac{8}{36}$, $\frac{3(a+1)}{36}$ **3.** $\frac{k(k+5)}{(k+5)^2}$, $\frac{3k}{(k+5)^2}$ **4.** $\frac{5y(2y+3)}{5y(y-6)}$, $\frac{20(y-6)}{5y(y-6)}$, $\frac{y^2(y-6)}{5y(y-6)}$ **5.** $\frac{8(x-2)}{(x+2)(x-2)}$, $\frac{x(x+2)}{(x+2)(x-2)}$ **6.** $-\frac{1}{16-x^2}$, $\frac{5(4+x)}{16-x^2}$, $\frac{x(4-x)}{16-x^2}$ **7.** $\frac{9}{5}$ **8.** $-\frac{11}{120}$ **9.** $-\frac{19}{60}$ **10.** $\frac{91}{120}$ **11.** $\frac{11}{24}$ **12.** $\frac{9}{20}$

Self-Test 3, page 498

1.

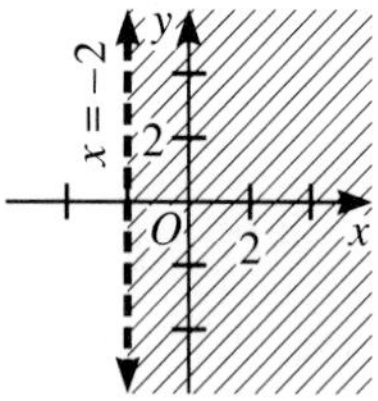

2.

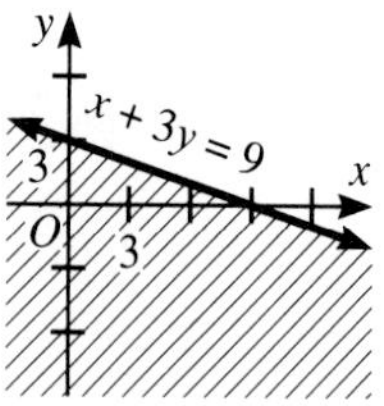

3.

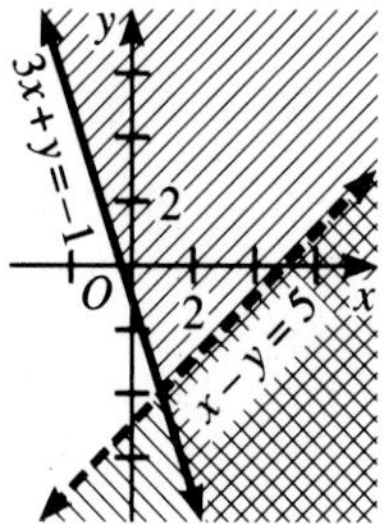

Calculator Key-In, page 498 **1.** F **3.** F

Application, page 500

1. a.

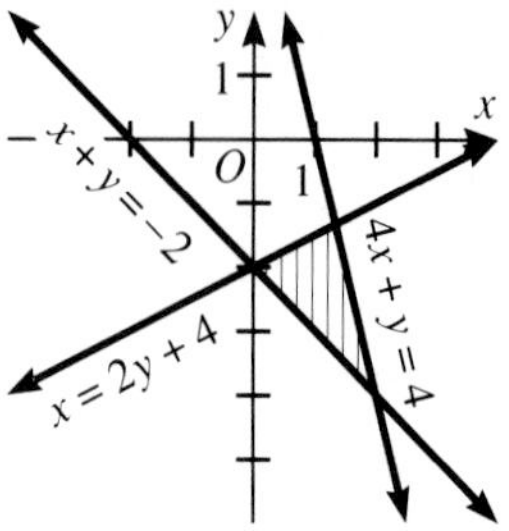

b. $\left(\frac{4}{3}, -\frac{4}{3}\right)$, (2, −4), (0, −2)

c. maximum: −4; minimum: −20

3. a. $6c + 12s \le 2400$; $12c + 16s \le 3600$; $c \ge 0$; $s \ge 0$

b.

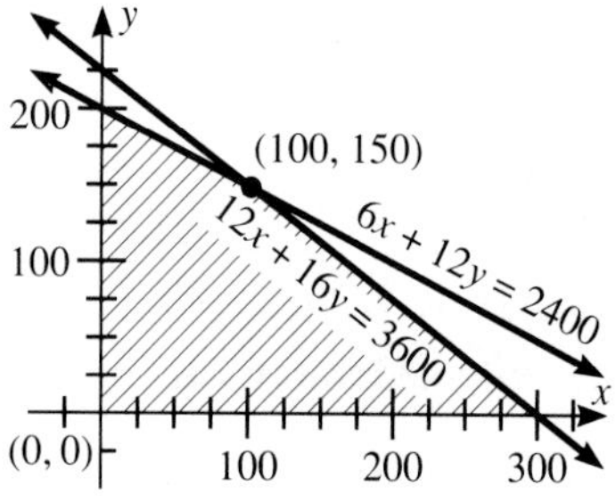

c. 100 acres of corn, 150 acres of soybeans; 0 acres of corn, 200 acres of soybeans

Chapter Review, pages 501–502 **1.** c **3.** c **5.** d **7.** b **9.** b **11.** b

Cumulative Review, page 503 **1.** $b - 3$ **3.** $27x^{14}y^{12}$ **5.** $3c^3 - 10c^2d + 16cd^2 - 16d^3$ **7.** $\frac{x-3}{3x+2}$ **9.** 2.4×10^{14} **11.** $\frac{y^2(y+1)}{y+5}$ **13.** $6(5z^2 + 40z + 16)$ **15.** $(4z - y - 5)(4z + y + 5)$ **17.** $x - 2y = -7$

19.

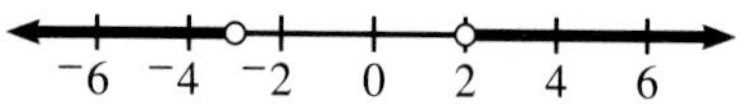

21. {7, −7} **23.** {−11, 9} **25.** {0} **27.** {−10, −1} **29.** {−5, 0, 2} **31.** $\left\{-\frac{4}{3}\right\}$ **33.** (1, 4) **35.** (−1, 2) **37.** {the real numbers less than −5} **39.** $7\frac{1}{2}$ h

Maintaining Skills, page 504 **1.** {−4, 10} **3.** {−6} **5.** $\left\{-1, \frac{1}{5}\right\}$ **7.** $\left\{-\frac{2}{5}, \frac{4}{3}\right\}$

9. $\left\{-\frac{16}{9}, 1\right\}$ **11.** {2} **13.** $\left\{-\frac{2}{5}\right\}$ **15.** no sol. **17.** {6} **19.** no sol. **21.** no sol.

Preparing for College Entrance Exams, page 505 **1.** D **3.** D **5.** C

Chapter 11 Rational and Irrational Numbers

Written Exercises, pages 510–511 **1.** $<$ **3.** $<$ **5.** $=$ **7.** $>$ **9.** $\frac{3}{8}, \frac{5}{9}, \frac{4}{7}$ **11.** $-5, 5.6, \frac{107}{18}$ **13.** $\frac{4}{15}, \frac{7}{24}, \frac{5}{16}, \frac{1}{2}$ **15.** $\frac{71}{126}$ **17.** $-\frac{17}{100}$ **19.** $-\frac{1}{2}$ **21.** increases **23.** decreases **25.** decreases **27.** $\frac{17}{45}$ **29.** $-\frac{31}{75}$ **31.** example: $\frac{13}{24}$ **33.** $\frac{29a}{168}$ **35. a.** yes **37.** $w < z$ and $wz > 0$; or $z < 0 < w$

Mixed Review Exercises, page 511
1. {2 and the real numbers less than 2}

2. {the real numbers between -10.5 and 9.5}

3. {0, 4, and the real numbers less than 0 or greater than 4}

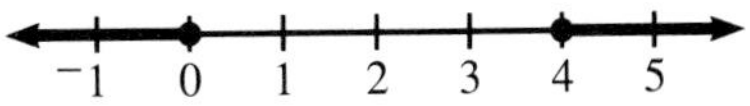

4. {-8, 2, and the real numbers less than -8 or greater than 2}

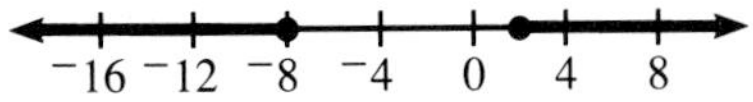

5. {0 and the real numbers between 0 and 1}

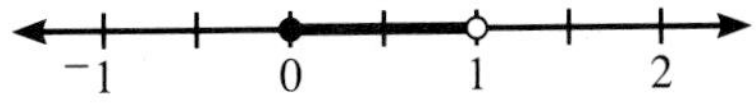

6. {-1 and the real numbers less than -1}

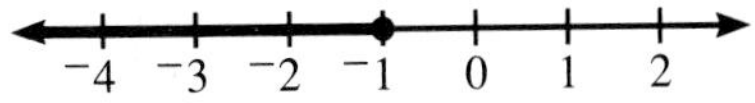

7. $\frac{7}{20}$ **8.** $\frac{3}{5}$ **9.** $\frac{22}{5}$ **10.** $\frac{3}{10{,}000}$ **11.** $\frac{5}{8}$ **12.** $\frac{1}{400}$

Written Exercises, pages 515–516 **1. a.** $0.\overline{6}$ **b.** $0.\overline{06}$ **3. a.** $-0.\overline{4}$ **b.** $-0.000\overline{4}$ **5.** 1.375 **7.** $1.\overline{36}$ **9.** $-0.3\overline{8}$ **11.** 3.45 **13.** $0.\overline{27}$ **15.** $-0.\overline{486}$ **17.** $\frac{1}{5}$ **19.** $\frac{13}{40}$ **21.** $\frac{4}{9}$ **23.** $-\frac{17}{60}$ **25.** $\frac{7}{99}$ **27.** $-\frac{7}{3}$ **29.** 0.2545 **31.** $0.44\overline{2}$ **33.** $0.831\overline{6}$ **35.** $\frac{3}{5}, \frac{3}{4}; \frac{9}{20}$ **37.** $\frac{2}{3}, \frac{7}{12}; \frac{7}{18}$ **39.** $\frac{11}{27}, \frac{5}{18}; \frac{55}{486}$ **41. a.** $0.\overline{1}; 0.\overline{5}; 0.\overline{8}$ **b.** $0.\overline{037}; 0.\overline{185}; 0.\overline{296}$ **c.** Each decimal in **(b)** is one third the corresponding decimal in **(a)**. **43. a.** $0.\overline{08}; 0.\overline{32}; 0.\overline{87}$ **b.** $1 = \frac{99}{99} = 99(0.\overline{01}) = .\overline{99} = 0.\overline{9}$ **c.** $10N = 9.\overline{9}$, $10N - N = 9.\overline{9} - 0.\overline{9}$, $9N = 9$, $N = 1$

Mixed Review Exercises, page 516 **1.** $2^3 \cdot 5^2$ **2.** $2 \cdot 7^2$ **3.** $3^2 \cdot 11^2$ **4.** $2 \cdot 3^2 \cdot 5^3$ **5.** $2^3 \cdot 7^2$ **6.** $2^6 \cdot 3^2$ **7.** {-3, 4} **8.** {-2, -8} **9.** no sol. **10.** {0, -4, 4} **11.** {-12, 8} **12.** {the real numbers less than 12}

Written Exercises, page 519 **1.** 6 **3.** 10 **5.** -20 **7.** 25 **9.** ± 50 **11.** $-\frac{9}{40}$ **13.** $\pm\frac{11}{5}$ **15.** $\frac{4}{7}$ **17.** $-\frac{11}{5}$ **19.** $\frac{19}{48}$ **21.** $-\frac{2}{3}$ **23.** $\frac{3}{2}$ **25.** $\pm\frac{5}{2}$ **27.** $\frac{1}{5}$ **29.** $\pm\frac{1}{2}$ **31.** $-\frac{20}{9}$ **33.** 0.2 **35.** -0.9 **37.** 1.1 **39.** ± 2.8 **41.** 0.14 **43.** 0.03 **45.** -1 **47.** -8

Mixed Review Exercises, page 520 **1.** $\frac{1}{8}$ **2.** $-\frac{32}{5}$ **3.** $\frac{1}{3}$ **4.** $\frac{214}{99}$ **5.** $\frac{1}{15}$ **6.** $-\frac{x}{42}$
7. $4(b + 3)(b - 6)$
8. $(4t - 1 + 3v)(4t - 1 - 3v)$
9. $k(8k + 1)(8k - 1)$ **10.** $(3w - 4y)^2$
11. $(2x + y)(x - 5y)$ **12.** $(3 - 5ab)(1 + ab)$

Challenge, page 520 (7, 6, 5)

Self-Test 1, page 520 **1.** $\frac{77}{144}$ **2.** $\frac{31}{24}$ **3.** $4\frac{31}{48}$ **4.** $>$ **5.** $<$ **6.** $<$ **7.** 0.48 **8.** 3.25 **9.** $0.2\overline{3}$ **10.** $0.6\overline{857142}$ **11.** $\frac{20}{99}$ **12.** 33 **13.** $\frac{8}{45}$ **14.** 1.6

Written Exercises, pages 522–523 **1.** $3\sqrt{7}$ **3.** $7\sqrt{2}$ **5.** $5\sqrt{3}$ **7.** 16 **9.** $8\sqrt{3}$ **11.** $30\sqrt{2}$ **13.** 23 **15.** $18\sqrt{5}$ **17.** 19 **19.** $50\sqrt{5}$ **21.** $8\sqrt{3}$ **23.** $50\sqrt{6}$ **25.** $42\sqrt{5}$ **27.** 75 **29.** $140\sqrt{3}$ **31.** 28.3 **33.** -26.5 **35.** -76.8 **37.** ± 88.3 **39.** 8.25 **41.** -0.71 **43.** ± 0.93 **45.** -0.26 **47.** 387 **49.** 648

Mixed Review Exercises, page 523 **1.** 20 **2.** -13 **3.** $\frac{5}{9}$ **4.** $-\frac{7}{15}$ **5.** 176 **6.** $\frac{3}{8}$ **7.** $289x^2$ **8.** $9y^8z^{18}$ **9.** $4x^2 + 12xy + 9y^2$ **10.** $225a^2 + 900a + 900$ **11.** $121a^8b^{22}c^2$ **12.** $36z^6 - 25y^8$

Written Exercises, page 526 **1.** $11|a|$ **3.** $2|x|\sqrt{7}$ **5.** $-3c^2$ **7.** $-5|d^3|$ **9.** $4|ab|\sqrt{5}$ **11.** $5r\sqrt{3r}$ **13.** $\pm 3|x|y\sqrt{6y}$ **15.** $-12|xz|$ **17.** $\pm\frac{10|f^5|}{11}$ **19.** $\frac{x^2|y^3|}{2|r|}$ **21.** $\frac{4|g^9|}{45h^{10}}$ **23.** $-1.8x^2$ **25.** $|y - 4|$ **27.** $\{5, -5\}$ **29.** $\{2, -2\}$ **31.** $\{10, -10\}$ **33.** $\{5, -5\}$ **35.** $\left\{\frac{4}{9}, -\frac{4}{9}\right\}$ **37.** $\left\{\frac{7}{9}, -\frac{7}{9}\right\}$ **39.** $\{24.9, -24.9\}$ **41.** $\{0.6, -0.6\}$ **43.** $\{14.6, -14.6\}$ **45.** $\{3.2, -3.2\}$ **47.** $\{7.5, -7.5\}$ **49.** $\{0.3, -0.3\}$ **51.** $\{8.5, -8.5\}$ **53.** $\{9.3, -9.3\}$

Problems, page 527 **1.** 17.3 cm **3.** 18 m **5.** 7.2 km **7.** 18 s **9.** $\frac{\sqrt{2}}{1} \approx \frac{1.4}{1}$ **11.** 131.9 m^2

Mixed Review Exercises, page 528 **1.** $\pm 5\sqrt{10}$ **2.** $-12\sqrt{19}$ **3.** $30\sqrt{11}$ **4.** $\frac{5}{36}$ **5.** $\frac{4}{3}$ **6.** $-\frac{2}{x^9}$ **7.** 97 **8.** 1296 **9.** 80 **10.** $\frac{1}{3}$ **11.** $\frac{3}{2}$ **12.** 16

Calculator Key-In, page 528 **1.** 37.95 cm^2 **3.** 71.55 m^2 **5.** 4.92 m^2 **7.** 51.51 cm^2

Written Exercises, page 532 **1.** 26 **3.** 9.43 **5.** 11.31 **7.** 20 **9.** 39.55 **11.** yes **13.** yes **15.** yes **17.** no **19.** yes **21.** 16.97 **23.** 18.97 **25.** 25.61 **27.** $a = b = 42.43$ **29.** $a = 9.49$; $b = 28.46$

Computer Exercises, page 532 **1.** yes **3.** yes

Problems, page 533 **1.** 65 cm **3.** 127.28 ft **5.** 22.25 cm **7.** 182 cm **9.** 77.94 cm **11.** 101.14 cm; yes

Mixed Review Exercises, page 534 **1.** $4x^8|y|$ **2.** $|c - 5|$ **3.** $5a^2|b + 4|\sqrt{2a}$ **4.** $\frac{9}{100{,}000{,}000}$ **5.** $\frac{4}{x^6y^{10}}$ **6.** $\frac{49}{64}$ **7.** $\frac{3 - a}{18}$ **8.** $5y - 1$ **9.** $\frac{r}{64x^2}$ **10.** $-\frac{k^6}{216}$ **11.** $r^2 + 2r$ **12.** $2s - 1$

Self-Test 2, page 534 **1.** 0.9 **2.** 41.2 **3.** -0.9 **4.** $12|mn|$ **5.** $-9x^4|y^3|$ **6.** $0.5a^2$ **7.** $\{-8, 8\}$ **8.** $\{-7, 7\}$ **9.** $\left\{-\frac{5}{6}, \frac{5}{6}\right\}$ **10.** 22.02 **11.** no

Challenge, page 534 8 roosters, 11 hens, and 81 chicks; or 12 roosters, 4 hens, and 84 chicks

Extra, page 536 **1.** 10 **3.** 6.7 **5.** 5 **7.** 9.8 **9.** 6.4 **11.** 8.5 **13.** $MA = MB = 13$, therefore M is equidistant from A and B.

Challenge, page 536

1.

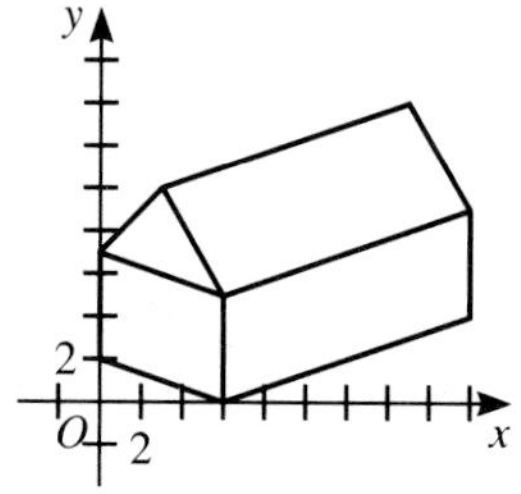

Written Exercises, pages 538–539 **1.** 30 **3.** 6 **5.** $2\sqrt{35}$ **7.** 9 **9.** 22 **11.** $36\sqrt{2}$ **13.** 1 **15.** $\frac{\sqrt{2}}{2}$ **17.** $\frac{\sqrt{6}}{3}$ **19.** 3 **21.** $\frac{\sqrt{65}}{13}$ **23.** $\frac{6\sqrt{5}}{5}$ **25.** $4\sqrt{3}$ **27.** 56 **29.** $5 - 2\sqrt{5}$ **31.** $-216\sqrt{3}$ **33.** $12ab$ **35.** $-x^2y^2\sqrt{xy}$ **37.** $m^2 + 6\sqrt{m}$ **39.** $30x^2$ **41.** $8x\sqrt{3}$ **43.** $20x$ **45.** $\frac{9x^2}{y}$ **47.** $6a - 4a\sqrt{6a}$ **49.** $24m^2 - 120m^3\sqrt{m}$ **51.** $24y^4\sqrt{3y}$ **53.** $50x^4y^2\sqrt{2} - 100x^2y^4$ **55.** $\frac{11}{\sqrt{33}}$ **57.** $\frac{6}{\sqrt{78}}$ **59.** $\frac{19}{2\sqrt{38}}$

Mixed Review Exercises, page 539 **1.** $\{13, -13\}$ **2.** $\{10, -10\}$ **3.** $\left\{\frac{4}{5}, -\frac{4}{5}\right\}$ **4.** $\{6\}$ **5.** $\{45\}$ **6.** $\{12\}$ **7.** $25x - 3$ **8.** $4a + 24$ **9.** $3b - 4$ **10.** $20c^3d^5$ **11.** $7m - 1$ **12.** $3x^2 - 5x - 4$

Written Exercises, page 541 **1.** $2\sqrt{3}$ **3.** $-20\sqrt{17}$ **5.** $15\sqrt{3}$ **7.** $12\sqrt{2} - 12\sqrt{7}$ **9.** $10\sqrt{7} - 6\sqrt{5}$ **11.** $-22\sqrt{2} - 14\sqrt{3}$ **13.** $10\sqrt{13} - 6\sqrt{11}$ **15.** $12\sqrt{7} - \sqrt{14}$ **17.** $-14\sqrt{2}$ **19.** $\frac{4\sqrt{55}}{11}$ **21.** $\frac{46\sqrt{2}}{5}$ **23.** $-\frac{6\sqrt{55}}{55}$ **25.** $\frac{17\sqrt{30}}{30}$ **27.** $\frac{\sqrt{3}}{3}$ **29.** $\frac{4\sqrt{14} - 7\sqrt{2}}{2}$ **31.** $15\sqrt{2} + 20\sqrt{6}$

33. $14x\sqrt{x} - 12x^2\sqrt{x}$ **35.** $\frac{x\sqrt{41}}{20}$
37. $\frac{x\sqrt{a^2 + b^2}}{ab}$

Mixed Review Exercises, page 542

1. $y = 3x + 5$ **2.** $y = \frac{1}{5}x - 2$ **3.** $y = 3x - 3$
4. $y = -x + \frac{4}{5}$ **5.** $y = \frac{1}{2}x - 3$ **6.** $y = \frac{2}{7}x$
7. $y = -x + 11$ **8.** $y = \frac{1}{11}x - \frac{7}{11}$
9. $y = -6x + 2$ **10.** (0, 0); $x = 0$ **11.** (3, 0); $x = 3$ **12.** (0, 5); $x = 0$ **13.** {0} **14.** {−2}
15. {1, 10} **16.** $\left\{\frac{1}{3}, -\frac{3}{2}\right\}$ **17.** {3, −1}
18. $\left\{-\frac{1}{2}\right\}$

Written Exercises, pages 545–546 **1.** 1
3. −21 **5.** 1 **7.** $11 + 4\sqrt{7}$ **9.** $17 - 12\sqrt{2}$
11. $33 - 4\sqrt{65}$ **13.** 25 **15.** 173
17. $9 + 2\sqrt{3}$ **19.** $-12 - 16\sqrt{35}$
21. $232 + 20\sqrt{22}$ **23.** $\frac{-1 + \sqrt{5}}{4}$
25. $3\sqrt{5} + 6$ **27.** $-3 - \sqrt{7}$
29. $\frac{\sqrt{21} - 2\sqrt{3} - 4\sqrt{7} + 8}{3}$ **31.** $\frac{14\sqrt{5} - 7}{19}$
33. $\frac{8\sqrt{5} + 12 + 4\sqrt{10} + 6\sqrt{2}}{11}$ **35.** $-1 - 5\sqrt{6}$
37. $-9 - 3\sqrt{2}$ **39.** $18 - 9\sqrt{11}$
41. Show that $(4 + \sqrt{7})^2 - 8(4 + \sqrt{7}) + 9 = 0$ and $(4 - \sqrt{7})^2 - 8(4 - \sqrt{7}) + 9 = 0$. **43.** Show that $3\left(\frac{2}{3} + \frac{\sqrt{7}}{3}\right)^2 - 4\left(\frac{2}{3} + \frac{\sqrt{7}}{3}\right) - 1 = 0$ and $3\left(\frac{2}{3} - \frac{\sqrt{7}}{3}\right)^2 - 4\left(\frac{2}{3} - \frac{\sqrt{7}}{3}\right) - 1 = 0$.
45. $x^2 - y$ **47.** $15a^2b + 4ac\sqrt{b} - 3c^2$

Mixed Review Exercises, page 546 **1.** $3x^4\sqrt{2}$
2. $60\sqrt{3x}$ **3.** $8\sqrt{2}$ **4.** $22\sqrt{7}$ **5.** $\frac{\sqrt{3}}{3}$
6. $\frac{5\sqrt{11}}{6}$ **7.** $9 - 30k^2 + 25k^4$
8. $4p^2 + 28pz + 49z^2$ **9.** $36a^2b^2 - x^2$ **10.** {15}
11. {5, 9} **12.** $\left\{\frac{2}{3}, -\frac{2}{3}\right\}$

Written Exercises, pages 548–549 **1.** {9}
3. {8} **5.** $\left\{\frac{1}{50}\right\}$ **7.** {16} **9.** $\left\{\frac{1}{9}\right\}$ **11.** {18}
13. {8} **15.** {8} **17.** {4} **19.** $\left\{\frac{1}{8}\right\}$ **21.** $\left\{\frac{38}{5}\right\}$
23. {63} **25.** {80} **27.** {18} **29.** {22}
31. {18} **33.** $\{3\sqrt{7}, -3\sqrt{7}\}$ **35.** {3, −3}
37. {6} **39.** {0} **41.** {4} **43.** {−8, 2} **45.** {0}
47. {4} **49.** (4, 25)

Problems, pages 549–550 **1.** 75 **3.** 576
5. 29 **7.** 8100π cm³ **9.** 1215 W **11.** 15.9 m

Mixed Review Exercises, page 550 **1.** 19
2. $9 + 4\sqrt{5}$ **3.** $-3 + \sqrt{11}$ **4.** $\frac{-7 - 3\sqrt{5}}{4}$
5. $15\sqrt{3} - 30$ **6.** $2 - 7\sqrt{3}$ **7.** $7(a - 1)^2$
8. $t(t - 9)(t + 5)$ **9.** $2(3x + 2)(x + 2)$
10. $(y^2 - 6)(y + 1)$ **11.** $4g(g^2 + 5)(g^2 - 5)$
12. $4(3x + y)^2$

Self-Test 3, pages 550–551 **1.** 30 **2.** 1
3. $7\sqrt{7} - 3\sqrt{13}$ **4.** $-4\sqrt{3}$ **5.** $15 - 6\sqrt{6}$
6. −1 **7.** $-3 - \sqrt{7}$ **8.** $\frac{-5 + 4\sqrt{5}}{11}$ **9.** {25}
10. $\left\{\frac{11}{5}\right\}$

Extra, page 553 **1.** $6^{1/2}$ **3.** $11^{1/3}$ **5.** $2^{1/4}$
7. $(-15)^{1/3}$ **9.** $10^{1/6}$ **11.** $4^{2/3}$ **13.** $2^{3/2}$
15. $3^{5/4}$ **17.** 8 **19.** 3 **21.** −4 **23.** not a real number **25.** 8 **27.** 243 **29.** not a real number
31. 216 **33.** 625 **35.** $\left\{\frac{1}{2}\right\}$ **37.** $\left\{\frac{1}{3}\right\}$ **39.** {3}

Calculator Key-In, page 554 **1.** 2.632148
3. 1.8707313 **5.** 1.3753959

Chapter Review, pages 555–556 **1.** b **3.** c
5. b **7.** b **9.** a **11.** c **13.** a **15.** d **17.** a

Cumulative Review, page 557 **1.** −25
3. $16a^6b^2 + 72a^3bc^2 + 81c^4$ **5.** 1.024×10^{-7}
7. $\frac{2(x - 1)}{x - 4}$ **9.** $-\frac{2(2t^2 + 6t - 1)}{t(t + 2)}$ **11.** $\sqrt{7}$
13. $\frac{5\sqrt{30}}{6}$ **15.** $\frac{2\sqrt{6} + \sqrt{30}}{6}$
17. $(2c - d - 3)(2c - d + 3)$
19.
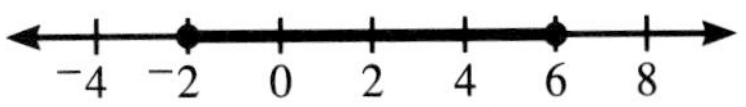

21.
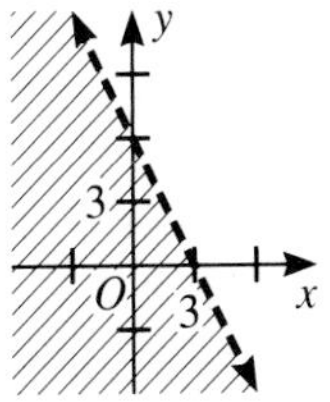

23. 0
25.
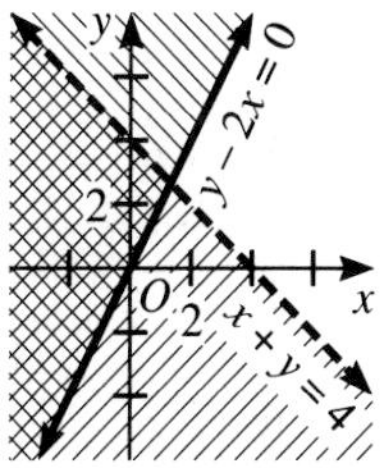

27. {16} **29.** $\left\{\frac{3}{2}\right\}$
31. {4, −1}

33. $\left(-1, -\frac{1}{5}\right)$ 35. {3, 5, and the real numbers between 3 and 5} 37. $\left\{\text{the real numbers greater than } -\frac{2}{3}\right\}$ 39. {1} 41. 7.48 cm

Maintaining Skills, page 558 1. $(-1, 2)$ 3. $(5, 5)$ 5. $\left(\frac{1}{2}, \frac{1}{3}\right)$ 7. $\left(-\frac{2}{3}, \frac{7}{3}\right)$ 9. $(7, 3)$ 11. $(12, -1)$ 13. $(0, 0)$ 15. $(7, -1)$ 17. $(-7, 12)$ 19. $(5, 6)$ 21. $(9, 4)$

Mixed Problem Solving Review, page 559
1. 1 km/h; 11 km/h 3. 12 cm 5. Saturn, 10 km/s; Mars, 24 km/s 7. \$1500 9. 30 min 11. no sol.; unrealistic result 13. $\frac{3x + 2}{3}$ dollars per kg

Chapter 12 Quadratic Functions

Written Exercises, page 563 1. $\{\pm 8\}$ 3. $\left\{\pm\frac{10}{13}\right\}$ 5. $\{\pm 6\}$ 7. $\{\pm 3\}$ 9. no sol. 11. $\{\pm\sqrt{3}\}$ 13. $\{\pm\sqrt{3}\}$ 15. $\{\pm\sqrt{7}\}$ 17. $\{6 \pm \sqrt{13}\}$ 19. $\{7 \pm 2\sqrt{7}\}$ 21. $\{2, 8\}$ 23. $\{-3 \pm \sqrt{7}\}$ 25. $\{1, -7\}$ 27. $\{9, 13\}$ 29. $\left\{\pm\frac{5}{7}\right\}$ 31. $\left\{\pm\frac{\sqrt{510}}{6}\right\}$ 33. $\{6, -24\}$ 35. $\left\{\pm\frac{\sqrt{2}}{2}\right\}$ 37. $\left\{\frac{27}{14}, \frac{29}{14}\right\}$ 39. $\left\{\frac{12 \pm 5\sqrt{7}}{20}\right\}$ 41. $\{0, \pm 5\}$ 43. $\left\{0, \pm\frac{1}{4}\right\}$ 45. $\{0, \pm 8\}$ 47. $\left\{0, \frac{1}{3}\right\}$ 49. a. 2 b. 2 c. none d. 1

Mixed Review Exercises, page 563
1. $x^2 - 22x + 121$ 2. $4x^2 + 20x + 25$ 3. $36x^2 - 84x + 49$ 4. $9c^2 - 24c + 16$ 5. $x^2 + x + \frac{1}{4}$ 6. $x^2 + \frac{2}{3}x + \frac{1}{9}$ 7. $\frac{1}{4}x^2 + \frac{2}{3}x + \frac{4}{9}$ 8. $\frac{1}{9}x^2 + \frac{1}{2}x + \frac{9}{16}$

Written Exercises, page 566
1. $\{\sqrt{21} + 2, -\sqrt{21} + 2\}$; $\{6.6, -2.6\}$ 3. $\{\sqrt{6} - 3, -\sqrt{6} - 3\}$; $\{-0.6, -5.4\}$ 5. $\{1, 19\}$ 7. $\{5\sqrt{11} - 9, -5\sqrt{11} - 9\}$; $\{7.6, -25.6\}$ 9. $\{\sqrt{6} + 2, -\sqrt{6} + 2\}$; $\{4.4, -0.4\}$ 11. $\left\{\frac{\sqrt{33} + 5}{2}, \frac{-\sqrt{33} + 5}{2}\right\}$; $\{5.4, -0.4\}$ 13. $\{5, 7\}$ 15. $\{-5, 7\}$ 17. $\left\{\frac{3}{2}, 3\right\}$ 19. $\{-2, 6\}$ 21. $\left\{-\frac{1}{2}, 6\right\}$ 23. $\left\{\frac{1 \pm \sqrt{37}}{3}\right\}$ 25. $\left\{\frac{-3 \pm \sqrt{41}}{8}\right\}$ 27. $\left\{\frac{-2 \pm \sqrt{3}}{3}\right\}$ 29. $\left\{\frac{b \pm \sqrt{b^2 - 4c}}{2}\right\}$

Mixed Review Exercises, page 566 1. $2\sqrt{47}$ 2. $20\sqrt{6}$ 3. $x^2y^4\sqrt{10y}$ 4. $2|a^3b^3|c^2\sqrt{30bc}$ 5. $\frac{z^2 - 2z + 24}{16 - z^2}$ 6. $\frac{b^2 + 2b + 1}{2b + 1}$ 7. $15x^2 + 40x + 12$

Written Exercises, page 569 1. $\{5, -2\}$ 3. $\left\{2, \frac{1}{5}\right\}$ 5. $\{-1, 6\}$ 7. $\{3 \pm 2\sqrt{5}\}$; $\{7.5, -1.5\}$ 9. $\{-4 \pm \sqrt{11}\}$; $\{-0.7, -7.3\}$ 11. $\left\{\frac{-1 \pm \sqrt{15}}{7}\right\}$; $\{0.4, -0.7\}$ 13. $\left\{\frac{1 \pm \sqrt{13}}{4}\right\}$; $\{1.2, -0.7\}$ 15. $\left\{\frac{3 \pm \sqrt{2}}{2}\right\}$; $\{0.8, 2.2\}$ 17. $\left\{\frac{-4 \pm \sqrt{22}}{3}\right\}$; $\{0.2, -2.9\}$ 19. $\left\{\frac{-0.7 \pm \sqrt{0.89}}{2}\right\}$; $\{0.1, -0.8\}$ 21. $\left\{\frac{0.3 \pm \sqrt{2.09}}{4}\right\}$; $\{0.4, -0.3\}$ 23. no real-number sol. 25. no real-number sol. 27. $\left\{\frac{3 \pm \sqrt{13}}{2}\right\}$; $\{-0.3, 3.3\}$ 29. $-\frac{b}{a}$ 31. $x^2 - 4x - 1 = 0$

Mixed Review Exercises, page 570
1. $\{-3, 11$, and the real numbers between -3 and $11\}$

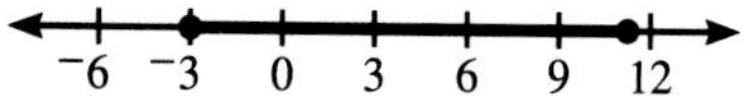

2. $\{-12, -2\}$

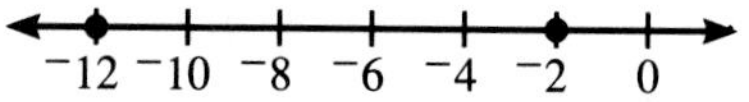

3. $\left\{\text{the real numbers between } -4 \text{ and } \frac{2}{3}\right\}$

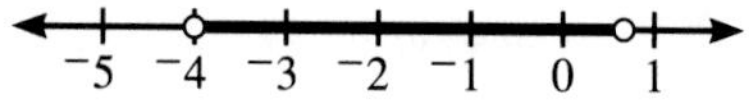

4. $\left\{4 \text{ and the real numbers between } -\frac{1}{2} \text{ and } 4\right\}$

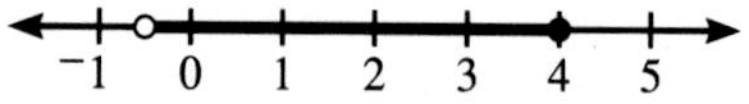

5. $\{81\}$

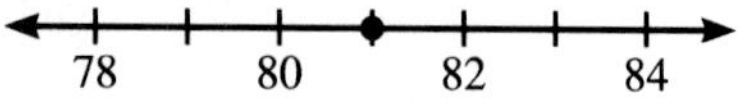

6. $\{4\}$

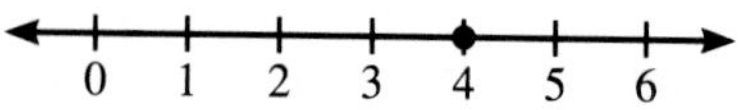

7. $\{12\}$ 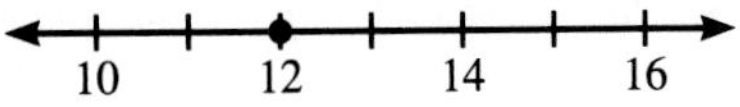

8. $\{-12, 3\}$

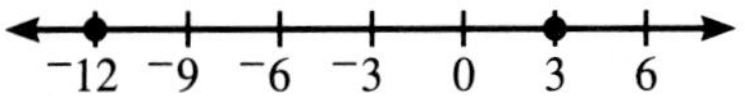

9. $\{-1, 9\}$

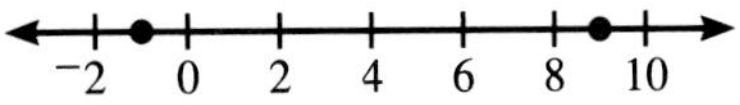

10. $\{2, 8\}$ **11.** $\{0, -6\}$ **12.** $\{-2, 3\}$

Computer Exercises, page 570 **3.** $\{1, 0.75\}$ **5.** $\{3.41, 0.59\}$ **7.** no real-number solution

Extra, page 571 **1.** -1 **3.** i **5.** $-i$ **7.** $7i$ **9.** $4\sqrt{6}$ **11.** $30i$ **13.** $18i\sqrt{6}$ **15.** $\frac{4i}{9}$ **17.** $-\frac{7i}{11}$ **19.** $\{\pm 10i\}$ **21.** $\{\pm 7i\sqrt{2}\}$

Written Exercises, page 574 **1.** 9; two **3.** 0; one **5.** 0; one **7.** 0; one **9.** 21; two **11.** 1.16; two **13.** two; below **15.** one; on **17.** two; above **19.** 4

Mixed Review Exercises, page 575 **1.** $\frac{\sqrt{2} - \sqrt{6}}{2}$ **2.** $\frac{3c^4}{5}$ **3.** 0 **4.** $\frac{2}{x^2 + x}$ **5.** $\frac{4b + 5}{4(b + 1)}$ **6.** 5.022×10^8 **7.** $(0, 0)$; $x = 0$ **8.** $(-5, 0)$; $x = -5$ **9.** $(0, 3)$; $x = 0$ **10.** $\left(4\frac{1}{2}, 17\frac{1}{4}\right)$; $x = 4\frac{1}{2}$ **11.** $\left(7\frac{1}{2}; -12\frac{3}{4}\right)$; $x = 7\frac{1}{2}$ **12.** $\left(\frac{3}{4}, 1\frac{1}{8}\right)$; $x = \frac{3}{4}$

Computer Exercises, page 575 **1.** 2 **3.** 0

Self-Test 1, page 575 **1.** $\{-3, 3\}$ **2.** $\{3 \pm \sqrt{7}\}$ **3.** $\{5, 7\}$ **4.** $\{-2, 8\}$ **5.** $\left\{2, -\frac{1}{2}\right\}$ **6.** $\left\{\frac{3 \pm \sqrt{33}}{2}\right\}$ **7.** none **8.** none

Written Exercises, pages 577–578 **1.** $\{-6, 1\}$ **3.** $\{\pm 2\}$ **5.** $\left\{\frac{-7 \pm \sqrt{41}}{2}\right\}$ **7.** $-3 \pm \sqrt{14}$ **9.** $\{0, 4\}$ **11.** $\{4 \pm 3\sqrt{2}\}$ **13.** $\left\{\frac{1}{5}, -4\right\}$ **15.** $\left\{\frac{1 \pm \sqrt{22}}{3}\right\}$ **17.** $\{-3 \pm 2\sqrt{5}\}$ **19.** $\left\{\frac{7 \pm \sqrt{161}}{28}\right\}$ **21.** $\left\{\frac{2}{3}, 3\right\}$ **23.** $\left\{\frac{1 \pm \sqrt{10}}{3}\right\}$ **25.** $\left\{\frac{32}{9}, 4\right\}$ **27.** $\left\{-\frac{8}{5}, \frac{2}{11}\right\}$ **29.** $\left\{\pm\frac{\sqrt{3}}{2}\right\}$ **31.** $\left\{\pm\frac{2\sqrt{6}}{3}\right\}$

Mixed Review Exercises, page 578 **1.** ± 10 **2.** $-2\sqrt{7}$ **3.** 7 **4.** $\sqrt{113}$ **5.** ± 17 **6.** no real-number sol. **7.** $\left\{-\frac{3}{2}, \frac{5}{2}\right\}$ **8.** $\left\{-7, \frac{11}{2}\right\}$ **9.** $\left\{-\frac{68}{39}\right\}$ **10.** $\{2 \pm \sqrt{6}\}$ **11.** $\left\{\frac{1}{3}, 1\right\}$ **12.** $\left\{\frac{-6 \pm \sqrt{51}}{6}\right\}$

Problems, pages 580–581 **1.** 20 m, 15 m **3.** 7 or -8 **5.** 9 cm **7.** 7 cm **9.** Olaf, 6 mi/h; Cindy, 8 mi/h **11.** Maria, 34.1 min; Johannes, 30.1 min **13.** 16 **15.** 12 h

Mixed Review Exercises, page 581 **1.** $\{45\}$ **2.** $\{84\}$ **3.** $\left\{\frac{4}{5}\right\}$ **4.** $\left\{10\frac{10}{13}\right\}$ **5.** $\{5, 9\}$ **6.** $\{8\}$ **7.** 12 **8.** 25 **9.** 3

Extra, page 582

1.

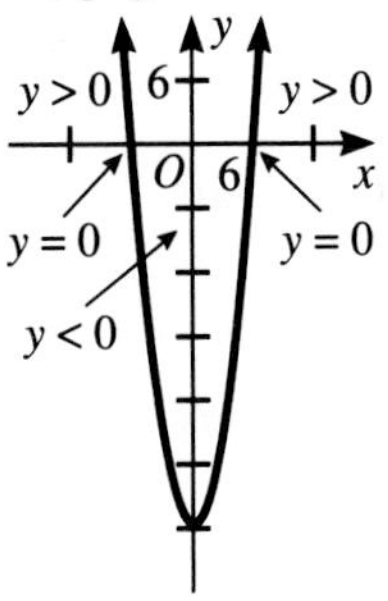

3.

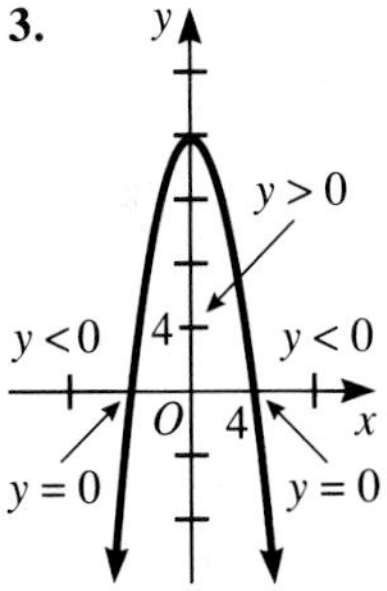

5.

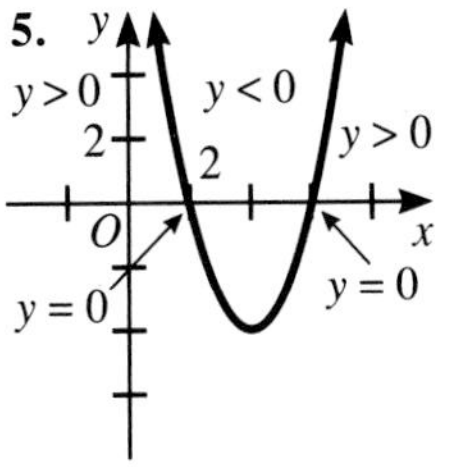

7. $x \le 0$ or $x \ge 3$ **9.** $x \le 3$ or $x \ge 7$

Self-Test 2, page 582 **1.** $\{-4, 0\}$ **2.** $\left\{\frac{-3 \pm \sqrt{3}}{2}\right\}$ **3.** $\{5 \pm 3\sqrt{5}\}$ **4.** $\{-3, 0\}$ **5.** 20 cm, 10 cm **6.** 50 m, 36 m

Application, page 583 **1.** 360 cm^3 **3.** 600 cm^3 **5.** 22.5 m^3

Problems, page 586–587 **1.** 18 cm **3.** 112 m **5.** 3 cm **7.** 1.2 s **9.** 1.4 **11.** 64:27

Mixed Review Exercises, page 587 **1.** $\frac{3x^2 - 1}{2}$ **2.** $\frac{2A}{b + c}$; $b \neq -c$ **3.** $\frac{2A - hc}{h}$; $h \neq 0$

4. $\frac{1}{a+1}$; $a \neq -1$ 5. $k^2 + tg$; $g \neq 0$
6. $\pm\frac{\sqrt{kE}}{E}$; $kE \geq 0$, $E \neq 0$ 7. $2x - y = 7$
8. $2x - 3y = 0$ 9. $x + 2y = 10$
10. $3x - y = -2$ 11. $x - 6y = 24$
12. $5x - 13y = 130$

Written Exercises, page 590 **1.** 48 **3.** ± 12 **5.** ± 4.2 **7.** quadrupled; no change **9.** h is 2.8 times as large

Problems, pages 590–592 **1.** 104 cm^3 **3.** 25 **5.** \$2.10 **7.** 12 s **9.** 5.30 **11.** 18 joules **13. a.** doubled **b.** quadrupled **c.** 18 times as large

Mixed Review Exercises, page 592 **1.** (1, 1) **2.** (12, −2) **3.** (9, 3) **4.** (−5, 10) **5.** (2, 2) **6.** (11, −8) **7.** $8x^2 + 8x + 2$ **8.** $48s^2 + 64s + 20$ **9.** $49t^2 - 4y^2$ **10.** $9p^2 - 24pk + 16k^2$ **11.** $r^2 - 4r + 4$ **12.** $3x^2y^2 - 2xy - 8$

Application, page 593 **1.** 10 lx **3.** 3 m **5.** 20 lx

Self-Test 3, page 594 **1.** 196 km **2.** 158.4 g

Chapter Review, pages 595–596 **1.** d **3.** c **5.** a **7.** b **9.** a **11.** b

Cumulative Review, pages 597–598 **1.** $-\frac{7}{2}$ **3.** 0 **5.** 1 **7.** −58 **9.** −133 **11.** $45x - 55 - 9c$ **13.** $12a^4b^3 + 9a^3b^4$ **15.** $\frac{3wx}{4y^2}$ **17.** $8u^3 + 1$ **19.** $45z^2 + 21z - 12$ **21.** $64r^6t^2 - 9v^2$ **23.** $\frac{2c - 3d}{2c - 6d}$ **25.** $9x^2 - 12x + 16$ **27.** $\frac{3z + 4}{(z + 1)(z + 3)}$ **29.** $2a - 3$ **31.** $\frac{5m - 21}{2(m + 3)(m - 3)}$ **33.** $90 - 27\sqrt{5}$ **35.** $12a$ **37.** $14\sqrt{5}$ **39.** $92 + 32\sqrt{10}$ **41.** $t^3(4t^2 + 9)$ **43.** $-16z^2(z^2 + 3z + 4)$ **45.** prime **47.** $(c - 4)^2$ **49.** $\left\{\frac{40}{3}\right\}$ **51.** {5} **53.** {300} **55.** {3, 6} **57.** $\left\{-\frac{2}{3}, \frac{1}{4}\right\}$ **59.** $\left(\frac{1}{2}, \frac{1}{8}\right)$ **61.** {−16} **63.** {−2, 8, and the real numbers less than −2 or greater than 8} **65.** $\left\{-\frac{3}{2}\right.$, 2, and the real numbers between $-\frac{3}{2}$ and $\left.2\right\}$ **67.** no sol. **69.** {5} **71.** $\left\{\frac{5 \pm \sqrt{13}}{6}\right\}$

73.
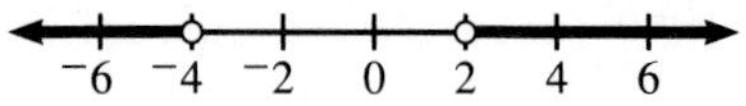

75.
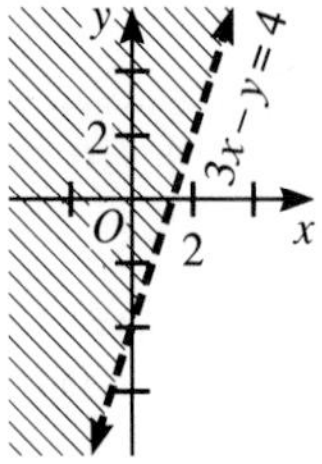

77.
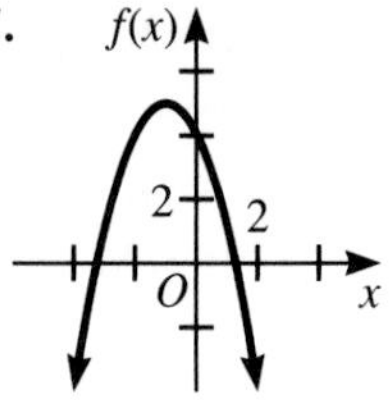

79.
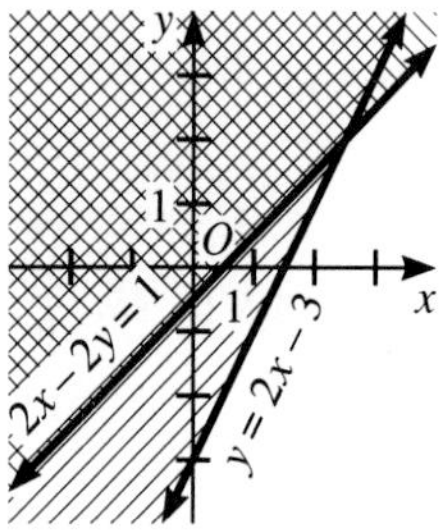

81. 12 h
83. less than 6 h

Preparing for College Entrance Exams, page 599 **1.** D **3.** B **5.** C **7.** E

Looking Ahead

Written Exercises, page 602 **1.** {A, B, C, D, E, F, G, H, I, J, K}; **a.** {A, E, I} **b.** {B, C, D, F, G, H, J, K} **c.** {C, F, H} **3.** {(2, 1), (2, 4), (2, 9), (4, 1), (4, 4), (4, 9), (8, 1), (8, 4), (8, 9), (15, 1), (15, 4), (15, 9)}; **a.** {(4, 4)} **b.** {(15, 1), (15, 9)} **c.** {(4, 9), (8, 9), (15, 1), (15, 4), (15, 9)} **d.** {(2, 1), (4, 1)} **5.** {(O, O, O), (O, O, F), (O, F, F), (O, F, O), (F, O, O), (F, O, F), (F, F, O), (F, F, F)}; **a.** {(O, O, O)} **b.** {(O, F, F), (F, F, O), (F, O, F), (F, F, F)} **c.** {(O, O, F), (O, F, F), (O, F, O), (F, O, O), (F, O, F), (F, F, O), (F, F, F)} **7.** {p, n, d, (p, n), (p, d), (n, d), (p, n, d)}; **a.** {d, (p, n), (p, n, d)} **b.** {p, n, (p, d), (n, d)} **c.** {n, d, (p, n), (p, d), (n, d)} **d.** {p, n, (p, n, d)}

Written Exercises, pages 604–605 **1. a.** $\frac{4}{15}$ **b.** $\frac{2}{3}$ **c.** $\frac{1}{3}$ **d.** $\frac{2}{3}$ **3. a.** $\frac{1}{24}$ **b.** $\frac{3}{8}$ **c.** $\frac{7}{24}$ **d.** $\frac{1}{6}$ **5. a.** $\frac{1}{8}$ **b.** $\frac{3}{8}$ **c.** $\frac{1}{2}$ **d.** $\frac{3}{4}$ **7. a.** $\frac{2}{15}$ **b.** $\frac{2}{5}$ **c.** $\frac{1}{5}$ **d.** $\frac{1}{15}$ **e.** $\frac{4}{15}$ **f.** $\frac{1}{3}$

Written Exercises, page 608 **1.** 44; 49; none; 38 **3.** 28.7; 30.5; 32; 23 **5.** 56; 56; 53 and 56 and 61; 9 **7.** 85.8; 84.5; 81 and 92; 11 **9.** 10.2; 10.5; 12; 5 **11.** 96% **13. a–d.** Each statistic is multiplied by 3. **15.** 38

Extra, page 610 **1.** The mean is 7 and the difference between each data point and the mean is 0. Therefore the variance and standard deviation are both 0. **3. a.** 41 **b.** 4.2

c.

x_i	standard score
36	−1.2
38	−0.7
41	0
45	1.0
48	1.7

5. Factory II; the standard deviation is lower, so there must have been less of a difference between each worker's productivity and the mean productivity.

Written Exercises, page 613 **1. a.** 51, 53, 54, 62, 63, 65, 68, 70, 71, 73, 76, 77, 79, 84, 84, 88, 90, 95 **b.** 72; 84; 44 **3. a.** 8 **b.** 6 **c.** 9 **d.** 10 **e.** 4 **f.** 6 **5.** 22; 21; 28; 30; 19

7.

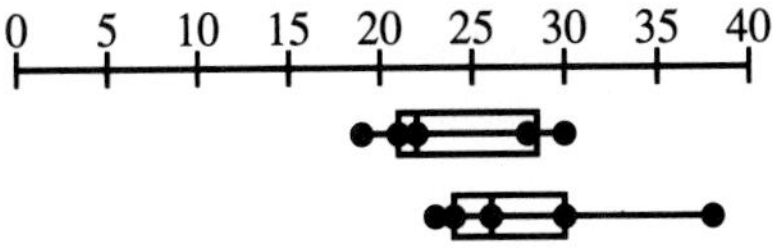

Application, page 615 **1.** no **3. a.** $22,000 **b.** $27,565 **c.** median; only two people earn more than $23,000

d. For the scale on the vertical axis, for example, make each unit $50 (in thousands).

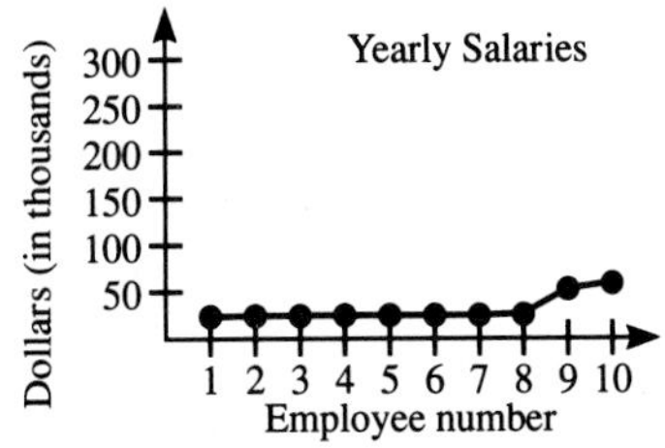

e. For the scale on the vertical axis, for example, make each unit $5 (in thousands).

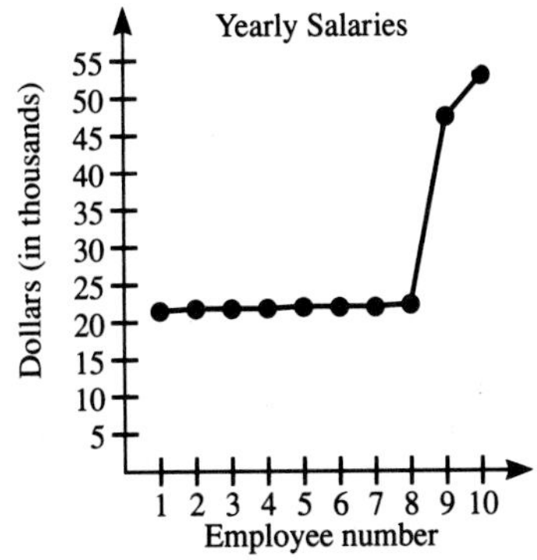

Written Exercises, page 618 **1.** Any 5 of: $\overline{WX}$, $\overline{WY}$, $\overline{WZ}$, $\overline{XY}$, $\overline{XZ}$, $\overline{YZ}$ **3.** Any 5 of: $\overline{AE}$, $\overline{BC}$, $\overline{EB}$, $\overline{ED}$, $\overline{DB}$, $\overline{AC}$, $\overline{AD}$, $\overline{DC}$ **5.** acute **7.** right **9.** obtuse **11.** acute

13. ray

15. point

17. point

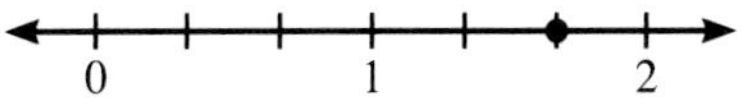

19. line segment

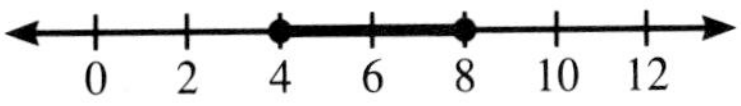

21. two rays

Written Exercises, page 620 **1.** $\angle HAD$, $\angle GBK$, $\angle EAB$ **3.** 30° **5.** 70° and 20° **7.** 127° **9.** 63°

Written Exercises, page 622 **1.** 93° **3.** 90° **5.** 66° **7.** no **9.** no **11.** yes **13.** 15 **15.** 18 **17.** 140° **19.** $4\sqrt{10}$ **21.** 8 **23.** $8\sqrt{5}$ **25.** $x\sqrt{2}$

Problems, page 623 **1.** 18° and 72° **3.** 10°, 70°, 100° **5.** 18°, 54°, 108° **7.** 60°, 60°, 60° **9.** 11°, 49°, 120° **11.** 72°, 37°, 71° **13.** 63°, 49°, 68°

Written Exercises, pages 625–626 **1. a.** $\angle S$, $\angle Z$; $\angle R$, $\angle Y$; $\angle T$, $\angle X$ **b.** $\overline{RS}$, $\overline{YZ}$; $\overline{ST}$, $\overline{ZX}$; $\overline{RT}$, $\overline{YX}$ **c.** YZX **3.** F **5.** T **7.** T **9.** $AB = 10$, $BC = 14$ **11.** $EF = 14$, $DF = 21$ **13.** $DE = 12$, $BC = 24$ **15.** $AB = 26$, $EF = 27$

Problems, page 626 **1.** 9 cm **3.** 36 m **5.** 225 m **7.** 6 m **9.** 11.25 m

Written Exercises, page 629 **1.** $\sin A = \frac{4}{5}$, $\cos A = \frac{3}{5}$, $\tan A = \frac{4}{3}$, $\sin B = \frac{3}{5}$, $\cos B = \frac{4}{5}$, $\tan B = \frac{3}{4}$ **3.** $\sin A = \frac{5\sqrt{34}}{34}$, $\cos A = \frac{3\sqrt{34}}{34}$, $\tan A = \frac{5}{3}$, $\sin B = \frac{3\sqrt{34}}{34}$, $\cos B = \frac{5\sqrt{34}}{34}$,

$\tan B = \frac{3}{5}$ **5.** $\sin A = \frac{4\sqrt{65}}{65}$, $\cos A = \frac{7\sqrt{65}}{65}$, $\tan A = \frac{4}{7}$, $\sin B = \frac{7\sqrt{65}}{65}$, $\cos B = \frac{4\sqrt{65}}{65}$, $\tan B = \frac{7}{4}$ **7.** $\sin A = \frac{\sqrt{2}}{2}$, $\cos A = \frac{\sqrt{2}}{2}$, $\tan A = 1$, $\sin B = \frac{\sqrt{2}}{2}$, $\cos B = \frac{\sqrt{2}}{2}$, $\tan B = 1$ **9.** $\sin A = \frac{3\sqrt{130}}{130}$, $\cos A = \frac{11\sqrt{130}}{130}$, $\tan A = \frac{3}{11}$, $\sin B = \frac{11\sqrt{130}}{130}$, $\cos B = \frac{3\sqrt{130}}{130}$, $\tan B = \frac{11}{3}$ **11.** $\cos A = \frac{b}{c}$; $\sin B = \frac{b}{c}$ **13.** $\tan A = \frac{a}{b}$; $\frac{\sin A}{\cos A} = \frac{\frac{a}{c}}{\frac{b}{c}} = \frac{a}{b}$

15. $\frac{\sqrt{55}}{8}$

Written Exercises, page 632 **1.** 0.3420, 0.9397, 0.3640 **3.** 0.2588, 0.9659, 0.2679 **5.** 0.9272, 0.3746, 2.4751 **7.** 0.4067, 0.9135, 0.4452 **9.** 0.0698, 0.9976, 0.0699 **11.** 0.7071, 0.7071, 1.0000 **13.** 78° **15.** 9° **17.** 57° **19.** 22° **21.** 35° **23.** 41° **25.** 20° **27.** 34° **29.** $>$ **31.** $=$

Challenge, page 632 **1.** no **3.** yes

Written Exercises, page 635 **1.** 18 **3.** 42 **5.** 16 **7.** $AC = 41$, $BC = 33$ **9.** $AB = 49$, $BC = 8$ **11.** $\angle D = 37°$, $\angle F = 53°$ **13.** $\angle F = 39°$, $\angle D = 51°$ **15.** $XY = 72$, $ZY = 62$

Problems, pages 635–636 **1.** 16 m **3.** 226 m **5.** 52 m **7.** 14° **9.** 9 m **11.** 21° **13.** 63 m; 83 m

Review, pages 637–638 **1.** c **3.** a **5.** c **7.** c **9.** a **11.** d **13.** c

EXTRA PRACTICE: Skills

Chapter 1, pages 639–640 **1.** 37 **3.** 100 **5.** 198 **7.** 12 **9.** 23 **11.** 24 **13.** 6 **15.** 9 **17.** 8 **19.** 3 **21.** 23 **23.** {6} **25.** {0, 1, 2, 3, 4, 5, 6} **27.** {0} **29.** {6} **31.** {4} **33.** {0, 5} **35.** {2} **37.** {0} **39.** $\frac{1}{2}z - 4$ **41.** $5w - 1$ **43.** $7x$ **45.** $x - 4$ **47.** $n - 5$ **49. a.** s **b.** $4s = 52$ **51.** Let x = Henry's age; $x(x - 4) = 140$ **53.** Cynthia, 30; Holly, 84 **55.** 400; 400 ft below sea level; -400 **57.** -10; ten wins; 10 **59.**

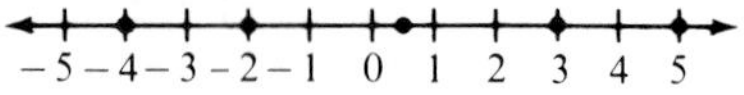

61. -3 **63.** 9 **65.** 3 **67.** 4 **69.** $>$ **71.** $<$ **73.** $<$

Chapter 2, pages 641–643 **1.** 350 **3.** 20 **5.** 16 **7.** $3m + 12$ **9.** $6w + 12$ **11.** $88n$ **13.** $60pqr$ **15.** $60hmw$ **17.** 0 **19.** -12 **21.** 20 **23.** -19 **25.** -5.6 **27.** -1 **29.** -153 **31.** -4 **33.** -12 **35.** 0 **37.** -10 **39.** 100 **41.** -83 **43.** 215 **45.** 17 **47.** -30 **49.** 4 **51.** 8 **53.** 34 **55.** 580 **57.** $7q$ **59.** $42a$ **61.** $7c + 27$ **63.** $8j - 15$ **65.** $8x + 20$ **67.** $2u + 5$ **69.** $2f + 10g$ **71.** 135 **73.** -180 **75.** -135 **77.** -480 **79.** 11 **81.** -270 **83.** $-7m + 42p$ **85.** $-24n + 36v$ **87.** $-8t - 4$ **89.** $-29x + 16y$ **91.** $-3c - 17d$ **93.** $x + (x + 1) + (x + 2) = 75$ **95.** $x + (x + 2) + (x + 4) = 138$ **97.** $x + 2 = 3x + 8$ **99.** -5 **101.** 7 **103.** -4 **105.** $11xy$ **107.** $8g$ **109.** $9h - 6$ **111.** $-6x + 9y$ **113.** $5p + 10q$ **115.** -8 **117.** 0 **119.** -40 **121.** 0 **123.** $-\frac{63}{2}a$ **125.** 11 **127.** $-x$ **129.** $5h$

Chapter 3, pages 643–645 **1.** {30} **3.** {8} **5.** {−15} **7.** {20} **9.** {−3} **11.** {−12} **13.** {2} **15.** {12} **17.** {−18} **19.** {−14} **21.** {−64} **23.** {50} **25.** {−128} **27.** {120} **29.** $\left\{\frac{1}{6}\right\}$ **31.** {7} **33.** {6} **35.** {8} **37.** {−13} **39.** {−27} **41.** {4} **43.** {6} **45.** {−3} **47.** 10 **49.** 21 **51.** 4 m, 6 m, 8 m **53.** {7} **55.** {−8} **57.** {−6} **59.** {−4} **61.** {15} **63.** $\left\{\frac{11}{8}\right\}$ **65.** {−7} **67.** {3} **69.** 75, 77, 79, 97 **71.** 16 cm by 10 cm; 14 cm by 13 cm **73.** 56 dozen **75.** 4 h **77.** Substitution principle, Assoc. prop. of add., Prop. of opposites, Ident. prop. of add.

Chapter 4, pages 645–646 **1.** 343 **3.** -48 **5.** 32 **7.** -26 **9.** 5 **11.** 68 **13.** 49 **15.** -2744 **17.** 1 **19.** $\frac{81}{4}$ **21.** $b - 2$ **23.** $4t - 10$ **25.** $10x^2 - 3xy + 2y^2$ **27.** $3a^2 + 3ab - b^2$ **29.** $5b + 10$ **31.** $-8t - 4$ **33.** $2x^2 - xy + 4y^2$ **35.** $7a^2 - 15ab + b^2$ **37.** $8f^7$ **39.** $-10g^4h^3$ **41.** $60j^5k^3l^5$ **43.** $-a^6$

45. 729 **47.** 2048 **49.** $4d^{10}$ **51.** x^{10} **53.** z^{2n} **55.** b^{3n} **57.** d^{3n} **59.** g^4h^4 **61.** $64\ m^3n^{15}$ **63.** $9a^{10}b^8$ **65.** $-512x^{15}$ **67.** $-200x^{13}$ **69.** $375x^7y^5$ **71.** $5y - 20$ **73.** $-8 - 32m$ **75.** $-12t + 8t^2$ **77.** $-40h^2 - 15h$ **79.** $-15b^4 + 10b^3 - 30b^2$ **81.** $5u^3v^2 - 2u^2v^3 + 4uv^4$ **83.** $n^2 + 2n - 15$ **85.** $5x^2 + 33x - 14$ **87.** $30m^2 + 38m + 12$ **89.** $3v^3 + v^2 + 3v - 7$ **91.** $21x^2 - 26xy + 8y^2$ **93.** $e^3 + 2e^2f + 2ef^2 + f^3$ **95.** $a = \frac{2A}{p}; p \neq 0$ **97.** $b_1 = \frac{2A - b_2h}{h}; h \neq 0$ **99.** $r = \sqrt{\frac{A}{\pi}}; A \geq 0$ **101.** $C = \frac{5}{9}(F - 32)$ **103.** $t = \frac{I}{Pr}; P \neq 0, r \neq 0$ **105.** 90 min **107.** 13.25 in. by 39.75 in.

Chapter 5, pages 647–649 **1.** 1, 42; 2, 21; 3, 14; 6, 7; −1, −42; −2, −21; −3, −14; −6, −7 **3.** 1, 91; 7, 13; −1, −91; −7, −13 **5.** 1, 52; 2, 26; 4, 13; −1, −52; −2, −26; −4, −13 **7.** $2^4 \cdot 5$ **9.** $2^3 \cdot 3^2$ **11.** 42 **13.** 13 **15.** $3x^4$ **17.** $-\frac{1}{3b^4}$ **19.** $\frac{1}{w^{12}}$ **21.** $-\frac{27}{y^3}$ **23.** $3e + 2$ **25.** $2x^2 + 6x + 1$ **27.** $3 - 5m - m^2$ **29.** $5(3w^2 - 2w + 1)$ **31.** $7u^2(u + 2)$ **33.** $3c(5c + d)$ **35.** $x^2 + 8x + 15$ **37.** $n^2 + 4n - 21$ **39.** $6 + 5m + m^2$ **41.** $8y^2 - 10y + 3$ **43.** $20n^2 - 22n + 6$ **45.** $12h^3 + 55h^2 + 63h$ **47.** $k^2 - 25$ **49.** $16d^2 - 64$ **51.** $25m^4 - n^2$ **53.** $(4e - 3)(4e + 3)$ **55.** $(9 - f)(9 + f)$ **57.** $(7 - 10y)(7 + 10y)$ **59.** $(s^3 - 2)(s^3 + 2)$ **61.** $g^2 + 14g + 49$ **63.** $4x^2 + 24x + 36$ **65.** $4m^2 + 12mn + 9n^2$ **67.** $e^2f^2 - 16ef + 64$ **69.** $(x - 3)^2$ **71.** $(2 - 7h)^2$ **73.** $(2m - 9n)^2$ **75.** $(k + 1)(k + 7)$ **77.** $(a - 1)^2$ **79.** $(n - 4)(n - 12)$ **81.** $(x + 6y)(x + 7y)$ **83.** $(e - 4f)(e - 11f)$ **85.** $(x - 7)(x + 5)$ **87.** $(h - 9)(h + 2)$ **89.** $(y - 9)(y + 5)$ **91.** $(u + 4v)(u - v)$ **93.** $(2x + 3)(x + 4)$ **95.** $(5d + 3)(2d - 1)$ **97.** prime **99.** $(5x + y)(3x + 2y)$ **101.** $(7m + 3n)(2m - n)$ **103.** $2(a + 2)(3a + 2)$ **105.** $(b - 3)(b + 1)^2$ **107.** $(7w + 3)(c - w)$ **109.** $(1 + m)(1 - m)(64 + m^4)$ **111.** $6y(5y + 1)(2y - 1)$ **113.** $16a^2(a - 3)(a + 3)$ **115.** $2w^5(14w^2 - 51)$ **117.** $-12(c - d)^2$ **119.** $\{-13, -8\}$ **121.** $\left\{2, \frac{5}{3}\right\}$ **123.** $\left\{0, -\frac{3}{4}\right\}$ **125.** $\{-1, -6\}$ **127.** $\{5, 9\}$ **129.** $\{4, -9\}$ **131.** $\left\{\frac{1}{4}, -6\right\}$ **133.** $\left\{-2, \frac{5}{2}\right\}$ **135.** $\left\{\frac{2}{3}, -\frac{2}{3}\right\}$ **137.** 7 or −8 **139.** 8 cm by 11 cm

Chapter 6, pages 649–651 **1.** $5, m \neq 3$ **3.** $\frac{c - d}{c + d}; c \neq -d$ **5.** $\frac{3}{u - v}; u \neq 0, v \neq 0, u \neq v$ **7.** $\frac{x + 8}{x + 7}; x \neq 8, x \neq -7$ **9.** $\frac{3}{5m - 2n}; m \neq -\frac{2}{5}n, m \neq \frac{2}{5}n$ **11.** $-1; k \neq 3, k \neq \frac{2}{7}$ **13.** $\frac{t - 7}{t + 2}; t \neq 2, t \neq -2$ **15.** $-\frac{1}{(x - 5w)^2}; w \neq \frac{x}{5}$ **17.** $\frac{4}{3}$ **19.** $\frac{3}{20}$ **21.** $\frac{e}{h}$ **23.** 2 **25.** $\frac{2uw^2}{3v^3}$ **27.** $\frac{1}{4xy(4 + y)}$ **29.** $25k^6$ **31.** $\frac{9x^2}{16}$ **33.** $-\frac{x^6}{125}$ **35.** $\frac{8c^5}{d^3}$ **37.** $\frac{1}{12}$ **39.** $\frac{2}{n^2}$ **41.** 1 **43.** $\frac{1}{(n - 3)(n - 5)}$ **45.** $\frac{(x - y)(x + y)(x - 4)}{2x}$ **47.** $\frac{(2t - 3s)(m^2 + n^2)}{7(4s - 5t)(m + n)}$ **49.** $\frac{x^2}{y^3}$ **51.** $\frac{c^2}{3}$ **53.** −1 **55.** $2h - 8$ **57.** $30m - 5n$ **59.** $12s^2t$ **61.** $5e + 5$ **63.** $5z$ **65.** $3ab$ **67.** $\frac{3x - 6}{48}, \frac{4x + 12}{48}$ **69.** $\frac{d}{3cd^2}, \frac{12}{3cd^2}$ **71.** $\frac{2wx + 6w}{3(x^2 - 9)}, \frac{3}{3(x^2 - 9)}$ **73.** $\frac{4}{x}$ **75.** $\frac{-k - 4}{5}$ **77.** $\frac{7}{g - 3}$ **79.** $\frac{5 + 3y}{y^2}$ **81.** $\frac{2 - 3x}{10wx}$ **83.** $\frac{2 + 3x}{3(x + 2)}$ **85.** $\frac{3(h + 1)}{10}$ **87.** $\frac{2x + 7}{(x + 2)(x + 3)}$ **89.** $\frac{u - 3}{u - 4}$ **91.** $\frac{5n + 1}{n}$ **93.** $\frac{x + 3y}{y}$ **95.** $\frac{8n - 14}{n - 2}$ **97.** $\frac{h(8h + 23)}{h + 3}$ **99.** $\frac{5e^2 - e - 8}{(e + 1)(e - 1)}$ **101.** $\frac{2w^2 - 7w - 3}{w - 3}$ **103.** $\frac{2v^2}{(v + u)(v - u)}$ **105.** $x + 5$ **107.** $a - 7 + \frac{11}{a + 2}$ **109.** $k + 1 + \frac{12}{k - 5}$ **111.** $b^2 - b + 1 - \frac{2}{b + 1}$ **113.** $w^2 + 2w + 4$ **115.** $n - 4$ **117.** $v^2 + 3v + 7 + \frac{15}{v - 2}$

Chapter 7, pages 651–653 **1.** 1:3 **3.** 200:3 **5.** 18*d*:5 **7.** 25:11 **9.** {9} **11.** $\left\{\frac{7}{6}\right\}$ **13.** {6} **15.** {18} **17.** {12} **19.** {72} **21.** {−9} **23.** {−7} **25.** {6} **27.** {2} **29.** {−6} **31.** 202.5 **33.** 30 **35.** 25% **37.** {40}

39. {800} **41.** {300} **43.** 8.4 kg **45.** \$127.50 **47.** 24 kg **49.** 30 min **51.** $\frac{1}{125}$ **53.** $\frac{1}{729}$ **55.** 36 **57.** 64 **59.** $\frac{1}{729y^3}$ **61.** $\frac{1}{a^2b^3}$ **63.** $\frac{e^2}{d^4f^2}$ **65.** $\frac{x^{12}y^{15}}{z^9}$ **67.** 1.47×10^8 **69.** 9.8×10^{-6} **71.** 1×10^{-11}

Chapter 8, pages 653–656 **1.** no; yes **3.** no; no **5.** yes; yes **7.** (0, 4), (2, 3), (4, 2), (6, 1), (8, 0) **9.** (0, 4), (3, 0) **11.** (2, 2), (6, 1), (10, 0)

13.

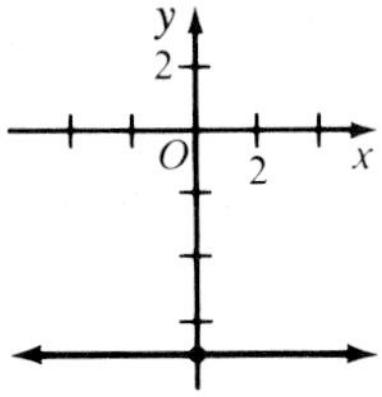

15.

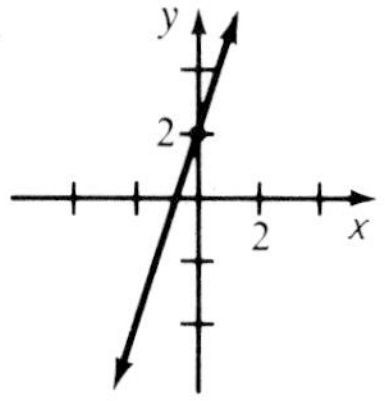

17.

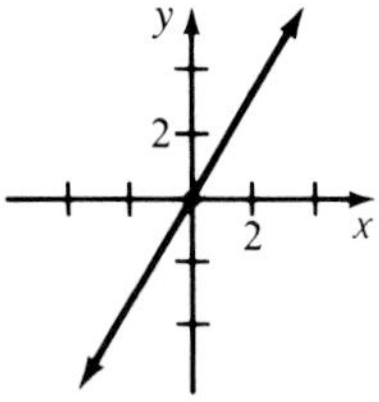

19.

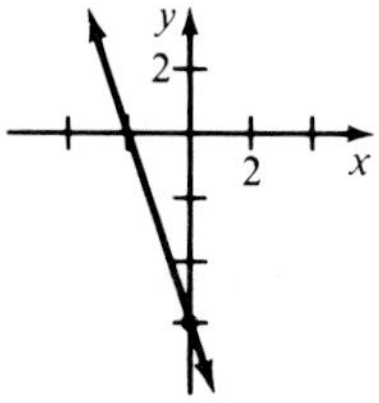

21.

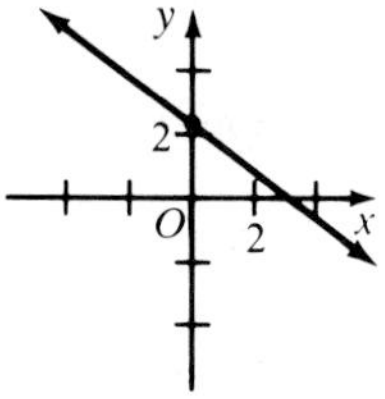

23. $\frac{1}{6}$ **25.** 0 **27.** $\frac{3}{13}$ **29.** no slope **31.** 0 **33.** −1 **35.** yes **37.** yes

39.

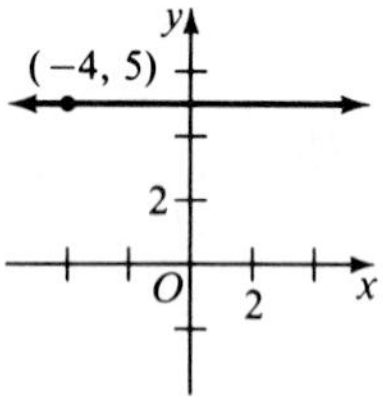

41.

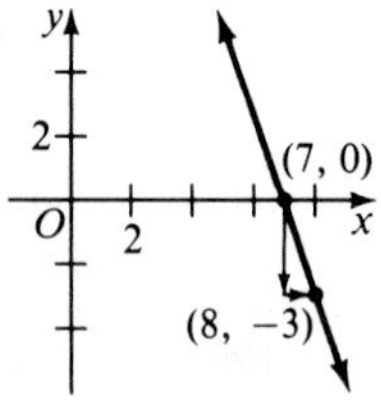

43.

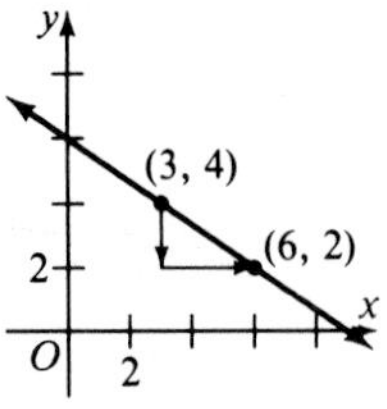

45. $y = \frac{7}{2}x$

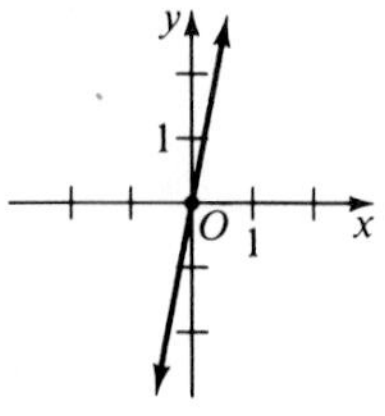

47. $y = -x + 3$

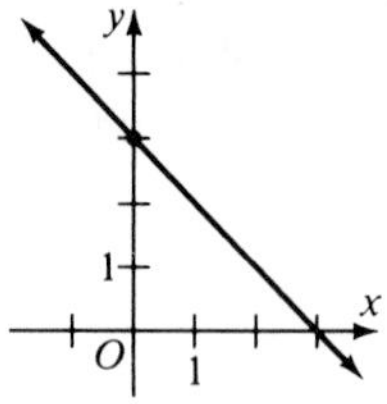

49. $y = \frac{3}{4}x - \frac{5}{4}$

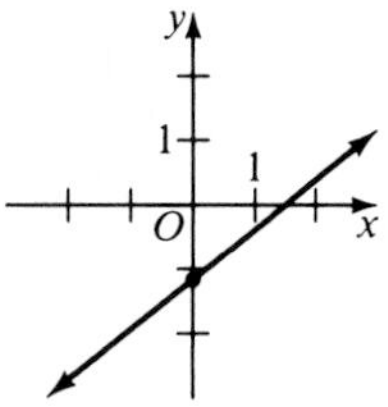

51. $y = \frac{3}{2}x - 3$, $y = \frac{3}{2}x - 6$; Both slopes are $\frac{3}{2}$, so the lines are parallel. **53.** $y = 3x + \frac{1}{2}$ **55.** $y = \frac{1}{3}x + 6$ **57.** $y = -\frac{3}{7}x + \frac{3}{8}$ **59.** $y = 3x + 4$ **61.** $y = \frac{3}{4}x - 2$ **63.** $y = -\frac{1}{5}x - 1$ **65.** $y = \frac{3}{4}x - \frac{1}{2}$ **67.** $y = -\frac{1}{6}x$ **69.** $y = -2x + 4$

71. D = {Mackinac Straits, Humber Estuary, Golden Gate, Ataturk, Verrazano Narrows}, R = {3800 ft, 4626 ft, 4200 ft, 3524 ft, 4260 ft}

73.

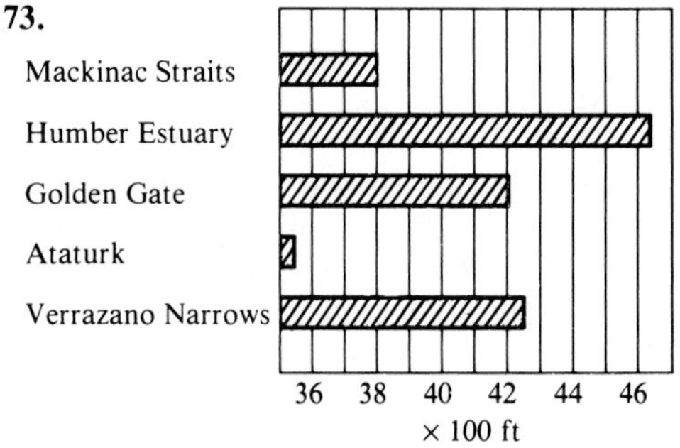

75. −7 **77.** 5 **79.** 0 **81.** $\frac{9}{8}$ **83.** {2, −3, −10} **85.** {5, 1, −3} **87.** {3, −1}

89. (0, 0); $x = 0$

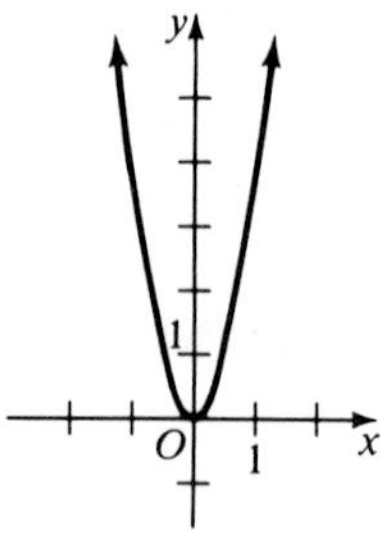

91. (0, 0); $x = 0$

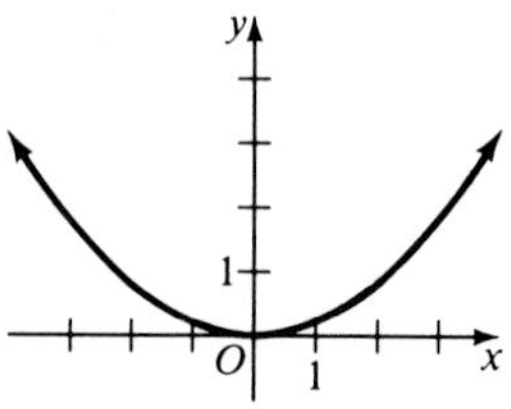

93. (1, 4); $x = 1$

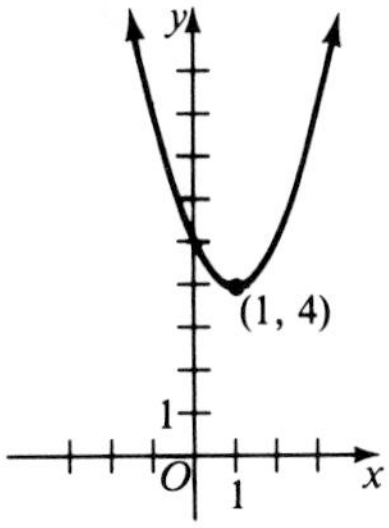

95. $\left(-\frac{7}{2}, -\frac{49}{4}\right); -\frac{49}{4}$

97. (0, 0); 0

99. (0, 2); 2 **101.** $\frac{1}{5}$

103. 900 **105.** 21

107. $\frac{3}{32}$

109. a. $e = km$ **b.** $\frac{e_1}{m_1} = \frac{e_2}{m_2}$

111. a. $rn = k$ **b.** $\frac{r_1}{n_2} = \frac{r_2}{n_1}$

113. a. $ns = k$ **b.** $\frac{n_1}{s_2} = \frac{n_2}{s_1}$

115.

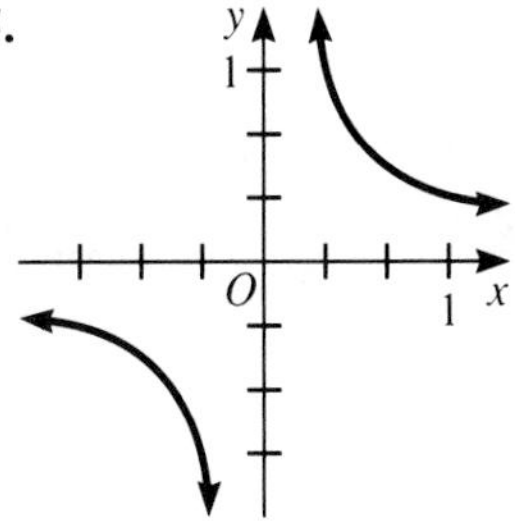

117.

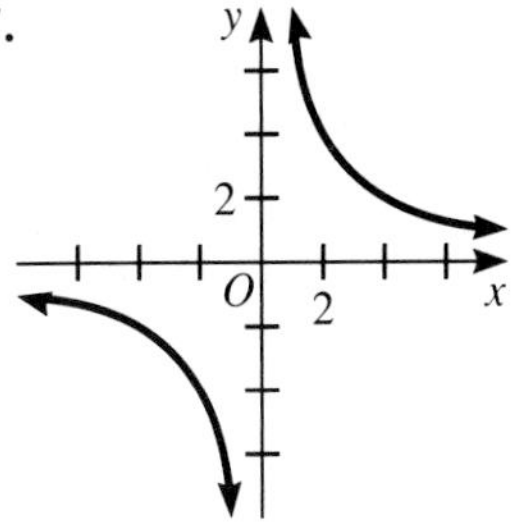

119. 1.8

Chapter 9, pages 656–657 **1.** (4, 2) **3.** (−2, 2) **5.** (3, 3) **7.** (1, 2) **9.** (3, −2) **11.** (5, −1) **13.** 7 men **15.** (3, 6) **17.** (8, 2) **19.** (5, −3) **21.** (4, −1) **23.** (2, 3) **25.** (4, 3) **27.** 20 km/h; 820 km/h **29.** Jenny, 17 years old; aunt, 28 years old

Chapter 10, pages 657–659 **1.** False **3.** True **5.** False **7.** False **9.** True **11.** {−4, −3} **13.** {−3, −2, −1, 0, 1, 2, 3}

15.

17.

19. {the real numbers less than 4}

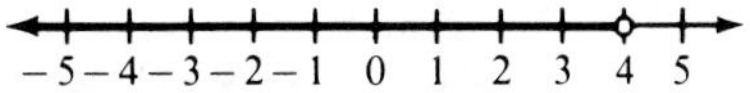

21. {the real numbers greater than −98}

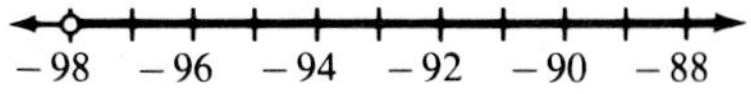

23. $\left\{\text{the real numbers less than } -\frac{25}{2}\right\}$

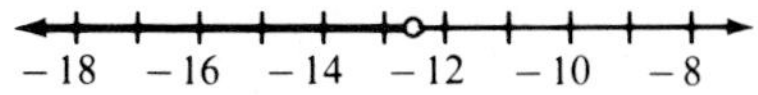

25. {the real numbers greater than 8}

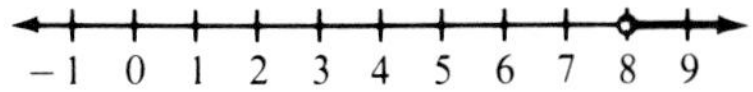

27. {the real numbers greater than 4}

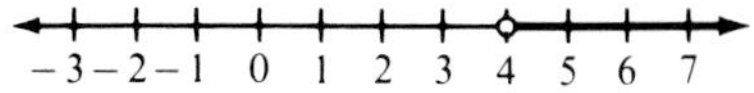

29. {the real numbers greater than −14}

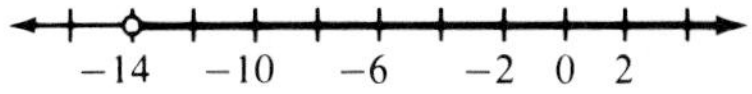

31. {the real numbers less than 4}

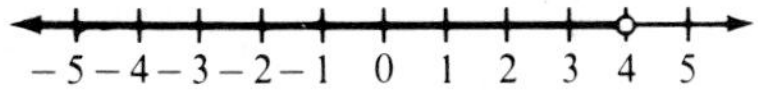

33. a. x **b.** $2x - 9 \leq 43$ **35. a.** y **b.** $\frac{1}{2}y - 10 \geq 25$ **37. a.** b **b.** $b - 6 < \frac{1}{2}b$

39. {8, and the real numbers between 0 and 8}

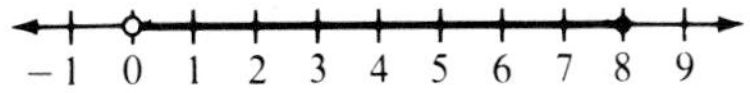

41. {−1, 2, and the real numbers between −1 and 2}

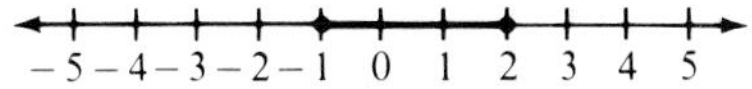

43. {−9, and the real numbers less than −9 or greater than −4}

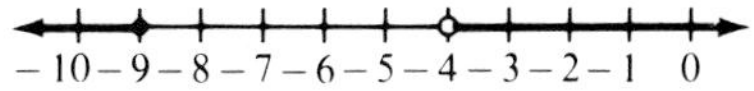

45. {−3, and the real numbers less than −3 or greater than 5}

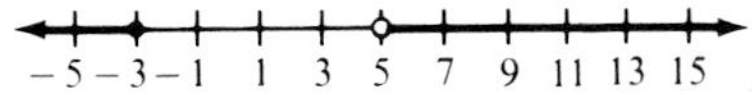

47. {6, 2, and the real numbers greater than 6 or less than 2}

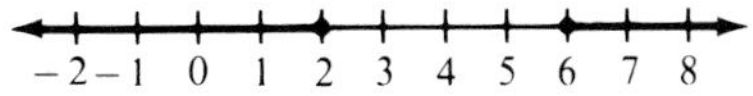

49. {3, 13}

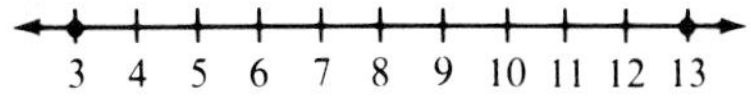

51. {−1.5, 1.5, and the real numbers between −1.5 and 1.5}

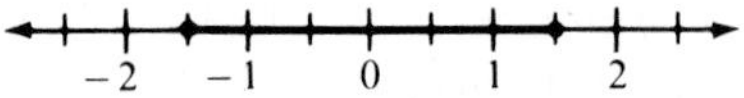

53. {−7, 1, and the real numbers between −7 and 1}

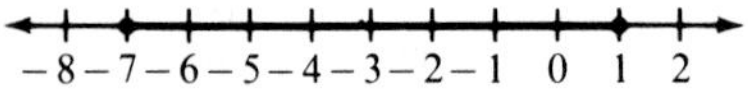

55. {the real numbers less than −11 or greater than 3}

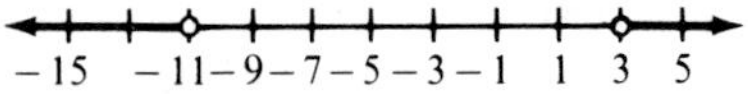

57. $\left\{-\frac{3}{2}, \frac{3}{2}\right.$, and the real numbers between $-\frac{3}{2}$ and $\left.\frac{3}{2}\right\}$

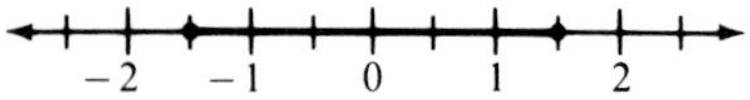

59. {the real numbers between −4 and 10}

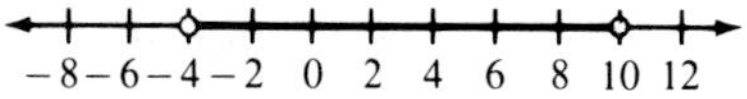

61. {−6, 6, and the real numbers less than −6 or greater than 6}

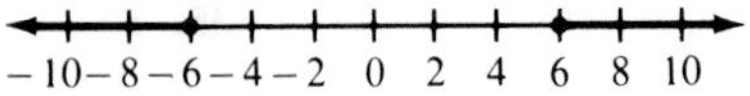

63. $\left\{4, -\frac{14}{5}\right\}$

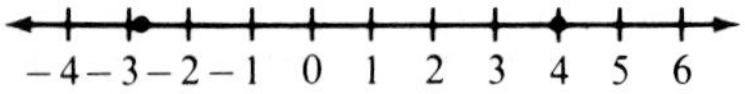

65. {the real numbers less than −1 or greater than 4}

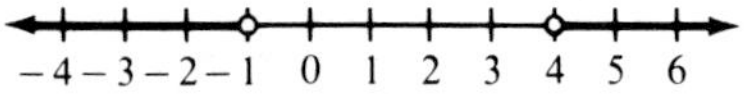

67. {−4, 8, and the real numbers between −4 and 8}

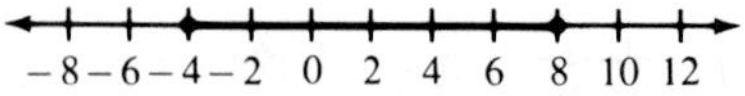

69. {the real numbers between −4 and 2}

71. No solution

73.

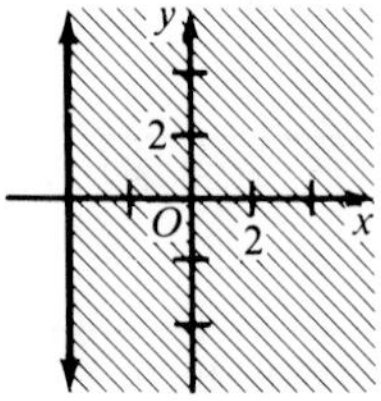

75.

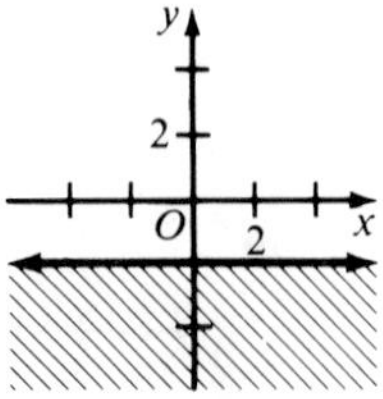

77.

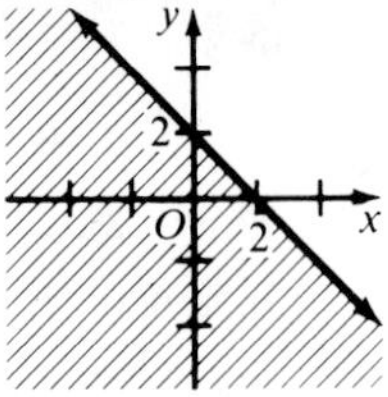

79.

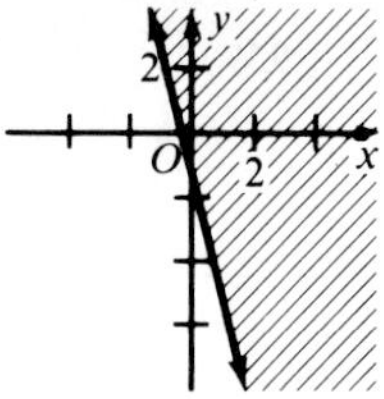

81. $y \le -4x - 2$

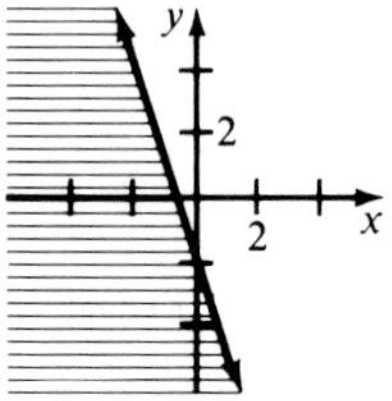

83. $y > 6x - 2$

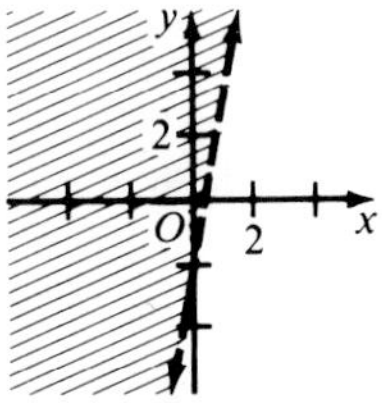

85. $y < \frac{5}{4}x$

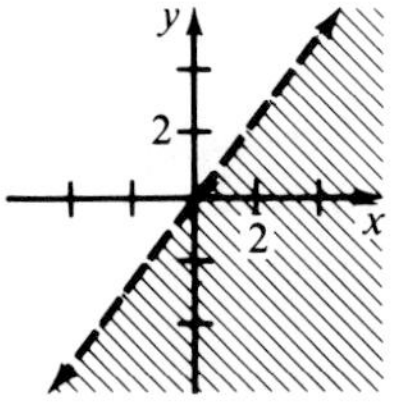

87. $y > 2x - \frac{2}{3}$

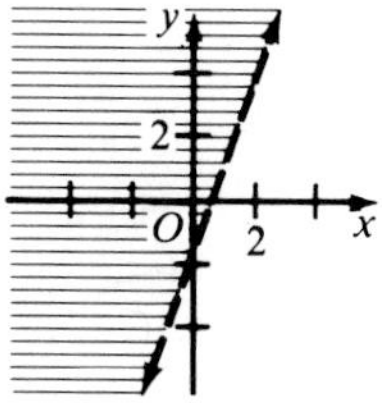

89.

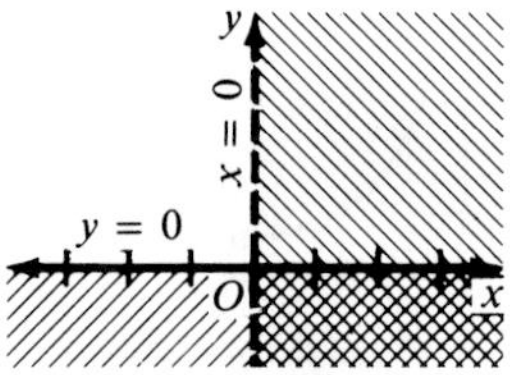

91.

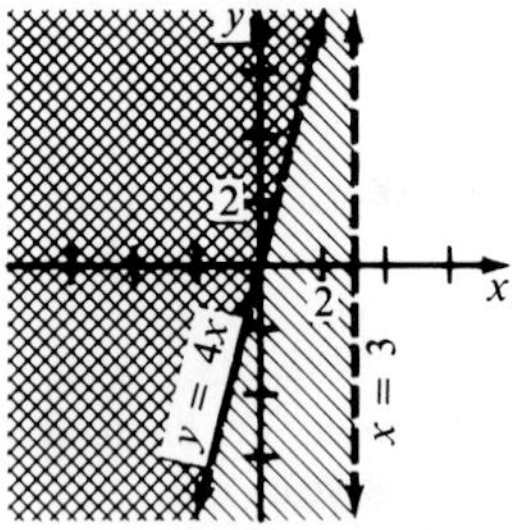

93.

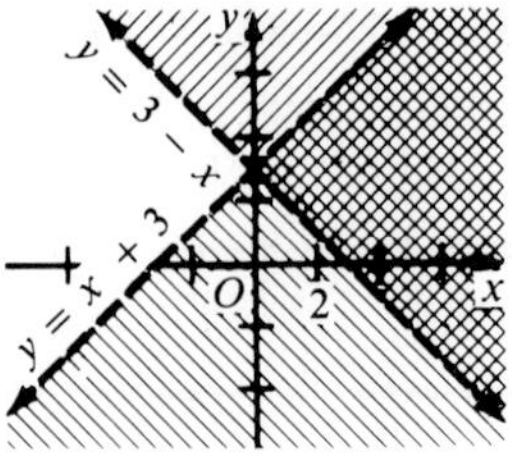

95. 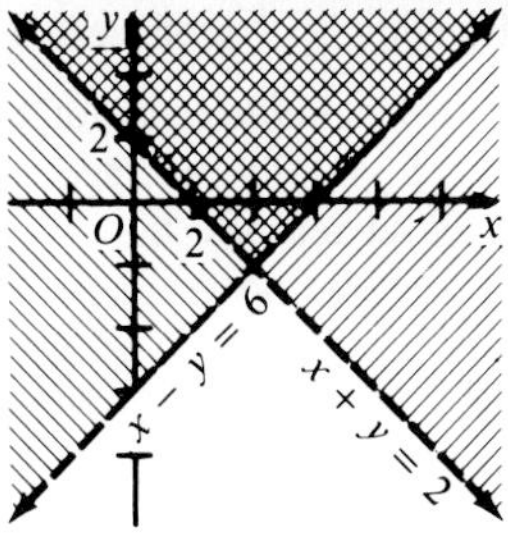

Chapter 11, pages 659–662 **1.** < **3.** <
5. $\frac{2}{3}, \frac{12}{17}, \frac{5}{7}, \frac{11}{15}$ **7.** $\frac{1135}{1517}$ **9.** $\frac{111}{56}$
11. increases **13.** decreases **15.** $0.\overline{4}$ **17.** 3.55
19. $0.7\overline{45}$ **21.** $\frac{2}{3}$ **23.** $\frac{235}{99}$ **25.** 0.6275
27. $0.6\overline{32}$ **29.** $\frac{4}{9}, \frac{2}{3}; \frac{8}{27}$ **31.** 21 **33.** 52
35. 104 **37.** 0.8 **39.** 0.12 **41.** $\frac{3}{5}$ **43.** $\frac{9}{22}$
45. $\frac{8}{9}$ **47.** $4\sqrt{11}$ **49.** $12\sqrt{11}$ **51.** $90\sqrt{2}$
53. $4\sqrt{42}$ **55.** $21\sqrt{6}$ **57.** −28.3 **59.** 91.7
61. $13|m|$ **63.** $5x^2\sqrt{5}$ **65.** $-6|t^3|$
67. $-12|xy|\sqrt{2x}$ **69.** $-2.2w^2$ **71.** $\frac{a^2|b^3|\sqrt{3}}{6|c|}$
73. $\frac{3k^4}{4}$ **75.** $\frac{15x^{20}}{4}$ **77.** $|a-2|$ **79.** $\{-7, 7\}$
81. $\left\{-\frac{4}{5}, \frac{4}{5}\right\}$ **83.** $\{-3, 3\}$ **85.** $\{-11.5, 11.5\}$
87. $\{-6.6, 6.6\}$ **89.** 9.43 **91.** 11.18
93. 22.36 **95.** 18.03 **97.** no **99.** no
101. no **103.** 30 **105.** 14 **107.** $72\sqrt{2}$
109. $\frac{3\sqrt{2}}{2}$ **111.** $\frac{\sqrt{2}}{4}$ **113.** $\frac{11\sqrt{3}}{7}$
115. $n^2 + 3\sqrt{n}$ **117.** $4\sqrt{3}$ **119.** $7\sqrt{6}$
121. $-50\sqrt{2}$ **123.** $2\sqrt{2} - \frac{\sqrt{30}}{6}$
125. $\frac{20\sqrt{7}}{7} + \frac{3\sqrt{2}}{4}$ **127.** $10\sqrt{3} - \sqrt{30}$
129. $3\sqrt{15}$ **131.** −29 **133.** $18 + 8\sqrt{2}$
135. $34 - 24\sqrt{2}$ **137.** $20\sqrt{3} - 24\sqrt{2}$
139. $252 + 133\sqrt{2}$
141. $-\frac{2 + \sqrt{3} + 2\sqrt{5} + \sqrt{15}}{4}$ **143.** $\left\{\frac{3}{8}\right\}$
145. $\left\{\frac{16}{25}\right\}$ **147.** $\{83\}$ **149.** $\{3\}$ **151.** $\left\{\frac{2}{5}\right\}$
153. $\{45\}$

Chapter 12, pages 662–664 **1.** $\left\{-\frac{5}{7}, \frac{5}{7}\right\}$
3. no solution **5.** $\{-4, 4\}$ **7.** $\{-\sqrt{3}, \sqrt{3}\}$
9. $\{-9, -1\}$ **11.** $\{-4 + 3\sqrt{3}, -4 - 3\sqrt{3}\}$
13. $\{-7 + \sqrt{21}, -7 - \sqrt{21}\}$
15. $\left\{\frac{1 + 2\sqrt{6}}{3}, \frac{1 - 2\sqrt{6}}{3}\right\}$ **17.** $\{-1, 13\}$
19. $\{-15, -1\}$ **21.** $\{6 + \sqrt{246}, 6 - \sqrt{246}\}$;
$\{21.7, -9.7\}$ **23.** $\left\{\frac{3 + \sqrt{29}}{2}, \frac{3 - \sqrt{29}}{2}\right\}$;
$\{4.2, -1.2\}$ **25.** $\{3, 7\}$ **27.** $\left\{2, -\frac{7}{2}\right\}$
29. $\left\{2, -\frac{5}{2}\right\}$ **31.** $\left\{\frac{-7 + \sqrt{37}}{2}, \frac{-7 - \sqrt{37}}{2}\right\}$;
$\{-0.5, -6.5\}$ **33.** $\left\{\frac{5 + \sqrt{37}}{2}, \frac{5 - \sqrt{37}}{2}\right\}$;
$\{5.5, -0.5\}$ **35.** $\left\{1, \frac{2}{3}\right\}$
37. $\left\{\frac{-3 + \sqrt{89}}{20}, \frac{-3 - \sqrt{89}}{20}\right\}$; $\{0.3, -0.6\}$
39. $\left\{\frac{7 + \sqrt{57}}{2}, \frac{7 - \sqrt{57}}{2}\right\}$; $\{7.3, -0.3\}$
41. −131; none **43.** −11.76; none **45.** 5; two
47. a. zero **b.** below **49.** $\{-3, -4\}$
51. $\left\{0, \frac{9}{5}\right\}$ **53.** $\{-4 + \sqrt{13}, -4 - \sqrt{13}\}$
55. $\left\{\frac{-2 + \sqrt{10}}{6}, \frac{-2 - \sqrt{10}}{6}\right\}$
57. $\left\{\frac{4 + 2\sqrt{31}}{9}, \frac{4 - 2\sqrt{31}}{9}\right\}$
59. $\left\{\frac{1 + \sqrt{7}}{6}, \frac{1 - \sqrt{7}}{6}\right\}$
61. $\left\{\frac{-5 + \sqrt{13}}{2}, \frac{-5 - \sqrt{13}}{2}\right\}$ **63.** length, 22.2 cm; width, 3.7 cm **65.** 14 m **67.** $hr^2 = k$
69. $L = krh$ **71.** $\frac{rt}{d} = k$

EXTRA PRACTICE: *Problem-Solving*

Chapter 1, page 665 ***(1-7)*** **1.** 225 km
3. 8 games **5.** 19

Chapter 2, page 665 ***(2-3)*** **1.** 38 yd **3.** \$205
5. 10:00 A.M. ***(2-4)*** **1.** 2.52° C **3.** 28 blocks
5. 397 m below sea level

Chapter 3, page 666 ***(3-1)*** **1.** −18 **3.** 58
5. \$747 ***(3-2)*** **1.** −34 **3.** 56¢ **5.** 12 cm
(3-4) **1.** 12 **3.** \$124 **5.** 8 quarters, 12 dimes, 16 nickels ***(3-5)*** **1.** −9 and −8 **3.** 12 **5.** 7, 9, 11 ***(3-6)*** **1.** Kevin, 18 h; Karen, 6 h **3.** 60
5. Becky, 6; Ryan, 4; Amy, 2 dimes
(3-7) **1.** 13 quarters, 35 dimes **3.** 7.5 h **5.** 36 quarters

Chapter 4, page 668 ***(4-8)*** **1.** 2.5 h
3. 2400 km **5.** 7:00 P.M. ***(4-9)*** **1.** 7 m by 11 m **3.** 5 m by 9 m **5.** 60 cm by 70 cm
(4-10) **1.** no solution **3.** no solution **5.** −5, −4, −3

Chapter 5, page 669 ***(5-13)*** **1.** 11 or -12 **3.** 12 cm by 20 cm **5.** 4 m by 8 m

Chapter 7, page 670 ***(7-1)*** **1.** 50, 75 **3.** 40, 60, 100 **5.** 180 coins ***(7-2)*** **1.** \$7.73 **3.** \$167.50 **5.** 180 lb ***(7-3)*** **1.** Juan, \$16; Sylvia, \$14 **3.** Bart, 14; mother, 42 years old **5.** 20 dimes ***(7-4)*** **1.** $\frac{3}{4}$ or $\frac{4}{3}$ **3.** $\frac{1}{3}$ **5.** 50 km/h ***(7-5)*** **1.** \$10.50 **3.** \$40 **5.** \$630 ***(7-6)*** **1.** 35% **3.** 1475 **5.** \$9600 ***(7-7)*** **Chemistry** **1.** 80 L **3.** 25.6% **Grocery** **1.** 40 L of cranberry juice; 80 L of apple juice **3.** \$1.75 **Investment and Wages** **1.** \$12.50 **3.** \$15,000 ***(7-8)*** **1.** $\frac{11}{15}$ **3.** 13 h 20 min **5.** 54 min ***(7-9)*** **1. a.** 10,000 **b.** 9709 **c.** 10,300 **3.** about 61 bacteria **5.** about 6701 people ***(7-10)*** **1.** 1.28 s **3.** 2.03×10^4 s **5.** 6.0×10^{-5} cm

Chapter 8, page 674 ***(8-9)*** **1.** 3.1 cm **3.** 33 kg **5.** 226,800 km^2 ***(8-10)*** **1.** 7 h **3.** \$1875 **5.** 0.55 m from the mass of 18 g or 0.45 m from the mass of 22 g

Chapter 9, page 675 ***(9-3)*** **1.** 32 quarters **3.** width, 10; length, 17 **5.** $\frac{5}{12}$ ***(9-4)*** **1.** 21, 15 **3.** 87 boys **5.** 18 quarters, 20 dimes ***(9-5)*** **1.** 19, 32 **3.** 150 ft **5.** 42 questions ***(9-6)*** **1.** boat, 23 km/h; current, 7 km/h **3.** current, 2 km/h; swimmer, 8 km/h **5.** 200 km/h

Chapter 10, page 677 ***(10-3)*** **1.** 40, 41 **3.** 260 **5.** 90 km/h

Chapter 11, page 677 ***(11-5)*** **1.** 13.6 cm **3.** 4.5 cm **5.** 3.3 m ***(11-6)*** **1.** 53.85 m **3.** 8 cm, 15 cm **5.** 9 cm, 12 cm ***(11-10)*** **1.** 784 **3.** 49 **5.** 30, 32

Chapter 12, page 679 ***(12-6)*** **1.** 5 or -6 **3.** 9 m by 60 m **5.** 72 h and 90 h ***(12-7)*** **1.** 85.75 m **3.** 1 unit **5.** It is $\frac{1}{9}$ as large as it was. ***(12-8)*** **1.** 6¢ **3.** $5\frac{1}{4}$ h

Explorations

Page 685 ***(1-8)*** **1. d.** No. The product approaches, but never reaches, zero. **3.** This process of multiplying by $\frac{1}{2}$ produces numbers that approach zero from *either* side of zero on the number line. **5. b.** The average approaches, but never reaches, the smaller number. **7. a.** yes **b.** no

Page 686 ***(2-3)*** **1. c.** 0 **e.** Use an equal number of red chips and blue chips. **3. b.** The signs of the addends and their sums are the same. **c.** no **5. a.** 8 **b.** -8 **c.** 2 **d.** -2

Page 687 ***(2-4)*** **1. c.** 1 **d.** $4 - 3 = 1$ **3. a.** by removing 3 red chips from 4 blue chips **d.** 7 blue chips **e.** $4 - (-3) = 7$ **5.** $-5 - (-3) = -2$ (2 red chips); $-3 - (-5) = 2$ (2 blue chips) **7.** true

Page 688 ***(3-1)*** **1. a.** The pans balance; $6 = 6$ **b.** The pans balance; 8; $6 + 2 = 6 + 2$, or $8 = 8$ **c.** The pans balance; 5; $8 - 3 = 8 - 3$, or $5 = 5$ **d.** The pans do not balance; $5 - 1 \neq 5 - 2$, or $4 \neq 3$, or $4 > 3$ **e.** If the same number of washers is added to or subtracted from each pan, the pans stay in balance. **3. a.** The pans balance; $y - 4 = 7$ **b.** $y = 11$

Pages 689–690 ***(4-5, 4-6)*** **1. a.** x; $x + 1$ **b.** $x(x + 1)$ **c.** x^2; x **d.** The area of the rectangle is the sum of the areas of the tiles. **e.** $x(x + 1) = x^2 + x$ **3. b.** three 1-by-1 tiles **c.** $x + 1$, $x + 3$ **d.** $x^2 + 4x + 3$ **e.** $x^2 + 4x + 3$ **5. a.** $2x^2 + 3x$ **b.** $6x^2 + 3x$ **c.** $3x^2 + 15x$

Page 691 ***(5-7)*** **1. a.** $x^2 + 3x$ **b.** $x + 3$; x **c.** $x(x + 3)$ **d.** $x^2 + 3x = x(x + 3)$ **3. a.** One x-by-x tile, seven 1-by-x tiles, and twelve 1-by-1 tiles **c.** $x + 4$, $x + 3$ **d.** $(x + 4)(x + 3)$ **5. a.** $x(2x + 1)$ **b.** $(x + 1)^2$ **c.** $(3x + 1)(x + 2)$

Page 692 ***(6-4)*** **1. a.** $2 \cdot 3$ **b.** 2^3, 3^2 **c.** $2^3 \cdot 3^2$ **d.** 2, 3 **e.** The factors not included in the GCF form the LCM, and those not included in the LCM form the GCF. **3. a.** abc^2 **b.** $a^2b^2c^3d$ **c.** $a^2b^2c^3d$ **d.** abc^2 **e.** The factors not included in the GCF form the LCM, and those not included in the LCM form the GCF. **5.** 12; 240

Page 693 ***(7-2)*** **3.** 1250 fish

Page 694 ***(8-4)*** **1. d.** The lines all go through the same point, (0, b); the slant, or slope, of the line is different; the equations are alike except for the value of m. **3.** For an equation of the form $y = mx + b$, the value of m determines the slant, or slope, of the line. **5. c.** The lines are parallel (have the same slope); each line goes through a different point (0, b) on the y-axis; the equations are alike except for the value of b. **7.** They both pass through the point (0, 5), but the second line is steeper.

Page 695 (9-1) **1. b.** The lines are parallel. **c.** The lines are parallel to the original line. **3. b.** The lines intersect in one point. **c.** yes; yes **d.** The lines all intersect the original line in one point. **5.** The graphs coincide. The first equation multiplied by −2 yields the second equation.

Page 696 (10-2) **1. a.** a is next door to a. **b.** If a is next door to b, then b is next door to a. **c.** If a is next door to b and b is next door to c, then a is next door to c. **3. a.** transitive **b.** symmetric, transitive **c.** symmetric **d.** transitive **5.** reflexive and transitive **7.** 5

Page 697 (11-2) **1. a.** 0.5 **b.** $0.\overline{3}$, 0.25, 0.2, $0.1\overline{6}$, $0.\overline{142857}$, 0.125, $0.\overline{1}$, 0.1, $0.\overline{09}$, $0.08\overline{3}$ **c.** $\frac{1}{2}, \frac{1}{4}, \frac{1}{5}, \frac{1}{8}, \frac{1}{10}$ **d.** $\frac{1}{3}, \frac{1}{6}, \frac{1}{7}, \frac{1}{9}, \frac{1}{11}, \frac{1}{12}$ **e.** The denominators for (c) have only 2 and/or 5 as prime factors. The denominators for (d) have other primes besides 2 and 5. **f.** Their decimal forms are terminating. **g.** Their decimal forms are repeating. **3. a.** $\frac{4}{10} = \frac{2}{5}$, $\frac{29}{100}$, $\frac{325}{1000} = \frac{13}{40}$, $\frac{4791}{10{,}000}$ **b.** 5, $2^2 \cdot 5^2$, $2^3 \cdot 5$, $2^4 \cdot 5^4$ **c.** Their only prime factors are 2 and 5; agree. **5.** They are the product of prime factors that include at least one prime other than 2 or 5.

Pages 698–699 (11-6) **1. a.** $\sqrt{2}$ **b.** $\sqrt{3}$ **c.** $\sqrt{4} = 2$ **d.** $\sqrt{5}$, $\sqrt{6}$, $\sqrt{7}$, $\sqrt{8} = 2\sqrt{2}$, $\sqrt{9} = 3$ **e.** The new hypotenuse is the square root of the number that is one more than the radicand of the longer leg. **3.** $x\sqrt{y + 1}$ **5. a.** $\sqrt{13}$ **b.** $\sqrt{5}$; yes **c.** Possible answer: 3, 5, $\sqrt{34}$ **d.** $2\sqrt{2}$ **e.** $\sqrt{29}$ **7.** yes; no

Page 700 (12-4) **1. b.** one **3. b.** none **c.** There are none. **5.** one, because $b^2 - 4ac = 0$; $x \approx 1.7$

Appendices

A–2, page 714 **1.** $y - 2 = 3(x - 1)$ **3.** $y - 4 = -\frac{1}{2}(x - 3)$ **5.** $y + 8 = 5(x + 3)$ **7.** $y - 2 = \frac{4}{7}(x - 0)$ **9.** $y = \frac{3}{4}x - \frac{7}{4}$; $3x - 4y = 7$ **11. a.** $y = -2x + 8$ **b.** $y = \frac{1}{2}x + \frac{19}{2}$

A–3, pages 716–717 **1.** deductive **3.** inductive **5.** Inductive: A chemistry experiment produces the same result 20 times. You conclude that it will always produce the same result. Deductive: a direct two-column proof in geometry. Inductive reasoning makes a general statement based on a number of observations. Deductive reasoning uses known facts, definitions, and properties in a logical order to reach a conclusion. **7. a.** $3 + 4 = 7$; $3 \cdot 4 = 12$ **b.** yes **c.** $(x + a)(x + b) = x^2 + (a + b)x + ab$ **d.** $(x + a)(x + b) = x^2 + xa + ab = x^2 + (a + b)x + ab$ **9.** $a = 2$, $b = -2$ **11.** $a = 0.5$ **13.** false; $10^2 = 100$ **15.** The sum of the first n positive even integers is $n(n + 1)$. $4n(n + 1) + 1 = 4n^2 + 4n + 1 = (2n + 1)^2$. Since $(2n + 1)^2$ is a perfect square, the statement is true.

A–4, page 719 **1.** hypothesis: The current month is September. conclusion: There are 30 days in the month. True; There are 30 days in September. **3.** hypothesis: Joe lives in Vermont. conclusion: Joe lives in New England. True; Vermont is a New England state. **5.** (1) If there are 30 days in the month, then the current month is September. False; April, June, and November all have 30 days. (2) If ab is positive, then a and b are negative. False; a and b could both be positive. (3) If Joe lives in New England, then he lives in Vermont. False; Joe could live in Maine, New Hampshire, Rhode Island, Connecticut, or Massachusetts. (4) If $|a + b| = |a| + |b|$, then a and b are both positive. False; a and b could both be 0. **9.** always true; true when a and b are both positive or both negative, or when one is zero, or when one is positive and one negative.

A–5, page 720 **1.** hypothesis and known fact: n^3 is negative. desired conclusion: n is negative. alternative conclusion: n is positive or 0. Assume temporarily that the alternative conclusion is true. If n is positive, then n^3 is positive since the cube of a positive number is positive. If $n = 0$, then $n^3 = 0$ since the cube of 0 is 0. This contradicts the known fact that n^3 is negative. The desired conclusion must be accepted and the original statement is true. **3.** hypothesis and known fact: $x > 3$. desired conclusion: $|x| - 3 > 0$. alternative conclusion: $|x| - 3 \leq 0$. Assume temporarily that the alternative conclusion is true. If $|x| - 3 \leq 0$, then $|x| \leq 3$ contradicts the known fact that x is greater than 3. The desired conclusion must be accepted and the original statement is true. **5.** hypothesis and known fact: n^2 is a multiple of 3. desired conclusion: n is a multiple of 3. alternative conclusion: n is not a multiple of 3. Assume temporarily that the alternative conclusion is true. Then either $n = 3k + 1$ or $n = 3k + 2$, where k is any integer. If $n = 3k + 1$, then $n^2 = (3k + 1)^2 = 9k^2 + 6k + 1$, or $3(3k^2 + 2k) + 1$. Since $3(3k^2 + 2k)$ is a multiple of 3, $3(3k^2 + 2k) + 1$, or n^2, is not a multiple of 3. If $n = 3k + 2$, then $n^2 = 9k^2 + 12k + 4$, or $3(3k^2 + 4k + 1) + 1$. Since $3(3k^2 + 4k + 1)$ is a multiple of 3, $3(3k^2 + 4k + 1) + 1$, or n^2, is not a multiple of 3. Both cases contradict the known fact that n^2 is a multiple of 3. The desired conclusion must be accepted and the original statement is true.